Introduction to

A Computer Integrated Approach

WEST PUBLISHING COMPANY

ST. PAUL · NEW YORK · LOS ANGELES · SAN FRANCISCO

MINITAB Commands Used Within the Text (continued)

C denotes a column, K denotes a constant

9. REGRESSION

REGRESS Y in C using K predictors in C, · · · , C
  Subcommands: COEF into C
  RESIDUALS into C
  PREDICT for K, · · · , K
  or PREDICT for C, · · · , C
  Example: REGRESS C1 2 C2 C3 C4 C5 will regress Y in C1 using 2 predictors in C2 and C3 as well as store the standardized residuals in C4 and the estimated Y values ($\hat{Y}$ values) in C5.
BRIEF output at level K
STEPWISE regression of C using predictors C, · · · , C
  Subcommands: FENTER = K
  FREMOVE = K
  FORCE C, · · · , C
  ENTER C, · · · , C
  REMOVE C, · · · , C

10. ANALYSIS OF VARIANCE

ONEWAY using data in C, levels in C
TWOWAY using data in C, levels in C, blocks in C

11. NONPARAMETRIC STATISTICS

CHISQUARE using C, · · · , C
RUNS above and below K for data in C
MANN-WHITNEY [alternative = K] using C and C
WTEST using C
  Subcommand: ALTERNATIVE = K
KRUSKAL-WALLIS test for data in C, levels in C
RANK the values in C, put ranks into C

12. TIME SERIES

ACF of C
DIFFERENCES [of lag K] using C, put into C
LAG [by K] using C, put into C

13. MISCELLANEOUS

IRANDOM K integers between K and K, put into C
ERASE C, · · · , C

14. SUBCOMMANDS

Some MINITAB commands have subcommands to convey additional information. To use a subcommand, include a semicolon at the end of the main command; the subcommands follow (one per line). End the final subcommand with a period.

Introduction to
Business Statistics

Business Statistics

ALAN H. KVANLI

C. STEPHEN GUYNES

ROBERT J. PAVUR

North Texas State University

Student Study Guide

A study guide has been developed to assist students in mastering the concepts presented in this text. It reinforces chapter material, presenting it in a concise format with review questions. An examination copy is available to instructors by contacting West Publishing Company. Students can purchase the study guide from local bookstores under the title *Study Guide to Accompany Introduction to Business Statistics: A Computer Integrated Approach,* prepared by Wilke English.

Cover: Compatible Graphics
Production Coordination: Julia Chitwood, Bookman Productions
Copy Editor: Lyn Dupré
Interior Design: Paula Schlosser
Illustrator: Carl Brown

Library of Congress Cataloging-in-Publication Data
Kvanli, Alan H.
     Introduction to business statistics.

     Bibliography: p.
     Includes index.
     1. Business statistics.   2. Statistics.   3. Business statistics—Data processing.   4. Statistics—Data processing.   I. Guynes, Carl S.   II. Pavur, Robert J. III. Title.
HF1017.K83   1986   519.5′024658   85-20295
ISBN 0-314-93192-9

To Ann, who provided the inspiration and quiet place to make it happen.

A. H. K.

To Jan, whose assistance made this task possible.

C. S. G.

To Gail, Robert, and Michael, whose support was so necessary.

R. J. P.

Contents

6   Discrete Probability Distributions   135

7   Continuous Probability Distributions   169

8   Statistical Inference and Sampling   201

9 Hypothesis Testing for the Mean and Variance of a Population 241

10 Inference Procedures for Two Populations 287

11 Estimation and Testing for Population Proportions   335

12 Analysis of Variance   361

13 Applications of the Chi-Square Statistic   407

14   Simple Linear Regression   445

15   Multiple Linear Regression   495

16 Time Series Analysis and Index Numbers

17 Quantitative Business Forecasting

18 Decision Making Under Uncertainty 701

19 Nonparametric Statistics 747

Appendixes 807

Answers to Odd-Numbered Exercises

Index

Preface

When we first considered this project, we had to ask ourselves if the world was screaming for another business statistics text. What we saw was a myriad of texts that did a fine job of explaining basic statistics to business and economics students. What we didn't see was a textbook that allowed the student full use of computers and statistical computer packages. We also saw texts that were comprehensive in their coverage but often intimidating to students with their "encyclopedia of statistics" writing style.

As a result, we became excited about this project because we believed that a need does exist for a new text. Since computer power within universities is growing at an accelerating (and cheaper) rate, a text integrating statistical software is a necessity in the marketplace. In an effort to appeal to all teaching styles, we decided to design a text which could be used by instructors wanting to fully utilize computer packages, yet one which could still be an excellent text for instructors who prefer a more standard, calculator-based approach.

The text is intended to be an undergraduate or M.B.A. introduction to basic statistics. We assume that the student has a good understanding of basic algebra. Reference is made on a few occasions to calculus applications, but no calculus background is required to read the material. The reading level is interesting and easy-to-understand without sacrificing any credibility in the descriptive material. It is a non-mathematical, but not a "black box," approach to teaching the appreciation and application of statistics.

We've included a large number of illustrative examples to better guide the student to an understanding of statistical concepts and applications.

To the Instructor

This text can be used for either a one- or two-semester introduction to business statistics. Suggested material to be covered in the first semester would be chapters 1 through 8, in order, which concludes with an introduction to statistical inference (confidence intervals for the mean). Chapters 9, 10, and 11 could be included in a second-semester course, along with those remaining chapters that you feel are particularly relevant and of interest to your students.

The text has intentionally been written in somewhat of a conversational (user-friendly) style to make it less intimidating to the student. Our intent was for the student to read the text; not just use it as a source of homework exercises.

The text fully integrates three popular statistical packages: MINITAB, SAS and SPSSX. The featured package throughout all of the chapter examples is MINITAB, since these commands are simple English statements and are illustrative of computer capabilities whether or not you use the MINITAB package in your course instruction. Corresponding SAS and SPSSX descriptions are contained at the ends of chapters—a feature unique to this text. We have fully integrated these packages throughout the text, making it possible for you to include computer usage as part of your course without having to spend a great deal of time explaining the mechanics of a particular package. An introduction to each of these three packages is presented at the end of the text. For instructors who wish to avoid computer usage, the text allows for a calculator-based approach—the exercises do not require a computer package and contain reasonably sized data sets.

Other features of the text include:

* a Look Back/Introduction at the start of each chapter to tie the chapter to the relevant material from the preceding chapters. Each chapter closes with a summary section.

* an abundance of exercises (over 1100) using realistic business situations. Many chapters also include case studies containing larger data sets and requiring an in-depth discussion.

* a full treatment of the use of p-values to make statistical decisions. These are derived and discussed throughout the entire text.

* three continuous distributions (normal, uniform, and exponential), along with three discrete distributions (binomial, hypergeometric, and Poisson).

* various sampling procedures, along with corresponding sample estimators and confidence intervals, as separate sections in two of the earlier chapters. In this way, the instructor is able to cover this often-neglected material without having to spend the time to cover an entire chapter.

* separate chapters for inference regarding normal parameters (μ, σ) and inference on a binomial parameter (p). Chapters 8, 9, and 10 are strictly devoted to normal inference, both one population (8 and 9) and two populations (10). Binomial inference (one and two populations) is covered in Chapter 11.

* an entire chapter devoted to forecasting using time series data. It includes several exponential smoothing models and discusses the pros and cons of using multiple regression versus time series modeling techniques for such data.

- an entire chapter on statistical decision theory. This chapter is placed near the end of the text (Chapter 18) but can be covered at any time, including the first semester, if desired.
- a large data base (1140 observations) containing data on family income, family size, total indebtedness, monthly utility expenditures, and other variables. This is an end-of-text appendix and is available to adopters in floppy disk or magnetic tape form.
- appendixes that provide an introduction to each of the three statistical packages utilized in the text.

The following material is also available:

- an instructor's manual containing solutions to all exercises and suggested applications of the data base to material covered within each chapter.
- a test bank containing true/false questions, completion exercises, and additional application problems.
- a student study guide written to put students at ease and guide them through applications of the chapter material.

We certainly hope that this text will meet your classroom needs. If you care to offer comments and suggestions, we would like to hear from you. Address any correspondence to Al Kvanli, College of Business Administration, North Texas State University, Denton, Texas 76203.

To the Student

We believe you will find this text to be a readable, easily understood treatment of business statistics. Our intent is to carefully explain the various statistical concepts and strategies without getting bogged down in unnecessary mathematics. We have included many examples within each chapter to allow you to see how each procedure works. At the beginning of each chapter you will find a Look Back/Introduction section which will set up the chapter and tie it in with the previous chapters. At the end of each chapter is a summary containing all of the key definitions and concepts introduced within the chapter. At the end of the book you will find introductions to the three computer packages integrated into the text: MINITAB, SPSSX, and SAS.

As the old adage goes, "practice makes perfect," and mastering statistics is no exception. To this end, we have included a large number of exercises to help you along the road to perfection. Also, you will find the solutions to the odd-numbered exercises at the end of the text. A study guide, which contains additional examples along with their solutions, has also been prepared. These solutions take you by steps through the applications of the various statistical techniques with many blanks where you supply the missing number or word.

Acknowledgments

We are very grateful to the large number of people who helped us along the way. We would like to especially thank Bill Bailey, who typed the entire first draft of the text, and Cheryl McQueen, Anis Kashani and Chris Haviland, who worked on the second draft. The editorial assistance of Ray Deveaux and Charles Place was always supportive and well-directed. Special thanks to Jan Guynes, who helped with the computer supplements, and to many of the graduate students at NTSU for their valuable input.

We certainly want to thank and acknowledge the many reviewers who shared in this project. From this group we would like to single out Barbara Fox, whose in-depth review was a giant help. Also, thanks to Ron LeBlanc, who in addition provided the chapter case studies. With special appreciation, we would like to thank Wilke English, who authored an entertaining and very helpful study guide to accompany the text.

The following list contains the names and affiliations of the many reviewers whose assistance was invaluable in the preparation of this text: Wayne Albrecht, Northern Illinois University; Janet Anaya, San Jose State University; Paul Berger, Boston University; Warren Boe, University of Iowa; Bruce Bowerman, Miami University; Kenneth Cogger, University of Kansas—Lawrence; Barbara Fox; Alan Goldberg, California State University—Hayward; Mike Hanna, University of Texas—Arlington; Edgar Hickman, University of South Carolina; Philip Jeffress, University of New Orleans; Jeffrey Jerrett, University of Rhode Island; Ron LeBlanc, Idaho State University; Carol Leininger, Research Triangle, Inc.; Susan Lenker, Central Michigan University; John McGill, Merrimack College; Alan Neebe, University of North Carolina; Paul Nelson, Kansas State University; Jeffrey Reed, University of North Dakota; Susan Reiland; Walter Rom, Cleveland State University; Craig Slinkman, University of Texas—Arlington; Vasanth B. Solomon, Drake University; Donna Stroup, University of Texas—Austin; Ron Suich, California State University—Fullerton; William Terrell, Wichita State University; John Wiorkowski, University of Texas—Dallas; and Tom Witt, West Virginia University.

Introduction to Business Statistics

CHAPTER 1

A First Look at Statistics

Until recently, many people thought a statistician was someone who helped figure batting averages during a baseball game broadcast. You might wonder how we can devote an entire textbook to compiling numbers and making simple calculations. Surely it cannot be that complicated!

Statistics is the science comprising rules and procedures for collecting, describing, analyzing, and interpreting numerical data. The application of statistics is evident everywhere. Hardly a day goes by without our being bombarded by such statements as:

Results show that Crest toothpaste helps prevent tooth decay.

The latest government figures indicate an upturn in the number of housing starts.

The state court has ruled that the XYZ Company is guilty of age discrimination in its termination procedure.

Or how about:

The Surgeon General has determined that cigarette smoking is dangerous to your health.

Besides using statistics to inform the public, statisticians help businesses make forecasts for planning and decision making.

The use of statistics began as early as the first century A.D., when governments used a census of land and properties for tax purposes. Census taking was gradually extended to include such local events as births, deaths, and marriages. The *science* of statistics, which uses a sample to predict or estimate some characteristics of a population, was developed during the nineteenth century.

Use of statistical methods underwent a dramatic change as computers entered the business environment. Companies could store and manipulate large numbers of data, and once-formidable statistical calculations were reduced to a few key strokes. Sophisticated computer software allows users merely to specify the type of analysis desired and input the necessary data. This textbook will concentrate on three of these statistical packages: MINITAB (a statistical computer package originally designed by Penn State University specifically for students), SAS (Statistical Analysis System), and SPSSX (Statistical Package for the Social Sciences).

Although most statistical functions are performed by professional statisticians, you may have to draw a valid interpretation from a statistical report. Statistics can obscure the truth or give an erroneous impression. Anyone who has ever changed their plans due to a 90% chance of rainy weather only to sit home on a sunny day can attest to the fact. You often can avoid a bad decision by recognizing statistical errors and bias in the material that you review.

In addition, you may be asked to perform a statistical analysis. Although you may elect to obtain outside assistance, you will need to know when to consult a statistician and how to tell him or her what you need.

1.1

Uses of Statistics in Business

Modern businesses have more need to predict future operations than did those in the past, when businesses were smaller. Small-business managers often can solve problems simply through personal contact. Managers in large corporations, however, must try to summarize and analyze the various data available to them. They do this by using modern statistical methods.

Areas of business that rely on statistical information and techniques include:

1. *Quality control.* Statistical quality-control procedures assure high product quality and enhance productivity.
2. *Product planning.* Statistical methods are used to analyze economic factors and business trends, and to prepare detailed sales budgets, inventory-control systems, and realistic sales quotas.
3. *Forecasting.* Statistics are used in business forecasting to predict sales, productivity, and employment trends.
4. *Yearly reports.* Annual stockholder reports are based on statistical treatment of the many cost and revenue factors analyzed by the business comptroller.
5. *Personnel management.* Statistical procedures are used in such areas as age- and sex-discrimination lawsuits, performance appraisals, and workforce-size planning.
6. *Market research.* Corporations that develop and market products or services use sophisticated statistical procedures to describe and analyze consumer purchasing behavior.

1.2

Some Basic Definitions

Statistics has specialized definitions for terms crucial to statistical reasoning. In **descriptive statistics,** you collect data and describe them. If you also analyze and interpret the data, you are using **inferential statistics.**

Figure 1.1

Population versus a sample.

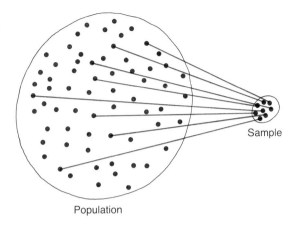

Sample

Population

Descriptive statistics are used to describe a large number of data. For example, you can reduce the set of data values to one or more single numbers, such as the average of 150 test scores, or you can construct a graph that represents some feature of the data.

You use inferential statistics to form conclusions about a large group—a population—by collecting a portion of it—a sample. Thus, a **population** is the set of people or objects that is of interest. A **sample** is the portion of the population about which information is gathered.

The analyst decides what the population is. Typically, this population is so large that it would be nearly impossible to obtain information about every item in it. Instead, we obtain information about selected population members and attempt to draw a conclusion about all members. In other words, we attempt to infer something about the population using information about only some of the members of this population. For this procedure to be valid, the sample must be typical of the entire population.

To make an early prediction of election results, analysts use a sample of certain voting precincts, as illustrated in Figure 1.1. The population is all the votes cast in the election. To make a valid statistical inference using a sample, it is crucial that the sample **represent** the population. One way to do this is to collect a sample of size n where each set of n people has the same chance of being selected for the sample. This is a **simple random sample** (Figure 1.1). It is akin to drawing names out of a hat; each name in the hat has the same chance of being pulled out. Thus, if our population is all votes cast on the night of a presidential election, a sample of votes cast in only New Jersey would not be representative. We would have no guarantee that these votes would represent the voting of the entire nation. A random sample obtained across the entire nation would better represent this population.

As another illustration, assume that Calcatron, a producer of electronic calculators, orders 50,000 components from GLC. Calcatron instructs GLC that they will accept the shipment if an outside laboratory that randomly selects 100 components from the batch finds that fewer than three are defective. Calcatron relies on inferential statistics; they infer that the population of components is of satisfactory quality if the sample is satisfactory. Note that it is possible that the sample will contain fewer than three defective components whereas the population will contain, say, 80% defective parts. Whenever we attempt to infer something about a population from a sample, there is always a chance of drawing an incorrect conclusion. The only way of being 100% sure is to sample the entire population. Such a sample is called a **census.**

1.3

Discrete and Continuous Numerical Data

Proper use of numerical data can be a great aid in making a critical decision. However, using an improper technique or "bad data" can lead you down the wrong path. Generally, the technique we use to analyze data in statistics will depend on the nature of the data. We can distinguish between two types of numerical data.

How do the following two sets of numbers differ?

3, 5, 2, 1, 4, 4, 3, 5, 5, 1, 2, 4

4.31, 11.62, 5.37, 1.55, 3.71, 6.88, 7.23, 9.52, 2.36, 7.42, 6.11, 4.85

The primary difference is that the values in the first data set consist of *counting numbers,* or *integers.* Such data are **discrete.** For example, these data may be the coded responses from 12 people who answered a particular question in a marketing survey, where: 1 = strongly agree, 2 = agree, 3 = uncertain, 4 = disagree, and 5 = strongly disagree. Note that discrete data may contain a decimal point. Nevertheless, such data have *gaps* in their possible values. For example, if you throw a single die twice and record the average of the two throws, the possible values are 1, 1.5, 2, 2.5, 3, 3.5, 4, 4.5, 5, 5.5, and 6.

Examples of discrete data that have integer values are: the number of automobiles that arrive at a drive-up window over a 5-minute period, the number of children in your family, and the total of the two numbers appearing on a throw of two dice. Note that although the first two have infinite (theoretically, at least) possible values the data are discrete. Your family cannot have 2.5 children.

Now consider the second data set in our original example. These data might represent the weight of 12 parcels received at a post office. A list of all the possible values of package weights would be long—if our scale was completely accurate, the list would be infinite and any value would be possible. Such data are **continuous:** *any value* over some particular range is possible. There are no gaps in possible continuous data values. For example, although we may say Sandra is 5.5 feet tall, we mean her height is about 5.5 feet. In fact, this value may be 5.50372 feet. Height data are continuous. Or consider the contents of a coffee cup filled by a vending machine. Will the machine release exactly 6 ounces every time? Probably not. In fact, if you were to observe the machine fill five such cups and measured (accurately) the contents, you might observe values of 6.031, 5.932, 5.871, 6.353, and 5.612 ounces. Here again, any value between, say, 5.5 oz. and 6.5 oz. is possible: these are continuous data.

1.4

Level of Measurement for Numerical Data

As well as classifying numerical data as discrete or continuous, we can also label these data as to their **level of measurement.** We will discuss them in order of strength, beginning with the weakest. **Nominal data** are really not numerical at all, but merely a label or assigned value. Examples include: sex (1 = male, 2 = female), manufacturer of automobile (1 = General Motors, 2 = Ford, 3 = Toyota), or color of eyes (1 = blue, 2 = green, 3 = brown). Assigning a **numerical code** to such data is merely a convenience so that, for example, one can store the information in a computer. However, it makes no sense to perform calculations with such numbers, such as finding their average. What would it mean to claim that, "The average eye color is 2.73"? This is a meaningless statement. Generally, we are interested in the **proportion** of such data in each category. Consider Calcatron's shipment, in which each component

Figure 1.2

Classifications of numerical data.

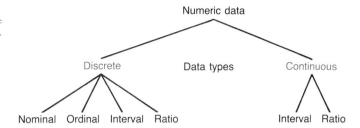

is either defective or not defective. We could assign the code: 1 = defective, 0 = not defective. The value of interest here is p, where p = proportion of defective components in the population of 50,000 components. If Calcatron believes p is too large, they will not accept the shipment. We will consider what is "too large" in Chapter 11.

Ordinal data can be arranged in order, such as worst to best or F to A (grades on an exam). A classic example of ordinal data is the results of a cross-country race, where ten people compete and 1 = the fastest (the winner), 2 = the runner-up, and so on, with 10 = the slowest. Here, the *order* of the values is important (3 finished before 4) but the *difference* of the values is not. For example, 2 − 1 = 1 and 10 − 9 = 1, but this does *not* imply that 1 and 2 were just as close in the final results as were 9 and 10.

The difference between values of **interval data** *does* have meaning. It is meaningful to add and average such data. The classic example is *temperature,* where it *is* true that the difference in heat between 60°F and 61°F is the same as that between 80°F and 81°F. Many of the techniques used to analyze data in statistics require data that are at least of this strength.

Ratio data differ from interval data in that there is a definite *zero point.* To decide if your data are interval or ratio, ask yourself whether twice the value is twice the strength. For example, is 100°F twice as hot as 50°F? The answer is no, so these data are interval. Is a 4-acre field twice as large as a 2-acre field? The answer is yes, so these are ratio data. Here the zero point is a field of zero acres. Typically, data consisting of areas, volumes, and weights are ratio data.

The techniques used in statistics generally do not distinguish between interval and ratio data. A summary of the various data classifications is shown in Figure 1.2. Notice that discrete data can have any of the four levels of measurement, whereas continuous data must be interval or ratio.

Summary

The science of statistics comprises a set of rules and procedures used to describe numerical data or to make decisions using these data. **Descriptive statistics** is concerned with only collecting and describing data. **Inferential statistics** is used when conclusions about a **population** are drawn on the basis of data about a representative **sample.** Most statistical methods assume that a simple random sample has been collected. A sample that contains the entire population is a **census.**

Numeric data are either discrete or continuous. **Discrete data** have limited, specific possible values. **Continuous data** can assume any value over some range. A further classification of data is their level of measurement. At the lowest level, **nominal data** are categorical data that are assigned numeric codes. **Ordinal data** are ranked—the order of the data values is meaningful. In **interval data,** both the order of the data and the difference between any two data values have meaning. Finally,

ratio data have all the properties of interval data and also contain a definite zero point. Most statistical techniques do not distinguish between interval and ratio data, but do require the data to have at least an interval level of measurement.

Review Exercises

1.1 A city planner is interested in the amount of money spent by the average tourist visiting the city. The city planner collects data from 100 randomly selected tourists. Explain what the sample is and what the population of interest is.

1.2 The manager of Easy Fly Airlines took a sample of 200 people who regularly fly on Easy Fly Airlines and collected information on the salaries of these people. The manager then graphed the data to get an idea of the distribution of the incomes. After studying the graph, the manager concluded that most Easy Fly Airlines customers are in the middle income bracket.

a. Explain how the manager used descriptive statistics.

b. Did the manager use inferential statistics?

1.3 Explain whether the following groups of people or objects would represent a population or a sample.

a. A list of 500 employees of General Motors.

b. Forty students who were randomly stopped and questioned on a university campus.

c. A marketing questionnaire mailed to 200 people selected randomly from the telephone book.

d. The list of all possible ways of choosing two cards from a deck of 52 cards.

1.4 Explain whether the following data are continuous or discrete.

a. The income of 20 executives.

b. The number of long distance calls made each month.

c. The length of time for each long distance call for a particular month.

d. The number of defective items in a manufacturing process.

1.5 Explain why inferential statistics is not needed if data are collected by taking a census.

1.6 What is the lowest level of measurement for a set of data that would permit the valid calculation of a proportion?

1.7 Your student record contains information about your age, sex, race, current grade point average, and current classification (freshman, sophomore, . . .). State whether each of these data is nominal, ordinal, interval or ratio.

1.8 Do you think nominal data would usually be continuous data or discrete data?

1.9 Give an example of ordinal data that would not be interval data.

1.10 What is the highest level of measurement for each of the following data sets?

a. The chain of command for officers in the army

b. The closing prices of the stocks in the Dow Jones Industrial Index

c. The temperatures in degrees Fahrenheit of several classrooms

d. The social security numbers of 12 randomly selected people

e. A listing of the college graduates and noncollege graduates of a company

2

Descriptive Graphs

A Look Back/Introduction

Chapter 1 introduced you to some of the basic terms used in statistics. One of the key concepts was the idea of acquiring data using a sample from a population. It was also emphasized that the proper use of statistics depends on the nature of the data involved. Are the data discrete or continuous? Are the values nominal, ordinal, interval, or ratio?

Once the data have been gathered, the problem becomes learning whatever we can from them. One method is to describe the data by means of a graph. A graph allows us to discuss intelligently the shape of the data.

Everyone has heard the expression that a picture is worth a thousand words or, more appropriately here, a thousand numbers. This is especially true in statistics, where it may be vital to reduce a large set of numbers to a graph (or picture) that illustrates the structure underlying your data. For example, in a business meeting a quick glance at a graph demonstrates a point much more easily than does a page filled with numbers and words.

To see why you may want to describe a data set by using a descriptive graph, assume the television department of Q-Mart sells color and black-and-white televisions and home videocassette recorders (VCRs). They decide to take a sample of 50 of their customers over a three-month period. For each sale, they record: (1) what the customer purchased, (2) the purchase price, and (3) the number of channels that each customer receives on his or her home set. The results are shown in Table 2.1.

Table 2.1

Data from Q-Mart survey

Item	No. of Sales	Purchase Price/No. of Channels						
Color TV	30	460.04	538.13	477.18	475.96	715.93	436.68	643.55
		3	9	6	12	5	8	9
		495.57	515.62	712.26	463.36	676.84	620.24	561.63
		18	6	15	10	8	12	4
		375.94	516.82	434.27	397.95	481.45	517.79	520.24
		16	10	5	13	8	7	12
		488.37	840.57	624.63	419.19	782.57	485.15	812.36
		8	11	20	15	6	9	8
		583.82	388.70					
		5	11					
Black and White TV	6	345.88	255.46	295.77	318.91	362.81	405.16	
		7	14	5	10	4	8	
VCR	14	478.03	715.71	450.36	488.34	582.36	657.41	684.71
		9	4	17	8	11	6	19
		631.78	521.48	515.61	540.44	528.57	564.16	745.28
		10	6	9	4	8	13	3

How can you summarize and present these data in a form that is easily understood? There are many graphical methods to do just that, depending on the nature of the data and what you are trying to demonstrate about them. When presenting data graphically, the first step usually is to combine the data values into a frequency distribution.

2.1

Frequency Distributions

We need to reduce a large set of data to a much smaller set of numbers that can be more easily comprehended. Assume you have recorded the population sizes of 500 randomly selected cities. There is no easy way to examine these 500 numbers visually and learn anything. It would be easier to examine a condensed version of this set of data, such as that presented in Table 2.2.

This type of summary, called a **frequency distribution,** consists of *classes* (such as "10,000 and under 15,000") and *frequencies* (the number of data values within each

Table 2.2

Frequency distribution of the populations of 500 cities

Class Number	Size of City	Frequency
1	Under 10,000	4
2	10,000 and under 15,000	51
3	15,000 and under 20,000	77
4	20,000 and under 25,000	105
5	25,000 and under 30,000	84
6	30,000 and under 35,000	60
7	35,000 and under 40,000	45
8	40,000 and under 45,000	38
9	45,000 and under 50,000	31
10	50,000 and over	5
		500

class). What do you gain using this procedure? You reduce 500 numbers to ten—the class frequencies. You can study the frequency distribution in Table 2.2 and learn a great deal about the shape of this data set. For example, approximately 50% of the cities in your sample have a population between 20,000 and 35,000. Also, only 1% of the cities contain 50,000 people or more.

Frequency Distribution for Continuous Data

A frequency distribution is typically condensed from data having an interval or ratio level of measurement. When you construct a frequency distribution for continuous data, you need to decide (1) how many classes to use (ten in Table 2.2) and (2) the class width (5,000 in Table 2.2).

There is no "correct" **number of classes (K)** to use in a frequency distribution. However, you can best condense a set of data using between 5 and 15 classes. The usual procedure is to choose what you think would be an adequate number of classes and to construct the resulting frequency distribution. A quick look at the resulting distribution will tell you if you have reduced the data too much (K is too small) or not enough (K is too large). If you have a very large set of data, you can use a larger number of classes than you would for smaller data sets. Whenever you construct frequency distributions using a computer, select several different values of K and look at the effects of the different choices.

Having chosen a value for K, the next step is to examine

$$\frac{\text{range}}{\text{number of classes}} = \frac{H - L}{K}$$

where H = the highest value in your data, L = the lowest value in your data, and K = the number of classes. Round the result to a clean number. This is the **class width (CW)**. The width of each class should be the same for each class. One exception to this rule is open-ended classes, which we will discuss later.

Assume that, for a particular set of data, you have elected to use $K = 10$ classes in your frequency distribution. Also, $H = 106$ and $L = 10$, and so

$$\frac{H - L}{K} = \frac{106 - 10}{10} = 9.6$$

So $CW = 10$.

Now let us use the 50 purchase prices in Table 2.1 to construct a frequency distribution of the purchase prices, using six classes. Your first step should be to arrange the data from smallest to largest. This is called an **ordered array.** The original (unordered) data are the **raw data.** The ordered purchase prices are listed in Table 2.3. Using the ordered data, $H = 840.57$ and $L = 255.46$. Since $K = 6$, you compute CW:

$$\frac{840.57 - 255.46}{6} = 97.5$$

The best choice here is $CW = 100$.

There are two rules to remember in selecting the first class: this class must contain

L, your lowest data value, and it should begin with a clean number. Because $L =$

Table 2.3

50 purchase prices from Q-Mart survey arranged as an ordered array

Raw Data					Ordered Data				
460.04	463.36	520.24	345.88	582.36	255.46	434.27	488.34	538.13	657.41
538.13	676.84	488.37	255.46	657.41	295.77	436.68	488.37	540.44	676.84
477.18	620.24	840.57	295.77	684.71	318.91	450.36	495.57	561.63	684.71
475.96	561.63	624.63	318.91	631.78	345.88	460.04	515.61	564.16	712.26
715.93	375.94	419.19	362.81	521.48	362.81	463.36	515.62	582.36	715.71
436.68	516.82	782.57	405.16	515.61	375.94	475.96	516.82	583.82	715.93
643.55	434.27	485.15	478.03	540.44	388.70	477.18	517.79	620.24	745.28
495.57	397.95	812.36	715.71	528.57	397.95	478.03	520.24	624.63	782.57
515.62	481.45	583.82	450.36	564.16	405.16	481.45	521.48	631.78	812.36
712.26	517.79	388.70	488.34	745.28	419.19	485.15	528.57	643.55	840.57

Table 2.4

Frequency distribution of purchase prices using six classes

Class Number	Class	Frequency
1	250 and under 350	4
2	350 and under 450	8
3	450 and under 550	20
4	550 and under 650	8
5	650 and under 750	7
6	750 and under 850	3
		50

Table 2.5

Frequency distribution of purchase prices using ten classes

Class Number	Class	Frequency	Relative Frequency
1	250 and under 310	2	.04
2	310 and under 370	3	.06
3	370 and under 430	5	.10
4	430 and under 490	12	.24
5	490 and under 550	10	.20
6	550 and under 610	4	.08
7	610 and under 670	5	.10
8	670 and under 730	5	.10
9	730 and under 790	2	.04
10	790 and under 850	2	.04
		50	

255.46, this class should begin with either 200 or 250—we will use 250. The resulting frequency distribution is shown in Table 2.4.

Perhaps you think that six classes is not enough; that is, you have condensed this set of data too much. One indication of this would be that a large portion of your data (say, nearly 50%) lies in one class. Table 2.5 summarizes this set of data using $K = 10$ classes. Here, the class width chosen is $CW = 60$ because

$$\frac{H - L}{10} = \frac{840.57 - 255.46}{10} = 58.5$$

As before, the first class begins at 250.

This table also contains each **relative frequency,** where

$$\text{relative frequency} = \frac{\text{frequency}}{\text{total number of values in data set}}$$

So, for example, in class 2, the relative frequency is .06; this class contains 3 out of the 50 values. The advantage of using relative frequencies is that the reader can tell immediately what percentage of the data values lie in each class.

Comments

Another alternative would be to use $CW = 50$ because an increment of 50 produces classes easier to comprehend. This would produce 12 classes, as shown in Table 2.6. We could argue that 12 are too many classes, considering that the data set has only 50 values. Many classes contain only one or two data values.

The highest and lowest values in a class are the **class limits.** For example, in Table 2.4, the lower class limit of class 2 is 350, whereas the upper class limit is 450. The **class midpoints** are those values in the center of the class. Each midpoint in a sense "represents" its class. These values often are used in a statistical graph as well as for calculations performed on the information contained within a frequency distribution. The midpoint of class 2 in Table 2.4 is $(350 + 450)/2 = 400$.

Often, a set of data will contain one or two very small or very large numbers quite unlike the remaining data values. Such values are called **outliers.** It is generally better to include these values in one or two **open-ended classes.** The distribution in Table 2.2 contains two open-ended classes: class 1 (under 10,000) and class 10 (50,000 and over). You may need an open-ended class if your data set includes one or more outliers or your present frequency distribution has too many empty classes on the low or high end.

Constructing a Frequency Distribution

1. Gather the sample data.
2. Arrange the data in an ordered array.
3. Select the number of classes to be used.
4. Determine the class width (use a clean number).
5. Determine the class limits for each class by first selecting clean numbers for the first class.
6. Count the number of data values in each class (the class frequencies).
7. Summarize the class frequencies in a frequency distribution table.

Frequency Distribution for Discrete Data

When your data are discrete, the procedure is almost the same as when they are continuous, except: (1) we define CW to be the difference between the lower class limits and not the difference between an upper and lower limit (this will also work for continuous data) and (2) the description of each class is slightly different because we no longer use the "and under" definition of each class. Thus, if $CW = 5$ and *the data are continuous,* our classes might be: 5 and under 10, 10 and under 15, and 15 and under 20. *If the data are discrete,* they might be 5 to 9, 10 to 14, and 15 to 19. Note that, for the continuous data, the class midpoints are 7.5, 12.5, and 17.5. For the discrete data, however, the midpoints are 7, 12, and 17.

Table 2.6

Frequency distribution of purchase prices using $CW = 50$

Class Number	Class	Frequency
1	250 and under 300	2
2	300 and under 350	2
3	350 and under 400	4
4	400 and under 450	4
5	450 and under 500	11
6	500 and under 550	9
7	550 and under 600	4
8	600 and under 650	4
9	650 and under 700	3
10	700 and under 750	4
11	750 and under 800	1
12	800 and under 850	2
		50

Table 2.7

Frequency distribution of the number of channels received

Class Number	Class	Frequency	Relative Frequency
1	3–5	10	.20
2	6–8	15	.30
3	9–11	12	.24
4	12–14	6	.12
5	15–17	4	.08
6	18–20	3	.06
		50	1.0

Using the data in Table 2.1, we can construct a frequency distribution using six classes for the number of channels each customer receives on his or her television set. First we develop an ordered array:

3, 3, 4, 4, 4, 4, 5, 5, 5, 5, 6, 6, 6, 6, 6, 7, 7, 8, 8, 8, 8, 8, 8, 8, 8, 8, 9, 9, 9, 9, 9, 10, 10, 10, 10, 11, 11, 11, 12, 12, 12, 13, 13, 14, 15, 15, 16, 17, 18, 19, 20

So, $H = 20$ and $L = 3$. Since

$$\frac{H - L}{K} = \frac{20 - 3}{6} = 2.83$$

we use $CW = 3$. The resulting frequency and relative frequency distribution is shown in Table 2.7.

Exercises

2.1 The following are the scores of the students of a junior college on a statistics exam:

69, 47, 82, 73, 99, 97, 55, 18, 100, 85, 77, 80, 94, 79, 66, 81, 81, 88, 94, 70, 62, 58, 43, 21, 85, 68, 50, 43, 91, 85, 60, 45, 88, 95, 46, 59, 75, 80, 74, 71, 70

a. Convert the raw data into an ordered array.

b. If you have to transform the data into a frequency distribution, what value of K would you use? (K = the number of classes).

c. Calculate the class width for the frequency distribution.

d. Present the data in the form of a frequency distribution.

e. What is the difference between cumulative relative and relative frequencies?

f. Calculate the relative frequencies and the cumulative relative frequencies of the scores of the junior college students.

g. What sorts of statements do the cumulative relative frequencies allow you to make about the exam scores?

2.2 The number of hours per day that the secretary of an accounting firm spends on the telephone is recorded. The following data are the number of hours per day over a 30-day period.

5.21, 2.12, 1.33, 7.10, 4.30, 4.20, 5.20, 2.50, 4.10, 1.50, 3.22, 3.51, 2.45, 2.54, 1.80, 1.70, 1.80, 7.10, 3.20, 2.50, 4.11, 6.20, 6.79, 1.67, 3.30, 2.90, 7.20, 5.00, 2.80, 3.90

a. Are these data discrete or continuous?

b. Construct a frequency and a relative frequency distribution.

c. What are the class midpoints?

2.3 A survey was conducted to find out how long homemakers spend food shopping each week. One-hundred homemakers were selected randomly by a telephone survey and asked to state the amount of time that they spent food shopping during the past week. The results were:

Hours Shopping	Frequency
0 and under 2	38
2 and under 4	31
4 and under 6	21
6 and under 8	6
8 and under 10	3
10 and over	1

a. Construct a relative frequency distribution.

b. What are the class limits?

c. What are the class midpoints?

d. Before the survey, the researchers believed that most homemakers spent no more than 2 hours per week food shopping. Do the data for these 100 homemakers support that opinion?

2.4 A retail store charges its customers 15% of the value of a check on any check that bounces. In 1 week, 30 checks bounced and the following fees were collected (in dollars):

1.02, .50, 6.00, 7.21, 2.34, 2.51, 10.91, 5.95, 2.59, 4.31, 6.31, 8.30, 1.03, 8.62, 9.71, 5.21, 25.91, 10.91, 7.30, 12.51, 8.51, 6.51, 7.31, 1.19, 11.60, 12.51, 2.24, 5.41, 7.20, 8.51

a. Construct a frequency distribution using class intervals of $0 and under $2, $2 and under $4, and so on.

b. Can the value of $25.91 be considered to be an outlier?

2.5 Harberts Wholesale Plumbing Supply receives special orders for parts not in stock at local retail stores. The following data are the number of special orders received per day over a 30-day period.

2, 4, 10, 1, 12, 15, 5, 6, 9, 18, 14, 13, 19, 22, 18, 6, 4, 10, 20, 7, 15, 10, 6, 2, 7, 17, 23, 11, 16, 4

a. Are the data discrete or continuous?

b. Construct a relative frequency distribution.

2.6 Comment on the "correct" number of classes to be used in a frequency distribution.

2.7 The following are the unemployment rates (percent of available labor) for the year 1984 for selected northern cities in the United States:

6.8, 2.6, 4.6, 5.4, 6.8, 4.3, 17.1, 6.7, 6.2, 6.4, 4.7, 5.1, 2.7, 16.8, 3.4, 2.2, 4.1, 9.8, 10.4, 11.5

a. Calculate the class width for a frequency distribution for the data.

b. What do you hope to achieve by tabulating the data in the form of a frequency distribution?

c. Prepare a frequency distribution table.

2.2

Histograms

After you complete a frequency distribution, your next step will be to construct a "picture" of these data values using a histogram. A **histogram** is a graphical representation of a frequency distribution. It describes the shape of the data. You can use it to answer quickly such questions as "Are the data symmetric?" and "Where do most of the data values lie?" For the frequency distribution in Table 2.4, the corresponding histogram is illustrated in Figure 2.1. The height of each box represents the frequency of that particular class. The edges of each box represent the class limits.

In a histogram of continuous data, the boxes must be adjoining (no gaps). For discrete data (such as that in Table 2.7), there will be a gap between each of the boxes. For example, a histogram of Table 2.7 will contain a box between 3 and 5 (with a height of 10), the next box between 6 and 8 (height of 15), and so forth.

Avoid constructing a "squashed" histogram by using the vertical axis wisely. The top of this axis (21 in Figure 2.1) should be a value close to your largest class frequency (20). Notice also that, for this example, you obtain a more concise picture by starting the horizontal axis at 250 rather than at zero.

A histogram can be constructed using the relative frequencies rather than the frequencies. A **relative frequency histogram** of the data in Table 2.4 is shown in Figure 2.2. Notice that the shape of a frequency histogram (Figure 2.1) and a relative frequency histogram (Figure 2.2) are the same. One advantage of using a relative frequency histogram is that the units on the vertical axis are always between zero and one, so the reader can tell at a glance what percentage of the data lies in each class.

Most standard statistical software packages will construct a histogram from your data. Using MINITAB, you can specify CW and the starting class midpoint, or you can let MINITAB select these values. Your output will contain the frequency distri-

Figure 2.1

Frequency histogram for the frequency distribution shown in Table 2.4.

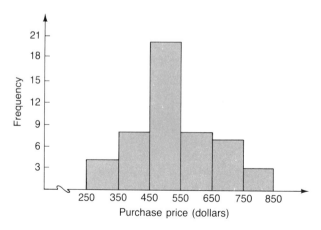

Figure 2.2

Relative frequency histogram of the frequency distribution in Table 2.4.

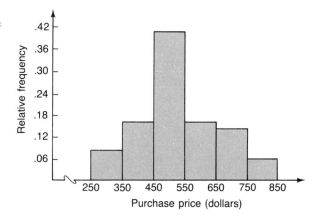

bution as well as a graphical representation in the form of a histogram (without the boxes). MINITAB will provide each class frequency next to the corresponding class midpoint (not class limits). Figure 2.3 contains the necessary MINITAB statements and the resulting output, where CW and the midpoint of the first class were not specified. Figure 2.4 specified $CW = 100$ and the first midpoint to be 300. One can use the output as it appears or use this information to construct Figure 2.1.

Figure 2.3

Histogram using MINITAB, where CW and the first class midpoint are not specified.

```
MTB > SET INTO C1
DATA> 460.04 538.13 477.18 475.96 715.93 436.68 643.55 495.57 515.62 712.26
                                     ⋮
DATA> 582.36 657.41 684.71 631.78 521.48 515.61 540.44 528.57 564.16 745.28
DATA> END
MTB > PRINT C1
C1
   460.04    538.13    477.18    475.96    715.93    436.68    643.55    495.57
   515.62    712.26    463.36    676.84    620.24    561.63    375.94    516.82
   434.27    397.95    481.45    517.79    520.24    488.37    840.57    624.63
   419.19    782.57    485.15    812.36    583.82    388.70    345.88    255.46
   295.77    318.91    362.81    405.16    478.03    715.71    450.36    488.34
   582.36    657.41    684.71    631.78    521.48    515.61    540.44    528.57
   564.16    745.28

MTB > HISTOGRAM OF C1

Histogram of C1   N = 50

Midpoint    Count
    250         1    *
    300         2    **
    350         2    **
    400         5    *****
    450         5    *****
    500        14    **************
    550         5    *****
    600         4    ****
    650         3    ***
    700         5    *****
    750         1    *
    800         2    **
    850         1    *
```

Figure 2.4

MINITAB histogram using specified classes. $CW = 100$, and the first midpoint is 300.

```
MTB > HISTOGRAM OF C1,FIRST MIDPOINT AT 300,CLASS WIDTH IS 100

Histogram of C1   N = 50

Midpoint    Count
    300         4    ****
    400         8    ********
    500        20    ********************
    600         8    ********
    700         7    *******
    800         3    ***
```

2.3

Frequency Polygons

Although a histogram does demonstrate the shape of the data, perhaps a clearer method of illustrating this is to use a **frequency polygon.** Here, you merely connect the centers of the histogram boxes (located at the class midpoints) with a series of straight lines. The resulting multisided figure is a frequency polygon. Figure 2.5 is an example; once again, the data in Table 2.4 were used.

Comments

The polygon can also be constructed from the relative frequency histogram. The shape will not change, but the units on the vertical axis will now represent relative frequencies.

Figure 2.5

Frequency polygon using the frequency distribution in Table 2.4.

Figure 2.6

Frequency histogram using footnotes to handle open-ended classes. The data are from Table 2.2.

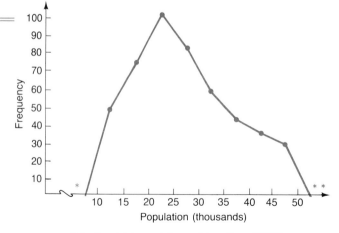

 * 4 cities had populations of less than 10,000.
 * * 5 cities had populations of 50,000 or greater.

Figure 2.7

Frequency polygon
showing annual salaries
for Texcom Electronics
management personnel.

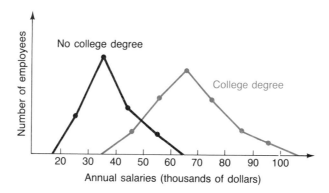

The polygon must begin and end at zero frequency (as in Figure 2.5). To accomplish this, imagine a class at each end of the corresponding histogram that is empty (contains no data values). Begin and end the polygon with the class midpoints of these imaginary classes. Thus, your vertical axis *must* begin at zero. This need not be true for the horizontal axis.

How do you handle an open-ended class? The easiest way is to construct a frequency polygon of the closed classes and place a footnote at each open-ended class location indicating the frequency of that particular class. Figure 2.6 demonstrates this, using the data from Table 2.2.

Frequency polygons are usually better than histograms for comparing the shape of two (or more) different frequency distributions. For example, Figure 2.7 demonstrates at a glance that salaries are higher (for the most part) for management personnel at Texcom Electronics who have a college degree.

Both histograms and frequency polygons represent the actual number of data values in each class. Assume that your annual salary is one of the values contained in a sample of 250 salaries. One question of interest might be, "What fraction of the people in the sample have a salary *less than* mine?" Such information can be displayed using a statistical graph called an ogive.

2.4

Cumulative Frequencies (Ogives)

Another method of examining a frequency distribution is to list the number of observations (data values) that are *less than* each of the class limits rather than how many are *in* each of the classes. You are then determining **cumulative frequencies.** Take another look at the frequency distribution in Table 2.4. Table 2.8 shows the cumulative frequencies. Notice that you can determine cumulative frequencies (column 2) or cumulative relative frequencies (column 4). The results in Table 2.8 can be summarized more easily in a simple graph called an **ogive** (pronounced oh'-jive). The ogive is useful whenever you want to determine what percentage of your data lie *below* a certain value. Figure 2.8 is constructed by noting that

$$4 \text{ values } (4/50 \ = .08) \text{ are less than } 350$$
$$4 + 8 = 12 \text{ values } (12/50 = .24) \text{ are less than } 450$$
$$12 + 20 = 32 \text{ values } (32/50 = .64) \text{ are less than } 550, \text{ and so on.}$$

Table 2.8

Purchase prices from
Table 2.3 with cumulative
frequencies analyzed

Class Number	Class	Frequency	Cumulative Frequency	Relative Frequency	Cumulative Relative Frequency
1	250 and under 350	4	4	.08	.08
2	350 and under 450	8	12	.16	.24
3	450 and under 550	20	32	.40	.64
4	550 and under 650	8	40	.16	.80
5	650 and under 750	7	47	.14	.94
6	750 and under 850	3	50	.06	1.00
		50		1.0	

Figure 2.8

Ogive for cumulative rel-
ative frequencies using
data from Table 2.8.

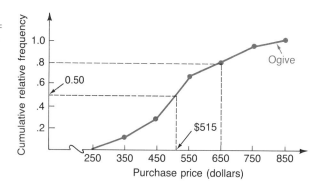

The ogive allows you to make such statements as "Eighty percent of the purchase prices were less than \$650" and "Fifty percent of the purchase prices were
under \$515."

You always begin at the lower limit of the first class (250 here). The cumulative
relative frequency at that point is always zero because the number of data values less
than this number is zero. You always end at the upper limit of the last class (850 here).
The cumulative relative frequency here is always one because all the data values are
less than this upper limit. This ogive value would be n = the number of data values
($n = 50$ here) if you are constructing a frequency ogive rather than a relative frequency
ogive. However, the shape of the ogive is the same for both procedures.

The ogives discussed here are *less than* ogives. Such an ogive always goes up or
is flat but never decreases. For example, the number of data values less than 450 must
be at least as large as the number of values less than 350. A *greater than* ogive plots
the percentage of data values greater than each class limit. Such an ogive always
decreases or remains flat if a particular class is empty.

Exercises

2.8 The following were the daily maximum temperatures in Dallas, Texas for the month of
June (in degrees Fahrenheit):

84, 84, 94, 97, 97, 89, 90, 95, 99, 94, 88, 91, 90, 97, 93, 91, 88, 89, 102, 100, 88, 85,
88, 106, 102, 86, 93, 90, 105, 99

a. Convert the data into an ordered array.

b. Present the data in the form of a frequency distribution.

c. Calculate the relative frequencies and the cumulative relative frequencies.

2.9 Construct a histogram for the data in exercise 2.2.

2.10 Draw a frequency polygon from the data in exercise 2.3.

2.11 Construct the cumulative frequency distribution for the data in exercise 2.4. Draw the ogive.

2.12 Does the shape of an ogive change if the cumulative relative frequencies are used instead of the cumulative frequencies?

2.13 The following is the distribution for a certain town of the population between age 5 and 39 for the year 1983:

Age	Number
5–9	30,116
10–14	14,633
15–19	29,424
20–24	40,146
25–29	29,424
30–34	44,555
35–39	40,100

a. Construct a histogram.

b. What does the shape of the histogram indicate?

c. If a histogram was constructed from the relative frequency distribution, would the shape of the histogram change? Try it, if you are not sure.

2.14 Draw a histogram that indicates the scores of the students on a statistics exam, given in exercise 2.1.

2.15 The price:earnings (P:E) ratio is important for investors. The following is a list of P:E ratios for some of the major U.S. corporations in the year 1985:*

Company	P:E Ratio
Burroughs Corp.	11
Gulf & Western	12
Borden	10
Anheuser-Busch Inc.	11
AT&T	17
International Paper	34
Texas Instruments	8
McGraw-Hill	16
General Instruments	18
Polaroid	36
Pennzoil	22
JC Penney	8
Phillips Petroleum	8
Control Data	35
Merrill Lynch	29
Uniroyal	14
Texaco	36
Coca-Cola	15
Walmart	24
IBM	12

*Source: *The Wall Street Journal*, 16 April 1985.

a. Construct a frequency distribution.

b. Construct a histogram for the P:E ratios.

2.16 For the data in exercise 2.15, draw a relative frequency histogram showing the distribution of the P:E ratios. Also, draw a frequency polygon using the relative frequencies.

2.17 For the unemployment rate data given in exercise 2.7:

a. Construct a histogram.

b. Draw an ogive.

2.18 A county library's records show the following information regarding the number of patrons who used the library during the past 30 days.

100, 87, 44, 53, 17, 34, 88, 67, 31, 40, 98, 77, 55, 41, 73, 62, 88, 28, 70, 51, 82, 44, 32, 50, 33, 49, 59, 67, 79, 84

a. Construct a cumulative frequency distribution.

b. Convert the cumulative frequency distribution in question a into an ogive graph.

c. The number of patrons attending the library was less than or equal to what value, 80% of the time?

2.19 The following is a frequency distribution of the number of daily automobile accidents reported for a month in Newark, New Jersey.

Accidents per Day	Frequency
0–3	12
4–7	10
8–11	7
12–15	1
16–19	1

a. Construct a cumulative relative frequency distribution for the data.

b. What percentage of the time do eight or more daily accidents occur?

2.20 The profitability index is widely used by big corporations in making capital investment decisions. It is defined as the ratio of the present value of a project to its cost and should be at least equal to one. The following is a schedule of profitability indices developed by J. Conway, financial analyst of Control Systems:

Profitability Index	Project Name
1.70	A
.41	B
2.44	C
2.98	D
4.00	E
1.01	F
5.13	G
2.96	H
3.50	I
1.41	J
2.20	K
5.98	L
6.90	M
1.78	N
6.00	O

a. Construct a cumulative relative frequency distribution of the profitability indices.

b. Construct a frequency histogram.

c. Are Control System's projects uniformly profitable? What can you say about them at the next capital investment committee meeting?

2.21 Price elasticity of electricity measures the responsiveness of consumers to changes in the price of electricity. It can be expressed as the percentage change in quantity demanded (of electricity) over percentage change in the price (of electricity). Because it is always a negative number, it is expressed only in absolute value. The following are the price elasticities (of electricity) for various utility companies in the country:

.40, .71, .33, .08, .14, .24, .38, .27, .44, .35, .22, .05, .39, .18, .22, .70, .52, .31, .21, .36, .15, .38, .41, .23, .55, .61, .52, .35, .48, .62

a. Construct a frequency polygon.

b. Construct an ogive curve for the data.

2.22 An econometric model is a statistical model that predicts an econometric measure such as gross national product (GNP), unemployment rate, or inflation rate for a specific time span. The effectiveness of an econometric model is judged by the percentage of wrong predictions made when using the model to forecast. The following is a frequency distribution for a list of 25 econometric models and the percentage of errors (wrong predictions) created by them:

Percentage of Wrong Predictions	Number of Models
1–5	7
6–10	10
11–15	4
16–20	2
21–25	1
≥ 26	1
	25

Construct a frequency polygon using this information.

2.23 The following are the test scores of freshmen on the first exam in an economics course at a local university:

62, 67, 74, 48, 100, 93, 49, 57, 77, 63, 82, 10, 78, 88, 99, 44, 51, 80, 71, 39, 58, 76, 89, 94, 70, 41, 66, 82, 18, 73

a. Construct a relative frequency histogram.

b. Draw an ogive curve.

c. How do you interpret the distribution of the test scores?

2.24 David Bannerman, the president of Bannerman Automobile Manufacturing, has gathered the following data concerning the company's new sports car, the Chariot. The data show the numbers of cars (in hundreds) sold by the 22 top dealers during the past year. Transform the data into an appropriate graph to help David make management decisions in areas such as advertising expenditure and plant expansion. How would you describe the distribution of the data in your report to David Bannerman?

Cars Sold	Dealers
1 and under 5	4
5 and under 10	8
10 and under 15	2
15 and under 20	2
20 and under 25	3
25 and under 30	2
30 and under 35	1

2.25 Metro Power manufactures a high-powered copper coil to be used in giant power transformers. Tensile strength (given in thousands of pounds per square inch) is of critical importance in the manufacture of the copper coil. The following data are from a sample of copper coils tested for tensile strength:

Coil Tensile Strength	Coil Tensile Strength
5	18
8	21
12	24
10	7
15	26
7	11
18	15
10	9
6	22
4	10

a. Construct an ogive.

b. Find an appropriate value, X, in units of pounds per square inch such that more than one-half of the coils sampled have tensile strengths greater than X.

2.26 The following list summarizes the number and value of stocks (in dollars) that make up the investment portfolio of a mutual fund corporation:

Value of Stocks	Number of Stocks
10000–14999	7
15000–19999	4
20000–24999	13
25000–29999	6
30000–34999	10

a. Draw a histogram.

b. Construct an ogive.

2.27 Return on sales is a popular measure of corporate performance. It is expressed as a percentage and is equal to (net income/sales) · 100. The following are the returns on sales for 15 U.S. corporations for the year 1980:*

Company	Return on Sales
Exxon	5.5
Texaco	5.2
Gulf Oil	5.3
IBM	13.6
Rockwell International	4.1
LTV	1.6
Ashland Oil	2.5
Marathon Oil	4.6
Aluminum Company of America	9.1
Kaiser Steel	20.9
Westinghouse Electric	4.7
Monsanto	2.3
Standard Oil (OH)	16.4
Occidental Petroleum	5.7
Western Electric	5.8

a. Construct a histogram.

*Source: Fortune 500 Listings, *Fortune*, 4 May 1981, p. 325.

b. Construct a frequency polygon.

c. Construct an ogive.

d. What is a "typical" return on sales?

e. Are there companies with exceptionally high returns? What can you say about them?

2.5

Bar Charts

Histograms, frequency polygons, and ogives are used for data having an interval or ratio level of measurement. For data having an ordinal level, we use a bar chart. A bar chart is similar to a histogram, except that the horizontal axis represents data that are **nominal** (such as eye color, sex, or national origin). Such a graph is most helpful when you have many categories to represent.

Consider the data in Table 2.1. If you are interested in the number of sales for each of the three products (color televisions, black-and-white televisions, and VCRs), a bar chart will do a good job of summarizing this information (Figure 2.9). Notice that a gap is inserted between each of the boxes in a bar chart. The data here are nominal, so the length of this gap is arbitrary.

Figure 2.10 is an example of a bar chart in which the boxes are constructed horizontally rather than vertically. This enables you to label each category *within* the box.

Figure 2.9

Bar chart for number of sales of each of three items. Data from Table 2.1.

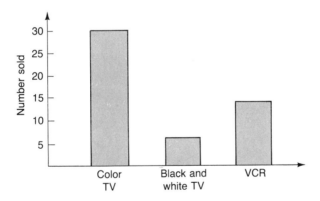

Figure 2.10

Bar chart drawn horizontally, which makes it easy to place labels within the boxes.

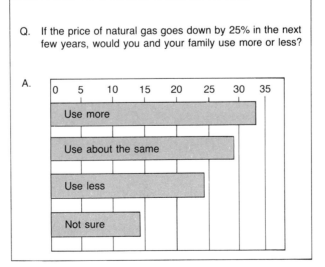

Figure 2.11

Pie chart of number of sales using data from Table 2.1.

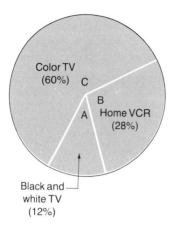

2.6
Pie Charts

A **pie chart** is used to split a particular quantity into its component pieces, typically at some specified point in time or over a specified time span. It is a convenient way of representing percentages or relative frequencies rather than frequencies. Figure 2.11 shows a pie chart of the 50 sales in Table 2.1. To construct a pie chart, draw a line from the center of the circle to the outer edge. Then construct the various pieces of the pie chart by drawing the corresponding angles. For example, the black-and-white televisions represent 12% of the total number of sales (6 out of 50). So angle A in Figure 2.11 is 12% of 360° or 43.2°. Angle B is 28% of 360°, or 100.8°, and angle C is 60% of 360°, or 216°.

Exercises

2.28 Consumers spend their incomes on a vast array of goods and services. The following figures provide a quick summary of how the average consumer dollar is spent:

Category	Percent of Income
Medical care	5
Clothing	5
Entertainment	4
Housing	46
Food	17
Transportation	19
Others	4
	100

a. Summarize the information in the form of a pie chart.

b. What area represents the largest piece of the pie? Is it very much larger than the next piece? How much?

2.29 Millions of business firms supply goods and services to us. Usually they are organized as proprietorships, partnerships, or giant corporations. In 1981, there were roughly 14.741 million firms producing goods and services, out of which 11.346 and 1.153 million were proprietorships and partnerships, respectively. The remainder were corporations. Present these data in the form of a pie diagram.

2.30 Using the data concerning econometric models in exercise 2.22, construct a pie chart.

2.31 Reexamine the investment portfolio of the mutual fund corporation in exercise 2.26. Present the information in the form of a pie chart.

2.32 The following are various current assets of nonfinancial corporations for the year 1983 (in billions of dollars):*

Current Assets	Amount
Cash	165.8
U.S. Government securities	30.6
Notes and account receivables	577.8
Inventories	599.3
Other assets	183.7
Total	1557.3

Summarize the above information using a pie chart.

2.33 The following data indicate the electricity consumption (in kilowatt-hours) for 20 typical two-bedroom apartments in a major city:

10, 12, 17, 11, 12, 10, 9, 14, 12, 10, 14, 12, 8, 10, 8, 13, 15, 14, 12, 8

a. Construct a frequency distribution.

b. Construct a histogram.

c. Is there much variation among the "typical" apartments?

2.34 The following data indicate the total motor fuel consumption in millions of gallons on the highway for the year 1983 for selected states:**

State	Fuel Consumption	State	Fuel Consumption
Wisconsin	1886	Kansas	1147
Arkansas	1082	Alabama	1790
Louisiana	2076	Iowa	1280
Washington	1788	Minnesota	1750
Tennessee	2263	Virginia	2424
Maryland	1849	Missouri	2369
Mississippi	1104	Georgia	2755

Construct a cumulative frequency distribution (ogive).

2.35 The number of suicides in hundreds for the past 20 years for a certain metropolitan area are summarized by age in years as follows:

Age Group	Number of Suicides
10–14	.8
15–19	8.0
20–24	16.9
25–29	17.6
30–34	15.7
35–39	15.6
40–44	16.1
45–49	16.7
50–54	17.6
55–59	17.8

*Source: *Economic Indicators*, January 1985, p. 29.
**Source: Adapted from *World Almanac and Book of Facts*, 1985.

a. Construct a histogram using the frequency distribution.

b. Draw a frequency polygon.

c. Comment on the shape of the distribution of the data.

2.36 A successful businessperson receives the following yearly incomes (in dollars) from seven business partnerships.

Business Partnership	Yearly Income
A	23,160
B	30,070
C	32,732
D	35,900
E	37,304
F	43,608
G	60,014
Total	262,788

Express the yearly incomes from each partnership as a percentage of the businessperson's total income and summarize this information using a pie chart.

2.37 The following data indicate the percentage of U.S. petroleum imports by source for the year 1983:*

Nation	Percentage of U.S. Petroleum Imports
Algeria	4.8
Indonesia	6.7
Saudi Arabia	6.7
Iran	0.9
Venezuela	8.4
United Arab Emirates	0.6
Canada	10.8
Mexico	16.4
Virgin Islands	5.6
Others	39.1
	100.0

Construct a pie chart to express the world production of crude oil.

2.38 The following table contains the traffic for the major airports in the United States in 1983 (total take-offs and landings, in thousands):**

Airport	Traffic
Chicago O'Hare	671.7
Long Beach	422.2
Santa Ana	457.8
Van Nuys	494.3
Atlanta	612.8
Los Angeles	506.1
Dallas/Ft. Worth	435.5
Oakland	356.8
Denver Stapleton	458.1

Present the data in the form of a bar graph.

*Source: *The World Almanac and Book of Facts,* 1985, p. 176.

**Source: *World Almanac,* 1985, p. 203.

2.39 The following are the gold reserves of the U.S. government for the years 1965–1979 (in million fine troy ounces):

Year	Gold Reserves	Year	Gold Reserves
1965	401.86	1973	275.97
1966	378.14	1974	275.97
1967	344.71	1975	274.71
1968	311.20	1976	274.68
1969	338.83	1977	277.55
1970	316.34	1978	276.41
1971	291.60	1979	264.60
1972	275.97		

a. Are the data discrete or continuous?

b. Present the data in the form of a bar chart.

2.7

Deceptive Graphs

You might be tempted to be creative in your graphical displays by using, for example, a three-dimensional figure. Such originality is commendable, but does your graph accurately represent the situation? Consider Figure 2.12, which someone drew in an attempt to demonstrate that there are twice as many men as women in management positions. The artist constructed a box for the *men* category twice as high—but also twice as deep—as that for the *women* category. The result is a rectangular solid for men that is, in fact, four times the volume of the one for women. So the illustration is misleading; it appears that there are four times as many men as women in management.

When data values correspond to specific time periods—such as monthly sales or annual expenditures—the resulting data collection is a **time series**. A time series is represented graphically by using the horizontal axis for the time increments. For example, Figure 2.13 contains a return-on-investment time series for two mutual funds, plotted over a 6-year period. A glance at this figure might lead you to believe that mutual fund A is performing nearly twice as well as mutual fund B. A closer look, however, reveals that *the vertical axis did not start at zero,* which can seriously distort the information contained in such a graph. The 1985 return for fund A appears to be roughly twice that for fund B. However, the actual returns are 15.8% for fund A and 14.5% for fund B. Granted, fund A *is* outperforming fund B, but not nearly as dramatically as Figure 2.13 seems to indicate.

Figure 2.12

The illustrator wished to show that there are twice as many men as women in management positions. However, box B is twice the height *and* twice the depth of box A, and thus is four times the volume.

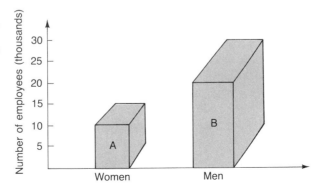

Figure 2.13

Time-series graph of the performance of two mutual funds. The graph is misleading because the vertical axis does not start at zero.

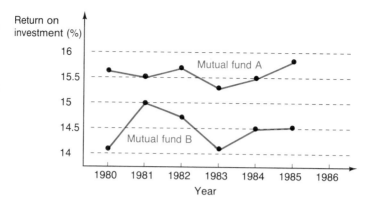

Figure 2.14

Two misleading bar charts. The vertical axis of the left chart does not begin at zero, and the bars in the right chart are chopped without a corresponding adjustment in the vertical axis.

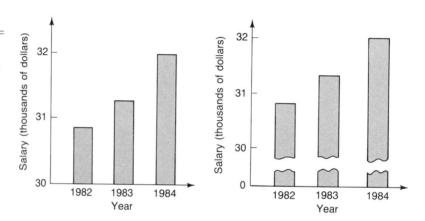

Such examples, and many others, are contained in an entertaining and enlightening book by Darrell Huff entitled *How to Lie with Statistics*.* Other deceptive graphs mentioned by Huff include bar charts similar to those in Figure 2.14. Here, you may be tempted to conclude that there is a significant difference in the bar heights, either because the vertical axis does not begin at zero (left side) or because the bars are chopped in the middle without a corresponding adjustment of the vertical axis (right side). As an observer, beware of such trickery. As an illustrator do not intentionally mislead your reader by disguising the results through the use of a misleading graph. It tends to give statisticians a bad name!

2.8

Computer Graphics on the Microcomputer

Now that you are ready to invest in graph paper, a straight edge, a protractor, and colored pens, you will be happy to learn that there is a much easier method of preparing professional-looking statistical graphs. Practically all microcomputers have available a package that allows you to construct a variety of multicolored bar charts, pie charts, and so on. Figure 2.15 was drawn with a Radio Shack microcomputer by using a few simple commands. If you think you will be having to create many graphic summaries, try to obtain access to a computer graphics package and its output. No good report is complete without at least one such graph!

*Darrell Huff, *How to Lie with Statistics* (New York: W. W. Norton, 1954).

Figure 2.15

This graph was drawn using a Radio Shack (Tandy Corporation) microcomputer.

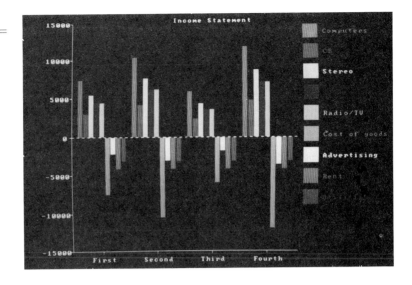

Summary

This chapter examined methods of summarizing and presenting a large number of data using a graph. The steps taken were: (1) place the data into an ordered array, (2) construct a frequency distribution of the data, and (3) construct the appropriate graph. We discussed four kinds of graphs:

1. A *histogram* or *frequency polygon* is a graphical view of a frequency distribution.
2. A *bar chart* summarizes categorical (nominal) data.
3. An *ogive* allows you to illustrate "less than" percentages or frequencies.
4. A *pie chart* presents a percentage breakdown of a particular quantity.

A frequency distribution provides a summary of the data by placing them into groups, called classes. The number of values in each class is the class frequency. For example, there may be ten values in the class "150 and under 250." The numbers "150" and "250" here are the class limits, and the difference between them (100) is the class width. The center of this class [(150 + 250)/2 = 200] is the class midpoint. All classes should have the same width, except the highest and lowest, which may be open-ended if you have a few outliers.

To construct a frequency distribution, place the data values into an ordered array, from smallest to largest. For comparisons, the same data can be summarized using relative frequencies, which indicate the fraction of data values in each class rather than actual counts (frequencies).

A histogram is a graphical representation of a frequency distribution and generally is used for data having an interval or ratio level of measurement. When the data are nominal, a bar chart provides a graphical summary. When constructing a bar chart, gaps are inserted between the boxes due to the nature of this data type.

An excellent way to indicate the shape of the data values is to use a frequency polygon. This is constructed by replacing the boxes in the histogram with straight lines connecting the center of each box.

An ogive allows you to make such statements as, "40% of the data values are *less than* 500." Like a frequency polygon, an ogive consists of many straight lines; in the ogive, the lines increase from zero to one on the vertical axis. The final graph we discussed is a pie chart. This circular graph can be used to represent percentages (relative frequencies) at some point in time or over a certain time period.

What's Next?

A graph, such as a frequency polygon, is an excellent method of describing a set of data, but it does have its limitations. For example, examine Figure 2.5 and answer the following question: Where is the middle (center) of the data? One person might argue that it is "somewhere around 500," whereas someone else might decide that it is some value closer to 550. The point is that we need to define what the word *middle* means and define some method of calculating this value, so that we all get the *same* result. Such a value is called a numerical measure.

The next chapter will examine a variety of such numerical measures. Rather than reducing a set of data to a graph we will reduce the data to a *number* that gives us some information about the data.

Review Exercises

2.40 The amount of time it takes in days to order a special automobile part from the manufacturer is of great concern to a local automobile dealer. The following data are the delivery times (in days) for 30 parts that were special ordered.

  2.50, 1.50, 4.25, 3.50, 2.25, 2.00, 1.50, 4.00, 3.50, 2.25, 3.75, 4.75, 3.25, 4.25, 2.00, 2.50, 1.75, 4.25, 3.00, 2.00, 5.25, 1.75, 2.00, 3.75, 3.00, 3.50, 4.50, 5.00, 3.50, 2.50

a. Order the data and construct a frequency distribution.

b. Based on the data, what would the dealer tell the next customer who asks how long his or her special order will take?

2.41 Quick Check-Out convenience store sells the following numbers of gallons of milk weekly over a 24-week period:

  28, 36, 41, 23, 45, 23, 24, 45, 20, 26, 53, 54, 57, 43, 21, 29, 60, 42, 33, 28, 39, 44, 49, 52

a. Construct a frequency distribution using class intervals of 20–24, 25–30, and so on.

b. Construct a histogram.

c. Draw the ogive.

2.42 An economist has a model to forecast the weekly money supply. The following values represent the difference between the forecasted money supply and the actual money-supply figures over a period of 25 weeks. Units are in hundreds of thousands of dollars.

  11.4, 2.5, −50.5, −12.4, −5.1, 4.5, 13.6, 29.8, 51.6, −10.8, −17.8, 30.1, 33.8, 39.6, 44.7, −40.1, −35.6, −37.1, 46.7, 21.6, 18.2, −24.5, −20.5, −15.4, 53.4

a. Construct a frequency distribution.

b. Construct a cumulative relative frequency distribution.

c. Draw the ogive.

2.43 A large real-estate firm has 20 agents. The following data are the yearly salaries of each agent. Units are in thousands of dollars.

  13.5, 19.6, 29.8, 43.4, 50.2, 18.7, 7.5, 24.6, 20.3, 27.4, 30.5, 34.6, 12.7, 31.7, 45.8, 41.4, 32.7, 22.6, 27.8, 20.1

a. Construct a frequency distribution.

b. Construct a cumulative relative frequency distribution.

c. Draw the ogive.

2.44 An investor owns several thousand shares of the stock Computer Graphics. Because the price of the stock is so volatile, the investor records the closing price of the stock every day to get an idea of the distribution of the price of the stock. The closing price of this stock for 25 days is

13.125, 13.5, 12.875, 12.25, 12.375, 13.00, 13.75, 13.375, 14.25, 15.00, 15.25, 15.375, 15.00, 14.75, 15.125, 15.375, 15.75, 16.125, 16.375, 16.50, 16.00, 15.50, 15.75, 16.25, 16.50

a. Construct a frequency distribution.

b. Construct a histogram.

c. Construct a frequency polygon.

2.45 A mutual fund has its assets spread over seven sectors of the economy. The following data are the total value (in millions of dollars) of the stocks in which the fund is invested for each sector.

Stock	Value
Electronics and electrical equipment	2.116
Aerospace and defense	10.375
Food and beverage	4.864
Utilities	2.713
Insurance and finance	6.538
Health care	3.675
Oil and gas	1.532

a. Express the amount invested in each sector of the economy as a percent.

b. Summarize the list in a pie chart.

2.46 The following data represent the scores on a computer-graded multiple-choice test. There are 20 questions, and each question is worth 5 points. Construct a frequency polygon for the grades of the 30 students.

95, 90, 80, 55, 90, 45, 50, 75, 75, 60, 55, 90, 50, 85, 95, 55, 60, 50, 45, 95, 70, 60, 50, 85, 90, 55, 45, 95, 100, 90

2.47 An independent oil firm recently hired ten engineers, five geologists, three accountants, one statistician, four computer scientists, and one chemist. Present these data in the form of a pie chart.

2.48 The numbers of hours that a repair machine is used daily at Pat's Shoe Repair are listed below for 20 days.

3.2, 4.6, 3.1, 3.6, 2.5, 4.3, 2.1, 5.7, 6.1, 4.3, 3.0, 2.5, 1.3, 1.7, 2.4, 5.6, 5.1, 4.2, 1.9, 2.6

a. Construct a frequency distribution.

b. Construct a cumulative relative frequency distribution.

c. What can you say about machine usage (in hours per day)?

2.49 The ages (in years) of the 20 loan officers, four vice-presidents, and the president of American Bank are

47, 52, 55, 65, 42, 37, 29, 52, 47, 36, 60, 50, 48, 42, 45, 35, 38, 45, 57, 43, 39, 41, 33, 58, 60

a. Construct a frequency distribution.

b. Construct a cumulative frequency distribution.

c. Write a summary statement about the distribution of the ages of the loan officers.

2.50 A psychologist has designed a technique to improve a person's memory. Certain material is given to 30 people to memorize before they learn the technique. Similar material is given to the 30 people after the technique has been taught to them. The difference in the amount of time that it took to memorize the material (before–after) is given below in minutes.

5, 10, 15, 11, 13, 20, 14, 5, 23, 18, 17, 4, 1, 5, 29, 18, 15, 21, 24, 16, 2, 15, 19, 30, 24, 21, 14, 18, 26, 10

a. Construct a frequency distribution.

b. Construct a histogram.

c. Construct a frequency polygon.

d. Take one class interval and write out, in words, exactly what it tells you.

2.51 A manufacturing firm would like to find out the distribution of defective fuses in each package of fuses that it manufactures. Twenty boxes of 50 fuses were randomly selected and the following number of defective fuses were noted for each box:

3, 5, 10, 12, 0, 6, 17, 1, 0, 7, 3, 15, 21, 9, 13, 24, 12, 10, 6, 16

a. Construct a frequency distribution.

b. Construct a cumulative relative frequency distribution.

c. Make several statements about the number of defectives usually found in a box of 50 fuses.

2.52 Custom House Products has seven stores. The following list indicates the total yearly sales for each store (in thousands of dollars):

Store	Sales
1	60.5
2	70.3
3	44.6
4	59.8
5	88.7
6	142.6
7	104.2

Draw a pie chart to represent the data.

2.53 The following are the number of workers absent each day recorded for 30 days in a steel factory:

10, 5, 2, 13, 17, 3, 16, 5, 7, 10, 3, 19, 22, 14, 11, 6, 9, 18, 23, 14, 7, 8, 20, 17, 13, 7, 24, 2, 6, 15

a. Construct a frequency distribution for the data.

b. Assume that the total work force is 100 people. If you were a supervisor, would you inform management of an absentee problem? If so, what would you say?

2.54 The number of cars rented daily at Rent-a-Cheapie is recorded over 40 days. Construct a frequency distribution and draw a histogram for these data.

15, 20, 22, 10, 13, 24, 9, 8, 13, 21, 6, 19, 17, 13, 26, 21, 22, 19, 13, 11, 5, 26, 27, 19, 16, 10, 4, 18, 22, 14, 24, 31, 28, 18, 12, 19, 26, 7, 18, 30

2.55 Twenty utility stocks were randomly selected from all utility stocks on the New York Stock Exchange. The following are the dividend rates (the dividend divided by the price of the stock) for each of the 20 utility stocks.

11.2, 9.35, 7.26, 13.55, 12.62, 6.71, 7.22, 5.73, 14.18, 15.35, 5.01, 16.81, 11.89, 13.64, 14.53, 5.97, 8.97, 10.06, 17.31, 10.69

a. Construct a cumulative relative frequency distribution.

b. Construct an ogive.

Example

Constructing a Histogram

You can use SPSSX to construct a histogram using the prices of television sets and VCRs purchased from the Q-Mart department store. The SPSSX program listing in Figure 2.16 requests a histogram of the data in Table 2.1. As you can see, it is almost identical to the procedure in the SPSSX Appendix at the end of the text, which was used to obtain test score averages. Each line represents one card image to be entered:

The TITLE command names the SPSSX run.
The DATA LIST command gives each variable a name, and describes the data as being in free form.
The FREQUENCIES statement specifies the variable from which we wish to produce a histogram, with the histogram statement generating the actual histogram.
The BEGIN DATA command indicates to SPSSX that the input data immediately follow.
The next ten lines are card images, which represent the prices of the items in the sample.
The END DATA statement indicates the end of the data card images.
The FINISH command indicates the end of the SPSSX program.

Figure 2.17 shows the output obtained by executing the listing in Figure 2.16.

Figure 2.16

SPSSX program listing requesting a histogram of data from Table 2.1.

```
TITLE       Q-MART PURCHASE PRICE
DATA LIST FREE   /TVDAT
FREQUENCIES      VARIABLES=TVDAT/
                 HISTOGRAM/
BEGIN DATA
460.04   463.36   520.24   345.88   582.36
538.13   676.84   488.37   255.46   657.41
477.18   620.24   840.57   295.77   684.71
475.96   561.63   624.63   318.91   631.78
715.93   375.94   419.19   362.81   521.48
436.68   516.82   782.57   405.16   515.61
643.55   434.27   485.15   478.03   540.44
495.57   397.95   812.36   715.71   528.57
515.62   481.45   583.82   450.36   564.16
712.26   517.79   388.70   488.34   745.28
END DATA
FINISH
```

S
P
S
S
X

Figure 2.17

SPSSX output obtained by executing the program listing in Figure 2.16.

VALUE LABEL	VALUE	FREQUENCY	PERCENT	VALID PERCENT	CUM PERCENT
	255.46	1	2.0	2.0	2.0
	295.77	1	2.0	2.0	4.0
	318.91	1	2.0	2.0	6.0
	345.88	1	2.0	2.0	8.0
	362.81	1	2.0	2.0	10.0
	375.94	1	2.0	2.0	12.0
	388.70	1	2.0	2.0	14.0
	397.95	1	2.0	2.0	16.0
	.				
	.				
	582.36	1	2.0	2.0	70.0
	583.82	1	2.0	2.0	72.0
	620.24	1	2.0	2.0	74.0
	624.63	1	2.0	2.0	76.0
	631.78	1	2.0	2.0	78.0
	643.55	1	2.0	2.0	80.0
	657.41	1	2.0	2.0	82.0
	676.84	1	2.0	2.0	84.0
	684.71	1	2.0	2.0	86.0
	712.26	1	2.0	2.0	88.0
	715.71	1	2.0	2.0	90.0
	715.93	1	2.0	2.0	92.0
	745.28	1	2.0	2.0	94.0

S
A
S

Example

Constructing a Histogram

You can also produce a histogram using SAS. The SAS program listing in Figure 2.18 was used to request a histogram of the data in Table 2.1. As you can see, it is almost identical to the procedure in the end-of-text SAS Appendix, which was used to obtain test score averages. Each line represents one card image to be entered:

The TITLE command names the SAS run.

The DATA command gives the data a name.

The INPUT command names and gives the correct order for the different fields on the data cards.

The CARDS command indicates to SAS that the input data immediately follow.

The next 50 lines are card images. The first line, for example, represents the price of the first item in the sample. The remaining lines indicate the prices of the other 49 items.

The ; indicates the end of the data card images.

The PROC PRINT command directs SAS to list the data that were just read in.

The PROC CHART command requests a SAS procedure to print a bar chart.

The VBAR PRICE generates a vertical bar chart of the variable PRICE. The resulting bar chart is actually a histogram centered at each of the class midpoints.

Figure 2.19 shows the output obtained from executing the program listing in Figure 2.18.

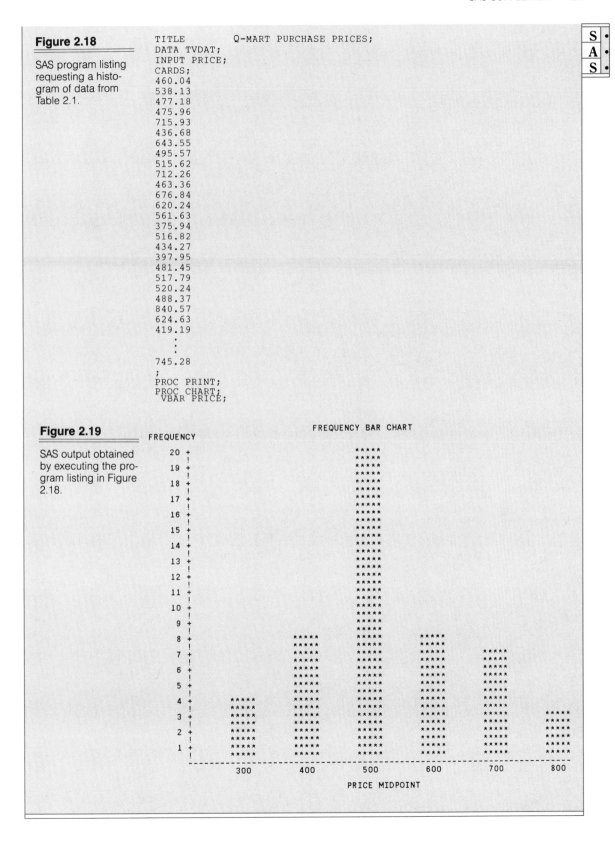

Figure 2.18

SAS program listing requesting a histogram of data from Table 2.1.

```
TITLE           Q-MART PURCHASE PRICES;
DATA TVDAT;
INPUT PRICE;
CARDS;
460.04
538.13
477.18
475.96
715.93
436.68
643.55
495.57
515.62
712.26
463.36
676.84
620.24
561.63
375.94
516.82
434.27
397.95
481.45
517.79
520.24
488.37
840.57
624.63
419.19
    .
    .
    .
745.28
;
PROC PRINT;
PROC CHART;
  VBAR PRICE;
```

Figure 2.19

SAS output obtained by executing the program listing in Figure 2.18.

```
                                        FREQUENCY BAR CHART
    FREQUENCY

    20 +                                      *****
       !                                      *****
    19 +                                      *****
       !                                      *****
    18 +                                      *****
       !                                      *****
    17 +                                      *****
       !                                      *****
    16 +                                      *****
       !                                      *****
    15 +                                      *****
       !                                      *****
    14 +                                      *****
       !                                      *****
    13 +                                      *****
       !                                      *****
    12 +                                      *****
       !                                      *****
    11 +                                      *****
       !                                      *****
    10 +                                      *****
       !                                      *****
     9 +                                      *****
       !                                      *****
     8 +                    *****             *****             *****
       !                    *****             *****             *****
     7 +                    *****             *****             *****             *****
       !                    *****             *****             *****             *****
     6 +                    *****             *****             *****             *****
       !                    *****             *****             *****             *****
     5 +                    *****             *****             *****             *****
       !                    *****             *****             *****             *****
     4 +       *****        *****             *****             *****             *****
       !       *****        *****             *****             *****             *****
     3 +       *****        *****             *****             *****             *****        *****
       !       *****        *****             *****             *****             *****        *****
     2 +       *****        *****             *****             *****             *****        *****
       !       *****        *****             *****             *****             *****        *****
     1 +       *****        *****             *****             *****             *****        *****
       !       *****        *****             *****             *****             *****        *****
       ----------------------------------------------------------------------------------------------
                  300          400              500              600              700          800

                                        PRICE MIDPOINT
```

CHAPTER 3

Descriptive Measures

A Look Back/Introduction

The first two chapters focused on different types of numerical data and methods of summarizing and presenting data. A frequency distribution is used to condense data from a sample into groups (called classes). Different types of statistical graphs can be used to illustrate sample data in different ways. The types of graphs we have discussed so far include the histogram, bar chart, ogive, frequency polygon, and pie chart. The purpose of these graphs is to convey information at a glance about the distribution of the values in your data set.

We have seen how to reduce a set of sample data to a graph. It also is helpful to reduce data to one or more numbers (such as an average). Such a number is called a descriptive measure. Because this number is derived from a sample, it also can be called a sample statistic. We will discuss many of the popular descriptive measures and explain what you can expect to learn from each one.

3.1

Various Types of Descriptive Measures

A **descriptive measure** is a *single* number that provides information about a data set. The class of descriptive measures described here consists of four types. Which one you select depends on what you want to measure. These types are:

1. *Measures of central tendency.* These answer the questions "Where is the 'middle' of my data?" and "Which data value occurs most often?"
2. *Measures of dispersion.* These answer the questions "How spread out are my data values?" and "How much do the data values jump around?"
3. *Measures of position.* These answer the questions "How does my value (score on an exam, for example) compare with those of everyone else?" and "Which data value was exceeded by 75% of the data values? by 50%? by 25%?"
4. *Measures of shape.* These answer the questions "Are my data values symmetric?" and "If not symmetric, just how nonsymmetric (skewed) are the data?"

3.2

Measures of Central Tendency

The purpose of a **measure of central tendency** is to determine the "center" of your data values or possibly the "most popular" data value. The measures of central tendency are the mean, median, midrange, and mode. We will illustrate each of these measures using as data the number of accidents (monthly) reported over a particular 5-month period:

Accident Data: 6, 9, 7, 23, 5

The Mean

The **mean** is the most popular measure of central tendency. It is merely the average of the data. The mean is easy to obtain and explain, and it has several mathematical properties that make it more advantageous to use than the other three measures.

Business managers often use a mean to represent a set of values. They select one value as typical of the whole set of values, such as average sales, average price, average salary, or average production per hour. In economics, the term *per capita* is a measure of central tendency. The income per capita of a certain district, the number of clothes washers per capita, and the number of televisions per capita are all examples of a mean.

The sample mean, $\bar{x}$ (read as "x bar"), is equal to the sum of the data values divided by the number of data values. For the accident data set,

$$\bar{x} = \frac{6 + 9 + 7 + 23 + 5}{5} = 10.0$$

In general, let an arbitrary data set be represented as:

$$x_1, x_2, x_3, \ldots, x_n$$

where n is the number of data values. (In the accident data set, $x_1 = 6$, $x_2 = 9$, $x_3 = 7$, $x_4 = 23$, $x_5 = 5$, and n is 5.) Then,

$$\bar{x} = \frac{x_1 + x_2 + \ldots + x_n}{n} = \frac{\Sigma x}{n} \tag{3-1}$$

The symbol Σ (sigma) means "the sum of." In this case, the sample mean, $\bar{x}$, is the sum of the x values divided by n.*

In subsequent chapters, we will be concerned with the mean of the *population*. The symbol for the population mean is μ (mu). For a population consisting of N elements, denoted by

$$x_1, x_2, x_3, \ldots, x_N$$

the population mean is defined to be

$$\mu = \frac{x_1 + x_2 + \ldots + x_N}{N} = \frac{\Sigma x}{N} \qquad (3\text{-}2)$$

- Population: $x_1, x_2, \ldots, x_N$
- Population Mean $= \mu = \dfrac{x_1 + x_2 + \ldots + x_N}{N} = \dfrac{\Sigma x}{N}$

- Sample Values (selected from the population): $x_1, x_2, \ldots, x_n$ where $n \leqslant N$
- Sample Mean $= \bar{x} = \dfrac{x_1 + x_2 + \ldots + x_n}{n} = \dfrac{\Sigma x}{n}$

The Median

The **median** of a set of data is the data value in the center of the values when the values are arranged from smallest to largest. Consequently, it is the center value of the ordered array.

Using the accident data set, the median **Md** is found by first constructing an ordered array:

5, 6, **7**, 9, 23

The value that has an equal number of items to the right and the left is the median. Thus, Md = 7.

In general, if n is odd, Md is the center data value of the ordered set:

$$\text{Md} = \left(\frac{n+1}{2}\right) \text{st ordered value}$$

If n is even, Md is the average of the two center values of the ordered set. Thus, the median of the array 3, 8, 12, 14 is $(8 + 12)/2 = 10.0$.

In our accident data set, one of the five values (23) is much larger than the remaining values—it is an outlier. Notice that the median was much less affected by this value than was the mean. When dealing with data that are likely to contain outliers (for

*Another application of this symbol is where we square each of the sample values and sum these values. For the accident data, this operation would be written as

$$\Sigma x^2 = 5^2 + 6^2 + 7^2 + 9^2 + 23^2$$
$$= 25 + 36 + 49 + 81 + 529$$
$$= 720$$

For these data, then, $\Sigma x = 50$ and $\Sigma x^2 = 720$.

example, personal incomes or prices of residential housing), the median usually is preferred to the mean as a measure of central tendency.

The Midrange

Although less popular than the mean and median, the **midrange (Mr)** provides an easy-to-grasp measure of central tendency. Notice that it also is severely affected (even more than $\bar{x}$) by the presence of an outlier in the data. In general:

$$\text{Mr} = \frac{(\text{smallest value}) + (\text{largest value})}{2} \qquad (3\text{-}3)$$

Using the accident data set,

$$\text{Mr} = \frac{5 + 23}{2} = 14.0$$

Compare this to $\bar{x} = 10$ and Md $= 7$.

The Mode

The **mode (Mo)** of a data set is the value that occurs the most often. The mode is not always a measure of central tendency; this value need not occur in the "center" of your data. One situation in which the mode is the value of interest is the manufacturing of clothing. The *most common* hat size is what you would like to know, not the *average* hat size. Can you think of other applications where the mode would provide useful information?

Note that there is no Mo for our accident data set because all values occur only once. Instead, consider the data set

4, 8, 7, 6, 9, 8, 10, 5, 8

Mo $= 8$ (occurs three times).

There may be more than one mode if several numbers occur the same (and the largest) number of times.

Example 3.1

A sample of ten was taken to determine the typical completion time (in months) for the construction of a particular model of Brockwood Homes:

4.1, 3.2, 2.8, 2.6, 3.7, 3.1, 9.4, 2.5, 3.5, 3.8

We find the average completion time as follows:

$$\bar{x} = \frac{4.1 + 3.2 + \ldots + 3.8}{10} = \frac{38.7}{10} = 3.87 \text{ months}$$

Notice that there is an outlier in the data, namely, 9.4 months. To be safe, you should double-check this figure to make sure that it is, in fact, correct. In the presence of one or two outliers, the median generally provides a more reliable measure of central tendency, so we construct an ordered array:

2.5, 2.6, 2.8, 3.1, **3.2, 3.5,** 3.7, 3.8, 4.1, 9.4

Figure 3.1

Dot array diagram of the measure of central tendency for a sample of ten housing construction times. See text for explanation.

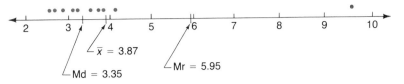

Construction time (months)

Consequently,

$$Md = \frac{3.2 + 3.5}{2} = 3.35 \text{ months}$$

Also, the midrange is given by

$$Mr = \frac{2.5 + 9.4}{2} = 5.95 \text{ months}$$

This value is severely affected by the presence of the outlier; the midrange of nearly 6 months is a poor measure of central tendency for this application.

Finally, no mode exists because there are no repeats in the data values. These results are summarized in the graph in Figure 3.1, a **dot array diagram.** Each data value is represented as a dot on the horizontal line. ●

Exercises

3.1 Compute the mean, median, and mode for the daily maximum temperatures in the Dallas data in exercise 2.8.

3.2 Compute the mean, median, and mode for the price:earnings–ratio data in exercise 2.15.

3.3 Compute the mean, median, and mode for the profitability-index data in exercise 2.20.

3.4 Compute the mean, median, and mode for the price elasticity of electricity in exercise

3.5 The distribution of family income (in dollars) in the United States in 1983 was as follows:*

Income Range	Percent Distribution of Families
under 5000	5.7
5000 and under 10000	10.2
10000 and under 15000	11.6
15000 and under 20000	11.8
20000 and under 25000	11.5
25000 and under 35000	19.5
35000 and under 50000	17.1
50000 and over	12.6
Total	100.0

Estimate the median. Give an interpretation of the value of the median.

3.6 Compute the mean, median, and mode for the student scores in exercise 2.23.

3.7 Compute the mean, median, and mode for the return-on-sales (ROS) data in exercise 2.27.

*Source: *Statistical Abstract of the United States 1985*, U.S. Department of Commerce, p. 446.

3.8 Compute the mean, median, and mode for the following data on the monthly commissions (in hundreds of dollars) for eight salespersons:

.5, 12.3, 15.9, 16.1, 16.2, 16.3, 16.4, 18.6

3.9 Compute the mean, median, and mode for the daily advertising expense of a car dealer using the following data. The daily advertising expense in dollars is given for 20 days.

38, 60, 20, 130, 55, 150, 47, 35, 86, 95, 31, 46, 112, 130, 55, 42, 130, 35, 60, 130

3.10 Compute the mean, median, and mode for the U.S. gold reserves in exercise 2.39.

3.11 The following are the largest foreign industrial corporations, ranked in the order of sales (in millions of dollars):*

Company	Sales
Royal Dutch	59,417
British Petroleum	38,713
Unilever	21,749
ENI	18,985
Fiat	18,300
Francaise	17,305
Peugeot	17,270
Volkswagen	16,766
Phillips	16,576
Renault	16,117
Siemens	15,070
Daimler Benz	14,942
Hoechst	14,785
Bayer	14,196
Basf	14,139
Toyota	14,012

Compute the mean and median of the sales values.

3.3

Measures of Dispersion

A measure of central tendency, such as the mean, is certainly useful and significant. However, the use of any single value to describe a complete distribution will fail to reveal important facts.

The more homogenous a set of data is, the better the mean will represent a "typical value." **Dispersion** is the tendency of data values to scatter about the mean, $\bar{x}$. If all the data values in a sample are identical, then the mean provides perfect information, and the dispersion is zero. This is rarely the case, however, so we need a measure of this dispersion that will increase as the scatter of the data values about $\bar{x}$ increases.

Knowledge of dispersion can sometimes be used to control the variability of your data values in the future. Industrial production operations maintain quality control by observing and measuring the dispersion of the units produced. If there is too much variation in the production process, the causes are determined and corrected using an inspection control procedure.

The measures of dispersion are the range, mean absolute deviation (MAD), variance, standard deviation, and coefficient of variation. To illustrate the various dispersion measures, we will use the accident data from the previous section: 6, 9, 7, 23, 5.

*Source: *The World Almanac and Book of Facts*, 1981, p. 173.

Figure 3.2

This presentation of the accident data shows their variation.

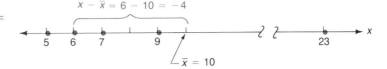

The Range

The simplest measure of dispersion is the **range** of the data, which is the numerical distance between the largest value and the smallest value. For the accident data,

Range $= 23 - 5 = 18$

The range is a rather crude measure of dispersion, but it is an easy number to calculate and contains valuable information for many situations. Stockmarket reports generally are given in terms of their ranges, citing the high and low prices of the day. The value of the range is strongly influenced by an outlier in the sample data.

Mean Absolute Deviation (MAD)

The purpose of a measure of dispersion is to determine the variability of your data. The more variation there is in your data, the larger this measure should become. Take a look at the accident data illustrated in Figure 3.2. To measure the variation about the sample mean, $\bar{x}$, consider the distance from each data value to $\bar{x}$ (that is, $x - \bar{x}$) and its absolute value:

Data value (x)	$x - \bar{x}$	$\lvert x - \bar{x} \rvert$
5	-5	5
6	-4	4
7	-3	3
9	-1	1
23	13	13
	$\Sigma(x - \bar{x}) = 0$	$\Sigma\lvert x - \bar{x}\rvert = 26$

As a possible measure, consider the average of the $(x - \bar{x})$ values:

$$\frac{\Sigma(x - \bar{x})}{5} = \frac{0}{5} = 0$$

This value is *always* zero for any set of data because the positive deviations always balance out the negative ones. To overcome this, use the actual distance from each data value to the sample mean, paying no attention to the side of the mean on which it lies, by taking the **absolute value** of each deviation. This average distance defines the **mean absolute deviation (MAD)**.

$$\text{MAD} = \frac{\Sigma\lvert x - \bar{x}\rvert}{n} \tag{3-4}$$

Using the accident data,

$$\text{MAD} = \frac{5 + 4 + 3 + 1 + 13}{5} = \frac{26}{5} = 5.2$$

What is the MAD without the value 23?

$$\bar{x} = \frac{5 + 6 + 7 + 9}{4} = 6.75$$

and so

$$\text{MAD} = \frac{|5 - 6.75| + |6 - 6.75| + |7 - 6.75| + |9 - 6.75|}{4}$$

$$= \frac{1.75 + .75 + .25 + 2.25}{4} = 1.25$$

Here the MAD is much lower than before. This indicates that the smaller data set has much less variation than does the one containing the outlier.

The Variance and Standard Deviation

By far the most widely used measures of dispersion are the **variance** and **standard deviation.** They resemble the MAD in that they are based on deviations of all the values from the sample mean, $\bar{x}$. The problem encountered earlier in examining the sum of each $(x - \bar{x})$ was that the negative deviations balanced out the positive ones. The MAD fixed this by taking the absolute value of each deviation. Another possibility is to *square* each of these deviations, thereby removing all the negative signs. We can illustrate this using our example data. Recall that $\bar{x} = 10$.

Data value (x)	$(x - \bar{x})^2$
5	25
6	16
7	9
9	1
23	169
	220

So $\Sigma(x - \bar{x})^2 = 220$.

The obvious thing to do next would be to find the average of these squared deviations:

$$\frac{1}{n} \cdot \Sigma(x - \bar{x})^2$$

One use of this particular statistic in subsequent chapters will be as an *estimator.* In particular, we will need to estimate the variation within an entire population, using sample data collected from the population. However, a better estimator is obtained by dividing the sum of the squared deviations by $n - 1$ rather than by n. This leads to the **sample variance, s^2.** In general,

$$s^2 = \frac{\Sigma(x - \bar{x})^2}{n - 1} \tag{3-5}$$

Using the accident data,

$$s^2 = \frac{220}{5 - 1} = \frac{220}{4} = 55.0$$

The square root of the variance is referred to as the sample standard deviation, **s.**

In general,

$$s = \sqrt{\frac{\Sigma(x - \bar{x})^2}{n - 1}} \tag{3-6}$$

Using the accident data,

$$s = \sqrt{55.0} = 7.416$$

As previously mentioned, the sample variance, s^2, is used to estimate the variance of the entire population. The symbol for the population variance is σ^2 (read as sigma squared). For a population consisting of N elements,

$$x_1, x_2, x_3, \ldots, x_N$$

the population variance is defined to be

$$\sigma^2 = \frac{\Sigma(x - \mu)^2}{N} \tag{3-7}$$

where μ is the population mean, defined in equation 3-2.

As we saw, the *population* variance can be obtained by dividing the sum of the squared deviations about μ by the population size N. The *sample* variance is calculated by dividing the sum of the squared deviations about $\bar{x}$ by the sample size (n) minus one. Had we chosen to divide by n rather than by $n - 1$, the resulting estimator would (on the average) underestimate σ^2. For this reason, we use $n - 1$ in the denominator of s^2.

- Population: $x_1, x_2, \ldots, x_N$
- Population Variance $= \sigma^2 = \dfrac{(x_1 - \mu)^2 + \ldots + (x_N - \mu)^2}{N}$

$$= \frac{\Sigma(x - \mu)^2}{N}$$

- Population Standard Deviation $= \sigma = \sqrt{\dfrac{\Sigma(x - \mu)^2}{N}}$

- Sample Values (selected from the population): $x_1, x_2, \ldots, x_n$ where $n \leqslant N$
- Sample Variance $= s^2 = \dfrac{(x_1 - \bar{x})^2 + \ldots + (x_n - \bar{x})^2}{n - 1}$

$$= \frac{\Sigma(x - \bar{x})^2}{n - 1}$$

- Sample Standard Deviation $= s = \sqrt{\dfrac{\Sigma(x - \bar{x})^2}{n - 1}}$

Now consider what the units are on s and s^2. The units on s are the same as the units on the data. If the data are measured in pounds, then the units on s are pounds.

Consequently, the units on the variance, s^2, would be (pounds)^2—a rather difficult unit to grasp.

For the accident data,

$$s = 7.416 \text{ accidents}$$

$$s^2 = 55 \text{ (accidents)}^2$$

For this reason, s (rather than s^2) is typically the preferred measure of dispersion.

There is another way to compute the sample variance. Using equation 3-5 to compute the value of s^2 may have appeared easy enough, but this was helped in part by the fact that the sample mean, $\bar{x}$, was an integer (10). When $\bar{x}$ is not a counting number, this is not the easiest way to find s^2. Instead, use

$$s^2 = \frac{\Sigma x^2 - (\Sigma x)^2/n}{n-1} \tag{3-8}$$

As before, the standard deviation is the square root of the variance. To illustrate the use of equation 3-8, consider the accident data:

x	x^2
5	25
6	36
7	49
9	81
23	529
50	720

So, $n = 5$, $\Sigma x = 50$, and $\Sigma x^2 = 720$. Consequently, using equation 3-8:

$$s^2 = \frac{720 - (50)^2/5}{5-1}$$

$$= \frac{720 - 500}{4} = 55.0 \text{ (as before)}$$

Also

$$s = \sqrt{55.0} = 7.416 \text{ (as before)}$$

Finally, you may wish to know the magnitude of the value of s or s^2, that is, whether your value of s (or s^2) is large or not. This is difficult to determine because the values of s and s^2 depend on the magnitude of the data values. In other words, large data values produce large values of s. For example, which of the following two data sets exhibits more variation?

Data set 1: 5, 6, 7, 9, 23 (accident reports)

Data set 2: 5000, 6000, 7000, 9000, 23,000

As we have already seen, for data set 1, $\bar{x} = 10.0$ and $s = 7.416$. For data set 2, $\bar{x} = 10,000$ and $s = 7416$ (we will discuss this later).

Does this mean that data set 2 has a great deal more variation, given that its standard deviation is 1000 times that of data set 1? Another look at the values reveals that the large value of s for data set 2 is due to the large values within this set. In fact, considering the size of the numbers within each data set, the relative variation within each group of values is the same. So comparing the standard deviations or variances of two data sets is not a good idea *unless* you know that their mean values ($\bar{x}$) are approximately equal. The next section deals with another statistical measure that *will* allow you to compare the relative variation within two data sets.

The Coefficient of Variation

Consider again our two data sets that appear to have the same variation (relative to the size of the data values) yet have vastly different standard deviations. These data sets are

Data set 1: 5, 6, 7, 9, 23 ($\bar{x} = 10$, $s = 7.416$)

Data set 2: 5000, 6000, 7000, 9000, 23,000 ($\bar{x} = 10,000$, $s = 7416$)

To compare their variation, we need a measure of dispersion that will produce the *same* value for both of them. The solution here is to measure the standard deviation in terms of the mean; that is, what percentage of $\bar{x}$ is s? This is the **coefficient of variation, CV.** In general,

$$CV = \frac{s}{\bar{x}} \cdot 100 \qquad\qquad (3\text{-}9)$$

For our example data sets:

Data set 1: $CV = \dfrac{7.416}{10} \cdot 100 = 74.16$

Data set 2: $CV = \dfrac{7,416}{10,000} \cdot 100 = 74.16$

So our conclusion here is that both data sets exhibit the same relative variation; s is 74.16% of the mean for both sets.

Example 3.2

To review the various measures of dispersion, use the data on housing construction time that you used in example 3.1.

4.1, 3.2, 2.8, 2.6, 3.7, 3.1, 9.4, 2.5, 3.5, 3.8 (completion time in months)

First, compute the range:

(largest value) − (smallest value)

$9.4 - 2.5 = 6.9$ months

To determine the MAD, recall that $\bar{x}$ is 3.87 months:

$$MAD = \frac{1}{10} \left(\,|\, 4.1 - 3.87 \,|\, + \,|\, 3.2 - 3.87 \,|\, + \ldots + \,|\, 3.8 - 3.87 \,|\, \right)$$

$$= \frac{1}{10} \,(11.52) = 1.152 \text{ months}$$

Now find the variance and the standard deviation:

$$\Sigma x = 4.1 + 3.2 + \ldots + 3.8 = 38.7$$

and

$$\Sigma x^2 = (4.1)^2 + (3.2)^2 + \ldots + (3.8)^2 = 186.25$$

then:

$$s^2 = \frac{186.25 - (38.7)^2/10}{10 - 1}$$

$$= \frac{186.25 - 149.77}{9} = 4.05 \ (\text{months})^2$$

and

$$s = \sqrt{4.05} = 2.01 \ \text{months}$$

To calculate the coefficient of variation, use the previously obtained values of s and $\bar{x}$, where

$$CV = \frac{2.01}{3.87} \cdot 100 = 51.9$$

The standard deviation is 51.9% of the sample mean.   ●

So far, you can reduce a set of sample data to a number that indicates a typical or average value (a measure of central tendency) or one that describes the amount of variation within the data values (a measure of dispersion). The next section will examine yet another set of statistics—measures of position.

Exercises

3.12   When making capital-investment decisions, firms frequently consider the dispersion of the estimated future cash flows. Usually, the project with lesser dispersion is preferred to the one with more dispersion. Given the estimated cash flows (after tax) for projects A and B, which one would you prefer? Why?

Month	Project A Cash Flow	Project B Cash Flow
Jan	4000	700
Feb	7200	1100
Mar	8800	600
Apr	2400	1300
May	7400	800
Jun	4100	650
Jul	10800	710
Aug	9100	450
Sep	2000	580
Oct	14000	640
Nov	7700	330
Dec	3900	210

3.13   The following are the scores made on an aptitude test by a group of job applicants:

53, 55, 43, 14, 64, 39, 65, 22, 17, 74, 36, 24, 13, 28, 40, 96, 92, 32, 92, 36, 18, 100, 84, 65

Calculate the:

a. Range.

b. Mean absolute deviation.

c. Variance.

d. Standard deviation.

e. Coefficient of variation.

3.14 The following are the average weekly earnings of production workers (in current dollars) for the years 1976 through 1983:*

Year	Earnings
1976	175
1977	189
1978	204
1979	219
1980	225
1981	255
1982	267
1983	281

Calculate the:

a. Mean.

b. Range.

c. Standard deviation.

3.15 For the price:earnings–ratio data in exercise 2.15, calculate the standard deviation.

3.16 Calculate the standard deviation of the price elasticity of electricity in exercise 2.21.

3.17 Determine the standard deviation and the variance for the U.S. gold reserves data in exercise 2.39.

3.18 For the data in exercise 3.11 concerning sales of multinational corporations, calculate the:

a. Range.

b. Standard deviation.

c. Variance.

3.19 The game of cricket, which originated in England, is popular in Australia, India, and the West Indies. The following are the runs (strikes) scored by two players, A and B, in various innings:

	Player A	Player B
	47	66
	0	10
	14	11
	33	22
	101	88
	68	32
	87	40
	14	38
	22	18
	46	41
Total	432	366

a. Who is the better player? On what basis?

b. Who is more consistent? Why?

*Source: *The World Almanac and Book of Facts,* 1985, p. 102.

3.20 The yield on a stock is equal to dividend per share / market price $\times$ 100. It is one of the popular measures used by individual investors when they make investment decisions. The following are the yield figures (in percent) for two stocks, A and B, for the past 10 years:

Stock A	Stock B
7	12
9	13
14	13
13	17
11	11
18	9
7	18
11	12
12	17
10	13

Which is a more stable stock in terms of yields? Why?

3.21 Calculate the variance for the daily advertising expense of the car dealer in exercise 3.9.

3.4

Measures of Position

Suppose that you think you are drastically underpaid as compared with other people with similar experience and performance. One way to attack the problem is to obtain the salary of these other employees and demonstrate that *comparatively* you are way down the list. To evaluate your salary as compared with the entire group, you would use a measure of position. **Measures of position** are indicators of how a particular value fits in with all the other data values. There are two measures of position: percentile and quartile, and Z score.

To illustrate these measures, we will suppose that the personnel manager of Texon Industries has administered an aptitude test to 50 applicants. The ordered data are shown in Table 3.1. The mean of the data is $\bar{x} = 60.36$, and the standard deviation is $s = 18.61$. Ms. Jenson received the score of 83. She wishes to measure her performance in relation to all of the applicant scores. We will return to this illustration in example 3.3.

Percentiles

A **percentile** is the most common measure of position. The value of, for example, the 40th percentile is essentially the data value that exceeds 40% of all the data values.

Table 3.1

Ordered array of aptitude test scores for 50 applicants ($\bar{x} = 60.36$, $s = 18.61$)

22	44	56	68	78
25	44	57	68	78
28	46	59	69	80
31	48	60	71	82
34	49	61	72	83
35	51	63	72	85
39	53	63	74	88
39	53	63	75	90
40	55	65	75	92
42	55	66	76	96

In other words, 40% of the data are below and 60% are above the 40th percentile. We will use the Texon Industries applicant data to determine the 35th percentile. Which data value is 35% of the way between the smallest and largest value? Here the number of data values is $n = 50$ and the percentile is $P = 35$. We define the *position* of the 35th percentile as follows:

$$n \cdot \frac{P}{100} = 50 \cdot .35 = 17.5$$

Note that whenever $n \cdot P/100$ is *not* a counting number, it should be rounded *up* to the next counting number. So, 17.5 is rounded up to 18, and the 35th percentile is the 18th value *of the ordered values*. Referring to Table 3.1, the 35th percentile = 53.

In general, to find the **location** of the Pth percentile, determine $n \cdot P/100$. If this is not a counting number, round it up. If $n \cdot P/100$ *is* a counting number, the Pth percentile is the average of the number in this location (of the ordered data) and the number in the next largest location.

Now we can use the applicant data to determine the 40th percentile. Here $n \cdot P/100 = (50)(.4) = 20$. Then

$$\text{40th percentile} = \frac{(\text{20th value}) + (\text{21st value})}{2} = \frac{55 + 56}{2} = 55.5$$

Notice here that the 40th percentile is *not* one of the data values but an average of two of them. Now work out the 50th percentile yourself. What measure of central tendency uses the same procedure? As should be obvious, the 50th percentile is the median.

Example 3.3   Recall that Ms. Jenson received a score of 83. What is her percentile value?

Solution Her value is the 45th largest value (out of a total of 50). An initial guess of the percentile here would be:

$$P = \frac{45}{50} \cdot 100 = 90$$

However, due to the percentile rules used here, this may be slightly incorrect. Your next step should be to examine this value of P, along with the next two smaller values. The following calculations of $P = 88$, $P = 89$, and $P = 90$ reveal that Ms. Jenson's score is the 89th percentile.

P	$n \cdot P/100$	**Pth percentile**
88	$50 \cdot .88 = 44$	$(82 + 83)/2 = 82.5$
89	$50 \cdot .89 = 44.5$	45th value $= 83$
90	$50 \cdot .90 = 45$	$(83 + 85)/2 = 84$

Example 3.4   What is the 50th percentile for the applicant data in Table 3.1?

Solution Here, $n \cdot P/100 = 50 \cdot .5 = 25$. The 50th percentile is an average of the 25th and 26th ordered data values:

$$\text{50th percentile} = \frac{61 + 63}{2} = 62$$

Quartiles

Quartiles are merely particular percentiles that divide the data into quarters, namely:

Q_1 = 1st quartile = 25th percentile

Q_2 = 2nd quartile = 50th percentile = median

Q_3 = 3rd quartile = 75th percentile

They are used as benchmarks, much like the use of A, B, C, D, and F on examination grades. Using the applicant data in Table 3.1, we can determine:

$n \cdot P/100 = 50 \cdot .25 = 12.5$

This is rounded up to 13, and Q_1 = 13th ordered value = 46.

Q_2 = median = 62

from Example 3.4. Finally,

$n \cdot P/100 = 50 \cdot .75 = 37.5$

This is rounded up to 38, and Q_3 = 38th ordered value = 75.

Z Scores

Another measure of position is a sample **Z score,** which is based on the mean $(\bar{x})$ and standard deviation of your data set. As with percentiles, a Z score determines the relative position of any particular data value x. The Z score of x is defined as

$$Z = \frac{x - \bar{x}}{s} \tag{3-10}$$

Recall from example 3.3 that Ms. Jenson had a score of 83 on the test. For this data set, $\bar{x} = 60.36$ and $s = 18.61$. Her score of 83 is in the 89th percentile. The corresponding Z score is

$$Z = \frac{83 - 60.36}{18.61} = 1.22$$

This means that Ms. Jenson's score of 83 is 1.22 standard deviations to the right of the mean, or above the group's average. Thus, if Z is positive, it indicates how many standard deviations x is to the *right* of the mean.

A negative value implies that x is to the *left* of the mean. Again referring to Table 3.1, what is the Z score for the individual who obtained a total of 35 on the aptitude examination?

$$Z = \frac{35 - 60.36}{18.61} = -1.36$$

This individual's score is 1.36 standard deviations to the *left* of the mean, or below the group's average.

Figure 3.3

Histogram constructed with symmetric data. The mean, median, and mode are equal.

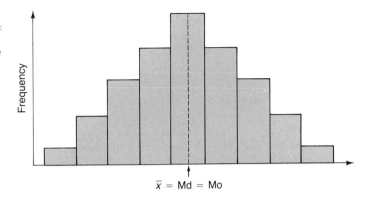

$$\bar{x} = \text{Md} = \text{Mo}$$

3.5

Measures of Shape

A basic question in many applications is whether your data exhibit a **symmetric** pattern. **Measures of shape** determine skewness and kurtosis.

Skewness

The histogram in Figure 3.3 demonstrates a perfectly symmetric distribution. When the data are symmetric, the sample mean, $\bar{x}$, the sample median, Md, and the sample mode, Mo, are the same. As the data tend toward a nonsymmetric distribution, referred to as **skewed,** the mean and median drift apart. The easiest method of determining the degree of skewness present in your sample data is to calculate a measure referred to as the **Pearsonian coefficient of skewness, Sk.** Its value is given by:

$$\text{Sk} = \frac{3(\bar{x} - \text{Md})}{s} \qquad (3\text{-}11)$$

where s is the standard deviation of the sample data.

The value of Sk ranges from -3 to 3. If the data are perfectly symmetric (a rare event), Sk = 0, because $\bar{x} = $ Md. For Figure 3.3, Sk is zero. If Sk is positive, then the mean is larger than the median, and we say that the data are *skewed right*. This merely means the data exhibit a pattern with a right tail, as illustrated in Figure 3.4.

Figure 3.4

Histogram showing right (positive) skew.

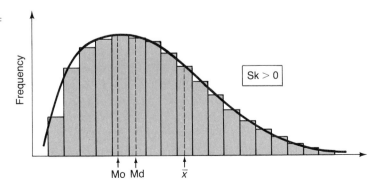

Sk > 0

Mo Md $\bar{x}$

Figure 3.5

Histogram showing left (negative) skew.

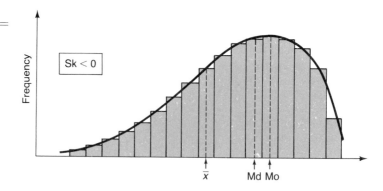

We know the mean is affected by extreme values, so we would expect the mean to move toward the right tail, above the median. This results in a positive value of Sk. Similarly, if Sk is negative, then the data are *skewed left* and the mean is smaller than the median. Figure 3.5 shows a data distribution exhibiting a left tail.

Using the aptitude examination scores in Table 3.1, we have $\bar{x} = 60.36$, $s = 18.61$, and Md $= 62$.

$$Sk = \frac{3(60.36 - 62)}{18.61} = -.26$$

Consequently, a histogram of these data should be just slightly skewed left.

Kurtosis

Sk measures the tendency of a distribution to stretch out in a particular direction. Another measure of shape, referred to as the **kurtosis,** measures the **peakedness** of your distribution. The calculation of this measure is a bit cumbersome, and the kurtosis value is not needed in the remaining text material.* Briefly, this value is small if the frequency of observations close to the mean is high and the frequency of observations far from the mean is low.

Exercises

3.22 The following table indicates the scores of the students at a junior college on a statistics exam:

18, 58, 71, 83, 89, 96, 21, 62, 74, 84, 90, 97, 43, 66, 75, 86, 92, 98, 47, 66, 77, 86, 94, 100, 55, 68, 78, 88, 95, 100

a. Calculate the fortieth percentile.

b. Calculate the seventy-seventh percentile.

c. Interpret the meaning of the numbers calculated for the two percentiles.

3.23 In exercise 3.22, how would you evaluate the performance of a student who scored 74 on the exam?

---

*The following texts contain an alternate method of computing sample skewness as well as a procedure for computing the sample kurtosis. L. Ott and D. K. Hildebrand, *Statistical Thinking for Managers* (Boston: Duxbury Press, 1983), p. 27; C. L. Olsen, and M. J. Picconi, *Statistics for Business Decision Making* (Glenview, IL: Scott, Foresman, 1983), pp. 127–129.

3.24 Using the data in exercise 3.22, calculate the first and third quartiles. State the results in words.

3.25 Considering the following data:

7, 8, 8, 9, 11, 14, 15, 16, 18, 19, 21, 27, 28, 30, 32, 35

Calculate the:

a. Ninetieth percentile.

b. Fifty-eighth percentile.

3.26 Calculate the three quartiles for the data in exercise 3.25.

3.27 Assume a particular set of sample data such that

$$\bar{x} = 49$$
$$s = 18$$

Consider one particular value of $x = 63$.

a. Calculate the Z score.

b. Interpret the Z score.

3.28 If the Z score for an observation is 1.50, the standard deviation is 14, and the observation is 32, what is the mean?

3.29 If the mean is 40, $x = 35$, and its Z score is -2, what is the value of the standard deviation?

3.30 If the Z score for an observation is -1.22, $\bar{x} = 83$ and the variance is 84, what is the value of the observation?

3.31 If the Z score is 1.78 and the variance is 64, what is $x - \bar{x}$?

3.32 Assume the following about a set of sample data:

$$s = 14$$
$$\bar{x} = 21$$
$$Md = 18.5$$

a. What do you observe about the pattern of the data?

b. Calculate the coefficient of skewness. What does this value suggest?

3.33 The gross national product (GNP) is the market value of all final goods and services produced by an economy in a given time period. It is probably the most important indicator of economic health of a country. The GNP (in billions of constant 1972 dollars) of the United States for the years 1970 through 1984 was as follows:*

Year	GNP	Year	GNP
1970	1085.6	1978	1438.6
1971	1122.4	1979	1479.4
1972	1185.9	1980	1475.0
1973	1254.3	1981	1512.2
1974	1246.3	1982	1480.0
1975	1231.6	1983	1534.7
1976	1298.2	1984	1639.0
1977	1369.7		

a. Calculate the mean, median, variance, and standard deviation of the GNP values.

b. Calculate the coefficient of skewness. Are the data skewed to the left?

*Source: *Economic Report of the President,* Feb. 1985.

3.6

Interpreting $\bar{x}$ and s

Now that you spent more time than you cared to determining the sample mean and standard deviation, what can you learn from these values? The type of question that you can answer is, "How many of the data values are within two standard deviations of the mean?"

Take a look at the data from Table 3.1. Here, $\bar{x} = 60.36$ and $s = 18.61$, and so we obtain

$$\bar{x} - s = 60.36 - 18.61 \qquad \bar{x} + s = 60.36 + 18.61$$
$$= 41.75 \qquad\qquad = 78.97$$

$$\bar{x} - 2s = 60.36 - 37.22 \qquad \bar{x} + 2s = 60.36 + 37.22$$
$$= 23.14 \qquad\qquad = 97.58$$

$$\bar{x} - 3s = 60.36 - 55.83 \qquad \bar{x} + 3s = 60.36 + 55.83$$
$$= 4.53 \qquad\qquad = 116.19$$

Examine these data and observe that (1) 33 out of the 50 values (66%) lie between $\bar{x} - s$ and $\bar{x} + s$; (2) 49 out of the 50 values (98%) lie between $\bar{x} - 2s$ and $\bar{x} + 2s$; and (3) 50 out of the 50 values (100%) lie between $\bar{x} - 3s$ and $\bar{x} + 3s$. Or, put another way: (1) 66% of the data values have a Z score between -1 and 1; (2) 98% have a Z score between -2 and 2, and (3) 100% have a Z score between -3 and 3.

What can we say in general for *any* data set? There are two types of statements we can make. One of these, **Chebyshev's inequality,** is usually conservative but makes *no assumption* about the population from which you obtained your data. Following are the components of Chebyshev's inequality.

Chebyshev's Inequality

1. At least 75% of the data values are between $\bar{x} - 2s$ and $\bar{x} + 2s$
2. At least 89% of the data values are between $\bar{x} - 3s$ and $\bar{x} + 3s$
3. In general, there are at least $(1 - 1/k^2)$ of your data values between $\bar{x} - ks$ and $\bar{x} + ks$, for $k = 2, 3, 4, \ldots$

Note that if $k = 1$, $1 - 1/k^2 = 0$; so Chebyshev's inequality provides no information on the number of data values to expect between $\bar{x} - s$ and $\bar{x} + s$.

The other type of statement is called the **empirical rule.** We make a key assumption here, namely that the population from which you obtain your sample has a *bell-*

Figure 3.6

A bell-shaped (normal) population.

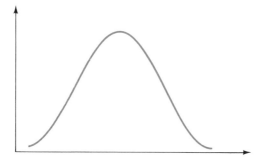

shaped distribution; that is, it is symmetric and tapers off smoothly into each tail. Such a population is called a **normal population** and is illustrated in Figure 3.6. Thus, the data set should have a skewness measure, Sk, near zero and a histogram similar to that in Figure 3.3. However, the empirical rule is still quite accurate if your distribution is not exactly bell-shaped. Following are the components of the empirical rule.

Empirical Rule

Under the assumption of a bell-shaped population:
1. Approximately 68% of the data values will lie between $\bar{x} - s$ and $\bar{x} + s$
2. Approximately 95% of the data values will lie between $\bar{x} - 2s$ and $\bar{x} + 2s$
3. Approximately 99.7% of the data values will lie between $\bar{x} - 3s$ and $\bar{x} + 3s$

Returning to Table 3.1, we can summarize our previous results along with the information provided by Chebyshev's inequality and the empirical rule. The actual percentage of the sample values in each interval, as well as the percentage specified using each of the two rules, are shown in Table 3.2.

As you can see, Chebyshev's inequality is very conservative, but it always works. The empirical rule predicted results close to what was observed. This is not surprising because the skewness measure is only slightly different from zero (Sk $= -.26$).

Example 3.5

In a random sample of 200 automotive insurance claims obtained from Pearson Insurance Company, $\bar{x} = \$615$ and $s = \$135$. (1) What statement can you make using Chebyshev's inequality? (2) If you assume that the population of all insurance claims is bell-shaped (normal), what does the empirical rule say about these 200 values?

Solution 1 Chebyshev's inequality provides information regarding the number of sample values within a specified number of standard deviations of the mean. For $k = 2$, we have:

$$\bar{x} - 2s = 615 - 2(135) = \$345$$
$$\bar{x} + 2s = 615 + 2(135) = \$885$$

We conclude that at least 75% of the sample values lie between \$345 and \$885. Because $.75 \cdot 200 = 150$, this implies that at least 150 of the claims are between \$345 and \$885.

Table 3.2

Summary of percentages of sample values by interval, using data from Table 3.1

Between	Actual Percentage	Chebyshev Inequality Percentage	Empirical Rule Percentage
$\bar{x} - s$ and $\bar{x} + s$	66% (33 out of 50)	–	$\approx 68\%$
$\bar{x} - 2s$ and $\bar{x} + 2s$	98% (49 out of 50)	$\geq 75\%$	$\approx 95\%$
$\bar{x} - 3s$ and $\bar{x} + 3s$	100% (50 out of 50)	$\geq 89\%$	$\approx 100\%$

For $k = 3$,

$$\bar{x} - 3s = 615 - 3(135) = \$210$$
$$\bar{x} + 3s = 615 + 3(135) = \$1020$$

and we conclude that at least 8/9 (89%) of the data values are between \$210 and \$1020. Here, $8/9 \cdot 200 = 177.8$, and so at least 178 of the claims are between \$210 and \$1020.

Solution 2   Under the assumption that all the automotive claims at Pearson Insurance Company are bell-shaped, the empirical rule allows us to draw stronger conclusions. In particular, for $k = 1$, we have

$$\bar{x} - s = 615 - 135 = \$480$$
$$\bar{x} + s = 615 + 135 = \$750$$

and we conclude that approximately 68% of the data values $(.68 \cdot 200 = 136)$ are between \$480 and \$750.
  For $k = 2$,

$$\bar{x} - 2s = \$345$$
$$\bar{x} + 2s = \$885$$

and we conclude that approximately 95% of the data values $(.95 \cdot 200 = 190)$ will lie between \$345 and \$885.   ●

Exercises

3.34 Use the mean, median, and standard deviation obtained for the data in exercise 3.33.

a. Using Chebyshev's inequality, find the range of GNP that will include 89% of the data.

3.35 The mean of the wages of a sample of production workers in a company is \$18,600, and the standard deviation is \$445. Assuming the corresponding population is normally distributed, estimate the range of wages within which about 95% of the employees in the sample are expected to lie.

3.36 In the annual spaghetti-eating contest of a small town, 100 people participated. The contestants' spaghetti consumption averaged 120 feet with a standard deviation of 14 feet.

a. At least how many contestants ate between 92 and 148 feet of spaghetti?

b. At least how many contestants ate between 78 and 162 feet of spaghetti?

c. Did you have to make any assumptions about the data to answer questions a and b?

3.37 What do you think will be the value of the coefficient of skewness for a symmetric distribution? Will the mean and median be equal?

3.38 Refer to the data on exam scores in exercise 2.1. Using Chebyshev's inequality, estimate the values that should contain at least 75% of the data.

3.39 Refer to the data in exercise 3.11.

a. Do the data appear to resemble a normal curve?

b. Using the empirical rule, estimate the range of values within which about 68% of the data values are expected to lie.

3.40 The mean score of students in an accounting class was 78.5, and the standard deviation was 22. Using the empirical rule, estimate the range of scores within which about 95% of the data values are expected to lie.

3.41 If the mean of a sample is 28.2 with a standard deviation of 6.2, what data values would lie within two standard deviations of the mean?

3.42 For the P:E ratio data in exercise 2.15, calculate the:

a. Coefficient of skewness

b. Using the empirical rule, find the range of values within which approximately 100% of the values are expected to lie.

3.43 Using Chebyshev's inequality, find the scores on the aptitude test in exercise 3.13 between which at least 89% of the data will fall.

3.44 The average number of visitors to the local museum is 48 per day and the standard deviation is 17. Using the empirical rule, estimate the range within which approximately 100% of the visitors will fall.

3.45 A shoe salesperson computes that his mean daily sales of shoes is $280 with a standard deviation of $40. Give two bounds within which the shoe salesperson can expect daily shoe sales to lie at least 75% of the time.

3.7

Grouped Data

You may have to work with data in the form of a frequency distribution, called **grouped data,** when the raw data are not available. This situation can arise when we find a histogram or frequency distribution in a magazine or newspaper article in which the actual raw data used to construct the histogram are not included. We do not have the data values used to make up this frequency distribution, so we are forced to estimate the sample statistics, in particular the mean, median, and standard deviation.

Estimating the Sample Mean, $\bar{x}$

Assume we obtain the frequency distribution shown in Table 3.3, containing the ages of 35 individuals who recently passed a CPA examination. The 35 data values are not available, so we cannot add them up. A procedure that works well for estimating $\bar{x}$ is simply to pretend that the 35 data values are equal to their respective class midpoints. Consequently, there are

$$5 \text{ values at } (20 + 30)/2 = 25$$
$$14 \text{ values at } (30 + 40)/2 = 35$$
$$\vdots$$
$$2 \text{ values at } (60 + 70)/2 = 65$$

Table 3.3

Age of 35 individuals who recently passed a CPA examination

Class Number	Class (age in years)	Frequency
1	20 and under 30	5
2	30 and under 40	14
3	40 and under 50	9
4	50 and under 60	5
5	60 and under 70	2
		35

The value of $\bar{x}$ is estimated by finding what it is approximately equal to ($\cong$).

$$\bar{x} \cong \frac{(25 + 25 + 25 + 25 + 25) + \ldots + (65 + 65)}{35}$$

$$= \frac{(5)(25) + (14)(35) + (9)(45) + (5)(55) + (2)(65)}{35}$$

$$= \frac{1425}{35} = 40.7$$

Our estimate of the average age of these 35 individuals is

$\bar{x} \cong 40.7$ years

In general,

$$\bar{x} \cong \frac{\Sigma f \cdot m}{n} \qquad\qquad (3\text{-}12)$$

where n = sample size, f = frequency of each class, and m = midpoint of each class.

Estimating the Sample Standard Deviation, s

Using the same fictitious data set at the various class midpoints, the variance, s^2, can be found in the usual way, using equation 3-8.

$$s^2 = \frac{\Sigma(\text{each data value})^2 - [\Sigma(\text{each data value})]^2/n}{n - 1}$$

$$\Sigma \, (\text{each data value})^2 \; = \; \overbrace{(25^2 + 25^2 + \ldots + 25^2)}^{5 \text{ times}}$$

$$+ \overbrace{(35^2 + 35^2 + \ldots + 35^2)}^{14 \text{ times}}$$

$$\vdots$$

$$+ (65^2 + 65^2)$$

$$= (5)(25^2) + (14)(35^2) + (9)(45^2) + (5)(55^2) + (2)(65^2)$$

$$= 62,075$$

Also, Σ (each data value) = 1425. This was determined previously when estimating $\bar{x}$.

$$s^2 \cong \frac{62,075 - (1425)^2/35}{34} = \frac{4057.14}{34} = 119.33$$

$$s \cong \sqrt{119.33} = 10.92$$

Table 3.4

Summary of calculations for grouped data

Class Number	Class	f	m	$f \cdot m$	$f \cdot m^2$
1	20 and under 30	5	25	125	3,125
2	30 and under 40	14	35	490	17,150
3	40 and under 50	9	45	405	18,225
4	50 and under 60	5	55	275	15,125
5	60 and under 70	2	65	130	8,450
				$\Sigma f \cdot m = 1{,}425$	$\Sigma f \cdot m^2 = 62{,}075$

In general,

$$s^2 \cong \frac{\Sigma f \cdot m^2 - (\Sigma f \cdot m)^2 / n}{n - 1} \tag{3-13}$$

where f, m, and n are as defined in equation 3-12.

The calculations necessary to estimate $\bar{x}$ and s are more easily performed using a table similar to Table 3.4.

Estimating the Sample Median, Md

Using the previous example, we have

$$Md \cong \left(\frac{35 + 1}{2}\right) \text{th ordered value} = 18\text{th ordered value}$$

Where is this value in the frequency distribution? The first class contains the five smallest values, and the first two classes contain the first 19 ordered values (5 + 14 = 19). So the 18th value is in the second class.

We can better approximate the median by assuming that the values in this class (and all classes) are spread *evenly* between the lower and upper limits. Because the first class contains five values, the median is 13 (18 − 5) values into the second class. This class begins at 30, has a width of 10, and has 14 values in it. So we want to go 13 values into a class of width 10 containing 14 values. The resulting estimate of the median is

$$Md \cong 30 + \frac{13}{14}(10) = 39.3$$

In general,

$$Md \cong L + \frac{k}{f} \cdot W \tag{3-14}$$

where L = lower limit of the class containing the median (called the **median class**); $k = (n + 1)/2 -$ (the number of data values preceding the median class); $f =$ frequency of the median class; and W = class width.

In the previous example, $L = 30$, $f = 14$, $W = 10$, and thus

$$k = \frac{35 + 1}{2} - 5 = 13$$

If n is even (say, $n = 100$), then $(n + 1)/2 = 50.5$, and you need to estimate the 50.5th ordered value. This is halfway between the 50th and the 51st value. The procedure to follow here is exactly the same, except k will not be a counting number.

Remember that these procedures for estimating the sample statistics are used only when the raw data are not available and your only information is a frequency distribution or corresponding histogram. If the actual data values are available, these statistics can be determined exactly, and the estimation procedures described in this section should not be used.

Exercises

3.46 The following data are the number of legal abortions (in thousands) by age of mother (in years) in the U.S. for the year 1981:*

Mother's Age	Number of Legal Abortions
under 15	15
15 and under 20	433
20 and under 25	555
25 and under 30	316
30 and under 35	167
35 and under 40	70
40 and above	21

Compute the median. Is the median an appropriate summary number for these data? Why or why not?

3.47 The following is the summarized information concerning family income (in dollars) for a specific neighborhood of a major city.

Income Level	Percent of Families
0 and under 10,000	11
10,000 and under 20,000	19
20,000 and under 30,000	30
30,000 and under 40,000	15
40,000 and under 50,000	10
50,000 and under 60,000	15

Find the median family income.

3.48 Advertising expenditures constitute one of the important components of the cost of goods sold. From the following data concerning advertising expenditures (in millions of dollars) of 50 companies, find the median advertising expenditure.

Advertising Expenditure	Number of Companies
25 and under 35	5
35 and under 45	11
45 and under 55	18
55 and under 65	6
65 and under 75	10
	50

*Source: *U.S. Statistical Abstracts*, U.S. Department of Commerce, 1985, p. 67.

3.49 Calculate the median age of the U.S. population for the year 1983 using the data in exercise 2.13.

3.50 Glen's Mufflers and Exhaust has been experiencing a steady growth in sales. The following grouped data show a breakdown of the frequency of sales volume (in hundreds of dollars):

Daily Sales	Number of Days
.5 and under 1	2
1 and under 1.5	2
1.5 and under 2	3
2 and under 2.5	11
2.5 and under 3	20
3 and under 3.5	12
3.5 and under 4	5
4 and under 4.5	3
4.5 and under 5	2

a. Calculate the mean daily sales.

b. Calculate the standard deviation of the mean daily sales.

3.51 The following is the final distribution of grades in an introductory economics course at a local university:

Grade	Number of Students
90–99	5
80–89	14
70–79	11
60–69	4
50–59	7
	41

a. Calculate the mean score.

b. Calculate the standard deviation.

c. Interpret the value of the mean and standard deviation.

3.52 The industrial engineer of the Bright Light company is interested in examining the average burning hours (life) of the 100-watt bulbs manufactured. Using the following data, determine the mean burning hours of a 100-watt bulb:

Burning Hours	Number of Bulbs
0 and under 40	231
40 and under 50	168
50 and under 60	244
60 and under 70	300
70 and under 80	111
80 and under 90	48
90 and under 100	98
	1200

3.8

Calculating Descriptive Statistics by Coding

When you use a calculator to determine the sample mean or standard deviation, one problem that can occur is that the data values are too large or too small to "fit" into your calculator. To avoid having the calculator self-destruct in your hands, a procedure referred to as **data adjusting** or **data coding** allows you to derive these statistics using more reasonable data values. You can then work backwards to get the desired

Figure 3.7

Data coding.

Subtracting or adding a constant

Actual data

Adjusted data

1005, 1006, 1007, 1009, 1023 ——— subtract 1000 ———→ 5, 6, 7, 9, 23

$\bar{x} = 1000 + 10 = 1010$ ←——— add 1000 ——— $\bar{x} = 10$

$s = 7.416$ ←——— is the same as ——— $s = 7.416$

Dividing or multiplying by a constant

Actual data

Adjusted data

5000, 6000, 7000, 9000, 23,000 ——— divide by 1000 ———→ 5, 6, 7, 9, 23

$\bar{x} = 1000 \times 10 = 10,000$ ←——— multiply by 1000 ——— $\bar{x} = 10$

$s = 1000 \times 7.416 = 7,416$ ←——— multiply by 1000 ——— $s = 7.416$

statistics. To code or adjust the data you subtract (or add) or divide (or multiply) your original data set by a fixed amount. Figure 3.7 demonstrates this procedure using data sets containing several large values. To adjust the data when subtracting (adding) a positive constant to each data value,

actual $\bar{x}$ = adjusted $\bar{x}$ plus (minus) the constant

actual s = adjusted s (no change)

When dividing (multiplying) by a positive constant,

actual $\bar{x}$ = adjusted $\bar{x}$ times (divided by) the constant

actual s = adjusted s times (divided by) the constant

When you derive sample statistics, you have essentially two options: use a calculator or use a computer. Calculators work well for small data sets but involve too much time (and opportunity for error) for moderate or large sample sizes. Practically all statistical computer packages will provide you with the basic sample statistics (mean, median, variance, and so on) in response to only a few commands once the data have been read in. Figure 3.8 contains the MINITAB commands (along with the output) necessary to derive the basic statistics for the data in Table 3.1. The appendices at the end of the chapter will demonstrate this procedure using SPSSX and SAS.

Figure 3.8

MINITAB procedure for describing sample data.

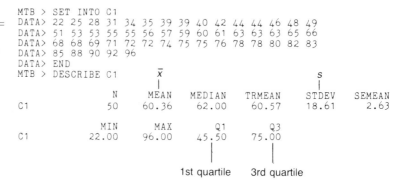

```
MTB > SET INTO C1
DATA> 22 25 28 31 34 35 39 39 40 42 44 44 46 48 49
DATA> 51 53 53 55 55 56 57 59 60 61 63 63 63 65 66
DATA> 68 68 69 71 72 72 74 75 75 76 78 78 80 82 83
DATA> 85 88 90 92 96
DATA> END
MTB > DESCRIBE C1
                         x̄                              s
                         |                              |
                N      MEAN    MEDIAN   TRMEAN   STDEV   SEMEAN
         C1    50     60.36    62.00    60.57    18.61    2.63

               MIN      MAX       Q1       Q3
         C1   22.00    96.00    45.50    75.00
                                  |        |
                              1st quartile  3rd quartile
```

Exercises

3.53 Using the subtraction rule, adjust the following data and calculate the mean and standard deviation.

413, 407, 411, 402, 425, 408, 410, 421

3.54 Using the multiplication rule, adjust the following data and calculate the mean and standard deviation:

0.00119, 0.00101, 0.00121, 0.00108, 0.0010, 0.00114, 0.00117, 0.00104, 0.00123, 0.00124

3.55 Using the division rule, calculate the mean and variance for the following data:

200, 600, 800, 1000, 400, 1200, 10,000, 1400, 1600, 400

3.56 Using the division rule, calculate the mean and standard deviation for the following data:

500, 3000, 600, 1000, 400, 300, 100, 2500, 700, 300

3.57 Using the multiplication rule, adjust the following data and calculate the mean and standard deviation:

0.001182, 0.001104, 0.001270, 0.001251, 0.001407, 0.001553, 0.001177, 0.001333, 0.001489, 0.001505

3.58 Using the subtraction rule, adjust the following data and calculate the mean:

1013, 1007, 1011, 1102, 1025, 1008, 1110, 1021, 1111, 1009

Summary

This chapter has introduced you to some of the more popular statistical measures used to describe a set of sample values. Measures of central tendency are used to describe a typical value within the sample. They are the mean, median, mode, and midrange. To measure the variation within a set of sample data, we use measures of dispersion: the range, mean absolute deviation, variance, standard deviation, and coefficient of variation. Percentiles, quartiles, and Z scores are used to indicate the relative position of a sample value and are thus measures of position. Finally, the shape of a data set can be described using various measures of shape; two such measures are the sample skewness and kurtosis.

The two most commonly used measures are the sample mean and standard deviation. These two statistics can be used together to describe the sample data by applying Chebyshev's inequality or the empirical rule. The latter procedure draws a stronger conclusion about the concentration of the data values but assumes that the population of interest is bell-shaped (normal).

We examined how to estimate the sample mean and standard deviation when the only information available is a frequency distribution, or grouped data. Finally, data coding can be used to calculate these two measures more easily when you encounter data sets containing extremely large or small values.

Review Exercises

3.59 Unemployment rate (U) represents the percent of the labor force that is unemployed. The following are the U.S. unemployment rates for the years 1951 through 1983:*

Year	U	Year	U
1951	3.3	1968	3.6
1952	3.0	1969	3.5
1953	2.9	1970	4.9
1954	5.6	1971	5.9
1955	4.4	1972	5.6
1956	4.1	1973	4.9
1957	4.3	1974	5.6
1958	6.8	1975	8.5
1959	5.5	1976	7.7
1960	5.5	1977	7.0
1961	6.7	1978	6.0
1962	5.6	1979	5.8
1963	5.6	1980	7.1
1964	5.2	1981	7.6
1965	4.5	1982	9.7
1966	3.8	1983	9.6
1967	3.9		

Calculate the:

a. Range.

b. Mean.

c. Median.

d. Mode.

e. Standard deviation.

f. Coefficient of variation.

g. First quartile.

h. Ninetieth percentile.

3.60 Interest rate measures the cost of borrowing over a specified period of time. Prime rate generally indicates the interest rate charged by banks to borrowers with the highest credit rating. Following are the prime rates charged by U.S. banks for the years 1974 through 1984:*

10.80, 7.86, 6.84, 9.06, 12.67, 15.26, 18.87, 14.86, 10.79, 11.51

Calculate the:

a. Mean.

b. Median.

c. Mode.

d. Mean absolute deviation.

e. Variance.

f. Third quartile.

g. Z score for the data value in question f. What does this suggest about the 1984 interest rate?

*Source: *Statistical Abstract of the United States,* U.S. Department of Commerce.

3.61 Using the data in exercise 3.60.

a. Do the data appear to be bell-shaped?

b. Calculate the coefficient of skewness.

c. Using the empirical rule, estimate the range of values within which about 68% of the data values are expected to lie.

d. Is the empirical rule appropriate? Compare actual percentages with the predicted percentages.

3.62 The following is the distribution of the annual incomes (in thousands of dollars) of the households in a neighborhood:

Annual Income	Number of Households
0 and under 10	21
10 and under 20	11
20 and under 30	9
30 and under 40	13
40 and under 50	17
50 and under 60	20
60 and under 70	14
70 and under 80	20
80 and under 90	7
90 and under 100	2
	134

a. Calculate the mean annual income.

b. Calculate the variance.

c. Estimate the proportion of data that lies within two standard deviations from the mean.

d. Calculate the coefficient of skewness.

3.63 The mean rate charged by the CPAs in a certain city is about $75 per hour, with a standard deviation of $15. Assuming that the data came from a normal population, estimate the range of rates within which about 95% of the charges by the CPAs are expected to lie.

3.64 The Z score is -1.50, the mean is 45, and $x = 15$, what is the value of the variance?

3.65 The mean is 81, the standard deviation is 9, and one particular x value is 45.

a. Calculate the Z score.

b. Interpret the Z score.

3.66 The mean GMAT score of the 65 applicants who were accepted into the MBA program of Xavier Business School was 520 with a standard deviation of 25. About how many applicants scored between 470 and 570 on the GMAT?

3.67 Calculate the mean and standard deviation for these data:

50.2, 53.8, 51.4, 52.2, 50.8, 59.1, 52.8, 57.7, 51.1, 54.3, 55.5, 52.1, 57.6, 55.9, 50.9, 54.7

3.68 Calculate the mean and standard deviation for the following data:

1000, 700, 400, 100, 800, 20,000, 4000, 300, 900, 600, 200, 500, 2000, 700, 2500, 5500

3.69 The industrial production index (IPI) is one of the useful indicators that helps to monitor the economy. Simply stated, it indicates the gross value of production in a given sector of an industry. Because it is expressed relative to a base year (such as 1967 = 100), it facilitates comparison over a period of time. The following are the IPIs for the month of July 1984 for various industries.*

Industry	IPI
Foods	164.9
Tobacco products	115.1
Textile mills	139.8
Paper and products	176.7
Printing and publishing	172.6
Chemicals	232.0
Petroleum products	124.7
Rubber and plastics	341.4
Leather products	60.6
Lumber products	146.0
Furniture and fixtures	192.6
Clay, glass, and stone products	160.9
Fabricated metal products	140.6
Electrical instruments	221.5
Motor vehicles and parts	169.0
Oil and gas extraction	122.8
Coal mining	176.5
Utilities	181.8
Stone and earth minerals	147.9

Calculate the values for questions a through l.

a. Mean.

b. Median.

c. Mode.

d. Variance.

e. Standard deviation.

f. Mean absolute deviation.

g. Range.

h. Coefficient of variation.

i. Coefficient of skewness.

j. First quartile.

k. Eighty-fifth percentile.

l. Z score for lumber products.

m. Using Chebyshev's inequality, find the values of the IPI between which at least 75% of the data values will fall.

n. Calculate the proportion of the data values that will have a Z score between -1 and $+1$, assuming that the empirical rule holds.

3.70 The following are the 20 largest U.S. industrial corporations, ranked by sales (in millions of dollars) in the year 1981:**

*Source: *Federal Reserve Bulletin*, February 1985, No. 2, Vol. 71, Washington, D.C.: Board of Governors of the Federal Reserve System.

**Source: *Fortune*, 3 May 1982, p. 260.

Rank	Company	Sales
1	Exxon	108,108
2	Mobil	64,488
3	GM	62,698
4	Texaco	57,628
5	Standard Oil (CA)	44,224
6	Ford Motor	38,247
7	Standard Oil (IN)	29,947
8	IBM	29,070
9	Gulf Oil	28,252
10	Arco	27,797
11	GE	27,240
12	Du Pont	22,810
13	Shell Oil	21,629
14	ITT	17,306
15	Phillips Petroleum	15,966
16	Tenneco	15,462
17	Sun	15,012
18	Occidental Petroleum	14,707
19	U.S. Steel	13,941
20	United Technologies	13,668

Calculate the values for questions a through i.

a. Mean.

b. Median.

c. Mode.

d. Standard deviation.

e. Range.

f. Coefficient of variation.

g. Coefficient of skewness.

h. Ninetieth percentile.

i. Z score for Arco.

j. Using Chebyshev's inequality, find the values of the sales figure between which at least 89% of the data will fall.

k. Why use Chebyshev's inequality instead of the empirical rule?

Case Study

Resorts of New England

The resort industry of New England asked its trade association, Resorts of New England, to update its information on the average vacationer. The association's promotional effort used a seasonal appeal, and the spring promotion had focused on white-water adventures. The white-water industry had grown tenfold in the last five years, and information on the average user of this service was outdated.

The association decided to conduct a scientific study of this group of vacationers and selected a random weekend in May to interview subjects. (Past surveys had indicated that the use of the rivers was stable in May.) They then interviewed a proportional number of vacationers from each take-out area, based on the volume of the river traffic.

The interviewer asked each vacationer how much money he or she had spent in the New England states during the visit. This information could be used to forecast future tourist spending as well as to make comparisons with vacationers in other areas.

Here is the array for the total dollars spent by the 100 people interviewed, rounded to the nearest ten dollars:

1440	1550	3530	1670	1650	1530	1530	1530	1450	3790
1460	1520	1710	1690	1670	1710	1690	1720	1730	1720
1740	1720	1810	1460	4130	1130	1440	1960	1170	1170
1730	1750	1560	1690	1710	1190	1480	1310	1430	1740
1810	1790	1930	3810	1690	1690	1690	1690	1690	1690
1820	1690	1740	1750	1690	1690	1530	1530	1550	1440
1370	1420	1380	1430	1820	1680	1690	1690	1690	1730
1690	2780	1550	1740	1760	4350	1770	3570	1140	1180
1150	1740	1120	1930	1630	1670	1710	4420	1640	1670
4690	1650	1540	1610	1760	1910	1710	1660	1190	1850

Case Study Questions

1. What is the shape of the distribution of costs of the raw data?
2. Does the shape of the distribution change if you use grouped data?
3. What is the mean cost of a vacation?
4. What is the modal cost?
5. What is the median cost?
6. Which measure of central tendency is the best measure of the typical cost of a white-water vacation? Why?
7. What is the variance of the set of costs?
8. What is the standard deviation of the costs?

Solution
Table 3.1

We can use SPSSX for the aptitude-test scores in Table 3.1. The SPSSX program listing in Figure 3.9 was used to request the calculation of the mean, standard deviation, and other descriptive statistics. Each line represents one card image to be entered:

Figure 3.9

SPSSX program listing requesting descriptive statistics on data in Table 3.1.

```
TITLE      DESCRIPTIVE STATISTICS
DATA LIST FREE      /APTEST
CONDESCRIPTIVE      APTEST
BEGIN DATA
22    44    56    68    78
25    44    57    68    78
28    46    59    69    80
31    48    60    71    82
34    49    61    72    83
35    51    63    72    85
39    53    63    74    88
39    53    63    75    90
40    55    65    75    92
42    55    66    76    96
END DATA
FINISH
```

The TITLE command names the SPSSX run.

The DATA LIST command gives each variable a name and describes the data as being in free form.

The CONDESCRIPTIVE statement requests an SPSSX procedure to print simple descriptive statistics for the variables in the applicant data set.

The BEGIN DATA command indicates to SPSSX that the input data immediately follow.

The next 10 lines are card images. Each line represents the test score of five of the 50 applicants.

The END DATA statement indicates the end of the data card images.

The FINISH command indicates the end of the SPSSX program.

Figure 3.10 gives the output obtained from executing the program listing in Figure 3.9.

Figure 3.10

Output obtained by executing the program listing in Figure 3.9.

```
NUMBER OF VALID OBSERVATIONS (LISTWISE) =       50.00

VARIABLE       MEAN      STD DEV     MINIMUM    MAXIMUM VALID N    LABEL

APTEST       60.360      18.605      22.00      96.00      50
```

Solution

Table 3.1

SAS will compute the descriptive statistics using the aptitude test scores in Table 3.1. The SAS program listing in Figure 3.11 was used to request the calculation of

Figure 3.11

SAS program listing requesting descriptive statistics on data in Table 3.1.

```
TITLE     DESCRIPTIVE STATISTICS;
DATA APTDAT;
INPUT APTEST;
CARDS;
22
25
28
31
34
35
39
39
40
42
44
44
46
48
49
51
53
53
55
55
56
57
59
 :
 :
96
;
PROC PRINT;
PROC MEANS;
```

the mean, standard deviation, and other descriptive statistics. Each line represents one card image to be entered:

The TITLE command names the SAS run.

The DATA command gives the data a name.

The INPUT command names and gives the correct order for the different fields on the data cards.

The CARDS command indicates to SAS that the input data immediately follow.

The next 50 lines are card images, with each line representing one applicant's aptitude test score.

The ; indicates the end of the data card images.

The PROC PRINT command directs SAS to list the data that were just read in.

The PROC MEANS command requests an SAS procedure to print simple descriptive statistics for the variable in the applicant file.

Figure 3.12 is the output obtained from executing the program listing in Figure 3.11.

Figure 3.12

Output obtained by executing program listing in Figure 3.11.

DESCRIPTIVE STATISTICS

VARIABLE	N	MEAN	STANDARD DEVIATION	MINIMUM VALUE	MAXIMUM VALUE	STD ERROR OF MEAN	SUM	VARIANCE	C.V.
APTEST	50	60.36000000	18.60520006	22.00000000	96.00000000	2.63117263	3018.0000000	346.15346939	30.824

4

Bivariate Data

A Look Back/Introduction

So far we have discussed ways of obtaining information from a set of numbers (sample). These included reducing the set of data to a numerical measure, such as the mean or the variance, and reducing the set of data to a graph. Both are concerned with reducing a set of numbers on one variable. A **variable** here is the characteristic of the population that is being measured or observed. For example, the variable of interest might be an individual's height or income. The sample consists of random observations of the variable in a given population.

We have assumed in these early chapters that someone gives you a sample of measurements of some kind (such as inches or dollars), and your job is to describe these data in some way. This chapter discusses how to describe data when you are given information on two variables.

4.1

The Nature of Bivariate Data

Bivariate data are data on two variables, say X and Y, where the observations are **paired.** This means that the first observation on X is paired (belongs) with the first value of Y, the second on X with the second on Y, and so on.

Assume that a personnel department has gathered sample data on the age (X) and annual income (Y) of eight employees. The data are:

Person	Age (X)	Income (Y) (in thousands of dollars)
1	35	37
2	26	29
3	45	52
4	48	55
5	31	35
6	50	60
7	32	38
8	40	46

Here $(X = 35, Y = 37)$, $(X = 26, Y = 29)$, and so on are **bivariate data;** the two variables being sampled are paired according to the person to whom they belong. An easier way to represent these data is to use **ordered pairs:** (35,37), (26,29), and so on. Notice that the X value is the *first* value within each ordered pair. As in Chapters 2 and 3, we can describe these data by constructing a picture (called a scatter diagram) and computing a number (numerical measure) that tells us something about the relationship between X and Y.

In a **scatter diagram,** each ordered pair in the sample is represented as a point. The X axis always is horizontal and the Y axis is vertical. A scatter diagram of the eight sample points from the personnel data is shown in Figure 4.1. In this diagram, we make better use of the space if we do not begin the X axis and Y axis at zero. If both axes had started at zero, the resulting array of dots would have been very crowded, and not as much information would have been conveyed. So spread the points out as much as possible by labeling the axes properly. Do not forget to label the axes. Here the labels are "Age" and "Income." What type of pattern, if any, do you observe in Figure 4.1?

What we are looking for in a scatter diagram is some underlying pattern. One thing is clear in Figure 4.1: as X increases, so does Y. This means that X and Y have a

Figure 4.1

Scatter diagram for the eight ordered pairs from the personnel data.

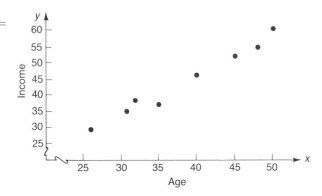

Figure 4.2

A straight line con-
structed through the
sample data.

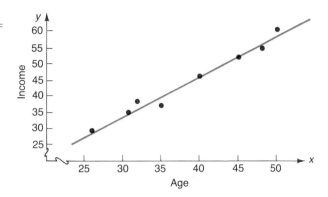

positive relationship. A **negative relationship** exists when Y decreases as X increases. Typically, demand (Y) versus selling price (X) data reveal such a negative relationship.

The pattern in Figure 4.1 is not only positive, it is also nearly **linear.** This means that there is some straight line that "slices through" these points, as shown in Figure 4.2. Remember that a linear pattern does not imply that there is a straight line that connects each of the points—that rarely happens in practice. It does mean that if ten people tried to draw a straight line through this array of dots, they would all draw the line in nearly the same location with nearly the same direction, or **slope.** Chapter 14 will discuss how to find the "best" line through a set of points that exhibit a strong linear pattern.

So the first step in examining a sample of bivariate data is to plot and examine a scatter diagram of the data. A careful inspection of such a plot can provide much useful information regarding the nature of the data and can help to prevent you from drawing an erroneous conclusion caused by examining computer outputs and skipping a *visual* inspection of the data.

Exercises

4.1 Would you expect the following pairs of variables to exhibit a positive relationship, negative relationship, or no relationship?

a. Age in years and weight.

b. Time of day and rainfall.

c. Sales and profits.

d. Hair color and type of car owned.

For exercises 4.2 to 4.8, set up scatter diagrams with headings and appropriately marked axes, and plot the points. Comment on the pattern observed.

4.2 The following data represent the educational level and annual income in thousands of dollars of ten business executives.

Executive	X (Years of college)	Y (Income)
1	4	50
2	2	37
3	0	35
4	3	45
5	4	57
6	4	49
7	5	60
8	5	47
9	2	39
10	2	50

4.3 Easy Fly Airlines has changed its ticket prices several times during the past few years. The following results were tabulated for the number of persons flying from Los Angeles to Denver at various ticket prices.

X (Price)	Y (Number of persons flying, in 100s)
99	1200
150	1000
130	1050
105	1150
219	700
167	850
180	900

4.4 In a study of automobile-repair cost, data have been collected on automobile age in months and annual repair cost.

Y (Repair cost)	X (Age, months)
30	6
24	24
67	12
123	15
89	48
234	74
45	18
36	13
67	19
87	23

4.5 The Texas State Racing Commission is interested in knowing the relationship between attendance and the amount of money wagered. The following are the data for seven racing days.

X (Attendance in hundreds)	Y (Amount wagered in millions)
117	2.07
128	2.09
122	3.14
119	3.33
131	3.76
110	3.00
104	2.20

4.6 A general practitioner in Butte, Montana, was trying to determine if the exodus of younger families due to poor economic conditions would have an effect on her practice to the extent that she would need to reduce her staff. She tabulated the age and number of visits for a sample of her clients for the preceding year.

X (1982 age)	Y (Number of visits/year)
60	5
80	15
72	9
55	5
44	2
5	1
17	1
12	3
1	6
39	3

4.7 The data given in the following table represent typing speed and number of keypunch errors in one hour for 11 data-entry computer operators.

Operator	X (Speed)	Y (Errors)
1	65	6
2	60	9
3	70	2
4	73	4
5	55	9
6	65	3
7	61	7
8	59	1
9	75	4
10	64	2
11	70	3

4.8 The manager of Hot and Crusty Pizza would like to establish a timetable to give the customers an idea of how long it will take to deliver a pizza. Twelve randomly selected deliveries were used to record the number of miles to the delivery site from Hot and Crusty Pizza and the times from the order to the delivery.

X (Distance, miles)	Y (Delivery time, minutes)
2.3	5
6.7	13
7.5	10
3.1	5
4.6	9
3.9	8
8.7	15
9.8	20
10.1	18
6.5	13
7.3	12
5.2	9

4.2

Correlation Coefficient

Our next objective is to determine a number (numerical measure) that will measure just how linear the pattern in the scatter diagram really is. If this number is "large," the pattern is nearly linear (as in Figure 4.1). If it is "small," X and Y have neither a positive relationship nor a negative relationship—in this case, X and Y are said to be **uncorrelated.** The numerical measure is called the sample correlation coefficient (r).

> ### Definition
>
> The **correlation coefficient, r,** for a sample of bivariate data is a measure of the strength of the linear relationship between the two variables, X and Y, and is computed using:
>
> $$r = \frac{\Sigma(x - \bar{x})(y - \bar{y})}{\sqrt{\Sigma(x - \bar{x})^2}\sqrt{\Sigma(y - \bar{y})^2}} \qquad (4\text{-}1)$$
>
> The possible values of r range from -1.0 to 1.0.

Here $\bar{x}$ and $\bar{y}$ are the means (averages) of the X and Y values, and the summation is over all n ordered pairs. An easier expression to compute r using a calculator is:

> $$r = \frac{\Sigma xy - (\Sigma x)(\Sigma y)/n}{\sqrt{\Sigma x^2 - (\Sigma x)^2/n}\sqrt{\Sigma y^2 - (\Sigma y)^2/n}} \qquad (4\text{-}2)$$

For extremely large data sets, the only reasonable way to calculate r is to use a computer. At the end of the chapter we will show you how to do this using SAS and SPSSX. A computer-generated scatter diagram using MINITAB is contained in Figure 4.3.

To determine r for the personnel data using equation 4-2, format your data and calculations in a table, as shown in Table 4.1.

Figure 4.3

Computer-generated scatter diagram for personnel data, using MINITAB.

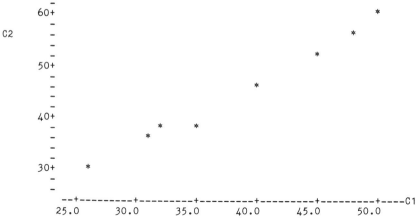

```
MTB > SET INTO C1
DATA> 35 26 45 48 31 50 32 40
DATA> END
MTB > SET INTO C2
DATA> 37 29 52 55 35 60 38 46
DATA> END
MTB > CORRELATION BETWEEN C1 AND C2

Correlation of C1 and C2 = 0.991

MTB > PLOT C2 VS C1
```

Table 4.1

Summary of calculations for finding r

X	Y	XY	X²	Y²
35	37	1295	1225	1369
26	29	754	676	841
45	52	2340	2025	2704
48	55	2640	2304	3025
31	35	1085	961	1225
50	60	3000	2500	3600
32	38	1216	1024	1444
40	46	1840	1600	2116
307	352	14,170	12,315	16,324

Using equation 4-2:

$$r = \frac{14,170 - (307)(352)/8}{\sqrt{12,315 - (307)^2/8}\ \sqrt{16,324 - (352)^2/8}}$$

$$= \frac{14,170 - 13,508}{(23.11)(28.91)} = .991$$

You could have found r using equation 4-1, where $\bar{x} = 307/8 = 38.375$ and $\bar{y} = 352/8 = 44.0$. However, equation 4-2 provides a computationally easier procedure.

The following are some important things to keep in mind regarding the correlation coefficient.

1. r ranges from -1.0 to 1.0.

2. The larger $|r|$ (absolute value of r) is, the stronger the linear relationship.

3. r near zero indicates that there is no linear relationship between X and Y, and the scatter diagram typically appears to contain a shotgun effect (Figure 4.4a). Here, X and Y are uncorrelated.

4. $r = 1$ or $r = -1$ implies that a perfect linear pattern exists between the two variables in the sample; that is, a single line will go *through* each point. Here we say that X and Y are **perfectly correlated** (Figure 4.4b and c).

5. Values of $r = 0$, 1, or -1 are rare in practice. Several other values of the correlation coefficient are illustrated in Figure 4.4d, e, and f.

6. The sign of r tells you whether the relationship between X and Y is a positive (direct) one or a negative (inverse) one.

7. The value of r tells you nothing about slope of the line through these points (except for the sign of r). If r is positive, the line through these points has positive slope, and, similarly, this line will have negative slope if r is negative. However, a set of data with $r = .9$ will not necessarily have a steeper line passing through it than will a set of data with $r = .4$. All you will observe in the first data set is a set of points that is very close to some straight line with positive slope, but you know nothing (except for the sign) about the slope of this line. See Figure 4.5, where both sets of data provide an r value of .9.

Figure 4.4

Scatter diagrams for various values of the sample correlation coefficient.

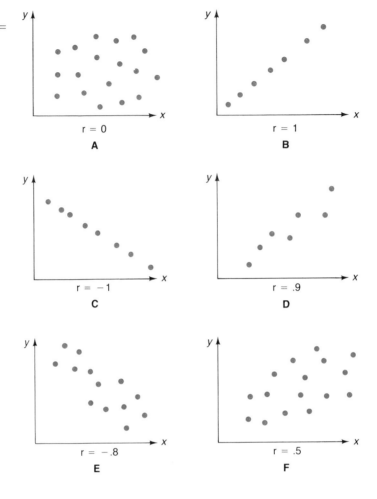

r = 0
A

r = 1
B

r = −1
C

r = .9
D

r = −.8
E

r = .5
F

Figure 4.5

Although **A** has a large slope and **B** has a small slope, both are scatter diagrams for r = .9.

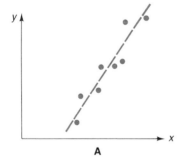

A

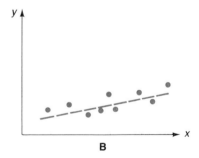

B

Example 4.1

Southern Power is interested in determining the relationship between the square footage of a home and the average monthly expenditure for electricity. A random sample of 12 homes was obtained, the results of which are shown in Figure 4.6. What is the value of *r* for these data?

Figure 4.6

Data and scatter diagram for relationship between home size and average expenditure for electricity.

	1	2	3	4	5	6	7	8	9	10	11	12
Home square footage (X) (hundreds)	17	24	17	11	19	28	35	13	23	15	29	38
Average electric bill (Y) (hundred dollars)	2.1	1.8	1.5	.5	1.1	3.0	2.0	2.0	2.8	1.5	2.2	3.1

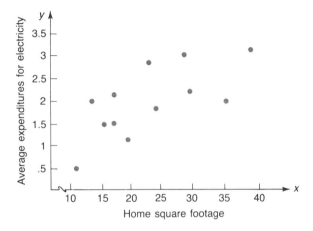

Solution Here we observe a basically positive relationship between home size and the average expenditure for electricity. So we expect to find a value of r that is positive but not as close to 1.0 as before. Table 4.2 shows the calculations we make. Then:

$$r = \frac{579.3 - (269)(23.6)/12}{\sqrt{6853 - (269)^2/12}\,\sqrt{52.90 - (23.6)^2/12}}$$

$$= \frac{50.27}{(28.687)(2.547)} = .688$$

Table 4.2

Summary of calculations for example 4.1 (see Figure 4.6)

X	Y	XY	X^2	Y^2
17	2.1	35.7	289	4.41
24	1.8	43.2	576	3.24
17	1.5	25.5	289	2.25
11	.5	5.5	121	.25
19	1.1	20.9	361	1.21
28	3.0	84.0	784	9.00
35	2.0	70.0	1225	4.00
13	2.0	26.0	169	4.00
23	2.8	64.4	529	7.84
15	1.5	22.5	225	2.25
29	2.2	63.8	841	4.84
38	3.1	117.8	1444	9.61
269	23.6	579.3	6,853	52.90

Table 4.3

Housing data for example 4.2 (X = number shown, Y = number sold)

Month	1	2	3	4	5	6	7	8	9	10	11	12	
X	155	320	490	131	228	512	182	430	408	140	350	280	
Y	15	38	25	18	8	13	19	28	15	16	5	10	
Month	13	14	15	16	17	18	19	20	21	22	23	24	
X	428	176	108	220	550	380	217	436	536	466	472	142	
Y	24	12	18	18	36	37	35	26	25	42	28	40	
Month	25	26	27	28	29	30	31	32	33	34	35	36	37
X	321	388	182	368	410	341	110	352	580	314	260	450	356
Y	36	37	8	38	31	18	37	21	35	45	7	14	41
Month	38	39	40	41	42	43	44	45	46	47	48	49	50
X	340	516	165	370	452	410	240	241	580	236	510	520	271
Y	40	40	38	41	42	25	20	30	22	20	20	30	21

Example 4.2

Brockwood Homes is a major developer of suburban homes. The president of the company wants to determine what relationship (if any) exists between the number of times their model homes were shown to prospective buyers and the number of homes sold. Data from 50 months were gathered and are shown in Table 4.3. Does it appear that there is a positive relationship (as you might expect) between these two variables?

Solution In Figure 4.7, we observe little, if any, pattern to the data, and so it appears that the number of houses sold for any given month is not related to the number of houses shown. Consequently, we would expect a value of r close to zero. A summary of the data here is:

$$\Sigma x = 17,040$$
$$\Sigma y = 1,308$$
$$\Sigma xy = 463,651$$
$$\Sigma x^2 = 6,712,964$$
$$\Sigma y^2 = 40,392$$

Figure 4.7

Scatter diagram for example 4.2; data are shown in Table 4.3.

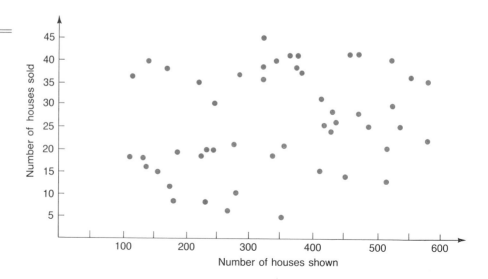

So

$$r = \frac{463,651 - (17,040)(1,308)/50}{\sqrt{6,712,964 - (17,040)^2/50}\;\sqrt{40,392 - (1,308)^2/50}}$$

$$= \frac{17,884.6}{(951.699)(78.579)} = .239$$

For this example, r is not close to either $+1$ or -1. Is there a linear relationship or not? At what point do we go from the conclusion that r is "large enough" to indicate that there is an underlying linear relationship between X and Y to the conclusion that no such linear association exists? In other words, would we put $r = .239$ into the "too small" category (no linear pattern exists) or the "large enough" category (there is a linear relationship to these data)?   ●

Significant is a popular word in the world of statistics. In later chapters, we will provide a more rigorous definition of *significance,* but for now consider example 4.2. Suppose that these two variables are *not* related in a linear manner (*are* uncorrelated). Does this mean that if we selected 50 such months of data, we would obtain a value of r (derived from the sample) *exactly* equal to zero? The answer is, "No, but it will be close to zero." The reason for this is simply that we are sampling here, and r will be slightly different from zero due to *random chance.*

Suppose the value of r in example 4.2 was .98 (very large). Is this large sample value due to random chance, or does it suggest that a strong linear relationship exists between these two variables in the population from which the sample was selected? We conclude the latter, because to get a value of r that large if X and Y were uncorrelated in the population would be very unlikely. So, we have two situations here:

Situation 1: r is different from zero only by random chance—in fact, X and Y are nearly (or exactly) uncorrelated.

Situation 2: r is *significantly* different from zero because there is a strong linear association between X and Y in the population.

Where would you classify $r = .239$? Is this value of r large enough to say that there is a linear pattern to these data? We know the linear pattern is not perfect because r is neither 1.0 nor -1.0. How we classify this r value depends on one important piece of information—n, the sample size. A value of, say, $r = .4$ may be considered large enough (far enough away from zero) for us to conclude that a linear relationship exists (Situation 2) for one sample size but not for another sample size (Situation 1).

One procedure for determining whether r is "large enough" is to use Table 4.4. If the value of $|r|$ exceeds the value in the table for that particular sample size, then we say that the underlying relationship between X and Y *is* a linear one. However, to apply this table, we need to make an assumption similar to the one that was necessary for applying the empirical rule in Chapter 3. The assumption is that the population of X values and the population of Y values are bell-shaped, or normal. Suppose that you make two histograms of the X values only and the Y values only. If either histogram is not approximately symmetrical and bell-shaped in appearance, you cannot use Table 4.4 to reach a valid conclusion. Thus, if $|r|$ exceeds the significant value in Table 4.4 for a specified value of n, then there is evidence of a linear relationship between these two variables; this assumes that both the X and Y populations are bell-shaped (normal).

In our personnel data (Figure 4.1), $r = .991$ (and $n = 8$), which exceeds the value of $r = .707$ from Table 4.4. This situation is illustrated in Figure 4.8. Since .991 >

Table 4.4

Significant values of *r*: this table will lead to the conclusion that a linear relationship exists, when in fact it does not, 5% of the time

n	Significant Value	*n*	Significant Value	*n*	Significant Value
5	.879	15	.514	30	.361
6	.811	16	.497	35	.334
7	.754	17	.482	40	.312
8	.707	18	.468	45	.294
9	.666	19	.456	50	.279
10	.632	20	.444	60	.254
11	.602	22	.423	70	.235
12	.576	24	.404	80	.220
13	.553	26	.388	90	.207
14	.532	28	.374	100	.196

Figure 4.8

Significant values of *r* for personnel data (*n* = 8).

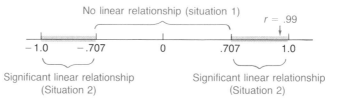

.707, we conclude that there *is* a significant linear association between age and income—the same conclusion we obtained by simply looking at Figure 4.1. Keep in mind, however, that this conclusion is based on the assumption that both the age and income populations are bell-shaped. Because the sample here consists of only eight values from each population, constructing a histogram to check the shape of these populations is difficult. Devising histograms is more practical for determining the shape of populations using larger sample sizes (*n*).

In example 4.1, the computed value of *r* was .688, which does exceed the value of .576 from Table 4.4 (using *n* = 12). Therefore, it appears that there is a significant linear relationship, although *not* an overwhelming one, in the population between home size and the average electric bill. This is a good example of how just looking at the scatter diagram (Figure 4.6) does not necessarily lead to the correct conclusion.

For the data from example 4.2, as expected, the value of *r* = .239 does *not* exceed the entry in Table 4.4 for *n* = 50, which is .279. So we conclude that there is not a strong linear association here and that the number of houses sold and the number shown are uncorrelated.

Drawing Conclusions from Table 4.4

There are three points of interest in regard to Table 4.4. First, using this procedure will lead to the conclusion that a linear relationship exists, when in fact there is no such relationship, 5% of the time. There is no way to get around this problem because we are using a *sample* of (*X, Y*) values to make a decision concerning a *population* of all (*X, Y*) values. However, this table provides only one possible approach. You could construct a table for which the chance of making such an incorrect conclusion is not 5% but is 1%, 10%, or whatever percent you desire. Be careful, though—there is a tradeoff. The smaller this percentage, the more likely you are to conclude that there is *not* a linear relationship when in fact there *is*. We will take a closer look at this situation in Chapter 9.

Second, remember that Table 4.4 requires the assumption that both the X and Y populations are bell-shaped, normal populations. When they are not, you should use a much more reliable measure of association between the X and Y variables: the rank correlation, discussed in the next section.

Third, just because there is a strong positive statistical relationship between two variables does not necessarily imply that an increase in X *causes* an increase in Y. As a simple example, consider X = percentage of gray hairs, and Y = blood pressure. One might expect to observe a high correlation between these two variables, but it is probably absurd to say that an additional gray hair will *cause* a person's blood pressure to increase. What is actually happening is that there is another variable, in this case age, that is causing both gray hair percentage and blood pressure to increase. In many business situations, this underlying variable is *time*. As time increases, a large number of business and economic variables also increase, due to growth, inflation, or other factors. So remember, a high statistical correlation does not imply that a causal relationship exists between the two variables.

Example 4.3

Mr. Roberts and Mr. Clauson each examined eight different brands of television sets and ranked them from 1 to 8. Determine the sample correlation between these two sets of rankings.

Brand	Roberts (X)	Clauson (Y)
A	1	2
B	4	3
C	2	1
D	6	6
E	8	7
F	3	5
G	7	8
H	5	4

Here:

$$\Sigma x = 36$$
$$\Sigma y = 36$$
$$\Sigma x^2 = 204$$
$$\Sigma y^2 = 204$$
$$\Sigma xy = 199$$

Using equation 4-2:

$$r = \frac{199 - (36)(36)/8}{\sqrt{204 - (36)^2/8}\,\sqrt{204 - (36)^2/8}} = .881$$

At this point, you may be tempted to use Table 4.4 to determine if this value of r is significantly large. As the next section will demonstrate, when dealing with *ordinal* data of this type, a better procedure is to use a table especially designed for such data. When we reexamine this set of data in Section 4.3, the conclusion will be that, based upon $r = .881$, there *is* a significant positive relationship between the rankings of the two testers. Another way of looking at this result is that the two testers agree (although not perfectly) with each other. So here r is a **measure of agreement** between the two sets of rankings. For a consumer-testing situation (or a contest) in which you compile multiple rankings, a large r between any two judges is desirable. Whenever the value of r is not significantly large, we are unable to conclude that there is agreement between judges.

Exercises

4.9 Are the following values of r for sample size n significant, according to Table 4.4, for testing that there is no linear relationship?

a. $r = 0.473$, $n = 50$.

b. $r = 0.223$, $n = 29$.

c. $r = 0.175$, $n = 75$.

d. $r = 0.819$, $n = 15$.

e. $r = 0.750$, $n = 5$.

4.10 Use the data from exercise 4.2 to estimate r for educational level and income of business executives.

a. Calculate r.

b. Does there appear to be a linear relationship using the scatter diagram?

c. Is the relationship significant using Table 4.4?

d. Do your answers to questions b and c agree?

4.11 Use the data from exercise 4.3 and answer a, b, c, d in exercise 4.10.

4.12 Use the data from exercise 4.4 and answer a, b, c, d in exercise 4.10.

4.13 Use the data from exercise 4.5 and answer a, b, c, d in exercise 4.10.

4.14 Use the data from exercise 4.6 and answer a, b, c, d in exercise 4.10.

4.15 The following data represent the utility bill for a particular month and the number of people in the household.

X (Utility bill)	Y (Number in household)
150	4
95	1
120	2
200	6
145	3
170	4
190	5

a. Plot the scatter diagram.

b. Calculate r.

c. Does there appear to be a positive or negative relationship?

d. Is the relationship significant?

4.16 Prepare a scatter diagram for the following set of paired data.

X	Y
5.1	3.2
6.9	4.3
7.8	5.1
10.11	5.5
12.1	6.5
15.8	7.1
18	9.3
18.5	10.1
19.2	11.3

a. Calculate r.

b. Is there a positive or negative linear relationship?

c. Is the relationship significant?

4.3
Rank Correlation

In example 4.3, Mr. Roberts ranked the sets from 1 to 8 without actually assigning each of them a score or number that measured its consumer value. For Mr. Roberts, brand A was "better" than brand C, maybe only slightly better or maybe a lot—we do not know which. The object here was to obtain a ranking of the eight brands, and this type of data is acceptable. In Chapter 1, this type of data was referred to as ordinal data.

Definition

When examining *ordinal* data consisting of two sets of rankings, the resulting correlation coefficient is referred to as Spearman's **rank correlation,** denoted as r_s. For such data, $r = r_s$. The value of r_s is always between -1.0 and 1.0.

It is sometimes desirable to analyze the relationship between two variables according to the rank of the values of each of the variables in the sample. The variables may be ranked on the basis of quality (as the televisions were) or any other standard. The use of ranks allows us to measure correlation using characteristics that cannot be expressed quantitatively but that lend themselves to being ranked. For example, it is difficult to measure the quality of a television picture quantitatively.

For data consisting of ranks, equation 4-2 can be used to determine r, but an easier expression is

$$r_s = 1 - \frac{6 \cdot \Sigma d^2}{n(n^2 - 1)} \tag{4-3}$$

where d represents the difference between each of the individual ranks. As a check of your calculations, Σd should always equal zero.

Using the television data in Example 4.3,

Brand	Roberts	Clauson	d	d^2
A	1	2	-1	1
B	4	3	1	1
C	2	1	1	1
D	6	6	0	0
E	8	7	1	1
F	3	5	-2	4
G	7	8	-1	1
H	5	4	1	1
			0	10

Here, $\Sigma d^2 = 10$, so:

$$r_s = 1 - \frac{(6)(10)}{8(64 - 1)} = .881 \text{ (as in example 4.3)}$$

The interpretation of r_s is similar to that for r, namely:

1. A value of r_s near 1.0 indicates a strong *positive* relationship.
2. A value of r_s near -1.0 indicates a strong *negative* relationship.

As mentioned earlier, it is sometimes much easier simply to rank a group of items without assigning a numerical value to the quality that is being measured. When dealing with rank data, we know that $r = r_s$. We determine the rank correlation for *interval* data by replacing each of the X values by its rank and each of the Y values by its rank. The resulting r_s value will *not* be the same as the original r value but will have the same sign and be of roughly the same magnitude.

Let us compute the rank correlation for the sample data in the personnel example. Look at the data in section 4.1. For the X values, 26 is the smallest value, so its rank is 1; 31 is the next largest and receives a rank of 2, and so on. For the Y values, 29 is replaced by its rank of 1, 35 receives a rank of 2, and so on. The ranked data are:

Person	Age (X) Ranks	Income (Y) Ranks	d	d^2
1	4	3	1	1
2	1	1	0	0
3	6	6	0	0
4	7	7	0	0
5	2	2	0	0
6	8	8	0	0
7	3	4	-1	1
8	5	5	0	0
			0	2

So $\Sigma d^2 = 2$ and

$$r_s = 1 - \frac{(6)(2)}{8(64 - 1)} = .976$$

For this data set, $r = .991$ and $r_s = .976$, both of which are near 1.0; this indicates a very strong positive relationship within the population. A computer calculation of the rank correlation for these data (using MINITAB) is contained in Figure 4.9.

Another important reason for using the rank correlation (r_s) rather than a correlation of the actual sample data (r) is that we are relieved of one of the key assumptions regarding the type of populations from which you obtained the sample. When using the sample correlation coefficient (r), we were forced to assume that the X and Y values came from a symmetrical, bell-shaped (normal) population. This can be checked by constructing a histogram of the sample X values and a histogram of the sample Y

Figure 4.9

MINITAB calculation of the rank correlation of the age and income paired data.

```
MTB > SET   INTO   C1
DATA> 35 26 45 48 31 50 32 40
DATA> END
MTB > SET   INTO   C2
DATA> 37 29 52 55 35 60 38 46
DATA> END
MTB > RANK C1,PUT INTO C3
MTB > RANK C2,PUT INTO C4
MTB > CORRELATION OF C3 AND C4

Correlation of C3 and C4 = 0.976
```

Figure 4.10

Examples of non–bell-shaped histograms.

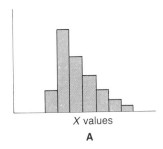

X values

A

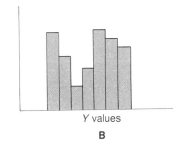

Y values

B

values. If they appear nearly symmetrical, with a bell-shaped appearance, then Table 4.4 offers a reliable procedure for determining if a linear relationship exists or not.

Suppose your histograms appear as in Figure 4.10. Since they are both clearly nonsymmetric and certainly not bell-shaped, using the rank correlation, r_s, to measure the relationship between X and Y will be much more reliable than using r. Only one of the histograms need be non–bell-shaped to violate the assumption necessary to apply Table 4.4. Also, keep in mind that there is nothing wrong with providing *both* r and r_s if the original data are interval data. In fact, an easy way to spot that the assumptions behind Table 4.4 are not being satisfied is that r and r_s *will have substantially different values*. If the assumptions are being met, these values should be nearly the same. However, just because these two values are nearly the same does *not* imply that the assumptions are being satisfied.

In example 4.2, the sample correlation between X = number of houses shown and Y = number of houses sold was found to be $r = .239$. We used Table 4.4 to determine whether a significant linear relationship existed between these two variables, without examining the assumption that the populations were normal.

In Figure 4.11, MINITAB was used to construct histograms of the X and Y values. Notice that *neither* histogram is bell-shaped. This suggests that the corresponding populations of *all X* values and *all Y* values are not bell-shaped (normal) either. Consequently, using Table 4.4 for this situation was *not* appropriate. Figure 4.11 also contains a computer solution for the rank correlation, namely, $r_s = .254$. Notice that the r (.239) and r_s values are nearly the same, but the assumption of bell-shaped populations appears to be on shaky ground here.

Significant Values of r_s

Table 4.4 was used to determine if a correlation coefficient was large enough to conclude that there was an underlying linear relationship between the two variables within the population. If $|r|$ exceeded the table value and if r was positive, a significant positive relationship existed; or if r was negative, the two variables had a significant negative relationship. Using Table 4.5 in the same way we use Table 4.4 for r, we can determine if $|r_s|$ is large due to a strong positive or negative association between a pair of variables within the population. As in Table 4.4, there is a 5% chance of concluding that a positive or negative relationship exists when in fact it does not.

In our personnel survey example, $r_s = .976$, which exceeds .7143 using $n = 8$, so we conclude there is a significant positive relationship between age and income. Notice we do not say *linear* here because r_s measures the amount of the positive or negative relationship between X and Y—not necessarily how linear that relationship

Figure 4.11

MINITAB histograms for the *X* and *Y* values from example 4.2.

```
MTB > HISTOGRAM C1 ◄─── Y values

Histogram of C1    N = 50

Midpoint    Count
       5        2    **
      10        4    ****
      15        5    *****
      20       11    ***********
      25        5    *****
      30        5    *****
      35        7    *******
      40       10    **********
      45        1    *

MTB > HISTOGRAM C2 ◄─── X values

Histogram of C2    N = 50

Midpoint    Count
     100        2    **
     150        5    *****
     200        5    *****
     250        6    ******
     300        4    ****
     350        7    *******
     400        5    *****
     450        7    *******
     500        5    *****
     550        2    **
     600        2    **

MTB > RANK C1,PUT INTO C3
MTB > RANK C2,PUT INTO C4
MTB > CORRELATION BETWEEN C3 AND C4

Correlation of C3 and C4 = 0.254
```

Table 4.5

Significant values of r_s: this table will lead to a conclusion that a positive or negative relationship exists, when in fact it does not, 5% of the time

n	Significant Value	n	Significant Value	n	Significant Value
5	.9000	15	.5179	30	.3620
6	.8286	16	.5000	35	.3313
7	.7450	17	.4853	40	.3138
8	.7143	18	.4716	45	.2955
9	.6833	19	.4579	50	.2800
10	.6364	20	.4451	60	.2552
11	.6091	22	.4241	70	.2360
12	.5804	24	.4061	80	.2205
13	.5549	26	.3894	90	.2078
14	.5341	28	.3749	100	.1970

is. For example, in Figure 4.12, both data sets will provide an r_s value of exactly 1.0 when the data values are converted to ranks. This is because every time X increases, so does Y for both data sets. However, the value of r will be *less* than 1.0 for both data sets because the pattern is not exactly linear.

In example 4.3, $n = 8$ and $r_s = .881$, which exceeds the table value of .7143. This implies that we do have general agreement between the two testers—a desirable result!

Figure 4.12

Two data sets where rank correlation equals 1.0. Note that the value of r for both data sets will be less than 1.0 because the pattern is not exactly linear.

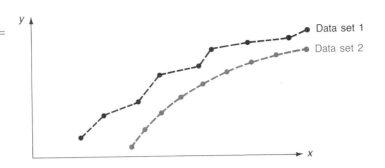

We can rank the data from example 4.1, replacing the X and Y values by their ranks:

House Number	Square Footage Rank	Average Electricity Rank	d	d^2
1	4.5	8	−3.5	12.25
2	8	5	3	9
3	4.5	3.5	1	1
4	1	1	0	0
5	6	2	4	16
6	9	11	−2	4
7	11	6.5	4.5	20.25
8	2	6.5	−4.5	20.25
9	7	10	−3	9
10	3	3.5	−0.5	0.25
11	10	9	1	1
12	12	12	0	0

Notice that some of the data are *tied* for assignment to certain ranks. In the X values, there is a tie between fourth place and fifth place because both have $X = 17$. This is easily resolved by giving each a rank of $(4 + 5)/2 = 4.5$. There are two ties for the Y values. $Y = 1.5$ occurs in both the third and the fourth ranked positions, so it gets a rank of 3.5 for these two values; $Y = 2.0$ occurs twice as a tie for the sixth and seventh ranked positions, and both values are assigned a rank of 6.5. One advantage to this procedure is that the sum of the d values is zero, as in situations without ties.

For these data, we have:

$$\Sigma d^2 = 12.25 + 9 + \ldots + 1 + 0 = 93$$

and so

$$r_s = 1 - \left[\frac{(6)(93)}{(12)(144 - 1)} \right] = .675$$

Since .675 is larger than .5804 (from Table 4.5), our conclusion (as before) is that there is a positive relationship in the population between home size and the average electricity expenditure. However, because r_s is not dramatically larger than the table value, we also add that this relationship is not a very strong one. Once again, $r_s (= .675)$ and $r (= .688)$ are very nearly the same.

From Figure 4.11, the rank correlation for the 50 observations in Table 4.1 is shown to be $r_s = .254$. It is more appropriate to use rank correlation to determine whether a relationship (positive or negative) exists between these two variables because the X and Y histograms are not bell-shaped. Based on Table 4.3, because $r_s = .254$, which is less than .2800 (corresponding to $n = 50$), we once again conclude that there is not a positive or negative relationship between the number of houses shown and the number of houses sold.

Exercises

4.17 For the following set of ranked data,

Number	X	Y
1	2	7
2	3	8
3	8	2
4	4	5
5	6	4
6	5	3
7	1	6
8	7	1

a. Calculate r_s.

b. Is there a positive or negative relationship?

c. Is it significant according to Table 4.5?

4.18 The following table illustrates the unemployment and inflation figures of the U.S. economy for the years 1975 through 1984:

Year	X (Unemployment, %)	Y (Inflation, %)
1975	8.5	9.3
1976	7.7	5.2
1977	7.1	5.8
1978	6.1	7.4
1979	5.8	8.6
1980	7.0	9.2
1981	7.5	9.6
1982	9.5	6.0
1983	9.5	3.8
1984	7.4	3.8

a. Plot a scatter diagram of the data.

b. Calculate the correlation coefficient between rate of unemployment and rate of inflation.

c. Determine the rank correlation.

d. Compare and comment on the results of questions a and b.

4.19 Use the data in exercise 4.3 and rank the ticket prices and number of passengers.

a. Calculate r_s.

b. Is there a positive or negative relationship?

c. Is it significant?

d. Does this r_s value lead to the same conclusion as the computations, based on the prices and number of people, in exercise 4.11?

4.20 At the 1983 Drum Corps International competitions, one set of final rankings by judges was compared with those made by the fans.

Band	X (Judges)	Y (Fans)
1	10	8
2	6	5
3	7	10
4	9	9
5	1	1
6	4	4
7	5	6
8	2	3
9	3	2
10	8	7

a. Compute r_s.

b. Is there a positive or negative relationship?

c. Is it significant according to Table 4.5?

4.21 The following table summarizes the rankings of the ten participants in a Texas baking contest by judges A and B.

Participant	X (Judge A)	Y (Judge B)
a	2	6
b	6	2
c	10	9
d	4	7
e	8	10
f	5	3
g	1	4
h	7	5
i	3	1
j	9	8

Calculate r_s and comment on the relationship of the rankings of judge A and judge B.

4.22 Answer a, b, c, d in exercise 4.20 for the data in exercise 4.4.

4.23 Answer a, b, c, d in exercise 4.20 for the data in exercise 4.5.

4.24 Answer a, b, c, d in exercise 4.20 for the data in exercise 4.15.

Summary

This chapter described methods of examining sample data collected on two variables. These are bivariate data, and the data occur in pairs. A graphical representation of a set of this type of data is a scatter diagram, where each pair of data values is represented as a point. Using the scatter diagram, we can determine whether (1) a positive relationship exists between the two variables (as one increases, the other increases), or (2) the variables exhibit a negative relationship (as one increases, the other decreases), or (3) the variables are uncorrelated (the scatter diagram does not exhibit a linear pattern).

To measure the amount of positive or negative association between two variables, we can use the sample correlation coefficient or the sample rank correlation. The sample correlation coefficient, r, measures the strength of the *linear* relationship between the variables. If r is near $+1.0$, then the variables are strongly positively related; if r is near -1.0, the variables are strongly negatively related. If r is near zero, the variables are (nearly) uncorrelated. Table 4.4 is used to determine if $|r|$ is significantly large enough to conclude that a linear relationship exists. This procedure assumes that both the X and Y populations are normal (bell-shaped) in appearance. The sample rank correlation, r_s is found using the ranks of the data and measures the amount of association between the variables. This relationship need not be linear for $|r_s|$ to be large. When dealing with rank data, the values of r and r_s are identical. Table 4.5 is used to determine significantly large values of r_s. The assumption of normal populations is not necessary here.

A key advantage to using the rank correlation as your measure of association is that it is not necessary to assume (as it is when using r) that the X and Y populations are normal. We illustrated how the rank correlation can be applied to interval type data by replacing each data value by its rank. You thus convert interval data to ordinal data, which require the use of r_s. So, for the same data set, if you compute r using the original interval data, it will not equal r_s computed on the *ranks* of that same data set because it uses different values. When you have only ranks, you will have r_s, no matter which of the two formulas you use.

Review Exercises

4.25 The following table describes the demand for oranges (in dozens) at various prices (in dollars).

X (Quantity demanded)	Y (Price per dozen)
250	6
300	5
400	4
500	3
550	2
600	1

a. Construct the scatter diagram for these data.

b. What do you infer about the nature of the relationship between quantity demanded and price?

c. Determine the sample correlation coefficient.

4.26 A survey of the students of Highpoint College gathered the following information with regard to their study time (hours per week) and grade point averages.

X (Study time)	Y (Grade point average)
16	4.0
15	3.8
14	3.5
12	3.0
10	2.8
8	2.2
6	1.5
4	1.0
2	0.5
0	0.2

a. Plot a scatter diagram of the data.

b. Calculate the sample correlation coefficient.

c. Interpret the r value.

d. Is there a significant relationship between study time and grade point average?

4.27 Estimate the sign and magnitude of the population correlation coefficient for each of the following pairs of variables.

a. The monthly utility bill of a home and the difference in absolute value between the average monthly temperature and 70°F.

b. The income of an individual and the value of the car owned by the individual.

c. The number of television sets sold in a department store and the number of fans sold in the same department store.

d. The rate of inflation and the interest rate.

e. The income of an individual and the number of times per year the individual is a passenger on an airplane.

4.28 Uniformity of judging is important in ice-skating contests. Two judges scored contestants 1 to 6 as follows.

Contestant	X (Judge A)	Y (Judge B)
1	85	80
2	81	82
3	89	87
4	96	92
5	94	94
6	92	90

a. Compute r.

b. Is it significant?

c. Do you think this pair of judges should be hired for this year's competition?

4.29 The University of Southern North Dakota is in the top ten party schools. A sample of freshman taking English placement examinations was correlated to the number of fraternity rush parties they attended during the first week of school.

X (Score on exam)	Y (Number of parties)
80	3
75	4
95	1
100	0
63	4
60	5
86	2
90	2
70	3
88	2

a. Plot a scatter diagram of the data.

b. Compute r.

c. Is it significant?

4.30 Using the data in exercise 4.25,

a. Calculate r_s.

b. Is it significant?

c. Compare the value of r_s with the value of r.

4.31 Using the data in exercise 4.29,

a. Calculate r_s.

b. Is it significant?

c. Compare the value of r_s with the value of r.

4.32 An instructor of introductory business statistics wanted to know the relationship between the number of absences for each student and the student's final grade. From the data below, make a scatter plot, and compute r. Is it significant?

X (Number of absences)	Y (Final grade)
0	90
10	65
5	77
7	45
9	60
6	72
3	85
1	95

4.33 The following pairs of observations represent the scores of a test given by a psychologist to a group before an experiment (X) and then to the same group after the experiment (Y).

X	Y	X	Y
2.1	9.4	2.4	12.9
3.4	35.6	1.9	5.2
1.6	3.5	1.3	3.4
2.7	15.4	0.2	0.1
3.2	30.1	1.5	4.6
4.5	52.7	2.1	9.3
1.8	17.4		

a. Calculate the correlation coefficient, r, between X and Y.

b. Take the log to the base 10 of Y. Calculate the correlation coefficient between X and log Y.

c. Compare the correlations in questions a and b.

4.34 Mr. Smart Fellow, the president of Well-Run Car, is examining the nature of the relationship between new car sales and annual advertising expenditure. His administrative assistant gathered the following information from the company's records.

Year	X (New car sales)	Y (Advertising dollars)
1971	4000	120,000
1972	4500	127,000
1973	4200	131,000
1974	4800	134,000
1975	5400	140,000
1976	5750	139,000
1977	6000	144,000
1978	6100	147,000
1979	6800	152,000
1980	7200	160,000
1981	7800	165,000
1982	9100	170,000

a. Calculate r.

b. Is this a significant relationship?

c. Calculate r_s.

d. Compare your findings from question c with the conclusion you reached in b.

4.35 The manager of a city zoo would like to use his staff more efficiently to accommodate large crowds. Fifteen days were randomly selected on which attendance and high temperature for the day were recorded. Do the data indicate a significant correlation between attendance and daily high temperature?

X (Attendance, 1000s)	Y (High temperature, °F)
1.9	82
0.8	104
1.2	90
1.4	92
2.4	75
2.8	70
1.5	86
1.4	87
2.6	76
0.7	105
1.3	90
1.6	85
2.1	78
1.8	83
2.3	77

4.36 Using the data in exercise 4.32,

a. Calculate r_s.

b. Is it significant?

c. Compare the value of r_s with the value of r.

4.37 Each week, a realtor advertises the houses he manages that are available for rent. The number of telephone calls from people inquiring about the advertisement were recorded for several weeks, during which various sizes of the advertisement were used. From the following data, compute r_s. Is it significant?

X (Height of ad, inches)	Y (Number of inquiries)
0.5	3
1.0	4
1.5	6
2.0	5
2.5	10
3.0	14
3.5	12
4.0	18

Solution

Section 4.1

The personnel survey of age and income problem requested a scatter diagram of a set of eight data points and the correlation coefficient between the two variables. You can use SPSSX to solve this problem. The SPSSX program listing in Figure 4.13 was used to request the scatter diagram and correlation coefficient. Each line represents one card image to be entered.

The TITLE command names the SPSSX run.

The DATA LIST command gives each variable a name and describes the data as being in free form.

The SCATTERGRAM command requests an SPSSX plot and specifies that the values for INC be on the vertical axis and the values for AGE be on the horizontal axis.

The STATISTICS command requests SPSSX calculate the correlation coefficient, along with other statistical data.

Figure 4.13

SPSSX program listing requesting scatter diagram and correlation coefficient.

```
TITLE           AGE VERSUS INCOME
DATA LIST FREE  /INC, AGE
SCATTERGRAM     INC WITH AGE
STATISTICS      ALL
BEGIN DATA
37 35
29 26
52 45
55 48
35 31
60 50
38 32
46 40
END DATA
FINISH
```

The BEGIN DATA command indicates to SPSSX that the input data immediately follow.

The next eight lines are card images. The first line, for example, indicates an income of $37,000 and an age of 35 years. The remaining card images are interpreted in the same manner.

The END DATA statement indicates the end of the data card images.

The FINISH command indicates the end of the SPSSX program.

Figure 4.14

Output obtained by executing the SPSSX program listing in Figure 4.13.

Figure 4.14 shows the output obtained by executing the program listing in Figure 4.13.

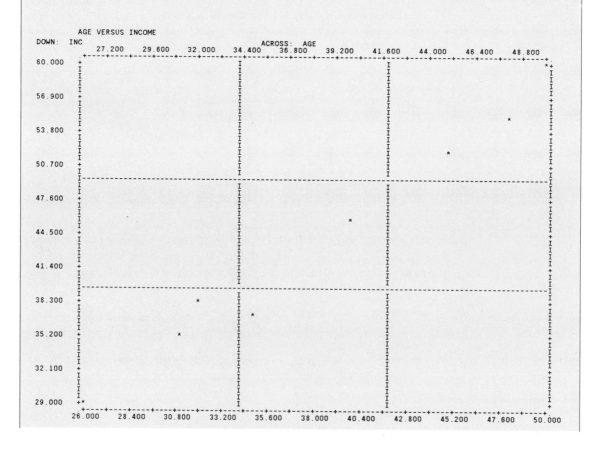

```
STATISTICS..

CORRELATION (R)-  =  .99091    R SQUARED     -     .98191    SIGNIFICANCE  -    .00000
STD ERR OF EST -      1.58778   INTERCEPT (A) -   -3.58464    SLOPE (B)     -   1.23999
PLOTTED VALUES -      8         EXCLUDED VALUES-   0          MISSING VALUES -   0

        '********' IS PRINTED IF A COEFFICIENT CANNOT BE COMPUTED.
```

S
A
S

Solution

Section 4.1

The personnel survey of age and income requested a scatter diagram of a set of eight data points and the correlation coefficient between the two variables. You can use SAS to solve this problem. The SAS program listing in Figure 4.15 was used to request the plot and correlation coefficient. Each line represents one card image to be entered.

The TITLE command names the SAS run.
The DATA command gives the data a name.
The INPUT command names and gives the correct order for the different fields on the data cards.
The CARDS command indicates to SAS that the input data immediately follow.

Figure 4.15

SAS program listing requesting scatter diagram and correlation coefficient.

```
TITLE      AGE VERSUS INCOME;
DATA       INCAGE;
INPUT      INCOME AGE;
CARDS;
37 35
29 26
52 45
55 48
35 31
60 50
38 32
46 40
;
PROC PRINT;
PROC PLOT;
     PLOT INCOME*AGE;
PROC CORR;
     VAR INCOME AGE;
```

The next eight lines are card images. The first line, for example, indicates an income of $37,000 and an age of 35 years. The remaining input data are interpreted in the same manner.
The ; indicates the end of the data card images.
The PROC PRINT command directs SAS to list the data that were just read in.
The PROC PLOT command requests an SAS procedure to plot. The following line, PLOT INCOME*AGE, requests that the values for INCOME be on the vertical axis and the values for AGE be on the horizontal axis of the plot.
The PROC CORR command requests an SAS procedure to compute a correlation coefficient. The following statement, VAR INCOME AGE, lists the variables to be used in this computation.

Figure 4.16 shows the output obtained by executing the program listing in Figure 4.15.

Figure 4.16

Output obtained by executing the SAS program listing in Figure 4.15.

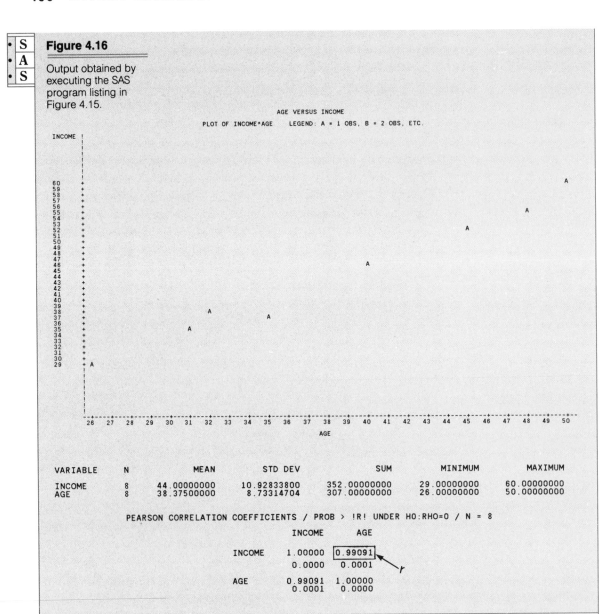

Probability Concepts

A Look Back/Introduction

You use descriptive statistics to summarize or present data that consist of observations that have already occurred. If these data are drawn from a population, then you describe your sample in some way. If you wish to infer something about the population using the smaller sample, you are now dealing with uncertainty. We need to measure the chance that something will occur, or its **probability.** The concepts of probability form the foundation of all decision making in statistics. By using probabilities, we are able to deal with uncertainty because we are able, at least, to measure it.

5.1

Events and Probability

An activity for which the outcome is uncertain is an **experiment.** This need not involve mixing chemicals in the laboratory; it could be as simple as throwing two dice and observing the total. An **event** consists of one or more possible outcomes of the experiment; it is usually denoted by a capital letter. The following are examples of experiments and their events:

1. *Experiment:* Rolling two dice; *events: A* = rolling a total of 7, *B* = rolling a total greater than 8, *C* = rolling two 4s.
2. *Experiment:* Taking a CPA exam; *events: A* = pass, *B* = fail.
3. *Experiment:* Observing the number of arrivals at a drive-up window over a five-minute period; *events: A_0* = no arrivals, *A_1* = one arrival, *A_2* = two arrivals, and so on.

When you estimate a probability, you determine the probability *of an event.* For example, when rolling two dice, the probability that you will roll a total of 7 (event *A*) is the probability that event *A* occurs. It is written: **$P(A)$.** The probability of any event is always between zero and one.

Notation

$P(A)$ = probability that event A occurs

Classical Definition of Probability

Suppose a particular experiment has *n* possible outcomes. Now, event *A* is not likely to occur every time. Suppose that it occurs in *m* of the *n* outcomes. The **classical definition** of the probability that event *A* will occur is

---

$$P(A) = m/n \qquad\qquad (5\text{-}1)$$

This definition assumes that all *n* possible outcomes have the same chance of occurring. Such outcomes (events) are said to be **equally likely,** and each has probability $1/n$ of occurring. If this is not the case, the classical definition does not apply.

Consider the experiment of tossing a nickel and a dime into the air and observing how they fall. Event *A* is observing one head and one tail. The possible outcomes are (H = head, T = tail):

Nickel	Dime
H	H
H	T
T	H
T	T

Thus, there are two combinations that are event *A* (*m* = 2) of the four possible outcomes (*n* = 4). These four outcomes are equally likely, so each occurs with probability 1/4. Consequently,

$$P(A) = 2/4 = .5$$

Relative Frequency Approach

Another method of estimating a probability is referred to as the **relative frequency** approach. This is based on observing the experiment n times and counting the number of times an event (say, A) occurs. If event A occurs m times, then your estimate of the probability that A will occur in the future is

$$P(A) = m/n \qquad\qquad (5\text{-}2)$$

Suppose that a particular production process has been in operation for 250 days; 220 days have been accident-free. Let A = a particular day in the future that will be free of accidents. Using the relative frequency definition, then

$$P(A) = 220/250 = .88$$

Subjective Probability

Another type of probability is **subjective probability.** This is a measure (between zero and one) of your belief that a particular event will occur. A value of one indicates that you believe this event will occur with complete certainty.

Examples of situations requiring a subjective probability are:

The probability that the Dow Jones closing index will be below 1000 at some time during the next six months.

The probability that your newly introduced product will capture at least 10% of the market.

The probability that your recently married cousin, divorced five times already, will once again go down alimony lane.

Although no two people may agree on a particular subjective probability, these probabilities are governed by the same rules of probability, which will be developed later in the chapter.

5.2

Basic Concepts

Datacomp has recently conducted a survey of 200 selected purchasers of their new microcomputer to obtain a sex-and-age profile of their customers. The results obtained are shown in Table 5.1, which is a **contingency** or **cross-tab table.** Such tables are a popular method of summarizing a group by means of two categories—in this case, age and sex. The numbers within the table represent the frequency, or number of individuals, within each pair of subcategories.

Table 5.1

Datacomp survey of microcomputer purchasers

	AGE (YEARS)			
Sex	< 30 (U)	30–45 (B)	> 45 (O)	Total
Male (M)	60	20	40	120
Female (F)	40	30	10	80
Total	100	50	50	200

There are 60 purchasers who are male *and* under 30; ten of the purchasers are female *and* over 45. One person from the total group of 200 is to be selected at random to receive a free software package. We can define the following events:

M = a male is selected

F = a female is selected

U = the person selected is under 30

B = the person selected is between 30 and 45

O = the person selected is over 45

Because there are 200 people, there are 200 possible outcomes to this experiment. All 200 outcomes are equally likely (the person is randomly selected), so the classical definition provides an easy way of determining probabilities.

The probability of any one single event used to define the contingency table is a **marginal probability.** When you use a contingency table, you can obtain the marginal probabilities by merely counting. For example, of the 200 purchasers, 120 are males. So the probability of selecting a male is

$P(M) = 120/200 = .6$

Similarly,

$P(F) = 80/200 = .4$

$P(U) = .5$

$P(B) = .25$

$P(O) = .25$

Notice that $P(O) = 50/200 = .25$, which implies that (1) if you repeatedly selected a person at random from this group, 25% of the time this individual would be over 45 years of age, and (2) 25% of the people in this group are over 45 years old. So, a probability here is simply a **proportion.**

Complement of an event   The complement of an event A is the event that A does *not* occur. This event is denoted $\overline{A}$. For example, A = it rains tomorrow, $\overline{A}$ = it does not rain tomorrow; or A = stock market rises tomorrow, $\overline{A}$ = stock market does not rise tomorrow.

In our Datacomp survey, $P(M) = .6$, and so

$P(\overline{M}) = P(F) = .4$

Notice that $P(M) + P(\overline{M}) = .6 + .4 = 1.0$. In general, for any event A, either A or $\overline{A}$ must occur. Consequently,

$P(A) + P(\overline{A}) = 1$

and so

$P(\overline{A}) = 1 - P(A)$

How can we determine what proportion of the purchasers are age 45 or younger?

$P(\overline{O}) = 1 - P(O) = 1 - .25 = .75$

Joint Probability

What if we wish to know the probability of selecting a purchaser who is female *and* under age 30? Such a person is selected if events F *and* U occur. This probability is written $P(F$ and $U)$ and is referred to as a **joint probability.*** There are 40 purchasers who are female and under 30, so

$P(F$ and $U)$ = 40/200 = .2

What proportion are males between 30 and 45? This is the same as

$P(M$ and $B)$ = 20/200 = .1

because 20 out of 200 satisfy both requirements.

Probability of *A* or *B*

In addition to calculating joint probabilities involving two events, we can also determine the probability that *either* of the two events will occur. In our discussion, "either *A* or *B*" will refer to the event that *A* occurred, *B* occurred, or both occurred. There is no accepted name for such a probability, but it will be written as

$P(A$ or $B)$

for any two events *A* and *B.*****

Now we will calculate the probability of selecting someone who is a male *or* under 30 years of age. This is $P(M$ or $U)$. How many people qualify? There are 120 males and there are 100 people under 30. Is the answer (120 + 100)/200 = 1.1? You should realize that this is not correct because *a probability is never greater than one.* What is the mistake here? The problem is that the 60 males under age 30 were counted *twice.* How many purchasers are male or under 30? The answer is the 120 males plus the 40 females under age 30. So

$P(M$ or $U)$ = (120 + 40)/200 = .8

What is $P(F$ or $B)$? The people in the shaded area in Table 5.1 qualify. So,

$P(F$ or $B)$ = (20 + 40 + 30 + 10)/200 = .5

Conditional Probability

Suppose that someone has some inside information about who has been selected from the group of 200 purchasers. This person informs you that the selected individual is under 30 years of age; that is, event U occurred. Armed with this information, we can calculate the probability that the selected person is a male. Given that event U occurred, we have immediately narrowed the number of possible outcomes from 200 to the 100 people under age 30. Each of these 100 people is equally likely to be chosen, and 60 of them are male. So the answer is 60/100 = .6.

Whenever you are given information and are asked to find a probability based on this information, the result is a **conditional probability.** This probability is written as

$P(A|B)$

where B is the event that you know occurred, and A is the uncertain event whose probability you need, given that event B has occurred. The vertical line indicates that

---

*The joint probability of events A and B is often written as $P(A \cap B)$, read as "the probability of A *intersect B.*"

**The probability $P(A$ or $B)$ can be written as $P(A \cup B)$, read as "the probability of A *union B.*"

the occurrence of event B is given, so the expression is read as the "probability of A given B." In the example, $P(M|U) = .6$.

Suppose that you were given *no information* about U and were asked to find the probability that a male is selected. This is a marginal probability. We earlier determined that $P(M) = .6$. For our example, note that

$$P(M) = P(M|U) = .6$$

This means that being given the information that the person selected is under 30 has *no effect* on the probability that a male is selected. In other words, whether or not U happens has no effect on whether or not M occurs. Such events are said to be independent. Thus, events A and B are **independent** if the occurrence of event A is unaffected by the occurrence or nonoccurrence of event B.

There are a number of ways to demonstrate that any two events A and B are independent.

Events A and B are independent if and only if

1. $P(A \mid B) = P(A)$, or $\hspace{3cm}$ (5-3)

2. $P(B \mid A) = P(B)$, or $\hspace{3cm}$ (5-4)

3. $P(A \text{ and } B) = P(A) \cdot P(B)$. $\hspace{2.5cm}$ (5-5)

You need not demonstrate all three conditions. If one of the equations is true, they are all true; if one is false, they are all false (in which case A and B are not independent). Events that are not independent are **dependent** events.

In our example, are events F and O independent? We previously showed that

$$P(O) = 50/200 = .25$$

Since $P(O|F) = 10/80 = .125$, then $P(O) \neq P(O|F)$, and these events are dependent. Put another way, if someone informs you that event F (a female) has occurred, this *does* have an effect on whether or not the person selected is over 45 years of age. If you are told that F occurred, the probability that the selected person is over 45 *drops* from $.25$ to $.125$. These events do affect each other and so are dependent events.

We could also approach this by showing that $P(F|O)$ is not the same as $P(F)$:

$$P(F|O) = 10/50 \ = .2$$

$$P(F) = 80/200 = .4$$

These are not the same values, so events F and O are not independent.

The final option is to show that $P(F \text{ and } O)$ is not the same as $P(F) \cdot P(O)$. This follows since

$$P(F \text{ and } O) = 10/200 \ = .05$$

$$P(F) \cdot P(O) = (.4)(.25) = .1$$

In our discussion of joint probabilities, we showed that

$$P(F \text{ and } U) = 40/200 = .2$$

Consequently, events F and U *can both occur* because their joint probability is not zero.

How would you calculate $P(F \text{ and } M)$? One cannot be both a male and a female, so $P(F \text{ and } M) = 0$. Because events M and F cannot both occur, these events are said to be mutually exclusive.

Definition

Events A and B are **mutually exclusive** if A and B cannot both occur simultaneously. To demonstrate that two events, A and B, are mutually exclusive, you must show that their joint probability is zero: $P(A \text{ and } B) = 0$.

Example 5.1

The Quality Control Department of Lectron has selected ten devices for testing purposes. Which of these outcomes are mutually exclusive?

A = exactly one device is defective
B = more than two devices are defective
C = less than four devices are defective

Solution

A and B are mutually exclusive events—they cannot both occur.
A and C are *not* mutually exclusive—if A occurs, so does event C.
B and C are *not* mutually exclusive—if three devices are defective, both events B and C will occur.

Note: By "not mutually exclusive" we do not mean that these events *must* both occur, only that they *could* both occur. ●

Exercises

5.1 Assume that there are two red marbles, two blue marbles, and two green marbles in a jar. One marble is picked at random. List the outcomes. Is each outcome equally likely? What is the probability of each outcome?

5.2 If there are 20 sophomores, ten juniors, and five seniors in a classroom, what is the probability of choosing a junior at random? Is this the relative frequency approach to estimating a probability?

5.3 Assume that 20 doctors are chosen at random from the Houston telephone directory. Of these 20, there are 15 who recommend Little's pills and five who do not. If a doctor was chosen at random from the city of Houston, estimate the probability that this doctor would recommend Little's pills.

5.4 Suppose a nickel, a dime, and a penny were tossed at the same time. List the possible outcomes by examining whether a head or tail appears on each coin. Is each outcome equally likely? What is the probability of getting a head on each of these three coins?

5.5 Which of the following values cannot be a probability? Why?

a. .02.
b. 0.
c. 5/4.
d. 985/1051.

5.6 Four hundred randomly sampled automobile owners were asked whether they selected the particular make and model of their present car mainly because of its appearance or because of its performance. The results were as follows:

Owner	Appearance	Performance	Totals
Male	95	55	150
Female	85	165	250
Both	180	220	400

a. What is the probability that an automobile owner buys a car mainly because of its appearance?

b. What is the probability that an automobile owner buys a car mainly because of its appearance and that the automobile owner is a male?

c. What is the probability that a female automobile owner purchases the car mainly because of its appearance?

5.7 A large sports chain wants to know whether it should concentrate its advertising on the serious athlete or on the "weekend" athlete. The sports store also wants to know which sports are the most popular. The marketing department gathered the followed information on 500 randomly selected customers:

Athlete	Tennis	Running	Basketball	Swimming	Soccer	Racquetball	Total
Serious	46	17	60	43	59	50	275
Weekend	54	63	20	37	11	40	225

a. What is the probability that a customer's favorite sport is basketball?

b. What is the probability that a customer is a weekend athlete?

c. What is the probability either that a customer is a serious athlete or that a customer's favorite sport is running?

d. What is the probability that a customer's favorite sport is not swimming?

5.8 The employment center at a university wanted to know the proportion of students who worked and also the proportion of those students who lived in the dorm. The following data were collected:

Living Arrangements	Work Full Time	Work Part Time	Do Not Work	Total
In dorm	19	22	20	61
Not in dorm	25	9	5	39
				100

a. What is the probability of selecting a student who works either full or part time?

b. Given that a student works, what is the probability that the student lives in the dorm?

c. What is the probability that a student either works full time or else does not live in the dorm?

d. Is the event that a student lives in the dorm independent of the event that a student works full time? Discuss what your answer means.

5.9 An investment-newsletter writer wanted to know in which investment areas her subscribers were most interested. A questionnaire was sent to 331 randomly selected professional clients, with the following results:

Business	Stocks	Bonds	Commercial Paper	Commodities	Stock Options	Total
Doctors	30	25	15	2	0	72
Lawyers	29	34	12	0	5	80
Bankers	50	35	29	5	10	129
Others	21	14	10	3	2	50
						331

a. What is the probability that an investment client is neither a doctor nor a lawyer?

b. What is the probability that an investment client is a banker and that the investment client's main investment interest is in commodities?

c. Given that an investment client's main investment interest is commodities, what is the probability that he or she is a banker?

d. What is the probability that an investment client's main investment interest is not in stock options?

e. Let A be the event that an investment client is a lawyer. Let B be the event that an investment client's main investment interest is in commodities. Are the events A and B mutually exclusive?

5.10 If events A and B are mutually exclusive, then is the occurrence of event A affected by the occurrence of event B? Can one say that if two events are mutually exclusive, they are not independent?

5.11 A large supermarket has 67 employees classified by job and by number of years of schooling. The following contingency table gives the categories:

Job	⩽8	9–10	11–12	13–14	15–16	Total
Stocker	1	5	8	1	0	15
Checker	0	5	6	3	0	14
Meat cutter	1	3	7	1	0	12
Cashier	0	0	4	10	5	19
Manager	0	0	1	3	3	7
						67

a. What is the probability that an employee selected at random has 11 or more years of schooling?

b. What is the probability that an employee is either a manager or has 13 or more years of schooling?

c. Given that an employee is a cashier, what is the probability that the employee has 15–16 years of schooling?

d. Let A be the event that an employee is a meat cutter. Let B be the event that an employee has 15–16 years of schooling. Are the events A and B mutually exclusive? Are the events A and B independent?

5.12 A statistics instructor wishes to find out the relationship between the classification of a student and the student's grade in the course. The following is a breakdown of three sections of an introductory statistics course:

Grade	Freshman	Sophomore	Junior	Senior	
A	0	8	9	10	
B	0	6	8	11	
C	1	7	9	12	
D	2	4	1	4	
F	0	6	2	1	
Total	3	31	29	38	101

a. What is the probability that the student is a junior and makes at least a B in the course?

b. What is the probability that the student does not make an A in the course, given that the student is a senior?

c. What is the probability that the student makes a D or F in the course?

d. Let A be the event that a sophomore is taking the course. Let B be the event that the student makes a C in the course. Are the events A and B independent? Are the events A and B mutually exclusive?

5.13 A local bank has 5276 accounts cross-classified by type of account and average account balance. The summarized results are (in dollars)

Account Balance	Checking Account	Savings Account	New Account	Money-Market Account	Total
< 500	1020	803	21	90	1934
500–1000	640	774	452	112	1978
> 1000	51	659	538	116	1364
					5276

a. What is the probability that an account balance does not have over $1000 in it and that the account is not a money-market account?

b. What is the probability that an account is a new account, given that the account balance is between $500 and $1000?

c. What is the probability that an account has less than $500 in it or that the account is a savings account?

d. Given that an account is not a savings account, what is the probability that the account has $1000 or less in it?

5.14 If the probability that it is going to rain today is 0.3, what can you say about the probability that it is not going to rain today?

5.15 Give an example of two events that are mutually exclusive. Explain why they are mutually exclusive. Give an example of two events that are independent. Explain why they are independent.

5.3

Going Beyond the Contingency Table

Our Datacomp survey served as an intuitive introduction to probability definitions. The classical approach was used to derive probabilities by dividing the number of outcomes favorable to an event by the total number of (equally likely) outcomes. Not all probability problems, however, are concerned with randomly selecting an individual from a contingency table.

When dealing with two or more events outside of a contingency table, one approach is to illustrate these events by means of a **Venn diagram.** A Venn diagram representing any two events A and B is shown in Figure 5.1.

In a Venn diagram, the probability of an event occurring is its corresponding area. This may sound complicated, but it really is not. The Venn diagram for $P(A) = .4$ is shown in Figure 5.2. The area of the rectangle is 1; it represents all possible outcomes. The shaded area is the complement of A. Here, $P(\overline{A}) = 1 - P(A) = 1 - .4 = .6$. No effort is made to construct a circle with an area of .4; it is simply labeled .4. The shaded area then represents $\overline{A}$, and the corresponding area must be .6.

Figure 5.3 shows $P(A \text{ and } B)$, and Figure 5.4 shows $P(A \text{ or } B)$.

If A and B are mutually exclusive (they cannot both occur), then $P(A \text{ and } B) = 0$. For example, an auto dealer has data that indicate that 20% of all new cars ordered

Figure 5.1

Venn diagram for events A and B. The rectangle represents all possible outcomes of an experiment.

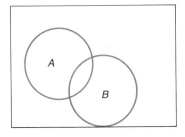

Figure 5.2

Venn diagram for
$P(A) = .4$.

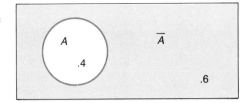

Figure 5.3

$P(A \text{ and } B)$. The points
in the shaded area are
in A and B.

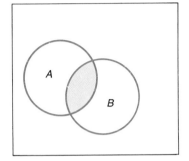

Figure 5.4

$P(A \text{ or } B)$. The points in
the shaded area are in A
or B.

Figure 5.5

Venn diagram of
mutually exclusive
events. $P(A \text{ and } B) = 0$.
$P(A) + P(B) = .2 + .25$
$= .45$.

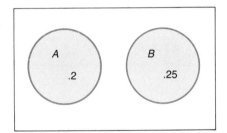

contain a red interior, whereas 25% have a blue interior. Only one color is allowed when selecting an interior color. Let A be the event that a red interior is selected and B be the event that a blue interior is selected. A Venn diagram for this situation is shown in Figure 5.5.

Each person can select only one color, so events A and B are mutually exclusive, and the resulting circles do not overlap in the Venn diagram. What is the probability that a person selects red *or* blue? This is $P(A \text{ or } B)$ and is represented by the shaded area in the circles in Figure 5.5. The Venn diagram allows us to see clearly that this shaded area is $P(A) + P(B) = .2 + .25 = .45$. In other words, 45% of the people will purchase either red or blue interiors. We thus have the following rule.

Figure 5.6

A Venn diagram illustrating $P(A$ or $B)$ and $P(A$ and $B)$.

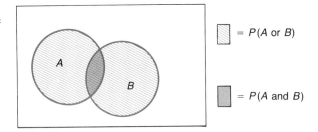

> **Rule**
>
> If events A and B are mutually exclusive, then
>
> $$P(A \text{ or } B) = P(A) + P(B) \qquad (5\text{-}6)$$

This rule does *not* work when A and B can both occur, but there is an easy way to devise another solution. Look at the Venn diagram for this situation, shown in Figure 5.6. By adding $P(A) + P(B)$, we do not obtain $P(A$ or $B)$ because we have counted $P(A$ and $B)$ *twice*. So we need to subtract $P(A$ and $B)$ to obtain the actual area corresponding to $P(A$ or $B)$. This is the **additive rule of probability.**

> **Additive Rule**
>
> For *any* two events, A and B,
>
> $$P(A \text{ or } B) = P(A) + P(B) - P(A \text{ and } B) \qquad (5\text{-}7)$$

Notice that if A and B are mutually exclusive, then $P(A$ and $B) = 0$, and we obtain the previous rule; namely, that $P(A$ or $B) = P(A) + P(B)$.

Example 5.2

Draw a single card from a deck of 52 playing cards. Let S be the event that the card is a seven and H be the event that the card is a heart.

1. Are these events mutually exclusive?
2. What is $P(S$ and $H)$?

Solution 1 Both S and H can occur. A seven of hearts is a possible outcome here. S and H are *not* mutually exclusive. There are (1) 52 equally likely outcomes (cards), (2) 4 sevens, and (3) 13 hearts, so

$$P(S) = 4/52$$
$$P(H) = 13/52$$

Solution 2 $P(S$ and $H)$ is the probability of selecting a seven of hearts from the deck. There is only one such card, so

$$P(S \text{ and } H) = 1/52$$

A Venn diagram for this situation is shown in Figure 5.7. Using the additive rule, the proportion of draws (probability) that a seven *or* a heart will be selected from the deck is

Figure 5.7

$P(S) = 4/52$; $P(H) = 13/52$.

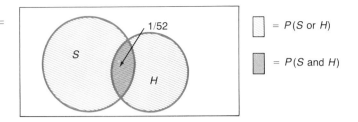

$$P(S \text{ or } H) = P(S) + P(H) - P(S \text{ and } H)$$
$$= 4/52 + 13/52 - 1/52$$
$$= 16/52$$

Refer back to Table 5.1. Does the additive rule work here also? It does—this rule work for *any* two events—but it certainly is a hard way to solve this problem. Suppose we want to find the probability (from our previous example) that the person selected is a male or is under age 30. By inspection, we previously found that

$$P(M \text{ or } U) = 160/200 = .8$$

Using the additive rule, we obtain the same result:

$$P(M \text{ or } U) = P(M) + P(U) - P(M \text{ and } U)$$
$$= 120/200 + 100/200 - 60/200$$
$$= 160/200 = .8$$

Conditional Probabilities

Using Table 5.1, we found that the probability that the person selected is a male (M), given the information that the person selected is under 30 (U), was $P(M|U) = .6$. Our reasoning here was: (1) there are 100 people under 30 years of age, (2) 60 of them are male, (3) each of these 100 people is equally likely to be selected, and so (4) the result is $60/100 = .6$. Notice that

$$P(U) = \frac{100}{200} = .5$$

$$P(M \text{ and } U) = \frac{60}{200} = .3$$

$$P(M|U) = \frac{P(M \text{ and } U)}{P(U)} = \frac{.3}{.5} = .6$$

This procedure for finding a conditional probability applies to *any* two events. Use the Venn diagram in Figure 5.8 to determine $P(A|B)$. Given the information that event B occurred, we are immediately restricted to the lined area (B). What is the probability that a point in B is also in A (that is, event A occurred) given this information? A point is also in A if it lies in the shaded area, and

$$P(A|B) = \frac{\text{shaded area}}{\text{striped area}}$$
$$= \frac{P(A \text{ and } B)}{P(B)}$$

This is the rule for conditional probabilities.

Figure 5.8

A Venn diagram illustrating a conditional probability.

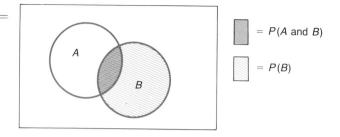

Rule for Conditional Probabilities

For any two events, A and B,

$$P(A|B) = \frac{P(A \text{ and } B)}{P(B)} \tag{5-8}$$

and

$$P(B|A) = \frac{P(A \text{ and } B)}{P(A)} \tag{5-9}$$

Independent Events

In the discussion of the Datacomp survey example, a summary of how to demonstrate that two events are independent was provided in equations 5-3, 5-4, and 5-5. One need demonstrate only that one of these equations holds to verify independence. These three methods of proving independence apply to *any two events*, not just to contingency table applications.

In many situations, it is unnecessary (or impossible) to prove independence of two events. However, one can often argue convincingly that two events are independent or dependent without resorting to a mathematical proof. Consider these events:

A = Procter and Gamble's new laundry detergent captures at least 5% of the market next year

and

B = General Motors will introduce a new line of compact automobiles next year.

Whether event B happens should have no effect on whether event A occurs. So $P(A|B) = P(A)$, and these events are independent. Next, change event A to be: Toyota automobile sales will drop next year. Now whether event B occurs definitely will have an effect on whether event A occurs. So it is not safe to assume that $P(A|B) = P(A)$ because it seems reasonable that $P(A|B)$ is *larger* than $P(A)$. Notice that we have not discussed the values of $P(A)$ and $P(A|B)$. The probability values are not necessary to show that the events are dependent. The important thing is that $P(A|B) \neq P(A)$, so these events are clearly dependent events.

Joint Probabilities

The rule for conditional probabilities in equations 5-8 and 5-9 can be rewritten as

---

Multiplicative Rule

For any two events, A and B,

$$P(A \text{ and } B) = P(A|B) \cdot P(B) \tag{5-10}$$

$$= P(B|A) \cdot P(A) \tag{5-11}$$

This is the **multiplicative rule of probability.** Using equation 5-5, we also have the following rule for two independent events.

Rule

For any two independent events, A and B,

$$P(A \text{ and } B) = P(A) \cdot P(B) \tag{5-12}$$

You may be wondering how we can use the same equation to define the rule for $P(A|B)$ (equation 5-8) and the rule for $P(A \text{ and } B)$ (equation 5-10). This is not a bad question! It appears that we have used the same rule twice to make two different statements—and in fact we have. However, for any application you encounter, either $P(A|B)$ or $P(A \text{ and } B)$ must be provided or can be determined without resorting to formulas. We can clarify this using our card-drawing example:

S = select a seven

H = select a heart

Here $P(S \text{ and } H)$ (the probability of selecting a seven of hearts) is 1/52. No formulas were necessary to determine this, only a little head scratching.

Now, what is $P(S|H)$? Using equation 5-8,

$$P(S|H) = \frac{P(S \text{ and } H)}{P(H)}$$

$$= \frac{1/52}{13/52}$$

$$= 1/13$$

Assume that you select a card from a deck, examine it, and then discard it. You then select another card. This is called **sampling without replacement.** Let

A = selecting a seven on the first draw

B = selecting a seven on the second draw

What is the probability of drawing two sevens [$P(A \text{ and } B)$]? If you selected a seven on the first draw, then, of the 51 cards remaining, three are sevens. So $P(B|A) = 3/51$. Again, we used no formulas.

Next, we use the multiplicative rule, equation 5-11:

$$P(A \text{ and } B) = P(B|A) \cdot P(A)$$

$$= 3/51 \cdot 4/52 = .0045$$

Notice that $P(A) = 4/52$ because there are four sevens available on the first draw. So you are likely to draw two sevens from a card deck 45 times out of 10,000, if you are drawing without replacement.

Now suppose you select a card from a deck but replace it before selecting the second card. This is called **sampling with replacement.** What is $P(B|A)$? There are still 52 cards in the deck when you select your second card, and four of these are sevens. So

$$P(B|A) = 4/52 = P(B)$$

If event A occurs, the probability of a seven on the second draw is unaffected. This probability is 4/52 *whether or not A* occurs; these events are now independent. For this situation,

$$\begin{aligned} P(A \text{ and } B) &= P(A|B) \cdot P(B) \\ &= P(A) \cdot P(B) \text{ (since they are independent)} \\ &= 4/52 \cdot 4/52 = .0059 \end{aligned}$$

The probability of getting two sevens is higher when drawing cards with replacement—not a surprising result.

5.4

Applying the Concepts

Example 5.3

In a particular city, 20% of the people subscribe to the morning newspaper, 30% subscribe to the evening newspaper, and 10% subscribe to both. Determine the probability that an individual from this city subscribes to the morning newspaper, the evening newspaper, or both.

Solution   The most important thing when solving a wordy probability problem is to set up the problem correctly. Your first step when solving any probability application should always be to *define* your events clearly, using capital letters. Your initial step should be to define

M = person subscribes to the morning newspaper

E = person subscribes to the evening newspaper

We do not need to define another event for a person subscribing to both newspapers, as we will see.

We now have

$$P(M) = .2$$
$$P(E) = .3$$

The probability that a selected individual subscribes to the morning *and* the evening newspaper is given as .10. This is a *joint* probability:

$$P(M \text{ and } E) = .1$$

We want to find the probability of M or E. Using the additive rule,

$$P(M \text{ or } E) = P(M) + P(E) - P(M \text{ and } E)$$
$$= .2 + .3 - .1$$
$$= .4$$

So 40% of the people in this city subscribe to at least one of the two newspapers.

Suppose we also know that 60% of the evening newspaper subscribers are also morning newspaper subscribers. How can you translate this statement into a probability? Another way of stating the above sentence is, "Given that you subscribe to the evening newspaper, the probability that you also subscribe to the morning newspaper is .6." In other words, this is a *conditional* probability:

$$P(M|E) = .6 \qquad \bullet$$

Example 5.4

Referring to example 5.3, what percentage of the evening subscribers do not subscribe to the morning newspaper?

Solution A Venn diagram for this problem is shown in Figure 5.9. Notice that M (the morning subscribers) is made up of two components, (1) those people in E (the evening subscribers) and (2) those not in E. Since $P(M \text{ and } E) = .1$, the area of M that is striped is

$$P(M) - P(M \text{ and } E) = P(M \text{ and } \overline{E})$$
$$= .2 - .1 = .1$$

Similarly, the area of E that is striped is

$$P(E) - P(M \text{ and } E) = P(E \text{ and } \overline{M})$$
$$= .3 - .1 = .2$$

Our question could be stated, "Given that a person subscribes to the evening newspaper, what is the probability that this person does not subscribe to the morning newspaper?" This is a *conditional* probability:

$$P(\overline{M}|E)$$

Look at the Venn diagram. You know that E occurred, so you are in the E circle. What is the probability that you are not in M? We know that the total area of E is .3 and that the area that is not in M but is in E is .2. So

$$P(\overline{M}|E) = .2/.3 = 2/3 \qquad \bullet$$

Figure 5.9

Venn diagram for example 5.4.

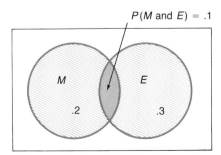

$P(M \text{ and } E) = .1$

M E

.2   .3

Helpful Hints for Probability Applications

1. Define each event using capital letters.
2. Translate each statement into a probability. Is a particular statement telling you $P(A)$? $P(B)$? $P(A$ and $B)$? $P(A$ or $B)$? $P(A|B)$? $P(B|A)$?
3. Determine the answer by identifying the probability rule that applies and by using a Venn diagram. Using both allows you to check your logic and your arithmetic.

Example 5.5

First City Bank conducted a survey of their automobile loans and found that 8% of the loan holders were presently unemployed. Past records indicated that 15% of all borrowers default and that 75% of unemployed borrowers default. First City Bank would like to know:

1. What is the probability that, for any loan, the borrower is unemployed and will default?
2. What is the probability that, for any loan, the borrower is unemployed or will default?
3. What percentage of borrowers who will default are unemployed?

Solution 1 The first step is to define each event.

A = borrower is presently unemployed

B = borrower defaults

We now translate each of the statements into a probability. We know that

$P(A) = .08$

$P(B) = .15$

The last statement in the problem can be written as, "Given that you are unemployed, the probability that you will default is .75." So

$P(B|A) = .75$

What is question 1 of First City Bank's questions asking for? $P(A$ or $B)$? $P(A|B)$? $P(A$ and $B)$? They wish to know the probability that someone is unemployed *and* will default. This is $P(A$ and $B)$. Using the multiplicative rule,

$P(A$ and $B) = P(B|A) \cdot P(A)$

$= .75 \times .08 = .06$

Solution 2 For question 2, we wish to know the probability that A or B occurs. By the additive rule,

$P(A$ or $B) = P(A) + P(B) - P(A$ and $B)$

$= .08 + .15 - .06 = .17$

Thus, 17% of the borrowers are unemployed, will default, or both.

Solution 3 Question 3 can be phrased as, "Given that an individual has defaulted, what is the probability that this person is unemployed?" This is $P(A|B)$.

$$P(A|B) = \frac{P(A \text{ and } B)}{P(B)} = \frac{.06}{.15} = .4$$

Therefore, 40% of those people who default are unemployed.

Exercises

5.16 Use the additive rule for the data in exercise 5.7c to find the probability that a customer is either a serious athlete or that a customer's favorite sport is running.

5.17 Use the additive rule for the data in exercise 5.8c to find the probability that a student either works full time or else does not live in the dorm.

5.18 Suppose one card is randomly picked from a deck of 52 playing cards. Event A is the occurrence of a king. Event B is the occurrence of a spade.

a. What is the probability of A and B?

b. What is the probability of A or B?

c. What is the probability of A given B?

5.19 An independent oil-drilling company drills "wild cat" oil wells. So far, 60% of the wells have been oil producing and 40% have been dry. A private investor wishes to go into a partnership with the oil company in two wells. Assuming that the outcome of one well does not affect the outcome of the other well, what is the probability that both of the oil wells in the partnership will produce oil? What is the probability that at least one of the two wells will produce oil?

5.20 If $P(A) = .5$, $P(B) = .2$, and $P(A \text{ or } B) = .7$, then are the events A and B mutually exclusive? Explain.

5.21 If $P(A) = .5$ and $P(B) = .6$, then are the events A and B mutually exclusive? Explain.

5.22 If the probability that a person orders the morning newspaper is .5 and the probability that a person orders the evening newspaper is .3, and if the probability that a person orders at least one of the two newspapers is .7, then what is the probability that a person orders both the morning and evening newspapers?

5.23 If $P(A) = .4$, $P(B) = .3$, and $P(A \text{ and } B) = .12$, then what is the probability of A given B? Are the events A and B independent?

5.24 A manufacturer of widgets historically has produced 80 good widgets out of every 100 widgets. If two widgets are randomly selected off the assembly line, what is the probability that both widgets will be nondefective? What is the probability that two randomly selected widgets will be defective?

5.25 If a penny, a nickel, and a dime are flipped, what is the probability of getting three heads, given that the flip of the penny resulted in a head?

5.26 A manufacturer claims that a customer has a 30% chance of noticing a particular flaw in a dress it makes. Two dresses, one without the flaw and one with the flaw, are given to two customers to see whether they can recognize the dress with the flaw.

a. What is the probability that a customer will notice the flaw if each of the two customers examines a different dress?

b. What is the probability that the flaw will be recognized if the two customers examine both dresses?

c. Assume that a customer randomly selects one of the two dresses and then examines the selected dress. What is the probability that the customer will find a flaw?

d. If both customers select and examine a dress in the manner described in question c, what is the probability that both customers will recognize the flaw?

5.27 If $P(A) = .5$, $P(B) = .3$, and $P(A|B) = .4$, what is $P(B|A)$?

5.28 At a certain university, 30% of the students major in mathematics. Of the students majoring in mathematics, 60% are males. Of all the students at the university, 70% are males.

a. What is the probability that a student selected at random in the university is a male majoring in mathematics?

b. What is the probability that a student selected at random in the university is a male or is majoring in mathematics?

c. What proportion of the males are majoring in mathematics?

5.29 At a semiconductor plant, 60% of the workers are skilled and 80% of the workers are full time. Ninety percent of the skilled workers are full time.

a. What is the probability that an employee, selected at random, is a skilled full-time employee?

b. What is the probability that an employee, selected at random, is a skilled worker or a full-time worker?

c. What percentage of the full-time workers are skilled?

5.30 A supermarket has 40% of its merchandise on sale. Twenty percent of its merchandise consists of nonedible items. Fifty percent of the sale items consists of nonedible items.

a. What is the probability that an item, selected at random in the supermarket, is nonedible and on sale?

b. What is the probability that an item, selected at random, is either nonedible or on sale?

c. What proportion of nonedible items are on sale?

5.31 For every person that visits a leasing office of an apartment community near a certain university, there is a 26% chance that the person will lease an apartment if the person is a student and a 17% chance that the person will lease an apartment if the person is not a student. If two people, one of whom is a student and the other is not, enter the office, what are the chances of leasing an apartment to at least one of the two people? What assumption did you have to make here?

5.32 Let $P(A) = .7$, $P(B) = .3$, and $P(A \text{ and } B) = .2$. Find the following probabilities:

a. $P(\bar{A})$.   c. $P(B|A)$.   e. $P(A|\bar{B})$.   g. $P(\overline{A \text{ and } B})$.

b. $P(A \text{ or } B)$.   d. $P(A \text{ and } \bar{B})$.   f. $P(\bar{A} \text{ and } \bar{B})$.

5.33 If a pair of dice is tossed, what is the probability that each of the two dice show the same number?

5.34 A jar contains four green marbles, six red marbles, and two blue marbles.

a. If three marbles are chosen without replacement, what is the probability of getting a red marble on the third draw if a green and a red marble were drawn on the first and second draw, respectively.

b. What is the probability in question a if the marbles are drawn with replacement?

5.35 If $P(A|B) = .8$ and $P(A \text{ and } B) = .6$, what is the $P(B)$?

5.5

Probabilities for More Than Two Events

We will illustrate what happens when you encounter more than two events by using three events, A, B, and C. The following rules can easily be extended to any number of events. In the applications of probability in the chapters that follow, we typically will be dealing with multiple events that are either mutually exclusive or independent.

Mutually Exclusive Events

Events A, B, and C are mutually exclusive if no two events can occur simultaneously. A Venn diagram of this situation is shown in Figure 5.10. When dealing with mutually exclusive events, we usually will be interested in the probability that *one* of these events will occur—that is $P(A \text{ or } B \text{ or } C)$. We can use a simple rule here:

Figure 5.10

Three mutually exclusive events.

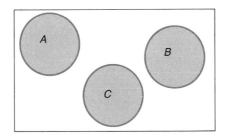

> For mutually exclusive events, A, B, and C,
>
> $P(A \text{ or } B \text{ or } C) = P(A) + P(B) + P(C)$ (5-13)

Thus, to determine "or" probabilities when the events are mutually exclusive, you add the respective probabilities.

Independent Events

Events A, B, and C are (pairwise) independent if the occurrence or nonoccurrence of any one event has no effect on the remaining events; $P(A|B) = P(A)$, $P(C|B) = P(C)$, and so on. When dealing with independent events, the probability of interest usually is that *all* of the events occur—that is, $P(A \text{ and } B \text{ and } C)$. Once again, a simple rule exists for this situation:

> For independent events, A, B, and C,
>
> $P(A \text{ and } B \text{ and } C) = P(A) \cdot P(B) \cdot P(C)$ (5-14)

Thus, to determine "and" probabilities when the events are independent, you multiply the respective probabilities.

Example 5.6

Dellex Industries makes memory units for a microcomputer. Dellex customers have agreed to select three units randomly from each shipment and test them. If none of the units is defective, the customer will accept the shipment.

Usually, 2% of all Dellex units are defective. Determine the probability that a shipment will be accepted—that is, that all three units tested will be nondefective.

Solution Let

A = first unit is nondefective

B = second unit is nondefective

C = third unit is nondefective

We know that 2% of the units produced are defective, so 98% of them are not defective; consequently, $P(A) = P(B) = P(C) = .98$.

We want to find $P(A \text{ and } B \text{ and } C)$. Are the events independent? There is no need to use fancy formulas here. The answer is yes, simply because the units are selected randomly from the entire shipment. Therefore,

$$P(A \text{ and } B \text{ and } C) = P(A) \cdot P(B) \cdot P(C)$$
$$= .98 \cdot .98 \cdot .98 = .94$$

So 94% of shipments will be accepted.

Exercises

5.36 In exercise 5.9, let A be the event that a subscriber is a banker. Let B be the event that a subscriber is a lawyer. Let C be the event that the subscriber is a doctor.

a. Are the events A, B, and C mutually exclusive?

b. What is the $P(A \text{ or } B \text{ or } C)$?

c. What is the $P(A \text{ and } B \text{ and } C)$?

5.37 In exercise 5.11, let A be the event that an employee has 8 years or less of schooling. Let B be the event that the employee has 9–10 years of schooling. Let C be the event that an employee has 15–16 years of schooling:

a. Are the events A, B, and C mutually exclusive?

b. What is $P(A \text{ or } B \text{ or } C)$?

c. What is $P(A \text{ and } B \text{ and } C)$?

5.38 In exercise 5.12, are the events "receiving the grade of A," "receiving the grade of B," and "receiving the grade of C or better" mutually exclusive? What is the probability that at least one of these events will occur?

5.39 Let $P(A) = .3$, $P(B) = .4$, $P(C) = .5$, and $P(A \text{ and } B \text{ and } C) = .06$. Are the events A, B, and C independent?

5.40 If three events are independent, then are the three events mutually exclusive? If the three events are mutually exclusive, then are the three events independent?

5.41 Three cards are picked with replacement from a deck of 52 playing cards. What is the probability that the first card will be a queen, that the second will be a spade, and that the third will be a king?

5.42 At a university, 40% of the accounting majors, 20% of the marketing majors, and 15% of the finance majors are from out of state. If a student is selected randomly from each of these three majors, what is the probability that all three are from out of state?

5.43 A retailer receives, on the average, one defective calculator of every 20. What is the probability that three calculators, randomly selected by the retailer, are nondefective?

5.6

Counting Rules

Counting rules determine the number of possible outcomes that exist for a certain experiment. They can be extremely useful in determining probabilities. For instance, consider an experiment that has 200 possible outcomes, all of which are equally likely to occur. The probability of any one such outcome is $1/200 = .005$.

The question we wish to answer here is, for a particular experiment, how many possible outcomes are there? No set of rules applies to all situations, but we will consider three very popular counting procedures: (1) filling slots, (2) permutations (a special case of filling slots), and (3) combinations.

Filling Slots

We use **counting rule 1** to fill k different slots. Let

n_1 = the number of ways of filling the first slot

n_2 = the number of ways of filling the second slot *after* the first slot is filled

n_3 = the number of ways of filling the third slot after the first two slots are filled

.
.
.

n_k = the number of ways of filling the kth slot after filling slots 1 through $k - 1$.

The number of ways of filling all k slots is

$$n_1 \cdot n_2 \cdot n_3 \cdot \ldots \cdot n_k$$

Example 5.7

When ordering a new car, you have a choice of eight interior colors, ten exterior colors, and four roof colors. How many possible color schemes are there?

Solution There are three slots to fill here, (eight) interior color, (ten) exterior color, and (four) roof color. To answer the question, you simply *multiply* the number of ways of filling each slot. So the answer is $8 \cdot 10 \cdot 4 = 320$ different color schemes.

The order in which you fill the slots is unimportant. So $n_2 = 10$, regardless of whether or not you have filled the first slot. For some applications, this is not the case. Consider the following example. ●

Example 5.8

A local PTA group is selecting their officers for the current year. There are 15 individuals in the group, whom we label as $I_1, I_2, \ldots, I_{15}$. They need to select a president, vice-president, secretary, and treasurer. How many possible groups of officers are there?

Solution We have four slots to fill here, president (n_1), vice-president (n_2), secretary (n_3), and treasurer (n_4). We know that n_1 is 15. After a president is elected, only 14 people remain, so $n_2 = 14$. By a similar argument, $n_3 = 13$ and $n_4 = 12$. The answer is $15 \cdot 14 \cdot 13 \cdot 12 = 32{,}760$ different slates of officers. ●

Permutations

Example 5.8 is a counting situation in which you select people *without replacement*. If a particular person, say I_3, is elected president, then I_3 is not available to fill the remaining slots. Another way of stating the result is that there are 32,760 ways of selecting four people out of 15, where the **order of selection** is important. For example,

I_2 = president

I_6 = vice-president

I_{12} = secretary

I_7 = treasurer

is not the same slate of officers as

I_7 = president

I_{12} = vice-president

I_2 = secretary

I_6 = treasurer

even though the same people are involved.

The number of ways of selecting k objects (or people) from a group of n distinct objects, where the order of selection is important, is referred to as the "number of permutations of n objects using k at a time." This is written

$$_nP_k$$

In example 5.8, $_{15}P_4 = 32{,}760$. Determining the number of permutations is just a special case of counting rule 1; this is also a slot-filling application.

The symbol **$n!$** is read as "n factorial." Its value is determined by multiplying n by all the numbers lower than n.

$$n! = (n)(n - 1)(n - 2) \ldots \tag{5-15}$$

For example,

$$5! = (5)(4)(3)(2)(1) = 120$$

$$1! = 1$$

$$0! = 1 \text{ (by definition)}$$

Notice that $n!$ is the number of ways of filling n slots using n objects. There are n ways of filling the first slot, $(n - 1)$ ways of filling the second slot, $(n - 2)$ ways for the third slot, and so on.

In example 5.8, the result was obtained by finding $15 \cdot 14 \cdot 13 \cdot 12 = 32{,}760$. This also can be written as

$$\frac{15 \cdot 14 \cdot 13 \cdot 12 \cdot 11 \cdot 10 \cdot 9 \cdot 8 \cdot 7 \cdot 6 \cdot 5 \cdot 4 \cdot 3 \cdot 2 \cdot 1}{11 \cdot 10 \cdot 9 \cdot 8 \cdot 7 \cdot 6 \cdot 5 \cdot 4 \cdot 3 \cdot 2 \cdot 1} = 32{,}760$$

This is an application of **counting rule 2**: The number of **permutations** of n objects using k objects at a time is

$$_nP_k = \frac{n!}{(n - k)!} = (n)(n - 1) \ldots (n - k + 1) \tag{5-16}$$

Example 5.9

How many two-digit numbers can you construct using the digits 1, 2, 3, and 4, without repeating any digit?

Solution The order of selection is certainly important here—the number 42 is not the same as 24. The answer is $_4P_2$, where

$$_4P_2 = \frac{4!}{(4 - 2)!} = \frac{(4)(3)(2!)}{2!} = 12$$

These 12 permutations are

12	21	31	41
13	23	32	42
14	24	34	43

●

Combinations

Take another look at example 5.8, where we selected four people from a group of 15. This time, however, choose a committee of four people from a group of 15 where the order of selection does *not* matter. Each such committee is one *combination* of the 15 people, using four at a time. For example,

$$I_2 \quad I_6 \quad I_{12} \quad I_7$$

and

$$I_7 \quad I_{12} \quad I_2 \quad I_6$$

are different permutations but are the same combination. These two arrangements are made up of the same individuals; hence they form the same committee or combination.

Clearly, there are not as many combinations (using I_2, I_6, I_{12}, I_7) as there are permutations. The two permutations above form the same combination. There are 24 other possible permutations of this combination ($4 \cdot 3 \cdot 2 \cdot 1 = 24$).

Now we wish to determine how many possible committees (combinations) of four there are for the group of 15. This is written as

$$_{15}C_4$$

Each combination has 24 permutations, so

$$_{15}C_4 = \frac{_{15}P_4}{24} = \frac{32,760}{24} = 1365$$

There are 1365 possible committee combinations. Notice that 24 is the number of *permutations* of these four numbers (2, 6, 7, and 12); that is $24 = {_4}P_4 = 4!$

Counting rule 3 is used to count the number of possible combinations. The number of **combinations** of n objects using k at a time is

$$_nC_k = \frac{_nP_k}{k!} = \frac{n!}{k!(n-k)!} \tag{5-17}$$

Example 5.10

A company must select five employees from a department of 40 people to attend a national conference. How many possible delegations are there?

Solution The order of selection is not a factor here, so this is a combination problem rather than a permutation problem. The answer is

$$_{40}C_5 = \frac{40!}{5!35!}$$

$$= \frac{(40)(39)(38)(37)(36)(35!)}{(5!)(35!)}$$

$$= \frac{(40)(39)(38)(37)(36)}{(5)(4)(3)(2)(1)}$$

$$= 658,008$$

Exercises

5.44 A cafeteria serves four different vegetables, five different main dishes consisting of either fish or meat, and three different desserts. If a customer chooses one serving from each of these three categories, how many different combinations of vegetables, main dishes, and desserts are possible?

5.45 A firm has 100 laborers, 20 salespeople, and ten executives. If an employee is chosen from each of these three categories, how many different combinations of three employees are possible?

5.46 How many different ways can you select four playing cards from a deck of 52 such that the first is a heart, the second is a diamond, the third is a club, and the fourth is a spade?

5.47 Five offices are available for five recently hired junior executives. How many different ways can the five junior executives be assigned to the offices?

5.48 Seven assistant professors have applied for tenure at a university. However, only two assistant professors can be granted tenure. How many different combinations of two assistant professors can be selected to receive tenure?

5.49 A shoe salesperson has ten different western boots to display in her showcase window. She can display only four at one time. How many different combinations of four western boots can the salesperson select?

5.50 Six chairs are available for the six typists at a certain firm. How many seating arrangements are possible?

5.51 A committee of ten people needs to select a committee chairperson and committee secretary. How many different ways can the chairperson and secretary be selected from this committee?

5.52 A builder has five different house styles and three lots on which to build. If each lot has a different style of house on it, how many combinations of the five house styles are possible on these three lots?

5.53 How many different three-digit numbers can be constructed using the digits 3, 5, 7, and 9 if no digit can be repeated?

5.54 To cut down on overhead, a small business decides to reduce the number of keypunchers employed. How many different combinations of five people can be selected from 25 keypunchers if the firm decides to reduce the number of keypunchers by five?

5.55 A person has six different-colored shirts and ten different-colored trousers. How many color schemes are possible if one shirt and one pair of trousers are chosen?

5.56 Eight balls are numbered and placed in a jar. How many different combinations of four balls can be selected from the jar, if the balls are chosen without replacement?

5.57 Ten employees have the option of selecting the day shift or the night shift. How many different combinations of employees can be found such that only two choose the night shift?

5.58 In exercise 5.56, if the balls are arranged in the order that they are selected, how many different arrangements of four balls are possible, assuming that the balls are chosen without replacement?

5.7

Simple Random Samples

Practically all of the applications in later chapters that use probabilities derived from sample results to make a decision concerning the population are based on the assumption of a simple random sample or, more simply, a random sample.

We introduced this concept in Chapter 1. A sample of size n, selected from a population of size N, constitutes a **simple random sample** if every possible sample of size n has the same probability of being selected.

In example 5.10, we determined that there were 658,008 possible delegations when selecting five people from a group of 40. If we view this group as the population of interest, then $n = 5$ and $N = 40$. Our concern here is to determine the probability that any specified group of five individuals will be the designated delegation if simple random sampling is used.

There are $_{40}C_5 = 658,008$ possible delegations, and each has the same probability of being selected. Therefore, the probability that any one combination of people will be picked is $1/658,008 = .000002$.

In general, when employing a simple random sample of size n, selected from a population of size N, the total number of possible random samples is

$$_NC_n$$

Also, each of these samples has a probability of being selected of

$$\frac{1}{_NC_n}$$

Example 5.11

Your task is to obtain a random sample of two individuals from a group of five employees (E_1, E_2, E_3, E_4, and E_5). What is the probability that you select E_2 and E_5 as your sample?

Solution There are

$$_5C_2 = \frac{5!}{2!3!} = 10$$

possible random samples. They are:

Sample Number	Sample
1	E_1, E_2
2	E_1, E_3
3	E_1, E_4
4	E_1, E_5
5	E_2, E_3
6	E_2, E_4
7	E_2, E_5
8	E_3, E_4
9	E_3, E_5
10	E_4, E_5

Each random sample (including the one containing E_2 and E_5) has a probability of being selected of $1/10 = .1$.

Obtaining a Random Sample

When N is small, we can put the N names in a hat and pick out n of them for our sample. This will constitute a random sample (if you do not have a hat, improvise). When N is moderately large (for example, 10,000), we need a more practical method of selecting n items from this population. A common procedure is to select n **random numbers** between 1 and 10,000 using a table of random numbers or a computer-generated list of n random numbers. A list of random numbers is provided in Table A-13 at the end of the text. To generate a list of random numbers between 1 and 10,000, one procedure you could use is to

1. Start in any arbitrary position, say, row 5 of column 3.
2. Select a list of random numbers by reading either across or down the table.

Figure 5.11

Generating 100 random numbers using MINITAB.

```
MTB > RANDOM 100 VALUES INTO C1;        Input: command to generate
SUBC> UNIFORM A=1 AND B=10000.             100 random numbers
MTB > PRINT C1                            between 1 and 10,000
C1
  7568.77    595.46   2672.86   1227.55   4916.36   3060.44   3936.49
  7746.85   1720.48   4319.06   3981.19   5096.07   6417.83   8504.57
  1941.75   9205.89   6385.97   7724.74   4084.04     44.40   7828.79
  1756.49   2090.23   5733.98    698.87   6247.64   2540.10    427.17
  7859.45   9273.34   5567.33   9495.70   5226.03   3578.34   8152.08
  3168.49   7077.12   9357.30   5021.09   7169.32   8283.48   9924.69
  7622.27   6490.57   2652.87     97.98   9149.57   5860.12   4116.25
  4652.27   1076.31   8019.35   4980.91   1696.44   4169.58   8395.87
  2955.91   3289.48   4465.25   2265.26   6177.87   3169.72   2151.65
  7995.29   2957.01   8919.00   8847.03   7475.97    451.86   3420.95
  6238.37   2309.68   4004.25   7940.04   6536.16   1873.23   6346.29
  6689.04   2735.05   6839.47   3396.54    202.00   4129.78   9249.82
   867.62   2374.91     70.60   7731.96   3404.84   3515.72   2412.03
  3959.48   5472.79   9236.27   4639.87   3945.08    706.78   2545.35
  3130.68   5262.95
```

Output: 100 random numbers

3. For each five-digit number selected, place a decimal before the final digit and round this value to the nearest counting number; for example, 24127 would become 2412.7, which is then rounded to 2413.

A computer-generated list of random numbers is easiest to use. Figure 5.11 contains the instructions for generating 100 random numbers between 1 and 10,000 using MINITAB. We will give you the necessary commands in SAS and SPSSX at the end of the chapter.

Using either procedure, let us assume that the resulting set of random numbers is 415, 6962, and 4815 (for $n = 3$). Then you must (1) code your population from 1 to 10,000 in some manner and (2) select individuals 415, 4815, and 6962 for your random sample. This topic and extensions of simple random sampling will be further discussed in Chapter 8.

MINITAB, SAS, and SPSSX all have options available that allow you to sample randomly from a stored data set and save the results for further analysis. You can find the necessary commands to carry out this procedure in the appropriate user's manual.

To obtain a representative sample when N is extremely large or unknown requires good judgment. Stopping the first ten people you meet on the street is a very poor way of representing your population.

You sometimes may be forced to select items for the sample that represent the population as accurately as possible, realizing that a poorly gathered sample can easily lead to an incorrect decision of significant importance. Accountants often encounter this problem when performing a statistical audit. However, when such a sample is *not* a random sample, it is not correct to use probability theory for your analysis.

Exercises

5.59 An instructor requires each of 35 students in a class to write a term paper comparing nonparametric with parametric statistics. Two students are selected to present their term papers in class. What is the probability that Georgia and Fred (two students in the class) will be picked?

5.60 There are eight identically shaped objects in a jar. Two objects are selected randomly without replacement. If the objects are numbered one through eight, what is the probability that a six and a seven are drawn?

5.61 A firm has 12 skilled technicians, eight of whom have college degrees. If a group of four technicians is chosen randomly to form a production team, what is the probability that none of the four will have a college degree? Do the four selected at random constitute a simple random sample?

5.62 Explain how to select a simple random sample for a population of 100,000 using the computer-generated random numbers in Table A-13.

5.63 The school-newspaper photographer takes ten different pictures of the homecoming queen at the school's football game. All ten pictures are excellent, so the photographer chooses two at random to place in the school newspaper. What is the probability that the first two pictures taken will be selected?

Summary

This chapter has examined methods of dealing with uncertainty by applying the concept of probability. An activity that results in an uncertain outcome is called an experiment; the possible outcomes are events. Uncertainty is measured in terms of the probabilities of events. To determine the value of a particular probability, we used the classical approach, the relative frequency method, and the subjective probability approach.

When examining more than one event, say A and B, several types of probabilities can be derived. The probability of A *and* B occurring is a joint probability and is written $P(A \text{ and } B)$. The multiplicative rule is a method of determining a joint probability. The probability of A *or* B (or both) occurring is written $P(A \text{ or } B)$ and can be obtained using the additive rule. When asked to find a probability given particular information about events, you determine a conditional probability. For example, the probability that B occurs given that A has occurred is a conditional probability, written $P(B|A)$. A variation of the multiplicative rule provides a method of determining a conditional probability. The probability of a single event, such as P(the person selected is a female) or P(an individual subscribes to *The Wall Street Journal*), is a marginal probability.

An effective method of determining a probability in complicated situations is to use a Venn diagram. When you represent the various events visually, you can often obtain a seemingly complex probability easily.

Two events are said to be independent if the occurrence of the one event has no effect on the probability that the other event occurs. If two events can never occur simultaneously, they are mutually exclusive. For example, these two events are certainly independent but are *not* mutually exclusive (since both events could occur): A, the stock market drops more than two points during a particular week, and B, your company's copying machine breaks down during the same week.

We discussed various counting rules, including permutations and combinations. These rules are used to count the number of possible outcomes for experiments that select a certain number of people or objects (k) from a large group of n such objects. When determining the corresponding number of permutations (written $_nP_k$), the *order* of selection is considered. The number of combinations for this situation (written $_nC_k$) ignores the order of selection and counts only the number of groups that can be obtained.

We also discussed the number of random samples that exists when the population size is known, and we examined methods of obtaining such a sample. In the chapters to follow, any results using a statistical sample assume that the sample is obtained randomly.

Review Exercises

5.64 For a marketing survey, 200 customers were classified according to their age (in years) and their favorite type of donut.

Age of Customer	Glazed	Chocolate Covered	Creme Filled	Cake	
< 21	3	25	10	7	
21–30	5	23	26	10	
31–45	15	12	3	20	
> 45	29	5	1	6	
Total	52	65	40	43	200

a. What is the probability that a person prefers creme-filled donuts and is age 45 years or less?

b. What is the probability that a person's favorite donut is not glazed or that the person is less than 21 years of age?

c. What is the probability that a person is between 21 and 30 years of age if that person favors chocolate-covered donuts?

d. Are age and favorite donut independent variables?

5.65 The probability that a person buys a car after receiving a sales pitch is .10. After a customer decides to buy a car, the probability that the customer will arrange financing through the dealer is .75. What is the probability that a customer who hears a sales pitch will buy a car and arrange financing through the dealer?

5.66 If you are selecting playing cards at random without replacement from a deck of 52 and you have already drawn a king of spades, queen of spades, ten of spades, and nine of spades, then what is the probability of drawing a jack of spades?

5.67 A marketing-research group conducted a survey to find out where people did their Christmas shopping. Out of a group of 110 randomly selected shoppers, 70 said that they shopped exclusively at the local mall, 30 said that they shopped exclusively in the downtown area, and 10 said that they shopped at both the local mall and the downtown area.

a. What is the probability that a customer shops in both the local mall and the downtown area?

b. What proportion of customers who shop at the local mall also shop in the downtown area?

c. What is the probability that a customer shops downtown but not at the local mall?

5.68 An electronics firm decides to market three different software packages for its personal computers. The marketing analyst gives each of the three packages an 80% chance of success. The outcomes for each of the software packages are independent.

a. What is the probability that all three will be a success?

b. What is the probability that only two of the packages will be a success?

c. What is the probability that none will be successful?

5.69 Six green beans and one lima bean are placed in a jar. Two beans are randomly selected from the jar, without replacement.

a. What is the probability of drawing a green bean on the first draw?

b. What is the probability of drawing a green bean on the second draw?

c. What is the probability of drawing a green bean on the first or second draw?

d. What is the probability of drawing a lima bean on the first or second draw?

5.70 If $P(A) = .4$ and $P(B) = .7$, are the events A and B mutually exclusive?

5.71 Assume events A and B are mutually exclusive. Find the following probabilities where $P(A) = .4$ and $P(B) = .15$.

a. $P(A \text{ or } B)$.

b. $P(A \text{ or } \overline{B})$.

c. $P(\overline{A} \text{ or } \overline{B})$.

d. $P(\overline{A} \text{ and } B)$.

e. $P(A|B)$.

f. $P(A|\overline{B})$.

5.72 Consider the experiment in which a single die is tossed.

a. What is the probability that an even number occurs?

b. What is the probability that an even number occurs, given that the number is greater than three?

c. What is the probability that an even number occurs or that a number greater than three occurs?

5.73 An instructor has 40 questions from which she can draw to make up a 30-question test. How many different tests can the instructor design?

5.74 A busy executive has to meet with five production managers during the day. The executive needs to decide in which order to see the managers. How many different orderings can the executive choose? What is the probability of the executive's choosing any one ordering, if the choice is random?

5.75 A defective tape recorder is inspected by two service representatives. If one representative has a 50% chance of finding the defect, and the other has a 60% chance, then what is the probability that at least one will find the defect if both check the tape recorder independently? What is the probability that neither will spot the defect?

5.76 A student forgot the combination for his bike lock. The combination consists of a sequence of three numbers and each number can range from zero to nine. How many different sequences are possible?

5.77 If $P(A|B) = .3$, $P(B) = .5$, and $P(A) = .4$, what is $P(A \text{ or } B)$?

5.78 Forty percent of the students in an economics class major in business and 70% are from St. Louis, Missouri. Also, 20% are neither business majors nor from St. Louis. What is the probability that a student in the economics class selected at random is a business major from St. Louis?

Solution

Random Number Generation

You can use SPSSX to generate random numbers. The SPSSX program listing in Figure 5.12 was used to request the generation of 100 random numbers between 1 and 10,000. Each line represents one card image to be entered.

Figure 5.12

SPSSX program listing requesting the generation of 100 random numbers between 1 and 10,000.

```
TITLE      RANDOM NUMBERS
INPUT PROGRAM
LOOP #1=1 TO 100
COMPUTE RANNUM=UNIFORM(10000)
END CASE
END LOOP
END FILE
END INPUT PROGRAM
PRINT      /RANNUM
EXECUTE
```

The TITLE command names the SPSSX run.

The INPUT PROGRAM statement allows you to build your own subprograms either to input or to generate data.

The LOOP statement sets up a loop that is terminated by an END LOOP statement. In this example, we are looping 100 times to COMPUTE 100 different random numbers.

The END CASE statement passes control of the loop to the END LOOP statement, which passes control to the loop until 100 random numbers have been generated.

The END FILE statement terminates loop processing.

The END INPUT PROGRAM statement terminates the INPUT PROGRAM.

The PRINT statement set up the 100 random numbers that were generated for printing.

The EXECUTE command causes the printing to occur.

Figure 5.13 shows the output obtained by executing the program listing in Figure 5.12.

Figure 5.13

Output obtained by executing SPSSX program listing in Figure 5.12.

```
7152.14    5270.75    1746.97
9283.01    6618.39    2883.52
5781.33    9358.01    6688.70
2618.57    3156.88    7612.06
7248.30    5227.24    8031.34
 370.92    7658.50    7028.58
1005.66    1270.73     479.13
7326.45    5593.55    3942.61
2254.11    9826.16    2286.20
2214.21    3252.62    7262.15
6100.88    5355.03    8824.65
9539.67    5076.78    1822.22
2369.01    2819.95    2796.90
3385.18    3472.06    6955.45
 528.11    9210.85    9025.72
7383.47    4081.48    1228.13
1198.11     957.39    5076.97
 588.94    3338.91    1172.83
1880.19    6207.71    9247.25
 995.58    6411.31    5172.83
6758.70    7521.35    2714.06
6926.52    2049.52    6446.36
8667.91    1432.59    6437.86
3512.31    4458.81    8528.29
4964.23    3690.64     651.50
7019.78    4852.80    4067.98
2060.08     992.68    5667.01
7733.91    7256.51    8432.90
 669.20     372.51
```

Solution

Random Number Generation

You can generate random numbers using SAS. The SAS program listing in Figure 5.14 was used to request the generation of 100 random numbers between 1 and 10,000. Each line represents one card image to be entered.

The TITLE command names the SAS run.

The PROC MATRIX command allows you to build a table to hold the generated random numbers.

Figure 5.14

SAS program listing requesting the generation of 100 random numbers between 1 and 10,000.

```
TITLE      RANDOM NUMBERS;
PROC MATRIX;
X=UNIFORM (J(20,5,0));
X = X * 10000;
PRINT X FORMAT=F6.0;
```

The X = UNIFORM (J(20,5,0)) command calls 100 random numbers and stores them in a table of 20 rows by 5 columns.

The X = X * 10000 statement scales the numbers up from a decimal number to an integer between 1 and 10,000.

The PRINT X FORMAT = F6.0 statement establishes the size of the numbers to be printed and then prints the 20-by-5 table.

Figure 5.15 shows the output obtained by executing the program listing in Figure 5.14.

Figure 5.15

Output obtained by executing SAS program listing in Figure 5.14.

RANDOM NUMBERS

X	COL1	COL2	COL3	COL4	COL5
ROW1	300	906	1933	2089	2891
ROW2	208	8650	2092	4109	6326
ROW3	1042	747	7167	2514	6847
ROW4	2403	604	2378	5214	4830
ROW5	3567	2680	8036	6593	1125
ROW6	5545	7115	7011	8491	2996
ROW7	876	8194	236	6486	6093
ROW8	2070	4512	1427	4599	2418
ROW9	2267	6722	5014	1898	1468
ROW10	9297	9453	4085	6314	3631
ROW11	5257	496	1462	6289	1702
ROW12	2626	1238	5452	1721	8974
ROW13	3862	5448	8624	7079	665
ROW14	6283	7815	550	305	8175
ROW15	3513	1094	7988	1081	469
ROW16	5552	9688	9233	682	7928
ROW17	1364	663	5124	6420	3179
ROW18	1742	454	5449	8718	6705
ROW19	740	2698	9209	2184	4173
ROW20	1134	2739	6742	4791	6045

Discrete Probability Distributions

A Look Back/Introduction

The early chapters were concerned with describing data that had been gathered from a previous experiment, a printed report, or some other source. The data were summarized using one or more numerical measures (for example, a sample mean, variance, or correlation) or using a statistical graph (such as a histogram, bar chart, or scatter diagram).

Chapter 5 introduced you to methods of dealing with uncertainty by using a probability to measure the chance of a particular event occurring. Rules were defined that enable you to derive the various probabilities of interest, such as a conditional or a joint probability. However, so far we have defined only the probability of a certain *event* happening.

Whenever an experiment results in a numerical outcome, such as the total value of two dice, one can represent the various possible outcomes and their corresponding probabilities much more conveniently by using a random variable. Suppose that your company manufactures a product that is sometimes defective and is returned for repair in 10% of the cases. An excellent way of describing the chance that three of 20 products will be returned before the warranty runs out is to use the concept of a random variable.

Random variables can be classified into two categories: discrete and continuous. This chapter will introduce both types but will concentrate mainly on the discrete type of random variable. Several commonly used discrete random variables will be discussed, as will methods of describing and applying them.

6.1

Random Variables

Discrete Random Variables

The probability laws developed in the previous chapter provide a framework for the discussion of random variables. We will still be concerned about the probability of a particular event; often, however, the set of possible events for an experiment can be more easily represented using a random variable. The result of a simple experiment can sometimes be summarized concisely by defining a discrete random variable to describe the possible outcomes.

Flip a coin three times. The number of possible outcomes for each flip is two—heads (H) or tails (T). According to counting rule 1 from Chapter 5, there are $2 \cdot 2 \cdot 2 = 8$ possible results here. Let

A = event of observing 0 heads in 3 flips (TTT)

B = event of observing 1 head in 3 flips (TTH, THT, HTT)

C = event of observing 2 heads in 3 flips (HHT, HTH, THH)

D = event of observing 3 heads in 3 flips (HHH)

We wish to find $P(A)$, $P(B)$, $P(C)$, and $P(D)$.

Consider one outcome, say, HTH. The coin flips are independent, so we use equation 5-14:

(probability of H on 1st flip) · (probability of T on 2nd flip) · (probability of H on 3rd flip) = $(1/2)(1/2)(1/2) = 1/8$

This same argument applies to all eight outcomes. These outcomes are all equally likely, and each occurs with probability 1/8.

Event A occurs only if you observe TTT. This has the probability of occurring one time out of eight:

$P(A) = 1/8$

Event B will occur if you observe HTT, TTH, or THT. It would be impossible for HTT and TTH *both* to occur, so $P(\text{HTT and TTH}) = 0$. This is true for any combination here, so these three events are all mutually exclusive. Consequently, according to equation 5-13,

$P(B) = P(\text{HTT or TTH or THT})$

$= P(\text{HTT}) + P(\text{TTH}) + P(\text{THT})$

$= 1/8 + 1/8 + 1/8$

$= 3/8$

By a similar argument,

$P(C) = 3/8$ (using HHT, HTH, THH)

$P(D) = 1/8$ (using HHH)

The variable of interest in this example is X, defined as

X = number of heads out of three flips

We defined all of the possible outcomes of X by defining the four events A, B, C, and D. This works but is cumbersome. Consider having to do this for 100 flips of a coin! A more convenient way to represent probabilities is to examine the value of X for each possible outcome.

Outcome	Value of X	
TTT	0	1 outcome
THT	1	
TTH	1	3 outcomes
HTT	1	
HHT	2	
HTH	2	3 outcomes
THH	2	
HHH	3	1 outcome

Each outcome has probability 1/8, so the probability that X will be 0 is 1/8, written:

$$P(X = 0) = 1/8 = P(0)$$

The probability that X will be 1 is 3/8, written:

$$P(X = 1) = 3/8 = P(1)$$

The probability that X will be 2 is 3/8, written:

$$P(X = 2) = 3/8 = P(2)$$

The probability that X will be 3 is 1/8, written:

$$P(X = 3) = 1/8 = P(3)$$

Notice that

$$P(X = 0) + P(X = 1) + P(X = 2) + P(X = 3)$$
$$= 1/8 + 3/8 + 3/8 + 1/8$$
$$= 1$$

because 0, 1, 2, and 3 represent *all the possible values* of X.

The values and probabilities for this random variable can be summarized by listing each value and its probability of occurring.

$$X = \begin{cases} 0 \text{ with probability } 1/8 \\ 1 \text{ with probability } 3/8 \\ 2 \text{ with probability } 3/8 \\ 3 \text{ with probability } 1/8 \end{cases}$$

This list of possible values of X and the corresponding probabilities is a **probability distribution.**

In any such formulation of a problem, the variable X is a **random variable.** Its value is not known in advance, but there is a probability associated with each possible value of X. Whenever you have a random variable of the form

$$X = \begin{cases} x_1 \text{ with probability } p_1 \\ x_2 \text{ with probability } p_2 \\ x_3 \text{ with probability } p_3 \\ \vdots \\ x_n \text{ with probability } p_n \end{cases}$$

where $x_1 \ldots x_n$ is a set of possible values of X, then X is a **discrete random variable.** In the coin-flipping example, $x_1 = 0$ and $p_1 = 1/8$; $x_2 = 1$ and $p_2 = 3/8$; $x_3 = 2$ and $p_3 = 3/8$, and $x_4 = 3$ and $p_4 = 1/8$.

Other examples of a discrete random variable include:

X = the number of cars that drive up to a bank within a five-minute period (X = 0, 1, 2, 3, . . .).

X = the number of people, out of a group of 50, who will suffer a fatal accident within the next ten years (X = 0, 1, 2, . . . , 50).

X = the number of people, out of 200, who make an airline reservation and then fail to show up (X = 0, 1, 2, . . . , 200).

X = the number of calls arriving at a telephone switchboard over a two-minute period (X = 0, 1, 2, 3, . . .).

Notice that, for each example, the discrete random variable is a *count* of the number of people, calls, accidents, and so on that can occur.

Example 6.1

You roll two dice, a red die and a blue die. What is a possible random variable X for this situation? What are its possible values and corresponding probabilities? (*Hint:* Roll the dice and observe a particular number. This number is your value of the random variable, X. What observations are possible from the roll of two dice?)

Solution There are many possibilities here, including

X = total of the two dice.

X = the higher of the two numbers that appear (possible values: 1, 2, 3, 4, 5, 6).

X = the number of sides with 3 appearing on the two dice (possible values: 0, 1, 2).

Consider that the random variable X equals the total of the two dice. The next step is to determine the possible values of X and the corresponding probabilities. When you roll the two colored dice, there are $6 \cdot 6 = 36$ possible outcomes, using counting rule 1 from Chapter 5.

Outcome	Red Die	Blue Die	Value of X	
1	1	1	2	
2	1	2	3	
3	1	3	4	
4	1	4	5	
5	1	5	6	$P(X = 3) = 2/36$
6	1	6	7	
7	2	1	3	
8	2	2	4	
9	2	3	5	
.	.	.	.	
.	.	.	.	
.	.	.	.	
34	6	4	10	
35	6	5	11	
36	6	6	12	

The 36 outcomes are equally likely because the number appearing on each die (1, 2, 3, 4, 5, or 6) has the same chance of appearing. Notice that we are *not* saying that each value of X is equally likely, as the following discussion will make clear. Each of the above 36 outcomes has probability 1/36 of occurring. If you write down all 36 outcomes and note what can happen to X, your random variable, you will observe:

Value of X	Number of Possible Outcomes
2	1 (rolling a 1,1)
3	2 (rolling a 1,2 or 2,1)
4	3 (rolling a 1,3 or 3,1 or 2,2)
5	4 (and so on)
6	5
7	6
8	5
9	4
10	3
11	2
12	1

Consequently,

$$
X = \begin{cases}
2 \text{ with probability } 1/36 \\
3 \text{ with probability } 2/36 \\
4 \text{ with probability } 3/36 \\
5 \text{ with probability } 4/36 \\
6 \text{ with probability } 5/36 \\
7 \text{ with probability } 6/36 \\
8 \text{ with probability } 5/36 \\
9 \text{ with probability } 4/36 \\
10 \text{ with probability } 3/36 \\
11 \text{ with probability } 2/36 \\
12 \text{ with probability } \underline{1/36} \\
\phantom{12 \text{ with probability }} 1.0
\end{cases}
$$

Because 2 through 12 represent all possible values of X, the total of all probabilities is equal to one. ●

Continuous Random Variables

The previous section introduced you to the discrete random variable where the possible values of X can be listed along with corresponding probabilities. Characteristic of this type of random variable is the presence of *gaps* in the list of possible values. For example, when throwing two dice, a total of 8.5 cannot occur.

The other type of random variable is the **continuous random variable,** where *any* value is possible over some range of values. For a random variable of this type, there are no gaps in the set of possible values. As a simple example, consider two random variables: X is the number of days that it rained in Boston during any particular month, and Y is the amount of rainfall during this month. X is a *discrete* random variable, because it counts the number of days, and consequently there are gaps in the possible values (7.4, for example, is not possible). Y, on the other hand, is a *continuous* random variable because the amount of rainfall can be any value between zero and some larger value.

Suppose the heights of all adult males in the United States range from 3′ to 7.5′. Your task is to describe these heights using such statements as

"15% of the heights are under 5.5′."
"88% of the heights are between 5′ and 6′."

Figure 6.1

Example of a continuous random variable. $X =$ height in feet of a randomly selected adult male in the United States.

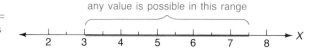

any value is possible in this range

We first define the random variable:

$X =$ height of a randomly selected adult male in the United States

Figure 6.1 shows the range of X.

We are unable to list all of the possible values of X since *any* height is possible over this range. However, we can still discuss probabilities associated with X. For example, the preceding two statements can be described by using the probability statements

$P(X < 5.5') = .15$

$P(X$ is between $5'$ and $6') = P(5' < X < 6') = .88$

For this situation, X is a continuous random variable. A probability for this type of random variable can be described only for a particular *interval*. (Probabilities of exact values are meaningful only for discrete random variables.) Determining probabilities for a continuous random variable will be discussed in Chapter 7.

In Chapter 1, we discussed discrete and continuous data. They are directly related to our present discussion. When you observe a discrete random variable, you obtain discrete data. When you observe a continuous random variable (such as 100 heights), you obtain continuous data.

Exercises

6.1 If a bank is interested in the business received from customers daily, what random variables would be of interest to the bank?

6.2 If a student is taking a multiple-choice test with ten questions and is interested in the final score, what random variable would be of interest to the student?

6.3 Classify the following random variables as discrete or continuous.

a. The number of pages in a statistics book.

b. The daily number of students visiting the university bookstore.

c. Tomorrow's temperature.

d. The speed at which a car is traveling on the freeway.

e. The daily consumption of water at your home.

6.4 Consider an experiment in which two dice are rolled. Let X be the total of the numbers on the two dice. What is the probability that X is equal to two or four?

6.5 Consider an experiment in which a coin is tossed and a die is rolled. Let X be the number observed from rolling the die. Let Y be the value one if a head appears and zero if a tail appears. List the values that the random variables X and Y can have, along with the corresponding probabilities.

6.6 Consider an experiment in which a coin is tossed four times. List all possible outcomes. Let X be the number of heads in each outcome. What is the value of $P(X = 2)$? of $P(X = 3)$?

6.7 If the random variable X can take on the values of two, three, four, and five with equal probability, what is the probability that X is equal to 3? Assume that X cannot take on any other values.

6.8 Consider an experiment in which two dice are rolled. Let X take on the value of one if both dice have the same number, and of zero otherwise. What is the probability that X is equal to one?

6.2

Representing Probability Distributions for Discrete Random Variables

There are three popular methods of describing the probabilities associated with a discrete random variable, X. They are

List each value of X and its corresponding probability.

Use a bar chart to convey the probabilities corresponding to the various values of X.

Use a function that assigns a probability to each value of X.

Remember our coin-flipping example, in which X = number of heads in three flips of a coin. We can list each value and probability:

$$X = \begin{cases} 0 \text{ with probability } 1/8 \\ 1 \text{ with probability } 3/8 \\ 2 \text{ with probability } 3/8 \\ 3 \text{ with probability } 1/8 \end{cases}$$

This works well when there are only a small number of possible values for X; it would not work well for 100 flips of a coin.

Using a bar chart also is a convenient way to represent the shape of a discrete distribution having a small number of possible values. For this situation, you construct a bar chart in which the height of each bar is the probability of observing that value of X (Figure 6.2). It is easier to determine the shape of the probability distribution by using such a chart. The distribution in Figure 6.2 is clearly symmetric and concentrated in the middle values.

Using a function to assign probabilities is the most convenient method of describing the probability distribution for a discrete random variable. For any given application of such a random variable, however, this function may or may not be known. Later in the chapter we will identify certain useful discrete random variables, each of which has a corresponding function that assigns these probabilities.

The function that assigns a probability to each value of X is called a **probability mass function (PMF)**. Denoting a particular value of X as x, this function is of the form

$$P(X = x) = \text{ some expression (usually containing } x\text{) that produces the probability of observing } x$$

$$= P(x)$$

Figure 6.2

A bar chart representation of a discrete random variable, where X = number of heads in three coin flips.

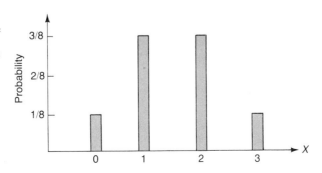

Not every function can serve as a PMF. The requirements for a PMF function are:

1. $P(x)$ is between 0 and 1 (inclusively) for each x
2. $\Sigma P(x) = 1$

Example 6.2

Consider a random variable X having possible values of 1, 2, or 3. The corresponding probability for each value is:

$$X = \begin{cases} 1 \text{ with probability } 1/6 \\ 2 \text{ with probability } 1/3 \\ 3 \text{ with probability } 1/2 \end{cases}$$

Determine an expression for the PMF.

Solution Consider the function

$$P(X = x) = P(x) = x/6 \qquad \text{for } x = 1, 2, 3.$$

This function provides the probabilities

$$P(X = 1) = P(1) = 1/6 \text{ (OK)}$$
$$P(X = 2) = P(2) = 2/6 = 1/3 \text{ (OK)}$$
$$P(X = 3) = P(3) = 3/6 = 1/2 \text{ (OK)}$$

This function satisfies the requirements for a PMF: Each probability is between 0 and 1, and $P(1) + P(2) + P(3) = 1/6 + 1/3 + 1/2 = 6/6 = 1$. Consequently, the function

$$P(X) = x/6 \qquad \text{for } x = 1, 2, 3$$

is the PMF for this discrete random variable. ●

Example 6.3

Consider Example 6.1, where X is the total of two dice. Determine the PMF for this discrete random variable.

Solution Consider the expression

$$P(x) = \frac{x - 1}{36} \qquad \text{for } x = 2, 3, 4, \ldots, 12$$

If this is the proper PMF, then, for example,

$$P(2) = P(X = 2) = \frac{2 - 1}{36} = 1/36$$

This does appear to be correct, so far. Also,

$$P(5) = P(X = 5) = \frac{5 - 1}{36} = 4/36$$

This also is correct. But now consider

$$P(10) = P(X = 10) = \frac{10 - 1}{36} = 9/36$$

According to our previous solution, we know that $P(10) = 3/36$, not 9/36. So this particular function is not the PMF for this random variable; the PMF must work for *all* values of X.

Consider the expression

$$P(x) = \frac{6 - |x - 7|}{36} \qquad \text{for } x = 2, 3, \ldots, 12$$

where | | represents the absolute value of a number. See if you can demonstrate that this function is a bona fide PMF for this example (it is). Do not worry about where this expression came from, but do verify that it works. The truth of the matter is that often PMFs are derived by trial and error until one that works is found. ●

Exercises

6.9 Let X be the value observed from rolling a die.

a. What is the probability mass function of X?

b. Construct a bar chart in which the height of each bar is the probability of X.

6.10 A salesperson calls on three customers who request to see his product. The salesperson has a probability of 50% of selling his product. What is the probability mass function of X, where X is the number of customers (out of three) who buy his product?

6.11 A jar contains four red marbles and three green marbles. Consider an experiment in which two marbles are chosen at random with replacement. Let X be the number of red marbles chosen. What is the probability distribution of X?

6.12 Is the following function a probability mass function? Why or why not?

$$P(X = x) = \begin{cases} (x - 2)/6 & \text{for } x = 1, 4, 7 \\ 0 & \text{otherwise} \end{cases}$$

6.13 Is the following function a probability mass function? Why or why not?

$$P(X = x) = \begin{cases} x^2/10 & \text{for } x = -2, -1, 1, 2 \\ 0 & \text{otherwise} \end{cases}$$

6.14 Let X be equal to the number of heads from tossing a coin twice. Verify that the following function is the probability mass function of X.

$$P(X = x) = \begin{cases} \dfrac{1}{2(2 - x)! \, x!} & \text{for } x = 0, 1, 2 \\ 0 & \text{otherwise} \end{cases}$$

6.15 A jar contains two red marbles, two green marbles, and two black marbles. Assume that a marble is drawn at random. Let the random variable X take on the value one if red appears, two if green appears, and three if black appears on a draw. Write the probability mass function of X.

6.16 Do you recognize the following probability mass function? What is it?

$$P(X = x) = \begin{cases} 1/6 & \text{if } x = 1, 2, 3, 4, 5, 6 \\ 0 & \text{otherwise} \end{cases}$$

6.17 Suppose, in exercise 6.15, that the random variable X was assigned the value of two if red appears on a draw, four if green appears on a draw, and six if black appears on a draw. Write the probability mass function of X.

6.18 Suppose a probability mass function is defined to be nonzero at three points, $X = 1, 2$, and 3. If $P(X = 1) = 0.2$ and $P(X = 2) = 0.3$, what is $P(X = 3)$?

6.19 There are six marbles in a jar. One marble is white, two are blue, and three are black. A marble is drawn at random. Let the random variable X be equal to one if white is drawn, two if blue is drawn, and three if black is drawn. Verify that the following function is the probability mass function of X.

$$P(X = x) = \begin{cases} x/6 & \text{if } x = 1, 2, 3 \\ 0 & \text{otherwise} \end{cases}$$

6.3

Mean and Variance of Discrete Random Variables

Mean of Discrete Random Variables

Chapter 3 introduced you to the mean and variance of a set of sample data consisting of n values. Suppose that these values were obtained by observing a particular random variable n times. The sample mean, $\overline{X}$, represents the *average* value of the sample data. In this section, we determine a similar value, the **mean of a discrete random variable**, written as μ. The value of μ represents the average value of the random variable if you were to observe this variable over an indefinite period of time.

Reconsider our coin-flipping example, where X is the number of heads in three flips of a coin. Suppose you flip the coin three times, record the value of X, flip the coin three times again, record the value of X, and repeat this process ten times. Now you have ten observations of X. Suppose they are

2, 1, 1, 0, 2, 3, 2, 1, 1, 3

The mean of these data is

$$\overline{X} = \frac{2 + 1 + 1 + \ldots + 1 + 3}{10}$$

$$= 1.6 \text{ heads}$$

If you observed X *indefinitely,* what would X be on the average?

$$X = \begin{cases} 0 \text{ with probability } 1/8 \\ 1 \text{ with probability } 3/8 \\ 2 \text{ with probability } 3/8 \\ 3 \text{ with probability } 1/8 \end{cases}$$

So you should observe the value 0, 1/8 of the time, the value 1, 3/8 of the time, the value 2, 3/8 of the time, and the value 3, 1/8 of the time. In a sense, each probability represents the *relative frequency* for that particular value of X. So the average value of X is

$$(0)(1/8) + (1)(3/8) + (2)(3/8) + (3)(1/8) = 1.5 \text{ heads}$$

Notice that X never is 1.5; this is merely the value of X on the average.

Definition

The average value of the discrete random variable X (if observed indefinitely) is the mean of X. The symbol for the mean is μ.

We found that $\mu = 1.5$ by multiplying each value of X by its corresponding probability and summing the results:

$$\mu = 1.5 = 0 \cdot P(0) + 1 \cdot P(1) + 2 \cdot P(2) + 3 \cdot P(3)$$

This procedure applies to any discrete random variable, and so

$$\mu = \Sigma x P(x) \tag{6-1}$$

Example 6.4

A personnel manager in a large production facility is investigating the number of reported on-the-job accidents over a period of one month. We define the random variable:

X = number of reported accidents per month

Based on past records, she has derived the following probability distribution for X:

$$X = \begin{cases} 0 \text{ with probability } .50 \\ 1 \text{ with probability } .25 \\ 2 \text{ with probability } .10 \\ 3 \text{ with probability } .10 \\ 4 \text{ with probability } \underline{.05} \\ \phantom{0 \text{ with probability }} 1.0 \end{cases}$$

During 50% of the months there were no reported accidents, 25% of the months had one accident, and so on. (Notice that deriving an expression for the PMF for this distribution would be extremely difficult, if not impossible. This poses no problem, however.)

What is the mean (average value) of X?

Solution Using equation 6-3,

$$\mu = (0)(.5) + (1)(.25) + (2)(.1) + (3)(.1) + (4)(.05)$$
$$= .95$$

There is .95 (nearly one) accident reported on the average per month. ●

Variance of Discrete Random Variables

We previously considered ten observations of the random variable that counted the number of heads in three flips of a coin. These data were: 2, 1, 1, 0, 2, 3, 2, 1, 1, 3. We used the notation from Chapter 3 to define the mean of these data, and we obtained $\overline{X} = 1.6$. The variance of these data, using equation 3-8, is $s^2 = .933$.

Once again, consider observing X indefinitely. For this situation, the average value of X is defined as the mean of X, μ. When we observe X indefinitely, this particular variance is defined to be the variance of the random variable, X, and is written σ^2 (read as "sigma squared").

σ^2 = variance of the discrete random variable, X

The **variance of a discrete random variable**, X, can be obtained by using one of the following expressions:

$$\sigma^2 = \Sigma (x - \mu)^2 \cdot P(x) \tag{6-2}$$
$$\sigma^2 = \Sigma x^2 P(x) - \mu^2 \tag{6-3}$$

Equation 6-3 generally provides an easier method of determining the variance and will be used in all of the examples to follow. For the coin-flipping example,

$$\sigma^2 = \Sigma x^2 P(x) - \mu^2$$
$$= [(0)^2 \cdot 1/8 + (1)^2 \cdot 3/8 + (2)^2 \cdot 3/8 + (3)^2 \cdot 1/8] - (1.5)^2$$
$$= 3 - 2.25 = .75$$

So our final results would be:

Using the Sample of Ten Observations		**For the Random Variable, X (indefinite number of observations)**	
$\overline{X} = 1.6$	$s^2 = .933$	$\mu = 1.5$	$\sigma^2 = .75$
mean	variance	mean	variance

In Chapter 3, the square root of the variance, s, was defined to be the standard deviation of the data. The same definition applies to a random variable. The **standard deviation of a discrete random variable,** X is denoted σ, where:

$$\sigma = \sqrt{\Sigma(x - \mu)^2 \cdot P(x)} \qquad (6\text{-}4)$$

$$\sigma = \sqrt{\Sigma x^2 P(x) - \mu^2} \qquad (6\text{-}5)$$

Example 6.5

Determine the variance and standard deviation of the random variable described in example 6.4 concerning on-the-job accidents.

Solution A convenient method of determining both the mean and variance of a discrete random variable is to summarize the calculations in tabular form:

x	$P(x)$	$x \cdot P(x)$	$x^2 \cdot P(x)$
0	.5	0	0
1	.25	.25	.25
2	.1	.2	.4
3	.1	.3	.9
4	.05	.2	.8
	1.00	.95	2.35

So

$$\mu = \Sigma x P(x) = .95 \text{ accident}$$

and

$$\sigma^2 = \Sigma x^2 P(x) - \mu^2 = 2.35 - (.95)^2$$
$$= 1.45$$

Also

$$\sigma = \sqrt{1.45} = 1.20 \text{ accidents}$$

Exercises

6.20 The supervisor of the employees who solder resistors on certain electrical components would like to know what the average number of absentees is daily and also what the standard deviation is of the daily employee absentee rate. Find these two values from the following probability mass function, which was constructed from historical data of the company:

X: Number of Daily Absentees	P(x)
0	0.50
1	0.23
2	0.12
3	0.10
4	0.02
5	0.02
6	0.01

6.21 Several students in a finance class subscribe to the *Wall Street Journal*. If two students are chosen at random, the probability of choosing no students who subscribe is 0.81. The probability of choosing one student who subscribes and one who does not subscribe is 0.18, and the probability of choosing two students who subscribe is 0.01. X is a random variable equal to the number of students who subscribe from the two chosen at random. Find the mean value of X and the variance of X.

6.22 Find the mean and variance of a random variable X the probability mass function of which is as follows:

X	P(x)
−2	.12
−1	.3
0	.1
1	.3
2	.18

6.23 Suppose that a coin is flipped three times. Define the random variable X to be equal to twice the number of heads that appear. Determine the mean and variance of X.

6.24 Show that $\Sigma(x - \mu) P(x) = 0$, where the summation is over all outcomes of X, for any discrete random variable.

6.25 Determine the mean and standard deviation of the random variable defined in exercise 6.11.

6.26 Determine the mean and standard deviation of the random variable the probability mass function of which is defined as follows:

$$P(X = x) = \begin{cases} (x - 2)/30 & \text{if } x = 3, 12, 21 \\ 0 & \text{otherwise} \end{cases}$$

6.27 Determine the mean and standard deviation of the random variable the probability mass function of which is defined as follows:

$$P(X = x) = \begin{cases} 1/5 & \text{if } x = 1, 2, 3, 4, 5 \\ 0 & \text{otherwise} \end{cases}$$

6.4

Binomial Random Variables

The random variable X representing the number of heads in three flips of a coin is a special type of discrete random variable, a **binomial** random variable.

Below we list the conditions for a binomial random variable in general and as applied to our coin-flipping example.

A Binomial Situation

1. Your experiment consists of n repetitions, called **trials.**

For Example 6.1

1. n = three flips of a coin.

2. Each trial has two mutually exclusive possible outcomes, referred
   to as **success** and **failure.**

2. Success = head, failure = tail
   (this is arbitrary).

3. The probability of a success for
   each trial is denoted p; the value
   of p remains the same for each
   trial.

3. p = the probability of flipping a
   head on a particular trial = $1/2$.

4. The n trials are *independent.*

4. The results on one coin flip do
   not affect the results on another
   flip.

5. The random variable X is the
   number of *successes* out of n trials.

5. X = the number of heads out of
   three flips.

You encounter a binomial random variable when a certain experiment is repeated many times (n trials), the trials are independent, and each experiment results in one of two mutually exclusive outcomes. For example, a randomly selected individual is either male or female, is on welfare or is not, will vote Republican or will not, and so on.

The two outcomes for each experiment are labeled as *success* or *failure.* A success need not be considered "good" or "desirable." Instead, it depends on what you are counting at the completion of the n trials. If, for example, the object of the experiment is to determine the probability that three people, out of 20 randomly selected individuals, *are* on welfare, then a success on each of the n = 20 trials will be the event that the person selected on each trial *is* on welfare.

Example 6.6

In example 5.3, it was noted that 30% of the people in a particular city read the evening newspaper. Select four people from this city. Consider the number of people out of these four that read the evening paper. Does this satisfy the requirements of a binomial situation? What is your random variable here?

Solution   Refer to conditions 1 through 5 in our list for a binomial situation.

1. There are n = 4 trials, where each trial consists of selecting one individual from this city.
2. There are two outcomes for each trial. We are interested in counting the number of people, out of the four selected, who *do* read the evening paper, so define

   success = read the evening newspaper

   failure = do not read the evening newspaper

3. p = probability of a success on each trial = .3.
4. The trials are independent since the people are selected randomly.
5. The random variable here is X, where

   X = number of successes in n trials

   = number of people (out of four) that read the evening newspaper

All of the requirements are satisfied. Thus, X is a binomial random variable (it is also discrete). ●

Counting Successes for a Binomial Situation

How many ways are there of getting two heads out of four flips of a coin? There are six: HHTT, HTHT, HTTH, THHT, THTH, and TTHH. How many ways can you select two people from a group of four people, where the order of selection is unimportant (say you are selecting a two-person committee)? Label the individuals as I_1, I_2, I_3, and I_4. You want to find the number of combinations of four people using two at a time:

$$_4C_2 = \frac{4!}{2!2!} = 6$$

Put these results side by side. The scheme for matching the two results is to select I_1 if H appears on the first flip, select I_2 if H appears on the second flip, and so on.

Two Heads out of Four Flips	Two People from a Group of Four
HHTT	I_1, I_2
HTHT	I_1, I_3
HTTH	I_1, I_4
THHT	I_2, I_3
THTH	I_2, I_4
TTHH	I_3, I_4

You should see a direct correspondence between the two solutions. Our conclusion is that the number of ways of getting two heads out of four flips of a coin is $_4C_2$. Extending this to any number of flips of a coin, the number of ways of getting k heads out of n flips of a coin is $_nC_k$. Finally, for any binomial situation, the number of ways of getting k successes out of n trials is $_nC_k$. We are thus able to determine the probability mass function (PMF) for any binomial random variable.

Once again, let X equal the number of heads out of three flips. Here X is a binomial random variable, with $p = .5$. Consider any value of X, say, $X = 1$. Then (1) 1/8 is the probability of any one outcome where $X = 1$, such as HTT, and (2) $_3C_1 = 3$ is the number of ways of getting one head (success) out of three flips (trials). Consequently, the probability that X will be one is:

$$P(1) = {_3C_1}1/8 = 3/8$$

The resulting PMF for this situation can be written as

$$P(x) = {_3C_x} \cdot 1/8 \quad \text{for } x = 0, 1, 2, 3$$

Using this function, we obtain the same results as before:

$$P(0) = {_3C_0}\,1/8 = 1 \cdot 1/8 = 1/8$$
$$P(1) = {_3C_1}\,1/8 = 3 \cdot 1/8 = 3/8$$
$$P(2) = {_3C_2}\,1/8 = 3 \cdot 1/8 = 3/8$$
$$P(3) = {_3C_3}\,1/8 = 1 \cdot 1/8 = \underline{1/8}$$
$$1.0$$

Example 6.7

In example 6.6, the binomial random variable X is the number of people (out of four) who read the evening newspaper. Also, there are $n = 4$ trials (people) with $p = .3$ (30% of the people read the evening newspaper). Let S denote a success and F a failure. Then define:

$S = $ a person reads the evening newspaper

$F = $ a person does not read the evening newspaper

What is the probability that exactly two people (out of four) will read the evening paper?

Solution This is $P(X = 2)$ or $P(2)$. Consider any one result where $X = 2$, such as *SFSF*. The probability of this result, using equation 5-14, is (probability of S on first trial) · (probability of F on second trial) · (probability of S on third trial) · (probability of F on fourth trial), which is

$$(.3)(.7)(.3)(.7) = (.3)^2(.7)^2$$

Also note that the probability of *each* result with two S's and two F's ($X = 2$) also is $(.3)^2(.7)^2 = p^2(1 - p)^2$. How many ways can we get two successes out of four trials? This is:

$$_4C_2 = \frac{4!}{2!2!} = 6$$

So, the final result here is

$$P(2) = \text{(number of ways of getting } X = 2)(\text{probability of each one})$$
$$= {}_4C_2\,(.3)^2(.7)^2$$
$$= (6)(.09)(.49) = .265$$

So, 26.5% of the time, exactly two people out of four will read the evening newspaper.

●

We can extend the results of example 6.7 to obtain the PMF for a binomial random variable:

$$P(x) = {}_nC_x p^x(1 - p)^{n-x} \qquad \text{for } x = 0, 1, 2, \ldots, n \qquad (6\text{-}6)$$

For the newspaper example, $x = 2$, $n = 4$, and $p = .3$. The complete list of probabilities for this example is:

$$X = \begin{cases} 0 \text{ with probability } {}_4C_0(.3)^0(.7)^4 = .240 \\ 1 \text{ with probability } {}_4C_1(.3)^1(.7)^3 = .412 \\ 2 \text{ with probability } {}_4C_2(.3)^2(.7)^2 = .265 \\ 3 \text{ with probability } {}_4C_3(.3)^3(.7)^1 = .076 \\ 4 \text{ with probability } {}_4C_4(.3)^4(.7)^0 = \underline{.008} \\ \phantom{0 \text{ with probability } {}_4C_0(.3)^0(.7)^4 = } 1.000 \end{cases}$$

Note that the total value may be slightly greater or less than 1.0, due to rounding. A graphical representation of this PMF is shown in Figure 6.3.

Using the Binomial Table

The binomial PMFs have been tabulated in Table A-1 (page 809) for various values of n and p. The maximum number of trials in this table is $n = 20$. For binomial situations where $n > 20$, one must use an approximation to a binomial probability. This will be considered in the next section and in Chapter 7.

For the binomial situation in Example 6.6, $n = 4$ and $p = .3$. To find $P(2)$, locate $n = 4$ and $x = 2$. Go across the table to $p = .3$ and you will find the corresponding

Figure 6.3

Probability mass function for $n = 4$, $p = .3$.

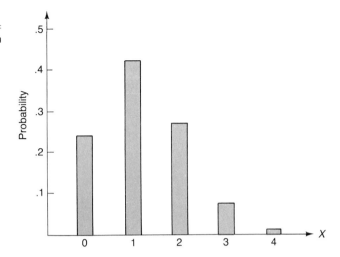

probability (after inserting the decimal in front of the number). This probability is .265. Similarly, $P(0) = .240$, $P(1) = .412$, $P(3) = .076$, and $P(4) = .008$, as before.

The probability that no more than two people will read the evening paper is written $P(X \leq 2)$, where

$$P(X \leq 2) = P(X = 0) + P(X = 1) + P(X = 2)$$
$$= P(0) + P(1) + P(2)$$
$$= .240 + .412 + .265 = .917$$

This is a **cumulative probability** and is obtained by summing the appropriate values of X.

Shape of the Binomial Distribution

Figure 6.4 contains a graphical representation of four binomial distributions. In particular, notice that:

1. When $p = .5$, the shape is perfectly *symmetrical* and resembles a bell-shaped (normal) curve.
2. When $p = .2$, the distribution is *skewed right*. This skewness increases as p decreases.
3. For $p = .8$, the distribution is *skewed left*. As p approaches 1, the amount of skewness increases.

Compare Figure 6.4c and d. Notice that, in both cases, p is .2; however, the number of trials increased from $n = 10$ (in c) to $n = 20$ (in d). For the larger value of n, the shape of this distribution is nearly bell-shaped, *despite the small value of p*. This implies that, regardless of the value of p, the shape of a binomial distribution approaches a bell-shaped distribution as the number of trials (n) increases. We will use this fact in the next chapter, when we demonstrate an approximation to the binomial distribution using a bell-shaped (normal) curve.

In summary, the shape of a binomial distribution is:

1. Skewed left for $p > 1/2$ and small n.
2. Skewed right for $p < 1/2$ and small n.
3. Approximately bell-shaped (symmetric) if p is near $1/2$ or if the number of trials is large.

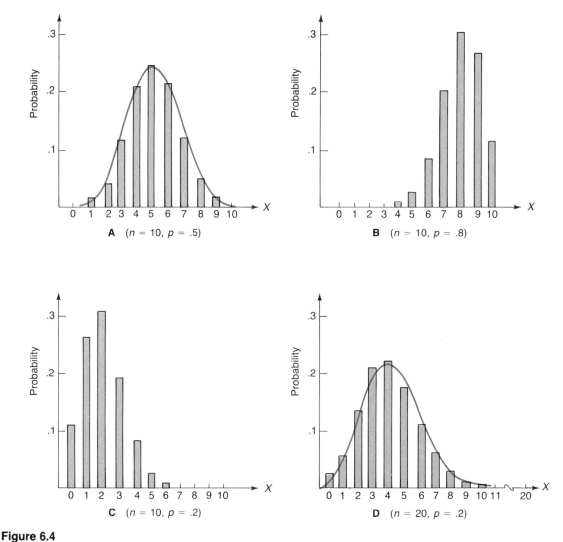

Figure 6.4

Shape of the binomial distribution.

Mean and Variance of Binomial Random Variables

In example 6.6, we examined the binomial random variable X representing the number of people (out of four) who read the evening newspaper. If you select four people, observe X, select four more people, observe X, and repeat this procedure indefinitely, what will X be on the average? This is the mean of X, where, using equation 6-1,

$$\mu = \Sigma x P(x)$$
$$= (0)(.240) + (1)(.412) + (2)(.265) + (3)(.076) + (4)(.008)$$
$$= 1.2 \text{ people}$$

Also, using equation 6-3, the variance of X is

$$\sigma^2 = \Sigma x^2 P(x) - \mu^2$$
$$= [(0)^2(.240) + (1)^2(.412) + (2)^2(.265) + (3)^3(.076) + (4)^2(.008)] - (1.2)^2$$
$$= 2.28 - 1.44 = .84$$

and so σ = standard deviation of $X = \sqrt{.84} = .92$ people. (Watch the units.)

The good news is that there is a convenient shortcut for finding the mean and variance of a binomial random variable. For this situation, you need not use equations 6-1 and 6-3. Instead, for any binomial random variable,

$$\mu = np \tag{6-7}$$

$$\sigma^2 = np(1 - p) \tag{6-8}$$

How these expressions were derived is certainly not obvious, but let us verify that they work for example 6.6. Here $n = 4$ and $p = .3$, so

$$\mu = (4)(.3) = 1.2 \text{ (OK)}$$

$$\sigma^2 = (4)(.3)(.7) = .84 \text{ (OK)}$$

Example 6.8

If you repeat Example 6.6 using $n = 50$ people (rather than $n = 4$ people), how many evening newspaper readers will you observe on the average?

Solution Now, X is the number of people (out of 50) who read the evening paper. Consequently,

$$\mu = np = (50)(.3) = 15$$

So, on the average, X will be 15 people. For this situation, the variance of X is

$$\sigma^2 = np(1 - p) = (50)(.3)(.7) = 10.5$$

Also,

$$\sigma = \sqrt{10.5} = 3.24 \text{ people}$$

Example 6.9

Airline overbooking is a common practice. Many people make reservations on several flights due to uncertain plans and then cancel at the last minute or simply fail to show up. Air Texas is a small commuter airline. Their planes hold only 15 people. Past records indicate that 20% of the people making a reservation do not show up for the flight.

Suppose that Air Texas decides to book 18 people for each flight. Determine the probability that:

1. On any given flight, at least one passenger holding a reservation will not have a seat.
2. There will be one or more empty seats for any one flight.

Solution 1 The binomial random variable for this situation is $X =$ the number of people (out of 18) who book a flight and actually do appear. For this binomial situation, $n = 18$ (18 reservations are made) and $p = 1 - .2 = .8$ (the probability that any one person will show up). At least one passenger will have no place to sit if X is 16 or more. Using Table A-1,

$$P(X \geq 16) = P(X = 16) + P(X = 17) + P(X = 18)$$
$$= .172 + .081 + .018$$
$$= .271$$

We see that, if the airline follows this policy, 27% of the time one or more passengers will be deprived of a seat—not a good situation.

Solution 2 We want to find the probability that the number of people who actually arrive (X) is 14 or less. Using Table A-1 (where $n = 18$, $p = .2$),

$$P(X \le 14) = .215 + .151 + \ldots + .003 + .001$$
$$= .50$$

(Notice that the four remaining probabilities are nearly zero.) With this booking policy, the airline will have flights with one or more empty seats approximately one-half of the time. ●

Example 6.10

A situation that requires the use of a binomial random variable is **lot acceptance sampling,** where you decide to accept or send back a lot (batch) consisting of many electrical components, machine parts, or whatever.

A shipment of 500 calculator chips arrives at Cassidy Electronics. The contract specifies that Cassidy will accept this lot if a sample size of ten from the shipment has no more than one defective chip. What is the probability of accepting the lot if, in fact, 10% of the lot (50 chips) are defective? If 20% are defective?

Solution This is approximately a binomial situation where:

1. There are $n = 10$ trials.
2. Each trial has two outcomes:

    success = chip is defective
    failure = chip is not defective

    (Note: since the object is to count the number of *defective* chips in the shipment, a success on each trial (chip) will be that the chip is defective. As mentioned earlier, a "success" need not be a desirable event.)
3. p = probability of a success = .10.*
4. The random variable here is X = number of successes out of n trials = number of defective chips out of ten. Cassidy accepts the lot of chips if X is 0 or 1. The corresponding probability is a cumulative probability:

    $$P(\text{accept}) = P(X \le 1)$$
    $$= P(0) + P(1)$$

Using Table A-1 (for $n = 10$, $p = .10$), you obtain

$$P(0) = .349, \text{ and } P(1) = .387$$

The resulting probability of accepting the lot is $.349 + .387 = .736$. This means that such a sampling procedure will result in Cassidy accepting the entire batch of chips 73.6% of the time.

If $p = .20$, then $P(0) = .107$ and $P(1) = .268$, again using Table A-1; Cassidy now accepts the lot with probability $.107 + .268 = .375$. ●

---

*If the lot size is large (= 500 here) and the sample size is small (= 10 here), then the value of p is nearly, although not completely, unaffected by the previous trials. For example, if 10% of the chips are defective, then, on the first trial, p is $50/500 = .10$. On the second trial, p is either $50/499 = .1002$ (if the first chip was nondefective) or $49/499 = .098$ (if the first chip was defective). We typically ignore this minor problem in lot sampling. Situations in which the value of p is severely affected by what occurred on previous trials will be dealt with in the next section, where we discuss the hypergeometric distribution.

The concept of lot acceptance sampling was originally presented in Chapter 1 to illustrate the distinction between a population and a sample. It also serves as a brief introduction to the area of inferential statistics, discussed at length in Chapter 8. In example 6.10, we inferred something about a population (the lot of 500 chips) using a sample (the ten chips selected for testing). The sample does not include all elements of the population, so there is a risk of making an incorrect decision, such as (1) accepting the lot of chips when in fact Cassidy should not have, or (2) rejecting the lot of chips when in fact it was satisfactory. Such possibilities for error *always* exist when a statistical sample is used as a basis for an assertion about a population.

Exercises

6.28 An investment advisor predicts that five stocks will grow over the next 18 months. From the advisor's records, 40% of the stocks she recommends are profitable.

a. What is the probability that exactly two of the five stocks are profitable?

b. What is the probability that at least three of the five stocks are profitable?

6.29 If four trials are independently conducted and each trial results in a success with probability one-third, what is the probability that exactly two of the four trials result in successes?

6.30 A survey reveals that 60% of the eligible people in a certain county vote during a county election.

a. If 20 people in the county who are eligible to vote are chosen at random, what is the probability that exactly 12 vote during the next county election?

b. What is the probability that exactly 10 people in the county vote during this election out of the 20 chosen at random?

6.31 The vice-president of a business firm has reviewed the records of the firm's personnel and has found that 70% of the employees read *The Wall Street Journal*. If the vice-president was to choose 12 employees at random, what is the probability that the number of these employees who read *The Wall Street Journal* is the following?

a. At least equal to five.

b. Between four and ten, inclusive.

c. No more than seven.

6.32 A lawyer estimates that 40% of the cases in which she represented the defendant were won. If the lawyer is presently representing ten defendants in different cases, what is the probability that at least five of the cases will be won?

6.33 A market-research firm has discovered that 30% of the people who earn between $25,000 and $50,000 per year have bought a new car within the past two years. In a sample of 12 people earning between $25,000 and $50,000 per year, what is the probability that between four and ten people, inclusive, have bought a new car within the past two years?

6.34 A newsstand owner has calculated that 80% of the midday newspapers are sold. If the owner orders 25 midday newspapers daily, what is the probability that on any day 23 or more of the newspapers will be sold?

6.35 The sales manager of an insurance company knows that the company's best salesperson can sell an insurance policy 60% of the time. If this salesperson were to make 15 calls to sell insurance, what is the probability that at least ten insurance policies would be sold?

6.36 Let the random variable X represent the number of loans that have gone into default from a sample of eight loans made five years ago. The probability of a loan going into default within five years is equal to 0.15.

a. What is the mean and standard deviation of the random variable X?

b. What is $P(X = 2)$?

6.37 Let the random variable X represent the number of correct responses on a multiple-choice test that has 15 questions. Each question has five multiple-choice answers.

a. What is the probability that the random variable X is greater than 8 if the person taking the test randomly guesses?

b. What is the mean value of X if the person randomly guesses?

c. What is the standard deviation of X if the person randomly guesses?

6.38 The *Professional Technician* recommends stocks each month. If 40% of the stocks recommended advance at least 20%, what is the probability that, of the five stocks most recently recommended, at least three will advance at least 20%?

6.39 If X is binomially distributed, with the number of trials equal to 18 and the probability of a success equal to 0.12, then what are the mean and standard deviation of X?

6.40 The manager of a retail store knows that 10% of all checks written are "hot" checks. Of the next 25 checks written at the retail store, what is the probability that no more than three checks are hot?

6.41 A nursery knows that 90% of its hedges will survive the winter. If 15 hedges are randomly selected and planted, what is the probability that at least 13 hedges will survive the winter?

6.5

Hyper-geometric and Poisson Discrete Distributions

As mentioned earlier, not all discrete random variables belong to a special category, such as binomial. One example is X = total value of two dice. This is a discrete random variable, but it is not binomial. There are two other widely used discrete distributions worthy of mention: the hypergeometric and Poisson random variables. (The total of two dice does not fall into one of these categories either; not all discrete random variables can be classified as one of these types.)

Hypergeometric Distribution

The conditions for a **hypergeometric random variable** are:

1. Population size = N. In this population, k members are S (successes) and $N - k$ are F (failures).
2. Sample size = n trials, obtained *without replacement*.
3. X = the number of successes out of n trials (a hypergeometric random variable).

The main distinction between a hypergeometric and a binomial situation is that the trials in the former *are not independent*. As a result, the probability of a success on each trial is affected by the results of the previous trials. This occurs when sampling *without replacement* from a *finite* population.

The situation surrounding a hypergeometric random variable is similar to the binomial situation in that you count "successes" in both cases. However, for the hypergeometric situation, you have a *finite* population (of size N) and you know the number of successes (k) and failures ($N - k$) that make up this population. For example, you might select a sample of $n = 8$ from a group of $N = 30$ unionized workers, of which $k = 20$ are in favor of a strike and $N - k = 10$ are not. For this situation, the hypergeometric random variable is X = the number of workers (of the eight) who favor the strike.

We can repeat example 6.10 using 50 chips (instead of 500), ten of which are selected for testing. Suppose that 10% of these chips (five chips) are defective. As before, define

S = success = chip is defective

F = failure = chip is not defective

In example 6.10, we used $p = P(S) = .10$ for each trial. Here, out of the 50 chips, five are defective. So

$P(S$ on first trial$) = 5/50 = .10$

The conditional probability of S on the second trial is:

$5/49 = .102$ if first chip was not defective

$4/49 = .082$ if first chip was defective

The probability of a success on the second trial is affected by what occurred on the first trial; this is a hypergeometric situation.

The PMF for the hypergeometric random variable is:

$$P(x) = \frac{{}_kC_x \cdot {}_{N-k}C_{n-x}}{{}_NC_n} \tag{6-9}$$

for $x = a, a + 1, a + 2, \ldots, b$, where a is the maximum of 0 and $n + k - N$ and b is the minimum of k and n.

Example 6.11

Determine the probability of observing exactly one defective chip out of a sample of size ten.

Solution Imagine two containers (the population). One contains five S's and the other has 45 F's. The sample consists of ten chips, randomly selected from these two containers. If x chips are selected from the success container, then $10 - x$ chips are selected from the failure container. For this situation, $N = 50$, $k = 5$ and $n = 10$. The possible values for X are from a = maximum of 0 and -35 (0) to b = minimum of 5 and 10 (5). The probability of obtaining one S and nine F's in your sample is

$$P(X = 1) = P(1) = \frac{{}_5C_1 \cdot {}_{45}C_9}{{}_{50}C_{10}}$$

As you will quickly see, the term ${}_NC_n$ gets very large—in fact, it becomes too large for most calculators. The only practical way to evaluate a hypergeometric probability, short of relying on a computer, is to cancel as many terms as possible in the expression.

The final result here is $P(1) = .431$: 43% of the time, you will obtain exactly one defective chip in your sample of size ten. ●

Example 6.12

A local group of 30 unionized workers contains 20 people who are in favor of a strike and ten who are not. Determine the probability that a random sample of eight workers contains five individuals who favor the strike and three that are opposed.

Solution This situation fits the requirements for a hypergeometric random variable, where X is the number of workers (out of eight) that favor a strike, $n = 8$, $N = 30$, and $k = 20$. Consequently

$$P(X = 5) = P(5) = \frac{_{20}C_5 \cdot {_{10}}C_3}{_{30}C_8}$$

$$= \frac{\dfrac{20!}{5!15!} \cdot \dfrac{10!}{3!7!}}{\dfrac{30!}{8!22!}}$$

$$= \frac{(15,504)(120)}{5,852,925} = .318$$

Approximately 32% of the time, in a sample of size eight from this group, five people would favor a strike.

●

Mean and Variance of a Hypergeometric Random Variable As we did with the binomial random variable, we could use the definition of the mean and variance of a discrete random variable contained in equations 6-1 and 6-3. For example,

$$\mu = \Sigma x P(x)$$

where $P(x)$ is the PMF given in equation 6-9.

As in the binomial situation, simpler expressions exist for both the mean and the variance of the hypergeometric random variable. These are:

$$\mu = \Sigma x P(x) = \frac{nk}{N} \tag{6-10}$$

and

$$\sigma^2 = \Sigma x^2 P(x) - \mu^2$$
$$= \frac{k(N - k)n(N - n)}{N^2(N - 1)} = \left[n\left(\frac{k}{N}\right)\left(1 - \frac{k}{N}\right) \right]\left(\frac{N - n}{N - 1}\right) \tag{6-11}$$

For example 6.11, $N = 50$, $k = 5$, $n = 10$. Consequently,

$$\mu = \frac{(10)(5)}{50} = 1 \text{ chip}$$

$$\sigma^2 = \frac{(5)(45)(10)(40)}{(50)^2(49)} = .735$$

and so

$$\sigma = \sqrt{.735} = .857 \text{ chip}$$

This means that, if we observed this process of sampling ten chips out of a batch of 50 indefinitely, we would obtain one ($= \mu$) defective chip on the average. Also, $\sigma = .857$ (or $\sigma^2 = .735$) is our measure of the variation in the observations of this random variable if we observe it over an indefinite period.

Using the Binomial to Approximate the Hypergeometric Whenever n/N < .05, the binomial distribution will provide a good approximation to the hypergeometric distribution. Here, define

$$p = \frac{\text{number of successes in population}}{\text{size of population}} = k/N$$

Then X is the number of successes in the sample. X is approximately a binomial random variable with n trials and probability of success p. Briefly, the binomial approximation works well if your sample size is *less than 5%* of your population size. This was the case in example 6.10, where $n/N = 10/500 = .02$.

What probability would you obtain had you treated example 6.11 as a binomial situation, where $p = k/N = 5/50 = .10$? Here you have a binomial situation with $n = 10$ and $p = .10$. Using equation 6-6,

$$P(1) = {}_{10}C_1(.1)^1(.9)^9$$

$$= (10)(.1)(.387) = .387$$

The same result is obtained using Table A-1.

For this example, .431 is the *exact* probability using the hypergeometric distribution and .387 is the *approximate* probability using the binomial distribution. We did not obtain a very good approximation here. The problem is that the population size is $N = 50$ and the sample size is $n = 10$, which is 20% of the population size.

The Poisson Distribution

The Poisson distribution, named after the French mathematician Simeon Poisson, is useful for counting the number of times a particular event occurs over a specified period of time. It also can be used for counting the number of times an event (such as a manufacturing defect) occurs over a specified area (such as a square yard of sheet metal) or in a specified volume. We will restrict our discussion to counting over time, although any unit of measurement is permissible.

The random variable X for this situation is the number of occurrences of a particular event over a specified period of time. The possible values are 0, 1, 2, 3, ... For X to be a **Poisson random variable,** three conditions must be present:

1. The number of occurrences in one interval of time is unaffected by (statistically independent of) the number of occurrences in any other nonoverlapping time interval. For example, what took place between 3:00 and 3:20 P.M. is unaffected by what took place between 9:00 and 10:00 P.M.
2. The expected (or average) number of occurrences over any time period is proportional to the size of this time interval. For example, we would expect half as many occurrences between 3:00 and 3:30 P.M. as between 3:00 and 4:00 P.M.

   This also implies that the probability of an occurrence must be constant over any intervals of the same length. A situation in which this is usually *not* true is at a restaurant from 12:00 noon to 12:10 P.M. and 2:00 to 2:10 P.M. Due to the differences in traffic flow for these two intervals, we would not expect the arrivals between, say, 11:30 A.M. and 2:30 P.M. to satisfy the requirements of a Poisson situation.
3. Events cannot occur exactly at the same time. More precisely, there is a unit of time sufficiently small (such as one second) during which no more than one occurrence of an event is possible.

Four example situations that usually meet these conditions are

The number of arrivals at a local bank over a five-minute interval.

The number of telephone calls arriving at a switchboard over a one-minute interval.

The number of daily accidents reported along a 20-mile stretch of an intercity toll road.

The number of trucks from a fleet that break down over a one-month period.

For each situation, the (discrete) random variable X is the number of occurrences over the time period T. If all the assumptions are satisfied, then X is a Poisson random variable. Define μ to be the expected (or average) number of occurrences over this period of time.* For any application, the value of μ must be specified or estimated in some manner. The Poisson PMF for X follows:

Poisson Probability Mass Function

X = number of occurrences over time period T.

$$P(x) = \frac{\mu^x e^{-\mu}}{x!} \qquad \text{for } x = 0, 1, 2, 3, \ldots \qquad (6\text{-}12)$$

where μ = expected number of occurrences over T.

Equation 6-12 contains the number e. This is an interesting and useful number in mathematics and statistics. To get an idea how this number is derived, consider the following sequence:

$(1 + 1/2)^2 = 2.25$

$(1 + 1/3)^3 = 2.37$

$(1 + 1/4)^4 = 2.44$

$(1 + 1/5)^5 = 2.49$

$\vdots$

$(1 + 1/100)^{100} = 2.705$

$\vdots$

$(1 + 1/1000)^{1000} = 2.717$

$\vdots$

This sequence of numbers is approaching e. The actual value is:

$e = 2.71828 \ldots$

One interesting application of the number e occurs when calculating compound interest. For example, if you invest $100 at 12%, compounded annually, then at the end of the year you will have $112. However, if your interest is compounded not monthly, not daily, but *continuously*, the amount in your account will be $(100)(e^{.12}) = (100)(1.1275) = \$112.75$. The difference in these amounts is not as large as you might expect!

We will use e again in Chapter 7.

---

*The symbol λ (lambda) often is used to denote this parameter.

Mean and Variance of a Poisson Random Variable Once again, we could use the definition of the mean and variance of a discrete random variable in equations 6-1 and 6-3. However, this is not necessary. It is fairly easy to show that, using equation 6-12,

$$\text{mean of } X = \Sigma x P(x)$$
$$= \mu$$

This is hardly a surprising result, given how μ was originally defined. Also,

$$\text{variance of } X = \sigma^2$$
$$= \Sigma x^2 P(x) - \mu^2$$
$$= \mu$$

So, both the mean and the variance of the Poisson random variable, X, are equal to μ.

Applications of a Poisson Random Variable

Example 6.13

Handy Home Center specializes in building materials for home improvements. They recently constructed an information booth in the center of the store. Define X to be the number of customers who arrive at the booth over a five-minute period. Assume that the conditions for a Poisson situation are satisfied with

$\mu = 4$ customers over a five-minute period

A graph of the Poisson probabilities for $\mu = 4$ is contained in Figure 6.5.

1. What is the probability that, over any five-minute interval, exactly four people arrive at the information booth?
2. What is the probability that more than one person will arrive?
3. What is the probability that you observe exactly six people over a ten-minute period?

Solution 1 First, this probability is not 1 because $\mu = 4$ is the *average* number of arrivals over this time period. The actual number of arrivals over some five-minute period may be fewer than four, more than four, or exactly four. The fraction of time that you observe exactly four people is, using Table A-3,

Figure 6.5

Poisson probabilities for $\mu = 4$.

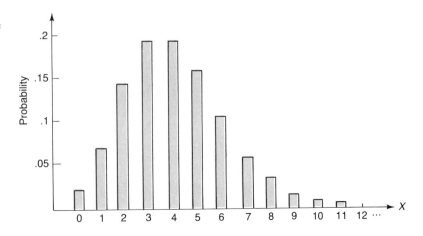

$$P(4) = \frac{4^4 e^{-4}}{4!} = .1954$$

If you stand in the booth for five minutes, 19.5% of the time you will observe four people arrive.

Solution 2 This is $P(X > 1) = P(X \geq 2)$. We could try

$$P(X \geq 2) = P(X = 2) + P(X = 3) + \ldots$$
$$= P(2) + P(3) + \ldots$$
$$= .1465 + .1954 + \ldots$$

There is an infinite number of terms here, however, so this is *not* the way to find this probability. A much better way is to use the fact that these probabilities sum to 1. Consequently,

$$P(X \geq 2) = 1 - P(X < 2)$$
$$= 1 - P(X \leq 1)$$
$$= 1 - [P(0) + P(1)]$$
$$= 1 - \left[\frac{4^0 e^{-4}}{0!} + \frac{4^1 e^{-4}}{1!} \right]$$
$$= 1 - [.0183 + .0733] = .9084$$

Solution 3 For this time interval,

μ = expected (average) number of people over a ten-minute time period

= 8 (we expect 4 people over a five-minute period)

Therefore, the probability of observing six people over a ten-minute period is

$$\frac{8^6 e^{-8}}{6!} = .1221$$

using Table A-3. ●

Example 6.14

Jim Higgins, owner of Burger Haven, is concerned about having enough standby employees who can report to work in the event that a regular employee fails to show up at his or her scheduled time. Past records indicate that no-shows occur randomly at the rate of one every five days. Assume that the number of no-shows in any five-day period is a Poisson random variable, with $\mu = 1$. Determine the probability that

1. Every regular employee will report to work during the next five days.
2. There will be more than five no-shows during the next 20 days.

Solution 1 The Poisson random variable X for this situation is the number of employees who fail to show up for work. The average number of no-shows over a five-day period is one, so

$$P(X = 0) = \frac{1^0 e^{-1}}{0!} = .3679$$

using Table A-3. This means that, 37% of the time, all of Higgins' employees will report to work over a five-day period.

Solution 2 The average number of no-shows over a 20-day period is four, given that the average is one over a five-day period. Therefore, using Table A-3 with $\mu = 4$:

$$P(X > 5) = 1 - P(X \leqslant 5)$$

$$= 1 - \left[\frac{4^0 e^{-4}}{0!} + \frac{4^1 e^{-4}}{1!} + \ldots + \frac{4^5 e^{-4}}{5!} \right]$$

$$= 1 - [.0183 + .0733 + .1465 + .1954 + .1954 + .1563]$$

$$= .2148$$

Mr. Higgins can expect more than five employees to fail to report over a 20-day period roughly 21% of the time.

Poisson Approximation to the Binomial There will be many times when you are in a binomial situation but n is too large to be tabulated. For such situations, you can use a computer. If that is not convenient, there are methods of *approximating* these probabilities without sacrificing much accuracy. One method is to pretend that your binomial random variable, X, is a Poisson random variable having the same mean. The corresponding Poisson probability may be much simpler to derive and will serve as an excellent approximation to the binomial probability.

A good approximation to a binomial probability is obtained using the Poisson distribution if n is large and p is small. For most situations, you can trust this approximation if $n > 20$ and $np \leqslant 7$. An illustration using $n = 20$ and $p = .10$ is shown in Figure 6.6.

Example 6.15

In example 6.10, Cassidy Electronics received a batch (lot) of 500 calculator chips, ten of which they sampled. Suppose instead that they receive a batch of 2500 chips and test 100 of them. They will accept the lot if the sample contains no more than one defective chip. If we assume that 5% of the chips are defective, what is the probability that they will accept the lot?

Solution We can treat this as a binomial situation (rather than the more complicated hypergeometric situation) because

$$\frac{n}{N} = \frac{100}{2500} = .04 < .05$$

Figure 6.6

Poisson distributions provide a good approximation of binomial probabilities where $n > 20$ and $np \leqslant 7$. Here, $n = 20$, $p = .10$.

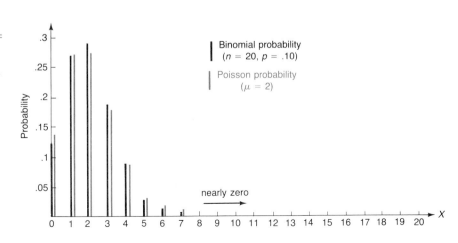

This is approximately a binomial situation with $n = 100$ trials and $p = .05$. The binomial random variable X here is the number of defective chips out of 100. So

$$P(\text{accept}) = P(X \leq 1) = P(0) + P(1)$$

Using the PMF in equation 6-6:

$$P(\text{accept}) = {}_{100}C_0 \cdot (.05)^0(.95)^{100} + {}_{100}C_1 \cdot (.05)^1(.95)^{99}$$

Table A-1 does not contain values of n larger than 20, so you need another means of determining these probabilities. A computer or a calculator will allow you to determine these exactly. The exact answer here is $P(\text{accept}) = .037$.

The other alternative is to pretend that X is a Poisson random variable with the same mean as the actual binomial random variable; that is,

$$\mu = np = (100)(.05) = 5$$

The approximation should work quite well because $n > 20$ and np is ≤ 7. Using Table A-3, with $\mu = 5$,

$$P(0) = .0067$$

and

$$P(1) = .0337$$

Therefore,

$$P(X \leq 1) = .0067 + .0337 = .0404$$

Using the Poisson approximation,

$$P(\text{accept}) \cong .0404$$

which is quite close to the binomial value of $.037$.

Summary of the Three Most Commonly Used Discrete Random Variables

Binomial Distribution
1. X denotes the number of successes out of n independent trials. Each trial results in a success (with probability p) or a failure (with probability $1 - p$).
2. PMF is $P(X = x) = P(x) = {}_nC_x p^x(1 - p)^{n-x}$ for $x = 0, 1, \ldots, n$.
3. Mean $= \mu = np$.
4. Variance $= \sigma^2 = np(1 - p)$ and standard deviation $= \sigma = \sqrt{np(1 - p)}$.
5. Probabilities for the binomial random variable are provided in Table A-1.

Hypergeometric Distribution
1. X represents the number of successes in a sample of size n when selecting from a population of size N, containing k successes and $N - k$ failures.
2. PMF is $P(x) = ({}_kC_x \cdot {}_{N-k}C_{n-x})/{}_NC_n)$ for $x = a, a + 1, \ldots, b$, where $a = \text{maximum } \{0, n + k - N\}$ and $b = \text{minimum } \{k, n\}$.
3. Mean $= \mu = n(k/N)$.
4. Variance $= \sigma^2 = [n(k/N)(1 - k/N)][(N - n)/(N - 1)]$.

Poisson Distribution
1. $X =$ the number of occurrences of a particular event.
2. PMF is $P(x) = (\mu^x e^{-\mu})/(x!)$ for $x = 0, 1, 2 \ldots$.
3. Mean $= \mu$.

4. Variance $= \mu$.

5. Probabilities for the Poisson random variable are provided in Table A-3.

Exercises

6.42 Ten people apply for a job as a bookkeeper. Six of the applicants have college degrees and the remainder do not. If four of the applicants are randomly selected for the job, what is the probability that exactly three have college degrees?

6.43 Six vegetables are available at a cafeteria. Four vegetables are green and the other two are not green. If three different vegetables are ordered at random, what is the probability that at least two of the vegetables are green?

6.44 A population consists of eight round and seven square objects. Let the random variable X be equal to the number of round objects selected randomly without replacement from a sample of nine objects.

a. Find the $P(2 \leqslant X \leqslant 5)$.

b. Find the $P(X > 4)$.

c. Find the mean of the random variable X.

d. Find the standard deviation of the random variable X.

6.45 A batch of 350 resistors is to be shipped if a random sample of 15 resistors has two or less defective resistors. If it is known that there are 50 defective resistors in the batch, what is the probability that two or less of the sample of 15 resistors will be defective?

6.46 The Good Olde Boys used-car lot has 20 cars for sale. It is known that eight of the cars get over 28 miles per gallon (mpg) on the highway and 12 do not. Let X be the random variable equal to the number of cars sold that get over 28 mpg out of the next five cars sold. Assume that each car is equally likely to sell.

a. What is $P(X \leqslant 2)$?

b. What is $P(1 \leqslant X \leqslant 3)$?

c. Find the mean and variance of X.

6.47 In a sample of ten men, it is found that six are physically fit. If four men are randomly selected from this sample of ten, what is the probability that no more than three are physically fit?

6.48 A box contains eight golf balls. Four of these balls are not perfectly round. If three balls are randomly selected without replacement from the eight golf balls, what is the probability that at least one is not perfectly round?

6.49 A factory manufactures rubber grommets to be placed on the stick shift of a car. A sample of ten grommets is chosen from a box of 200. Let the random variable X be the number of defective rubber grommets. Assume that it is known that there are ten defective grommets in the box.

a. What is the probability that X is greater than two?

b. What is the probability that X is equal to zero?

c. What is the standard deviation of X?

6.50 A textbook copy editor is reviewing a manuscript for grammatical errors. Let the random variable X represent the number of grammatical errors made in a particular chapter. Assume that the conditions of a Poisson distribution are satisfied with an average of ten grammatical errors per chapter.

a. What is the probability that X is less than seven?

b. What is the mean value of X?

c. What is the standard deviation of X?

6.51 Let the random variable X be binomially distributed with $n = 60$ and $p = 0.05$. Use the Poisson distribution to approximate the probability that X is greater than or equal to three.

6.52 A police officer writes an average of two speeding tickets per hour. What is the probability that, in 1 hour, the police officer writes no more than one speeding ticket? What assumptions need to be made?

6.53 The auto parts department of an automotive dealership sends out an average of eight special orders daily. The number of special orders is assumed to follow a Poisson distribution.

a. What is the probability that, for any day, the number of special orders sent out will be more than four?

b. What is the standard deviation of the number of special orders sent out daily?

6.54 A survey indicates that 10% of the people who earn less than $20,000 per year are homeowners.

a. If a sample of 40 people who earn less than $20,000 per year is randomly selected, what is the probability that more than four people are homeowners?

b. What is the probability that exactly four people are homeowners from the sample of 40 people who earn less than $20,000 per year?

6.55 The owner of Fashion Designs knows that only six customers can be handled effectively in a 15-minute period. If the average number of customers in a 15-minute interval is five, what is the probability that more than six customers will arrive in a 15-minute interval? Assume a Poisson distribution.

Summary

When an experiment results in a numerical outcome, a convenient way of representing the possible values and corresponding probabilities is to use a random variable. If the possible values of this variable can be listed along with the probability for each value, this variable is said to be a discrete random variable. Conversely, if *any* value of this variable can occur over a specific range, then it is a continuous random variable. This chapter concentrated on the discrete type, whereas Chapter 7 will discuss the continuous random variable.

For a discrete random variable, the set of possible values and corresponding probabilities is a probability distribution. There are several ways of representing such a distribution, including a list of each value and its probability, a bar chart, or an expression called a probability mass function (PMF), which assigns a probability to each value of the random variable.

In Chapter 3, we introduced ways of describing a set of sample data, including the sample mean and variance. Similarly, we can describe a random variable using its mean and variance. The mean of a discrete random variable, μ, is the average value of this variable if observed over an indefinite period. The mean is found by summing the product of each value and its probability of occurring. The variance of a discrete random variable, σ^2, is a measure of the variation for this variable. The standard deviation, σ, also measures this variation and is the square root of the variance.

The most commonly used discrete random variables are the binomial, hypergeometric, and Poisson random variables. Often, the probabilities for one of these discrete distributions are difficult to calculate due to the magnitude of the numbers involved. In many situations, you can use one discrete distribution to *approximate* the probability for another. Figure 6.7 summarizes how this is done.

Figure 6.7

Summary of how the three most common types of discrete random variables can be used to approximate values for one another.

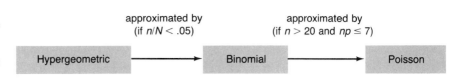

Review Exercises

6.56 Is the following function a probability mass function? Why or why not?

$$P(X = x) = \begin{cases} x^3/153 & \text{for } x = 1, 3, 5 \\ 0 & \text{otherwise} \end{cases}$$

6.57 Let the variable X be equal to minus one if stock XYZ declines, zero if stock XYZ remains unchanged, and one if stock XYZ increases in price. If the $P(X = x)$ is equal to $(x + 2)/6$, what are the mean and standard deviation of X?

6.58 Assume that a die has one blue face, two white faces, and three black faces. Define the random variable X as follows:

$$X = \begin{cases} 1 \text{ if blue} \\ 2 \text{ if white} \\ 3 \text{ if black} \end{cases}$$

Find the probability mass function of X. Construct a bar chart in which the height of each bar is the probability of X.

6.59 Find the mean and variance of the following random variable X with probability mass function $P(x)$.

X	$P(x)$
-3	0.2
0	0.1
3	0.2
5	0.3
10	0.2

6.60 A bakery knows that historically the number of cakes sold daily has the following probability distribution:

X: Number of Cakes Daily	$P(x)$
0	0.40
1	0.30
2	0.15
3	0.10
4	0.05

a. Find the probability that at least two cakes are sold daily.

b. Find the mean and standard deviation of the number of cakes sold daily.

6.61 For a binomially distributed random variable X with 12 trials and with the probability of a success equal to .3, find the following.

a. $P(X = 7)$.   c. $P(X > 5)$.

b. $P(4 < X \leq 6)$.   d. $P(X < 2)$.

6.62 A manager has ten research projects to assign to either engineer 1 or engineer 2. If each research project is randomly assigned to either one of the two engineers, what is the probability that engineer 1 will be assigned no more than five research projects?

6.63 Let the random variable X be equal to the number of apartments vacant in a 20-unit apartment complex. If the apartment complex has a 20% vacancy rate, what is the probability that more than one but less than five apartments are vacant?

6.64 An average of five books per week are returned to a bookstore. Assume that the number of returned books is Poisson distributed.

a. What is the probability that less than four books will be returned in one week?

b. What is the standard deviation of the number of books returned in one week?

6.65 A medical-research firm finds that 8% of the people who have high blood pressure do not know it. If 35 people who have high blood pressure are randomly selected, what is the probability that at least three people do not know they have high blood pressure?

6.66 Ten employees are being reviewed for promotion. Four of the employees are females. If each employee is equally likely to get promoted, what is the probability that two females and three males will be promoted if a total of five promotions are given?

6.67 There are 90 drill bits in a box at a machine shop. Fifty of the drill bits are 3/8-inch diameter, and 40 are 7/16-inch diameter. If four drill bits are selected at random, what is the probability that two drill bits of 3/8-inch diameter and two drill bits of 7/16-inch diameter will be chosen?

6.68 A population consists of 15 employees, six of whom have less than 2 years experience. Let X be equal to the number of employees with less than 2 years experience from a sample of eight employees drawn from this population.

a. Find $P(X = 3)$.

b. Find $P(X \leq 2)$.

c. Find the average value of X.

d. Find the standard deviation of X.

6.69 Blair's Moving Company loads an average of three boxes of damaged merchandise daily. What is the probability that exactly three boxes of damaged merchandise are shipped daily? What is the standard deviation of the number of boxes of damaged merchandise that are shipped daily? Assume a Poisson distribution.

6.70 A person has written seven songs, three of which are ballads. If the songwriter chooses two at random, what is the probability of the following?

a. Exactly one is a ballad.

b. None are ballads.

c. Both are ballads.

Continuous Probability Distributions

A Look Back/Introduction

After we described the use of descriptive statistics, we introduced you to the area of uncertainty by using probability concepts and random variables. Random variables offer you a convenient method of describing the various outcomes of an experiment and their corresponding probabilities.

When each value of the random variable as well as its probability of occurring can be listed, the random variable is discrete. The other type, a continuous random variable, can assume any value over a particular range. This includes such variables as X = height, X = weight, and X = time. For this kind of situation, it is impossible to list all values of X, yet you can still make probability statements regarding X if you can make certain assumptions about the type of population.

Making decisions from sample information in statistics is called **statistical inference.** In subsequent chapters, we will develop a formal set of rules to offer you a guide in making statistical decisions. The making of such a decision typically involves one or more assumptions about the population from which the sample was obtained. One such assumption, widely used in statistics, is that the data came from a normal population, which means that you are dealing with a normal random variable.

The concept of a continuous random variable was introduced in Chapter 6. What distinguishes a discrete random variable from one that is continuous is the presence of *gaps* in the possible values of the former. To illustrate, X = total of two dice is a

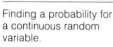

Figure 7.1

Finding a probability for a continuous random variable.

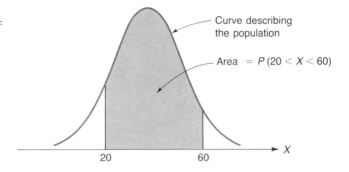

discrete random variable; there are many gaps over the range of possible values and a value of 10.4, for example, is not possible. One can list the possible values of a discrete variable, along with the probability that each value will occur.

Describing probabilities for a continuous random variable is quite different. For such a variable, any value is possible over a specific range. This means that we are unable to list all of the possible values of this variable. Probability statements for a continuous random variable are not concerned with specific values (such as the probability that X will equal 50) but rather deal with probabilities over a range of values, such as the probability that X is *between* 40 and 50, *greater than* 65, or *less than* 20.

Such probabilities can be determined by first making an assumption regarding the nature of the population involved. We assume that the population can be described by a curve having a particular shape—such as normal, uniform, or exponential. Once this curve is specified, a probability can be determined by finding the corresponding *area* under this curve. As an illustration, Figure 7.1 demonstrates a particular curve (called the normal curve) for which the probability of observing a value of X between 20 and 60 is the area under this curve between these two values. The entire range of probability is covered using such a curve since, for any continuous random variable, the total area under the curve is equal to 1.

The following sections will examine the normal, uniform, and exponential distributions since these are the most widely encountered random variables in practice.

7.1
Normal Random Variables

The normal distribution is the most important of the continuous distributions. You will find that this distribution plays a key role in the application of many statistical techniques. When attempting to make an assertion about a population by using sample information, a major assumption often is that the population has a normal distribution.

When discussing measurements such as height, weight, thickness, or time, the resulting population of all measurements often can be assumed to have a probability distribution that is normally distributed.

A histogram constructed from a large *sample* of such measurements can help determine whether this assumption is realistic. Assume, for example, that data were collected on the length of life of 200 Everglo light bulbs. Let X represent the length of life (in hours) of an Everglo bulb. One thing we are interested in is the *shape* of the distribution of the 200 lifetimes. Where are they centered? Are they symmetric? The easiest way to approach such questions is to construct a histogram of the 200 values, as illustrated in Figure 7.2. This histogram indicates that the data are nearly symmetric and are centered at approximately 400.

Figure 7.2

Histogram of 200 Everglo light bulb lifetimes (in hours). The curve represents all possible values (population). The histogram represents the sample (200 values).

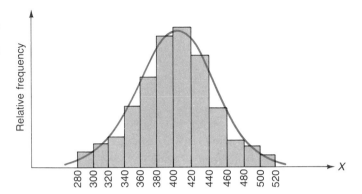

The curve in Figure 7.2 is said to be a **normal curve** because of its **shape.** A normal curve is characterized by a **symmetric, bell-shaped appearance,** with **tails** that "die out" rather quickly. We use such curves to represent the **assumed population** of all possible values. This example contained 200 values taken from a *sample.* Consequently,

1. A histogram represents the shape of the sample data.
2. A smooth curve represents the assumed shape (distribution) of the population.

If all possible values of a variable, *X,* follow an assumed normal curve, then *X* is said to be a **normal random variable,** and the population is **normally distributed.**

When you assume that a particular population follows a normal distribution, you assume that *X,* an observation randomly obtained from this population, is a normal random variable. Based on the histogram in Figure 7.2, it appears to be a reasonable assumption that the smooth curve describing the population of *all* Everglo bulbs can be approximated using a normal curve centered at 400 hours. Therefore, we will assume that *X* is a normal random variable, centered at 400 hours.

There are two numbers used to describe a normal curve (distribution); namely, where the curve is centered and how wide it is. The **center** of a normal curve is called the *mean* and is represented by the symbol μ (mu). The **width** of a normal curve can be described using the *standard deviation,* represented by the symbol σ (sigma).

These are illustrated in Figure 7.3, which shows the normal curve representing the lifetime of Everglo light bulbs. Another way of stating this situation is: *X* is a normal random variable with $\mu = 400$ hours and $\sigma = 50$ hours. Notice that the units of μ and σ are the same as the units of the data (hours).

Figure 7.3

Distribution of the lifetime of Everglo bulbs showing the mean ($\mu = 400$), the standard deviation ($\sigma = 50$), and the inflection point (*P*).

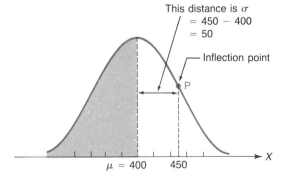

In Figure 7.3, there is a point P on the normal curve. Above this point P, the curve resembles a bowl that is upside down, and below P the curve is "right side up." In calculus, this point is referred to as an **inflection point**. The distance from μ to P is the value of σ. For purposes of illustration, we will generally represent the inflection point as being approximately halfway down the curve.

Because μ and σ represent the location and spread of the normal distribution, they are called **parameters**. The parameters are used to define the distribution completely. The values of μ and σ of a normal population are all you need to separate it from all other normal populations that have the same bell shape but different location and variability. The values of the parameters must be specified in order to make probability statements regarding X.

In Chapter 6, we discussed the mean of (say) ten observations of the random variable, X, written as $\overline{X}$. If you were to observe X indefinitely, then you could obtain the mean of the population, μ. The same concept applies to continuous random variables where, for the Everglo example, $\overline{X}$ represents the mean of the 200 bulbs (the sample) and μ is the mean of all Everglo bulbs (the population).

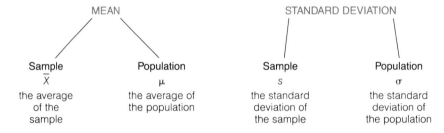

In our Everglo example, the average lifetime of all bulbs is *assumed* to be $\mu = 400$ hours. The standard deviation of the population, σ, just like s, is a measure of **variability**. The larger σ is, the more variation (jumping around) we would see if X were observed indefinitely. For both the sample and the population, the standard deviation is referred to as the variance. It is another measure of the variability of X. The **variance** of a random variable, X, is represented by σ^2.

Consider whether the sample average ($\overline{X}$) of the 200 values in our example is the *same* as μ. It is not. Do not confuse the average lifetime of all lightbulbs (μ) with the average lifetime of just 200 bulbs ($\overline{X}$). This is an important distinction in statistics. However, if our assumed normal distribution (with $\mu = 400$ and $\sigma = 50$) is correct, then $\overline{X}$ most often will be "close to" μ. We will examine this again in Chapter 8.

Figure 7.4

Two normal curves with unequal means and equal standard deviations.

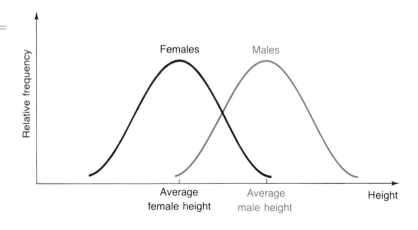

Figure 7.5

Two normal curves
with equal means and
unequal standard
deviations.

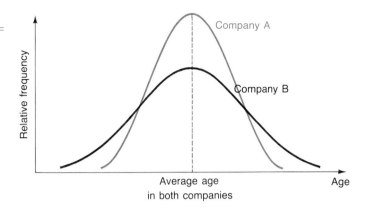

The curve in Figure 7.3 is an illustration of a normal random variable with a mean of 400 hours and a standard deviation of 50 hours. We can compare normal curves that may differ in mean, standard deviation, or both. The normal curves in Figure 7.4 indicate that, on the average, males are taller than females. The mean of the male curve is to the right of the mean of the female curve. The male heights "jump around" about as much as female heights. In other words, there is about the same amount of *variation* in male and female heights. This is because the standard deviation of each curve is the same; that is, each curve is equally wide.

In Figure 7.5, the two normal curves represent the ages of the employees at two large companies. It appears that

1. The average age of employees for the two companies is the same.
2. The ages in Company B have more variability. This simply means that there are more old people and more young people in Company B than in Company A.

7.2
Determining a Probability for a Normal Random Variable

So you have assumed that the lifetime of an Everglo light bulb is a normal random variable with $\mu = 400$ and $\sigma = 50$. Now what? This brings us back to the subject of probability. Before we describe probabilities for a normal random variable, consider one important property of *any* normal curve (or of any probability distribution, for that matter), namely, that the total area under the curve is 1 (see Figure 7.6). When we described the normal curve as bell-shaped, we also determined that it was symmetrical. If the halves are identical, then the probability above the middle (μ) is equal to .5 and is the same as the probability below the mean. Thus, in Figure 7.3, the shaded area is equal to the nonshaded area under the curve.

Returning to the Everglo bulb example, what percentage of the time will the burnout time, X, be less than 360? This probability can be written as

$P(X < 360)$

We will discuss how to determine this area (a simple procedure) later in the chapter, but for now, just remember that, when dealing with a normal random variable, a **probability** is represented by an **area** under the corresponding normal curve. The value of $P(X < 360)$ is illustrated in Figure 7.7. It appears that roughly 20% of the

Figure 7.6

Area under a normal curve.

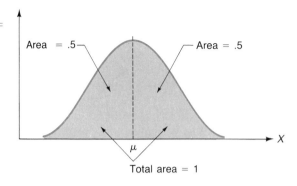

Area = .5   Area = .5

μ

Total area = 1

Figure 7.7

Normal curve for Everglo light bulbs showing $P(X < 360)$. The shaded area is the percentage of time that X will be less than 360. (X = lifetime of Everglo bulb.)

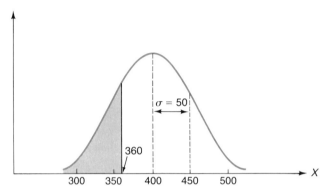

$\sigma = 50$

360

300   350   400   450   500

total area has been shaded, so we conclude that (1) roughly 20% of the Everglo bulbs will burn out in less than 360 hours, and (2) the probability that X is less than 360 is .2.

7.3

Finding Areas Under a Normal Curve

Areas Under the Standard Normal Curve

We will begin our discussion by finding the area under a special normal curve—namely, one that is centered at zero ($\mu = 0$) and has a standard deviation of one ($\sigma = 1$). This random variable is represented by the letter Z and is referred to as the **standard normal random variable.** As Figure 7.8 demonstrates, Z will be positive 50% of the time and negative 50% of the time. Although you probably never will observe a random variable like Z in practice, it is a useful normal random variable. In fact, an area under *any* normal curve (as in Figure 7.7) can be determined by finding the corresponding area under the standard normal curve.

Figure 7.8

Standard normal curve.

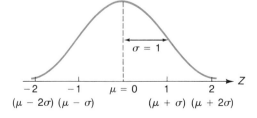

$\sigma = 1$

-2 -1 $\mu = 0$ 1 2 Z

$(\mu - 2\sigma)$ $(\mu - \sigma)$ $(\mu + \sigma)$ $(\mu + 2\sigma)$

Figure 7.9

Shaded area = .4474,
from Table A-4.

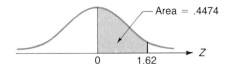

To derive the area under the standard normal curve requires the use of integral calculus. Unfortunately, the integral of the function describing the standard normal curve does not have a simple (closed form) expression. By using excellent approximations of this integral, however, we can tabulate these areas—see Table A-4 and Figure 7.9.

For example, say that we want to determine the probability that a standard normal random variable will be between 0 and 1.62. This is written as

$$P(0 < Z < 1.62)$$

The value for this probability is obtained from Table A-4 by noting that it contains the area under the curve between the mean of zero and the particular value of Z. The far left column of Table A-4 identifies the first decimal place for Z, and you read across the table to obtain the second decimal place.

In our example, we find the intersection between 1.6 on the left and .02 on the top, because $Z = 1.62$. Look at Table A-4; the value .4474 is the *area* between 0 and 1.62. In other words, Z will lie between 0 and 1.62 44.74% of the time.

You can begin to see why it is a good idea to sketch the curve and shade in the area when dealing with normal random variables. It gives you a clear picture of what the question is asking and cuts down on mistakes.

Example 7.1

What is the probability that Z will be greater than 1.62?

Solution We wish to find $P(Z > 1.62)$. Examine Figure 7.10. The area under the right half of the Z curve is .5, so, using our value from Table A-4, the desired area here is

$$.5 - .4474 = .0526$$

So Z will exceed 1.62 about 5% of the time. ●

What, if we wish to know the probability that Z is equal to a particular value, such as $P(Z = 1.62)$? There is no area under the curve corresponding to $Z = 1.62$, so

$$P(Z = 1.62) = 0$$

In fact,

$$P(Z = \text{any value}) = 0$$

One nice thing about this fact is that $P(Z \geqslant 1.62)$ is the *same* as $P(Z > 1.62)$ (that is, .0526). So putting the equal sign on the inequality ($\geqslant$ or $\leqslant$) has *no* effect on the interpretation of the resulting probability.

Figure 7.10

The shaded area represents the probability that Z will be greater than 1.62 [$P(Z > 1.62)$].

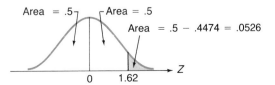

Figure 7.11

Area under the Z curve for $P(Z < 1.62)$.

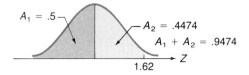

Figure 7.12

Area under the Z curve for $P(1.0 < Z < 2.0)$.

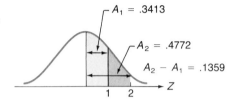

By looking at the Z curve in Figure 7.11, you can see that

$$P(Z < 1.62) = .5 + .4474 = .9474$$

As before, this also is $P(Z \leq 1.62)$.

Figure 7.12 shows $P(1.0 < Z < 2.0)$ (areas from Table A-4). We see that

$$P(1.0 < Z < 2.0) = P(0 < Z < 2.0) - P(0 < Z < 1.0)$$
$$= .4772 - .3413$$
$$= .1359$$

By subtracting the two areas, we find that Z will lie between 1.0 and 2.0 13.59% of the time.

We use Figure 7.13 and Table A-4 to determine $P(-1.25 < Z < 1.15)$:

$$P(-1.25 < Z < 1.15) = P(-1.25 < Z < 0) + P(0 < Z < 1.15)$$
$$= A_1 + A_2$$

Using the symmetry of the Z curve and Figure 7.14, the area of A_1 is the same as $P(0 < Z < 1.25)$, and thus is .3944. The area of A_2, from Table A-4, is .3749. So we add A_1 and A_2:

$$.3944 + .3749 = .7693$$

Finally, we can determine $P(Z < -1.45)$ using Figure 7.15. This can be written as $P(Z < 0) - P(-1.45 < Z < 0)$. Using the discussion from Figure 7.14, the area between zero and -1.45 is .4265 (from Table A-4). As a result, Z will be less than (or equal to) -1.45 approximately 7.35% of the time.

Figure 7.13

Area under the Z curve for $P(-1.25 < Z < 1.15)$.

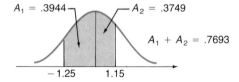

Figure 7.14

Z curve for $P(0 < Z < 1.25) = P(-1.25 < Z < 0)$.

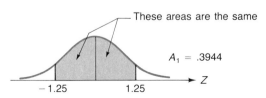

Figure 7.15

Area under the Z curve for $P(Z < -1.45)$.

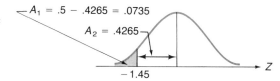

$A_1 = .5 - .4265 = .0735$

$A_2 = .4265$

-1.45

Z

Exercises

7.1 Explain how the parameters μ and σ determine the graph of a normal distribution.

7.2 Find the area under the standard normal curve for the following Z values. Sketch the corresponding area.

a. $Z \leq 0$ c. $Z \geq 1.0$

b. $Z \leq 1.0$ d. $Z \leq -1.0$

7.3 Find the area under the standard normal curve between the following Z values. Sketch the corresponding area.

a. $Z = 0$ to 1.0 c. $Z = -1.0$ to 1.0

b. $Z = 1.0$ to 1.5 d. $Z = -2.5$ to -1.5

7.4 Find the following probabilities. Sketch the corresponding area.

a. $P(Z \leq 1.75)$ c. $P(-1.0 \leq Z \leq 2.5)$

b. $P(Z \geq 1.96)$ d. $P(-0.5 \leq Z \leq 0.5)$

7.5 Find the probability that an observation taken from a standard normal population will be

a. between -3 and 1.6 c. between 0.76 and 1.96

b. less than -2.1 d. between -1.65 and 1.65

7.6 Find the value of z for the following probability statements and sketch the corresponding area.

a. $P(Z \leq z) = 0.95$ c. $P(Z \geq z) = 0.025$

b. $P(Z \leq z) = 0.10$ d. $P(Z \geq z) = 0.55$

7.7 Find the value of z for the following probability statements and sketch the corresponding area.

a. $P(-1.8 \leq Z \leq z) = 0.6$ c. $P(1.0 \leq Z \leq z) = 0.1$

b. $P(0 \leq Z \leq z) = 0.25$ d. $P(-2.8 \leq Z \leq z) = 0.05$

7.8 Find the two Z values such that

a. the area bounded by them is equal to the middle 40% of the standard normal distribution.

b. the area bounded by them is equal to the middle 80% of the standard normal distribution.

7.9 Find the Z values such that the area under the standard normal curve between the Z value and 1.0 is equal to 0.10. Find both Z values that make this possible.

7.10 The output from a monitor that measures the amperage of an electronic circuit follows a normal distribution with mean 0 and variance 1. What proportion of the data would be outside the interval from -2 to 2?

Areas Under Any Normal Curve

Take another look at the histogram of the 200 Everglo light bulb lifetimes in Figure 7.2. A normal curve with $\mu = 400$ hours and $\sigma = 50$ hours was used to describe the

Figure 7.16

Histogram obtained by subtracting μ = 400 (compare with Figure 7.2).

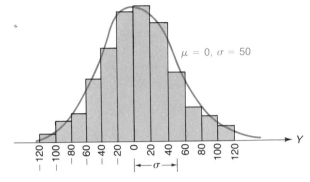

$\mu = 0,\ \sigma = 50$

population of *all* Everglo lifetimes. So, X = Everglo lifetime is a normal random variable with $\mu = 400$ and $\sigma = 50$.

What happens to the shape of the data if we take each of the 200 lifetimes in this example and subtract 400 (that is, subtract μ)? As you can see in Figure 7.16, the histogram (and corresponding normal curve) is merely shifted to the left by 400. It resembles the normal curve for X, except here $\mu = 0$. The random variable defined by $Y = X - 400$

1. Is a normal random variable.
2. Has mean, μ, equal to zero.
3. Has standard deviation, σ, equal to that of X; that is, 50.

Figure 7.17 shows what happens to the shape of the 200 Y values if each of them is *divided* by 50 (that is, by σ). Notice the horizontal axis in the histogram and the corresponding normal curve. The resulting normal curve resembles a normal curve with a mean of zero and a standard deviation equal to 1.

Thus, if X is a normal random variable with mean 400 and standard deviation 50, then the random variable defined by

$$Z = \frac{X - 400}{50}$$

1. Is a normal random variable.
2. Has a mean equal to zero.
3. Has a standard deviation equal to 1.

This means that, in general, for *any normal* random variable X,

$$Z = \frac{X - \mu}{\sigma}$$

Figure 7.17

Histogram obtained by subtracting μ and dividing by σ (compare with Figures 7.2 and 7.16).

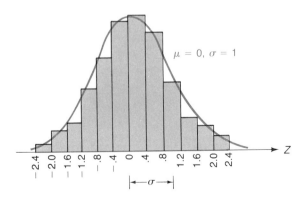

$\mu = 0,\ \sigma = 1$

is a **standard normal random variable.** This procedure of subtracting μ and dividing by σ is referred to as **standardizing** the normal random variable X. It allows us to determine probabilities for *any* normal random variable by first standardizing it and then using Table A-4. So the standard normal distribution turns out to be much more important than you might have expected!

Example 7.2

The normal curve in Figure 7.7 represented the lifetime of all Everglo bulbs, with μ = 400 hours and σ = 50 hours. What percentage of the bulbs will burn out in less than (or equal to) 360 hours? Or, put another way, what is the probability that any particular bulb will last less than 360 hours?

Solution This is a probability and is written as

$$P(X < 360)$$

This random variable is continuous, so $P(X < 360) = P(X \leq 360)$. To determine the probability, you need to standardize this variable:

$$P(X < 360) = P\left(\frac{X - 400}{50} < \frac{360 - 400}{50}\right)$$
$$= P(Z < -.8)$$

where $Z = (X - 400)/50$ (Figure 7.18).

Earlier, by examining Figure 7.7, we estimated this area to be roughly 20%. The actual area, from Figure 7.18, is .2119; that is, it is 21.19% of the total area. The conclusion here is that

$$P(X < 360) = .2119$$

and so 21% of the Everglo bulbs will have a lifetime of less than 360 hours. ●

Figure 7.18

Compare the areas for the X (**A**) and Z (**B**) normal curves to find $P(X < 360)$.

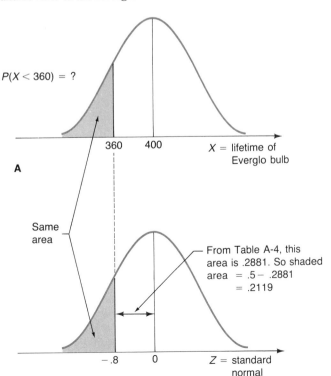

Interpreting Z

What does a Z value of $-.8$ imply in Example 7.2? It simply means that 360 is .8 standard deviations to the left (Z is negative) of the mean. So,

$$\mu - .8(\sigma) = 400 - .8(50)$$
$$= 360$$

Recall that a Z score was defined in exactly the same way in Chapter 3 using a sample mean ($\overline{X}$) and standard deviation (s). In this chapter, we use the population mean (μ) and standard deviation (σ). In general,

1. A *positive* value of Z designates how many standard deviations (σ) to the *right* of the mean (μ) you are.
2. A *negative* value of Z designates how many standard deviations to the *left* of the mean you are.

Example 7.3

The weight of a randomly selected axle is assumed to follow a normal distribution with $\mu = 120$ lbs and $\sigma = 20$ lbs. Determine the probability that an axle will weigh between 80 lbs and 110 lbs.

Solution This probability can be written as

$$P(80 < X < 110)$$

Using the standard procedure,

$$P(80 < X < 110) = P\left[\frac{80 - 120}{20} < \frac{X - 120}{20} < \frac{110 - 120}{20}\right]$$
$$= P(-2.0 < Z < -.5),$$

where Z once again represents the *standardized* normal random variable, which, for this example, is defined by

$$Z = \frac{X - 120}{20}$$

Refer to Table A-4 and Figure 7.19. Comparing Figures 7.19a and b, the areas are equal:

$$.4772 - .1915 = .2857$$

So 29% of the axles will weigh between 80 and 110 lbs. Notice that:

1. 80 is two standard deviations to the left of the mean: $Z = -2$ and $80 = 120 - 2(20)$.
2. 110 is .5 standard deviation to the left of the mean: $Z = -.5$ and $110 = 120 - .5(20)$.
3. $P(X = 80) = P(X = 110) = 0$, so $P(80 < X < 110) = P(80 \leqslant X \leqslant 110) = .2857$.
●

Example 7.4

Actuarial scientists in an insurance company formulate insurance policies that will be both profitable and marketable. For a particular policy, the lifetimes of the policy holders follow a normal distribution with $\mu = 66.2$ years and $\sigma = 4.4$ years. One of the options with this policy is to receive a lump sum at age 65 years and a payment every five years thereafter.

Figure 7.19

A: The probability that X is between 80 and 110 lbs. **B:** The probability that Z is between −2.0 and −.5.

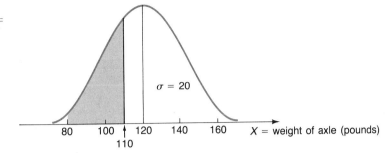

A

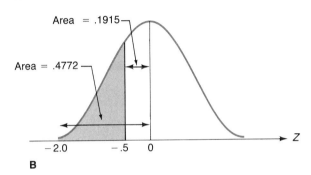

B

1. What percentage of policy holders will receive at least one payment using this option?
2. What percentage will receive two or more?
3. What percentage will receive exactly two?

Solution 1 The normal curve for the policy-holder lifetimes is shown in Figure 7.20. To receive at least one payment, the policy holder must live beyond 65 years of age. So we need to determine (see Figure 7.21):

$$P(X > 65) = P[(X - 66.2)/4.4 > (65 - 66.2)/4.4]$$
$$= P(Z > -.27)$$
$$= .1064 + .5$$
$$= .6064$$

So nearly 61% of the policy holders will receive at least one payment.

Figure 7.20

The normal curve for policy-holder lifetimes. X = age at death (in years)

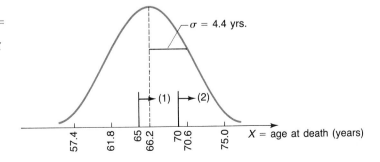

Figure 7.21

Z curve for $P(Z > -.27)$.

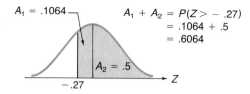

$A_1 = .1064$ $A_1 + A_2 = P(Z > -.27)$
                   $= .1064 + .5$
                   $= .6064$

$A_2 = .5$

$-.27$ Z

Figure 7.22

Z curve for $P(Z > .86)$.

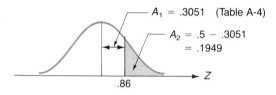

$A_1 = .3051$ (Table A-4)

$A_2 = .5 - .3051$
    $= .1949$

$.86$ Z

Figure 7.23

Z curve for
$P(.86 < Z < 2.00)$.

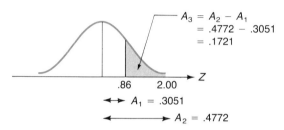

$A_3 = A_2 - A_1$
   $= .4772 - .3051$
   $= .1721$

$.86$ 2.00 Z

$A_1 = .3051$

$A_2 = .4772$

Solution 2   Because the policy holder receives a payment every five years, he or she will receive two or more payments provided he or she lives to be older than 70 years of age. This means that the probability of two or more payments is determined by (see Figure 7.22):

$$P(X > 70) = P[(X - 66.2)/4.4 > (70 - 66.2)/4.4]$$
$$= P(Z > .86)$$
$$= .5 - .3051$$
$$= .1949$$

So 19.5% of the policy holders will survive long enough to collect two payments.

Solution 3   To receive exactly two payments, the policy holder must live longer than 70 years and less than 75 years. This probability is

$$P(70 < X < 75)$$

Using the same standardization procedure (see Figure 7.23):

$$P(70 < X < 75) = P[(70 - 66.2)/4.4 < (X - 66.2)/4.4 < (75 - 66.2)/4.4]$$
$$= P(.86 < Z < 2.00)$$
$$= .4772 - .3051$$
$$= .1721$$

So approximately 17% of the policy holders will receive exactly two payments.

7.4

Applications Where the Area Under a Normal Curve Is Provided

Another twist to dealing with normal random variables is a situation where you are given the area under the normal curve and asked to determine the corresponding value of the variable. This is a common application of a normal random variable. For example, the manufacturer of a product may want to determine a warranty period during which the product will be replaced if it becomes defective, so that at most 5% of the items are returned during this period. Or, in a grocery store on any given day, the demand for a freshly made food item may or may not exceed the supply. The owner may want to determine how much to supply each day, such that the demand (a normal random variable) will exceed this value 10% of the time (in other words, the customers will be disappointed no more than 10% of the time).

Example 7.5

Referring to example 7.2, 80% of the Everglo bulbs will burn out before what period of time? Recall that $\mu = 400$ and $\sigma = 50$.

Solution The first step here is to sketch this curve (Figure 7.24a) and estimate the value of X (say X_0) so that

$$P(X < X_0) = .8$$

Because .8 is larger than .5, X_0 must lie to the *right* of 400.

Next, find the point on a standard normal (Z) curve such that the area to the left is also .8 (Figure 7.24b). Using Table A-4, the area between 0 and .84 is .2995. This means that

$$P(Z < .84) = .5 + .2995$$
$$= .7995$$
$$= .8 \text{ (approximately)}$$

Figure 7.24

A: $P(X < X_0) = .8.$
B: $P(Z < .84) = .8.$

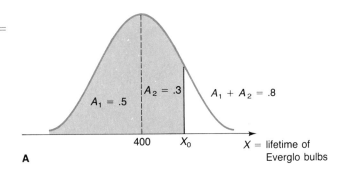

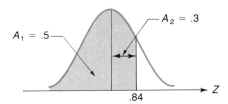

By standardizing X, we conclude that

$$\frac{X_0 - 400}{50} = .84$$

$$X_0 - 400 = 42$$

$$X_0 = 400 + 42 = 442$$

So 80% of the Everglo bulbs will burn out within 442 hours.   ●

Example 7.6

A bakery shop sells loaves of freshly made French bread. Any unsold loaves at the end of the day are either discarded or sold elsewhere at a loss. The demand for this bread has followed a normal distribution with $\mu = 35$ loaves and $\sigma = 8$ loaves.

How many loaves should the bakery make each day so that they can meet the demand 90% of the time?

Solution   The normal random variable X here is the demand for French bread (measured in loaves) (Figure 7.25a). To meet the demand 90% of the time, the bakery must determine an amount, say X_0 loaves, such that:

$$P(X \leq X_0) = .90$$

Proceeding as before, examine a Z curve having an area to the *left* $= .90$ (Figure 7.25b). Using Table A-4,

$$P(0 \leq Z \leq 1.28) = .4 \text{ (actually .3997)}$$

which means that

$$P(Z \leq 1.28) = .4 + .5 = .9$$

So

$$\frac{X_0 - 35}{8} = 1.28$$

and

$$X_0 = 35 + (1.28)(8) = 45.24$$

To be conservative, round this value up to 46 loaves. By stocking 46 loaves each day, the bakery will meet the demand for this product 90% of the time.   ●

Figure 7.25

A: $P(X \leq X_0) = .90$.
B: $P(Z \leq 1.28) = .90$.

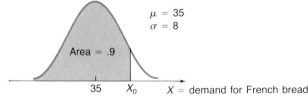

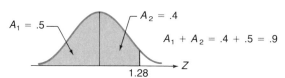

Figure 7.26

Z curve for
$P(-1 < Z < 1) = .68.$

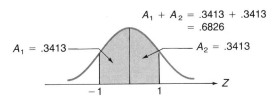

$$A_1 + A_2 = .3413 + .3413$$
$$= .6826$$

$A_1 = .3413$ —   — $A_2 = .3413$

7.5

Another Look at the Empirical Rule

In Chapter 3, the empirical rule specified that, when sampling from a bell-shaped distribution (which means a normal distribution):

1. Approximately 68% of the data values should lie between $\overline{X} - s$ and $\overline{X} + s$.
2. Approximately 95% of them should lie between $\overline{X} - 2s$ and $\overline{X} + 2s$.
3. Approximately 100% of them should lie between $\overline{X} - 3s$ and $\overline{X} + 3s$.

Nothing was said at that time about the origin of these numbers. They actually came directly from Table A-4. To see this, consider Figure 7.26, in which

$$P(-1 < Z < 1) = .68$$

This implies that, for any normal random variable X,

$$P[-1 < (X - \mu)/\sigma < 1] = .68$$

That is,

$$P[(\mu - \sigma) < X < (\mu + \sigma)] = .68$$

Thus, for a set of data from a normal population, where $\overline{X}$ is the sample mean and s is the sample standard deviation, approximately 68% of the data will be between $\overline{X} - s$ and $\overline{X} + s$.

Similarly, $P(-2 < Z < 2) = .4772 + .4772 = .9544$, so you can expect (approximately) 95% of the data points from a normal (bell-shaped) population to lie between $\overline{X} - 2s$ and $\overline{X} + 2s$.

Finally, $P(-3 < Z < 3) = .4987 + .4987 = .9974$, which leads to the third conclusion of the empirical rule.

Exercises

7.11 Let the random variable X be normally distributed with mean 5 and variance 4. Find the following probabilities.

a. $P(X \geq 5.7)$
b. $P(X \leq 3.4)$
c. $P(2.8 \leq X \leq 5.1)$
d. $P(5.7 \leq X \leq 6.8)$

7.12 Find the value of x if the random variable X is normally distributed with mean 10 and variance 9.

a. $P(X \leq x) = 0.51$
b. $P(X \geq x) = 0.805$
c. $P(10 \leq X \leq x) = 0.05$
d. $P(8 \leq X \leq x) = 0.13$

7.13 High-Tech, Inc. produces an electronic component, GX-7, that has an average life span of 4500 hours. The life span is normally distributed with a standard deviation of 500 hours. The company is considering a 3800 hours warranty on GX-7. If this warranty policy is adopted, what proportion of GX-7 components should High-Tech expect to replace under warranty?

7.14 The estimated miles-per-gallon (on the highway) ratings of a class of trucks are normally distributed with a mean of 12.8 and a standard deviation of 3.2. What is the probability that one of these trucks selected at random would get

a. between 13 and 15 mpg?

b. between 10 and 12 mpg?

7.15 Given a normal distribution of values with a mean of 64 and a variance of 9, find the proportion of values that are greater than 70.

7.16 The diameter of ½-inch bolts produced by a workshop is normally distributed with a mean of 0.5 inch and a standard deviation of 0.04 inch. What is the probability that a bolt selected at random will fit in a hole whose diameter is between 0.475 and 0.525 inch?

7.17 To become a member of MENSA, the nationwide organization for people with high I.Q.'s, one has to pass the qualifying examination. If the scores on the exam are normally distributed with a mean of 80 and a standard deviation of 25 and if only 20% of the people taking this exam are admitted to the organization, what is the passing score?

7.18 The weights of students in a junior college are normally distributed with a mean of 160 lbs. and a standard deviation of 18 lbs. What is the probability that a student drawn at random will weigh less than 150 lbs.?

7.19 The mechanics at Quick Brown Fox can tune up a car in an average of 30 minutes with a standard deviation of 5 minutes. If a car arrives for a tune-up 25 minutes before closing, what is the probability that the car will be serviced by closing, assuming that the time it takes for a tune-up is normally distributed.

7.20 The vice-president of Offshore Oil and Gas, a consulting firm, notices that the average length of time that a consultant spends on the telephone with a client at any one time is 40 minutes with a standard deviation of 18 minutes. Assuming that the length of time a consultant talks is normally distributed, what percent of the time would a consultant spend longer than 50 minutes on the phone?

7.21 The yearly cost of dental claims for the employees of D.S. Inc. is normally distributed with a mean of $75 and a standard deviation of $30. At least what yearly cost would be expected for 40 percent of the employees?

7.22 Find the value of k such that $P(\mu \leq X \leq \mu + k\sigma) = 0.251$, for a random variable X having a normal distribution with mean μ and standard deviation σ.

7.23 If X is a normally distributed random variable with standard deviation of 10, find the mean μ given that $P(X \leq 0.35) = 0.182$.

7.24 If X is normally distributed with a mean of 100, find the standard deviation given that $P(X \geq 110) = 0.123$.

7.25 If X is a normally distributed random variable with $P(X \geq 2) = 0.1$ and $P(X \leq 1) = 0.3$, find both the mean and standard deviation.

7.6

Normal Approximation to the Binomial

The binomial random variable was introduced in Chapter 6. It is a discrete random variable used to count the number of successes in a binomial situation.

Characteristics of a Binomial Situation

---

1. You have n independent (identical) trials.
2. Each trial is a success (with probability p) or a failure (with probability $1 - p$).
3. The binomial random variable X is the number of successes out of n trials.
4. The mean of X is $\mu = np$, and the standard deviation of X is $\sigma = \sqrt{np(1 - p)}$.

Examples included:

X = the number of heads (successes) out of three flips (trials) of a coin.

X = the number of people that read the evening newspaper (successes) out of a sample of 50 people (trials).

X = the number of defectives (successes) out of a sample of ten electrical components (trials).

Table A-1 contains values of n (the number of trials) only up to $n = 20$. In Chapter 6, we used the Poisson approximation to determine binomial probabilities for values of $n > 20$. In other words, we pretend that X is a Poisson random variable *having the same mean* as the actual binomial random variable. This is a good approximation, provided n is large (> 20) and p is small ($np \leqslant 7$).

We can also use the **normal approximation** to the binomial random variable. Here you pretend that X is a normal random variable *having the same mean and standard deviation* as the actual binomial random variable. This approximation works well when p is near .5 and in general offers a good estimate when *both $np > 5$ and $n(1 - p) > 5$*.

Approximations to the Binomial

- Poisson Approximation: Use when $n > 20$ and $np \leqslant 7$.
- Normal Approximation: Use when $np > 5$ and $n(1 - p) > 5$.

Consider 12 flips of a coin. We want to determine (1) the probability of observing no more than four heads and (2) the probability of observing more than five heads. First, notice that a normal approximation is not necessary here. This is a binomial situation with $n = 12$ and $p = .5$, and Table A-1 does contain probabilities for this set of values. We chose this illustration to compare the actual binomial probability to the approximated probability using the normal distribution. Look at Figure 7.27, which demonstrates how we estimate binomial probabilities using a normal curve.

To solve question 1, let X = the number of heads in 12 flips, so X is a binomial random variable. We want to determine $P(X \leqslant 4)$. We can obtain an exact solution using Table A-1:

Figure 7.27

Approximating binomial probabilities using a normal curve.

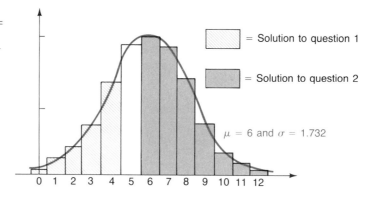

$$P(X \le 4) = P(0) + P(1) + P(2) + P(3) + P(4)$$
$$= 0 + .003 + .016 + .054 + .121 = .194$$

In Figure 7.27, this value is the sum of the areas of the boxes corresponding to $X = 0, 1, 2, 3$, and 4.

We can also obtain an approximate solution. For this binomial random variable,

$$\mu = np = (12)(.5) = 6$$

and

$$\sigma = \sqrt{np(1 - p)}$$
$$= \sqrt{3} = 1.732$$

To obtain an approximation, treat X as a normal random variable with $\mu = 6$ and $\sigma = 1.732$, illustrated in Figure 7.27. The area under the normal curve that approximates $P(X \le 4)$ is the area to the left of 4.5. So we obtain a better approximation here if we find the area under the normal curve to the left of 4.5, not 4.0. This .5 adjustment is referred to as an **adjustment for continuity**. This adjustment is necessary whenever you approximate a *discrete* random variable (such as binomial) using a *continuous* distribution (such as normal). Remember that the discrete distribution has gaps, whereas the continuous does not, so we must assign a portion of the space (probability) *between* 4 and 5 when we use a continuous distribution to approximate a discrete one. Using Table A-4,

Binomial	**Normal**
($n = 12, p = .5$)	($\mu = 6, \sigma = 1.732$)
$P(X \le 4) \cong$	$P(X \le 4.5)$

$$= P\left[Z \le \frac{4.5 - 6}{1.732}\right]$$
$$= P(Z \le -.87) = .1992$$

Notice that the approximate solution of .1992 is very close to the actual probability of .194. This is helped in part by the fact that $p = .5$ for this situation, which means that the binomial distribution is perfectly symmetric. As the value of p moves away from .5, larger values of n are necessary to achieve an approximation this good.

Now consider question 2, the probability of observing more than five heads in 12 flips, or $P(X > 5) = P(X \ge 6)$. Using Table A-1, we can obtain an exact solution:

$$P(X \geq 6) = P(6) + P(7) + \ldots + P(11) + P(12)$$
$$= .226 + .193 + \ldots + .003 + 0 = .613$$

We can also obtain an approximate solution. Using Figure 7.27, the area under the normal curve that corresponds to the lined area representing the exact solution is the area to the right of 5.5. So, using Table A-4:

Binomial	**Normal**
$(n = 12, p = .5)$	$(\mu = 6, \sigma = 1.732)$
$P(X \geq 6) \cong$	$P(X \geq 5.5)$

$$= P\left(Z \geq \frac{5.5 - 6}{1.732}\right)$$
$$= P(Z \geq -.29) = .6141$$

Again, we obtain a very good approximation, helped by the fact that we are using a perfectly symmetrical binomial distribution.

How to Adjust for Continuity

If X is a binomial random variable with n trials and probability of success $= p$, then

1. $P(X \leq b) \cong P\left(Z \leq \dfrac{b + .5 - \mu}{\sigma}\right)$

2. $P(X \geq a) \cong P\left(Z \geq \dfrac{a - .5 - \mu}{\sigma}\right)$

3. $P(a \leq X \leq b) \cong P\left(\dfrac{a - .5 - \mu}{\sigma} \leq Z \leq \dfrac{b + .5 - \mu}{\sigma}\right)$

where

$$\mu = np, \ \sigma = \sqrt{np(1 - p)},$$

and Z is a standard normal random variable

4. Be sure to convert a $<$ probability to a $\leq$, and convert a $>$ probability to a $\geq$ *before* switching to the normal approximation.

Example 7.7

In Chapter 6, we discussed a binomial situation (approximated by the Poisson) in which we had a sample of 100 chips to be tested. Each chip was either defective (a success) or not defective (a failure). Therefore, X was the number of defective chips (out of 100) and was a binomial random variable. We assumed that $p = .05$, which resulted in a very good Poisson approximation because n was large and p was small. Suppose, instead, that 10% of these chips are defective; that is, $p = .10$. Now, $np = 10$ and, because this is greater than 7, the Poisson distribution cannot be expected to provide a good approximation. However, we can obtain a good normal approximation here because $np = 10$ and $n(1 - p) = 90$, both of which are > 5.

For this situation, what is the probability that you observe one or fewer defective chips in a sample of 100, in which case the lot of chips is accepted?

Solution X is a binomial random variable with

$$\mu = np = (100)\,(.10) = 10$$

and

$$\sigma = \sqrt{np(1-p)} = \sqrt{9} = 3$$

Therefore, using Table A-4:

Binomial	**Normal**
($n = 100$, $p = .10$)	($\mu = 10$, $\sigma = 3$)
$P(X \leqslant 1) \cong$	$P(X \leqslant 1.5)$

$$= P\left[Z \leqslant \frac{1.5 - 10}{3}\right]$$

$$= P(Z \leqslant -2.83) = .0023$$

Consequently there is a very small chance of accepting the lot since you can expect to accept it only 23 times out of 10,000 using this procedure. ●

Example 7.8

In Chapter 6, we discussed a binomial situation in which Air Texas was intentionally overbooking their flights. On a particular flight from Dallas to El Paso, they use a much larger aircraft that holds 200 people. As in our previous example, 20% of the people do not show up for a reserved flight. If Air Texas accepts 235 reservations, what is the probability that at least one passenger will end up without a seat on this flight?

Solution The binomial random variable X here is the number of people (out of 235) who show up for the flight. For this situation, $n = 235$, and $p = .8$ represents the probability that any one passenger *will* show up. The mean of this random variable is

$$\mu = (235)(.8) = 188$$

and the standard deviation is

$$\sigma = \sqrt{(235)(.8)(.2)} = 6.13$$

At least one person holding a reservation will be deprived of a seat if $X \geqslant 201$ because the plane holds only 200 people. Once again, we use the normal approximation (Table A-4) to obtain the following probability:

Binomial	**Normal**
($n = 235$, $p = .8$)	($\mu = 188$, $\sigma = 6.13$)
$P(X \geqslant 201) \cong$	$P(X \geqslant 200.5)$

$$= P\left[Z \geqslant \frac{200.5 - 188}{6.13}\right]$$

$$= P(Z \geqslant 2.04)$$

$$= .5 - .4793$$

$$= .0207$$

So on approximately two flights out of 100, at least one person will be unable to secure a seat. ●

Exercises

7.26 A random variable X has a binomial distribution with the probability of a success, p, equal to 0.25.

a. Would it be appropriate to use the normal approximation to the binomial if $n = 30$? if $n = 15$?

b. With $n = 40$, use the normal approximation to find $P(2 \leqslant X \leqslant 10)$.

c. What is the smallest value that n can be and still have the normal distribution to be appropriate for approximating the binomial distribution?

7.27 Let the random variable X indicate the number of female students chosen (with replacement) in a sample of 15 from a student body with 40% female students.

a. Using the binomial table, find the probability that X is greater than 4 and less than 9.

b. Use the normal approximation to answer part a.

c. Compare the answers in part a and part b.

7.28 Thirty percent of the computer programmers who are hired to work for Techronics do not have work experience in programming. If a random sample of 35 computer programmers is selected, what is the probability that less than 20 have had experience in computer programming before being hired by Techronics?

7.29 A travel agency promotes vacation packages by phoning households at random in the evening hours. Historically, only 65% of heads of households are at home when the agency phones. If 30 households are phoned on a given evening, what is the probability that the agency will find between 15 and 25 households, inclusively, with the head of the household at home?

7.30 Thirty percent of the customers at Ranch Steak House present the coupon from the local newspaper for a discount on the main dish. If a sample of 28 customers is randomly selected, what is the probability that more than 12 customers will present the coupon?

7.31 The percentage of cars sold at Lance Holey's used-car lot that required financing is 58%. If 30 car buyers at this lot are randomly selected, what is the probability that between 15 and 25 buyers (inclusive) financed their car?

7.32 A fair coin is flipped 50 times. What is the probability that between 20 and 30 heads (inclusive) will be recorded?

7.33 If a pair of fair dice are rolled 70 times, what is the probability that a pair of snake eyes (a one on each die) will appear between five and ten times, inclusively?

7.7

Other Continuous Distributions

The normal distribution is one example of a continuous distribution. A normal random variable, X, is a continuous random variable. This simply means that over some specific range, *any* value of X is possible. We used X to represent the lifetime of an Everglo bulb to illustrate a continuous random variable because any value between 280 hours and 520 hours (see Figure 7.2) is possible. In fact, any value less than 280 or more than 520 is also possible, although not likely to occur.

For the Everglo example, a normal distribution seemed appropriate because the histogram of 200 sample bulbs in Figure 7.2 revealed a concentration of burnout times in the "middle" and not nearly as many burnout times around 300 or 500. This is why the normal curve has a "mound" in the center and "tails" on each end.

There are many continuous distributions that do not resemble a normal curve in appearance. For example, consider these two situations in which a random variable, X, ranges from one to ten.

Situation 1: The chance that X is between 1.0 and 1.5

    = the chance that X is between 1.5 and 2.0
    = the chance that X is between 2.0 and 2.5

      .
      .
      .

    = the chance that X is between 9.0 and 9.5
    = the chance that X is between 9.5 and 10.0

Situation 2: The larger X is, the less likely it is to occur. Thus, the chance that X is between 1.0 and 1.5

    > the chance that X is between 1.5 and 2.0
    > the chance that X is between 2.0 and 2.5

      .
      .
      .

    > the chance that X is between 9.0 and 9.5
    > the chance that X is between 9.5 and 10.0

These two cases can be represented by two other popular continuous distributions. Situation 1 can be represented by a uniform random variable, whereas Situation 2 could be described using an exponential random variable.

Although there are other random variables that apply to these two situations, the uniform and exponential distributions most often fit the applications encountered in business.

The Uniform Distribution

Consider spinning the minute hand on a clock face. Define a random variable X to be the stopping point of the minute hand. It seems reasonable to assume that, for example, the probability that X is between two and four is *twice* the probability of observing a value of X between eight and nine. In other words, the probability that X is in any particular interval is *proportional* to the width of that interval.

A random variable of this nature is a **uniform random variable.** The values of such a variable are evenly distributed over some interval because the random variable occurs *randomly* over this interval. Unlike the normal random variable, values of the uniform random variable do not tend to be concentrated about the mean.

Assume that the manager of Dixie Beverage Service is concerned about the amount of soda that is released by the dispensing machine that the company is now using. She is considering the purchase of a new machine that electronically controls the cut-off time and is supposed to be very accurate. The present machine cuts off mechanically, and she suspects that the device shuts off the fluid flow *randomly* at anywhere between six and eight ounces. To test the present system, a sample of 150 cups is taken from the machine, and the amount of soda released into each cup is recorded. The relative frequency histogram made from these 150 observations is shown in Figure 7.28.

Would you be tempted to describe the population of *all* cup contents using a normal curve? We hope not, because there is no evidence of a declining number of observations

Figure 7.28

Relative frequency histogram of a sample of 150 cups of soda.

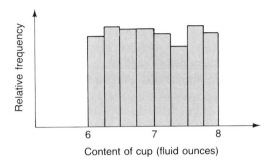

in the tails. As a word of warning here, we often have a tendency to think of all continuous random variables as being normally distributed. As this application demonstrates, this is certainly not the case. Instead, this distribution is a flat or uniform distribution. The random variable, X = content of soda, is a uniform random variable. The corresponding smooth curve describing the population is shown in Figure 7.29.

Notice the total area here is given by a rectangle, and, as is true of all continuous random variables, this total area must be 1. The area of a rectangle is given by (length) · (height). By making the height of this curve (a straight line, actually) equal to .5, the total area is

$$(8 - 6) \cdot .5 = 1.0$$

In general, the curve defining the probability distribution for a uniform random variable is shown in Figure 7.30. The total area is

$$(b - a) \left[\frac{1}{b - a} \right] = 1.0$$

Mean and Standard Deviation Refer to Figure 7.30. The average value of X (μ) is the value midway between a and b, namely,

$$\mu = \frac{a + b}{2}$$

The standard deviation of X is, as before, a measure of how much variation there would be in X if you were to observe it indefinitely. Unlike when using the normal

Figure 7.29

Uniform distribution for X = soda content (compare with Figure 7.28).

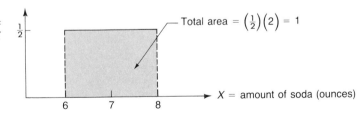

Figure 7.30

Total area for a uniform distribution.

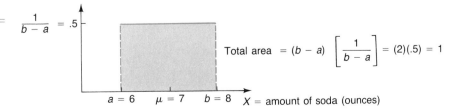

Figure 7.31

The probability that X exceeds 7.5. The shaded area represents the percentage of cups containing more than 7.5 oz.

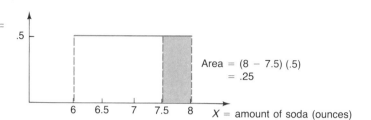

distribution, σ is hard to represent graphically here as a particular distance on the probability curve. Its value, however, is given by

$$\sigma = \frac{b - a}{\sqrt{12}}$$

Determining Probabilities As for all continuous random variables, a probability using a uniform random variable is determined by finding an area under a curve. Suppose, for example, the manager of Dixie Beverage Service would like to know what percentage of the cups will contain more than 7.5 ounces, using the present machines. In Figure 7.31, the shaded area is a rectangle, so its area is easy to find:

$$\text{Area} = (\text{length}) \cdot (\text{height})$$
$$= (8 - 7.5) \cdot .5$$
$$= .25$$

So 25% of the cups will contain more than 7.5 ounces.

Example 7.9

What is the probability that a cup will contain between 6.5 and 7.5 ounces? What is the average contents?

Solution The first result is the same as the percentage of cups containing between 6.5 and 7.5 ounces. Based on Figure 7.32, we conclude that

$$P(6.5 < X < 7.5) = .5$$

The average cup content (mean of X) is

$$\mu = \frac{6 + 8}{2} = 7$$

The standard deviation of X is

$$\sigma = \frac{8 - 6}{\sqrt{12}} = .58$$

Figure 7.32

The probability that X is between 6.5 and 7.5.

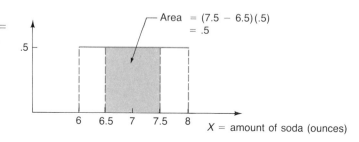

Notice that, as with the normal random variable, the probability that X is equal to any particular value is zero. So,

$$P(X = 6.5) = P(X = 7.5) = 0$$

As a result,

$$P(6.5 \leq X \leq 7.5) = P(6.5 < X < 7.5) = .5$$

Simulation is an area of statistics that relies heavily on the uniform distribution. In fact, this distribution is the underlying mechanism for this often complex procedure. So, although not as many "real world" populations resemble this distribution as they do the normal one, the uniform distribution is important in the application of statistics.

The Exponential Distribution

The final continuous distribution we will discuss is the **exponential distribution.** Similar to the uniform random variable, the exponential random variable is used in a variety of applications in statistics. One application is observing the time between arrivals at, for example, a drive-up bank teller. Another situation that often fits the exponential distribution is observing the lifetime of certain components in a machine.

Chapter 6 discussed the Poisson random variable, which often is used to describe the *number* of arrivals over a specified time period. If the random variable Y, representing the number of arrivals over time period T, follows a Poisson distribution, then X representing the *time between* successive arrivals, will be an **exponential random variable.** The exponential random variable has many applications when describing any situation in which people or objects have to wait in line. This line is called a **queue.** People, machines, or telephone calls may wait in a queue.

The Exponential Random Variable The shape of the exponential distribution is represented by a curve that steadily decreases as the value of the random variable, X, increases. Thus, the larger X is, the probability of observing a value of X at least this large decreases exponentially. This type of curve is illustrated in Figure 7.33.

Determining Probabilities Determining areas for exponential random variables is not as simple as for uniform ones, but it is easier than for normal random variables because exponential probabilities can be derived on a calculator. Table A-2 on page 813 also can be used to determine the probability for an exponential random variable.

As Figure 7.34 illustrates, for an exponential random variable, X, the probability that X exceeds or is equal to a specific value, X_0, is

$$P(X \geq X_0) = e^{-A \cdot X_0}$$

The parameter A is related to the Poisson random variable we used when discussing arrivals. In fact, the Poisson distribution for arrivals per unit time and the exponential

Figure 7.33

Curve showing the distribution of an exponential random variable.

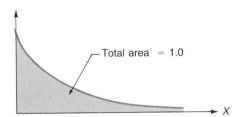

Total area $= 1.0$

X

Figure 7.34

Curve used for determining a probability for an exponential random variable.

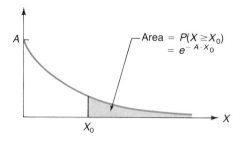

distribution for time *between* arrivals provide two alternative ways of describing the same thing. For example, if the number of arrivals per unit time follows a Poisson distribution with $\mu = 6$ per hour, then an alternate way of describing this situation is to say that the time between arrivals is exponentially distributed with mean time between arrivals equal to $A = 1/\mu = 1/6$ hour (10 minutes).

In general, $1/A$ is the average (mean) value of the exponential random variable, X. It is *also* equal to the standard deviation of X. So,

$$\mu = 1/A$$
$$\sigma = 1/A$$

In applications using this distribution, the value of A either will be given or can be estimated in some way.

Example 7.10

A manufacturer of color televisions has determined that the lifetime of the picture tube follows an exponential distribution with an average lifetime of ten years. Determine the fraction of picture tubes that

1. Fail after 15 years.
2. Fail before the warranty period of two years.

Solution 1 Since $\mu = 10$ years and $\mu = 1/A$, then $A = 1/\mu = .1$. We want to determine $P(X > 15)$, which is illustrated in Figure 7.35.

We see that $X_0 = 15$ and $A = .1$. Values of e^{-X} are contained in Table A-2. Using this table or your calculator,

$$
\begin{aligned}
P(X > 15) &= P(X \geqslant 15) \\
&= e^{-A \cdot X_0} \\
&= e^{-(.1)\,(15)} \\
&= e^{-1.5} \\
&= .22
\end{aligned}
$$

So 22% of the television picture tubes will survive longer than 15 years.

Figure 7.35

Curve showing the probability that X exceeds 15 $[P(X > 15)]$.

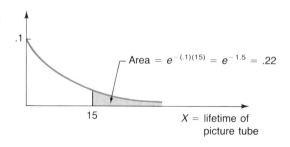

Figure 7.36

Curve showing the probability that X is less than 2 [P(X < 2)].

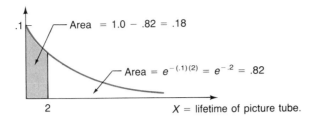

Area $= 1.0 - .82 = .18$

Area $= e^{-(.1)(2)} = e^{-.2} = .82$

2   X = lifetime of picture tube.

Solution 2 Here the problem is to find $P(X < 2) = P(X \leqslant 2)$, which is $1 - P(X > 2)$. Using Table A-2 and Figure 7.36,

$$P(X > 2) = e^{-(.1)(2)}$$
$$= e^{-.2}$$
$$= .82$$

The total area under the curve is 1.0, so

$$P(X < 2) = P(X \leqslant 2) = 1 - .82 = .18$$

The manufacturer will be forced to replace 18% of the tubes during the two-year warranty period.   ●

Exercises

7.34 A random variable X has a uniform distribution between the values 0 and 4.

a. What is the mean of X?

b. What is the standard deviation of X?

c. What is the height of the probability distribution of X?

d. What is the probability that X is greater than 1.23?

7.35 The errors from a forecasting technique appear to be uniformly distributed between -3 and 3.

a. Find the probability that the errors deviate by no more than 1.5 from the mean.

b. Find the value x such that sixty percent of the errors occur between $-x$ and x.

7.36 The temperature of a warming tray is uniformly distributed between the values of 100° and 104° Fahrenheit.

a. What percent of the time is the warming tray less than 101.5°?

b. What is the mean temperature of the warming tray?

c. What is the standard deviation of the temperature of the warming tray?

7.37 The rate at which a swimming pool is filled is uniformly distributed between 20 and 26.3 gallons per minute.

a. What is the probability that the rate at which the swimming pool is filled at any one time is between 21.3 and 24.6 gallons per minute?

b. What is the mean rate at which the swimming pool is filled?

c. What is the standard deviation of the rate at which the swimming pool is filled?

7.38 A quality control engineer records that a certain machine uniformly produces between 10 and 15 precision ball bearings per hour. At least how many precision ball bearings are produced per hour 75% of the time?

7.39 If X is a uniform distribution with mean 0 and variance 2.083, what is the probability that X is greater than 1?

7.40 If the amount of time that a customer spends in Ricky's Hide-Away restaurant follows an exponential distribution and if the average time spent by a customer is 0.75 hours, what is the probability that a customer will spend more than an hour in the restaurant? What is the standard deviation of the amount of time spent by a customer in the restaurant?

7.41 Yellow Rose taxi company estimates that it makes an average of $415 in profits per day. Assuming that the daily profit follows an exponential distribution, what is the probability that on a given day at least $500 in profits will be made?

7.42 The president of Bright-Light Candles estimates that the average burning time of their "medium-K" candles is 40 hours. Assuming that burning time follows an exponential distribution, calculate the probability that a given "medium-K" candle will burn for at least 50 hours?

7.43 If the amount of time ships spend at the Philadelphia dockyard follows an exponential distribution and if the average ship spends 3.1 days there, what is the probability that a given ship spends no more than 1.5 days at the dockyard?

7.44 The Mylapore County fire department has determined that the amount of time per month spent fighting fires follows an exponential distribution. If the average fire-fighting time per month is 10.4 hours, what is the probability that in a given month no more than 15 hours will be spent fighting fires?

7.45 If the amount of time spent by visitors in a certain zoo follows an exponential distribution and if it is known that the average visitor spends 1.9 hours at the zoo, calculate the probability that a given visitor will spend at least 1.5 hours at the zoo?

Summary

A random variable that can assume any value over a specific range is a continuous random variable. Many business applications have continuous probability distributions that can be approximated using a normal, uniform, or exponential random variable. Each of these distributions has a unique curve that can be used to determine probabilities by finding the corresponding area under this curve. Table A-4 gives the probabilities of areas under the standard normal (or Z) distribution. You can also use this table to determine a probability for *any* normal random variable if you first standardize the variable by defining $Z = (X - \mu)/\sigma$.

We discussed examples illustrating the shape of each distribution, along with the mean and standard deviation of each random variable. These two parameters completely specify the location and variability for each of the distributions. The normal distribution is characterized by a bell-shaped curve with values concentrated about the mean. The uniform distribution is flat; values of this random variable are evenly distributed over a specified interval. An exponential random variable is one whose probabilities steadily decrease as the values of the variable increase, according to an exponential type of curve.

The normal distribution can be used to approximate binomial probabilities for a large number of trials, n. Because the normal distribution is continuous and the binomial is discrete, the approximation can be significantly improved by adjusting for continuity before applying the normal approximation.

Review Exercises

7.46 Determine each of the following for a standard normal curve. Sketch the corresponding area.

a. $P(0 < Z < 1.5)$ c. $P(Z < -1.88)$

b. $P(Z > -3)$ d. $P(-2.5 < Z < 2.5)$

7.47 Calculate and sketch the area under the standard normal curve between the following Z values.

a. $Z = 2.2$ and 3.25   b. $Z = -1.5$ and 1.5   c. $Z = -0.75$ and 0

7.48 A commodities broker has a record of being correct 30 percent of the time in transactions which the broker solicits. From a random sample of 35 different recommendations to clients, what is the probability that less than 11 of the recommendations by the broker are profitable?

7.49 A quality control engineer noted that about two percent of all smoke detectors do not go off when a fire is present. Out of a sample of 600 smoke detectors that were in homes that caught fire, what is the probability that more than eight smoke detectors did not sound an alarm?

7.50 The mean length of certain gauges manufactured by a firm is 20 inches with a standard deviation of 0.44 inches. A random sample of 100 gauges was taken. Assuming that the length of gauges manufactured is approximately normally distributed, what percentage of these gauges measured less than 20 inches in length?

7.51 Let X be a normally distributed random variable. Find the values of X which bound the middle fifty percent of the distribution of X if the mean is 5 and the variance is 9.

7.52 Scores on the English screening exam for international students are distributed normally with a mean of 68 and a standard deviation of 11. Calculate the following:

a. The percentage of scores between 70 and 80

b. The percentage of scores that are less than 60

7.53 The examination committee of the Institute of Chartered Accountants passes only 20% of those who take the examination. If the scores follow a normal distribution with an average of 72 and a standard deviation of 18, what is the passing score?

7.54 The shelf-life of cookies made by a small bakery is considered to be exponentially distributed with a mean equal to 3 days. What percentage of the boxes of cookies placed on the shelf today would still be considered marketable after 2.75 days?

7.55 The time that a certain drug has an effect on a normal human being is considered to be exponentially distributed when a standard dose is taken. If the average length of time that the drug has an effect is 30 hours, what is the probability that any given normal person will be affected by the drug for at least 32 hours? What is the standard deviation for the length of time that the drug affects a person?

7.56 The weights of the students in a class are normally distributed with a mean of 160 lbs. and a standard deviation of 15 lbs. What proportion of the class weighs

a. more than 180 lbs?

b. less than 130 lbs?

c. between 140 and 160 lbs?

7.57 Clearvision Company manufactures picture tubes for color television sets and claims that the life spans of their tubes are exponentially distributed with a mean of 1800 hours. What percentage of the picture tubes will last less than or equal to 1600 hours?

7.58 The amount of time each day that the copying machine is used at a certain business is approximately exponentially distributed with a mean of 3.5 hours. What is the probability that the copying machine will be used at least 2 hours a day?

7.59 The diameter of a special aluminum pipe made by Everything Aluminum Inc. is normally distributed with a mean of 3.00 cm and a standard deviation of 0.1 cm. Calculate the proportion of pipes whose diameters are more than 3.15 cm.

7.60 A hot dog vendor knows that on the average he can sell 200 hot dogs daily with a standard deviation of 28.9. If the number sold daily is approximately normally distributed, what is the probability that on any given day more than 250 hot dogs will be sold?

7.61 A manufacturer of heating elements for hot water heaters ships boxes that contain 100 elements. A quality-control inspector randomly selects a box in each shipment and accepts the shipment if there are 5 or less defective heating elements in the box. Assuming that the manufacturer has had a rate of 6 percent defective items, what is the probability that a shipment of heating elements will pass the inspection?

7.62 A box of marbles contains 20 red marbles and 40 blue marbles. If 30 marbles are randomly selected with replacement, what is the probability that there are between 5 and 12 red marbles, inclusively?

7.63 A paint sprayer coats a metal surface with a layer of paint between 0.5 and 1.5 millimeters thick. The thickness of the coat of paint is approximately uniformly distributed.

a. What is the mean and standard deviation of the thickness of the coat of paint on the metal surface?

b. What is the probability that paint from this sprayer on any given metal surface will be between 1.0 and 1.3 millimeters thick?

7.64 The rate at which a sack of soybeans is filled varies uniformly from 50 lbs. per hour to 65 lbs. per hour. What percent of the time is the rate greater than 55 lbs. per hour?

7.65 If X is a uniform random variable that represents the percentage of time each day that a machine does not work, what is the probability that X is greater than the mean percentage of time that the machine does not work?

7.66 If the random variable X has a uniform distribution between -10 and 10, find the value of x such that $P[X \geq x] = 0.25$.

7.67 The marketing division of Goodlife Tires determined the average (mean) life of tires to be 30,000 miles with a standard deviation of 5,000 miles. Given that tire life is a normally distributed random variable, find the following:

a. the probability that tires last between 25,000 and 35,000 miles

b. the probability that tires last between 28,000 and 33,000 miles

c. the probability that tires last less than 28,000 miles

d. the probability that tires last more than 35,000 miles

7.68 The random variable X is normally distributed with mean μ and variance σ^2. Find k if $P(\mu - k\sigma \leq X \leq \mu + k\sigma) = 0.67$.

7.69 If the random variable X is normally distributed with mean 25, find the variance if $P(X \geq 29) = 0.27$.

7.70 The random variable X is normally distributed such that $P(X \leq 10) = 0.12$ and $P(X \geq 15) = 0.4$. Find the mean and variance of the random variable X.

CHAPTER 8

Statistical Inference and Sampling

A Look Back/Introduction

The previous three chapters laid the foundation for using statistical methods in decision making. Any such decision will have uncertainty associated with it, but we can attempt to measure this uncertain outcome using a probability. Random variables (both discrete and continuous) allow one conveniently to represent certain outcomes of an experiment and their corresponding probabilities. If the experiment fits a binomial situation, you can easily determine the probability of certain events or determine the mean (average) outcome for this situation. Similar procedures exist for situations requiring a Poisson or hypergeometric random variable.

If the random variable of interest is continuous, you can make probability statements after assuming the probability distribution involved (such as normal, exponential, uniform, or others not discussed). Both discrete and continuous random variables come into play in all areas of decision making. They allow us to make decisions concerning a large population using a much smaller sample.

This is the area of **statistical inference,** which this chapter will introduce by demonstrating how to estimate something about the population (such as the average value, μ) by using the corresponding value from a sample (such as the sample average, $\overline{X}$). Recall that μ (belonging to the population) is a parameter and $\overline{X}$ (belonging to the sample) is a statistic. When dealing with a normal population, for example, what does one do if the population mean, μ, is unknown? So far in the text, this value has been specified for you. We will discuss answers to this type of question, along with several methods of gathering and using your sample data.

8.1

Random Sampling and the Distribution of the Sample Mean

In Chapter 3, you learned how to calculate the mean of a sample, $\overline{X}$. This sample is drawn from a population having a particular distribution, such as normal, exponential, or uniform. If you were to obtain another sample (you probably will not, as most decisions are made from just one sample), would you get the same value of $\overline{X}$? Assuming the new sample was made up of different individuals than was the first sample, then almost certainly the two $\overline{X}$'s would not be the same. So, $\overline{X}$ itself is a random variable. We will demonstrate that, if a sample is large enough, $\overline{X}$ is always a *normal* random variable. That is, if you were to obtain many samples, calculate the resulting $\overline{X}$'s, and then make a histogram of these $\overline{X}$'s, this histogram would always resemble a bell-shaped (normal) curve.

Simple Random Samples

In Chapter 5, the concept of a simple random sample was introduced. The mechanics of obtaining a random sample range from drawing names out of a hat to using a computer to generate lists of random numbers. For extremely large populations, one is often forced to select individuals (elements) from the population in a *nearly* random manner.

The underlying assumption behind a random sample of size n is that any sample of size n has the same chance (probability) of being selected. To be completely assured of obtaining a random sample from a *finite* population, one should number the members of the population from 1 to N (the population size) and, using a set of n random numbers, select the corresponding sample of n population elements for your sample.

This procedure was described in Chapter 5 and is often used in practice, particularly when you have a sampling situation that needs to be legally defensible. Such is the case in many statistical audits. However, for situations in which the population is extremely large, this strategy may be impractical, and instead you can use a sampling plan that is nearly random. Several other sampling procedures will be discussed in the last section of this chapter.

The main point of all this lengthy discussion is that practically all the procedures presented in subsequent chapters related to decision making and estimation assume that one is using a random sample. In the chapters that follow, the word *sample* will mean *simple random sample*.

Estimation

The idea behind statistical inference has two components:

1. The *population* consists of everyone of interest. By "everyone" we mean all people, machine parts, daily sales, or whatever else you are interested in measuring or observing. The mean value (for example, average height, average income) of everyone in this population is μ and generally is not known.
2. The *sample* is randomly drawn from this population. Elements of the sample thus are part of the population—but certainly not all of it. The exception to this is a *census*, a sample that consists of the entire population.

The sample values should be selected randomly, one at a time, from the entire population. Figure 8.1 emphasizes our central point—namely, an unknown population **parameter** (such as μ = the mean value for the entire population) can be **estimated**

Figure 8.1

The sample mean, $\bar{X}$, is used to estimate the population mean, μ. In general, sample statistics are used to estimate population parameters.

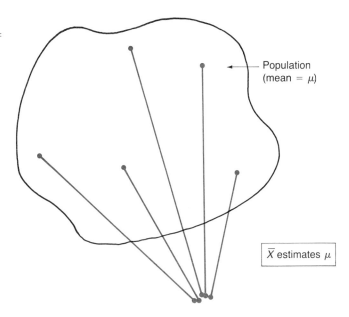

Population (mean = μ)

$\bar{X}$ estimates μ

using the corresponding sample **statistic** (such as $\bar{X}$ = the mean of your sample).

It makes sense, doesn't it? It would be most desirable to know the average value for everyone in the population, but this may be impossible. It may take too much time or money, we may not be able to obtain values for them all even if we want to, or the process of measuring the individual items may destroy them (such as measuring the lifetime of a light bulb). In many instances, estimating the population value using a sample estimate is the best we can do.

Example 8.1

In Chapter 7, the weight of a randomly selected axle was *assumed* to follow a normal distribution with a mean of μ = 120 lbs and a standard deviation of σ = 20 lbs. There is no way of *knowing* that μ = 120 lbs unless you check all existing axles. Assume that

X = weight of a randomly selected axle

is a normal random variable, but do not assume anything about the mean and standard deviation. Ignoring the standard deviation, estimating μ involves obtaining a random sample of axles and recording their weights. Suppose you obtain a sample of size n = 10, with the following results:

118.9, 123.4, 119.6, 123.8, 122.6, 118.8, 121.5, 123.2, 119.8, 122.7

What is the estimate of μ, based on these values?

Solution The sample mean would be $\bar{x}$ = 121.4 lbs. Thus, based on ten sample values, our best estimate of μ is $\bar{x}$ = 121.4 lbs. ●

Distribution of $\bar{X}$

Referring to example 8.1, the value of $\bar{X}$ would certainly change if you were to obtain another sample. The question of interest here is, if we *were* to obtain many values of $\bar{X}$, how would they behave? If we observed values of $\bar{X}$ indefinitely, where would they center; that is, what is the **mean** of the distribution for the random variable, $\bar{X}$? Is

Table 8.1

20 samples of ten Everglo bulbs

	Sample 1	Sample 2	Sample 3	Sample 4	Sample 5	Sample 6	Sample 7
	312	431	416	372	348	405	371
	423	448	361	450	379	391	403
	393	380	389	328	443	391	492
	436	371	497	459	413	455	343
	366	387	400	480	477	387	395
	306	410	489	349	390	386	440
	444	400	406	430	311	385	372
	434	426	333	355	451	352	437
	379	381	307	409	398	393	359
	387	361	375	352	474	397	366
$\overline{X} =$	388.0	399.5	397.3	398.4	408.4	394.2	397.8
$s =$	49.30	28.54	60.51	53.99	54.25	25.45	46.10

	Sample 8	Sample 9	Sample 10	Sample 11	Sample 12	Sample 13	Sample 14
	446	401	351	327	432	457	443
	386	348	443	471	289	395	381
	394	563	340	334	385	412	370
	425	352	455	354	383	374	483
	371	356	401	383	426	355	442
	499	410	465	363	391	404	424
	362	439	413	417	332	389	372
	399	338	337	446	441	370	375
	413	357	406	457	426	436	367
	313	444	405	447	381	450	403
$\overline{X} =$	400.8	400.8	401.6	399.9	388.6	404.2	406.0
$s =$	50.32	68.93	46.28	54.12	47.91	34.60	40.12

	Sample 15	Sample 16	Sample 17	Sample 18	Sample 19	Sample 20
	450	487	444	333	403	419
	425	349	341	429	407	359
	418	371	430	447	326	436
	384	532	424	422	470	420
	422	443	351	403	427	466
	441	411	413	391	455	428
	409	318	397	365	389	466
	422	346	414	441	355	449
	407	449	318	354	524	299
	308	339	339	348	420	399
$\overline{X} =$	408.6	404.5	387.1	393.3	417.6	414.1
$s =$	39.73	71.46	45.28	41.35	56.78	51.48

the variation of the $\overline{X}$ values more, less, or the same as the variation of individual observations? This is measured by the **standard deviation** of the distribution for $\overline{X}$.

In example 7.2, it was assumed that the average lifetime of an Everglo light bulb was $\mu = 400$ hours, with a population standard deviation of $\sigma = 50$ hours. This does not imply that, if you obtain a random sample of these bulbs, the resulting sample mean, $\overline{X}$, always will be 400. Rather, a little head-scratching should convince you that $\overline{X}$ will not be exactly 400, but $\overline{X}$ should be *approximately* 400.

Twenty samples of ten bulbs and the calculated $\overline{X}$ for each sample are shown in Table 8.1. We will assume that the population parameters are $\mu = 400$ hours and $\sigma = 50$ hours (Figure 8.2).

Figure 8.2

Assumed distribution of Everglo bulbs.

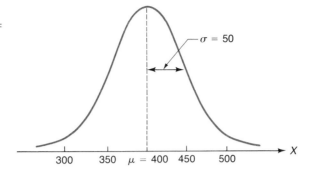

Figure 8.3

Histogram of 20 sample means generated by MINITAB. Compare with Figure 8.2.

```
MTB > SET INTO C1
DATA> 388.0 399.5 397.3 398.4 408.4 394.2 397.8 400.8
DATA> 400.8 401.6 399.9 404.2 406.0 388.6 408.6 404.5
DATA> 387.1 393.3 417.6 414.1
DATA> END
MTB > HISTOGRAM OF C1

Histogram of C1    N = 20

Midpoint    Count
    385        1    *
    390        2    **
    395        3    ***
    400        7    *******
    405        3    ***
    410        2    **
    415        1    *
    420        1    *
```

The 20 values of $\overline{X}$ are:

388.0, 399.5, 397.3, 398.4, 408.4, 394.2, 397.8, 400.8, 400.8, 401.6, 399.9, 388.6, 404.2, 406.0, 408.6, 404.5, 387.1, 393.3, 417.6, 414.1

They are not all 400, but they are all close to 400. Using a calculator or computer, you would also find that (1) the average (mean) of these 20 values if 400.54 (this is close to $\mu = 400$) and (2) the standard deviation of these 20 values is 8.14 (this is *much smaller* than $\sigma = 50$).

The $\overline{X}$ values appear to be centered at $\mu = 400$ hours but have *much less variation* than the individual observations in each of the samples. A histogram of these 20 values generated by MINITAB is contained in Figure 8.3. Based on the shape of this histogram, it seems reasonable to assume that the values of $\overline{X}$ follow a normal distribution, but one that is much *narrower* than the population of individual lifetimes in Figure 8.2.

8.2
The Central Limit Theorem

Our last example illustrates a useful result, the **Central Limit Theorem (CLT)**.

Central Limit Theorem (CLT)

When using a random sample of size n from a population with mean μ and standard deviation σ, the resulting sample mean, $\overline{X}$, has a *normal distribution* with mean μ and standard deviation $\sigma/\sqrt{n}$. This is true for any sample size, n, *if* the underlying population is normally distributed, and it is approximately true for large sample sizes (generally $n > 30$) obtained from *any* population.

In other words, the distribution of *all possible* $\overline{X}$ values has an exact or approximate normal distribution, with mean μ and standard deviation $\sigma/\sqrt{n}$.

Comments

The second part of the CLT is an extremely strong result; it says that you can assume that $\overline{X}$ follows an approximate normal distribution *regardless* of the shape of the population from which the sample was obtained. For example, if you repeatedly sampled from a population with an exponential distribution, the resulting $\overline{X}$'s would follow a *normal* (not an exponential) curve.

In Table 8.1, 20 samples of size ten were obtained, and the corresponding values of $\overline{X}$ were determined. Suppose samples of size ten were obtained *indefinitely* and we wished to describe the shape of the resulting $\overline{X}$'s. According to the CLT, $\overline{X}$ will be a normal random variable. We are assuming that the individual lifetimes follow a normal curve (see Figure 8.2), so this will be true for any sample size—in particular, $n = 10$. So the resulting $\overline{X}$'s will describe a normal curve, similar to the curve in Figure 8.3.

Where is the curve centered? According to the CLT, the mean of this normal random variable is the *same* as that in Figure 8.2; that is, it is the mean of the population from which you are sampling. This is $\mu = 400$, and so, on the average, the value of $\overline{X}$ is $\mu_{\overline{X}} = 400$ hours. Notice that the average of the 20 values of $\overline{X}$ that we did observe was 400.54. This value will get closer to, or **tend toward,** 400 as we take more samples of size ten.

What is the standard deviation of the normal curve for $\overline{X}$? As we noted earlier, the 20 values of $\overline{X}$ jump around (vary) much less than do the individual observations in each of the samples. Consequently, the standard deviation of the $\overline{X}$ normal curve will

Figure 8.4

Normal curves for population and sample mean.

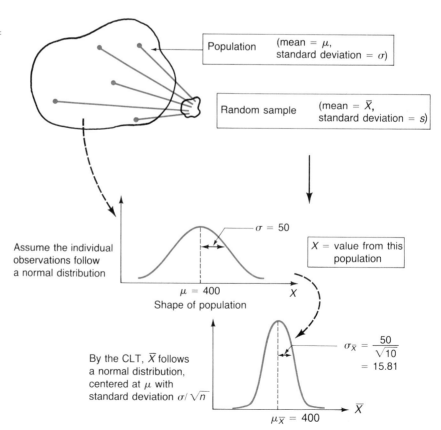

Figure 8.5

Normal curves for the sample mean ($n = 10$, 20, 50, 100).

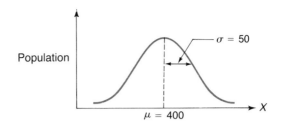

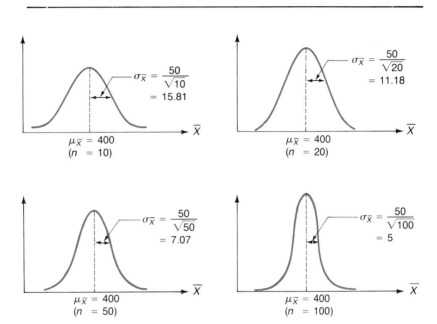

be much less than that of the population curve (describing individual lifetimes) in Figure 8.2. In fact, according to the CLT, this will be

$$\sigma_{\overline{X}} = \frac{\sigma}{\sqrt{n}} \qquad\qquad (8\text{-}1)$$

where σ is the standard deviation of the population ($\sigma = 50$ in Figure 8.2). Consequently,

$$\sigma_{\overline{X}} = \frac{50}{\sqrt{10}} = 15.81$$

Recall that the standard deviation of the 20 observed $\overline{X}$ values was 8.14. This value will tend toward 15.81 if we take more samples of size ten. These results are summarized in Figure 8.4, where $\mu_{\overline{X}} = 400$ and $\sigma_{\overline{X}} = 15.81$.

Basically, the CLT says that the normal curve (distribution) for $\overline{X}$ is centered at the same value as the population distribution but has a much smaller standard deviation. Notice that as the sample size, n, increases, $\sigma/\sqrt{n}$ decreases, and so the width of the $\overline{X}$ curve (that is, the variation in the $\overline{X}$ values) decreases. If we repeatedly obtained lsamples of size 100 (rather than ten), the corresponding $\overline{X}$ values would lie even closer to $\mu_{\overline{X}} = 400$ because now $\sigma_{\overline{X}}$ would equal $50/\sqrt{100} = 5$. This is illustrated in Figure 8.5.

For the 20 values of $\overline{X}$ in Table 8.1, it was assumed that the population mean was *known* to be $\mu = 400$, so each of the $\overline{X}$ values estimates μ with a certain amount of error. The more variation in the $\overline{X}$ values, the more error we encounter using $\overline{X}$ as an estimate of μ. Consequently, the standard deviation of $\overline{X}$ also serves as a measure of the error that will be encountered using a sample mean to estimate a population mean. The standard deviation of the $\overline{X}$ distribution is often referred to as the **standard error** of $\overline{X}$.

---

standard error of $\overline{X}$ = standard deviation of the probability distribution for $\overline{X}$

$$= \frac{\sigma}{\sqrt{n}}$$

Example 8.2

Electricalc has determined that the assembly time for a particular electrical component is normally distributed with a mean of 20 minutes and a standard deviation of three minutes.

1. What is the probability that an employee in the assembly division takes longer than 22 minutes to assemble one of these components?
2. What is the probability that the average assembly time for 15 such employees exceeds 22 minutes?
3. What is the probability that the average assembly time for 15 employees is between 19 and 21 minutes?

Solution 1 The random variable X here is the assembly time for a component. This was assumed to be a normal random variable, with $\mu = 20$ minutes and $\sigma = 3$ minutes (Figure 8.6). We wish to determine $P(X > 22)$. Standardizing this variable and using Table A-4, we obtain

$$P(X > 22) = P\left[\frac{X - 20}{3} > \frac{22 - 20}{3}\right]$$
$$= P(Z > .67)$$
$$= .5 - .2486 = .2514$$

Therefore, an employee will require longer than 22 minutes to assemble the component 25% of the time.

Solution 2 Figure 8.6 does *not* apply to this question because we are concerned with the *average* of 15 employees, not an individual employee. Using the CLT, we know that the curve describing $\overline{X}$ (an average of 15 employees) is normal with

Figure 8.6

Assembly time for electrical components. See example 8.2.

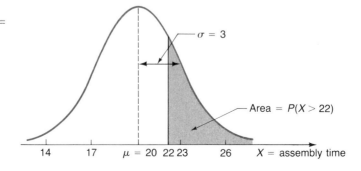

Figure 8.7

Curve for $\bar{X}$ = average of 15 employees' assembly times. Shaded area shows $P(\bar{X} > 22)$.

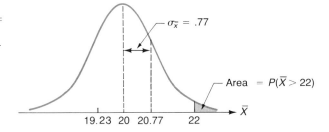

$\sigma_{\bar{x}} = .77$

Area $= P(\bar{X} > 22)$

19.23 20 20.77   22

$$\text{mean} = \mu_{\bar{X}} = \mu = 20 \text{ minutes}$$

$$\text{standard deviation (standard error)} = \sigma_{\bar{X}} = \sigma/\sqrt{n}$$

$$= 3/\sqrt{15} = .77 \text{ minutes} \qquad \text{(Figure 8.7).}$$

The procedure is the same as in Solution 1, except now the standard deviation of this curve is .77, rather than 3:

$$P(\bar{X} > 22) = P\left[\frac{\bar{X} - 20}{.77} > \frac{22 - 20}{.77}\right]$$

$$= P(Z > 2.60)$$

$$= .5 - .4953 = .0047$$

So an average assembly time for a sample of 15 employees will be more than 22 minutes less than 1% of the time.

Solution 3 The curve for this solution is shown in Figure 8.8. We wish to find $P(19 < \bar{X} < 21)$.

$$P(19 < \bar{X} < 21) = P\left[\frac{19 - 20}{.77} < \frac{\bar{X} - 20}{.77} < \frac{21 - 20}{.77}\right]$$

$$= P(-1.30 < Z < 1.30)$$

$$= .4032 + .4032 = .8064$$

Thus, a sample of 15 employees will produce an average assembly time between 19 and 21 minutes about 81% of the time. ●

In example 8.2, it was assumed that the individual assembly times followed a normal distribution. However, remember that the strength of the CLT is that this assumption is not necessary for large samples. We can answer questions 2 and 3 for *any* population whose mean is 20 minutes and standard deviation is three minutes, provided we take

Figure 8.8

Curve for average assembly time of 15 employees. Shaded area shows $P(19 < \bar{X} < 21)$.

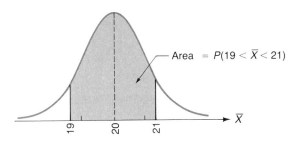

Area $= P(19 < \bar{X} < 21)$

19   20   21

a *large* sample ($n > 30$). In this case, the normal distribution of $\overline{X}$ is not exact, but it provides a very good approximation.

Example 8.3

The price/earnings (P/E) ratio of a stock is usually considered by analysts who put together financial portfolios. Suppose a population of all P/E ratios has a mean of 10.5 and a standard deviation of 4.5.

1. What is the probability that a sample of 40 stocks will have an average P/E ratio less than nine?
2. What assumptions are necessary about the population of all P/E ratios in your answer to question 1?

Solution 1 By the CLT, $\overline{X}$ is approximately a normal random variable with mean $= \mu = 10.5$ and standard deviation $= \sigma/\sqrt{n} = 4.5/\sqrt{40} = .71$. So

$$Z = \frac{\overline{X} - 10.5}{.71}$$

is approximately a standard normal random variable, and consequently

$$P(\overline{X} < 9) = P\left[\frac{\overline{X} - 10.5}{.71} < \frac{9 - 10.5}{.71}\right]$$
$$= P(Z < -2.11) = .0174$$

Solution 2 No assumptions regarding the shape of the P/E ratio population are necessary. This population may be normal or it may not—it simply does not matter because we are using a large sample ($n = 40$). The distribution of $\overline{X}$ is approximately normal, regardless of the shape of the population of all P/E ratios. Our only assumptions in Solution 1 were that $\mu = 10.5$ and $\sigma = 4.5$. ●

Exercises

8.1 The manager of Homer and Gordon Realty finds that their four realtors have sold 0, 1, 3, and 4 homes, respectively, in the past month. All four outcomes have occurred with equal probability.

a. List the number of homes sold by two realtors selected with replacement for all possible samples of size two.

b. Calculate the sample mean for each sample of size two. Construct the probability distribution for the sample mean.

c. Draw a histogram showing the distribution of the same mean ($\overline{X}$).

8.2 A southwestern bank issues travelers checks in denominations of $10, $20, $50, $100, and $500. All five amounts have occurred with equal probability.

a. List all possible samples of three from these five denominations. (Denominations may not be repeated.)

b. Calculate the sample mean for each sample of size three.

c. Construct the probability distribution for the sample mean.

d. Draw a histogram showing the distribution of the sample mean ($\overline{X}$).

8.3 Five machines produce electronic components. The number of components produced per hour is normally distributed with a mean of 25 and a standard deviation of four.

a. What percentage of the time does a machine produce more than 27 components per hour?

b. What percentage of the time is the average rate of output of the five machines more than 27 components per hour?

8.4 If a sample of size 22 is selected from a normally distributed population with mean 100 and variance 25, what is the probability that the mean of this sample is less than 99?

8.5 Let $\overline{X}$ be the average of a sample of size 18 from a normally distributed population with mean 37 and variance 16. Find the following probabilities.

a. $P(\overline{X} \leqslant 35)$.

b. $P(\overline{X} \geqslant 38)$.

c. $P(34 \leqslant \overline{X} \leqslant 36.5)$.

d. $P(36 \leqslant \overline{X} \leqslant 38)$.

8.6 A survey of fees charged by attorneys found that the hourly charge was approximately normally distributed with a mean of $80 and a standard deviation of $20.

a. If an attorney is selected at random, what is the probability that the attorney charges a fee less than $70 per hour?

b. What is the probability that the average fee of 30 attorneys selected at random is less than $70 per hour?

8.7 The mean number of defectives found in a box of electrical resistors is ten with a population standard deviation of four. If 11 boxes are selected at random, what is the probability that the average number of defectives will be between nine and 12? What are you assuming about the probability distribution here?

8.8 Avionics employs 2000 engineers. If the mean yearly salary of an engineer at Avionics is $50,000 with a standard deviation of $10,000, what is the probability that the average yearly salary of 50 engineers selected at random will be between $46,000 and $52,000?

Applying the Central Limit Theorem to Normal Populations

The CLT tells us that $\overline{X}$ tends toward a normal distribution as the sample size increases. If you are dealing with a population that has an assumed normal distribution (as in Example 8.2), then $\overline{X}$ is normal regardless of the sample size. However, as the sample size increases, the variability of $\overline{X}$ decreases, as is illustrated in Figure 8.5. This means that, for large sample sizes, if you were to get many samples and corresponding values of $\overline{X}$, these values of $\overline{X}$ would be more concentrated around the middle, with very few extremely large or extremely small values.

Look at Figure 8.5, which illustrates the assumed normal distribution of all Everglo bulbs. We know that (using Table A-4) 95% of a normal curve is contained within 1.96 standard deviations of the mean. For a sample size of $n = 10$ from a normal population with $\mu = 400$ and $\sigma = 50$, $\sigma_{\overline{X}} = 15.81$. Now,

$$\mu_{\overline{X}} - 1.96\sigma_{\overline{X}} = 400 - 1.96(15.81) = 369.0$$

and

$$\mu_{\overline{X}} + 1.96\sigma_{\overline{X}} = 400 + 1.96(15.81) = 431.0$$

Thus, if we repeatedly obtain samples of size ten, 95% of the resulting $\overline{X}$ values will lie between 369.0 and 431.0.

This result and the corresponding results using $n = 20$, 50, and 100 are contained in Table 8.2. This reemphasizes that, for larger samples, you are much more likely to

Table 8.2

Sampling from a normal population with $\mu = 400$ and $\sigma = 50$; 95% of the time, the value of X will be between $\mu_{\bar{x}} - 1.96\sigma_{\bar{x}}$ and $\mu_{\bar{x}} + 1.96\,\sigma_{\bar{x}}$

Sample size	$\sigma_{\bar{x}}$	$\mu_{\bar{x}} - 1.96\sigma_{\bar{x}}$	$\mu_{\bar{x}} + 1.96\sigma_{\bar{x}}$	Conclusion
$n = 10$	15.81	369.0	431.0	95% of the time, the value of $\overline{X}$ will be between 369.0 and 431.0
$n = 20$	11.18	378.1	421.9	95% of the time, the value of $\overline{X}$ will be between 378.1 and 421.9
$n = 50$	7.07	386.1	413.9	95% of the time, the value of $\overline{X}$ will be between 386.1 and 413.9
$n = 100$	5	390.2	409.8	95% of the time, the value of $\overline{X}$ will be between 390.2 and 409.8

get a value of $\overline{X}$ that is close to $\mu = 400$. In practice, you typically do not know the value of μ. However, by using a larger sample size, you are more apt to obtain an $\overline{X}$ that is a good estimate of the unknown μ.

Applying the Central Limit Theorem to Nonnormal Populations

The real strength of the CLT is that $\overline{X}$ will tend toward a normal random variable regardless of the shape of your population. You need a large sample ($n > 30$) to obtain a nearly normal distribution for $\overline{X}$. The CLT also holds when sampling from a discrete population.

Figures 8.9, 8.10, and 8.11 illustrate the distribution of $\overline{X}$ for three nonnormal populations. Notice that the uniform population (Figure 8.9) is at least symmetric about the mean, so the distribution of the sample mean, $\overline{X}$, tends toward a normal distribution for much smaller sample sizes. The U-shaped distribution (Figure 8.11) is another

Figure 8.9

Distribution of $\overline{X}$ for a uniform population.

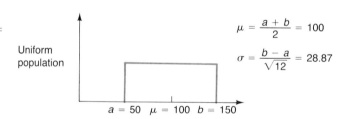

Uniform population

$$\mu = \frac{a + b}{2} = 100$$

$$\sigma = \frac{b - a}{\sqrt{12}} = 28.87$$

$a = 50 \quad \mu = 100 \quad b = 150$

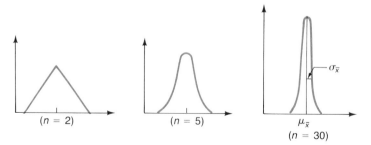

$(n = 2)$ $(n = 5)$ $(n = 30)$

By the CLT, $\mu_{\bar{x}} = \mu = 100$

$$\sigma_{\bar{x}} = \frac{\sigma}{\sqrt{n}} = \frac{28.87}{\sqrt{30}}$$

$$= 5.27$$

Figure 8.10

Distribution of $\overline{X}$ for an exponential population.

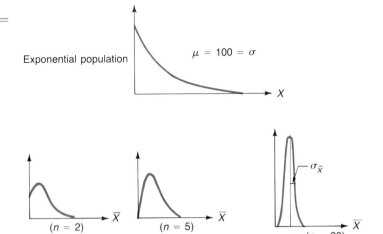

Exponential population

$\mu = 100 = \sigma$

$(n = 2)$

$(n = 5)$

$\sigma_{\overline{X}}$

$\mu_{\overline{X}}$ $(n = 30)$

By the CLT, $\mu_{\overline{X}} = \mu = 100$

$$\sigma_{\overline{X}} = \frac{\sigma}{\sqrt{n}} = \frac{100}{\sqrt{30}}$$

$$= 18.26$$

continuous distribution. It is characterized by many small and large values, with few values in the middle. This distribution is symmetric about the mean, but its shape is opposite to that of a normal distribution. Here, $\overline{X}$ requires a large sample ($n > 30$) to attain a normal distribution.

Sampling from a Finite Population

In the previous discussion, we assumed that the population was large enough that the sample was extremely small by comparison. We will now consider whether our results,

Figure 8.11

Distribution of $\overline{X}$ for a U-shaped population.

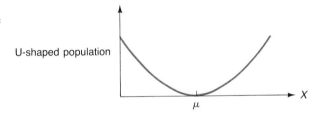

U-shaped population

μ

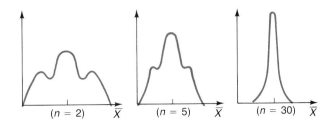

$(n = 2)$ $\overline{X}$

$(n = 5)$ $\overline{X}$

$(n = 30)$ $\overline{X}$

including the CLT, apply when the exact size of the population is known and the sample is a significant portion of the population.

Sampling with Replacement When you return each element of the sample to the population before taking the next sample element, you are sampling with replacement. This is not a common sampling procedure; people generally obtain their sample all at once, which makes it impossible to sample with replacement. When sampling with replacement, it is possible to obtain the same element more than once. For example, the same person could be chosen all three times in a sample of size $n = 3$.

When sampling with replacement, the CLT applies exactly as before, without any adjustments necessary.

Central Limit Theorem: Sampling with Replacement from a Finite Population

When sampling with replacement from a finite population with mean μ and standard deviation σ, the sample mean $\overline{X}$ tends toward a normal distribution with

mean $= \mu_{\overline{x}} = \mu$

standard deviation (standard error) $= \sigma_{\overline{x}} = \dfrac{\sigma}{\sqrt{n}}$ (8-2)

where n = sample size.

Sampling Without Replacement We first encountered the problem of sampling without replacement from a finite population in Chapter 6, where the hypergeometric distribution considered the population size (N), and the binomial distribution did not. It is easy to show that, for this situation,

$$\begin{bmatrix} \text{variance of hypergeometric} \\ \text{random variable} \end{bmatrix} = \begin{bmatrix} \text{variance of corresponding} \\ \text{binomial random variable} \end{bmatrix} \cdot \begin{bmatrix} \dfrac{N-n}{N-1} \end{bmatrix}$$

because

$$\frac{k(N-k)n(N-n)}{N^2(N-1)} = n\,\frac{k}{N}\left[1 - \frac{k}{N}\right] \cdot \left[\frac{N-n}{N-1}\right]$$

$$= np(1-p) \cdot \left[\frac{N-n}{N-1}\right]$$

where $p = k/N$. Here, $(N-n)/(N-1)$ is called the **finite population correction (fpc) factor.** When the sample size, n, is very small as compared with the population size, N, the fpc factor is nearly 1 and can be ignored. In fact, as discussed in Chapter 6, the binomial distribution serves as a good approximation to the hypergeometric whenever $n/N < .05$. The same result applies to sampling situations as well. We can express this as a rule: the fpc can be ignored whenever $n/N < .05$.

We can also use the CLT in this situation.

> **Central Limit Theorem: Sampling Without Replacement from a Finite Population**
>
> When sampling without replacement from a finite population (of size N), with mean μ and standard deviation σ, the sample mean $\overline{X}$ tends toward a normal distribution with
>
> $$\text{mean} = \mu_{\overline{x}} = \mu$$
>
> $$\text{standard deviation (standard error)} = \sigma_{\overline{x}} = \frac{\sigma}{\sqrt{n}} \cdot \sqrt{\frac{N-n}{N-1}} \qquad (8\text{-}3)$$
>
> where n = sample size.

Example 8.4

A group of women managers at Compumart is considering filing a sex-discrimination suit. A recent report stated that the average annual income of all employees in middle-management positions at Compumart is $48,000, and the standard deviation is $8500. A random sample of 45 women in these positions taken from a population of 350 female middle-managers at Compumart had an average income of $\overline{X}$ = $43,900. If the population of all female incomes at this level is assumed to have the same mean ($48,000) and standard deviation ($8500) as the distribution of incomes for all employees, what is the probability of observing a value of $\overline{X}$ this low?

Solution Because we have a large sample, we can assume (using the CLT) that the curve describing $\overline{X}$ is normal, as shown in Figure 8.12. Here, n = 45 and N = 350. We need to find $P(\overline{X} \leq 43{,}900)$. Standardizing and using Table A-4 we find that

$$P(\overline{X} \leq 43{,}900) = P\left[Z \leq \frac{43{,}900 - 48{,}000}{1184.75} \right]$$

$$= P(Z \leq -3.46)$$

$$= .0003$$

So, if the female population has an average salary of $48,000 (and standard deviation of $8500), then the chance of obtaining an $\overline{X}$ as low as $43,900 is extremely small. If we assume that the standard deviation is correct, then, based strictly on this set of data, our conclusion would be that the average salary for women at this level is not $48,000 but is less than $48,000. ●

Figure 8.12

Distribution of sample mean of annual salaries (assuming μ = $48,000, σ = $8500). The shaded area represents the solution to example 8.4, $P(\overline{X} \leq 43{,}900)$.

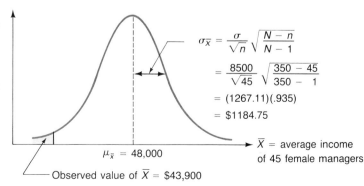

$$\sigma_{\overline{x}} = \frac{\sigma}{\sqrt{n}} \sqrt{\frac{N-n}{N-1}}$$

$$= \frac{8500}{\sqrt{45}} \sqrt{\frac{350-45}{350-1}}$$

$$= (1267.11)(.935)$$

$$= \$1184.75$$

$\mu_{\overline{x}}$ = 48,000

Observed value of $\overline{X}$ = $43,900

$\overline{X}$ = average income of 45 female managers

With the type of question asked in example 8.4, there is always the chance that we will reach an incorrect decision using the sample data; there is always the chance of error due to sampling. This possible error will be a concern whenever you test a hypothesis. For now, remember that, when dealing with sample data, statistics never *prove* anything. They do, however, *support* or *fail to support* a claim (such as $\mu <$ $48,000$).

Exercises

8.9 From a finite population of size 300 that is approximately normally distributed with a mean of 50 and a standard deviation of 10, what is the probability that a random sample of size 30 without replacement will yield a sample mean larger than 55? What is the probability that a random sample of size 30 with replacement will yield a sample mean larger than 55?

8.10 Advanced Machinery manufactured 1584 diagnostic machines. The machines can pinpoint electrical problems in a certain type of machinery in 5 minutes on the average with a standard deviation of 2 minutes. If a random sample of 300 diagnostic machines are selected without replacement, what is the probability that the sample mean of the time it takes to pinpoint the electrical problems is greater than 6 minutes?

8.11 The electric bill for 250 households in a small midwestern town was found to have a mean of $120 with a standard deviation of $25 for the month of November. If ten households are selected at random from the 250 households, what is the probability that the sample mean will be between $110 and $130? What are you assuming about the population?

8.12 General Appliances has 70 microwave ovens that need repair. The mean cost of repair for the 70 microwaves is $80. The standard deviation of the cost is $35. The cost can be considered to be approximately normally distributed.

a. If a sample of ten from the 70 microwaves is selected without replacement, what is the probability that the mean cost for the sample is greater than $100?

b. If a sample of ten from the 70 microwaves is selected with replacement, what is the probability that the mean cost for the sample is greater than $100?

8.13 The mean daily time spent on the telephone by the 60 personnel managers of Retail Products is 1.25 hours; the standard deviation is 0.62 hours. Assuming that the time spent on the telephone is approximately normally distributed, what is the probability that the mean daily time spent on the telephone by ten different personnel managers selected at random is greater than 1.5 hours?

8.14 As the finite population size gets large for a fixed sample size, explain how the finite population correction factor is affected.

8.15 National Distributing employs 500 salespersons in 200 territories throughout the United States. The average yearly commission earned by a salesperson is $47,000 and the standard deviation of the yearly commission is $8540. If a random sample of 60 salespersons is selected, what is the probability that the sample mean of their yearly commission is less than $45,000?

8.16 An aptitude test on the theory of electronics was given to all the 275 repairpeople of A.N.P. Micronics. The mean score on the test was 112 and the standard deviation of the test scores was 18.6. Twenty repairpeople were selected at random. What is the probability that the sample mean would be between 110 and 120? What are you assuming about the distribution of the exam scores?

8.17 One-hundred and fifty construction workers drive an average of 11.23 miles to a construction site. The standard deviation of this distance is 4.13 miles. If a random sample of 35 workers is selected, what is the probability that the sample mean of the distance driven to the construction site is greater than 16 miles?

8.18 Two hundred boxes of meat patties are loaded into a truck. The mean weight of the 200 boxes is 8.2 pounds. The standard deviation of the weight is 0.5 pounds. If a fast-food restaurant randomly selects 40 boxes of meat patties, what is the probability that the mean weight of the 40 boxes is less than 8.0 pounds?

8.3

Confidence Intervals for the Mean of a Normal Population (σ Known)

Return to the situation where we have obtained a sample from a normal population with unknown mean, μ. We will first consider a case in which we know the variability of the normal random variable, the value of σ (Figure 8.13). (The situation where both μ and σ are unknown will be dealt with in the next section.)

We know that, to estimate μ, the average of the entire population, we obtain a sample from this population and calculate $\overline{X}$, the average of the sample. $\overline{X}$, the estimate of μ, is also called a **point estimate** because it consists of a single number.

In example 8.2, it was assumed that the assembly time for a particular electrical component followed a normal distribution, with $\mu = 20$ minutes and $\sigma = 3$ minutes. What if μ is not known for *all* workers? A random sample of 25 workers' assembly times was obtained with the following results (in minutes):

22.8, 29.3, 27.2, 30.2, 24.0, 23.2, 22.9, 30.3, 27.1, 31.2, 27.0, 32.0, 28.6, 24.1, 28.9, 26.8, 26.6, 23.4, 25.1, 26.6, 25.7, 28.1, 31.5, 24.8, 25.2

Based on these data,

$$\text{estimate of } \mu = \text{sample mean, } \overline{X}$$
$$= \frac{22.8 + 29.3 + \ldots + 25.2}{25}$$
$$= 26.9 \text{ minutes}$$

Is this large value of $\overline{X}$ ($= 26.9$) due to random chance? We know that, 50% of the time, $\overline{X}$ will be larger than 20, even if $\mu = 20$ (Figure 8.14). Or is this value large because μ is a value larger than 20? In other words, does this value of $\overline{X}$ provide just cause for concluding that μ is larger than 20? We will tackle this type of question in Chapter 9.

How accurate is a derived estimate of the population mean, μ? This depends, for one thing, on the sample size. We can measure the precision of this estimate by using a **confidence interval (CI)**. By providing the CI, one can make such statements as "I am 95% confident that the average assembly time, μ, is between 25.7 minutes and 28.1 minutes." For this illustration, (25.7, 28.1) is called a 95% CI for μ.

Figure 8.13

An example where the standard deviation σ is known, but the mean μ is unknown.

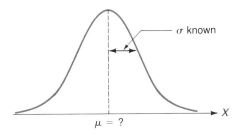

Figure 8.14

Distribution of $\overline{X}$ if μ = 20 minutes.

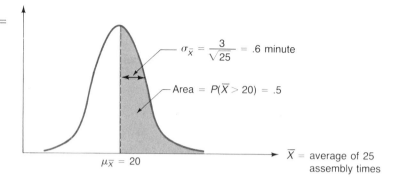

$$\sigma_{\overline{x}} = \frac{3}{\sqrt{25}} = .6 \text{ minute}$$

Area $= P(\overline{X} > 20) = .5$

$\mu_{\overline{x}} = 20$

$\overline{X}$ = average of 25 assembly times

Using the CLT, we know that $\overline{X}$ is approximately a normal random variable with

$$\mu_{\overline{x}} = \mu$$
$$\sigma_{\overline{x}} = \sigma / \sqrt{n}$$

where μ and σ represent the mean and standard deviation of the population. To standardize $\overline{X}$, you subtract the mean of $\overline{X}$ (μ) and divide by the standard deviation of $\overline{X}$ ($\sigma / \sqrt{n}$). Consequently,

$$Z = \frac{\overline{X} - \mu}{\sigma / \sqrt{n}}$$

is a standard normal random variable. Consider the following statement and refer to Figure 8.15.

$$P(-1.96 \leq Z \leq 1.96) = .95$$

so

$$P\left(-1.96 \leq \frac{\overline{X} - \mu}{\sigma / \sqrt{n}} \leq 1.96\right) = .95$$

After some algebra and rearrangement of terms, we get

$$P(\overline{X} - 1.96\sigma / \sqrt{n} \leq \mu \leq \overline{X} + 1.96\sigma / \sqrt{n}) = .95$$

How does the last statement apply to a *particular* sample mean, $\overline{x}$? Consider the interval

$$(\overline{x} - 1.96\,\sigma / \sqrt{n}, \ \overline{x} + 1.96\,\sigma / \sqrt{n}) \qquad (8\text{-}4)$$

Figure 8.15

$P(-1.96 \leq Z \leq 1.96) = .95$.

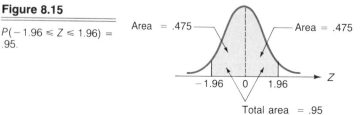

Area $= .475$

Area $= .475$

$-1.96 \quad 0 \quad 1.96 \qquad Z$

Total area $= .95$

Using the values from our assembly-time example, we have $\bar{x} = 26.9$, $\sigma = 3$, and $n = 25$. The resulting 95% confidence interval is

$$(26.9 - 1.96 \cdot 3/\sqrt{25}, \ 26.9 + 1.96 \cdot 3/\sqrt{25})$$

or

$$(25.72, \ 28.08)$$

Since μ is unknown, then it is unknown whether μ lies between 25.72 and 28.08. However, if you were to obtain random samples repeatedly, calculate $\bar{x}$, and determine the interval defined in equation 8-4, then 95% of these intervals would contain μ, and 5% would not. For this reason, equation 8-4 is called a **95% confidence interval** for μ. Using our assembly-time illustration, we are 95% confident that the average assembly time, μ, lies between 25.72 and 28.08.

Notation Let Z_a denote the value of Z with an area *to the right* of this value equal to a. How can we determine $Z_{.025}$, $Z_{.05}$, and $Z_{.1}$ (Figure 8.16)? Using Table A-4, $Z_{.025} = 1.96$, $Z_{.05} = 1.645$, and $Z_{.1} = 1.28$.

When defining a CI for μ, one can define a 99% CI, a 95% CI, a 90% CI, or whatever. The specific percentage represents the **confidence level**. The *higher* the confidence level, the *wider* the CI. The confidence level is written as $(1 - \alpha) \cdot 100\%$, where $\alpha = .01$ for a 99% CI, $\alpha = .05$ for a 95% CI, and so on. Thus, a $(1 - \alpha) \cdot 100\%$ CI for the mean of a normal population, μ, is

$$\left[\bar{x} - Z_{\alpha/2}(\sigma/\sqrt{n}), \ \bar{x} + Z_{\alpha/2}(\sigma/\sqrt{n}) \right] \tag{8-5}$$

According to the CLT, equation 8-5 provides an *approximate* CI for the mean of *any* population, provided the sample size, n, is large ($n > 30$).

Example 8.5

Determine a 90% and a 99% CI for the average assembly time of all workers, using the 25 observations given on page 217.

Solution The sample mean here was $\bar{x} = 26.9$. The population standard deviation is assumed to be three minutes. The resulting 90% CI for the population mean μ is

$$26.9 - Z_{.05}(3/\sqrt{25}) \text{ to } 26.9 + Z_{.05}(3/\sqrt{25})$$
$$= 26.9 - 1.645(3/\sqrt{25}) \text{ to } 26.9 + 1.645(3/\sqrt{25})$$
$$= 26.9 - .99 \text{ to } 26.9 + .99$$
$$= 25.91 \text{ minutes to } 27.89 \text{ minutes}$$

Figure 8.16

$1.28 = Z_{.1}$, $1.645 = Z_{.05}$, and $1.96 = Z_{.025}$.

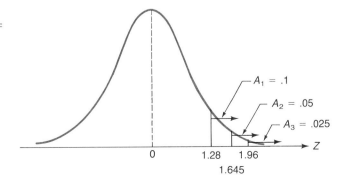

The 99% CI for μ is

$$26.9 - Z_{.005}(3/\sqrt{25}) \text{ to } 26.9 + Z_{.005}(3/\sqrt{25})$$
$$= 26.9 - 2.575(3/\sqrt{25}) \text{ to } 26.9 + 2.575(3/\sqrt{25})$$
$$= 26.9 - 1.54 \text{ to } 26.9 + 1.54$$
$$= 25.36 \text{ minutes to } 28.44 \text{ minutes}$$

Discussing a Confidence Interval

The narrower your CI the better, for the same level of confidence. Suppose Electricalc spent $50,000 investigating the average time necessary to assemble their electrical components. Part of this study included obtaining a CI for the average assembly time, μ. Which statement would they prefer to see?

1. I am 95% confident that the average assembly time is between 2 minutes and 50 minutes.
2. I am 95% confident that the average assembly time is between 25 minutes and 27 minutes.

The information contained in the first statement is practically worthless, and that's $50,000 down the drain. The second statement contains useful information; μ is narrowed down to a much smaller range.

Given the second statement, can you tell what the corresponding value of $\overline{X}$ was that produced this CI? For any CI for μ, $\overline{X}$ (the estimate of μ) is always *in the center*. So $\overline{X}$ must have been 26 minutes.

For the 90% CI in example 8.5, the following conclusions are valid:

1. I am 90% confident that the average assembly time lies between 25.91 and 27.89 minutes.
2. If I repeatedly obtained samples of size 25, then 90% of the resulting CIs would contain μ and 10% would not. (Question from the audience: Does this CI [25.91,27.89] contain μ? Your response: I don't know. All I can say is that this procedure leads to an interval containing μ 90% of the time.)
3. I am 90% confident that my estimate of μ (namely, $\bar{x} = 26.9$) is within .99 minute of the actual value of μ.

Here .99 is equal to 1.645 $(\sigma/\sqrt{n})$. This is referred to as the **maximum error, E.**

$$E = \text{maximum error} = Z_{\alpha/2}(\sigma/\sqrt{n}) \tag{8-6}$$

Be careful! The following statement is *not* correct: "The probability that μ lies between 25.91 and 27.89 is .90." What is the probability that the number 27 lies in this CI? How about 24? The answer to the first question is 1, and to the second, 0, because 27 lies in the CI and 24 does not. So what is the probability that μ lies in the CI? Remember that μ is a fixed number; we just do not know what its value is. It is *not* a random variable, unlike its estimator, $\overline{X}$. As a result, this probability is either 0 or 1, not .95. Therefore, remember that, once you have inserted your sample results into equation 8-5 to obtain your CI, the word *probability* can no longer be used to describe the resulting CI.

Example 8.6

Refer to the 20 samples of Everglo bulbs in Table 8.1. Using sample 1, what is the resulting 80% CI for the population mean, μ? Assume that σ is 50 hours.

Solution Here, $n = 10$ and $\bar{x} = 388.0$. The confidence level is 80%, so $Z_{\alpha/2} = Z_{.1} = 1.28$ (from Table A-4). Therefore, the resulting 80% confidence interval for μ is

$$388.0 - 1.28(50/\sqrt{10}) \text{ to } 388.0 + 1.28(50/\sqrt{10})$$

$$= 388.0 - 20.2 \text{ to } 388.0 + 20.2$$

$$= 367.8 \text{ to } 408.2$$

So we are 80% confident that μ lies between 367.8 and 408.2 hours. Also, we are 80% confident that our estimate of μ ($\bar{x} = 388.0$) is within 20.2 hours of the actual value.   ●

Exercises

8.19 A random sample of 125 observations is obtained from a normally distributed population with a standard deviation of five. Given that the sample mean is 20.6, construct a 90% CI for the mean of the population.

8.20 The following data are the values of a random sample from a normally distributed population. Assume that the population variance is 10.2. Construct a 99% CI for the mean of the population.

50.6, 52.3, 48.6, 45.3, 51.8, 50.8, 46.7, 56.1, 47.7, 49.3, 44.9, 57.0, 50.7, 42.6, 49.8, 46.1, 48.7, 51.8, 54.3, 48.4, 50.5

8.21 A random sample of size 60 from a normally distributed population yields a mean of 100. The standard deviation of the population is 30. Construct a 95% CI for the mean of the population.

8.22 The monthly advertising expenditure of Discount Hardware Store is normally distributed with a standard deviation of $100. If a sample of 10 randomly selected months yields a mean advertising expenditure of $380 monthly, what is a 90% CI for the mean of the store's monthly advertising expenditure?

8.23 A vending machine containing laundry detergent produces a total profit of $1800 over 7 randomly selected months. If the monthly profit from the vending machine is considered to be normally distributed with a standard deviation of $300, what would be a 90% CI for the mean monthly profit from this machine?

8.24 A real-estate firm takes a random sample of 40 homes from a small suburb of Memphis. The standard deviation of the total square feet of living space per home is 150. Construct a 98% CI for the mean square footage of living space, assuming that the random sample yielded a mean of 1600.

8.25 A manufacturer of ten-speed racing bicycles believes that the average weight of the bicycle is normally distributed with a mean of 22 pounds and a standard deviation of 1.5 pounds. A random sample of 30 bicycles is selected. If the mean from this sample is 22.8, what is a 96% CI for the mean weight of the bicycle?

8.26 A quality-control engineer is concerned about the breaking strength of a metal wire manufactured to stringent specifications. A sample of size 25 is randomly obtained and the breaking strengths are recorded. The breaking strength of the wire is considered to be normally distributed with a standard deviation of three. Find a 95% CI for the mean breaking strength of the wire.

26, 27, 18, 23, 24, 20, 21, 24, 19, 27, 25, 20, 24, 21, 26, 19, 21, 20, 25, 20, 23, 25, 21, 20, 21

8.27 An investor would like to bid on a tract of forest land and then clear the land selectively to market the timber. To arrive at an estimate of the total weight of the lumber, a random sample of 50 trees is selected and their diameters are measured. The sample yields a mean diameter of 13.2 inches. Find a 90% CI for the mean diameter of the trees if the diameter of the tree on the tract of land is considered to be normally distributed with a variance of 4.3 inches squared.

8.28 As the sample size increases, would a CI given by equation 8-5 get smaller or larger? For a given random sample, would the CI given by equation 8-5 for a 90% CI be larger or smaller than that for an 80% CI?

8.29 A medical researcher would like to obtain a 99% CI for the mean length of time that a particular sedative is effective. Thirty subjects are randomly selected. The mean length of time that the sedative was effective is found to be 8.3 hours for the sample. Find the 99% CI, assuming that the length of time that the sedative is effective is considered to be approximately normally distributed with a standard deviation of .93 hours.

8.30 A safety council is interested in the age at which a person first obtains his or her driver's license. If the ages of people who obtain their first driver's license is considered to be normally distributed with a standard deviation of 2.5 years, what is an 80% CI for the mean age, given that a random sample of 20 new drivers yields a mean age of 19.3 years?

8.4

Confidence Intervals for the Mean of a Normal Population (σ Unknown)

If σ is unknown, then it is impossible to determine a confidence interval for μ using equation 8.5 because we are unable to evaluate the standard error $\sigma/\sqrt{n}$. Let us take another look at how we estimate the parameters of a normal population.

When a population mean is unknown, we can estimate it using the sample mean. The logical thing to do if σ is unknown is to replace it by its estimate, the standard deviation of the sample, s. But consider what happens when

$$\frac{\overline{X} - \mu}{\sigma/\sqrt{n}}$$

is replaced by

$$\frac{\overline{X} - \mu}{s/\sqrt{n}}$$

This is no longer a standard normal random variable, Z. However, it does follow another identifiable distribution, the **t distribution**. Its complete name is *Student's t distribution*, named after W. S. Gosset, a statistician in a Guinness brewery who used the pen name *Student*. The distribution of

$$\frac{\overline{X} - \mu}{s/\sqrt{n}}$$

will follow a t distribution, *provided* the population from which you are obtaining the sample is normally distributed.

The t distribution is similar in appearance to the standard normal (Z) distribution, in that it is symmetric about zero. Unlike the Z distribution, however, its shape depends on the sample size, n. Consequently, when you use the t distribution, you must state the sample size. This is accomplished by using **degrees of freedom**. For this application using the t distribution,

degrees of freedom $= df = n - 1$

The value of $df = n - 1$ can be explained by observing that, for a given value of $\bar{X}$, only $n - 1$ of the sample values are free to vary. For example, in a sample of size $n = 3$, if $\bar{x} = 5.0$, $x_1 = 2$, and $x_2 = 7$, then x_3 *must* be 6 because this is the only value providing a sample mean equal to 5.0.

Two t distributions are illustrated in Figure 8.17. Notice that the t distributions are symmetrically distributed about zero but have wider tails than does the standard normal, Z. Observe that as n increases, the t distribution tends toward the standard normal, Z. In fact, for $n > 30$, there is little difference between these two distributions. Areas under a t curve are provided in Table A-5 on page 819 for various df. So, for large samples ($n > 30$), it does not matter whether σ is known (Z distribution, Table A-4) or σ is unknown (t distribution, Table A-5) because the t and Z curves are practically the same. For this reason, the t distribution often is referred to as the **small sample distribution** for $\bar{X}$. The Z table can be used as an approximation whenever σ is unknown and n is larger than 30.

Using the t distribution, then, a $(1 - \alpha) \cdot 100\%$ CI for μ is

$$\bar{x} - t_{\alpha/2,n-1}(s/\sqrt{n}) \text{ to } \bar{x} + t_{\alpha/2,n-1}(s/\sqrt{n})$$

where $t_{\alpha/2,n-1}$ denotes the t value from Table A-5 using a t curve with $n - 1$ df and a right tail area of $\alpha/2$.

Do you remember our sample of 25 assembly times that produced a point estimate for μ having a value of $\bar{x} = 26.9$ minutes? This estimate was used in example 8.5, where it was assumed that the population standard deviation was $\sigma = 3$, in constructing a CI for μ. Furthermore, the assembly times were assumed to follow a *normal* distribution.

Suppose that we do not know σ, either. Then the point estimate of the population standard deviation is

$$s = \sqrt{\frac{(22.8^2 + 29.3^2 + \ldots + 25.2^2) - (22.8 + 29.3 + \ldots + 25.2)^2/25}{24}}$$

$$= \sqrt{\frac{18,285.14 - (672.6)^2/25}{24}}$$

$$= \sqrt{7.896} = 2.81 \text{ minutes}$$

Using Table A-5 to find a 90% CI for μ, you first determine that

$$t_{\alpha/2,n-1} = t_{.05,24} = 1.711$$

The resulting 90% CI is

$$26.9 - 1.711(2.81/\sqrt{25}) \text{ to } 26.9 + 1.711(2.81/\sqrt{25})$$
$$= 26.9 - .96 \text{ to } 26.9 + .96$$
$$= 25.94 \text{ to } 27.86$$

Figure 8.17

The t distribution.

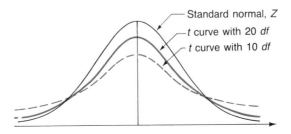

Figure 8.18

MINITAB solution to example 8.7.

```
MTB > SET INTO C1
DATA> 9.4 8.6 11.1 7.5 9.1 10.4 8.8 10.8 11.4 6.8 7.8
DATA> 11.8 12.1 10.7 8.4 9.5 9.3 10.1
DATA> END
MTB > TINTERVAL WITH 95 PERCENT CONFIDENCE USING C1

            N      MEAN    STDEV   SE MEAN    95.0 PERCENT C.I.
C1         18     9.644    1.515    0.357    ( 8.891,  10.398)
```

Using these data, we are 90% confident that the estimate for the mean of this normal population ($\bar{x} = 26.9$) is within .96 minutes of the actual value. Comparing this result with example 8.5, we notice little difference in the two 90% CIs. This is due mostly to the fact that the estimate of σ ($s = 2.81$) is very close to the assumed value of $\sigma = 3$.

Example 8.7

Metro Moving Company is considering the purchase of a new large moving van. The sales agency has agreed to lease the truck to Metro for three weeks (18 working days) on a trial basis. Of primary concern to Metro is the miles per gallon (mpg) that the van obtains on a typical moving day. The mpg values for the 18 trial days are

9.4, 8.6, 11.1, 7.5, 9.1, 10.4, 8.8, 10.8, 11.4, 6.8, 7.8, 11.8, 12.1, 10.7, 8.4, 9.5, 9.3, 10.1

What is the 95% CI for the average mpg for this van, assuming that the daily mpg follows a normal distribution?

Solution Your (point) estimate of σ is $s = 1.52$ mpg. Also, your point estimate of μ is $\bar{x} = 9.64$ mpg. A 95% CI for the average mpg of the new van (if daily mpg were recorded indefinitely) is

$$9.64 - t_{.025, 17}(1.52/\sqrt{18}) \text{ to } 9.64 + t_{.025, 17}(1.52/\sqrt{18})$$

$$= 9.64 - 2.11(1.52/\sqrt{18}) \text{ to } 9.64 + 2.11(1.52/\sqrt{18})$$

$$= 9.64 - .756 \text{ to } 9.64 + .756$$

$$= 8.88 \text{ to } 10.40 \text{ mpg}$$

We are thus 95% confident that the daily mpg of the van is between 8.88 and 10.40 mpg. Notice here that the maximum error is

$$E \doteq 2.11(1.52/\sqrt{18}) = .756 \text{ mpg}$$

which implies that we are 95% confident that $\overline{X}$ is within .756 mpg of the actual average mpg. The MINITAB solution for this example is shown in Figure 8.18. ●

Exercises

8.31 Find the t values for the following α levels and degrees of freedom.

a. $t_{.10, 29}$

b. $t_{.025, 13}$

c. $t_{.05, 18}$

d. $t_{.90, 20}$

e. $t_{.95, 25}$

f. $t_{.10, 40}$

8.32 For a sample of size 21 used to test a hypothesis about a sample mean, what is the t value from a t distribution such that the following are true?

a. Ninety percent of the area under the t distribution is to the right of the t value.

b. Ten percent of the area under the t distribution is to the right of the t value.

c. Five percent of the area under the t distribution is to the left of the t value.

8.33 A random sample of size 15 is selected from a normally distributed population. The sample mean is 30 and the sample variance is 16. Find a 95% CI for the population mean.

8.34 The price per month of back orders at Harlington Industries is considered to be normally distributed. A random sample of back orders for 12 randomly selected months yields a mean of $115,320 with a standard deviation of $35,000. Construct a 90% CI for the mean price of back orders per month at Harlington Industries.

8.35 The mean monthly expenditure on gasoline per household in Middletown is determined by selecting a random sample of 36 households. The sample mean is $68 with a sample standard deviation of $17.

a. What is a 95% CI for the mean monthly expenditure per household on gasoline in Middletown?

b. What is a 90% CI for the mean monthly expenditure per household on gasoline in Middletown?

8.36 Second Federal Savings and Loan would like to estimate the mean number of years in which 30-year mortgages are paid off. Eighteen paid-off 30-year mortgages are randomly selected and the numbers of years in which the loans were paid in full are

19.6, 20.8, 29.6, 6.3, 3.1, 10.6, 30.0, 21.7, 10.5, 26.3, 10.7, 6.1, 7.3, 12.6, 9.8, 27.4, 20.1, 10.8

Assuming that the number of years in which 30-year mortgages are paid off is normally distributed, construct an 80% CI for the mean number of years in which the mortgages are paid off.

8.37 An apartment-finder service would like to estimate the average cost of a one-bedroom apartment in Kansas City. A random sample of 41 apartment complexes yielded a mean of $310 with a standard deviation of $29. Construct a 90% CI for the mean cost of one-bedroom apartments in Kansas City.

8.38 Sacks of grapefruit are packaged mechanically for commercial distribution. A random sample of 31 sacks yields a sample mean of 5.2 lbs. of grapefruit and a sample standard deviation of 0.8 lbs. Find a 90% CI for the mean weight.

8.39 An investment advisor believes that the return on interest-sensitive stocks is approximately normally distributed. A sample of 24 interest-sensitive stocks was selected and their yearly return (including dividends and capital appreciation) was as follows (in percentages):

11.1, 12.5, 13.6, 9.1, 8.7, 10.6, 12.5, 15.6, 13.8, 8.0, 10.9, 7.6, 5.2, 1.2, 12.8, 16.7, 13.9, 10.1, 9.6, 10.8, 11.6, 12.3, 12.9, 11.6

Find a 90% CI for the mean yearly return on interest-sensitive stocks.

8.40 The president of Secure Savings and Loan Association would like to estimate the average salaries of vice-presidents of savings and loans associations. After selecting a random sample of 41 vice-presidents, the following statistics were calculated regarding annual salaries:

$\bar{x} = 52,100$

$s = 10,350$

Construct a 95% CI for the mean annual salaries of vice-presidents.

8.41 A quality-control engineer conducted a test of the tensile strength of 20 aluminum wires. The coded data represent the tensile strength of 20 aluminum wires selected at random. Find a

90% CI for the mean value of the coded data. What are you assuming about the distribution of the tensile strengths?

105, 113, 95, 90, 112, 93, 106, 80, 95, 90, 88, 101, 93, 91, 86, 107, 103, 93, 84, 97

8.42 MAXIX has been selling automatic toll-collection systems in the United States at various prices depending on the competition. It is believed that the price at which the systems are sold can be approximated by a normal distribution. A sample of 15 systems was sold at the following values (in dollars):

16,500, 13,200, 14,560, 12,320, 13,640, 12,980, 13,350, 12,130, 11,980, 13,590, 15,670, 16,350, 11,860, 13,400, 13,860

Find a 90% CI for the mean price at which the automatic toll-collection systems are sold.

8.5

Selecting the Necessary Sample Size

Sample Size for Known σ

How large a sample do you need? This is often difficult to determine, although a carefully chosen *large* sample generally provides a better representation of the population than does a smaller sample. Acquiring large samples can be costly and time-consuming; why obtain a sample of size $n = 1000$ when a sample size of $n = 500$ will provide sufficient accuracy for estimating a population mean? This section will show you how to determine what sample size is necessary when the maximum error, E, is specified in advance.

In example 8.6, we assumed that the lifetime of Everglo bulbs is normally distributed with standard deviation $\sigma = 50$ hours but unknown mean μ. Based on the results of sample 1 from Table 8.1, the conclusion was that we were 80% confident that the estimate of μ ($\bar{x} = 388.0$) was within 20.2 hours of the actual value of μ for $n = 10$. How large of a sample is necessary if we want our point estimate ($\bar{X}$) to be within ten hours of the actual value of μ, with 80% confidence? The value ten here is the maximum error, E, defined in equation 8-6. We would like the estimate of μ (that is, $\bar{X}$) to be within ten of the actual value, so

$$E = 10 = Z_{\alpha/2}(50/\sqrt{n})$$

Because the confidence level is 80%, $Z_{\alpha/2} = Z_{.1} = 1.28$. Consequently,

$$10 = (1.28)\frac{50}{\sqrt{n}}$$

$$\sqrt{n} = \frac{(1.28)\,(50)}{10} = 6.4$$

Squaring both sides of this statement produces

$$n = (6.4)^2 = 40.96$$

Rounding this value *up* (always), then a sample size of $n = 41$ will produce a CI with $E = 10$ hours. As a result, your point estimate of μ, $\bar{X}$, will be within ten hours of the actual value, with 80% confidence.

This sequence of steps can be summarized using the following expression:

$$n = \left[\frac{Z_{\alpha/2} \cdot \sigma}{E} \right]^2 \qquad\qquad (8\text{-}7)$$

Sample Size for Unknown σ

Equation 8-7 works if σ is known but does not apply to situations where both μ and σ are unknown. There are two approaches to the latter situation.

A Preliminary Sampling If you have already obtained a small sample, then you have an estimate of σ, namely, the sample standard deviation, s. Replacing σ by s in equation 8-7 gives you the desired sample size, n. Assuming that the resulting value of n is greater than 30, the $Z_{\alpha/2}$ notation in equation 8-7 is still valid because the actual t distribution here will be closely approximated by the standard normal.

When you do obtain the CI using the larger sample, the resulting maximum error, E, may not be exactly what you originally specified because the new sample standard deviation will not be the same as that belonging to the smaller original sample.

Example 8.8 In example 8.7, Metro Moving Company obtained 18 observations consisting of daily miles per gallon (mpg) on a large moving van. For these data,

$$\bar{x} = 9.64 \text{ mpg}$$
$$s = 1.52 \text{ mpg}$$

How large of a sample would they need for $\overline{X}$ to be within .5 mpg of the actual average mpg, with 95% confidence?

Solution Based on the results of the original sample, $s = 1.52$, so

$$n = \left[\frac{Z_{\alpha/2} \cdot s}{E} \right]^2 = \left[\frac{(1.96)(1.52)}{.5} \right]^2$$
$$= 35.5$$

We round this up to 36. Assuming a six-day work week, Metro would need six weeks of driving time to make a statement with this much precision, that is, within .5 mpg. Of course, they already have three weeks of data that can be included in the larger sample. ●

Obtaining a Rough Approximation of σ We know from the empirical rule and Table A-4 that 95.4% of the population will lie between $\mu - 2\sigma$ and $\mu + 2\sigma$. Because $(\mu + 2\sigma) - (\mu - 2\sigma) = 4\sigma$, this is a span of four standard deviations. One method of obtaining an estimate of σ is to ask a person who is familiar with the data to be collected these questions:

1. What do you think will be the highest value in the sample (H)?
2. What will be the lowest value (L)?

The approximation of σ is then obtained by assuming that $\mu + 2\sigma \cong H$ and $\mu - 2\sigma \cong L$, so

$$H - L \cong (\mu + 2\sigma) - (\mu - 2\sigma) = 4\sigma$$

Consequently,

$$\sigma \cong \frac{H - L}{4} \tag{8-8}$$

We can use this estimate of σ in equation 8-7 to determine the necessary sample size, n.

Example 8.9

The quality-control manager of a division that produces hair dryers is interested in the average number of switches that can be tested by his employees. Assuming that the number of switches that are tested each hour by an employee follows a normal distribution (centered at μ), he wants to estimate μ with 90% confidence. Also, he wants this estimate to be within one unit (switch) of μ. He estimates that H is 45 switches and L is 25 switches. How large of a sample will be necessary?

Solution Based on $H = 45$ switches and $L = 25$ switches,

$$\sigma \cong \frac{45 - 25}{4} = 5 \text{ switches}$$

The sample size necessary to obtain a maximum error of $E = 1$ is

$$n = \left[\frac{(1.645)(5)}{1} \right]^2 = 67.7$$

Thus, a sample size of 68 should produce a value of E close to one switch. The value will not be exactly one because the sample standard deviation, s, probably will not be exactly five. Estimating σ in this manner, however, produces a value that is "in the neighborhood" of σ. ●

Exercises

8.43 A 99% CI is to be constructed such that $\overline{X}$ is within 1.5 units of the mean of a normal population. Assuming that the population variance is 30, what sample size would be necessary to achieve this maximum error?

8.44 To be 95% confident that $\overline{X}$ is within .65 of the actual mean of a normal population with a standard deviation of 2.5, what sample size would be necessary?

8.45 The Chamber of Commerce of Tampa, Florida would like to estimate the mean amount of money spent by a tourist to within $100 with 95% confidence. If the amount of money spent by tourists is considered to be normally distributed with a standard deviation of $200, what sample size would be necessary for the Chamber of Commerce to meet their objective in estimating this mean amount?

8.46 Security Savings and Loan Association's manager would like to estimate the mean deposit by a customer into a savings account to within $500. If the deposits into savings accounts are considered to be normally distributed with a standard deviation of $1250, what sample size would be necessary to be 90% confident?

8.47 If a sample size of 70 was necessary to estimate the mean of a normal population to within 1.2 with 90% confidence, what is the approximate value of the standard deviation of the population?

8.48 The marketing agency for computer software of Personal Micro Systems would like to estimate with 95% confidence the mean time that it takes for a beginner to learn to use a standard software package. Past data indicate that the learning time can be approximated by a normal distribution with a standard deviation of 20 minutes. How large a sample size should the marketing agency choose if the mean time to learn to use the software package is to be estimated within 8 minutes with 90% confidence?

8.49 Past data indicate that the distribution of the daily price-earnings ratio of National Health and Medical Services can be approximated by a normal distribution with a variance of 17. How large a sample size would be necessary to estimate the mean price-earnings ratio of National Health and Medical Services to within 2 units with 98% confidence?

8.50 A chemist at International Chemical would like to measure the adhesiveness of a new wood glue. From past experiments, a measure used to indicate adhesiveness has ranged from 7.3 to 11.1 units. To be 98% confident, how large a sample would be necessary to estimate the mean adhesiveness to within .5 units?

8.51 An investor would like to obtain an idea of the profitability of a soft-drink vending machine by taking a random sample of several days and recording the daily number of soft drinks sold. A preliminary sample shows that the highest number of drinks sold daily is 106 and the least sold in a day is 36. What sample size would be necessary to estimate the mean number of soft drinks sold to within six soft drinks with 99% confidence?

8.52 If past data indicate that the maximum value of a random variable X is 155 and the lowest value of X is 120, what is the sample size necessary to be 95% confident in estimating the mean of X to within one? Assume that X is approximately normally distributed.

8.53 An economist would like to estimate the rise in personal income for a particular quarter. A preliminary study shows that the rise is between 1% and 6%. What sample size would be necessary to obtain a 95% CI to estimate the mean rise in personal income for the quarter to within .1%?

8.6

Other Sampling Procedures

To discuss methods of sampling other than simple random sampling, we need to define several terms. These definitions also apply to simple random sampling.

1. **Population.** As before, this refers to the collection of people or objects of interest about which we desire to learn something. It may be as large as the set of all voting adults in the United States or as small as the set of all top-level managers in a particular company. In this section, we will assume that we are sampling from a *finite* population.
2. **Sampling unit.** This is a collection of elements or an individual element selected from the population. Elements within one sampling unit must not overlap with the elements in other sampling units.
3. **Cluster.** This is a sampling unit that is a group of elements from the population, such as all adults in a particular city block.
4. **Sampling frame.** This is a list of population elements from which the sample is to be selected. Ideally, the sampling frame should be identical to the population. In many situations, however, this is impossible, in which case the frame must be *representative* of the population.
5. **Strata.** These are nonoverlapping subpopulations. For example, the population of all cigarette smokers can be split into two strata—men and women. You can then use **stratified sampling,** in which your total sample consists of a sample selected from each individual stratum.
6. **Sampling design.** This is a plan that specifies the manner in which the

sampling units are to be selected for your sample. Examples include simple random sampling, systematic sampling, stratified sampling, and cluster sampling.

Simple Random Sampling

The results obtained when using a simple random sample were presented earlier and will be summarized here for the usual case of sampling without replacement, where every sample of n elements (from a population of size N) has an equal chance of being selected.

According to the CLT, for large samples the distribution of the sample mean, $\overline{X}$, is approximately normal, without making any assumptions concerning the shape of the population being sampled. The resulting CI for the population mean, μ, is an *approximate* CI for this parameter. If you assume that the population has a normal distribution with mean μ, the CI is exact.

Simple Random Sampling

- Population Mean: μ
- Estimator:

$$\overline{X} = \frac{\Sigma x}{n} \tag{8-9}$$

- Variance of the estimator:

$$\sigma_{\overline{X}}^2 = \frac{\sigma^2}{n} \cdot \frac{N-n}{N-1} \tag{8-10}$$

The fpc is $(N-n)/(N-1)$ and can be ignored if n/N is $< .05$.

- Approximate Confidence Interval: $\overline{X} \pm Z_{\alpha/2}\, \sigma_{\overline{X}}$

Systematic Sampling

For large populations, obtaining a random sample can be quite cumbersome. Perhaps you have just informed a group of bank tellers that you need a random sample of their customers over the next few days. For them to select people randomly would be nearly impossible. A much easier scheme would be to have them select every kth customer to be included in the sample. This is systematic sampling.

Other situations where systematic sampling is advantageous include:

1. The population consists of N records on a magnetic tape or disk. The sample of n is obtained by sampling every kth record, where k is an integer approximately equal to N/n. For example, if there are $N = 9435$ records and you need a sample of size $n = 100$, then selecting every $9435/100 \cong 94$th record would result in a systematic sample. Typically, a random starting point (record) is determined, and then every kth record is selected for your sample.

2. The population consists of a collection of files stored consecutively by date of birth. A quick (although not necessarily reliable) method of obtaining a

"nearly random" sample would be to select every kth file for your sample. What could cause the sample selected from such a list to be *not* random?

There are many situations in which it is dangerous to use systematic sampling. If there are obvious patterns contained in the sample frame listing, your sample may be far from random. If elements are stored according to days, for example, your sample could consist of data that all belong to Tuesday. If the data are cyclic, your sample might consist of all the peaks or all the valleys of the population. Basically, systematic sampling works best when the order of your population is fairly random with respect to the measurement of interest.

Despite its dangers, systematic sampling can provide an easy method of obtaining a representative sample. If the order of your population is in fact random (no cycles, no obvious patterns of any kind), then a systematic sample can be analyzed as though it were a simple random sample.

Stratified Sampling

Suppose that you own a chain of four tire stores in four different cities, and you are interested in the average amount due on delinquent accounts. The population sizes of these four cities differ considerably, ranging from a small store in an east Texas town to a large store in downtown Houston. To obtain a random sample, you could combine the delinquent accounts from all four stores into one large population and obtain your random sample from this group of accounts. On the other hand, because of the different sizes, locations, and credit policies of the stores, you might want to sample the stores individually. You could obtain the largest sample from the Houston store and smaller samples from the smaller stores. This is proportional stratified sampling.

Stratified sampling is used when the population can be physically or geographically separated into two or more groups (strata), where the variation within the strata is less than the variation within the entire population. The cost of obtaining the stratified sample may be less than that of collecting a random sample of the same size, especially if the sampling units are determined geographically.

The advantages of stratified sampling are:

1. By stratifying, one can obtain more information from the sample because data are more homogeneous within each stratum; consequently, CIs are narrower than those obtained through random sampling.
2. One does obtain a cross-section of the entire population.
3. One does obtain an estimate of the mean within each stratum as well as an estimate of μ for the entire population.

We use the following notation:

n_i = sample size in stratum i

N_i = number of elements in stratum i

N = total population size = ΣN_i

n = total sample size = Σn_i

$\overline{X}_i$ = sample mean in stratum i

s_i = sample standard deviation in stratum i

Stratified Sampling

- Population Mean: μ

- Estimator : $\overline{X}_S = \dfrac{\Sigma N_i \overline{X}_i}{N}$ (8-11)

- Variance of the estimator: $\sigma_{\overline{X}_S}^2 = \dfrac{\Sigma N_i^2 \left(\dfrac{N_i - n_i}{N_i - 1}\right) \dfrac{s_i^2}{n_i}}{N^2}$ (8-12)

- Approximate Confidence Interval: $\overline{X}_S \pm Z_{\alpha/2}\, \sigma_{\overline{X}_S}$

One method often used to determine the strata sample sizes, n_i, is to select each sample size **proportional to** stratum size. Consequently,

$$n_i = n\left(\frac{N_i}{N}\right)$$

In this way, you obtain larger samples from the larger strata.

Because you desire an estimator with *small* variance (that is, one that will not drastically vary from one data set to the next), you should attempt to create strata such that the individual variances, s_i^2, are as small as possible.

Assume you would like to obtain a sample of size 20 from the chain of four tire stores. You want to use a stratified sample with proportional sample sizes because each of the stores has a different volume of customers, credit policy, and credit ceiling. Here, N_i is the number of delinquent accounts at each store; $N_1 = 72$, $N_2 = 39$, $N_3 = 25$, and $N_4 = 44$. So

$$N = 72 + 39 + 25 + 44 = 180 \text{ delinquent accounts}$$

Your sample sizes are:

$$n_1 = 20\left(\frac{72}{180}\right) \qquad\qquad n_3 = 20\left(\frac{25}{180}\right)$$
$$\cong 8 \qquad\qquad\qquad\qquad \cong 3$$
$$n_2 = 20\left(\frac{39}{180}\right) \qquad\qquad n_4 = 20\left(\frac{44}{180}\right)$$
$$\cong 4 \qquad\qquad\qquad\qquad \cong 5$$

The randomly selected accounts are analyzed to find the dollar amounts due on delinquent accounts. The sample results are:

	Store 1	Store 2	Store 3	Store 4
	$150	$ 82	$186	$321
	175	106	162	285
	216	98	174	306
	205	110		356
	182			332
	240			
	195			
	213			
$\overline{X}_i$	$197.00	$ 99.00	$174.00	$320.00
s_i	$ 27.91	$ 12.38	$ 12.00	$ 26.75

To estimate μ from these data,

$$\overline{X}_s = \frac{(72)(197) + (39)(99) + (25)(174) + (44)(320)}{180}$$

$$= \$202.64$$

Also

$$\sigma^2_{\overline{X}_S} = \left[(72)^2 \left(\frac{72 - 8}{72 - 1} \right) \frac{(27.91)^2}{8} + (39)^2 \left(\frac{39 - 4}{39 - 1} \right) \frac{(12.38)^2}{4} \right.$$

$$\left. + (25)^2 \left(\frac{25 - 3}{25 - 1} \right) \frac{(12.00)^2}{3} + (44)^2 \left(\frac{44 - 5}{44 - 1} \right) \frac{(26.75)^2}{5} \right] \div (180)^2$$

$$= 787,475.21 \div 32,400 = 24.305$$

Consequently,

$$\sigma_{\overline{X}_S} = \sqrt{24.305} = \$4.93$$

The corresponding approximate 95% CI for the average overdue amount, μ, is

$$\$202.64 - (1.96)(4.93) \text{ to } \$202.64 + (1.96)(4.93) = \$192.98 \text{ to } \$212.30$$

So we are 95% confident that the average delinquent amount for the four stores is between $192.98 and $212.30.

Cluster Sampling

We can sample clusters (groups) within the population rather than collecting individual elements one at a time. For example, to determine the opinions of the members of a particular labor union, you might interview everyone attending several of the local meetings. Of course, the danger here is that possibly (1) the people attending the local meetings that were sampled (clusters) do not represent the population of all voting members, and (2) the people attending the local meetings do not provide an adequate representation of the local members. As a general rule, it is advisable to select many small clusters rather than a few large clusters to obtain a more accurate representation of your population.

Cluster sampling is preferred to (and less costly than) random and stratified sampling when

1. The only sampling frame that can be constructed consists of clusters (for example, all people in a particular household, city block, or ZIP code area).
2. The population is extremely spread out, or it is impossible to obtain data on all the individual members.

When using cluster sampling, you should *randomly* select a set of clusters (once they have been clearly defined) for sampling. You can then include all individuals within each cluster selected for the sample (**single-stage cluster sampling**) or randomly select individuals from the sampled clusters to be included in the sample (**two-stage cluster sampling**).

We use the following notation:

M = total number of clusters in the population

m = number of clusters randomly selected for the sample

n_i = number of elements in sample cluster i

$\bar{n}$ = average cluster size of the sampled clusters ($\bar{n} = \Sigma n_i / m$)

N = total population size (N = total of all M cluster sizes that make up the population)

$\bar{N}$ = average cluster size for the population ($\bar{N} = N/M$)

T_i = total of all observations within cluster i (required for the sampled clusters only)

Cluster Sampling (Single Stage)

- Population Mean: μ

- Estimator: $\bar{X}_C = \dfrac{\Sigma T_i}{\Sigma n_i}$ (8-13)

- Variance of estimator: $\sigma_{\bar{X}_C}^2 = \left(\dfrac{M - m}{mM\bar{N}^2}\right) \dfrac{\Sigma (T_i - \bar{X}_C n_i)^2}{m - 1}$ (8-14)

If $\bar{N}$ is unknown, this can be replaced by its estimate, $\bar{n}$.

- Approximate Confidence Interval: $\bar{X}_C \pm Z_{\alpha/2}\, \sigma_{\bar{X}_C}$

As marketing director for a cable-television company in a large city, you are trying to decide whether to begin a major advertising campaign to reach tenants in local high-rise apartment buildings. Your staff disagree about whether or not this is a good idea. One group of your employees feels that people living in high-rise apartments are always on the go and are not likely to spend much time watching television—cable or network. The others tend to believe that such tenants have very little grass to mow and leaves to rake and so have a great deal of time to spend watching television.

Rather than drawing a sample from all high-rise tenants, you construct a sampling frame consisting of all 18 ($= M$) high-rise apartment complexes. From these, you randomly select a sample of $m = 4$ complexes (clusters). Each tenant in these four complexes is then asked how many hours per week he or she watches television. You obtain the following results:

	Complex 1	Complex 2	Complex 3	Complex 4
Number of Units (n_i)	260	220	310	274
Total Number of Hours per Cluster (complex)	2475	2750	3160	4110

N = the total number of units in the 18 high-rise complexes (population) = 4590, so $\bar{N}$ = 4590/18 = 255.

You begin by noting:

$$\Sigma(T_i - \bar{X}_c n_i)^2 = \Sigma T_i^2 - 2\bar{X}_c \Sigma T_i n_i + \bar{X}_c^2 \Sigma n_i^2 \qquad (8\text{-}15)$$

Using the sample data,

$$\Sigma T_i = 2475 + \ldots + 4110 = 12{,}495$$

$$\Sigma n_i = 260 + \ldots + 274 = 1064$$

$$\Sigma T_i^2 = (2475)^2 + \ldots + (4110)^2 = 40{,}565{,}825$$

$$\Sigma T_i n_i = (2475)(260) + \ldots + (4110)(274) = 3,354,240$$

$$\Sigma n_i^2 = (260)^2 + \ldots + (274)^2 = 287,176$$

As a result,

$$\overline{X}_c = \frac{\Sigma T_i}{\Sigma n_i} = \frac{12,495}{1064} = 11.743$$

Also, using equation 8-15,

$$\frac{\Sigma(T_i - \overline{X}_c n_i)^2}{m - 1} = [40,565,825 - (2)(11.743)(3,354,240)$$
$$+ (11.743)^2 (287,176)] \div 3$$
$$= 463,051.49$$

Consequently,

$$\sigma_{\overline{X}_C}^2 = \frac{18 - 4}{(4)(18)(255)^2} \cdot 463,051.49 = 1.385$$

and so

$$\sigma_{\overline{X}_C} = \sqrt{1.385} = 1.177$$

The resulting approximate 95% CI for the average number of television hours (for all 18 complexes) is

$$11.743 - 1.96(1.177) \text{ to } 11.743 + 1.96(1.177)$$
$$= 9.44 \text{ hours to } 14.05 \text{ hours}$$

Therefore, we are 95% confident that μ lies between 9.44 and 14.05 hours and that we have estimated μ to within 2.3 hours. This example has illustrated single-stage cluster sampling where everyone in the selected clusters (apartment complexes) was used in the sample. Another look at this example indicates that a two-stage cluster procedure might be more practical where each of the four sample clusters is also sampled to obtain the final sample.

Exercises

8.54 A realtor would like to estimate the average price of a home in the suburbs of a major metropolitan city. The realtor decides to use stratified random sampling. The population of homes is stratified into the five major suburbs. The results of the stratified sample yield the following statistics. Construct a 95% CI for the mean price of a home in units of one thousand.

Stratum	N_i: Number of Houses	n_i: Sample Size	$\overline{X}_i$ (in thousands)	s_i^2
Suburb 1	150	22	101.2	64.2
Suburb 2	220	33	80.7	24.3
Suburb 3	140	21	61.4	20.8
Suburb 4	70	11	139.6	53.5
Suburb 5	90	13	76.8	30.1
	670	100		

8.55 An advertising firm would like to estimate the amount of money spent per month on advertising by certain retail stores in an industrial sector of northeast New Jersey. Three sizes of retail stores were chosen—small, medium, and large. The random sample for each stratum yielded the following values. Construct a 90% CI for the mean monthly advertising expenditure of retail stores.

Stratum	N_i: Number of Stores	n_i: Sample Size	Monthly Advertising Expenditure (in thousands)
Large	40	8	2.1 1.6 1.8 1.2 0.7 2.6 0.9 0.8
Medium	112	22	0.5 0.7 0.9 1.1 0.6 1.4 1.7 0.4
			0.8 0.7 0.9 0.7 0.9 1.3 1.1 1.2
			0.4 0.3 0.8 0.6 0.9 1.1
Small	80	15	0.3 0.4 0.3 0.6 0.5 0.4 0.3 0.4
	232	45	0.1 0.3 0.2 0.4 0.5 0.2 0.7

8.56 Basic Microcomputers would like to market its version of the professional computer. To price the professional computer and its peripheral equipment properly, a survey is taken among the lower-middle, upper-middle, and high income groups to find out what a businessperson would be willing to pay. The survey was restricted to a certain city in an industrial area. A stratified sample among these three groups yielded the following statistics. Construct a 90% CI for the mean price that a professional businessperson would be willing to pay, in units of one thousand.

Income Level	N_i	n_i	$\overline{X}_i$	s_i^2
Lower-middle	8641	56	2.3	1.6
Upper-middle	14683	95	4.6	1.9
High	7457	49	4.8	1.4
	30781	200		

8.57 A market-research firm would like to estimate the average number of hours that a householder spends shopping each week. Four neighborhoods were selected from a total of 24 neighborhoods for sampling purposes. Find a 90% CI interval for the mean number of hours that a householder spends shopping each week from the following data (units are in hours per week):

1	2	3	4
2.3	5.4	1.6	5.6
1.1	4.2	0.9	4.1
4.3	3.6	4.6	2.3
0.5	7.2	5.4	7.3
3.7	8.4	5.6	6.1
4.6	11.8	4.6	4.7
10.1	2.1	7.1	5.8
6.3	1.5	3.2	4.8
7.8	8.1	4.5	5.3
8.4	4.1	3.1	1.9
7.9	3.4	2.6	8.4
10.6			

8.58 In what situation is the use of systematic sampling appropriate? Explain how a systematic sample would be taken from a file of students listed by social security number.

8.59 The administration of Digital Systems would like to obtain an estimate of the amount of time workers spend on physical exercise. Five departments out of 20 in Digital Systems were selected for sampling purposes. Find a 95% CI for the mean time that an employee spends on physical fitness per week given the following data (units are in hours per week):

1	2	3	4	5
1.1	2.3	3.5	7.9	0.1
0.2	0.4	4.6	1.3	0.0
2.3	0.3	1.5	2.5	7.6
4.6	1.0	0.7	5.7	5.1
0.1	4.6	3.6	7.8	4.0
0.0	8.3	9.5	10.3	3.0
2.6	7.1	0.8	0.6	6.5
6.8	0.2			
1.1	2.7			

Summary

This chapter introduced you to statistical inference, an extremely important area of statistics. We described procedures used to estimate a certain unknown parameter (such as the mean, μ, or the standard deviation, σ) of a population by using the corresponding sample statistic (such as the sample mean, $\overline{X}$, or the sample standard deviation, s).

The central limit theorem (CLT) states that, for large samples, the sample mean, $\overline{X}$, always follows an approximate normal distribution. If, in addition, you assume that the population is normally distributed, then $\overline{X}$ will follow an exact normal distribution. The strength of the CLT is that no assumptions need be made concerning the shape of the population, provided the sample is large ($n > 30$). The CLT allows you to make probability statements concerning $\overline{X}$, such as $P(\overline{X} < 150)$. When sampling without replacement from a finite population, the standard deviation of the normal distribution for $\overline{X}$ (the standard error) is obtained by including a finite population correction factor (fpc).

The sample mean, $\overline{X}$, provides a point estimate of μ because it consists of a single number. A confidence interval (CI) for μ measures the precision of the point estimate. If the population standard deviation σ is known, then the standard normal table (Table A-4) is used to derive the CI. If σ is unknown, it can be replaced by its estimate— the sample standard deviation, s. This provided an introduction to the t distribution. The corresponding CI for μ is constructed using the t table (Table A-5) and assumes that the sampled population is normally distributed (that is, that μ is the mean of a normal population).

For many applications, the precision of the point estimate, $\overline{X}$, is specified using the maximum error, E. The sample size n necessary to achieve a desired accuracy can be obtained using E. The population standard deviation can be estimated from a pre-liminary sample, or a rough approximation procedure can be used.

Finally, nonrandom sampling procedures, such as systematic, stratified, and cluster sampling, can provide an estimate for the population mean μ, along with an approximate CI for this parameter.

Review Exercises

8.60 Medical Products Consolidated wishes to estimate the yearly maintenance costs of the mechanical ventilators that hospitals buy from them. Fifteen hospitals were randomly chosen from a total of 45. From the data, construct a 90% CI for the mean yearly maintenance costs (in thousands of dollars) of the ventilators.

Hospital	Number of Ventilators	Maintenance cost
1	2	1.2
2	5	2.3
3	2	0.6
4	7	4.1
5	6	3.0
6	5	2.0
7	4	1.3
8	2	0.9
9	5	2.3
10	4	1.9
11	5	2.8
12	7	3.8
13	6	3.4
14	4	1.8
15	5	2.7

8.61 An accounting firm has six secretaries. It is assumed that the time it takes a secretary to type a certain legal document is normally distributed with a mean time of 30 minutes and a standard deviation of 4 minutes.

a. What is the probability that a secretary will spend less than 27 minutes typing the legal document?

b. If the six secretaries can be considered to be a random sample, what is the probability that the average time that it takes them to type the legal document is less than 27 minutes?

8.62 The tensile strength of a high-powered copper coil used in giant power transformers is believed to follow a normal distribution. A sample of 14 high-powered copper coils yields the following tensile strength (in units of thousands of pounds per square inch). Construct a 90% CI for the mean tensile strength of copper coils.

   6.1, 2.6, 3.5, 4.3, 3.1, 5.2, 3.6, 3.5, 5.4, 4.2, 3.2, 2.8, 4.0, 3.7

8.63 The ages of applicants for the position of manager of a particular fast-food restaurant are considered to be approximately normally distributed. A sample of the ages of 36 applicants selected at random yielded a sample mean of 29.4 years with a sample standard deviation of 2.1 years. Construct a 95% CI for the mean age of applicants for this position.

8.64 A local merchant would like to estimate the mean amount of money that a family spends at the state fair to within $15. If the amount spent by a family is considered to be normally distributed with a standard deviation of $27, what sample size would be necessary to be 90% confident?

8.65 A random variable is found to range from a high of 50 to a low of 25 from past data. The distribution of the random variable can be approximated by a normal distribution. To estimate the mean of the random variable to within 2.1, what sample size would be necessary in selecting a random sample to achieve a 99% confidence level?

8.66 A wholesale furniture store has 160 dining tables that have a mean weight of 47.3 pounds with a standard deviation of 9.8 pounds. If 15 tables are randomly selected, what is the probability that the average weight of the 15 tables will be between 41 and 56 pounds? What are you assuming about the distribution of the table weights?

8.67 The research and development department of a large oil company employs 253 engineers who have an average of 6.2 years of practical experience with a standard deviation of 2.1 years.

a. If a sample of 35 engineers is selected randomly without replacement, what is the probability that the average number of years of experience of the sample will be greater than 6.8 years?

b. If a sample of 35 engineers is selected randomly with replacement, what is the probability that the average number of years of experience will be greater than 6.8 years?

8.68 A CI for the mean of a normally distributed population is found to range from 70.1 to 80.2. What is the level of confidence for the CI if the sample size is 36 and the population standard deviation is 13.2?

8.69 A personnel administrator for Teltronix would like to estimate the amount of term life insurance that an employee carries. Three strata are used for finding a stratified random sample of all employees. From the data, construct a 95% CI for the mean amount of term life insurance that an employee carries (given in units of one thousand dollars).

Stratum	N_i: Total Number in Company	n_i	$\overline{X}_i$	s_i
Employees paid by the hour	350	67	28.5	5.7
Engineers and technicians	112	22	80.6	10.3
Management	57	11	125.2	13.6
	519	100		

8.70 A machine at a manufacturing plant fills sacks with 10 pounds of oats. Each case contains ten sacks of oats. The quality-control engineer would like to find a 99% CI for the mean weight per sack of oats. Using cases as clusters, construct the CI if eight cases are chosen at random. Assume that there is a total of 50 cases from which to choose.

Cases	Sacks per Case	Weight of Case
1	10	96.7
2	10	99.8
3	10	103.5
4	10	92.7
5	10	110.8
6	10	104.6
7	10	93.5
8	10	112.3

Hypothesis Testing for the Mean and Variance of a Population

A Look Back/Introduction

We have seen that statistical inference is used to estimate a population parameter using a sample statistic. For the rest of this book, the mean (μ) and standard deviation (σ) of your population will be unknown and will have to be estimated from the sample. Do not forget that even though you have estimated μ or σ, these values still are unknown and will remain unknown forever.

As a measure of how reliable your point estimate of the population mean μ really is, you can determine a confidence interval for this parameter. For a given confidence level, the narrower your resulting CI is, the more faith you can have in the ability of your sample mean $\overline{X}$ to provide an accurate estimate of the population mean. Also, with the Central Limit Theorem, you need not worry about the shape of your population (normal, exponential, etc.) before making probability statements regarding $\overline{X}$, provided you have a large sample. When you do, the distribution of $\overline{X}$ closely approaches the normal. This allows you to construct CIs for the population mean without worrying about the nature of your population, simply because it doesn't matter.

Next, we turn to the situation where someone makes a claim regarding the value of μ. For example, when dealing with the lifetime of Everglo light bulbs in Chapter 7, we assumed that the population average of *all* bulbs was $\mu = 400$ hours. Where did this value come from? Suppose that Everglo advertisements claim that the average lifetime of the bulbs is 400 hours. By testing a sample of bulbs, can we *prove* this statement? The answer is an emphatic no; the only way to know the value of μ exactly is to obtain data for *all* Everglo bulbs.

The sample, however, may allow us to reject the claim that μ is 400 hours, although since the sample is only a portion of the population, this conclusion may be incorrect. Such is the nature of hypothesis testing.

9.1

Hypothesis Testing on the Mean of a Population: Large Sample

A newspaper article claims that the average height of adult males in the United States is not the same as it was 50 years ago; it says the height is now 5.9′ (approximately 5′11″). Your firm manufactures clothing, so the value of this population mean is of vital interest to you. To investigate the article's claim, you randomly select 75 males and measure their heights.* Your results for $n = 75$ are $\bar{x} = 5.76'$ and $s = .48'$.

Let μ represent the population average (mean) of all U.S. male heights. We do have a point estimate of μ; namely, $\bar{x}$ = estimate of μ = 5.76′. Keep in mind that the actual value of μ is unknown (although it *does exist*) and will remain that way. All we can do is estimate it using our sample data. This situation can be summarized by considering the following pair of hypotheses.

Null hypothesis:

H_0: $\mu = 5.9'$

Alternative hypothesis:

H_a: $\mu \neq 5.9'$

H_0 asserts that the value of μ that has been claimed to be correct is in fact correct. H_a asserts that μ is some value other than 5.9′. The alternative hypothesis typically contains the conclusion that the researcher is attempting to demonstrate using the sample data. In our height example, if you do not believe that the average height is 5.9′, and you expect the data to demonstrate that μ has some other value, H_a is $\mu \neq 5.9'$.

The task of *all* tests of hypothesis is to **reject H_0** or **fail to reject (FTR) H_0**. Notice that we do not say "reject H_0 or accept H_0." This is an important distinction.

In our study of male heights, the (point) estimate of μ is $\bar{x} = 5.76'$. Should we reject H_0, given that it claims that μ is 5.9′? First, we need not worry about the shape of the underlying population of male heights because, by the CLT, $\bar{X}$ (for large samples) is approximately normally distributed, regardless of the shape of this population. So, $\bar{X}$ is approximately a normal (and thus continuous) random variable. What is the probability that *any* continuous random variable is equal to a certain value? In particular, what is the probability that $\bar{X}$ is exactly equal to 5.9′? The answer to both questions is zero. Thus we see that we cannot reject H_0 simply because $\bar{X}$ is not equal to 5.9′. What we do is to allow H_0 to stand, provided $\bar{X}$ is "close to" 5.9′, and reject H_0 otherwise. To define what "close" means, we need to take an in-depth look at what happens when you test hypotheses.

Type I and Type II Errors

Because the sample does not consist of the entire population, there always is the possibility of drawing an incorrect conclusion when inferring the value of a population

---

*The size of this sample is unrealistically small (yet large, statistically).

parameter using a sample statistic. When testing hypotheses, there are two types of possible error:

Type I error. This occurs if you reject H_0 when in fact it is true. For example, this would occur if you reject the claim (hypothesis) that the population mean is 5.9′ when in fact it really is true.

Type II error. This occurs if you fail to reject (FTR) H_0 when in fact H_0 is not true.

Actual Situation

Conclusion	H_0 **True**	H_0 **False**
FTR H_0	Correct decision	Type II error
Reject H_0	Type I error	Correct decision

For any test of hypothesis, define

α = the probability of rejecting H_0 when it is true = P(Type I error)

β = the probability of failing to reject H_0 when it is false = P(Type II error)

For any test of hypothesis, you would like to have control over n (the sample size), α (the probability of a Type I error), and β (the probability of a Type II error). However, in reality, you can control only two of these: n and α, n and β, or α and β. In other words, for a *fixed* sample size (n controlled), you cannot control both α and β.

Suppose you decide to set α = .02. This means that the procedure you use to test H_0 versus H_a will reject H_0 when it is true (Type I error) 2% of the time. You may wonder why we do not set α = 0, so we would never have a Type I error. The thought of never rejecting a correct H_0 sounds appealing, but the bad news is that β (the probability of a Type II error) is then equal to 1; that is, you will *always* fail to reject H_0 when it is false. If we set α = 0, then the resulting test of H_0 versus H_a will automatically fail to reject H_0: μ = 5.9′ whenever μ is, in fact, any value other than 5.9′. If, for example, μ is 7.5′ (hardly the case, but interesting), we would still fail to reject (FTR) H_0—not a good situation at all. We therefore need a value of α that offers a better compromise between the two types of error probabilities. (Note that, for the situation where α = 0 and β = 1, $\alpha + \beta$ = 1. As later examples will demonstrate, this is *not true* in general.)

The value of α you select depends on the relative importance of the two types of error. For example, consider the following hypotheses, and decide if the Type I error or the Type II error is the more serious.

You have just been examined by a physician using a sophisticated medical device, where

H_0: device indicates that you do not have a serious disease

H_a: device indicates that you do have the disease

α = P(rejecting H_0 when it is true) = P(device indicates that you have the disease when you do not have it)

β = P(FTR H_0 when in fact it is false) = P(devices indicates that you do not have the disease when you do have it)

For this situation, the Type I error (measured by α) is not nearly as serious as the Type II error (measured by β). Provided the treatment for the disease does you no serious harm if you are well, the Type I error is not serious. But the Type II error means you fail to receive the treatment even though you are ill.

We never set β in advance, only α. The smaller α is, the larger β is. Consequently, if you want β to be small, then you choose a large value of α. For most situations, the range of acceptable α values is .01 to .1.

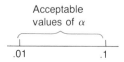

For the medical-device problem, you could choose a large value of α near .1 (or possibly larger) due to the seriousness of a Type II error. On the other hand, if you are more worried about Type I errors for a particular test (such as rejecting an expensive manufactured part that really is good), then a small value of α is in order. What if there is no basic difference in the effect of these two errors? If there is no significant difference between the effects of a Type I error versus a Type II error, researchers often choose an α of .05.

Performing a Statistical Test

The claim that the average adult male height is 5.9′ resulted in the following hypotheses:

H_0: $\mu = 5.9'$

H_a: $\mu \neq 5.9'$

We decide to use a test that will reject H_0 when it is correct, 5% of the time. So $\alpha = .05$. In hypothesis testing, α is referred to as the **significance level** of your test. Using $n = 75$, $\bar{x} = 5.76'$, and $s = .48'$, we wish to carry out the resulting statistical test of H_0 versus H_a. We decided to let H_0 stand (not reject it) if $\bar{X}$ was "close to" 5.9′. In other words, we will reject H_0 if $\bar{X}$ is "too far away" from 5.9′. We write this as follows:

Reject H_0 if $|\bar{X} - 5.9|$ is "too large"

or, by standardizing $\bar{X}$, we can

Reject H_0 if $\left| \dfrac{\bar{X} - 5.9}{s/\sqrt{n}} \right|$ is "too large"

We rewrite the last statement as

Reject H_0 if $\left| \dfrac{\bar{X} - 5.9}{s/\sqrt{n}} \right| > k$, for some k

What is the value of k? Here is where the value of α has an effect. If H_0 *is* true, and the sample size is large, then (using the CLT) $\bar{X}$ is approximately a normal random variable with

$$\text{mean} = \mu = 5.9'$$

$$\text{standard deviation} \cong \frac{s}{\sqrt{n}}$$

So, if H_0 is true, $(\bar{X} - 5.9)/(s/\sqrt{n})$ is approximately a standard normal random variable, Z, for large samples.† In this case, we reject H_0 if $|Z| > k$, for some k. Suppose $\alpha = .05$. Then,

$$.05 = \alpha = P(\text{rejecting } H_0 \text{ when it is true})$$

$$= P\left(\left|\frac{\bar{X} - 5.9}{s/\sqrt{n}}\right| > k, \text{ when } \mu = 5.9'\right)$$

$$= P(|Z| > k)$$

To find the value of k that satisfies this statement, consider Figure 9.1. When $|Z| > k$, either $Z > k$ or $Z < -k$, as illustrated. Since $P(|Z| > k) = .05$, then the total shaded area is .05, with .025 in each tail due to the symmetry of this curve. Consequently, the area between 0 and k is .475, and, using Table A-4, $k = 1.96$. So our test of H_0 versus H_a is

$$\text{Reject } H_0 \text{ if } \left|\frac{\bar{X} - 5.9}{s/\sqrt{n}}\right| > 1.96$$

and FTR H_0 otherwise. So,

$$\text{Reject } H_0 \text{ if } \frac{\bar{X} - 5.9}{s/\sqrt{n}} > 1.96$$

or

$$\text{Reject } H_0 \text{ if } \frac{\bar{X} - 5.9}{s/\sqrt{n}} < -1.96.$$

This test will reject H_0 when it is true, 5% of the time.

Using the sample data, we obtained $n = 75$, with $\bar{x} = 5.76'$ and $s = .48'$. Is $\bar{x} = 5.76'$ far enough away from $5.9'$ for us to reject H_0? This was not at all obvious at first glance; it may have seemed that this value of $\bar{X}$ is "close enough to" 5.9 for us to not reject H_0. Such is not the case, however, because

$$Z = \frac{\bar{X} - 5.9}{s/\sqrt{n}} = \frac{5.76 - 5.9}{.48/\sqrt{75}} = -2.53 = Z^*$$

where Z^* is the **computed value** of Z. Because $-2.53 < -1.96$, we reject H_0. We thus conclude that, based on the sample results and a value of $\alpha = .05$, the average population male height (μ) is not equal to $5.9'$.

Figure 9.1

The shaded area represents the significance level, α.

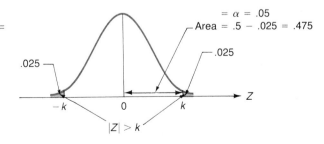

and FTR H_0 otherwise. So,

Figure 9.2

Distribution of $\overline{X}$ if H_0 is true (H_0: μ = 5.9′).

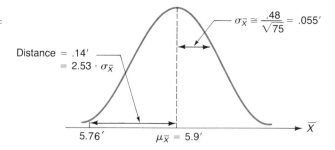

Another way of phrasing this result is to say that, if H_0 is true (that is, if μ = 5.9′), the value of $\overline{X}$ obtained from the sample (5.76′) is 2.53 standard deviations to the left of the mean using the normal curve for $\overline{X}$ (Figure 9.2). Because a value of $\overline{X}$ this far away from the mean is very unlikely (that is, with probability less than α = .05), our conclusion is that H_0 is not true, and so we reject it.

When testing μ = (some value) versus μ ≠ (some value), the null hypothesis, H_0, always contains the =, and the alternative hypothesis, H_a, always contains the ≠. In our example, this resulted in splitting the significance level, α, in half and including one-half in each tail of the test statistic, Z. Consequently, when testing H_0: μ = (some value) versus H_a: μ ≠ (some value), we refer to this as a **two-tailed test.**

Example 9.1

Using the data from our example of male heights, what would be the conclusion using a significance level α of .01?

Solution   The only thing that we need to change from our previous solution is the value of k. Now,

$$P(|Z| > k) = \alpha = .01$$

as shown in Figure 9.3. Using Table A-4, k = 2.575, and the test is (see Figure 9.4):

Reject H_0 if $Z > 2.575$ or $Z < -2.575$

What is the value of $(\overline{X} - 5.9′)/(s/\sqrt{n})$? Our data values have not changed, so the value of this expression is the same: $Z^* = -2.53$.

The shaded area in Figure 9.4 is the **rejection region.** The value of k (2.575) defining this region is the **critical value.** Z^* fails to fall in this region, so we FTR H_0. In other words, for α = .01, the value of $\overline{X}$ is "close enough" to 5.9 to let H_0 stand; there is insufficient evidence to conclude that μ is different from 5.9′.   ●

Figure 9.3

The shaded area is α = .01.

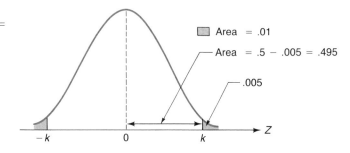

Figure 9.4

We reject H_0 if Z^* falls within either shaded area—the rejection region.

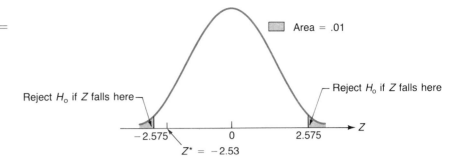

Reject H_o if Z falls here —

Area = .01

— Reject H_o if Z falls here

-2.575 0   2.575

$Z^* = -2.53$

Accepting H_0 or Failing to Reject (FTR) H_0?

Many researchers (and textbooks) fail to make a distinction between accepting and failing to reject (FTR) H_0, but there is a significant difference between these decisions. When you test a hypothesis, H_0 is *presumed innocent until it is demonstrated to be guilty*. In example 9.1, using $\alpha = .01$, we decided to FTR H_0. Now, how certain are we that μ is *exactly* 5.9'? After all, our estimate of μ is 5.76'. Clearly, we do not believe that μ is precisely 5.9'. There simply was not enough evidence to *reject* the claim that $\mu = 5.9'$.

For any hypothesis-testing application, the only hypothesis that can be *accepted* is the alternative hypothesis, H_a. Either there is sufficient evidence to *support* H_a (we reject H_0) or there is not (we fail to reject H_0). The focus of our attention is whether there is sufficient evidence within the sample data to conclude that H_a is correct. By failing to reject H_0, we are simply saying that the data do not allow us to support the claim made in H_a (such as $\mu \neq 5.9'$) and not that we accept the statement made in H_0 (such as $\mu = 5.9'$).

The Five-Step Procedure for Hypothesis Testing

The discussion up to this point has concentrated on hypothesis testing on the unknown mean of a particular population. We want to emphasize that the shape of your population is not important, provided you have a large sample. In other words, the population may be a normal (bell-shaped) one or it may not—it simply does not matter for large samples. The steps carried out when attempting to reject or failing to reject (FTR) a claim regarding the population mean μ are:

Step 1. *Set up the null hypothesis, H_0, and the alternative hypothesis, H_a.* If the purpose of the hypothesis test is to test whether the population mean is equal to a particular value (say, μ_0), the "equal hypothesis" always is stated in H_0 and the "unequal hypothesis" always is stated in H_a.

Step 2. *Define the test statistic.* This is evaluated, using the sample data, to determine if the data are compatible with the null hypothesis. For tests regarding the mean of a population using a large sample, the test statistic is approximately a standard normal random variable given by the equation

$$Z = \frac{\overline{X} - \mu_0}{s/\sqrt{n}} \qquad (9\text{-}1)$$

where μ_0 is the value of μ specified in H_0.

> **Step 3.** *Define* a *rejection region*, having determined a value for α, the significance level. In this region the value of the test statistic will result in rejecting H_0.
>
> **Step 4.** *Calculate the value of the test statistic, and carry out the test.* State your decision: to reject H_0 or to FTR H_0.
>
> **Step 5.** *Give a conclusion in the terms of the original problem or question.* This statement should be free of statistical jargon and should merely summarize the results of the analysis.
>
> Steps 1 through 5 apply to *all* tests of hypothesis in this and subsequent chapters. The form of the test statistic and rejection region change for different applications, but the sequence of steps always is the same.

Example 9.2

Remember that Everglo light bulbs are advertised as lasting 400 hours on average. As manager of the quality control department, you need to examine this claim closely. If the average lifetime is in fact less than 400 hours, you can expect at least a half-dozen government watchdog agencies knocking on your door. If the light bulbs last longer than the 400 hours (on the average) claimed, you want to revise your advertising accordingly. To check this claim, you have tested the lifetimes of 100 bulbs, each under the same circumstances (power load, room temperature, and so on). The results of this sample are $n = 100$, $\bar{x} = 411$ hours, and $s = 42.5$ hours. What conclusion would you reach using a significance level of .1?

Solution

Step 1. *Define the hypotheses.* We will test H_0: $\mu = 400$ versus H_a: $\mu \neq 400$.

Step 2. *Define the test statistic.* The proper test statistic for this problem is

$$Z = \frac{\bar{X} - 400}{s/\sqrt{n}}$$

Step 3. *Define the rejection region.* The steps for finding the rejection region (shaded) are shown in Figure 9.5. We conclude:

$$\text{Reject } H_0 \text{ if } Z > 1.645 \quad \text{or} \quad Z < -1.645.$$

Step 4. *Calculate the value of the test statistic and carry out the test.* The computed value of Z is

$$Z^* = \frac{411 - 400}{42.5/\sqrt{100}} = \frac{11}{4.25} = 2.59$$

Since $2.59 > 1.645$, our decision is to reject H_0. In Figure 9.5, Z^* falls in the rejection region.

Step 5. *State a conclusion.* Based on the sample data, there is sufficient evidence to conclude that the average lifetime of Everglo bulbs is not 400 hours. ●

Comments

In example 9.2, $\bar{X}$ was "far enough away from" 400 for us to reject the claim that the average lifetime is equal to 400 hours (H_0). However, remember that you cannot decide what is "far enough away from" without also considering the value of the standard deviation ($s = 42.5$ hours in example 9.2). This is why the value of s (or σ, if it is known) is a vital part of the test statistic.

Figure 9.5

See example 9.2; the rejection region is shaded.

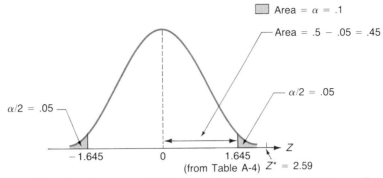

Examine the test statistic in example 9.2. Observe that the *smaller s* becomes, the *easier* it is to reject H_0. As s becomes smaller, the absolute value of the test statistic, Z, becomes larger, and the test statistic is more likely to be in the rejection region, for a given value of α.

Confidence Intervals and Hypothesis Testing

What is the relationship, if any, between a 95% CI and performing a *two-tailed* test using $\alpha = .05$? There is a very simple relationship here, namely, when testing $H_0: \mu = \mu_0$ versus $H_a: \mu \neq \mu_0$, using the five-step procedure and a significance level, α, H_0 will be rejected if and only if μ_0 does *not* lie in the $(1 - \alpha) \cdot 100\%$ CI for μ.

The five-step procedure and the CI procedure always lead to the same result. In fact, you can think of a CI as that set of values that would not be rejected by a two-tailed test of hypothesis.

In our heights of U.S. males example, a sample of 75 heights produced $\bar{x} = 5.76'$ and $s = .48'$. The resulting 95% CI for μ is

$$\bar{X} - k\left[\frac{s}{\sqrt{n}}\right] \qquad \text{to} \qquad \bar{X} + k\left[\frac{s}{\sqrt{n}}\right]$$

What is the value of k? The population standard deviation (σ) is unknown, so we need to use the t table (Table A-5). We do have a large sample, however, so the t value will be closely approximated by the corresponding Z value (Table A-4). Keep in mind that, when dealing with large samples, it really does not matter if σ is known or replaced by s. In either case, the standard normal table (Table A-4) gives us the probabilities we need.

The value of k that provides a 95% CI here is the *same* value of k that provides a two-tailed area under the Z curve equal to $1 - .95 = .05$. In other words, we use the same k value that we used in a two-tailed test of H_0 versus H_a—namely, $k = 1.96$. So the 95% CI for μ is

$$\bar{X} - 1.96(s/\sqrt{n}) \qquad \text{to} \qquad \bar{X} + 1.96(s/\sqrt{n})$$
$$= 5.76 - 1.96(.48/\sqrt{75}) \qquad \text{to} \qquad 5.76 + 1.96(.48/\sqrt{75})$$
$$= 5.76 - .11 \qquad \text{to} \qquad 5.76 + .11$$
$$= 5.65 \qquad \text{to} \qquad 5.87$$

The value of μ we are investigating here is $\mu = 5.9'$, and the resulting hypotheses were $H_0: \mu = 5.9$ and $H_a: \mu \neq 5.9'$. Using $\alpha = .05$, our result using the two-tailed test was to reject H_0. Using the CI procedure, we obtain the same result because 5.9 does not lie in the 95% CI.

Thus, if you already have computed a CI for μ, you can tell at a glance whether to reject H_0 for a two-tailed test, provided the significance level, α, for the hypothesis test and the confidence level, $(1 - \alpha) \cdot 100\%$, match up.

Example 9.3

Repeat the heights of U.S. males example using a 99% CI. Is the result the same as in example 9.1, where we failed to reject H_0: $\mu = 5.9$ using $\alpha = .01$?

Solution Using $\alpha = .01$, we failed to reject H_0 because the absolute value of the test statistic did not exceed the critical value of $k = 2.575$. The corresponding 99% CI for μ is

$$\overline{X} - 2.575(s/\sqrt{n}) \quad \text{to} \quad \overline{X} + 2.575(s/\sqrt{n})$$

$$= 5.76 - 2.575(.48/\sqrt{75}) \quad \text{to} \quad 5.76 + 2.575(.48/\sqrt{75})$$

$$= 5.76 - .143 \quad \text{to} \quad 5.76 + .143$$

$$= 5.617 \quad \text{to} \quad 5.903.$$

Because 5.9 does (barely) lie in this confidence interval, our decision is to FTR H_0—the same conclusion reached in example 9.1. ●

The Power of a Statistical Test

Up to this point, the probability of a Type II error, β, has remained a phantom—we know it is there, but we don't know what it is. One thing we *can* say is that a *wide* CI for μ means that the corresponding two-tailed test of H_0 versus H_a has a *large* chance of failing to reject a false H_0; that is, β is large. Now,

$$\beta = P(\text{FTR } H_0 \text{ if it is false})$$

which means that

$$1 - \beta = P(\text{rejecting } H_0 \text{ if it is false})$$

The value of $1 - \beta$ is referred to as the **power** of the test. Since we like β to be small, we prefer the power of the test to be large. Notice that $1 - \beta$ represents the probability of making a *correct* decision in the event that H_0 is false, because in this case we *should* reject it. The more powerful your test is, the better.

Determining the power of your test (hence, β) is not difficult. We will illustrate this procedure for the previous two-tailed test of H_0: $\mu = \mu_0$ versus H_a: $\mu \neq \mu_0$, for some μ_0. We will first consider the case where σ is known and then discuss the situation where σ is unknown.

Power of the Test: σ Known In example 9.2 we looked at the data on Everglo light bulbs, where the hypotheses were H_0: $\mu = 400$ hours and H_a: $\mu \neq 400$ hours. Assume that the actual population standard deviation is known to be $\sigma = 50$ hours. For this situation, our test statistic is (using a sample size of $n = 100$):

$$Z = \frac{\overline{X} - 400}{\sigma/\sqrt{n}} = \frac{\overline{X} - 400}{50/\sqrt{100}} = \frac{\overline{X} - 400}{5}$$

Proceeding as in example 9.2, using $\alpha = .10$, we reject H_0 if $Z > 1.645$ or $Z < -1.645$; that is, $|Z| > 1.645$. So, reject H_0 if $(\overline{X} - 400)/5 > 1.645$ (same as $\overline{X} > 400 + (1.645)(5) = 408.225$) or if $(\overline{X} - 400)/5 < -1.645$ (same as $\overline{X} < 400 - (1.645)(5) = 391.775$). This way of representing the rejection region is illustrated in Figure 9.6, using the shaded area under curve A.

Figure 9.6

The shaded area is the probability of rejecting H_0 if $\mu = 400$ (that is, $\alpha = .10$), and the striped area is the probability of rejecting H_0 if $\mu = 403$ (that is, the power of the test $1 - \beta$ when $\mu = 403$).

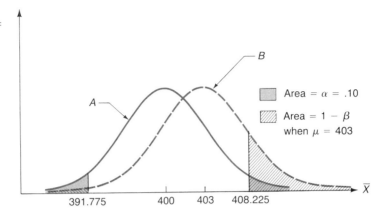

The power of this test is

$$1 - \beta = P(\text{rejecting } H_0 \text{ if } H_0 \text{ is false})$$
$$= P(\text{rejecting } H_0 \text{ if } \mu \neq 400)$$

What is the power of this test if μ is not 400 but is 403? What you have here is a value of $1 - \beta$ for *each* value of $\mu \neq 400$.

Recall that we reject H_0 if $\overline{X} > 408.225$ or $\overline{X} < 391.775$. The probability of this occurring *if* $\mu = 403$ is illustrated as the lined area under curve B in Figure 9.6. Now, if $\mu = 403$ and $\sigma = 50$ (assumed), then

$$Z = \frac{\overline{X} - 403}{50/\sqrt{n}} = \frac{\overline{X} - 403}{5}$$

is a standard normal random variable. So, in Figure 9.6, the striped area to the right of 408.225 is

$$P(\overline{X} > 408.225) = P\left[\frac{\overline{X} - 403}{5} > \frac{408.225 - 403}{5}\right]$$
$$= P\left[Z > \frac{5.225}{5}\right]$$
$$= P(Z > 1.04) = .5 - .3508$$
$$= .1492$$

Also, the striped area to the left of 391.775 is

$$P(\overline{X} < 391.775) = P\left[\frac{\overline{X} - 403}{5} < \frac{391.775 - 403}{5}\right]$$
$$= P(Z < -2.24) = .5 - .4875$$
$$= .0125$$

Adding these two areas, we find that, if $\mu = 403$, the power of the test of H_0: $\mu = 400$ versus H_a: $\mu \neq 400$ is

$$1 - \beta = .1492 + .0125 = .1617$$

This means that, if $\mu = 403$, the probability of making a Type II error (not rejecting H_0) is $\beta = 1 - .1617 = .8383$ (rather high).

The power of your test increases (β decreases) as μ moves away from 400. This is illustrated in Figure 9.7. Using the five-step procedure, which uses the test statistic $Z = (\overline{X} - 400)/(\sigma/\sqrt{n})$, the resulting power curve is the solid line curve in Figure 9.7. It is symmetric, and its lowest point is located at $\mu = 400$. For this value of μ, H_0 is actually true, so that a Type II error was *not* committed. Nevertheless, the value on the power curve corresponding to $\mu = 400$ is always

$$P(\text{rejecting } H_0 \text{ if } \mu = 400) = \alpha = .10 \text{ (for this example)}$$

The *steeper* your power curve is, the better. You are more apt to reject H_0 as μ moves away from 400—certainly a nice property. If we assume that the sampled population is normally distributed, Figure 9.7 illustrates that the power curve using the five-step procedure lies above (is steeper than) the power curve for *any* other testing procedure. To illustrate briefly another testing procedure, rather than basing the test statistic on the sample mean $\overline{X}$, we could derive a test statistic using the sample *median*. The resulting power curve for this procedure will lie *below* the one using $\overline{X}$, indicating that the test using the sample median is less powerful and thus inferior. So, in this sense, the five-step procedure defines the best (most powerful) test of H_0: $\mu = \mu_0$ versus H_a: $\mu \neq \mu_0$.

Power of the Test: σ Unknown When σ is unknown, we are forced to *approximate* the power of the test by replacing σ with the sample estimate, s. We are dealing with large samples, so we can use Table A-4 (the Z table).

In our discussion of the power of our test for Everglo bulb lifetimes, we treated the population standard deviation, σ, as known. If we make no assumptions about this parameter, we need to approximate the power of the test for $\mu = 403$. We assume $s = 42.5$ hours (as before) and use $\alpha = .10$.

We will now reject H_0 if

$$\overline{X} > 400 + 1.645\left[\frac{s}{\sqrt{n}}\right] \quad \text{or} \quad \overline{X} < 400 - 1.645\left[\frac{s}{\sqrt{n}}\right]$$

So, H_0 is rejected, provided

$$\overline{X} > 400 + 1.645\left[\frac{42.5}{\sqrt{100}}\right] = 406.99$$

or

$$\overline{X} < 400 - 1.645\left[\frac{42.5}{\sqrt{100}}\right] = 393.01$$

Figure 9.7

Power curve for H_0: $\mu = 400$ versus H_a: $\mu \neq 400$.

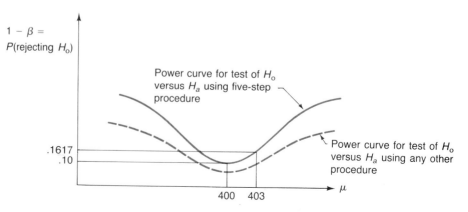

The resulting power of the test for $\mu = 403$ is approximately equal to

$$P(\bar{X} > 406.99 \text{ if } \mu = 403) + P(\bar{X} < 393.01 \text{ if } \mu = 403)$$

$$= P\left[Z > \frac{406.99 - 403}{42.5/\sqrt{100}}\right] + P\left[Z < \frac{393.01 - 403}{42.5/\sqrt{100}}\right]$$

$$= P(Z > .94) + P(Z < -2.35)$$

$$= (.5 - .3264) + (.5 - .4906) = .1736 + .0094$$

$$= .183$$

Exercises

9.1 The vice-president of Metropolitan Bank must decide whether to grant a large loan to an independent energy-exploration company. Consider the null hypothesis: the energy-exploration company will pay back the entire loan.

a. Describe the four possible outcomes from deciding either to fail to reject the null hypothesis or to reject the null hypothesis.

b. Which of the two errors, type I or type II, is more serious?

c. If the energy-exploration company does not qualify for the loan, does this "prove" that the energy-exploration company would not pay back the entire loan?

9.2 State what type of error can be made in the following situations:

a. The conclusion is to reject the null hypothesis.

b. The conclusion is to fail to reject the null hypothesis.

c. The calculated value of the test statistic does not fall in the rejection region.

9.3 Explain why the following situations are true or false.

a. The probability of the type I error and the probability of the type II error always add to one.

b. Increasing the value of α increases the value of β.

c. A large value for the power at a specified value of the alternative hypothesis indicates a small value for the probability of a type II error given the specified value stated in the alternative hypothesis.

d. The smaller the specified value of α is, the larger the rejection region.

9.4 Hallman Industrial is interested in testing the null hypothesis that a particular applicant is qualified for the position of marketing strategist.

a. Explain what the type I and type II errors are for this situation.

b. Which of the two errors in question a is more serious?

9.5 The mean of a normally distributed population is believed to be equal to 50.1. A sample of 36 observations is taken and the sample mean is found to be 53.2. The alternative hypothesis is that the population mean is not equal to 50.1. Complete the hypothesis test, assuming that the population standard deviation is equal to four. Use a .05 significance level.

9.6 Given the following statistics, perform the hypothesis test that the mean of a normally distributed population is equal to 30:

$n = 75$

$\bar{x} = 27.4$

$s^2 = 9$

Use a significance level of .05.

9.7 The weights of fish in a certain pond that is regularly stocked are considered to be normally distributed with a standard deviation of 1.1 pounds. A random sample of size 30 is selected from the pond and the sample mean is found to be 2.4 pounds. Test the null hypothesis that the mean weight of fish in the pond is 3.1 pounds. Use a 10% significance level.

9.8 An all-natural breakfast cereal claims that there is .4 milligrams of sodium per ounce of cereal. To test the claim, the following statistics are gathered from 60 randomly selected boxes of cereal:

$n = 60$

$\bar{x} = .35$ milligrams per ounce

$s = .03$ milligrams per ounce

Test this hypothesis at the .05 significance level.

9.9 A 95% CI for the mean time that it takes a city bus to complete its route is 2.2 hours to 2.6 hours. The time that it takes the bus to complete its route is normally distributed. Test the null hypothesis that the mean time to complete the route is 2.0 hours, using a 5% significance level.

9.10 The life span of an electronic chip used in a high-powered microcomputer is estimated to be 625.35 hours from a random sample of 40 chips. The life of an electronic chip is considered to be normally distributed with a population variance of 400 hours.

a. Find a 90% CI for the mean life of the electronic chips.

b. Using the answer to question a, test the null hypothesis that the mean life of the electronic chips is equal to 633 hours. Use a 10% significance level.

9.11 The manufacturer of a special-purpose industrial pipe is interested in testing the hypothesis that the mean diameter of the pipes is 12.75 inches. A sample of 100 pipes was randomly selected and the diameters were measured. The sample mean was found to be 12.73 inches and the sample standard deviation was found to be .01.

a. Find a 99% CI for the mean diameter of the pipes.

b. Test the null hypothesis that the mean diameter of the pipes is 12.75 inches, using a 1% significance level.

9.12 The hypotheses for a situation are

$H_0: \mu = 20$

$H_a: \mu \neq 20$

If the population of interest is normally distributed, what is the power of the test for the mean if μ is actually equal to 22? Assume that a sample of size 49 is used and the sample standard deviation is 4.2. Use a significance level of .05.

9.13 Find the power of the test for the mean for the following situations if the true population mean is 30 and the population variance is 25. Use a 10% significance level.

a. $H_0: \mu = 26, H_a: \mu \neq 26, n = 20$

b. $H_0: \mu = 36, H_a: \mu \neq 36, n = 25$

c. $H_0: \mu = 33, H_a: \mu \neq 33, n = 25$

9.14 An electro-optical firm currently uses a laser component in producing sophisticated graphic designs. The time it takes to produce a certain design with the current laser component is 70 seconds, with a standard deviation of 8 seconds. A new laser component is bought by the firm because it is believed that the time it takes this laser to produce the same design is not equal to 70 seconds, and has a standard deviation of 8 seconds. The research-and-development department is interested in constructing the power curve for testing the claim that the time it takes to produce the same design by the new laser component is not equal to 70 seconds. Graph the power function for a sample of size 25 and a significance level of .05.

9.15 Fermet's Soup is interested in knowing how much the average homemaker spends on soup and ingredients to make soup per month. The company's marketing analyst takes a sample of 100 homemakers from a certain city and finds the standard deviation of the amount spent monthly on soup to be $1.50. What would be the power of the test for the hypothesis that the monthly expenditure on soup is equal to $8 if the true monthly expenditure on soup was $10? Assume a significance level of .05.

9.16 Explain why the sample mean, rather than the sample median, is used as a basis for testing the hypothetical mean of a normally distributed population.

9.2

One-Tailed Test for the Mean of a Population: Large Sample

There are many situations in which you are interested in demonstrating that the mean of a population is *larger* or *smaller* than some specified value. For example, as a member of a consumer-advocate group, you may be attempting to demonstrate that the average weight of a bag of sugar for a particular brand is not ten lbs (as specified on the bag) but is in fact less than ten lbs. Because the situation that you are attempting to demonstrate goes into the alternative hypothesis, the resulting hypotheses would be H_0: $\mu \geq 10$ and H_a: $\mu < 10$. Remember that we said it is standard practice always to put the *equal sign* in the *null* hypothesis. Another approach to stating H_0 is to consider only its **boundary value,** and so the hypotheses would be written

$$H_0: \mu = 10$$
$$H_a: \mu < 10$$

In this way, we can identify the distribution of $\overline{X}$ when H_0 is *true*—namely, $\overline{X}$ is a normal random variable centered at ten with standard deviation $s/\sqrt{n}$ (or $\sigma/\sqrt{n}$ if σ is known). Because the focus of our attention is on H_a (can we support it or not?), which of the two ways you use to write H_0 is not an important issue. The procedure for testing H_0 versus H_a is the same regardless of how you state H_0.

The resulting test is referred to as a **one-tailed test,** and it uses the same five-step procedure as the two-tailed test. The only change we make is to modify the rejection region.

Example 9.3

A foreign car manufacturer advertises that its newest model, the Bullet, rarely stops at gas stations. In fact, they claim its EPA rating for highway driving is at least 32.5 mpg. However, the results of a recent independent study determined the mpg for 50 identical models of the Bullet, with these results: $n = 50$, $\overline{x} = 30.4$ mpg, and $s = 5.3$ mpg. This report failed to offer any conclusion, and you have been asked to interpret these results by someone who has always felt that the 32.5 figure is too high. What would be your conclusion using a significance level of $\alpha = .05$?

Solution

Step 1. An important point to be made here is that H_0 and H_a (as well as α) must be defined *before* you observe any data. In other words, *do not let the data dictate your hypotheses;* this would introduce a serious bias into your final outcome. For this application, we want to demonstrate that the population mean, μ, is less than 32.5 mpg, and so this goes into H_a. The appropriate hypotheses then are H_0: $\mu \geq 32.5$ and H_a: $\mu < 32.5$.

Step 2. The test statistic for a one-tailed test is the same as that for a two-tailed test, namely,

$$Z = \frac{\overline{X} - \mu_0}{s/\sqrt{n}} \quad \text{or, if } \sigma \text{ is known,} \quad \frac{\overline{X} - \mu_0}{\sigma/\sqrt{n}}$$

$$= \frac{\overline{X} - 32.5}{s/\sqrt{n}}$$

Step 3. What happens to Z when H_a is true? Here we would expect $\overline{X}$ to be < 32.5 (because μ is), so the value of Z should be negative. Consequently, our procedure will be to reject H_0 if Z lies "too far to the left" of zero; that is,

$$\text{Reject } H_0 \text{ if } Z = \frac{\overline{X} - 32.5}{s/\sqrt{n}} < k \text{ for some } k < 0$$

Since $\alpha = .05$, we will choose a value of k (the critical value) such that the resulting test will reject H_0 (shoot down the mpg claim) when it is true, 5% of the time. This amounts to defining a rejection region in the *left tail* of the Z curve, the shaded area in Figure 9.8. Using Table A-4, we see that the critical value is $k = -1.645$, and the resulting test of H_0 versus H_a is

$$\text{Reject } H_0 \text{ if } Z = \frac{\overline{X} - 32.5}{s/\sqrt{n}} < -1.645$$

Step 4. Using the sample results, the value of the test statistic is

$$Z^* = \frac{30.4 - 32.5}{5.3/\sqrt{50}} = -2.80$$

Because $-2.80 < -1.645$, the decision is to reject H_0.

Step 5. The results of this study support the claim that the average mileage for the Bullet is *less than* 32.5 mpg. This would provide just cause for claiming false advertising by the auto manufacturer. ●

One-Tailed Test or Two-Tailed Test?

The decision to use a one-tailed test or a two-tailed test depends on what you are attempting to demonstrate. For example, when the quality-control department of a manufacturing facility receives a shipment from one of its vendors and wants to determine if the product meets minimal specifications, a one-tailed test is appropriate. If the product does not meet specifications, it will be rejected. This problem was first

Figure 9.8

The shaded area is the one-tailed rejection region. We reject H_0 if Z = $(\overline{X} - 32.5)/(s/\sqrt{n}) <$ -1.645.

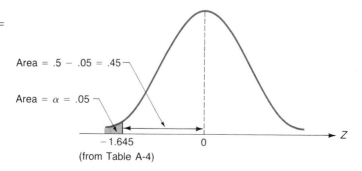

Area = .5 − .05 = .45

Area = α = .05

−1.645

0

Z

(from Table A-4)

encountered in Chapter 6, when we examined lot acceptance sampling. Here, the product is *not* checked to see whether it *exceeds* specifications because any product that exceeds specifications is acceptable.

On the other hand, the vendors who supply the products would generally run two-tailed tests to determine two things. First, they must know if the product meets the minimal specifications of their customers before they ship it. Second, they must determine whether the product greatly exceeds specifications because this can be very costly in production. If they are making a product that in effect is too well built, this costs them extra money.

The testing of electric fuses is a classic example of a two-tailed test. A fuse must break when it reaches the prescribed temperature or a fire will result. However, the fuse must not break before it reaches the prescribed temperature or it will shut off the electricity when there is no need to do so. Therefore, the quality-control procedures for testing fuses must be two-tailed.

Example 9.4

The mean consumption of electricity for the month of June at the Southern States Power Company (SSPC) historically has been 918 kilowatt-hours per residential customer. As part of its request for a rate increase, SSPC is arguing that the power consumption for June of the current year is substantially higher. To demonstrate this, they hired an independent consulting firm to examine a random sample of customer accounts. The results of the sample were: $n = 60$ customers, $\bar{x} = 952.36$ kilowatt-hours, and $s = 173.92$ kilowatt-hours. Can you conclude that the average consumption for all users during June of this year (denoted as μ) is larger than 918? Use $\alpha = .01$.

Solution

Step 1. The hypotheses here are H_0: $\mu \leq 918$ and H_a: $\mu > 918$.

Step 2. The correct test statistic is

$$Z = \frac{\bar{X} - 918}{s/\sqrt{n}}$$

Step 3. For this situation, what happens to Z if H_a is true? The value of $\bar{X}$ should then be *larger* than 918 (on the average), resulting in a *positive* value of Z. So we

$$\text{Reject } H_0 \text{ if } Z = \frac{\bar{X} - 918}{s/\sqrt{n}} > k \text{ for some } k > 0$$

Examine the standard normal curve in Figure 9.9, where the area corresponding to α is the shaded part of the *right tail;* using Table A-4, the critical value is $k = 2.33$. The test of H_0 versus H_a will be

$$\text{Reject } H_0 \text{ if } Z > 2.33$$

Figure 9.9

One-tailed rejection region; reject H_0 if $Z > 2.33$.

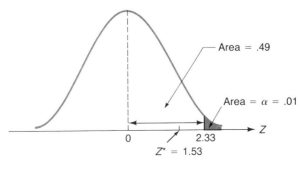

Area = .49

Area = α = .01

0   2.33

$Z^* = 1.53$

Step 4. The value of your test statistic is

$$Z^* = \frac{952.36 - 918}{173.92/\sqrt{60}} = 1.53$$

Step 5. Using this value of α, there is insufficient evidence to support the power company's claim that the power consumption for June has increased.

    This result is very much tied to the value of α. Using $\alpha = .10$ in example 9.4, we would obtain the *opposite* conclusion—which you may find somewhat disturbing. You often hear the expression that "statistics lie." This is not true—statistics are merely mistreated, either intentionally or accidentally. One can often obtain the desired conclusion by choosing the value of α that produces a desired conclusion. We therefore reemphasize that you must choose α by weighing the seriousness of a Type I versus a Type II error *before* seeing the data. A partial remedy for this dilemma will be discussed in section 9.3.

Large Samples Taken from a Finite Population

For applications in which we take a large sample from a finite population, we make a slight adjustment to the standard error of $\overline{X}$ by including the finite population correction (fpc) factor.

    For the finite population case, the standard error (standard deviation) of $\overline{X}$ is not $s/\sqrt{n}$ but instead

$$\text{standard error of } \overline{X} = s_{\overline{X}} = \frac{s}{\sqrt{n}} \sqrt{\frac{N - n}{N - 1}} \tag{9-2}$$

Once again using the results of the CLT, the test statistic is an *approximate* standard normal random variable, given by

$$Z = \frac{\overline{X} - \mu_0}{s_{\overline{X}}}$$

As a result, the five-step procedure can be carried out exactly as before.

Example 9.5

In example 8.4, we considered a sample of 45 incomes from a group of female managers at Compumart. The women wished to demonstrate that the average income of the population of 350 female middle managers was less than \$48,000. For this illustration, it was assumed that the population standard deviation was known. Because this assumption is *not necessary* (and perhaps incorrect), a safer procedure would be to use the sample estimate, s. The results of the sample were: $n = 45$, $\bar{x} = \$43,900$, and $s = \$7140$.

    What would be your conclusion from these results, using a significance level of $\alpha = .05$?

Solution

Step 1. The hypotheses are H_0: $\mu \geqslant 48,000$ and H_a: $\mu < 48,000$ where $\mu =$ the average annual income for all females in middle-management positions at Compumart.

Step 2. The corresponding test statistic here is

$$Z = \frac{\overline{X} - 48,000}{s_{\overline{X}}}$$

where

$$s_{\overline{X}} = \frac{s}{\sqrt{n}} \sqrt{\frac{N - n}{N - 1}}$$

Step 3. Using Figure 9.8, the rejection region is: Reject H_0 if $Z < -1.645$

Step 4. Here,

$$s_{\overline{X}} = \frac{7140}{\sqrt{45}} \sqrt{\frac{350 - 45}{350 - 1}} = 995.01$$

so our computed test statistic is

$$Z^* = \frac{43,900 - 48,000}{995.01} = -4.12$$

Since $-4.12 < -1.645$, we (strongly) reject H_0 in favor of H_a.

Step 5. The sample results strongly support the assertion that the female middle managers are underpaid. We reached the same conclusion in example 8.4, where we based this decision on the extremely small probability of observing a value of $\overline{X}$ this small if μ was in fact $48,000. ●

Comment

As mentioned in Chapter 8, the fpc factor of $(N - n)/(N - 1)$ can be ignored whenever your sample size is less than 5% of the population size; that is, when $n/N < .05$. Such is also the case when using the fpc in hypothesis testing.

Large Sample Tests on a Population Mean

TWO-TAILED TEST

$H_0\colon \mu = \mu_0$

$H_a\colon \mu \neq \mu_0$

Reject H_0 if $|Z| > Z_{\alpha/2}$ where $Z = (\overline{X} - \mu_0)/s_{\overline{x}}$ ($Z_{\alpha/2} = 1.96$ for $\alpha = .05$)

ONE-TAILED TEST

$H_0\colon \mu \leq \mu_0$	$H_0\colon \mu \geq \mu_0$
$H_a\colon \mu > \mu_0$	$H_a\colon \mu < \mu_0$
Reject H_0 if $Z > Z_\alpha$	Reject H_0 if $Z < -Z_\alpha$
($Z_\alpha = 1.645$ for $\alpha = .05$)	($-Z_\alpha = -1.645$ for $\alpha = .05$)

For a finite population with $n/N > .05$,

$$s_{\overline{x}} = \frac{s}{\sqrt{n}} \sqrt{\frac{N - n}{N - 1}}$$

Otherwise,

$$s_{\overline{x}} = \frac{s}{\sqrt{n}}$$

Exercises

9.17 Find the rejection region of the Z statistic in a hypothesis test of the population mean for the following situations:

a. It is believed that the mean monthly advertising expenditure for a company was greater than $2000. A significance level of .05 is used.

b. It is believed that the average length of sick time taken by an employee for firm XYZ is equal to 5.2 days per year. A significance level of .10 is used.

c. It is believed that the mean age of an applicant applying for a particular job is less than 25 years. A significance level of .01 is used.

9.18 A sample of size 20 is drawn from a finite population of size 225. The finite population can be approximated by a normal distribution. The sample of size 20 yields a sample mean of 75.8. The population variance is equal to 16. Test the null hypothesis that the mean of the population is equal to 82.5. Use a 10% significance level and a two-tailed test.

9.19 Carry out the hypothesis test for the mean of the normally distributed population given the following information:

H_0: $\mu \geq 4.5$ $\bar{x} = 3.9$

H_a: $\mu < 4.5$ $\sigma = 1.12$

$n = 30$ $\alpha = .07$

9.20 Given the following statistics, perform the hypothesis test that the mean of a normally distributed population is greater than 10.31:

$n = 48$ $\bar{x} = 12.03$ $s = 1.8$

Use a significance level of .05.

9.21 A delivery company claims that the mean time it takes to deliver frozen food between two particular cities is less than 3.7 hours. A random sample of 50 deliveries yielded a sample mean of 3.3 hours with a sample standard deviation of .2 hours. Test the delivery company's claim using a 10% significance level.

9.22 An auditing firm would like to test the hypothesis that the average customer of a small town's utility service pays the utility bill in less than 15 days after receipt of the bill. The town has only 12,352 customers. A sample of size 1325 yields a sample mean of 14.6 days in which a customer payed the utility bill. The sample standard deviation is 6 days. Test the hypothesis using a 5% significance level.

9.23 Two-hundred and fifty applicants apply for the same position at an assembly plant. A random sample of 25 applicants is reviewed carefully. The average experience of the 25 applicants is 3.4 years. Can it be concluded that the mean experience of the 250 applicants is greater than 2.5 years at a significance level of .05? Assume that the population standard deviation of the experience of the 250 applicants is 1.3 years.

9.24 The quality-control engineer of a battery-manufacturing firm has been asked to verify that the marketing department's claim that the mean life of the multipurpose battery made by the firm is greater than 47 hours. The quality-control engineer takes a random sample of 80 batteries and finds the sample mean to be 47.5 hours with a sample standard deviation of 1.6 hours. Can the marketing department's claim be rejected at the .05 significance level?

9.25 The owners of a shopping center are contemplating increasing the parking space in front of the shopping center. The owners would like to demonstrate that the average driver parks for more than .75 hours. The length of time parked is considered to be normally distributed. A random sample of 45 parked cars is observed; the average time parked was .80 hours with a standard deviation of .12. Test the hypothesis using a 10% significance level.

9.26 Bobby Marks is seriously considering investing in the grocery business in the southeast United States. He believes that the industry's average return on sales (ROS) is 5%. A random sample of 46 such businesses in various sectors of southeast United States revealed that

$$\bar{x} = 4.6\% \qquad s = 1.2\%$$

Test Marks' belief concerning the ROS of the grocery business in the southeast United States, using a 4% significance level.

9.3

Reporting Testing Results Using a *p*-Value

In example 9.1, we noted that for one value of α we rejected H_0, and for another (seemingly reasonable) value of α we failed to reject H_0. Is there a way of summarizing the results of a test of hypothesis that allows you to determine whether these results are barely significant (or insignificant) or overwhelmingly significant (or insignificant)? Did we barely reject H_0, or did H_0 go down in flames?

A convenient way to summarize your results is to use a *p*-value, often called the *achieved* α or *achieved significance level*.

> The **p-value** is the value of α at which the hypothesis test procedure changes conclusions. It is the *smallest* value of α for which you can reject H_0 (that is, at which the test is significant).

Consequently, the *p*-value is the point at which the five-step procedure leads us to switch from rejecting H_0 to failing to reject H_0.

Determining the *p*-Value

The *p*-value for *any* test is determined by replacing the area corresponding to α by the area corresponding to the *computed* value of the test statistic. In our discussion and example 9.1, using $\alpha = .05$ you reject H_0, and using $\alpha = .01$ you fail to reject H_0. We know that the *p*-value here is between .01 and .05. For this example, the computed value of the test statistic was $Z^* = -2.53$, where the hypotheses are H_0: $\mu = 5.9'$ and H_a: $\mu \neq 5.9'$. The Z curve for this situation is shown in Figure 9.10.

For which value of α does the testing procedure change the conclusions here? In Figure 9.10, if you were using a predetermined significance level α, you would split α in half and put $\alpha/2$ into each tail. So the total tail area represents α. Using Figure 9.11, we reverse this procedure by finding the *total* tail area corresponding to a two-

Figure 9.10

Rejection regions for $\alpha = .01, .05$.

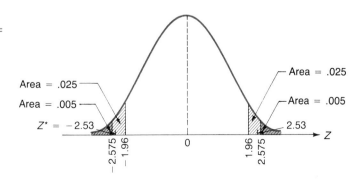

Figure 9.11

p-value is determined by replacing the area corresponding to α (see Figure 9.10) by the area corresponding to Z^*. Here $Z^* = -2.53$, and the p-value $= 2 \cdot .0057 = .0114$ (total shaded area).

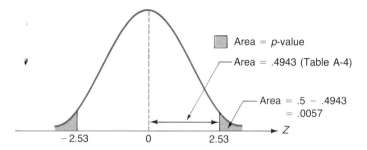

Area = p-value

Area = .4943 (Table A-4)

Area = $.5 - .4943$
  $= .0057$

tailed test with $Z^* = -2.53$; we add the area to the left of -2.53 (.0057) to that to the right of 2.53 (also .0057). This total area is .0114, which is the p-value for this application. Thus, if you choose a value of $\alpha > .0114$ (such as .05), you will reject H_0. If you choose a value of $\alpha < .0114$ (such as .01), you will fail to reject H_0.

Procedure for Finding the p-Value

1. For H_a: $\mu \neq \mu_0$

$p = 2$ (area outside of Z^*)

Reason: When using a significance level α, the value of α represents a *two*-tailed area.

2. For H_a: $\mu > \mu_0$

$p =$ area to the right of Z^*

Reason: When using a significance level α, the value of α represents a *right*-tailed area.

3. For H_a: $\mu < \mu_0$

$p =$ area to the left of Z^*

Reason: When using a significance level α, the value of α represents a *left*-tailed area.

Example 9.6

What is the p-value for example 9.4?

Solution The results of the sample were $n = 60$, $\bar{x} = 952.36$ kilowatt-hours, and $s = 173.92$ kilowatt-hours. The corresponding value of the test statistic was

$$Z^* = \frac{952.36 - 918}{173.92/\sqrt{60}} = 1.53$$

The alternative hypothesis is H_a: $\mu > 918$, so the p-value will be the area to the *right* of the computed value, 1.53, as illustrated in Figure 9.12. The p-value here is .063, which is consistent with the results of example 9.4, where we concluded that for $\alpha = .01$, you fail to reject H_0, and for $\alpha = .10$, you reject H_0. That is, the p-value is between .01 and .10. ●

Most statistical computer packages will provide you with the computed p-value when testing the mean of a population. The MINITAB solution to example 9.4 is

Figure 9.12

p-value for $Z^* = 1.53$.

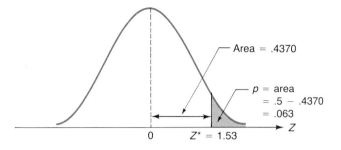

Figure 9.13

MINITAB solution for example 9.4.

```
MTB > SET INTO C1
DATA> 950.14 1006.79 1119.31 1115.08  ...
      .
      .    (the 60 data values)
      .

DATA> END


MTB > AVERAGE OF C1
   MEAN    =      952.36
MTB > STDEV OF C1
   ST.DEV. =      173.92
MTB > TTEST OF MU=918 USING C1;
SUBC> ALTERNATIVE=1.

TEST OF MU = 918.0 VS MU G.T. 918.0

             N      MEAN    STDEV   SE MEAN        T   P VALUE
  C1        60     952.4    173.9      22.4     1.53     0.066
```

Box pointing to ALTERNATIVE=1:
= 1 for H_a: $\mu > \mu_o$
= -1 for H_a: $\mu < \mu_o$
This step is not necessary for H_a: $\mu \neq \mu_o$

provided in Figure 9.13. This procedure assumes that the population standard deviation (σ) is unknown, and so it uses the command TTEST (as in *t* test). The *p*-value in Figure 9.13 is slightly different than the value obtained in example 9.6 since MINITAB uses the *t* distribution to obtain this value. We will discuss this point further in Section 9.4, but for now remember that the *t* random variable is closely approximated by the standard normal, *Z,* when using a large sample.

Interpreting the *p*-Value

We will consider two ways of using the *p*-value to arrive at a conclusion. The first is the classical approach that we have used up to this point: We choose a value for α and base our decision on this value. When using a *p*-value in this manner, the procedure is:

Reject H_0 if *p*-value $< \alpha$

FTR H_0 if *p*-value $\geq \alpha$

The second approach is a general rule of thumb that applies to most applications of hypothesis testing on μ. We previously stated that typical values of α range from .01 to .10. This implies that for most applications we will not see values of α smaller than .01 or larger than .1. With this in mind, the following rule can be defined:

Reject H_0 if the *p*-value is small ($p < .01$)

FTR H_0 if the *p*-value is large ($p > .1$)

Consequently, if $.01 \leq$ *p*-value $\leq .1$, the data are *inconclusive*.

The advantage of this approach is that you avoid having to choose a value of α; the disadvantage is that you may arrive at an inconclusive result.

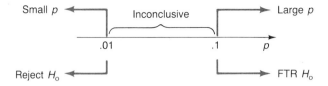

Now for a brief disclaimer: This rule does not apply to all situations. If a Type I error would be serious, and you prefer a very small value of α (using the classical approach), then you can lower the .01 limit. Similarly, you might raise the .1 limit if the Type II error is extremely critical and you prefer a large value for α. However, this gives a working procedure for most applications in business.

What can you conclude if the p-value is $p = .0001$? This value is extremely small as compared with *any* reasonable value of α. So we would strongly reject H_0. Consequently if, for example, you are making an investment decision based on these results, you can breathe a little easier. This data set supports H_a overwhelmingly. On the other hand, if $p = .65$, this value is large as compared with any reasonable value of α. Without question, we would fail to reject H_0.

There is yet one other interpretation of the p-value, summarized in the box below.

Another Interpretation of the p-Value

1. For a two-tailed test where $H_a: \mu \neq \mu_0$, the p-value is the probability that the value of the test statistic, Z^*, will be at least as large (in absolute value) as the observed Z^*, if μ is in fact equal to μ_0.
2. For a one-tailed test where $H_a: \mu > \mu_0$, the p-value is the probability that the value of the test statistic, Z^*, will be at least as large as the observed Z^*, if μ is in fact equal to μ_0.
3. For a one-tailed test where $H_a: \mu < \mu_0$, the p-value is the probability that the value of the test statistic, Z^*, will be at least as small as the observed Z^*, if μ is in fact equal to μ_0.

In example 9.6, we determined the p-value to be .063; the computed value of the test statistic was $Z^* = 1.53$; the hypotheses were $H_0: \mu \leq 918$ and $H_a: \mu > 918$. So the probability of observing a value of Z^* as large as 1.53 (≥ 1.53) if μ is 918 is $p = .063$.

Based on this description of the p-value, if p is small, conclude that H_0 is not true and reject it. We obtain precisely the same result using the classical and "rule-of-thumb" options of the p-value. Small values of p favor H_a, and large values favor H_0.

Example 9.7

In example 9.5, we performed a one-tailed test of $H_0: \mu \geq 48,000$ and $H_a: \mu < 48,000$. The sample results were $n = 45$, $\bar{x} = \$43,900$, and $s = \$7140$. The calculated value of the test statistic was

$$Z^* = \frac{43,900 - 48,000}{s_{\bar{x}}}$$

where

$$s_{\bar{x}} = \frac{s}{\sqrt{n}} \sqrt{\frac{N-n}{N-1}}$$

$$= \frac{7140}{\sqrt{45}} \sqrt{\frac{350-45}{350-1}} = 995.01$$

so $Z^* = -4.12$.

1. What is your conclusion based on the corresponding p-value, using $\alpha = .05$?
2. Without specifying a value of α, what would be your conclusion based on the calculated p-value?
3. Interpret the p-value for this application.

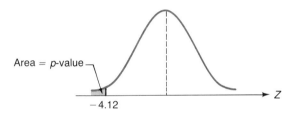

Area = p-value

-4.12

Z

Solution 1 We are unable to determine the p-value exactly using Table A-4; however, this area is roughly the same as the area to the left of -4.0 under the Z curve—namely, $.5 - .49997 = .00003$. So $p \cong .00003$. Because p is less than $\alpha = .05$, we reject H_0. Our conclusion is the same as that of example 9.5 (which also used $\alpha = .05$), where we concluded that the female managers were underpaid.

Solution 2 We use the general rule of thumb for interpreting the p-value. Since $p \cong .00003$; it is extremely small, so we strongly reject H_0 (same conclusion as Solution 1).

Solution 3 We can make the following statements:

1. The significance level at which the conclusion indicated by the testing procedure changes is $\alpha = .00003$.
2. The smallest significance level for which you can reject the null hypothesis is $\alpha = .00003$.
3. The probability of observing a value of the test statistic as small as the one obtained (≤ -4.12) is $.00003$, if in fact the population mean is \$48,000. ●

Practical Versus Statistical Significance

Researchers often calculate what appears to be a conclusive result without considering the practical significance of their findings. For example, consider a situation similar to the one described in example 9.3; this time, a sample of 1000 Bullets, tested under normal highway conditions, results in a sample average of $\bar{x} = 32.32$ mpg, with a standard deviation of $s = 2.15$ mpg. Advertising for this car claims that the mpg under test conditions is at least 32.5 mpg. Is there sufficient evidence to reject this claim?

The hypotheses are $H_0: \mu \geq 32.5$ and $H_a: \mu < 32.5$. The value of the test statistic is

$$Z^* = \frac{\overline{X} - 32.5}{s/\sqrt{n}} = \frac{32.32 - 32.5}{2.15/\sqrt{1000}} = -2.65$$

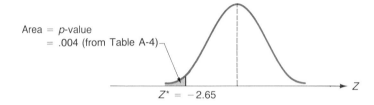

Area = p-value
= .004 (from Table A-4)

$Z^* = -2.65$

The p-value here is the area to the left of -2.65 under the Z curve, which (from Table A-4) is .004. Based on this small p-value, we reject H_0 and conclude (as we did in example 9.3) that the mpg for these cars under normal highway conditions is *less* than 32.5. Statistically speaking, this is correct, and the data do provide sufficient evidence to support the statement that their mpg claim is overstated. As a consumer, however, how concerned would you be that the sample average ($\overline{x} = 32.32$) is (only) .18 mpg under the advertised level? In other words, in a practical sense, how misleading is the Bullet advertising?

What we have seen is that $\overline{X}$ is far enough away from 32.5 (in a statistical sense) to conclude that μ is less than 32.5 mpg. However, perhaps in the eyes of a consumer about to invest $15,000 in a new car, this value of $\overline{X}$ is really "close enough" to 32.5.

Moral: You can begin to see that you must be careful when you interpret statistical results. Do not confuse a statistically significant result with one that is significant in a practical sense. In the latter case, what is a significant result is, of course, subjective. The responsibility for determining practical significance lies with the person who wishes to act on the basis of the conclusions obtained from the sample data.

Exercises

9.27 State whether you would reject or fail to reject the null hypothesis in each of the following cases.

a. $p = .12$, $\alpha = .05$.

b. $p = .03$, $\alpha = .05$.

c. $p = .001$, $\alpha = .01$.

d. $p = .01$, $\alpha = .001$.

9.28 Using the rule-of-thumb option (not selecting a value of α) in the interpretation of the p-value, state whether the test statistic would be statistically significant in the following situations.

a. $p = .57$.

b. $p = .008$.

c. $p = .12$.

d. $p = .04$.

9.29 Explain the difference between "significance" in a statistical sense and "significance" in a practical sense.

9.30 Find p-values for the following situations with calculated test statistics given by Z^*.

a. H_0: $\mu = 30$, H_a: $\mu \neq 30$, $Z^* = 2.38$

b. H_0: $\mu \leq 20$, H_a: $\mu > 20$, $Z^* = 1.645$

c. H_0: $\mu \geq 15$, H_a: $\mu < 15$, $Z^* = -2.54$

d. H_0: $\mu = 50$, H_a: $\mu \neq 50$, $Z^* = -1.85$

9.31 Test the null hypothesis that the mean of a normally distributed population is less than or equal to 20, assuming that a sample of size 60 yields the statistics

$$\bar{x} = 20.4$$
$$s = 3.0$$

Use the p-value criteria.

9.32 The producer of Take-a-Bite, a snack food, claims that each package weighs 175 grams. A representative of a consumer advocate group selected a random sample of 70 packages. From this sample, the mean and standard deviation were found to be 172 grams and 8 grams, respectively.

a. Find the p-value for testing the claim that the mean weight of Take-a-Bite is less than 175 grams.

b. Interpret the p-value in question a.

9.33 A marketing-research analyst is interested in examining the statement made by the makers that brand A cigarettes contain less than 3 milligrams of tar. The marketing-research analyst randomly selected 60 cigarettes and found the mean amount of tar to be 2.75 milligrams with a standard deviation of 1.5 milligrams. Test the claim and find the p-value.

9.34 Find the p-value for the test conducted in exercise 9.23.

9.35 Find the p-value for the test conducted in exercise 9.24.

9.36 Find the p-value for the test conducted in exercise 9.26.

9.4

Hypothesis Testing on the Mean of a Normal Population: Small Sample

Our approach to hypothesis testing with small samples when the standard deviation, σ, is unknown uses the same technique we used for dealing with CIs on the mean of a population: We switch from the standard normal distribution, Z, to the t distribution. However, we need to examine the distribution of the population when the sample is small—the population distribution determines the procedure that we use. In this section, we will assume the population has a normal distribution. When it does not, we use a nonparametric procedure, which will be discussed in Chapter 19.

Certain variations from a normal population *are* permissible with the small-sample test. If a test of hypothesis is still reliable when slight departures from the assumptions are encountered, this test is said to be **robust.** If your population appears to be reasonably symmetric, the level of your CI and Type I error (α) will be quite accurate, even if the population has heavy tails (unlike the normal distribution), as shown in Figure 9.14a. However, when using small samples, the small-sample test is *not* robust for populations that are heavily skewed (see Figure 9.14b). A nonparametric procedure offers a much better solution for this situation. A histogram of your data often can detect whether a population is heavily skewed in one direction.

To reemphasize, the discussion in this section will assume a normal population. In other words, if X is an observation from this population, then X is a normal random variable with unknown mean μ. Also, we will assume that σ is unknown. [If σ is known, your resulting test statistic is $Z = (\bar{X} - \mu_0)/(\sigma/\sqrt{n})$, and the five-step procedure of section 9.1 allows you to do hypothesis testing on μ.]

Figure 9.14

A: Small-sample test is valid. **B:** Small-sample test is not valid.

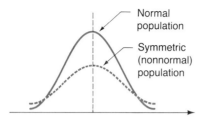

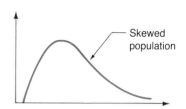

The only distinction between using a small and a large sample is the form of the test statistic. Using the discussion from Chapter 8, if we define the test statistic as

$$t = \frac{\overline{X} - \mu_0}{s/\sqrt{n}} \qquad\qquad (9\text{-}3)$$

we now have a t distribution with $n - 1$ degrees of freedom (df). The procedure to use for testing H_0: $\mu = \mu_0$ and H_a: $\mu \neq \mu_0$ is the same five-step procedure, except that the rejection region is defined using the t table (Table A-5) rather than the Z table (Table A-4). This also applies to a one-tailed test. Because we are looking at very small samples (typically $n < 30$), we can ignore the fpc factor.

Example 9.8

You may recall from example 8.7 that Metro Moving Company is considering the purchase of a new moving van. They will purchase the van if it can be demonstrated that its average miles per gallon (mpg) is greater than 9 mpg. Using the $n = 18$ data values from example 8.7, how would you advise Metro? Assume that the daily mpg follow a normal distribution.

Solution

Step 1. What you are attempting to demonstrate goes into the alternative hypothesis, H_a, so the hypotheses are H_0: $\mu \leq 9$ and H_a: $\mu > 9$.

Step 2. The test statistic here is

$$t = \frac{\overline{X} - 9}{s/\sqrt{n}}$$

Step 3. The implications of making a Type I error (rejecting a correct H_0) and a Type II error (FTR an incorrect H_0) appear to be the same, so you decide on a significance level of $\alpha = .05$.

As before, we will reject H_0 when the value of the test statistic lies in the right tail (Figure 9.15):

Reject H_0 if $t > t_{.05,17} = 1.74$

because $df = n - 1 = 17$.

Step 4. For this data set, $n = 18$, $\bar{x} = 9.64$ mpg, and $s = 1.52$ mpg. The value of your test statistic is

$$t^* = \frac{9.64 - 9}{1.52/\sqrt{18}} = 1.79$$

Because $1.79 > 1.74$, we reject H_0.

Step 5. The average daily mpg of this van is larger than 9. ●

Figure 9.15

t distribution; the rejection region is the shaded area to the right of 1.74, for example 9.8.

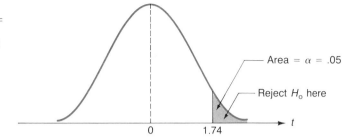

Area = α = .05

Reject H_o here

0   1.74

What is the *p*-value in example 9.8, and what can we conclude based on this value? We run into a slight snag when dealing with the *t* distribution, because we are not able to determine precisely the *p*-value. You can see this in Figure 9.16, using Table A-5 (17 *df*). The *p*-value is the area to the right of $t^* = 1.79$. The best we can do here is to say that *p* is *between* .025 and .05. (*Note:* A reliable computer package will provide the exact *p*-value. Using MINITAB, this value is $p = .0456$.)

Using the classical approach and $\alpha = .05$ (despite not knowing *p* exactly), we can say that *p* is less than .05. Consequently, we reject H_0. This procedure always produces the same result as the five-step procedure. Notice that this conclusion does *not* tell us *how strongly* we reject H_0, since the value of t^* barely fell in the rejection region.

Suppose we choose not to select a significance level (α) but prefer to base our conclusion strictly on the calculated *p*-value. We use the rule of thumb and decide whether *p* is small (< .01), large (> .1), or in between. Despite not having an exact value of *p*, we can say that this *p*-value falls in the inconclusive range. These data values do not provide us with any strong conclusion. Our advice to Metro would be to obtain some additional data.

Example 9.9

Roy's Texaco wants to keep the price of its unleaded gasoline competitive with that of other stations in the area. Roy's is currently charging $1.29 per gallon. To check that the average price for this gasoline for all stations within a 15-mile radius is higher than his price, Roy randomly samples the price of unleaded gasoline at ten stations located in this area. He obtains the following data for the price per gallon (in dollars):

1.24, 1.53, 1.46, 1.22, 1.36, 1.47, 1.35, 1.41, 1.31, 1.44

So $n = 10$, $\bar{x} = 1.379$, and $s = .1016$. Set up the appropriate hypotheses and test them using a significance level of $\alpha = .05$.

Figure 9.16

t curve with 17 *df*. The *p*-value is the area to the right of $t^* = 1.79$, so we can say only that it is between .025 and .05.

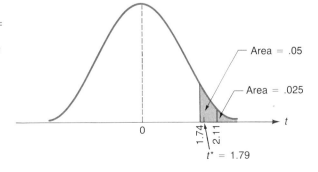

Area = .05

Area = .025

0

1.74
2.11

$t^* = 1.79$

Solution

Step 1. The hypotheses are H_0: $\mu \leq 1.29$ and H_a: $\mu > 1.29$, where μ is the average price per gallon of unleaded gasoline at *all* stations within a 15-mile radius.

Steps 2, 3.

$$\text{Reject } H_0 \text{ if } t = \frac{\overline{X} - 1.29}{s/\sqrt{n}} > t_{.05, 9} = 1.833$$

where the *df* are $n - 1 = 9$.

Step 4. The calculated t is

$$t^* = \frac{1.379 - 1.29}{.1016/\sqrt{10}} = 2.77$$

Because 2.77 exceeds the tabulated value of 1.833, we reject H_0. Also, the *p*-value (using Table A-5 and 9 *df*) is the area to the *right* of 2.77. This is between .01 and .025, which is less than $\alpha = .05$, and so (as before) we reject H_0.

Step 5. These data support the claim that the average price of unleaded gasoline in this area is higher than what Roy is currently charging.

A MINITAB solution for this example is contained in Figure 9.17. Note that the calculated (exact) *p*-value is .011. ●

Small-Sample Tests on a Normal Population Mean

TWO-TAILED TEST

H_0: $\mu = \mu_0$

H_a: $\mu \neq \mu_0$

Reject H_0 if $|t| > t_{\alpha/2, n-1}$

where n = sample size and

$$t = \frac{\overline{X} - \mu_0}{s/\sqrt{n}}$$

ONE-TAILED TEST

H_0: $\mu \leq \mu_0$ H_0: $\mu \geq \mu_0$

H_a: $\mu > \mu_0$ H_a: $\mu < \mu_0$

Reject H_0 if $t > t_{\alpha, n-1}$ Reject H_0 if $t < -t_{\alpha, n-1}$

Figure 9.17

MINITAB Solution for example 9.9.

```
MTB > SET INTO C1
DATA> 1.24 1.53 1.46 1.22 1.36 1.47 1.35 1.41 1.31 1.44
DATA> END
MTB > TTEST OF MU=1.29 USING C1;
SUBC> ALTERNATIVE=1.

TEST OF MU = 1.2900 VS MU G.T. 1.2900

            N      MEAN    STDEV    SE MEAN        T    P VALUE
C1         10    1.3790   0.1016    0.0321     2.77      0.011
```

Exercises

9.37 Find the rejection region of the t test used to test the following situations for a normally distributed population:

a. Twenty observations are randomly selected to test the claim that mean yearly maintenance expense on a certain type of lawn mower is less than $28 per year. A significance level of .05 is used.

b. Twenty-five observations are randomly selected to test the claim that managers of convenience stores have an annual income of more than $30,000. A significance level of .10 is used.

c. Fifteen observations are randomly selected to test the claim that the tensile strength of steel rods is equal to the tensile strength specified by the firm ordering the steel rods. A significance level of .05 is used.

9.38 Find the p-value for the following situations with calculated test statistics given by t^*.

a. H_0: $\mu = 40$, H_a: $\mu \neq 40$, $t^* = 2.30$, $n = 12$.

b. H_0: $\mu \leq 13.6$, H_a: $\mu > 13.6$, $t^* = 2.73$, $n = 19$.

c. H_0: $\mu \geq 100.80$, H_a: $\mu < 100.80$, $t^* = 1.25$, $n = 20$.

d. H_0: $\mu = 35.6$, H_a: $\mu \neq 35.6$, $t^* = 1.57$, $n = 11$.

9.39 Carry out the hypothesis test for the mean of a normally distributed population given the following information:

H_0: $\mu \leq 1.6$

H_a: $\mu > 1.6$

$n = 15$ $\bar{x} = 1.8$ $s^2 = 1.7$ $\alpha = .10$

9.40 A sample of size 12 is drawn from a finite population of size 300. The finite population can be approximated by a normal distribution. The sample mean and sample standard deviation are 100.6 and 3.7, respectively. Test the null hypothesis that the mean of the population is equal to 107. Use a 10% significance level.

9.41 Refer to exercise 9.40. Test the null hypothesis that the mean of the population is equal to 107, if it is known that the population standard deviation is equal to 4.

9.42 The senior executive of a publishing firm would like to train his employees to read faster than 1000 words per minute. A random sample of 21 employees underwent a special speed-reading course. This sample yielded a mean of 1018 words per minute with a standard deviation of 30 words per minute. Using a significance level of .05, test the belief that the speed-reading course will enable the employees to read more than 1000 words per minute. Assume that the reading speeds of persons who have taken the course are normally distributed.

9.43 It is believed that the mean score on an aptitude test of engineers graduating from Safire University is greater than 180. Assuming the scores are normally distributed, test the belief if a random sample of 26 engineers yielded a mean score of 186 with a standard deviation of 10.2. Use the p-value.

9.44 Gopal and Krause, an investment firm, have made public a new growth and income mutual fund. To enjoy the fruits of this well-managed fund, an initial deposit of $10,000 is required. After the account is opened, the balance can fall as low as $5000. Gopal and Krause believe that the account balances in this mutual fund are normally distributed with a mean greater than $10,000. To test this belief, a random sample of 23 accounts is selected. The sample mean is $10,963 and the sample standard deviation is $446. Test the claim that the mean account balance in this fund is greater than $10,000. Use a .05 significance level.

9.45 The controller of National Insurance states that the average claim against the company for an automobile accident is less than $4500. A random sample of 14 claims yielded a mean amount of $4200 with a sample standard deviation of $171. It is believed that the claims are normally distributed. Use the p-value criteria to test the controller's statement.

9.46 In exercise 9.25, test the hypothesis that the average driver is parked for more than .75 hours, assuming that the sample size was only 15 instead of 45. Use the same values for the sample statistics. Let the significance level be the same as in exercise 9.25 (10%).

9.5

Inference for the Variance and Standard Deviation of a Normal Population

Our discussion in Chapters 8 and 9 has been concerned with the mean of a particular random variable or population. In other words, we are trying to decide (or estimate) what is occurring *on the average.* Suppose you are involved with a production process that is manufacturing two-inch bolts, and you have been informed that, without a doubt, these bolts are two inches long, on the average. Is there anything else you might like to know about this process? Suppose that one-half of the bolts produced are one inch long and the other half are three inches. The report was accurate—on the average, they *are* two inches long. * However, such a production process certainly will not satisfy your customers, and you soon will be out of the bolt business.

What was missing in the report was the amount of *variation* in this production process. If the variation was zero, then *every* bolt would be exactly two inches long— an ideal situation. In practice, there always will be a certain amount of variation in any mechanical or production process. So we are concerned about not only the mean length μ of the population of bolts but also the variance σ^2 or standard deviation σ of the lengths of these bolts. If the variance is *too large,* the process is not operating correctly and needs adjustment.

The variance of a population also is of vital interest to someone making investment decisions. Here the *risk* of a venture (or portfolio) often is measured by the variance of the return paid by the venture in the past. Often, financial analysts prefer a financial package with a relatively small average return (based on past history) that appears to be low risk on the basis of only small fluctuations in its past performance.

In the inference procedures for a population variance (and standard deviation) to follow, we will assume that the population of interest is normally distributed. Unlike the *t* test, the hypothesis testing procedures and CIs for the variance are very sensitive to departures from the normal population—notably, heavy tails in the distribution or heavy skewness will have a large effect. In other words, the following tests of hypothesis are less robust than are those we discussed earlier.

Confidence Interval for the Variance and Standard Deviation

The point estimate of a population variance is the obvious one—namely, the sample variance. This was discussed in Chapter 8, where we used the variance of a sample, s^2, to estimate the variance of the much larger population, σ^2.

When constructing a CI for μ using a small sample, we used the *t* distribution. Such a distribution is referred to as a **derived distribution** because it was derived to describe the behavior of a particular test statistic. This type of distribution is not used to describe a population, as is the normal distribution in many applications. For example, you will *not* hear a statement such as "assume that these *data* follow a *t* distribution—normal, exponential, uniform, maybe—but not a *t* distribution. The *t* random variable merely offers us a method of testing and constructing CIs for the

---

*A statistician often is described as someone who thinks that if one-half of you is in an oven and the other half is in a deep freeze, on the average you are very comfortable.

Figure 9.18

Shape of a chi-square distribution.

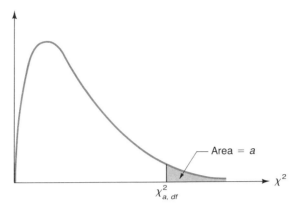

mean of a *normal* population when the standard deviation is unknown, and is replaced by its estimate.

Another such continuous derived distribution allows us to determine CIs and perform tests of hypothesis on the variance and standard deviation of a normal population. This is the **chi-square** (pronounced *ky*) distribution, written as χ^2. The shape of this distribution is illustrated in Figure 9.18. Notice that, unlike the Z and t curves, the χ^2 distribution is not symmetric and is definitely skewed right.

For chi-square, as with all continuous distributions, a probability corresponds to an area under a curve. Also, the shape of the chi-square curve, like that of its cousin the t distribution, depends on the sample size n. As before, this will be specified by the corresponding degrees of freedom (*df*).

When using the χ^2 distribution to construct a CI or perform a test of hypothesis on a population variance (or standard deviation), the **degrees of freedom** are given by

$$df = n - 1$$

Let $\chi^2_{a, df}$ be the χ^2 value whose area to the right is a, using the proper *df*.

Example 9.10

Using a chi-square curve with 12 *df*, determine $P(\chi^2 > 18.5494)$ and $P(\chi^2 < 6.30380)$.

Solution Tabulated values for the χ^2 distribution are contained in Table A-6 on page 820. This table contains *right tail* areas (probabilities). Based on this table (see Figure 9.19),

$$P(\chi^2 > 18.5494) = .1$$

This can be written as

$$\chi^2_{.1, 12} = 18.5494$$

Figure 9.19

χ^2 curve with 12 *df*. The shaded area represents $P(\chi^2 > 18.5494)$.

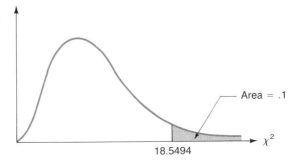

For $\chi^2 = 6.30380$, Table A-6 informs us that the area to the right of 6.30380 is .900. Consequently, the area to the left of 6.30380 is $1 - .900 = .1$ (because the total area is 1), and so $P(\chi^2 < 6.30380) = .1$. As a result, we can say that

$$P(6.30380 \leqslant \chi^2 \leqslant 18.5494) = 1 - .1 - .1 = .8$$

That is, 80% of the time a χ^2 value (with 12 df) will be between 6.30380 and 18.5494.

Example 9.11

Using example 9.10, determine a and b that satisfy

$$P(a < \chi^2 < b) = .95$$

Choose a and b so that an equal area occurs in each tail.

Solution Figure 9.20 shows the areas for a and b. Using Table A-6,

$a = $ the χ^2 value whose left-tailed area is .025

$\quad = $ the χ^2 value whose area to the right is .975

$\quad = 4.40$

and

$b = $ the χ^2 value whose right-tailed area is .025

$\quad = 23.3$

To derive a CI for σ^2, we need to examine the sampling distribution of s^2. If we repeatedly obtained a random sample from a normal population (with mean μ and variance σ^2), calculated the sample variance s^2, and made a histogram of these s^2 values, what would be the resulting shape of this histogram? It can be shown that the shape will depend on the sample size n and the value of σ^2 but *not* on the value of the population mean μ. In fact, the values of n and σ^2, along with the random variable s^2, can be combined to define a chi-square random variable, given by

$$\chi^2 = \frac{(n-1)s^2}{\sigma^2} \tag{9-4}$$

having a chi-square distribution with $n - 1$ degrees of freedom (df). Therefore, the sampling distribution for s^2 can be defined using the chi-square distribution in equation 9-4.

Figure 9.20

χ^2 curve with 12 df.

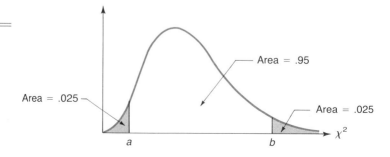

Area = .95

Area = .025

Area = .025

For example, using 12 df (a sample size of $n = 13$), it follows that (from example 9.11)

$$P(4.40 < \chi^2 < 23.3) = .95$$

So,

$$P\left[4.40 < \frac{12s^2}{\sigma^2} < 23.3\right] = .95 \text{ using equation 9-4}$$

or

$$P\left[\frac{12s^2}{23.3} < \sigma^2 < \frac{12s^2}{4.40}\right] = .95$$

This means that a 95% CI for σ^2 is

$$\frac{12s^2}{23.3} \quad \text{to} \quad \frac{12s^2}{4.40}$$

In general, the following procedure can be used to construct a CI for σ^2 or σ. A $(1 - \alpha) \cdot 100\%$ CI for σ^2 is

$$\frac{(n - 1)s^2}{\chi^2_{\alpha/2,\ n-1}} \quad \text{to} \quad \frac{(n - 1)s^2}{\chi^2_{1-\alpha/2,\ n-1}} \tag{9-5}$$

The corresponding CI for σ is

$$\sqrt{\frac{(n - 1)s^2}{\chi^2_{\alpha/2,\ n-1}}} \quad \text{to} \quad \sqrt{\frac{(n - 1)s^2}{\chi^2_{1-\alpha/2,\ n-1}}} \tag{9-6}$$

Example 9.12
: Vitamix Dog Chow comes in 10-, 25-, and 50-lb bags. The owners are concerned about the variation in the weight of the 50-lb bags because they have recently acquired a new mechanical packaging device. A random sample of 15 bags was obtained, with the following results:

Weight of bag (lbs): 51.2, 47.5, 50.8, 51.5, 49.5, 51.1, 51.3, 50.7, 46.7, 49.2, 52.1, 48.3, 51.6, 49.2, 51.5

For these data, $\bar{x} = 50.15$ lbs and $s = 1.65$ lbs. Determine a 90% CI for σ^2 and for σ. Assume that the bag weights are normally distributed.

Solution The corresponding 90% CI interval for σ^2 is

$$\frac{(15 - 1)\ (1.65)^2}{\chi^2_{.05,14}} \quad \text{to} \quad \frac{(15 - 1)\ (1.65)^2}{\chi^2_{.95,14}}$$

$$= \frac{(14)(1.65)^2}{23.7} \quad \text{to} \quad \frac{(14)(1.65)^2}{6.57}$$

$$= 1.61 \quad \text{to} \quad 5.80$$

The 90% CI for σ would be

$$\sqrt{1.61} \quad \text{to} \quad \sqrt{5.80}$$

that is, 1.27 lbs to 2.41 lbs.

Hypothesis Testing for the Variance and Standard Deviation

For many applications, we are concerned that the variance of our population may be exceeding some specified value. If this claim is supported, then, for example, we may wish to shut down a production process and make adjustments that will reduce this excessive variation. As you could with the tests of hypothesis examined so far, you can (although this is not the usual case) perform a two-tailed test where either too much variation or too little variation is the topic of concern.

Hypothesis Testing on σ^2

TWO-TAILED TEST

$H_0: \sigma^2 = \sigma_0^2$

$H_a: \sigma^2 \neq \sigma_0^2$

Test statistic: $\chi^2 = \dfrac{(n-1)s^2}{\sigma_0^2}$

Reject H_0 if $\chi^2 > \chi_{\alpha/2,\, n-1}^2$

or if $\chi^2 < \chi_{1-\alpha/2,\, n-1}^2$

ONE-TAILED TEST

$H_0: \sigma^2 \leq \sigma_0^2$	$H_0: \sigma^2 \geq \sigma_0^2$
$H_a: \sigma^2 > \sigma_0^2$	$H_a: \sigma^2 < \sigma_0^2$
Reject H_0 if $\chi^2 > \chi_{\alpha,\, n-1}^2$	Reject H_0 if $\chi^2 < \chi_{1-\alpha,\, n-1}^2$

Example 9.13

Example 9.12 was concerned with the variation of the actual weight of a (supposedly) 50-lb bag of Vitamix Dog Chow. Based on earlier production tests, management is convinced that the average weight of all bags being produced is, in fact, 50 lbs. However, the production supervisor has been informed that at least 95% of the bags produced *must* be within one lb of the specified weight (50 lbs). Using a significance level of $\alpha = .1$, what can we conclude? Assume a normal distribution for the bag weights.

What is the supervisor being told about σ? Remember that, for a normal population, 95% of the observations will lie within two standard deviations of the mean (empirical rule, Chapter 3). So, if two standard deviations are the same as one lb, then the supervisor is being told that σ must be no more than .5 lb. Is there any evidence to conclude that this is not the case—that is, that σ is larger than .5 lb? Let's investigate.

Solution

Step 1. The appropriate hypotheses are $H_0: \sigma \leq .5$ and $H_a: \sigma > .5$ (production is not meeting required standards).

(Note that these hypotheses are precisely the same as $H_0: \sigma^2 \leq .25$ and $H_a: \sigma^2 > .25$. Whether you write H_0 and H_a in terms of σ or σ^2 does not matter; the testing procedure is the same in either case.)

Step 2. The test statistic is

$$\chi^2 = \frac{(15 - 1)s^2}{(.5)^2} = \frac{14s^2}{.25}$$

which has a chi-square distribution with 14 df.

Step 3. The rejection region for this test (using $\alpha = .1$ and Table A-6) is

Reject H_0 if $\chi^2 > 21.1$

Step 4. The computed value using the sample data is

$$\chi^{*2} = \frac{(15 - 1)(1.65)^2}{(.5)^2} = 152.5$$

Since $152.5 > 21.1$, we reject H_0. This is hardly a surprising result; the point estimate of σ is $s = 1.65$, quite a bit larger than .5.

Step 5. We conclude rather convincingly that σ is larger than .5 lb. The bagging procedure has far too much variation in the weight of the bags produced. ●

Note that the p-value for the test of hypothesis in example 9.13 is the area to the right of 152.5 under the χ^2 curve with 14 df.

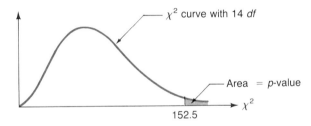

All we are able to determine about this value using Table A-6 is that it is much smaller than .005 (the smallest tabulated value). Using this information, we arrive at the same decision—namely, reject H_0—because (1) using the classical approach, p is less than $\alpha = .10$, or (2) the p-value is extremely small ($<.01$) by the general rule of thumb described in section 9.4.

Exercises

From the tabulated values for the chi-square distribution, find the following values and indicate graphically where the values fall with respect to other values of the chi-square distribution.

a. $\chi^2_{.10, 10}$ **c.** $\chi^2_{.95, 15}$

b. $\chi^2_{.025, 30}$ **d.** $\chi^2_{.01, 26}$

9.48 A sample of size 25 from a normally distributed population yields a sample standard deviation of 12.8. At the 10% significance level, test the null hypothesis that the population standard deviation is less than or equal to 11.3.

9.49 A sample of size 15 from a normally distributed population yields the sample statistic

$$\Sigma(x - \bar{x})^2 = 180.3$$

a. Construct a 90% CI for the population variance.

b. Construct a 90% CI for the population standard deviation.

c. Test the null hypothesis that the population variance is equal to ten. Use a 10% significance level.

9.50 A sample of size five from a normally distributed population yields the following sample statistics:

$$\Sigma x^2 = 135$$
$$\Sigma x = 23$$

a. Construct a 95% CI for the population variance.

b. Construct a 95% CI for the population standard deviation.

c. Test the null hypothesis that the population standard deviation is equal to 2.8. Use a 5% significance level.

9.51 The production manager of Crystal-Clear Picture Tubes believes that the life of the picture tubes is 25,000 hours. However, to maintain the company's reputation for quality, the manager would like to keep the standard deviation of the life span of the picture tubes to less than 1000 hours. A sample of 24 picture tubes was randomly selected and the sample standard deviation was found to be 928 hours. Test that the population standard deviation is less than 1000 hours. Use a 10% significance level. What assumption must be made about the distribution of the life span of the picture tubes?

9.52 For a random variable χ^2, which has chi-square distribution with 18 degrees of freedom, determine the values of a and b such that $P(a \leqslant \chi^2 \leqslant b) = .90$ and such that the areas in each tail are equal, that is, $P(0 \leqslant \chi^2 < a) = P(b < \chi^2)$.

9.53 A production manager in charge of manufacturing plastic discs must maintain a standard deviation of no more than 2 millimeters for the diameter of the disc. A sample of 26 plastic discs randomly selected reveals a standard deviation of 1.85 millimeters. Assuming that the diameters of the disc are normally distributed, test the null hypothesis that the standard deviation of the disc is at least 2 millimeters. Use the p-value criteria.

9.54 The salaries for mathematics teachers in secondary schools in Connecticut are believed to be normally distributed with a variance greater than $3000. Test this belief using the following sample statistics:

$$\Sigma(x - \bar{x})^2 = 45,130$$
$$n = 14$$

where X represents a math teacher's salary. Use a 1% significance level.

9.55 A medical researcher selects 15 rats at random and gives each the same dose of an antihypertensive drug. The blood pressure of the rats is then recorded. It is believed that the blood pressures are normally distributed. From the sample, the standard deviation of the blood pressures is found to be 3.86. The standard deviation of blood pressures for rats without the drug is known to be 4.16.

a. Test the hypothesis that the standard deviation of blood pressures for rats given the drug is less than 4.16. Use a significance level of .01.

b. Is there sufficient evidence to indicate that the standard deviation of blood pressures for rats given the drug is less than that for rats not given the drug?

9.56 A realtor believes that the standard deviation of the prices of homes in Bloomington Hill Estates is less than $6,000. A random sample of 25 homes in Bloomington Hill Estates yields a sample standard deviation of $5,030. Test the realtor's belief using the p-value criteria.

Summary

Chapter 8 introduced the concept of statistical inference by discussing the concept of estimating a population parameter (such as μ or σ) by using a corresponding sample estimate. The reliability of using the sample mean to estimate μ was measured using a confidence interval (CI). This chapter presented the other side of statistical inference—hypothesis testing regarding this population parameter, along with a CI for the population standard deviation, σ.

For testing a hypothetical value of the population mean (μ), we introduced a procedure that used the standard normal (Z) distribution for large samples ($n > 30$) and the t distribution for small samples. For small samples, the hypotheses are concerned with the mean of a normal population. However, we are able to discuss the mean of any continuous population when we have large samples by using the CLT.

The two hypotheses under investigation are the null hypothesis, H_0, and the alternative hypothesis, H_a. Typically, a claim that one is attempting to demonstrate goes into the alternative hypothesis.

Since any test of hypothesis uses a sample to infer something about a population, errors can result. Two specific errors are of great concern when you use the hypothesis-testing procedure. A Type I error occurs when you reject a null hypothesis when in fact it is true; a Type II error occurs when you fail to reject a null hypothesis when in fact is is not true.

The probability of a Type I error is the significance level of the test and is written as α. The probability of a Type II error is β; β increases as α decreases. To define a test of hypothesis, you select a value of α that considers the cost of rejecting a correct H_0 and failing to reject (FTR) an incorrect H_0. Typical values of α range from .01 to .1.

The power of a statistical test is defined as $1 - \beta$ and is equal to the probability of rejecting H_0 when it is in fact false. The value of β (and so $1 - \beta$) depends on the actual value of the parameter under investigation, and so the power of the test can be obtained for each possible value of this parameter. The resulting set of power values defines a power curve for this test of hypothesis.

A five-step procedure was defined for any test of hypothesis. The steps are:

Step 1. Set up H_0 and H_a.

Step 2. Define the test statistic, which is evaluated using the sample data.

Step 3. Define a rejection region, using the value of α, such that the value of the test statistic will result in rejecting H_0.

Step 4. Calculate the value of the test statistic from the sample data and carry out the test. This will result in rejecting H_0 or failing to reject H_0.

Step 5. Give a conclusion in the language of the problem.

A test such as H_0: $\mu = 50$ versus H_a: $\mu \neq 50$ is called a two-tailed test because we reject H_0 whenever the sample estimate of μ ($\overline{X}$) is either too large (test statistic is in the right tail) or too small (test statistic is in the left tail). Similarly, a test on the population variance (or standard deviation) such as H_0: $\sigma^2 = .2$ versus H_a: $\sigma^2 \neq .2$ also is a two-tailed test.

$$H_0\text{: } \mu \leq 50 \text{ versus } H_a\text{: } \mu > 50 \qquad \text{or } H_0\text{: } \mu \geq 50 \text{ versus } H_a\text{: } \mu < 50$$

$$\text{or } H_0\text{: } \sigma^2 \leq .2 \text{ versus } H_a\text{: } \sigma^2 > .2 \qquad \text{or } H_0\text{: } \sigma^2 \geq .2 \text{ versus } H_a\text{: } \sigma^2 < .2$$

are all examples of one-tailed tests of hypothesis.

The tests on a population variance introduced the chi-square distribution, χ^2. This distribution was used to construct CIs for σ^2 and σ as well as to define a distribution for the test statistic when performing a test of hypothesis on the variance or standard deviation.

Finally, we discussed why you should always include a p-value in the results of any hypothesis test. This value measures the strength of your point estimate (such as $\overline{X}$ or s^2). When using a predetermined significance level, α, you reject H_0 whenever the p-value is less than α and FTR H_0 otherwise. Another option you can use is *not* to select the somewhat arbitrary value of α but simply to reject H_0 whenever the p-value is "small" (say, $< .01$), FTR H_0 if it is "large" (say, $> .1$), or decide that the data are inconclusive if the p-value lies between these two values. You can also use the p-value to measure the enthusiasm (p-value very small) with which you reject H_0 or the authority (p-value quite large) with which you FTR H_0.

Review Exercises

9.57 Explain how changes in the α level affect the following.

a. The rejection region.

b. The type II error.

9.58 The manager of Jack-Be-Nimble candle company would like to claim that a certain type of their candles burns more than 14 hours. To test this claim, the manager randomly selects 50 candles and finds that the sample mean is equal to 14.75 hours with a standard deviation of 1.8 hours.

a. What are the null and alternative hypotheses?

b. Which error would you consider to be more serious, type I or type II?

c. At a significance level of .05, what is your conclusion?

9.59 Given the following statistics from a normally distributed population, perform the hypothesis test that the mean of the population is equal to 235.6:

$n = 21$

$\overline{x} = 234.1$

$\sigma = 2.3$

Use the p-value to draw your conclusion.

9.60 The manager of the Train Depot restaurant believes that the average time customers wait before being served is 10 minutes. To test the belief, the manager selects 50 customers at random and records that the average waiting time is 11.9 minutes with a standard deviation of 1.4 minutes.

a. Find a 95% CI for the mean waiting time of a customer.

b. Test the null hypothesis that the mean waiting time is equal to 10 minutes, using a 5% significance level.

9.61 Calculate the power of the test for the mean of a normally distributed population with known population variance for the following situations, assuming that the true population mean is 10 and the known population standard deviation is 3.1. Use a significance level of .05.

a. H_0: $\mu = 11$, H_a: $\mu \neq 11$, $n = 14$.

b. H_0: $\mu = 9.5$, H_a: $\mu \neq 9.5$, $n = 25$.

c. H_0: $\mu = 8$, H_a: $\mu \neq 8$, $n = 40$.

9.62 The Miser, an economy car, has an EPA gas mileage of 35 miles per gallon on the highway. A local dealer would like to verify that the car's realistic gas mileage is not significantly less than that when the car is driven under "ideal" conditions. A random sample of 55 cars yields a sample mean of 34.4 with a sample standard deviation of 1.8 miles per gallon. Using a significance level of .05, is there sufficient evidence that the mean gas mileage of the Miser is less than 35 miles per gallon on the highway?

9.63 A manufacturer of drugs and medical products claims that a new antiinflammatory drug will be effective for 4 hours after the drug is administered in the prescribed dosage. A random sample of 50 volunteers demonstrated that the average effective time is 3.70 hours with a sample standard deviation of .606 hours. Use the p-value criteria to test the null hypothesis that the mean effective time of the drug is 4 hours.

9.64 Indicate what the p-values are for the following situations in which the mean of a normally distributed population is being tested.

a. H_0: $\mu = 31.6$, H_a: $\mu \neq 31.6$ (population variance is known), $Z^* = 2.16$.

b. H_0: $\mu = 4.07$, H_a: $\mu \neq 4.07$ (population variance is known), $Z^* = -1.35$.

c. H_0: $\mu = 87.6$, H_a: $\mu \neq 87.6$ (population variance is unknown), $t^* = 2.51$, $n = 15$.

d. H_0: $\mu = 195.3$, H_a: $\mu \neq 195.3$ (population variance is unknown), $t^* = -1.71$, $n = 25$.

9.65 Using the following information, perform the hypothesis test for the mean of a normally distributed population:

H_0: $\mu \geq 7.19$

H_a: $\mu < 7.19$

$\bar{x} = 6.21$

$s^2 = .26$

$n = 23$

$\alpha = .10$

9.66 The vice-president of academic affairs at a small private college believes that the average full-time student who lives off campus spends about \$300 per month for housing. A random sample of 200 full-time students living off campus spent an average of \$305 per month with a standard deviation of \$70 a month.

a. Find the p-value to determine whether there is sufficient evidence to indicate that a full-time student spends more than \$300 per month on housing.

b. Would you reject the null hypothesis for the test in question a if $\alpha = .01$? if $\alpha = .05$? if $\alpha = .10$?

9.67 A marketing analyst is looking at the feasibility of opening a new movie theater in a small town. The town currently has only two movie theaters. The movie theater would be a practical investment if the average family in the town spends at least 14 hours at the movies each year. A random sample of 80 households yielded a sample mean of 14.5 hours per year with a standard deviation of 1.4.

a. Find the 95% CI for the mean time that a family spends per year at the movies.

b. Is there sufficient evidence to indicate that the mean time that a family spends at the movies is greater than 14 hours per year? Use a .05 significance level.

9.68 From a finite population of size 425, a random sample of size 20 is drawn. The finite population can be approximated by a normal distribution. From the sample, it is found that

$\bar{x} = 43.7$

$s^2 = 6.7$

Test the null hypothesis that the mean of the population is less than or equal to 40. Use a 1% significance level.

9.69 The manager of a real-estate firm is concerned about the yearly vacancy rate of apartments in a large city. There are 125 apartment complexes in the city. A random sample of 25 apartment complexes reveals that the average yearly vacancy rate is 13.6% The vacancy rate for the apartment complexes is considered to follow a normal distribution. The sample standard deviation for the vacancy rate is 1.9%.

a. Is there sufficient evidence to indicate that the vacancy rate is greater than 10% for apartment complexes in the city? Use a 1% significance level.

b. Find the p-value for the test in question a.

9.70 There are 210 students in a particular dormitory at City University. The manager would like to know how much time the average student uses the dormitory's recreational facilities. Twenty-eight students are randomly selected and questioned. The sample mean is 2.6 hours per week with a standard deviation of .4.

a. Find a 90% CI for the mean time per week that a student spends using the dormitory's recreational facilities.

b. Test the null hypothesis that the mean time per week that a student spends using the dormitory's recreational facilities is equal to 2.0 hours. Use a 10% significance level.

9.71 From a normally distributed population, a random sample yields the following statistic:

$$\Sigma(x - \bar{x})^2 = 1.67$$
$$n = 22$$

a. Find a 95% CI for the population variance.

b. Find a 95% CI for the population standard deviation.

c. Test the null hypothesis that the population variance is equal to .07 at the .05 significance level.

9.72 Find values for a and b such that the following statement is true for a chi-square random variable with 13 degrees of freedom:

$$P(a \leqslant \chi^2 \leqslant b) = .99$$
$$P(0 \leqslant \chi^2 < a) = P(b < \chi^2)$$

9.73 Using a significance level of 0.05, perform the hypothesis test for the standard deviation of a normally distributed population given the following information:

$$H_0: \sigma \geqslant 20.6$$
$$H_a: \sigma < 20.6$$
$$\Sigma(x - \bar{x})^2 = 6100$$
$$n = 18$$

9.74 Eastern State Bank currently operates five drive-in teller windows. Management is concerned about the variability of the time spent by a customer using the windows. A sample of 24 customers was taken and the sample standard deviation was found to be 4.7 minutes. Management would like to keep the standard deviation below 4 minutes and may consider adding another drive-in teller window.

a. Test the null hypothesis that the standard deviation of the waiting time by a customer is less than or equal to 4 minutes. Use a 10% significance level.

b. What assumption should be made about the distribution of the waiting time of a customer who uses the drive-in teller windows?

9.75 An investment counselor would like to know how much variability there is in the yield of money-market funds. The yields of the funds can be considered to be approximately normally distributed for the time frame of interest. A sample of 21 money-market funds yields a sample standard deviation of .7%. At the .05 significance level, is there sufficient evidence to indicate that the standard deviation of the yields of money-market funds is greater than .6%?

Case Study

Hot Tubs Inc.

Ron White, the marketing manager of Hot Tubs Inc., was reviewing the sales information on the company. He was particularly pleased with the continued growth in sales but realized that this was in part the result of a rapidly expanding industry, which also meant an increased level of competition. Ron was interested in keeping the company at the front edge of the competitive action in the industry. One of the decisions that Ron had to make was in which magazine to run the company's new advertising campaign.

The two magazines he was interested in were both national publications with regional issues for the sales territory. The publications were also equal in a number of other important aspects, such as cost of advertising space and number of subscribers. There was one important difference, however: the readers. The first magazine's readership had a mean age of 25 years; the second had a mean of 35 years. So Ron needed to determine which age group was more likely to buy hot tubs. He used the company's sales records to find the average age of their customers.

First, Ron collected a random set of 60 customers from the 1350 sales records. He obtained the following information:

Age	Frequency	Age	Frequency
23	3	36	4
25	2	37	6
26	2	38	2
27	3	39	3
28	4	40	4
30	2	41	1
31	2	42	4
32	2	43	2
33	6	44	1
34	3	48	1
35	3		

Ron calculated the measures of central tendency—the mean, median, and mode—as well as the measures of variability—the variance, standard deviation, and range.

Case Study Questions

1. Prepare Ron's memorandum summarizing his findings and recommending that one (or both?) of the publications be used for advertising. Be sure that you say why he favors the choice.

Also prepare a statistical supplement that contains all the evidence that Ron gathered to support his choice. Show the calculations, plot the data, translate the statistics—do whatever is useful to make the data understandable. If the supplement includes computer output, be sure to annotate it, saying which number serves what purpose.

2. If Ron decided to take another sample and wanted to know the average age of Hot Tub's customers within ± 1 year, how large a sample would he need to take? Justify your answer.

•	S
•	P
•	S
•	S
•	X

There is no direct method for computing the *t*-statistic, as we did in example 9.9, when using SPSSX. It is possible, however, to determine the value of the *t*-statistic by using the output from the CONDESCRIPTIVE procedure described in Chapter 3.

•	S
•	A
•	S

Solution

Example 9.9

Example 9.9 was concerned with the computation of means and a *t*-statistic to determine average gasoline prices. You can use SAS to solve this problem. The SAS program listing in Figure 9.21 was used to request the calculation of the mean, *t*-statistic, and *p*-value. Note that SAS automatically assumes a two-tailed test; this was a one-tailed test, so the calculated *p*-value needs to be divided by two. Each line represents one card image to be entered:

Figure 9.21

SAS program listing used to request calculation of the mean, *t*-statistic, and *p*-value.

```
TITLE     GASOLINE;
DATA PRICEDAT;
INPUT PRICES;
  HO1=PRICES-1.29;
CARDS;
1.24
1.53
1.46
1.22
1.36
1.47
1.35
1.41
1.31
1.44
PROC PRINT;
PROC MEANS N MEAN T PRT;
  VAR HO1;
  TITLE TWO-TAILED TEST;
```

The TITLE command names the SAS run.

The DATA command gives the data a name.

The INPUT command names and gives the correct order for the different fields on the data cards.

The HO1 = PRICES − 1.29 statement is used to compute a new variable, HO1, which is the difference between the variable PRICES and 1.29.

The CARDS command indicates to SAS that the input data immediately follow.

The next 10 lines are card images, with each line representing one competitor's gasoline price.

The PROC PRINT command directs SAS to list the data that were just entered.

The PROC MEANS command requests a SAS procedure to print the number of observations, the mean, the t-statistic, and the p-value.

The VAR statement specifies that the variable HO1 is the variable to be used in computing the statistics.

The TITLE statement specifies the heading for the printout.

Figure 9.22 shows the output obtained by executing the program listing in Figure 9.21.

Figure 9.22

Output obtained by executing the SAS program listing in Figure 9.21. This SAS routine assumes a two-tailed test, but, because this example is for a one-tailed test, the desired p-value is actually one-half of the value stated on the output listing. The p-value is really $.0217/2 = .011$.

OBS	PRICES	HO1
1	1.24	-0.05
2	1.53	0.24
3	1.46	0.17
4	1.22	-0.07
5	1.36	0.07
6	1.47	0.18
7	1.35	0.06
8	1.41	0.12
9	1.31	0.02
10	1.44	0.15

TWO-TAILED TEST

VARIABLE	N	MEAN	T	PR>!T!
HO1	10	0.08900000	2.77	0.0217

Inference Procedures for Two Populations

A Look Back/Introduction

We have learned to describe and summarize data from a single population using a statistic (such as the sample mean, $\overline{X}$), or a graph (such as a histogram). Chapters 8 and 9 introduced you to statistical inference, where we (1) attempted to estimate a parameter (such as the mean, μ) from this population by using the corresponding sample statistic and (2) arrived at a conclusion about this parameter (such as $\mu > 5.9'$) by performing a test of hypothesis. The concept behind hypothesis testing was described, and we paid special attention to the errors (Type I and Type II) that can occur when we use a sample to infer something about a population.

Next, we will learn how to examine two populations. Questions that will be of interest here include:

1. Are the values in population 1 larger, on the average, than those in population 2? (for example, are men taller, on the average, than women?).
2. Do the values in population 1 exhibit more variation than those in population 2? (for example, do male heights vary more than female heights?).

The two populations under observation may or may not be normally distributed. For large samples, once again using the CLT, it simply does not matter. For small samples, we need to assume that both populations *are* normally distributed so we can use the t distribution to construct CIs and perform tests of hypothesis.

This chapter will discuss two different sampling situations. In the first, random samples from two populations are obtained *independently* of each other; in the second, corresponding data values from the two samples are matched up, or paired. Paired samples are *dependent.*

10.1

Indepen-dent Versus Dependent Samples

When making comparisons between the means of two populations, we need to pay particular attention to how we intend to collect sample data. For example, how would you determine if tire brand A lasts longer than brand B? You might decide to put one of each brand on the rear wheels of ten cars and measure the tires' wear. Or you might randomly select ten brand-A and ten brand-B tires and attach them to a machine that wears them down for a certain time, and then measure the resulting tire wear. If you use the first procedure (putting both brands of tire on the same car), you obtain *dependent* samples; in the latter situation, you obtain *independent* samples.

Consider another situation. Suppose you are interested in male heights as compared with female heights. You obtain a sample of $n_1 = 50$ male heights and $n_2 = 50$ female heights. You obtain these data:

Observation	Male Heights	Female Heights
1	5.92′	5.36′
2	6.13′	5.64′
3	5.78′	5.44′
.	.	.
.	.	.
.	.	.
50	5.81′	5.52′

Is there any need to match up 5.92 with 5.36, 6.13 with 5.64, 5.78 with 5.44, and so on? The male heights were randomly selected and the female heights were obtained independently, so there is no reason to match up the first male height with the first female height, the second male height with the second female height, and so on. Nothing relates male 1 with female 1 other than the accident of their being selected first—these are **independent samples.**

What if you wish to know whether husbands are taller than wives? To collect data, you select 50 married couples. Suppose you obtain the 100 observations from the previous male and female height example. Now, there *is* a reason to compare the first male height with the first female height, the second with the second, and so on. The answer is a definite yes since each pair of heights belongs to a married couple. The resulting two samples are **dependent** or **paired samples.**

In summary,

1. If there is a definite reason for pairing (matching) corresponding data values, the two samples are **dependent** samples.
2. If the two samples were obtained independently and there is no reason for pairing the data values, the resulting samples are **independent** samples.

Why does this distinction matter? If you are trying to decide whether male heights are, on the average, larger than female heights, the procedure that you use for testing this depends on whether the samples are independent or dependent.

Applications of dependent samples in a business setting include data from the following situations.

1. Comparisons of *before versus after*. Sample 1: person's weight before a diet plan is begun. Sample 2: person's weight six months after starting the diet. Why pair the data? Each pair of observations belongs to the same person.
2. Comparisons of people with *matching characteristics*. Sample 1: salary for a male employee at Company ABC. Sample 2: salary for a female employee at Company ABC, where the woman has education and job experience equal to the man's. Why pair the data? The two paired employees are identical in their job qualifications.
3. Comparisons of observations *matched by location*. Sample 1: sales of brand-A tires for a group of n stores. Sample 2: sales of brand-B tires for the same group of stores. Why pair the data? Both observations were obtained from the same store. Your data consist of sales (weekly, monthly, and so on) from a sample of stores selling these two brands.
4. Comparisons of observations *matched by time*. Sample 1: sales of restaurant A during a particular week. Sample 2: sales of restaurant B during this week. Why pair the data? Each pair of observations corresponds to the same week of the year.

Exercises

10.1 For each of the following claims determine whether the paired samples or the independent samples procedure would be appropriate.

a. The mean of the scores attained by students before a tutorial session is less than the mean of the scores attained by the same students after the tutorial session.

b. There is no difference between the mean grade point averages of females and males in the MBA program.

c. The average wage for Japanese auto workers is less than that for European auto workers.

10.2 Two private colleges decided to compare the mean SAT scores of their incoming freshmen. One college gathered 98 scores and the other took a sample of 52 scores. Do the two sets of data represent dependent or independent samples?

10.3 A medical institution is examining the effectiveness of a newly developed drug. The drug was administered to 18 patients whose health condition before and after taking the drug was recorded. Is this a case of dependent or independent samples?

10.4 The advertising division of a chemical company would like to see how two different dishwashing detergents are rated by homemakers. Homemakers are chosen at random. They assign a value from zero to ten to each product. They assign a value of zero to the product if they think the detergent is worthless and ten to the detergent if they believe it is the best on market. How can dependent samples be chosen? How can independent samples be chosen?

10.5 The career placement center at Safire University conducts a survey of beginning salaries for MBAs with no on-the-job experience. Ten pairs of men and women are chosen randomly such that each pair of one man and one woman have nearly identical qualifications. Can the sample of observations from men be independent of the sample of observations from women?

10.6 A retail store would like to compare sales from two different arrangements of displaying its merchandise. Sales are recorded for a 30-day period with one arrangement and then sales are recorded for another 30-day period for the alternative arrangement. Can the data for each of the two 30-day periods be independent or dependent?

10.7 Fifty people were randomly selected to rate particular brand of soft drink on a scale from one to ten, with ten being the highest rating. If 25 people rated brand A and the other 25 people rated brand B, would the samples from these two groups be independent or dependent?

10.8 In exercise 10.7, suppose the 50 people were each asked to rate both brand A and brand B. Would the sample of 50 observations of brand A be independent of the sample of 50 observations of brand B?

10.2

Comparing Two Means Using Two Large Independent Samples

When comparing the means of two independent samples from different populations, we can use Figure 10.1 to help visualize the situation. The two populations are shown to be normally distributed, but, because we will be using large samples from these populations, this is *not* a necessary assumption. For these populations,

μ_1 = mean of population 1

μ_2 = mean of population 2

σ_1 = standard deviation of population 1

σ_2 = standard deviation of population 2

For example, if we wished to compare U.S. adult male and female heights:

μ_1 = average of all male heights

μ_2 = average of all female heights

σ_1 = standard deviation of all male heights

σ_2 = standard deviation of all female heights

The point estimates discussed in earlier chapters apply here as well—we simply have two of everything because we are dealing with two populations.

The procedure we follow is to obtain a random sample of size n_1 from population 1 and then obtain another sample of size n_2, completely independent of the first sample, from population 2. So, $\overline{X}_1$ is our best (point) estimate of μ_1. Likewise, $\overline{X}_2$ estimates μ_2. The sample standard deviations (s_1 and s_2) provide the best estimates of the population standard deviations (σ_1 and σ_2).

Constructing a Confidence Interval for $\mu_1 - \mu_2$

Ace Delivery Service operates a fleet of delivery vans in the Houston area. They prefer to have all their drivers charge their gasoline using the same brand of credit card. Presently, they all use a Texgas credit card. Ace management has decided that perhaps Quik-Chek, a chain of convenience stores also selling gasoline but not accepting credit cards, is worth investigating. A random sample of gas prices at 35 Texgas

Figure 10.1

Example of two populations. Is $\mu_1 = \mu_2$?

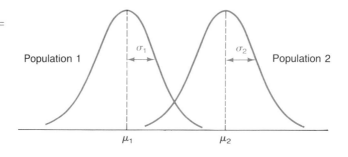

stations and 40 Quik-Chek stores in the Houston area is obtained. The cost of one gallon of regular gasoline is recorded; the data are summarized:

Sample 1 (Texgas) **Sample 2 (Quik-Chek)**
$n_1 = 35$ $n_2 = 40$
$\bar{x}_1 = \$1.48$ $\bar{x}_2 = \$1.39$
$s_1 = \$ .12$ $s_2 = \$ .10$

Let μ_1 be the average price of regular gasoline at *all* Texgas stations in the Houston area, and let μ_2 be the average price of regular gasoline at *all* Quik-Check stores in the Houston area.

When dealing with two populations, the parameter of interest is $\mu_1 - \mu_2$ rather than the individual values of μ_1 and μ_2. Here, $\mu_1 - \mu_2$ represents how much the gasoline at the Texgas stations is as compared with that at the Quik-Chek stores (on the average). If we conclude that $\mu_1 - \mu_2 > 0$, then this means that $\mu_1 > \mu_2$. In this case, the gasoline *is* more expensive at the Texgas stations.

The point estimate of $\mu_1 - \mu_2$ is the obvious one: $\bar{X}_1 - \bar{X}_2$. For our data, the (point) estimate of $\mu_1 - \mu_2$ is $\bar{x}_1 - \bar{x}_2 = 1.48 - 1.39 = .09$. How much more expensive is the gasoline from all of the Texgas stations, on the average? We do not know, because this is $\mu_1 - \mu_2$, but we *do* have an estimate of this value—namely, nine cents.

What kind of random variable is $\bar{X}_1 - \bar{X}_2$? First, because the samples are large, we know by using the CLT that $\bar{X}_1$ is approximately a normal random variable with mean μ_1 and variance σ_1^2/n_1 and that $\bar{X}_2$ is approximately a normal random variable with mean μ_2 and variance σ_2^2/n_2. These are two independent samples, so $\bar{X}_1 - \bar{X}_2$ is also approximately a normal random variable with mean $\mu_1 - \mu_2$ and variance $(\sigma_1^2/n_1) + (\sigma_2^2/n_2)$. Note that the variance of $\bar{X}_1 - \bar{X}_2$ is obtained by *adding* the variances for $\bar{X}_1$ and $\bar{X}_2$.

By standardizing this normal distribution, we obtain an approximate standard normal random variable defined by

$$Z = \frac{(\bar{X}_1 - \bar{X}_2) - (\mu_1 - \mu_2)}{\sqrt{\dfrac{\sigma_1^2}{n_1} + \dfrac{\sigma_2^2}{n_2}}} \tag{10-1}$$

We do not need normal populations. The results of equation 10-1 are valid *regardless* of the shape of the two populations, provided both samples are large (from the CLT). We pointed out that the two populations illustrated in Figure 10.1 need not follow a normal distribution. In fact, they can have any shape, such as exponential, uniform, or possibly a discrete distribution of some sort.

This enables us to derive a CI for $\mu_1 - \mu_2$. We know, by using Table A-4, that

$$P(-1.96 < Z < 1.96) = .95$$

Using equation 10-1 (after rearranging the inequalities), we can make the following statement prior to obtaining the sample data:

$$P\left[(\bar{X}_1 - \bar{X}_2) - 1.96\sqrt{\frac{\sigma_1^2}{n_1} + \frac{\sigma_2^2}{n_2}} < \mu_1 - \mu_2 < (\bar{X}_1 - \bar{X}_2) + 1.96\sqrt{\frac{\sigma_1^2}{n_1} + \frac{\sigma_2^2}{n_2}} \right] = .95$$

This produces a $(1 - \alpha) \cdot 100\%$ CI for $\mu_1 - \mu_2$ (large samples), where σ_1 and σ_2 are *known*, of:

$$(\bar{X}_1 - \bar{X}_2) - Z_{\alpha/2}\sqrt{\frac{\sigma_1^2}{n_1} + \frac{\sigma_2^2}{n_2}}$$

$$\text{to} \quad (\bar{X}_1 - \bar{X}_2) + Z_{\alpha/2}\sqrt{\frac{\sigma_1^2}{n_1} + \frac{\sigma_2^2}{n_2}} \tag{10-2}$$

If σ_1 and σ_2 are *unknown*, we have:

$$(\bar{X}_1 - \bar{X}_2) - Z_{\alpha/2}\sqrt{\frac{s_1^2}{n_1} + \frac{s_2^2}{n_2}}$$

$$\text{to} \quad (\bar{X}_1 - \bar{X}_2) + Z_{\alpha/2}\sqrt{\frac{s_1^2}{n_1} + \frac{s_2^2}{n_2}} \tag{10-3}$$

Notice that if σ_1 and σ_2 are unknown (the usual case), you simply substitute the sample estimates in their place *provided* you have large samples ($n_1 > 30$ and $n_2 > 30$). For this case, the Z table provides an approximate CI for $\mu_1 - \mu_2$.

Example 10.1

Using the data from the two gas-price samples, construct a 90% CI for $\mu_1 - \mu_2$.

Solution To begin with, the estimate of μ_1 is $\bar{X}_1 = \$1.48$, and the estimate of μ_2 is $\bar{X}_2 = \$1.39$. We are constructing a 90% CI, so (using Table A-4) we find that $Z_{.05} = 1.645$ (Figure 10.2). The resulting 90% CI for $\mu_1 - \mu_2$ is

$$(\bar{X}_1 - \bar{X}_2) - 1.645\sqrt{\frac{s_1^2}{n_1} + \frac{s_2^2}{n_2}} \quad \text{to} \quad (\bar{X}_1 - \bar{X}_2) + 1.645\sqrt{\frac{s_1^2}{n_1} + \frac{s_2^2}{n_2}}$$

$$= (1.48 - 1.39) - 1.645\sqrt{\frac{(.12)^2}{35} + \frac{(.10)^2}{40}} \quad \text{to} \quad (1.48 - 1.39) + 1.645\sqrt{\frac{(.12)^2}{35} + \frac{(.10)^2}{40}}$$

$$= .09 - (1.645)(.0257) \quad \text{to} \quad .09 + (1.645)(.0257)$$

$$= .09 - .042 \quad \text{to} \quad .09 + .042$$

$$= .048 \quad \text{to} \quad .132$$

We can summarize this result in several ways:

1. We are 90% confident that $\mu_1 - \mu_2$ lies between .048 and .132.
2. We are 90% confident that the average price of Texgas regular gasoline is

Figure 10.2

Finding the pair of Z values containing 90% of the area under the curve. The values are -1.645 and 1.645.

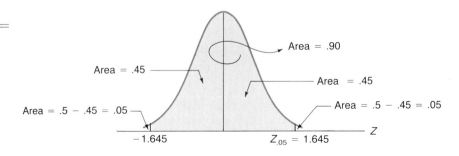

between 4.8 cents and 13.2 cents higher than the regular gasoline at Quik-Chek.

3. We are 90% confident that our estimate of $\mu_1 - \mu_2$ $(\overline{X}_1 - \overline{X}_2 = .09)$ is within 4.2 cents of the actual value. ●

The CIs defined in equations 10-2 and 10-3 will contain $\mu_1 - \mu_2$, 90% of the time. In other words, if you repeatedly obtained independent samples and repeated the procedure in example 10.1, 90% of the corresponding CIs would contain the unknown value of $\mu_1 - \mu_2$, and 10% of them would not.

Sample Sizes

The amount that you add to and subtract from your point estimate to obtain the CI is the **maximum error, E.** For example 10.1, this value is $E = .042$ (4.2 cents). If you think that E is too large and you would like it to be smaller, one recourse is to *obtain larger samples* from your two populations. To determine how large of a sample you need, one procedure is simply to experiment with different values of n_1 and n_2 until you obtain the desired value of E.

For example, if you would like the maximum error to be 2 cents $(E = .02)$, then try using several larger values of n_1 and n_2.

$$E = 1.645 \sqrt{\frac{s_1^2}{n_1} + \frac{s_2^2}{n_2}} \qquad (s_1 = .12, \ s_2 = .10)$$

$n_1 = 100 \qquad n_2 = 100 \qquad E = .026$

$n_1 = 150 \qquad n_2 = 125 \qquad E = .022$

$n_1 = 200 \qquad n_2 = 150 \qquad E = .019$

Somewhere in the range between the second and third values of n_1 and n_2 will be an adequate sample from each of the populations. For example, consider using sample sizes $n_1 = 190$ and $n_2 = 139$. The resulting maximum error is

$$E = 1.645 \sqrt{\frac{(.12)^2}{190} + \frac{(.10)^2}{139}} = .02$$

Keep in mind that there will be many other values of n_1 and n_2 that also provide a value of $E = .02$.

In this illustration, the total sample size is $n = n_1 + n_2 = 190 + 139 = 329$. A better way to proceed here is to find the values of n_1 and n_2 that **minimize the total sample size, n.** The values of n_1 and n_2 that accomplish this are

$$n_1 = \frac{Z_{\alpha/2}^2 s_1 (s_1 + s_2)}{E^2} \qquad (10\text{-}4)$$

$$n_2 = \frac{Z_{\alpha/2}^2 s_2 (s_1 + s_2)}{E^2} \qquad (10\text{-}5)$$

For this illustration, $Z_{\alpha/2} = Z_{.05} = 1.645$, $s_1 = .12$, $s_2 = .10$, and $E = .02$. Consequently,

$$n_1 = \frac{(1.645)^2 (.12)(.22)}{(.02)^2} \cong 179$$

$$n_2 = \frac{(1.645)^2(.10)(.22)}{(.02)^2} \cong 149$$

and the total sample size is $n = 179 + 149 = 328$.

A derivation of this result is contained in Appendix B, on page 847. Notice that the advantage of using this procedure is that you need not experiment with different values of n_1 and n_2 to find those likely to provide the specified value for the maximum error, E. Keep in mind that, when using these values of n_1 and n_2, the resulting value of E may not be exactly what you previously specified—because the values of s_1 and s_2 in the new samples will change.

Using equations 10-4 and 10-5, observe that, if $s_1 = s_2$, your total sample size $(n_1 + n_2)$ will be the smallest when $n_1 = n_2$. If $s_1 > s_2$, you will select $n_1 > n_2$, and if $s_1 < s_2$, you will select $n_1 < n_2$.

Hypothesis Testing for μ_1 and μ_2 (Large Samples)

Are men on the average taller than women? How do you answer such a question? We know that we can start by getting a sample of male heights and a sample of female heights. Figure 10.3 shows two such samples.

We proceed as before and put the claim that we are trying to demonstrate into the *alternative* hypothesis. The resulting hypotheses are

H_0: $\mu_2 \leq \mu_1$ (men are not taller, on the average)

H_a: $\mu_2 > \mu_1$ (men are taller, on the average)

We have estimates of μ_1 and μ_2, namely, $\overline{X}_1$ and $\overline{X}_2$. A sensible thing to do would be to reject H_0 if $\overline{X}_2$ is "significantly larger" than $\overline{X}_1$. In this case, the obvious conclusion is that μ_2 (the average of all male heights in your population) is larger than μ_1 (for female heights).

To define "significantly larger," we need to know what chance we are willing to take in rejecting H_0 when in fact it is true. This is α (the significance level) and, as before, is determined prior to seeing any data. Typical values range from .01 to .1, with $\alpha = .05$ a good choice in the situation where there is an equal tradeoff between the Type I and Type II errors. The test statistic here is the same as the one used to derive a CI for $\mu_1 - \mu_2$. We are dealing with large samples ($n_1 > 30$ and $n_2 > 30$), so this is approximately a standard normal random variable, defined by

$$Z = \frac{\overline{X}_1 - \overline{X}_2}{\sqrt{\dfrac{s_1^2}{n_1} + \dfrac{s_2^2}{n_2}}} \tag{10-6}$$

Figure 10.3

Hypothesis testing for two populations. Sample 1: size, n_1, mean, $\overline{X}_1$, and standard deviation, s_1. Sample 2: size, n_2, mean, $\overline{X}_2$, and standard deviation, s_2. Is $\mu_2 > \mu_1$?

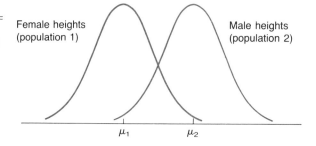

Female heights (population 1)

Male heights (population 2)

μ_1 μ_2

Example 10.2

The Ace Delivery people suspected that the gasoline at the Quik-Chek stores was less expensive than that at Texgas before they obtained any data. (*Note:* This is important! Do not let the data dictate your hypotheses for you. If you do, you introduce a serious bias into your testing procedure, and the "true" significance level may no longer be the predetermined α). Here, μ_1 represents the average price at all of the Texgas stations and μ_2 is the average price at the Quik-Chek stores in the area. Is $\mu_2 < \mu_1$? Or, put another way, is $\mu_1 > \mu_2$? Use a significance level of .05.

Solution

Step 1. *Define the hypotheses.* The question is whether or not the data support the claim that $\mu_1 > \mu_2$, so we put this statement in the alternative hypothesis.

$H_0: \mu_1 \leq \mu_2$ (Texgas is less expensive or the same)

$H_a: \mu_1 > \mu_2$ (Quik-Chek is less expensive)

Note that, as in Chapter 9, when defining a one-tailed test, the equals sign goes into H_0. In other words, the case where $\mu_1 = \mu_2$ is contained in the null hypothesis.

Step 2. *Define the test statistic.* This is the statistic that you evaluate using the sample data. Its value will either support the alternative hypothesis or it will not. The test statistic for this situation is equation 10-6:

$$Z = \frac{\overline{X}_1 - \overline{X}_2}{\sqrt{\dfrac{s_1^2}{n_1} + \dfrac{s_2^2}{n_2}}}$$

Notice that the $\mu_1 - \mu_2$ term used in equation 10-1 drops out here because, if H_0 is true, the difference between these two means is zero.

Step 3. *Define the rejection region.* In Figure 10.4, where should the null hypothesis H_0 be rejected? We simply ask, what happens to Z when H_a is true? In this case ($\mu_1 > \mu_2$), we *should* see $\overline{X}_1 > \overline{X}_2$. In other words, Z will be positive. So we reject H_0 if Z is "too large"; that is,

Reject H_0 if $Z > k$ for some $k > 0$

Using $\alpha = .05$, we use Table A-4 to find the corresponding value of Z (that is, k). The resulting shaded area in Figure 10.4 is the rejection region.

In Figure 10.4, $k = 1.645$. This is the same value and rejection region we obtained in Chapter 9 when using Z for a one-tailed test in the right tail. The test is

Reject H_0 if $Z > 1.645$

Figure 10.4

Z curve showing rejection region for example 10.2.

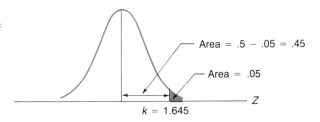

Area = .5 − .05 = .45

Area = .05

Z

$k = 1.645$

Step 4. *Evaluate the test statistic and carry out the test.* The data collected showed $n_1 = 35$, $\bar{x}_1 = 1.48$, $s_1 = .12$ (from the Texgas sample) and $n_2 = 40$, $\bar{x}_2 = 1.39$, $s_2 = .10$ (from the Quik-Chek sample). Based on these sample results, can we conclude that $\bar{x}_1 = 1.48$ is significantly *larger* than $\bar{x}_2 = 1.39$? If we can, the decision will be to reject H_0. The following value of the test statistic will answer our question.

$$Z = \frac{\overline{X}_1 - \overline{X}_2}{\sqrt{\dfrac{s_1^2}{n_1} + \dfrac{s_2^2}{n_2}}} = \frac{1.48 - 1.39}{\sqrt{\dfrac{(.12)^2}{35} + \dfrac{(.10)^2}{40}}}$$

$$= \frac{.09}{.0257} = 3.50 = Z^*$$

Because $3.50 > 1.645$, we reject H_0; $\bar{x}_1$ is significantly larger than $\bar{x}_2$.

Step 5. *State a conclusion.* We conclude that the Quik-Chek stores *do* charge less for gasoline (on the average) than do the Texgas stations. If the locations of these stores are equally convenient to Ace Delivery Service, buying gas from Quik-Chek appears to be a money-saving alternative.   ●

Using the corresponding p-value for the data in example 10.2, what would you conclude using the classical approach (with $\alpha = .05$)? For this example, the p-value will be the area under the Z curve (Z is our test statistic) to the right (we reject H_0 in the right tail for this example) of the calculated test statistic, $Z^* = 3.50$. In general,

$$p = p\text{-value} = \begin{cases} \text{area to the right of } Z^* \text{ for } H_a\colon \mu_1 > \mu_2 \\ \text{area to the left of } Z^* \text{ for } H_a\colon \mu_1 < \mu_2 \\ 2 \text{ (tail area of } Z^*) \text{ for } H_a\colon \mu_1 \neq \mu_2 \end{cases} \qquad (10\text{-}7)$$

These three alternative hypotheses are your choices for this situation. Once again, $H_0\colon \mu_1 = \mu_2$ versus $H_a\colon \mu_1 \neq \mu_2$ is a two-tailed test, and the first two alternative hypotheses represent one-tailed tests.

Returning to our example, we can see from Figure 10.5 that the resulting p-value is $p = .0002$ (very small). Using the classical approach, because $p < \alpha = .05$, we reject H_0—the same conclusion as before. In fact, this procedure *always* leads to the same conclusion as the five-step solution, as we saw in Chapter 9.

If we elect not to select a significance level α and instead use only the p-value to make a decision, we proceed as before:

Figure 10.5

Z curve showing *p*-value
for *Z* ★ = 3.50.

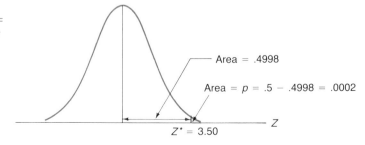

Area = .4998

Area = p = .5 − .4998 = .0002

Z

Z^* = 3.50

Reject H_0 if p is small ($< .01$).
FTR H_0 if p is large ($> .1$).
Data are inconclusive if p is neither small nor large ($.01 \leqslant p \leqslant .1$).

For this example, $p = .0002$ is clearly small, and so we again reject H_0. The Quik-Chek gasoline definitely appears to be less expensive than the Texgas gasoline. As was pointed out in the previous chapter, you often encounter a result that is *statistically* significant but may not be significant in a *practical* sense. To illustrate, suppose that the p-value of .0002 was the result of two very large samples and that the difference in gasoline price for the two samples was $\bar{x}_1 - \bar{x}_2 = .008$. You might not view this difference (less than 1 cent) as being worth the inconvenience of having to pay cash for all gasoline purchases.

Comment

There may well be situations where the severity of the Type I error requires a significance level smaller than .01 on the low end, or the impact of a Type II error dictates a significance level larger than .1 on the upper end. This rule is thus only a general yardstick that applies to most, but certainly not all, business applications.

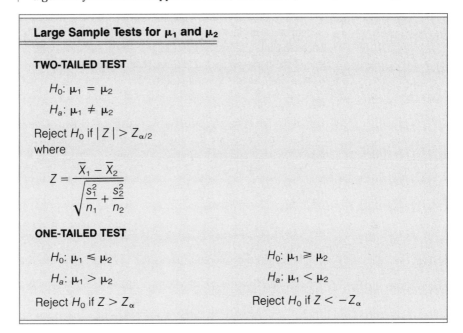

Large Sample Tests for μ_1 and μ_2

TWO-TAILED TEST

H_0: $\mu_1 = \mu_2$

H_a: $\mu_1 \neq \mu_2$

Reject H_0 if $|Z| > Z_{\alpha/2}$
where

$$Z = \frac{\bar{X}_1 - \bar{X}_2}{\sqrt{\dfrac{s_1^2}{n_1} + \dfrac{s_2^2}{n_2}}}$$

ONE-TAILED TEST

H_0: $\mu_1 \leqslant \mu_2$ H_0: $\mu_1 \geqslant \mu_2$

H_a: $\mu_1 > \mu_2$ H_a: $\mu_1 < \mu_2$

Reject H_0 if $Z > Z_\alpha$ Reject H_0 if $Z < -Z_\alpha$

Two-Sample Procedure for any Specified Value of $\mu_1 - \mu_2$

The two-tailed hypotheses for large sample tests for μ_1 and μ_2 can be written as

H_0: $\mu_1 - \mu_2 = 0$

H_a: $\mu_1 - \mu_2 \neq 0$

The right-sided one-tailed hypotheses are

H_0: $\mu_1 - \mu_2 \leqslant 0$

H_a: $\mu_1 - \mu_2 > 0$

The left-tailed hypotheses can be written in a similar manner. The point is that H_0 (so far) claims that $\mu_1 - \mu_2$ is equal to *zero* or lies to one side of zero (the one-tailed tests).

Suppose the claim is that $\mu_1 - \mu_2$ is more than ten. To demonstrate that this is true, we must make our alternative hypothesis H_a: $\mu_1 - \mu_2 > 10$, and the corresponding null hypothesis is H_0: $\mu_1 - \mu_2 \leq 10$.

In general, to test that $\mu_1 - \mu_2 =$ (some specified value, say D_0), the five-step procedure still applies, except the test statistic is now

$$Z = \frac{(\bar{X}_1 - \bar{X}_2) - D_0}{\sqrt{\dfrac{s_1^2}{n_1} + \dfrac{s_2^2}{n_2}}} \tag{10-8}$$

Equation 10-8 applies to both one-tailed and two-tailed tests. It can be used to compare two means directly (for example, H_0: $\mu_1 = \mu_2$ versus H_a: $\mu_1 \neq \mu_2$) by setting $D_0 = 0$, as in example 10.2.

Example 10.3

In example 10.2, we decided that Ace Delivery Service would save money if they purchased their gasoline from Quik-Chek because that store's average gasoline price appeared to be less than that of the Texgas stations. The owner of Ace says that, because Quik-Chek does not accept credit cards, he is willing to purchase their gasoline only if their average price is more than six cents per gallon less than Texgas's. Do the data indicate that it is (α is still .05)?

Solution So, now the hypotheses are whether the data support the claim that the difference between the two means (Texgas and Quik-Chek) is larger than six cents. So the hypotheses are H_0: $\mu_1 - \mu_2 \leq .06$ and H_a: $\mu_1 - \mu_2 > .06$, where μ_1 is Texgas's mean and μ_2 is Quik-Chek's mean.

The test statistic is

$$Z = \frac{(\bar{X}_1 - \bar{X}_2) - .06}{\sqrt{\dfrac{s_1^2}{n_1} + \dfrac{s_2^2}{n_2}}}$$

The computed value of Z is

$$Z^* = \frac{(1.48 - 1.39) - .06}{\sqrt{\dfrac{(.12)^2}{35} + \dfrac{(.10)^2}{40}}} = \frac{.03}{.0257}$$

$$= 1.17$$

The testing procedure is exactly as it was previously—reject H_0 if $Z^* > 1.645$. Because $1.17 < 1.645$, we FTR H_0. The difference between the two sample means (nine cents) was *not* significantly larger than the hypothesized value of six cents.

These data provide insufficient evidence to conclude that Quik-Chek is more than six cents less expensive (on the average) than Texgas. If Ace's owner thinks that not using credit cards would be too much trouble for less than a six-cent per gallon savings, Ace should use the Texgas gasoline. ●

Exercises

10.9 Determine the value of the test statistic and the p-value that would result from the hypothesis test in each of the following cases:

a. H_0: $\mu_1 - \mu_2 \leq 100$, H_a: $\mu_1 - \mu_2 > 100$, $n_1 = 31$, $n_2 = 34$, $\bar{x}_1 = 190$, $\bar{x}_2 = 80$, $s_1 = 25.1$, $s_2 = 20$.

b. H_0: $\mu_1 - \mu_2 = 0$, H_a: $\mu_1 - \mu_2 \neq 0$, $n_1 = 40$, $n_2 = 64$, $\bar{x}_1 = 4.5$, $\bar{x}_2 = 5.8$, $\sigma_1 = 19.1$, $\sigma_2 = 49.3$.

c. H_0: $\mu_1 - \mu_2 \geq 406$, H_a: $\mu_1 - \mu_2 < 406$, $n_1 = 100$, $n_2 = 100$, $\bar{x}_1 = 1050$, $\bar{x}_2 = 650$, $s_1 = 900$, $s_2 = 330$.

10.10 The computer center managers in Becker Industries would like to know if there is a difference in the weekly computer time (in seconds) used by the employees within the financial-planning department and that used by those in the legal-aid department. Test the hypothesis that there is no difference in computer usage for the two departments. Let the significance level be .05. Use the sample statistics that follow, in which 40 weeks were randomly selected for each department.

Statistic	n	$\bar{x}$	$\Sigma(x - \bar{x})^2$
Financial Planning	40	2503	2180.4
Legal	40	2510	2291.6

10.11 Fort Worth and Dallas are two large cities that, despite their geographical closeness, have somewhat different economies. To find out the difference in the amount of unemployment, a statistician randomly interviewed 120 unemployed workers from Fort Worth and 150 unemployed workers from Dallas. These people indicated the number of weeks they had been out of work over the past 52 weeks. The data are as follows. Total number of weeks: Fort Worth, 2,031; Dallas, 3,713. Standard deviation: Fort Worth, 1.3; Dallas, 2.1. Find a 90% CI for the mean difference in the number of weeks unemployed for the work forces of Fort Worth and Dallas.

10.12 First National Bank and City National Bank are competing for customers who would like to open IRAs (individual retirement accounts). Thirty-two weeks are randomly selected for First National Bank and another 32 weeks are randomly selected for City National. The total amount of deposits from IRAs is noted for each week. A summary of data (deposits in thousands of dollars) from the survey is as follows. First National: $\bar{x} = 4.1$, $s = 1.2$. City National: $\bar{x} = 3.5$, $s = 0.9$. Use a 98% CI to estimate the difference in the mean weekly deposits from IRAs for each bank.

10.13 Two discount stores in a popular shopping mall have their merchandise laid out differently. Both stores claim that the arrangement of goods in their store makes the customer buy more on impulse. A survey of 100 customers from each store is taken. Each customer is asked how much money he or she spent on merchandise he or she did not originally intend to buy before walking into the store. The results are as follows. Discount store 1, $\bar{x} = \$15.5$, $s = \$3.2$. Discount store 2: $\bar{x} = \$19.4$, $s = \$4.8$. Find a 90% CI for the difference in the mean amount of cash spent per customer on impulse buying for the two different stores. Is layout affecting impulse buying? How do you know?

10.14 If a 99% CI is found in exercise 10.13, instead of a 90% CI, would the former CI be larger or smaller than the latter? Explain.

10.15 A personnel director wants to know if the mean length of employment in years with the company is about the same for assembly and clerical workers. A sample 35 employees was randomly drawn from each of these two groups of workers. Test the hypothesis that the mean length of employment with the company is the same for both groups. Use a significance level of .03. Assembly workers: $n = 35$, $\bar{x} = 4.1$, $s^2 = 30.2$. Clerical workers: $n = 35$, $\bar{x} = 3.2$, $s^2 = 28.1$.

10.16 Construct the 90% CI for the difference in the mean length of employment from the two groups of workers in exercise 10.15.

10.17 Consider the following two independent random samples: $n_1 = 37$, $s_1 = 210$, $\bar{x}_1 = 1360$, and $n_2 = 64$, $s_2 = 108$, $\bar{x}_2 = 1270$. Test the hypotheses: H_0: $\mu_1 - \mu_2 \leq 75$ and H_a: $\mu_1 - \mu_2 > 75$. Use a 10% significance level.

10.18 Alan Nakkupuchi, a designer for high-quality stereo systems, is interested in constructing a 95% CI for the difference between the signal/noise ratios for the two models he developed. Data were obtained from each model as follows. Model A: $\bar{x} = 54$, $n = 45$, $s = 8$. Model B: $\bar{x} = 62$, $n = 60$, $s = 17$. Find the 95% CI.

10.19 Test the null hypothesis of no difference in the mean signal/noise ratios for models A and B in exercise 10.18, using a .02 significance level.

10.20 The systems manager of Ace Manufacturing is about to purchase a microcomputer and has narrowed her choices to the Alpha and Gemini models. She is seriously concerned about the cost of maintenance of these two models. After interviewing 40 experts on the Alpha model and a different 40 experts on the Gemini model, she obtained the following information on the cost of maintenance. Average annual cost of maintenance: Alpha, $46.50; Gemini, $37.20. Standard deviation: Alpha, 4.20; Gemini, 6.10. Do the data indicate a significant difference in the cost of maintenance for the two models? Use the p-value to justify your answer.

10.21 The financial analyst of Hogan Securities believes that there is no difference in the annual average returns for steel industry stocks and mineral industry stocks. Using the following information, test the hypothesis that there is no significant difference in the average returns for these two types of stocks. Steel industry stocks: $\bar{x} = 9\%$, $n = 33$, $s = 2.4\%$. Mineral industry stocks: $\bar{x} = 11\%$, $n = 41$, $s = 4\%$. Use a 10% significance level.

10.22 Calculate the p-value for exercise 10.21 and interpret it.

10.23 An education analyst is studying the performance of high-school seniors on the SAT examination. He is specifically testing whether there is any difference between the mean SAT scores of seniors who attended public schools and those who attended private schools. He believes that this difference should be at least 50 points. Using the following information, what would be your conclusion at a significance level of 0.05? Do you agree with the analyst? Seniors— public schools: $\bar{x} = 590$, $s = 67$, $n = 40$. Seniors—private schools: $\bar{x} = 680$, $s = 110$, $n = 55$.

10.24 For exercise 10.23, construct a 95% CI for the mean difference in the SAT scores for seniors for the two types of schools. What does this tell you?

10.3

Comparing Two Normal Population Means Using Two Small Independent Samples

When dealing with *small* samples from two populations, we need to consider the assumed distribution of the populations because the CLT no longer applies. This section is concerned with comparing two population means when two small independent random samples are used. It differs from the previous section in two respects:

1. We are dealing with *small samples*.
2. We must assume that the two populations of interest are *normal* populations. In Figures 10.1 and 10.3, where we had large sample sizes, this was *not* a necessary assumption. When you use small samples from two populations, one or both of which appear to be *not* normally distributed, a nonparametric procedure is the proper method for analyzing such data. This will be discussed in Chapter 19.

In Chapter 9, we showed that, when going from large samples to small samples, the CI and hypothesis-testing procedures both remained exactly the same, except we use the t distribution, rather than the Z distribution, to describe the test statistic. We will use the same approach for small samples from two populations.

Confidence Interval for $\mu_1 - \mu_2$ (Small Independent Samples)

When using large samples from the two populations to compare μ_1 and μ_2, we used the Z statistic defined by

$$Z = \frac{\overline{X}_1 - \overline{X}_2}{\sqrt{\dfrac{s_1^2}{n_1} + \dfrac{s_2^2}{n_2}}}$$

When using small samples ($n_1 < 30$ or $n_2 < 30$), this statistic no longer approximately follows a standard normal distribution. To make matters more complicated, it is not a t random variable either. However, this expression is *approximately* a t random variable with a somewhat complicated expression used to derive the degrees of freedom (df). So we define

$$t' = \frac{\overline{X}_1 - \overline{X}_2}{\sqrt{\dfrac{s_1^2}{n_1} + \dfrac{s_2^2}{n_2}}} \tag{10-9}$$

This statistic approximately follows a t distribution with degrees of freedom df given by

$$df \text{ for } t' = \frac{\left[\dfrac{s_1^2}{n_1} + \dfrac{s_2^2}{n_2}\right]^2}{\dfrac{\left(\dfrac{s_1^2}{n_1}\right)^2}{n_1 - 1} + \dfrac{\left(\dfrac{s_2^2}{n_2}\right)^2}{n_2 - 1}} \tag{10-10}$$

Admittedly, equation 10-10 is complex, but a good calculator or computer package makes this calculation relatively painless. To be on the conservative side, if df as calculated is not an integer (1, 2, 3, . . .), it should be rounded *down* to the nearest integer.

When finding the df, you can scale *both* s_1 and s_2 any way you wish, provided you scale them both the same way. By scaling, we mean that you can use s_1 and s_2 as is, or you can move the decimal point to the right or left. The resulting df will be the same *regardless* of the scaling used. However, when you evaluate the test statistic, t', or later perform a test of hypothesis, you must return to the *original* values of s_1 and s_2.

To derive an approximate CI for $\mu_1 - \mu_2$, we use the same logic as in the previous (large samples) procedure. Thus, a $(1 - \alpha) \cdot 100\%$ CI for $\mu_1 - \mu_2$ (small samples) is:

$$(\overline{X}_1 - \overline{X}_2) - t_{\alpha/2, df}\sqrt{\dfrac{s_1^2}{n_1} + \dfrac{s_2^2}{n_2}}$$

$$\text{to} \quad (\overline{X}_1 - \overline{X}_2) + t_{\alpha/2, df}\sqrt{\dfrac{s_1^2}{n_1} + \dfrac{s_2^2}{n_2}} \tag{10-11}$$

where *df* is specified in equation 10-10. If *df* is not an integer, round this value *down* to the nearest integer.

Example 10.4

Checkers Cab Company is trying to decide which brand of tires to use for the coming year. Based on current price and prior experience, they have narrowed their choice to two brands, Beltex and Roadmaster. A recent study examined the durability of these tires by using a machine with a metallic device that wore down the tires. The time it took (in hours) for the tire to blow out was recorded.

Because the test for each tire took a great deal of time and the tire itself was ruined by the test, small samples of 15 of each brand were used. Notice that these are *independent* samples; there is no reason to match up the first Beltex tire with the first Roadmaster tire in the sample, the second Beltex with the second Roadmaster, and so on. As discussed in Section 10.1, they would be dependent samples if the tires were tested by putting one of each brand on the rear wheels of 15 different cars.

The blowout times (hours) were as follows:

Beltex	Roadmaster	Beltex	Roadmaster
3.82	4.16	2.84	3.65
3.11	3.92	3.26	3.82
4.21	3.94	3.74	4.55
2.64	4.22	3.04	3.82
4.16	4.15	2.56	3.85
3.91	3.62	2.58	3.62
2.44	4.11	3.15	4.88
4.52	3.45		

Construct a 90% CI for $\mu_1 - \mu_2$, letting μ_1 be the average blowout time for *all* Beltex tires and μ_2 be the average blowout time for *all* Roadmaster tires.

Solution Here is a summary of the data from these two samples.

Sample 1 (Beltex)   **Sample 2 (Roadmaster)**
$n_1 = 15$ $n_2 = 15$
$\bar{x}_1 = 3.33$ hours $\bar{x}_2 = 3.98$ hours
$s_1 = .68$ hours $s_2 = .38$ hours

Your next step is to get a *t* value from Table A-5. To do this, you first must calculate the correct *df* using equation 10-10. This is

$$df = \frac{\left[\dfrac{(.68)^2}{15} + \dfrac{(.38)^2}{15}\right]^2}{\dfrac{\left(\dfrac{(.68)^2}{15}\right)^2}{14} + \dfrac{\left(\dfrac{(.38)^2}{15}\right)^2}{14}}$$

$$= \frac{(.0404)^2}{.0000679 + .00000662} = 21.9$$

Rounding this down, we have *df* = 21. Using Table A-5:

$$t_{.10/2, 21} = t_{.05, 21} = 1.721$$

The resulting 90% CI for $\mu_1 - \mu_2$ is

$$(\bar{X}_1 - \bar{X}_2) - t_{.05,21}\sqrt{\frac{s_1^2}{n_1} + \frac{s_2^2}{n_2}} \quad \text{to} \quad (\bar{X}_1 - \bar{X}_2) + t_{.05,21}\sqrt{\frac{s_1^2}{n_1} + \frac{s_2^2}{n_2}}$$

$$= (3.33 - 3.98) - 1.721\sqrt{\frac{(.68)^2}{15} + \frac{(.38)^2}{15}} \quad \text{to} \quad (3.33 - 3.98) + 1.721\sqrt{\frac{(.68)^2}{15} + \frac{(.38)^2}{15}}$$

$$= -.65 - .35 \quad \text{to} \quad -.65 + .35$$

$$= -1.00 \text{ hour} \quad \text{to} \quad -.30 \text{ hour}$$

So we are 90% confident that the average blowout time for the Beltex tires is between 18 minutes (.3 hours) and 1 hour *less* than for the Roadmaster tires. Based on these results, Roadmaster appears to be the better (longer-wearing) tire. ●

Hypothesis Testing for μ_1 and μ_2 (Small Independent Samples)

The five-step procedure for testing hypotheses concerning μ_1 and μ_2 with large samples also applies to the small-sample situation. The only difference is that Table A-5 is used (rather than Table A-4) to define the rejection region.

Example 10.5

In example 10.4, a CI was constructed for the difference between average blowout times for Beltex and Roadmaster tires. Can we conclude that these average blowout times are in fact not the same? Use a significance level of .10.

Solution

Step 1. We are testing for a difference between the two means (not that Roadmaster is longer-wearing than Beltex, or vice versa). The corresponding appropriate hypotheses are H_0: $\mu_1 = \mu_2$ and H_a: $\mu_1 \neq \mu_2$.

Step 2. The test statistic is

$$t' = \frac{\bar{X}_1 - \bar{X}_2}{\sqrt{\frac{s_1^2}{n_1} + \frac{s_2^2}{n_2}}}$$

which approximately follows a t distribution with df given by equation 10.10.

Step 3. You next need the df in order to determine your rejection region. In example 10.4, we found that $df = 21$. Because H_a: $\mu_1 \neq \mu_2$, we will reject H_0 if t' is too large ($\bar{X}_1$ is significantly *larger* than $\bar{X}_2$) or if t' is too small ($\bar{X}_1$ is significantly *smaller* than $\bar{X}_2$). As in previous two-tailed tests using the Z or t statistic, H_0 is rejected if the absolute value of t exceeds the value from the table corresponding to $\alpha/2$. Using Table A-5, the rejection region for this situation will be

Reject H_0 if $| t' | > t_{\alpha/2,df} = t_{.05,21} = 1.721$

Step 4. The value of the test statistic is

$$t'^* = \frac{3.33 - 3.98}{\sqrt{\frac{(.68)^2}{15} + \frac{(.38)^2}{15}}} = \frac{-.65}{.20} = -3.25$$

Because $|t'^*| = 3.25 > 1.721$, we reject H_0. Consequently, the difference between the sample means $(-.65)$ *is* significantly large (in absolute value), which leads to a rejection of the null hypothesis.

Step 5. There *is* a significant difference in the average blowout times for the two brands. ●

Comments

The hypotheses in example 10.4 could be written as H_0: $\mu_1 - \mu_2 = 0$ and H_a: $\mu_1 - \mu_2 \neq 0$. Having already determined a 90% CI for $\mu_1 - \mu_2$, a much simpler way to perform this two-tailed test (using $\alpha = .10$) would be to reject H_0 if 0 does not lie in the CI for $\mu_1 - \mu_2$, and FTR H_0 otherwise. The CI here is $(-1.00, -.30)$, which does not contain zero, and so we reject H_0 (as before).

This alternate method of testing H_0 versus H_a holds only for a two-tailed test in which the significance level of the test, α, and the confidence level $[(1 - \alpha) \cdot 100\%]$ of the CI "match up." For example, a significance level of $\alpha = .05$ would correspond to a 95% confidence interval, a value of $\alpha = .10$ would correspond to a 90% confidence interval, and so on.

A MINITAB solution to example 10.4 is provided in Figure 10.6. The calculated p-value is $p = .0038$. Based on this extremely small value, we again reject H_0.

Notice that the procedure in this section for testing μ_1 versus μ_2 and constructing CIs for $\mu_1 - \mu_2$ was not concerned with the population variances, σ_1^2 and σ_2^2. In particular, no mention was made as to whether these variances (or standard deviations) were equal or not. In fact, we can say that this procedure did not assume that $\sigma_1 = \sigma_2$; it also did *not* assume that $\sigma_1 \neq \sigma_2$. Next, we will examine a special case where we have reason to believe that the standard deviations *are* equal. For this situation, we will define another t test to detect any difference between the population means.

Special Case of Equal Variances

There are some situations in which we are willing to assume that the population variances (σ_1^2 and σ_2^2) are equal. This is not a common occurrence when dealing with data from a business application. One exception might be a long-running production

Figure 10.6

MINITAB solution to example 10.4.

```
MTB > SET INTO C1
DATA> 3.82 3.11 4.21 2.64 4.16 3.91 2.44 4.52 2.84
DATA> 3.26 3.74 3.04 2.56 2.58 3.15
DATA> END
MTB > SET INTO C2
DATA> 4.16 3.92 3.94 4.22 4.15 3.62 4.11 3.45 3.65
DATA> 3.82 4.55 3.82 3.85 3.62 4.88
DATA> END
MTB > TWOSAMPLE TEST WITH 90% CONFIDENCE USING C1 AND C2

TWOSAMPLE T FOR C1 VS C2
          N      MEAN     STDEV    SE MEAN         No subcommands
C1   15       3.332     0.679      0.18           are necessary
C2   15       3.984     0.377      0.097          for a two-tailed test

90 PCT CI FOR MU C1 - MU C2: (-1.00, -0.307)
TTEST MU C1 = MU C2 (VS NE): T=-3.25 P=0.0038 DF=21.9
                                    |          |
                                   t'*      p-value
```

process for which, based on past experience, you are convinced that the variation within population 1 is the same as the variation within population 2.

Another situation in which we may assume $\sigma_1 = \sigma_2$ arises when we obtain two *additional* samples from the two populations, which we use strictly to determine if the population standard deviations are equal. If there is not sufficient evidence to indicate that $\sigma_1 \neq \sigma_2$, then there is no harm in assuming that $\sigma_1 = \sigma_2$. A procedure for testing the population standard deviations will be discussed in Section 10.4.

Why make the assumption that $\sigma_1 = \sigma_2$? Remember, we are still interested in the means, μ_1 and μ_2. As before, we would like to obtain a CI for $\mu_1 - \mu_2$ and to perform a test of hypothesis. If, in fact, σ_1 *is* equal to σ_2, we can construct a slightly stronger test of μ_1 versus μ_2. By "stronger," we mean that we are *more likely* to reject H_0 when it is actually false. This test is said to be more **powerful.**

For this case, because we believe that $\sigma_1{}^2 = \sigma_2{}^2 = \sigma^2$ (say), it makes sense to combine—or **pool**—our estimate of $\sigma_1{}^2$ (s_1^2) with the estimate of $\sigma_2{}^2$ (s_2^2) into one estimate of this common variance (σ^2). The resulting estimate of σ^2 is called the **pooled sample variance** and is written s_p^2. This estimate is merely a *weighted average* of s_1^2 and s_2^2, defined by

$$s_p^2 = \frac{(n_1 - 1)s_1^2 + (n_2 - 1)s_2^2}{n_1 + n_2 - 2} \qquad (10\text{-}12)$$

Constructing Confidence Intervals for $\mu_1 - \mu_2$ To construct the CI, we make two changes in the previous procedure. First, t' is replaced by

$$t = \frac{\overline{X}_1 - \overline{X}_2}{\sqrt{\dfrac{s_p^2}{n_1} + \dfrac{s_p^2}{n_2}}} \qquad (10\text{-}13)$$

$$= \frac{\overline{X}_1 - \overline{X}_2}{s_p \sqrt{\dfrac{1}{n_1} + \dfrac{1}{n_2}}} \qquad (10\text{-}14)$$

Here (unlike with the previous test statistic), t exactly follows a t distribution (assuming the two populations follow a normal distribution).

Second, the *df* for t are much easier to derive:

$$df = n_1 + n_2 - 2$$

So you avoid the difficult *df* calculation in equation 10-10, but you need to derive the pooled variance, s_p^2, using the individual sample variances, s_1^2 and s_2^2.

As a check, your resulting pooled value for s_p should be between s_1 and s_2.

Hypothesis Testing for μ_1 and μ_2 In hypothesis testing for μ_1 and μ_2, the previous procedure applies except that t' is replaced by t, where the *df* used in Table A-5 are $df = n_1 + n_2 - 2$ rather than $df =$ value from equation 10-10.

In examples 10.4 and 10.5, we examined the blowout times for two brands of tires as measured by a machine performing a stress test of the sampled tires. Assume we have determined from previous tests that the *variation* of the blowout times is not affected by the tire brand. Assuming that σ_1^2 (Beltex) $= \sigma_2^2$ (Roadmaster), how can we construct a 90% CI for $\mu_1 - \mu_2$ and determine whether there is a difference in the mean blowout times?

Sample 1 (Beltex)

$n_1 = 15$

$\bar{x}_1 = 3.33$ hours

$s_1 = .68$ hour

Sample 2 (Roadmaster)

$n_2 = 15$

$\bar{x}_2 = 3.98$ hours

$s_2 = .38$ hour

Our first step is to pool the sample variances:

$$s_p^2 = \frac{(15 - 1)(.68)^2 + (15 - 1)(.38)^2}{15 + 15 - 2}$$

$$= \frac{8.495}{28} = .303$$

$$s_p = \sqrt{.303} = .55 \text{ hour}$$

Is .55 between .68 and .38? Yes. Consequently, $s_p^2 = .303$ is our estimate of the common variance (σ^2) of the two tire populations. To find the 90% CI for $\mu_1 - \mu_2$, we use

$$(\bar{X}_1 - \bar{X}_2) - t_{\alpha/2, df} \sqrt{\frac{s_p^2}{n_1} + \frac{s_p^2}{n_2}}$$

$$\text{to} \quad (\bar{X}_1 - \bar{X}_2) + t_{\alpha/2, df} \sqrt{\frac{s_p^2}{n_1} + \frac{s_p^2}{n_2}} \tag{10-15}$$

where $df = n_1 + n_2 - 2$ and $\alpha = .10$.

Because $n_1 + n_2 - 2 = 28$, we find (from Table A-5) that $t_{.05, 28} = 1.701$. Next,

$$\sqrt{\frac{s_p^2}{n_1} + \frac{s_p^2}{n_2}} = s_p \sqrt{\frac{1}{n_1} + \frac{1}{n_2}}$$

$$= .55 \sqrt{\frac{1}{15} + \frac{1}{15}} = .20$$

The resulting CI is

$$(3.33 - 3.98) - (1.701)(.20) \quad \text{to} \quad (3.33 - 3.98) + (1.701)(.20)$$

$$= -.65 - .34 \quad \text{to} \quad -.65 + .34$$

$$= -.99 \quad \text{to} \quad -.31$$

Comparing this result to the CI in example 10.4, you see little difference. This is *not always* the case; it depends on the relative sizes of n_1 and n_2 as well as the relative values of s_1^2 and s_2^2.

Now we wish to test $H_0: \mu_1 = \mu_2$ versus $H_a: \mu_1 \neq \mu_2$. For this particular example, we can, as noted earlier, reject H_0 (using $\alpha = .10$) because zero does not lie in the previously derived CI for $\mu_1 - \mu_2$. When using the five-step procedure, there are only two changes we need to make when using the pooled sample variances. First, when defining our rejection region, we use $n_1 + n_2 - 2 = 28$ df. From Table A-5, the rejection region is

Reject H_0 if $|t| > t_{\alpha/2, df}$

where $t_{.05, 28} = 1.701$.

Second, the value of our test statistic is now

$$t = \frac{\overline{X}_1 - \overline{X}_2}{s_p \sqrt{\dfrac{1}{n_1} + \dfrac{1}{n_2}}} \qquad (10\text{-}16)$$

Here,

$$t = \frac{3.33 - 3.98}{.55 \sqrt{\dfrac{1}{15} + \dfrac{1}{15}}} = \frac{-.65}{.20}$$

$$= -3.25$$

Because $|-3.25| = 3.25 > 1.701$, we reject H_0, once again the two sample means are significantly different. We conclude that there is a difference in the mean blowout times for the two brands of tires.

A MINITAB solution for this example is provided in Figure 10.7. Notice that the computed t value ($t = -3.25$) is the same as in Figure 10.6, but, due to the different df, the p-value is slightly smaller. For this particular example, we observe little difference in the two solutions.

To Pool or Not to Pool? You might think, based on the previous examples, that it really does not matter whether you assume $\sigma_1 = \sigma_2$ or not. The two CIs were nearly the same and the tests of hypothesis results were extremely close, differing only in their df for the test statistic. However, this is not always the case. For situations where s_1^2 is very different from s_2^2, and n_1 and n_2 are not the same, these two results can differ considerably.

Unless, from prior experience, you have strong evidence that the variances are the same, *do not pool the sample variances,* and use the test statistic defined in equation 10-9. If you assume that $\sigma_1 = \sigma_2$ and use the t test statistic in equation 10-16, but in fact $\sigma_1 \neq \sigma_2$, your results will be unreliable. This test is quite sensitive to this particular

Figure 10.7

MINITAB pooled variances solution using data from example 10.4.

```
MTB > TWOSAMPLE TEST WITH 90% CONFIDENCE USING C1 AND C2;
SUBC> POOLED.                                          This subcommand
                                                       is necessary when
TWOSAMPLE T FOR C1 VS C2                               you assume σ₁ = σ₂
        N     MEAN    STDEV    SE MEAN
C1  15      3.332    0.679      0.18
C2  15      3.984    0.377      0.097

90 PCT CI FOR MU C1 - MU C2: (-0.99, -0.311)
TTEST MU C1 = MU C2 (VS NE): T=-3.25 P=0.0030 DF=28.0
                                |             |
                               t'*        p-value
```

assumption. Also, if σ_1 and σ_2 *are* the same, then we would expect s_1 and s_2 to be nearly the same. If, in addition, $n_1 = n_2$ (or nearly so), then the computed values of t' and t will be practically identical (including the df). What this means is that you have little to gain by pooling the variances (and using t), but a great deal to lose if your assumption is incorrect.

We will show you in the next section how to use two samples to test the hypothesis that $\sigma_1 = \sigma_2$. With those results in hand, one possible procedure to use when testing the *means* would be: (1) if you reject H_0: $\sigma_1 = \sigma_2$, then use t' to test H_0: $\mu_1 = \mu_2$, and (2) if you FTR H_0: $\sigma_1 = \sigma_2$, then use t to test H_0: $\mu_1 = \mu_2$.

At first glance this may look reasonable, but it has some problems. The main one is that these two tests use the same data, and so the tests are not performed independently of one another. Also, your actual significance level may not be the α that you had previously chosen before you saw any data. This *can* be a valid procedure if you obtain separate samples—one to test the σ values and the other to test the μ values.

The next section provides a procedure for testing the variances from two normal populations using independent samples. By using the technique on separate data from the two populations, one can decide whether the pooling procedure should be used when using additional data to test μ_1 versus μ_2. If you reject H_0: $\sigma_1 = \sigma_2$, then the t' statistic in equation 10-9 is the proper test statistic to use on a test for the means because it does *not* assume that the population standard deviations are equal. On the other hand, if you fail to reject H_0, then the t statistic in equation 10-16, which *does* assume that $\sigma_1 = \sigma_2$, is the recommended test statistic for testing μ_1 versus μ_2.

Small Sample Tests for μ_1 and μ_2

TWO-TAILED TEST

$$H_0: \mu_1 - \mu_2 = D_0$$
$$H_a: \mu_1 - \mu_2 \neq D_0$$
$$(D_0 = 0 \text{ for } H_0: \mu_1 = \mu_2)$$

Reject H_0 if $|T| > t_{\alpha/2, df}$
where, not assuming $\sigma_1 = \sigma_2$:

$$T = t' = \frac{(\bar{X}_1 - \bar{X}_2) - D_0}{\sqrt{\dfrac{s_1^2}{n_1} + \dfrac{s_2^2}{n_2}}}$$

Or, assuming $\sigma_1 = \sigma_2$:

$$T = t = \frac{(\bar{X}_1 - \bar{X}_2) - D_0}{s_p\sqrt{\dfrac{1}{n_1} + \dfrac{1}{n_2}}}$$

and, for t':

$$df = \frac{\left[\dfrac{s_1^2}{n_1} + \dfrac{s_2^2}{n_2}\right]^2}{\dfrac{\left(\dfrac{s_1^2}{n_1}\right)^2}{n_1 - 1} + \dfrac{\left(\dfrac{s_2^2}{n_2}\right)^2}{n_2 - 1}}$$

and, for t:

$$df = n_1 + n_2 - 2$$

where

$$s_p = \sqrt{\frac{(n_1 - 1)s_1^2 + (n_2 - 1)s_2^2}{n_1 + n_2 - 2}}$$

ONE-TAILED TEST

$H_0: \mu_1 - \mu_2 \leq D_0$ $H_0: \mu_1 - \mu_2 \geq D_0$

$H_a: \mu_1 - \mu_2 > D_0$ $H_a: \mu_1 - \mu_2 < D_0$

$(D_0 = 0$ for $H_0: \mu_1 \leq \mu_2)$ $(D_0 = 0$ for $H_0: \mu_1 \geq \mu_2)$

Reject H_0 if $T > t_{\alpha, df}$ Reject H_0 if $T < -t_{\alpha, df}$

Exercises

10.25 Achieving a high score on the LSAT examination is a prerequisite to getting accepted to law school. Scores on the LSAT are considered to be normally distributed. Two law schools decided to compare the mean scores on the LSAT for students enrolled in their schools. Is there sufficient evidence to indicate that the average scores differ between the two schools? Law school 1: $\bar{x} = 680$, $s = 84$, $n = 15$. Law school 2: $\bar{x} = 634$, $s = 92$, $n = 21$. Use a 1% significance level. Assume that the population variances are equal for law school 1 and law school 2.

10.26 Construct a 95% CI for $\mu_1 - \mu_2$ in exercise 10.25. Assume that the population variances are equal for the two law schools.

10.27 The president of a personnel agency is interested in examining the annual mean salary differences between vice-presidents of banks and vice-presidents of savings and loan institutions. A random sample of eight of each kind of vice-president was selected. Their annual salaries (in dollars) were as follows:

n	**Banks**	**Savings and Loan Institutions**
1	84,320	73,420
2	67,440	49,580
3	98,590	58,750
4	111,780	101,400
5	48,940	88,670
6	56,790	59,640
7	77,610	65,590
8	62,000	74,810

Test the hypothesis that there is no significant difference in the average salary for the two vice-president groups. The salaries for both groups are considered to be approximately normally distributed. Use a significance level of .05. Do not assume that the population variances are equal.

10.28 Construct a 90% CI for the difference in the means of the salaries for vice-presidents in the banking industry and for vice-presidents of savings and loan institutions for exercise 10.27. Do not assume that the population variances are equal.

10.29 Using the data in exercise 10.27, test the same hypothesis, but assume that the population variances *are* equal.

10.30 The production supervisor of Dow Plast is conducting a test of the tensile strength of two types of copper coils. The relevant data are as follows. Coil A: $\bar{x} = 118$, $s = 17$, $n = 9$. Coil B: $\bar{x} = 143$, $s = 24$, $n = 16$. The tensile strengths for the two types of copper coils are approximately normally distributed. Based on the p-value, would you reject the hypothesis that $\mu_A - \mu_B = 0$ at a significance level of 7%? Do not assume that the population variances are equal.

10.31 Construct a 99% CI for $\mu_A - \mu_B$ in exercise 10.30. Do not assume that the population variances are equal.

10.32 Using a pooled estimate of the variance in exercise 10.30, test the hypothesis that $\mu_A - \mu_B = 0$. Compare the two answers.

10.33 Do the following sample data support the hypothesis H_a: $\mu_1 - \mu_2 < 10$? The data are sampled from two normally distributed populations. Sample 1: $\bar{x} = 88$, $s = 9$, $n = 12$. Sample 2: $\bar{x} = 80$, $s = 5$, $n = 19$. Use a significance level of .01. Assume that the variances for the two populations are equal.

10.34 A machine operator is interested in whether there is a significant difference in the time to produce a particular item of output between machine 1 and machine 2. The time that it takes to output an item is normally distributed. Ten items produced by machine 1 and then another ten items produced by machine 2 were recorded. The resulting times in minutes were:

Machine 1		Machine 2	
40.3	39.7	43.7	41.6
35.6	40.2	42.1	42.3
42.7	38.2	41.8	40.9
41.9	39.6	42.8	43.8
38.6	40.3	40.2	42.7

Without assuming equal population variances, test the hypothesis that there is no significant difference in the time for machine 1 and machine 2 to produce one item of output. Use a significance level of .05.

10.35 Construct a 95% CI for $\mu_1 - \mu_2$ for exercise 10.34.

10.36 Using the information in exercise 10.34, and using the pooled estimate of the variance, test the hypothesis that $\mu_1 - \mu_2 = 0$. Calculate the p-value.

10.4

Comparing the Variances of Two Normal Populations Using Independent Samples

Once again we concentrate on independent samples from two normal populations, only this time we focus our attention on the *variation* of these populations rather than on their averages. This is illustrated in Figure 10.8. When estimating and testing σ_1 versus σ_2, we will not be concerned about μ_1 and μ_2. They may be equal, or they may not—it simply does not matter.

In business applications, you may want to compare the variation of two different production processes or compare the risk involved with two proposed investment portfolios. As mentioned previously, when testing for population *means* using small independent samples, you must pay attention to the population standard deviations (variances). Based on your belief that σ_1 does or does not equal σ_2, you select your corresponding test statistic for testing the means, μ_1 and μ_2. As a reminder, it is *not* a safe procedure to use the *same data set* to test both $\sigma_1 = \sigma_2$ and $\mu_1 = \mu_2$. A proper procedure would be to test σ_1 and σ_2 using one set of samples (as outlined in this section) and to obtain another set of samples *independently* of the first to test the means.

Figure 10.8

Comparing two standard
deviations. Is $\sigma_1 = \sigma_2$?

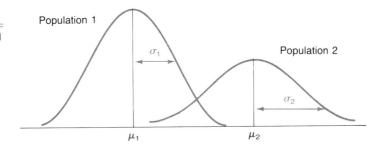

In the previous section, when trying to decide if $\mu_1 = \mu_2$, we examined the *difference* between the point estimates, $\overline{X}_1 - \overline{X}_2$. If $\overline{X}_1 - \overline{X}_2$ was large enough (in absolute value), we rejected H_0: $\mu_1 = \mu_2$. When looking at the variances, we use the **ratio of the sample variances,** s_1^2 and s_2^2, to derive a test of hypothesis and construct CIs. We do this because $s_1^2 - s_2^2$ is difficult to describe mathematically, but s_1^2/s_2^2 does have a recognizable distribution when in fact $\sigma_1{}^2$ and $\sigma_2{}^2$ are equal. So we define

$$F = \frac{s_1^2}{s_2^2} \qquad\qquad (10\text{-}17)$$

If you were to obtain sets of two samples repeatedly, calculate s_1^2/s_2^2 for each set, and make a histogram of these ratios, the shape of this histogram would resemble the curve in Figure 10.9. This is the **F distribution.** Its shape resembles the chi-square curve—it is nonsymmetric, skewed right (right-tailed), and never negative. There are many F curves, depending on the sample sizes, n_1 and n_2. The shape of the F curve becomes more symmetric as the sample sizes, n_1 and n_2, increase. As later chapters will demonstrate, the F distribution has a large variety of applications in statistics. Right-tail areas for this random variable have been tabulated in Table A-7.

When using the t and χ^2 statistics, we needed a way to specify the sample size(s) because the shape of these curves changes as the sample size changes. The same applies to the F distribution. There are two samples here, one from each population, and we need to specify *both* sample sizes. As before, we use the degrees of freedom (*df*) to accomplish this, where

$$v_1 = df \text{ for numerator} = n_1 - 1$$

$$v_2 = df \text{ for denominator} = n_2 - 1$$

So, the F statistic shown in Figure 10.9 follows an F distribution with v_1 and v_2 *df* provided $\sigma_1{}^2 = \sigma_2{}^2$ ($\sigma_1 = \sigma_2$). What happens to F when $\sigma_1 \neq \sigma_2$? Suppose that σ_1

Figure 10.9

Shape of the F
distribution.

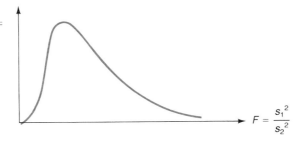

$> \sigma_2$? Then we would expect s_1 (the estimate of σ_1) to be larger than s_2 (the estimate of σ_2); we should see

$$s_1^2 > s_2^2$$

or

$$F = \frac{s_1^2}{s_2^2} > 1$$

Similarly, if $\sigma_1 < \sigma_2$, then we expect an F value < 1. We will use this reasoning to define a test of hypothesis for σ_1 versus σ_2.

Hypothesis Testing for σ_1 and σ_2

Is $\sigma_1 = \sigma_2$? We use another five-step procedure for testing a hypothesis concerning the two variances. Your choice of hypotheses is (as usual) a two-tailed test or a one-tailed test. For the two-tailed test, H_0: $\sigma_1 = \sigma_2$ ($\sigma_1^2 = \sigma_2^2$), and H_a: $\sigma_1 \neq \sigma_2$ ($\sigma_1^2 \neq \sigma_2^2$). For the one-tailed test, H_0: $\sigma_1 \leq \sigma_2$ ($\sigma_1^2 \leq \sigma_2^2$), and H_a: $\sigma_1 > \sigma_2$ ($\sigma_1^2 > \sigma_2^2$) (Figure 10.10a) or H_0: $\sigma_1 \geq \sigma_2$ ($\sigma_1^2 \geq \sigma_2^2$), and H_a: $\sigma_1 < \sigma_2$ ($\sigma_1^2 < \sigma_2^2$) (Figure 10.10b).

Notice that the hypotheses can be written in terms of the standard deviations (σ_1 and σ_2) or the variances (σ_1^2 and σ_2^2); if $\sigma_1 = \sigma_2$, then $\sigma_1^2 = \sigma_2^2$.

Right-tail areas under an F curve are provided in Table A-7. Notice that we have a table for areas of .1 (Table A-7a), .05 (Table A-7b), .025 (Table A-7c), and .01 (Table A-7d). These are the most commonly used values. For each table, the df for the numerator (v_1) run across the top, and the df for the denominator (v_2) run down the left margin.

Suppose we want to know which F value has a right-tail area of .05, using 10 and 12 df. Let the F value whose right-tail area is a, where the df are v_1 and v_2, be

$$F_{a,v_1,v_2}$$

For example, $F_{.05,10,12} = 2.75$ (Figure 10.11).

Notice that Table A-7 contains *right-tail* areas only. Later, we will show you how to find left-tail areas. We can, however, define each of our tests of hypothesis as a right-tailed test by simply and arbitrarily putting the larger variance in the numerator for a two-tailed test. Then F always will be ≥ 1. This procedure is summarized in the accompanying box.

Figure 10.10

Unequal population variances.

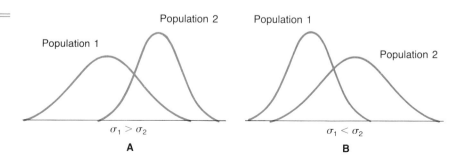

Population 1   Population 2   Population 1   Population 2

$\sigma_1 > \sigma_2$ $\sigma_1 < \sigma_2$

A   **B**

Figure 10.11

F curve with 10 and 12 df for probability that F exceeds 2.75 (2.75 is from Table A-7b).

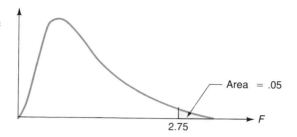

Area = .05

2.75

F

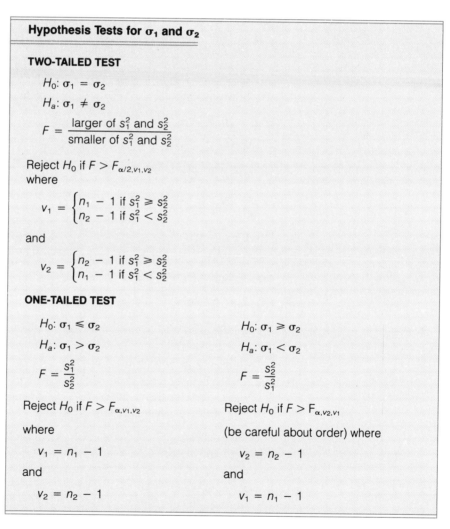

Hypothesis Tests for σ_1 and σ_2

TWO-TAILED TEST

$H_0: \sigma_1 = \sigma_2$

$H_a: \sigma_1 \neq \sigma_2$

$$F = \frac{\text{larger of } s_1^2 \text{ and } s_2^2}{\text{smaller of } s_1^2 \text{ and } s_2^2}$$

Reject H_0 if $F > F_{\alpha/2, v_1, v_2}$
where

$$v_1 = \begin{cases} n_1 - 1 & \text{if } s_1^2 \geq s_2^2 \\ n_2 - 1 & \text{if } s_1^2 < s_2^2 \end{cases}$$

and

$$v_2 = \begin{cases} n_2 - 1 & \text{if } s_1^2 \geq s_2^2 \\ n_1 - 1 & \text{if } s_1^2 < s_2^2 \end{cases}$$

ONE-TAILED TEST

$H_0: \sigma_1 \leq \sigma_2$ $H_0: \sigma_1 \geq \sigma_2$

$H_a: \sigma_1 > \sigma_2$ $H_a: \sigma_1 < \sigma_2$

$F = \dfrac{s_1^2}{s_2^2}$ $F = \dfrac{s_2^2}{s_1^2}$

Reject H_0 if $F > F_{\alpha, v_1, v_2}$ Reject H_0 if $F > F_{\alpha, v_2, v_1}$

where   (be careful about order) where

$v_1 = n_1 - 1$ $v_2 = n_2 - 1$

and   and

$v_2 = n_2 - 1$ $v_1 = n_1 - 1$

Example 10.6   The management of Case Automotive Products is considering the purchase of some new equipment that will fill one-quart containers with a recently introduced radiator additive. They have narrowed their choice of brand of filling machine down to Brand 1 and Brand 2. Although Brand 1 is considerably less expensive than Brand 2, they suspect that the contents delivered by the Brand 1 machine will have *more variation* than that obtained using Brand 2. In other words, Brand 1 is more apt to slightly (or severely) overfill or underfill containers. (The Case people realize that they must use a container slightly larger than one quart in any event, to allow for heat expansion and overfill of their product.)

The Case production department was able to obtain data on the performance of both brands for a sample of 25 containers using Brand 1 and 20 containers using Brand 2. Using their summary information, can you confirm Case's suspicions? Use $\alpha = .05$. All mean and standard deviation measures are fluid ounces.

Brand 1   **Brand 2**

$n_1 = 25$ $n_2 = 20$

$\bar{x}_1 = 31.8$ $\bar{x}_2 = 32.1$

$s_1 = 1.21$ $s_2 = .72$

Solution

Step 1. The purpose of the test is to determine if one standard deviation (or variance) is *larger* than the other; this calls for a one-tailed test. The suspicion is that σ_1 is larger than σ_2, so this statement is put in the alternative hypothesis. The resulting hypotheses are

$$H_0: \sigma_1 \leq \sigma_2$$

$$H_a: \sigma_1 > \sigma_2$$

Step 2. The appropriate test statistic is

$$F = \frac{s_1^2}{s_2^2}$$

Step 3. Because the *df* are $v_1 = 25 - 1 = 24$ and $v_2 = 20 - 1 = 19$, we find $F_{.05, 24, 19} = 2.11$. The test of H_0 versus H_a will be to

Reject H_0 if $F > 2.11$

Step 4. The computed F value is

$$F^* = \frac{(1.21)^2}{(.72)^2} = 2.82$$

Because $2.82 > 2.11$, we reject H_0.

Step 5. On the basis of these data and this significance level, Case is correct in their belief that the variation in the containers filled by Brand 1 exceeds that of the containers filled by Brand 2. ●

Note that, in example 10.6, nothing was said regarding the *average* contents delivered by Brands 1 and 2; that is, μ_1 and μ_2.

Example 10.7

We have, perhaps to the point of overkill, let you know that to use a single data set to examine variances and then (based on the results of this test) to use the appropriate *t* statistic to test the means is not a reliable procedure. Using the data from example 10.4, examine the variances *only*. Can you conclude that there is a difference in the two population variances, using a significance level of .05?

Solution From these data, we determined that $s_1 = .68$ hour and $s_2 = .38$ hour, with $n_1 = n_2 = 15$.

Step 1. We are trying to detect a *difference* in the two variances (not whether one exceeds the other); a two-tailed test should be used. We define

$$H_0: \sigma_1 = \sigma_2 \text{ (or } \sigma_1{}^2 = \sigma_2{}^2)$$
$$H_a: \sigma_1 \neq \sigma_2 \text{ (or } \sigma_1{}^2 \neq \sigma_2{}^2)$$

Step 2. The test statistic here is

$$F = \frac{\text{larger of } s_1^2 \text{ and } s_2^2}{\text{smaller of } s_1^2 \text{ and } s_2^2}$$

Step 3. We need $F_{.025,14,14}$ from Table A-7c. Unfortunately, it is not there; this table contains only selected *df.* In this situation, we pick the nearest *df,* which, for this example, is $F_{.025,15,14} = 2.95$. So our test of H_0 versus H_a is to

Reject H_0 if $F > 2.95$

Step 4. Since $s_1^2 = (.68)^2$ is larger than $s_2^2 = (.38)^2$, the computed value of the test statistic is

$$F* = \frac{(.68)^2}{(.38)^2} = 3.20 > 2.95$$

Therefore, reject H_0 in favor of H_a.

Step 5. There *is* sufficient evidence to conclude that the two variances are unequal. If additional data are obtained to test the population *means* (such as $H_0: \mu_1 \geq \mu_2$ versus $H_a: \mu_1 < \mu_2$) using small samples, the correct procedure would be to use the t' statistic described earlier, which does *not* assume that σ_1 and σ_2 are equal. ●

Confidence Interval for $\sigma_1{}^2/\sigma_2{}^2$

Consider an F curve with v_1 and v_2 *df.* To construct a 95% CI for $\sigma_1{}^2/\sigma_2{}^2$, you first need to find the values of F_L and F_U, where (Figure 10.12)

F_L has a left-tail area $= .025$

F_U has a right-tail area $= .025$

F_U can be found directly from Table A-7c. It is F_L that poses a problem, however, because Table A-7 contains only right-tail areas and the F distribution is *not symmetric.* However,

$$F_L = \frac{1}{F_{.025,v_2,v_1}} \tag{10-18}$$

Figure 10.12

F curve with v_1 and v_2 *df* showing lower and upper limits for a 95% CI.

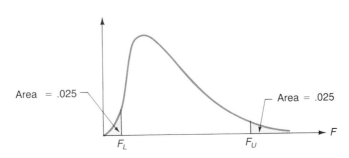

Notice that we *switched* the *df* used when finding F_U because F_U can be written

$$F_U = F_{.025, v_1, v_2}$$

The CI for σ_1^2/σ_2^2 is then

$$\frac{s_1^2/s_2^2}{F_U} \quad \text{to} \quad \frac{s_1^2/s_2^2}{F_L}$$

In general, we have a $(1 - \alpha) \cdot 100\%$ CI for σ_1^2/σ_2^2 (independent samples):

$$\frac{s_1^2/s_2^2}{F_U} \quad \text{to} \quad \frac{s_1^2/s_2^2}{F_L} \qquad\qquad\qquad (10\text{-}19)$$

where

$$F_U = F_{\alpha/2, v_1, v_2}$$
$$F_L = 1/F_{\alpha/2, v_2, v_1}$$
$$v_1 = n_1 - 1$$
$$v_2 = n_2 - 1$$

Example 10.8

Using the data from example 10.6, determine a 95% CI for σ_1^2/σ_2^2.

Solution Here, $n_1 = 25$, $s_1 = 1.21$, and $n_2 = 20$, $s_2 = .72$. So we need

$$F_U = F_{.025, 24, 19} = 2.45$$
$$F_L = 1/F_{.025, 19, 24}$$
$$\cong 1/2.33 \;(\text{using } F_{.025, 20, 24})$$
$$= .43$$

The 95% CI for σ_1^2/σ_2^2 is

$$\frac{(1.21)^2/(.72)^2}{2.45} \quad \text{to} \quad \frac{(1.21)^2/(.72)^2}{.43}$$
$$= 1.15 \quad \text{to} \quad 6.57$$

As a result, we are 95% confident that σ_1^2/σ_2^2 is between 1.15 and 6.57. This means that we are 95% confident that σ_1^2 is between 1.15 and 6.57 *times as large* as σ_2^2. ●

Example 10.9

For the data from example 10.6, determine a 95% CI for σ_1/σ_2. Use the results of example 10.8.

Solution This is obtained simply by finding the *square root* of each end-point of the CI for σ_1^2/σ_2^2. Your 95% CI for σ_1/σ_2 will be

$$\sqrt{1.15} \quad \text{to} \quad \sqrt{6.57}$$
$$= 1.07 \quad \text{to} \quad 2.56 \text{ (fluid ounces)}$$

●

Exercises

10.37 In evaluating capital-investment projects, the variability of the cash flows of the returns is carefully assessed. The higher the variability, the higher the risk associated with that project. Boone Enterprises is currently evaluating two projects. The mean expected net cash flow for the next 11 years for project 1 is $134,000, as against $166,000 for project 2 for the next eight years. The standard deviations of the net cash flows are $28,000 and $37,000 for project 1 and project 2 respectively. Assume that cash flows are normally distributed. Do these sample standard deviations present sufficient evidence to indicate that project 1 and project 2 are not equally risky? Use a significance level of 5%.

10.38 Using the sample statistics in exercise 10.18, test the following hypotheses with a significance level of .10: H_0: $\sigma_1^2 \geq \sigma_2^2$ and H_a: $\sigma_1^2 < \sigma_2^2$.

10.39 Construct a 95% CI for σ_1^2/σ_2^2 in exercise 10.18.

10.40 A computer program generates data that are approximately normal. Two different samples are generated:

Sample 1		Sample 2	
17	26	24	29
25	34	32	34
30	19	29	26
28	25	25	30

Using a significance level of .05, would you reject the null hypothesis that the variance of the population from which Sample 1 was taken is less than or equal to the variance of the population from which Sample 2 was taken?

10.41 Construct a 95% CI for the ratio of the population variances in exercise 10.40.

10.42 The statistical quality-control department of a company that manufacturers wall clocks is studying the variability of two types of wall clocks that have been recently developed. Using the following information, test the hypothesis that H_0: $\sigma_1 = \sigma_2$, using a significance level of .05. Assume that the samples are taken from populations that are approximately normally distributed. Clock 1: $n = 25$, $s = 1.8$. Clock 2: $n = 21$, $s = 1.39$.

10.43 Construct a 95% CI for σ_1^2/σ_2^2 using the data in exercise 10.42.

10.44 The following is a summary of the mean annual return ($\overline{X}$) and variance (s^2) of the annual return of common stocks for three different industries. Computer industry: $n = 16$, $\overline{X} = 14.3\%$, $s^2 = 5.6$. Steel industry: $n = 9$, $\overline{X} = 8.5\%$, $s^2 = 11.2$. Oil-and-gas industry: $n = 13$, $\overline{X} = 11.8\%$, $s^2 = 16.4$. Using these data, can we conclude that computer stocks are less risky than oil and gas stocks? Use a significance level of .05. Assume that the mean annual return for the industries are approximately normally distributed.

10.45 Using the data in exercise 10.44, test the hypothesis that the steel industry's stocks are just as risky as the computer industry's stocks. Use a significance level of .05.

10.46 The manager of a vending-machine company decided to buy one of two types of dispenser to put in her vending machines. Both dispensers claim to dispense, on the average, six ounces of fluid in a plastic cup when used. The amount dispensed is approximately normally distributed. However, to test this claim, the manager would first like to know whether the variability in the amount of fluid dispensed is the same for both dispensers. Using a significance level of .05, is the manager justified in using a pooled estimate of the population variance, if 15 replications on each dispenser give the following results? Dispenser 1: $s = 1.5$, $n = 16$. Dispenser 2: $s = 3.4$, $n = 16$. If so, derive the pooled estimate.

10.5

Comparing the Means of Two Normal Populations Using Paired Samples

This final section examines the situation in which the two samples are *not* obtained independently. All discussion up to this point has assumed that the two samples *are* independent. By not independent, we mean that the corresponding elements from the two samples are *paired*. Perhaps each pair of observations corresponds to the same city, the same week, the same married couple, or even the same person. This discussion focuses on comparing the two population means for this situation where two *dependent* samples are obtained from the two populations.

When attempting to estimate or test for the difference between two population means, your first question always should be, is there any reason to pair the first observation from sample 1 with the first observation from sample 2, the second with the second, and so on? If there is no reason to pair these data and the samples were obtained independently, the previous methods for finding CIs and testing μ_1 versus μ_2 apply. If the data were gathered such that pairing the values is necessary, then it is *extremely* important that you recognize this and treat the data in a different manner. We can still determine CIs and perform a test of hypothesis, but the procedure is different.

We will assume here that the populations follow a *normal* distribution (as we did in Sections 10.3 and 10.4). As a result, we need not worry about large samples versus small samples because we will use the t distribution for our CIs and test of hypothesis, regardless of the sample sizes. Of course, if the samples are large ($n_1 > 30$ and $n_2 > 30$), this distribution is very closely approximated by the standard normal distribution.

If you have reason to suspect that your two populations are *not* normally distributed, then one alternative is to use a nonparametric procedure—in particular, the Wilcoxon signed rank test (discussed in Chapter 19.)

Assume that the city council of a large western city is taking a close look at the number of people who visit two local museums, one displaying the history of humanity, the other containing space-exploration exhibits. They believe that the space museum is attracting more people, even though the history museum has a national reputation. If this is correct, the space museum will receive additional funding for the coming year. The following data were gathered based on the number of adult admissions (in thousands) for 12 randomly selected weeks during the past year. Sample 1 is the space museum; sample 2 is the history museum.

Week	1	2	3	4	5	6	7	8	9	10	11	12
Space Museum	.6	.8	.7	1.2	1.4	2.3	3.8	4.4	1.5	1.3	1.1	.8
History Museum	.5	1.0	.5	.8	1.2	2.5	2.8	3.5	1.2	1.4	.8	.6
d	.1	$-.2$	.2	.4	.2	$-.2$	1.0	.9	.3	$-.1$	.3	.2
d^2	.01	.04	.04	.16	.04	.04	1.0	.81	.09	.01	.09	.04

$\Sigma d^2 = .01 + .04 + \ldots + .04 = 2.37$

$\Sigma d = .1 + (-.2) + \ldots + .2 = 3.1$

Each pair of data values was collected during the same week, so these data values clearly need to be paired—these are dependent samples. It seems reasonable to examine the difference of the two values for each week, so these differences (d), along with the d^2 values, are also shown. We have thus reduced the problem from two sets of values to a single new set. The following discussion will demonstrate how to use these differences to construct a CI for $\mu_1 - \mu_2$ or perform a test of hypothesis.

Confidence Interval for $\mu_1 - \mu_2$ Using Paired Samples

The statistic used to derive a CI for $\mu_1 - \mu_2$ and perform a test of hypothesis using *dependent* samples is

$$t_D = \frac{\overline{X}_1 - \overline{X}_2}{s_d/\sqrt{n}} = \frac{\overline{d}}{s_d/\sqrt{n}} \tag{10-20}$$

where

$$n = \text{the number of paired observations}$$

$$s_d = \text{the standard deviation of the } n \text{ differences}$$

$$= \sqrt{\frac{\Sigma d^2 - (\Sigma d)^2/n}{n-1}}$$

$$df \text{ for } t_D = n - 1$$

This is a *t random variable* with $n - 1$ *df*. Notice that the numerator of t_D is the same as before—namely, $\overline{X}_1 - \overline{X}_2$, which is also represented by $\overline{d} = \Sigma d/n$, the mean of the differences. The mean of the differences $\overline{d}$ always is equal to $\overline{X}_1 - \overline{X}_2$. Notice that this can help you in checking your arithmetic when computing the d's.

Using this t statistic, we obtain a $(1 - \alpha) \cdot 100\%$ CI for $\mu_1 - \mu_2$ (paired samples):

$$\overline{d} - t_{\alpha/2, n-1} \frac{s_d}{\sqrt{n}} \quad \text{to} \quad \overline{d} + t_{\alpha/2, n-1} \frac{s_d}{\sqrt{n}} \tag{10-21}$$

Example 10.10 Using the data from the history and space museums, derive a 95% CI for $\mu_1 - \mu_2$, where

$$\mu_1 = \text{average weekly attendance at the space museum}$$

$$\mu_2 = \text{average weekly attendance at the history museum}$$

Solution We have

$$\overline{d} = \frac{\Sigma d}{n} = \frac{3.1}{12} = .258$$

Notice that

$$\overline{x}_1 = \frac{.6 + .8 + \ldots + .8}{12} = 1.658$$

and

$$\overline{x}_2 = \frac{.5 + 1.0 + \ldots + .6}{12} = 1.4$$

so $\overline{d} = \overline{x}_1 - \overline{x}_2 = .258$. It checks! Also,

$$s_d = \sqrt{\frac{\Sigma d^2 - (\Sigma d)^2/n}{n-1}} = \sqrt{\frac{2.37 - (3.1)^2/12}{11}}$$

$$= \sqrt{\frac{1.569}{11}} = \sqrt{.143} = .378$$

The resulting 95% CI for $\mu_1 - \mu_2$ is

$$\bar{d} - t_{.025,11} \frac{s_d}{\sqrt{n}} \quad \text{to} \quad \bar{d} + t_{.025,11} \frac{s_d}{\sqrt{n}}$$

$$= .258 - 2.201 \frac{.378}{\sqrt{12}} \quad \text{to} \quad .258 + 2.201 \frac{.378}{\sqrt{12}}$$

$$= .258 - .240 \quad \text{to} \quad .258 + .240$$

$$= .018 \quad \text{to} \quad .498$$

Based on these data, we are 95% confident that the number of admissions per week to the space museum is between 18 and 498 *more* than that to the history museum. ●

Hypothesis Testing Using Paired Samples

The test statistic for testing the means is the t statistic given in equation 10-20.* When testing H_0: $\mu_1 = \mu_2$ ($\mu_1 - \mu_2 = 0$) versus H_a: $\mu_1 \neq \mu_2$ ($\mu_1 - \mu_2 \neq 0$), reject H_0 if $|t_D| > t_{\alpha/2, n-1}$. Here, $t_{\alpha/2, n-1}$ is obtained from Table A-5 using $n - 1$ *df*. One-tailed tests are performed in a similar manner by placing α in either the right tail (H_a: $\mu_1 > \mu_2$) or in the left tail (H_a: $\mu_1 < \mu_2$). A summary is provided in the box on paired sample tests for μ_1 and μ_2.

Example 10.11   Consider the data on the admissions per week at the space and history museums. Can you confirm the suspicion that the average attendance at the space museum (μ_1) is greater than that at the history museum (μ_2)? Use a significance level of $\alpha = .05$.

Solution

Step 1. We are attempting to demonstrate that μ_1 is larger than μ_2; this claim goes into the alternative hypothesis. The resulting hypotheses are

$$H_0: \mu_1 \leq \mu_2 \ (\mu_1 - \mu_2 \leq 0)$$
$$H_a: \mu_1 > \mu_2 \ (\mu_1 - \mu_2 > 0)$$

Step 2. We are dealing with paired data, so the correct test statistic is

$$t_D = \frac{\bar{d}}{s_d/\sqrt{n}}$$

Step 3. What happens to t_D when H_a is true? if $\mu_1 > \mu_2$, then we would expect their estimates to behave in the same way; that is $\bar{X}_1 > \bar{X}_2$. In other words, $\bar{d} = \bar{X}_1 - \bar{X}_2$ should be *positive*. So,

Reject H_0 if $t_D > k$, for some $k > 0$

What is k? As before, this depends on α and, in the usual manner, we have

Reject H_0 if $t_D > t_{\alpha, n-1}$

where $t_{\alpha, n-1}$ is obtained from Table A-5.

---

*Hypotheses using paired (dependent) data are often written in terms of the mean difference between the two populations; $\mu_d = \mu_1 - \mu_2$. The corresponding two-tailed hypotheses can then be written H_0: $\mu_d = 0$ and H_a: $\mu_d \neq 0$.

Figure 10.13

MINITAB solution to example 10.11. This is the correct way to analyze these data.

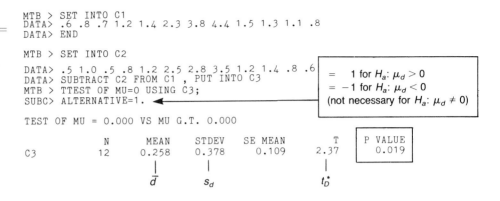

```
MTB > SET INTO C1
DATA> .6 .8 .7 1.2 1.4 2.3 3.8 4.4 1.5 1.3 1.1 .8
DATA> END

MTB > SET INTO C2
DATA> .5 1.0 .5 .8 1.2 2.5 2.8 3.5 1.2 1.4 .8 .6
DATA> SUBTRACT C2 FROM C1 , PUT INTO C3
MTB > TTEST OF MU=0 USING C3;
SUBC> ALTERNATIVE=1.
```

```
= 1 for $H_a$: $\mu_d > 0$
= -1 for $H_a$: $\mu_d < 0$
(not necessary for $H_a$: $\mu_d \neq 0$)
```

```
TEST OF MU = 0.000 VS MU G.T. 0.000

            N      MEAN     STDEV   SE MEAN       T      P VALUE
C3          12    0.258     0.378     0.109     2.37      0.019
                    |         |                   |
                    $\bar{d}$  $s_d$             $t_D^*$
```

For this situation, $t_{.05,11} = 1.796$, and so we

$$\text{Reject } H_0 \text{ if } t_D > 1.796$$

Step 4. Using the sample data,

$$t_D^* = \frac{.258}{.378/\sqrt{12}} = 2.36$$

Because $2.36 > 1.796$, we reject H_0.

Step 5. The average attendance at the space museum *is* higher than that at the history museum. ●

A MINITAB solution to example 10.11 is provided in Figure 10.13. Notice that the differences are first derived, and then a standard *t* test (described in section 9.4) is used to test that the mean difference ($\mu_d = \mu_1 - \mu_2$) is ≤ 0 versus the alternative H_a: $\mu_d > 0$. The resulting *p*-value is $p = .019$, which, using $\alpha = .05$, again results in rejecting H_0 because $p < \alpha$.

What happens if you fail to pair these observations and perform a regular two-sample *t* test, as we did in section 10.3 for small *independent* samples? The results are summarized in Figure 10.14, where we observe an interesting result. The *t* value (using the test statistic from equation 10-9) now is .57, with a corresponding *p*-value of $p = .29$. This means that, using this test, we now *fail to reject* H_0. We are unable to demonstrate a difference between the average weekly attendances, which, according to Figure 10.13, is *not* a correct conclusion. Figure 10.14 shows convincingly that failing to pair the observations when you should can cause you to obtain an incorrect result. More important, there is nothing to warn you that this has occurred.

Figure 10.14

MINITAB solution to example 10.11. This is THE INCORRECT WAY to analyze these data. Compare with Figure 10.13.

```
MTB > TWOSAMPLE TEST USING C1 AND C2;
SUBC> ALTERNATIVE=1.

TWOSAMPLE T FOR C1 VS C2
        N      MEAN     STDEV   SE MEAN
C1      12     1.66     1.23      0.36
C2      12     1.400    0.991     0.29

95 PCT CI FOR MU C1 - MU C2: (-0.69, 1.21)
TTEST MU C1 = MU C2 (VS GT): T=0.57 P=0.29 DF=21.0
                                          |
                                       p-value
```

Example 10.12   Turner Management Corporation owns and operates a chain of steak houses and seafood restaurants across the United States. In a move to improve profitability, they are currently examining the average monthly utility payment (mostly the electricity used for heating and cooling) at a representative sample of ten pairs of steak houses and seafood restaurants. Each pair was selected from the same city because the climate must be held constant for each pair in order to observe true differences in temperature-control efficiency. Using these data, can you conclude that the average utility payment (given in thousands of dollars) is different for the two restaurant types? Use $\alpha = .05$ to define your test.

CITY	1	2	3	4	5	6	7	8	9	10
STEAK HOUSES	1.8	2.1	1.2	1.7	2.4	1.6	1.7	2.0	1.6	2.2
SEAFOOD RESTAURANTS	1.5	1.7	1.8	1.4	2.2	1.9	2.0	1.7	1.8	1.7

Solution The data were gathered by collecting a pair of observations from each city, so this is a clear-cut case of dependent samples. Your next step should be to determine the paired differences.

CITY	1	2	3	4	5	6	7	8	9	10	TOTAL
d	.3	.4	−.6	.3	.2	−.3	−.3	.3	−.2	.5	.6
d^2	.09	.16	.36	.09	.04	.09	.09	.09	.04	.25	1.3

Step 1. We are attempting to detect a difference in the two means; a two-tailed test is in order. Let

$$\mu_1 = \text{average utility payment for all steak houses}$$
$$\mu_2 = \text{average utility payment for all seafood restaurants}$$

The correct hypotheses are

$$H_0: \mu_1 = \mu_2 \ (\mu_1 - \mu_2 = 0)$$
$$H_a: \mu_1 \neq \mu_2 \ (\mu_1 - \mu_2 \neq 0)$$

Steps 2, 3. Using the t_D test statistic, the test will be to

$$\text{Reject } H_0 \text{ if } |t_D| > t_{\alpha/2, n-1}$$

where $t_{\alpha/2, n-1} = t_{.025, 9} = 2.262$.

Step 4. Using the sample data,

$$\bar{d} = \frac{\Sigma d}{n} = \frac{.6}{10} = .06$$

$$s_d = \sqrt{\frac{\Sigma d^2 - (\Sigma d)^2/n}{n-1}}$$

$$= \sqrt{\frac{1.3 - (.6)^2/10}{9}} = \sqrt{\frac{1.264}{9}}$$

$$= .375$$

From these values, we obtain

$$t_D^* = \frac{\overline{d}}{s_d/\sqrt{n}} = \frac{.06}{.375/\sqrt{10}} = .506$$

Because $.506 < 2.262$, we fail to reject H_0.

Step 5. Based on these data, there is *insufficient evidence* to conclude that there is a difference in the average utility payments for the two restaurant types. ●

Paired Sample Tests for μ_1 and μ_2

TWO-TAILED TEST

H_0: $\mu_1 - \mu_2 = D_0$

H_a: $\mu_1 - \mu_2 \neq D_0$

($D_0 = 0$ for H_0: $\mu_1 = \mu_2$)

Reject H_0 if $|t_D| > t_{\alpha/2, n-1}$
where

1. each difference, d, is $X_1 - X_2$

2. $t_D = \dfrac{\overline{d} - D_0}{s_d/\sqrt{n}}$

3. $\overline{d} = \overline{X}_1 - \overline{X}_2 = \dfrac{\Sigma d}{n}$

4. $s_d = \sqrt{\dfrac{\Sigma d^2 - (\Sigma d)^2/n}{n-1}}$

5. df for $t_D = n - 1$

ONE-TAILED TEST

H_0: $\mu_1 - \mu_2 \leq D_0$ H_0: $\mu_1 - \mu_2 \geq D_0$

H_a: $\mu_1 - \mu_2 > D_0$ H_a: $\mu_1 - \mu_2 < D_0$

($D_0 = 0$ for H_0: $\mu_1 \leq \mu_2$)   ($D_0 = 0$ for H_0: $\mu_1 \geq \mu_2$)

Reject H_0 if $t_D > t_{\alpha, n-1}$ Reject H_0 if $t_D < -t_{\alpha, n-1}$

Exercises

10.47 A hospital is experimenting with the effectiveness of a newly developed drug that controls blood pressure. The blood-pressure level is measured using a sphygmometer before and after administration of the drug to a sample of hypertensive patients with a history of elevated blood pressure. The question is whether there is a measured decrease in systolic blood pressure (in mm Hg) after administration of the drug. The difference in blood pressure before and after is believed to be approximately normally distributed.

Patient	Before Drug	After Drug
1	110	94
2	88	81
3	84	82
4	94	88
5	108	97
6	82	85
7	96	77
8	97	89
9	134	110

a. Using a significance level of .10, can you conclude that the blood-pressure level is lower after the drug is administered?

b. Should you use an independent or dependent samples t statistic to analyze this experiment?

10.48 Construct a 99% CI for $\mu_1 - \mu_2$ using the data in exercise 10.47 (1 = before, 2 = after).

10.49 Suppose that, in exercise 10.47, the manufacturer of the drug claims that the new drug is effective in reducing the average blood-pressure scores by more than eight mm Hg. Would you support that statement at a significance level of .01?

10.50 The controller of a fast-food chain is interested in determining whether there is any difference in the weekly sales of restaurant 1 and restaurant 2. The weekly sales are approximately normally distributed. The sales, in dollars, for seven randomly selected weeks are:

Week	Restaurant 1	Restaurant 2
1	4100	3800
2	1800	4600
3	2200	5100
4	3400	3050
5	3100	2800
6	1100	1950
7	2200	3400

a. Should this problem be analyzed using an independent or dependent samples t statistic?

b. Using a significance level of .01, test the hypothesis that there is no significant difference in the weekly sales of the two restaurants.

10.51 Calculate the p-value for exercise 10.50 and interpret it.

10.52 Construct a 95% CI for the difference in the mean of the weekly sales of the two restaurants in exercise 10.50.

10.53 Smart Look, an exercise program developed by Joni Beauty consultants, is claimed to be effective in reducing the weight of a typical overweight woman by more than 17 pounds. In order to examine the validity of this hypothesis, the program was tried on a group of middle-aged women, and their weights (in pounds) were recorded before and after completion of the exercise program. Assume that the difference in a woman's weight after the program is approximately normally distributed.

Woman	Before	After	Woman	Before	After
1	140	115	5	175	165
2	160	130	6	145	125
3	110	100	7	115	101
4	132	109	8	122	105

a. Using a significance level of .10, what would be your conclusion?

b. Why did you select the particular test statistic you used to analyze this problem?

10.54 Using the data from exercise 10.53, test the hypothesis that $H_0: \mu_1 - \mu_2 = 0$ at a .01 level (1 = before, 2 = after).

10.55 The effectiveness of an advertisement is usually judged by the extent to which it increases the sales of a certain product. Weekly sales before and after an advertisement are:

Week	Before Campaign	After Campaign
1	3400	4340
2	4100	5270
3	5000	6100
4	3800	4010
5	6200	5750
6	4400	4810
7	3700	3600

Weekly sales are considered to be normally distributed. Construct a 95% CI for $\mu_1 - \mu_2$ (1 = after, 2 = before).

10.56 In exercise 10.55, the advertising department claims that the campaign increased sales by more than $400 a week. Is there sufficient evidence to support this claim? Base your decision on the resulting p-value.

Summary

This chapter has presented an introduction to statistical inference for two populations. We examined tests of hypothesis and CIs for the means and variances (for example, whether they are equal) of the two populations, using both independent and dependent samples.

When we used large independent samples to test the population means, we defined a test statistic having an approximate standard normal distribution, which we also used to define a CI for $\mu_1 - \mu_2$. For small independent samples ($n_1 < 30$ or $n_1 < 30$), hypothesis testing on μ_1 versus μ_2 is concerned with means from two normal populations. For this situation, although we are concerned with the means, we must pay special attention to whether we assume that the population standard deviations (σ_1 and σ_2) are equal.

If we do not assume that the σ values are equal, we use a test statistic for μ_1 versus μ_2 having an *approximate* t distribution. This statistic also results in an approximate CI for $\mu_1 - \mu_2$. If we assume that the σ values are equal, then we use a procedure that pools the sample variances and results in a test statistic having an *exact* t distribution. We also derived CIs for $\mu_1 - \mu_2$ for this situation.

To determine whether two population variances (or standard deviations) are the same, we introduced the F distribution. This distribution is nonsymmetric (right skew) and assumes that two independent samples were obtained. Probabilities (areas under the curve) for the F random variable are contained in Table A-7. Using this distribution, we can perform two-tailed tests (such as $H_a: \sigma_1 \neq \sigma_2$) or one-tailed tests (such as $H_a: \sigma_1 > \sigma_2$) on the two standard deviations. We also use it to construct a CI for σ_1^2/σ_2^2 or σ_1/σ_2.

When two samples are obtained such that corresponding observations are paired (matched), the resulting samples are dependent or paired. When using two such samples, we defined a t statistic to test the population means and to construct a CI for $\mu_1 - \mu_2$. We need not be concerned about whether the population standard deviations are equal for this situation because the test statistic uses the differences between the paired observations, a new variable.

Review Exercises

10.57 To evaluate the expected life of two types of tires, a car manufacturer decided to use a randomly selected set of 20 similar cars for testing the mean difference in the amount of wear (in thousandths of an inch) for the two brands of tires after 10,000 miles. The manufacturer placed two tires of the first brand and two tires of the second brand on each car. Will the resulting samples be independent samples or dependent samples? Discuss.

10.58 A sandwich shop wishes to test the effectiveness of its coupons. The manager believes that the business brought in by the responses to the coupon in the *Highland Village Daily* is equal to the business brought in by the responses to the coupon placed in the *Green Sheet*. The amount spent by each customer using a coupon is recorded (in dollars) and can be considered to be normally distributed. Test the manager's belief with a significance level of .01. *Highland Village Daily:* $n = 32$, $\bar{x} = 9.50$, $\bar{s} = 26.3$. *Green Sheet:* $n = 39$, $\bar{x} = 11.80$, $\bar{s} = 29.4$.

10.59 Dairy Castle would like to boost the sales of their "Country Baskets." They think that it might be helpful to hang posters that picture the item. They recorded the number of Country Baskets sold during lunch time for one week at its various stores. They repeated the sampling for another week when the poster advertising was used. Assume that weekly sales are normally distributed. Is there sufficient evidence to say that hanging the posters improved sales of the Country Baskets? Use a .05 significance level.

Store	Before	After
1218	215	240
1224	180	220
1236	150	190
1252	180	175
1270	201	220
1282	207	215
1292	195	219
1304	180	195

10.60 Denver Hydro-Mulch Company helps lawns grow by spraying a prepared mixture on top of each lawn. A chemical company sales representative would like to convince Denver Hydro-Mulch that her company has a better fertilizer mixture. She has agreed to give the company enough fertilizer mixture to spray on eight randomly selected lawns. An additional set of eight randomly selected lawns are sprayed with the fertilizer mix that the company currently is using. At the end of four weeks, the eight lawns prepared with the new mixture had an average growth of 32 cm and a standard deviation of 7.8 cm. The eight lawns sprayed with the fertilizer mixture that the company is currently using had an average growth of 25 cm and a standard deviation of 6 cm. The growth of the grass at the end of the four-week period is considered to be normally distributed. Test the claim that the new fertilizer mixture is superior to the current one. Use a 10% significance level. Do not assume that the population variances are equal.

10.61 Test the claim in exercise 10.60, but assume that the variances of the grass growth for the two different fertilizer mixtures are equal.

10.62 An insurance company wants to compare the amount of damage (dollar value) from a rear-end collision of cars equipped with 5 mph bumpers to those equipped with 1983 2.5 mph bumpers. Twenty cars are tested, ten with the 5-mph bumpers and the other ten with 2.5 mph bumpers. The cars are put through ten different tests. Do the following data show that there is no significant difference in the dollar value of damage between the two types of bumpers? Use a .05 significance level. What assumption needs to be made about the distribution of the damage from a rear-end collision?

Collision	2.5 Mph Bumper	5.0 Mph Bumper
1	750	435
2	675	600
3	825	739
4	439	325
5	980	650
6	650	700
7	575	405
8	450	350
9	580	470
10	625	485

10.63 Construct a 90% CI for the difference in the mean dollar value of the damage between the two types of bumpers using the data given in exercise 10.62.

10.64 A financial analyst measures the risk in investing in a particular type of mutual fund by the variance in the rate of return for funds with similar goals. The distribution of the rate of return for the funds is considered to be approximately normally distributed. Based on the following data, in which 31 maximum capital gain funds and 41 long-term growth funds were sampled, can you conclude that the long-term growth funds are riskier at the .05 level of significance? Maximum capital gains: $n = 31$, $s = 112$. Long-term growth: $n = 41$, $s = 209$.

10.65 Find a 90% CI for the ratio of the population variances for the data in exercise 10.64.

10.66 Determine which of the following sets of hypotheses are equivalent.

a. H_0: $\sigma_1^2/\sigma_2^2 \leq 1$ and H_a: $\sigma_1^2/\sigma_2^2 > 1$.

b. H_0: $\sigma_2^2/\sigma_1^2 \geq 1$ and H_a: $\sigma_2^2/\sigma_1^2 < 1$.

c. H_0: $\sigma_2^2 \geq \sigma_1^2$ and H_a: $\sigma_2^2 < \sigma_1^2$.

d. H_0: $\sigma_1 \leq \sigma_2$ and H_a: $\sigma_1 > \sigma_2$.

10.67 A study is designed to determine the effect of an office-training course on typing productivity. Ten typists are randomly selected and are asked to type 15 pages of equally difficult text before and after completing the training course. Their productivity is measured by the total number of errors made.

Typist	Before	After
1	30	27
2	19	14
3	36	31
4	42	37
5	35	29
6	33	31
7	28	22
8	30	25
9	27	30
10	34	33

Assume that the total number of errors can be approximated by a normal distribution. Test the claim that taking the office-training course leads to a reduction in the average number of errors made by a typist. Use a significance level of .05.

10.68 Suppose that a sample of size 16 is chosen from population 1 and a sample of size 26 is drawn from population 2. Assume that both populations are normally distributed. If a 90% CI for the ratio of the variance of population 1 to the variance of population 2 is .367 to 1.753, what is the point estimate of the ratio of the two population variances?

Case Study

Gulf Coast Machine Tools

Shortly after the oil embargo disrupted the world's oil supplies, Al Jones formed Gulf Coast Machine Tools in anticipation of the increased activity in the Texas Gulf Coast oil industry. His hunch was right and the company did well making parts for the oil companies. Consumer reaction to the oil embargo, however, was more dramatic than expected. Demand for gasoline dropped substantially and stabilized at a much lower level than Al had originally anticipated. The sales and profits of Gulf Coast have been stagnant for several years.

Al now wants to take advantage of the high-technology industry that has begun to move into the area by providing specialized parts for these new companies. Three high-technology firms are ready to place orders for new parts. Al knows that he will have to invest in additional machinery to meet the new production demands. He discussed with his purchasing agent the anticipated cost of adding five machines of a type similar to one they had purchased the year before. These machines were versatile enough to manufacture a wide variety of parts and components for the high-technology companies.

The purchasing agent reported to Al that they had chosen the old machine because of its low overall cost of operation. All machines available then had been evaluated on a number of criteria, including total delivered price, rate of producing units, energy consumption, cost of replacement parts, maintenance schedules, and availability of factory-supported repair service.

Two new companies that made similar machines claimed their machines were an even better buy. Both companies agreed to lend Al one of their machines for a test of productive ability. The two machines were randomly assigned jobs of the same type. The number of parts finished by each machine was recorded at the end of each day. All partially finished items were included in the count as work in progress and counted as percent complete. The number of parts completed on each new machine (A and B) were recorded. In addition, the Gulf Coast records of the last two weeks provide the production information on the old machine (C).

Case Study Questions

Machine A	Machine B	Machine C
18.3	13.2	9.5
7.5	10.4	7.4
6.1	8.1	9.9
7.3	9.2	7.7
4.5	10.4	9.8
8.8	7.8	12.3
5.9	9.5	14.6
5.1	7.6	6.7
3.6	8.3	8.1
11.9	5.1	11.3
10.5	13.6	12.5
18.9	13.8	14.9
11.1	12.7	13.8
18.6	10.7	10.4

1. You are the research expert. What type of test will you use? Why?

2. Are machines A and B equal in productive capacity? Explain.
3. How does the old machine (C) compare with the better of the new machines (A or B) in productive capacity?
4. Is there any problem associated with the sampling procedure used to get information on the old machine? Explain.
5. Which machine should Al buy?

Solution

Example 10.4

S	•
P	•
S	•
S	•
X	•

Example 10.4 was concerned with a t test for two independent samples to determine two population means. The problem was to determine if the average blowout times using the test apparatus were different for Beltex and Roadmaster tires. (H_0: $\mu_1 = \mu_2$). The SPSSX program listing in Figure 10.15 was used to test the variances and means for two independent samples. For the test on the means, the value of the test statistic and the p-value are provided for the case where the population variances are assumed equal and the case where it is not assumed that the variances are equal. We urge you not to use the same data to test both the means *and* variances at a predefined significance level. Each line represents one card image to be entered.

Figure 10.15

SPSSX program listing requesting a two-sample test for the variances and means.

```
TITLE    BELTEX-ROADMASTER TIRES
DATA LIST FREE/BRAND(A) WEAR
RECODE BRAND ('B'=1) ('R'=2) INTO XBRAND
PRINT /BRAND WEAR
T-TEST GROUPS=XBRAND/VARIABLES=WEAR
BEGIN DATA
B 3.82
B 3.11
B 4.21
B 2.64
B 4.16
B 3.91
B 2.44
B 4.52
B 2.84
B 3.26
B 3.74
B 3.04
B 2.56
B 2.58
B 3.15
R 4.16
R 3.92
R 3.94
R 4.22
R 4.15
R 3.62
R 4.11
R 3.45
R 3.65
R 3.82
R 4.55
R 3.82
R 3.85
R 3.62
R 4.88
END DATA
```

• S
• P
• S
• S
• X

The TITLE command names the SPSSX run.

The DATA LIST command gives each variable a name and describes the data as being in free form. The (A) after BRAND indicates that "brand" is character data.

The PRINT command requests a printout of the input data.

The RECODE statement recodes the two brands B and R to the numeric values of 1 and 2, respectively, and merges them into the variable XBRAND.

The TTEST command compares two sample means. The GROUPS and VARI- ABLES subcommands divide the cases into two groups for a comparison of sample means.

The BEGIN DATA command indicates to SPSSX that the input data immediately follow.

The next 30 lines are card images, with each line representing the brand (Roadmaster or Beltex) and the wear factor. The first line, for example, represents brand B (Beltex) and a wear factor of 3.82.

Figure 10.16

Output obtained by executing the SPSSX program listing in Figure 10.15.

The END DATA statement indicates the end of the data card images.

Figure 10.16 shows output obtained by executing the program listing in Figure 10.15.

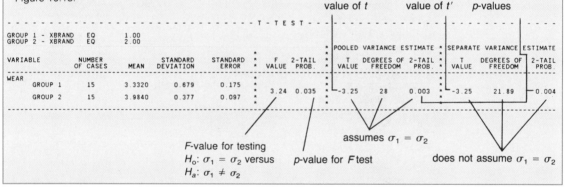

• S
• P
• S
• S
• X

Solution

Example 10.11

Example 10.11 was concerned with the computation of the t statistic for the means of two populations using paired (dependent) samples. The problem was to determine whether the average weekly attendance at the space museum exceeded that at the history museum (H_a: $\mu_1 > \mu_2$). The SPSSX program listing in Figure 10.17 was used to request a mean, t score, and p-value. Note that SPSSX assumes a two-tailed test. This was a one-tailed test, so the calculated p-value must be divided by two. Each line represents one card image to be entered.

The TITLE command names the SPSSX run.

The DATA LIST command gives each variable a name and describes the data as being in free form.

The PRINT command requests that the input data be printed.

The T-TEST command compares two sample means. The PAIRS subcommand names the variables being compared.

The BEGIN DATA command indicates to SPSSX that the input data immediately follow.

Figure 10.17

SPSSX program listing used to request a two-sample *t* test for two population means using paired (dependent) samples.

```
TITLE    MUSEUM ATTENDANCES
DATA LIST FREE/SPACE HISTORY
PRINT /SPACE HISTORY
T-TEST PAIRS=SPACE HISTORY
BEGIN DATA
0.6  0.5
0.8  1.0
0.7  0.5
1.2  0.8
1.4  1.2
2.3  2.5
3.8  2.8
4.4  3.5
1.5  1.2
1.3  1.4
1.1  0.8
0.8  0.6
END DATA
```

The next 12 lines are card images, which represent the attendance in thousands at the space and history museums, respectively. The first card, for example, says that there were 600 guests at the space museum and 500 guests at the history museum.

The END DATA statement indicates the end of the data card images.

Figure 10.18

Output obtained by executing the SPSSX program listing in Figure 10.17.

Figure 10.18 shows the output obtained by executing the program listing in Figure 10.17.

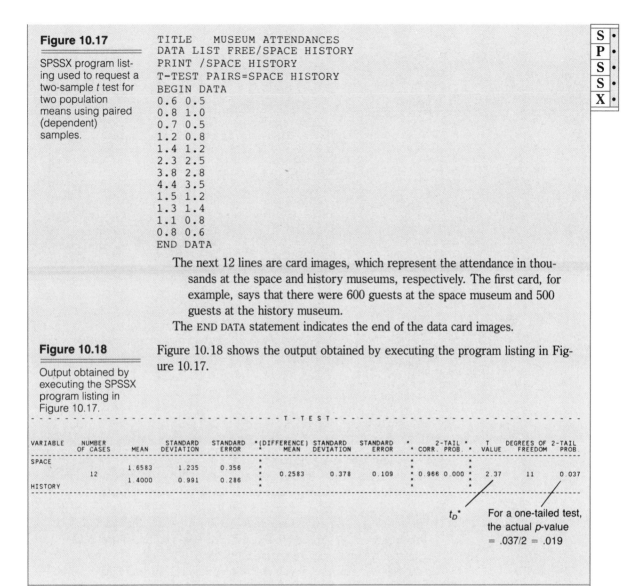

For a one-tailed test, the actual *p*-value = .037/2 = .019

Solution

Example 10.4

Example 10.4 was concerned with a *t* test for two independent samples to determine two population means. The problem was to determine if the average blowout times using the test apparatus were different for Beltex and Roadmaster tires (H_0: $\mu_1 = \mu_2$). The SAS program listing in Figure 10.19 was used to request the variances and the means for two independent samples. For the test on the means, the value of the test statistic and the *p*-value are provided for the case where the population variances are assumed equal and the case where it is not assumed that the variances are equal. We urge you not to use the same data to test both the means *and* variances at a predefined significance level. Each line represents one card image to be entered.

Figure 10.19

SAS program listing used to request a two-sample test for the variances and means.

```
TITLE      BELTEX-ROADMASTER TIRES;
DATA BLOWOUT;
INPUT BRAND $ WEAR;
CARDS;
B 3.82
B 3.11
B 4.21
B 2.64
B 4.16
B 3.91
B 2.44
B 4.52
B 2.84
B 3.26
B 3.74
B 3.04
B 2.56
B 2.58
B 3.15
R 4.16
R 3.92
R 3.94
R 4.22
R 4.15
       .
       .
       .
R 3.62
R 4.88
PROC PRINT;
PROC TTEST;
 CLASS BRAND;
 TITLE INDEPENDENT SAMPLES TTEST;
```

The TITLE command names the SAS run.

The DATA command gives the data a name.

The INPUT command names and gives the correct order for the different fields on the data cards. The $ indicates that BRAND is a character data.

The CARDS command indicates to SAS that the input data immediately follow.

The next 30 lines are card images, with each line representing the brand (Roadmaster or Beltex) and the wear factor. The first line, for example, represents brand B and a wear factor of 3.82.

The PROC PRINT command directs SAS to list the data that were just entered.

The PROC TTEST command compares the means of two groups of observations. The subcommand CLASS identifies BRAND as the variable to be classified in this example. The subcommand TITLE provides a report heading for the output.

Figure 10.20

Output obtained by executing SAS program listing in Figure 10.19.

Figure 10.20 shows the output obtained by executing the program listing in Figure 10.19.

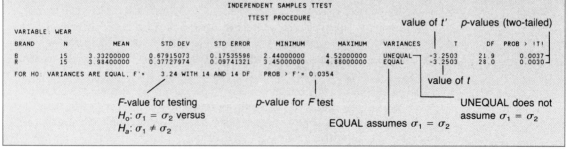

INDEPENDENT SAMPLES TTEST

TTEST PROCEDURE

VARIABLE: WEAR										
BRAND	N	MEAN	STD DEV	STD ERROR	MINIMUM	MAXIMUM	VARIANCES	T	DF	PROB > ┆T┆
B	15	3.33200000	0.67915073	0.17535596	2.44000000	4.52000000	UNEQUAL	-3.2503	21.9	0.0037
R	15	3.98400000	0.37727974	0.09741321	3.45000000	4.88000000	EQUAL	-3.2503	28.0	0.0030

FOR HO: VARIANCES ARE EQUAL, F'= 3.24 WITH 14 AND 14 DF   PROB > F'= 0.0354

value of *t'*   *p*-values (two-tailed)

value of *t*

F-value for testing
$H_0: \sigma_1 = \sigma_2$ versus
$H_a: \sigma_1 \neq \sigma_2$

p-value for *F* test

EQUAL assumes $\sigma_1 = \sigma_2$

UNEQUAL does not assume $\sigma_1 = \sigma_2$

Solution

Example 10.11

Example 10.11 was concerned with the computation of the t statistic for the means of two populations using point (dependent) samples. The problem was to determine whether the average weekly attendance at the space museum exceeded that at the history museum (H_a: $\mu_1 > \mu_2$). The SAS program listing in Figure 10.21 was used to request a mean, t score, and p-value. Note that SAS assumes a two-tailed test. This was a one-tailed test, so the calculated p-value must be divided by two. Each line represents one card image to be entered.

The TITLE command names the SAS run.

The DATA command gives the data a name.

The INPUT command names and gives the correct order for the different fields on the data cards.

The DIFF = SPACE − HISTORY statement is used to compute a new variable, DIFF, which is the difference between the value of SPACE and the value of HISTORY.

The CARDS command indicates to SAS that the input data immediately follow.

The next 12 lines are card images. Each card image represents the attendance in thousands at the space and history museums, respectively. The first card, for example, indicates that there were 600 guests at the space museum and 500 guests at the history museum.

The PROC PRINT command directs SAS to list the data that were just entered.

The PROC MEANS command requests an SAS procedure to print simple descriptive statistics for the variable in the following subcommand VAR DIFF. The TITLE subcommand names the output.

Figure 10.22 shows the output obtained by executing the program listing in Figure 10.21.

Figure 10.21

SAS program listing used to request a two-sample t test for two population means using paired (dependent) samples.

```
TITLE     MUSEUM ATTENDANCE;
DATA MUSEUM;
INPUT SPACE HISTORY;
DIFF=SPACE-HISTORY;
CARDS;
0.6 0.5
0.8 1.0
0.7 0.5
1.2 0.8
1.4 1.2
2.3 2.5
3.8 2.8
4.4 3.5
1.5 1.2
1.3 1.4
1.1 0.8
0.8 0.6
PROC PRINT;
PROC MEANS N MEAN T PRT;
 VAR DIFF;
  TITLE TWO DEPENDENT SAMPLES;
```

Figure 10.22

Output obtained by executing the SAS program listing in Figure 10.21.

TWO DEPENDENT SAMPLES

VARIABLE	N	MEAN	T	PR>!T!
DIFF	12	0.25833333	⌐ 2.37	0.0372 ⌐

t_D^*

For a one-tailed test, the actual p-value = .037/2 = .019

Estimation and Testing for Population Proportions

A Look Back/Introduction

By now you should be comfortable with the concepts of estimation and hypothesis testing. You make an assumption about the nature of your population, such as "assume that male heights follow a normal distribution," and then estimate the necessary parameters (such as the mean and standard deviation) using the corresponding sample statistics. You should be well aware that there always is the risk of arriving at an incorrect conclusion when using sample information to infer something about an entire population. Due to the Central Limit Theorem, the assumptions regarding your population can be relaxed when using larger samples.

Chapters 8, 9, and 10 have mostly concentrated on normal populations. We provided you with CIs for the mean and the variance of a single normal population. We examined how to check a statement regarding one of these parameters (such as $\mu < 100$ or $\sigma > .5$) using a test of hypothesis. Then this concept was extended to comparing the means or variances of two normal populations.

Now we return to the *binomial* situation, in which we are interested in the *proportion* of your population that has a certain attribute. This would include personal attributes, such as willingness to buy a product or being in favor of a proposed labor contract. We can also examine proportions as they relate to a particular physical attribute, such as the proportion of defective components in a batch.

We are interested in a single parameter, referred to as **p**, which is the **proportion** of the population having this attribute. For example, suppose that a recent report claims that only 10% of all registered voters in a certain area are in favor of forced busing for school children ($p = .10$). Or suppose it has been reported that a lower proportion of families with children favor busing than do those without children. How can we estimate the actual proportions here and test these claims?

11.1

Estimation and Confidence Intervals for a Population Proportion

When testing a population *proportion*, we are dealing with a binomial situation. Using the definitions from Chapter 6, each member of your population is either a *success* or a *failure*. These words can be misleading; it is necessary only that each person (or object) in your population either have a certain attribute (a success) or not have it (a failure). So we define **p** to be the proportion of successes in the population; that is, the proportion that have a certain attribute.

Do not confuse the notation p = a population proportion with the previously used shorthand for a *p*-value. They do not mean the same thing. We hope that the particular application will make it clear which of the two p is describing.

In Chapter 6, we assumed that p is known. For any binomial situation, perhaps p *is* known, or (more likely) it was estimated in some way. This chapter will examine how you can estimate p by using a sample from the population. Also, we can support (or fail to support) claims concerning the value of p. The final section in this chapter will compare two samples from two separate populations.

Point Estimate for a Population Proportion

Assume that the management of Cassidy Electronics, a manufacturer of calculators and microcomputers, is considering offering a dental plan to their employees. Because the monthly premium will be deducted from employee paychecks, perhaps not all employees will wish to join the plan. The insurance company is interested in the proportion of employees who will want to join. A random sample of 200 employees was interviewed. Of these, 137 said they would purchase the dental insurance if it were offered. What can you say about the proportion (p) of all employees who wish to join?

We view this problem as a binomial situation and define success as a person who will sign up for the dental insurance, and failure as a person who will not sign up for the dental insurance. Consequently, p is the proportion of successes in the population (proportion of all employees who favor the dental insurance). Remember that p, like μ and σ previously, will remain *unknown* forever. To *estimate* p, we obtain a random sample and observe the proportion of successes in our sample. We use $\hat{p}$ (read as "p hat") to denote the estimate of p, which is the proportion of successes in the sample. Here, $\hat{p}$ = proportion of employees in the sample who will sign up for the dental insurance, so $\hat{p} = 137/200 = .685$.

In general,

$\hat{p}$ = estimate of p

= proportion of sample having a specified attribute   (11-1)

= x/n

where n = sample size and x = the number of sample observations having this attribute.

The symbol ˆ is used to denote an *estimate*. Distinguish between $\hat{p}$ (obtained from sample information) with p (what $\hat{p}$ is estimating, its value unknown). This is the same difference that we previously recognized between a sample mean, $\overline{X}$, and a population mean, μ.

Confidence Intervals for a Population Proportion (Using a Small Sample)

The calculations involved in determining a CI for p using a small sample are fairly complex. To make them easier, we have listed 90% and 95% CIs for sample sizes of n = 5, 6, . . . , 20 in Table A-8 on page   . For sample sizes other than these, you can (1) use the large sample CI (described next) or (2) extend Table A-8 by consulting your local statistician. Or you can use a computer subroutine to derive additional values for this table. An explanation of the method used to generate these confidence limits is included at the end of the table.

Using Table A-8 is much like using Table A-1, the table of binomial probabilities. Let n = sample size and x = the observed number of successes in your sample. Based on these values, the CI (p_L, p_U) can be obtained directly from the table.

Example 11.1

A private company is considering the purchase of 200 Beagle microcomputers to monitor seismic activity. These computers will be placed in outdoor stations where they must be able to operate in extremely cold weather. If the computers will operate in temperatures as low as $-10°F$, the company will purchase them. Beagle, anxious to demonstrate the reliability of their system, has agreed to subject 15 computers to a "cold test." Let p = proportion of *all* Beagle computers that will function at $-10°F$.

Of the 15 sample computers, three of them stopped operating at above $-10°F$. What can you say about p? Construct a 95% CI interval for p.

Solution Let a success be that a computer *survives* the cold test (still functions at $-10°F$). We observe 12 successes out of 15 in the sample. So,

$$\hat{p} = 12/15 = .8$$

Using Table A-8 for n = 15, x = 12, and α = .05, we find p_L = .519 and p_U = .957. The corresponding 95% CI for p is

$$p_L \quad \text{to} \quad p_U = .519 \quad \text{to} \quad .957$$

So we are 95% confident that the actual (population) percentage of Beagle computers that can function at $-10°F$ is between 51.9% and 95.7%. ●

Confidence Intervals for a Population Proportion (Using a Large Sample)

When dealing with large samples, the CLT once again provides us with a reliable method of determining CIs. For each element in your sample, assign a value of one if this observation is a success (has the attribute) or zero if this observation is a failure (does not have the attribute). Using the dental-plan example to illustrate, for *each* person in the sample, we assign 1 if this person wants the dental insurance and 0 if this person does not want the dental insurance. So what is $\hat{p}$? We can write this as

$$\hat{p} = \frac{\overbrace{1 + 1 + \ldots + 1}^{137 \text{ times}} + \overbrace{0 + 0 + \ldots + 0}^{63 \text{ times}}}{200} = \frac{137}{200} = .685$$

In this sense, then, $\hat{p}$ is a **sample average**: it is an average of zeros and ones. As a result, we can apply the CLT to $\hat{p}$ and conclude that $\hat{p}$ is (approximately) a *normal random variable* for large samples. This works reasonably well provided both np and $n(1 - p)$ are > 5. So the distribution of $\hat{p}$ [large sample; $np > 5$ and $n(1 - p) > 5$] can be summarized: $\hat{p}$ is (approximately) a normal random variable with

mean $= p$

standard deviation (standard error) $= \sqrt{\dfrac{p(1 - p)}{n}}$

By standardizing this result, we have

$$Z = \frac{\hat{p} - p}{\sqrt{\dfrac{p(1 - p)}{n}}} \tag{11-2}$$

which is approximately a standard normal random variable. This allows us to use Table A-4 to construct a CI for p. Thus, a $(1 - \alpha) \cdot 100\%$ CI for p [large sample; np and $n(1 - p) > 5$] is

$$\hat{p} - Z_{\alpha/2} \sqrt{\frac{\hat{p}(1 - \hat{p})}{n}} \quad \text{to} \quad \hat{p} + Z_{\alpha/2} \sqrt{\frac{\hat{p}(1 - \hat{p})}{n}} \tag{11-3}$$

where $\hat{p}$ = sample proportion. Notice that we have used $\hat{p}$ and $1 - \hat{p}$ under the square root in equation 11-3 rather than p and $1 - p$. This was necessary because p is *unknown* and must be replaced by its estimate, $\hat{p}$. As we observed in previous chapters, such a procedure (replacing an unknown parameter by its estimate) works well provided our sample is large enough. For this situation, both np and $n(1 - p)$ must be greater than five.

Example 11.2   Using the data regarding employees' desire to join the dental plan, what is a 90% CI for the proportion of all employees who would participate in the dental insurance program?

Solution   Using Table A-4, $Z_{\alpha/2} = Z_{.05} = 1.645$. Also, $\hat{p} = 137/200 = .685$. So the 90% CI for p is

$$.685 - 1.645 \sqrt{\frac{(.685)(.315)}{200}} \quad \text{to} \quad .685 + 1.645 \sqrt{\frac{(.685)(.315)}{200}}$$

$$= .685 - .054 \quad \text{to} \quad .685 + .054$$

$$= .631 \quad \text{to} \quad .739$$

Based on the sample data, we are 90% confident that the percentage of employees who would purchase the dental insurance is between 63.1% and 73.9%.   ●

Example 11.3

Remember that, in lot acceptance sampling, we either accept or reject a batch (lot) of components, parts, or assembled products based on tests using a random sample drawn from the lot.

   Suppose we draw a sample of size 150 from a lot of calculators. We test each of the sampled calculators and find 13 defectives. Determine a 95% CI for the proportion of defectives in the entire batch.

Solution Let p = proportion of defective calculators in the batch. Based on the sample of 150 calculators, we have

$$\hat{p} = 13/150 = .0867$$

Because $Z_{.025} = 1.96$, the 95% CI for p is

$$.0867 - 1.96 \sqrt{\frac{(.0867)(.9133)}{150}} \quad \text{to} \quad .0867 + 1.96 \sqrt{\frac{(.0867)(.9133)}{150}}$$

$$= .0867 - .045 \quad \text{to} \quad .0867 + .045$$

$$= .042 \quad \text{to} \quad .132$$

   Consequently, we are 95% confident that our estimate of p ($\hat{p} = .0867$) is within .045 of the actual value of p. In other words, this sample estimates the actual percentage of defective calculators to within 4.5%, with 95% confidence. ●

Choosing the Sample Size (One Population)

Suppose that you want your point estimate, $\hat{p}$, to be within a certain amount of the actual proportion, p. In example 11.3, the *maximum error, E,* was $E = .045$. What if the buyer's specifications necessitate that we estimate the parameter p to within 2% with 95% confidence? Now,

$$E = 1.96 \sqrt{\frac{p(1 - p)}{n}} \tag{11-4}$$

We have an earlier estimate of p ($\hat{p} = .0867$) using the sample of size 150; this can be used in equation 11-4. The purpose is to extend this sample in order to obtain this specific maximum error, E. The specified value of E is .02, so,

$$E = .02 = 1.96 \sqrt{\frac{(.0867)(.9133)}{n}}$$

Therefore,

$$\sqrt{\frac{(.0867)(.9133)}{n}} = \frac{.02}{1.96}$$

Squaring both sides and rearranging leads to

$$n = \frac{(1.96)^2(.0867)(.9133)}{(.02)^2} = 760.5$$

Rounding up (*always*), we come to the conclusion that a sample of size $n = 761$ calculators will be necessary to estimate p to within 2%.

Figure 11.1

Curve of values of $\hat{p}(1 - \hat{p})$.

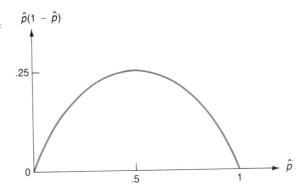

In general, the following equation provides the necessary sample size to estimate p with a specified maximum error, E, and confidence level $(1 - \alpha) \cdot 100\%$:

$$n = \frac{Z_{\alpha/2}^2 \, \hat{p}(1 - \hat{p})}{E^2} \tag{11-5}$$

In this illustration, we used an estimate of p from a prior sample to determine the necessary sample size using equation 11-5. If the sample of size n, based on this equation, is our first and only sample, then we *have no estimate*, $\hat{p}$. There is a conservative procedure we can follow here that will guarantee the accuracy (E) that we require. Look at the curve of different values of $\hat{p}(1 - \hat{p})$ in Figure 11.1. Consider these values:

$\hat{p}$	$\hat{p}(1 - \hat{p})$
.2	.16
.4	.24
.5	.25
.7	.21
.9	.18

Note that the largest value of $\hat{p}(1 - \hat{p})$ is .25.

If we make $\hat{p}(1 - \hat{p})$ in equation 11-5 *as large as possible*, this will provide a value of n that will result in a maximum error that is sure to be less than the specified value. So we can formulate this rule: If no prior estimate of p is available, a conservative procedure to determine the necessary sample size from equation 11-5 is to use $\hat{p} = .5$.

Example 11.4

Suppose that the insurance company underwriting the dental plan wishes to obtain a single sample that will estimate, to within 2% with 90% confidence, the proportion (p) of employees who would purchase the dental insurance. How large of a sample is required? (We are assuming now that we have not yet obtained the sample of size 200.)

Solution We have no prior knowledge of p, so we use $\hat{p} = .5$ to obtain a sample size of

$$n = \frac{(1.645)^2(.5)(.5)}{(.02)^2} = 1691.3$$

To obtain an estimate of p with a maximum error of $E = .02$, we will need a sample size of $n = 1692$ employees. With a sample of this size, we can safely say that the point estimate, p, will be within 2% of the actual value, with 90% confidence (however, this is a very large sample). ●

Exercises

11.1 Mary Pharmaceuticals is interested in estimating the proportion (p) of its employees who would accept a substantial increase in benefits instead of an annual raise in salary for a particular year. A random sample of 20 employees was obtained, and 12 welcomed the idea. How can you estimate the proportion in the population who would welcome this plan? Construct a 90% CI for p. Use Table A-8.

11.2 In exercise 11.1, let the maximum error of the estimating proportion be 4%. Estimate the necessary sample size for a 95% CI. Use the estimate of p from exercise 11.1 for the value of p.

11.3 In exercise 11.2, assume that you have no prior knowledge of p. Estimate the sample size that is required to estimate the proportion (p) of employees who would accept the plan with a 95% confidence level, using the same maximum error of estimate for the proportion.

11.4 A company wishes to estimate the proportion, p, of its employees who went on sick leave during the past six months. A random sample of 18 employees was taken; of them, ten went on sick leave. Construct a 90% CI for p. Use Table A-8.

11.5 Using the information in exercise 11.4, construct an approximate 90% CI for the proportion of all employees who went on sick leave during the past six months. Use the normal approximation to the binomial. How does it compare with the exact CI in exercise 11.4?

11.6 A math workshop will be offered only if the student demand is sufficiently high. What is the required sample size necessary to estimate with 90% confidence the proportion of students who would register for the workshop if we specify a value of .03 for the maximum error E?

11.7 In exercise 11.6, if a previous study indicated that the proportion of students who would register for the workshop was .68, estimate the necessary sample size for a maximum error, E, of 3%.

11.8 Winthrop Boat Lines is exploring the possibility of offering a ferry service between the cities of Patna and Madura, provided there is sufficient demand to make it feasible. The firm randomly interviewed 210 commuters from the two cities, and 146 of them indicated they would patronize the ferry service instead of the present bus service. Estimate the population proportion p of commuters from the two cities who prefer the ferry service. Construct a 95% CI for p.

11.9 In exercise 11.8, if the maximum error is $E = .01$, estimate the necessary sample size at the 95% confidence level. Use the value obtained in exercise 11.8 for the estimate of p.

11.10 Suppose a small sample $(n = 12)$ was drawn from a lot of electric bulbs. Each bulb was tested; four defectives were found. Determine the 90% CI for the proportion of defectives in the entire batch.

11.11 A manufacturer of microcomputers purchases electronic chips from a supplier who claims her chips are defective only 5% of the time. Determine the sample size that would be required to estimate the true proportion of defective chips if we wanted our estimate $\hat{p}$ to be within 1.25% of the true proportion, with 95% confidence.

11.12 A credit union randomly selected 110 savings-account customers and found that 85 of them also had checking accounts with the union. Construct a 95% CI for the true proportion of savings-account customers who also have checking accounts.

11.13 Blackburry Candies is considering the withdrawal from the market of its product Nutty Bar if Nutty Bar has not captured at least 5% of the candy bar market. A random sample of 115 candy-bar buyers was taken; four bought the Nutty Bar. Find a 95% CI for the proportion, p, of the population of candy-bar buyers who choose Nutty Bar.

11.14 Construct a 99% CI for the proportion in exercise 11.13. Compare the two CIs.

11.15 Using the data in exercise 11.13, what is the required sample size necessary to estimate with 95% confidence, and to be within .03, the proportion of candy-bar buyers who would choose the candy bar? Assume that we have no prior knowledge of p.

11.2

Hypothesis Testing for a Population Proportion

How can you statistically reject a statement such as, "At least 60% of all heavy smokers will contact a serious lung or heart ailment before age 65"? Perhaps someone merely took a wild guess at the value of 60%, and it is your job to gather evidence that will either shoot down this claim or let it stand if there is insufficient evidence to conclude that this percentage actually is less than 60%. We set up hypotheses and test them much like before, only now we are concerned about a population proportion, p, rather than the mean or standard deviation of a particular population.

Hypothesis Testing Using a Small Sample

Because CIs can be used to perform a test of hypothesis, we will use Table A-8 to conduct such a test. Table A-8 contains sample sizes of $n = 5$ to 20 and $\alpha = .05$ and .10. If $np > 5$ and $n(1 - p) > 5$, the large-sample approximation will provide an accurate test. For sample sizes contained in Table A-8, use the procedure outlined in the accompanying box.

Hypothesis Testing (Small Sample; n Is Between 5 and 20)

TWO-TAILED TEST

$H_0: p = p_0$

$H_a: p \neq p_0$

1. Obtain the $(1 - \alpha) \cdot 100\%$ CI from Table A-8; that is, (p_L, p_U), using $x =$ the observed number of successes.
2. Reject H_0 if p_0 does not lie between p_L and p_U.
3. Fail to reject H_0 if $p_L \leq p_0 \leq p_U$.

ONE-TAILED TEST

$H_0: p \leq p_0$ $\qquad\qquad\qquad\qquad$ $H_0: p \geq p_0$

$H_a: p > p_0$ $\qquad\qquad\qquad\qquad$ $H_a: p < p_0$

1. Obtain the $(1 - 2\alpha) \cdot 100\%$ CI from Table A-8; that is, (p_L, p_U), using $x =$ the observed number of successes.
2. Reject H_0 if $p_0 < p_L$.
3. Fail to reject H_0 if $p_0 \geq p_L$.

1. Obtain the $(1 - 2\alpha) \cdot 100\%$ CI from Table A-8; that is, (p_L, p_U), using $x =$ the observed number of successes.
2. Reject H_0 if $p_0 > p_U$.
3. Fail to reject H_0 if $p_0 \leq p_U$.

Notice that, for a one-tailed test, we *double* α when finding the CI for p from Table A-8. For example, if $\alpha = .05$, then $2\alpha = .10$, and so we retrieve a 90% CI from the table. As a result, this particular binomial table can be used only when $\alpha = .025$ or .05 for a one-tailed test.

Example 11.5

In example 11.1, suppose that the company interested in the Beagle microcomputers will purchase them if Beagle's claim that the proportion, p, of all Beagle computers that can survive these cold temperatures is greater than .75 (75%) can be shown to be true. Do the data support this claim using $\alpha = .05$?

Solution The claim under investigation goes into the alternative hypothesis. The appropriate hypotheses are

$H_0: p \leq .75$ and $H_a: p > .75$

We observed, in the sample of 15 computers, $x = 12$ successes (computers that survived). Because $\alpha = .05$, we double this ($2\alpha = .10$) and refer to Table A-8 for a 90% CI for p when $n = 15$, $x = 12$. This is

$(p_L, p_U) = (.560, .943)$

We will reject H_0 provided $p_0 = .75$ lies to the left of p_L. Because $p_0 = .75$ is greater than $p_L = .560$, we fail to reject H_0.

Based on the evidence gathered from this sample, we cannot demonstrate that p is greater than the required 75%. Notice that we are not *accepting* H_0—we simply *fail to reject* it. In other words, we are not convinced that this percentage is $\leq 75\%$. This means that the point estimate $\hat{p} = 12/15 = .8$ is *not enough larger* than .75 to justify this claim. The fact that $\hat{p}$ exceeds .75 apparently is due to the sampling error we always encounter when using a sample statistic ($\hat{p}$) to infer something about a population parameter (p). ●

Hypothesis Testing Using a Large Sample

The standard five-step procedure will be outlined for testing H_0 versus H_a when attempting to support a claim regarding a binomial parameter, p, using a large sample.

Hypothesis Testing [Large Sample; np_0 and $n(1 - p_0) > 5$]

TWO-TAILED TEST

$H_0: p = p_0$

$H_a: p \neq p_0$

Reject H_0 if $|Z| > Z_{\alpha/2}$ where

$$Z = \frac{\hat{p} - p_0}{\sqrt{\dfrac{p_0(1 - p_0)}{n}}}$$

ONE-TAILED TEST

$H_0: p \leq p_0$ $H_0: p \geq p_0$

$H_a: p > p_0$ $H_a: p < p_0$

Reject H_0 if $Z > Z_{\alpha}$ Reject H_0 if $Z < -Z_{\alpha}$

To define a test statistic for this situation, the approximate standard normal random variable contained in equation 11-2 is used.

The rejection region for this test is defined by determining the distribution of the test statistic, given that H_0 is true. This means that the unknown value of p in equation 11-2 is replaced by the value of p specified in H_0 (say, p_0). For a one-tailed test, the boundary value of p in H_0 is used. This procedure is summarized in the box on page 343.

Example 11.6

In example 11.2, we estimated the proportion of employees at Cassidy Electronics who would sign up for the dental insurance. The insurance company is not willing to offer such a plan unless more than 60% of the employees will participate. Using the sample of 200 employees, can you conclude that this percentage is greater than the required 60%? Use a significance level of $\alpha = .10$.

Solution

Step 1. Your hypotheses should be

$$H_0: p \leq .6$$
$$H_a: p > .6$$

Step 2. Since $np_0 = (200)(.6) = 120$ and $n(1 - p_0) = (200)(.4) = 80$ are both > 5, the large-sample test statistic can be used, namely,

$$Z = \frac{\hat{p} - p_0}{\sqrt{\dfrac{p_0(1 - p_0)}{n}}}$$

$$= \frac{\hat{p} - .6}{\sqrt{\dfrac{(.6)(.4)}{200}}}$$

Step 3. The rejection region, using $\alpha = .10$, will be

$$\text{Reject } H_0 \text{ if } Z > Z_{.10} = 1.28$$

Step 4. Using the sample data, $\hat{p} = 137/200 = .685$, so

$$Z^* = \frac{.685 - .6}{\sqrt{\dfrac{(.6)(.4)}{200}}} = \frac{.085}{.0346} = 2.45$$

Because $2.45 > 1.28$, we reject H_0 in favor of H_a.

Step 5. This sample indicates that the proportion of employees who would participate in the dental insurance plan *is* greater than 60%.

In example 11.6, the computed test statistic was $Z^* = 2.45$. Figure 11.2 shows the Z curve and the calculated p-value, which is .0071. Using the classical approach, because $.0071 < \alpha = .10$, we reject H_0. If we choose to base our conclusion strictly on the p-value (without choosing a significance level, α), this value would be classified as *small*—it is less than .01. Consequently, using this procedure, we once again reject H_0.

Figure 11.2

Z curve showing p-value
for example 11.6.

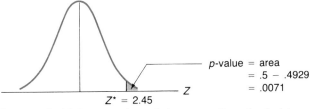

p-value = area
= .5 − .4929
= .0071

$Z^* = 2.45$

Example 11.7

In example 11.3, we estimated the proportion of calculators that were defective in a batch (lot). The company has determined that a good target for this defective percentage is 4%. The sample of 150 had 13 defectives. Can we conclude that the actual proportion of defective calculators is different from 4%? Use $\alpha = .05$.

Solution

Step 1. We wish to see if p is *different* from 4%, so we should use a two-tailed test with hypotheses

$$H_0\colon p = .04$$

$$H_a\colon p \neq .04$$

Step 2. Here $np_0 = (150)(.04) = 6$ and $n(1 - p_0) = (150)(.96) = 144$. Both are > 5, so the appropriate test statistic is

$$Z = \frac{\hat{p} - p_0}{\sqrt{\dfrac{p_0(1 - p_0)}{n}}} = \frac{\hat{p} - .04}{\sqrt{\dfrac{(.04)(.96)}{150}}}$$

Step 3. With $\alpha = .05$, the test of H_0 versus H_a will be

Reject H_0 if $|Z| > 1.96$

Step 4. Using $\hat{p} = 13/150 = .0867$,

$$Z^* = \frac{.0867 - .04}{\sqrt{\dfrac{(.04)(.96)}{150}}} = \frac{.0467}{.016} = 2.92$$

Because $2.92 > 1.96$, we reject H_0.

Step 5. The company is *not* meeting their target percentage of defectives. As a reminder, because $\alpha = .05$, this particular test will reject H_0 when in fact it is true, 5% of the time. ●

In example 11.7, $Z^* = 2.92$. What is the p-value? This is a two-tailed test, so we need to *double* the right-tail area, as illustrated in Figure 11.3. So $p = 2 \cdot .0018 = .0036$. Thus, using either the classical procedure (comparing the p-value to $\alpha = .05$) or basing our decision strictly on the p-value, we reject H_0 because of this extremely small p-value.

Figure 11.3

Z curve showing p-value
(twice the shaded area)
for example 11.7.

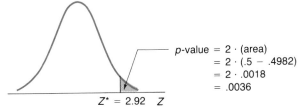

p-value = 2 · (area)
= 2 · (.5 − .4982)
= 2 · .0018
= .0036

$Z^* = 2.92$ Z

Exercises

11.16   Using the data in exercise 11.13, test the hypothesis that Nutty Bar captures less than 5% of the market share using a .05 level of significance.

11.17   Calculate the p-value for exercise 11.16. Based on the p-value, would you reject the null hypothesis at the .05 level?

11.18   Using the data in exercise 11.4, test the hypothesis that less than 55% of the employees went on sick leave, using a .10 level of significance. Use Table A-8.

11.19   Using the data in exercise 11.8, test the hypothesis that less than 75% of the commuters would patronize the proposed ferry service. Use a significance level of .05. What is the p-value?

11.20   Using the data in exercise 11.10, test the hypothesis that the defective rate is more than 10%, using a .05 level of significance. Use Table A-8.

11.21   In order for $np \geqslant 5$ and $n(1 - p) \geqslant 5$, how large must n be if $p = .03$.

11.22   Using the data in exercise 11.1, test the hypothesis that more than half of the employees prefer the proposed benefit plan at the .05 level of significance.

a.   What is the rejection region using Table A-8?

b.   What is the rejection region using the large-sample procedure?

11.23   The editor of a famous weekly magazine is concerned about typographical errors and believes that about 1.5% of the number of lines printed have at least one error. An examination of 650 different lines revealed 11 lines that had at least one error. Do the data support the editor's belief? Use a significance level of .10.

11.24   A manager at National Insurance believes that, out of the total number of automobile-accident claims settled in a particular month, there are more claims related to speeding by the driver than there are claims that are not related to speeding. From a random sample of 75 claims, 40 were found to be associated with speeding. Test the manager's belief. Use a significance level of .05.

11.25   Calculate the p-value for exercise 11.24 and interpret it.

11.26   An instructor believes that, of the students who take a certain course, there are more students who have not taken the prerequisites for the course than students who have taken the prerequisites. The instructor randomly selected 70 students and found that only 30 students had taken the prerequisites for the course. Do these data support the instructor's belief? Use a significance level of .10.

11.27   Based on the p-value for exercise 11.26, would you reject the null hypothesis at the .01 level?

11.28   A labor-union leader stated that at least 40% of the members of the union had a college degree. A random sample of 440 members revealed that only 170 had a college degree. Test the hypothesis that H_0: the proportion of union members with a college degree is greater than or equal to 40%. Use a .05 level of significance.

11.29   KNNN, a television news channel, claimed that more than 65% of its subscribers had an annual income of \$40,000 or more. A random sample of 160 subscribers was interviewed; 71% of them had incomes of \$40,000 or more. Does this information support KNNN's claim? Use a significance level of .05.

11.30   Calculate and interpret the p-value for exercise 11.29.

11.3

Comparing Two Population Proportions (Large Independent Samples)

Consider the following questions:

Is the divorce rate higher in California than it is in New York?

Is there any difference in the proportion of cars manufactured by Henry Motor Company requiring an engine overhaul before 100,000 miles and the proportion of General Auto automobiles requiring one?

Is there a higher rate of lung cancer among cigarette smokers than there is among nonsmokers?

These questions are concerned with proportions from *two* populations. Our method of estimating these proportions will be exactly as it was for one population. We simply have two of everything—two populations, two samples, two estimates, and so on. In this section, it will be assumed that the two samples are obtained *independently*.

For example, consider the question concerning the proportion of cars requiring an engine overhaul. Population 1 is all Henry cars, with p_1 = proportion of Henry Autos requiring an engine overhaul before 100,000 miles, n_1 = Henry sample size, and x_1 = number of Henry cars requiring an overhaul before 100,000 miles. Population 2 is all GA cars, with p_2 = proportion of GA cars requiring an engine overhaul before 100,000 miles, n_2 = GA sample size, and x_2 = number of GA cars requiring an overhaul before 100,000 miles.

Define a success to be that a car requires an overhaul before 100,000 miles. (Keep in mind that "success" is merely a label for the trait you are interested in. It need not be a desirable trait.) Our point estimate of p_1 will be (as before)

$$\hat{p}_1 = \frac{\text{observed number of successes in the sample}}{\text{sample size}}$$

$$= \frac{\text{number of cars in the Henry sample requiring an overhaul}}{n_1}$$

That is, the point estimate of p_1 is

$$\hat{p}_1 = x_1/n_1 \qquad\qquad (11\text{-}6)$$

Similarly, our point estimate of p_2, obtained from the second sample, is

$$\hat{p}_2 = x_2/n_2 \qquad\qquad (11\text{-}7)$$

For the two-population case, the parameter of interest will be the *difference* between the two population proportions, $p_1 - p_2$. The next section will discuss a method of estimating $p_1 - p_2$ by using a point estimate along with a corresponding CI.

Confidence Interval for $p_1 - p_2$ (Large Independent Samples)

The logical estimator of $p_1 - p_2$ is $\hat{p}_1 - \hat{p}_2$, the difference between the sample estimates. What kind of random variable is $\hat{p}_1 - \hat{p}_2$? We are dealing with large independent samples (where $n_1\hat{p}_1$, $n_1(1 - \hat{p}_1)$, $n_2\hat{p}_2$, and $n_2(1 - \hat{p}_2)$ are each larger than five,) so the CLT assures us that $\hat{p}_1 - \hat{p}_2$ is (approximately) a normal random variable with

mean $= p_1 - p_2$

and

standard deviation $= \sqrt{\dfrac{p_1(1 - p_1)}{n_1} + \dfrac{p_2(1 - p_2)}{n_2}}$

In a previous section, we observed that $\hat{p}_1$ can be thought of as a sample mean, where the sample consists of observations that are either a 1 (a particular event occurred) or a 0 (this event did not occur). Because the two samples are obtained independently, the results extend to this situation, leading to the approximate normal distribution for $\hat{p}_1 - \hat{p}_2$. Notice that the variance of $\hat{p}_1 - \hat{p}_2$ is obtained by *adding* the variance of $\hat{p}_1$, or $p_1(1 - p_1)/n_1$ and the variance of $\hat{p}_2$, or $p_2(1 - p_2)/n_2$.

To evaluate the CI, we are forced to approximate the confidence limits by replacing p_1 by $\hat{p}_1$ and p_2 by $\hat{p}_2$ under the square root. This approximation works well provided both sample sizes are large. So we derive a $(1 - \alpha) \cdot 100\%$ CI for $p_1 - p_2$ [large independent samples; $n_1\hat{p}_1$, $n_1(1 - \hat{p}_1)$, $n_2\hat{p}_2$, and $n_2(1 - \hat{p}_2)$ are each > 5]:

$$(\hat{p}_1 - \hat{p}_2) - Z_{\alpha/2}\sqrt{\dfrac{\hat{p}_1(1 - \hat{p}_1)}{n_1} + \dfrac{\hat{p}_2(1 - \hat{p}_2)}{n_2}}$$

$$\text{to} \quad (\hat{p}_1 - \hat{p}_2) + Z_{\alpha/2}\sqrt{\dfrac{\hat{p}_1(1 - \hat{p}_1)}{n_1} + \dfrac{\hat{p}_2(1 - \hat{p}_2)}{n_2}} \tag{11-8}$$

where $\hat{p}_1 = x_1/n_1$ and $\hat{p}_2 = x_2/n_2$ are the sample proportions.

Example 11.8

Of a random sample of 100 cars manufactured by Henry (population 1), 28 needed an engine overhaul before reaching 100,000 miles. A second sample, obtained independently of the first, consisted of 150 cars produced by GA; 48 of them required an engine overhaul before 100,000 miles. Both sets of cars were subjected to the same weather conditions, maintenance program, and driving conditions. Construct a 99% CI for $p_1 - p_2$.

Solution We have $\hat{p}_1 = 28/100 = .28$ and $\hat{p}_2 = 48/150 = .32$. Also, $Z_{\alpha/2} = Z_{.005} = 2.575$, using Table A-4. The resulting CI for $p_1 - p_2$ is

$$(.28 - .32) - 2.575\sqrt{\dfrac{(.28)(.72)}{100} + \dfrac{(.32)(.68)}{150}}$$

$$\text{to} \quad (.28 - .32) + 2.575\sqrt{\dfrac{(.28)(.72)}{100} + \dfrac{(.32)(.68)}{150}}$$

$= -.04 - .15 \quad \text{to} \quad -.04 + .15$

$= -.19 \quad \text{to} \quad .11$

This CI leaves us unable to conclude that either manufacturer produces a better engine. We are 99% confident that the percentage of Henry engines requiring an overhaul before 100,000 miles is between 19% *lower* to 11% *higher* than for the GA engines.

Example 11.9

Boone Advertising Agency handles the advertising for Slick cigarettes. They recently completed a six-month advertising campaign in an attempt to increase the market share for Slick. A private marketing consulting firm was chosen to estimate the market share before and after the campaign. A set of vendors who supply cigarettes nationwide was used to determine market share. Prior to the campaign, a random sample of 1200 cartons supplied by these vendors was selected. Following the campaign, a second random sample of 1200 cartons was selected (independently of the first sample). The results were as follows. After the advertising campaign: $n_1 = 1200$ cartons, and x_1 = number of Slick cartons = 90. Before the advertising campaign: $n_2 = 1200$ cartons, and x_2 = number of Slick cartons = 54. Let p_1 = proportion of cartons sold *after* the advertising campaign that were Slick cigarettes, and p_2 = proportion *before* the campaign. Determine a 95% CI for $p_1 - p_2$.

Solution Our proportion estimates are

$$\hat{p}_1 = 90/1200 = .075$$

$$\hat{p}_2 = 54/1200 = .045$$

The 95% CI for $p_1 - p_2$ is

$$(.075 - .045) - 1.96 \sqrt{\frac{(.075)(.925)}{1200} + \frac{(.045)(.955)}{1200}}$$

$$\text{to} \quad (.075 - .045) + 1.96 \sqrt{\frac{(.075)(.925)}{1200} + \frac{(.045)(.955)}{1200}}$$

$$= .03 - .019 \text{ to } .03 + .019$$

$$= .011 \text{ to } .049$$

So we are 95% confident that (1) our estimate of the difference in proportion (after minus before), namely $\hat{p}_1 - \hat{p}_2 = .03$, is within 1.9% of the actual difference, and (2) the proportion increase after the advertising campaign is between 1.1% and 4.9%. ●

Choosing the Sample Sizes (Two Populations)

In Chapter 10, we discussed how to select samples from two populations when the desired accuracy of the point estimate of the difference between two population means is specified—this is the maximum error, E. If E is, say, 10 lbs, then what sample sizes (n_1 and n_2) are necessary for the point estimate of $\mu_1 - \mu_2$ (namely, $\overline{X}_1 - \overline{X}_2$) to be within 10 lbs of the actual value, with 95% (or whatever) confidence? Using the results contained in Appendix B on page , values of n_1 and n_2 were provided in Chapter 10 that minimized the total sample size, $n_1 + n_2$, for this specific value of E.

We encounter a similar situation when dealing with two population proportions, p_1 and p_2. If a maximum error of, say, $E = .10$ is specified, then the question of interest is: What sample sizes (n_1 and n_2) are necessary for the point estimate of $p_1 - p_2$ (namely, $\hat{p}_1 - \hat{p}_2$) to be within .10 of the actual value, with 95% (or whatever) confidence?

The maximum error, E, always is the amount that you *add to* and *subtract from* the point estimate when determining a CI. When dealing with two proportions, this is

$$E = Z_{\alpha/2} \sqrt{\frac{p_1(1 - p_1)}{n_1} + \frac{p_2(1 - p_2)}{n_2}} \tag{11-9}$$

To evaluate this expression, you will need estimates of p_1 and p_2. You have two options. If you have previously obtained small samples from these two populations, then you can use the resulting sample estimates $\hat{p}_1$ and $\hat{p}_2$. The purpose then will be to extend these samples to obtain better accuracy in the point estimate, $\hat{p}_1 - \hat{p}_2$. If no information regarding p_1 and p_2 is available, then you can use the conservative approach discussed in Section 11.1 by letting $\hat{p}_1 = \hat{p}_2 = .5$.

By applying the results of Appendix B to this situation, the sample sizes n_1 and n_2 that minimize the total sample size $n_1 + n_2$ are given by

$$n_1 = \frac{Z_{\alpha/2}^2 (A + B)}{E^2} \qquad (11\text{-}10)$$

$$n_2 = \frac{Z_{\alpha/2}^2 (C + B)}{E^2} \qquad (11\text{-}11)$$

where

$$A = p_1(1 - p_1)$$
$$B = \sqrt{p_1 p_2 (1 - p_1)(1 - p_2)}$$
$$C = p_2(1 - p_2)$$

To determine A, B, and C, estimates of p_1 and p_2 should be substituted for p_1 and p_2 by using one of the two options described.

Example 11.10

Using the data from example 11.8, determine what sample sizes are necessary for the estimate of the difference between the proportion of cars needing an overhaul before 100,000 miles to be within .10 of the actual value, with 99% confidence, if (1) the results from example 11.8 are available and (2) no sample information is available.

Solution 1 The specified maximum error is $E = .10$. Sample data have been collected regarding these proportions, so we use the corresponding estimates to determine the sample sizes necessary to obtain this degree of accuracy. Using Table A-4, $Z_{\alpha/2} = Z_{.005} = 2.575$. Here, $\hat{p}_1 = .28$ and $\hat{p}_2 = .32$. Consequently,

$$A = \hat{p}_1(1 - \hat{p}_1)$$
$$= .2016$$
$$B = \sqrt{\hat{p}_1 \hat{p}_2 (1 - \hat{p}_1)(1 - \hat{p}_2)}$$
$$= .2094$$
$$C = \hat{p}_2(1 - \hat{p}_2)$$
$$= .2176$$

To obtain the *smallest possible* total sample size, the two sample sizes should be

$$n_1 = \frac{(2.575)^2(.2016 + .2094)}{(.10)^2}$$
$$\cong 273$$

(remember—always round *up*)—and

$$n_2 = \frac{(2.575)^2(.2176 + .2094)}{(.10)^2} \cong 284$$

providing a total sample size of $n_1 + n_2 = 557$ cars.

Solution 2 If no prior estimates of $p_1 = p_2$ are available, using $\hat{p}_1 = \hat{p}_2 = .5$ will result in sample sizes n_1 and n_2 that, when obtained, will provide a maximum error *no larger than* the specified value of $E = .10$. Here, $A = (.5)(.5) = .25$. Similarly, $B = C = .25$, so

$$n_1 = n_2 = \frac{(2.575)^2(.25 + .25)}{(.10)^2} \cong 332$$

Consequently, a total sample size of $n_1 + n_2 = 664$ cars will be necessary for $\hat{p}_1 - \hat{p}_2$ to be within .10 of the actual value of $p_1 - p_2$, with 99% confidence. ●

Hypothesis Testing for p_1 and p_2 (Large Independent Samples)

Suppose that a recent report stated that, based on a sample of 500 people, 35% of all cigarette smokers had at some time in their life developed disease Q. On the other hand, 25% of the nonsmokers in the sample acquired disease Q. Can we conclude from this sample that, because $\hat{p}_1 = .35 > \hat{p}_2 = .25$, the proportion ($p_1$) of all smokers who will acquire disease Q exceeds the proportion (p_2) for nonsmokers? In other words, is $\hat{p}_1$ *significantly* larger than $\hat{p}_2$? After all, even if $p_1 = p_2$, there is a 50–50 chance that $\hat{p}_1$ will be larger than $\hat{p}_2$ because for large samples, the distribution of $\hat{p}_1 - \hat{p}_2$ is approximately a bell-shaped (normal) curve centered at $p_1 - p_2$—which, if $p_1 = p_2$, would be zero.

Are the results of the sample significant, or are they due simply to the sampling error that we always encounter when estimating from a sample? Your alternative hypothesis can be that two proportions are *different* (a two-tailed test) or that one *exceeds* the other (a one-tailed test). As before, we will assume that the two random samples are obtained *independently*. The possible hypotheses are these: for a two-tailed test,

$H_0: p_1 = p_2$

$H_a: p_1 \neq p_2$

and for a one-tailed test,

$H_0: p_1 \leq p_2$

$H_a: p_1 > p_2$

or

$H_0: p_1 \geq p_2$

$H_a: p_1 < p_2$

One possible test statistic to use here would be the standard normal (Z) statistic that was used to derive a CI for $p_1 - p_2$, namely,

$$Z = \frac{\hat{p}_1 - \hat{p}_2}{\sqrt{\dfrac{\hat{p}_1(1 - \hat{p}_1)}{n_1} + \dfrac{\hat{p}_2(1 - \hat{p}_2)}{n_2}}} \qquad (11\text{-}12)$$

In all previous tests of hypothesis, we always examined the distribution of the test statistic when H_0 was *true*. For a one-tailed test, we assumed the boundary condition of H_0, which in this case would be $p_1 = p_2$. Because of this, whenever we obtained a value of the test statistic in one of the tails, our decision was (because this value would be very unusual if H_0 were true) to reject H_0. This reasoning was used for test statistics that followed a Z, t, χ^2, or F distribution.

We use the same approach here. If $p_1 = p_2 = p$ (say), we can improve the test statistic in equation 11-12. For this situation, p is the proportion of successes in the combined population. Our best estimate of p is the proportion of successes in the *combined sample*. So define

$$\bar{p} = \frac{x_1 + x_2}{n_1 + n_2}$$

Thus, assuming $p_1 = p_2$, $\hat{p}_1 - \hat{p}_2$ is approximately a normal random variable with

$$\text{mean} = p_1 - p_2 = 0$$

and

$$\text{standard deviation} = \sqrt{\frac{p_1(1 - p_1)}{n_1} + \frac{p_2(1 - p_2)}{n_2}}$$

$$\cong \sqrt{\frac{\bar{p}(1 - \bar{p})}{n_1} + \frac{\bar{p}(1 - \bar{p})}{n_2}}$$

The resulting test statistic for p_1 versus p_2 [large independent samples; $n_1\hat{p}_1$, $n_1(1 - \hat{p}_1)$, $n_2\hat{p}_2$, and $n_2(1 - \hat{p}_2)$ are each > 5] is

$$Z = \frac{\hat{p}_1 - \hat{p}_2}{\sqrt{\dfrac{\bar{p}(1 - \bar{p})}{n_1} + \dfrac{\bar{p}(1 - \bar{p})}{n_2}}} \qquad (11\text{-}13)$$

where

$$\hat{p}_1 = x_1/n_1$$

$$\hat{p}_2 = x_2/n_2$$

$$\bar{p} = \frac{x_1 + x_2}{n_1 + n_2}$$

The test procedure is the standard routine when using the Z distribution. For a two-tailed test,

H_0: $p_1 = p_2$

H_a: $p_1 \neq p_2$

Reject H_0 if $|Z| > Z_{\alpha/2}$

where Z is defined in equation 11-13. For a one-tailed test,

$H_0: p_1 \leq p_2$

$H_a: p_1 > p_2$

Reject H_0 if $Z > Z_\alpha$

or

$H_0: p_1 \geq p_2$

$H_a: p_1 < p_2$

Reject H_0 if $Z < -Z_\alpha$

Example 11.11   Use the data from example 11.8 and determine whether there is any difference between the proportion of Henry cars and that of GA cars that required an engine overhaul before 100,000 miles. Let $\alpha = .01$.

Solution   The five-step procedure is the correct one. The CI derived in example 11-8 would produce the same result as the five-step procedure *if* the test statistic were the one defined in equation 11-12. A better procedure here is to use the Z statistic in equation 11-13 as your test statistic.

Step 1.   Since we are looking for a difference between p_1 and p_2, define

$H_0: p_1 = p_2$

$H_a: p_1 \neq p_2$

Step 2.   The test statistic is

$$Z = \frac{\hat{p}_1 - \hat{p}_2}{\sqrt{\dfrac{\bar{p}(1 - \bar{p})}{n_1} + \dfrac{\bar{p}(1 - \bar{p})}{n_2}}}$$

Step 3.   Using $\alpha = .01$, then $Z_{\alpha/2} = Z_{.005} = 2.575$. The test will be

Reject H_0 if $|Z| > 2.575$

Step 4.   Since $n_1 = 100$, $x_1 = 28$, and $n_2 = 150$, $x_2 = 48$, then

$$\bar{p} = \frac{x_1 + x_2}{n_1 + n_2}$$

$$= \frac{76}{250} = .304$$

Therefore, our estimate of the proportion of cars needing an overhaul in the combined population (if $p_1 = p_2$) is $\bar{p} = .304$ (30.4%). Also, $\hat{p}_1 = 28/100 = .28$, and $\hat{p}_2 = 48/150 = .32$. The value of the test statistic is

$$Z^* = \frac{.28 - .32}{\sqrt{\dfrac{(.304)(.696)}{100} + \dfrac{(.304)(.696)}{150}}}$$

$$= \frac{-.04}{.059} = -.68$$

Because $|Z^*| = .68 < 2.575$, we fail to reject H_0.

Figure 11.4

Z curve showing p-value
(twice the shaded area)
for example 11.11.

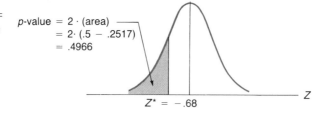

p-value $= 2 \cdot$ (area)
$= 2 \cdot (.5 - .2517)$
$= .4966$

$Z^* = -.68$

Z

Helv12pt.

Step 5. There is *insufficient evidence* to conclude that a difference exists
between the Henry and GA cars as far as engine durability is
concerned.

    The Z curve and calculated p-value for example 11.11 are shown in Figure 11.4.
The p-value is twice the shaded area (this was a two-tailed test) and is .4966, which
is extremely large. Using the classical approach, because $.4966 > \alpha = .01$, we fail to
reject H_0—there is insufficient evidence to indicate a difference in engine durability.
(As a reminder, this reasoning *always* leads to the same conclusion as the five-step
procedure.) Because .4966 exceeds *any* reasonable value of α, we fail to reject H_0
quite strongly for this application.

Example 11.12

In example 11.9, we derived a CI for Slick cigarettes' proportion sold after the campaign (p_1) and their proportion sold before the campaign (p_2). Based on these data,
can you conclude that the proportion sold increased as a result of this campaign? Use
a significance level of $\alpha = .05$.

Solution

Step 1. We wish to know whether the data warrant the conclusion that p_1 is
larger than p_2. Placing this in the alternative hypothesis leads to

$$H_0: p_1 \le p_2$$
$$H_a: p_1 > p_2$$

Steps 2, 3. Using the test statistic in equation 11-13, the resulting one-tailed
test would be

Reject H_0 if $Z > Z_{.05} = 1.645$

Step 4. We have

$$\hat{p}_1 = 90/1200 = .075$$

and

$$\hat{p}_2 = 54/1200 = .045$$

Also,

$$\bar{p} = \frac{(90 + 54)}{(1200 + 1200)} = \frac{144}{2400} = .06$$

Figure 11.5

Z curve showing the cal-
culated p-value for
example 11.12.

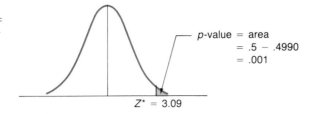

p-value = area
= .5 − .4990
= .001

$Z^* = 3.09$

Consequently,

$$Z^* = \frac{.075 - .045}{\sqrt{\dfrac{(.06)(.94)}{1200} + \dfrac{(.06)(.94)}{1200}}}$$

$$= \frac{.03}{.0097} = 3.09$$

Because $3.09 > 1.645$, we reject H_0.

Step 5. There *is* evidence of an increase in the proportion of Slick cigarettes
sold following the advertising campaign.

The Z curve and calculated p-value for example 11.12 (a one-tailed test) are shown
in Figure 11.5. The p-value is .001. This is definitely a very small p-value and (as
before) leads to rejecting H_0 using a significance level of .05. Based on this p-value
alone, we arrive at the same conclusion—namely, that the market share *did* increase
following the six-month advertising campaign.

Exercises

11.31 A manufacturer of storm windows sampled 250 new (less than five years of age) homes
and found that 142 of them had storm windows. Another sample of size 320 of older (at least
five years of age) homes was taken; 150 of them had storm windows. The manufacturer believes
that the proportion of new homes that have storm windows is larger than the proportion of older
homes that have storm windows. Do the sample statistics support the manufacturer's claim at
the .05 significance level?

11.32 Using the data in exercise 11.31, construct a 90% CI for the difference between the
proportion of new homes with storm windows and the proportion of older homes with storm
windows.

11.33 How does the value of the test statistic given in equation 11-13 change if p_1, the
proportion of successes for population 1, is replaced by the proportion of failures for population
1, and if p_2, the proportion of successes for population 2, is replaced by the proportion of failures
for population 2?

11.34 An educational analyst was interested in examining the proportions of foreign students
in two colleges, Xavier and Safire. A random sample of 68 students was taken from Safire College;
nine of them were foreign students. A similar random sample of 110 students was taken at Xavier
College; 14 of them were foreign students. Can we conclude from the data that the proportions
of foreign students in the two colleges differ? Use a significance level of .05.

11.35 Construct a 95% CI for the difference of the two proportions in exercise 11.34.

11.36 A random sample of 125 manufacturing firms showed that 64% of them spent more
than 75% of their total revenue on salaries and wages. A random sample of 100 wholesale firms

showed that 57% of them spent more than 75% of their total revenue on salaries and wages. Let $\alpha = .05$ and test $H_0: p_1 \leq p_2$ and $H_a: p_1 > p_2$ where p_1 and p_2 are the proportions of manufacturing and wholesale firms, respectively, that spent more than 75% of their total revenue on salaries and wages.

11.37 Construct a 99% CI for $p_1 - p_2$ using the information in exercise 11.36.

11.38 A financial analyst compared the performances of individual stocks with the performance of the industry average (in terms of rate of return). The industry average is the average of all stocks that belong to the same industry and are listed on the New York Stock Exchange. The analyst believed that the proportion of stocks that perform better than the industry average is the same for both the oil and the steel industry. In a random sample of 37 oil-industry stocks, 17 performed better than the industry average. Similarly, in a random sample of 30 steel-industry stocks, 11 did better than the industry average. Using a .05 significance level, test the validity of the financial analyst's belief.

11.39 For exercise 11.38, construct a 99% CI for the difference in the proportion of the stocks in the oil industry and in the steel industry that have performed better than the industry average.

Summary

You will often encounter a situation in which you are concerned with a population proportion rather than a population mean or variance. For example, the parameter of interest might be the proportion (p) of executives earning more than $100,000 annually— rather than the average salary (μ) or the standard deviation (σ) of the salaries. The usual procedure of estimating a population parameter (p, here) using the sample estimate, $\hat{p}$, allows us to derive a point estimate and construct a CI for p. When the sample is small, Table A-8 provides an exact CI for p. For large samples, the CLT can be applied to determine an approximate CI, provided that *both* np and $n(1 - p)$ are > 5.

When the desired accuracy of the point estimate, $\hat{p}$, is specified in advance, you can determine the sample size necessary to obtain this degree of accuracy for a certain confidence level. To derive this sample size, an estimate of p is necessary. You can calculate this value using a previous sample estimate, or, if no information is available, using a conservative procedure and making $\hat{p} = .5$.

When you investigate a statement concerning a population proportion, you can use a statistical test of hypothesis. For small samples, the confidence interval from Table A-8 provides an exact procedure for either a one- or two-tailed test. For tests of hypothesis when a large sample is used, a test statistic having an approximate standard normal distribution defines the rejection region.

To compare two population proportions (p_1 and p_2), two *independent* random samples are obtained, one from each population. Procedures for large independent samples generally provide an accurate CI or test of hypothesis whenever $n_1\hat{p}_1$, $n_1(1 - \hat{p}_1)$, $n_2\hat{p}_2$, and $n_2(1 - \hat{p}_2)$ each exceed five. Using a standard normal approximation, we can construct a CI for $p_1 - p_2$. If the accuracy of this estimate is specified, the sample sizes necessary to obtain this level of accuracy, as well as to minimize the total sample size $n_1 + n_2$, can be obtained.

Two population proportions can be compared by using two large independent samples to evaluate a test statistic having an approximate standard normal distribution. We examined procedures for a one-tailed test (for example, $H_a: p_1 > p_2$) or a two-tailed test ($H_a: p_1 \neq p_2$). The rejection region for these tests are defined using the areas from Table A-4.

Review Exercises

11.40 Ten of the 17 employees who took an in-house speed-reading course can show that the course has substantially increased their efficiency on the job.

a. Are there significantly more employees who have benefited from the course than have not at the .05 significance level? Use Table A-8.

b. Find a 95% CI for the proportion of employees who have benefited from the course. Use Table A-8.

11.41 An advertising agent for Computerized Telephone Systems claims that the proportion of installed telephone systems that have maintenance problems during the first three years is less than 10%. A random sample of 19 computerized telephone systems that were installed within the last three years was taken, and one of the telephone systems was found to have needed repairs.

a. Test the advertising agent's claim at the .05 significance level. Use Table A-8.

b. Find a 90% CI for the true proportion of installed telephone systems that have maintenance problems.

11.42 Fifteen male customers were asked which of two electric shavers, brand 1 or brand 2, they preferred. Nine of them preferred brand 2.

a. At the .05 level of significance, can it be concluded that brand 1 was preferred to brand 2 by male shoppers? Use Table A-8.

b. Find a 95% CI for the proportion of male shoppers who preferred brand 2 over brand 1. Use Table A-8.

c. Assume you have no prior knowledge of p (the proportion of males who preferred brand 2 over brand 1). Estimate the sample size that is required to estimate p, with 90% confidence, assuming a maximum error of .08.

11.43 A small sample ($n = 15$) is drawn from a lot of dry-cell batteries. Each of the batteries was tested; seven were defective. Determine a 95% CI for the proportion of defectives in the entire batch. Use Table A-8.

11.44 William's Packaging is interested in estimating the proportion of its employees who would attend an alcohol-awareness program. In a random sample of 70 employees, 39 said that they would attend the program. Calculate the estimate of the proportion of all employees who would attend the program. Find a 90% CI for this proportion.

11.45 Using the data from exercise 11.44, test the hypothesis that at least 40% of the employees would attend the proposed program. Based on the p-value alone, would you reject this null hypothesis?

11.46 Using the data from exercise 11.44, if the maximum error of the estimate for the proportion is 4%, estimate the sample size needed for a 95% confidence level. Use the value of $\hat{p}$ from exercise 11.44.

11.47 *People's Choice*, a monthly magazine, claimed that more than 40% of its subscribers had an annual income of $50,000 or more. In a random sample of 62 subscribers, 30 had incomes of $50,000 or more. Does this information substantiate the magazine's claim? Use a significance level of .10.

11.48 Calculate and interpret the p-value for exercise 11.47.

11.49 A statistician reported to a car insurance company a CI for the proportion of convertible cars that had been involved in major accidents during the past year. The 95% CI for p was reported to be the interval from .10 to .36.

a. What is the statistician's estimate of p?

b. What is the maximum error of estimate (E) of the proportion for this CI?

c. Approximately what sample size did the statistician use?

11.50 A CI is reported for the proportion of male YLU students who belong to the $\alpha\sigma\mu$ fraternity. The CI is based on a sample of 1000 students and is given to be .22 to .44. What level of confidence was used in obtaining this interval?

11.51 Must a CI for a proportion contain the true proportion of the population? Explain what the "level of confidence" means for a CI.

11.52 A market-research firm believed that the proportion of households with more than four family members in county 1 was greater than the proportion of households with more than four family members in county 2. The firm gathered random samples of 180 and 155 from counties 1 and 2, respectively. The number of households with more than four members were 74 from county 1 and 61 from county 2. From these data, can we conclude that the proportion of households with more than four members is higher in county 1 than in county 2? Use a significance level of .01.

11.53 Calculate the p-value for exercise 11.52. Using the p-value, would you reject the null hypothesis at the .05 level?

11.54 Construct a 95% confidence interval for the difference of the two proportions in exercise 11.52.

11.55 A market-research firm is interested in testing the hypothesis that the proportion of students who own a car is the same for the local state university campus and a local private college. They interviewed 240 students from the state university and 270 from the private college. The number of students who did not own a car was 78 at the state university and 82 at the private college. Using a .02 significance level, test the hypothesis.

11.56 For exercise 11.55, construct a 95% CI for the difference of the true proportions of students who own a car at the two campuses.

11.57 For exercise 11.55, calculate the p-value and interpret it.

Case Study

Braun Systems

The competition in the military–industrial complex in high-technology products for the armed services is severe. Braun Systems often was not competitive, in terms of the price of the contract, on government contracts because the cost of their meticulous quality-control program made their price comparatively high.

Braun's newest project was developing a tracking system for the Coast Guard. After evaluating 19 proposals, the Coast Guard provided funds to two firms, one of which was Braun, to develop a working prototype. The two prototypes would be tested by the Coast Guard on operational vessels at sea.

Braun had eight months to develop a system. Their prototype's design required that they test new microprocessors. Braun had developed two methods of handling the technical problems associated with the complex tracking system. Both generated microprocessors that met the performance specifications of the Coast Guard, but their costs were significantly different. Braun's management knew that the Coast Guard would examine the cost over the useful life of the product (about four years). If the lower-cost microprocessors could be used in the tracking system, Braun would have a much better chance of getting the contract, provided the lower-cost system was as reliable as the one with the higher-cost microprocessor.

Braun engineers performed destructive tests on a randomly selected sample of 100 of each microprocessor to see whether there was a significant difference in the performance level, over time, between the two types of microprocessors. Each unit was randomly assigned to the test stands. The 30-day test subjected the parts to stress equivalent to four years of normal wear. The quality-control criterion was a failure rate that did not exceed 1%. A statistical evaluation would compare the failure rates for the two products.

The results of the testing process were as follows. Microprocessor type 1: passed = 98, failed = 2; Microprocessor type 2: passed = 97, failed = 3. Type 2 was the microprocessor that had the lower production cost.

The conclusions of the statistical analysis would determine the type of microprocessor that the company would use in its product. Braun's testing procedures required that a 99% level of confidence be used for all statistical tests.

Case Study Questions

1. Do each of the microprocessors pass the 1% failure rate of the quality-control criterion?
2. Is there a significant difference in the failure rates between type 1 and type 2 microprocessors?
3. Which of the microprocessors should Braun use? Why?
4. Would the more commonly used 95% level of confidence have resulted in a different decision? Why or why not?

12

Analysis of Variance

A Look Back/Introduction

In Chapter 10, we considered a question of the type, "Do men have the same height as women?" By this we mean, is the *average* height of males equal to the average height of females? We were interested in the means of two populations and performed a test of hypothesis, using, for example, H_0: $\mu_M = \mu_F$ and H_a: $\mu_M \neq \mu_F$. This works well when dealing with two populations, but how can we compare the means of *more than two* populations? For example, we might wish to examine the (average) sales of five different training programs to see whether they are the same. Our hypotheses become

H_0: $\mu_1 = \mu_2 = \mu_3 = \mu_4 = \mu_5$

H_a: not all μ's are equal

We test such a hypothesis by first collecting five samples, one from each of the training programs (populations). We will see that to compare these five means one pair at a time is *not* the correct approach. This results in ten different pairwise tests, and what was intended to be a testing procedure with, say, 95% confidence, results in a much lower confidence level. In other words, the overall significance level, α, is *larger* than the predetermined value. The correct procedure for this situation is to examine the *variation* of the sales values, both (1) within each of the samples (examining the variability of each sample alone) and (2) among the five samples (for example, are the values in sample 1 larger or smaller, on the average, than the values in the other samples?).

In Chapter 10, we saw that, when trying to decide if $\overline{X}_1$ is "significantly different" from $\overline{X}_2$, a key part of the answer rested on the values of s_1 and s_2, the variation *within* the two samples. Both s_1 and s_2 affect the width of the CI for $\mu_1 - \mu_2$. Consequently, we infer something about the *means* of several populations by examining the *variation* of the resulting samples. Hence the term *analysis of variance*—our next topic.

12.1

Comparing Two Means: Another Look

We will begin with an example. The manager of a convenience store wants to know whether the sales of two particular brands of cigarettes (brand 1 and brand 2) are the same. Based on past experience, he believes that weekly sales follow a *normal* distribution. By using past sales records, he obtains the number of cartons sold per week for brand 1 using a randomly selected five-week period. The sales for brand 2 are randomly obtained for a *different* five-week period, with the following results (in numbers of cartons):

Brand 1	Brand 2
43	30
48	26
38	37
41	31
51	34

Let μ_1 be the average weekly sales (if observed indefinitely) for brand 1 and μ_2 be the average for brand 2. We wish to determine whether the data allow us to conclude that $\mu_1 \neq \mu_2$, using $\alpha = .10$.

We examined the same type of question in Chapter 10; we are dealing with two small independent samples. In Chapter 10, we advised against assuming that σ_1 was equal to σ_2. As a result, you generally used a t test that did *not* pool the sample variances. However, when examining more than two normal populations (the main concern of this chapter), the testing procedure for detecting a difference in the population means requires that the populations have the *same* distribution under H_0: the means are equal. Consequently, it will be necessary to assume that the *population variances are equal*. The analysis of variance procedure is *not* extremely sensitive to departures from this assumption, especially if equal-sized samples are obtained from each population. A procedure for verifying this assumption (similar to the F test used to compare two variances in Chapter 10) will be discussed in this chapter.

As a result, we will assume the variation of the brand 1 sales is the same as for brand 2 sales; that is, $\sigma_1 = \sigma_2$. Using the approach discussed in Chapter 10, we first find

$$s_p^2 = \text{pooled variance} = \frac{(n_1 - 1)s_1^2 + (n_2 - 1)s_2^2}{n_1 + n_2 - 2}$$

where n_1, n_2 = sample size for brand 1, brand 2 and s_1^2, s_2^2 = sample variance for brand 1, brand 2. Using the sample data,

Brand 1	Brand 2
$n_1 = 5$	$n_2 = 5$
$\bar{x}_1 = 44.2$	$\bar{x}_2 = 31.6$
$s_1 = 5.263$	$s_2 = 4.159$

Consequently,

$$s_p^2 = \frac{(4)(5.263)^2 + (4)(4.159)^2}{8}$$

$$= \frac{180.0}{8}$$

$$= 22.5$$

and so

$$s_p = \sqrt{22.5} = 4.74$$

The appropriate hypotheses are H_0: $\mu_1 = \mu_2$ and H_a: $\mu_1 \neq \mu_2$. The resulting test statistic is

$$t = \frac{\overline{X}_1 - \overline{X}_2}{s_p \sqrt{\dfrac{1}{n_1} + \dfrac{1}{n_2}}}$$

$$= \frac{44.2 - 31.6}{4.74 \sqrt{\dfrac{1}{5} + \dfrac{1}{5}}} = \frac{12.6}{2.998}$$

$$= 4.20$$

That is, $t^* = 4.20$.

We are dealing with a two-tailed test using a t statistic with $n_1 + n_2 - 2 = 8\ df$, so the test is to

$$\text{Reject } H_0 \text{ if } | t^* | > t_{\alpha/2, df} = t_{.05, 8} = 1.86$$

Comparing $t^* = 4.20$ to 1.86, we reject H_0 and conclude that the mean sales for the two brands are not the same. Looking at the sample data, we can say that $\bar{x}_1 = 44.2$ *is* significantly different from $\bar{x}_2 = 31.6$

The Analysis of Variance Approach

We need to introduce two new terms. The previous example examined the effect of one **factor** (brand), consisting of two **levels** (brand 1 and brand 2). If you want to extend this to four brands (say, brands 1, 2, 3, and 4), then you still have *one* factor but now have four levels.

The purpose of **analysis of variance (ANOVA)** is to determine if this factor has *a significant effect* on the variable being measured (sales, in our example). If, say, the brand factor *is* significant, then the mean sales within each of the different brands will not be equal. Consequently, testing for equal means among the various brands is the same as attempting to answer the question, "Is there a significant effect on sales due to this factor?"

This section examines the effect of a single factor on the variable being measured, **one-factor ANOVA**. Extensions of this technique include ANOVA procedures that determine the effect of two or more factors operating simultaneously. These factors may be *qualitative* (such as brand in the previous illustration) or *quantitative* (such as several levels of advertising expenditure).

All ten values in the cigarette-sales example are different, and we observe a variation in these values. We will look at two *sources of variation:* (1) variation *within* the samples (levels), and (2) variation *between* the samples.

Within-Sample Variation When you obtain a sample, you (usually) obtain different values for each observation. The five sample values for brand 1 vary about the mean $\bar{x}_1 = 44.2$ cartons, as measured by $s_1 = 5.26$ cartons. Likewise, the five values in the second sample also exhibit some variation ($s_2 = 4.16$) about $\bar{x}_2 = 31.6$ cartons. This is the **within-sample variation.** It is used when estimating the common population variance, say σ^2. This procedure provides an accurate estimate of σ^2, whether or not the sample means are equal.

Between-Sample Variation When you compare the two samples, you observe that the values for brand 1 are *larger* on the average than are those for brand 2. This is observed in the sample means, where $\bar{x}_1 = 44.2$ appears to be considerably larger than $\bar{x}_2 = 31.6$. So there is a variation in the ten values due to the *brand;* that is, due to the factor. This is **between-sample variation.** In general, if this variation is large, we expect considerable variation among the sample means. The between-sample variation is also used in another estimate of the common variance σ^2, *provided the population means are equal.* In other words, if the means are equal, the between-sample and within-sample estimates of σ^2 should be nearly the same. As we will see later in this section, we can derive a test of hypothesis procedure for determining whether the means are equal by comparing these two estimates.

Measuring Variation When using the ANOVA approach, we measure these two sources of variation by calculating various **sums of squares, SS.** We determine

SS(factor) measures: between-sample variation [also called SS(between)]

SS(error) measures: within-sample variation [also called SS(within)]

$$SS(\text{total}) = SS(\text{between}) + SS(\text{within})$$
$$= SS(\text{factor}) + SS(\text{error})$$

In addition, each of the first two sums of squares will have corresponding degrees of freedom, *df*, which are determined from the number of terms that make up this particular SS. The *df* are given by

$$df \text{ for factor} = (\text{number of levels}) - 1$$
$$= (\text{number of brands}) - 1$$
$$= 2 - 1 = 1$$
$$df \text{ for error} = (n_1 - 1) + (n_2 - 1)$$
$$= n_1 + n_2 - 2$$
$$= 5 + 5 - 2 = 8$$

We will show how to determine these sums of squares and how we combine them, and their *df*, into another test statistic for testing H_0: $\mu_1 = \mu_2$ against H_a: $\mu_1 \neq \mu_2$. The beauty of this approach is that it extends nicely to the situation in which you wish to compare more than two means using a *single* test.

Determining SS(factor) SS(factor) is the sum of squares that determines whether the values in one sample are larger or smaller (on the average) than the values in the second sample.

$$SS(\text{factor}) = n_1(\bar{x}_1 - \bar{x})^2 + n_2(\bar{x}_2 - \bar{x})^2 \qquad (12\text{-}1)$$

where $\bar{x}_1$, $\bar{x}_2$ are the two sample means and

$$\bar{x} = \frac{\Sigma(\text{all data values})}{n} = \frac{n_1\bar{x}_1 + n_2\bar{x}_2}{n_1 + n_2}$$

and $n = n_1 + n_2 = $ total sample size.

A method of determining this sum of squares that is much easier using a calculator is

$$\text{SS(factor)} = \left[\frac{T_1^2}{n_1} + \frac{T_2^2}{n_2}\right] - \frac{T^2}{n} \tag{12-2}$$

where $T_1 = $ total of the sample 1 observations, $T_2 = $ total of the sample 2 observations, $T = $ grand total $= T_1 + T_2$.

Determining SS(total) SS(total) is a measure of the variation in all $n = n_1 + n_2$ data values. You obtain its value as though you were finding the *variance* of these n values, except that you do not divide by $n - 1$. So,

$$\text{SS(total)} = \Sigma(x - \bar{x})^2 \tag{12-3}$$

or (after some algebra similar to that used in Chapter 3),

$$\begin{aligned} \text{SS(total)} &= \Sigma x^2 - \frac{(\Sigma x)^2}{n} \\ &= \Sigma x^2 - \frac{T^2}{n} \end{aligned} \tag{12-4}$$

Determining SS(error) SS(error) is the measure of the variation *within* each of the samples. Its value simply is the *numerator of the pooled variance, s_p^2*, obtained using the previous t test. Thus,

$$\text{SS(error)} = \underset{\text{first sample}}{\Sigma(x - \bar{x}_1)^2} + \underset{\text{second sample}}{\Sigma(x - \bar{x}_2)^2} \tag{12-5}$$

and therefore,

$$\text{SS(error)} = \Sigma x^2 - \left[\frac{T_1^2}{n_1} + \frac{T_2^2}{n_2}\right] \tag{12-6}$$

Given that

$$\text{SS(total)} = \text{SS(factor)} + \text{SS(error)}$$

a much easier way to find this value is

$$\text{SS(error)} = \text{SS(total)} - \text{SS(factor)} \tag{12-7}$$

Let us return to the cigarette sales example. To find the SS(factor) here, we first determine

$$T_1 = 43 + 48 + 38 + 41 + 51$$
$$= 221$$
$$T_2 = 30 + 26 + 37 + 31 + 34$$
$$= 158$$
$$T = T_1 + T_2 = 221 + 158 = 379$$

So, using equation 12-2,

$$\text{SS(factor)} = \frac{221^2}{5} + \frac{158^2}{5} - \frac{379^2}{10}$$
$$= 14{,}761 - 14{,}364.1$$
$$= 396.9$$

To find SS(total), the only new term we need to evaluate is

$$\Sigma x^2 = \text{sum of each data value squared}$$
$$= 43^2 + 48^2 + \ldots + 31^2 + 34^2$$
$$= 14{,}941$$

So, using equation 12-4 [the value 14,364.1 was obtained in SS(factor)],

$$\text{SS(total)} = \Sigma x^2 - \frac{T^2}{n}$$
$$= 14{,}941 - 14{,}364.1$$
$$= 576.9$$

Finally, we find SS(error) by subtraction:

$$\text{SS(error)} = \text{SS(total)} - \text{SS(factor)}$$
$$= 576.9 - 396.9$$
$$= 180.0$$

ANOVA Test for $H_0: \mu_1 = \mu_2$ Versus $H_a: \mu_1 \neq \mu_2$ To begin with, the procedure we are about to define is valid for a *two-tailed test only*. In other words, the alternative hypothesis must be that the two means differ, not that one is larger than the other (a one-tailed test). (When examining more than two means the alternative hypothesis will be that *at least* two of the means are unequal and H_0 will be that all the means are equal.) The next step, when using the ANOVA procedure, is to determine something resembling an "average" sum of squares, referred to as a **mean square.** We compute a mean square for only SS(factor) and SS(error), not for SS(total).

$$\text{MS(factor)} = \text{SS(factor)}/df \text{ for factor}$$
$$= \text{SS(factor)}/1$$

(12-8)

Note that the *df* for this term always is (number of levels) $-$ 1. In this section, we are dealing with two levels (populations), and so this *df* is *always* 1.

$$\text{MS(error)} = \text{SS(error)}/df \text{ for error}$$
$$= \text{SS(error)}/(n_1 + n_2 - 2)$$

(12-9)

We denote the common variance of the two normal populations as σ^2. So, $\sigma^2 = \sigma_1^2 = \sigma_2^2$. If the null hypothesis—H_0: the means are equal—is true, then, because the populations have identical means and variances, this implies that under H_0 we are dealing with a *single population*. The ANOVA procedure is based on a comparison between two separate estimates of the variance, σ^2. The first estimate is derived using the variation among the sample means (only two in the previous example). The other estimate is determined using the variation *within* each of the samples.

The ANOVA procedure is based on a comparison of these two estimates of σ^2 because they should be approximately equal *provided H_0 is true*. We have derived these two estimates:

MS(factor) = estimate of σ^2 based on the variation among the sample means

MS(error) = estimate of σ^2 based on the variation within each of the samples.

Our new test statistic for testing H_0: $\mu_1 = \mu_2$ versus H_a: $\mu_1 \neq \mu_2$ is the *ratio* of these two estimates:

$$F = \frac{\left(\begin{array}{l}\text{estimated population variance based on the variation} \\ \text{among the sample means}\end{array}\right)}{\left(\begin{array}{l}\text{estimated population variance based on the variation} \\ \text{within each of the samples}\end{array}\right)}$$

(12-10)

$$= \frac{\text{MS(factor)}}{\text{MS(error)}}$$

This test statistic follows an F distribution, which was first introduced in Chapter 10 as a ratio of two variance estimates. The degrees of freedom (df) for the F statistic in equation 12-10 are the df for factor and the df for error; that is, the df for F are 1 and $(n_1 + n_2 - 2)$. Because the F statistic is based on a comparison of two variance estimates, this technique is called analysis of variance.

This is our second encounter with the F distribution. In Chapter 10, we used this distribution to compare two population variances (σ_1^2 and σ_2^2). The shape of this distribution is illustrated in Figure 12.1 and is tabulated in Table A-7. Remember that the shape of the F curve is affected by both the df for the numerator (= 1 here) and the df for the denominator (= $n_1 + n_2 - 2$ here).

Figure 12.1

Shape of the F distribution shown by F curve with 1 and $n_1 + n_2 - 2$ df.

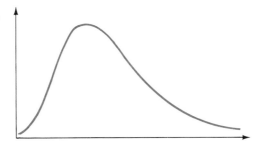

Defining the Rejection Region What happens to the F statistic when H_a is true; that is, when $\mu_1 \neq \mu_2$? In this case, we would expect $\overline{X}_1$ and $\overline{X}_2$ to be "far apart." As a result, the estimate of the variance σ^2 using the *between-sample* variation [measured by MS(factor)] will be *larger* than the estimate of σ^2 based on the *within-sample* variation [measured by MS(error)]. This implies that we should reject H_0 (in favor of H_a) whenever F (the ratio of these two estimates) is large—in which case it is in the right tail. Consequently, the test will be to

Reject H_0 if $F^* > F_{\alpha, v_1, v_2}$

where $v_1 = df$ for numerator $= 1$, $v_2 = df$ for denominator $= n_1 + n_2 - 2$, and F_{α, v_1, v_2} is obtained from Table A-7 with a right-tail area $= \alpha$.

Example 12.1

Using the data from the cigarette sales example and the previously calculated sums of squares, test H_0: $\mu_1 = \mu_2$ versus H_a: $\mu_1 \neq \mu_2$, where $\mu_1 =$ average weekly number of cartons sold for brand 1, if observed indefinitely, and $\mu_2 =$ average for brand 2. Use a significance level of $\alpha = .10$.

Solution

Step 1. The hypotheses are as defined—H_0: $\mu_1 = \mu_2$ and H_a: $\mu_1 \neq \mu_2$.

Step 2. The test statistic is

$$F = \frac{\text{MS(factor)}}{\text{MS(error)}}$$

Step 3. The rejection region (using Table A-7a) is

Reject H_0 if $F > F_{.10, 1, 8} = 3.46$

Step 4. From the previous calculations, SS(factor) $= 396.9$ and SS(error) $= 180$. So,

$$\text{MS(factor)} = \text{SS(factor)}/1$$
$$= 396.9$$

and

$$\text{MS(error)} = \text{SS(error)}/(n_1 + n_2 - 2)$$
$$= 180.0/8$$
$$= 22.5$$

The resulting value of the test statistic is

$$F^* = \frac{396.9}{22.5} = 17.64$$

Because $17.64 > 3.46$, we reject H_0.

Step 5. These data indicate that the mean sales for brand 1 and brand 2 are *not* the same. ●

Comment

Compare our first treatment of the cigarette sales problem with example 12.1 Both solutions led to the same conclusion, namely, that the two average sales are not the same. In fact, both solutions *always* lead to the same conclusion when comparing *two* means. Furthermore, the p-values for both solutions *are the same,* as illustrated in Figure 12.2. The values were obtained using a computer program (available in

Figure 12.2

p-values for the solution to the cigarette sales example. **A:** Solution using pooled variance t test. **B:** Solution using ANOVA (see example 12.1).

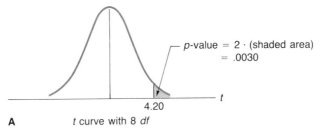

A   t curve with 8 df

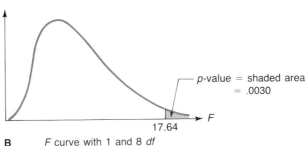

B   F curve with 1 and 8 df

many statistical packages) that provides an exact p-value for a t or F statistic, given the computed value and corresponding degrees of freedom.

The computed value of the F statistic is equal to (the computed value of the t statistic)^2 because $17.64 = (4.20)^2$. This is true whenever you have an F statistic or table value with 1 df in the numerator. So,

$$F_{\alpha,1,v} = t^2_{\alpha/2,v}$$

for any $v \geq 1$. In example 12.1,

$$F_{.10,1,8} = 3.46 = (1.86)^2 = t^2_{.05,8}$$

We see that the two tests are *identical;* they produce the same conclusion and p-value. Furthermore, the computed value and the table value for the F statistic are the square of the corresponding values using the t statistic. This comparison applies *only* when the F statistic has 1 df in the numerator—that is, when there are 2 factor levels (as in this illustration). As mentioned previously, the advantage of the ANOVA approach is that it extends very easily to the situation of comparing means for more than two populations (covered in the next section).

The ANOVA Table   Rather than carrying out the five-step procedure using the F statistic, an easier method is to use an **ANOVA table** of the various sums of squares. The format of this table is as follows:*

Source	df	SS	MS	F
Factor	1	SS(factor)	MS(factor)	MS(factor)/MS(error)
Error	$n-2$	SS(error)	MS(error)	
Total	$n-1$	SS(total)		

*The headings under the "Source" column will vary, depending on the computer package. SS(factor) often is labeled "between groups" (SAS) or "among groups"; SS(error) often is labeled "within groups" (SAS) or "residual" (SPSSX) or "error" (MINITAB).

To fill in this table, you compute the necessary sums of squares along with the mean squares and insert them. Notice that $n = n_1 + n_2 =$ total sample size and that column 3 (MS) = column 2 (SS) divided by column 1 (df).

The ANOVA table for example 12.1 follows.

Source	df	SS	MS	F
Factor	1	396.9	396.9	17.64
Error	8	180.0	22.5	
Total	9	576.9		

Summary of the ANOVA Approach for One-Factor Tests In example 12.1, we concluded that a difference existed between the two *means* because the variation *between* the two samples [measured by MS(factor)] was much greater than the variation *within* the samples [measured by MS(error)]. Thus, the ratio of these values (F^*) was very large and fell in the rejection region. Consequently, we rejected H_0: $\mu_1 = \mu_2$. What this means in the language of ANOVA is that there *is* a significant effect on sales due to the brand factor.

To carry out the F test, we first randomly obtain observations, called **replicates,** from each population. Example 12.1 used five replicates (monthly sales) from each of the two cigarette populations. It is *not necessary* to obtain the same number of replicates from each population.

Figure 12.3 is a dot-array diagram of the replicates (data) in example 12.1, where the symbol A represents a value from brand 1 and B represents brand 2. You do not need to be an expert statistician to observe that a clear difference exists between the sales of the two brands of cigarettes. The variation within the A's alone and the B's alone is your within-sample variation. Because the distances from the A values to the B values are much larger than the distances among the A values alone, the between-sample variation is quite large, as we have already observed.

Suppose instead that your dot-array diagram looks like Figure 12.4. Now the two sources of variation appear to be nearly the same and there is no obvious difference between the two brands. The resulting F statistic here would not lie within the rejection region and we would not be able to demonstrate, using the ANOVA approach, a difference between the two mean sales.

Figure 12.3

Dot-array diagram of replicates in example 12.1

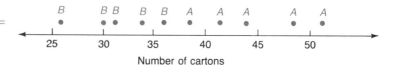

Figure 12.4

Dot-array diagram where between-sample and within-sample variations are nearly the same. The F statistic would not lie in the rejection region.

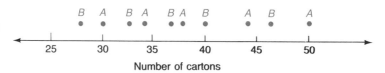

12.2

One-Factor ANOVA Comparing More Than Two Means

In the previous section, we examined a single *factor* with two *levels*. Our concern was whether there was any difference between the two levels of this factor. This amounted to performing a test of hypothesis on the means of two populations. Because we were dealing with the effect of a single factor, this was a one-factor (or one-way) ANOVA.

In general, one-factor ANOVA techniques can be used to study the effect of any single factor on sales, performance, or whatever. This factor can consist of any number of levels—say, k levels. To determine if the levels of this factor affect our measured observations, we examine the hypotheses

H_0: $\mu_1 = \mu_2 = \ldots = \mu_k$

H_a: not all μ's are equal

Suppose we are interested in the average sales for not two but five brands of cigarettes. Is there any difference in these five mean sales? To answer this question, we test

H_0: $\mu_1 = \mu_2 = \mu_3 = \mu_4 = \mu_5$

H_a: not all μ's are equal

We have a single factor (brand) consisting of five levels (brand 1, brand 2, . . . , brand 5). One possibility is to examine these samples one pair at a time using the t statistic discussed in the previous section. This appears to be a safe way to proceed here, although there are $_5C_2 = 10$ such pairs of tests to perform this way. The main problem with this approach when performing many tests of this nature is determining the probability of making an incorrect decision. In particular, what is α = probability of rejecting H_0: all μ's are equal, when in fact it is true? You set α in advance but, after performing, say, ten of these pairwise tests ($\mu_1 = \mu_2$, $\mu_1 = \mu_3$, . . .), what is your *overall* probability of concluding that at least one pair of means are not equal when they actually are? This is a difficult question. The overall probability is *not* the significance level, α, with which you started for just one pair. So we need an approach that will test for the equality of these five means using a single test. This is what the ANOVA approach does.

Assumptions Behind the ANOVA Analysis

When using the ANOVA procedure, there are three key assumptions that must be satisfied. They are basically the same assumptions that were necessary when testing two means using small independent samples and the pooled variance approach. These assumptions are:

1. The replicates are obtained *independently* and *randomly* from each of the populations. The value of one observation has no effect on any other replicates within the same sample or within the other samples.
2. The observations (replicates) from each population follow (approximately) a *normal* distribution.
3. The normal populations all have a *common variance*, σ^2. We expect the values in each sample to vary about the same amount. The ANOVA procedure will be much less sensitive to this assumption when we obtain samples of equal size from each population.

Deriving the Sum of Squares

When examining, say, k populations, the data will be configured somewhat like this:

	Level 1	**Level 2**	. . .	**Level k**
	.	.		.
	.	.		.
	.	.		.
	n_1 replicates	n_2 replicates		n_k replicates
	.	.		.
	.	.		.
Totals	T_1	T_2		T_k

This resembles the data from example 12.1, where $k = 2$ and $n_1 = n_2 = 5$ replicates. To derive the sum of squares for this situation, we will extend the results in equations 12-2, 12-4, and 12-6 to

$$SS(factor) = \left[\frac{T_1^2}{n_1} + \frac{T_2^2}{n_2} + \ldots + \frac{T_k^2}{n_k}\right] - \frac{T^2}{n} \tag{12-11}$$

$$SS(total) = \Sigma x^2 - \frac{T^2}{n} \tag{12-12}$$

$$SS(error) = \Sigma x^2 - \left[\frac{T_1^2}{n_1} + \frac{T_2^2}{n_2} + \ldots + \frac{T_k^2}{n_k}\right] \tag{12-13}$$

$$= SS(total) - SS(factor) \tag{12-14}$$

Here, n = the total number of observations = $n_1 + n_2 + \ldots + n_k$, and $T = \Sigma x$ = the sum of all n observations = $T_1 + T_2 \ldots + T_k$. Also, to find Σx^2, you square each of the n observations and sum the results.

The ANOVA Table

The good news is that the format of the ANOVA table is the same regardless of the number of populations (levels), k. The only change from the two-population case is that

df for factor = $k - 1$

df for error = $n - k$

As before, the total df are $n - 1$. The resulting ANOVA table follows.

Source	df	SS	MS	F
Factor	$k - 1$	SS(factor)	MS(factor)	MS(factor)/MS(error)
Error	$n - k$	SS(error)	MS(error)	
Total	$n - 1$	SS(total)		

Note that

$$MS(factor) = SS(factor)/df \text{ for factor}$$
$$= \frac{SS(factor)}{k - 1} \qquad (12\text{-}15)$$

$$MS(error) = SS(error)/df \text{ for error}$$
$$= \frac{SS(error)}{n - k} \qquad (12\text{-}16)$$

The test statistic for testing H_0: $\mu_1 = \mu_2 = \ldots = \mu_k$ versus H_a: not all μ's are equal is

$$F = \frac{MS(factor)}{MS(error)}$$

which has an F distribution with $k - 1$ and $n - k$ df.

As in the two-sample case, the procedure is to reject H_0 when the variation among the sample means [measured by MS(factor)] is *large* compared to the variation within the samples [measured by MS(error)]. Consequently, the test will be to reject H_0 whenever F lies in the *right-tailed* rejection region, defined by the significance level, α.

Example 12.2

A convenience-store manager has asked you to examine the sales for the four brands of ice cream that she carries. Space in her refrigerated storage area is limited, so she would like to eliminate one or more of the brands that sells less well. She wants to know whether there is any difference among the average sales of these four brands. Past sales records showed data for the sales from six randomly selected weeks for *each* brand (gallons sold per week). Overall, the sales from 24 randomly selected weeks were used. Past experience has indicated that sales follow a normal distribution.

	Brand 1	Brand 2	Brand 3	Brand 4
	41	32	35	33
	35	37	30	27
	48	46	24	36
	40	53	26	35
	45	41	28	27
	52	43	31	25
Total (T)	261	252	174	183
Average ($\overline{X}$)	43.5	42.0	29.0	30.5
Variance (s^2)	37.1	52.8	15.2	22.3

The four sample averages are $\bar{x}_1 = 43.5$, $\bar{x}_2 = 42.0$, $\bar{x}_3 = 29.0$, $\bar{x}_4 = 30.5$. Brands 1 and 2 appear to be outselling brands 3 and 4. In other words, it appears that there is a significant *between-group variation*. But do these sample means provide sufficient evidence to reject H_0: $\mu_1 = \mu_2 = \mu_3 = \mu_4$ where each μ_i represents the average of *all* weekly sales of brand i? Use the ANOVA procedure to answer this question with $\alpha = .05$.

Solution The assumptions behind this analysis are that (1) the samples were obtained randomly and independently from each of the four populations and (2) the number of gallons of each brand that are sold each week follow a *normal* distribution, with a *common variance*, say, σ^2.

$$\text{SS(factor)} = \left[\frac{T_1^2}{n_1} + \frac{T_2^2}{n_2} + \frac{T_3^2}{n_3} + \frac{T_4^2}{n_4}\right] - \frac{T^2}{n}$$

So $n = n_1 + n_2 + n_3 + n_4 = 24$, and

$$
\begin{aligned}
T = \Sigma x &= T_1 + T_2 + T_3 + T_4 \\
&= 261 + 252 + 174 + 183 \\
&= 870
\end{aligned}
$$

Therefore,

$$
\begin{aligned}
\text{SS(factor)} &= \frac{261^2}{6} + \frac{252^2}{6} + \frac{174^2}{6} + \frac{183^2}{6} - \frac{870^2}{24} \\
&= 32{,}565 - 31{,}537.5 \\
&= 1027.5
\end{aligned}
$$

$$
\begin{aligned}
\text{SS(total)} &= \Sigma x^2 - \frac{T^2}{n} \\
&= [41^2 + 35^2 + \ldots + 27^2 + 25^2] - \frac{870^2}{24} \\
&= 33{,}202 - 31{,}537.5 \\
&= 1664.5
\end{aligned}
$$

$$
\begin{aligned}
\text{SS(error)} &= \text{SS(total)} - \text{SS(factor)} \\
&= 1664.5 - 1027.5 \\
&= 637
\end{aligned}
$$

This is the ANOVA table for this analysis.

Source	df	SS	MS	F
Factor	$k - 1 = 3$	1027.5	1027.5/3 = 342.5	342.5/31.85 = 10.75
Error	$n - k = 20$	637	637/20 = 31.85	
Total	23	1664.5		

The computed F value using the ANOVA table is $F^* = 10.75$. Since $\alpha = .05$, we use Table A-7 to find that $F_{.05, 3, 20} = 3.10$. Comparing these two values, $F^* = 10.75 > 3.10$, so we reject H_0.

We conclude that the average sales for the four brands are not the same. This confirms our earlier suspicion based on the variation among the four sample means. Our results indicate that the brand factor *does* have a significant effect on sales. ●

The Assumptions Behind ANOVA and a Test for Equal Variances

Use of *independent random samples* is of extreme importance when using the ANOVA procedure. The F test used for comparing the population means in the ANOVA table is very sensitive to departures from this assumption, so the safest way to guard against incorrect conclusions is to use random sampling techniques. In many situations, however, this may be difficult or impossible, such as when using the same set of people for before–after experiments. One solution to this problem is to modify your study design, such as by using a randomized block design, discussed in the next section.

Lack of **normality** within the populations is not a critical matter provided the departure is not too extreme. The F test used to test the means is not severely affected by populations that are somewhat nonnormal in nature. One way of making the ANOVA procedure even less sensitive to this assumption is to use *large samples*.

If the *variances* of the population *are not equal*, the F test used in the ANOVA procedure for testing the means is only slightly affected, provided the *sample sizes are equal* (or nearly so). However, for this case, there is a very simple test of hypothesis for verifying this assumption.

In Chapter 10, an F test was defined for determining whether two normal population variances (or standard deviations) are equal. A similar test is used when you are comparing more than two normal population variances, provided the sample sizes are equal. * Here the hypotheses are

H_0: $\sigma_1^2 = \sigma_2^2 = \ldots = \sigma_k^2$

H_a: at least two variances are unequal (the k variances are not the same)

We warned you in Chapter 10 about the dangers of using the same data to test both the variances *and* the means. This argument applies to tests of more than two populations. A better procedure is to use a different data set for testing H_0: the variances are equal. Another possibility is to split a single data set into two segments— one for testing the variances and the other for testing the means. This requires a much larger data set than is necessary if you use the same data for both tests.

The test for equal variances is the **Hartley test;** the test statistic is defined to be

$$H = \frac{\text{maximum } s^2}{\text{minimum } s^2} \qquad (12\text{-}17)$$

which is simply the ratio of the largest sample variance divided by the smallest of these k variances.

If H_0 is false, then the test statistic will be "large," so the testing procedure is to reject H_0 if the computed value of H lies in the right tail. The rejection region for a 5% level of significance can be obtained from Table A-14 on page 843. This region depends on the number (k) of populations or levels and the number of observations in *each* sample.

Suppose we use the data from example 12.2 only for testing the hypotheses

H_0: $\sigma_1^2 = \sigma_2^2 = \sigma_3^2 = \sigma_4^2$

H_a: at least two variances are unequal

Using $\alpha = .05$ and Table A-14, because $k = 4$ and there are six observations in each sample, the test is to

Reject H_0 if $H > 13.7$

---

*When the sample sizes are unequal, a computationally more difficult test for equal variances can be performed, derived by M.S. Bartlett. For details, see J. Neter and W. Wasserman, *Applied Linear Statistical Models.* (Homewood, IL: Richard D. Irwin, 1974), pp. 509–512.

Using the data summary in example 12.2, the minimum s^2 is 15.2 and the maximum s^2 is 52.8. Consequently,

$$H = \frac{52.8}{15.2} = 3.47$$

which is less than 13.7, and so the conclusion is that we have no reason to suspect unequal variances for this situation.

If other data are available for testing the means, the assumption of equal variances behind the ANOVA procedure appears to be safe.

Confidence Intervals in One-Factor ANOVA

When we deal with normal populations, as we are here, we can supply

1. A point estimate of each mean, μ_i; for example, an estimate of μ_2 is $\overline{X}_2$.
2. A point estimate of each mean difference, $\mu_i - \mu_j$; for example, an estimate of $\mu_1 - \mu_3$ is $\overline{X}_1 - \overline{X}_3$.

When using the ANOVA procedure, the populations have a common variance, say σ^2. To estimate this variance, we use an estimate of σ^2 that does not depend on whether the population means are equal. This is the *within*-sample variation, measured by MS(error). The point estimate of σ^2 is

s_p^2 = pooled variance

   = MS(error)

where MS(error) is defined in equation 12-16.

In previous chapters, we always supplied a CI along with a point estimate to provide a measure of how reliable this estimate really is. The narrower the CI, the more faith you have in your point estimate. A $(1 - \alpha) \cdot 100\%$ CI for μ_i is

$$\overline{X}_i - t_{\alpha/2, n-k} \frac{s_p}{\sqrt{n_i}} \qquad \text{to} \qquad \overline{X}_i + t_{\alpha/2, n-k} \frac{s_p}{\sqrt{n_i}}$$

where

k = number of populations (levels)

n_i = number of replicates in the ith sample

n = total number of observations

s_p = $\sqrt{\text{MS(error)}}$

$t_{\alpha/2, df}$ is the value from Table A-5 with $df = df$ for error $= n - k$, and right-tail area $= \alpha/2$

A $(1 - \alpha) \cdot 100\%$ CI for $\mu_i - \mu_j$ is

$$(\overline{X}_i - \overline{X}_j) - t_{\alpha/2, n-k} \, s_p \sqrt{\frac{1}{n_i} + \frac{1}{n_j}}$$

$$\text{to} \qquad (\overline{X}_i - \overline{X}_j) + t_{\alpha/2, n-k} \, s_p \sqrt{\frac{1}{n_i} + \frac{1}{n_j}}$$

Example 12.3   Using the data from example 12.2, construct a 95% CI for the average sales of brand 1. Also determine a 95% CI interval for the difference between the average sales of brands 1 and 3.

Solution First, your point estimate of μ_1 is $\bar{x}_1 = 43.5$. Using the ANOVA table from example 12.2,

$$s_p^2 = MS(error) = 31.85$$

and so

$$s_p = \sqrt{31.85} = 5.64$$

Because $n = 24$ and $k = 4$, the resulting 95% CI for μ_1 is

$$43.5 - t_{.025, 20} \,(5.64)\sqrt{\frac{1}{6}} \quad \text{to} \quad 43.5 + t_{.025, 20}\,(5.64)\sqrt{\frac{1}{6}}$$

$$= 43.5 - (2.086)(5.64)(.408) \quad \text{to} \quad 43.5 + (2.086)(5.64)(.408)$$

$$= 43.5 - 4.80 \quad \text{to} \quad 43.5 + 4.80$$

$$= 38.7 \quad \text{to} \quad 48.3$$

As a result, we are 95% confident that the average sales of the brand 1 ice cream is between 38.7 and 48.3 gallons per week.

The 95% CI for $\mu_1 - \mu_3$ is

$$(\bar{X}_1 - \bar{X}_3) - t_{.025, 20}\, s_p \sqrt{\frac{1}{n_1} + \frac{1}{n_3}}$$

$$\text{to} \quad (\bar{X}_1 - \bar{X}_3) + t_{.025, 20}\, s_p \sqrt{\frac{1}{n_1} + \frac{1}{n_3}}$$

$$= (43.5 - 29.0) - (2.086)(5.64)\sqrt{\frac{1}{6} + \frac{1}{6}}$$

$$\text{to} \quad (43.5 - 29.0) + (2.086)(5.64)\sqrt{\frac{1}{6} + \frac{1}{6}}$$

$$= 14.5 - (2.086)(5.64)(.577) \quad \text{to} \quad 14.5 + (2.086)(5.64)(.577)$$

$$= 14.5 - 6.79 \quad \text{to} \quad 14.5 + 6.79$$

$$= 7.71 \quad \text{to} \quad 21.29$$

A Word of Warning The procedure we used in example 12.3 for determining confidence intervals is reliable, providing you decide which intervals you want computed *before* you observe your data. For example, constructing a CI for the difference of two population means having the corresponding largest and smallest sample means is not an accurate procedure. If you do this, you let the data dictate which CI you determine.

If you want to construct CIs for all pairs of the μ's ($\mu_1 - \mu_2$, $\mu_1 - \mu_3$, $\mu_1 - \mu_4$, $\mu_2 - \mu_3$, . . .) and be, say, 95% confident of your overall results, this procedure is *not* recommended. The overall confidence of this procedure is not 95%; it is something much less than 95%. CIs developed by Tukey (Too'-key) and Scheffe (Sheh-fay') are *wider* than the CIs determined using the t table. However, they have an overall confidence level equal to 95%.

Tukey's method is generally preferred for situations containing an equal number of replicates in each sample. These procedures will not be discussed here, but are contained in textbooks that present a more advanced treatment of analysis of variance.*

---

*For an excellent discussion of these procedures, see J. Neter and W. Wasserman, *Applied Linear Statistical Methods*. (Homewood, IL: Richard D. Irwin, 1974), pp. 473–482.

Example 12.4

The personnel director of Comptek, a computer software development firm, is interested in the effect of educational level on the job knowledge of the company's employees. He administers an exam to a randomly selected group of people having various educational backgrounds.

In the sample of 15 employees, 6 have only a high-school diploma, 5 have only a bachelor's degree, and 4 have a master's degree. The exam scores are:

	High-school Diploma	Bachelor's Degree	Master's Degree
	81	94	88
	84	83	89
	69	86	78
	85	81	85
	84	78	
	95		
Total (T)	498	422	340
Average ($\overline{X}$)	83.0	84.4	85.0

What would be your conclusion using a significance level of .10?

Solution Examining the sample means, you might be tempted to conclude that the higher a person's level of education, the higher their performance. But is there a *significant* difference among these three means? An ANOVA analysis will determine this.

The assumptions necessary here are:

1. The scores were obtained randomly and independently from each of the three populations.
2. The exam scores for each of the 3 populations follow a normal distribution, with means μ_1, μ_2 and μ_3. The scores in each of the samples are assumed to have the *same* amount of variation. Because the sample sizes are not the same, the Hartley test for equal variances cannot be used here. As discussed earlier, we prefer not to use the same data for testing both the means and variances, and so a better procedure would be to obtain additional data (with equal sample sizes) for testing the equality of these three variances.

$$SS(\text{factor}) = \left[\frac{T_1^2}{n_1} + \frac{T_2^2}{n_2} + \frac{T_3^2}{n_3}\right] - \frac{T^2}{n}$$

where

$$T = \Sigma x = T_1 + T_2 + T_3$$
$$= 498 + 422 + 340 = 1260$$
$$n = n_1 + n_2 + n_3$$
$$= 6 + 5 + 4 = 15$$

So,

$$SS(\text{factor}) = \frac{498^2}{6} + \frac{422^2}{5} + \frac{340^2}{4} - \frac{1260^2}{15}$$
$$= 105,850.8 - 105,840.0$$
$$= 10.8$$

$$SS(\text{total}) = \Sigma x^2 - \frac{T^2}{n}$$

$$= [81^2 + 84^2 + \ldots + 78^2 + 85^2] - \frac{1260^2}{15}$$

$$= 106{,}424 - 105{,}840$$

$$= 584$$

$$SS(\text{error}) = 584 - 10.8 = 573.2$$

Finally, because $k = 3$ and $n = 15$,

$$df \text{ for factor} = k - 1 = 2$$
$$df \text{ for error} = n - k = 12$$
$$df \text{ for total} = n - 1 = 14$$

The resulting ANOVA table is

Source	df	SS	MS	F
Factor	2	10.8	5.4	.11
Error	12	573.2	47.8	
Total	14	584		

The hypotheses are

$$H_0\colon \mu_1 = \mu_2 = \mu_3$$
$$H_a\colon \text{not all } \mu\text{'s are equal}$$

where each μ represents the average score of *all* employees having this particular educational level at Comptek.

We will reject H_0 if

$$F^* > F_{.10,2,12} = 2.81$$

Because $.11 < 2.81$, we fail to reject H_0.

We conclude that there is not sufficient evidence to indicate that the average performance on the exam is different among the three groups. As usual, we do not *accept* H_0; that is, we do *not* conclude that these three means *are* equal. There is simply not enough evidence to support the claim that employees with a higher educational level are better performers at this particular company. ●

The factor in example 12.4 was the educational level of the employee; it had three levels. The results show that we are unable to demonstrate that this factor has a significant effect on exam performance.

Example 12.5 In example 12.4, before the exam was given, Comptek decided to construct a 95% CI for the average exam score of all people holding a master's degree and the difference between the exam scores for personnel with a master's degree and those with only a high-school diploma. What are the CIs?

Solution The point estimates are

for μ_3: $\bar{x}_3 = 85.0$

for $\mu_3 - \mu_1$: $\bar{x}_3 - \bar{x}_1 = 85.0 - 83.0$

$$= 2.0$$

To construct the CIs, you first need an estimate of the common variance of these three populations. Based on the results of example 12.4, this is

$$s_p^2 = \text{MS(error)}$$

$$= 47.8$$

so

$$s_p = \sqrt{47.8} = 6.91$$

Because $n = 15$, $k = 3$, and $n_3 = 4$, the 95% CI for μ_3 is

$$\bar{X}_3 - t_{.025,\,12}\, s_p \sqrt{\frac{1}{n_3}} \quad \text{to} \quad \bar{X}_3 + t_{.025,\,12}\, s_p \sqrt{\frac{1}{n_3}}$$

$$= 85.0 - (2.179)(6.91)(.5) \quad \text{to} \quad 85.0 + (2.179)(6.91)(.5)$$

$$= 85.0 - 7.53 \quad \text{to} \quad 85.0 + 7.53$$

$$= 77.47 \quad \text{to} \quad 92.53$$

The 95% CI for $\mu_3 - \mu_1$ is

$$(\bar{X}_3 - \bar{X}_1) - t_{.025,\,12}\, s_p \sqrt{\frac{1}{n_3} + \frac{1}{n_1}} \quad \text{to} \quad (\bar{X}_3 - \bar{X}_1) + t_{.025,\,12}\, s_p \sqrt{\frac{1}{n_3} + \frac{1}{n_1}}$$

$$= (85.0 - 83.0) - (2.179)(6.91)(.645) \quad \text{to} \quad (85.0 - 83.0) + (2.179)(6.91)(.645)$$

$$= 2.0 - 9.71 \quad \text{to} \quad 2.0 + 9.71$$

$$= -7.71 \quad \text{to} \quad 11.71$$

Figure 12.5

MINITAB solution for examples 12.4 and 12.5.

```
MTB > READ INTO C1 C2
DATA> 81  1          Factor level:  1 = H.S. diploma
DATA> 84  1                         2 = Bachelors degree
DATA> 69  1                         3 = Masters degree
DATA> 85  1
DATA> 84  1
DATA> 95  1
DATA> 94  2
DATA> 83  2
DATA> 86  2
DATA> 81  2
DATA> 78  2
DATA> 88  3
DATA> 89  3
DATA> 78  3
DATA> 85  3
DATA> END
     15 ROWS READ
MTB > ONEWAY USING DATA IN C1,LEVELS IN C2

ANALYSIS OF VARIANCE ON C1
SOURCE     DF        SS        MS         F
C2          2      10.8       5.4      0.11
ERROR      12     573.2      47.8
TOTAL      14     584.0
                                     INDIVIDUAL 95 PCT CI'S FOR MEAN
                                     BASED ON POOLED STDEV
LEVEL       N      MEAN     STDEV    ------+---------+---------+--------
  1         6    83.000     8.367    (-----------*-----------)
  2         5    84.400     6.107       (-------------*------------)
  3         4    85.000     4.967       (------------*-------------)
                                     ------+---------+---------+--------
POOLED STDEV =     6.911             80.0      85.0      90.0
```

Consequently, we are 95% confident that the average exam score of all employees with master's degrees is between 7.71 *lower* to 11.71 *higher* than those with a high-school diploma only. This implies that the data do *not* allow us to say that the employees with master's degrees performed better than those with high-school degrees. ●

A MINITAB solution to this example is shown in Figure 12.5. The output contains summary information for each sample, the ANOVA table, and a graphical representation of the CI for each population mean.

One-Factor ANOVA Procedure

ASSUMPTIONS

1. The replicates are obtained *independently* and *randomly* from each of the populations. The value of one observation has no effect on any other replicates within the same sample or within the other samples.
2. The observations (replicates) from each population follow (approximately) a *normal* distribution.
3. The normal populations all have a *common variance*, σ^2. We expect the values in each sample to vary about the same amount. The ANOVA procedure will be much less sensitive to this assumption when we obtain samples of equal size from each population.

HYPOTHESES

$H_0: \mu_1 = \mu_2 = \ldots = \mu_k$

$H_a:$ not all μ's are equal

Note that H_a is not the same as $H_a':$ all μ's are unequal; H_a states that *at least two* of the μ's are different.

SUM OF SQUARES

$$SS(\text{factor}) = \left[\frac{T_1^2}{n_1} + \frac{T_2^2}{n_2} + \ldots + \frac{T_k^2}{n_k} \right] - \frac{T^2}{n}$$

where: $n = n_1 + n_2 + \ldots + n_k$ and $T = \Sigma x = T_1 + T_2 + \ldots + T_k$.

$$SS(\text{total}) = \Sigma x^2 - \frac{T^2}{n}$$

$$SS(\text{error}) = SS(\text{total}) - SS(\text{factor})$$

$$= \Sigma x^2 - \left[\frac{T_1^2}{n_1} + \frac{T_2^2}{n_2} + \ldots + \frac{T_k^2}{n_k} \right]$$

DEGREES OF FREEDOM

df for factor $= k - 1$

df for error $= n - k$

df for total $= n - 1$

Note that $(k - 1) + (n - k) = n - 1$.

(continued)

ANOVA TABLE

Source	df	SS	MS	F
Factor	$k - 1$	SS(factor)	MS(factor)	MS(factor)/MS(error)
Error	$n - k$	SS(error)	MS(error)	
Total	$n - 1$	SS(total)		

where MS = mean square = SS/df.

TESTING PROCEDURE

Reject H_0 if $F^* > F_{\alpha, k-1, n-k}$

where $F_{\alpha, k-1, n-k}$ is obtained from Table A-7.

Exercises

12.1 A shoe manufacturer wanted to test whether there is a difference in the amount of wear on three different designs of rubber soles for a particular jogging shoe. Eighteen joggers were selected for the experiment. Each type of design was randomly assigned to six joggers. After running 200 miles, the joggers turned in their shoes. The manufacturer used an index to indicate the amount of rubber left on the sole. The measures obtained were:

Design 1	3.2	4.1	6.2	5.3	4.9	3.5
Design 2	4.7	6.3	4.0	5.4	7.1	4.5
Design 3	3.9	6.0	5.5	4.2	3.1	5.1

a. State the null and alternative hypotheses.

b. What assumptions are necessary to use the ANOVA procedure on these data?

c. What are the point estimates of the mean wear for each of the three designs?

d. What is the within-groups mean square?

e. Set up an ANOVA table and state the conclusion. Use a significance level of .05.

12.2 In exercise 12.1, subtract 3.0 from each of the observations in the table. Perform the ANOVA procedure. Are the sum of squares the same for the coded data as for the original data? Why or why not? What happens when any set of data is coded by adding or subtracting the same number to each observation value in terms of the sum of squares?

12.3 A manufacturer introduces a new car that gets 40 mpg with a standard deviation of 3 mpg. The manufacturer's competitor introduces a similar economy car and claims it also gets the same mpg with the same standard deviation. A random sample of 15 observations of mpg is taken for each manufacturer's car. Is there any difference in the mean mpg for these two cars?

Manufacturer	41	40	40	39	36	41	40	42	42	39	40	41	39	38	41
Competitor	38	39	37	40	42	43	41	39	38	37	37	38	39	39	38

12.4 A consumer would like to know if there is any difference in the mean drained weight of tuna canned in oil and tuna canned in spring water. What conclusions can be drawn from these data?

Spring water	6.0	5.5	5.9	5.8	6.1	5.8	5.9	6.1	5.7	5.6
Oil	6.1	6.3	6.0	5.9	5.9	6.0	6.2	6.0	6.1	6.0

Assume that the variance of each group is the same and perform an ANOVA procedure. Use a significance level of .05.

12.5 Use the two-sample t test for the data in exercise 12.4 to test for any difference in the weights of the two types of canned tuna. What is the relationship between the t test of this exercise and the F test of exercise 12.4?

12.6 A psychologist wanted to know whether there was any difference in three types of diet therapy for overweight men. Ten men were chosen for method 1, 12 for method 2, and 13 for method 3. The method 3 group received no treatment; it was a control group. The percent of body weight lost using each method follows. A negative value indicates weight was gained.

Method 1	Method 2	Method 3
5	1	1
7	2	-2
8	5	3
4	-2	-1
10	3	0
11	4	1
6	6	-1
8	1	4
-3	4	3
1	-3	2
	-1	1
	1	-2
		0

a. What is the between-sample variation?

b. What is the within-sample variation?

c. Test the null hypothesis that all three methods work equally well using a .10 significance level.

12.7 A sales manager wanted to know whether there was a significant difference in the monthly sales of her three sales representatives. John is strictly on commission. Randy is on commission and a small salary, and Ted is on a small commission and a salary. Eight months were chosen at random. The data represent monthly sales.

John	969	905	801	850	910	1030	780	810
Randy	738	773	738	805	850	800	690	720
Ted	751	764	701	810	840	790	720	735

a. Using a significance level of .05, test the hypothesis that there is no difference in the mean monthly sales. (Coding the data may make the computations easier.)

b. What is the p-value?

c. Find a 95% CI for the mean of each of the three sales representatives.

d. Find a 95% CI for the mean of the difference between John's and Randy's monthly sales.

e. Find a 95% CI for the mean of the difference between Randy's and Ted's monthly sales.

f. Compare the CIs in questions d and e.

12.8 An instructor wanted to test whether there was a difference in effectiveness of four different teaching techniques. Four groups of students were taught using one of the four teaching techniques. If the instructor examined the groups for mean differences one pair at a time, how many t tests would have to be performed? What is the advantage of using an ANOVA procedure instead?

12.9 Astral Airlines recently introduced a nonstop flight between Houston and Chicago. The vice-president of marketing for Astral decided to run a test to see whether Astral's passenger load was similar to that of its two major competitors. Ten daytime flights were picked at random from each of the three airlines and the percent of unfilled seats on each flight was as follows:

Astral	10	14	12	10	8	13	11	8	12	9
Competitor 1	12	9	8	9	9	10	12	7	11	10
Competitor 2	15	10	15	8	14	9	8	11	10	12

Use a significance level of .05 and perform an ANOVA procedure. Find the p-value.

12.10 Find a 95% CI for each of the pairwise mean differences for the airlines in exercise 12.9.

12.11 What assumptions do the data need to satisfy in exercise 12.9 to ensure that the ANOVA procedure is valid?

12.12 The workers at a calculator assembly plant wish to bargain for more breaks during the work day. The manager believes that increasing the number of 15-minute breaks will adversely affect productivity. The workers currently receive three breaks during the eight-hour work day. The manager decides to run a test by choosing four groups of five workers each and giving one group three breaks, the next group four breaks, and so on. The number of calculators assembled per day is recorded for five days. Test the manager's claim using an ANOVA procedure with a .10 significance level. Find the p-value.

3 Breaks	200	205	197	210	205
4 Breaks	210	203	201	197	199
5 Breaks	198	190	185	188	180
6 Breaks	197	180	190	192	175

12.13 EZ Car Wash would like to know whether its three car-wash machines are dispensing the same mean number of gallons of soapy water to wash each car. The number of gallons is recorded after each machine has completed a wash cycle. Six replications were used for each machine. Is there sufficient evidence to reject, at the .01 level, the hypothesis that the mean number of gallons dispensed by the three machines are equal?

Machine 1	12	12	14	13	11	13
Machine 2	10	11	10	9	10	9
Machine 3	9	11	10	11	12	10

12.14 Independent samples of size 16 are drawn from each of four normally distributed populations. The resulting sample standard deviations are: $s_1 = 2.0$, $s_2 = 2.5$, $s_3 = 2.2$, $s_4 = 2.5$. Do the data provide sufficient evidence that a significant difference exists in the population standard deviations of the four populations? Use a .10 significance level.

12.15 Three machines package 50-lb sacks of pinto beans. A preliminary test is performed using data from a pilot study to determine whether a significant difference exists among the variances of the amount of beans packaged for each machine. Use a 5% significance level in conducting a test for equality of variances for each of the machines from the sample data, in pounds:

Machine 1	Machine 2	Machine 3	Machine 1	Machine 2	Machine 3
52	50	48			
51	49	46	49	50	52
48	51	51	56	49	50
50	50	50	51	51	51
46	52	52	56	50	49
55	53	50	45	49	50
53	55	51	50	48	50

12.16 A sales manager would like to determine whether there is a significant difference in the variance of sales of three salespersons. Three independent samples of daily sales (in hundreds of dollars) are collected. Using a 5% significance level, determine whether the data indicate a difference in the variance of the sales of the three salespersons.

Salesperson 1	Salesperson 2	Salesperson 3
1.2	2.5	1.4
1.1	2.1	1.8
1.4	2.3	1.5
1.6	2.0	1.6
1.4	2.3	1.4
1.0	2.2	1.7
1.3	2.3	1.3
1.8	2.4	1.2
1.4	2.3	1.5
1.5	2.5	1.6

12.17 A target-shooting club performed an experiment on a randomly selected group of 21 beginning shooters to determine whether shooting accuracy is affected by the method of sighting: right eye only open, left eye only open, or both eyes open. The 21 beginners were randomly divided into three groups of seven each. Each group went through the same training and practicing procedures with one exception—the use of eyes for sighting. The scores from each shooter were coded and are:

Right Eye	2	0	8	2	5	3	1
Left Eye	3	6	0	9	0	4	2
Both Eyes	1	7	2	7	1	5	2

a. Do the data provide sufficient evidence to indicate that a difference exists among the mean scores of the three methods? Use a .10 significance level. Find the p-value.

b. Find a 95% CI to estimate the mean score of the coded data for each method.

12.18 In a small company, upper management wants to know if there is a difference in the three types of methods used to train its machine operators. One method uses a hands-on approach but is very expensive. A second method uses a combination of classroom instruction and some on-the-job training. The third method is the least expensive and is confined completely to the classroom. Eight trainees are assigned to each training technique. The following table gives the results of a test administered after completion of the training. Do the data provide sufficient evidence to indicate a difference in the methods of training at the .01 level of significance?

Method 1	Method 2	Method 3
95	85	88
100	90	94
90	95	90
91	88	80
81	93	81
85	86	84
96	94	90
95	95	87

12.3

Random-ized Block Design

The previous section introduced you to the one-factor ANOVA. In this type of analysis, you randomly obtain samples from each of your k populations (levels) describing a single factor. The type of sampling plan you use to obtain data is a particular **experimental design**. The one-factor ANOVA utilizes the **completely randomized design**, in which replicates are obtained in a completely random manner from each population.

Consider another situation. The editors of ten automotive magazines are asked to evaluate the new-car warranty for Henry and GA automobiles. Several criteria are included, leading to a composite score ranging from 0 to 100. A higher score indicates the editor thinks it is a better warranty. The scores are:

Person	Henry	GA
1	68	72
2	40	43
3	82	89
4	56	60
5	70	75
6	80	91
7	47	58
8	55	68
9	78	77
10	53	65

Once again, there is a single factor of interest, namely, *brand* of automobile. But are the twenty sample observations in fact replicates? Replicates (by definition) are obtained under (nearly) identical circumstances, so any variation in the values within any one sample is due strictly to chance. For this situation, the person from whom the values were obtained influences heavily each sample value. Also, each pair of values is supplied by the same person, and so these samples are *not independent,* violating a key assumption of the completely randomized design.

This situation fits the *paired sample* design discussed in Section 10.5, provided we assume that both populations are normally distributed, as we have been assuming throughout this chapter. Our discussion now becomes an extension of Section 10.6, except that we can now consider more than two populations.

The samples are organized into homogeneous units, referred to as **blocks.** In this illustration, each person represents a block. *Within* each block, any predictable difference in the observations is due to the effect of the factor of interest—in this case, brand of automobile.

To determine if there is a factor (brand) effect in these 20 ratings, we must first account for the block (person) effect. If we ignore this effect, we could easily come to an incorrect conclusion regarding a brand difference. This same point was made in Chapter 10, where a crucial question was whether to pair (block) the data. Figures 10.13 and 10.14 illustrated how one can arrive at an incorrect conclusion by failing to block the data.

Now assume that the warranty analysis was extended to three brands of automobiles by also including the warranty provided by the manufacturers of Roadster automobiles, using the same ten people. The results were:

Person	Henry	GA	Roadster
1	68	72	65
2	40	43	42
3	82	89	84
4	56	60	50
5	70	75	68
6	80	91	86
7	47	58	50
8	55	68	52
9	78	77	75
10	53	65	60

Table 12.1

The randomized block design

Block	FACTOR LEVEL (POPULATION)					Total
	1	2	3	. . .	k	
1	X	X	X	. . .	X	S_1
2	X	X	X	. . .	X	S_2
3	X	X	X	. . .	X	S_3
.						
.						
.						
b	X	X	X	. . .	X	S_b
Total	T_1	T_2	T_3	. . .	T_k	T
Sample Mean	$\overline{X}_1$	$\overline{X}_2$	$\overline{X}_3$	. . .	$\overline{X}_k$	

The data from the warranty example constitute a randomized block design with a single factor (brand) containing three levels (Henry, GA, Roadster) as well as ten blocks (person 1, . . . , person 10). The general appearance of such a design is shown in Table 12.1.

When using the randomized block design, the various levels should be applied in a *random* manner within each block. In our warranty example, each person should *not* always examine the Henry warranty first, the GA warranty second, and the Roadster warranty last. Instead these three companies should be assigned in a randomized order to each person—hence the name "randomized block design."
The assumptions for the randomized block design are:

1. The observations within each factor level/block combination are obtained from a normal population.
2. These normal populations have a common variance, σ^2.

The analysis using the randomized block design is similar to that for the one-factor ANOVA, except that the total sum of squares [SS(total)] has an additional component. Now,

$$SS(total) = SS(factor) + SS(block) + SS(error)$$

where SS(block) measures the variation due to the blocks.
If you use the randomized block design when blocking is not necessary, SS(block) will be very small in comparison to the other sums of squares. Referring to Table 12.1, this will occur when $S_1, S_2, \ldots, S_b$ are nearly the same. If all the S's are equal, then SS(block) = 0. The effect of the blocks will be significant whenever you observe a lot of variation in these block totals.
The sum of squares for the randomized block design is thus

$$SS(factor) = \frac{1}{b}\left[T_1^2 + T_2^2 + \ldots + T_k^2 \right] - \frac{T^2}{bk}$$

where

n = number of observations = bk

$T_1, T_2, \ldots, T_k$ represent the totals for the k factor levels

$S_1, S_2, \ldots, S_b$ are the totals for the b blocks

$$T = T_1 + T_2 + \ldots + T_k$$
$$= S_1 + S_2 + \ldots + S_b$$
$$= \text{total of all observations.}$$

$$SS(\text{blocks}) = \frac{1}{k}\left[S_1^2 + S_2^2 + \ldots + S_b^2\right] - \frac{T^2}{bk}$$

$$SS(\text{total}) = \Sigma x^2 - \frac{T^2}{bk}$$

where Σx^2 = sum of the squares for each of the $n(= bk)$ observations.

$$SS(\text{error}) = SS(\text{total}) - SS(\text{factor}) - SS(\text{blocks})$$

The degrees of freedom are

df for factor $= k - 1$

df for blocks $= b - 1$

df for error $= (k - 1)(b - 1)$

df for total $= bk - 1$

The ANOVA table for a blocked design is very similar to the one-factor ANOVA table. There is one additional row because you now include the effect of the various blocks in your design:

Source	df	SS	MS	F
Factor	$k - 1$	SS(factor)	MS(factor)	F_1 = MS(factor)/MS(error)
Blocks	$b - 1$	SS(blocks)	MS(blocks)	F_2 = MS(blocks)/MS(error)
Error	$(k - 1)(b - 1)$	SS(error)	MS(error)	
Total	$bk - 1$	SS(total)		

where

$$MS(\text{factor}) = SS(\text{factor})/(k - 1)$$

$$MS(\text{blocks}) = SS(\text{blocks})/(b - 1)$$

$$MS(\text{error}) = SS(\text{error})/[(k - 1)(b - 1)]$$

Hypothesis Testing

Is there a difference in the average rating of the three warranties in our illustration? In other words, does the brand have a significant effect on the warranty ratings? The hypotheses for this situation are H_0: $\mu_1 = \mu_2 = \mu_3$ and H_a: not all the means are equal. We determine the test statistic exactly as we did for the one-factor ANOVA:

$$F_1 = \frac{MS(\text{factor})}{MS(\text{error})} \qquad (12\text{-}18)$$

where the mean square values are obtained from the ANOVA table. Notice that the MS(factor) value is the *same* regardless of whether you block or not. However, when you use the block effect in the design, the MS(error) is smaller. You are thus more likely to detect a difference in these k means when a difference does exist. Had you *not* included the block effect, the block variation would have been included in SS(error), resulting in a smaller F value. This value often becomes small enough not to fall in the rejection region, leading you to conclude that no difference exists. But perhaps there *is* a difference among these means (the factor *does* have a significant effect) that will go undetected if an incorrect experimental design is used.

There are many other such designs that we will not discuss in this text. Choosing the correct design is an art. For now, remember to ask, do I have replicates at each factor level or do I need to include a block effect? If there is no need for blocking the data, use the one-factor ANOVA technique for determining whether the factor of interest is significant.

Here, our test will be

Reject H_0 if $F_1 > F_{\alpha, v_1, v_2}$

where $v_1 = k - 1$ and $v_2 = (k - 1)(b - 1)$. So, once again, we reject H_0 if the F statistic falls in the right-tail rejection region, this time using Table A-7 with $v_1 = k - 1$, the *df* for factor, and $v_2 = (k - 1)(b - 1)$, the *df* for error.

Now suppose we wish to determine whether the effect of the person evaluating the warranties is significant. We are attempting to determine whether there is a block effect, so the hypotheses are

H_0': there is no effect due to the evaluators (blocks) (the block means are equal)

H_a': there *is* an effect due to the evaluators (the block means are not all equal)

The corresponding test uses the "other" F statistic from the randomized block ANOVA table, namely,

$$F_2 = \frac{MS(\text{blocks})}{MS(\text{error})} \qquad (12\text{-}19)$$

and the test is

Reject H_0' if $F_2 > F_{\alpha, v_1', v_2'}$

where $v_1' = b - 1$ and $v_2' = (k - 1)(b - 1)$.

Let us reexamine our data. We will use $\alpha = .05$. Here, $k = 3$ levels (brands), $b = 10$ blocks (people), and $n = bk = 30$ observations.

Person	Henry	GA	Roadster	Totals
1	68	72	65	205
2	40	43	42	125
3	82	89	84	255
4	56	60	50	166
5	70	75	68	213
6	80	91	86	257
7	47	58	50	155
8	55	68	52	175
9	78	77	75	230
10	53	65	60	178
Total	629	698	632	1959
$\overline{X}$	62.9	69.8	63.2	

$$\text{SS(factor)} = \frac{1}{10}\left[629^2 + 698^2 + 632^2\right] - \frac{1959^2}{30}$$
$$= 128,226.9 - 127,922.7$$
$$= 304.2$$

$$\text{SS(blocks)} = \frac{1}{3}\left[205^2 + 125^2 + \ldots + 178^2\right] - \frac{1959^2}{30}$$
$$= 133,627.7 - 127,922.7$$
$$= 5,705.0$$

$$\text{SS(total)} = \left[68^2 + 40^2 + \ldots + 75^2 + 60^2\right] - \frac{1959^2}{30}$$
$$= 134,107 - 127,922.7$$
$$= 6,184.3$$

$$\text{SS(error)} = \text{SS(total)} - \text{SS(factor)} - \text{SS(blocks)}$$
$$= 6,184.3 - 304.2 - 5,705.0$$
$$= 175.1$$

So

$$\text{MS(factor)} = \text{SS(factor)}/(k - 1)$$
$$= 304.2/2 = 152.1$$

$$\text{MS(blocks)} = \text{SS(blocks)}/(b - 1)$$
$$= 5705.0/9 = 633.9$$

$$\text{MS(error)} = \text{SS(error)}/[(k - 1)(b - 1)]$$
$$= 175.1/18 = 9.73$$

The resulting ANOVA table is

Source	df	SS	MS	F
Factor	2	304.2	152.1	152.1/9.73 = 15.63 (F_1)
Blocks	9	5705.0	633.9	633.9/9.73 = 65.15 (F_2)
Error	18	175.1	9.73	
Total	29	6184.3		

We first consider the hypotheses

H_0: $\mu_1 = \mu_2 = \mu_3$

H_a: not all μ's are equal

where

μ_1 = average rating of Henry warranty (estimate is $\bar{x}_1 = 62.9$)

μ_2 = average rating of GA warranty (estimate is $\bar{x}_2 = 69.8$)

μ_3 = average rating of Roadster warranty (estimate is $\bar{x}_3 = 63.2$)

Because $F_1 = 15.63 > F_{.05,2,18} = 3.55$, we reject H_0 and conclude that there *is* a difference in the perceived quality of the three warranties. This is not a surprising

Figure 12.6

MINITAB solution for car
warranties data.

```
MTB > READ INTO C1-C3
DATA> 68 1 1
DATA> 40 1 2
DATA> 82 1 3
DATA> 56 1 4
DATA> 70 1 5
DATA> 80 1 6
DATA> 47 1 7
DATA> 55 1 8
DATA> 78 1 9
DATA> 53 1 10
DATA> 72 2 1
DATA> 43 2 2
DATA> 89 2 3
DATA> 60 2 4
DATA> 75 2 5
DATA> 91 2 6
DATA> 58 2 7
DATA> 68 2 8
DATA> 77 2 9
DATA> 65 2 10
DATA> 65 3 1
DATA> 42 3 2
DATA> 84 3 3
DATA> 50 3 4
DATA> 68 3 5
DATA> 86 3 6
DATA> 50 3 7
DATA> 52 3 8
DATA> 75 3 9
DATA> 60 3 10
DATA> END
      30 ROWS READ
MTB > TWOWAY USING DATA IN C1, LEVELS IN C2, BLOCKS IN C3

ANALYSIS OF VARIANCE   C1
```

C_3 contains block values: 1 = person 1
                                2 = person 2, etc.

C_2 contains factor (brand) levels

$\quad\quad$ 1 = K
$\quad\quad$ 2 = L
$\quad\quad$ 3 = J

SOURCE	DF	SS	MS	
C2	2	304.20	152.10	F value not provided
C3	9	5704.97	633.89	F_1 = 152.10/9.73 = 15.63 (factor)
ERROR	18	175.13	9.73	F_2 = 633.89/9.73 = 65.15 (block)
TOTAL	29	6184.30		

result because it appears that the GA warranty scored much higher than Henry and Roadster warranties. This means that the factor (car brand) *does* have a significant effect on the warranty rating.

We also wish to test

H_0': there is no block effect

H_a': there is a block effect

$S_1, S_2, \ldots, S_{10}$ appear to contain considerable variation, so our initial guess is that there is a block effect. Carrying out the statistical test, we see that

$$F_2 = 65.15 > F_{.05,9,18} = 2.46$$

Consequently, we strongly reject H_0', in favor of H_a'. The effect of the person doing the three evaluations *is* significant.

A MINITAB solution for this problem is shown in Figure 12.6.

What would the result have been had we treated these 30 observations as replicates, ten from each of the three brands? In other words, what would happen if we failed to recognize that blocking was necessary and we incorrectly used the one-factor ANOVA?

Because both SS(factor) and SS(total) *do not change,* the only difference is a new SS(error). Therefore,

$$SS(error) = SS(total) - SS(factor)$$
$$= 6184.3 - 304.2$$
$$= 5880.1$$

Also,

$$df \text{ for error} = (df \text{ for total}) - (df \text{ for factor})$$
$$= 29 - 2 = 27$$

The resulting F value will be

$$F = \frac{MS(\text{factor})}{MS(\text{error})} = \frac{304.2/2}{5880.1/27} = .70$$

Because $F^* = .70$ is *much less* than $F_{.05,2,27} = 3.35$, *we fail to detect a difference in the three means,* μ_1, μ_2, and μ_3. This is the effect of assuming independence among the samples when it does not exist. This emphasizes that failing to recognize the need for a randomized block design can have serious consequences!

Constructing a Confidence Interval for the Difference Between Two Population Means

We can construct a CI for the difference between any pair of means, $\mu_i - \mu_j$. Remember, however, that we must determine which CIs we will construct *before* observing the data. Do not fall into the trap of letting the data dictate which CIs you construct.

When using the randomized block design, our estimate of the common variance, σ^2, is now

$$s^2 = \text{estimate of } \sigma^2$$
$$= MS(\text{error}) = \frac{SS(\text{error})}{(k-1)(b-1)} \qquad (12\text{-}20)$$

Thus, a $(1 - \alpha) \cdot 100\%$ CI for $\mu_i - \mu_j$ is

$$(\overline{X}_i - \overline{X}_j) - t_{\alpha/2,df} \cdot s \cdot \sqrt{\frac{1}{b} + \frac{1}{b}} \quad \text{to} \quad (\overline{X}_i - \overline{X}_j) + t_{\alpha/2,df} \cdot s \cdot \sqrt{\frac{1}{b} + \frac{1}{b}}$$

where df = degrees of freedom for the t statistic (Table A-5) = $(k-1)(b-1)$; b = number of blocks; k = number of factor levels; and s is determined from equation 12-20.

Example 12.6

Assume you have not yet observed the data from the car-warranty example, and you decided to construct a 95% CI for the difference between the average GA and Roadster warranty ratings. What does it tell you?

Solution Using the ANOVA table for these data,

$$s^2 = MS(\text{error}) = 9.73$$

and so $s = 3.12$. Also, $t_{.025, 18} = 2.101$ using Table A-5. The resulting 95% CI for $\mu_2 - \mu_3$ is

$$(\bar{X}_2 - \bar{X}_3) - t_{.025, 18}\, s\sqrt{\frac{1}{10} + \frac{1}{10}} \quad \text{to} \quad (\bar{X}_2 - \bar{X}_3) + t_{.025, 18}\, s\sqrt{\frac{1}{10} + \frac{1}{10}}$$

$$= (69.8 - 63.2) - (2.101)(3.12)(.447)$$
$$\text{to} \quad (69.8 - 63.2) + (2.101)(3.12)(.447)$$
$$= 6.6 - 2.93 \quad \text{to} \quad 6.6 + 2.93$$
$$= 3.67 \quad \text{to} \quad 9.53$$

We are thus 95% confident that the average GA warranty rating is between 3.67 and 9.53 points *higher* than that for the Roadster warranty. The GA warranty appears to be superior to the Roadster warranty. ●

Deciding When to Block

If a particular experiment includes a block effect that, according to the block F test, is insignificant, is it safe not to include the block effect the next time you encounter this same situation? After all, by omitting the block effect, you do obtain additional degrees of freedom in the error term, which should make the test for the means more powerful. The main problem with this argument is that you perform the ANOVA procedure only *once,* so in essence your decision never to include the block effect again for this application is based on a sample of size *one.* There is no guarantee that, for the next set of data, the block effect will once again turn out to be insignificant.

A general rule of thumb here is that, if you have any doubt about whether the block effect is significant, include it. This assumes that there are sufficient data available that the loss in the degrees of freedom for the error term when including a block effect will not be substantial. As we have seen, treating the sample observations as replicates (that is, assuming independent samples) when in fact blocks were used when obtaining the samples can have serious consequences.

Exercises

12.19 A real-estate firm used two independent property appraisers. The firm wanted to know whether the two appraisers were consistent in determining the market value of local buildings. The appraisers each appraised 11 buildings and the following data were collected (values in dollars):

Building	Appraiser 1	Appraiser 2
1	25,000	25,500
2	28,000	30,000
3	41,200	41,100
4	48,300	47,600
5	51,350	50,100
6	32,450	34,125
7	29,950	30,590
8	38,100	39,500
9	31,350	32,750
10	25,890	24,900
11	48,500	47,300

a. Use a paired t test to test for differences due to the appraisers. Use a .05 significance level.

b. Use the F test in the randomized block design to test for no differences in appraisers. Use a .05 significance level.

c. What is the relationship between the t test in question a and the F test in question b?

12.20 A study compared the price of regular gas at Exgas stations and at Argas stations. Ten locations were randomly chosen in which both Exgas and Argas service stations were located. The price per gallon (in dollars) was:

Location	1	2	3	4	5	6	7	8	9	10
Exgas	1.08	1.05	1.09	1.04	1.10	1.09	1.05	1.06	1.09	1.10
Argas	1.07	1.04	1.04	1.07	1.08	1.10	1.05	1.03	1.06	1.07

a. Use a paired t test to test for differences in the mean price of regular gas of the two companies. Use a .01 significance level.

b. Use the F test in the randomized block design to test for the difference in the mean price of regular gas at the Exgas and Argas service stations. Use a .01 significance level. Is the F value equal to the square of the t value in question a?

12.21 A particular application contains four blocks and four levels for the factor of interest. The totals for each of the four blocks are given as: $S_1 = 170$, $S_2 = 184$, $S_3 = 182$, $S_4 = 240$, and the totals for each of four levels of the factor are given as: $T_1 = 120$, $T_2 = 240$, $T_3 = 210$, $T_4 = 206$. Construct the ANOVA table for the randomized block design and assume that the total sum of squares is 2836.

12.22 Complete the following ANOVA table for a randomized block design. Find the p-value.

Source	df	SS	MS	F
Factor	7			
Blocks	3	105.6		
Error		90.8		
Total		336.5		

12.23 Explain the difference between a completely randomized design and a randomized block design. What is the purpose of using blocks in a design?

12.24 Suppose in exercise 12.1 that, instead of 18 joggers, only six joggers are selected. Each jogger wears each of the three types of jogging shoes. After 200 miles of wear on each of the shoes, the joggers turn in their shoes. The amount of rubber left on the soles of each pair of shoes is:

Shoe 1	3.1	4.1	6.1	3.9	5.1	3.6
Shoe 2	3.4	4.5	6.5	4.4	5.8	3.8
Shoe 3	3.5	3.8	4.8	3.7	4.9	3.5

a. State the null and alternative hypotheses for testing whether there is a difference in the amount of wear on the three different designs of rubber soles.

b. Test the hypotheses in question a at a .05 significance level. Find the p-value.

c. What is the error mean square?

d. Find a 90% CI for the difference in the average amount of rubber left on the soles for designs 1 and 2.

e. How does this experimental design differ from that in exercise 12.1?

12.25 In exercise 12.24, subtract 3.0 from each of the observations in the table. Perform the ANOVA procedure and test the hypothesis of no effect due to shoe design at the .05 confidence level. Is the sum of squares the same for the coded data as for the original data? If any set of ·

data is coded by adding or subtracting the same number to the value of each observation, how will the sum of squares be affected?

12.26 A computer firm compared the performance of four of its compilers. Five different programs were tested. The time required to compile each of the five programs was recorded. The observations are given in seconds. Do the data provide sufficient evidence to indicate that there is a difference in the performance of the compilers at the .05 significance level? Is there a significant difference due to blocks?

	1	2	3	4
Program 1	31.103	24.315	33.058	22.013
Program 2	30.111	25.216	34.698	21.001
Program 3	29.903	25.347	33.872	20.314
Program 4	30.013	24.136	35.671	24.316
Program 5	31.981	24.977	34.751	22.591

12.27 In a randomized block design, if the degrees of freedom for the error sum of squares is given as 12 and the degrees of freedom for the factor sum of squares is 3, can you find the number of blocks used in the experiment? If yes, how many were used? If the total sum of squares is given as 520, the error sum of squares as 110, and the sum of squares due to blocks as 280, can you find the F test for this experiment? If yes, what is it?

12.28 A machine-shop supervisor is interested in knowing whether there is a significant difference among the production times of three machines running six different jobs.

	1	2	3	4	5	6
Machine 1	4.2	2.1	1.3	7.1	6.0	3.4
Machine 2	6.1	2.9	2.0	7.8	6.8	4.3
Machine 3	5.3	2.1	1.4	7.3	5.8	3.1

a. At the .01 level, test the hypothesis that there is no mean differences in the production time for each of the three machines.

b. Is the test for blocks at the .05 level significant?

c. Find a 90% CI for the difference in mean production time for machine 1 and machine 2.

12.29 The Green Thumb lawn-care company is testing three different formulas for a fertilizer specially designed for lawns in Denton County. To adjust for variation in the soil, the formulas are tested in 13 locations. The growth rate of the grass is recorded. Do the coded results indicate a difference in the lawn growth due to the formulas at the .05 level of significance?

Location	Formula 1	Formula 2	Formula 3
1	3.1	3.0	2.7
2	2.6	2.4	2.5
3	2.9	2.1	2.3
4	3.5	3.4	3.1
5	3.8	3.7	3.2
6	2.9	2.5	2.6
7	3.1	3.3	3.2
8	3.4	2.9	3.1
9	3.1	3.2	3.2
10	3.3	3.0	2.9
11	2.7	2.4	2.2
12	2.8	2.3	2.1
13	3.4	3.0	3.1

12.30 Linoleum Unlimited is experimenting with three types of adhesives for laying linoleum. Each glue is tested on five different surfaces. The adhesiveness of the glue is measured and the coded results are as follows. Construct the ANOVA table and test the hypothesis that there is no difference in the three types of adhesives at the .10 level of significance.

Surface	Adhesive 1	Adhesive 2	Adhesive 3
1	1.5	2.1	2.4
2	1.6	1.8	1.9
3	2.4	2.5	2.4
4	3.1	3.4	3.1
5	4.5	4.2	4.0

12.31 Suppose the following results were given from a computer printout: SS(factor) = 293.1, SS(blocks) = 5160.2, and SS(error) = 170.2. Assume four factor levels and ten blocks were used. Develop the ANOVA table and test for the effect of the factor and also for the effect of blocks. Use a significance level of .05.

12.32 What assumptions need to be made about the distribution of the population from which data are obtained in a randomized block design?

12.33 A consumer wished to know whether three leading brands of bread were priced approximately the same. Twelve supermarkets were selected as blocks. The following data were collected:

Supermarket	Brand 1	Brand 2	Brand 3
1	45	40	38
2	40	39	38
3	41	40	37
4	42	41	37
5	40	40	40
6	39	40	40
7	46	42	38
8	43	40	39
9	42	40	40
10	43	41	36
11	40	38	37
12	39	38	37

Test the hypothesis H_0: $\mu_1 = \mu_2 = \mu_3$ at the .01 signifiance level. Is the test for blocks significant at the .01 level?

Summary

The analysis of variance (ANOVA) procedure is a method of detecting differences between the means of two or more normal populations. The various populations represent the *levels* of a *factor* under observation. The factor might consist of, for example, different locations (does the crime rate differ among five cities?), brands (does one brand outsell the others?), or time periods (is average attendance the same during each day of the week?).

Samples for this analysis must be obtained independently of each other. The ANOVA technique measures sources of variation among the sample data by computing various sums of squares. The variation from one level (population) to the next is measured by the factor sum of squares [SS(factor)], which is large when there is great variation among the sample means. The variation *within* the samples is measured by the error sum of squares [SS(error)]. Each of these SS has a corresponding degree of freedom (*df*), which is divided into the SS to produce a mean square, MS.

The ratio of MS(factor) to MS(error) produces an F statistic that is used to test for equal means within the various populations. If the F value is large (significant), then we conclude that the means are not all the same, which implies that the factor of interest *does* have a significant effect on the variable under observation.

When we analyze the effect of a single factor, we perform a one-factor ANOVA and use a completely randomized design. The results of this analysis, including the various sums of squares, mean squares, and degrees of freedom, are summarized in an ANOVA table.

When samples are not obtained in an independent manner, a randomized block design often can be used to test for differences in the population means. Again, there is a single factor of interest, but, to determine the effect of this factor, the sample data are organized into *blocks*. For this situation, the samples are not independently obtained, but data within the same block may be gathered from the same city or person or at the same time. By including a block effect in the ANOVA procedure, we can analyze the factor of interest (the population means) using an F test. In addition, another F statistic can be used for determining whether there is a significant block effect within the sample data.

Review Exercises

12.34 A random sample is taken from each of four independent and normally distributed populations with a common variance. Do the data provide sufficient evidence to reject the null hypothesis that the means of the four populations are the same with a significance level of .05?

Population 1	Population 2	Population 3	Population 4
10.0	11.3	9.6	10.4
12.1	11.4	9.7	10.5
11.2	11.1	9.8	10.0
9.5	10.4	10.5	10.1
10.1	10.9	11.1	9.3
13.8	10.1	9.5	11.2
10.2	9.8	9.9	11.3
9.8	9.1	10.8	9.9
	11.8		10.1
	12.1		10.3

12.35 To compare the effectiveness of three motivational lectures, 21 employees hired in the past seven months were randomly divided into three groups. Each group heard one lecture. The increase in productivity of the 21 employees was measured over the two weeks following the lectures. The coded values for the increase in productivity were:

Lecture 1	5	6	7	4	6	5	6
Lecture 2	3	4	8	3	5	4	4
Lecture 3	1	2	6	7	2	4	3

a. State the null and alternative hypotheses for this experiment.

b. What is the between-sample variation?

c. What is the within-sample variation?

d. Test the null hypothesis at the .05 significance level and find the p-value.

12.36 For the data in exercise 12.35, find the 95% CI for each of the three pairwise differences in the mean increase of productivity after the three lectures.

12.37 The manager of Cut-Ups beauty salon wants to know if there is evidence that the texture of a person's hair has an effect on how long a permanent wave lasts. Thirty people were selected with three types of hair texture. The number of months the permanent waves lasted was:

Texture 1	1.2	1.5	1.8	1.9	1.3	1.4	1.2	.9	1.1	1.0
Texture 2	.3	.8	.9	1.1	.9	1.1	1.1	.8	1.2	.9
Texture 3	.6	.7	1.0	1.2	.8	1.0	1.0	1.0	1.3	.9

Test the null hypothesis that how long a permanent wave lasts is not affected by the person's hair texture.

12.38 The cycling club would like to know whether there is any difference in the wear of three different tubeless bicycle tires. Thirty-six cyclists are randomly assigned one of the types of tires, so that 12 tires of each type are used. Each cyclist rides 600 miles. The following coded data represent the amount of tread left on the tires.

Tire 1	1.2	3.1	1.9	1.8	2.1	3.1	1.9	1.8	3.0	3.1	1.8	3.1
Tire 2	2.1	2.2	2.1	1.9	2.2	1.1	1.2	1.7	2.1	1.9	2.9	2.0
Tire 3	3.1	1.9	3.4	2.0	1.9	3.0	1.7	1.7	1.8	2.5	1.6	2.3

Test the null hypothesis that there is no difference in the mean wear for the three types of tires at the .01 level.

12.39 Suppose in exercise 12.38 that only 12 cyclists were available for the experiment. Each cyclist rides 600 miles with each of the three types of tires. The data from this experiment are:

Cyclist	1	2	3	4	5	6	7	8	9	10	11	12
Tire 1	2.1	1.9	2.5	1.8	2.8	3.0	3.1	2.7	1.9	2.4	2.7	2.1
Tire 2	2.2	1.1	2.3	1.6	2.5	3.0	2.5	2.5	1.3	2.1	2.3	1.6
Tire 3	2.3	1.8	2.7	1.9	2.7	3.1	3.0	2.6	1.7	2.3	2.5	2.4

a. Test the null hypothesis that there is no difference in the mean wear for the three types of tires at the .01 level.

b. Is there an effect due to blocking at the .01 level?

12.40 To test the merit of relaxation therapy, eight men over age 40 were selected. Their heart rate was recorded before and after the therapy. The results were:

Subject	1	2	3	4	5	6	7	8
Before	74	75	79	81	73	85	88	70
After	70	68	69	72	69	70	82	62

a. Use a paired t test to test for the difference in the mean heart rate before and after the therapy at the .05 level.

b. Use the F test in the randomized block design to test for the difference in the mean heart rate before and after the therapy at the 0.05 level. What is the relationship between the paired t test and the F test?

12.41 Assume four samples of size ten are taken from four normally distributed populations with a common variance. The total sum of squares is 221.6 and the error mean square is 3.7. Test the null hypothesis that there is no difference in the mean of each population at the .05 level. Find the p-value.

12.42 Assume that, in exercise 12.41, you are given the additional information that the sample means of populations 1 and 2 are 33.5 and 37.9, respectively. Find the 95% CI for the difference in the means of populations 1 and 2.

12.43 Complete the following table for a randomized block design.

Source	df	SS	MS	F
Factor	9			
Blocks		250		
Error	18	149		
Total		589		

12.44 Suppose it is known in a randomized block design that the mean square for blocks is 75, the error mean square is 291, the total sum of squares is 5083, and five blocks and four factor levels are used in the experiment. What would be the value of the F test for testing the hypothesis that there is no difference in the mean levels of the factor?

12.45 The block totals (S's) and totals (T's) for each level of the factor for a randomized block design are given as follows:

$$S_1 = 30 \quad S_2 = 46 \quad S_3 = 38 \quad S_4 = 40$$
$$S_5 = 40 \quad S_6 = 48 \quad S_7 = 38 \quad S_8 = 36$$
$$T_1 = 102, \quad T_2 = 82, \quad T_3 = 122$$

Construct the ANOVA table for the randomized block design and assume that the total sum of squares is 274.

12.46 Fifteen university campuses of similar size were selected to determine which of three methods of advertising a blood-donation drive was most effective. Five randomly selected campuses advertised in the university newspaper (method 1). Another five advertised only by posters and signs around campus (method 2). The remaining five had each professor credit five points to the student's last test if the student contributed (method 3). The table gives the percentage of the student body that contributed.

Method 1	.10	.15	.19	.21	.25
Method 2	.20	.18	.20	.23	.19
Method 3	.29	.20	.25	.30	.25

Do these data provide sufficient evidence at the .01 level of significance to reject the null hypothesis that there is no difference in the effectiveness of the three methods of advertising?

12.47 Sample data from three normally distributed populations were generated by a computer program for a simulation study. Do the data provide evidence to indicate that at least two of the population variances are not equal? Use a .05 significance level.

Sample 1	Sample 2	Sample 3
38	45	28
37	47	27
35	43	31
40	44	30
39	42	31
35	44	32
34	45	29
33	47	30
32	45	31
39	43	32
37	42	31
36	44	29
35	45	30

12.48 A randomized block design was used to compare the chemical breakdown of three high-quality motor oils. Four different automobiles used each of the three motor oils for 7000 miles. The coded data represent a measure of breakdown by the three types of motor oil:

Motor oil 1	2.1	1.8	1.9	1.7
Motor oil 2	1.8	2.2	2.1	2.0
Motor oil 3	1.9	2.0	2.0	2.1

Is there evidence that the mean breakdowns of the three motor oils differ? Use a .05 significance level. Find the p-value.

12.49 Using the data in exercise 12.48, construct a 95% CI for the difference between the average breakdown for motor oil 1 and motor oil 2. What does the CI tell you?

12.50 Four workers at a manufacturing plant were given ten different tasks to perform. The time in minutes for each task was:

Task	Worker 1	Worker 2	Worker 3	Worker 4
1	20	21	19	23
2	25	22	26	23
3	37	40	31	35
4	105	100	95	101
5	90	95	88	100
6	10	12	13	11
7	38	35	31	36
8	45	40	42	42
9	41	42	36	38
10	10	12	11	9

A MINITAB computer printout provides the following analysis. Can it be concluded at a .05 significance level that the time it takes to perform the tasks is different for the four workers?

```
MTB > READ INTO C1-C3      DATA> 36 4 7
DATA> 20 1 1               DATA> 42 4 8
DATA> 25 1 2               DATA> 38 4 9
DATA> 37 1 3               DATA> 9 4 10
DATA> 105 1 4              DATA> END
DATA> 90 1 5                    40 ROWS READ
DATA> 10 1 6               MTB > TWOWAY ANOVA,DATA IN C1,WORKER IN C2,JOB IN C3
DATA> 38 1 7
DATA> 45 1 8
DATA> 41 1 9               ANALYSIS OF VARIANCE   C1
DATA> 10 1 10
DATA> 21 2 1               SOURCE      DF       SS        MS
DATA> 22 2 2               C2          3      56.50     18.83
DATA> 40 2 3               C3          9   35231.00   3914.56
DATA> 100 2 4              ERROR      27     214.00      7.93
DATA> 95 2 5               TOTAL      39   35501.50
DATA> 12 2 6
DATA> 35 2 7
DATA> 40 2 8
DATA> 42 2 9
DATA> 12 2 10
DATA> 19 3 1
DATA> 26 3 2
DATA> 31 3 3
DATA> 95 3 4
DATA> 88 3 5
DATA> 13 3 6
DATA> 31 3 7
DATA> 42 3 8
DATA> 36 3 9
DATA> 11 3 10
DATA> 23 4 1
DATA> 23 4 2
DATA> 35 4 3
DATA> 101 4 4
DATA> 100 4 5
DATA> 11 4 6
```

12.51 A MINITAB program using the ANOVA procedure to test the equality of tensile strengths for three designs of an electrical coil provided the following computer printout for the coded data. From the printout, state the statistical conclusion assuming a .10 significance level.

```
MTB > READ INTO C1 C2
DATA> 12 1
DATA> 10 1
DATA> 18 1
DATA> 7 1
DATA> 20 1
DATA> 14 1
DATA> 20 1
DATA> 15 1
DATA> 14 2
DATA> 7 2
DATA> 11 2
DATA> 15 2
DATA> 16 2
DATA> 18 2
DATA> 15 2
DATA> 13 2
DATA> 10 3
DATA> 11 3
DATA> 12 3
DATA> 6 3
DATA> 5 3
DATA> 13 3
DATA> 15 3
DATA> 14 3
DATA> END
      24 ROWS READ
MTB > ONEWAY ANOVA,DATA IN C1,GROUP IN C2

ANALYSIS OF VARIANCE ON C1
SOURCE      DF        SS        MS        F
C2           2       61.6      30.8      1.98
ERROR       21      327.4      15.6
TOTAL       23      389.0
                                    INDIVIDUAL 95 PCT CI'S FOR MEAN
                                    BASED ON POOLED STDEV
LEVEL       N       MEAN      STDEV   ----+---------+---------+---------+--
   1        8      14.500     4.721                 (--------*---------)
   2        8      13.625     3.378              (--------*--------)
   3        8      10.750     3.615   (---------*--------)
                                    ----+---------+---------+---------+--
POOLED STDEV =     3.948             9.0      12.0      15.0      18.0
```

Case Study

Specialty Products

Specialty Products decided to start manufacturing a new drink mixer. Specialty's design engineers were asked to develop two prototype mixers. One had fewer speeds and cost less to manufacture than the other. The first also had a more expensive case.

Specialty conducted an extended test by randomly assigning 100 of each of the two prototypes to 200 test households. The more expensive mixer received significantly higher ratings, and Specialty began to manufacture enough mixers to sell in a test market of nine cities. The demographic profile of the test-market cities was the same as that of the total population. Specialty was testing the effectiveness of three different point-of-purchase displays. The test market was set up as a randomized block design experiment. The nine cities were grouped into three categories from smallest to largest to remove the influence that the size of the city might have on the buying patterns of customers. The point-of-purchase displays were randomly assigned to the three cities in each block. The data from the test market in unit sales (thousands) were:

Small cities	15(A)	17(B)	14(C)
Medium cities	16(C)	14(A)	19(B)
Large cities	21(B)	16(A)	17(C)

where A, B, and C are the three types of displays.

Case Study Questions

1. Which display should Specialty use? Why?
2. Did the city size have any effect on the sale of the product? What reason can you give for the lack of effect or the effect?
3. Explain how Specialty could have used a test market of 20 cities to test five different displays.

S
P
S
S
X

Solution

Example 12.4

Example 12.4 was concerned with using one-factor ANOVA procedures when testing for a difference in two or more population means. The purpose was to test for a difference in job knowledge among three groups. The groups were (1) employees with a high-school diploma only, (2) employees with a bachelor's degree only, and (3) employees with a master's degree. The SPSSX program listing in Figure 12.7 was used to request the ANOVA table and in particular the F value and the p-value for F. Each line represents one card image to be entered:

The TITLE command names the SPSSX run.
The DATA LIST command gives each variable a name and describes the data as being in free form.

Figure 12.7

SPSSX program listing used to request ANOVA table, F value, and p-value for F.

```
TITLE    JOB KNOWLEDGE
DATA LIST FREE/EDUC GRADE
PRINT /EDUC GRADE
ONEWAY GRADE BY EDUC(1,3)/
BEGIN DATA
1 81
1 84
1 69
1 85
1 84
1 95
2 94
2 83
2 86
2 81
2 78
3 88
3 89
3 78
3 85
END DATA
```

The PRINT command requests a printout of the input data.

The ONEWAY command specifies a one-way analysis of variance model. GRADE is the dependent variable and EDUC is the independent variable. EDUC has minimum and maximum values of 1 and 3, respectively.

The BEGIN DATA command indicates to SPSSX that the input data immediately follow.

The next 15 lines are card images, which represent the level of education and the respective grade on the test. The first line indicates that the individual had a level 1 (high-school) education and scored 81 on the exam.

The END DATA statement indicates the end of the data card images.

Figure 12.8

Output obtained by executing the SPSSX program listing in Figure 12.7.

Figure 12.8 shows the output obtained by executing the program listing in Figure 12.7.

```
- - - - - - - - - - - - - - O N E W A Y - - - - - - - - - - - - - - -

       Variable  GRADE              ANALYSIS OF VARIANCE
    By Variable  EDUC

                              SUM OF        MEAN         F      F
           SOURCE      D.F.   SQUARES       SQUARES     RATIO  PROB.

  BETWEEN GROUPS        2     10.8000       5.4000      .1130  .8940

  WITHIN GROUPS        12    573.2000      47.7667

  TOTAL                14    584.0000                    F*    p-value
```

Solution

Section 12.3

The car-warranty example was based on a randomized block design. The purpose was to analyze ten individual assessments of new car warranties for three brands of automobiles. The three brands of automobiles represented three factor levels; the ten individuals represented ten blocks. Each observation consisted of an individual's assessment of the new car warranty for a particular brand. The SPSSX program listing in Figure 12.9 was used to request the ANOVA table and in particular

Figure 12.9

SPSSX program listing used to request the randomized block ANOVA table.

```
TITLE    WARRANTY ASSESSMENTS
DATA LIST FREE/PERSON BRAND SCORES
PRINT /PERSON BRAND SCORES
MANOVA SCORES BY PERSON(1,10) BRAND(1,3)/
  DESIGN=PERSON,BRAND/
BEGIN DATA
1 1 68        6 3 86
1 2 72        7 1 47
1 3 65        7 2 58
2 1 40        7 3 50
2 2 43        8 1 55
2 3 42        8 2 68
3 1 82        8 3 52
3 2 89        9 1 78
3 3 84        9 2 77
4 1 56        9 3 75
4 2 60       10 1 53
4 3 50       10 2 65
5 1 70       10 3 60
5 2 75       END DATA
5 3 68
6 1 80
6 2 91
```

the sum of squares for error, block, factor, and total. We were also interested in the F values for the brands and individuals, and their respective p-values. Each line represents one card image to be entered:

The TITLE command names the SPSSX run.

The DATA LIST command gives each variable a name and describes the data as being in free form.

The PRINT command requests a printout of the input data.

The MANOVA command specifies a multivariate ANOVA model. SCORES is the dependent variable; PERSON and BRAND are the factor variables. The PERSON and BRAND variables have minimum and maximum values of 1 to 10 and 1 to 3, respectively. The DESIGN subcommand specifies that only the main effect terms are to be included in the analysis.

The BEGIN DATA command indicates to SPSSX that the input data immediately follow.

The next 30 lines are card images. In this example, each line of data represents one rater's scoring of the warranty of one brand of automobile. For example, in line one the first 1 represents the first rater, the second 1 represents the first brand, and the 68 represents the warranty rating or score.

The END DATA statement indicates the end of the data card images.

Figure 12.10

Output obtained by executing the SPSSX program listing in Figure 12.9.

Figure 12.10 shows the output obtained by executing the program listing in Figure 12.9.

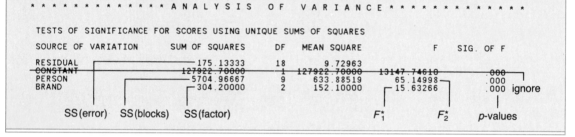

Solution

Example 12.4

Example 12.4 was concerned with using one-factor ANOVA procedures when testing for a difference in two or more population means. The purpose was to test for a difference in job knowledge among three groups. The groups were (1) employees with a high-school diploma only, (2) employees with a bachelor's degree only, (3) employees with a master's degree. The SAS program listing in Figure 12.11 was used to request the ANOVA table and in particular the F value and the p-value for F. Each line represents one card image to be entered:

The TITLE command names the SAS run.

The DATA command gives the data a name.

The INPUT command names and gives the correct order for the different fields on the data cards.

The CARDS command indicates to SAS that the input data immediately follow.

Figure 12.11

SAS program listing used to request ANOVA table, *F* value, and *p*-value for *F*.

```
TITLE    JOB KNOWLEDGE;
DATA EDUCEXP;
INPUT EDUC GRADE;
CARDS;
1  81
1  84
1  69
1  85
1  84
1  95
2  94
2  83
2  86
2  81
2  78
3  88
3  89
3  78
3  85
PROC PRINT;
PROC GLM;
 CLASS EDUC;
 MODEL GRADE=EDUC;
 MEANS EDUC;
```

S
A
S

The next 15 lines are card images. Each card image represents the level of education and the respective grade on the test. The first line indicates that the individual had a level 1 (high-school) education and scored 81 on the exam.

The PROC PRINT command directs SAS to list the data that were just entered.

The PROC GLM command requests the general linear regression model be executed. The CLASS subcommand identifies EDUC as the variable to be classified in this example. The MODEL subcommand indicates that the exam grade is the dependent variable and the education level is the independent variable.

Figure 12.12

Output obtained by executing the SAS program listing in Figure 12.11.

Figure 12.12 shows the output obtained by executing the program listing in Figure 12.11.

GENERAL LINEAR MODELS PROCEDURE

DEPENDENT VARIABLE: GRADE

SOURCE	DF	SUM OF SQUARES	MEAN SQUARE	F VALUE	PR > F	R-SQUARE	C.V.
MODEL	2	10.80000000	5.40000000	0.11	0.8940	0.018493	8.2278
ERROR	12	573.20000000	47.76666667		ROOT MSE		GRADE MEAN
CORRECTED TOTAL	14	584.00000000		F^*	6.91134333 *p*-value		84.00000000

SOURCE	DF	TYPE I SS	F VALUE	PR > F	DF	TYPE III SS	F VALUE	PR > F
EDUC	2	10.80000000	0.11	0.8940	2	10.80000000	0.11	0.8940

Solution

Section 12.3

The car warranty example was based on a randomized block design. The purpose was to analyze ten individual assessments of new car warranties for three brands of automobiles. The three brands of automobiles represented three factor levels; the ten individuals represented ten blocks. Each observation consisted of an individual's assessment of the new car warranty for a particular brand. The SAS program listing in Figure 12.13 was used to request the ANOVA table and in particular the sum of squares for error, block, factor, and total. We were also interested in the *F* values for the brands and individuals and their respective *p*-values. Each line represents one card image to be entered:

Figure 12.13

SAS program listing requesting the randomized block ANOVA table.

```
TITLE    WARRANTY ASSESSMENTS;
DATA AUTO;
  INPUT PERSON $ @;
  DO BRAND=1 TO 3;
    INPUT AUTO @;
    OUTPUT;
  END;
CARDS;
  1 68 72 65
    .
    .
    .
  10 53 65 60
PROC PRINT;
PROC GLM;
  CLASS BRAND PERSON;
  MODEL AUTO=PERSON BRAND/SOLUTION;
```

The TITLE command names the SAS run.

This DATA command gives the data to be analyzed the name AUTO.

This INPUT statement reads the PERSON field from the current record. (The $ means character data, the @ means that more data are still to come for this record.)

The DO command allows multiple brands for each person. The INPUT subcommand following the DO statement reads the three brand ratings from the same current record. The OUTPUT subcommand causes the observations to be transferred to the data set named AUTO. The END subcommand ends the loop through the ten individual raters.

The CARDS command indicates to SAS that the input data immediately follow.

The next ten lines are card images. In this example, each line of data represents one individual's assessment of the three brands. For example, the first individual's rating of the brand 1 warranty was 68, the brand 2 warranty was 72, and the brand 3 warranty was 65.

The PROC PRINT command directs SAS to list the data that were just read in.

The PROC GLM command requests the general linear regression model be executed. The CLASS subcommand identifies BRAND and PERSON as variables to be classified in our study. The MODEL subcommand indicates that AUTO (rating) is the dependent variable; PERSON and BRAND are the independent variables. The SOLUTION subcommand requests that the procedure print the parameter estimates.

Figure 12.14

Output obtained by executing the SAS program listing in Figure 12.13.

Figure 12.14 shows the output obtained by executing the program listing in Figure 12.13.

WARRANTY ASSESSMENTS
GENERAL LINEAR MODELS PROCEDURE

DEPENDENT VARIABLE: AUTO

SOURCE	DF	SUM OF SQUARES	MEAN SQUARE	F VALUE	PR > F	R-SQUARE	C.V.
MODEL	11	6009.16666667	546.28787879	56.15	0.0001	0.971681	4.7768
ERROR	18	175.13333333	9.72962963		ROOT MSE		AUTO MEAN
CORRECTED TOTAL	29	6184.30000000			3.11923542		65.30000000

SOURCE	DF	TYPE I SS	F VALUE	PR > F	DF	TYPE III SS	F VALUE	PR > F
PERSON	9	5704.96666667	65.15	0.0001	9	5704.96666667	65.15	0.0001
BRAND	2	304.20000000	15.63	0.0001	2	304.20000000	15.63	0.0001

SS(total)   SS(error)   SS(blocks)   SS(factor) F_1^* F_2^*

p-values

13

Applications of the Chi-Square Statistic

A Look Back/Introduction

We have examined several topics in both *descriptive* and *inferential* statistics. The descriptive area introduced you to the numeric (for example, mean, median, and variance) and the graphic (for example, histogram and scatter diagram) methods of describing data. In inferential statistics, we discussed point estimation, confidence intervals, and tests of hypothesis. In the remaining chapters, we will turn our attention to other applications of the material from these earlier chapters.

In Chapter 9, we introduced the chi-square (χ^2) distribution. We tested, for example, H_0: $\sigma^2 = 2.0$ versus H_a: $\sigma^2 \neq 2.0$. The corresponding test statistic had a chi-square distribution. This chapter will introduce you to additional applications of statistics by using the chi-square distribution to answer such questions as

Do reported percentages of market share accurately describe the product mix for the new cars sold this past year in Minneapolis, Minnesota?

Does a person's age have an influence on buying behavior?

13.1

Chi-Square Goodness-of-Fit Tests

The Binomial Situation

The binomial situation was introduced in Chapter 6, where the three following conditions had to be satisfied:

1. The experiment consists of n repetitions, called *trials*.
2. Each trial has two (and only two) outcomes, referred to as *success* and *failure*.
3. The probability of a success each trial is p, where p remains the same for each trial. In addition, the trials are *independent*. For a large finite population, p is the *proportion* of successes in this population.

Consequently, the binomial distribution applies to applications where there are only two possible outcomes, such as

the person selected is a male or a female.
the product tested is either defective or it is not.
a new-car buyer buys either an American-made car or a foreign-made car.

Inferences for the Binomial Situation   Estimating the binomial parameter, p, was covered in Chapter 11. We obtained a (random) sample of size n and observed the number of successes, x. Our estimate of p, the proportion of successes in the *population*, was $\hat{p} = x/n =$ the proportion of successes in the sample. We also discussed hypothesis testing for p. For example, we discussed a binomial situation in which a calculator was either defective (with probability p) or was not defective. The hypothetical value of p was 4%, and we determined whether the results of the sample (13 defectives out of 150) indicated a departure from this percentage. Here, $\hat{p} = 13/150 = .0867$. So, 8.67% of the sampled calculators were defective. Is this a large enough percentage for us to conclude that p is different from 4%, or is this large value of $\hat{p}$ just due to the fact that we tested a sample and not the entire population—that is, is this a sampling error?

The resulting value of the test statistic was

$$Z^* = \frac{\hat{p} - .04}{\sqrt{\dfrac{(.04)(.96)}{150}}}$$

$$= \frac{.0867 - .04}{.016} = 2.92$$

By comparing $Z^* = 2.92$ with the value in Table A-4 (1.96 using $\alpha = .05$), we rejected H_0; that is, the proportion of defective calculators was *not* 4%. The corresponding p-value was .0036.

Another Test for H_0: $p = p_0$ versus H_a: $p \neq p_0$ There is another test for a *two-tailed* test on p. This new test will extend easily to a situation in which there are *more than two possible outcomes* for each trial: the **multinomial situation**.

To demonstrate this new testing procedure, a **chi-square goodness-of-fit** test, look at the lot sampling example. Note that the population consists of two **cate-**

gories—defective (category 1) and nondefective (category 2). Let p_1 = the proportion of defectives (category 1) in the population ($= p$ in the previous solution) and p_2 = the proportion of nondefectives (category 2) in the population ($= 1 - p$ in the previous solution).

We *observed* 13 sample values in category 1 (defective) and 137 in category 2. So define

$$O_1 = 13$$

$$O_2 = 137$$

How many units do we *expect* to see in each category if H_0 is *true*? The hypotheses here can be written

$$H_0: p_1 = .04, \ p_2 = .96$$

$$H_a: p_1 \neq .04, \ p_2 \neq .96$$

This means that if H_0 is true, then, on the average, 4% of the sample values should be defective (category 1) and 96% should be nondefective (category 2). Define

E_1 = expected number of sample values in category 1 (if H_0 is true)
  $= (150)(.04) = 6$

E_2 = expected number of sample values in category 2 (if H_0 is true)
  $= (150)(.96) = 144$

We next define a test statistic that has an approximate chi-square distribution

$$\chi^2 = \sum \frac{(O - E)^2}{E} \tag{13-1}$$

where the summation is over all categories ($= 2$ here). In previous uses of this distribution, its shape depended on the sample size, specified by the degrees of freedom (df). Now the shape depends on the number of categories, where

$$df = \text{number of categories} - 1$$

For the binomial situation this is

$$df = 2 - 1 = 1$$

Therefore, for any *binomial* application, the test statistic in equation 13-1 has a *chi-square distribution with 1 df*.

Example 13.1

Analyze the lot sampling data using the chi-square test statistic and a significance level of $\alpha = .05$.

Solution

Step 1. The hypotheses are

$$H_0: p_1 = .04, \ p_2 = .96$$

$$H_a: p_1 \neq .04, \ p_2 \neq .96$$

Step 2. The test statistic is

$$\chi^2 = \sum \frac{(O - E)^2}{E}$$

$$= \frac{(O_1 - E_1)^2}{E_1} + \frac{(O_2 - E_2)^2}{E_2}$$

Step 3. If H_0 is not true (H_a is true), we expect the observed values to be different from the expected values. This would result in a *large* value for χ^2, so the procedure is to reject H_0 if the chi-square test statistic lies in the *right* tail. Consequently, the rejection region is

Reject H_0 if $\chi^2 > \chi^2_{.05,1}$

where $\chi^2_{.05,1}$ is the χ^2 value having a right-tail area of .05 with 1 *df*. Using Table A-6, this is 3.84. Therefore, the test is

Reject H_0 if $\chi^2 > 3.84$

Step 4. We have

$$O_1 = 13, \quad E_1 = 6$$

$$O_2 = 137, E_2 = 144$$

(Note that $O_1 + O_2 = E_1 + E_2 = n = 150$.) The calculated value of the test statistic is

$$\chi^{2*} = \frac{(13 - 6)^2}{6} + \frac{(137 - 144)^2}{144}$$

$$= 8.17 + .34$$

$$= 8.51$$

This value is larger than 3.84, so we reject H_0.

Step 5. We conclude, as before, that the proportion of defectives (p_1) is not 4%. ●

The *p*-value for example 13.1 using the chi-square analysis is shown in Figure 13.1; it is the shaded area to the right of 8.51. Using Table A-6, all we can say is that this value is less than .005. The actual value is .0036 (calculated using a statistical software package). This is the *same p*-value as obtained when Z^* was used to perform this test of hypothesis.

Figure 13.1

p-value for example 13.1 using the chi-square analysis.

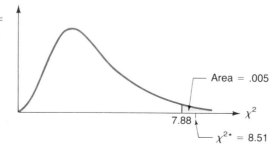

In the lot sampling examples, we observe some utterly fascinating (would you believe, interesting?) parallels with Chapter 12. In Chapter 12, we noted that, when using the F test from the ANOVA procedure to test H_0: $\mu_1 = \mu_2$, we obtained an F value that was the *square* of the t value obtained using the corresponding t test. Also, the value from the F table used to define the rejection region was the square of the corresponding t value. This relationship held only when testing the equality of two means. Finally, the p-values from the two tests were identical; it made no difference which test we used for a two-tailed test on two means because the results were the same for both procedures. However, the ANOVA technique also could be used for comparing the means of more than two populations.

Using the results from the lot sampling example in this chapter, we again find that:

1. $\chi^{2*} = 8.51 \cong (2.92)^2 = (Z^*)^2$.
2. The table values for the rejection region for Z test $= 1.96$ and for χ^2 test $= 3.84 = (1.96)^2$.
3. The p-value for each test was the same.

So again we have two testing procedures that produce identical conclusions. The chi-square test, however, extends easily to the multinomial situation. The chi-square goodness-of-fit test is an *extension* of the Z test used to test a binomial parameter. Furthermore, there is a definite relationship between the standard normal distribution (Z) and the chi-square distribution: the *square* of Z always is a chi-square random variable with 1 df.

Testing H_0: $p = p_0$ Versus H_a: $p \neq p_0$

USING Z TEST

Test statistic

$$Z = \frac{\hat{p} - p_0}{\sqrt{\dfrac{p_0(1 - p_0)}{n}}}$$

Rejection region

Reject H_0 if $|Z| > Z_{\alpha/2}$

(use Table A-4)

USING χ^2 TEST

Test statistic

$$\chi^2 = \frac{(O_1 - E_1)^2}{E_1} + \frac{(O_2 - E_2)^2}{E_2}$$

$$= \sum \frac{(O - E)^2}{E}$$

Rejection region

Reject H_0 if $\chi^2 > \chi^2_{\alpha,1}$

(use Table A-6)

The Multinomial Situation

The multinomial situation is identical to the binomial situation, except that there are k possible outcomes on each trial rather than two. Here k is any integer that is greater than 2.

Assume that a recent survey indicated the following percent of market share for U.S. auto manufacturers:

GA	62.5
K	22.6
L	11.5
M	1.4
Other	2.0
	100

An executive at GA questions whether these percentages apply to the new cars sold during the past year in Minneapolis, Minnesota. Obtaining a random sample of 500 new car registrations from that year, she observes the following frequencies of cars sold:

GA	290
K	125
L	65
M	10
Other	10
	500

The assumptions necessary for a multinomial situation are:

1. The experiment consists of n independent repetitions (trials).
2. There are k possible outcomes (categories) on each trial.
3. The probabilities of the k outcomes are denoted $p_1, p_2, \ldots, p_k$, where these proportions remain the same on each trial. Also, $p_1 + p_2 + \ldots + p_k = 1$.

The k random variables for this situation are the k observed values, where

O_1 = the observed number of sample values in category 1

O_2 = the observed number of sample values in category 2

.

.

.

O_k = the observed number of sample values in category k

For this example, $n = 500$ trials, where each trial consists of obtaining a new car registration and observing in which of the $k = 5$ categories this new car lies. Assuming these registrations are obtained in a *random* manner (not the first 500 cars in May, for example), then these trials are independent. Also,

p_1 = the proportion of cars sold in Minneapolis that were GA cars for that year

p_2 = the proportion of cars sold in Minneapolis that were K cars for that year

.

.

.

The five random variables here are

O_1 = the number of GA cars in the sample

O_2 = the number of K cars in the sample

.

.

.

Thus, this example fits the assumptions for the multinomial situation.

Hypothesis Testing for a Multinomial Situation The hypotheses for the Minneapolis market share example would be

H_0: $p_1 = .625$, $p_2 = .226$, $p_3 = .115$, $p_4 = .014$, $p_5 = .02$

H_a: at least one of the p_i's is incorrect

Notice that H_a is *not* $p_1 \neq .625$, $p_2 \neq .226$, . . . , $p_5 \neq .02$. This is too strong and is not the complement of H_0.

Let $p_{1,0}$ be any specified value of p_1, $p_{2,0}$ any specified value of p_2, and so on. The multinomial goodness-of-fit hypotheses are

H_0: $p_1 = p_{1,0}$, $p_2 = p_{2,0}$, . . . , $p_k = p_{k,0}$

H_a: at least one of the p_i's is incorrect

Using the observed values (O_1, O_2, . . .), the point estimates here are

$\hat{p}_1$ = estimate of $p_1 = O_1/n$

$\hat{p}_2$ = estimate of $p_2 = O_2/n$

and so on.

To test H_0 versus H_a, we use the previously stated chi-square statistic. To define the rejection region, notice that, when H_a is true, we would expect the O's and E's to be "far apart" because the E's are determined by assuming that H_0 is true. In other words, if H_a is true, the chi-square test statistic should be *large*. Consequently, we always reject H_0 when χ^{2*} lies in the *right tail* when using this particular statistic.

To test H_0 versus H_a, compute

$$\chi^2 = \sum \frac{(O - E)^2}{E} \qquad (13\text{-}2)$$

where

1. The summation is across all categories (outcomes).
2. The O's are the *observed* frequencies in each category using the sample.
3. The E's are the *expected* frequencies in each category if H_0 is true, so

$E_1 = np_{1,0}$

$E_2 = np_{2,0}$

$E_3 = np_{3,0}$

.

.

.

4. The df for the chi-square statistic are $k - 1$, where k is the number of categories.

To carry out the test,

Reject H_0 if $\chi^2 > \chi^2_{\alpha, df}$

Notice that the hypothetical proportions (probabilities) for each of the categories *are specified in H_0*. Consequently, we will complete the analysis by concluding that at least one of the proportions is incorrect (we reject H_0) or that there is not enough evidence to conclude that these proportions are incorrect (we fail to reject H_0). (We do not *accept H_0*; we never conclude that these specified proportions *are* correct. We act like the juror who acquits a defendant, not because he or she is convinced that this person is innocent but rather because there was not sufficient evidence for conviction.)

When we introduced the ANOVA technique, we mentioned that this procedure allowed us to determine whether many population means were equal using a *single* test. This was preferable to using many t tests to test the equality of two means, one pair at a time; these tests are not independent, and the overall significance level is difficult to determine. We encounter the same situation here. It is much better to use a chi-square goodness-of-fit test to test *all* of the proportions at once rather than using many Z tests to test the individual proportions.

Example 13.2

What do the observed number of cars sold in our market share example tell us about the mix of new car sales in Minneapolis for that year? Do they conform to the percentages for all U.S. auto sales? Use a significance level of $\alpha = .05$.

Solution

Step 1. Let p_1 = proportion of all Minneapolis new car sales that are GA, p_2 are K, p_3 are L, p_4 are M, and p_5 are all other new (U.S. made) cars. The hypotheses under investigation are

H_0: $p_1 = .625$, $p_2 = .226$, $p_3 = .115$, $p_4 = .014$, $p_5 = .02$

H_a: at least one of these p_i's is incorrect

Step 2. The test statistic will be

$$\chi^2 = \sum \frac{(O - E)^2}{E}$$

where the summation is over the five categories.

Step 3. Your rejection region here is

Reject H_0 if $\chi^2 > \chi^2_{\alpha, df}$

The df are (number of categories) $- 1$, so $df = 5 - 1 = 4$. The chi-square value from Table A-6 is $\chi^2_{.05, 4} = 9.49$, and the test is

Reject H_0 if $\chi^2 > 9.49$

Step 4. The observed values are

$O_1 = 290, O_2 = 125, O_3 = 65, O_4 = 10, O_5 = 10$

The expected values when H_0 is true are obtained by multiplying $n = 500$ by each of the proportions in H_0. So,

$$E_1 = (500)(.625) = 312.5$$
$$E_2 = (500)(.226) = 113$$
$$E_3 = (500)(.115) = 57.5$$
$$E_4 = (500)(.014) = 7$$
$$E_5 = (500)(.02) = \underline{10}$$
$$500$$

Note that we do not round off the expected values because they are *averages*.

The computed value of the chi-square test statistic is

$$\chi^{2*} = \frac{(290 - 312.5)^2}{312.5} + \frac{(125 - 113)^2}{113} + \frac{(65 - 57.5)^2}{57.5} + \frac{(10 - 7)^2}{7} + \frac{(10 - 10)^2}{10}$$

$$= 5.16$$

Because 5.16 does not exceed 9.49, we fail to reject H_0.

Step 5. There is no evidence to suggest that the Minneapolis car sales differ from the U.S. mixture. In other words, the observed values were "close enough" to the expected values under H_0 to let this hypothesis stand. ●

In example 13.2, the proportions under investigation were directly specified. We can also use the chi-square statistic when the proportions are implied.

Example 13.3

A manufacturer of patio furniture is interested in whether people have a preference among the three available chair colors—yellow, green, and blue. A random sample of the orders from last year revealed the following number of chairs ordered of each color: yellow, 485; green, 405; blue, 310; total = 1200. What can you conclude, using $\alpha = .01$?

Solution

Step 1. Let p_1 = proportion of all chairs ordered that were yellow, p_2 = proportion green, and p_3 = proportion blue. If there is no color preference, then each of these proportions will be 1/3. This provides the values for H_0:

$$H_0: p_1 = 1/3, \, p_2 = 1/3, \, p_3 = 1/3$$
$$H_a: \text{at least one of these proportions is incorrect}$$

Steps 2, 3. The test will be to

$$\text{Reject } H_0 \text{ if } \chi^2 > \chi^2_{.01,2} = 9.21$$

because $df = k - 1 = 3 - 1 = 2$. The value of χ^2 is determined from equation 13-2.

Step 4. The observed and expected values are

O	E (if H_0 is true)	$\hat{p}$
$O_1 = 485$	$E_1 = (1200)(1/3) = 400$	$485/1200 = .404$
$O_2 = 405$	$E_2 = (1200)(1/3) = 400$	$405/1200 = .338$
$O_3 = \underline{310}$	$E_3 = (1200)(1/3) = \underline{400}$	$310/1200 = \underline{.258}$
1200	1200	1.0

$$\chi^{2*} = \frac{(485 - 400)^2}{400} + \frac{(405 - 400)^2}{400} + \frac{(310 - 400)^2}{400}$$

$$= 18.06 + .06 + 20.25$$

$$= 38.4$$

So we reject H_0 because $38.4 > 9.21$.

Step 5. There *is* a significant color preference. Your next step should be to examine the three values making up this large χ^2 value. This large value is due to the 18.06 (yellow was *more* popular than expected under H_0) and the 20.25 (blue was *less* popular than expected under H_0). This can also be seen in the $\hat{p}$ values from step 4. ●

The p-value for the results in example 13.3 is shown in Figure 13.2. Using Table A-6 and 2 *df,* the largest value here is 10.6, with a corresponding right-tail area of .005. All you can say using this table is that the p-value is $< .005$. At any rate, it is very small and would lead you to reject H_0 for *any* reasonable value of α.

Pooling Categories When using the chi-square procedure of comparing observed and expected values, we determine the difference between these two values for each category, square it, and *divide by the expected value, E.* If the value of E is very small (say, less than 5), then this produces an extremely *large* contribution to the final χ^2 value from this category. In other words, this small expected value produces an inflated chi-square value, with the result that we reject H_0 when perhaps we should not have. To prevent this from occurring, we use the rule: When using equation 13-2, each expected value, E, should be at least 5.

If you encounter an application where one or more of the expected values are less than 5, you can handle this situation by *pooling* your categories such that each of the new categories has an expected value that is at least 5.

Example 13.4

The analysis in example 13.2 was repeated for a much smaller community using 200 observations (rather than $n = 500$). The following mixture was observed (number of cars sold):

GA	95
K	50
L	41
M	5
Other	9
	200

Figure 13.2

Shaded area is p-value for example 13.3.

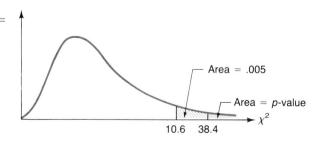

Do the data from this community appear to fit the U.S. proportions of 62.5% for GA, 22.6% for K, and so on? Use $\alpha = .05$.

Solution

Category	Observed (O)	Expected (E), if H_0 is true
GA	$O_1 = 95$	$E_1 = (200)(.625) = 125$
K	$O_2 = 50$	$E_2 = (200)(.226) = 45.2$
L	$O_3 = 41$	$E_3 = (200)(.115) = 23$
M	$O_4 = 5$	$E_4 = (200)(.014) = 2.8$
Other	$O_5 = \underline{\ \ 9}$	$E_5 = (200)(0.02) = \underline{\ \ 4}$
	200	200

Notice that the last two expected values are less than 5. These two categories need to be pooled (combined) into a new category, which we will label category 4: other. The new summary is

Category	Observed (O)	Expected (E), if H_0 is true
GA	95	125
K	50	45.2
L	41	23
Other	14 (= 5 + 9)	6.8 (= 2.8 + 4)

Now each of the expected values is at least 5, and we can continue the analysis. The hypotheses using the four categories will be

H_0: $p_1 = .625$, $p_2 = .226$, $p_3 = .115$, $p_4 = .034$

H_a: at least one of the proportions is incorrect

The value of p_4 represents the proportion of all other cars (including those from M) sold in this community. The hypothetical value of p_4 becomes $.014 + .020 = .034$.
The computed chi-square value is now

$$\chi^{2*} \frac{(95 - 125)^2}{125} + \frac{(50 - 45.2)^2}{45.2} + \frac{(41 - 23)^2}{23} + \frac{(14 - 6.8)^2}{6.8}$$

$$= 7.2 + .51 + 14.09 + 7.62$$

$$= 29.4$$

This exceeds the Table A-6 value of $\chi^2_{.05,3} = 7.81$, so we reject H_0 and conclude that we do have a significant departure from the U.S. percentages in this community. The largest contributor to this chi-square value is from the L category, which exceeds expectations by 18 cars (78% more than expected if H_0 is true). ●

Testing a Hypothesis about a Distributional Form

In this discussion of the goodness-of-fit test, we will examine such questions as:

Is it true that these data came from a binomial distribution?
Does this particular set of data violate the assumption that the number of defects in this product follow a Poisson distribution?
Is there any reason to doubt the assumption that the weight of all Rice Krinkle cereal boxes follows a normal distribution using a recently obtained sample of boxes?

The first two questions concern *discrete* distributions (binomial and Poisson). The final question is concerned with whether the data came from a particular *continuous* (in this case, normal) distribution. We will illustrate the chi-square technique using a goodness-of-fit test for a discrete situation. (Goodness-of-fit tests for the normal distribution will be illustrated in exercises 13.13, 13.14, and 13.15.

Assume that Blitz laundry detergent is well known for its obnoxious commercials, which advertise that 20% of all Blitz boxes contain a valuable discount coupon. A recent study obtained a random sample of ten Blitz boxes from each of 100 different stores. The results were

Of 10 Boxes, Number Containing Coupons	Number of Stores
0	9
1	31
2	29
3	18
>3	13
	100

We wish to know whether these data appear to come from a binomial distribution with $p = .2$, using $\alpha = .05$.

Your immediate reaction may well be that this problem does not fit a multinomial situation. However, there are 100 independent trials, each trial consisting of randomly selecting ten boxes of Blitz detergent. Also, we can set up 5 categories here, namely:

Category 1: Observe 0 coupons in the ten boxes (probability p_1)
Category 2: Observe 1 coupon in the ten boxes (probability p_2)
Category 3: Observe 2 coupons in the ten boxes (probability p_3)
Category 4: Observe 3 coupons in the ten boxes (probability p_4)
Category 5: Observe >3 coupons in the ten boxes (probability p_5)

So we *do* have a multinomial situation here. The hypotheses can be stated as

H_0: the data follow a binomial distribution with $p = .2$

H_a: the data do not follow a binomial distribution with $p = .2$

If H_0 is true, then how often should we observe zero coupons in ten boxes? Each multinomial trial fits a binomial situation, where a success consists of a box containing a coupon. We repeat the trial ten times and count the number of successes (coupons). According to Table A-1, with $n = 10$ and probability of success $p = .2$, you should observe zero coupons out of ten boxes 10.7% of the time. So, if H_0 is true, $p_1 = .107$. Similarly, if H_0 is true, we should see one success out of ten trials 26.8% of the time. In other words, $p_2 = .268$. Therefore, another way to state your hypotheses is

H_0: $p_1 = .107$, $p_2 = .268$, $p_3 = .302$, $p_4 = .201$, $p_5 = .122$

H_a: at least one of these p_i's is incorrect

We obtain p_5 by finding the probability of more than three successes in ten trials. This is

$$1 - (\text{probability of 3 or less}) = 1 - (p_1 + p_2 + p_3 + p_4) = 1 - .878 = .122$$

So this is a multinomial test of hypothesis in disguise. Next, we compute the expected values, E.

Category	Observed (*O*)	Expected (*E*), if H_0 is true
0 boxes	9	$(100)(.107) = 10.7$
1 box	31	$(100)(.268) = 26.8$
2 boxes	29	$(100)(.302) = 30.2$
3 boxes	18	$(100)(.201) = 20.1$
> 3 boxes	13	$(100)(.122) = 12.2$
	100	100

Make sure that all the *E*'s (do not worry about the *O*'s) are at least 5. In this case, all *E*'s are greater than 5, so no pooling of categories is necessary.

To define the rejection region, we notice that there are $k = 5$ categories. So the degrees of freedom in the chi-square statistic is $df = k - 1 = 4$. Also, $\chi^2_{.05,4} = 9.49$, and so the test will be

Reject H_0 if $\chi^2 > 9.50$

The value of our test statistic is

$$\chi^{2*} = \frac{(9 - 10.7)^2}{10.7} + \frac{(31 - 26.8)^2}{26.8} + \cdots + \frac{(13 - 12.2)^2}{12.2}$$

$$= 1.25$$

Because 1.25 is less than 9.49, we fail to reject H_0 and conclude that there is no evidence to suggest that these data have violated the binomial assumption. These 100 observations suggest that we have no reason to accuse Blitz of false advertising for their claim that 20% of their boxes contain coupons.

In summary, suppose you are trying to perform a test of hypothesis on a binomial parameter, *p*—say, H_0: $p = .2$.

1. If we are using a *single* sample of size *n*, then the results of Chapter 11 apply; we are dealing with a binomial situation.
2. If we are using *many* samples of size *n*, then the results of this section apply; this problem can be expressed as a multinomial situation. The previous example provides an illustration of this type of situation.

Distributional Form with Unknown Parameters In the Blitz cereal example, H_0 not only stated that the data followed a binomial distribution, it also specified a value of the binomial parameter *p* (namely, $p = .2$). Your only concern often is whether the data follow a particular distribution (such as binomial, Poisson, or normal), and the value of the corresponding parameters is not important.

For example, say that the manager of Case Electronics has always assumed that the weekly sales of his top-of-the-line telephone answering machine followed a Poisson distribution. Data from a 50-week period were gathered, with the following results:

Units Sold	Number of Weeks	Units Sold	Number of Weeks
0	1	6	5
1	3	7	3
2	6	8	4
3	11	> 8	0
4	10		50
5	7		

How can we test the hypothesis that the number of units sold follows a Poisson distribution, using $\alpha = .1$?

The correct hypotheses here are

H_0: weekly sales follow a Poisson distribution

H_a: weekly sales do not follow a Poisson distribution

The probability function for the Poisson distribution has one parameter, μ, because this function (from equation 6-12) is given by

$$P(X = x) = \frac{\mu^x e^{-\mu}}{x!}$$

for $x = 0, 1, 2, \ldots$, where $X =$ the number of units sold during a particular week.

However, the value of μ was not specified in H_0. In this case, we estimate any unknown parameter (μ, here) from the sample information and replace each parameter by its estimate in the probability function. In this way, we can estimate all of the expected frequencies ($E_1, E_2, E_3, \ldots$).

Whenever you estimate unknown parameters for use with the chi-square test, you need to *adjust the corresponding degrees of freedom, df.* In general, the df for the chi-square goodness-of-fit statistic is given by

$$df = (\text{number of classes}) - 1 - (\text{number of estimated parameters})$$

For the Poisson situation, you are estimating only one parameter, μ, and so the *df* $= (\text{number of classes}) - 1 - 1 = (\text{number of classes}) - 2$. The same argument would hold true for a test of hypothesis on a binomial distribution where the single parameter, p, was unspecified in H_0 and was instead estimated from the sample information.

Estimating μ   Because μ is the mean of the telephone answering machine sales population, we estimate it using the average (mean) of the sample. In the sample, we observe one value of zero, three values of one, six values of two, and so on for all 50 values. This means that the sample average, our estimate of μ, will be

$$\hat{\mu} = \frac{(0)(1) + (1)(3) + (2)(6) + \ldots + (8)(4)}{50}$$

$$= \frac{206}{50} = 4.12$$

Rounding this to $\hat{\mu} = 4.1$, the estimated probability function is

$$P(X = x) = \frac{(4.1)^x e^{-4.1}}{x!}$$

for $x = 0, 1, 2, \ldots$.

We can now use Table A-3 (the Poisson table) to estimate the expected number of weeks with 0 sales, with one sale, and so on. We are *estimating* each expected value, so we denote each of them as $\hat{E}$.

X	$P(X = x)$	$\hat{E}$		O
0	.0166	$(.0166)(50) =$	.83	1
1	.0679	$(.0679)(50) =$	3.39	3
2	.1393	$(.1393)(50) =$	6.97	6
3	.1904	$(.1904)(50) =$	9.52	11

X	$P(X = x)$	$\hat{E}$		O
4	.1951	$(.1951)(50) =$	9.76	10
5	.1600	$(.1600)(50) =$	8.00	7
6	.1093	$(.1093)(50) =$	5.46	5
7	.0640	$(.0640)(50) =$	3.20	3
8	.0328	$(.0328)(50) =$	1.64	4
> 8	.0246	$(.0246)(50) =$	1.23	0
	1		50	50

Notice that, for the category $X > 8$, the corresponding probability is $1 - (.0166 + .0679 + \ldots + .0640 + .0328) = .0246$.

The next step always is to check your expected frequencies $(\hat{E})$ to see if pooling is necessary. Each $\hat{E}$ value must be at least 5, so it is necessary to pool the first three classes $(.83 + 3.39 + 6.97)$ and the last three classes $(3.20 + 1.64 + 1.23)$. Now you can evaluate the chi-square statistic.

X	$\hat{E}$	O	$(O - \hat{E})$	$(O - \hat{E})^2/\hat{E}$
≤ 2	11.19	10	-1.19	.127
3	9.52	11	1.48	.230
4	9.76	10	.24	.006
5	8.00	7	-1.00	.125
6	5.46	5	$-.46$	.039
≥ 7	6.07	7	.93	.142
	50	50	0	.669
			(check)	

$$\chi^2 = \sum \frac{(O - \hat{E})^2}{\hat{E}} = .669$$

The degrees of freedom for the corresponding test will be

$df =$ (number of classes) $- 1 -$ (number of estimated parameters)

$\quad = 6 - 1 - 1 = 4$

The resulting test, using Table A-6 and $\alpha = .1$, will be

Reject H_0 if $\chi^2 > 7.779$

Because $.669 < 7.779$, we fail to reject H_0 and conclude that there is not enough evidence to indicate that the Poisson distribution assumption is incorrect.

Exercises

13.1 After the label, "Warning: The Surgeon General Has Determined That Cigarette Smoking Is Dangerous to Your Health" was added to cigarette packages, a chapter of the American Heart Association wished to know whether the proportion of the population that were current smokers in a particular metropolitan area was equal to 35%. A random sample of 100 observations was taken and the estimate of the proportion of smokers was 0.31. Let the significance level be .05.

a. Test the belief that the population proportion of smokers is equal to 35%. Use the Z test from section 11.2.

b. Use the chi-square goodness-of-fit test to test the hypothesis in question a.

c. What is the relationship between the test statistics in questions a and b?

13.2 A car-insurance–company owner believes that 20% of drivers under 25 years of age have been in exactly one automobile accident in the past 2 years. She also believes that 15% of the drivers under 25 have been in exactly two automobile accidents in the past 2 years. Finally, she believes that 10% of the drivers under 25 have been in more than two automobile accidents in the past 2 years. A survey of 300 randomly selected drivers under 25 years of age was taken. Test the beliefs using the following data and letting the significance level be 0.10.

No Accident	1 Accident	2 Accidents	>2 Accidents
153	68	51	28

13.3 In exercise 13.2, the equality of proportions for any two categories can be tested using the Z test in section 11.2. Is there any difference in testing the equality of two proportions one pair at a time and testing all the proportions at once using the chi-square goodness-of-fit test? Is the overall significance level the same in both cases?

13.4 Barton's Food Store carries three brands of milk. Recently, Barton had been getting numerous complaints about the milk being spoiled after being sold to the customer. Barton decided to categorize 30 randomly selected complaints to see whether they were equally divided among the three brands of milk. Using the accompanying data, test that the complaints are equally divided among the three brands. Let the significance level be .05.

Brand A	Brand B	Brand C
7	13	14

13.5 A stockbroker believes that, when too many of the stockmarket newsletters are bullish on the market (that is, they predict that stock prices will go higher), the stockmarket will most likely fall. Thirty-two randomly selected stockmarket newsletters were each placed in one of three categories:

Bearish on Stockmarket	Neutral on Stockmarket	Bullish on Stockmarket
9	10	13

Test the null hypothesis that the newsletters are equally divided among the three categories. Use a .05 significance level.

13.6 A manufacturer of bleach sold the same bleach to three different companies, placing their respective brand names on the bottle. A marketing-research firm wanted to know whether the same amount of bleach would be sold from each of the three brands, provided the price was the same for each brand. Supplies of the three brands of bleach were placed on a supermarket shelf. By the end of the month, 335 bottles of bleach were sold, as follows:

Bleach X	Bleach Y	Bleach Z
105	133	97

Test the null hypothesis that each brand sells equally well. Use a significance level of .10.

13.7 A soft-drink company believes that people are particular about the type of sweetener used in the soft drinks. The manager of the marketing department believes that 50% of the people prefer sugar, 35% prefer aspartame, 10% prefer saccharin, and 5% have no preference. Thirty people who regularly drank sweetened soft drinks were randomly selected. Using the following data and a significance level of 5%, test the manager's claim. (Do any of the categories need to be pooled?)

Sugar	Aspartame	Saccharin	No Preference
12	11	5	2

13.8 A nutritionist surveyed 200 randomly selected athletes to find out how concerned the athletes were about their food intake. These athletes responded that they were very, somewhat, little, or not at all concerned about the quality of food they ate; the results were 65, 50, 45, and 40, respectively. Test the hypothesis that athletes are equally divided among the four categories. Use a 10% significance level.

13.9 Electrical fuses are packaged in lots of 20. The quality-control department claims that only about 10% of the fuses are defective on the average for each package of 20 fuses. A random sample of 40 packages was selected and the results were:

Defective Fuses	Packages
0	7
1	12
2	10
3	7
4	1
5	1
>5	2

Do these data appear to have come from a binomial distribution with $p = .10$? Use a significance level of .05.

13.10 An auditor believes that the number of errors per 25 invoices contained in the records of a discount furniture store chain follow a Poisson distribution with a mean of 2.2. To test the auditor's belief, 25 stores were randomly selected and the number of errors were tabulated.

Errors per 25 Invoices	Stores
0	3
1	5
2	7
3	4
4	2
5	2
6	1
>6	1

Do these data appear to have come from a Poisson distribution with a mean of 2.2? Use a .10 significance level.

13.11 On each flight of Astral Airways, 12 randomly selected passengers are asked if they would be willing to pay a 5% air fare increase to fly on an airline that had an open bar in the airplane. Results of the survey from 50 different flights were as follows:

Yes Answers	Flights
0	3
1	10
2	13
3	12
4	7
5	3
6	2
>6	0

Use a chi-square goodness-of-fit test to determine whether these data came from a binomial distribution. Let the significance level be .05. [Hint: p must be estimated using (total number of people who said yes)/(total number asked).]

13.12 In an effort to monitor the service of its employees, a parcel-delivery firm keeps a tally of the number of packages misrouted each week at each of its 25 distribution centers, with the following results:

Misrouted Packages	Distribution Centers
0	5
1	6
2	8
3	6
>3	0

Do these data appear to come from a Poisson distribution? Use a .05 significance level.

13.13 To perform certain statistical tests on a set of data, the assumption of normality is required. It is thought that the percentage gain over the past 3 years in mutual funds that have balanced portfolios of both long-term–growth stocks and income-oriented stocks is normally distributed, with a mean of 35% and a standard deviation of 10%. A sample of 75 mutual funds of this type is selected. To test this assumption of normality, a chi-square goodness-of-fit test can be used. For the intervals listed, probabilities can be found from the normal table (Table A-4). To find the expected frequencies in the third column, the sample size is multiplied by each probability. If the differences between the observed and expected frequencies are large, then the chi-square statistic based on the observed and expected frequencies would be large and would cause the null hypothesis, which is that the data was sampled from a normally distributed population with mean = 35 and standard deviation = 10, to be rejected.

Interval	Probability	Expected Frequency	Observed Frequency
less than 20	.0668	5.01	7
20 and less than 30	.2417	18.1275	15
30 and less than 40	.3830	28.725	26
40 and less than 50	.2417	18.1275	21
50 or more	.0668	5.01	6

At the 5% significance level, complete the chi-square goodness-of-fit test by calculating the chi-square statistic presented in the chapter and by using a tabulated chi-square value for the critical value of the rejection region. The degrees of freedom is taken to be equal to the number of intervals minus one.

13.14 The monthly maintenance time on a particular machine at a manufacturing plant is believed to be normally distributed with a mean of 6 hours and a standard deviation of 1.5 hours. A sample of 45 months is selected and the maintenance time is recorded (in hours). From the following data, use the chi-square goodness-of-fit procedure in exercise 13.13 to test whether there is enough evidence to support the hypothesis that the maintenance time is not normally distributed with a mean of 6 and a standard deviation of 1.5. Use a 10% significance level.

Interval	Observed Frequency
less than 5	10
5 hours but less than 6	6
6 hours but less than 6.5	5
6.5 hours but less than 7	7
7 hours but less than 8	6
8 hours or more	11

13.15 The weekly traffic flow between 8 A.M. and 6 P.M. at a certain intersection in Oklahoma City is believed to be normally distributed, with a mean of 65,000 cars and a standard deviation of 12,000. Fifty weeks are randomly selected over the past 3 years. Using the following data and the chi-square goodness-of-fit test procedure in exercise 13.13, is there sufficient evidence to conclude that the traffic flow (in thousands of cars) is not normally distributed with a mean of 65 (thousand) and a standard deviation of 12 (thousand)? Use a .10 significance level.

Traffic flow	Observed Frequency
less than 50	9
50 and less than 60	10
60 and less than 70	11
70 and less than 80	10
80 or more	10

13.2

Chi-Square Tests of Independence

In the previous section, we classified each member of a population into one of many categories. This was a one-dimensional situation because each member was classified using only *one* criterion (brand, color, and so on). In this section, we extend this idea to a two-dimensional situation in which each element in the population is classified according to two criteria, such as sex and income level (high, medium, or low). The question of interest will be, are these two variables (classifications) *independent*? For example, if sex and income level are not independent, then perhaps there is sex discrimination present in the salary structure of a company. If a person's salary was not affected by (related to) sex, then these two classifications *would* be independent.

In Chapter 5, we examined a survey concerned with the age and sex of the purchasers of a recently released microcomputer. The results were summarized in a *contingency* (or *cross-tab*) table. This table consists of **cells**, where each cell contains the **frequency** of people in the sample that satisfy each of the various cross-classifications.

Sex	Age < 30	Age 30–45	Age > 45	Total
MALE	60	20	40	120
FEMALE	40	30	10	80
TOTAL	100	50	50	200

This is a 2 × 3 contingency table. It shows that there were 60 people who were both male *and* under 30. In Chapter 5, we selected a person at random from this group of 200 and determined various probabilities, such as the probability that this person is both a male and over 45 years. Here we will not select a person at random. Instead, we will view these data as the results of a particular experiment (survey) and attempt to determine whether the variables—age and sex—are independent for this application. Put another way, is the age structure of the male buyers the same as that for the female purchasers? The hypotheses are

H_0: the classifications (age and sex) are independent

H_a: the classifications are dependent

Deriving a Test of Hypothesis for Independent Classifications

Calculating the Expected Values We want to decide whether the data about the purchasers exhibit random variation or a pattern of some type due to a dependency between age and sex. If these classifications *are* independent (H_0 is true), how many people would you expect in each cell? Consider the upper right cell, which shows males over 45 years. The expected number of sample observations in this cell is $200 \cdot P$(sampled purchaser is a male and over 45). Assuming independence, this is $200 \cdot P$(sampled purchaser is a male) $\cdot P$(sampled purchaser is over 45).

What is P(sampled purchaser is a male)? We do not know, because we do not have enough information to determine what percentage of *all* purchasers are male. However, from these data, we can *estimate* this probability using the percentage of males in the sample. This is $120/200 = .6$.

Similarly, P(sampled purchaser is over 45) can be estimated by the fraction of people over 45 in the sample—namely, $50/200$. So, our estimate of the expected number of observations for this cell is

$$\hat{E} = 200 \cdot \frac{120}{200} \cdot \frac{50}{200} = \frac{(120)(50)}{200}$$

$$= 30$$

So, for this cell, the observed frequency is $O = 40$, and our estimate of the expected frequency (if H_0 is true) is $\hat{E} = 30$. In general,

$$\hat{E} = \frac{(\text{row total for this cell}) \cdot (\text{column total for this cell})}{n}$$

where n = total sample size.

A summary of the calculations can be tabulated as

Sex	Age	Observed (O)	Expected ($\hat{E}$) if H_0 is true
Male	<30	60	$120 \cdot 100/200 = 60$
	30–45	20	$120 \cdot 50/200 = 30$
	>45	40	$120 \cdot 50/200 = 30$
Female	<30	40	$80 \cdot 100/200 = 40$
	30–45	30	$80 \cdot 50/200 = 20$
	>45	10	$80 \cdot 50/200 = 20$
		200	200

The easiest way to represent these 12 values is to place the observed value on top and the expected value estimate underneath in each cell:

Sex	Age < 30		Age 30–45		Age > 45		Total
MALE	60	60	20	30	40	30	120
FEMALE	40	40	30	20	10	20	80
TOTAL	100		50		50		200

Pooling At this point, you need to check your expected values. If any of them are less than 5, you need to combine the column (or row) in which this small value occurs with any adjoining column (or row). The observed and expected values for this new column (row) are obtained by summing the values for the two columns (rows).

The Test Statistic The test statistic for testing H_0: the classifications are independent versus H_a: the classifications are dependent is the usual chi-square statistic, which in this case compares each *observed* frequency with the corresponding *expected* frequency estimate.

$$\chi^2 = \sum \frac{(O - \hat{E})^2}{\hat{E}} \tag{13-3}$$

where the summation is over all cells of the contingency table.

Degrees of Freedom For the multinomial situation, the degrees of freedom for the chi-square statistic were $k - 1$, where k = the number of categories (outcomes). For this situation, there were k values of $(O - \hat{E})$. However, because the sum of the observed frequencies is the same as the sum of the expected frequencies, the sum of the k values of $(O - \hat{E})$ is *always zero*. This means that, of these k values, only $k - 1$ are free to vary. This resulted in $k - 1$ *df* for the chi-square statistic.

Take a close look at the observed and expected frequencies in the contingency table for age and sex of purchasers. Notice that (1) for each row, sum of O's = sum of $\hat{E}$'s, and (2) for each column, sum of O's = sum of $\hat{E}$'s. In general, if classification 1 has c categories and classification 2 has r categories, you construct an **$r \times c$ contingency table** (Figure 13.3). Of the c values of $(O - \hat{E})$ in each row, only $c - 1$ are free to vary. Similarly, only $r - 1$ of the values in each column are free to assume any value. So, for this contingency table, only $(r - 1)(c - 1)$ values are free to vary. Therefore, for the chi-square test of independence,

$$df = (r - 1)(c - 1) \tag{13-4}$$

Testing Procedure When H_0 is not true, the expected frequencies and observed frequencies will be very different, producing a large χ^2 value. We again reject H_0 if the value of the test statistic falls in the *right-tail* rejection region, so we

Reject H_0 if $\chi^2 > \chi^2_{\alpha, df}$

where $df = (r - 1)(c - 1)$.

In summary, the chi-square test for independence hypotheses are

H_0: the (row and column) classifications are independent

H_a: the classifications are dependent

Figure 13.3

Expected value estimates for an $r \times c$ contingency table.

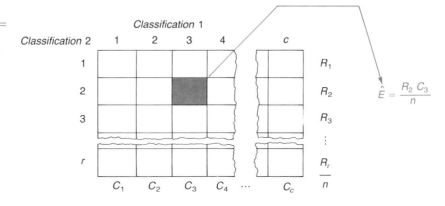

The test statistic is

$$\chi^2 = \sum \frac{(O - \hat{E})^2}{\hat{E}}$$

where

1. The summation is over all cells of the contingency table consisting of r rows and c columns.
2. O is the observed frequency in this cell.
3. $\hat{E}$ is the estimated expected frequency for this cell.

$$\hat{E} = \frac{\begin{pmatrix} \text{total of row in} \\ \text{which the cell lies} \end{pmatrix} \cdot \begin{pmatrix} \text{total of column in} \\ \text{which the cell lies} \end{pmatrix}}{(\text{total of all cells})}$$

4. The degrees of freedom for the chi-square statistic are $df = (r - 1)(c - 1)$.

The test procedure is (using Table A-6):

Reject H_0 if $\chi^2 > \chi^2_{\alpha, df}$

We can now return to our question of whether age and sex of purchasers are independent. Step 1 (statement of hypotheses) and step 2 (definition of test statistic) of our five-step procedure have been discussed already. Assume a significance level of $\alpha = .1$ was specified. For step 3, the df are $(2 - 1)(3 - 1) = 2$. Using Table A-6, $\chi^2_{.1, 2} = 4.61$. So our test procedure will be to reject H_0 if $\chi^2 > 4.61$. For step 4, referring to the contingency table,

$$\chi^{2*} = \frac{(60 - 60)^2}{60} + \frac{(20 - 30)^2}{30} + \frac{(40 - 30)^2}{30} + \frac{(40 - 40)^2}{40} + \frac{(30 - 20)^2}{20} + \frac{(10 - 20)^2}{20}$$

$$= 0 + 3.33 + 3.33 + 0 + 5 + 5$$

$$= 16.66$$

This exceeds the table value of 4.61, so we reject H_0. We thus conclude that the age and sex classifications are *not* independent (step 5). We obtained more men (and fewer women) over 45 years than we would expect if there was no dependency. Similarly, there were fewer men (and more women) between 30 and 45 years.

We can find the p-value for this also, given $\chi^{2*} = 16.66$. Using a χ^2 curve with 2 df, the area to the right of 16.66, using Table A-6, is $< .005$. The p-value indicates the **strength** of the dependency between two classifications. The *smaller* the p-value is, the more you tend to support the alternative hypothesis, which indicates a *stronger* dependency between the two variables. For the age and sex illustration, $p < .005$ so we conclude that the age and sex of these purchasers are strongly related.

Example 13.5

In example 12.4, a personnel director attempted to determine whether an employee's educational level had an effect on his or her job performance. An exam was given to a sample of the employees, and we used the ANOVA procedure to test for a difference among the three groups: (1) those with a high-school diploma only, (2) those with a bachelor's degree only, and (3) those with a master's degree.

The director decided to expand this procedure by testing 120 employees; rather than recording the exam scores, she rated each person's exam performance as high, average, or low. The results of this study are:

	High	Average	Low	Total
MASTER'S	4	20	11	35
BACHELOR'S	12	18	15	45
HIGH-SCHOOL DIPLOMA	9	22	9	40
TOTAL	25	60	35	120

Does job performance as measured by the exam appear to be related to the level of an employee's education at this particular firm? Use $\alpha = .05$.

Solution

Step 1. This calls for a chi-square test of independence, with hypotheses

H_0: exam performance is independent of educational level

H_a: these classifications are dependent

Steps 2, 3. Your test statistic is the chi-square statistic in equation 13-3. The table of frequencies here is a 3×3 contingency table, which means that the degrees of freedom are $df = (3 - 1)(3 - 1) = 4$. From Table A-6, we determine that $\chi^2_{.05,4} = 9.49$, so the testing procedure is

Reject H_0 if $\chi^2 > 9.49$

Step 4. Computing the expected frequency estimates in the usual way, we arrive at the following table:

	High		Average		Low		Total
MASTER'S	4	7.29	20	17.5	11	10.21	35
BACHELOR'S	12	9.38	18	22.5	15	13.12	45
HIGH-SCHOOL DIPLOMA	9	8.33	22	20.0	9	11.67	40
TOTAL	25		60		35		120

To illustrate the calculations, the 11.67 in the lower right cell is $(40 \cdot 35)/120$.

The computed chi-square value is

$$\chi^{2*} = \frac{(4 - 7.29)^2}{7.29} + \frac{(20 - 17.5)^2}{17.5} + \cdots + \frac{(9 - 11.67)^2}{11.67}$$

$$= 4.67$$

This value is < 9.49, and so we fail to reject H_0.

Step 5. We see no evidence of a relationship between job performance and level of education. (This is probably somewhat disturbing to those employees who spent many years obtaining an advanced degree.)

We do not conclude that these data demonstrate that the two classifications are clearly *independent* because this amounts to accepting H_0. We are simply unable to demonstrate that a relationship exists.

Figure 13.4

MINITAB solution to
example 13.5 (test for
independence).

```
MTB > READ INTO C1-C3
DATA> 4 20 11
DATA> 12 18 15
DATA> 9 22 9
DATA> END
      3 ROWS READ
MTB > CHISQUARE USING C1-C3

Expected counts are printed below observed counts

              C1        C2        C3     Total
   1           4        20        11        35        Observed (O)
             7.3      17.5      10.2                   Expected (E)

   2          12        18        15        45
             9.4      22.5      13.1

   3           9        22         9        40
             8.3      20.0      11.7

Total         25        60        35       120

ChiSq =     1.49 +    0.36 +    0.06 +
            0.74 +    0.90 +    0.27 +
            0.05 +    0.20 +    0.61 = 4.67

df = 4
```

A MINITAB solution to example 13.5 is contained in Figure 13.4. Notice that the format of this table is similar to that of the one we constructed, with the expected value (assuming H_0) below the observed value within each cell.

Comments

In example 13.5, the personnel director recorded the exam performance as high, average, or low rather than listing the actual exam score. Why would anyone take *interval/ratio* data (the exam scores) and convert them to seemingly weaker *ordinal* data (the exam performance classifications)? Do you lose useful information by doing this? When using the ANOVA procedure, we were forced to assume that these data came from *normal* populations with equal variances. In this chapter, aside from the randomness of the sample, *no* assumptions regarding the populations were necessary. So, by converting the exam scores to a form suitable for a contingency table and using the chi-square test of independence, we can avoid the assumptions of normality and equal variances.

This introduces **nonparametric statistics,** often called *distribution-free* statistics. The beauty of these procedures is that they require only very weak assumptions regarding the populations. However, if the data *do* satisfy the requirements of the ANOVA procedure (or nearly so), the nonparametric test is less sensitive to differences among the populations (such as educational level) and so is less powerful than the ANOVA F test. Additional nonparametric tests of hypothesis will be discussed in Chapter 19.

Test of Independence with Fixed Marginal Totals (Test of Homogeneity)

A slightly different interpretation of the previous chi-square procedure occurs when we determine *in advance* the number of observations to be sampled within each column (or row). In the previous discussion, the row and column totals were random variables because we had no way of knowing what they would be before the sample was obtained. In this discussion, the contingency table is the same, except that the column (or row) totals are predetermined.

Assume Lextron International, a manufacturer of electronic components, has facilities located in Dallas, Boston, Seattle, and Denver. Over the years, Lextron has gone to great lengths to discourage the formation of labor unions at these plants, including constructing employee recreational centers and offering better-than-average employee benefits. Management suspects, however, that there is growing interest among the employees in forming a union. Of particular interest is whether employee interest in a union differs among the four plants.

The Dallas and Denver plants are considerably larger than the other two, so Lextron obtains a random sample of 200 employees from each of these two plants and of 100 from each of the two smaller facilities. The results of the survey are:

	Dallas	Boston	Seattle	Denver	Total
Interested	120	41	45	112	318
Not interested	35	38	40	36	149
Indifferent	45	21	15	52	133
Total	200	100	100	200	600

In the previous tests of independence, we had a *single* population, where each member was classified according to two criteria, such as age and sex. Now we have four distinct populations, namely, the Lextron employees in each of the four cities. Consequently, we obtained a random sample from each one. The column totals (sample sizes) were determined in advance. This differs from our previous examples, where we had no idea what the row or column totals would be before the sample was obtained.

The question of interest here becomes, is interest in a labor union the same in each of the four cities? In other words, we are trying to determine whether these four populations can be viewed as belonging to the *same* population (in terms of this criterion). Identical populations are said to be **homogeneous.** Consequently, the test of hypothesis here is a **test of homogeneity** as well as a test for independence. The null hypothesis can be written as

H_0: the four populations are homogeneous in their interest in a union

or as

H_0: plant location and employee interest are independent classifications

The procedure for analyzing a contingency table is the *same* whether or not the column (or row) totals are fixed in advance.

A MINITAB solution using $\alpha = .05$ is provided in Figure 13.5. The expected cell frequencies are computed by finding

$$\hat{E} = \frac{(\text{row total})(\text{column total})}{600}$$

The computed chi-square value is

$$\chi^{2*} = \frac{(120 - 106.0)^2}{106} + \frac{(41 - 53.0)^2}{53} + \cdots + \frac{(52 - 44.3)^2}{44.3}$$
$$= 34.16$$

The degrees of freedom here are $(3 - 1)(4 - 1) = 6$. This means that we reject H_0 if $\chi^2 > 12.59$, where 12.59 is $\chi^2_{.05,6}$. The computed value (34.16) exceeds the table value, so we reject H_0. We conclude that these four populations are *not* homogeneous. The employee interest in a labor union is not identical at each of the four locations. We can also say that the location and union interest classifications are not independent. Comparing the observed and expected frequencies, we note that the larger plants

Figure 13.5

MINITAB solution to test of H_0: plant location and employee interest are independent class-ifications (test of homogeneity).

```
MTB > READ INTO C1-C4
DATA> 120 41 45 112
DATA> 35 38 40 36
DATA> 45 21 15 52
DATA> END
     3 ROWS READ
MTB > CHISQUARE USING C1-C4

Expected counts are printed below observed counts

              C1       C2       C3       C4     Total
      1       120       41       45      112      318
            106.0     53.0     53.0    106.0

      2        35       38       40       36      149
             49.7     24.8     24.8     49.7

      3        45       21       15       52      133
             44.3     22.2     22.2     44.3

Total        200      100      100      200      600

ChiSq =    1.85 +    2.72 +    1.21 +    0.34 +
           4.33 +    6.98 +    9.26 +    3.76 +
           0.01 +    0.06 +    2.32 +    1.33 = 34.16
df = 6
```

(Dallas and Denver) had a higher proportion of employees interested in forming a union. In Dallas, for example, if these classifications were independent, we would expect 106 employees to be interested; instead, we observed 120. The same argument applies to the Denver plant.

From Table A-6, the p-value here is $< .005$. Because of this extremely small value, we can conclude that, at these four plants, employees have considerably different views in regard to the formation of a labor union. The small p-value also implies that there is an extremely strong dependence between the two classifications.

Exercises

13.16 Suppose you are interested in determining whether there is a relationship between one's educational preference (major) and one's sex. A random sample of 172 students at Hamilton College yields the following data:

Major	Female	Male	Total
Liberal Arts	35	25	60
Home Economics	6	9	15
Physics	18	21	39
Business	26	32	58
Total	85	87	172

a. Formulate the necessary hypotheses.

b. Using the chi-square test, test the hypotheses to determine whether educational preference is independent of sex, using a significance level of .10.

c. Find and interpret the p-value for the chi-square test.

13.17 A lawn-equipment shop is considering adding a brand of lawnmowers to its merchandise. The manager of the shop believes that the highest-quality lawnmowers are Trooper, Lawneater, and Nipper and needs to decide whether it makes a difference which of these three the shop will add to its existing merchandise. Twenty owners of each of these three types of lawnmowers are randomly sampled and asked how satisfied they are with their lawnmowers.

Lawnmower	Very Satisfied	Satisfied	Not Satisfied	Total
Trooper	11	6	3	20
Lawneater	13	4	3	20
Nipper	13	6	1	20

Are the owners of the lawnmowers homogeneous in their response to the survey? Use a 5% significance level.

13.18 A real-estate firm wanted to know whether the type of house purchased is associated with the amount of education of the head of the household. Fox and Jones Construction builds four styles of homes. A random sample of 175 homeowners who own a Fox and Jones house was taken and the education level of the household head was noted.

Type of House	No College Degree	Bachelor's Degree	Master's Degree	Doctoral Degree	Total
1	12	5	1	0	18
2	13	10	8	2	33
3	10	20	25	10	65
4	2	18	30	9	59

Do the data provide sufficient evidence to indicate that the type of house owned is related to the education level of the head of the household? Use a .05 level of significance.

13.19 A marketing-research analyst of a major retail firm is studying the shopping habits of her customers. She is interested in examining whether there is a relationship between method of payment and gender. She has obtained the following data:

Customer	Cash	Charge
Male	52	38
Female	28	47

Using a significance level of .05, test the hypothesis that there is no relationship between method of payment and gender. Also calculate the p-value.

13.20 An insurance company claims that big cars are more prone to automobile accidents and hence should be subject to a higher insurance premium. To test the validity of the claim, an auto firm gathered a random sample.

Car Size	At Least One Accident	No Accidents
Big	24	13
Compact	36	117
Small	108	214

Formulate the necessary hypotheses and test at the 10% significance level. Also calculate the p-value. Based on this value, would you reject the null hypothesis that car size and occurrence of accidents are independent at the 1% level?

13.21 Do the data in exercise 5.64 indicate that there is a relationship between a customer's age and a customer's favorite donut? Use the p-value to test the hypothesis.

13.22 Kingston Pencils is considering a new bonus plan. Under the current bonus plan, the amount of bonus is not linked to the production but only linked to the profits. According to the proposed bonus plan, the amount of bonus will be linked to the quantity produced but will be subject to the amount of profits. The controller of Kingston is interested in examining whether employee opinion of the bonus plan is independent of job classification.

Employee	Favorable	Unfavorable
White Collar	67	28
Blue Collar	43	19

Calculate the p-value and interpret it.

13.23 A research team conducts a study to see whether voting for the candidates in the recent local election is homogeneous within age groups (given in years). One-hundred voters were randomly selected from each of five age classifications. Do the data indicate that voting is homogeneous with respect to age group? Use a 5% significance level.

Age	Candidate A	Candidate B	Candidate C	Total
Less than 25	48	22	30	100
25 and less than 35	55	20	25	100
35 and less than 45	50	28	22	100
45 and less than 55	45	21	34	100
Over 55	49	21	30	100

Summary

When performing a two-tailed test of hypothesis on a binomial parameter (for example, $p = .75$) we can use a chi-square test statistic. The advantage of this approach is that it extends easily to the multinomial situation, where each trial can result in any specified number of outcomes. An example is the roll of a single die, which has six possible outcomes on each roll.

For the multinomial situation, the probability of observing each possible outcome may be specified (such as $\frac{1}{6}$ for each outcome in the single die illustration). To test the hypothesis, a random sample of observations is obtained, and a chi-square test statistic is evaluated either to reject or to fail to reject this set of probabilities (percentages). The form of this chi-square test statistic is

$$\chi^2 = \sum \frac{(O - E)^2}{E}$$

where

1. O represents the observed frequency of observations in a particular category (such as the observed number of 3's in 60 rolls of a single die).
2. E is the expected frequency for this category. For example, we would expect to see $60 \cdot \frac{1}{6} = 10$ values of 3 in the die illustration.
3. The chi-square value is obtained by summing over all categories of the multinomial random variable.
4. Categories must be combined (pooled) together whenever an expected value (E) for a particular category is less than 5.

The same chi-square statistic can be used to determine whether a certain set of sample data came from a specified probability distribution. For example, you might attempt to determine whether the number of defects in a particular product follow a Poisson distribution. By collecting a random sample and counting the number of defects in each product, you can compare the observed values (how many zeroes, how many ones, and so on) with what you would expect if the null hypothesis—H_0: the data are from a Poisson distribution—is true. If the calculated chi-square value is significantly large (in the right tail), this hypothesis will be rejected. Whenever any of the parameters for this distribution are unknown (such as μ for the Poisson illustration), they can be estimated using the sample data. The degrees of freedom of the chi-square test statistic are reduced by one for *each* estimated parameter.

Finally, this chi-square statistic can be used to test whether two classifications (such as age and performance) used to define a contingency table are independent. This is the chi-square test of independence. The expected value within each cell of the contingency table is determined under the assumption that H_0 is true, where H_0:

the row and column classifications are independent. This also leads to a right-tailed rejection region using the chi-square statistic. This procedure can be used as a test for homogeneity when fixed sample sizes are used for each row or column of the table.

Review Exercises

13.24 The manager of the Grandiose Hotel guarantees that a customer's room will be ready at 6:00 P.M. if a reservation is made. Otherwise, the customer stays at the hotel for free. The manager believes that this policy should be continued; he believes that a room is not available on time only 5% of the time. A random sample of 200 past reservations was selected and the estimate of the proportion of times when a room was not available on time was .065.

a. Letting the significance level be .05, test the belief that the proportion of occurrences when a room is not available on time is .05. Use the Z test from section 11.2.

b. Use the chi-square goodness-of-fit test instead of the Z test in question a.

c. What is the relationship between the test statistics in questions a and b?

13.25 A student wanted to know whether the answers a, b, c, d, and e on the standardized departmental multiple choice test occurred equally as often. Several old departmental tests were randomly selected and the occurrences of each answer were tabulated.

Answer	Times Used As Answer
a	39
b	26
c	43
d	42
e	25

Test the belief that all answer choices occur equally as often. Use a significance level of .10.

13.26 A manufacturer of clothes dryers believes that historically 40% of its sales are for the basic 18-pound-capacity clothes dryer, 35% are for the 20-pound-capacity dryer and 25% are for the 22-pound-capacity dryer. A random sample of 200 clothes dryers sold during the past 6 months was obtained, with the following results (capacity in pounds):

Capacity	Number Sold
18	72
20	68
22	60

Using a significance level of .10, is there sufficient evidence to indicate that the manufacturer was wrong in its statement of these percentages?

13.27 A construction company sells and installs solid vinyl siding. Siding comes in five basic colors: white, brown, avocado, reddish-tan and yellow. Historically, the percentages of sales for each color are 50%, 27%, 12%, 8% and 3%, respectively. A random sample of 100 recent sales gives the following data:

Color	Number Sold
White	43
Brown	29
Avocado	14
Reddish-tan	13
Yellow	1

Does the sales distribution of these colors appear to be the same as the historical distribution? Test at the 1% significance level.

13.28 A large department store in New York City has five entrances and exits. It is believed that the proportion of shoppers entering or leaving the store is approximately the same for each of the five doorways on any single day. The number of customers entering or leaving the store is tallied at each doorway for 3 randomly selected days.

Doorways	Customers
1	150
2	123
3	126
4	163
5	152

Do the data justify the statement that all five entrances and exits are used equally often? Use a 5% significance level.

13.29 The police department in a suburb of Los Angeles believes that 50% of the rapes occur between the hours of 10 P.M. and midnight, 20% occur between 6 P.M. and 10 P.M., and 20% occur between midnight and 3 A.M. One-hundred randomly selected rape cases were chosen and the times were noted.

Time	Number of Occurrences
6 P.M. to 10 P.M.	24
10 P.M. to midnight	44
midnight to 3 A.M.	22
other times	10

Do the data justify the percentages given by the police department? Use a 1% significance level.

13.30 A car-rental company has 15 cars to rent. The owner believes that the number of cars rented daily is binomially distributed. He also believes that each car has a 30% chance of being rented each day. Forty-five randomly selected days are chosen and the number of cars rented are indicated. From the data, test the hypothesis that the daily rental of cars is binomially distributed with $p = .30$. Use a 5% significance level.

Cars Rented	Days Occurred
0	0
1	3
2	3
3	6
4	9
5	12
6	6
7	3
≥ 8	3

13.31 An advertising firm believes that the number of daily responses to an advertisement in the *Wall Street Journal* follows a Poisson distribution. Forty days were randomly selected and the following data were collected:

Responses	Days
0	0
1	8
2	8
3	10
4	6
5	6
6	2

Can you conclude that the data did come from a Poisson distribution? Use a 1% level of significance.

13.32 The assistant dean of the College of Business at Oceanside University believes that the number of students dropping a class is Poisson distributed. Fifty classes, all containing the same number of students, were randomly selected. The number of withdrawals from the classes was recorded. Based on the following data, what conclusion can be drawn about whether or not these data come from a Poisson distribution? Use a significance level of .05 to justify your conclusion.

Drops	Classes
0	0
1	2
2	6
3	10
4	18
5	4
6	6
7	4
>7	0

13.33 A temporary-help employment agency regularly has ten workers who are ready to work. An employer telephones the agency when he or she needs temporary help. The owner of the agency believes that the number of workers used each day by the employers in the community is binomially distributed. Thirty days of operation were used to compile the following:

Workers (out of 10) Used	Days Used
≤ 4	0
5	12
6	12
7	12
8	14
9	8
10	2
Total	60

With a significance level of .10, test the goodness-of-fit of the data to a binomial distribution.

13.34 A computer generates 100 observations from a normally distributed population with mean 35 and standard deviation 2. The results of the 100 observations generated are:

Interval	Observed Frequency
less than 32	6
32 but less than 33	9
33 but less than 34	12
34 but less than 35	23
35 but less than 36	19
36 but less than 37	15
37 but less than 38	11
38 or more	5

Use the chi-square goodness-of-fit procedure in exercise 13.13 to test that there is enough evidence to support the conclusion that the generated numbers did not come from a normally distributed population with mean $= 35$ and standard deviation $= 2$. Use a 1% significance level.

13.35 Using the data in exercise 5.8, test that the percent of time a student works is independent of whether the student lives in the dorm. Use the p-value to support your conclusion.

13.36 Using the data in exercise 5.11, test that the number of years of schooling is independent of the job description. Use the p-value to support your conclusion.

13.37 Using the data in exercise 5.13, test that the account balance is independent of the type of account. Use a 1% significance level.

13.38 A national skiing magazine surveys 500 skiers. It prepares the following tabulation by sex and skill level. Do these data provide sufficient evidence to indicate that skiing ability is related to gender? Use a 5% significance level.

Skiing Ability	Male	Female	Total
Advanced	98	22	120
Intermediate	189	147	336
Beginner	30	14	44
			500

13.39 Microtron, a maker of semiconductors, has plants in four states: Texas, Georgia, California, and New York. Management would like to evaluate the effect of a mandatory retirement age of 60. The largest plants are in California and New York, so they sample 300 employees from each of these states and 200 employees each in Texas and Georgia.

Response	Texas	Georgia	California	New York
Favor	81	85	122	128
Against	119	115	178	172

Do the data support the hypothesis that employees within different states have different opinions about the mandatory retirement age? Use a 5% significance level.

13.40 A marketing survey was taken of 277 frequent flyers by recording their socioeconomic class and airline preference. Do the sample data provide sufficient evidence to reject the null hypothesis of independence of airline preference and social class at the .05 significance level?

Socioeconomic Class	Delta	Southwest	American	Other	Total
Low	20	45	23	4	92
Middle	25	40	20	20	105
Upper	18	15	30	17	80

13.41 A record company wanted to survey its customers regarding music preferences. A random sample of 258 frequent customers of the record company was taken and information was gathered on their music preference and job classification. From the following data, can the null hypothesis of independence between type of music preferred and working status be rejected at the 10% significance level?

Job Classification	Country and Western	Rock	Classical	Jazz	Total
Clerical	25	40	17	5	87
Managerial	21	25	29	15	90
Blue Collar	27	33	14	7	81
	73	98	60	27	258

13.42 The personnel department of a particular firm wants to know if an employee's age is associated with productivity (given in items per hour). The manager of the personnel department draws a random sample of 60 employees from each of the age classifications listed. Do the data support the hypothesis that the five age categories are not homogeneous with respect to productivity? Use a 10% significance level.

Age	4–5 Items	6–7 Items	≥ 8 Items	Total
20 and under 30	15	25	20	60
30 and under 40	13	29	18	60
40 and under 50	16	26	18	60
50 and under 60	19	26	15	60
60 and under 70	22	24	14	60

13.43 An aspiring politician decided to sample 300 citizens from each of two major cities to find out whether the two populations were homogeneous with regard to their opinion on gun control. Do the following data indicate a lack of homogeneity? Use a 10% significance level.

City	Favor Gun Control	Against Gun Control
A	126	174
B	148	152

13.44 Axiom Market Research published the following data concerning education level and attendance at "regular" theater performances. A sample size of 950 was selected. Do the data indicate, at the .05 significance level, a relationship between level of education and regular theater attendance?

Education	Attend More Than Once Per Year	Attend No More Than Once Per Year	Total
College graduate	82	120	202
Some college	75	131	206
High-School graduate	106	215	321
Not a high-school graduate	51	170	221

Case Study

Mountain West Sales

Mountain West Sales was formed in the late 1960s by a group of college friends. The company initially had only one product, limited editions of art prints. Gradually, the company added other products to the line and increased its sales force. Jim Lang, one of the founders, decided to work full time for Mountain West as the sales manager.

Jim is developing his plan for the next sales year. He has to decide whether he has allocated the sales representatives to the correct sales territories. Jim has obtained historical sales data for each territory from the accounting department. The percent of sales by territory was

Territory 1	25%
Territory 2	10%
Territory 3	16%
Territory 4	11%
Territory 5	18%
Territory 6	20%

Jim also looked at the previous year's sales for the territories in dollars; total sales were over $2.7 million:

Territory 1	809,925
Territory 2	280,765
Territory 3	320,721
Territory 4	390,936
Territory 5	408,367
Territory 6	554,536

Jim wants to know whether there has been a significant shift in sales among the territories.

Case Study Questions

1. What statistical technique should Jim use?
2. Define the rejection region for this test.
3. What can you conclude about the sales in these six territories using a significance level of .05?

<table>
<tr><td>• S</td></tr>
<tr><td>• P</td></tr>
<tr><td>• S</td></tr>
<tr><td>• S</td></tr>
<tr><td>• X</td></tr>
</table>

Solution

Example 13.4

Example 13.4 was concerned with a multinomial goodness-of-fit test. One of the expected values was less than 5, and it was necessary to pool the categories and create a new category with an expected value of at least 5. The problem was to determine whether the percentage of sales in the sample community fit the U.S. proportions.

H_0: $p_1 = .625$, $p_2 = .226$, $p_3 = .115$, $p_4 = .034$

H_a: at least one of the proportions is incorrect

The SPSSX program listing in Figure 13.6 was used to request a computed chi-square value when the categories were pooled. Each line represents one card image to be entered:

The TITLE command names the SPSSX run.

The DATA LIST command gives each variable a name and describes the data as being in free form.

The VALUE LABELS statement assigns the labels GENERAL AUTO to type 1 records, K to type 2 records, L to type 3 records, and OTHER to type 4 records.

The PRINT command requests a printout of the input data.

The WEIGHT command is used to weight the cases by the number of observed cars sold.

The NPAR TESTS CHISQUARE = statement requests a chi-square test between the observed and expected sales. For instance, 0.625 is the expected market share for the variable labeled GENERAL AUTO.

The BEGIN DATA command indicates to SPSSX that the input data immediately follow.

Figure 13.6

SPSSX program listing requesting a chi-square value for pooled categories.

```
TITLE    NEW CAR SALES MIXTURE
DATA LIST FREE/TYPE CARSSOLD
VALUE LABELS TYPE 1 'GA' 2 'K' 3 'L' 4 'OTHER'/
PRINT /TYPE CARSSOLD
WEIGHT BY CARSSOLD
NPAR TESTS CHISQUARE=TYPE/EXPECTED=0.625,0.226,0.115,0.034
BEGIN DATA
1 95
2 50
3 41
4 14
END DATA
```

Figure 13.7

Output obtained by executing the SPSSX program listing in Figure 13.6.

```
- - - - - CHI-SQUARE TEST
    TYPE
                                         ┌─O      ┌─E       ┌─O-E
                                         │ CASES  │         │
                              CATEGORY  OBSERVED  EXPECTED  RESIDUAL
    GA                          1.00       95     125.00    -30.00
    K                           2.00       50      45.20      4.80
    L                           3.00       41      23.00     18.00
    OTHER                       4.00       14       6.80      7.20
                                          ---
                              TOTAL       200

          CHI-SQUARE                D.F.          SIGNIFICANCE
            29.420                    3               0.000
```

$$\chi^2 = \Sigma \frac{(O-E)^2}{E}$$

The next four lines are card images, with each line representing a type (1 = GENERAL AUTO, and so on) and the observed number of cars sold.
The END DATA statement indicates the end of the data card images.

Figure 13.7 shows the output obtained by executing the program listing in Figure 13.6.

Solution

Example 13.5

Example 13.5 was concerned with a chi-square test of independence. The problem was to determine whether an employee's educational level had an effect on job performance, as measured by an exam.

H_0: there is no relationship between educational level and job performance

H_a: there is a relationship between educational level and job performance

The SPSSX program listing in Figure 13.8 requests the chi-square and p-value statistics from the data obtained by testing 120 employees. Each line represents one card image to be entered:

Figure 13.8

SPSSX program listing requesting the chi-square and p-value statistics.

```
TITLE    EDUCATIONAL LEVEL VERSUS JOB KNOWLEDGE
DATA LIST FREE/LEVEL PERFORM COUNT
VALUE LABELS LEVEL 1 'MASTERS' 2 'BACHELOR' 3 'HIGH SCHOOL'/
             PERFORM 1 'HIGH' 2 'AVERAGE' 3 'LOW'
PRINT / LEVEL PERFORM COUNT
WEIGHT BY COUNT
CROSSTABS TABLES=LEVEL BY PERFORM
STATISTICS 1
OPTIONS 14
BEGIN DATA
1  1  4
1  2  20
1  3  11
2  1  12
2  2  18
2  3  15
3  1  9
3  2  22
3  3  9
END DATA
```

The TITLE command names the SPSSX run.

The DATA LIST command gives each variable a name and describes the data as being in free form.

The VALUE LABELS statement assigns codes to different categories (LEVEL and PERFORM) of data. These are positional categories. The first position of the input data stream is the LEVEL category; the second position is the PER-FORM category. A 1 in the first position of the data stream indicates that the employee has a master's degree, a 2 indicates a bachelor's degree, and a 3 indicates a high-school degree. For the second position of the data stream, a 1 indicates that the employee scored high on the exam, 2 indicates average, and 3 indicates low.

The PRINT command requests a printout of the input data.

The WEIGHT command requests that the data be weighted by the variable COUNT. This variable indicates the total number of employees who satisfy the criteria in the adjacent LEVEL and PERFORM categories. In the first row of data, 4 employees had master's degrees and scored high on the exam.

The CROSSTABS command produces a cross-tabulation of the variables LEVEL and PERFORM.

The STATISTICS 1 command requests the chi-square test.

The OPTIONS 14 command requests that the expected frequencies be printed.

The BEGIN DATA command indicates to SPSSX that the input data immediately follow.

The next nine lines are card images, representing an educational level code, a performance level code, and the number of observations that compose the two adjacent categories.

The END DATA statement indicates the end of the data card images.

Figure 13.9 shows the output obtained by executing the program listing in Figure 13.8.

Figure 13.9

Output obtained by executing the SPSSX program listing in Figure 13.8.

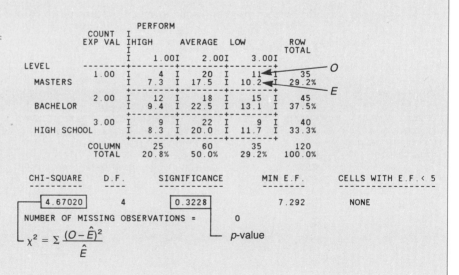

S ·
A ·
S ·

Solution

Example 13.5

Example 13.5 was concerned with a chi-square test of independence. The purpose was to determine whether an employee's educational level had an effect on job performance, as measured by an exam.

H_0: there is no relationship between educational level and job performance

H_a: there is a relationship between educational level and job performance

The SAS program listing in Figure 13.10 requests the chi-square and p-value statistics from the data obtained by testing 120 employees. Each line represents one card image to be entered:

The TITLE command names the SAS run.

The DATA command gives the data a name.

Figure 13.10

SAS program listing requesting the chi-square and p-value statistics.

```
TITLE     EDUCATIONAL LEVEL VERSUS JOB KNOWLEDGE;
DATA EXAM PERFORM;
 INPUT LEVEL $ PERFORM $ COUNT@@;
CARDS;
MASTERS HIGH 4 MASTERS AVERAGE 20 MASTERS LOW 11
BACHELORS HIGH 12 BACHELORS AVERAGE 18 BACHELORS LOW 15
HIGHSCHOOL HIGH 9 HIGHSCHOOL AVERAGE 22 HIGHSCHOOL LOW 9
PROC PRINT;
PROC FREQ;
 WEIGHT COUNT;
 TABLES LEVEL*PERFORM/CHISQ;
```

Figure 13.11

Output obtained by executing the SAS program listing in Figure 13.10.

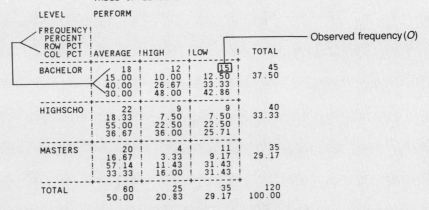

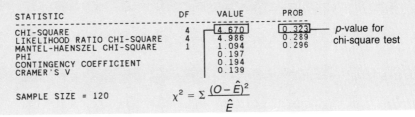

$$\chi^2 = \Sigma \frac{(O - \hat{E})^2}{\hat{E}}$$

The INPUT command names and gives the correct order for the different fields on the data cards. The $ indicates that both LEVEL and PERFORM are character data. The @@ indicates that each card image contains two additional sets of data.

The CARDS command indicates to SAS that the input data immediately follow.

The next three lines are card images. The first line, for example, indicates that four employees with a master's degree scored high on the exam, 20 scored average, and 11 scored low.

The PROC PRINT command directs SAS to list the data that were just entered.

The PROC FREQ command and WEIGHT COUNT subcommand specify that the values of the variable COUNT are relative weights for the observations.

The TABLES subcommand produces a cross-tabulation of the variables LEVEL and PERFORM.

The CHISQ command generates chi-square statistics.

Figure 13.11 shows the output obtained by executing the program listing in Figure 13.10.

Simple Linear Regression

A Look Back/Introduction

Chapter 4 introduced bivariate data. These are data on two variables, such as age and income, which can be graphically represented using a scatter diagram. We also measured the amount of the linear relationship between these two variables using a coefficient of correlation. Our discussion was descriptive; we measured and illustrated how these two variables reacted together in a sample from a bivariate situation. If you believe that a significant linear relationship exists, your next step is to construct the best line through the points.

We now turn our attention to the question of what we are estimating when using a bivariate sample. How can we determine whether a significant linear relationship exists? We will answer this by introducing the concept of a **statistical model** and the assumptions behind it. Various tests of hypothesis will examine the adequacy of this model (Is it a good one?), and an assortment of CIs will measure the reliability of the corresponding estimates using this model.

14.1

Bivariate Data and Correlation

In bivariate data, each observation consists of data on two variables. For example, you obtain a sample of people and record their age (X) and liquid assets (Y). Or, for each month, you record the average interest rate (X) and the number of new housing starts (Y). These data are *paired.*

Assume a real-estate developer is interested in determining the relationship between family income (X, in thousands of dollars) of the local residents and the square footage of their homes (Y, in hundreds of square feet). A random sample of ten families is obtained with the following results:

Income (X)	22	26	45	37	28	50	56	34	60	40
Square Footage (Y)	16	17	26	24	22	21	32	18	30	20

Figure 14.1a provides a scatter diagram of these data. In this graph, each observation is represented by a point. The underlying pattern here appears to be that larger incomes (X) are associated with larger home sizes (Y). This means that X and Y have a **positive relationship.** (A **negative relationship** occurs when Y decreases as X increases; for example, when Y is the demand for a particular consumer product and X is the selling price).

We next try to determine whether we can estimate this relationship by means of a straight line. One possible line is sketched in Figure 14.1b, which passes through the interior of these points and has a positive slope. To measure the strength of the linear relationship between these two variables, we determine the coefficient of correlation.

Coefficient of Correlation

It is often difficult to determine whether a significant linear relationship exists between X and Y by inspecting a scatter diagram of the data. A second procedure is to include a *measure* of this linearity—the sample coefficient of correlation. It is computed from the sample data by combining these pairs of values into a single number, written as r. Thus, the sample **coefficient of correlation, r,** measures the amount of linearity that exists within a sample of n bivariate data. Its value is given by

Figure 14.1

Scatter diagram of real-estate data. **A:** Scatter diagram of sample data. **B:** Line through sample data.

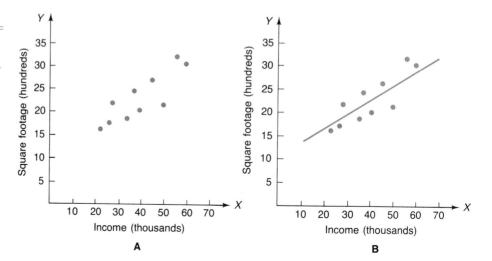

$$r = \frac{\Sigma(x - \bar{x})(y - \bar{y})}{\sqrt{\Sigma(x - \bar{x})^2}\ \sqrt{\Sigma(y - \bar{y})^2}} \qquad (14\text{-}1)$$

$$= \frac{\Sigma xy - (\Sigma x)(\Sigma y)/n}{\sqrt{\Sigma x^2 - (\Sigma x)^2/n}\ \sqrt{\Sigma y^2 - (\Sigma y)^2/n}} \qquad (14\text{-}2)$$

where Σx = sum of X values, Σx^2 = sum of X^2 values, Σy = sum of Y values, Σy^2 = sum of Y^2 values, Σxy = sum of XY values, $\bar{x} = \Sigma x/n$, and $\bar{y} = \Sigma y/n$.

Possible values for r range from -1 to 1. A value of -1 indicates a perfect linear relationship (negative), 0 indicates no linear relationship, and 1 indicates a perfect linear relationship (positive).

Sum of Squares We will introduce a shorthand notation at this point, related to the notation in Chapter 12 for ANOVA. Let

$$\begin{aligned}
\text{SS}_X &= \text{sum of squares for } X \\
&= \Sigma(x - \bar{x})^2 \qquad\qquad (14\text{-}3) \\
&= \Sigma x^2 - (\Sigma x)^2/n \\
\text{SS}_Y &= \text{sum of squares for } Y \\
&= \Sigma(y - \bar{y})^2 \qquad\qquad (14\text{-}4) \\
&= \Sigma y^2 - (\Sigma y)^2/n \\
\text{SS}_{XY} &= \text{sum of squares for } XY \\
&= \Sigma(x - \bar{x})(y - \bar{y}) \qquad (14\text{-}5) \\
&= \Sigma xy - (\Sigma x)(\Sigma y)/n
\end{aligned}$$

Using this notation, we can write r as

$$r = \frac{\text{SS}_{XY}}{\sqrt{\text{SS}_X}\ \sqrt{\text{SS}_Y}} \qquad (14\text{-}6)$$

Example 14.1   Determine the correlation coefficient for the real-estate data in Figure 14.1.

Solution   Your calculations can be summarized best as follows:

Family	X (Income)	Y (Square Footage)	XY	X²	Y²
1	22	16	352	484	256
2	26	17	442	676	289
3	45	26	1,170	2,025	676
4	37	24	888	1,369	576
5	28	22	616	784	484
6	50	21	1,050	2,500	441
7	56	32	1,792	3,136	1,024
8	34	18	612	1,156	324
9	60	30	1,800	3,600	900
10	40	20	800	1,600	400
	398	226	9,522	17,330	5,370

Using the totals from this table,

$$SS_X = 17,330 - (398)^2/10 = 1489.6$$

$$SS_Y = 5,370 - (226)^2/10 = 262.4$$

$$SS_{XY} = 9,522 - (398)(226)/10 = 527.2$$

The value of the correlation coefficient is

$$r = \frac{SS_{XY}}{\sqrt{SS_X}\ \sqrt{SS_Y}}$$

$$= \frac{527.2}{\sqrt{1489.6}\ \sqrt{262.4}} = \frac{527.2}{625.2}$$

$$= .843$$

Interpreting the Correlation Coefficient Having calculated a value of r, you next need to interpret the result. In example 14.1, is $r = .843$ large enough to conclude that a significant linear relationship exists between income level and home size? In Chapter 4, we used a table to answer this question. We did not discuss the assumptions behind this table, as well as the probability of concluding that a linear relationship exists when in fact it does not. Both topics will be discussed later in this chapter, when we introduce the idea of statistical modeling. We will outline another test of hypothesis that enables you to determine if the value of r leads to a conclusion that a significant (positive or negative) linear relationship exists between the two variables.

Covariance

Another commonly used measure of the association between two variables, X and Y, is the sample covariance, written $cov(X, Y)$. It is similar to the correlation between these two variables. For one thing, the covariance and correlation always have the *same sign*. Consequently, if large values of X are associated with large values of Y, then both the covariance and correlation are positive. Similarly, both values are negative whenever large values of X are associated with small values of Y. For any two variables, X and Y, the sample **covariance** between these variables is

$$cov(X, Y) = \frac{1}{n - 1}\Sigma(x - \bar{x})(y - \bar{y}) \qquad (14\text{-}7)$$

$$cov(X, Y) = \frac{1}{n - 1}SS_{XY} \qquad (14\text{-}8)$$

In example 14.1, the covariance between income (X) and home size (Y) is

$$cov(X, Y) = \frac{1}{n - 1}SS_{XY}$$

$$= \frac{1}{9}(527.2) = 58.58$$

To see how the sample covariance and sample correlation (r) are related, let

s_X = standard deviation of the X values

$$= \sqrt{\frac{SS_X}{n-1}}$$

and

s_Y = standard deviation of the Y values

$$= \sqrt{\frac{SS_Y}{n-1}}$$

Then

r = correlation between X and Y

$$= \frac{cov(X,Y)}{s_X s_Y} \qquad\qquad (14\text{-}9)$$

In example 14.1,

$$s_X = \sqrt{\frac{1489.6}{9}} = 12.865$$

$$s_Y = \sqrt{\frac{262.4}{9}} = 5.400$$

and so

$$r = \frac{58.58}{(12.865)(5.400)} = .843 \text{ (as before)}$$

The correlation between two variables is used more often than is the covariance because r always ranges from -1 to 1. The covariance, on the other hand, has no limits and can assume any value. So, in a sense, the correlation is a scaled version of the covariance. The covariance does have its applications, however, particularly in financial analyses, such as determining the risk associated with a number of interrelated investment opportunities.

As a final look at these two measures, you can consider the correlation between two variables to be the covariance between the **standardized** variables. By defining

$$X' = \frac{X - \overline{X}}{s_X}$$

and

$$Y' = \frac{Y - \overline{Y}}{s_Y}$$

then

$$cov(X', Y') = \text{correlation between } X \text{ and } Y$$
$$= r$$

Least Squares Line

Assuming that we believe two variables do exhibit an underlying linear pattern, how can we determine a straight line that best passes through these points? So far, we

Figure 14.2

Vertical distances from line L to real-estate data (example 14.1), represented by $d_1, d_2, \ldots, d_{10}$.

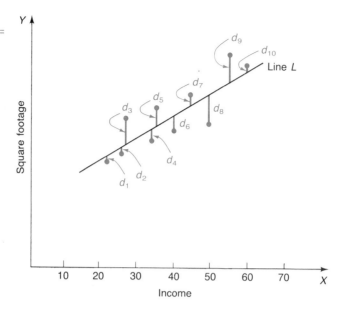

have demonstrated only the calculations necessary to compute a correlation coefficient. We will next illustrate how to construct a line through a set of points exhibiting a linear pattern; we will look at the assumptions behind this procedure in the next section.

Look at the scatter diagram in Figure 14.1b, which shows one possible line through these points. This diagram, as well as the vertical distances from each point to the line ($d_1, d_2, \ldots$) are contained in Figure 14.2.

Is line L the best line through these points? Because we would like the distances $d_1, d_2, \ldots, d_{10}$ to be *small*, we define the best line to be the one that minimizes

$$\Sigma d^2 = d_1^2 + d_2^2 + d_3^2 + \cdots + d_{10}^2 \tag{14-10}$$

We square each distance because some of these distances are positive (the point lies *above* line L) and some are negative (the point lies *below* line L). If we did not square each distance, d, the positive d's might cancel out the negative ones. This means that using ($d_1 + d_2 + \ldots + d_{10}$) as a *measure of fit* is *not* a good idea. A better method is to determine which line makes equation 14-10 as small as possible; this is called the **least squares line.** Deriving this line in general requires the use of calculus (derivatives, in particular).*

---

*For the mathematically curious, we provide a condensed derivation of these coefficients. In order to minimize Σd^2, first write this expression as

$$f(b_0, b_1) = \Sigma d^2 = \Sigma(y - \hat{y})^2$$
$$= \Sigma(y - b_0 - b_1 x)^2$$

because $\hat{y} = b_0 + b_1 x$.

To minimize this function, determine the partial derivatives with respect to b_0 (written f_{b_0}) and with respect to b_1 (written f_{b_1}). These are

$$f_{b_0} = 2\Sigma(y - b_0 - b_1 x)(-1)$$
$$f_{b_1} = 2\Sigma(y - b_0 - b_1 x)(-x)$$

Setting $f_{b_0} = f_{b_1} = 0$ and solving for b_0 and b_1 results in equations 14-11 and 14-12.

Because we intend to use this line to *estimate* Y for a particular value of X, we use the notation $\hat{Y}$ (Y hat) to describe the equation of the line. We can now define, for the least squares line, the b_0 and b_1 that minimize $(d_1^2 + d_2^2 + \cdots d_n^2)$, given by

$$b_1 = \frac{SS_{XY}}{SS_X} \tag{14-11}$$

$$b_0 = \bar{y} - b_1\bar{x} \tag{14-12}$$

where SS_X and SS_{XY} are as defined in equations 14-3 and 14-5. Also, $\bar{x} = \Sigma x/n$ and $\bar{y} = \Sigma y/n$. The resulting least squares line is

$$\hat{Y} = b_0 + b_1 X$$

In Figure 14.3, notice that each distance, d, is actually $Y - \hat{Y}$, and consists of the **error** or **residual**, encountered by using the straight line to estimate the value of Y at this point. So

$$\Sigma d^2 = \Sigma(y - \hat{y})^2$$

This term is the **sum of squares of error** (or *residual sum of squares*) and is written **SSE.** Consequently, the least squares line is the one that makes SSE as small as possible.

$$SSE = \Sigma d^2 = \Sigma(y - \hat{y})^2 \tag{14-13}$$

There is another method of determining SSE when using the least squares line, which avoids having to determine the value of $\hat{Y}$ at each point.

$$SSE = SS_Y - \frac{(SS_{XY})^2}{SS_X} \tag{14-14}$$

Figure 14.3

The least squares line for example 14.1. Each $d = Y - \hat{Y}$, the error encountered by using the straight line to estimate the value of Y at the corresponding point.

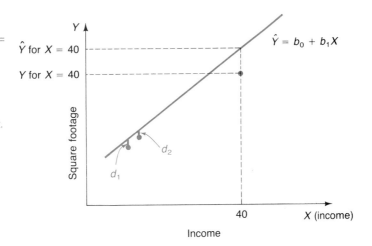

Example 14.2

Determine the least squares line for the real-estate data we used in example 14.1. What is the SSE?

Solution Using the calculations from example 14.1, $SS_{XY} = 527.2$, $SS_X = 1489.6$, and $SS_Y = 262.4$. This leads to

$$b_1 = \frac{SS_{XY}}{SS_X}$$

$$= \frac{527.2}{1489.6} = .354$$

and

$$b_0 = \bar{y} - b_1\bar{x}$$

$$= 22.6 - (.354)(39.8) = 8.51$$

because

$$\bar{y} = \Sigma y/n$$

$$= 226/10 = 22.6$$

and

$$\bar{x} = \Sigma x/n$$

$$= 398/10 = 39.8$$

So the equation of the best (least squares) line through these points is

$$\hat{Y} = 8.51 + .354\,X$$

This equation tells us that an increase of $1000 in income ($X$ increases by one) is accompanied by an increase of 35.4 square feet in home size (Y increases by .354), on the average. For this illustration (and many others in practice), the *intercept*, b_0, has no real meaning because it corresponds to an income of zero dollars. The *slope*, b_1, generally is the more informative value.

Figure 14.4

Least squares line for real-estate data (example 14.2).

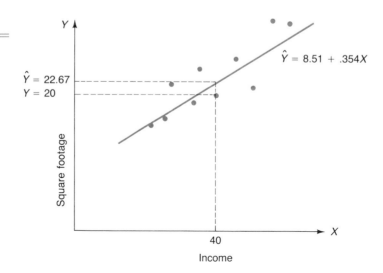

In Figure 14.4, the actual value of Y (in the sample data) for $X = 40$ is $Y = 20$ (the last pair of X, Y values). Your estimate of Y using the least squares line would be

$$\hat{Y} = 8.51 + .354(40) = 22.67$$

So, the error, or residual, at this point is

$$\text{Error} = Y - \hat{Y} = 20 - 22.67 = -2.67$$

Repeating this for the other nine points leads to the following results. Notice that the sum of the errors when using the least squares line is zero. This is always true.

X	Y	$\hat{Y}$	$Y - \hat{Y}$	$(Y - \hat{Y})^2$
22	16	16.30	$-$ .30	.090
26	17	17.71	$-$ .71	.504
45	26	24.44	1.56	2.434
37	24	21.61	2.39	5.712
28	22	18.42	3.58	12.816
50	21	26.21	-5.21	27.144
56	32	28.33	3.67	13.469
34	18	20.54	-2.54	6.452
60	30	29.75	.25	.063
40	20	22.67	-2.67	7.129
			0	75.81

As you can see, calculating the SSE ($= 75.81$) using the table and equation 14-13 is tedious. Using equation 14-14 instead leads to

$$\text{SSE} = 262.4 - \frac{(527.2)^2}{1489.6}$$

$$= 262.4 - 186.59$$

$$= 75.81 \text{ (the same as before)}$$

Remember, however, that equation 14-13 applies to *any* line that you choose to construct through these points, whereas equation 14-14 applies only to the SSE for the least squares line. ●

In example 14.2, we attempted to estimate the size of a home (Y) using the corresponding income (X). The variable Y is the **dependent variable** because we are implying that the value of Y *depends* on the value of X, the **independent variable.** By passing a straight line through the sample points with Y as the dependent variable, we are **regressing** Y on X. In linear regression, you regress the dependent variable, Y, which you are trying to estimate, on the independent (or predictor or explanatory) variable, X.

Exercises

14.1 It is believed that a strong linear relationship exists at a steel factory between the production of net tonnage of steel at an open hearth furnace (in thousands of net tons) and the number of hours worked at the furnace (in thousands). The following data were collected for analysis.

Year	Y: Production	X: Hours of Labor
1983	456	126
1982	950	350
1981	1701	650
1980	1510	480
1979	1250	412
1978	1112	356
1974	1160	362
1973	941	341
1972	840	250

a. Draw a scatter diagram of the X and Y values. What would you estimate the coefficient of correlation to be (without calculating it)?

b. Calculate the coefficient of correlation, r.

14.2 The manager of Computeron believes that there is a strong relationship between the total cost of operations and the amount of inventory on the balance sheet. A sample of 12 randomly selected months provides the following information:

Y: Total Cost of Operations	X: Total Cost of Inventory
120	31
90	22
81	20
110	27
160	39
155	38
108	27
105	23
113	28
95	26
105	25
140	35

a. Calculate the coefficient of correlation.

b. Find the least squares line.

c. Graph the data and the least squares line, as a check on your calculations.

d. Verify that the sum of the deviations from the least squares line is zero.

e. Interpret the coefficients of the least squares line.

14.3 Tony's used-car lot has been paying car salespeople the highest commission in town. Tony decides to compile data to substantiate his belief that yearly net earnings increase when the car salespeople are highly paid. Fifteen months are chosen:

Y: Net Earnings	X: Total Commissions Paid	Y: Net Earnings	X: Total Commissions Paid
10,780	3,680	11,915	3,161
15,120	5,160	25,160	7,540
18,195	5,180	26,151	8,216
21,690	7,150	18,630	6,051
14,691	5,030	15,551	4,980
16,151	5,210	16,980	5,801
11,015	2,991	24,130	7,160
10,151	3,151		

a. Graph the data and draw a line through them, using the "eyeball" method.

b. Calculate the least squares line. How does it compare to the line in question a?

14.4 The supervisor of a group of assembly-line workers wanted to compare last year's productivity (X) to this year's productivity (Y) for each of the 20 employees that she supervises. In the past, an approximate linear relationship has existed between these two variables. The average productivity last year per worker was 9.5 items per hour. This year, the average productivity per worker is 12.1 items per hour. The supervisor found the following sums for her 20 employees:

$$SS_{xy} = 0.4$$
$$SS_x = 0.3$$
$$SS_y = 0.8$$

a. Calculate the correlation coefficient.

b. Calculate the least squares line.

c. Calculate the sum of squares for error.

14.5 Because $b_0 = \bar{y} - b_1\bar{x}$ we can replace b_0 in $\hat{Y} = b_0 + b_1X_1$ by $\bar{y} - b_1\bar{x}$. Hence, we have $\hat{Y} = \bar{y} + b_1 (X - \bar{x})$. From this equation, show that the point $(\bar{x},\bar{y})$ falls on the least squares line.

14.6 Compare the formulas for the sample correlation, r, and the slope of the least squares line, b_1, and verify that $b_1 = r \sqrt{SS_y/SS_x}$. What can we say about the sign of r and b_1?

14.7 Lucky Jack's retail store advertises sale items each month to increase its sales. The manager believes that there is a linear relationship between the amount spent on advertising $(X$, in thousands of dollars) and the amount of merchandise sold $(Y$, in thousands). Data were collected for 10 months.

Y	X
21	5.3
16	3.8
13	3.1
12	2.9
18	4.4
20	4.9
23	5.1
24	5.4
14	3.2
19	5.1

a. Calculate the line of best fit.

b. Use the prediction equation to predict the amount of merchandise sold if $4,700 are spent on advertising.

14.8 The owner of Grandmother's Cake Shop would like to predict the quantity of cakes sold when they are marked at low prices. There are no restrictions on the quantity, because the shop can easily bake several cakes in an hour if the demand is stronger than predicted. Past data show the following results.

Y: Number of Cakes Sold	X: Price of Cake	Y: Number of Cakes Sold	X: Price of Cake
14	2.30	16	1.99
16	2.10	17	1.90
17	1.80	15	2.25
17	1.89	14	2.39
13	2.50	13	2.70
12	2.80		

a. Find the least squares line for X and Y.

b. Graph the data and the least squares line.

c. Suppose that the manager believes that there was a strong linear relationship between Y and X^2. Find the prediction equation for Y using X^2 only.

d. Compare the SSE for the least squares line found in question a with the least squares line found in question c.

14.9 The owner of an ice-cream stand believes that there is a linear relationship between the temperature (X) and the number of ice creams sold (Y). Data are collected during the noon hour every day for 20 days. The average number of ice creams sold during this hour is 35.6 and the average temperature over the 20 days at noon is 87.4. The following sample statistics were collected.

$$SS_{xy} = 8.4$$
$$SS_x = 28.1$$
$$SS_y = 3.9$$

a. Calculate the correlation coefficient.

b. Calculate the least squares line.

c. Calculate the error sum of squares.

14.10 In most developing countries, suicide is an important problem. One of the major causes is the economic pressure. The following are the unemployment rate (X) and the suicide rate (Y) for a certain third world country over the past 12 years. X is the number of unemployed per 100 people and Y represents the number of suicides per 10,000 people.

Y	X	Y	X
15.4	12.4	15.4	13.8
19.6	17.8	18.6	16.9
14.3	12.7	12.8	10.5
10.1	7.2	16.4	13.8
13.3	12.1	13.3	11.5
16.7	14.3	9.9	7.0

a. Calculate the least squares line. Interpret the coefficients of the least squares line in the context of the problem.

b. Calculate the error sum of squares.

c. Graph the data and draw the least squares line through them.

14.11 It is well known that the federal funds rate influences the yield on 13-week treasury bills. The federal funds rate is the rate at which reserves are traded among commercial banks for overnight use. Treasury bills are short-term government bills sold at an auction at a discount from the face value. The following data were collected.

Y: Treasury Bill Yield	X: Federal Funds Rate	Y: Treasury Bill Yield	X: Federal Funds Rate
12.89	14.23	8.79	9.43
12.36	14.51	9.39	9.56
9.71	11.01	9.05	9.45
7.93	9.29	8.71	9.48
8.08	8.65	8.71	9.34
8.42	8.80	8.96	9.47
9.19	9.46		

Find the least squares line and predict what the treasury bill rate would be if the federal funds rate was 9.67. Interpret the coefficient of the X variable in the least squares line.

14.12 The following equation is used to predict total yearly maintenance cost (Y) from the number of breakdowns (X) that a certain machine had during the year.

$$\hat{Y} = 3712 + 1279.5X$$

Interpret the value of the coefficient 1279.5.

14.2

The Simple Linear Regression Model

When we previously constructed a straight line through a set of data points, we were attempting to predict the behavior of a dependent variable, Y, using a straight line equation with one predictor (independent) variable, X. Examples 14.1 and 14.2 examined the relationship in a particular community between the square footage (Y) of a particular home and the income of the owner (X).

Another application would be attempting to predict the sales (Y) of a certain brand of shampoo using the amount of advertising expenditure (X) as the independent variable. We expect that, as more advertising dollars are spent, the sales will increase. In other words, we expect a *positive* relationship for this situation.

Regression analysis is a method of studying the relationship between two (or more) variables, the purpose being to arrive at a method for predicting a value of the dependent variable. In **simple linear regression,** you use only *one* predictor variable, X, to describe the behavior of the dependent variable, Y. Also, the relationship between X and Y is assumed to be basically linear.

You have learned the mechanics of constructing a line through a set of bivariate sample values. We are now ready to introduce the concept of a statistical model.

Defining the Model

Return to example 14.2 and Figure 14.4. This set of sample data contained a value of $X = 40$ and $Y = 20$. Consider the population of *all* houses in this community where the owner's income is 40 (that is, \$40,000). Will they all have the same square footage? Unless this is a very boring-looking neighborhood, certainly not. Does this mean that the straight line predictor is of no use? The answer, again, is no, because very few things in this world are that perfectly predictable. When you use the straight line to predict the square footage, you should be aware that there will be a certain amount of *error* present in this estimate. This is similar to the situation dealing with estimating the mean, μ, of a population where the sample mean, $\overline{X}$, always estimates this parameter with a certain amount of error.

When we elect to use a straight line predictor, we employ a **statistical model** of the form

$$Y = \beta_0 + \beta_1 X + e \tag{14-15}$$

where (1) $\beta_0 + \beta_1 X$ is the *assumed* line about which *all* values of X and Y will fall, called the **deterministic** portion of the model; and (2) e is the error component, referred to as the **random** part of the model.

In other words, there exists some (unknown) line about which all X, Y values can be expected to fall. Notice that we said "about which," not "on which"—hence the necessity of the error term, e, which is the unexplained error that results from the simple linear model. Because this model considers only one independent variable, the effect of the other variables (perhaps unknown to the analyst) is contained in this error term.

We emphasize that the deterministic portion, $\beta_0 + \beta_1 X$, refers to the straight line for the *population* and will remain unknown. However, by obtaining a random sample of bivariate data from this population, we are able to estimate the unknown parameters, β_0 and β_1. Thus b_0 is the **intercept** of the sample regression line and is the estimate of the population intercept, β_0. The value of b_0 can be calculated using equation 14-12. Similarly, b_1 is the **slope** of the sample regression line and is the estimate of the population slope, β_1. The value of b_1 can be calculated using equation 14-11.

Assumptions for the Simple Linear Regression Model

We can construct a least squares line through *any* set of sample points, whether or not the pattern is linear. We could construct a least squares line through a set of sample data exhibiting no linear pattern at all. However, to have an effective predictor and a model that will enable us to make statistical decisions, certain assumptions are necessary.

We treat the values of X as fixed (nonrandom) quantities when using the simple linear regression model. For any given value of X, the only source of variation comes from the error component, e, which is a random variable. In fact, there are many random variables here, one for each possible value of X. The assumptions used with this model are concerned with the nature of these random variables.

The first three assumptions are concerned with the behavior of the error component for a fixed value of X. The fourth assumption deals with the manner in which the error components (random variables) affect each other.

Assumption 1 *The mean of each error is zero.* This is the key assumption behind simple linear regression. Look at Figure 14.5, where we once again examine a value of $X = 40$. If we consider all homes in this community whose owners have an income

Figure 14.5

Illustration of assumption 1; see text.

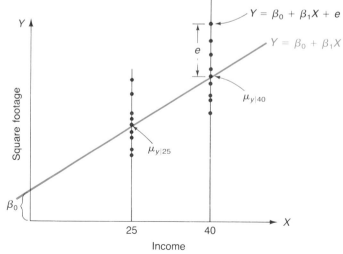

Figure 14.6

A violation of assumption 3; see text.

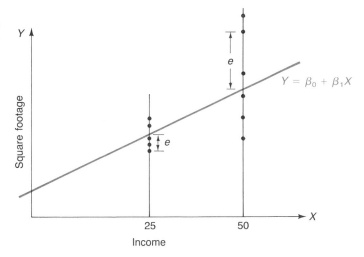

of \$40,000 ($X = 40$), we have already decided the homes do not all have the same square footage, Y. In fact, the square footage values will be scattered about the (unknown) line $Y = \beta_0 + \beta_1 X$, with some values lying above the line (e is positive) and some falling below it (e is negative). Consider the average of *all* Y values with $X = 40$. This is written as

$$\mu_{Y|40}$$

which is the mean of Y *given* $X = 40$. Our assumption here is that $\mu_{Y|40}$ *lines on this line;* that is, for *any* value of X, $\mu_{Y|X}$ lies on the line $Y = \beta_0 + \beta_1 X$ (such as $\mu_{Y|25}$ in Figure 14.5). Put another way, the error is, *on the average,* equal to zero.

Assumption 2 *Each error component (random variable) follows an approximate normal distribution.* In our sample of ten homes and incomes, we had one family with $X = 40$ and $Y = 20$. Figure 14.5 illustrates what we might expect if we *were* to examine other homes whose owners had an income of \$40,000. We assume here that if we were to obtain, say, 100 homes whose owners had this income, a histogram of the resulting errors (e) would be bell-shaped in appearance. So we would expect a concentration of errors near zero (from assumption 1), with one-half of them positive and one-half of them negative.

Assumption 3 *The variance of the error component, σ_e^2, is the same for each value of X.* For each value of X, the errors illustrated in Figure 14.5 have so far been assumed to follow a normal distribution, with mean = zero. So each error, e, is from such a normal population. The variance of this population is σ_e^2. The assumption here is that σ_e^2 *does not change* as the value of X changes. This is the assumption of **homoscedasticity.** A situation where this assumption is violated is illustrated in Figure 14.6, where we once again consider what might occur if we *were* to obtain (we will not, actually) many values of Y for $X = 25$ and $X = 50$. If Figure 14.6 were the result, assumption 3 would be violated because the errors would be much larger (in absolute value) for the \$50,000-income homes than they would for the \$25,000-income homes. This is **heteroscedasticity,** which does pose a problem when we try to infer results from a linear regression equation.

You might argue that, proportionally, the errors for $X = 50$ seem about the same as those for $X = 25$, which means that you would expect larger errors for larger

Figure 14.7

Illustration of assumptions 1, 2, 3; see text.

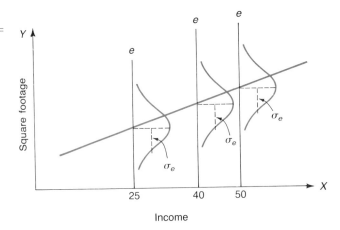

values of X here. If this is the case, then the CIs and tests of hypothesis that we are about to develop for the simple linear regression model are *not appropriate*. There are methods of "repairing" this situation, by applying a *transformation* to the dependent variable, Y, such as $\sqrt{Y}$ or $\log(Y)$. By using this "new" dependent variable rather than the original Y, the resulting errors often will exhibit a nearly constant variance. Such transformations, however, are beyond the scope of this text.

A summary of the first three assumptions is shown in Figure 14.7. Note that the distribution of errors is *identical* for each illustrated value of X; namely, it is a normal distribution with mean = zero and variance σ_e^2.

Assumption 4 *The errors are independent of each other.* This implies that the error encountered in predicting Y for one value of X is unaffected by the error for any other value of X. To illustrate, consider the real-estate data and suppose that the sample is *not* random but that instead the sampled houses are all located on a certain street. The first house has a positive error when predicting the square footage. If the probability is greater than .5 that the next house in the sample also has a positive error (that is, if its location makes it probable that it will be a certain size), then the assumption of independence is violated. In other words, the sample was poorly chosen because the houses on one street are likely to be more or less the same size and their owners are likely to have similar incomes. The nonrandom sample led to a violation of assumption 4.

We can draw two conclusions from these assumptions. First, each value of the dependent variable, Y, is a normal random variable with mean = $\beta_0 + \beta_1 X$ and variance σ_e^2. Second, the error components come from the same normal population, *regardless of the value* of X. In other words, it makes sense to examine the residuals resulting from each value of X in the sample, to construct a histogram of these residuals, and to determine whether its appearance is bell-shaped (normal), centered at zero. A key assumption when using simple linear regression is that the residuals (errors) follow a normal distribution with a mean of zero. Constructing a histogram of the residuals provides an easy method of determining whether this assumption is satisfied for a particular application.

We will further discuss methods of examining each of these assumptions in Chapter 15, where we will learn how to use more than one independent variable in a linear regression equation.

Estimating the Error Variance, σ_e^2

The variance of the error component, σ_e^2, measures the variation of the error terms resulting from the simple linear regression model. The value of σ_e^2 severely affects our ability to use this model as an effective predictor for a given situation. Suppose, for example, that σ_e^2 is very large in Figure 14.7. This means that, if we were to obtain many observations (square footage values, Y) for a *fixed* value of X (say, income = \$40,000), these Y values would vary a great deal. This decreases the accuracy of our model; we would prefer that these values were grouped closely about the mean, $\mu_{Y|40}$.

In practice, σ_e^2 typically is unknown and must be estimated from the sample. To estimate this variance, we first determine the sum of squares of error, SSE, using SSE = $\Sigma(y - \hat{y})^2$ or equation 14-14. Estimating β_0 and β_1 for the simple regression model results in a loss of 2 degrees of freedom, leaving $n - 2$ *df* for estimating the error variance. Consequently,

$$s^2 = \hat{\sigma}_e^2 = \text{estimate of } \sigma_e^2$$

$$= \frac{\text{SSE}}{n - 2} \qquad\qquad (14\text{-}16)$$

where

$$\text{SSE} = \Sigma(y - \hat{y})^2$$

$$= \text{SS}_Y - \frac{(\text{SS}_{XY})^2}{\text{SS}_X}$$

We can determine the estimate of σ_e^2 and σ_e for the real-estate data in example 14.2, where we calculated the value of SSE to be 75.81. Our estimate of σ_e^2 is

$$s^2 = \frac{\text{SSE}}{n - 2} = \frac{75.81}{8} = 9.476$$

and so $s = \sqrt{9.476} = 3.078$ provides an estimate of σ_e. The values of s^2 and s are a measure of the variation of the Y values about the least squares line.

Comments

We know from the empirical rule that approximately 95% of the data from a normal population should lie within two standard deviations of the mean. For this example, this implies that:

1. Approximately 95% of the error values should lie within 2(3.078) = 6.16 of the mean. In the table in example 14.2, the sample errors are in the fourth column. Their sum is *always* zero, when using the least squares line; therefore, their mean is zero. So, approximately 95% of these values should be no larger (in absolute value) than 6.16. In fact, all of them are less than 6.16—not a surprising result, given that we had only ten values to work with.
2. Approximately 95% of the $\hat{Y}$ values should lie within 6.16 of the actual value, Y. The table in exercise 14.2 shows that 100% of the estimates lie within this distance.

Exercises

14.13 A stock broker collected data on company XYZ's quarterly earnings (X) and also on the company's closing price (Y) on the day that the quarterly earnings were reported.

Y: Closing Price	X: Quarterly Earnings
10.125	1.09
10.0	1.10
10.25	1.12
10.75	1.80
10.5	1.95
14.0	2.0
14.25	2.10
14.37	2.50
15.0	2.85
14.55	2.65

a. Find the least squares line. Then graph the data and the least squares line.

b. Find the residual $(Y - \hat{Y})$ for each value of Y.

c. Is there any indication that the error terms may be correlated?

14.14 The following data were collected for labor hours (X, in hundreds) spent on maintenance and total cost (Y in thousands of dollars) of maintenance.

X: Labor Hours	Y: Total Cost
2.1	5.5
2.9	6.4
4.9	11.2
3.8	7.9
2.8	6.3
1.4	6.2
6.1	12.9
5.0	13.5
6.2	12.8
4.3	10.7
4.1	9.4
2.3	4.7
6.7	14.9
7.2	13.3
4.8	13.0
5.3	12.9
5.2	12.2
1.2	2.5
4.5	8.6
3.8	8.4

a. Calculate the least squares line. Interpret the coefficients of the least squares line in the context of the problem.

b. Find the residuals $(Y - \hat{Y})$ for each value of Y.

c. Construct a histogram for the residuals. Do they appear to follow a normal distribution?

14.15 An experiment was performed in which different amounts (in milligrams) of an anti-hypertension drug were given to a rat. The decrease in systolic blood pressure (Y) was recorded for X number of milligrams. The following sample statistics were collected from 25 observations.

$$SS_{xy} = -10.3 \qquad SS_y = 15.3 \qquad SS_x = 13.2$$

Determine an estimate for the variance of the error component for the linear model $Y = \beta_0 + \beta_1 X_1 + e$.

14.16 What assumptions need to be made about the error component of a linear model in order that statistical inference can be used?

14.17 The following is a list of sample errors $(Y - \hat{Y})$ from a linear regression application:

2.1, $-.3$, 1.4, -2.8, -3.9, 4.2, 3.6, 4.3, 1.8, -2.7, $-.8$, 1.2, .9, -1.1, -4.5, -5.2, -1.3, .5, .9, $-.6$, 1.5, 2.1, -2.2, .9

Do the data appear to conform to the empirical rule that approximately 95% of the errors should lie within two standard deviations of the mean? Construct a histogram for the residuals.

14.18 Let X be the distance an employee lives from his or her job. Let Y be the average time that it takes the employee to drive to work. Data from 30 employees gave the following sample statistics.

$$SS_{xy} = 8.4 \qquad SS_x = 9.4 \qquad SS_y = 12.2$$

a. Find the estimate of the error variance.

b. Find the interval in which approximately 68.26% of the error values should fall.

14.19 The following are residuals resulting from a regression analysis:

$Y - \hat{Y}$	X
.2	1
$-$ .2	1.5
$-$ .5	1.75
.6	2.00
$-$ .5	2.50
$-$ .8	3.00
1.0	4.00
-1.5	5.00
-1.7	6.00
2.1	7.00
-2.5	8.00
3.8	9.00

From these data, where Y is the dependent variable and X is the independent variable, does it appear that any of the standard assumptions of regression analysis are violated?

14.20 Why is $\Sigma(y - \hat{y})^2$ used in estimating the variance of the error term instead of $\Sigma(y - \hat{y})$?

14.21 In the statistical model $Y = \beta_0 + \beta_1 X_1 + e$, is X a random variable? Comment on your answer.

14.22 Let X be a person's income. Let Y be the amount of life insurance that this person has. Data from 20 people were collected (in thousands of dollars):

X: Income	Y: Life Insurance	X: Income	Y: Life Insurance
15.4	33.2	28.6	53.7
19.8	39.5	38.7	67.6
20.6	42.2	41.5	75.4
29.4	52.5	40.1	68.3
22.3	44.3	36.5	65.2
19.5	42.3	27.4	51.2
30.8	57.6	28.6	54.9
25.5	49.2	21.4	41.0
20.4	41.6	19.8	40.9
18.4	36.7	20.1	40.2

a. Calculate the least squares line.

b. Find the residual $Y - \hat{Y}$ for each value of Y.

c. Construct a histogram of the residuals.

d. Do the residuals appear to follow a normal distribution?

14.3

Inference on the Slope, β_1

Performing a Test of Hypothesis on the Slope of the Regression Line

Under the assumptions of the simple linear regression model outlined in the previous section, we are now in a position to determine whether a linear relationship exists between the variables X and Y. Examining the estimate of the slope, b_1, will provide information as to the nature of this relationship.

Consider the *population* slope, β_1. Three possible situations are demonstrated in Figure 14.8. What can you say about using X as a predictor of Y in Figure 14.8a? When $\beta_1 = 0$, the population line is perfectly horizontal. As a result, the value of Y is the *same* for each value of X, and so X is not a good predictor of Y; the value of X provides no information regarding the value of Y.

To determine whether X provides information in predicting Y, the hypotheses would be

$H_0: \beta_1 = 0$ (X provides no information)

$H_a: \beta_1 \neq 0$ (X does provide information)

Other Alternative Hypotheses If we are attempting to demonstrate that a significant *positive* relationship exists between X and Y, the appropriate alternative hypothesis would be $H_a: \beta_1 > 0$. For example, do the data in example 14.1 support the hypothesis that owners with large incomes are associated with larger homes?

When the purpose of the analysis is to determine whether a *negative* relationship exists between X and Y, the alternative hypothesis should be $H_a: \beta_1 < 0$. For example, you would expect such a relationship between the number of new housing starts (Y) and the interest rate (X). As the interest rate increases, you would expect the number of new houses under construction to decrease.

The Test Statistic We use the point estimate of β_1 (that is, b_1) in the test statistic to determine the nature of β_1. What is b_1? A constant? A variable? Suppose that we obtained a different set of data and recalculated b_1. The new value would not be exactly the same as the previous value, which implies that b_1 is actually a variable. To be more precise, under the assumptions of the previous section, b_1 is a *normal* random variable with mean $= \beta_1$ and variance $= \sigma_{b_1}^2 = (\sigma_e^2)/(SS_X)$.

If we replace the unknown σ_e^2 by its estimate, s^2, then the *estimated* variance of b_1 is $s_{b_1}^2 = s^2/SS_X$. Consider

$$t = \frac{b_1 - \beta_1}{s/\sqrt{SS_X}} = \frac{b_1 - \beta_1}{s_{b_1}} \qquad (14\text{-}17)$$

Figure 14.8

Three possible population slopes (β_1).

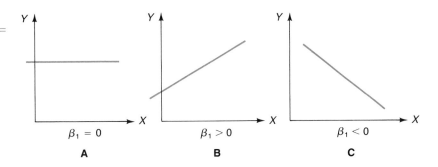

This will have a t distribution with $n - 2$ df. If the null hypothesis is H_0: $\beta_1 = 0$, the test statistic becomes

$$t = \frac{b_1}{s/\sqrt{SS_X}}$$ (14-18)

A summary of the testing procedure is shown in the accompanying box. As usual, for a one-tailed test, the null hypothesis can be written as an inequality (≤ 0 or ≥ 0), or as an equality using the boundary condition ($= 0$).

Test of Hypothesis on the Slope of the Regression Line

TWO-TAILED TEST

H_0: $\beta_1 = 0$

H_a: $\beta_1 \neq 0$

Test statistic

$$t = \frac{b_1}{s_{b_1}}$$

where $s_{b_1} = s/\sqrt{SS_X}$ and the $df = n - 2$

Test

Reject H_0 if $|t| > t_{\alpha/2, n-2}$

ONE-TAILED TEST

H_0: $\beta_1 = 0$ (≤ 0)	H_0: $\beta_1 = 0$ (≥ 0)
H_a: $\beta_1 > 0$	H_a: $\beta_1 < 0$

Test statistic

$$t = \frac{b_1}{s_{b_1}} \qquad\qquad t = \frac{b_1}{s_{b_1}}$$

where $s_{b_1} = s/\sqrt{SS_X}$ and the $df = n - 2$ (left); where $s_{b_1} = s/\sqrt{SS_X}$ and the $df = n - 2$ (right)

Test

Reject H_0 if $t > t_{\alpha, n-2}$ (left)   Reject H_0 if $t < -t_{\alpha, n-2}$ (right)

Example 14.3

Is there sufficient evidence, using the real-estate data in example 14.1, to conclude that a significant positive relationship exists between income (X) and home size (Y)? Use $\alpha = .05$.

Solution

Step 1. The hypotheses here should be

$$H_0: \beta_1 = 0$$
$$H_a: \beta_1 > 0$$

Step 2. The test statistic is

$$t = \frac{b_1}{s_{b_1}}$$

which has a t distribution with $n - 2 = 8$ df.

Step 3. The testing procedure (rejection region) will be

$$\text{Reject } H_0 \text{ if } t > t_{.05,8} = 1.860$$

This area is sketched in Figure 14.9.

Step 4. We previously determined that $SS_X = 1489.6$, $b_1 = .354$, and $s = 3.078$. The calculated test statistic is then

$$t^* = \frac{.354}{3.078/\sqrt{1489.6}} = \frac{.354}{.0797} = 4.44$$

where $s_{b_1} = .0797$.

Because $4.44 > 1.86$, we reject H_0.

Step 5. Based on these ten observations, we conclude that a positive linear relationship does exist between income and home size. ●

A MINITAB solution using the real estate data is shown in Figure 14.10. This output contains nearly all the calculations performed so far. In particular, note that

1. The least squares equation is $\hat{Y} = 8.51 + .354X$.
2. The standard deviation of b_1 is $s_{b_1} = .07976$.
3. The value of the test statistic is $t^* = b_1/s_{b_1} = 4.44$.
4. The standard deviation of the error component is $s = 3.078$.
5. The value of SSE is 75.81, contained in the ANOVA table (construction of this table will be discussed in Chapter 15).
6. The column of estimated Y's $(\hat{Y}$'s) and the corresponding errors (residuals) are in the column labeled $Y - \hat{Y}$.

Figure 14.9

t curve with 8 df showing rejection region (shaded) for example 14.3.

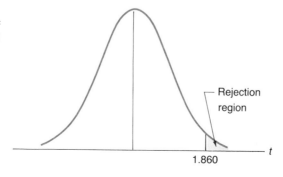

Rejection region

1.860

t

Figure 14.10

MINITAB solution to
example 14.3.

```
MTB > SET INTO C1
DATA> 22 26 45 37 28 50 56 34 60 40
DATA> END
MTB > SET INTO C2
DATA> 16 17 26 24 22 21 32 18 30 20
DATA> END
MTB > BRIEF 3
MTB > REGRESS Y IN C2 USING 1 PREDICTOR IN C1
```

The regression equation is
C2 = 8.51 + 0.354 C1 ← —— Least squares line

Predictor	Coef	Stdev	t-ratio
Constant	8.514	3.320	2.56
C1	0.35392	0.07976	4.44

s_{b_1} $t = b_1/s_{b_1}$ (Example 14.3)

(Section 14.2) → s = 3.078   R-sq = 71.1%   R-sq(adj) = 67.5%

Analysis of Variance

SOURCE	DF	SS	MS
Regression	1	186.59	186.59
Error	8	75.81	9.48
Total	9	262.40	

SSE

Obs.	C1	C2	Fit	Stdev.Fit	Residual	St.Resid
1	22.0	16.000	16.300	1.721	-0.300	-0.12
2	26.0	17.000	17.716	1.469	-0.716	-0.26
3	45.0	26.000	24.440	1.058	1.560	0.54
4	37.0	24.000	21.609	0.999	2.391	0.82
5	28.0	22.000	18.424	1.354	3.576	1.29
6	50.0	21.000	26.210	1.269	-5.210	-1.86
7	56.0	32.000	28.334	1.618	3.666	1.40
8	34.0	18.000	20.547	1.078	-2.547	-0.88
9	60.0	30.000	29.749	1.882	0.251	0.10
10	40.0	20.000	22.671	0.974	-2.671	-0.91

$\hat{Y}$ $Y - \hat{Y}$

Example 14.4   The personnel director at Blackburn Industries is interested in knowing whether a relationship exists between the age of the company's secretaries and the number of days they are absent. She does not know whether younger or older secretaries are more likely to have high absenteeism. A random sample of 12 secretaries was selected, and the following data were obtained. Absenteeism is given as the number of days absent during the past 12 months.

Age (X)	Absenteeism (Y)
19	14
52	2
28	10
40	10
50	6
21	9
45	5
38	7
24	12
30	13
42	9
35	15

A scatter diagram of these 12 observations is provided in Figure 14.11, with a summary of the calculations. Using $\alpha = .10$, do you think that a secretary's age provides useful information for predicting this person's absenteeism?

Solution To derive the least squares regression line, we determine

$$b_1 = \frac{SS_{XY}}{SS_X} = \frac{-346.33}{1342.67} = -.258$$

and

$$b_0 = \bar{y} - b_1\bar{x}$$
$$= 9.33 - (-.258)35.33 = 18.44$$

Consequently, the least squares line is

$$\hat{Y} = 18.44 - .258X$$

Notice that the slope of this line is negative. As the following test of hypothesis will conclude, this slope is significant. Consequently, higher absenteeism is associated with the *younger* secretaries. According to these data, each additional year of age is accompanied by a decrease of .258 day in absenteeism, on the average.

To carry out a test of hypothesis, we follow the usual five-step procedure.

Step 1. Because the suspected direction of the relationship between these two variables (positive or negative) is unknown before the data are obtained, a two-tailed test is appropriate. The hypotheses are

$$H_0: \beta_1 = 0$$
$$H_a: \beta_1 \neq 0$$

Step 2. The test statistic is $t = b_1/s_{b_1}$, which has $n - 2 = 10$ df.
Step 3. The rejection region is defined by

$$\text{Reject } H_0 \text{ if } |t| > t_{.10/2,10} = t_{.05,10} = 1.812$$

Figure 14.11

Scatter diagram of age and absenteeism data from example 14.4, with a summary of the calculations.

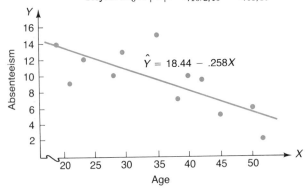

$$SS_X = 1342.67 \qquad SS_Y = 164.67 \qquad SS_{XY} = -346.33$$
$$\bar{x} = 35.33 \qquad \bar{y} = 9.33$$
$$r = \frac{SS_{XY}}{\sqrt{SS_X}\sqrt{SS_Y}} = -.737$$

Step 4. Based on the data summary in Figure 14.11, and using equation 14-14,

$$SSE = SS_Y - \frac{(SS_{XY})^2}{SS_X}$$

$$= 164.67 - \frac{(-346.33)^2}{1342.67}$$

$$= 164.67 - 89.33$$

$$= 75.34$$

Consequently,

$$s^2 = \frac{SSE}{n - 2}$$

$$= \frac{75.34}{10} = 7.534$$

and so

$$s_{b_1} = \frac{s}{\sqrt{SS_X}}$$

$$= \frac{\sqrt{7.534}}{\sqrt{1342.67}} = .0749$$

This means that the computed value of the test statistic is

$$t^* = \frac{b_1}{s_{b_1}}$$

$$= \frac{-.258}{.0749} = -3.44$$

Because $|\,t^*\,| = 3.44$ exceeds the table value of 1.812, we reject H_0 in support of H_a.

Step 5. Our conclusion is that age is a good (although imperfect) predictor of absenteeism.

Remember that, as we have seen in previous tests of hypothesis, *statistical* significance does not always imply *practical* significance. In other words, rejection of H_0: $\beta_1 = 0$ (statistical significance) does not mean that precise prediction (practical significance) will follow. It *does* demonstrate to the researcher that, within the sample data at least, this particular independent variable has an association with the dependent variable. ●

Confidence Interval for β_1

Following our usual procedure of providing a CI with a point estimate, we use the t distribution of the previous test statistic and equation 14-17 to define a CI for β_1. The narrower this CI is, the more faith we have in our estimate of β_1 and in our model as an accurate, reliable predictor of the dependent variable. A $(1 - \alpha) \cdot 100\%$ CI for β_1 is

$$b_1 - t_{\alpha/2, n-2}\, s_{b_1} \qquad \text{to} \qquad b_1 + t_{\alpha/2, n-2}\, s_{b_1}$$

Example 14.5

Construct a 90% CI for the population slope, β_1, using the real-estate data in example 14.1.

Solution All the necessary calculations have been completed; $b_1 = .354$ and $s_{b_1} = .0797$ (from example 14.3). Using $t_{.05,8} = 1.860$, the resulting CI is

$$.354 - (1.860)(.0797) \quad \text{to} \quad .354 + (1.860)(.0797)$$
$$= .354 - .148 \quad \text{to} \quad .354 + .148$$
$$= .206 \quad \text{to} \quad .502$$

So we are 90% confident that the value of the estimated slope ($b_1 = .354$) is within .148 of the actual slope, β_1. The large width of this interval is due in part to the lack of information (small sample size) used to derive the estimates; a larger sample would decrease the width of this CI. •

Comments

A failure to reject H_0 when performing a hypothesis test on β_1 does not always indicate that no relationship exists between the two variables. Some form of non-linear relationship may exist between these variables. For example, in Figure 14.12, there is clearly a strong curved (**curvilinear**) relationship between X and Y. How-ever, the least squares line through these points is flat, leading to a small t value and a failure to reject H_0. Furthermore, the sample correlation coefficient, r, for these data is zero.

Of course, you may fail to reject H_0 as the result of a type II error. In other words, you failed to reject H_0 when in fact a significant linear relationship does exist. This situation is more apt to occur when using a small sample to test the null hypothesis.

More often, a failure to reject H_0 will occur when there is no visible relationship between the two variables within the sample data. To determine whether there is no relationship, or that there is a nonlinear one, you should inspect either a scatter diagram of the data or, better yet, a scatter diagram of the residuals, or both. The latter diagram is a picture of the residuals ($Y - \hat{Y}$) plotted against the independent variable, X. Residual plots will be discussed further in Chapter 15.

In many situations, a business analyst has the opportunity to select the values of the independent variable, X, *before* the sample is obtained. At first glance, it might appear that the accuracy of our model is unaffected by the X values. This is partially true but not completely true.

Because a narrow CI for β_1 lends credibility to our model, we may choose to decrease the width of this CI by decreasing s_{b_1}. Now, $s_{b_1} = s/\sqrt{SS_X}$, so, if we make SS_X large, the resulting s_{b_1} will be small. Therefore, given the opportunity, select a set of X values having a *large variance*. You can accomplish this by choosing a

Figure 14.12

Curvilinear relationship. The horizontal line is the least squares line.

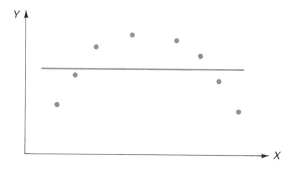

great many X values on the lower end of your range of interest, a large number of values at the upper end, and some values in between to detect any curvature that exists (as in Figure 14.12).

Exercises

14.23 A banker is interested in the relationship between a person's income and the amount of money the person has in tax-free investment instruments (such as municipal bonds or IRAs). Data on 20 working individuals were collected. The results are as follows (in thousands of dollars):

X: Income	Y: Money In Tax-Free Investments	X: Income	Y: Money In Tax-Free Investments
20.2	5.1	24.1	5.2
33.2	7.5	25.1	4.4
35.1	8.1	34.2	7.1
29.4	6.7	33.0	5.1
33.0	7.4	45.1	12.4
40.1	9.4	41.0	9.8
41.0	9.7	45.1	8.9
45.1	10.1	40.1	8.8
42.3	9.1	31.2	6.9
45.3	11.4	24.0	4.2

a. Is there sufficient evidence using the observed data to conclude that a positive relationship exists between X and Y? Use a 5% significance level.

b. Find the p-value for the test statistic in question a. What is your conclusion based on this value?

14.24 The regression equation $\hat{Y} = 2.3 + 1.5X$ was arrived at by fitting a least squares line to 25 data points. The standard deviation (error) of the estimate of the slope was found to be 0.812. Test the null hypothesis at the .01 level of significance that the slope of the line is equal to zero.

14.25 It is believed that the size of the U.S. population (X) is a variable that influences personal consumption expenditure for housing (Y). However, the relationship historically does not appear to be linear. Therefore, a log transformation of housing expenditure is used. Fifteen observations are taken over previous years. The units of Y are millions and the units of X are billions.

X	Log Y	X	Log Y
183.69	3.935	202.68	4.465
186.54	4.001	205.05	4.542
189.24	4.060	207.66	4.631
191.89	4.117	209.90	4.722
194.30	4.182	211.91	4.818
196.56	4.241	213.85	4.923
198.71	4.305	215.97	5.009
200.71	4.379		

From the data, does there appear to be a significant positive relationship between X and log Y? Use a significance level of .05.

14.26 The life of a lawn-mower engine can be extended by frequent oil changes. An experiment was conducted in which 20 lawn mowers were used over many years with different time intervals between oil changes. Let X be the number of hours of operation between oil changes. Let Y be the number of years that the engine was able to perform adequately.

X	Y	X	Y
11.25	12.1	23.5	8.8
15.5	11.8	24.0	7.1
17.5	11.5	24.5	7.2
20.5	10.1	25.0	5.8
19.5	9.9	25.5	6.1
18.5	9.7	26.0	5.4
21.5	10.1	26.5	4.8
22.0	9.5	27.0	4.6
22.5	9.2	28.0	4.8
23.0	8.4	30.0	4.1

a. Graph the data and the least squares line.

b. Is there sufficient evidence to conclude, at the 10% significance level, that a negative relationship exists between Y and X? What is the critical region?

14.27 Using a 10% significance level, test that the total cost of inventory in exercise 14.2 provides significant information for predicting the total cost of operations. Find a 95% CI for the slope.

14.28 A medical researcher was interested in the amount of weight loss caused by a particular diuretic. In a controlled experiment with 18 rats, the amount of weight loss was recorded after 1 month of daily dose of the diuretic. Let X be the amount, in milligrams, of diuretic given. Let Y be the weight loss in pounds.

X	Y	X	Y
0.10	0.05	0.30	0.42
0.10	0.08	0.35	0.43
0.15	0.11	0.35	0.42
0.15	0.13	0.40	0.44
0.20	0.19	0.40	0.47
0.20	0.21	0.45	0.51
0.25	0.35	0.45	0.52
0.25	0.31	0.50	0.54
0.30	0.41	0.50	0.53

Is there sufficient evidence to conclude that a significant positive relationship exists between the amount of diuretic given and the amount of weight loss? Use a significance level of 10%. Find a 90% CI for the slope of the regression equation used to predict Y.

14.29 Using the data in exercise 14.4, find a 95% CI for the slope of the regression equation used to predict the current year's productivity from the previous year's productivity for each employee.

14.30 An investment counselor wanted to know the relationship between the price:earnings ratio (Y) and the yield (X) for high-yield stocks. If a stock yielded over 5.5%, it was considered to be a high-yield stock. Twenty-five high-yield stocks were randomly selected. The following sample statistics were found:

$$SS_{xy} = -10.4$$

$$SS_x = 11.4$$

$$SS_y = 21.4$$

a. Test that the slope of the regression equation used to predict the price:earnings ratio from the yield of a stock is negative. Use a 10% significance level.

b. Find a 95% CI for the slope in question a.

14.31 In exercise 14.9, find the 90% CI for the slope of the regression equation used to predict the number of ice creams sold by using the independent variable, temperature.

14.32 In exercise 14.10, find the 95% CI for the slope of the regression equation used to predict the suicide rate from the unemployment rate.

14.4

Measuring the Strength of the Model

We have already used the sample coefficient of correlation, r, as a measure of the amount of linear association within a sample of bivariate data. The value of r is given by

$$r = \frac{SS_{XY}}{\sqrt{SS_X}\,\sqrt{SS_Y}} \qquad (14\text{-}19)$$

The possible range for r is -1 to 1.

Comparing the equations for r and b_1, we see that

$$r = b_1 \sqrt{\frac{SS_X}{SS_Y}}$$

Because SS_X and SS_Y are *always greater than zero*, r and b_1 have the same sign. Thus, if a positive relationship exists between X and Y, then both r and b_1 will be greater than zero. Similarly, they are both less than zero if the relationship is negative.

When you determine r, you use a sample of observations; r is a *statistic*. What does r estimate? It is actually an estimate of ρ (rho, pronounced "roe"), the **population correlation coefficient.** To grasp what ρ is, imagine obtaining a sample of *all* possible X, Y values and using equation 14-19 to determine a correlation. The resulting value is ρ.

The population slope, β_1, and ρ are closely related. In particular, $\beta_1 = 0$ if and only if $\rho = 0$. This leads to another method of determining whether the simple linear regression model (using X to predict Y) is satisfactory. The hypotheses are

H_0: $\rho = 0$ (no linear relationship exists between X and Y)

H_a: $\rho \neq 0$ (linear relationship does exist)

The test statistic uses the point estimate of ρ (that is, r) and is defined by

$$t = \frac{r}{\sqrt{\dfrac{1 - r^2}{n - 2}}} \qquad (14\text{-}20)$$

where $n =$ the number of observations in the sample. This is also a t statistic with $n - 2$ df. Although equations 14-18 and 14-20 appear to be unrelated, *their values are always the same.*

Thus, the t test for H_0: $\beta_1 = 0$ and H_0: $\rho = 0$ produce identical results, provided both tests use the same level of significance. These tests are therefore redundant; they both produce the same conclusion. Remember, if you have already computed the sample correlation coefficient, r, equation 14-20 offers a much easier method of determining whether the simple linear model is statistically significant.

Example 14.6

Use equation 14-20 to determine whether a positive linear relationship exists between X = income and Y = home square footage, based on the data from example 14.1. Use $\alpha = .05$.

Solution The hypotheses to be used here are $H_0: \rho \leq 0$ versus $H_a: \rho > 0$. In example 14.1, we found that $r = .843$. This leads to a computed test statistic value of

$$t^* = \frac{r}{\sqrt{\dfrac{1 - r^2}{n - 2}}}$$

$$= \frac{.843}{\sqrt{\dfrac{1 - (.843)^2}{8}}}$$

$$= \frac{.843}{.190}$$

$$= 4.44$$

Because this value is the same as the one obtained in example 14.3 (testing $H_0: \beta_1 \leq 0$ versus $H_a: \beta_1 > 0$), we draw the same conclusion. A positive linear relationship *does* exist between these two variables. In other words, r *is* large enough to justify this conclusion.

Remember, there is no harm in using equation 14-20 as a substitute for equation 14-18 with $H_0: \beta_1 = 0$ (or ≤ 0, or ≥ 0), particularly if you have already determined the value of r.

Danger of Assuming Causality

In Chapter 4, when we introduced the correlation coefficient, we cautioned you that high statistical correlation does not imply *causality*. Even if the correlation between X and Y is extremely high (say, $r = .95$), a unit increase in X does not necessarily *cause* an increase in Y. All we know is that, in the past, as X increased, so did Y.

In many business and economics applications, we observe highly correlated variables when each pair of observations corresponds to a particular time period. For example, we would expect a high correlation between average annual wages (X) and the U.S. gross national product (GNP; Y) when measured over time. Even though wages may be a good predictor of GNP, this does not imply that an increase in wages *causes* an increase in GNP. It is much more likely that a third factor—inflation—caused both wages and GNP to increase.

Coefficient of Determination

In our earlier discussion of ANOVA techniques, we used the expression SS(total) = $\Sigma(y - \bar{y})^2$ to measure the tendency of a set of observations to group about the mean.

If this value was large, then the observations (data) contained much variation and were *not* all clustered about the mean, $\bar{y}$.

In the simple linear regression model, $SS_Y = \Sigma(y - \bar{y})^2$ is computed in the same way, and (as before) measures the total variation in the values of the dependent variable.

SS_Y = total variation of the dependent variable observations

When comparing the sum of squares of error, SSE, to the total variation, SS_Y, we use the ratio SSE/SS_Y. If all $\hat{Y}$ values are equal to their respective Y values, there is a perfect fit, with SSE = 0 and r = 1 or -1. Our model explains 100% of this total variation, and the unexplained variation is zero.

In general, SSE/SS_Y (expressed as a percentage) is the **percentage of unexplained variation.** Recall from equations 14-14 and 14-19 that

$$SSE = SS_Y - \frac{(SS_{XY})^2}{SS_X}$$

$$r^2 = \frac{SS_{XY}^2}{SS_X SS_Y}$$

and thus

$$r^2 = 1 - \frac{SSE}{SS_Y}$$

As a result, r^2 is a measure of the *explained variation* in the dependent variable using the simple linear model; r^2 is the **coefficient of determination.**

---

r^2 = coefficient of determination

$$= 1 - \frac{SSE}{SS_Y} \qquad (14\text{-}21)$$

= the percentage of explained variation in the dependent variable using the simple linear regression model

---

For this model, we can determine r^2 simply by squaring the coefficient of correlation. In Chapter 15, we will predict the dependent variable, Y, using *more than one* predictor (independent) variable. To derive the coefficient of determination for this case, we must first calculate SSE and then use equation 14-21. So, although this definition may appear to be unnecessary, it will enable us to compute this value when we use a multiple linear regression model.

Example 14.7

What percentage of the total variation of the home sizes is explained by means of the single predictor, income, using the real-estate data from example 14.1?

Solution We previously calculated r to be .843, so the coefficient of determination is

$$r^2 = (.843)^2 = .71$$

Therefore, we have accounted for 71% of the total variation in the home sizes by using income as a predictor of home size.

Notice that we could have determined this value by using the calculations from examples 14.1 and 14.2, where

$$r^2 = 1 - \frac{\text{SSE}}{\text{SS}_Y}$$

$$= 1 - \frac{75.81}{262.4} = .71$$

●

Total Variation, SS_Y

In Chapter 12, when discussing the ANOVA procedure, the total variation of the observations, measured by SS(total), was partitioned into two other sums of squares—namely, SS(factor) and SS(error). The resulting equation was

$$\text{SS(total)} = \text{SS(factor)} + \text{SS(error)}$$

In a similar fashion, we can partition the total variation of the Y values in linear regression, measured by SS_Y, into two other sums of squares. In Figure 14.13, notice that the value of $y - \bar{y}$ can be written as the sum of two deviations, namely

$$y - \bar{y} = (\hat{y} - \bar{y}) + (y - \hat{y})$$

By squaring and summing over *all* the data points in the sample, we can show that

$$\Sigma(y - \bar{y})^2 = \Sigma(\hat{y} - \bar{y})^2 + \Sigma(y - \hat{y})^2$$

The summation on the left of the equals sign is SS_Y. The second summation on the right is the sum of squares of error, SSE. The first summation on the right is defined to be the **sum of squares of regression, SSR.**

$$\Sigma(\hat{y} - \bar{y})^2 = \text{SSR}$$

As a result, we have

$$\text{SS}_Y = \text{SSR} + \text{SSE} \tag{14-22}$$

Figure 14.13

Splitting $(y - \bar{y})$ into two deviations, $(\hat{y} - \bar{y}) + (y - \hat{y})$.

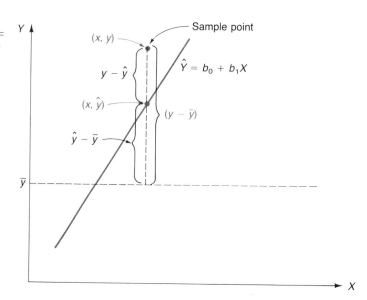

The regression sum of squares, SSR, measures the variation in the Y values that would exist if differences in X were the *only* cause of differences among the Y's. If this were the case, then all the (X, Y) points would lie exactly on the regression line. In practice, this rarely happens when using a simple linear regression model because generally there are factors other than the one independent variable in the model that influence the behavior of the dependent variable. Consequently, the sample points can be expected to lie about the regression line, rather than on this line. This variation *about* the regression line is measured by the error sum of squares, SSE.

Exercises

14.33 The sales manager of a real-estate firm believes that experience is the best predictor for determining the yearly sales of the various salespeople in the real-estate industry. Data were collected from 15 salespeople. Let X be the number of years of prior experience. Let Y be the annual sales (in thousands).

Y: Sales	X: Experience	Y: Sales	X: Experience
50	1.3	78	2.2
161	5.1	124	3.4
195	6.2	131	7.1
172	5.4	64	2.1
132	3.9	80	4.5
133	4.1	110	3.8
181	6.1	127	4.4
69	1.9		

Using a 10% significance level, test whether the population correlation coefficient between the variables X and Y is zero.

14.34 The manager of a company that relies on traveling salespersons to sell the company's products wants to examine the relationship between sales and the amount of time a salesperson spends with each established customer who regularly orders the company's products. The manager collects data on 12 salespersons. Let Y represent sales per month and X represent hours spent with customers per month.

X	Y	X	Y
3.2	412	5.6	610
4.6	500	5.3	600
3.9	450	5.1	570
5.3	610	7.1	800
6.1	715	6.5	725
4.2	500	7.8	850

Can one conclude that the population correlation coefficient between X and Y is positive? Use a 10% significance level. Can one conclude that spending more time with customers increases sales?

14.35 Using the data in exercise 14.3, test that there is no linear relationship between the total commissions paid and the net earnings of Tony's used-car lot. Use a 5% significance level.

14.36 Refer to exercise 14.23. Use equation 14-20 to test whether there is a positive relationship between a person's investment in tax-free investments and a person's income. Use a significance level of .05. Is the conclusion the same as that in exercise 14.23?

14.37 Ten cards numbered 1 through 10 are shuffled and a person is asked to pick one card. The card is replaced and the deck is reshuffled. Then the person is asked to draw a second card. If the second card is higher than the first, the dealer gives 85 cents to the player. If the second card is not higher than the first, the player pays $1.15 to the dealer. A sample of 15 pairs of draws is taken to see whether there is any correlation between the first and the second cards.

a. Would you expect to observe significant correlation here? Why or why not?

b. Find the coefficient of determination for the following data and test using a 5% significance level that there is no correlation between the first and second cards. Interpret the value of the coefficient of determination.

X: First Card	Y: Second Card	X: First Card	Y: Second Card
7	3		
3	10	10	5
8	2	3	6
5	8	4	3
2	7	6	1
7	9	7	8
9	4	8	4
1	1	2	6

14.38 Refer to exercise 14.25. Use equation 14-20 to test that there is no linear relationship between the size of the U.S. population and the logarithm of personal consumption expenditure on housing. Use a significance level of 5%.

14.39 For the data in exercise 14.26, test that there is no linear relationship between the number of hours of operation between oil changes and the number of years that the engine was able to perform adequately. Use equation 14-20 and test with a 10% significance level. Is the result the same as in exercise 14.26?

14.40 A sample of 35 pairs of observations is taken and a sample correlation coefficient is computed to be $r = .48$. Do the data provide sufficient evidence to reject the null hypothesis of no correlation? Use a 1% significance level.

14.41 Fifty people were asked to record their expenditure on vacation during the year and their yearly income. A correlation value of .39 was found. Do the data provide sufficient evidence to reject the null hypothesis of no correlation between the two variables? Use a 5% significance level.

14.42 Using the sample data of price:earnings ratios and yields in exercise 14.30, what percentage of the total variation in price:earnings ratios is explained by the predictor variable?

14.5

Estimation and Prediction Using the Simple Linear Model

We have concentrated on predicting an individual value of Y for a given value of X. In the previous examples, we used a person's income, X, to predict the size of that person's home (Y). Notice in Figure 14.5 that we can also use the least squares line to estimate the *average* value of Y for a specified value of X. So we can use this line to handle two different situations.

Situation 1 The regression equation $\hat{Y} = b_0 + b_1 X$ estimates the average value of Y for a specified value of the independent variable, X. For $X = x_0$, this would be written $\mu_{Y|x_0}$ (the mean of Y given $X = x_0$).

For example, the least squares line passing through the real-estate data in example 14.1 is $\hat{Y} = 8.51 + .354X$. The average square footage for *all* homes in the population with an income of $40,000 ($X = 40$) is $\mu_{Y|40}$. Its estimate is provided by the corresponding value on the least squares line, namely

$$\hat{Y} = 8.51 + .354(40)$$

$$= 22.67$$

So the estimate of the average square footage of all such homes is 2267 square feet (Figure 14.4).

Situation 2 An individual predicted value of Y also uses the regression equation $\hat{Y} = b_0 + b_1X$ for a specified value of X. This is denoted Y_{x_0} for $X = x_0$. This is the more common application in business because a regression equation is generally used for individual forecasts.

For example, assume the Jenkins family resides in our sample community and has an income of $40,000. An estimate of their home size is (once again)

$$\hat{Y} = 8.51 + .354(40)$$

$$= 22.67$$

which is 2267 square feet (Figure 14.4).

We see that the least squares line can be used to predict *average values* (situation 1) or *individual values* (situation 2). The difference between these two estimation procedures lies in determining a *confidence interval* (situation 1) or a *prediction interval* (situation 2).

Confidence Interval for $\mu_{Y|x_0}$ (Situation 1)

We have already established that the point estimate of $\mu_{Y|x_0}$ is the corresponding value of $\hat{Y}$. The reliability of this estimate depends on (1) the number of observations in the sample, (2) the amount of variation in the sample, and (3) the value of $X = x_0$. A CI for $\mu_{Y|x_0}$ reflects all three considerations.

A $(1 - \alpha) \cdot 100\%$ CI for $\mu_{Y|x_0}$ is

$$\hat{Y} - t_{\alpha/2, n-2}\, s\, \sqrt{\frac{1}{n} + \frac{(x_0 - \bar{x})^2}{SS_X}}$$

$$\text{to} \quad \hat{Y} + t_{\alpha/2, n-2}\, s\, \sqrt{\frac{1}{n} + \frac{(x_0 - \bar{x})^2}{SS_X}} \tag{14-23}$$

Example 14.8 Determine a 95% CI for the average home size of families with an income of $35,000, using the data from example 14.1.

Solution We previously determined that $n = 10$, $\bar{x} = 39.8$, $SS_X = 1489.6$, and $s = 3.078$. The point estimate for the average square footage, $\mu_{Y|35}$, is

$$\hat{Y} = 8.51 + .354(35)$$

$$= 20.90 \ (2,090 \text{ square feet})$$

Obtaining $t_{.025, 8} = 2.306$ from Table A-5, the 95% CI for $\mu_{Y|35}$ is

$$20.90 - (2.306)(3.078)\sqrt{\frac{1}{10} + \frac{(35 - 39.8)^2}{1489.6}}$$

$$\text{to} \quad 20.90 + (2.306)(3.078)\sqrt{\frac{1}{10} + \frac{(35 - 39.8)^2}{1489.6}}$$

$$= 20.90 - (2.306)(3.078)(.340) \quad \text{to} \quad 20.90 + (2.306)(3.078)(.340)$$

$$= 20.90 - 2.41 \quad \text{to} \quad 20.90 + 2.41$$

$$= 18.49 \quad \text{to} \quad 23.31$$

We are thus 95% confident that the average home size for families earning $35,000 is between 1849 and 2331 square feet. ●

Using MINITAB to Construct Confidence Intervals The MINITAB solution for the real-estate problem is contained in Figure 14.10. To construct CIs the column of interest is labeled as Stdev. Fit, which, when translated, means the standard deviation of the predicted Y. Writing this as $s_{\hat{Y}}$,

$$s_{\hat{Y}} = s\sqrt{\frac{1}{n} + \frac{(x_0 - \bar{x})^2}{SS_X}}$$

For each value of X *in the sample* (say, x_0), the corresponding CI for $\mu_{Y|x_0}$ is

$$\hat{Y} - t \cdot s_{\hat{Y}} \quad \text{to} \quad \hat{Y} + t \cdot s_{\hat{Y}}$$

where $t = t_{\alpha/2, n-2}$, as before, and $\hat{Y}$ is contained in the column to the left of the standard deviations. For values of X not in the sample, you can (1) approximate this CI by using the value of $s_{\hat{Y}}$ corresponding to an X value *near* this particular value or (2) use the computer procedure that will be discussed in Chapter 15, which will provide an exact value for $s_{\hat{Y}}$ belonging to this particular X value.

Using the MINITAB output in Figure 14.10, we can derive the CIs corresponding to X values of 22, 40, and 60. The remaining seven CIs are constructed in a similar manner.

For $X = 22$, the CI is

$$16.300 - (2.306)(1.721) \quad \text{to} \quad 16.300 + (2.306)(1.721)$$
$$= 12.33 \quad \text{to} \quad 20.27$$

For $X = 40$, the CI is

$$22.671 - (2.306)(.974) \quad \text{to} \quad 22.671 + (2.306)(.974)$$
$$= 20.42 \quad \text{to} \quad 24.92$$

For $X = 60$, the CI is

$$29.749 - (2.306)(1.882) \quad \text{to} \quad 29.749 + (2.306)(1.882)$$
$$= 25.41 \quad \text{to} \quad 34.09$$

Notice that the CIs are much wider for $X = 22$ and $X = 60$ than for $X = 40$.

By connecting the upper end of the CIs for all ten data points and connecting the lower limits, we obtain Figure 14.14. Equation 14-23 indicates that the CI is narrowest when $(x_0 - \bar{x})^2 = 0$; that is, at $X = x_0 = \bar{x}$. For values of X to the left or right of $\bar{x}$, the CI is wider. In other words, the farther x_0 is from $\bar{x}$, the less reliable is the estimate.

Figure 14.14

95% CIs for the real-
estate data derived from
MINITAB output shown
in Figure 14.10.

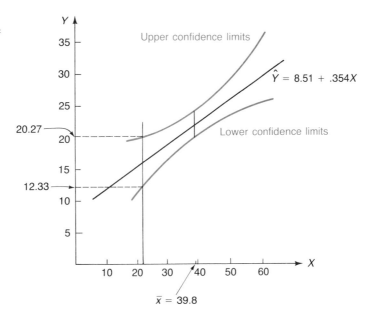

The Danger of Extrapolation Extrapolation is calculating an estimate corresponding to a value of X outside the range of the data used to derive the prediction equation (the least squares line). For example, in Figure 14.14, the least squares line could be used to estimate the average home size for families with an income of $100,000. Although we *can* estimate $\mu_{Y|100}$, the corresponding CI for this parameter will be extremely wide, which means that the point estimate, $\hat{Y}$, has little practical value.

To use the simple regression model effectively for estimation, you need to stay within the range of the sampled values for the independent variable, X. This is **interpolation.** If you use values far outside this range, you need to be aware that, given *another* set of data, you would quite likely obtain a considerably different estimate. Furthermore, you have no assurance that the linear relationship still holds outside the range of your sample data.

Prediction Interval for Y_{xo} (Situation 2)

The procedure of predicting individual values is most often used in business applications. The regression equation is generally used to **forecast** (predict) a value of the dependent variable for a particular value of the independent variable. When attempting to predict a single value of the dependent variable, Y, using the simple linear regression model, we begin, as before, with $\hat{Y}$. Substituting $X = x_0$ into the regression equation provides the best estimate of Y. For example, if the Johnson family has an income of $35,000, our best guess as to their home size (using this particular model) is $\hat{Y}$ for $X = 35$. From the results of example 14.8, this is 20.90, or 2090 square feet.

We do not use the term *confidence interval* for this procedure because what we are estimating (Y) is not a parameter. It is a value of a random variable, so we use the term **prediction interval.**

The variability of the error in predicting a single value of Y is more than that for estimating the average value of Y (situation 1). It can be shown that an estimate of the variance of the error ($Y - \hat{Y}$), when using $\hat{Y}$ to estimate an individual Y for $X = x_0$, is

$$s^2\left(1 + \frac{1}{n} + \frac{(x_0 - \bar{x})^2}{SS_X}\right) \tag{14-24}$$

This result can be used to construct a $(1 - \alpha) \cdot 100\%$ prediction interval for Y_{x_0}, as follows:

$$\hat{Y} - t_{\alpha/2, n-2}\, s \sqrt{1 + \frac{1}{n} + \frac{(x_0 - \bar{x})^2}{SS_X}}$$

$$\text{to} \quad \hat{Y} + t_{\alpha/2, n-2}\, s \sqrt{1 + \frac{1}{n} + \frac{(x_0 - \bar{x})^2}{SS_X}} \tag{14-25}$$

Notice that the only difference between this prediction interval and the CI in equation 14-23 is the inclusion of "1 +" under the square root sign. The other two terms under the square root are usually quite small, so this "1 +" has a large effect on the width of the resulting interval. Be aware that our warning about extrapolating too far outside the range of the data applies here as well. In equations 14-24 and 14-25, the distance from the mean $(x_0 - \bar{x})$ is squared, which increases the risk of predicting beyond the range of the sampled data.

Example 14.9

We previously determined that the Johnson family has an income of \$35,000, and so the best estimate of their home size is $\hat{Y} = 20.90$. Determine a 95% prediction interval for this situation.

Solution We can use the calculations from example 14.8 to derive the prediction interval for Y_{35}. The result is

$$20.90 - (2.306)(3.078)\sqrt{1 + \frac{1}{10} + \frac{(35 - 39.8)^2}{1489.6}}$$

$$\text{to} \quad 20.90 + (2.306)(3.078)\sqrt{1 + \frac{1}{10} + \frac{(35 - 39.8)^2}{1489.6}}$$

$$= 20.90 - (2.306)(3.078)(1.056) \quad \text{to} \quad 20.90 + (2.306)(3.078)(1.056)$$

$$= 20.90 - 7.49 \quad \text{to} \quad 20.90 + 7.49$$

$$= 13.41 \quad \text{to} \quad 28.39$$

Comparing this interval to the CI for $\mu_{Y|35}$ in example 14.8, we see that individual predictions are considerably less accurate than estimations for the mean home size. Of course, we could reduce the width of this interval by obtaining additional data. Expecting accurate results from a sample of ten observations is being a bit optimistic.

●

Using MINITAB for Constructing Prediction Intervals We can use the MINITAB output in Figure 14.10 for example 14.9. The values in the column labeled Stdev.Fit assume that Y is estimating $\mu_{Y|x}$; we previously used $s_{\hat{Y}}$ as a symbol for this standard deviation.

A prediction interval for a value of $X = x_0$ in the sample is provided by

$$\hat{Y} - t\sqrt{s_{\hat{Y}}^2 + s^2} \quad \text{to} \quad \hat{Y} + t\sqrt{s_{\hat{Y}}^2 + s^2}$$

where $t = t_{\alpha/2, n-2}$ is obtained from Table A-5 and $\hat{Y}$ is obtained from the column labeled FIT. For values of X *not* in the sample, you can derive a prediction interval by using the computer procedure to be discussed in Chapter 15. The following calculations determine the prediction intervals for three of the sample X values, namely, $X = 22$, 40, and 60.

For $X = 22$, the 95% prediction interval is

$16.300 - 2.306\sqrt{(1.721)^2 + (3.078)^2}$

to $\quad 16.300 + 2.306\sqrt{(1.721)^2 + (3.078)^2}$

$= 16.300 - 8.132 \quad$ to $\quad 16.300 + 8.132$

$= 8.17 \quad$ to $\quad 24.43$

For $X = 40$, the 95% prediction interval is

$22.671 - 2.306\sqrt{(.974)^2 + (3.078)^2}$

to $\quad 22.671 + 2.306\sqrt{(.974)^2 + (3.078)^2}$

$= 22.671 - 7.445 \quad$ to $\quad 22.671 + 7.445$

$= 15.23 \quad$ to $\quad 30.12$

For $X = 60$, the 95% prediction interval is

$29.749 - 2.306\sqrt{(1.882)^2 + (3.078)^2}$

to $\quad 29.749 + 2.306\sqrt{(1.882)^2 + (3.078)^2}$

$= 29.749 - 8.320 \quad$ to $\quad 29.749 + 8.320$

$= 21.43 \quad$ to $\quad 38.07$

Figure 14.15 shows the prediction intervals for all ten data points; the upper and lower limits have been connected. The increased width of a prediction interval versus a CI is quite apparent from this graph. Also, as with that of a CI, the width of a prediction interval increases as the value of X strays from $\bar{x}$.

Figure 14.15

The 95% prediction and confidence intervals for the real-estate data.

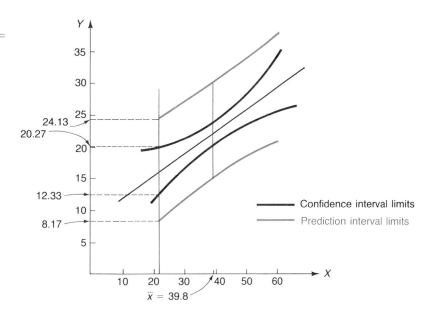

Exercises

14.43 The marketing division of Astral Airlines wants to determine the relationship between the amount of money a person spends yearly on air transportation and the yearly income of the person. They randomly selected 20 airline passengers. The data (in thousands of dollars) are:

Y: Yearly Expenditure	X: Yearly Income
423	22.5
396	31.4
120	18.1
140	19.1
550	26.4
690	44.5
740	37.1
320	16.8
1200	50.5
470	21.8
640	29.8
675	33.4
745	38.4
425	21.8
380	22.5
725	30.4
950	38.7
925	40.6
210	18.8
425	21.7

a. Determine a 95% CI for the average yearly airline expenditure for people with an annual income of $30,000.

b. Find a 95% prediction interval for the yearly airline expenditure of a person with an annual income of $30,000.

c. Interpret and compare the intervals in questions a and b.

14.44 A statistics instructor believes that there is a strong correlation between a student's grade in college algebra and a student's grade in introductory statistics. The following statistics were collected from 20 randomly selected students. Let X be the student's grade in college algebra. Let Y be the student's grade in introductory statistics (A $=$ 4.0, B $=$ 3.0, and so on).

$$SS_{xy} = 31.8$$
$$SS_x = 32.3$$
$$SS_y = 45.4$$
$$\bar{x} = 2.3$$
$$\bar{y} = 2.5$$
$$n = 20$$

a. Determine a 95% CI for the average grade in introductory statistics for students who make a B (equal to 3.0) in college algebra.

b. Find the 95% prediction interval for the grade in introductory statistics for a student who obtained a B in college algebra.

14.45 Using the data in exercise 14.23, find a 90% prediction interval for the predicted amount of money an individual places in tax-free investment instruments if the individual has an annual income of $40,000.

14.46 For the data in exercise 14.26, find the 99% CI for the average number of years that a lawn mower will be able to function properly if the number of hours of operation between oil changes is 23 hours. What is the standard deviation for a predicted value of the number of years that a single lawn mower will be able to perform adequately, for which the number of hours of operation between oil changes is 23?

14.47 For a fixed value of X, which interval is larger, the CI for the mean value of Y at X (equation 14-23) or the prediction interval for a predicted value of Y at X (equation 14-25)? What value can you assign to X to achieve the smallest CI for the mean value of Y at X or for the predicted value of Y at X?

14.48 A sample of 200 executives who work in Chicago was taken to find out how much of their own money the executives invest each year in stock of the company that they work for. The following regression equation was developed, where X is the income (in thousands) of an executive and Y is the amount of money (in thousands) he or she invests each year in the company. The prediction equation is

$$\hat{Y} = 9.5 + 0.05X$$

Based on the regression equation, can the following statement be made? A Chicago-area executive who earns \$15,000 a year would invest about \$10,250 in company stock. Comment.

14.49 The manager of an engineering firm believes that an employee's overall performance is related to the employee's score on Randall and Cantrell's job-aptitude test. Fourteen employees were selected randomly and the following data were collected. Evaluation of job performance was rated by the manager on a one to ten scale, with ten being the score of a perfect employee.

Y: Evaluation of Job Performance	X: Score on Aptitude Test
9.5	90
6.0	71
2.0	33
6.5	49
7.5	82
5.0	61
7.5	73
4.5	59
5.5	63
7.0	84
9.0	94
8.5	83
6.0	74
7.5	51

a. Determine a 95% CI for the average job performance evaluation for employees with a score of 75.

b. Find a 95% prediction interval for the job performance of an employee with a score of 75.

c. What score would give the smallest 95% prediction interval for an employee?

14.50 Using the following sample statistics, find a 90% CI for the mean value of Y at $X = .5$.

$$\text{SS}_{xy} = 31.4$$
$$\text{SS}_x = 40$$
$$\text{SS}_y = 45$$
$$\bar{x} = 7.5$$
$$\bar{y} = 10.0$$
$$n = 31$$

14.51 For the data in exercise 14.28, find a 99% prediction interval for the monthly weight loss of an individual rat that has a daily dose of 0.30 milligrams of the diuretic.

14.52 The owner of a used car lot would like to explain, to potential car buyers, the relationship between the horsepower rating of a car and the gasoline mileage. The owner collects the following data on 20 1985 automobiles with the objective of showing that horsepower rating gives a good indication of gasoline mileage.

Y: Gasoline Mileage	X: Horsepower Rating
16.0	180
14.9	195
14.1	160
18.5	235
15.3	175
21.9	285
15.2	210
18.2	230
17.0	235
16.9	200
16.8	195
20.0	290
14.8	150
13.0	100
20.3	290
18.2	255
17.1	220
19.8	235
17.5	260
21.4	275

a. Construct a scatter diagram of the data.

b. Find the least squares line for the data.

c. Test the hypothesis that there is no linear relationship between the variables Y and X at the 0.10 significance level.

Summary

When dealing with a pair of variables (say, X and Y), we generally are interested in determining whether the variables are related in some manner. If a relationship does exist, perhaps the independent variable can be used to predict values of the dependent variable. If a significant linear relationship exists within the sample data, both the direction (positive or negative) and the strength of this linear relationship can be measured using the sample coefficient of correlation, r. Another commonly used measure of association between two variables is the sample covariance.

Whenever a sample of bivariate data contains a significant linear pattern, we determine the least squares line through the data points. This generates an equation that can be used to predict values of the dependent variable. To describe accurately the assumptions behind this procedure, we introduced the concept of a statistical model consisting of a deterministic portion (the straight line) and a random error component. When we perform any test of hypothesis regarding the underlying bivariate population, we must be careful to satisfy the necessary assumptions behind this procedure. These assumptions will be examined more closely in Chapter 15.

Various methods for determining the strength of the model as a predictor of the dependent variable include: (1) a t test for detecting a significant slope, b_1—a value of $\beta_1 = 0$ indicates that X has no predictive ability; (2) a t test for determining whether the sample correlation, r, is significantly large—a value of $\rho = 0$ indicates that there is no linear relationship between the two variables; and (3) a CI for the slope, β_1. The two t tests appear to be quite different, but their computed values (and df) are *identical;* there is no point in performing both tests.

Another measure of how well the model provides estimates that fit the sample data is given by the coefficient of determination, r^2. For simple linear regression (one independent variable), this is the square of the correlation coefficient. Another definition of the coefficient of determination also can be used to examine more than one independent variable (called multiple linear regression), namely, $r^2 = 1 - (SSE/SS_Y)$. Here, SSE is the sum of squared errors and SS_Y represents the total variation in the sample Y values. For example, if $r^2 = .85$, then 85% of the variation in the sample Y values has been explained using this model.

To evaluate the predictive ability of the model for a specific value of X (say, $X = x_0$), a CI for the *average* value of Y, given this value of X (written $\mu_{Y|x_0}$), can be derived. Similarly, we can derive a prediction interval for a particular value of the dependent variable, given this specific value of X (written Y_{x_0}).

Summary of Linear Regression and Correlation Formulas

DESCRIPTION	FORMULA
Correlation between two variables	$r = \dfrac{SS_{XY}}{\sqrt{SS_X}\,\sqrt{SS_Y}}$

where

$$SS_{XY} = \Sigma xy - (\Sigma x)(\Sigma y)/n$$
$$SS_X = \Sigma x^2 - (\Sigma x)^2/n$$
$$SS_Y = \Sigma y^2 - (\Sigma y)^2/n$$

Least squares line	$\hat{Y} = b_0 + b_1 X$

where

$$b_1 = SS_{XY}/SS_X$$

and

$$b_0 = \bar{y} - b_1\bar{x}$$

Estimate of the residual variance	$\hat{\sigma}_e^2 = s^2 = \dfrac{SSE}{n-2}$

where

$$SSE = \Sigma(y - \hat{y})^2$$
$$= SS_Y - \dfrac{(SS_{XY})^2}{SS_X}$$

t statistic for detecting a significant slope	$t = \dfrac{b_1}{s_{b_1}}$

$(df = n - 2)$ where

$$s_{b_1} = s/\sqrt{SS_X}$$

CI for the slope, β_1	$b_1 - t_{\alpha/2,n-2}\, s_{b_1}$ to $\quad b_1 + t_{\alpha/2,n-2}\, s_{b_1}$
t statistic for detecting a significant correlation	$t = \dfrac{r}{\sqrt{\dfrac{1 - r^2}{n - 2}}}$ $(df = n - 2)$
Coefficient of determination	$r^2 = $ square of correlation coefficient $= 1 - \dfrac{SSE}{SS_Y}$
CI for the average value of Y at a specific value of X (say, x_0)	$\hat{Y} \mp t_{\alpha/2,n-2}\, s\, \sqrt{\dfrac{1}{n} + \dfrac{(x_0 - \bar{x})^2}{SS_X}}$ or, for MINITAB, $\hat{Y} \pm t_{\alpha/2,n-2}\, s_{\hat{Y}}$
Prediction interval for a particular value of Y at a specific value of X (say, x_0)	$\hat{Y} \mp t_{\alpha/2,n-2}\, s\, \sqrt{1 + \dfrac{1}{n} + \dfrac{(x_0 - \bar{x})^2}{SS_X}}$ or, for MINITAB, $\hat{Y} \pm t_{\alpha/2,n-2}\, \sqrt{s_{\hat{Y}}^2 + s^2}$

Review Exercises

14.53 Fans Unlimited finds that competition in the fan business has increased over the past year. The manager decides to perform an experiment by pricing the company's most popular 52-inch ceiling fan at various prices (in dollars) each week and then observing the demand. After 8 weeks, the following data had been recorded:

Week	X: Fan Cost	Y: Number Sold
1	175	13
2	160	15
3	145	18
4	129	18
5	115	20
6	99	24
7	110	20
8	89	29

a. Find the least squares line for the data, with X as the independent variable and Y as the dependent variable.

b. Find the coefficient of determination.

c. Find a 90% CI for the slope of the regression line.

d. Find a 90% CI for the mean number of fans that will be sold if the price is $120 per fan.

e. Find a 99% prediction interval for the satisfaction of a particular worker if the measure of productivity of this worker is 7.

14.54 For the data in exercise 14.30, find a 90% CI for the average price:earnings ratio for a stock that yields 7.0%. Assume that the average of the price:earnings ratios for the 25 stocks sampled is 8.1 and that the average for the yields of the 25 stocks is 7.6%.

14.55 Dolls-R-Us believes that television advertising is the most effective way to market their new line of dolls. The sales manager recorded the amount of money spent on advertising and the amount of sales for 20 randomly selected months. The average cost for television advertising for the 20 months was $110,000. The average sales volume for the 20 months was $675,000. The following sample statistics were found from the data for the 20 months:

$$SS_{xy} = 198.4$$
$$SS_x = 205.3$$
$$SS_y = 341.6$$

where Y represents the sales volume (in thousands), and X represents the television advertising costs (in thousands of dollars).

a. Calculate the least squares line.

b. Calculate the coefficient of determination.

c. Calculate the sum of squares of error.

d. What is the estimate of the variance of the error component for the model?

e. Is there sufficient evidence from the data to conclude at the .01 significance level that a positive relationship exists between X and Y?

f. Find a 95% prediction interval for the monthly sales volume if the television advertising expenditure during one particular month is $120,000.

14.56 A car rental agency has a fleet of 200 cars available for rent at Kennedy airport in New York City. The owner of the agency uses a regression equation for estimating the company's daily revenue based on the number of incoming flights that day. The regression equation is $\hat{Y} = 2500 + 21.4X$, where X is the number of daily incoming flights and Y is the daily revenue in dollars. The data used to find the least squares line are based on a sample of 100 randomly selected days in 1984. Can the following statement be made based on regression analysis? If Kennedy airport increases its daily incoming flights by 50 flights next year, then the car agency can expect to make an additional daily revenue of $1,070. Comment.

14.57 Refer to exercise 14.2. Determine a 95% CI for the average total cost of operations if the total cost of inventory is $29,000. What value would need to be assigned to the total cost of inventory to make the 95% CI for the average total cost of operation the smallest in length?

14.58 Refer to exercise 14.7. What percentage of the total variation in the amount of merchandise sold at Lucky Jack's retail store is explained by the least squares line for the data?

14.59 The following data were collected for a certain regression analysis.

$$SS_{xy} = -138.6$$
$$SS_x = 112.3$$
$$SS_y = 325.2$$
$$\bar{x} = 86.2$$
$$\bar{y} = 112.9$$
$$n = 41$$

a. Find the least squares line.

b. Test, using a 1% significance level, that the population correlation coefficient between the variables X and Y is negative.

c. Find a 90% CI for the slope of the regression equation.

14.60 One management policy is based on the hypothesis that, the more productive a worker is, the more satisfied the worker will be. A scale from one to ten is used to measure productivity, with ten being assigned to an extremely productive worker. A second scale from one to ten is used to measure satisfaction. The worker assigns him- or herself a ten if he or she is satisfied in every aspect of the job. Twenty employees were selected randomly from the production-and-research department of Tellon Oil. The results of the data collection are as follows:

Y: Satisfaction	X: Productivity	Y: Satisfaction	X: Productivity
5	4	9	7
2	3	7	5
9	8	4	4
9	9	8	7
5	6	9	8
3	5	10	9
5	4	5	6
7	7	1	2
9	8	7	8
2	3	9	9

a. Draw a scatter diagram of the data.

b. Test the hypothesis, at a 5% significance level, that productivity does not positively influence a worker's satisfaction.

c. Find a 99% CI for the slope of the regression equation.

d. Calculate the coefficient of determination.

e. Find a 99% prediction interval for the satisfaction of a particular worker if the measure of productivity of this worker is 7.

14.61 Using the sample statistics in exercise 14.9, calculate the coefficient of determination using equation 14-21.

14.62 Using the data in exercise 14.11, test the hypothesis that the federal funds rate contributes to predicting the treasury bill yield. Use a 10% significance level.

14.63 A regression line is fitted to a set of data and the values of $Y - \hat{Y}$ are calculated. Does the following set of sample errors appear to conform to the empirical rule that 95% of the data should lie within two standard deviations of the mean? Construct a histogram for the residuals. Comment on the slope of the histogram.

1.1, −0.8, 2.6, 1.5, 0.2, −0.4, 0.8, −1.8, −2.3, 0.9, −2.7, 3.1, −1.0, 0.9, 4.5, −3.4, −0.1, −0.2, 2.4, −1.7, −0.7

14.64 Diane's Beauty Salon is currently hiring beauticians at its new location in a popular mall. Diane wants to know what percentage of commission to pay the beauticians based on experience. A survey of 12 licensed beauticians was taken with the following results.

Y: Percentage of Commission	X: Years of Experience
24	2
18	1
30	5
41	10
35	8
35	7
25	4
44	12
33	8
24	3
20	1
40	10

a. Find the least squares line.

b. Caiculate the sum of squares due to error.

c. Test the null hypothesis that there is no linear relationship between years of experience and percentage of commissions paid. Use a significance level of .05.

d. Find a 90% CI for the slope of the least squares line.

Case Study

Blackburn Advertising

Blackburn Advertising is a small company that specializes in large-volume direct-mail advertising. A new contract with Western Insurance Company specifies that the insurance company will promise a free gift to anyone who returns an enclosed postcard indicating that this person will allow an agent to present various insurance plans. The main problem for Blackburn is to decide what the value of this gift should be. They suspect that a more expensive gift would increase the number of responses, whereas a token gift might not motivate the potential customer to return the postcard allowing an agent to call on them. In checking with Western, Glen Wilkens, the project director at Blackburn, discovers that Western finds the gift idea attractive, but the company has very little experience with such an idea and so cannot offer any suggestions as to the value of the gift.

Glen decides to conduct a pilot experiment by sending out 100 such Western advertising brochures in each of ten different test markets (cities). The value of the promised gift ranges from $5 to $50. Within each city, he randomly assigns one of ten possible gift values to ten different people, for a total of 100 brochures in each city. The ten cities were chosen in such a way that a good representation of the entire Western Insurance Company market was obtained, ranging from a small city in Arizona with a population of 8000 to a large California city with a population of nearly one million people.

Three weeks after the mailing, the number of respondents was tabulated. These results are shown below.

Value of Gift ($)	Number of Respondents (out of 100)
5	3
10	4
15	6
20	8
25	11
30	16
35	22
40	30
45	40
50	52

Case Study Questions

1. What is the correlation between the value of the gift (X) and the number of respondents (Y)?

2. Based on this correlation and a significance level of .10, does a linear model seem appropriate here?

3. Using such a model, what would be your predicted number of responses when the gift has a value of $32?

4. Determine a prediction interval for the response rate in an individual city receiving 100 brochures containing a promised gift worth $32.
5. Construct a scatter plot of the data here. Does the pattern appear to be linear? Can you suggest a better model? If so, what is it?

Solution

Example 14.2

Example 14.2 was concerned with computing the regression equation $\hat{Y} = b_0 + b_1 X$. The problem was to determine the relationship between family income of local residents and the square footage of their homes. The SPSSX program listing in Figure 14.16 was used to request the SSE, b_0, and b_1 values as well as other statistics. Each line represents one card image to be entered:

The TITLE command names the SPSSX run.
The DATA LIST command gives each variable a name and describes the data as being in free form.
The PRINT command requests a printout of the input data.
The REGRESSION statement defines the variables, SQFOOT and INCOME, as the regression variables, and specifies that SQFOOT is to be the dependent variable. The ENTER subcommand indicates that all independent variables are to be entered into the regression analysis. In this example, however, there is only one independent variable, INCOME.
The BEGIN DATA command indicates to SPSSX that the input data immediately follow.
The next ten lines are card images that represent square footage in hundreds and income in thousands of dollars. For example, the first card image (16 22) represents a family living in a 1600-square-foot home with an income of $22,000 per year.
The END DATA statement indicates the end of the data card images.

Figure 14.17 shows the output obtained by executing the program listing in Figure 14.16.

Figure 14.16

SPSSX program listing used to request the SSE, b_0, and b_1 values.

```
TITLE    REAL ESTATE EXAMPLE USING ONE PREDICTOR
DATA LIST FREE/SQFOOT INCOME
PRINT / SQFOOT INCOME
REGRESSION VARIABLES=SQFOOT,INCOME/DEPENDENT=SQFOOT/ENTER/
BEGIN DATA
16  22
17  26
26  45
24  37
22  28
21  50
32  56
18  34
30  60
20  40
END DATA
```

Figure 14.17

Output obtained by executing the SPSSX program listing in Figure 14.16.

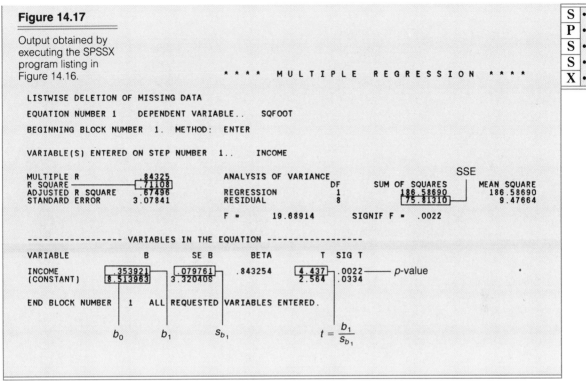

```
                            * * * *   M U L T I P L E   R E G R E S S I O N   * * * *

LISTWISE DELETION OF MISSING DATA

EQUATION NUMBER 1   DEPENDENT VARIABLE..   SQFOOT

BEGINNING BLOCK NUMBER  1.  METHOD:  ENTER

VARIABLE(S) ENTERED ON STEP NUMBER  1..   INCOME
```

						SSE
MULTIPLE R	.84325		ANALYSIS OF VARIANCE			
R SQUARE	.71108			DF	SUM OF SQUARES	MEAN SQUARE
ADJUSTED R SQUARE	.67496		REGRESSION	1	186.58690	186.58690
STANDARD ERROR	3.07841		RESIDUAL	8	75.81310	9.47664
			F =	19.68914	SIGNIF F =	.0022

```
------------------ VARIABLES IN THE EQUATION ------------------
```

VARIABLE	B	SE B	BETA	T	SIG T	
INCOME	.353921	.079761	.843254	4.437	.0022	─── *p*-value
(CONSTANT)	8.513963	3.320405		2.564	.0334	

```
END BLOCK NUMBER   1   ALL REQUESTED VARIABLES ENTERED.
```

$$b_0 \quad\quad b_1 \quad\quad s_{b_1} \quad\quad\quad t = \frac{b_1}{s_{b_1}}$$

Solution

Example 14.2

Example 14.2 was concerned with computing the regression equation $\hat{Y} = b_0 + b_1 X$. The problem was to determine the relationship between family income of local residents and the square footage of their homes. The SAS program listing in Figure 14.18 was used to request the SSE, b_0, and b_1 values as well as other statistics. Each line represents one card image to be entered:

Figure 14.18

SAS program listing used to request the SSE, b_0, and b_1 values.

```
TITLE    REAL ESTATE EXAMPLE USING ONE PREDICTOR;
DATA REAL ESTATE;
 INPUT SQFOOT INCOME;
 CARDS;
16  22
17  26
26  45
24  37
22  28
21  50
32  56
18  34
30  60
20  40
PROC PRINT;
PROC REG;
 MODEL SQFOOT=INCOME;
```

The TITLE command names the SAS run.

The DATA command gives the data a name.

The INPUT command names and gives the correct order for the different fields on the data cards.

The CARDS command indicates to SAS that the input data immediately follow.

The next ten lines are card images that represent square footage in hundreds and income in thousands of dollars. For example, the first card image (16 22) represents a family living in a 1600-square-foot home with an income of $22,000 per year.

The PROC PRINT command requests a printout of the input data.

The PROC REG command and MODEL subcommand indicate that SQFOOT and INCOME are the regression variables, with SQFOOT being the dependent variable and INCOME the independent variable.

Figure 14.19 shows the output obtained by executing the program listing in Figure 14.18.

Figure 14.19

Output obtained by executing the SAS program listing in Figure 14.18.

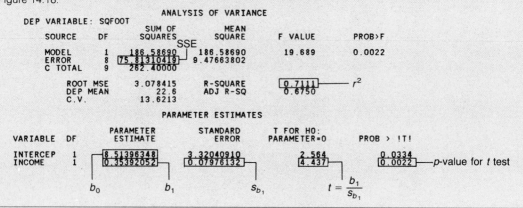

CHAPTER 15

Multiple Linear Regression

A Look Back/Introduction

We used the technique of simple linear regression in Chapter 14 to explain the behavior of a dependent variable using a single predictor (independent) variable. For example, one can attempt to explain the amount of new housing construction using the interest rate as a predictor variable.

To define this procedure in statistical terms, we introduced the concept of a statistical model. This model consists of two parts. The first is the deterministic component. This was assumed to be $Y = \beta_0 + \beta_1 X$ (a straight line), implying that the underlying pattern for the X and Y variables is linear. If a simple linear regression model is appropriate for the construction illustration, a scatter diagram of the new housing starts (Y) and the corresponding interest rates (X) should reveal a basic linear pattern. We never expect all of the sample data to lie *exactly* on a straight line; we realize that with any statistical model, there is error involved. This makes up the random component. The actual model used for simple linear regression is $Y = \beta_0 + \beta_1 X + e$, where e represents the distance from the actual Y value to the line passing through all X, Y values. The value of e is the error, or residual. The assumptions behind the use of this model were concerned about the behavior of these error terms—are they normally distributed, centered at zero, with the same variance? Are they independent?

In the construction example, it seems reasonable to assume that the volume of housing construction is affected not only by the interest rate, but also by many other factors (variables) as well, including cost of materials, geographic location, and unemployment rate in the area. We will next look at statistical models used to predict the dependent variable (such as Y = the number of new housing starts) as a function of *more than one* independent variable. The concept and assumptions are the same as before—we merely now are concerned with more than one predictor variable. When we include these additional variables, the predictive ability of the model should be significantly improved. This procedure is called multiple linear regression and is one of the more popular statistical techniques.

15.1

The Multiple Linear Regression Model

Prediction Using More Than One Variable

To explain or predict the behavior of a certain dependent variable using more than one predictor variable, we use a **multiple linear regression** model. The form of this model is

$$Y = \beta_0 + \beta_1 X_1 + \beta_2 X_2 + \ldots + \beta_k X_k + e \qquad (15\text{-}1)$$

where $X_1, X_2, \ldots, X_k$ are the k independent (predictor) variables, and e is the error associated with this model.

Notice that equation 15-1 is similar to that used in the simple linear regression model, except that the *deterministic component* is now

$$\beta_0 + \beta_1 X_1 + \ldots + \beta_k X_k \qquad (15\text{-}2)$$

rather than $\beta_0 + \beta_1 X$. Once again the error term, e, is included to provide for deviations about this component.

What is the appearance of the deterministic portion in equation 15-2? In Chapter 14, where we discussed simple linear regression, this was a straight line. For the multiple case, this is more difficult (usually impossible) to represent graphically. If your model contains two predictor variables, X_1 and X_2, the straight line becomes a plane, as shown in Figure 15.1. Consequently, the key assumption behind the use of this particular model is that the Y values will lie in this plane, *on the average*, for any particular values of X_1 and X_2.

In Chapter 14, we examined the relationship between the square footage of a home (Y) and the corresponding household income (X). The results were:

Least squares line: $\hat{Y} = 8.51 + .354X$
Correlation between X and Y: $r = .843$
Coefficient of determination: $r^2 = .711$
There is a significant linear relationship.

We now want to include two additional variables in the model. The real-estate developer performing the study suspects that (1) larger families have larger homes and (2) the size of the home is affected by the amount of formal education (years of college) of the wage earner(s) in the home. This results in three independent variables.

X_1 = annual income (thousands of dollars)

X_2 = family size

X_3 = combined years of formal education (beyond high school) for all household wage earners

The same ten families were used in the study, but data were collected on the two additional variables, X_2 and X_3.*

Family	Y (home square footage)	X_1 (income)	X_2 (family size)	X_3 (years of formal education)
1	16	22	2	4
2	17	26	2	8
3	26	45	3	7
4	24	37	4	0
5	22	28	4	2
6	21	50	3	10
7	32	56	6	8
8	18	34	3	8
9	30	60	5	2
10	20	40	3	6

The data configuration now has four columns (including Y) and ten rows (called "observations"). Our task is to use the data on all *three* variables (X_1, X_2, and X_3) to provide a better estimate of home size (Y).

The Least Squares Estimate Using Figure 15.1, we will proceed as we did for simple regression and determine an estimate of the β's that makes the sum of squares of the errors (e) as small as possible. In other words, we attempt to find the b_0, b_1, . . . , b_k that minimize the sum of squares of error,

$$\text{SSE} = \Sigma(Y - \hat{Y})^2 \tag{15-3}$$

Figure 15.1

The multiple linear regression model (two independent variables).

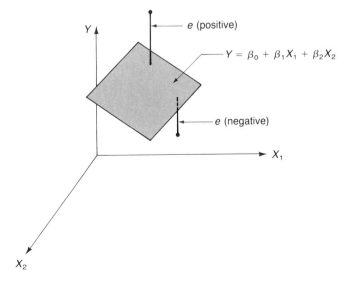

*A sample of size ten is unrealistically small in practice.

where now $\hat{Y} = b_0 + b_1X_1 + b_2X_2 + \ldots + b_kX_k$ and $b_0, b_1, \ldots, b_k$ are called the **least squares estimates** of $\beta_0, \beta_1, \ldots, \beta_k$.

By determining the estimated *regression coefficients* ($b_0, b_1, \ldots, b_k$) that minimize SSE, rather than $\Sigma(Y - \hat{Y})$, we once again avoid the problem of positive errors canceling out negative ones. Another advantage of this procedure is that, by means of a little calculus, one can show that a fairly simple expression exists for these sample regression coefficients. Because this expression involves the use of *matrix notation*, we will omit this result.*

There is only one way to solve a multiple regression problem in practice, and that is with the help of a computer. All computer packages determine the values of $b_0, b_1, \ldots, b_k$ in the same way—namely, by minimizing SSE. As a result, these values will be identical (except for numerical rounding errors) regardless of which computer program you use.

In the example attempting to predict home size using the three predictor variables, the prediction equation is

$$\hat{Y} = b_0 + b_1X_1 + b_2X_2 + b_3X_3$$

where

$$\hat{Y} = \text{estimate of the home size } (Y)$$
$$X_1 = \text{income}$$
$$X_2 = \text{family size}$$
$$X_3 = \text{years of education,}$$

and b_0, b_1, b_2 and b_3 are the least squares estimates of $\beta_0, \beta_1, \beta_2$ and β_3.

Figure 15.2 contains the MINITAB solution using the data we presented. According to this output, the best prediction equation (in the least squares sense) of home size is

$$\hat{Y} = 7.60 + .194X_1 + 2.34X_2 - .163X_3$$

So this solution minimizes SSE. But what is the SSE here? We need to determine how well this equation "fits" the ten observations in the data set. Consider the first family, where $X_1 = 22$ (income $= \$22,000$), $X_2 = 2$ (family size $= 2$; such as, an adult couple with no children), and $X_3 = 4$ (combined years of college $= 4$). The predicted home size here is

$$\hat{Y} = 7.60 + .194(22) + 2.34(2) - .163(4)$$
$$= 15.89$$

Consequently, the estimate of the home size is 1589 square feet. The actual square footage for this observation is 1600 ($Y = 16$), so the sample error (residual) here is $Y - \hat{Y} = 16 - 15.89 = .11$.

---

*Information on this expression is presented in W. Mendenhall and J. T. McClave, *A Second Course in Business Statistics: Regression Analysis* (San Francisco: Dellen, 1981); J. Neter, W. Wasserman, and M. Kutner, *Applied Linear Regression Models* (Homewood, IL: Richard D. Irwin, 1983); M.S. Younger, *Handbook for Linear Regression* (North Scituate, MA: Duxbury, 1979).

Figure 15.2

MINITAB multiple regression solution to house size using three predictor variables. See text.

```
MTB > READ INTO C1-C4
DATA> 16 22 2 4
DATA> 17 26 2 8
DATA> 26 45 3 7
DATA> 24 37 4 0
DATA> 22 28 4 2
DATA> 21 50 3 10
DATA> 32 56 6 8
DATA> 18 34 3 8
DATA> 30 60 5 2
DATA> 20 40 3 6
DATA> END
        10 ROWS READ
MTB > REGRESS Y IN C1 USING 3 PREDICTORS IN C2-C4
```

The regression equation is
C1 = 7.60 + 0.194 C2 + 2.34 C3 - 0.163 C4

Predictor	Coef		Stdev	t-ratio
Constant	7.596	$\leftarrow b_0$	2.595	2.93
C2	0.19388	$\leftarrow b_1$	0.08770	2.21
C3	2.3381	$\leftarrow b_2$	0.9078	2.58
C4	-0.1628	$\leftarrow b_3$	0.2441	-0.67

s = 2.035 $\leftarrow s$ R-sq = 90.5%   R-sq(adj) = 85.8%

Analysis of Variance

SOURCE	DF	SS	MS
Regression	3	237.542	79.181
Error	6	24.858	4.143
Total	9	262.400	

SSE

Using this procedure on the remaining nine observations, we find the following results:

Y	$\hat{Y}$	$Y - \hat{Y}$	$(Y - \hat{Y})^2$
16	15.89	0.11	.0121
17	16.01	0.99	.9801
26	22.19	3.81	14.5161
24	24.12	-0.12	.0144
22	22.05	-0.05	.0025
21	22.68	-1.68	2.8224
32	31.18	0.82	.6724
18	19.90	-1.90	3.6100
30	30.59	-0.59	.3481
20	21.39	-1.39	1.9321
		0	24.91 ≈ SSE

The computed value for the error sum of squares is SSE = 24.91. This value also is contained in the MINITAB output in Figure 15.2. The MINITAB value for SSE is 24.86, which differs slightly from the previous result because the computer uses much more accurate calculations than those in the table. SSE = 24.86 is more accurate, so we will use this value in the remaining discussion.

This implies that for *any* other values of b_0, b_1, b_2, and b_3, if we were to find the corresponding $\hat{Y}$'s and the resulting SSE = $\Sigma(Y - \hat{Y})^2$ using these values, this new SSE would be *larger* than 24.86. Thus, $b_0 = 7.60$, $b_1 = .194$, $b_2 = 2.34$, and $b_3 = -.163$ minimize the error sum of squares, SSE. Put still another way, these values of b_0, b_1, b_2, and b_3 provide the **best fit** to our data.

Using only income (X_1) as a predictor, in Chapter 14 we found the SSE to be 75.81 in our table. By including the additional two variables, the SSE has been reduced from

75.81 to 24.86 (a 67% reduction). It appears that either family size (X_2), years of education (X_3), or both contribute significantly to the prediction of Y.

Interpreting the Regression Coefficients   When using a multiple linear regression equation, such as $Y = \beta_0 + \beta_1 X_1 + \beta_2 X_2 + \beta_3 X_3 + e$, what does β_2 represent? Very simply, it reflects the change in Y that can be expected to accompany a change of one in X_2 *provided all other variables* (namely, X_1 and X_3) *are held constant.*

In the previous example, the sample estimate of β_2 was $b_2 = 2.34$. Can we expect an increase of 2.34 every time X_2 (the family size) increases by one if X_1 and X_3 are held constant? This type of argument is filled with problems, as we will demonstrate later. The primary problem is that a change in one of the predictor variables (such as X_2) always (or almost always) is accompanied by a change in one of the other predictors (say, X_1) in the sample observations. Consequently, variables X_1 and X_2 are related in some manner, such as $X_1 \cong 1 + 5X_2$. In other words, a situation in which, say, X_2 changed and the others remained constant would not be observed within the sample data.

In the other case (typically not observed in business applications), the predictor variables *are* totally unrelated. In this situation, a unit change in, say, X_2 can be expected to be accompanied by a change of β_2 in the dependent variable.

In general, it is *not* safe to assume that the predictor variables are unrelated. As a result, the b's usually do not reflect the true "partial effects" of the predictor variables and you should avoid such conclusions. Section 15.4 will discuss methods of dealing with this type of situation.

The Assumptions Behind the Multiple Linear Regression Model

The form of the multiple linear regression model is given by equation 15-1, which contains a linear combination of the k predictor (independent) variables as well as the error component, e. The assumptions for the case of $k > 1$ predictors are exactly the same as for $k = 1$ independent variable (simple linear regression). These assumptions, discussed in Chapter 14, are:

1. The errors (residuals) follow a normal distribution, centered at zero, with constant variance, σ_e^2.
2. The errors are (statistically) independent.

For the case of $k = 2$ predictor variables, this can be represented graphically, as shown in Figures 15.1 and 15.3. Using Figure 15.3, consider the situation in which $X_1 = 20$ and $X_2 = 15$. If you *were* to obtain repeated values of Y having these values for X_1 and X_2, you would obtain some Y's above the plane and some below. The assumption is that the *average* value of Y with $X_1 = 20$ and $X_2 = 15$ lies *on* the plane. Moreover, these errors are normally distributed.

The final part of assumption 1 is that the variation about this plane does not depend on the values of X_1 and X_2. You should see roughly the same amount of variation if you obtain repeated values of Y corresponding to $X_1 = 30$ and $X_2 = 5$ as you observed for $X_1 = 20$ and $X_2 = 15$. The variance of these residuals, if you observe Y indefinitely, is σ_e^2.

Finally, assumption 2 means that the residual encountered at, say, $X_1 = 30$ and $X_2 = 5$ is not affected by a known residual at any other point, such as $X_1 = 20$ and $X_2 = 15$. The error for one value of X_1 and X_2 has no effect on any other residual.

Figure 15.3

The residuals in multiple
linear regression ($k = 2$).

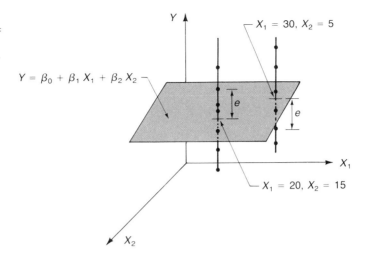

An Estimate of σ_e^2 When using a straight line to model a relationship between Y and a single predictor, the estimate of σ_e^2 was given by equation 14-16, where

$$s^2 = \hat{\sigma}_e^2 = \frac{\text{SSE}}{n - 2}$$

In general, for k predictors and n observations, the estimate of this variance is

$$s^2 = \hat{\sigma}_e^2 = \frac{\text{SSE}}{n - (k + 1)}$$
$$= \frac{\text{SSE}}{n - k - 1}$$

(15-4)

The value of s^2 is critical in determining the reliability and usefulness of the model as a predictor. If $s^2 = 0$, then SSE $= 0$, which implies that $Y = \hat{Y}$ for each of the observations in the sample data. This rarely happens in practice, but it does point out that a small s^2 is desirable. As s^2 increases, you can expect more error when predicting a value of Y for specified values of $X_1, X_2, \ldots, X_k$. In the next section, we will use s^2 as a key to determining whether the model is satisfactory and which of the independent variables is useful in the prediction of the dependent variable.

The square root of this estimated variance is the **residual standard deviation.**

$$s = \sqrt{\frac{\text{SSE}}{n - k - 1}}$$

(15-5)

In the MINITAB solution in Figure 15.2, the value of s is shown in the box containing $s = 2.035$.

Example 15.1

Determine the estimate of σ_e^2 and the residual standard deviation for the real-estate data in the previous example.

Solution This example contained $n = 10$ observations and $k = 3$ predictor variables. The resulting error sum of squares was SSE $= 24.86$ (from Figure 15.2).

Therefore,

$$s^2 = \hat{\sigma}_e^2$$

$$= \frac{24.86}{10 - 3 - 1} = \frac{24.86}{6} = 4.14$$

Also,

$$s = \sqrt{4.14} = 2.03$$

That is, the residual standard deviation is 203 square feet.

Assuming a normal distribution of the errors, the empirical rule implies that, when using this model, approximately 68% of the home sizes that you observe will lie within 203 square feet of the estimated value, $\hat{Y}$. Also, approximately 95% of the observed home sizes will be within $2s = (2)(2.03) = 4.06$ (406 square feet) of the predicted value.

If a particular regression model meets all the required assumptions, then the next question of interest is whether this set of independent variables provides an accurate method of predicting the dependent variable, Y. The next section shows how to calculate the predictive ability of your model and determine which variables contribute significantly to an accurate prediction of Y. ●

Exercises

15.1 A management-consulting firm uses a regression model where variable X_1 stands for previous experience, variable X_2 for number of years at current job, and variable X_3 for score on a job-aptitude test. These variables are used in a regression model to predict job satisfaction. Job satisfaction ranges from one to 20, with 20 indicating an employee is satisfied with every aspect of his or her job. The prediction equation is:

$$\hat{Y} = 1.7 - 0.15X_1 + 0.25X_2 + 0.14X_3$$

a. What would the consulting firm predict for the job satisfaction of an employee who has 15 years of prior experience, 10 years of employment at the present job, and an aptitude-test score of 85?

b. If an employee's score on the aptitude test is increased by 20, with the years of prior experience and years of employment at the current job remaining constant, what would be the net change in the employee's predicted satisfaction score?

15.2 The marketing department at Computeron would like to predict its sales volume of software for its personal computers. They believe that the sales volume of software (given in thousands) increases when the number of units of personal computers increases and when advertising expenditure (given in thousands of dollars) increases. The following data were collected for 14 months:

Y: Sales of Software	X_1: Units of Personal Computers Sold	X_2: Advertising Expenditure	Y: Sales of Software	X_1: Units of Personal Computers Sold	X_2: Advertising Expenditures
7.2	12	4.2	3.4	10	2.1
5.4	11	3.1	7.0	12	3.8
7.7	14	5.1	12.1	22	5.8
5.6	11	3.5	8.4	14	4.9
9.1	17	5.4	9.7	19	5.5
8.8	17	4.4	8.3	15	4.6
6.2	11	3.5	7.1	13	4.0

a. Using the least squares line $\hat{Y} = -1.21768 + 0.3141X_1 + 1.016X_2$, find the estimate of the variance of the error component.

b. Interpret the coefficients of the regression equation in the context of the problem. Would it be reasonable to expect sales of software to increase by 1.016 thousand if X_2 increased by one?

15.3 An oil-service company decided to fit a least squares equation to a set of data to predict the total cost of building a well. The independent variables are $X_1 = $ drilling days, $X_2 = $ total depth, and $X_3 = $ intermediate casing depth. After calculating the least squares equation, the residuals were calculated to find out whether the assumptions of regression analysis are satisfied. The following are the residuals from 20 observations:

$$-0.8,\ 1.5,\ -3.7,\ 4.1,\ -3.1,\ -5.2,\ 4.3,\ -2.1,\ -1.6,\ 4.1,\ 0.9,\ -0.3,\ 4.5,\ -4.2,\ 3.2,$$
$$-2.7,\ 1.7,\ -2.2,\ 3.4,\ -1.8$$

Do the residuals $Y - \hat{Y}$ appear to conform to the empirical rule that approximately 95% of the data should lie within two standard deviations of the mean?

15.4 What assumptions need to be made about the error component of a multiple linear regression model in order that the results of statistical inference can be used?

15.5 Tony owns a used-car lot. He would like to predict monthly sales volume. Tony believes that sales volume (given in thousands) is directly related to the number of salespeople employed and the number of cars on the lot for sale. The following data were collected over a period of 10 months:

Y: Monthly sales volume	X_1: Salespeople	X_2: Cars
5.8	4	20
7.5	5	15
11.4	7	25
7.0	3	17
5.1	2	18
8.1	4	25
13.3	8	30
15.0	9	35
8.3	5	20
6.8	4	23

a. Using a computerized statistical package, determine the least squares prediction equation here.

b. Find the value of SSE.

15.6 Using the multiple regression model $\hat{Y} = b_0 + b_1X_1 + b_2X_2 + b_3X_3$, where do you expect the average value of Y to fall for $X_1 = 3$, $X_2 = 4.1$, and $X_3 = 5.6$?

15.7 A regression analysis was performed for data with three independent variables. The following residuals were found for the 20 observations of the dependent variable:

$$5.4,\ 8.1,\ -7.4,\ 2.5,\ -3.5,\ -4.1,\ -8.1,\ 6.5,\ 4.3,\ -7.8,\ 2.8,\ 7.1,\ -6.2,\ 5.6,\ -5.1,$$
$$2.9,\ 2.8,\ -7.2,\ 8.3,\ -6.9$$

Find the residual standard deviation.

15.8 A veterinarian uses three independent variables to predict the weight of a doberman pinscher from birth to 2 years of age. The variables are $X_1 = $ age, $X_2 = $ height, and $X_3 = X_1X_2$. Thirty-five observations are used to find the least squares prediction equation. The veterinarian's standard error of estimate for the collected data was 4.25. What is the value of SSE?

15.2

Hypothesis Testing and Confidence Intervals for the β Parameters

Multiple linear regression is a popular tool in the application of statistical techniques to business decisions. However, this modeling procedure does not always result in an accurate and reliable predictor. When the independent variables that you have selected account for very little of the variation in the values of the dependent variable, the model (as is) serves no useful purpose.

The first thing we will demonstrate is how to determine whether your overall model is satisfactory. We will begin by summarizing a regression analysis in an ANOVA table, much as we did in Chapter 12.

The ANOVA Table

The summary ANOVA table contains the usual headings.

Source	df	SS	MS	F
Regression	k	SSR	MSR	MSR/MSE
Residual	$n - k - 1$	SSE	MSE	
Total	$n - 1$	SST		

where n = number of observations and k = number of independent variables

$$
\begin{aligned}
\text{SST} &= \text{total sum of squares} \\
&= \text{SS}_Y \\
&= \Sigma(Y - \bar{Y})^2 = \Sigma Y^2 - (\Sigma Y)^2/n
\end{aligned}
\tag{15-6}
$$

$$
\begin{aligned}
\text{SSE} &= \text{sum of squares for error} \\
&= \Sigma(Y - \hat{Y})^2
\end{aligned}
\tag{15-7}
$$

$$
\begin{aligned}
\text{SSR} &= \text{sum of squares for regression} \\
&= \Sigma(\hat{Y} - \bar{Y})^2 \\
&= \text{SST} - \text{SSE}
\end{aligned}
\tag{15-8}
$$

$$
\begin{aligned}
\text{MSR} &= \text{mean square for regression} \\
&= \text{SSR}/k
\end{aligned}
\tag{15-9}
$$

$$
\begin{aligned}
\text{MSE} &= \text{mean square for error} \\
&= \text{SSE}/(n - k - 1)
\end{aligned}
\tag{15-10}
$$

Practically all computer packages will provide you with this ANOVA summary as part of the standard output. The ANOVA section of the MINITAB solution for the real-estate model is highlighted in Figure 15.4.

Notice that

$$
\begin{aligned}
\text{SST} &= \text{SS}_Y \\
&= (16^2 + 17^2 + \ldots + 20^2) - (16 + 17 + \ldots + 20)^2/10 \\
&= 262.4
\end{aligned}
$$

Figure 15.4

ANOVA section of MINI-TAB output (see Figure 15.2).

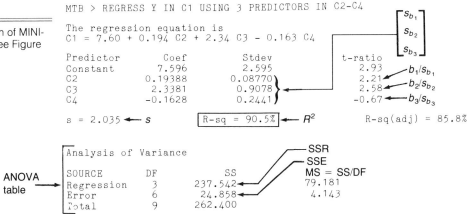

```
MTB > REGRESS Y IN C1 USING 3 PREDICTORS IN C2-C4

The regression equation is
C1 = 7.60 + 0.194 C2 + 2.34 C3 - 0.163 C4

Predictor        Coef        Stdev       t-ratio
Constant        7.596        2.595          2.93
C2            0.19388      0.08770          2.21
C3            2.3381       0.9078           2.58
C4           -0.1628       0.2441          -0.67

s = 2.035          R-sq = 90.5%          R-sq(adj) = 85.8%

Analysis of Variance

SOURCE         DF          SS        MS = SS/DF
Regression      3      237.542       79.181
Error           6       24.858        4.143
Total           9      262.400
```

$\begin{bmatrix} S_{b_1} \\ S_{b_2} \\ S_{b_3} \end{bmatrix}$

b_1/S_{b_1}
b_2/S_{b_2}
b_3/S_{b_3}

$\leftarrow s$ R^2

ANOVA table

SSR
SSE

This is the same value of SS_Y we obtained for the same example in Chapter 14, when we used only income (X_1) as the predictor variable. This is hardly surprising because *this value is strictly a function of the Y values* and is unaffected by the model that you are using to predict Y. The total sum of squares (SST) measures the total variation in the values of the dependent variable. Its value is the same, regardless of which predictor variables are included in the model.

The *df* for the regression source of variation = k = the number of predictor variables in the analysis. The *df* for the error sum of squares = $n - k - 1$ where n = the number of observations in the sample data.

As in the case of simple linear regression, the sum of squares of regression (SSR) measures the variation *explained* by the model—the variation in the Y values that would exist if differences in the values of the predictor variables were the only cause of differences among the Y's. On the other hand, the sum of squares of error (SSE) represents the variation *unexplained* by the model. The easiest way to determine the sum of squares of regression is to use SSR = SST − SSE.

The error mean square is MSE = SSE/($n - k - 1$) = 4.14. This is the same as the *estimate* of σ_e^2 determined in example 15.1. So

$$s^2 = \hat{\sigma}_e^2 = \text{MSE}$$

A Test for H_0: all β's = 0

We have yet to make use of the F value calculated in the ANOVA table, where

$$F = \frac{\text{MSR}}{\text{MSE}} \tag{15-11}$$

When using the simple regression model, we previously argued that one way to determine whether X is a significant predictor of Y is to test H_0: $\beta_1 = 0$, where β_1 is the coefficient of X in the model $Y = \beta_0 + \beta_1 X + e$. If you reject H_0, the conclusion is that the independent variable X *does* contribute significantly to the prediction of Y. For example, in example 14.3, we concluded that income (X_1) was a satisfactory predictor of home size (Y) using the simple linear model, by rejecting H_0: $\beta_1 = 0$.

We use a similar test as the first step in the multiple regression analysis, where we examine the hypotheses

$$H_0: \beta_1 = \beta_2 = \ldots = \beta_k = 0$$
$$H_a: \text{at least one of the } \beta\text{'s} \neq 0.$$

If we *reject* H_0, we can conclude that our model is satisfactory because at least one (but maybe not all) of the independent variables contributes significantly to the prediction of Y. If we *fail to reject* H_0, we are unable to demonstrate that any of the independent variables (or combination of them) help explain the behavior of the dependent variable, Y. For example, in our housing example, if we were to fail to reject H_0, this would imply that we are unable to demonstrate that the variation in the home sizes (Y) *can* be explained by the effect of income, family size, and years of education.

Test Statistic for H_0 Versus H_a The test statistic used to determine whether our multiple regression model is adequate is the F statistic from the preceding ANOVA table.

When testing H_0: all β's $= 0$ (this is a poor set of predictor variables) versus H_a: at least one $\beta \neq 0$ (at least one of these variables is a good predictor), the test statistic is

$$F = \frac{\text{MSR}}{\text{MSE}}$$

which has an F distribution with k and $n - k - 1$ *df*.

Notice that the *df* for the F statistic comes directly from the ANOVA table. The testing procedure (rejection region) will be to

$$\text{Reject } H_0 \text{ if } F > F_{\alpha, v_1, v_2}$$

where (1) $v_1 = k$, $v_2 = n - k - 1$, and (2) F_{α, v_1, v_2} is the corresponding F value in Table A-7, having a *right-tail area* $= \alpha$ (Figure 15.5).

Example 15.2

Using the real-estate data and the model we developed, what can you say about the predictive ability of the independent variables, income (X_1), family size (X_2), and years of education, X_3? Use $\alpha = .10$.

Solution

Step 1. The hypotheses are

$$H_0: \beta_1 = \beta_2 = \beta_3 = 0$$
$$H_a: \text{at least one } \beta \neq 0.$$

Remember that our intent here is to reject H_0. If you are unable to demonstrate that any of your independent variables have any predictive ability, then you will fail to reject H_0.

Figure 15.5

F curve with k and $n - k - 1$ *df*. The shaded area is the rejection region.

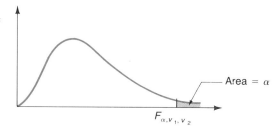

Step 2. The test statistic is

$$F = \frac{MSR}{MSE}$$

The mean squares are obtained from the ANOVA summary of the regression analysis (see Figure 15.4).

Step 3. The degrees of freedom for the F statistic are $k = 3$ and $n - k - 1 = 10 - 3 - 1 = 6$. So we will

Reject H_0 if $F > F_{.10,3,6} = 3.29$

Step 4. Using the results in Figure 15.4, the computed F value is

$$F^* = \frac{79.18}{4.14} = 19.1$$

Because $F^* > 3.29$, we reject H_0.

Step 5. The three independent variables *as a group* are good predictors of home size. This does *not* imply that all three variables have significant predictive ability; however, at least one of them does. The next section will show how you can tell *which* of these predictor variables significantly contributes to the prediction of home size. ●

A Test for H_0: $\beta_i = 0$

Assuming that you rejected the null hypothesis that all of the β's are zero, the next logical question would be, which of the independent variables contributes to the prediction of Y?

In example 15.2, we rejected the null hypothesis, so at least one of these three independent variables affects the variation of the ten home sizes in the sample. To determine the contribution of each variable, we will perform three separate t tests.

H_0: $\beta_1 = 0$ (X_1 does not contribute)

H_a: $\beta_1 \neq 0$ (X_1 does contribute)

H_0: $\beta_2 = 0$ (X_2 does not contribute)

H_a: $\beta_2 \neq 0$ (X_2 does contribute)

H_0: $\beta_3 = 0$ (X_3 does not contribute)

H_a: $\beta_3 \neq 0$ (X_3 does contribute)

One-tailed tests also can be used here, but we will demonstrate this procedure using two-tailed tests. This means that we are testing to see whether this particular X contributes to the prediction of Y, but we are not concerned about the direction (positive or negative) of this relationship.

When income (X_1) was the only predictor of home size (Y), we used a t test to determine whether the simple linear regression model was adequate. In example 14.3, the value of the test statistic was derived, where

$$t = \frac{b_1}{s_{b_1}} \tag{15-12}$$

Also, b_1 is the estimate of β_1 in the simple regression model, and s_{b_1} is the (estimated) standard deviation of b_1.

All computer packages provide both the estimated coefficient (b_1) and its standard deviation (s_{b_1}). In example 14.3, the computed value of this t statistic was $t^* = 4.44$. This led us to conclude that income *was* a good predictor of home size because a significant positive relationship existed between these two variables.

We use the same t statistic procedure to test the effect of the individual variables in a multiple regression model. When examining the effect of an individual independent variable, X_i, on the prediction of a dependent variable, the hypotheses are

$$H_0: \beta_i = 0$$

$$H_a: \beta_i \neq 0$$

The test statistic is

$$t = \frac{b_i}{s_{b_i}}$$

where (1) b_i is the estimate of β_i, (2) s_{b_i} is the (estimated) standard deviation of b_i, and (3) the *df* for the t statistic are $n - k - 1$.

The test of H_0 versus H_a is to

Reject H_0 if $|t| > t_{\alpha/2, n-k-1}$

where $t_{\alpha/2, n-k-1}$ is obtained from Table A-5.

We can now reexamine the real-estate data in example 15.2.

$X_1 =$ **Income** Consider the hypotheses

$$H_0: \beta_1 = 0$$

$$H_a: \beta_1 \neq 0$$

As in example 15.2, we will use $\alpha = .10$.

According to Figure 15.4, $b_1 = .194$ and $s_{b_1} = .0877$. Also contained in the output is the computed value of

$$t^* = \frac{b_1}{s_{b_1}} = \frac{.194}{.0877} = 2.21$$

Why is this value of t^* *not* the same as the value of t calculated previously in Chapter 14 for this variable, when income was the only predictor of Y? When there are three predictors in the model, t^* for income is 2.21. When income is the only predictor in the model, $t^* = 4.44$. The difference in the two values is simply that $t^* = 2.21$ provides a measure of the contribution of $X_1 =$ income, *given that X_2 and X_3 already have been included in the model*. A large value of t^* indicates that X_1 contributes significantly to the prediction of Y, even if X_2 and X_3 have been included previously as predictors.

The hypotheses can better be stated as

$H_0:$ = income *does not* contribute to the prediction of home size, *given* that family size and years of education already have been included in the model

$H_a:$ = income *does* contribute to this prediction, given that family size and years of education already have been included in the model or as

$H_0: \beta_1 = 0$ (if X_2 and X_3 are included)

$H_a: \beta_1 \neq 0$

Because $t^* = 2.21$ exceeds the table value of $t_{\alpha/2, n-k-1} = t_{.05, 10-3-1} = t_{.05, 6} = 1.943$, we conclude that income contributes significantly to the prediction of home size and should be kept in the model.

X_2 = Family Size Using a similar argument, the following test of hypothesis will determine the contribution of family size, X_2, as a predictor of the home square footage, given that X_1 and X_3 already have been included. The hypotheses here are

$H_0: \beta_2 = 0$ (if X_1 and X_3 are included)

$H_a: \beta_2 \neq 0$

According to Figure 15.4, the computed t statistic here is

$$t^* = \frac{b_2}{s_{b_2}}$$

$$= \frac{2.34}{.9078} = 2.58$$

This also exceeds $t_{.05, 6} = 1.943$, and so family size provides useful information in predicting the square footage of a home. We conclude that we should keep X_2 in the model.

X_3 = Years of Education To test

$H_0: \beta_3 = 0$ (if X_1 and X_2 are included)

$H_a: \beta_3 \neq 0$

we once again use the t statistic.

$$t = \frac{b_3}{s_{b_3}}$$

Using Figure 15.4, the computed value of this statistic is

$$t^* = \frac{-.163}{.2441} = -.67$$

Because $|t^*| = .67$, and this does *not* exceed $t_{.05, 6} = 1.943$, we fail to reject H_0. We conclude that, given the values of X_1 = income and X_2 = family size, the level of a family's education appears not to contribute to the prediction of the size of their home. This means that X_3 can be ignored in the final prediction equation, leaving only X_1 and X_2. As a word of warning, you should *not* simply remove this term from the equation containing all three variables. In Figure 15.4, the final prediction equation is not $\hat{Y} = 7.60 + .194X_1 + 2.34X_2$. Instead, the coefficients of X_1 and X_2 should be derived by repeating the analysis using only these two variables.

A Confidence Interval for β_i

Based on the previous t statistic, you can easily construct a $(1 - \alpha) \cdot 100\%$ CI for β_i:

$$b_i - t_{\alpha/2, n-k-1} \, s_{b_i} \qquad \text{to} \qquad b_i + t_{\alpha/2, n-k-1} \, s_{b_i}$$

Example 15.3

Using the results from example 15.2, construct a 90% CI for β_2, the coefficient for $X_2 =$ family size.

Solution Given $t_{\alpha/2, n-k-1} = t_{.05,6} = 1.943$, using Figure 15.4, the CI for β_2 is

$$2.34 - (1.943)(.9078) \qquad \text{to} \qquad 2.34 + (1.943)(.9078)$$
$$= 2.34 - 1.76 \quad \text{to} \quad 2.34 + 1.76$$
$$= .58 \quad \text{to} \quad 4.10$$

Therefore, we are 90% confident that the estimate of β_2 (that is, $b_2 = 2.34$) is within 1.76 of the actual value of β_2. Notice that this is an extremely wide CI—in fact, it is so wide that it is of little value. As usual, increasing the sample size would help to reduce the width of this CI. ●

Example 15.4

The managers of Brockwood Homes, a major developer, are attempting to predict their monthly sales of new homes. In Chapter 4, we examined the relationship between $X =$ number of times homes were shown to prospective buyers during a month and $Y =$ number of homes sold during this month. The resulting sample correlation was

Figure 15.6

MINITAB output for example 15.4.

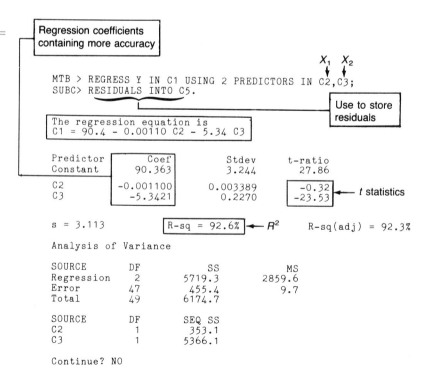

not significant. In reviewing this situation, suppose Brockwood decides to include the effect of the average interest rate for the month. Let

Y = number of homes sold during a month

X_1 = number of times homes were shown during this month

X_2 = average interest rate during this month.

The model used for this application is

$Y = \beta_0 + \beta_1 X_1 + \beta_2 X_2 + e$

Fifty months of data were randomly gathered on all three variables, as shown in the following table. The least squares equation and the complete MINITAB output are contained in Figure 15.6.

Month	Y: (number sold)	X_1: (number shown)	X_2: (interest rate)
1	15	155	14.0
2	38	320	10.1
3	25	490	11.5
4	18	131	12.8
5	8	228	16.5
6	13	512	14.1
7	19	182	13.0
8	28	430	11.3
9	15	408	14.0
10	16	140	13.5
11	5	350	16.4
12	10	280	14.2
13	24	428	12.2
14	12	176	13.9
15	18	108	13.4
16	18	220	12.9
17	36	550	11.5
18	37	380	10.0
19	35	217	11.1
20	26	436	11.6
21	25	536	12.0
22	42	466	9.6
23	28	472	11.5
24	40	142	9.5
25	36	321	10.2
26	37	388	10.0
27	8	182	16.2
28	38	368	10.0
29	31	410	10.9
30	18	341	13.7
31	37	110	9.5
32	21	352	12.1
33	35	580	9.4
34	45	314	9.5
35	7	260	16.5

(continued)

Month	Y: (number sold)	X_1: (number shown)	X_2: (interest rate)
36	14	450	13.8
37	41	356	9.4
38	40	340	9.9
39	40	516	9.7
40	38	165	9.6
41	41	370	9.8
42	42	452	9.5
43	25	410	11.8
44	20	240	13.0
45	30	241	11.0
46	22	580	11.9
47	20	236	12.7
48	20	510	12.0
49	30	520	11.6
50	21	271	13.1

Determine the estimated number of houses sold for a month during which 385 houses are shown and the average interest rate is 12.5%. What can you say about the predictive ability of these two independent variables? Use a significance level of $\alpha = .10$.

Solution The least squares equation from Figure 15.6 is

$$\hat{Y} = 90.36 - .0011X_1 - 5.342X_2$$

The predicted number of new home sales is

$$\hat{Y} = 90.36 - .0011(385) - 5.342(12.5)$$
$$= 90.36 - .423 - 66.775$$
$$= 23.16$$

That is, approximately 23 houses. Note that, similar to the argument in Chapter 14, 23.16 also serves as an estimate of the *average* number of homes sold for all months having $X_1 = 385$ and $X_2 = 12.5$.

The first test of hypothesis will determine whether these two variables *as a group* provide a useful model for predicting the amount of new home sales.

$$H_0: \beta_1 = \beta_2 = 0$$

$$H_a: \beta_1 \neq 0, \beta_2 \neq 0, \text{ or both} \neq 0$$

Using the ANOVA table in Figure 15.6, the value of the F statistic is

$$F^* = \frac{\text{MSR}}{\text{MSE}} = \frac{2859.6}{9.7} = 294.8$$

The *df* here are $v_1 = k = 2$ and $v_2 = n - k - 1 = 50 - 2 - 1 = 47$. Because $F_{.10,2,47}$ is not in Table A-7, we use the nearest value, $F_{.10,2,40} = 2.44$. The computed F^* exceeds this value, so we reject H_0 and conclude that at least one of these two independent variables is a significant predictor of new home sales. ●

The *t* Tests Because we rejected H_0 in example 15.4, the next step is to examine the *t* tests to determine which of the two independent variables are useful predictors. The *t* value from Table A-5 is $t_{\alpha/2, n-k-1} = t_{.05,47} = 1.645$. The computed *t* values in Figure 15.6 lead to the following conclusions. First, the t value for X_1 = number of times their homes were shown is $t^* = -.32$. The absolute value of t^* is *less than* 1.645, which means that, given the presence of X_2 in the model, X_1 does not contribute useful information to the prediction of new home sales. It can be removed from the model without seriously affecting the accuracy of a sales prediction, Y. Second, for X_2 = average interest rate for the month, the computed t value is $t^* = -23.53$. Now, $|t^*| = 23.53 > 1.645$, which means that the interest rate *is* an excellent predictor of the volume of new home sales. It was the contribution of this variable, and not of X_1, that produced the extremely large F value we obtained.

As we have seen, a quick glance at the computer output allows you to determine whether your model is satisfactory as a whole and, furthermore, which variables are useful predictors. But beware—the analysis is not over! Before you form your conclusions from this analysis and make critical decisions based on several tests of hypotheses, you need be sure that none of the assumptions of the multiple linear regression model (discussed earlier) has been violated. We will discuss this problem in the final section of this chapter, where we will conclude the analysis by examining the sample *residuals*, $Y - \hat{Y}$.

The use of t tests allows you to determine the predictive contribution of each independent variable, provided you want to examine the contribution of *one* such variable while assuming that the remaining variables are included in the equation. The next section will show you how to extend this procedure to a situation in which you wish to determine the contribution of any *set* of predictor variables by using a single test.

Exercises

15.9 The job placement center at Ozark Technological University would like to predict the starting salaries (given in thousands of dollars) for the college graduates in the engineering department. Two variables are used. The variable X_1 represents the student's overall grade point average (GPA). The variable X_2 represents the number of years of prior job-related experience. Data for fifteen randomly selected graduating students are:

Y: Starting Salary	X₁: Overall GPA	X₂: Years of Job-related Experience
27.1	3.7	0
23.3	2.9	1.1
21.4	2.4	1.5
24.2	3.2	0.5
26.1	3.6	0.8
19.8	2.7	0
22.8	3.1	0
20.5	2.2	2.1
32.3	3.8	2.5
18.1	2.1	1.4
22.5	3.0	0.3
23.8	3.4	0.5
20.9	2.8	0
20.0	2.5	1.0
27.8	3.3	2.1

The least square equation for the data is:

$$\hat{Y} = 2.189 + 6.5144X_1 + 1.9259X_2$$

a. Find the F value using an ANOVA table to test the hypothesis that $\beta_1 = 0$ and $\beta_2 = 0$ at the 5% level of significance.

b. Interpret the coefficients in the context of the problem.

15.10 Complete the following ANOVA table to test the usefulness of a model with five independent variables that attempted to explain the variation in the dependent variable:

Source	df	SS	MS	F
Regression				
Error		180		
Total	50	215		

15.11 The Department of Public Safety of Tennessee wanted to convince people to drive more slowly on wet highways. A highway patrol officer slammed the brakes at 12 different speeds on a wet highway and on a dry highway to measure the distance in feet that it took to stop; 24 observations were collected. Let X_1 be the speed in miles per hour. Let X_2 be 1 if the highway surface is wet and 0 if the surface is dry. A computer package gave the following sample statistics:

$$b_0 = 6.3 \qquad b_1 = 3.1 \qquad b_2 = 16.5 \qquad s_{b_1} = 1.12 \qquad s_{b_2} = 2.54$$

a. Given that X_2 is in the model, does the variable X_1 contribute to predicting the dependent variable at the .05 significance level?

b. Given that X_1 is in the model, does the variable X_2 contribute to predicting the dependent variable at the .05 significance level?

15.12 Brown and Gilbert's law firm would like to predict the salary for a legal secretary based on years of college education (X_1), typing speed in words per minute (X_2), and years of experience (X_3). The following data were collected:

Y	X_1	X_2	X_3
15,120	2	65	2
12,500	1	45	2
26,000	3.5	85	9
19,000	0	55	11
16,000	4	85	1
15,000	0	65	1
12,500	0	45	0.5
15,800	2.5	60	2
19,600	1	70	3
21,800	3	75	6
12,400	0	60	0.5
22,500	2	75	7

a. Using a computerized statistical package, determine the least squares prediction equation.

b. What is the value of the standard error of an estimate for the data?

c. Do the variables X_1, X_2, and X_3 contribute to predicting salaries at the .10 significance level?

d. Find a 90% CI for β_1.

e. Test the null hypothesis that $\beta_1 = 0$ at the 10% significance level.

f. Interpret the results of the hypothesis test in question e.

15.13 The following sample statistics were computed for a regression analysis:

$$b_0 = 10.2 \qquad b_1 = 5.6 \qquad b_2 = 100.4 \qquad s_{b_1} = 1.04 \qquad s_{b_2} = 17.95$$

Assume that twenty observations were taken.

a. Test that X_2 significantly contributes to the prediction of Y given that X_1 is in the model. Use a 5% significance level.

b. Find a 95% CI for β_1.

15.14 The model $\hat{Y} = 3.2 + 6.1X_1 + 5.2X_2$ was calculated to fit 20 data points pertaining to the growth rate of a hog. The variable X_1 represents the daily food consumption of the hog and X_2 represents the age of the hog. If the standard deviation of the estimate of β_1 is 2.5, what is a 95% CI for the parameter β_1?

15.15 Complete the following ANOVA table to test the null hypothesis that the independent variables are not useful predictors of the dependent variable.

Source	df	SS	MS	F
Regression				
Error		55	2.75	
Total	27	255		

15.16 Datamatics Equipment, a Seattle-based electronics firm, is interested in identifying variables in the manufacturing environment that have a linear relationship with the number of line shortages on the manufacturing floor. The sample data used in a regression analysis are as follows:

Week	Y	X_1	X_2	X_3
1	293	205	5.936	343
2	348	215	5.815	259
3	416	227	4.983	250
4	445	301	4.841	236
5	453	362	4.755	243
6	392	358	4.775	303
7	382	302	4.813	411
8	365	246	4.909	420
9	420	365	4.780	453
10	407	329	4.905	460
11	397	345	5.009	426
12	430	249	4.869	408
13	497	356	4.791	324
14	534	424	4.754	330
15	547	430	4.598	283

where

Y = number of line shortages with back-order status for a given week

X_1 = number of delinquent purchase orders for a given week

X_2 = inventory level (in millions of dollars) for prior weeks

X_3 = number of purchased items for prior weeks

The least squares regression equation was found to be:

$$\hat{Y} = 710.9 + 0.4767X_1 - 70.90X_2 - 0.2525X_3$$

a. Does the complete model significantly contribute to predicting the dependent variable? Use a 10% significance level.

b. If s_{b_2} is 36.886, find a 95% CI for β_2.

c. Interpret the results of the hypothesis test in question a and interpret the CI in question b.

15.17 The least squares line of $\hat{Y} = 3.4 + 1.2X_1 + 4.3X_2$ was obtained. The sample residuals of the 20 observations used in fitting the regression line are:

4.1, -3.2, 1.5, 6.7, 6.4, 3.8, -4.2, -2.4, 1.6, -8.7, -3.1, 1.2, -5.1, 2.1, 0.6, 5.4, 3.4, -7.1, -6.2, 3.2

Given that the value of SST is 510, test the null hypothesis that the variables X_1 and X_2 contribute to predicting the variation in the dependent variable. Use a 5% significance level.

15.18 Do the number of units of personal computers sold and the advertising expenditures contribute significantly to predicting the variation in the sales of software in exercise 15.2? Use a 5% level of significance.

15.19 Refer to exercise 15.5. Test the null hypothesis that the number of salespeople and the number of cars do not contribute to predicting the variation in the monthly sales of cars at Tony's used-car lot. Find a 90% CI for β_1, if s_{b_1} is 0.2116.

15.20 If the standard error of an estimate for a set of data is 3.82 and the total sum of squares is 269, what is the F test for testing that a model with five independent variables does not contribute to predicting the variation in the dependent variable? Assume that 15 observations of the dependent variable were taken.

15.3

Determining the Predictive Ability of Certain Independent Variables

We can extend the procedure we used to examine the contribution of each independent variable, one at a time, using a t test.

Assume that the personnel director of an accounting firm has developed a regression model to predict an individual's performance on the CPA exam. The multiple linear regression model contains eight independent variables, three of which (say, X_6, X_7, X_8) describe the physical attributes of each individual (say, height, weight, and age). Can all three of these variables be removed from the analysis without seriously affecting the predictive ability of the model?

To answer this question, we return to a statistic, described in Chapter 14, that measures how well the model captures the variation in the values of your dependent variable.

Coefficient of Determination

The total variation of the sampled dependent variable is determined by

$$\text{SST} = \text{total sum of squares}$$
$$= \text{SS}_Y$$
$$= \Sigma(Y - \overline{Y})^2$$
$$= \Sigma Y^2 - (\Sigma Y)^2/n$$

where $n = $ number of observations. To determine what percentage of this variation has been explained by the predictor variables in the regression equation, we determine the **coefficient of determination, R^2.**

$$R^2 = 1 - \frac{\text{SSE}}{\text{SST}} \tag{15-13}$$

The range for R^2 is 0 to 1. If $R^2 = 1$, then 100% of the total variation has been explained because, in this case, (1) SSE $= \Sigma(Y - \hat{Y})^2 = 0$, and so $Y = \hat{Y}$ for each observation in the sample; that is, the model provides a *perfect predictor.*

This will not occur in practice, but the main point is that a large value of R^2 is desirable for a regression application.

H_0: all β's $= 0$ A test statistic for testing H_0: all β's $= 0$ was introduced in equation 15-11, which used the ratio of two mean squares from the ANOVA table. Another way to calculate this F value is to use

$$F = \frac{R^2/k}{(1 - R^2)/(n - k - 1)} \qquad (15\text{-}14)$$

This version of the F statistic is used to answer the question, is the value of R^2 significantly large? If H_0 is rejected, then the answer is yes, and so this group of predictor variables provides at least an adequate method of predicting Y.

The F value computed in this way will be exactly the *same* (except for possible roundoff error) as the one computed using $F = $ MSR/MSE. This will be illustrated in example 15.5.

Once again, remember that *statistical* significance does not always imply *practical* significance. A large value of R^2 (rejecting H_0) does not imply that precise prediction (practical significance) will follow. However, it does inform the researcher that these predictor variables, as a group, are associated with the dependent variable.

Example 15.5

In example 14.7, we determined that $X = $ income explained 71% of the total variation of the new home sales values in the sample. What percentage is explained using all three predictors (income, family size, and years of education)?

Solution   The coefficient of determination using X_1 only is .71. The coefficient of determination using X_1, X_2 and X_3 is (see Figure 15.4)

$$R^2 = 1 - \frac{\text{SSE}}{\text{SST}}$$

$$= 1 - \frac{24.858}{262.4} = .905$$

Consequently, 90.5% of this variation has been explained using the three independent variables. This value is also shown in the MINITAB solution in Figure 15.4.

The F value determined in example 15.2 for testing H_0: $\beta_1 = \beta_2 = \beta_3 = 0$ can be duplicated using equation 15-14 because

$$F = \frac{.905/3}{(1 - .905)/(10 - 3 - 1)} = \frac{.905/3}{.095/6}$$

$$= 19.1 \text{ (as before)} \qquad \bullet$$

Comments

In example 15.5, notice that the value of R^2 *increased* when we went from using one independent variable to using three. As you add variables to your regression model, R^2 *always increases.* However, the increase may not be a significant one. If adding ten more predictor variables to your model causes R^2 to increase from .91 to .92, this is not a *significant* increase. Therefore, do not include these ten variables; they merely clutter up your model and add little predictive ability to it.

How can we tell if adding (or removing) a certain set of X variables causes a *significant* increase (or decrease) in R^2?

The Partial F Test

Consider the situation in which the personnel director is trying to determine whether to retain three variables (X_6, X_7, X_8) as predictors of a person's performance on a CPA exam. We know one thing—R^2 *will* be higher with these three variables included in the model. If we do not observe a *significant* increase, however, our advice would be to *remove* these variables from the analysis. To determine the extent of this increase, we use another F test.

We define two models—one contains X_6, X_7, X_8, and one does not.

Complete model: uses all predictor variables, including X_6, X_7, and X_8
Reduced model: uses the same predictor variables as the complete model except X_6, X_7, and X_8

Also, let

R_c^2 = the value of R^2 for the complete model

R_r^2 = the value of R^2 for the reduced model

Do X_6, X_7, and X_8 contribute to the prediction of Y? We will test

H_0: $\beta_6 = \beta_7 = \beta_8 = 0$ (they do not)

H_a: at least one of the β's $\neq 0$ (at least one of them does)

The test statistic here is

$$F = \frac{(R_c^2 - R_r^2)/v_1}{(1 - R_c^2)/v_2} \tag{15-15}$$

where v_1 = number of β's in H_0, and $v_2 = n - 1 -$ (number of X's in the complete model).

For this illustration, $v_1 = 3$ because there are three β's contained in H_0. Assuming that there are eight variables in the complete model, then $v_2 = n - 1 - 8 = n - 9$. Here, n is the total number of observations (rows) in your data. This F statistic measures the *partial* effect of these three variables; it is a **partial F statistic.**

Equation 15-15 resembles the F statistic given in equation 15-14, which we used to test H_0: all β's $= 0$. If all the β's are zero, then the reduced model consists of only a constant term and the resulting R^2 will be zero; that is, $R_r^2 = 0$. Setting $R_r^2 = 0$ in equation 15-15 produces equation 15-14, where $v_1 = k$ and $v_2 = n - k - 1$.

These variables (as a group) contribute significantly if the computed partial F value in equation 15-15 exceeds F_{α, v_1, v_2} from Table A-7.

Example 15.6

The personnel director gathered data from 30 individuals using all eight of the independent variables. These data were entered into a computer, and a multiple linear regression analysis was performed. The resulting R^2 was .857.

Next, variables X_6, X_7, and X_8 were omitted, and a second regression analysis was performed. The resulting R^2 was .824. Do the variables X_6, X_7, and X_8 (height, weight, and age) appear to have any predictive ability? Use $\alpha = .10$.

Solution Here, $n = 30$ and

$$R_c^2 = .857 \text{ (complete model)}$$

$$R_r^2 = .824 \text{ (reduced model)}$$

Based on the previous discussion, the value of the partial F statistic is

$$F^* = \frac{(.857 - .824)/3}{(1 - .857)/(30 - 1 - 8)}$$

$$= \frac{.033/3}{.143/21}$$

$$= 1.61$$

The procedure is to reject H_0: $\beta_6 = \beta_7 = \beta_8 = 0$ if $F^* > F_{.10,3,21} = 2.36$. The computed F value does not exceed the table value, so we fail to reject H_0. We conclude that these variables should be removed from the analysis because including them in the model fails to produce a significantly larger R^2. ●

The partial F test also can be used to determine the effect of adding a *single* variable to the model.

Example 15.7

Using the real-estate data analyzed in example 15.2, determine whether $X_2 =$ family size contributes to the prediction of home size, given that $X_1 =$ income and $X_3 =$ years of education are included in the model. Use a significance level of $\alpha = .10$.

Solution We will test the hypotheses

$$H_0: \beta_2 = 0 \text{ (if } X_1 \text{ and } X_3 \text{ are included)}$$

$$H_a: \beta_2 \neq 0.$$

The complete model uses X_1, X_2, and X_3. Using Figure 15.4,

$$R_c^2 = .905$$

The reduced model uses X_1 and X_3 only. Figure 15.7 shows the MINITAB output for this, and

$$R_r^2 = .801$$

Figure 15.7

MINITAB output using $X_1 =$ income and $X_3 =$ years of education as predictors.

```
MTB > REGRESS Y IN C1 USING 2 PREDICTORS IN C2, C4  ←—X₃
                                                     ↳—→X₁
The regression equation is
C1 = 10.5 + 0.373 C2 - 0.494 C4

Predictor        Coef        Stdev      t-ratio
Constant       10.465        3.148         3.32
C2            0.37315      0.07168         5.21
C4            -0.4938       0.2787        -1.77

s = 2.735          R-sq = 80.1%  ←—R²   R-sq(adj) = 74.4%

Analysis of Variance

SOURCE          DF          SS           MS
Regression       2       210.06       105.03
Error            7        52.34         7.48
Total            9       262.40
```

The value of the partial F statistic is

$$F^* = \frac{(.905 - .801)/1}{(1 - .905)/(10 - 1 - 3)}$$

$$= \frac{.104/1}{.095/6} = 6.6$$

(The one in the numerator indicates that there is one β in H_0; subtracting the 3 in the denominator 6 indicates that there are three X's in the complete model.)

This value does exceed $F_{.10,1,6} = 3.78$, and so $X_2 =$ family size does (as suspected from the earlier t test) significantly improve the model's predictive ability when included with X_1 and X_3. In other words, there *is* a significant increase in R^2 (from .801 to .905) when X_2 is added to the model. ●

Comments

Both example 15.7 and the t test for X_2 discussed earlier dealt with testing H_0: $\beta_2 = 0$ versus H_a: $\beta_2 \neq 0$. Both tests attempted to determine whether X_2 should be included as a predictor given that X_1 and X_3 were already included as predictor variables. Note two things: (1) the partial F value $= 6.6 = (2.578)^2 = (t \text{ value})^2$, and (2) the p-value using the t test (not shown) $=$ the p-value using the F test (not shown).

We can see that these tests are *identical:* They result in exactly the same p-value and the same conclusion. This means that, to determine the predictive ability of an individual independent variable, we can compute the partial F statistic or the somewhat simpler t statistic. Some computer packages use the F statistics to summarize the individual predictors, whereas others (such as MINITAB) use the t values to measure the influence of each predictor. You should use whatever is provided (the F statistic or t statistic) to measure the partial effect of each variable; both sets of statistics accomplish the same thing.

Using Curvilinear Models: Polynomial Regression

Mr. Bentley owns several furniture stores in a large metropolitan area. He is interested in the relationship between his monthly advertising expenditures (X) and the corresponding monthly sales (Y). He suspects that sales will increase as the amount spent on advertising increases but after a certain point will slow down (that is, continue to increase but at a slower rate). In other words, after spending a certain amount on advertising, he will reach a point where there will be little gain in sales, even though he spends a much larger amount on advertising.

Data were gathered from the company records covering 15 (nonconsecutive) months of sales (in tens of thousands of dollars) and advertising expenditures (in hundreds of dollars).

Month	Y (sales)	X (advertising expenditures)	Month	Y (sales)	X (advertising expenditures)
1	6.9	18.1	9	8.8	29.2
2	8.5	27.3	10	10.2	50.5
3	1.2	10.1	11	9.8	37.3
4	9.4	34.8	12	9.3	40.2
5	3.2	11.8	13	9.8	43.1
6	5.2	15.0	14	9.8	45.0
7	8.0	22.9	15	9.2	31.5
8	7.2	20.4			

Figure 15.8

MINITAB scatter diagram of data for advertising example.

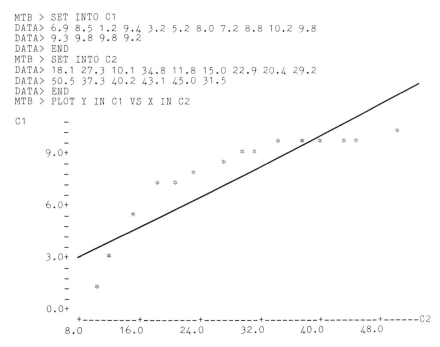

```
MTB > SET INTO C1
DATA> 6.9 8.5 1.2 9.4 3.2 5.2 8.0 7.2 8.8 10.2 9.8
DATA> 9.3 9.8 9.8 9.2
DATA> END
MTB > SET INTO C2
DATA> 18.1 27.3 10.1 34.8 11.8 15.0 22.9 20.4 29.2
DATA> 50.5 37.3 40.2 43.1 45.0 31.5
DATA> END
MTB > PLOT Y IN C1 VS X IN C2
```

The scatter diagram is shown in Figure 15.8. Mr. Bentley is correct—the sales do appear to level off after a certain amount of advertising expense.

Does the simple linear model $Y = \beta_0 + \beta_1 X + e$ capture the relationship between advertising expense (X) and sales (Y)? Although Y does increase as X increases here, the linear model does not capture the "slowing down" of Y for larger values of X. The least squares line (sketched in Figure 15.8) will underestimate sales for the middle range of X but overestimate sales for small or large values of X.

Figure 15.9 shows **quadratic curves** rather than straight lines. If we include X^2 in the model, we can describe the curved relationship that seems to exist between sales and advertising. More specifically, the left half of Figure 15.9b closely resembles the shape of the scatter diagram in Figure 15.8. Consider the model

$$Y = \beta_0 + \beta_1 X + \beta_2 X^2 + e \tag{15-16}$$

Is this a linear regression model? At first glance, it would appear not to be. However, by the word *linear* we really mean that the model is *linear in the unknown β's, not X.*

Figure 15.9

Quadratic curves. **A** Graph of $Y = 34 - 12X + 2X^2$. In general, this is the shape of $Y = \beta_0 + \beta_1 X + \beta_2 X^2$, where $\beta_2 > 0$. **B** Graph of $Y = 6 + 12X - 2X^2$. In general, this is the shape of $Y = \beta_0 + \beta_1 X + \beta_2 X^2$, where $\beta_2 < 0$.

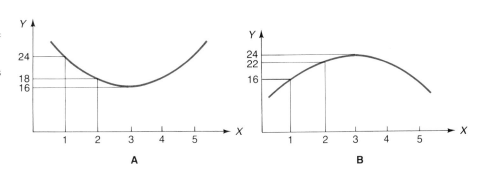

In equation 15-16, there are no terms such as β_1^2, $\beta_1\beta_2$, $\sqrt{\beta_0}$, and so on. So the model *is* linear in the β's, and this *is* a (multiple) linear regression application.

The model in equation 15-16 is a **curvilinear model** and is an example of **polynomial regression.** Such models are very useful when a particular independent variable and dependent variable exhibit a definite increasing or decreasing relationship that is nonlinear.

Solving for β_0, β_1 and β_2 Equation 15-16 represents a multiple regression model containing two predictors, namely, $X_1 = X$ and $X_2 = X^2$. The data for the model then are

Y	X_1	X_2
6.9	18.1	327.61 ($= 18.1^2$)
8.5	27.3	745.29 ($= 27.3^2$)
1.2	10.1	102.01
.	.	.
.	.	.
.	.	.
9.8	45.0	2025.0
9.2	31.5	992.25

These data will be your input to the multiple linear regression computer program. You can simplify this task by letting the computer build the $X_2 = X^2$ column of data by squaring the entries in the $X_1 = X$ column.

Example 15.8

Look at the MINITAB solution using the model $Y = \beta_0 + \beta_1X + \beta_2X^2 + e$ for the sales and advertising expenditure, shown in Figure 15.10.

1. Predict the sales for a month in which Mr. Bentley spends $3,000 on advertising.
2. What do the F and t tests tell you about this model? Use $\alpha = .10$.

Figure 15.10

MINITAB solution using $Y = \beta_0 + \beta_1X + \beta_2X^2$.

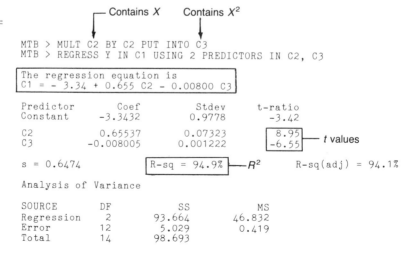

```
                      ┌ Contains X    Contains X²
                      │               │
                      ▼               ▼
MTB > MULT C2 BY C2 PUT INTO C3
MTB > REGRESS Y IN C1 USING 2 PREDICTORS IN C2, C3

┌──────────────────────────────────────────┐
│ The regression equation is                 │
│ C1 = - 3.34 + 0.655 C2 - 0.00800 C3        │
└──────────────────────────────────────────┘

Predictor       Coef         Stdev      t-ratio
Constant       -3.3432       0.9778      -3.42

C2              0.65537      0.07323     ┌ 8.95┐
C3             -0.008005     0.001222    └-6.55┘ ── t values

s = 0.6474              ┌R-sq = 94.9%┐──R²     R-sq(adj) = 94.1%

Analysis of Variance

SOURCE          DF           SS           MS
Regression      2          93.664       46.832
Error          12           5.029        0.419
Total          14          98.693
```

Solution 1 The predicted sales for $X_1 = 30$ (hundred) is

$$\hat{Y} = -3.34 + .655(30) - .008(30)^2$$
$$= 9.1$$

That is, it is $91,000.

Solution 2 We will first examine the F test. Our first test of hypothesis determines whether the overall model has predictive ability.

H_0: $\beta_1 = \beta_2 = 0$

H_a: at least one of the β's $\neq 0$

Using the R^2 value from Figure 15.10 and equation 15-14,

$$F = \frac{.949/2}{.051/(15 - 2 - 1)} = \frac{.949/2}{.051/12}$$
$$= 111.6$$

As we might have suspected, this model is quite satisfactory; $F^* = 111.6$ exceeds $F_{\alpha,k,n-k-1} = F_{.10,2,12} = 2.81$ from Table A-7.

Now we want to look at the t tests (same as partial F tests). Here, we examine each variable in the model, namely, X and X^2. The t value from Table A-5 is $t_{.10,12} = 1.356$ for a one-tailed test. We want to determine first whether $X_1 =$ advertising expenditure should be included in the model. Increased advertising should be associated with increased sales, so β_1 should be greater than zero. As a result, we will use a one-tailed procedure to test H_0: $\beta_1 \leq 0$ versus H_a: $\beta_1 > 0$.

According to Figure 15.10, the computed t statistic is $t^* = b_1/$(standard deviation of b_1) $= 8.95$. $t^* = 8.95 > 1.356$, which means that the advertising variable should be retained as a predictor of sales.

Next, we want to determine whether $X_2 =$ (advertising expenditures)^2 contributes significantly to the prediction of sales. We are asking whether including the *quadratic term* was necessary. If this model is the correct one, then, according to Figure 15.9b, β_2 should not only be unequal to zero, but also, more specifically, should be less than zero.

The appropriate hypotheses are

H_0: $\beta_2 = 0$ (or ≥ 0)

H_a: $\beta_2 < 0$.

We will reject H_0 if $t < -t_{.10,12} = -1.356$.

From Figure 15.10, we see that $t^* = b_2/$(standard deviation of b_2) $= -6.55$. This lies in the rejection region, so we conclude that β_2 is < 0, which means that the quadratic term, X^2, contributes significantly, and in the correct direction. ●

Comments

There are three things you should note about the curvilinear model.

1. Curvilinear models often are used for situations in which the rate of increase or decrease in the dependent variable (when plotted against a particular independent variable) is not constant. The use of X^2 (and in some cases, X^3) in your model allows you to capture this nonlinear relationship between your variables.

Figure 15.11

Error resulting from extrapolation. See text and Figure 15.9b.

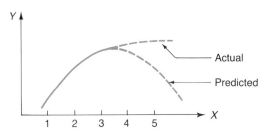

2. There are other methods available for modeling a nonlinear relationship, including

$$Y = \beta_0 + \beta_1(1/X) + error$$

and

$$Y = \beta_0 + \beta_1 e^{-X} + error$$

These models also are (simple, here) linear regressions; they are linear in the unknown parameters. These models, unlike the quadratic one discussed previously, involve a **transformation** to the independent variable, X. When replacing X by the transformed X (such as $1/X$ or e^{-X}) in the model, one has many other curvilinear models that may better fit a set of sample data displaying a nonlinear pattern.

3. Avoid using the model $Y = \beta_0 + \beta_1 X + \beta_2 X^2 + e$ for values of X outside the range of data used in the analysis. Extrapolation is extremely dangerous when using this modeling technique. Consider Figure 15.9b and suppose values of X between 1 and 3 were used to derive the estimate of β_0, β_1 and β_2. Figure 15.11 shows the results. For values of X larger than 3, the predicting equation will turn down, whereas the actual relationship (probably) will continue to level off. So this model works for interpolation (for values of X between 1 and 3, here) but is extremely unreliable for extrapolation.

Exercises

15.21 If all the values of the dependent variable Y fell on the plane $\hat{Y} = 2 + 5.2X_1 + 10X_2$ and the variables X_1 and X_2 were used in a least squares fit to the data, what would be the value of the coefficient of determination?

15.22 If the standard error of an estimate is 1.5 for a regression model with five independent variables and 26 observations, what is the value of R^2, assuming that SST is 231.95? Interpret the value of R^2.

15.23 A botanist would like to study the growth rate of a variety of grass that will withstand the dry heat of southern Arizona. Three variables are used:

$X_1 = $ gallons of water per week

$X_2 = $ temperature in Fahrenheit

$X_3 = $ kilograms of fertilizer per month

After observing 50 growth rates under different values of X_1, X_2, and X_3, the botanist wishes to test that X_2 and X_3 do not contribute to predicting the variation in the growth rates. The coefficient of determination for the model involving just Y and X_1 is .71. The coefficient of determination for the complete model with X_1, X_2, and X_3 is .82. Do the additional independent variables X_2 and X_3 contribute significantly to the model? Use a 5% significance level.

15.24 Refer to exercise 15.12. The least squares line to fit the data involving only Y and X_1 is found to be

$$\hat{Y} = 14812.135 + 1603.915X_1$$

a. Find the coefficient of determination for the least squares line

$$\hat{Y} = 1557.551 - 112.10X_1 + 244.152X_2$$

b. Find the coefficient of determination for the complete model involving X_1, X_2, and X_3.

c. Show that the F statistic for testing that X_1 does not contribute to predicting the variation in the dependent variable, given that X_2 and X_3 are in the model, is equal to the square of the t test used in question e of exercise 15.12.

15.25 The dean of the college of business at Fargo University would like to see whether several variables affect a student's grade point average. Thirty first-year students were randomly selected and data were collected on the following variables:

Y = grade point average for the first year

X_1 = average time spent per month at fraternity or sorority functions

X_2 = average time spent per month working part time

X_3 = total number of hours of coursework attempted

The SSE for the least squares line involving only Y and X_1 was found to be 5.21. The SSE for the complete model was found to be 4.31. The SST is 24.1. At the 5% significance level, test the null hypothesis that the independent variables X_2 and X_3 do not contribute to predicting the variation in Y given that X_1 is already in the model.

15.26 Refer to exercise 15.2. Does advertising expenditure contribute significantly to predicting the variation in the sales volume of software given that the number of units of personal computers sold is in the model? Use a 10% level of significance.

15.27 An independent research firm wants to investigate what motivates people to commit suicide. The variables used in this experiment are as follows:

Y = number of suicides

X_1 = number of psychiatric admissions per 1000 population

X_2 = number of persons below the poverty level (in millions)

X_3 = the number of unemployed persons (in millions)

X_4 = the number of divorces (in thousands)

X_5 = the number of crimes in the country (in millions)

Yearly data were collected for 15 years. The coefficient of determination for the model involving only the independent variables X_1 and X_3 is .53. The coefficient of determination for the model involving all five independent variables is .75. Do the variables X_2, X_4, and X_5 contribute to predicting the variation in the number of yearly suicides given that X_1 and X_3 are in the model?

15.28 An economist would like to examine the relationship between personal savings and the following independent variables:

X_1 = total personal income

X_2 = yield on U.S. Government securities

X_3 = consumer price index

The following data were collected for 14 randomly selected months:

Y	X_1	X_2	X_3
80.2	2077.2	12.036	233.2
91.6	2086.4	12.814	236.4
87.4	2101.0	15.526	239.8
104.9	2102.1	14.003	242.5
116.2	2114.1	9.150	244.9
109.1	2127.1	6.995	247.6
110.1	2161.2	8.126	247.8
107.4	2179.4	9.259	249.4
116.8	2205.7	10.321	252.7
102.1	2234.3	11.580	253.9
97.9	2257.6	13.888	256.2
93.3	2276.6	15.661	258.4
83.6	2300.7	14.724	260.5
91.0	2318.2	14.905	263.2

a. Using a computerized statistical package, determine the least squares equation for these data.

b. Use only the variables X_1 and X_2. What is the new prediction equation?

c. Does the variable X_3 contribute to predicting the variation in personal savings, given that X_1 and X_2 are in the model? Use a 10% significance level.

15.29 Refer to exercise 15.12. Test the null hypothesis that X_3 does not contribute to predicting salaries for legal secretaries, given that years of college education (X_1) and typing speed (X_2) are in the model. Assume that the SSE for the model with only X_1 and X_2 is 106, 309, 296. Use a 1% level of significance.

15.30 The amount of money that a family spends monthly on food is believed to be related to the number of family members (X_1), the joint income of the husband and wife (X_2), and the age of the oldest child (X_3). A regression procedure was run with 50 observations on the model with X_1, X_2, and X_3. The SSE was 121,580 and the SST was 486,321. Another computer run also included the variables $\sqrt{X_1}$ and $\sqrt{X_3}$. The SSE for this complete model was 77,811. Do the variables $\sqrt{X_1}$ and $\sqrt{X_3}$ contribute to predicting the amount that a family spends on food? Use a 5% level of significance.

15.4

The Problem of Multicollinearity

Another possible title for this section is "What do the individual b_i's tell you?" We will discuss one of the common problems in the use (or misuse) of multiple linear regression—namely, trying to extract more information from the results than they actually contain.

We will examine the validity of such statements as "Because $b_1 = 10$, increasing X_1 by one while *holding X_2 constant* will result in an increase of 10 in Y."

Assume that a sample of ten employees at Bellaire Industries was examined in an effort to determine the ability of age (X_1) and years of experience (X_2) to predict an employee's salary (Y). The following data were obtained:

Employee	Y (salary)	X_1 (age)	X_2 (years of experience)
1	52	52	33
2	35	47	21
3	45	38	14
4	28	25	3

(continued)

Employee	Y (salary)	X_1 (age)	X_2 (years of experience)
5	42	44	18
6	60	55	30
7	31	36	8
8	38	40	15
9	33	32	7
10	48	50	27

First, we can ask, how well does X_1 (age) predict Y (salary)?

A MINITAB solution using the model $Y = \beta_0 + \beta_1$ (age) $+ e$ is shown in Figure 15.12. Notice the computed t value. Now, $k = 1$ because this model considers only one independent variable, so the tabulated value for comparison (using $\alpha = .10$) is $t_{\alpha/2, n-k-1} = t_{.05, 10-1-1} = t_{.05, 8} = 1.860$. The value of $t^* = 4.60$ is considerably larger than 1.86, so X_1 (age) is an excellent predictor of Y (salary).

What is the *correlation* between X_1 and Y? It seems reasonable that this would be quite large because age has been shown to be a good predictor. In fact, according to Figure 15.12, this value is .852. So there is a *positive* relationship between age and salary, as one would expect.

Next, we determine how well X_2 (years of experience) predicts Y (salary). The solution using $Y = \beta_0 + \beta_1$ (years of experience) $+ e$ is shown in Figure 15.13. Once again, the computed t value $= t^* = 5.21$ is much larger than $t_{.05, 8} = 1.860$. Also, the correlation between these two variables is .879. This is not surprising; we might expect people with more years of experience to have higher salaries. Consequently, a significant positive relationship appears to exist between these two variables. Finally, we turn to the question, how well do both X_1 (age) and X_2 (years of experience) predict

Figure 15.12

MINITAB solution to Y (salary) $= b_0 + b_1$ (age).

```
MTB > READ INTO C1-C3
DATA> 52 52 33
DATA> 35 47 21
DATA> 45 38 14
DATA> 28 25 3
DATA> 42 44 18
DATA> 60 55 30
DATA> 31 36 8
DATA> 38 40 15
DATA> 33 32 7
DATA> 48 50 27
DATA> END
     10 ROWS READ
MTB > REGRESS Y IN C1 USING 1 PREDICTOR IN C2

The regression equation is
C1 = 2.97 + 0.912 C2

Predictor      Coef        Stdev      t-ratio
Constant       2.971       8.499        0.35

C2             0.9124      0.1983       4.60  ◄──── t value

s = 5.634       R-sq = 72.6%      R-sq(adj) = 69.1%

Analysis of Variance

SOURCE      DF          SS          MS
Regression   1       671.69      671.69
Error        8       253.91       31.74
Total        9       925.60
```

Instructions for obtaining the sample correlation between any two variables

```
MTB > CORRELATION BETWEEN C1 AND C2

Correlation of C1 and C2 = 0.852
```
                    Y X_1

Figure 15.13

MINITAB solution to Y (salary) = $b_0 + b_1$ (years of experience).

```
MTB > REGRESS Y IN C1 USING 1 PREDICTOR IN C3

The regression equation is
C1 = 25.8 + 0.878 C3

Predictor        Coef        Stdev       t-ratio
Constant       25.754        3.378          7.62

C3              0.8776       0.1684          5.21   ←— t value

s = 5.130      R-sq = 77.3%    R-sq(adj) = 74.4%

Analysis of Variance

SOURCE          DF            SS             MS
Regression       1         715.10         715.10
Error            8         210.50          26.31
Total            9         925.60

MTB > CORRELATION BETWEEN C1 AND C3

Correlation of C1 and C3 = 0.879
                            Y  X₂
```

salary? The model here is $Y = \beta_0 + \beta_1 X_1 + \beta_2 X_2 + e$. The least squares solution is shown in Figure 15.14.

$$\hat{Y} = 26.1 - .014X_1 + .890X_2$$

A few seemingly bizarre things show up here.

The coefficient of X_1 is $b_1 = -.014$. This would appear to indicate that larger values of X_1 (older people) produce smaller salaries. But we know from our first analysis that the *opposite* is true. We would have expected a *positive* value of b_1 here, and so the coefficient of X_1 appears to have the wrong sign.

Figure 15.14

MINITAB Solution to Y (salary) = $b_0 + b_1$ (age) + b_2 (years of experience).

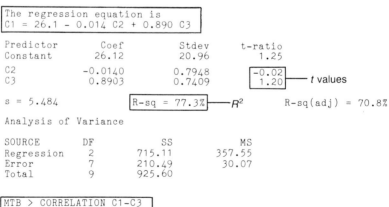

```
MTB > REGRESS Y IN C1 USING 2 PREDICTORS IN C2, C3

The regression equation is
C1 = 26.1 - 0.014 C2 + 0.890 C3

Predictor        Coef        Stdev       t-ratio
Constant        26.12       20.96          1.25
C2            -0.0140        0.7948        -0.02
C3             0.8903        0.7409         1.20   ←— t values

s = 5.484      R-sq = 77.3%  —R²    R-sq(adj) = 70.8%

Analysis of Variance

SOURCE          DF            SS             MS
Regression       2         715.11         357.55
Error            7         210.49          30.07
Total            9         925.60
```

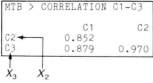

```
MTB > CORRELATION C1-C3

                 C1            C2
C2             0.852
C3             0.879         0.970
X₃             X₂
```

The small t values also are puzzling. The value of the F statistic (using Figure 15.14) is

$$F^* = \frac{R^2/2}{(1 - R^2)/(10 - 1 - 2)} = \frac{.773/2}{.227/7}$$

$$= 11.9$$

As before, you can compute this value using the ANOVA table, where

$$F^* = \frac{\text{MSR}}{\text{MSE}} = \frac{357.55}{30.07}$$

$$= 11.9$$

Using $\alpha = .10$, this is much larger than $F_{.10,2,7} = 3.26$, and so the model does provide a very good predictor of Y. The coefficient of determination is $R^2 = .77$; it explains 77% of the total variation in the ten salary values.

The t values are very small; both are smaller than $t_{\alpha/2, n-k-1} = t_{.05, 10-2-1} = t_{.05,7} = 1.895$. Does this imply that both predictors are weak and should be removed from the model? Certainly not, as our previous analyses made clear.

This is the problem of **multicollinearity.** In multiple regression models, it is desirable for each independent variable, X, to be highly correlated with Y, but it is not *desirable* for the X's to be highly correlated *with each other.* In business applications of multiple linear regression, the independent variables typically have a certain amount of pairwise correlation (usually positive). Extremely high correlation between any pair of variables can cause a variety of problems, as we will show.

The (sample) correlation between X_1 and X_2 is

$$r = \frac{\Sigma X_1 X_2 - (\Sigma X_1)(\Sigma X_2)/n}{\sqrt{\Sigma X_1^2 - (\Sigma X_1)^2/n} \; \sqrt{\Sigma X_2^2 - (\Sigma X_2)^2/n}}$$

This value, using Figure 15.14, is $r = .970$. Notice in the data set that nearly every time X_1 increases, so does X_2; X_1 and X_2 are highly correlated. As a result, this problem contains a great deal of multicollinearity.

Implications

First of all, the correlation of X_1 and X_2 explains the small t values. Remember that each t value describes the contribution of that particular independent variable *after* all other independent variables have been included in the model. X_1 is very nearly a linear combination of X_2 (due to $r = .970$), so it contributes very little to the prediction of Y, given that X_2 is in the model. The same argument applies to X_2. This means that neither X_1 nor X_2 is a strong predictor given that the other variable is included—not that each one is a weak predictor by itself.

The second implication of the multicollinearity is that the situation "increasing X_1 by one while holding X_2 constant" never occurred in the sample data. In the past, as X_1 increased by one, X_2 always changed also, because X_1 and X_2 are so highly correlated.

Finally, the sample coefficients of our independent variables (b_1 and b_2) have a very large variance. If we took another sample from this population, the values of b_1 and b_2 probably would change dramatically—which is not a good situation. In fact, as this example has demonstrated, these coefficients can even have *the wrong sign* (a sign different from that obtained when regressing X_1 or X_2 alone on Y).

Eliminating the Effects of Multicollinearity

The easiest way out of this dilemma is to remove some of the correlated predictors from the model. For this illustration, we should remove either X_1 or X_2 (but not both). Our best bet would be to retain $X_2 =$ years of experience because it has the highest correlation with Y.

One method of eliminating correlated predictor variables is to use a **stepwise** selection procedure. This technique of selecting the variables to be used in a multiple linear regression equation will be discussed in the next section. Essentially, it selects variables one at a time and generally (although not always) does not insert into the regression equation a variable that is highly correlated with a variable already in the equation. In the previous example, a stepwise procedure would have selected variable X_2 (the single best predictor of Y) and then informed the user that X_1 did *not* significantly improve the prediction of Y, given that X_2 is already included in the prediction equation.

Whenever you perform a multiple regression analysis, it is always a good idea to examine the pairwise correlations between all of your variables, including the dependent variable. In this way, you often can detect easily the two independent variables that are contributing to the multicollinearity problem. These correlations can be obtained using a single command with most computer packages. The MINITAB command to generate a table (often called a matrix) of pairwise correlations is shown in the bottom box in Figure 15.14. This output indicates that the correlation between Y and X_1 is .852, between Y and X_2 is .879, and between X_1 and X_2 is .970.

Other, more advanced methods of detecting and treating this situation are beyond the scope of this text. One of the more popular procedures is *ridge regression.**

We have seen that the problem of multicollinearity enters into our regression analysis when an independent variable is highly correlated with one or more other independent variables. Multicollinearity produces inflated regression coefficients that can even have the wrong sign. Also, the resulting t statistics can be small, making it difficult to determine the predictive ability of an individual variable. Therefore, b_1, b_2, . . . tell us nothing about the partial effect of each variable, unless we can demonstrate that there is no correlation among our predictor variables. In business applications, correlation (in particular, *positive* correlation) among the independent variables is far from unusual.

Exercises

15.31 What might cause the following situation to occur for a regression model with two independent variables? The t values for both β_1 and β_2 are nonsignificant. However, the F test for both $\beta_1 = \beta_2 = 0$ is highly significant.

15.32 If it is known that multicollinearity exists between three independent variables, how would you choose the independent variables that should remain in the model?

15.33 Refer to exercise 15.2. Find the correlation between the number of units of personal computers sold and the advertising expenditure. Is multicollinearity a concern?

15.34 A least squares equation was fit to a set of data for an experiment and was found to be $\hat{Y} = 30 - 501X_1 + 300X_2$. The experiment was repeated and a new set of data from the same

---

*For an excellent discussion of this topic, see J. Neter, W. Wasserman, and M. Kutner, *Applied Linear Regression Models* (Homewood, IL: Richard D. Irwin, 1983).

population was fit with the least squares line $\hat{Y} = -20 + 309X_1 - 151X_2$. Is there any explanation for these two different prediction equations?

15.35 The following set of data was collected:

Y	X_1	X_2
2.02	1.01	0.97
7.95	2.34	5.50
2.61	1.21	1.49
0.31	0.23	0.05
1.63	0.85	0.72
4.20	1.61	2.62
2.62	1.19	1.42
0.07	0.07	0.01
1.53	0.80	0.67
6.19	2.03	4.17

a. Find the correlation between X_1 and X_2.

b. Find the coefficient of determination for the model using only X_1. Then find it using only X_2.

c. The coefficient of determination for the complete model is 0.9996. Does it appear that both variables, X_1 and X_2, should stay in the model?

15.36 Consider the following set of data of 12 emerging growth-oriented companies. Y represents the growth rate of a company for the current year, X_1 represents the growth rate of the company for the previous year, and X_2 represents the percent of the market that does not use the company's product or a similar product. All values are percentages.

Y	X_1	X_2
20	10	30
24	12	35
18	15	25
33	30	40
27	19	32
20	24	20
30	15	60
36	42	38
47	45	40
35	32	32
28	24	31
32	20	50

a. Find the coefficient of determination for the model with only X_1 included in the model.

b. Find the coefficient of determination for the model with only X_2 in the model.

c. The coefficient of determination for the complete model is 0.896. Does it appear from observing the values of the coefficient of determination in questions a and b that both variables X_1 and X_2 should stay in the model?

15.37 The marketing department of a local industry used a regression equation to predict monthly sales based on total advertising expenditure and television advertising expenditure (both in thousands of dollars). The least squares equation used to predict monthly sales is $\hat{Y} = 103.2 - 0.20X_1 + 3.4X_2$, where X_1 = total advertising expenditure and X_2 = television advertising expenditure. Can you assume that, if television advertising expenditure stays constant and total advertising increases, monthly sales will decrease?

15.38 Refer to exercise 15.9. Find the correlation between students' overall grade point average and years of job-related experience. Does multicollinearity appear to be a concern?

15.5

Additional Topics in Multiple Linear Regression

The Use of Dummy Variables

The use of **dummy** or **indicator** variables in regression analysis allows you to include *qualitative* variables in the model. For example, if you wanted to include an employee's sex as a predictor variable in a regression model, define

$$X_1 = \begin{cases} 1 \text{ if female} \\ 0 \text{ if male} \end{cases}$$

Note that the choice of which sex is assigned the value of 1, male or female, is arbitrary. The estimated value of Y will be the same, regardless of which coding procedure is used.

Returning to the data we used in example 15.2, the real-estate developer noticed that all the houses in the population were from three neighborhoods, A, B, and C. Taking note of which neighborhood each of the sampled houses was from led to the following data (in the discussion following example 15.2, X_3 = years of education was shown to be a weak predictor, and so is removed from the model here):

Family	Y (home square footage)	X_1 (income)	X_2 (family size)	Neighborhood
1	16	22	2	B
2	17	26	2	C
3	26	45	3	A
4	24	37	4	C
5	22	28	4	B
6	21	50	3	C
7	32	56	6	B
8	18	34	3	B
9	30	60	5	A
10	20	40	3	A

Using these data, we can construct the necessary dummy variables and determine whether they contribute significantly to the prediction of home size (Y).

One way to code neighborhoods would be to define

$$X_3 = \begin{cases} 0 \text{ if neighborhood } A \\ 1 \text{ if neighborhood } B \\ 2 \text{ if neighborhood } C \end{cases}$$

However, this type of coding has many problems. First, because $0 < 1 < 2$, the codes imply that neighborhood A is smaller than neighborhood B, which is smaller than neighborhood C. Furthermore, any difference between neighborhoods A and C receives twice the weight (because $2 - 0 = 2$) of any difference between neighborhoods A and B, or B and C. So this coding transforms data that are actually *nominal* to data that are *interval* (a much stronger type). A better procedure is to use the necessary number of dummy variables (coded 0 or 1) to represent the neighborhoods.

We needed one dummy variable with two categories (male and female) to specify a person's sex. To represent the three neighborhoods, we use two dummy variables, by letting

$$X_3 = \begin{cases} 1 \text{ if house is in } A \\ 0 \text{ otherwise} \end{cases}$$

and

$$X_4 = \begin{cases} 1 \text{ if house is in } B \\ 0 \text{ otherwise} \end{cases}$$

Note that, as with the male/female dummy variable, this coding is arbitrary as far as the prediction, $\hat{Y}$, is concerned. We could have assigned $X_3 = 0$ and $X_4 = 0$ to neighborhood A, with $X_3 = 1$ for B and $X_4 = 1$ for C.

What happened to neighborhood C? It is not necessary to develop a third dummy variable here because we have the following scheme:

House Is in Neighborhood	X_3	X_4
A	1	0
B	0	1
C	0	0

In fact, it can be shown that a third dummy variable is not only unnecessary, it is very important that you not include it. If you attempted to use three such dummy variables in your model, you would receive a message in your computer output informing you that "no solution exists" for this model. Suppose we had introduced a third dummy variable (say, X_5) that was equal to 1 if the house was in neighborhood C. For each observation in the sample we would have

$$X_5 = 1 - X_3 - X_4$$

Whenever any one predictor variable is a linear combination (including a constant term) of one or more other predictors, then mathematically *no solution exists* for the least squares coefficients. To arrive at a usable equation, any such predictor variable must not be included.

The final array of data (ready for input into a computer program) is

Row	Y	X_1	X_2	X_3	X_4
1	16	22	2	0	1
2	17	26	2	0	0
3	26	45	3	1	0
4	24	37	4	0	0
5	22	28	4	0	1
6	21	50	3	0	0
7	32	56	6	0	1
8	18	34	3	0	1
9	30	60	5	1	0
10	20	40	3	1	0

where $Y =$ square footage of home, $X_1 =$ income, $X_2 =$ family size, $X_3 = 1$ if neighborhood A, and $X_4 = 1$ if neighborhood B.

A MINITAB solution is shown in Figure 15.15. To determine whether the particular neighborhood has any effect on the prediction of home size, we test

H_0: $\beta_3 = \beta_4 = 0$ (if X_1 and X_2 are included)

H_a: at least one $\beta \neq 0$

In the complete model, the variables are X_1, X_2, X_3, and X_4, and, from Figure 15.15a,

$$R_c^2 = .921$$

Figure 15.15

MINITAB solution to real-estate dummy variable problem. **A** Solution using variables X_1, X_2, X_3, and X_4. **B** Solution using variables X_1, X_2.

```
MTB > READ INTO C1-C5
DATA> 16 22 2 0 1
DATA> 17 26 2 0 0
DATA> 26 45 3 1 0
DATA> 24 37 4 0 0
DATA> 22 28 4 0 1
DATA> 21 50 3 0 0
DATA> 32 56 6 0 1
DATA> 18 34 3 0 1
DATA> 30 60 5 1 0
DATA> 20 40 3 1 0
DATA> END
        10 ROWS READ
MTB > REGRESS Y IN C1 USING 4 PREDICTORS IN C2-C5

The regression equation is
C1 = 7.77 + 0.082 C2 + 3.27 C3 + 1.61 C4 - 0.90 C5

Predictor       Coef        Stdev      t-ratio
Constant        7.772       2.557        3.04
C2              0.0819      0.1059       0.77
C3              3.2696      0.9870       3.31
C4              1.613       1.801        0.90
C5             -0.900       1.841       -0.49

s = 2.036     R-sq = 92.1%      R-sq(adj) = 85.8%
A                            R_c^2
```

```
MTB > REGRESS Y IN C1 USING 2 PREDICTORS IN C2, C3

The regression equation is
C1 = 6.74 + 0.165 C2 + 2.66 C3

Predictor       Coef        Stdev      t-ratio
Constant        6.740       2.164        3.11
C2              0.16485     0.07306      2.26
C3              2.6569      0.7405       3.59

s = 1.953     R-sq = 89.8%      R-sq(adj) = 86.9%
B                            R_r^2
```

In the reduced model, the variables are X_1 and X_2 only, and, from Figure 15.15b,

$$R_r^2 = .898$$

At first glance, it does not appear that X_3 and X_4 produced a significant increase in R^2. The partial F test will determine whether this is true.

$$F = \frac{(R_c^2 - R_r^2)/(\text{number of } \beta\text{'s in } H_0)}{(1 - R_c^2)/[n - 1 - (\text{number of } X\text{'s in the complete model})]}$$

$$= \frac{(.921 - .898)/2}{(1 - .921)/(10 - 1 - 4)}$$

$$= \frac{.023/2}{.079/5} = .73$$

Using $\alpha = .10$, this is considerably less than $F_{.10,2,5} = 3.78$, so there is no evidence that the neighborhood dummy variables significantly improve the prediction of home size.

In this example, the dummy variables were not significant predictors in the model. However, do not let this mislead you. In many business applications, dummy variables representing location, weather conditions, yes/no situations, time, and many other variables can have a tremendous effect on improving the results of a multiple regression model.

Stepwise Procedures

Assume you wish to predict annual divisional profits for a large corporation using, among other techniques, a multiple linear regression model. Your strategy is to consider any variable that you think *could* have an effect on these profits. You have identified twelve such variables.

One possibility is to include all of these in your model and to use the t tests to decide which variables are significant predictors. However, this procedure invites multicollinearity (including correlated predictors) and can severely hinder the interpretation of your model. In particular, two independent variables that are very highly correlated will both have small t values (as we saw in the employee example), causing you possibly to discard both of them from the model. This is *not* the right thing to do because possibly you should have retained one of them.

A better way to proceed here is to use one of the several stepwise selection procedures. These techniques either choose or eliminate variables, one at a time, in an effort not to include those variables that either have no predictive ability or are highly correlated with other predictor variables. A word of caution—these procedures do not provide a guarantee against multicollinearity; however, they greatly reduce the chances of including a large set of correlated independent variables.

These procedures consist of three different selection techniques: (1) forward regression, (2) backward regression, and (3) stepwise regression.

Forward Regression The forward regression method of model selection puts variables into the equation, one at a time, beginning with that variable having the highest correlation (or R^2) with Y. Call this variable (for sake of argument) X_1.

Next, it examines the remaining variables for the variable that, when included with X_1, has the highest R^2. That predictor (with X_1) is inserted into the model. This procedure continues until adding the "best" variable at that stage results in an insignificant increase in R^2 (according to the partial F test).

Backward Regression Backward regression is the opposite of forward regression: It begins with *all* variables in the model and, one by one, removes them. It begins by finding the "worst" variable—the one that, when removed from the complete model, causes the smallest decrease in R^2. If the decrease is insignificant, this variable is removed, and the process continues.

The variable, among those remaining in the model, that causes the smallest decrease in the new R^2 is considered next. You continue this procedure of removing variables until a significant drop in R^2 is obtained, at which point you replace this significant predictor and terminate the selection.

Will the model resulting from a backward regression be the same as that obtained using forward regression? Not necessarily; usually, however, the resulting models are very similar. Of course, if two variables are highly correlated, the forward procedure could choose one of the correlated predictors, whereas the backward procedure could choose the other.

Figure 15.16

Stepwise regression on
divisional profits data.

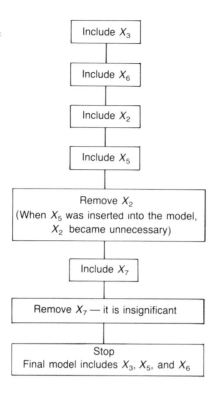

Stepwise Regression   Stepwise regression is a modification of forward regression. It is the most popular (and flexible) of the three selection techniques. It proceeds exactly as does forward regression, except that, at each stage it can *remove* any variable whose partial F value indicates that this variable does not contribute, given the present set of independent variables in the model. As with forward regression, it stops when the "best" variable among those remaining produces an insignificant increase in R^2.

Figure 15.16 illustrates this procedure using the data from our earlier example concerned with predicting divisional profits. Data from *all* twelve independent variables, as well as from Y, are used as input to a stepwise regression program. One possible outcome from this analysis is shown by Figure 15.16.

The stepwise solution for the data we used to predict home size is contained in the end-of-chapter MINITAB appendix. As we previously determined, X_3 = educational level does not contribute significantly, and so the resulting prediction equation includes only X_1 = income and X_2 = family size. This equation is

$$\hat{Y} = 6.74 + .165X_1 + 2.66X_2$$

Using Dummy Variables in Forward or Stepwise Regression   We emphasized that $C - 1$ dummy variables should be used to represent C categories if *all* of the dummy variables were to be inserted into the regression equation. When using a forward (or stepwise) regression procedure, this may not be the best way to proceed, as the following illustration will point out.

Suppose you are using nine dummy (indicator) variables to represent ten cities. The dependent variable (Y) is monthly sales, and the purpose is to determine which city (or cities) exhibits very large or very small sales. If a forward (or stepwise) selection procedure is used, then including one of these dummy variables would indicate that specifying this particular city significantly improves the prediction of sales.

In other words, this is an indication that sales for this city are not just average but are much higher (its coefficient will be positive) or lower (its coefficient will be negative).

When you use the forward or stepwise techniques, you probably will not include all nine dummy variables in the model. Your ability to predict sales (Y) is unaffected by not defining a tenth dummy variable, and in fact, as pointed out earlier, the regression analysis will not accept all ten dummy variables.

For this situation, however, there is the danger of not detecting extremely high or low sales in the tenth city that did not receive a dummy variable. When including these variables one at a time in the regression equation using a forward or stepwise procedure, we *can* allow the regression model to examine the effect of all ten cities. We do this defining ten such dummy variables, one for each city.*

Because a forward regression procedure generally will not attempt to include all ten dummy variables, you are able to investigate the existence of high or low sales in each of the ten cities. When using dummy variables in a forward (or stepwise) regression procedure, it is perfectly acceptable to use C such variables to represent C categories.

Checking the Assumptions: Examination of the Residuals

When you use a multiple linear regression model, you should keep two things in mind. First, no assumptions are necessary to derive the least squares estimates of β_1, β_2, β_3, ... The regression coefficients b_1, b_2, b_3, . . . determined by a computer solution are the "best" estimates, in the least squares sense.

Second, several key assumptions *are* required to construct CIs and perform any test of hypothesis. If these assumptions are violated, you may still have an accurate prediction, $\hat{Y}$, but the validity of these inference procedures will be very questionable.

Your final step in any regression analysis should be to verify your assumptions.

Assumption 1 The errors are normally distributed, with a mean of zero.

An easy method to determine whether the errors follow a normal distribution, centered at zero, is to let the computer construct a histogram of the sample residuals (e). This plot should reveal whether the distribution of residuals is severely skewed.

Consider the 50 residuals resulting from the analysis in example 15.4. The computer solution for this problem is shown in Figure 15.6. Notice that the RESIDUALS subcommand following the REGRESS command can be used to store the residuals in any column (such as column C5 in Figure 15.6).

A MINITAB histogram of these values is shown in Figure 15.17. The distribution of these residuals appears to be centered at zero and, except for a slight rise in the second class, is bell-shaped (normally distributed) in appearance. Remember that an *exact* normal distribution is not necessary here; problems arise only when the distribution is severely skewed and does not resemble a normal distribution.

More sophisticated methods of checking this assumption involve the use of a *probability plot* or a *chi-square goodness-of-fit test*. We will not discuss the probability plot technique here, except to say that you plot the residuals in a specialized type of graph. If the resulting graph is basically linear in appearance, the normality assumption has been verified. The goodness-of-fit test was discussed in Chapter 13, where we used a chi-square statistic to test the hypothesis that a particular set of data (in this case,

---

*This problem is discussed in D. Dorsett and J. T. Webster, Guidelines for Variable Selection Problems When Dummy Variables Are Used, *The American Statistician*, 37(4):337, 1983.

Figure 15.17

Histogram of residuals for real-estate data (see Figure 15.6).

```
MTB > HISTOGRAM OF C5

Histogram of C5    N = 50

Midpoint     Count
    -2.0         1    *
    -1.5         6    ******
    -1.0         3    ***
    -0.5        10    **********
     0.0        12    ************
     0.5         7    *******
     1.0         5    *****
     1.5         3    ***
     2.0         2    **
     2.5         1    *
```

the regression residuals) came from a specific distribution. The end-of-chapter exercises in Chapter 13 discuss how to use the chi-square test for a suspected *normal* population.

If you have reason to believe that this assumption of your model has been violated, then your model is inadequate. You need to search for additional predictor variables that may have been overlooked. As your model tends to "improve," you should observe the residuals tending toward a normal distribution.

Assumption 2 The variance of the errors remains constant. For example, you should not observe larger errors associated with larger values of $\hat{Y}$.

When the residuals ($\hat{e} = Y - \hat{Y}$) are plotted against the predicted values ($\hat{Y}$), one hopes to observe *no pattern* (a "shotgun blast" appearance) in this graph, as in Figure 15.18a. Remember—the assumptions are essentially that the errors consist of what engineers call *noise,* with no observable pattern.

A common violation of the assumption of equal variance occurs when the value of the residual increases as $\hat{Y}$, or an individual predictor, increases. This is illustrated in Figure 15.18b. In this Figure, the variance of the residual is increasing with $\hat{Y}$. This has a serious effect on the validity of the hypothesis tests developed in this chapter, which determine the strength of the regression model and the individual predictors.

When you encounter a violation of this type, you need to resort to more advanced modeling techniques, including *weighted least squares* or *transformations* of your dependent variable.*

Figure 15.18

Examination of the residuals. **A** The shotgun effect (no violation of assumptions 1 and 2). **B** A violation of the equal variance assumption (assumption 2).

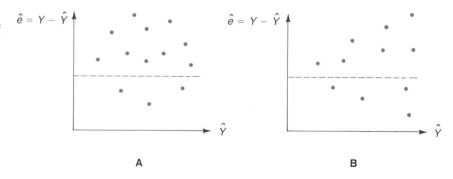

*See J. Neter, W. Wasserman, and M. Kutner, *Applied Linear Regression Models* (Homewood, IL: Richard D. Irwin, 1983).

Assumption 3 The errors are independent.

To examine these assumptions after the regression equation has been determined involves using the residual from each of the sample observations. For given values of $X_1, X_2, \ldots, X_k$, the actual error is

$$e = Y - (\beta_0 + \beta_1 X_1 + \beta_2 X_2 + \ldots + \beta_k X_k)$$

The β's are unknown, so we estimate the error by using the residual for this particular observation,

$$\hat{e} = Y - \hat{Y} = Y - (b_0 + b_1 X_1 + b_2 X_2 + \ldots + b_k X_k)$$

The residuals for the real-estate data are shown in the third column of the table, labeled $Y - \hat{Y}$, on page 499. In general, a close examination of these values will reveal any departures from the regression assumptions.

When your regression data consist of *time series* data, your errors often are not independent. This type of data has the appearance

Time	Y	X_1	X_2	$\ldots$	X_k
1970	x	x	x		x
1971	x	x	x		x
1972	x	x	x		x
.	.	.	.		.
.	.	.	.		.
.	.	.	.		.

Also remember that the error component *includes the effect of missing variables* in your model. In many business applications, there is a positive relationship between time-related predictor variables, such as prices and wages, because they both increase over time. This can produce a set of residuals in your regression analysis that are not independent of one another but, instead, display a pattern similar to that illustrated in Figure 15.19. This plot contains the sample residuals on the vertical axis and time on the horizontal axis. If this assumption were *not* violated here, we should observe the shotgun appearance. Instead we notice that adjacent errors have roughly the same value, and so are correlated with each other. This is **autocorrelation.** To be more specific, the pattern in Figure 15.19 is one of *positive* autocorrelation. Negative autocorrelation exists when most of the neighboring $\hat{e}$'s are very unequal in size.

The amount of autocorrelation that exists in your residuals is measured by the **Durbin–Watson statistic.** It ranges from zero to four, with a value near zero

Figure 15.19

Autocorrelated errors.

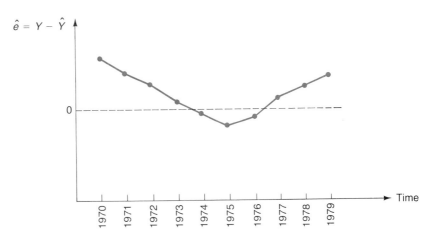

indicating strong *positive* autocorrelation and a value close to four meaning that there is a significant *negative* autocorrelation. A value near two indicates that there is no (or very little) autocorrelation—the ideal situation. Chapter 17 will discuss the calculation of this statistic and its use in detecting autocorrelated residuals.

The problem of autocorrelated errors is the most difficult of the three assumptions to correct. The error term is not noise, as we originally assumed, but instead has a definite pattern (as in Figure 15.19). Several ways of treating this problem will be discussed in Chapter 17.

Prediction Using Multiple Regression

Once a regression equation has been derived, its primary application generally is to derive predicted values of the dependent variable. Computer packages provide an easy method of deriving such an estimate. To illustrate, consider the regression equation we developed for the real-estate data.

$$\hat{Y} = 7.60 + .194X_1 + 2.34X_2 - .163X_3$$

Consider a situation in which

$X_1 = $ income $= 36$ (thousands of dollars)

$X_2 = $ family size $= 4$

$X_3 = $ years of formal education $= 8$ (years)

The predicted home size (Y) here is

$$\hat{Y} = 7.60 + .194(36) + 2.34(4) - .163(8)$$
$$= 22.64 \ (2264 \text{ square feet})$$

We can derive this estimate using MINITAB, SAS, or SPSSX. When using the latter two packages, we can derive a predicted value by adding one additional row to our input data containing these specific values of the predictor variables and a *missing value* for the dependent variable value. The computer routine will ignore this row when deriving the regression equation (and all subsequent tests of hypotheses) but will attach this row when listing the predicted values. The procedure when using MINITAB is slightly different, as described below.

Using MINITAB The MINITAB solution for the preceding illustration is shown in Figure 15.20. By using the subcommand PREDICT following the REGRESS command, you can easily derive a predicted value for the input values of the independent variables. The output will contain the predicted (fitted) Y value, the standard deviation of the predicted Y, a 95% confidence interval, and a 95% prediction interval. The resulting predicted value for $X_1 = 36$, $X_2 = 4$ and $X_3 = 8$ is $\hat{Y} = 22.625$, which is more accurate than the previously derived value of 22.64.

Using SPSSX A solution for this illustration using SPSSX is presented at the end of the chapter. A numeric value (such as -9) is used for the missing Y value, and then SPSSX is informed that such a value represents a missing value using the MISSING VALUES command. This command instructs SPSSX that a value of -9 appearing as a value for SQFOOT (the Y variable) should be interpreted as a missing value. The resulting predicted value of $\hat{Y} = 22.625$ appears at the end of the list of predicted values.

Figure 15.20

Prediction for new
data using MINITAB.
For the input data,
see Figure 15.2.

```
MTB > BRIEF 3
MTB > REGRESS Y IN C1 USING 3 PREDICTORS IN C2-C4;
SUBC> PREDICT FOR 36 4 8.

The regression equation is
C1 = 7.60 + 0.194 C2 + 2.34 C3 - 0.163 C4

Predictor        Coef       Stdev      t-ratio
Constant        7.596       2.595        2.93
C2            0.19388     0.08770        2.21
C3             2.3381      0.9078        2.58
C4            -0.1628      0.2441       -0.67

s = 2.035      R-sq = 90.5%     R-sq(adj) = 85.8%

Analysis of Variance

SOURCE        DF          SS           MS
Regression     3      237.542       79.181
Error          6       24.858        4.143
Total          9      262.400
```

```
Obs.      C2          C1      Fit  Stdev.Fit   Residual   St.Resid
  1     22.0      16.000   15.886      1.193      0.114       0.07
  2     26.0      17.000   16.010      1.161      0.990       0.59
  3     45.0      26.000   22.195      0.975      3.805       2.13R
  4     37.0      24.000   24.121      1.300     -0.121      -0.08
  5     28.0      22.000   22.051      1.371     -0.051      -0.03
  6     50.0      21.000   22.676      1.331     -1.676      -1.09
  7     56.0      32.000   31.179      1.854      0.821       0.98
  8     34.0      18.000   19.900      0.949     -1.900      -1.05
  9     60.0      30.000   30.593      1.608     -0.593      -0.48
 10     40.0      20.000   21.388      0.767     -1.388      -0.74

R denotes an obs. with a large st. resid.

   Fit   Stdev.Fit          95% C.I.              95% P.I.
22.625      1.355    ( 19.308, 25.943)    ( 16.640, 28.611)
```

$\hat{Y}$ using $X_1 = 36$, $X_2 = 4$, $X_3 = 8$

Using SAS Similar to SPSSX, SAS predicts values by including an additional row containing a missing value for the dependent variable. Any single *letter* (A to Z) can be used to represent the missing value; SAS is informed that such a character represents a missing value by using the MISSING statement after the DATA statement. This row is then automatically ignored during subsequent calculations, but, once again, the predicted value of $\hat{Y} = 22.625$ is generated for this set of X values at the end of the list of predicted values.

Confidence and Prediction Intervals In the preceding illustration, what does $\hat{Y} = 22.625$ estimate? For ease of notation, let X_0 represent the set of X values used for this estimate; that is, $X_0 = (36,4,8)$, where $X_1 = 36$, $X_2 = 4$, and $X_3 = 8$. This value of $\hat{Y}$ estimates (1) the *average* home size of all families with this specific set of X values, written $\mu_{Y|X_0}$ and (2) the home size for an *individual* family having this specific set of X values, written Y_{X_0}.

Using the notation from Chapter 14, let

$s_{\hat{Y}} =$ the standard deviation of the predicted Y value

These values can be computed and included in the output by each of the computer packages. To determine the reliability of this particular point estimate, $\hat{Y}$, you can (1) derive a *confidence interval* for $\mu_{Y|X_0}$ if your intent is to estimate the *average* value of Y given X_0 (not the usual situation) or (2) derive a *prediction interval* for Y_{X_0} if the purpose is to forecast an *individual* value of Y given this specific set of values for the predictor variables. In business applications, deriving a specific forecast is, by far, the more popular use of linear regression.

These intervals are summarized as follows. A $(1 - \alpha) \cdot 100\%$ CI for $\mu_{Y|X_0}$ is

$$\hat{Y} - t_{\alpha/2, n-k-1} \, s_{\hat{Y}} \quad \text{to} \quad \hat{Y} + t_{\alpha/2, n-k-1} \, s_{\hat{Y}} \tag{15-17}$$

A $(1 - \alpha) \cdot 100\%$ prediction interval for Y_{X_0} is

$$\hat{Y} - t_{\alpha/2, n-k-1} \sqrt{s^2 + s_{\hat{Y}}^2} \quad \text{to} \quad \hat{Y} + t_{\alpha/2, n-k-1} \sqrt{s^2 + s_{\hat{Y}}^2} \tag{15-18}$$

where $s^2 = $ MSE.

Using MINITAB [$X_0 = (36,4,8)$] Prediction and confidence intervals are easy to derive using MINITAB by using the PREDICT subcommand as illustrated in Figure 15.20. The resulting CI for the average home size, given X_0, is $(19.308, 25.943)$. As usual, the 95% prediction interval for an individual family with this set of X values, namely $(16.640, 28.611)$, is wider than the corresponding CI.

Using SPSSX [$X_0 = (36,4,8)$] These intervals are not directly available on this package but can be obtained easily using equations 15-17 and 15-18 and the regression output. SPSSX provides the estimated value, $\hat{Y}$, and the standard deviation of the predicted value, $s_{\hat{Y}}$. Referring to the discussion at the end of the chapter, these values are $\hat{Y} = 22.625$ and $s_{\hat{Y}} = 1.355$.

Using equation 15-17, a 95% CI for $\mu_{Y|X_0}$ is derived by first using Table A-5 to obtain $t_{\alpha/2, n-k-1} = t_{.025, 10-3-1} = t_{.025, 6} = 2.447$. The resulting CI is

$$22.625 - (2.447)(1.355) \quad \text{to} \quad 22.625 + (2.447)(1.355)$$
$$= 22.625 - 3.316 \quad \text{to} \quad 22.625 + 3.316$$
$$= 19.309 \quad \text{to} \quad 25.941$$

Consequently, we have estimated the average home size for families with $X_1 = 36$, $X_2 = 4$, and $X_3 = 8$ to within 331.6 square feet of the actual mean with 95% confidence. This CI is slightly different from that obtained with MINITAB due to rounding error.

The prediction interval from equation 15-18 is derived by using MSE $= 4.143$ from the computer solution to obtain

$$22.625 - 2.447\sqrt{4.143 + (1.355)^2}$$
$$\text{to} \quad 22.625 + 2.447\sqrt{4.143 + (1.355)^2}$$
$$= 22.625 - 5.983 \quad \text{to} \quad 22.625 + 5.983$$
$$= 16.642 \quad \text{to} \quad 28.608$$

This means that we have predicted the home size of an individual family with $X_1 = 36$, $X_2 = 4$, and $X_3 = 8$ to within 598.3 square feet of the actual value with 95% confidence. Once again, this result differs slightly from that obtained with MINITAB due to rounding error.

Using SAS [$X_0 = (36, 4, 8)$] SAS provides an easy method of determining these intervals by including CLI (for an individual Y_{X_0}) or CLM (for a mean $\mu_{Y|X_0}$) or both in the final SAS statement. According to the output at the end of the chapter, the 95% CI for the average home size, given X_0, is $(19.309, 25.942)$, with a corresponding prediction interval of $(16.641, 28.609)$.

Exercises

15.39 A real-estate agency was interested in the amount of rent paid (monthly) for commercial buildings near downtown Houston. The broker of the real-estate agency used the following independent variables:

X_1 = age of building

$X_2 = \begin{cases} 1 \text{ if low-rise building} \\ 0 \text{ if not} \end{cases}$

$X_3 = \begin{cases} 1 \text{ if mid-rise building} \\ 0 \text{ if not} \end{cases}$

X_4 = square footage of building

The data from 20 commercial buildings yielded the least squares equation $\hat{Y} = 130 - 50X_1 + 70X_2 - 20X_3 + 0.31X_4$.

a. What is the predicted rent for a 5-year-old high-rise commercial building that has 25,000 square feet of space?

b. Test the hypothesis that the dummy variables significantly improve the prediction of monthly rent for commercial buildings. Assume that R^2 for the model including only X_1 and X_4 is .65 and that R^2 for the complete model including X_1, X_2, X_3, and X_4 is .85.

15.40 The executive committee of Mini-Mart convenience-food-store chain would like to examine the yearly profit from its large number of stores. The following independent variables were used in analyzing the profits (Y) of each store:

X_1 = average yearly household income of nearby area

$X_2 = \begin{cases} 1 \text{ if there is a supermarket within 1 mile} \\ 0 \text{ otherwise} \end{cases}$

$X_3 = \begin{cases} 1 \text{ if weekly auto traffic volume is high} \\ 0 \text{ otherwise} \end{cases}$

The following least squares equation was obtained from observing 18 randomly selected stores:

$\hat{Y} = 7508 + 1.5X_1 - 6235X_2 + 5987X_3$

a. Interpret the coefficients of this equation.

b. Given that the standard deviations of the estimate of the coefficients of X_2 and X_3 are 2521 and 1873, respectively, test the hypothesis that the variable X_2 contributes to the prediction of Y, given that X_1 and X_3 are in the model. Also test that X_3 contributes to the prediction of Y given that X_1 and X_2 are in the model. Use a .01 significance level.

15.41 Nebraska Associated Insurance handles workers'-compensation insurance for three large manufacturing firms. The insurance company believes that the following independent variables are important in determining the total amount of compensation paid for each claim from the three manufacturers:

Age
Sex
Marital status
Length of employment
Type of injury (to a limb, to the head, or to other parts of the body)
Manufacturer employing the worker

Set up an appropriate regression model to predict total amount of compensation paid based on the independent variables. Define your variables.

15.42 Data are collected for the variables, Y, X_1, and X_2. A computer printout of the correlation table is:

	Y	X_1	X_2
Y	1	.49	.30
X_1	.49	1	.12
X_2	.30	.12	1

a. Which independent variable, X_1 or X_2, would be selected first in a forward regression procedure?

b. Which independent variable, X_1 or X_2, would be a better predictor of Y? Why?

15.43 The following is a correlation matrix for three independent variables and one dependent variable:

	Y	X_1	X_2	X_3
Y	1	.25	.36	.59
X_1	.25	1	.54	.22
X_2	.36	.54	1	.31
X_3	.59	.22	.31	1

a. Which independent variable would be chosen for the first stage of a forward-regression procedure?

b. Which independent variable would be chosen for the first step of a stepwise-regression procedure?

15.44 The least squares regression equation

$$\hat{Y} = 1.5 + 3.5X_1 + 7.5X_2 - 150X_3$$

has the following t values for the independent variables:

Null hypothesis	t statistic
$\beta_1 = 0$	4.5
$\beta_2 = 0$	1.89
$\beta_3 = 0$	1.52

Twenty observations were used in calculating the least squares equation. In the first stage of a backward-selection procedure, which independent variable would be eliminated first? Use a 5% level of significance.

15.45 Describe the main difference between the forward-selection procedure and the stepwise-selection procedure in regression analysis.

15.46 If a statistician would like to include dummy variables to indicate one of three cities and also one of four salespeople in a regression model, how many dummy variables would be needed in the model?

15.47 Which of the standard assumptions of regression appear to have been violated from the following table, which lists the dependent variable and the residual values?

$\hat{Y}$	$Y - \hat{Y}$
1.5	0.12
2.1	$-.70$
3.5	$-.91$
4.0	1.02
4.5	-1.18
5.0	-1.45
5.5	1.61
6.0	1.79
7.0	-2.40
7.5	2.10

15.48 How should a plot of the residuals $(Y - \hat{Y})$ plotted against the predicted values $\hat{Y}$ look if the standard assumptions of regression are satisfied?

15.49 A set of 20 observations is used to obtain the least squares line

$$\hat{Y} = 1.5 + 3.6X_1 + 4.9X_2$$

a. Given that the estimated standard deviation of Y at $X_1 = 1.0$ and $X_2 = 2.0$ is 3.4, find a 90% CI for the mean value of Y at $X_1 = 1.0$ and $X_2 = 2.0$.

b. Given that the MSE from this analysis is 21.5, then, using the information in question a, find a 90% prediction interval for an individual value of Y at $X_1 = 1.0$ and $X_2 = 2.0$.

15.50 Fifteen months are randomly selected to estimate the monthly sales, Y (in thousands of dollars), of a retail store based on monthly advertising expenditure, X (in thousands of dollars). The prediction equation is found to be

$$\hat{Y} = .2 + 1.5X + .4X^2$$

a. Find a 95% CI for the mean monthly sales with a monthly advertising expenditure of $1.4 thousand if the estimated standard deviation of the monthly sales for $X = 1.4$ is .8.

b. Using the information in question a, find a 95% prediction interval for the monthly sales of a month that has an advertising expenditure of $1.4 thousand if the MSE from the analysis is 1.55.

15.51 Explain the difference between a CI for the mean value of Y at particular values of the independent variables and a prediction interval for a future value of Y at particular values of the independent variables. Will the prediction interval for Y always be larger than the corresponding CI for particular values of the independent variables?

15.52 A real-estate firm would like to determine the monthly income (Y) of homeowners in a certain section of town by using the monthly mortgage payment (X_1), the market value of the homeowner's car(s) (X_2), and the age of the homeowner (X_3). The following data are collected from 15 randomly selected households (Y, X_1, and X_2 are in dollars; X_3 in years):

Y	X_1	X_2	X_3	Y	X_1	X_2	X_3	Y	X_1	X_2	X_3
2963	820	7,800	32	2225	725	4,380	30	3180	635	9,450	36
2100	710	5,100	33	1630	538	3,760	27	3350	758	12,600	31
2820	520	10,500	26	3070	679	7,350	37	3267	810	10,630	29
3350	630	9,500	30	2950	975	6,580	34	2120	710	5,340	28
2640	925	6,260	35	3460	1120	7,900	33	2280	504	4,690	32

Use a computerized statistical package to answer the following questions:

a. What is the mean income for a homeowner with $X_1 = 800$, $X_2 = 7000$, and $X_3 = 30$?

b. Find a 95% CI for the mean monthly income of a homeowner with $X_1 = 800$, $X_2 = 7000$, and $X_3 = 30$.

c. Find a 95% prediction interval for the income of a homeowner with $X_1 = 800$, $X_2 = 7000$, and $X_3 = 30$.

15.53 The operations manager in charge of a production process is interested in the amount of time in minutes, Y, that it takes an assembly-line worker to perform a certain task relative to his or her score, X, on an aptitude test. The proposed model is

$$Y = \beta_0 + \beta_1 X + \beta_2 X^2 + e$$

Twelve assembly line workers were randomly selected with the following results:

Y	X
49	58
37	67
12	95
60	43
33	72
22	83
19	85
17	89
50	52
67	41
39	67
35	70

a. Using a computerized statistical package and the proposed model, construct a 99% confidence interval for the mean time that it takes assembly-line workers to complete the task if the aptitude score is 80.

b. Using a computerized statistical package and the proposed model, construct a 99% prediction interval for the time it takes a worker to complete the task if the aptitude score of that worker is 80.

c. Compare the answers in questions a and b.

15.54 A researcher at the Institute for Human Fitness is interested in how a runner's present body fat, X_1 (in percent), and a runner's resting pulse, X_2 (in beats per minute), determine the time Y (in minutes) that it takes the runner to finish 10,000 meters. A random sample of 18 runners was selected and the following data were collected.

Y	X_1	X_2	Y	X_1	X_2
38.0	10.4	56	35.4	9.6	53
40.2	12.4	51	30.7	8.1	43
34.3	9.6	47	31.2	7.6	39
32.7	8.3	50	33.7	6.5	53
37.8	13.6	47	36.3	10.8	50
39.1	11.5	58	37.4	12.6	49
32.5	6.8	42	34.1	10.4	52
32.3	5.7	50	33.8	9.6	54
30.2	8.1	42	32.4	8.2	47

Use a computerized statistical package to answer the following questions.

a. Find a 90% CI for the mean value of Y at $X_1 = 9.0$ and $X_2 = 50$.

b. Interpret the CI in question a in the context of this exercise.

c. Find a 90% prediction interval for the value of Y at $X_1 = 9.0$ and $X_2 = 50$.

d. Interpret the prediction interval in question c in the context of this exercise.

Summary

Multiple linear regression offers you a method of predicting (or modeling) the behavior of a particular dependent variable (Y) using two or more independent (predictor) variables. As in the case of simple linear regression, which uses one predictor variable, the regression coefficients are those that minimize

$$
\begin{aligned}
\text{SSE} &= \text{sum of squares of error} \\
&= \Sigma(Y - \hat{Y})^2
\end{aligned}
$$

To use this technique properly, you must pay special attention to the assumptions behind it. These are that (1) the regression errors follow a normal distribution, centered at zero, with a common variance, and (2) the errors are statistically independent. An estimate of this common variance is

$$
\hat{\sigma}_e^{\,2} = s^2 = \text{MSE} = \frac{\text{SSE}}{n - k - 1}
$$

To determine the adequacy of the regression model, you can test the entire set of predictor variables using an F test with k and $n - k - 1$ degrees of freedom,

$$
F = \frac{\text{MSR}}{\text{MSE}} = \frac{R^2/k}{(1 - R^2)/(n - k - 1)}
$$

The contribution of an individual predictor variable (say, X_i) can be tested using a t statistic with $n - k - 1$ degrees of freedom:

$$
t = \frac{b_i}{s_{b_i}}
$$

where s_{b_i} represents the (estimated) standard deviation of b_i. Here, b_i is the (least squares) estimate of the population parameter, β_i, and centers the CI for this parameter.

The coefficient of determination, R^2, describes the percentage of the total variation in the sample Y values explained by this set of predictor variables. To determine the contribution of a particular subset of the predictor variables—say, X_2 and X_4—R^2 is computed with X_2 and X_4 included and then with X_2 and X_4 excluded from the regression equation. A partial F test is then used to determine whether the resulting decrease in R^2 is significant.

When a curvilinear pattern exists between two variables, X and Y, this nonlinear relationship often can be modeled by including an X^2 term in the regression equation. The resulting equation is

$$
\hat{Y} = b_0 + b_1 X + b_2 X^2
$$

This type of model often works well in situations where Y (for example, sales) appears to increase more slowly as the independent variable, X (for example, the amount of shelf space devoted to this product) continues to increase.

The problem of multicollinearity arises in the application of multiple linear regression when two or more independent variables are highly correlated. The resulting regression equation contains coefficients that are highly inflated (have a large variance) with t statistics that are extremely small, despite the fact that one or more of these seemingly insignificant variables are very useful predictors. An easy means of correcting this problem is to remove certain variables from the regression equation or to use a stepwise regression procedure.

Stepwise techniques allow you to insert variables one at a time into the equation (forward regression), remove them one at a time after initially including all variables in the equation (backward regression), or perform a combination of the two by inserting variables one at a time but removing a variable that has become redundant at any stage (stepwise regression).

Dummy variables can be used in a regression application to represent the categories of a qualitative variable (such as city). If all dummy variables are to be inserted into the equation, then $C - 1$ such variables should be defined to represent C categories. If a forward or stepwise selection procedure is used to define the final regression equation, then a better procedure is to define C dummy variables to represent this situation.

Use of a computer package is essential in the derivation of a multiple regression equation. In this chapter, we used MINITAB , SPSSX, and SAS. They provide the sampling coefficients (b_0, b_1, b_2, . . .), the statistics necessary to perform any test of hypothesis, and those needed for the prediction and confidence intervals for any specific set of predictor variable values.

Formulas Used in Multiple Linear Regression

H_0: all β's = 0

H_a: at least one $\beta \neq 0$

$$F = \frac{MSR}{MSE}$$

$$= \frac{R^2/k}{(1 - R^2)/(n - k - 1)}$$

$(df = k$ and $n - k - 1)$

H_0: $\beta_i = 0$

H_a: $\beta_i \neq 0$

(or H_a: $\beta_i > 0$)

(or H_a: $\beta_i < 0$)

$$t = \frac{b_i}{s_{b_i}}$$

$(df = n - k - 1)$

CI for β_i

$$b_i - t_{\alpha/2, n-k-1} \, s_{b_i}$$
$$\text{to} \quad b_i + t_{\alpha/2, n-k-1} \, s_{b_i}$$

Coefficient of determination

$$R^2 = 1 - (SSE/SST)$$

where

$$SST = \Sigma(Y - \bar{Y})^2$$
$$= \Sigma Y^2 - (\Sigma Y)^2/n$$

and

$$SSE = \Sigma(Y - \hat{Y})^2$$

H_0: $X_i, X_{i+1}, \cdots, X_j$ do not
    contribute

$$F = \frac{(R_c^2 - R_r^2)/v_1}{(1 - R_c^2)/v_2}$$

| H_a: at least one of them contributes | where (1) R_c^2 is the R^2 including the variables in H_0 (the complete model), (2) R_r^2 is the R^2 excluding the variables in H_0 (the reduced model), (3) v_1 = the number of β's in H_0, (4) $v_2 = n - 1 -$ (the number of X's in the complete model), and (5) the degrees of freedom for the F statistic are v_1 and v_2. |

Review Exercises

15.55 An automobile dealer decided to collect data to predict the demand for automobiles using regression analysis. Using historical data, the multiple regression method gave the least squares equation:

$$\hat{Y} = -307.2 + 1.994X_1 + 0.0207X_2 + 0.00876X_3 - 10.48X_4$$

where

Y = amount spent on new automobiles (in billions of dollars)

X_1 = U.S. population (in millions)

X_2 = disposable personal income (in billions of dollars)

X_3 = number of marriages (in thousands)

X_4 = financial interest rate (in percent) for automobile loans

a. Would you expect any multicollinearity to be present in these variables? Discuss.

b. If disposable personal income increased by $200 billion and the value of the other independent variables remained constant, how much would you expect the demand for automobiles to increase? Is your conclusion valid if multicollinearity exists?

15.56 A company has opened several ice-skating rinks and would like to know what factors affect the attendance at the rinks. The manager believes that the following variables affect attendance:

X_1 = temperature (forecasted high)

X_2 = wind speed (forecasted high)

X_3 = 1 if weekend and 0 otherwise

$X_4 = X_1X_2$

the following least squares model was found from 30 days of data:

$$\hat{Y} = 250 + 4.8X_1 - 30X_2 + 1.3X_2X_3 + 35X_4$$

a. What is the predicted attendance on a weekend if the forecasted high temperature is 28°F and the forecasted high wind speed is 12 mph?

b. If the coefficient of determination for the model is 0.67, test that the overall model contributes to predicting the attendance at the ice-skating rinks. Use a 5% significance level.

c. If the standard deviation of the estimate of the coefficient of X_2 is 2.01, does the variable wind speed contribute to predicting the variation in attendance, assuming that the variables X_1, X_3, and X_4 are in the model?

15.57 The manager of Stay Trim Health Studios would like to determine the average number of times per month a member attends the health studio (Y). The following independent variables were used in the analysis:

X_1 = weight at initial visit (in pounds)

$X_2 = X_1^2$

X_3 = age at initial visit

X_4 = length of membership (in years)

$X_5 = \begin{cases} 1 \text{ if employed} \\ 0 \text{ if not} \end{cases}$

The manager collected the following data:

Y	X_1	X_3	X_4	X_5
11	202	30	1	1
9	180	22	2	1
7	130	19	1	0
14	175	32	4	1
12	225	41	2	1
19	191	52	5	1
7	142	40	1	1
11	208	33	2	1
13	245	35	1	0
15	215	24	3	0
11	185	43	2	1
12	165	27	3	1
12	195	38	1	0
11	217	42	1	1
10	205	40	1	1

The least squares equation was found to be:

$$\hat{Y} = -11.218 + 0.15178X_1 - 0.0003X_2 + 0.08286X_3 + 1.9138X_4 - 2.299X_5$$

a. Does the overall model contribute significantly to predicting the monthly attendance at Stay Trim Health Studios? Use a 10% significance level.

b. Does weight squared contribute significantly to predicting the monthly attendance, assuming that the variables X_1, X_3, X_4, and X_5 are in the model? Use a 10% significance level.

c. Find a 95% CI for the coefficient of age.

d. Find a 95% CI for the coefficient of length of membership.

e. Use the model to predict the monthly attendance of a 35-year-old member who weighs 200 pounds, has a 2-year membership, and is currently employed.

f. Construct a histogram for the residuals of the complete model.

15.58 A realtor wanted to explore the feasibility of using multiple regression analysis in appraising the value of single-family homes within a certain community. The following variables were used:

Y = selling price of a house (in dollars)

X_1 = total living area (in square feet)

$X_2 = \begin{cases} 1 \text{ if in neighborhood 1} \\ 0 \text{ if not} \end{cases}$

$X_3 = \begin{cases} 1 \text{ if in neighborhood 2} \\ 0 \text{ if not} \end{cases}$

$X_4 = \begin{cases} 1 \text{ if lot size is larger than the typical house lot} \\ 0 \text{ if not} \end{cases}$

The data are as follows:

Y	X_1	X_2	X_3	X_4
63,000	2020	1	0	1
36,000	980	1	0	0
44,000	1230	0	0	1
37,000	980	0	1	0
28,000	640	0	1	0
28,000	720	0	1	0
56,000	2400	1	0	1
28,600	670	0	1	0
31,350	640	0	1	0
49,400	1910	0	0	1
31,000	900	1	0	0
56,000	1890	1	0	0
63,500	1900	0	0	1
49,000	2080	1	0	1
63,000	1900	0	0	1

Using a computerized statistical package, find the following:

a. The least squares equation.

b. The 95% CI for the coefficient of total living area.

c. The 95% prediction interval for selling price given that $X_1 = 1800$, $X_2 = 1$, $X_3 = 0$, and $X_4 = 0$.

d. The overall F test for the model and the resulting conclusion using a 5% significance level.

15.59 The following data were collected for the purpose of performing a regression analysis. Use a computerized statistical package.

Y	X_1	X_2	X_3	X_4
29	65	6.1	1	0
38	80	3.2	0	1
35	71	1.5	1	1
30	34	4.2	0	0
29	39	1.8	0	1
31	44	2.0	0	1
53	56	1.1	1	0
27	75	3.2	1	1
19	90	1.5	0	1
45	58	2.3	1	0
12	45	3.1	0	0
17	31	1.2	1	1
40	42	2.4	1	1
10	39	1.8	0	0
12	40	3.0	0	0

a. Find the least squares fit to the data.

b. Find the coefficient of determination for the complete model. Interpret the value of the coefficient of determination.

c. Find the coefficient of determination for the model using only X_1 and X_2 in the model.

d. Do a forward regression analysis using a significance level of .10.

e. Do a stepwise regression analysis using a significance level of .10.

f. Construct a histogram for the residuals of the complete model.

g. Find a 90% CI for the mean value of Y at $X_1 = 70$, $X_2 = 4.0$, $X_3 = 1$, and $X_4 = 0$.

h. Find the 90% prediction interval for an individual value of Y at $X_1 = 70$, $X_2 = 4.0$, $X_3 = 1$, and $X_4 = 0$.

15.60 The owner of a photographic laboratory would like to explore the relationship between her weekly profits (Y) and

X_1 = number of rolls of film sold

X_2 = number of enlargements given out free for advertising purposes

X_3 = number of prints

X_4 = number of reprints

Several weeks were selected randomly to collect the following data:

Y	X_1	X_2	X_3	X_4
350	50	15	130	50
414	61	18	150	39
385	71	12	125	45
429	86	21	141	36
415	90	22	133	40
358	62	17	125	35
392	55	19	150	36
415	59	24	157	44
380	63	28	140	38

Use a computerized statistical package.

a. Find the least squares prediction equation.

b. Test the null hypothesis that X_4 does not contribute to predicting the variation in Y given that X_1, X_2, and X_3 are already in the model. Use a .05 significance level.

c. Find the 90% CI for the mean value of Y given $X_1 = 85$, $X_2 = 20$, $X_3 = 135$, and $X_4 = 37$.

d. Find the coefficient of determination for the complete model and interpret its value.

15.61 Use a computerized statistical package to analyze the following data:

Y	X_1	X_2	X_3
154	30	1	1
223	41	3	9
201	33	5	25
177	31	4	16
143	25	3	9
155	29	2	4
220	34	5	25
210	38	4	16
230	44	3	9
265	51	2	4
306	55	5	25
170	31	4	16

a. Find the least squares prediction equation.

b. Find the coefficient of determination for the model.

c. Test at the .10 significance level that X_2 and X_3 contribute to the prediction of Y, given that X_1 is in the model.

d. Test at the .10 significance level that X_1 contributes to the prediction of Y, given that X_2 and X_3 are in the model.

e. Plot the residuals of the complete model versus the predicted values. Do the residuals appear to be random?

15.62 Complete the following ANOVA table for testing whether a model with five independent variables contributes significantly to the prediction of the dependent variable:

Source	df	SS	MS	F
Regression		95.6		
Error	20	159.0		
Total				

Case Study

Investment Designs

The management of Investment Designs was interested in the application of the 80–20 rule of thumb to its clientele. This rule says that 80% of the company's revenue should be generated by 20% of its clientele. This also should explain the variability among the sales of the brokers. Management wanted to forecast the demand for a portfolio of high-risk securities. The initial analysis suggested that the 80–20 rule of thumb was applicable: the record of investments in the high-risk portfolio indicated that 77% of the investments were made by 22% of the investors. This was the high-volume (HV) group.

The first step in the forecast development was to develop a model of buyer behavior. This meant trying to describe what factors influenced purchase decisions. It was generally agreed that the income of the investor should be a major factor in predicting his or her annual investment. This independent variable in a regression model should explain a major portion of the variability in the amount of money invested overall.

The managers also agreed that income alone probably would not explain enough of the variability to produce a good forecast model. The investor's willingness to assume risk also was influenced by that investor's view of present and future economic conditions. The more confidence the investor had in present and future economic conditions, the greater his or her investment in high-risk securities.

No information was available on the perceptions of the individual investors. On the assumption that the investors would use economic forecasts and economists' indices of future expectations, the group decided to analyze these data for their model.

The economic outlook data were in index form. The index could take any value from 0 to 100. The index value was tied to the expected increase in interest rates and borrowing levels, the expected increase in manufacturing costs because of the rate of inflation, and the expected level of price inflation at the retail level. This meant that the lower the index, the better the future economic conditions were expected to be.

The managers then randomly selected 24 high-risk portfolio customers from the group of HV investors and collected data on their income and investment history. The multiple regression model required that these data be randomly selected from the HV investment group to ensure a representative sample of investments at different points in time. This allowed the group to assess the economic index's influence on the investor. The data collected to test the model follow. The income figures represent annual income and the economic index values are the index values at the time the investment was made.

Observation	Investment	Income	Economic Index
1	1400	40000	72
2	1600	46000	87
3	1500	44000	84
4	1600	49000	81
5	1900	50000	95
6	1700	47000	86
7	1800	48000	91
8	2000	49000	08
9	1800	47000	03
10	1900	49000	10
11	1900	49000	10
12	1900	48000	12
13	2000	49000	18
14	2000	51000	27
15	2000	50000	15
16	2000	51000	18
17	1900	47000	09
18	1900	47000	10
19	2000	49000	21
20	2100	51000	25
21	2100	51000	21
22	2100	51000	13
23	2200	54000	18
24	2100	51000	20

Case Study Questions

1. What is the regression model, and the estimated coefficients?

2. Is this relationship consistent with the underlying model? Explain.

3. How much of the variability in the amount invested is explained by income alone?

4. What is the additional amount of explained variability in the amount invested when the economic index is added to the model? Is the contribution of this explained variance significant at $\alpha = .10$?

5. What is the change in the forecast level of investment when the economic index is held constant and income changes by $1000?

6. What is the change in the forecast level of investment when the income level is held constant and the economic index changes by 10 points?

7. What is the correlation among the independent variables? Do you think multi-collinearity is a problem? Why?

8. Are the conclusions you reached in questions 5 and 6 still valid? Why or why not?

Solution

Example 15.2

At the beginning of the chapter, we computed the regression equation for predicting the estimate of home size, based on the three predictor variables: income, family size, and level of education. Two methods of computing the results were used— multiple regression and stepwise multiple regression. The SPSSX program listing in Figure 15.21 uses multiple regression. Figure 15.22 uses stepwise regression. The listing in Figure 15.23 is used to determine predicted values of the dependent

Figure 15.21

SPSSX program listing requesting a multiple regression analysis of the real estate example.

```
TITLE    REAL ESTATE EXAMPLE USING TWO PREDICTORS
DATA LIST FREE/SQFOOT INCOME SIZE EDUC
PRINT / SQFOOT INCOME SIZE EDUC
REGRESSION VARIABLES=SQFOOT,INCOME,SIZE,EDUC/
         DEPENDENT=SQFOOT/ENTER/
BEGIN DATA
16  22  2  4
17  26  2  8
26  45  3  7
24  37  4  0
22  28  4  2
21  50  3  10
32  56  6  8
18  34  3  8
30  60  5  2
20  40  3  6
END DATA
```

Figure 15.22

SPSSX program listing requesting a stepwise regression analysis of the real estate example.

```
TITLE    REAL ESTATE EXAMPLE USING STEPWISE
DATA LIST FREE/SQFOOT INCOME SIZE EDUC
PRINT / SQFOOT INCOME SIZE EDUC
REGRESSION VARIABLES=SQFOOT,INCOME,SIZE,EDUC/
         CRITERIA=PIN(0.1)/
         DEPENDENT=SQFOOT/STEPWISE/
BEGIN DATA
16  22  2  4
17  26  2  8
26  45  3  7
24  37  4  0
22  28  4  2
21  50  3  10
32  56  6  8
18  34  3  8
30  60  5  2
20  40  3  6
END DATA
```

Figure 15.23

SPSSX program listing requesting predicted values for the input data and an additional row of predictor variable values.

```
TITLE    PREDICTION FOR REAL ESTATE EXAMPLE
DATA LIST FREE/SQFOOT INCOME SIZE EDUC
MISSING VALUES SQFOOT(-9)
PRINT / SQFOOT INCOME SIZE EDUC
REGRESSION VARIABLES=SQFOOT,INCOME,SIZE,EDUC/
         DEPENDENT=SQFOOT/ENTER/
         CASEWISE=ALL PRED SEPRED/
BEGIN DATA
16  22  2  4
17  26  2  8
26  45  3  7
24  37  4  0
22  28  4  2
21  50  3  10
32  56  6  8
18  34  3  8
30  60  5  2
20  40  3  6
-9  36  4  8
END DATA
```

```
                           * * * *   M U L T I P L E   R E G R E S S I O N   * * * *

  LISTWISE DELETION OF MISSING DATA

  EQUATION NUMBER 1   DEPENDENT VARIABLE..   SQFOOT

  BEGINNING BLOCK NUMBER  1.  METHOD:  ENTER

  VARIABLE(S) ENTERED ON STEP NUMBER  1..      EDUC
                                      2..      INCOME
                                      3..      SIZE
```

MULTIPLE R	.95145	ANALYSIS OF VARIANCE
R SQUARE	[.90527]	
ADJUSTED R SQUARE	.85790	
STANDARD ERROR	2.03545	

SSE — MSE $= s^2 = \hat{\sigma}_e^2$

	DF	SUM OF SQUARES	MEAN SQUARE
REGRESSION	3	237.54155	79.18052
RESIDUAL	6	[24.85845]	[4.14307]

F = [19.11154]   SIGNIF F = [.0018] ———— p-value for F test

F value used to test H_o : all b's = 0

```
---------------- VARIABLES IN THE EQUATION -----------------
```

	B	SE B	BETA		T	SIG T
VARIABLE	b_3 b_1			(3)		
EDUC	-.162771	.244071	-.099727	(1)	-.667	.5296
INCOME	.193878	.087700	.461936		2.211	.0691
SIZE	2.338108	.907791	.549625	(2)	2.576	.0420
(CONSTANT)	7.595501	2.594776			2.927	.0264

b_2 b_0

———— p-values for t tests

```
  END BLOCK NUMBER   1   ALL REQUESTED VARIABLES ENTERED.
```

(1) Used to test $H_0 : \beta_1 = 0$
(2) Used to test $H_0 : \beta_2 = 0$
(3) Used to test $H_0 : \beta_3 = 0$

Figure 15.24

SPSSX output obtained by executing the program listing in Figure 15.21.

variable for predictor values not in the data, along with information that can be used to construct prediction and confidence intervals. Each line represents one card image to be entered.

This explanation is presented in complete form for the multiple regression example, and in abbreviated form for the stepwise regression example. The only change between the two examples is the REGRESSION command. Complete program listings and output are shown for both.

The TITLE command names the SPSSX run.
The DATA LIST command gives each variable a name, and describes the data as being in free form.
The PRINT command requests a printout of the input data.
The REGRESSION statement requests that the independent variables INCOME, SIZE, and EDUC be entered in the regression equation to predict the dependent variable SQFOOT.
The BEGIN DATA command indicates to SPSSX that the input data immediately follow.

The next 10 lines are card images and represent the four variables to be considered in the regression analysis. The first card image represents a home with 1600 square feet, an income of $22,000, a family of two people, and 4 years of educational experience at the college level.

The END DATA statement indicates the end of the data card images.

Figure 15.24 shows the output obtained by executing the program listing in Figure 15.21.

Example 15.2

Using the STEPWISE Method

The REGRESSION statement for performing stepwise regression is similar. Notice that the word STEPWISE is substituted for ENTER, and that a new line has been added. Instead of forcing all variables into the equation with an ENTER command, STEPWISE selects the variables that meet the entry criteria. The CRITERIA = PIN(0.1) statement specifies that each independent variable must contribute at least a .1 probability of rejecting the null hypothesis before it is allowed to enter into the regression equation.

Figure 15.25 shows the output obtained by executing the program listing in Figure 15.22.

Figure 15.25

SPSSX output obtained by executing the program listing in Figure 15.22.

```
            * * * *   M U L T I P L E   R E G R E S S I O N   * * * *

LISTWISE DELETION OF MISSING DATA
EQUATION NUMBER 1    DEPENDENT VARIABLE..   SQFOOT
BEGINNING BLOCK NUMBER  1.   METHOD:  STEPWISE

VARIABLE(S) ENTERED ON STEP NUMBER  1..    SIZE — 1st variable entered (X₂)
MULTIPLE R         .90787       ANALYSIS OF VARIANCE
R SQUARE           .82422                      DF    SUM OF SQUARES    MEAN SQUARE
ADJUSTED R SQUARE  .80225       REGRESSION      1        216.27586      216.27586
STANDARD ERROR    2.40115       RESIDUAL        8         46.12414        5.76552
        R² using X₂ only        F =    37.51196    SIGNIF F =   .0003
```

R^2 using X_2 only

```
------------------ VARIABLES IN THE EQUATION ------------------     ------------- VARIABLES NOT IN THE EQUATION -------------

VARIABLE          B        SE B       BETA       T   SIG T      VARIABLE   BETA IN  PARTIAL  MIN TOLER     T   SIG T

SIZE          3.862069   .630573   .907867   6.125  .0003      INCOME    .392779  .648925   .479796    2.257  .0586
(CONSTANT)    9.082759  2.333971             3.892  .0046      EDUC      .064336  .148525   .936811     .397  .7029
```

1st variable entered (X_2)

Enter income into the equation because this value is $< \alpha$ where $\alpha = .1$

```
            * * * * * * * * * * * * * * * * * * * * * * * * * * *

VARIABLE(S) ENTERED ON STEP NUMBER  2..    INCOME — 2nd variable entered (X₁)
MULTIPLE R         .94776       ANALYSIS OF VARIANCE
R SQUARE           .89824                      DF    SUM OF SQUARES    MEAN SQUARE
ADJUSTED R SQUARE  .86917       REGRESSION      2        235.69890      117.84945
STANDARD ERROR    1.95306       RESIDUAL        7         26.70110        3.81444
     R² using X₂ and X₁          F =    30.89559    SIGNIF F =   .0003
```

R^2 using X_2 and X_1

2nd variable entered (X_1)

```
------------------ VARIABLES IN THE EQUATION ------------------     ------------- VARIABLES NOT IN THE EQUATION -------------

VARIABLE          B        SE B       BETA       T   SIG T      VARIABLE   BETA IN  PARTIAL  MIN TOLER     T   SIG T

SIZE          2.656940   .740463   .624574   3.588  .0089      EDUC     -.099727 -.262698    .346723    -.667  .5296
INCOME         .164853   .073055   .392779   2.257  .0586
(CONSTANT)    6.739579  2.163852             3.115  .0170
```

Final Equation : $\hat{Y} = 6.74 + .16$(income) $+ 2.66$(size)

Do not enter education because this value is $> \alpha$ where $\alpha = .1$

Example

Section 15.5

In the real-estate example in section 15.5, we wished to determine the predicted square footage (Y) for values of $X_1 = 36$, $X_2 = 4$ and $X_3 = 8$. Of course, one way to do this is to insert them manually into the regression equation resulting from the ten observations in the previous SPSSX example. An easier way is to attach these values at the end of the input data along with a numeric value for Y (we used -9 here), which will be identified as a *missing value* using the MISSING

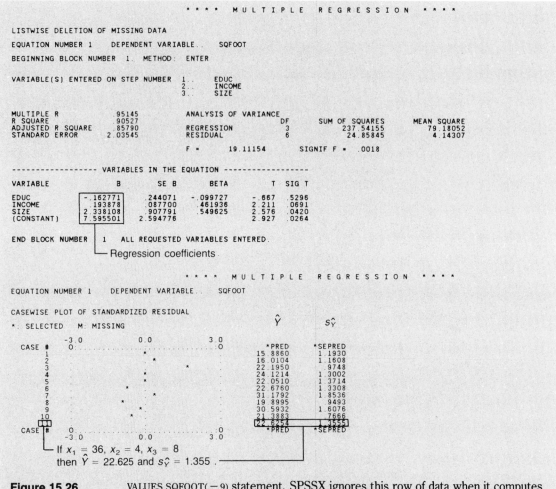

Figure 15.26

SPSSX output obtained by executing the program listing in Figure 15.23.

VALUES SQFOOT(− 9) statement. SPSSX ignores this row of data when it computes the regression equation but then includes this row when it summarizes the predicted values.

The predicted values as well as their standard errors ($s_{\hat{Y}}$) are calculated and included in the output using the CASEWISE = ALL PRED SEPRED statement. This informs SPSSX that you would like to see the predicted values (and their standard errors) for *all* of the cases in the input data, including the row(s) with the missing *Y* value.

Figure 15.26 shows the output obtained by executing the program listing in Figure 15.23.

Solution

Example 15.2

At the beginning of the chapter, we computed the regression equation for predicting the estimate of desired home size, based on the three predictor variables: income, family size, and level of education. Two methods of computing the results were used—multiple regression and stepwise multiple regression. The SAS program listing in Figure 15.27 is of multiple regression, while the listing in Figure 15.28

Figure 15.27

SAS program listing requesting a multiple regression analysis of the real estate example.

```
TITLE    REAL ESTATE EXAMPLE USING TWO PREDICTORS;
DATA REAL ESTATE;
 INPUT SQFOOT INCOME SIZE EDUC;
 CARDS;
16  22  2  4
17  26  2  8
26  45  3  7
24  37  4  0
22  28  4  2
21  50  3  10
32  56  6  8
18  34  3  8
30  60  5  2
20  40  3  6
PROC PRINT;
PROC REG;
 MODEL SQFOOT=INCOME SIZE EDUC;
```

Figure 15.28

SAS program listing requesting a stepwise regression analysis of the real estate example.

```
TITLE    REAL ESTATE EXAMPLE USING STEPWISE;
DATA REAL ESTATE;
 INPUT SQFOOT INCOME SIZE EDUC;
 CARDS;
16  22  2  4
17  26  2  8
26  45  3  7
24  37  4  0
22  28  4  2
21  50  3  10
32  56  6  8
18  34  3  8
30  60  5  2
20  40  3  6
PROC PRINT;
PROC STEPWISE;
 MODEL SQFOOT=INCOME SIZE EDUC/
        SLENTRY=0.1;
```

Figure 15.29

SAS program listing requesting predicted values for the input data and an additional row of predictor variable values.

```
TITLE    PREDICTION FOR REAL ESTATE EXAMPLE;
DATA REAL ESTATE;
    MISSING A;
 INPUT SQFOOT INCOME SIZE EDUC;
 CARDS;
16  22  2  4
17  26  2  8
26  45  3  7
24  37  4  0
22  28  4  2
21  50  3  10
32  56  6  8
18  34  3  8
30  60  5  2
20  40  3  6
A  36  4  8
PROC PRINT;
PROC REG;
 MODEL SQFOOT=INCOME SIZE EDUC/ CLI CLM;
```

uses stepwise regression. The listing in Figure 15.29 is used to determine predicted values of the dependent variable for predictor values not in the observed data, along with prediction and confidence intervals. Each line represents one card image to be entered.

This explanation is presented in complete form for the multiple regression example, and in abbreviated form for the stepwise regression example. The only change between the two examples is the PROC REG to PROC STEPWISE command. Complete program listings and output are shown for both.

Figure 15.30

SAS output obtained by executing the program listing in Figure 15.27.

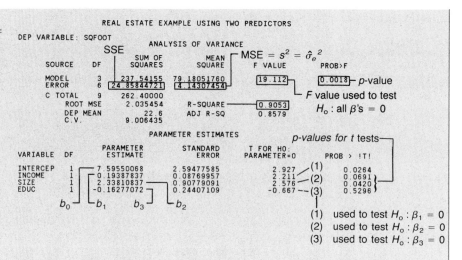

REAL ESTATE EXAMPLE USING TWO PREDICTORS

The TITLE command names the SAS run.

The DATA command gives the data a name.

The INPUT command names and gives the correct order for the different fields on the data cards.

The CARDS command indicates to SAS that the input data immediately follow.

The next 10 lines are card images and represent the four variables to be considered in the regression analysis. The first card image represents a home with 1600 square feet, an income of $22,000, a family of two people, and 4 years of educational experience at the college level.

The PROC PRINT command requests a printout of the input data.

The PROC REG command and MODEL subcommand request that the independent variables INCOME, SIZE, and EDUC be entered in the regression equation to predict the dependent variable SQFOOT.

Figure 15.30 shows the output obtained by executing the program listing in Figure 15.27.

Example

Using the STEPWISE Method

The STEPWISE statement for performing stepwise regression is very similar. Notice that the word STEPWISE is substituted for REG, and that a new line has been added. Instead of forcing all variables into the equation with the REG command, STEPWISE selects the variables that meet the entry criteria. The SLENTRY = 0.1 statement specifies that each independent variable must contribute at least a .1 probability of rejecting the null hypothesis before it is allowed to enter into the regression equation.

Figure 15.31 shows the output obtained by executing the program listing in Figure 15.28.

Figure 15.31

SAS output obtained by executing the program listing in Figure 15.28.

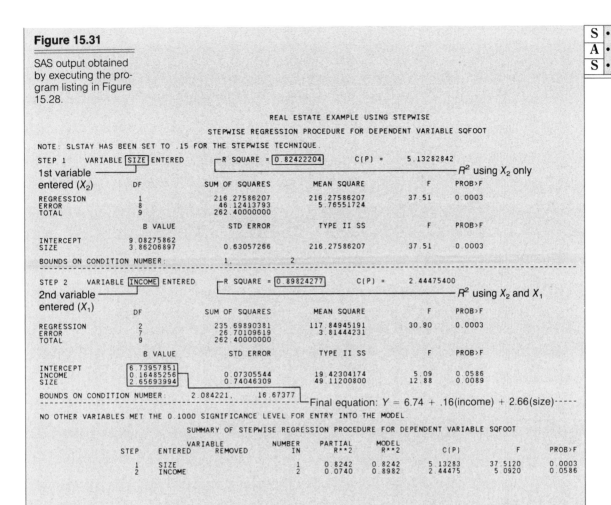

REAL ESTATE EXAMPLE USING STEPWISE

STEPWISE REGRESSION PROCEDURE FOR DEPENDENT VARIABLE SQFOOT

NOTE: SLSTAY HAS BEEN SET TO .15 FOR THE STEPWISE TECHNIQUE.

STEP 1   VARIABLE [SIZE] ENTERED   ┌─R SQUARE = [0.82422204]   C(P) =   5.13282842

1st variable ──────┘   ── R^2 using X_2 only
entered (X_2)   DF   SUM OF SQUARES   MEAN SQUARE   F   PROB>F

REGRESSION   1   216.27586207   216.27586207   37.51   0.0003
ERROR   8   46.12413793   5.76551724
TOTAL   9   262.40000000

                    B VALUE   STD ERROR   TYPE II SS   F   PROB>F

INTERCEPT   9.08275862
SIZE   3.86206897   0.63057266   216.27586207   37.51   0.0003

BOUNDS ON CONDITION NUMBER: 1.   2

STEP 2   VARIABLE [INCOME] ENTERED   ┌─R SQUARE = [0.89824277]   C(P) =   2.44475400

2nd variable ────┘   ── R^2 using X_2 and X_1
entered (X_1)   DF   SUM OF SQUARES   MEAN SQUARE   F   PROB>F

REGRESSION   2   235.69890381   117.84945191   30.90   0.0003
ERROR   7   26.70109619   3.81444231
TOTAL   9   262.40000000

                    B VALUE   STD ERROR   TYPE II SS   F   PROB>F

INTERCEPT   [6.73957851]
INCOME   [0.16485256]   0.07305544   19.42304174   5.09   0.0586
SIZE   [2.65693994]   0.74046309   49.11200800   12.88   0.0089

BOUNDS ON CONDITION NUMBER: 2.084221,   16.67377
                                                    └─Final equation: $Y = 6.74 + .16(\text{income}) + 2.66(\text{size})$ ─────

NO OTHER VARIABLES MET THE 0.1000 SIGNIFICANCE LEVEL FOR ENTRY INTO THE MODEL.

SUMMARY OF STEPWISE REGRESSION PROCEDURE FOR DEPENDENT VARIABLE SQFOOT

| | VARIABLE | | NUMBER | PARTIAL | MODEL | | | |
STEP	ENTERED	REMOVED	IN	R**2	R**2	C(P)	F	PROB>F
1	SIZE		1	0.8242	0.8242	5.13283	37.5120	0.0003
2	INCOME		2	0.0740	0.8982	2.44475	5.0920	0.0586

Example

Section 15.5

In the real-estate example in section 15.5, we wished to determine the predicted square footage (Y) for values of $X_1 = 36$, $X_2 = 4$, and $X_3 = 8$. Of course, one way to do this is to insert them manually into the regression equation resulting from the ten observations in the previous SAS example. An easier way is to attach these values at the end of the input data along with any single character from A to Z for the value of the dependent variable, indicating to SAS that this value is missing. Which character you use is arbitrary, but it should be specified in the MISSING statement immediately following the DATA statement (refer to the computer output for this example). SAS ignores this row of data when it computes the regression equation but then includes this row when it summarizes the predicted values.

The predicted values as well as the corresponding confidence intervals and prediction intervals are calculated and included in the output by inserting /CLI and CLM; in the final (MODEL) SAS statement. The CLI command generates the prediction intervals for an *individual*, whereas CLM will produce CIs for the *mean*. The row(s) containing the missing value(s) will be included in this summary.

Figure 15.32 shows the output obtained by executing the program listing in Figure 15.29.

S A S

Figure 15.32

SAS output obtained by executing the program listing in Figure 15.29.

PREDICTION FOR REAL ESTATE EXAMPLE

DEP VARIABLE: SQFOOT

ANALYSIS OF VARIANCE

SOURCE	DF	SUM OF SQUARES	MEAN SQUARE	F VALUE	PROB>F
MODEL	3	237.54155	79.18051760	19.112	0.0018
ERROR	6	24.85844721	4.14307454		
C TOTAL	9	262.40000			

ROOT MSE	2.035454	R-SQUARE	0.9053
DEP MEAN	22.6	ADJ R-SQ	0.8579
C.V.	9.006435		

PARAMETER ESTIMATES

VARIABLE	DF	PARAMETER ESTIMATE	STANDARD ERROR	T FOR H0: PARAMETER=0	PROB > !T!
INTERCEP	1	7.59550068	2.59477585	2.927	0.0264
INCOME	1	0.19387837	0.08769957	2.211	0.0691
SIZE	1	2.33810272	0.90779091	2.576	0.0420
EDUC	1	-0.16277072	0.24407109	-0.667	0.5296

OBS	ACTUAL	$\hat{Y}$ PREDICT VALUE	$s_{\hat{Y}}$ STD ERR PREDICT	LOWER95% MEAN	UPPER95% MEAN	LOWER95% PREDICT	UPPER95% PREDICT	$Y - \hat{Y}$ RESIDUAL
1	16.0000	15.8860	1.1930	12.9669	18.8050	10.1130	21.6589	0.1140
2	17.0000	16.0104	1.1608	13.1700	18.8508	10.2768	21.7440	0.9896
3	26.0000	22.1950	0.9748	19.8098	24.5801	16.6727	27.7172	3.8050
4	24.0000	24.1214	1.3002	20.9399	27.3030	18.2114	30.0315	-0.1214
5	22.0000	22.0510	1.3714	18.6953	25.4067	16.0454	28.0566	-0.0510
6	21.0000	22.6760	1.3308	19.4197	25.9324	16.7254	28.6267	-1.6760
7	32.0000	31.1792	1.8536	26.6436	35.7147	24.4429	37.9154	0.8208
8	18.0000	19.8995	0.9493	17.5766	22.2225	14.4039	25.1752	-1.8995
9	30.0000	30.5932	1.6076	26.6595	34.5269	24.2465	36.9399	-0.5932
10	20.0000	21.3883	0.7666	19.5125	23.2642	16.0662	26.7105	-1.3883
11	A	22.6254	1.3555	19.3086	25.9422	16.6415	28.6093	

SUM OF RESIDUALS 5.39568E-14
SUM OF SQUARED RESIDUALS 24.85845
PREDICTED RESID SS (PRESS) 69.29215

CI for $\mu_{Y|x}$ Prediction interval for Y_x

$\hat{Y}$ and $s_{\hat{Y}}$ for $x_1 = 36, x_2 = 4, x_3 = 8$

M I N I T A B

Instructions for Multiple and Stepwise Regression

The REGRESS Command

The MINITAB REGRESS command is illustrated in many of the examples contained in this chapter. By using various subcommands you can store the residuals and the values of $b_0, b_1, \ldots, b_k$.

For example, consider the sequence

REGRESS Y IN C1 USING 2 PREDICTORS IN C2 C3;

RESIDUALS IN C4;

COEF IN C5.

This sequence stores the residuals in column C4 and the estimated regression coefficients in column C5. Also, the abbreviated form of the REGRESS command here would be

REGRESS C1 2 C2 C3;

If you wish merely to examine the residuals but not to store them, type the command BRIEF 3 at some point before performing the regression analysis. This will provide additional output (including the residuals) when the REGRESS command is used. This is illustrated in Figure 15.33.

Figure 15.33

Multiple regression analysis of the real estate example.

```
MTB > BRIEF 3
MTB > REGRESS Y IN C1 USING 3 PREDICTORS IN C2-C4

The regression equation is
C1 = 7.60 + 0.194 C2 + 2.34 C3 - 0.163 C4

Predictor        Coef          Stdev      t-ratio
Constant        7.596          2.595        2.93
C2            0.19388        0.08770        2.21
C3             2.3381         0.9078        2.58
C4            -0.1628         0.2441       -0.67

s = 2.035       R-sq = 90.5%     R-sq(adj) = 85.8%

Analysis of Variance

SOURCE          DF            SS             MS
Regression       3       237.542         79.181
Error            6        24.858          4.143 ─MSE
Total            9       262.400

Continue? YES
SOURCE          DF         SEQ SS
C2               1        186.587
C3               1         49.112
C4               1          1.843

Obs.     C2         C1        Fit Stdev.Fit  Residual  St.Resid
  1    22.0     16.000     15.886     1.193     0.114      0.07
  2    26.0     17.000     16.010     1.161     0.990      0.59
  3    45.0     26.000     22.195     0.975     3.805      2.13R
  4    37.0     24.000     24.121     1.300    -0.121     -0.08
  5    28.0     22.000     22.051     1.371    -0.051     -0.03
  6    50.0     21.000     22.676     1.331    -1.676     -1.09
  7    56.0     32.000     31.179     1.854     0.821      0.98
  8    34.0     18.000     19.900     0.949    -1.900     -1.05
  9    60.0     30.000     30.593     1.608    -0.593     -0.48
 10    40.0     20.000     21.388     0.767    -1.388     -0.74

R denotes an obs. with a large st. resid.
```

Stepwise Regression

MINITAB also performs stepwise regression using the command

STEPWISE REGRESSION OF Y IN C1 USING PREDICTORS C2 C3 C4 . . .

Abbreviated statement:

STEP C1 C2 C3 C4 . . .

where C2, C3, C4 . . . are the predictor variables.

This procedure will enter a variable if its corresponding (partial) F value exceeds FENTER = 4 and remove any variable whose (partial) F value falls below FREMOVE = 4. An illustration of this procedure using the real-estate data is shown in Figure 15.34. Only two of the three variables being considered were selected (using the default values of FREMOVE = FENTER = 4). The resulting equation is

$$\hat{Y} = 6.74 + .165X_1 + 2.66X_2$$

To change the values of FENTER and/or FREMOVE, use the following sequence of commands. The semicolon (;) at the end of the REGRESS command informs MINITAB that subcommands are needed. The period following the final subcommand indicates that there are no further subcommands.

MTB > STEPWISE REGRESSION OF Y IN C1 USING C2, C3, C4, C5, C6;

SUBC > FENTER = 3.5;

SUBC > FREMOVE = 3.5.

To perform a forward selection, you simply do not allow any variable to be removed once it is included in the model. Setting FREMOVE = 0 will accomplish this. The procedure ends when the (partial) F statistic for an entering variable is below FENTER.

Similarly, you can perform backwards regression by first using the subcommand ENTER:

SUBC > ENTER C2-C6;

where C2-C6 are all of your predictor variables. This enters all of your predictor variables into the model. Next, use

SUBC > FENTER = 10000.

or any large value. This procedure stops when no variable in the model has an F value less than FREMOVE.

Figure 15.34

MINITAB stepwise regression procedure.

```
MTB > STEPWISE OF Y IN C1 USING PREDICTORS IN C2-C4

    STEPWISE REGRESSION OF     C1    ON  3 PREDICTORS, WITH N =   10

        STEP          1        2        ── Equation using one variable
    CONSTANT      9.083    6.740        is Ŷ = 9.083 + 3.86X₂

    C3             3.86     2.66
    T-RATIO        6.12     3.59        ── Equation using two variables
                                           is Ŷ = 6.74 + .165X₁ + 2.66X₂
    C2                      0.165
    T-RATIO                 2.26
                                        ── R² using
    S              2.40     1.95           X₂ only

    R-SQ          82.42    89.82        ── R² using
                                           X₁ and X₂
    MORE? (YES, NO, SUBCOMMAND, OR HELP)
    SUBC> NO
```

Time Series Analysis and Index Numbers

A Look Back/Introduction

The previous two chapters introduced you to a method of predicting the value of a dependent variable using the technique of *linear regression*. You determined a set of one or more predictor (independent) variables (X_1, X_2, . . .) that could be used to model the behavior of the dependent variable, Y.

When the dependent variable is measured over *time*, there is another method of describing the behavior of this variable—**time series analysis.** For example, consider the following data, where Y = the amount of electrical power consumed in Pine Bluff over a 10-year period.

	Power Consumption
Year	**(million kWh)**
1975	95
1976	145
1977	174
1978	200
1979	224
1980	245
1981	263
1982	275
1983	283
1984	288

This is an example of a (very short) time series. Typically, a time series covers many more periods, especially when measured for each month, week, or even day. To describe the behavior of the variable, Y, we examine the past data and, rather than searching for a number of predictor variables, we try to capture the patterns that exist only in the Y observations over a period of time. In other words, we assume that *time-related patterns can serve as predictors*. In this illustration, one pattern is clear—the power consumption values increase from one year to the next.

This prediction technique has both advantages and disadvantages. The primary advantage of using time series analysis is that often you can describe your variable of interest, Y, by using only a sample containing past observations. The disadvantage is that the past observations often contain patterns that are difficult to extract and, as a result, the models can become very complex.

In this chapter, we will not discuss the more sophisticated modeling techniques; instead, we will concentrate on methods of *describing* a time series by determining the various components that make up each observation.

16.1

Components of a Time Series

A **time series** represents a variable observed across time. The time increment can be years, quarters, months, or even days. The values of the time series can be presented in a table or illustrated using a scatter diagram. Usually, the points in the graph are connected by straight lines, making it easier to detect any existing patterns; this is a **line graph.**

The time series for the power consumption data is shown in Figure 16.1. As we noted, the power consumption values increase steadily from one year to the next. This long-term movement in the time series is called a *trend.* These values exhibit a definite increasing trend (or growth). Trend is only one of several components that describe the behavior of any time series. The **components** of a time series are:

Trend (TR)
Seasonal variation (S)
Cyclical variation (C)
Irregular activity (I)

Figure 16.1

Power consumption in Pine Bluff.

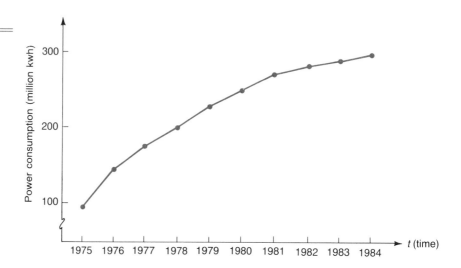

The purpose of time series analysis is to describe a particular data set by estimating the various components that make up this time series. We will examine each of these components individually, although time series data usually contain a mixture of all four.

Trend (TR)

The **trend** is a steady increase or decrease in the time series. If a particular time series is neither increasing nor decreasing over its range of time, it contains *no trend*. The trend reflects any long-term growth or decline in the set of observations. This pattern may be due to, for example, inflation, increases in the population, increases in personal income, market growth or decline, or changes in technology. Each of these could have a long-term effect on the variable of interest and would be reflected in the trend in the corresponding time series.

This long-term growth or decay pattern can take a variety of shapes. If the rate of change in Y from one time period to the next is relatively constant, this is a **linear trend**

$$TR = b_0 + b_1 t$$

(for some b_0 and b_1) where the predictor variable is time, t.

When the time series appears to be slowing down or accelerating as time increases, then a **nonlinear trend** may be present. It may be a **quadratic trend**

$$TR = b_0 + b_1 t + b_2 t^2$$

or a **decaying trend**

$$TR = b_0 + b_1 (1/t)$$

or

$$TR = b_0 + b_1 e^{-t}$$

These trend equations can be derived from the linear regression equations developed in Chapter 14 (for linear trend) and Chapter 15 (for quadratic trend). The linear trend equation is an application of *simple* linear regression, whereas the quadratic trend uses a *multiple* regression equation using two predictors, t and t^2. Simple linear regression techniques also can be used to derive b_0 and b_1 for the decay trend equations where values of t are replaced by the values of $1/t$ or e^{-t} in the data input.

The number of employees from 1977 to 1984 at Video-Comp, an expanding microcomputer-software firm, is recorded in the following table and illustrated in Figure 16.2.

Year	Number of Employees (thousands)
1977	1.1
1978	2.4
1979	4.6
1980	5.4
1981	5.9
1982	8.0
1983	9.7
1984	11.2

The underlying long-term growth in this time series appears to be nearly *linear*, as represented by the dotted line in Figure 16.2. To determine the equation of this line, we use the technique of simple linear regression, where $X =$ the predictor

Figure 16.2

Number of employees at Video-Comp (an example of linear trend).

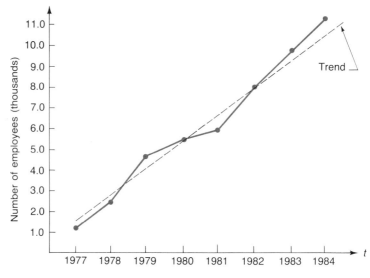

Figure 16.3

A Increasing linear trend: $TR = b_0 + b_1t$ $(b_1 > 0)$. **B** Decreasing linear trend: $TR = b_0 + b_1t$ $(b_1 < 0)$.

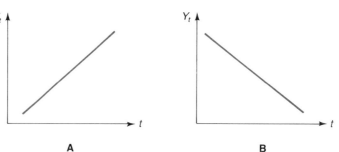

variable = time, and Y = the number of employees. We can estimate the existing trend using

$$\hat{y}_t = b_0 + b_1t$$

where t represents the time variable and y_t is the value of Y at time period t. Here b_0 and b_1 are the least squares regression coefficients for a straight line predictor. The procedure of deriving these least squares estimates will be developed later in the chapter. Figure 16.3 shows an *increasing* linear trend (y_t increases over time) and a *decreasing* linear trend (y_t decreases over time).

Example 16.1

What type of trend exists in the power-consumption data (Figure 16.1)?

Solution Although this time series increases steadily, it *increases at a decreasing rate:* it starts off with large increases from one time period to the next, but these increments gradually become smaller. When the growth is linear, the values increase at a nearly constant rate. Figure 16.1 is an illustration of **quadratic trend,** where the time series randomly fluctuates about a quadratic (or curvilinear) level over time. This trend is captured by the equation

$$\hat{y}_t = b_0 + b_1t + b_2t^2$$

To derive these estimates, we use the multiple linear regression approach discussed in Chapter 15 (curvilinear models). Section 16.2 will demonstrate this technique.

The four types of quadratic trend are summarized in Figure 16.4.

Figure 16.4

Quadratic trend. **A** Y increases at a decreasing rate. **B** Y decreases at an increasing rate. **C** Y decreases at a decreasing rate. **D** Y increases at an increasing rate.

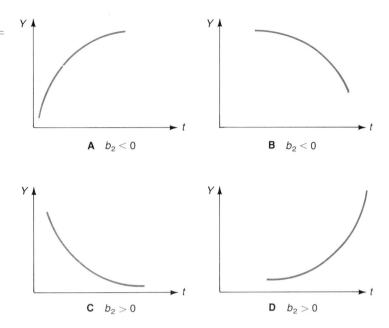

Seasonality (S)

Seasonal variation, or **seasonality,** refers to periodic increases or decreases in a time series that occur *within a calendar year.* They are very predictable because they occur every year. When a time series consists of annual data (as in Figure 16.1), you cannot see what is going on within each year. Data reported in annual increments therefore cannot be used to examine seasonality. Seasonality may or may not exist; the data are not in a form that will show whether it does.

When time series data are quarterly or monthly, seasonal variation may be evident. For example, if the power-consumption data were available for each month over these 10 years, then the resulting time series would contain $12 \cdot 10 = 120$ observations. A plot of monthly data for the last 3 years (36 observations) is shown in Figure 16.5. The seasonal effects here consist of

Extremely high power consumption during the hot summer months (July and August)

Very high consumption during the coldest part of the winter (December and January)

Gradually declining consumption during the spring, reaching a low level in April and then increasing until July

Gradually declining power consumption during the fall, but beginning to increase in November

The key is that these movements in the time series *follow the same pattern each year,* and so probably are due to seasonality. An analysis of seasonal variation is often a crucial step in planning sales and production. Just because your sales drop from one month to the next does not necessarily mean that it is time to panic. If a review of the past observations indicates that sales *always* drop between these 2 months, then quite likely there is no cause for concern. On the production side, if sales always are extremely high in December, then you will need to increase production in the months prior to

Figure 16.5

Illustration of seasonal variation. These are monthly observations; compare with annual data in Figure 16.1.

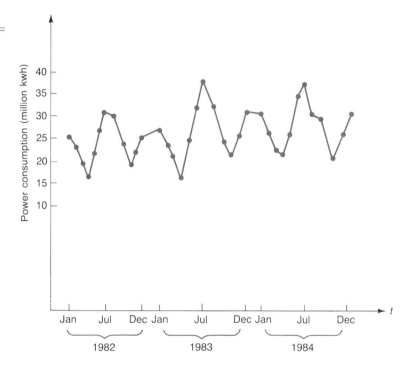

December so that you will have the necessary inventory level for this peak month. Measurement of this seasonal component will be discussed later.

As mentioned earlier, a time series often contains the effect of trend *and* seasonality (as well as cyclical and irregular activity). The sales of Wildcat sailboats, illustrated in Figure 16.6, contains a strong linear trend as well as definite seasonal variation. In particular, the highest sales occur in the summer months of each year.

Figure 16.6

A time series containing trend and seasonal variation.

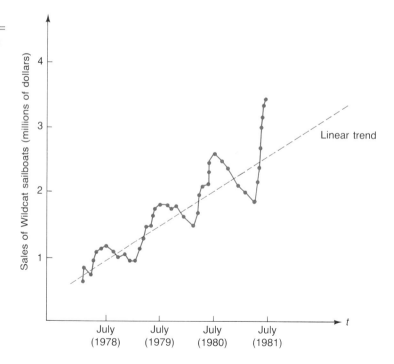

Figure 16.7

The cycle can be measured from P_1 to P_2, from V_1 to V_2, or from Z_1 to Z_2.

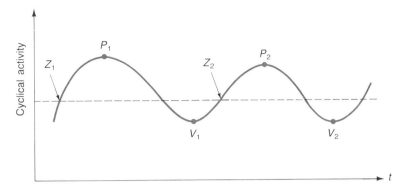

As manager of Wildcat Enterprises, would you be concerned that the sales of these boats in December 1981 were lower than those in July 1981? There may or may not be a problem; due to seasonal effects, this pattern exists in Figure 16.6 despite an overall growth. More data would be required to determine whether the December sales were lower than expected for that month. What would you think if sales in July 1982 were lower than those in July 1981? This should definitely concern you. This is a year-to-year comparison, and seasonal variation or not, we would expect the sales for July 1982 to be *larger* than for July 1981 if the long-term growth trend in Figure 16.6 is still present. Lower sales in July 1982 would indicate a possible leveling off, or a drop, in boat sales in 1982.

Cyclical Variation (*C*)

Cyclical variation describes a gradual cyclical movement about the trend; it is generally attributable to business and economic conditions. The length of a cycle is the **period** of that cycle. The period of a cycle can be measured from one **peak** to the next, one **trough** (valley) to the next, or from the time value at which the cycle crosses the horizontal line where no cyclic activity exists to the value where it completes the cycle and returns to this point. Figure 16.7, shows that the cycle length can be measured from P_1 to P_2, from V_1 to V_2, or from Z_1 to Z_2. In the illustrations to follow, we will use the Z_1 to Z_2 approach.

In business applications, cycles typically are long-term movements, with a period ranging from two to ten years. The primary difference between the cyclical and seasonal factors is the period length. Seasonal effects take place *within* one year, whereas the period for cyclical activity is *more than* one year.

Cyclical activity need not follow a definite, recurrent pattern. The cycles generally represent conditions within the economy, where a peak occurs at the height of an expansion (prosperity) period. This is generally followed by a period of contraction in economic activity. The low point (trough) of each cycle usually takes place at the low point of an economic recession or depression. This low point is then followed by a gradual increase during the recovery period.

Example 16.2

The annual corporate taxes paid by Lindale (a clothing manufacturer) over a 25-year period are shown in Figure 16.8. How many cycles do you observe?

Solution The year 1962 began a cycle lasting approximately eight years. There are three cycles contained within the time series, ending in the midst of an "up cycle." Notice that the cycle lengths are not the same. ●

Figure 16.8

Annual taxes paid by Lindale (illustration of cyclical activity; example 16.2).

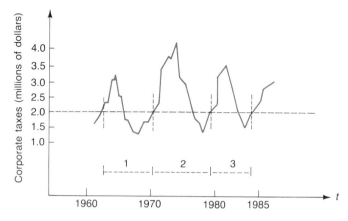

Irregular Activity (*I*)

Irregular activity consists of what is "left over" after accounting for the effect of any trend, seasonality, or cycl ical activity. These values should consist of "noise," much like the error term in the linear regression models discussed in the previous chapters. The irregular activity should contain no observable, or predictable, pattern. An extremely large irregular component can be caused by a measurement error in the variable. Such an outlier should always be checked to ensure its accuracy.

The irregular component will (1) measure the random movement in your time series, and (2) represent the effect introduced by unpredictable rare events, such as earthquakes, oil embargoes, or strikes.

If a noticeable "jump" in the resulting irregular components (when plotted across time) can be attributed to a particular rare event, you may wish to eliminate such data from the time series. You can then examine the remaining data to measure more accurately the other time series components.

Combining the Components

The time series components can be combined in various ways to describe the behavior of a particular time series. One method is to describe the time series variable, y_t, as a *sum* of these four components

$$y_t = TR_t + S_t + C_t + I_t$$

This is called the **additive structure.** The implication here is that any seasonal effects are additive from one year to the next. For example, if the seasonal effect of December for a time series representing sales is an increase of 250 units over the average yearly sales, then this same increase will occur each year *regardless* of the sales volume. Whether the average yearly sales are 1000 units or 10,000 units, December should show a sales volume of approximately 1250 (the first case) or 10,250 (the latter case).

Better success has been achieved by describing a time series using the **multiplicative structure,** where

$$y_t = TR_t \cdot S_t \cdot C_t \cdot I_t$$

Here, the seasonal effect increases or decreases according to the underlying trend and cyclical effect. Using the previous illustration, the difference between the December sales and the yearly average will be *higher* for the latter case where the yearly average is 10,000 units. For example, for the first case, the December sales might be 1250 (a 25% increase over the yearly average) and, for the latter situation, 12,500 (also a 25% increase). This follows from the implication in the multiplicative structure that, as the sales increase from one year to the next, the changes in volume due to seasonality also increase. For our illustration, this shift was 250 units for the first case and 2500 units for the second case.

Exercises

16.1 The management of a pharmaceutical firm would like to predict the effects of a technological breakthrough in an antiulcer drug in order to plan for company growth and capital expenditure. Would a time series analysis be appropriate? Why or why not?

16.2 Describe in words the trends for the quarterly sales figures (in thousands of dollars) of the companies A, B and C. Graph the data over time.

Year	Quarter	Company A	Company B	Company C
1983	1	13.1	8.3	5.1
	2	10.2	7.3	7.1
	3	11.1	8.0	6.4
	4	16.5	7.3	5.3
1984	1	14.1	7.1	5.4
	2	11.3	6.4	7.2
	3	12.5	7.0	6.3
	4	17.8	6.4	5.1
1985	1	15.1	6.2	5.0
	2	12.2	5.3	7.0
	3	13.4	6.0	6.1
	4	18.3	5.2	5.3

16.3 Construction in the housing industry usually appears to peak in the middle of the summer and to bottom out around January. If the number of new housing starts are the same for the month of March and the month of July in a particular year, of what concern would these figures be to housing construction companies? Would they be pleased, worried, or indifferent? Why?

16.4 The end-of-year inventory levels, in dollars, of West Coast Distributing are given in the following table. Estimate the period of the cyclical component by graphing the data.

Year	Inventory
1973	80
1974	75
1975	71
1976	73
1977	82
1978	76
1979	78
1980	80
1981	83
1982	80
1983	77
1984	79
1985	84

16.5 To which of the four components of a time series would each of the following influences on housing starts contribute?

a. Presidential election year.

b. Start of the school year in September.

c. Long-term growth of the housing industry.

d. Shortage of lumber because of a strike.

16.6 Describe in words both the trend and the seasonal components for the following sales (in thousands of dollars): (Hint: draw a graph for each.)

Month	1984	1985
January	1.2	2.2
February	1.4	2.4
March	1.3	2.3
April	1.5	2.4
May	1.5	2.5
June	2.3	3.5
July	2.9	3.8
August	3.2	4.0
September	2.5	3.5
October	2.4	3.0
November	2.3	2.8
December	2.1	2.5

16.2

Measuring Trend: No Seasonality

Suppose that you have a time series containing trend and cyclical activity but no seasonality. For example, the employment data in Figure 16.2 are annual, and so contain no seasonality. The same is true for the annual power-consumption data in Figure 16.1. When data are collected on a yearly basis, we are not concerned with any seasonality in the data; we need data from quarterly or shorter intervals to identify any seasonality. Yearly data may have trend (TR), cyclical activity (C), or irregular activity (I).

If we observe a strong linear trend (as in Figure 16.2) or a quadratic trend (Figure 16.4), we can estimate it using the least squares technique developed in Chapters 14 and 15. We use simple linear regression for linear trends and multiple linear regression for quadratic trends.

Linear Trend

We begin by **coding** the time variable to make the calculations (or computer input) easier.

In Figure 16.2, we can find an equation for the trend line passing through the eight observations in the time series. The least squares trend line through these eight values is sketched in Figure 16.9. The equation of the trend line is

$$\hat{y}_t = TR_t = b_0 + b_1 t$$

where t represents the time variable. For this equation, TR_t represents the trend component of the sample observation at time period t, and is simply a new name for the trend effect that this equation allows us to estimate.

We could use $t = 1977, 1978, \ldots$ to represent time, but a much simpler method is to *code* the data, as illustrated in Figure 16.9. By using $t = 1, 2, \ldots$ the estimate,

Figure 16.9

Least squares trend line using coded time data (compare with Figure 16.2). $\hat{y}_t = b_0 + b_1 t$.

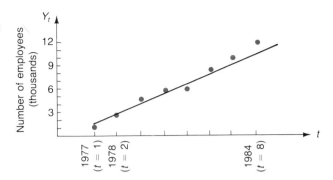

$\hat{y}_t$, is not affected and the calculations are easier. You are able to code the predictor variable, t, because the sample values are equally spaced—they are 1 year apart. As we saw in Chapter 14, this is not the case in all simple regression applications. Continuing the scheme in Figure 16.9, $t = 9$ would represent the year 1985 and the estimated number of employees for 1985 (using trend only) would be

$$\hat{y}_9 = b_0 + b_1(9)$$

To derive the "best" line through the time series data, we use the least squares estimates discussed in Chapter 14; the independent variable here is time, t. The data are

t	Y_t
1	1.1 ($= y_1$)
2	2.4 ($= y_2$)
3	4.6
4	5.4
5	5.9
6	8.0
7	9.7
8	11.2

The calculations are

$$\Sigma t = 1 + 2 + \ldots + 8 = 36$$
$$\Sigma t^2 = 1 + 4 + \ldots + 64 = 204$$
$$\Sigma y_t = 1.1 + 2.4 + \ldots + 11.2 = 48.3$$
$$\Sigma y_t^2 = (1.1)^2 + (2.4)^2 + \ldots + (11.2)^2 = 375.63$$
$$\Sigma t y_t = (1)(1.1) + (2)(2.4) + \ldots + (8)(11.2) = 276.3$$

In Chapter 14, when we regressed the variable Y on a single variable X, the estimate for the slope of the least squares line (from equation 14-11) was given by

$$b_1 = \frac{SS_{XY}}{SS_X}$$
$$= \frac{\Sigma xy - (\Sigma x)(\Sigma y)/n}{\Sigma x^2 - (\Sigma x)^2/n}$$

where n was the number of sample observations. To determine a linear trend line for a time series, this equation becomes

$$b_1 = \frac{\Sigma t y_t - (\Sigma t)(\Sigma y_t)/T}{\Sigma t^2 - (\Sigma t)^2/T} \qquad (16\text{-}1)$$

where T = the number of observations in the time series.
The sample estimate of the intercept will be

$$b_0 = \bar{y} - b_1\bar{x} = \bar{y}_t - b_1\bar{t} \qquad (16\text{-}2)$$

where $\bar{y}_t = (y_1 + y_2 + \ldots + y_t)/T$.

Because the time variable, t, *always* is 1, 2, ..., T, there is an easier way to calculate Σt, Σt^2 and $\bar{t}$.

$$\Sigma t = 1 + 2 + \ldots + T$$
$$= \frac{T(T + 1)}{2} \qquad (16\text{-}3)$$

$$\Sigma t^2 = 1 + 4 + \ldots + T^2$$
$$= \frac{T(T + 1)(2T + 1)}{6} \qquad (16\text{-}4)$$

$$\bar{t} = \frac{\Sigma t}{T} = \frac{T + 1}{2} \qquad (16\text{-}5)$$

We will use these equations to derive the least squares line in Figure 16.9. Using equations 16-3 and 16-4,

$$\Sigma t = \frac{T(T + 1)}{2} = \frac{(8)(9)}{2} = 36$$

and

$$\Sigma t^2 = \frac{T(T + 1)(2T + 1)}{6} = \frac{(8)(9)(17)}{6} = 204$$

Also,

$$\bar{t} = \frac{\Sigma t}{T} = \frac{36}{8} = 4.5$$

which can also be found using equation 16-5,

$$\bar{t} = \frac{T + 1}{2} = \frac{9}{2} = 4.5$$

So we can now calculate

$$b_1 = \frac{\Sigma t y_t - (\Sigma t)(\Sigma y_t)/T}{\Sigma t^2 - (\Sigma t)^2/T}$$

$$= \frac{276.3 - (36)(48.3)/8}{204 - (36)^2/8}$$

$$= \frac{58.95}{42} = 1.4036$$

and

$$b_0 = \bar{y}_t - b_1\bar{t}$$

$$= \frac{48.3}{8} - (1.4036)(4.5)$$

$$= 6.0375 - 6.3162 = -.279$$

The trend line for this time series is

$$\hat{y}_t = -.279 + 1.404t$$

We conclude that the number of employees appears to increase at the rate of 1404 per year, on the average.

The trend line is derived using the same least squares procedure as discussed in Chapter 14—you can use the computer instructions contained in the simple linear regression illustrations. A computer solution (using MINITAB) is shown in Figure 16.10. It produces the same results we obtained.

Figure 16.10 contains the t statistic; you may be tempted to use it to determine whether time is a significant predictor of Y = number of employees. However, to use this statistic, you must assume that the errors about the trend line are completely *independent* of one another and contain *no observable pattern*. Do not forget that there may well be considerable cyclical activity about the trend line, and this will be contained in the residuals of the regression analysis. This means that there probably will be a cyclical pattern to these residuals, so the assumption of complete independence is not met. This implies that the errors are *autocorrelated* and any test of hypothesis is invalid.

Figure 16.10

MINITAB solution of least squares trend line.

```
MTB > SET INTO C1
DATA> 1:8 ──────────┐ This command generates
DATA> END            │ integers 1 through 8
MTB > SET INTO C2
DATA> 1.1 2.4 4.6 5.4 5.9 8.0 9.7 11.2
DATA> END
MTB > REGRESS Y IN C2 USING 1 PREDICTOR IN C1;
SUBC> DW.

┌─────────────────────────────┐
│ The regression equation is  │
│ C2 = - 0.279 + 1.40 C1      │
└─────────────────────────────┘

Predictor      Coef        Stdev      t-ratio
Constant     -0.2786      0.3596       -0.77
C1            1.40357     0.07122      19.71


s = 0.4616      R-sq = 98.5%      R-sq(adj) = 98.2%

Analysis of Variance

SOURCE       DF          SS          MS
Regression    1       82.741      82.741
Error         6        1.278       0.213
Total         7       84.019


Durbin-Watson statistic = 1.88
```

This poses no serious problems at this point, however, because our intent is simply to describe the time series by measuring the various components, and not to perform a statistical test of hypothesis. If, however, the residuals about the trend line appear to be extremely large, then this suggests that a *linear* trend component is not appropriate.

Quadratic Trend

The nature of a quadratic trend is illustrated in Figure 16.4. This type of trend is common for a time series that increases or decreases rapidly and then gradually levels off over the observed values. We discussed a similar situation in Chapter 15, where a quadratic model of the form

$$\hat{Y} = b_0 + b_1X + b_2X^2$$

was used to capture a curvilinear relationship between two variables. We use exactly the same technique to describe a quadratic trend; now X is replaced by time, t.

The power-consumption time series in Figure 16.1 indicates that, as time increases, the amount of power consumption (y_t) also increases, but at a decreasing rate. More specifically, the increase for 1980 to 1981 $= 18$; for 1981 to 1982 $= 12$ $(12 < 18)$; for 1982 to 1983 $= 8$ $(8 < 12)$; and for 1983 to 1984 $= 5$ $(5 < 8)$.

When you observe a series where the *changes* from one year to the next are not (approximately) constant but seem to be either increasing or decreasing with time, this indicates a quadratic trend.

The equation of this curvilinear (quadratic) trend is

$$\hat{y}_t = b_0 + b_1t + b_2t^2$$

To derive the least squares estimates b_0, b_1, and b_2, we use the multiple linear regression procedure of Chapter 15.

What would be the input to a computer program (such as MINITAB, SAS or SPSSX) for the power-consumption data? For the regression program, you have two predictor variables, $X_1 = t$ and $X_2 = t^2$. The resulting data configuration is

y_t	t	t^2
95	1	1 (for 1975)
145	2	4 (for 1976)
174	3	9 (for 1977)
200	4	16 (and so on)
224	5	25
245	6	36
263	7	49
275	8	64
283	9	81
288	10	100

(Note that here the time series data (y_t) are put in the first column of the input data. This placement is arbitrary.)

The solution for these data (shown in Figure 16.11) is

$$\hat{y}_t = 58.6 + 44.048t - 2.1212t^2$$

To illustrate this equation, for the second time period the actual value is $y_2 = 145$ and the predicted value is

$$\hat{y}_2 = 58.6 + 44.048(2) - 2.1212(2)^2$$
$$= 138.21$$

Figure 16.11

MINITAB solution for
quadratic trend (power-
consumption data).

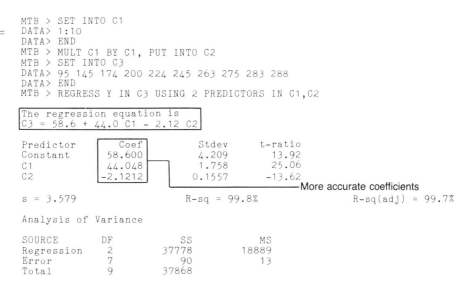

```
MTB > SET INTO C1
DATA> 1:10
DATA> END
MTB > MULT C1 BY C1, PUT INTO C2
MTB > SET INTO C3
DATA> 95 145 174 200 224 245 263 275 283 288
DATA> END
MTB > REGRESS Y IN C3 USING 2 PREDICTORS IN C1,C2
```

The regression equation is
C3 = 58.6 + 44.0 C1 - 2.12 C2

Predictor	Coef	Stdev	t-ratio
Constant	58.600	4.209	13.92
C1	44.048	1.758	25.06
C2	-2.1212	0.1557	-13.62

———More accurate coefficients

s = 3.579   R-sq = 99.8%   R-sq(adj) = 99.7%

Analysis of Variance

SOURCE	DF	SS	MS
Regression	2	37778	18889
Error	7	90	13
Total	9	37868	

A First Look at Forecasting: Extending the Trend

Whenever a time series contains very little seasonality (such as *annual* data, which have *no* seasonality) and a strong trend, an easy method of providing future forecasts is to project the observed growth pattern, as measured by the trend equation, into the future. For example, if a city's tax revenues have increased steadily by approximately $15,000 per year over the past 10 years, it seems reasonable to expect that this pattern will continue, at least for a short time. (Of course, assuming that such a growth will continue indefinitely is a hazardous gamble at best!)

The process of extending a trend equation is called **forecasting** or **extrapolation.** The following examples will illustrate that extending a straight line trend equation can provide useful estimates of future values. A quadratic trend equation is, however, useful only *within* the range of the sample data; that is, for **interpolation.**

This method of forecasting is but one of many possible ways of predicting the future time series values by capturing patterns present in the past observations. Chapter 17 will examine other methods of using the past observations to forecast future values.

Example 16.3

Using the trend line from Figure 16.9, estimate the number of employees in 1985.

Solution $t = 9$ corresponds to the year 1985, so your *forecast* for this year will be

$$\hat{y}_9 = -.279 + 1.404(9)$$
$$= 12.357$$

that is, 12,357 employees. ●

As mentioned earlier, your basic assumption when using the trend line to determine a forecast is that this same pattern *will continue* into the future. This may or may not be true. Very often a time series will increase at a more-or-less constant rate and then begin to level off. One example would be the sales of an innovative product. Such a time series will grow from one year to the next as people think that they just have to have this product, but eventually you reach a saturation point, and the sales grow at a much smaller rate. If the historical data used to determine the trend line are collected during the growth stage, then you will stop short of and miss the "slowing down" of the time series and severely *overestimate* the sales. This is not a flaw in the technique; any time series model makes predictions by capturing the pattern(s) in the past observations and extending this pattern beyond the last year of the data. It does, however, place a great deal of responsibility on the person who uses the data to predict beyond the data range. If you do not know what underlying factors are driving the trend, serious errors can result.

Very often, a nonlinear growth rate can be described accurately by including a quadratic term in the trend equation. However, using such an equation to forecast *future* values is not a reliable procedure, as the following section will demonstrate.

Example 16.4

Using the trend equation from Figure 16.11

$$\hat{y}_t = TR_t = 58.6 + 44.048t - 2.1212t^2$$

what is your forecast for the power consumption during 1985? During 1986? Use only the trend equation.

Solution 1985 corresponds to $t = 11$ (the last year of your data is $t = 10$ for 1984). Your forecast for 1985 is

$$\hat{y}_{11} = 58.6 + 44.048(11) - 2.1212(11)^2$$
$$= 286.46$$

That is, 2,864,600 kwh. For 1986, your forecast is

$$\hat{y}_{12} = 58.6 + 44.048(12) - 2.1212(12)^2$$
$$= 281.72$$ ●

The sermon we delivered about projecting a trend line beyond the range of the data applies to a quadratic trend as well: by forecasting with such an equation, you assume that this quadratic (curved) pattern observed in the time series observations will continue.

In addition, there is another danger when forecasting with a quadratic trend equation. Every such equation looks like

In other words, the curve reaches a peak (or trough) and then reverses. The problem is that you really do not know what your equation will do outside the range of your data.

The forecasts for power consumption (example 16.4) for 1985 and 1986 provide a good illustration of this problem. Notice that the predicted value for 1985 is less than the actual value for 1984, despite a steadily increasing pattern in the time series data. Even worse, the 1986 estimate is less than that for 1985. These values imply that the trend equation is decreasing during the years after 1984. This simply means that the trend equation forecasts appear to be poor estimates—we have no reason to suspect a downturn in the amount of power consumption for these future years. The trend is appropriately described by the quadratic curve, but only within the range of the data. Beyond this range, the curve turns down. Because we have no reason to believe that the demand for electrical power will decrease, the quadratic equation is no longer appropriate.

To describe the trend *within* the years of your time series data, the quadratic trend equation may work well. However, remember that, as a forecasting procedure, it is very dangerous; do not use it for this purpose.

This section has demonstrated how you can derive linear or quadratic trend equations by using linear regression techniques. Extending such a trend equation into the future is a method of statistical forecasting, a subject that will be discussed at length in Chapter 17.

Exercises

16.7 A company that supplies quotation machines to stockbroker firms has had increased sales volume every year for the past 10 years. Given in thousands of dollars, the sales figures are:

Year	Sales
1975	60
1976	80
1977	110
1978	130
1979	160
1980	170
1981	190
1982	230
1983	240
1984	270

a. Using the simple regression formula, find the least squares line to describe sales from time, t, where t is equal to 1975, 1976, . . . , 1984.

b. Do the calculations in question a with $t = 1, 2, \ldots , 10$.

c. Compare the prediction equations given in questions a and b. Do these two equations give the same predicted values?

16.8 The community of Farlington has seen its population grow dramatically over the past 8 years. Data on the community's population is given in the following table. Units are in thousands.

Year	Population
1978	3.1
1979	6.3
1980	10.1
1981	17.3
1982	22.4
1983	33.5
1984	49.3
1985	52.1

a. Is the time series increasing at an increasing rate?

b. Using a computerized statistical package, find the multiple regression equation to predict the population such that a quadratic curvature is taken into account. Do you think this community can continue to grow at this rate?

16.9 Explain why a prediction equation with a quadratic trend may be dangerous to use in forecasting even though a quadratic trend fits the historic data very well?

16.10 The amount of money deposited into savings accounts at a local bank has grown steadily over the years, as the following data indicate (Money = in savings accounts at the end of the year times $100,000):

Year	Money
1978	2.1
1979	4.2
1980	6.4
1981	8.5
1982	10.3
1983	13.3
1984	14.9
1985	16.7

a. Does it appear that a quadratic trend exists in the data?

b. Calculate the equation you would use to describe the trend.

16.11 An insurance company would like to find the trend line for the amount of insurance sold annually (in millions of dollars) across time. The variable time is represented by t and is equal to 1, 2, . . . , 8 for the past 8 years. The following statistics were collected:

$$\Sigma ty_t = 394.5$$
$$\Sigma y_t = 29.4$$

Find the trend line for these time series data.

16.12 Due to rising competition from overseas, an electronics firm has been losing its share of the market. The following data show the percent of the market that the firm has captured for the past 7 years.

Year	Share of market
1978	4.7
1979	4.3
1980	3.9
1981	3.8
1982	3.6
1983	3.0
1984	2.9

a. Does the trend appear to be linear?

b. Find the equation to estimate the trend for the time series data.

c. What would be your estimate of the electronics firm's share of the market in 1985?

16.13 Luz Chemicals, which manufactures a special-purpose baking soda, is interested in estimating the equation of the trend line for their monthly sales data (in tons) for the year 1985:

Month		Month	Baking Soda Sales
Jan	28	Jul	34
Feb	33	Aug	34
Mar	39	Sep	35
Apr	33	Oct	36
May	38	Nov	31
Jun	31	Dec	37

a. Without considering the seasonality present in the monthly sales, estimate the trend line equation.

b. Using the equation obtained in question a, estimate the sales (in tons) for the month of February 1986.

16.14 Refer to exercise 16.13.

a. Estimate the trend line equation assuming that a quadratic trend is present. Use a computerized statistical package.

b. Using the equation obtained in question a, estimate the sales (in tons) for the month of February, 1986.

c. What are the differences in the estimate obtained from questions b of this problem and of exercise 16.13? Is one method preferable to the other? Why? What are the assumptions made in each case about the baking soda sales of Luz Chemicals?

16.15 The GNP (gross national product) is an important statistic in measuring the economic growth of a country. The GNP is the value of all goods and services sold on the market during a particular time interval. The nominal GNP of the United States for the years 1970 through 1984 is:*

Year	Nominal GNP
1970	992.7
1971	1077.6
1972	1185.9
1973	1326.4
1974	1434.2
1975	1549.2
1976	1718.0
1977	1918.3
1978	2163.9
1979	2417.8
1980	2631.8
1981	2957.8
1982	3069.3
1983	3304.8
1984	3662.8

a. Estimate the trend line equation for the data assuming that a linear trend is present.

b. Estimate the trend line equation for the data assuming that a quadratic trend is present. Use a computerized statistical package.

c. Using the equations obtained in questions a and b, estimate the nominal GNP for the year 1985.

d. Look up the actual GNP values for 1985 in a reference book. How good were the estimates? What might account for the differences?

16.16 There is a variety of indexes of stock prices currently available. The Dow Jones industrial average (DJIA) probably is the most widely quoted and used stock price measure. The DJIA is an unweighted arithmetic average of the prices of 30 blue-chip stocks. The DJIA (high) for the years 1955 through 1984 is:†

Year	DJIA	Year	DJIA	Year	DJIA	Year	DJIA
1955	488.40	1963	767.20	1971	950.80	1979	897.60
1956	521.10	1964	891.70	1972	1036.30	1980	1000.20
1957	520.80	1965	969.30	1973	1051.70	1981	1024.10
1958	583.70	1966	995.20	1974	891.70	1982	1070.50
1959	679.40	1967	943.10	1975	879.00	1983	1287.20
1960	685.40	1968	985.20	1976	1015.00	1984	1206.10
1961	734.90	1969	968.90	1977	999.00		
1962	726.00	1970	842.00	1978	907.70		

*Source: *Statistical Abstract of the United States 1985,* 105th ed., U.S. Department of Commerce, Bureau of the Census, p. 431.

†Source: Standard & Poor's Statistical Service, *Security Price Index Record,* 1984, p. 197.

a. Estimate the trend line equation for the data assuming that a linear trend is present.

b. Assuming that a quadratic trend is present, estimate the trend. Use a computerized statistical package.

c. Use the equation found in question b to estimate the DJIA (high) for 1984. Compare the actual DJIA figure for 1984 with the estimate. Comment on the difference.

16.3

Measuring Cyclical Activity: No Seasonality

Practically every time series in a business setting contains a certain amount of cyclical activity. This is a gradual movement about the trend. It is generally due to economic or other long-term conditions. The overall U.S. economy tends to fluctuate through "good times" and "bad times," producing (rather unpredictable) upward and downward variation about the long-term growth or decline in a time series.

One way of describing the cyclical activity component is to represent it as a fraction of the trend. This procedure provides accurate measures of the cyclical activity provided the time series contains *little irregular activity*. Assuming that each time series observation is the *product* of its components, then

$$y_t = TR_t \cdot C_t \cdot I_t$$

because we are dealing with data containing no seasonality.

If we represent a small irregular activity component as i_t (rather than I_t), then a time series containing little irregular variation (noise) can be written as

$$y_t = TR_t \cdot C_t \cdot i_t$$

The cyclical components are then obtained by dividing each observation, y_t, by its corresponding estimate using trend only, $\hat{y}_t$.

$$\text{ratio of data to trend} = \frac{y_t}{\hat{y}_t}$$

$$= \frac{\cancel{TR_t} \cdot C_t \cdot i_t}{\cancel{TR_t}} = C_t \cdot i_t$$

where y_t = actual time series observation at time period t, and $\hat{y}_t = TR_t$ = the estimate of y_t using trend only.

Notice that the resulting ratios still contain some irregular activity. A method of reducing the irregular activity within these values will be illustrated later.

An estimate of the cyclical components can be obtained by ignoring the irregular activity components in these ratios and defining

$$C_t \cong \frac{y_t}{\hat{y}_t} \tag{16-6}$$

Assuming that we are dealing with data containing no seasonality (such as annual data), equation 16-6 provides a convenient method of determining the cycles present in the data. If $C_t > 1$, the actual y_t is larger than that predicted by trend alone. Consequently, this value is somewhere in a cycle *above* the trend line. A similar argument indicates a cycle below the trend line whenever $C_t < 1$ (Figure 16.12).

Figure 16.12

A complete cycle within a time series.

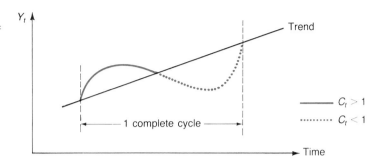

Example 16.5

For the data in Figure 16.9, we determined a least squares trend line for the number of employees (y_t) over an eight-year period at Video-Comp. We observed a linear trend with the corresponding equation

$$\hat{y}_t = -.279 + 1.404t$$

where $t = 1$ represents 1977, $t = 2$ is for 1978, and so on. Determine and graph the cyclical activity over this period.

Solution We can obtain Table 16.1 based on the preceding trend line. Here $\hat{y}_1 = -.279 + 1.404(1) = 1.125$, $\hat{y}_2 = -.279 + 1.404(2) = 2.529$, and so on.

To examine the cyclical activity, you can describe each component as a percentage of the trend. For example, in Table 16.1, during the first time period, the actual number of employees is 97.7% of the trend value: C_1 is .977. An illustration of the trend and cyclical activity is shown in Figure 16.13. The cycles fluctuate about the trend line. Between the years $t = 2$ (1978) and $t = 3$ (1979), $y_t = \hat{y}_t$ and a cycle begins. This cycle is completed somewhere between $t = 6$ (1982) and $t = 7$ (1983), where once again, $y_t = \hat{y}_t$. As discussed earlier, you can also measure cycles from peak to peak, or from trough to trough.

A summary of the cyclical variation (components) over the eight years is contained in Table 16.1 and Figure 16.14. The four-year cycle we described is more evident in this graph. The graph clearly indicates the beginning of the cycle, where $C_t = 1$. The cycle's peak occurs at the beginning of $t = 3$ (1979), the trough is at the beginning of $t = 5$ (1981), and the cycle is finally complete when C_t is again equal to 1, toward the end of 1982. ●

Table 16.1

Trend and cyclical activity (example 16.5)

t	y_t	$\hat{y}_t$	$C_t \cong y_t/\hat{y}_t$
1	1.1	1.125	.977
2	2.4	2.529	.949
3	4.6	3.933	1.169
4	5.4	5.337	1.012
5	5.9	6.741	.875
6	8.0	8.145	.982
7	9.7	9.549	1.016
8	11.2	10.953	1.022

The third column is the trend component, and the fourth column is the cyclical component as a fraction of the trend.

Figure 16.13

Cyclical activity about trend line (example 16.5).

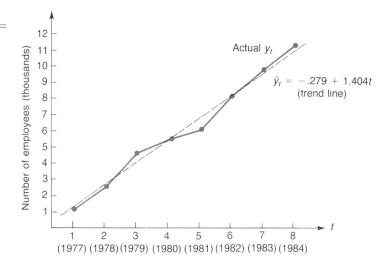

Figure 16.14

Cyclical components (example 16.5).

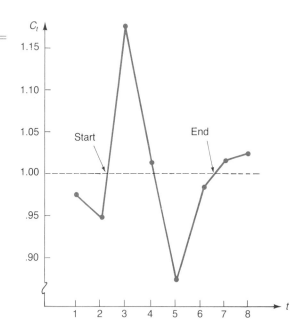

In summary, cyclical variation represents an upward or downward movement about the overall growth or decline (that is, the trend) in the time series data. Such cycles last more than one year. For annual data, these components can be estimated by dividing each observation (y_t) by its corresponding estimate using the trend equation ($\hat{y}_t$).

Exercises

16.17 Using 15 years of data, a forecaster for an oil company found a trend line for the amount of the company's yearly contracts for oil service projects. For the past 5 years, the table gives the predicted value (in thousands of dollars) of the amount of annual contracts as well as the actual amount of annual contracts. The predicted value was arrived at by using the trend line based on 15 years of past data. Find the cyclical component for each of the past 5 years. Does the period of the cycle appear to be longer than 5 years or less than 5 years? Why?

t	y_t	$\hat{y}_t$
11	52	53
12	54	59
13	57	61
14	59	60
15	62	60

16.18 Explain the relationship between the actual value y_t and the value $\hat{y}_t$, from the trend line when $C_t > 1$ and $C_t < 1$, where C_t is defined in equation 16-6.

16.19 A food-store chain has the following record over the past 9 years of yearly sales volume (in hundreds of thousands of dollars):

Year	Sales Volume
1975	7
1976	15
1977	10
1978	5
1979	11
1980	17
1981	12
1982	8
1983	17

a. Find the trend line.

b. Find the cyclical component.

c. Estimate the period of the cycle.

16.20 Residential Construction of America has been growing over the long term. Because the construction company is sensitive to cyclical variations in the economy, the level of employment for the company changes from year to year, as can be seen by the following data:

Year	Full-time Employees (in hundreds)
1973	2.4
1974	9.2
1975	11.1
1976	8.5
1977	10.5
1978	6.8
1979	5.4
1980	11.7
1981	17.3
1982	23.1
1983	28.7
1984	29.3
1985	25.2

a. Find the trend line.

b. Find the cyclical components.

c. Estimate the period of the cycle.

16.21 For the data in exercise 16.4, estimate the cyclical components.

16.22 Using the data from exercise 16.15, determine and graph the cyclical activity for the years 1970 through 1984.

16.23 The president of Techronics is concerned about changes in the wholesale price of raw materials. The president gathers the following data on the wholesale price index for raw materials (WPI):

Year	WPI
1975	105.0
1976	106.0
1977	105.0
1978	104.9
1979	105.6
1980	108.5
1981	107.7
1982	107.7
1983	106.0
1984	105.8

a. Estimate the trend line equation

b. Determine the cyclical activity, C_t, where $C_t = y_t / \hat{y}_t$.

16.24 Using the data from exercise 16.16, determine and graph the cyclical activity for the years 1955 through 1984.

16.25 Sales (in millions of dollars) of Konoco for the years 1976 through 1985 are as follows:

Year	Sales
1976	151
1977	194
1978	177
1979	157
1980	188
1981	163
1982	171
1983	199
1984	214
1985	169

Determine and graph the cyclical activity, C_t, where $C_t = y_t / \hat{y}_t$.

16.26 The capacity utilization rate (CUR, given in percent) of the U.S. manufacturing firms for the years 1970 through 1983 is:*

Year	CUR
1970	83
1971	82
1972	88
1973	92
1974	88
1975	74
1976	82
1977	85
1978	88
1979	90
1980	80
1981	81
1982	69
1983	76

Determine the cyclical component for each year.

*Source: U. S. Statistical Abstracts, 1985

16.4

Types of Seasonal Variation

Another type of variation about the trend in a time series is due to seasonality. Seasonality generally is present when the data are quarterly or monthly. It can also occur for weekly or even daily data. For example, recurrent daily effects can be expected to occur in the check-processing volume in a bank. Seasonality is any recurrent, constant source of variation caused by events at the particular time of year, rather than by any long-term influence (as in cyclical activity). For example, one would expect to sell more snowmobiles in January than in July. In a sense, the seasonal variation appears as a cycle within a year; we do not refer to this as cyclical variation, however, due to its recurrent nature.

We will discuss two types of seasonal variation: additive and multiplicative.

Additive Seasonal Variation

One encounters **additive seasonal variation** when the amount of the variation due to seasonality *does not depend on the level* y_t.

This type of seasonal variation is illustrated in Figure 16.15, which shows the sales of snowmobiles over a three-year period at The Outdoor Shop. Notice that the amount of variation for each of the winter quarters remains the same (100 units), even as the unit sales increase over the three years. For an actual application, we assume an additive effect of seasonality if these increments are of *nearly* the same magnitude over the observed time series.

Assume that the sales data for Jetski snowmobiles from sales area 1 were recorded quarterly over a five-year period. The following trend line was derived:

$$TR_t = \hat{y}_t = 100 + 20t$$

The seasonal indexes for a seasonal time series represent the incremental effect of the seasons alone, apart from any trend or cyclical activity. For the Jetski data in sales area 1, these indexes were found to be

$S_1 = +60$ (winter quarter) $S_3 = -40$ (summer quarter)

$S_2 = +30$ (spring quarter) $S_4 = -20$ (fall quarter)

Figure 16.15

Snowmobile sales at The Outdoor Shop (additive seasonal variation).

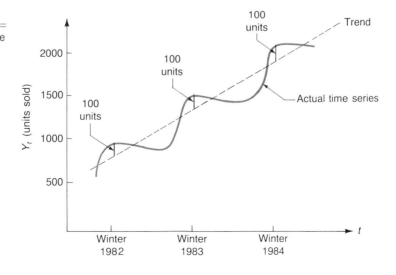

In a time series decomposition (where we actually derive these seasonal indexes), additive seasonal variation assumes that the seasonal index for, say, the winter quarter is the *same* for each year. Using the additive model, this implies that the store will sell 60 more Jetski units in the winter quarter than would be predicted by trend alone, during any year. This implies that $S_1 = S_5 = S_9 = \ldots = +60$.

To estimate y_t using only the trend and seasonality, we *add* the two corresponding components.

t (time)	$TR_t + S_t$ (sales estimate)
1 (winter, 1980)	$[100 + 20(1)] + 60 = 180$
2 (spring, 1980)	$[100 + 20(2)] + 30 = 170$
3 (summer, 1980)	$[100 + 20(3)] - 40 = 120$
4 (autumn, 1980)	$[100 + 20(4)] - 20 = 160$
5 (winter, 1981)	$[100 + 20(5)] + 60 = 260$
6 (spring, 1981)	$[100 + 20(6)] + 30 = 250$
7 (summer, 1981)	$[100 + 20(7)] - 40 = 200$
8 (autumn, 1981)	$[100 + 20(8)] - 20 = 240$
⋮	⋮

A graph of the estimated sales is shown in Figure 16.16. Notice that as the overall level of sales increases, the deviation from the trend line (due to seasonality) remains the same. If the past observations in the time series indicate that higher levels of sales produce wider seasonal fluctuations, this is an indication of multiplicative seasonal variation.

Multiplicative Seasonal Variation

Figure 16.6 showed **multiplicative seasonal variation** in the time series for the sale of Wildcat sailboats. Notice that, in each successive year, the difference between the actual value and the trend value for July is larger. In multiplicative seasonal variation, the seasonal fluctuation is *proportional* to the trend level for each observation.

Figure 16.16

Jetski sales from sales area 1 (additive seasonal variation).

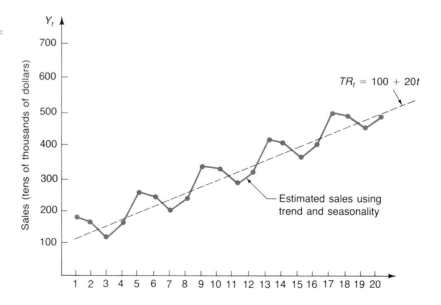

Figure 16.17

Heat-pump sales at Handy Home Center (An illustration of multiplicative seasonal variation).

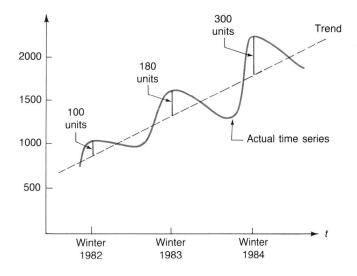

Figure 16.17 is a general illustration of multiplicative seasonality; it shows the sales of heat pumps over a 3-year period at Handy Home Center.

Considering only the effects of trend and seasonality, an estimate for a time series observation is given by

$$\text{estimate of } y_t = TR_t \cdot S_t$$

As with additive seasonal variation, the seasonal indexes, S_t, remain constant from one year to the next. When dealing with quarterly data, this means that $S_1 = S_5 = S_9 = \ldots$, $S_2 = S_6 = S_{10} = \ldots$, and so on. The next section will discuss a method for determining these indexes for the case of multiplicative seasonality.

Example 16.6

Suppose that the sales of Jetski snowmobiles from sales area 2 contain multiplicative seasonal effects with trend $= TR_t = 100 + 20t$ (as before) and seasonal indexes

$S_1 = 1.4$ (winter quarter)

$S_2 = 1.2$ (spring quarter)

$S_3 = .6$ (summer quarter)

$S_4 = .8$ (autumn quarter)

Determine the estimated sales using the trend and seasonal components.

Solution The calculations for the first two years are

t (time)	$TR_t \cdot S_t$ (estimate)
1 (winter 1980)	$[100 + 20(1)] \, 1.4 = 168$
2 (spring 1980)	$[100 + 20(2)] \, 1.2 = 168$
3 (summer 1980)	$[100 + 20(3)] \; .6 = 96$
4 (autumn 1980)	$[100 + 20(4)] \; .8 = 144$
5 (winter 1981)	$[100 + 20(5)] \, 1.4 = 280$
6 (spring 1981)	$[100 + 20(6)] \, 1.2 = 264$
7 (summer 1981)	$[100 + 20(7)] \; .6 = 144$
8 (autumn 1981)	$[100 + 20(8)] \; .8 = 208$

.
.
.

Figure 16.18

Jetski sales from sales area 2 (multiplicative seasonal variation).

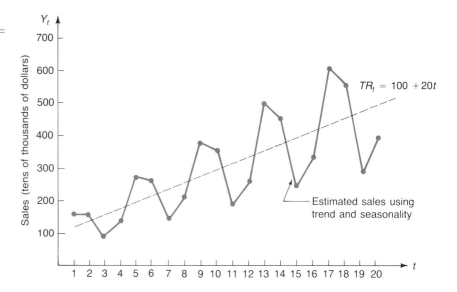

A graph of the estimated sales over a five-year period is shown in Figure 16.18. Notice that seasonal patterns do exist, but (unlike additive variation) these fluctuations increase as the sales level rises. For a time series representing sales, this type of variation seems to make sense. If the volume of sales doubles, it is reasonable to expect a larger effect due to seasonality than occurred previously.

Remember that, in practice, few time series exhibit exact additive or multiplicative seasonal effects. However, you can classify a great many time series as essentially belonging to one or the other of these two classes. ●

In the discussion to follow, we will assume that any seasonality in the time series is *multiplicative*. Most analysts (including those in the U.S. Census Bureau) have had better success describing a time series in this manner. The decomposition method to be discussed will assume that each observation is the *product* of its various components. So, the *component structure* is assumed to be

$$y_t = TR_t \cdot S_t \cdot C_t \cdot I_t \tag{16-7}$$

where the components representing seasonality, trend, cyclical variation and noise are multiplied by one another.*

Four-Step Procedure (Multiplicative Components)

Based on the multiplicative component structure in equation 16-7, the following four-step procedure can be used to decompose a time series containing the effects of all four components.

---

*Similar methods for determining the components of a time series containing additive seasonality also exist. Chapter 17 contains a small discussion of this topic. For a complete discussion of such techniques, see B.L. Bowerman and R.T. O'Connell, *Forecasting and Time Series* (North Scituate, MA: Duxbury, 1979), pp. 299–305.

Step 1 *Determine a seasonal index, S_t, for each time period.* For quarterly data, this involves determining four such indexes, S_1, S_2, S_3 and S_4. When the time series contains monthly observations, 12 seasonal indexes (S_1 through S_{12}) must be calculated, one for each month.

Step 2 *Deseasonalize the data.* This is often referred to as "adjusting for seasonality"; you eliminate the seasonal component. Because we are using a multiplicative structure, we divide each observation by its corresponding seasonal index.

So

deseasonalized observation $= d_t$

$$= y_t/S_t$$

where

$$S_t = \begin{cases} S_1, \, S_2, \, S_3, \text{ or } S_4 \text{ (quarterly data)} \\ S_1, \, S_2, \, \ldots \, , \text{ or } S_{12} \text{ (monthly data)} \end{cases}$$

Because $y_t = TR_t \cdot S_t \cdot C_t \cdot I_t$,

$$d_t = \frac{y_t}{S_t} = \frac{TR_t \cdot \cancel{S_t} \cdot C_t \cdot I_t}{\cancel{S_t}}$$

$$= TR_t \cdot C_t \cdot I_t$$

Step 3 *Determine the trend component, TR_t.* The trend is estimated by passing a least squares line through the *deseasonalized* data. The technique is identical to that discussed in section 16.2 (which assumed no seasonality), except that we use the d_t values, rather than the original time series. This will be illustrated in the next section.

Step 4 *Determine the cyclical component, C_t.* You obtain C_t by first dividing each deseasonalized observation, d_t, by the corresponding trend value from step 3. So the cyclical estimates are derived by first calculating (for each time period)

$$\frac{d_t}{\hat{d}_t} = \frac{d_t}{TR_t} = \frac{\cancel{TR_t} \cdot C_t \cdot I_t}{\cancel{TR_t}}$$

$$= C_t \cdot I_t$$

Notice that the resulting series contains cycles and irregular activity (but no trend or seasonality). A method for reducing the irregular component in these ratios will be demonstrated later. The resulting values are the cyclical components, C_t.

We will not use the cyclical components to attempt to forecast future values of the time series because their behavior (and period) generally cannot be predicted. The cyclical components can be used in forecasting if one is willing to assume a particular phase in the business cycle. If one assumes, for example, that the cycle is in the midst of an upturn, a value of C_t (such as $C_t = 1.2$) can be assigned to this particular time period. In the discussion to follow, the cyclical components will be obtained strictly as a means of *describing* the cyclical activity within a recorded time series.

Exercises

16.27 Explain the effect that seasonality has on the trend assuming additive and multiplicative seasonality. Would seasonality changes have a larger effect on an additive model or on a multiplicative model?

16.28 Riney, owner of Riney's Shoe Store, usually has a rush on shoe sales around September, when children are going back to school. Sales data (in thousands) for Riney's Shoe Store were recorded quarterly over a 4-year period (1982 to 1985). The following trend line was calculated from the data:

$$TR_t = 4 + 1.6t$$

where $t = 1,2,3, \ldots , 16$. Seasonal indexes were found to be the following:

quarter 1 $S_1 =$ 1.3
quarter 2 $S_2 = -1.4$
quarter 3 $S_3 =$ 4.2
quarter 4 $S_4 =$ 2.6

Assuming an additive model, estimate the quarterly sales y_t using only trend and seasonality for the 4 quarters of 1983.

16.29 For a 6-year period, (1979 to 1984), quarterly sales data (in thousands) were used to arrive at the following trend line and seasonal indexes:

$$TR_t = 35 + 2.3t \text{ for } t = 1,2, \ldots ,24$$
$$S_1 = -8.7$$
$$S_2 = 2.5$$
$$S_3 = 8.4$$
$$S_4 = 3.1$$

Estimate the sales figures for the 4 quarters in 1983 using an additive equation containing only the trend and seasonality components.

16.30 Advanced Digital Components has experienced rapid growth during the past several years. The quarterly data for the past 4 years give the following trend line and seasonal indexes. Sales units are in tens of thousand.

$$TR_t = 0.85 + 0.8t \text{ for } t = 1,2, \ldots ,16$$
$$S_1 = 0.82$$
$$S_2 = 1.36$$
$$S_3 = 1.20$$
$$S_4 = 0.62$$

Estimate the sales figures for the 4 quarters in the most recent year using a multiplicative equation containing only the trend and seasonality components.

16.31 Monthly data from the years 1981 through 1985 were used to find the following trend line and seasonal indexes:

$$TR_t = 1.3 + 0.5t \text{ for } t = 1,2, \ldots ,60$$

S_1	$= 0.5$	S_7	$= 2.4$
S_2	$= 0.8$	S_8	$= 3.1$
S_3	$= 0.6$	S_9	$= 0.3$
S_4	$= 1.3$	S_{10}	$= 0.2$
S_5	$= 1.1$	S_{11}	$= 0.2$
S_6	$= 1.4$	S_{12}	$= 0.1$

Assuming a multiplicative model containing only the trend and seasonality components, estimate the data for the 12 months of 1984.

16.32 Refer to exercise 16.13. Assuming that the sales of Luz Chemicals are subject to multiplicative seasonal variation, determine the deseasonalized sales for the 12 months of the year 1985. The seasonal indexes are as follows:

$S_1 = 0.8$ $S_7 = 0.9$
$S_2 = 0.8$ $S_8 = 0.9$
$S_3 = 1.2$ $S_9 = 0.7$
$S_4 = 1.2$ $S_{10} = 1.2$
$S_5 = 1.1$ $S_{11} = 0.9$
$S_6 = 1.0$ $S_{12} = 1.3$

16.33 Rework exercise 16.32 assuming that the sales are subject to additive seasonal variation. The seasonal indexes are as follows:

$S_1 = -25$
$S_2 = -50$
$S_3 = -60$
$S_4 = 25$
$S_5 = 25$
$S_6 = 28$
$S_7 = 25$
$S_8 = 25$
$S_9 = -30$
$S_{10} = -40$
$S_{11} = -40$
$S_{12} = -30$

16.34 The nominal GNP quarterly estimates (in billions of dollars) for the years 1978 to 1980 are:

Year	Quarter	Nominal GNP
1978	1	2032.4
	2	2129.6
	3	3190.5
	4	2271.9
1979	1	2340.6
	2	2374.6
	3	2444.1
	4	2496.3
1980	1	2571.7
	2	2564.8
	3	2637.3
	4	2732.3

Assuming multiplicative seasonality, calculate the deseasonalized data, given the following seasonal indexes:

$S_1 = 1.30$
$S_2 = 0.80$
$S_3 = 1.20$
$S_4 = 0.70$

16.5

Measuring Seasonality

Seasonality often is present in time series data collected over months or quarters. This effect is observed when, for example, some months are always higher than the average for the year. If, during the recorded values of the time series, July sales are 25% higher than the average for the year, the July index should be 1.25 using the multiplicative structure.

We derive a seasonal index for each period during the year (four for quarterly data, 12 for monthly data). We begin by developing a new series that contains *no seasonality*. This new series is obtained from the original time series and consists of the **centered moving averages.** This provides an excellent way of isolating the seasonal components from the original time series. In addition to containing no seasonality, the centered moving averages are *smoother* (contain less irregular activity) than the original time series. Consequently, the moving averages give you a clearer picture of any existing trend within a time series containing significant seasonality and irregular activity. Other methods of smoothing a time series will be discussed in Chapter 17.

Centered Moving Averages

To illustrate the calculation of a moving average, consider a time series containing quarterly observations, as shown in Table 16.2. Here,

$$(1) = \text{sum of } y_1 \text{ through } y_4$$

$$= 85 + 41 + 92 + 45 = 263$$

$$(2) = \text{sum of } y_2 \text{ through } y_5$$

$$= 41 + 92 + 45 + 90 = 268$$

$$(3) = \text{sum of } y_3 \text{ through } y_6$$

$$= 92 + 45 + 90 + 43 = 270$$

and so on.

Because each total contains four observations (one from each quarter), any quarterly seasonal effects have been removed. Consequently, there is no seasonality within the moving totals 263, 268, 270, and so on, in Table 16.2.

The first moving total in Table 16.2 is equal to $(y_1 + y_2 + y_3 + y_4)$. If we were to position this total in the center of these values, it would lie between $t = 2$ and $t = 3$,

Table 16.2

Time series with quarterly observations

Time	Quarter	t	y_t		Moving Totals
1981	1	1	85	(1)	263
	2	2	41	(2)	268
	3	3	92	(3)	270
	4	4	45	and so on	
1982	1	5	90		
	2	6	43		
	3	7	95		
	4	8	47		
1983	1	9	92		
	.	.	.		
	.	.	.		
	.	.	.		

at $t = 2.5$. The second moving total is equal to $(y_2 + y_3 + y_4 + y_5)$; again, we position this total in the center between $t = 3$ and $t = 4$, at $t = 3.5$.

We then add the first two moving totals. Notice that four values went into each of these totals, so that a total of *eight* values makes up this sum. The sum of first two moving totals is $263 + 268 = 531$. The average for the eight months in the first two moving totals is $531/8 = 66.38$. This is a **centered moving average**. The position of this moving average is midway between $t = 2.5$ and $t = 3.5$, at $t = 3$. We therefore conclude that 66.38 is the centered moving average corresponding to $t = 3$.

Example 16.7   Continue the procedure using Table 16.2 and determine the centered moving average for (1) $t = 4$ and (2) $t = 5$.

Solution 1 Here we obtain

$$268 = y_2 + y_3 + y_4 + y_5$$

(positioned at $t = 3.5$) and

$$270 = y_3 + y_4 + y_5 + y_6$$

(positioned at $t = 4.5$) So the average of the eight numbers making up $268 + 270 = 538$ would be positioned midway between 3.5 and 4.5, at $t = 4$. Consequently, the centered moving average for $t = 4$ is

$$\frac{268 + 270}{8} = 67.25$$

Solution 2 Proceeding as before,

$$270 = y_3 + y_4 + y_5 + y_6$$

(positioned at $t = 4.5$) and

$$273 = y_4 + y_5 + y_6 + y_7$$

(positioned at $t = 5.5$) Therefore, the centered moving average for $t = 5$ is

$$\frac{270 + 273}{8} = 67.88$$

Assume quarterly sales data at Video-Comp were recorded over a four-year period. We now want to determine the centered moving averages for these data, shown in Table 16.3. There appears to be a definite seasonal effect within this time series; the highest sales occur in the fourth quarter of each year. Table 16.4 shows the centered moving averages for these data. The first *moving total* is

Table 16.3

Sales data for Video-Comp (millions of dollars)

Year	Quarter 1	Quarter 2	Quarter 3	Quarter 4
1981	20	12	47	60
1982	40	32	65	76
1983	56	50	85	100
1984	75	70	101	123

Table 16.4

Moving averages for
Video-Comp sales data

Year	Quarter	t	y_t	Moving Total	Centered Moving Average	Ratio to Moving Average
1981	1	1	20		—	—
	2	2	12		—	—
				139		
	3	3	47		37.25	1.26
				159		
	4	4	60		42.25	1.42
				179		
1982	1	5	40		47.00	.85
				197		
	2	6	32		51.25	.62
				213		
	3	7	65		55.25	1.18
				229		
	4	8	76		59.50	1.28
				247		
1983	1	9	56		64.25	.87
				267		
	2	10	50		69.75	.72
				291		
	3	11	85		75.13	1.13
				310		
	4	12	100		80.00	1.25
				330		
1984	1	13	75		84.50	.89
				346		
	2	14	70		89.38	.78
				369		
	3	15	101		—	—
	4	16	123		—	—

$$139 = y_1 + y_2 + y_3 + y_4$$
$$= 20 + 12 + 47 + 60$$

Its actual location is $t = 2.5$; it is positioned between $t = 2$ and $t = 3$. Similarly, the next moving total is centered at $t = 3.5$, and so appears between $t = 3$ and $t = 4$ in the table. This total is

$$159 = y_2 + y_3 + y_4 + y_5$$
$$= 12 + 47 + 60 + 40$$

Each moving total is centered midway between the values making up this total. For example, the last moving total, 369, is centered between $t = 14$ and $t = 15$ at $t = 14.5$. Here,

$$369 = y_{13} + y_{14} + y_{15} + y_{16}$$
$$= 75 + 70 + 101 + 123$$

The *centered moving average* at time t is the average of the moving total immediately preceding this time value and the total immediately following it. This means that, for $t = 3$

$$37.25 = \frac{139 + 159}{8}$$

For $t = 4$

$$42.25 = \frac{159 + 179}{8}$$

and so on. Consequently, for $t = 3$, $y_3 = 47$ and the centered moving average = 37.25.

This procedure produces 12 centered moving averages; we are unable to compute this value for $t = 1$, 2, 15, or 16. Notice that first two values of t are for quarters 1 and 2, whereas the remaining two correspond to quarters 3 and 4. In general, if your time series contains T observations, you will derive $T - 4$ centered moving averages using quarterly data or $T - 12$ averages for monthly data.

The moving totals and centered moving averages are formed by summing over the four quarters (seasons), so there is no seasonality present in these values. Furthermore, the irregular component has been reduced because averages always contain less random variation (noise) than do the individual values making up these averages. Representing this reduced irregular activity component as i_t (rather than I_t), we can represent a centered moving average at time t as

centered moving average at time $t = TR_t \cdot C_t \cdot i_t$

Because of this averaging procedure, the moving averages contain much less irregular activity and so are much "smoother" than the original time series. This procedure thus is referred to as **smoothing** the time series to get a clearer picture of any existing trend, as well as of its shape (straight line or curve).

The centered moving averages in Table 16.4 show a steadily increasing trend. Because the differences between any two adjacent moving averages are nearly the same, this trend is very *linear*. This is more apparent in Figure 16.19, which contains the original data with the moving averages.

To determine the four quarterly seasonal indexes, the first step is to divide each observation, y_t, by its corresponding moving average (last column in the table).

for $t = 3$: ratio = 47/37.25 = 1.26
(belongs to quarter 3, 1981)

Figure 16.19

Smoothing a time series using moving averages (Video-Comp sales data).

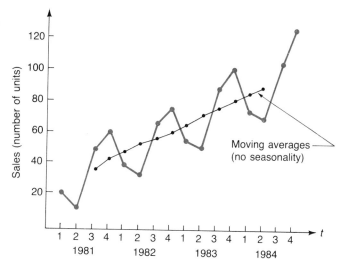

for $t = 4$: ratio $= 60/42.25 = 1.42$
(belongs to quarter 4, 1981)

.
.
.

for $t = 14$: ratio $= 70/89.39 = .78$
(belongs to quarter 2, 1984)

When we divide y_t by its corresponding centered moving average, we obtain

$$\text{ratio} = \frac{y_t}{\text{centered moving average}} = \frac{\mathcal{TR}_t \cdot S_t \cdot \mathcal{C}_t \cdot I_t}{\mathcal{TR}_t \cdot \mathcal{C}_t \cdot i_t}$$

$$= S_t \cdot I_t$$

Consequently, these ratios contain the seasonal effects, as well as the irregular activity (noise) components. The following discussion will illustrate how you can reduce the effect of the irregular activity factor by combining these ratios into a set of four seasonal indexes, one for each quarter.

Computing a Seasonal Index

The purpose of a seasonal index is to indicate how the time series value for each quarter (or month) compares with the average for the year. The following discussion will assume that we are dealing with a time series containing quarterly data. In the next section, we will illustrate this procedure using monthly data.

We begin by collecting the ratios to moving average, placing each of them in its respective quarter. In Table 16.4, we see that 1.26 belongs to quarter 3, 1.42 to quarter 4, .85 to quarter 1, and so on. Table 16.5 is the result. Notice that there are three ratios for each quarter. In general, you always will obtain (total number of years − 1) ratios under each quarter (or month). The time series in this example contains four years; therefore, it has three ratios. To obtain a "typical" ratio for each quarter, you have several options, including

1. Determine an average of these ratios.
2. Find the median of these values.
3. Eliminate the largest and smallest ratio within each quarter and compute a mean of the remaining ratios; this is called a **trimmed mean.**

We will follow the first procedure and calculate a mean ratio for each quarter, as illustrated in Table 16.5. When the time series contains five or more years of data, a

Table 16.5

Ratios for each quarter

		Quarter 1	Quarter 2	Quarter 3	Quarter 4
		—	—	1.26	1.42
		.85	.62	1.18	1.28
		.87	.72	1.13	1.25
		.89	.78	—	—
	TOTAL	2.61	2.12	3.57	3.95
	AVERAGE	.870	.707	1.190	1.317

trimmed mean offers you protection against an outlier ratio dominating the index for this quarter. Using the median ratios also helps guard against this type of situation.

A Final Adjustment The last step in computing the seasonal indexes is to make sure that the four computed ratio averages **sum to 4** (or 12, for monthly indexes). This is accomplished by (1) adding the four averages computed in the table (call this *SUM*) and (2) multiplying each average by 4/*SUM*. The modified average is the seasonal index for that quarter.

Example 16.8   Using Table 16.5, determine the four seasonal indexes.

Solution First,

$$SUM = .870 + .707 + 1.190 + 1.317$$
$$= 4.084$$

This means that we need to multiply each of the four averages in Table 16.5 by 4/4.084 = .9794.

Quarter	Seasonal Index
1	(.870)(.9794) = .852
2	(.707)(.9794) = .692
3	(1.190)(.9794) = 1.166
4	(1.317)(.9794) = 1.290
	4.0

The indexes for quarters 1 and 2 are below 1.0, so the sales during these quarters typically are below the yearly average. On the other hand, quarters 3 and 4 have seasonal indexes of 1.166 and 1.290, so the sales for these quarters are higher than the average for the year.

This procedure for determining seasonal effects works well, provided the ratios in Table 16.5 are reasonably *stable*. In example 16.8, all of the ratios for quarter 2 are small (near .7) and all of the ratios for quarter 4 are large (near 1.3). If strong seasonality is present, such will be the case.

Seasonal indexes can be updated as you obtain an additional year's observations on the variable of interest. You have the option of deleting the most distant year's observations prior to recalculating these values. This procedure leads to seasonal indexes that change slowly over the years.

In summary, to calculate the seasonal indexes

1. Derive the *moving totals* by summing the observations for four (quarterly data) or 12 (monthly data) consecutive time periods.
2. Average and center the totals by finding the *centered moving averages*.
3. Divide each observation by its corresponding centered moving average.
4. Place the ratios from step 3 in a table headed by the 4 quarters or 12 months.
5. For each column in this table, determine the mean of these ratios; these are the unadjusted seasonal indexes.
6. Make a final adjustment to guarantee that the final seasonal indexes sum to 4 (quarterly data) or 12 (monthly data); these adjusted means are the seasonal indexes.

Table 16.6

Deseasonalized sales

Year	t	y_t	Seasonal Index (S_t)	Deseasonalized Values $d_t = y_t/S_t$
1981	1	20	.852	23.47
	2	12	.692	17.34
	3	47	1.166	40.31
	4	60	1.290	46.51
1982	5	40	.852	46.95
	6	32	.692	46.24
	7	65	1.166	55.75
	8	76	1.290	58.91
1983	9	56	.852	65.73
	10	50	.692	72.25
	11	85	1.166	72.90
	12	100	1.290	77.52
1984	13	75	.852	88.03
	14	70	.692	101.16
	15	101	1.166	86.62
	16	123	1.290	95.35

Deseasonalizing the Data

To remove the seasonality from the data, we deseasonalize the time series. The resulting series contains no seasonal effects and consists of the trend, cyclical activity, and, of course, irregular activity. We write deseasonalized data as d_t.

$$d_t = \frac{y_t}{\text{corresponding seasonal index}}$$
$$= \frac{TR_t \cdot \acute{S}_t \cdot C_t \cdot I_t}{\acute{S}_t}$$
$$= TR_t \cdot C_t \cdot I_t$$

The deseasonalized sales values from Table 16.3 are contained in Table 16.6. These values contain trend, cyclical effects, and irregular activity. Notice how the trend is much more apparent in the deseasonalized values than in the original time series.

In Table 16.6, we obtained deseasonalized values for *all* 16 of the original observations, including the 2 quarters on each end. We will use the "new" deseasonalized series to determine the trend and cyclical components of the original time series. This will be illustrated in the next section, where we apply the four-step procedure by (1) computing seasonal indexes, (2) deseasonalizing the data, (3) computing the trend components from the deseasonalized time series (d_t), and finally (4) calculating the cyclical activity.

Exercises

16.35 Mid-Cities Appliance store is interested in determining an approximate inventory level in dollars to control its overhead. Quarterly inventory levels (in ten thousands) for 5 years are:

Year	Quarter 1	Quarter 2	Quarter 3	Quarter 4
1980	1	7	12	6
1981	4	11	17	9
1982	9	14	20	14
1983	12	16	24	18
1984	16	21	27	22

Find the four-quarter centered moving averages and ratios to moving average.

16.36 Several counties in Oregon and Washington depend heavily on the lumber industry. When there is little demand for lumber, the softness in the industry causes unemployment to increase. The following data represent the unemployment percentage of workers for certain counties in Oregon and Washington.

Year	Jan	Feb	Mar	Apr	May	Jun	Jul	Aug	Sep	Oct	Nov	Dec
1982	10.8	9.6	8.7	7.5	6.4	5.4	6.1	7.3	8.5	8.9	10.1	10.9
1983	9.6	8.5	7.5	6.3	5.2	4.1	5.9	6.1	7.4	8.1	9.8	9.8
1984	6.9	7.4	6.3	7.5	4.9	3.7	4.2	5.4	6.5	7.7	8.0	9.1
1985	7.0	6.7	5.7	4.2	3.3	2.8	3.4	4.0	4.4	5.3	6.7	7.4

Find the 12-month centered moving averages and ratios to moving average.

16.37 Explain why a moving average is a smoothing technique.

16.38 The following table presents the ratio to moving average figure for sales at Zano Systems, a supplier of photocopy machines. Find the seasonal indexes.

Year	Quarter 1	Quarter 2	Quarter 3	Quarter 4
1978			.88	.87
1979	1.14	1.25	.83	.86
1980	1.19	1.22	.94	.88
1981	1.23	1.35	.90	.72
1982	1.16	1.32	.94	.81
1983	1.10	1.21		

16.39 The following table presents the ratio to moving average figure for the cost of a bushel of grapefruit in a certain county in Florida. Find the seasonal indexes.

Year	Jan	Feb	Mar	Apr	May	Jun	Jul	Aug	Sep	Oct	Nov	Dec
1979							1.06	1.10	1.12	1.02	1.03	.99
1980	.90	.87	.95	.93	1.00	1.04	1.08	1.14	1.15	1.06	1.04	.97
1981	.87	.84	.81	.88	1.01	1.02	1.01	1.15	1.07	1.03	1.00	.90
1982	.81	.75	.82	.89	1.05	1.04	1.10	1.21	1.18	1.10	1.07	.97
1983	.87	.81	.77	.98	1.01	1.06						

16.40 The sale of grass sod is a seasonal business. Green Garden Supplies does most of its business in May, June, July, and August. The following table presents the monthly sales (in thousands of dollars) of Green. Find the seasonal indexes. For what month is the seasonal index the largest?

Year	Jan	Feb	Mar	Apr	May	Jun	Jul	Aug	Sep	Oct	Nov	Dec
1981	.1	.1	1.2	2.2	4.1	4.5	5.5	5.3	3.5	1.1	.2	.1
1982	.1	.2	1.4	2.0	4.0	4.2	5.3	5.0	3.2	1.0	.1	.1
1983	.1	.2	1.3	2.2	4.3	4.4	5.6	5.3	3.5	1.1	.2	.1
1984	.1	.3	1.4	2.3	4.4	4.6	5.8	5.5	3.7	1.3	.3	.1
1985	.1	.3	1.5	2.3	4.6	4.8	6.0	5.6	3.7	1.4	.4	.1

16.41 The following table represents the ratio to moving average figure for the number of people below the poverty level in a certain county. Find the seasonal indexes.

Year	Quarter 1	Quarter 2	Quarter 3	Quarter 4
1981			.84	.83
1982	1.12	1.29	.91	.89
1983	1.17	1.24	.92	.90
1984	1.15	1.30	.92	.88
1985	1.13	1.26		

16.42 Seaside University has four quarterly semesters during the school year. Enrollment for each of these quarters is as follows. Find the seasonal indexes.

Year	Quarter 1	Quarter 2	Quarter 3	Quarter 4
1980	9,385	9,020	9,350	9,060
1981	9,970	9,671	9,928	9,701
1982	10,328	9,950	10,121	9,922
1983	10,411	9,995	10,250	9,998
1984	10,535	10,240	10,506	10,279

16.43 A major department store usually has a strong fourth quarter because of the Christmas season. Earnings per share of the company are as follows. Find the seasonal indexes.

Year	Quarter 1	Quarter 2	Quarter 3	Quarter 4
1981	.75	.60	.80	1.40
1982	.80	.55	.82	1.51
1983	.83	.59	.81	1.63
1984	.84	.62	.83	1.75
1985	.84	.61	.82	1.79

16.44 The number of defaults per month of business loans at First State Bank are given below over a five year period. Find the seasonal indexes.

Year	Jan	Feb	Mar	Apr	May	Jun	Jul	Aug	Sep	Oct	Nov	Dec
1980	54	53	52	50	48	46	48	50	52	56	58	60
1981	58	54	53	50	50	45	46	49	51	55	57	62
1982	53	52	48	47	47	44	45	48	49	52	55	60
1983	58	51	50	49	45	43	44	49	50	51	58	63
1984	59	58	56	52	54	49	50	51	54	58	60	64

16.6

A Time Series Containing Seasonality, Trend, and Cycles

During the summer of 1984, the owner of an import/export company decided to investigate the past behavior of U.S. retail trade figures for the years 1980 through 1983. He collected the data in Table 16.7 using monthly figures released by the U.S. Department of Commerce. He suspected that these data would indicate high retail trade during December (due to Christmas sales) with much lower activity during January and, possibly, February. For the remaining months, he had no idea whether seasonal effects would be present or not. He also suspected there would be a steadily increasing trend, due to inflation and population growth.

We will perform a decomposition of the data in Table 16.7 and discuss the results. The four-step procedure for decomposing (a gruesome term, we'll admit) a time series into the seasonal, trend, and cyclical components was introduced in section 16.4. We will demonstrate this method of describing a time series using the monthly retail trade data.

Step 1 *Determine the seasonal indexes.* The first step is to determine the moving totals and centered moving averages for the 48 observations in Table 16.7. These calculations are summarized in Table 16.8. Notice that, for the monthly data, there is no moving average for $t = 1$ through $t = 6$ (months 1 through 6, 1980) and for $t = 43$ through $t = 48$ (months 7 through 12, 1983). The first moving total is

$$956.66 = y_1 + y_2 + \ldots + y_{12}$$

$$= 70.56 + 70.62 + \ldots + 100.76$$

Table 16.7

Total U.S. retail trade
(sales and inventories)
(in billions of dollars)

Month	1980	1981	1982	1983
Jan	70.56	76.68	77.34	81.34
Feb	70.62	73.73	76.21	78.88
Mar	76.00	83.97	86.57	93.76
Apr	75.15	85.21	87.96	93.97
May	79.20	86.90	90.81	97.84
Jun	77.37	87.31	88.96	100.61
Jul	79.86	88.25	91.21	99.56
Aug	81.74	89.05	89.64	100.23
Sep	77.58	85.52	88.16	97.97
Oct	84.00	88.78	91.42	100.66
Nov	83.82	87.33	94.20	103.86
Dec	100.76	106.07	113.19	124.99

Source: *Current Business Reports* (Vols. BR-81-12, BR-82-12, and BR-83-12), U.S. Department of Commerce, Bureau of the Census.

Table 16.8

Moving averages for
monthly retail trade

Year	Month	(1) t	(2) y_t	(3) Moving Total	(4) Centered Moving Average	(5) Ratio to Moving Average
1980	Jan	1	70.56			
	Feb	2	70.62			
	Mar	3	76.00			
	Apr	4	75.15			
	May	5	79.20			
	Jun	6	77.37			
				956.66		
	Jul	7	79.86		79.98	1.00
				962.78		
	Aug	8	81.74		80.36	1.02
				965.89		
	Sep	9	77.58		80.82	0.96
				973.86		
	Oct	10	84.00		81.57	1.03
				983.92		
	Nov	11	83.82		82.31	1.02
				991.62		
	Dec	12	100.76		83.05	1.21
				1001.56		
1981	Jan	13	76.68		83.81	0.91
				1009.95		
	Feb	14	73.73		84.47	0.87
				1017.26		
	Mar	15	83.97		85.10	0.99
				1025.20		
	Apr	16	85.21		85.63	1.00
				1029.98		
	May	17	86.90		85.98	1.01
				1033.49		
	Jun	18	87.31		86.35	1.01

Table 16.8

(continued)

				1038.80		
	Jul	19	88.25		86.59	1.02
				1039.46		
	Aug	20	89.05		86.72	1.03
				1041.94		
	Sep	21	85.52		86.94	0.98
				1044.54		
	Oct	22	88.78		87.16	1.02
				1047.29		
	Nov	23	87.33		87.44	1.00
				1051.20		
	Dec	24	106.07		87.67	1.21
				1052.85		
1982	Jan	25	77.34		87.86	0.88
				1055.81		
	Feb	26	76.21		88.01	0.87
				1056.40		
	Mar	27	86.57		88.14	0.98
				1059.04		
	Apr	28	87.96		88.36	1.00
				1061.68		
	May	29	90.81		88.76	1.02
				1068.55		
	Jun	30	88.96		89.34	1.00
				1075.67		
	Jul	31	91.21		89.81	1.02
				1079.67		
	Aug	32	89.64		90.08	1.00
				1082.34		
	Sep	33	88.16		90.49	0.97
				1089.53		
	Oct	34	91.42		91.04	1.00
				1095.54		
	Nov	35	94.20		91.59	1.03
				1102.57		
	Dec	36	113.19		92.37	1.23
				1114.22		
1983	Jan	37	81.34		93.20	0.87
				1122.57		
	Feb	38	78.88		93.99	0.84
				1133.16		
	Mar	39	93.76		94.84	0.99
				1142.97		
	Apr	40	93.97		95.63	0.98
				1152.21		
	May	41	97.84		96.42	1.01
				1161.87		
	Jun	42	100.61		97.31	1.03
				1173.67		
	Jul	43	99.56			
	Aug	44	100.23			
	Sep	45	97.97			
	Oct	46	100.66			
	Nov	47	103.86			
	Dec	48	124.99			

This value is positioned midway between $t = 1$ and $t = 12$, at $t = 6.5$. The next moving total is

$$962.78 = y_2 + y_3 + \ldots + y_{13}$$
$$= 70.62 + 76.00 + \ldots + 76.68$$

which is centered at $t = 7.5$. So the first moving *average* will be centered midway between $t = 6.5$ and $t = 7.5$, at $t = 7$. This is

$$79.98 = \frac{956.66 + 962.78}{24}$$

Notice that we divide by 24 because 24 observations went into the sum of these two moving totals.

The final moving average is

$$97.31 = \frac{1161.87 + 1173.67}{24}$$

and corresponds to $t = 42$.

Table 16.8 also contains each ratio to moving average (column 4 divided by column 2). To illustrate,

$$1.00 = 79.86/79.98$$
$$1.02 = 81.74/80.36$$

and so on. These ratios are summarized in Table 16.9, which also shows the average of the three values for each time period.

The final step is to adjust each of the averages in Table 16.9 so that they sum to 12 (because there are 12 time periods per year). Here,

$$SUM = .89 + .86 + \ldots + 1.22 = 12.01$$

and so

$$S_1 = \text{seasonal index for January}$$
$$= (.89) \cdot (12/12.01) = .89$$
$$S_2 = \text{seasonal index for February}$$
$$= (.86) \cdot (12/12.01) = .86$$

.
.
.

$$S_{12} = \text{seasonal index for December}$$
$$= (1.22) \cdot (12/12.01) = 1.22$$

The final collection of seasonal indexes follows Table 16.9.

Table 16.9

Summary of ratios

Year	Month 1	2	3	4	5	6	7	8	9	10	11	12
1							1.00	1.02	0.96	1.03	1.02	1.21
2	0.91	0.87	0.99	1.00	1.01	1.01	1.02	1.03	0.98	1.02	1.00	1.21
3	0.88	0.87	0.98	1.00	1.02	1.00	1.02	1.00	0.97	1.00	1.03	1.23
4	0.87	0.84	0.99	0.98	1.01	1.03						
Average	0.89	0.86	0.99	0.99	1.02	1.01	1.01	1.01	0.97	1.02	1.02	1.22

Month	Seasonal Index		Month	Seasonal Index
Jan	.89		Jul	1.01
Feb	.86		Aug	1.01
Mar	.99		Sep	.97
Apr	.99		Oct	1.02
May	1.02		Nov	1.02
Jun	1.01		Dec	1.22

For this application, the final adjustment failed to change any of the previous averages (to two decimal places). This means that $S_1 + S_2 + \ldots + S_{12}$ still sum to 12.01, which, due to the rounding of these values, is perfectly acceptable.

We observe (1) a large seasonal index for December ($S_{12} = 1.22$) indicating large retail trade for this month, (2) low indexes for January and February, and (3) very little seasonality for any of the remaining months.

Step 2 *Deseasonalize the data.* We obtain the deseasonalized values (which contain *no* seasonality) by dividing each observation by its corresponding seasonal index. These values are shown in Table 16.10. The trend is more apparent now because the deseasonalized values tend to increase over time.

Step 3 *Determine the trend components.* A common method (and the one we will use) of estimating trend is to construct a least squares trend line (or curve) through the deseasonalized data. From the moving averages in Table 16.8, it appears that a straight line trend equation will be appropriate; these values tend to increase at a fairly steady rate.

The calculations for the trend line are identical to those discussed in section 16.2, using the d_t values in place of the original observations, y_t. A summary of this procedure is given in Table 16.11. The least squares line through the deseasonalized data is given by

$$TR_t = \hat{d}_t = b_0 + b_1 t$$

where

$$
\begin{aligned}
b_1 &= \frac{\Sigma t d_t - (\Sigma t)(\Sigma d_t)/T}{\Sigma t^2 - (\Sigma t)^2/T} \\
&= \frac{108,249 - (1176)(4240.1)/48}{38,024 - (1176)^2/48} \\
&= \frac{4366.55}{9212} = .474
\end{aligned}
$$

and

$$
\begin{aligned}
b_0 &= \bar{d}_t - b_1 \bar{t} \\
&= \frac{4240.1}{48} - (.474)\left(\frac{1176}{48}\right) \\
&= 88.34 - 11.61 \\
&= 76.73
\end{aligned}
$$

Consequently, the trend equation is given by

$$
\begin{aligned}
TR_t &= \hat{d}_t \\
&= 76.73 + .474t
\end{aligned}
$$

Table 16.10

Deseasonalized monthly retail trade data values

Year	Month	t	y_t	S_t	$d_t = y_t/S_t$
1980	Jan	1	70.56	0.89	79.35
	Feb	2	70.62	0.86	82.18
	Mar	3	76.00	0.99	77.10
	Apr	4	75.15	0.99	75.83
	May	5	79.20	1.02	77.94
	Jun	6	77.37	1.01	76.34
	Jul	7	79.86	1.01	78.99
	Aug	8	81.74	1.01	80.70
	Sep	9	77.58	0.97	79.77
	Oct	10	84.00	1.02	82.56
	Nov	11	83.82	1.02	82.57
	Dec	12	100.76	1.22	82.85
1981	Jan	13	76.68	0.89	86.23
	Feb	14	73.73	0.86	85.80
	Mar	15	83.97	0.99	85.18
	Apr	16	85.21	0.99	85.99
	May	17	86.90	1.02	85.52
	Jun	18	87.31	1.01	86.15
	Jul	19	88.25	1.01	87.29
	Aug	20	89.05	1.01	87.91
	Sep	21	85.52	0.97	87.94
	Oct	22	88.78	1.02	87.26
	Nov	23	87.33	1.02	86.03
	Dec	24	106.07	1.22	87.22
1982	Jan	25	77.34	0.89	86.97
	Feb	26	76.21	0.86	88.69
	Mar	27	86.57	0.99	87.82
	Apr	28	87.96	0.99	88.76
	May	29	90.81	1.02	89.37
	Jun	30	88.96	1.01	87.77
	Jul	31	91.21	1.01	90.22
	Aug	32	89.64	1.01	88.49
	Sep	33	88.16	0.97	90.65
	Oct	34	91.42	1.02	89.86
	Nov	35	94.20	1.02	92.80
	Dec	36	113.19	1.22	93.08
1983	Jan	37	81.34	0.89	91.47
	Feb	38	78.88	0.86	91.80
	Mar	39	93.76	0.99	95.12
	Apr	40	93.97	0.99	94.83
	May	41	97.84	1.02	96.29
	Jun	42	100.61	1.01	99.27
	Jul	43	99.56	1.01	98.47
	Aug	44	100.23	1.01	98.95
	Sep	45	97.97	0.97	100.74
	Oct	46	100.66	1.02	98.94
	Nov	47	103.86	1.02	102.31
	Dec	48	124.99	1.22	102.78

This equation implies that, apart from seasonal fluctuations, the U.S. retail trade is increasing at an average rate of $474 million each month. A graph of the deseasonalized data and corresponding trend line is shown in Figure 16.20. Also, a MINITAB solution for the trend line using the deseasonalized data as input is contained in Figure 16.21.

Table 16.11

Calculations for trend line (U.S. monthly retail trade data)

t	d_t	$t \cdot d_t$	t^2
1	79.35	79.35	1
2	82.18	164.36	4
3	77.10	231.30	9
4	75.83	303.32	16
.	.	.	.
.	.	.	.
.	.	.	.
45	100.74	4533.30	2025
46	98.94	4551.24	2116
47	102.31	4808.57	2209
48	102.78	4933.44	2304
1176	4240.15	108,249	38,024

Figure 16.20

Deseasonalized data and trend line (monthly U.S. retail trade data).

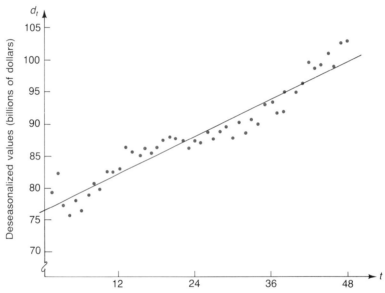

Figure 16.21

MINITAB solution for trend line (deseasonalized monthly U.S. retail trade data).

```
MTB > SET INTO C1
DATA> 1:48          ┌─────────────────────────┐
DATA> END           │ This command generates  │
MTB > SET INTO C2   │ integers 1 through 48   │
DATA> 79.35 82.18 77.10 75.83 77.94 76.34 78.99 80.70 79.77 82.56
DATA> 82.57 82.85 86.23 85.80 85.18 85.99 85.52 86.15 87.29 87.91
DATA> 87.94 87.26 86.03 87.22 86.97 88.69 87.82 88.76 89.37 87.77
DATA> 90.22 88.49 90.65 89.86 92.80 93.08 91.47 91.80 95.12 94.83
DATA> 96.29 99.27 98.47 98.95 100.74 98.94 102.31 102.78
DATA> END
MTB > REGRESS Y IN C2 USING 1 PRED IN C1, RES IN C3, DHATS IN C4

The regression equation is
C2 = 76.7 + 0.474 C1

Predictor       Coef        Stdev      t-ratio
Constant      76.7266      0.5873      130.64
C1            0.47387      0.02087      22.71

s = 2.003     R-sq = 91.8%    R-sq(adj) = 91.6%

Analysis of Variance

SOURCE      DF        SS          MS
Regression   1      2068.6      2068.6
Error       46       184.5         4.0
Total       47      2253.1
```

Step 4 *Determine the cyclical activity.* We begin by following the procedure outlined in Section 16.3. We divide each deseasonalized observation by the corresponding trend value,

$$\frac{d_t}{TR_t} = \frac{d_t}{\hat{d}_t} = \frac{\cancel{TR_t} \cdot C_t \cdot I_t}{\cancel{TR_t}}$$

$$= C_t \cdot I_t$$

The resulting values contain cyclical effects, as well as an irregular activity component. One method of reducing the irregular activity effect is to compute a series of three-period moving averages on the $C_t \cdot I_t$ values. This procedure greatly reduces the irregular activity effect, and the moving averages provide a much better estimate of the cyclical movement. The choice of using a *three-period* moving average is somewhat arbitrary, but when we use an odd number of terms, the moving averages need not be centered.

A partial solution is shown in Table 16.12. We see that the cyclical component for $t = 2$ is C_2, where

$$C_2 = \frac{1.03 + 1.06 + .99}{3} = 1.03$$

and the cyclical component for $t = 3$ is

$$C_3 = \frac{1.06 + .99 + .96}{3} = 1.00$$

Similarly, $C_4 = (.99 + .96 + .99)/3 = .98$ and $C_5 = (.96 + .99 + .96)/3 = .97$.

The complete set of cyclical components is contained in Table 16.13 and plotted in Figure 16.22. We observe an approximate two-and-one-half-year cycle between September 1980 and April 1983. Also, the year 1983 ended in the midst of an above-normal cycle.

A MINITAB solution for determining the cyclical components is shown in Figure 16.23. MINITAB computes the $C_t \cdot I_t$ components (cycles and irregular activity) for you. You can obtain the three-month moving averages by using your calculator.

Table 16.12

Calculating the cyclical components for the U.S. monthly retail trade data

t	d_t	$\hat{d}_t$	$d_t/\hat{d}_t$ $(C_t \cdot I_t)$	Three-month moving average (C_t)
1	79.35	76.73 + .474(1) = 77.20	1.03	—
2	82.18	76.73 + .474(2) = 77.67	1.06	1.03
3	77.10	76.73 + .474(3) = 78.15	.99	1.00
4	75.83	76.73 + .474(4) = 78.62	.96	.98
5	77.94	76.73 + .474(5) = 79.10	.99	.97
6	76.34	76.73 + .474(6) = 79.57	.96	.
.		.	.	.
.		.	.	.
.		.	.	.

Table 16.13

Cyclical components (monthly U.S. retail trade data)

Year	Month	d_t	$\hat{d}_t$ (TR_t)	$d_t/\hat{d}_t$ $(C_t \cdot I_t)$	Three-Month Moving Average (C_t)
1980	Jan	79.35	77.20	1.03	—
	Feb	82.18	77.67	1.06	1.03
	Mar	77.10	78.15	.99	1.00
	Apr	75.83	78.62	.96	.98
	May	77.94	79.10	.99	.97
	Jun	76.34	79.57	.96	.98
	Jul	78.99	80.04	.99	.98
	Aug	80.70	80.52	1.00	.99
	Sep	79.77	80.99	.98	1.00
	Oct	82.56	81.47	1.01	1.00
	Nov	82.57	81.94	1.01	1.01
	Dec	82.85	82.41	1.01	1.02
1981	Jan	86.23	82.89	1.04	1.03
	Feb	85.80	83.36	1.03	1.03
	Mar	85.18	83.83	1.02	1.02
	Apr	85.99	84.31	1.02	1.02
	May	85.52	84.78	1.01	1.01
	Jun	86.15	85.26	1.01	1.01
	Jul	87.29	85.73	1.02	1.02
	Aug	87.91	86.20	1.02	1.02
	Sep	87.94	86.68	1.01	1.01
	Oct	87.26	87.15	1.00	1.00
	Nov	86.03	87.63	.98	.99
	Dec	87.22	88.10	.99	.98
1982	Jan	86.97	88.57	.98	.99
	Feb	88.69	89.05	1.00	.99
	Mar	87.82	89.52	.98	.99
	Apr	88.76	90.00	.99	.99
	May	89.37	90.47	.99	.98
	Jun	87.77	90.94	.97	.98
	Jul	90.22	91.42	.99	.97
	Aug	88.49	91.89	.96	.98
	Sep	90.65	92.36	.98	.97
	Oct	89.86	92.84	.97	.98
	Nov	92.80	93.31	.99	.98
	Dec	93.08	93.79	.99	.98
1983	Jan	91.47	94.26	.97	.98
	Feb	91.80	94.73	.97	.98
	Mar	95.12	95.21	1.00	.99
	Apr	94.83	95.68	.99	1.00
	May	96.29	96.16	1.00	1.01
	Jun	99.27	96.63	1.03	1.01
	Jul	98.47	97.10	1.01	1.02
	Aug	98.95	97.58	1.01	1.02
	Sep	100.74	98.05	1.03	1.01
	Oct	98.94	98.52	1.00	1.02
	Nov	102.31	99.00	1.03	1.02
	Dec	102.78	99.47	1.03	—

Figure 16.22

Plot of cyclical activity
(monthly U.S. retail trade
data).

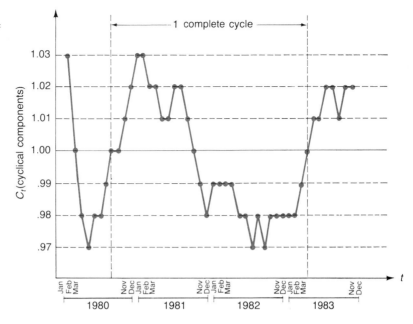

Figure 16.23

MINITAB solution for C_t ·
I_t components (monthly
U.S. retail trade data).

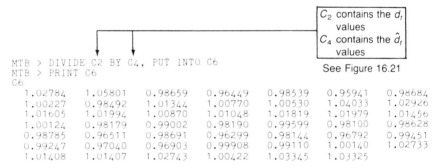

| | C_2 contains the d_t values |
| | C_4 contains the $\hat{d}_t$ values |

```
MTB > DIVIDE C2 BY C4, PUT INTO C6
MTB > PRINT C6
C6
    1.02784    1.05801    0.98659    0.96449    0.98539    0.95941    0.98684
    1.00227    0.98492    1.01344    1.00770    1.00530    1.04033    1.02926
    1.01605    1.01994    1.00870    1.01048    1.01819    1.01979    1.01456
    1.00124    0.98179    0.99002    0.98190    0.99599    0.98100    0.98628
    0.98785    0.96511    0.98691    0.96299    0.98144    0.96792    0.99451
    0.99247    0.97040    0.96903    0.99908    0.99110    1.00140    1.02733
    1.01408    1.01407    1.02743    1.00422    1.03345    1.03325
```

See Figure 16.21

Example 16.9   Once the steps in the previous sections have been completed, the various components can be combined for any specified value of t. Determine the four components for (1) May 1980 and (2) June 1983.

Solution 1 The value of t for May 1980 is $t = 5$. The seasonal index for May is $S_5 = 1.02$. The trend component (from Table 16.13) is $TR_5 = 79.10$. The cyclical component (from Table 16.13) is $C_5 = .97$. The product of $S_5 \cdot TR_5 \cdot C_5 = (1.02)(79.10)(.97) = 78.26$.

The actual observation during May 1980 is $y_5 = 79.20$. Since $y_5 = S_5 \cdot TR_5 \cdot C_5 \cdot I_5$,

$$I_5 = \frac{y_5}{S_5 \cdot TR_5 \cdot C_5}$$

$$= \frac{79.20}{78.26} = 1.012$$

and the final decomposition is

$$y_5 = 79.20 = S_5 \cdot TR_5 \cdot C_5 \cdot I_5$$

$$= (1.02)(79.10)(.97)(1.012)$$

Solution 2 For $t = 42$ (June 1983), we have S_{42} = seasonal index for June = S_6 = 1.01. Also, $TR_{42} = 96.63$ and $C_{42} = 1.01$ from Table 16.13. Consequently,

$$I_{42} = \frac{y_{42}}{S_{42} \cdot TR_{42} \cdot C_{42}}$$

$$= \frac{100.61}{(1.01)(96.63)(1.01)} = 1.021$$

Table 16.14

Time series components for U.S. retail trade data

Year	Month	y_t	TR_t	S_t	C_t	I_t
1980	Jan	70.56	77.20	.89	—	—
	Feb	70.62	77.67	.86	1.03	1.03
	Mar	76.00	78.15	.99	1.00	.98
	Apr	75.15	78.62	.99	.98	.98
	May	79.20	79.10	1.02	.97	1.01
	Jun	77.37	79.57	1.01	.98	.98
	Jul	79.86	80.04	1.01	.98	1.01
	Aug	81.74	80.52	1.01	.99	1.02
	Sep	77.58	80.99	.97	1.00	.99
	Oct	84.00	81.47	1.02	1.00	1.01
	Nov	83.82	81.94	1.02	1.01	.99
	Dec	100.76	82.41	1.22	1.02	.98
1981	Jan	76.68	82.89	.89	1.03	1.01
	Feb	73.73	83.36	.86	1.03	1.00
	Mar	83.97	83.83	.99	1.02	.99
	Apr	85.21	84.31	.99	1.02	1.01
	May	86.90	84.78	1.02	1.01	1.00
	Jun	87.31	85.26	1.01	1.01	1.00
	Jul	88.25	85.73	1.01	1.02	1.00
	Aug	89.05	86.20	1.01	1.02	1.00
	Sep	85.52	86.68	.97	1.01	1.01
	Oct	88.78	87.14	1.02	1.00	1.00
	Nov	87.33	87.63	1.02	.98	1.00
	Dec	106.07	88.10	1.22	.98	1.01
1982	Jan	77.34	88.57	.89	.99	.99
	Feb	76.21	89.05	.86	.99	1.01
	Mar	86.57	89.52	.99	.99	.99
	Apr	87.96	90.00	.99	.99	1.00
	May	90.81	90.47	1.02	.98	1.00
	Jun	88.96	90.94	1.01	.98	.99
	Jul	91.21	91.42	1.01	.97	1.02
	Aug	89.64	91.89	1.01	.98	.99
	Sep	88.16	92.36	.97	.97	1.01
	Oct	91.42	92.84	1.02	.98	.98
	Nov	94.20	93.31	1.02	.98	1.01
	Dec	113.19	93.79	1.22	.98	1.01
1983	Jan	81.34	94.26	.89	.98	.99
	Feb	78.88	94.73	.86	.98	.99
	Mar	93.76	95.21	.99	.99	1.00
	Apr	93.97	95.68	.99	1.00	.99
	May	97.84	96.16	1.02	1.01	.99
	Jun	100.61	96.63	1.01	1.01	1.02
	Jul	99.56	97.10	1.01	1.02	.99
	Aug	100.23	97.58	1.01	1.02	1.00
	Sep	97.97	98.05	.97	1.01	1.02
	Oct	100.66	98.52	1.02	1.02	.98
	Nov	103.86	99.00	1.02	1.02	1.01
	Dec	124.99	99.47	1.22	—	—

The combined decomposition for this observation is

$$y_{42} = 100.61 = S_{42} \cdot TR_{42} \cdot C_{42} \cdot I_{42}$$

$$= (1.01)(96.63)(1.01)(1.021)$$ ●

Summary of Time Series Decomposition

The time series decomposition procedure allows you to examine the presence of

Trend (a long-term growth or decline)
Seasonality (a within-year recurrent pattern)
Cyclical activity (upward and downward variation about the trend)

The remaining component (what is left after removing the effect of these three factors) is irregular activity. Having determined these components, you are able to describe a particular time series by carefully examining and plotting the calculated components.

A summary of the components for the U.S. retail trade time series is contained in Table 16.14. The irregular activity components (I_t) are determined by continuing the procedure in example 16.9. Graphs of these components are shown in Figure 16.24. Notice that the graph of the irregular activity components contains no obvious pattern, as we would expect. By combining the various graphs of the time series components into a *single* set of graphs (Figure 16.24), you can tell at a glance what is the nature of this series. The conclusions we can reach from this figure include

1. There is a strong linear trend that increases over the four-year period.
2. There is a strong retail trade peak each December followed by weak trading in January and February.
3. There is a cycle between the latter part of 1980 and the early part of 1983.

As we discussed in Chapter 2, graphs offer you an easy-to-comprehend method of summarizing data. It is time-consuming to construct this particular graph using pen and paper, but practically all microcomputer software packages have graph capabilities. Other methods of time series analysis will be discussed in Chapter 17, where we will examine time series forecasting.

Exercises

16.45 A real estate broker, in order to understand the nature of the real estate market in a growing suburb of New Orleans, collected data from the past four years on the price per square foot for the houses that had three bedrooms, two baths, and a two-car garage. The data are given below.

Year	Jan	Feb	Mar	Apr	May	Jun	Jul	Aug	Sep	Oct	Nov	Dec
1982	27.5	28.3	29.1	29.4	30.4	30.5	29.5	29.0	28.1	28.3	27.1	27.3
1983	27.1	28.6	29.5	30.4	31.4	31.8	31.3	30.7	30.4	29.5	29.6	29.0
1984	29.7	30.7	30.9	31.5	34.3	34.1	33.6	33.4	32.7	32.5	32.1	31.9
1985	31.8	32.7	35.6	36.1	36.8	36.7	35.4	36.5	35.0	34.8	34.7	34.7

a. Determine the seasonal indexes.

b. Determine the trend.

c. Determine the cyclical components for 1984 using a three-period moving average.

d. Determine the irregular components for the first three months of 1984.

Figure 16.24

Illustration of time series components (monthly U.S. retail trade data).

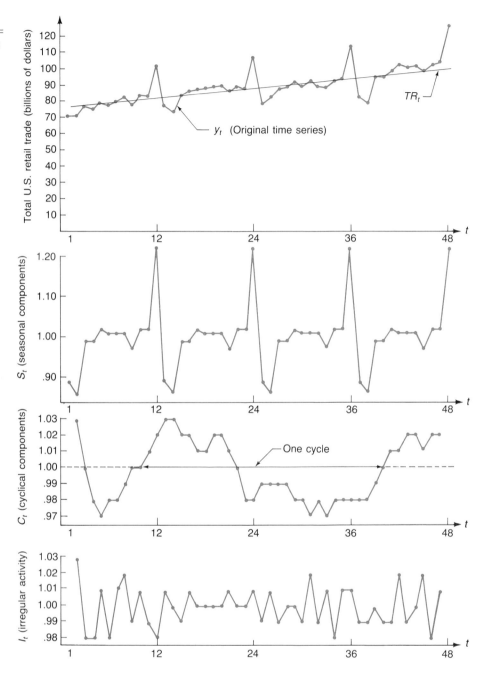

16.46 For the month of July 1985, a researcher finds that the seasonal index is 1.14, the trend value is 65.4, and the cyclical component is 0.86. What is the irregular component if the actual observation for July of 1985 is 80.42?

16.47 The following values represent deseasonalized observations. Find the corresponding trend values and cyclical components for each quarter.

Year	Quarter 1	Quarter 2	Quarter 3	Quarter 4
1981	1.79	1.77	1.75	1.68
1982	1.67	1.66	1.60	1.62
1983	1.63	1.71	1.72	1.70
1984	1.83	1.84	1.95	2.10
1985	2.13	2.11	2.15	2.16

16.48 Halston, a supplier of institutional food, sells to a restaurant in the metropolitan area of Memphis, Tennessee. Monthly data on sales (in ten thousands) are gathered over the past five years to help describe the company's growth pattern.

Year	Jan	Feb	Mar	Apr	May	Jun	Jul	Aug	Sep	Oct	Nov	Dec
1981	4.1	4.3	4.4	4.2	4.5	4.8	4.7	4.6	4.5	4.4	4.5	4.4
1982	4.3	3.6	4.7	4.9	5.3	5.5	5.9	5.7	5.5	5.3	5.2	5.0
1983	5.0	5.4	5.8	6.1	6.7	6.8	7.2	6.3	6.1	6.0	6.1	5.9
1984	5.8	6.3	6.7	6.9	7.4	7.9	8.5	7.9	7.8	7.7	7.4	7.3
1985	7.2	7.4	8.9	8.4	8.7	8.9	9.4	9.1	8.5	8.4	8.1	8.0

a. Compute the seasonal indexes.

b. Calculate the cyclical components for 1984 using a three-month moving average.

c. Calculate the irregular components for the last three months of 1984.

16.49 The manager of a large private golf course in southern California would like to examine the growth pattern of the number of golfers (given in hundreds) who would use the golf course. Monthly data were collected over a four-year period.

Year	Jan	Feb	Mar	Apr	May	Jun	Jul	Aug	Sep	Oct	Nov	Dec
1982	4.3	4.4	4.7	4.5	4.8	5.1	5.4	5.6	5.7	5.0	4.7	4.7
1983	4.8	4.9	4.8	6.1	5.0	5.4	5.9	6.0	6.1	6.0	5.8	5.5
1984	5.0	5.1	5.2	5.3	5.5	5.7	6.1	6.3	6.1	5.9	5.7	5.3
1985	5.1	5.7	5.8	6.1	6.3	6.4	4.7	6.8	6.3	6.2	6.1	5.7

a. Determine the seasonal indexes.

b. Determine the trend.

c. Determine the cyclical components for 1984, using a five-period moving average.

d. Determine the irregular components for the first three months of 1984.

16.50 The following table lists the number of building permits per month for nonresidential construction during the four-year period 1982 through 1985 in Parkins, Nebraska.

Year	Jan	Feb	Mar	Apr	May	Jun	Jul	Aug	Sep	Oct	Nov	Dec
1982	21	22	23	24	25	28	29	30	27	26	20	20
1983	21	24	23	25	26	25	29	32	32	27	20	18
1984	17	18	21	24	22	28	29	30	27	26	22	20
1985	17	21	23	23	24	29	31	22	28	22	21	29

a. Determine the seasonal indexes.

b. Determine the cyclical components for 1984 using a three-month moving average.

c. Determine the irregular component for July of 1984.

16.51 Find the cyclical components using a three-quarter moving average and the irregular components for the four quarters of 1981, using the data in exercise 16.35.

16.52 Deseasonalize the data in exercise 16.36. Find the cyclical components using a three-month moving average for 1983. Find the irregular component for February of 1983.

16.7

Index Numbers

How many times have you heard a remark such as, "I can remember that twenty years ago we could have bought that house for $20,000. Now it's worth $90,000." Or, "My weekly grocery bill used to be $25. Today, it's almost $100." Many people like to talk about the prices back in the "good old days," but were goods and services actually less expensive in those days?

Perhaps a particular item consumed a greater proportion of the typical consumer's consumable income (purchasing power) in years past. To compare effectively the change in the price or value of a certain item (or group of items) between any two time periods, we use an index number. An **index number** (or index) measures the change in a particular item (typically a product or service) or a collection of items between two time periods.

The average hourly wage for production employees at Kessler Toy Company during 1965, 1970, 1975, and 1980 is shown in Table 16.15. Suppose that we wish to compare the average wages for 1970, 1975, and 1980 with those for 1965. By computing a ratio for each pair of wages (expressed as a *percentage* of the 1965 wage), we obtain set of index numbers:

$$\text{index number for 1970: } \left(\frac{7.05}{6.40}\right) \cdot 100 = 110.2$$

$$\text{index number for 1975: } \left(\frac{8.50}{6.40}\right) \cdot 100 = 132.8$$

$$\text{index number for 1980: } \left(\frac{10.90}{6.40}\right) \cdot 100 = 170.3$$

When calculating an index number, we will follow standard practice and round to the nearest tenth (as in Table 16.15) and omit the percent sign. For this application, all wages were compared to those in 1965, which is the **base year.** The index number for the base year always is 100.

When each index number uses the same base year, the resulting set of values are an index time series. An **index time series** is a set of index numbers determined from the same base year. The purpose of such a time series is to measure the yearly values in *constant* units (dollars, people, and so on). Because these values define a time series, they can be analyzed and decomposed by using the methods described previously. Our purpose in this section will be simply to describe how to *construct* a time series of this type.

Price Indexes

Index numbers are derived for a variety of products (goods or services), as well as locations. You may wish to compare, for example, the relative costs of consumer items in Los Angeles and Minneapolis, if you are considering a move. Such information is readily available or can be determined from a number of business publications or

Table 16.15

Average hourly wage of production employees at Kessler Toy Company

	1965	1970	1975	1980
WAGE	6.40	7.05	8.50	10.90
INDEX (base = 1965)	100	110.2	132.8	170.3

Table 16.16

Prices of four items in 1975 and 1985

Item	1975	1985
Eggs	.75 (doz)	1.35 (doz)
Chicken	.95 (lb)	1.79 (lb)
Cheese	.89 (lb)	1.85 (lb)
Auto battery	$31 (each)	$55 (each)

government reports. The Department of Labor and the Bureau of Labor Statistics release reports (many of them monthly) on the price and quantity of many consumer items and agricultural commodities. Often, these are recorded for specific U.S. cities, providing geographical comparisons.

We will focus our attention on a comparison of *prices* from one year to the next; these are **price indexes.** The most popular of these indexes is the Consumer Price Index (CPI), which combines a large number (over 400) of prices for consumer goods (such as food and housing) and family services (such as health care and recreation) into a single index. It is often called the cost of living index.

An index that includes more than one item is an **aggregate index.** We will examine two methods of calculating an aggregate price index.

Say that we wish to measure the change in the prices of several items from 1975 to 1985, using a single price index. Table 16.16 shows four items; 1975 is the base year. Let P_0 denote the price for a particular item in the base year (1975) and P_1 represent this price during the reference year (1985). So

$$\Sigma P_0 = \text{sum of sampled prices for 1975}$$

$$= .75 + .95 + .89 + 31$$

$$= \$33.59$$

and

$$\Sigma P_1 = \text{sum of sampled prices for 1985}$$

$$= 1.35 + 1.79 + 1.85 + 55$$

$$= \$59.99$$

The ratio of these sums represents the **simple aggregate price index** for this application.

$$\text{simple aggregate price index} = \left(\frac{\Sigma P_1}{\Sigma P_0}\right) \cdot 100 \qquad (16\text{-}8)$$

For our example,

$$\text{Index} = \left(\frac{59.99}{33.59}\right) \cdot 100 = 178.6$$

It might be tempting to conclude that, based on the prices of these four items, all prices increased by 78.6% between 1975 and 1985. Two problems arise here. The first is whether or not these sampled items are *representative* of the population of all price changes over this ten-year period. This is not a new problem—the same concern arose when we first introduced statistical sampling.

The second problem is that this index does not take into account the *amounts* of these items that are typically purchased by consumers. A significant change in the price for any single item will have a dramatic effect on the simple aggregate index, regardless of the demand for this product. The increase of $24 in the price of an automobile battery dominated the computed value of the aggregate price index; however, a typical consumer will spend much more annually on chicken than on car batteries. The simple aggregate price index assumes that equal amounts of each item are purchased.

For this reason, the next step is to include a measure of the quantity (Q) of each item in the price index. (We will discuss methods of selecting the item quantities later.) The resulting index is known as a **weighted aggregate price index.**

$$\text{weighted aggregate price index} = \left(\frac{\Sigma P_1 Q}{\Sigma P_0 Q}\right) \cdot 100 \tag{16-9}$$

Example 16.10   Assume that a representative family each year purchases one automobile battery and each month consumes six dozen eggs, 15 pounds of chicken, and eight pounds of cheese. Using 1975 as the base year and equation 16-9, determine the weighted aggregate price index for 1985. Use the data in Table 16.16.

Solution   The choice of time units on the quantities, Q, is arbitrary, but it is essential that you be consistent across all items. Converting the family purchases to annual units, we have $6 \cdot 12 = 72$ dozen eggs, $15 \cdot 12 = 180$ pounds of chicken, $8 \cdot 12 = 96$ pounds of cheese, and 1 car battery (Table 16.17).

The weighted aggregate price index for 1985 (using 1975 as the base year) is

$$\text{index} = \left(\frac{\Sigma P_1 Q}{\Sigma P_0 Q}\right) \cdot 100 = \left(\frac{652}{341.44}\right) \cdot 100$$

$$= 191.0$$

In this index, the increase of 91% between 1975 and 1985 is not as severely affected by the price change for the car battery as was the simple aggregate price index, which ignored annual demand for each item. All widely used business price indexes are based on some variation of the weighted aggregate price index in equation 16-9.   ●

Selection of the Quantity, Q   Because the weights in a weighted aggregate price index usually reflect the quantities consumed, a problem arises when these quantities cannot be assumed to remain constant over the time span of the index. In example

Table 16.17

Calculated aggregate price index

Item	1975			1985		
	P_0	Q	$P_0 Q$	P_1	Q	$P_1 Q$
Eggs	.75	72	$ 54.00	1.35	72	97.20
Chicken	.95	180	171.00	1.79	180	322.20
Cheese	.89	96	85.44	1.85	96	177.60
Auto battery	31	1	31.00	55	1	55.00
			$\Sigma P_0 Q = 341.44$			$\Sigma P_1 Q = 652.00$

16.10, the same quantities, Q, were applied to both time periods, which means we are assuming an equal demand for the two years.

We have two options here: (1) use the quantities for the base year (1975, here) or (2) use the quantities for the reference year (1985, here). The first method is the **Laspeyres index;** the second is the **Paasche index.**

$$\text{Laspeyres index} = \left(\frac{\Sigma P_1 Q_0}{\Sigma P_0 Q_0}\right) \cdot 100 \tag{16-10}$$

where Q_0 represents a base-year quantity.

$$\text{Paasche index} = \left(\frac{\Sigma P_1 Q_1}{\Sigma P_0 Q_1}\right) \cdot 100 \tag{16-11}$$

where Q_1 represents a reference year quantity.

Each of these indexes has strengths and weaknesses. The main advantage of the Laspeyres index is that the same base-year quantities apply to all future reference years. This greatly simplifies updating of this index, particularly given that most aggregate business indexes contain a large number of items. Its main disadvantage is that it tends to give more weight to those items that show a dramatic price increase. When a particular commodity's price increases sharply, this is typically accompanied by a decrease in the demand (measured by Q) for this item, or perhaps another item may be substituted by the consumer. The Laspeyres index fails to adjust for this situation. The advantages of this index outweigh its disadvantages, however, and it is more popular than the Paasche index.

The complexity of updating the reference year quantities for the Paasche index make it difficult (and often impossible) to apply. Furthermore, because it reflects *both* price and quantity changes, we cannot use it to reflect price changes between two time periods. Its obvious advantage is that it uses current-year quantities, which provide a more realistic and up-to-date estimate of total expense.

We have seen that there is no completely reliable and accurate method of describing aggregate price changes. All such indexes include inaccuracies introduced by using a sample of items in the index, as well as by the quantities to be used for weighting. Nevertheless, we treat such an index like any other sample estimate: We use the index as an estimate of relative price changes and realize that it is subject to a certain amount of error.

Exercises

16.53 Lemer's Clothing Store has been selling the same style of men's slacks for six years. The average retail price (in dollars) for the years 1979 to 1984 are as follows:

Year	Price
1979	12.75
1980	12.95
1981	13.95
1982	16.95
1983	19.95
1984	23.95

Compare the average prices for the years 1979, 1980, 1981, 1982, 1983, and 1984, using index numbers with 1979 as a base year.

16.54 The total annual profits (in millions of dollars) of car dealers in a large suburb of Chicago over a seven-year period are summarized as follows:

Year	Total Annual Profits	Year	Total Annual Profits
1978	2.13	1982	3.33
1979	2.59	1983	4.15
1980	3.60	1984	4.54
1981	3.12		

Each total annual profit is an aggregate of profits. Find the simple aggregate price index for the years 1980, 1983, and 1984 using 1978 as the base year.

16.55 A typical family in Jackson, Mississippi had the following weekly buying patterns in 1979 and 1984. Use 1979 as a base year. Price is in dollars.

Item	1979 Unit Price	1979 Quantity	1984 Unit Price	1984 Quantity
Meat	1.03	2	1.25	2
Milk	0.97	3	1.19	2
Fish	0.98	2	1.05	3
Oranges	0.65	3	0.75	4
Bread	0.40	1	0.62	2

a. Find the simple aggregate price index.

b. Construct the Laspeyres index.

c. Construct the Paasche index.

16.56 Explain the meaning, including the advantages and disadvantages, of the Paasche and Laspeyres weighted indexes. Comment on whether the indexes can be used as a representation of buying pattern.

16.57 The following table reflects the typical family's buying habits per six months on repairs for the family car. Use 1979 as a base year.

Item	1979 Price	1979 Quantity	1983 Price	1983 Quantity
Lube job	3.50	2	5.00	1
Oil change	9.50	3	13.00	2
Tune up	29.95	1	39.95	1
New tires	35.95	2	49.00	2

a. Find the simple aggregate price index.

b. Construct the Laspeyres index.

c. Construct the Paasche index.

16.58 A conglomerate is considering buying one or more of three companies. The closing prices of the stocks of these three companies for the years 1977 to 1985 are:

Year	Better Foods	Friendly Insurance	Chock Full of Computer Chips
1977	13.500	20.125	39.25
1978	13.750	20.250	35.50
1979	14.250	20.500	31.75
1980	15.125	21.750	34.25
1981	15.500	21.500	37.75
1982	16.000	21.750	39.75
1983	16.125	22.500	40.00
1984	16.250	23.750	39.50
1985	16.750	23.500	42.25

Find an appropriate index to measure the change in the price of these three stocks for the years 1980, 1981, 1983, and 1985 using 1977 as a base year.

16.59 Suppose that, for a certain basket of goods, the Paasche index for 1985 is 115 and the Laspeyres index is 97. Assuming that the base year is 1978, interpret the meaning of the value of the two indexes.

16.60 The number of housing starts for four counties for the years 1982, 1983, and 1984 is:

County	1982	1983	1984
Brooks	1304	1505	1580
Litton	1264	1759	1987
Riverbed	1135	1443	1565
Tannon	1401	1605	1615

a. Compare the housing starts for Litton county for the years 1983 and 1984 using 1982 as a base year.

b. Compare the aggregate of housing starts for the years 1983 and 1984 for the four counties using 1982 as a base year.

16.61 The total revenue (in millions of dollars) of institutions of higher education for four southern states is:*

State	1978–1979	1979–1980
Alabama	826	937
Mississippi	487	544
Georgia	925	1032
Louisiana	658	807

a. For 1979–1980, find the simple aggregate index for the total revenue of institutions of higher education for the four states.

b. What can you conclude from the index calculated in question a?

16.62 A nursery purchases four different chemical ingredients to blend a certain popular fertilizer mixture. The data indicate the price per unit (PPU) paid for each ingredient and the quantity bought in 1981, 1982, and 1983.

Ingredients	1981 PPU	1982 PPU	1983 PPU	1981 Quantity	1982 Quantity	1983 Quantity
A	.80	.81	.85	385	375	380
B	.51	.55	.60	345	360	379
C	.45	.50	.53	200	250	280
D	.37	.39	.40	150	180	195

a. Calculate the Laspeyres index for 1982 and 1983 using 1981 as a base year.

b. Calculate the Paasche index for 1982 and 1983 using 1981 as a base year.

c. Compare the two indexes in questions a and b.

Summary

A variable recorded over time is a time series. You obtain a sample of values for this variable by recording its past observations. Because this is not a random sample, it is extremely difficult (if not impossible) to obtain any tests of hypothesis or CIs. Consequently, we resort to describing the past observations by deriving the components of the time series. This is time series decomposition. The components of a time series are (1) trend (a long-term growth or decline in the observations), (2) seasonality

*Source: U.S. Department of Education, National Center of Education Statistics.

(within-year recurrent fluctuations), (3) cyclical activity (upward and downward movements of various lengths about the trend) and (4) irregular activity (what remains after the other three components have been removed).

We described methods for estimating these components for a time series. We first specify how we believe the components interact with one another, thus describing the time series variable, y_t. The additive structure assumes that each observation is the *sum* of its components. In particular, this implies that seasonal fluctuations during a particular year are not affected by the base volume for that year. In the multiplicative structure, each value of y_t is the *product* of the four components. Within this framework, the seasonal fluctuation for a specific month (or quarter) is more apt to be a constant *percentage* of the base volume for that year; for example, sales in December might be 35% higher than the average (base) sales for that particular year. The multiplicative structure was assumed for practically all of the illustrations in this chapter and is used more commonly in practice. The Bureau of the Census uses a variation of this procedure for their time series decomposition analyses.*

We described a four-step procedure for deriving these components for a particular time series, based on the multiplicative structure. The steps were: (1) determine a seasonal index for each month (monthly data) or quarter (quarterly data); (2) deseasonalize the data by dividing each observation by its corresponding seasonal index; (3) determine the trend components by deriving a least squares line or quadratic curve through the deseasonalized values; and (4) determine the cyclical components by, for each time period, dividing each deseasonalized value by its estimate using the trend equation and smoothing these values by computing three-period moving averages.

An index time series, often used by business analysts, is a time-related sequence of index numbers, where each value is a measure of the change in a particular item (or group of items) from one year to the next. Price indexes are used to compare prices over time.

An aggregate price index is used to compare the relative price of a set of items for any year to the price during the base year. The index for the base year always is 100. The prices for the items can be averaged (simple aggregate price index) or weighted by the corresponding quantity of each item (weighted aggregate price index). Methods of selecting these quantities include using base-year quantities (the Laspeyres index) or using the reference-year quantities (the Paasche index).

Further Reading

Bowerman, B. L. and R. T. O'Connell, *Forecasting and Time Series*. North Scituate, MA.: Duxbury, 1979.

Makridakis, S. and S. C. Wheelwright, *Forecasting: Methods and Applications*, New York: Wiley, 1978.

Mendenhall, W. and J. E. Reinmuth, *Statistics for Management and Economics*, 4th ed. Boston: Duxbury, 1982), Chapter 13.

Review Exercises

16.63 Each of the following influences on the variation in profits of a national chain of department stores would contribute to which of the four components of a time series?

a. The long-term growth of the economy.

---

*The Bureau of the Census procedure is called the X-11 program and is available on SAS/ETS. Consult the Econometric Time Series (ETS) user's guide (available from SAS) for a description of this procedure.

b. The resignation of top managers in the company.

c. Annual demand in spring and summer for garden equipment.

d. The closing of several other department stores.

16.64 A manufacturer of tractors has built a record number of tractors for every year for the past seven years. Given in thousands, the figures show the number of tractors built from 1979 to 1985.

Year	Tractors built
1979	10.75
1980	11.78
1981	12.59
1982	13.4
1983	14.3
1984	15.7
1985	16.8

Find the least squares prediction equation that you would use to forecast the trend. What would you estimate the number of tractors built in 1986 to be?

16.65 The average monthly utility bill for the residents of the small community of Ridgecrest for the years 1982 to 1985 is:

Year	Jan	Feb	Mar	Apr	May	Jun	Jul	Aug	Sep	Oct	Nov	Dec
1982	190	180	179	130	135	145	148	153	145	153	170	185
1983	197	193	185	150	151	159	163	165	160	159	180	185
1984	215	205	193	175	171	179	185	184	180	180	173	190
1985	235	225	205	180	182	190	195	198	188	185	195	201

a. Determine the seasonal indexes.

b. Determine the trend.

c. Determine the cyclical components for 1983 using a three-period moving average.

d. Determine the irregular components for June and July 1983.

16.66 Telemex, a supplier of telephone systems, has experienced moderate to rapid growth over a 12-year period. The data show the annual sales figure (in tens of thousands of dollars).

Year	Sales
1974	3.1
1975	6.3
1976	10.5
1977	10.2
1978	11.5
1979	14.7
1980	18.8
1981	18.4
1982	20.0
1983	21.3
1984	29.0
1985	28.3

a. Find the trend line.

b. Find the cyclical components.

c. Graph the data and estimate the period of the cycle.

16.67 Ranton Houses Inc., has been building a certain style of house for the past four years. This house has sold for various prices over the years 1982 to 1985, as shown (in thousands of dollars).

Year	Jan	Feb	Mar	Apr	May	Jun	Jul	Aug	Sep	Oct	Nov	Dec
1982	49.5	51.3	51.3	51.5	52.0	57.3	57.4	58.3	57.2	56.3	55.4	58.6
1983	55.3	55.6	55.7	56.3	57.4	62.7	62.8	63.8	62.3	61.4	60.5	60.0
1984	60.5	61.3	62.4	62.7	63.0	68.6	68.9	70.1	68.6	68.4	67.4	67.0
1985	67.4	67.5	67.6	68.1	68.3	72.1	72.4	73.4	72.1	71.3	71.0	70.8

a. Determine the seasonal indexes.

b. Determine the trend.

c. Determine the cyclical components for 1984 using a three-period moving average.

d. Determine the irregular components for the months of September and October 1984.

16.68 Suppose that, for the month of September 1985, the marketing department of a firm finds that the seasonal index is 1.20, the trend-line value is $17,000 in sales, and the cyclical component is 0.79. What is the irregular component if the actual sales figure for September 1985 is $16,500?

16.69 Sales figures (in tens of thousands of dollars) for Dataphonics for a ten-year period follow. Find the corresponding trend values and cyclical components for each quarter of 1982 and 1983.

Year	Quarter 1	Quarter 2	Quarter 3	Quarter 4
1975	2.48	4.39	5.68	2.49
1976	2.76	4.86	5.69	2.73
1977	2.80	4.91	5.75	2.91
1978	2.90	5.10	5.85	2.95
1979	3.10	5.20	5.96	3.01
1980	3.15	5.21	6.04	3.10
1981	3.18	5.24	6.10	3.15
1982	3.20	5.30	6.14	3.19
1983	3.22	5.35	6.20	3.24
1984	3.25	5.36	6.23	3.25

16.70 The Treasury bill rate for each quarter from 1980 through 1983 follows.*

Year	Quarter 1	Quarter 2	Quarter 3	Quarter 4
1980	13.46	10.05	9.28	13.71
1981	14.37	14.83	15.09	12.02
1982	12.89	12.36	9.71	7.93
1983	8.08	8.42	9.19	8.79

a. Determine the seasonal indexes.

b. Determine the trend components.

c. Determine the cyclical components using a three-period moving average.

d. Determine the irregular components for the quarters of 1981.

16.71 The following data are the total assets of the Fortune 500 companies for 1970, 1975, 1980, and 1983 (in millions of dollars).†

Year	Total Assets
1970	432.1
1975	668.4
1980	1175.0
1983	1353.0

*Source: *International Financial Statistics,* April 1984

†Source: *The Fortune Directory,* Time Inc.,

The total amount of assets is an aggregate. Find the simple aggregate price index for the years 1975, 1980, and 1983, using 1970 as the base year.

16.72 The weekly buying pattern of a typical family in a suburb of Atlanta, Georgia for 1980 and 1985 follows. Use 1980 as a base year.

Item	1980 Unit Price	1980 Quantity	1985 Unit Price	1985 Quantity
Chicken	2.40	1	2.75	2
Milk	1.02	3	1.19	2
Bread	0.39	2	0.45	2
Ground beef	1.59	3	1.89	2
Tomatoes	0.39	2	0.78	2

a. Find the simple aggregate price index.

b. Calculate the Laspeyres index.

c. Calculate the Paasche index.

d. Compare the indexes in questions b and c.

16.73 The president of R & B Home Builders uses a housing index to obtain information about the direction of the housing market. The index for the four quarters of 1982, 1983, 1984, and 1985 yields these data:

Year	Quarter 1	Quarter 2	Quarter 3	Quarter 4
1982	157	155	154	147
1983	142	145	140	142
1984	143	153	152	150
1985	163	165	162	160

a. Determine the seasonal indexes for each quarter.

b. Determine the trend line.

c. Determine the cyclical components for 1983 using a three-period moving average.

d. Determine the irregular components for the first and second quarter of 1983.

Case Study

Carver Industries

Dave Carver, president of Carver Industries, was making up his plan of operations for the next year. This plan was Dave's basic managerial tool for overseeing his company and directing its growth. The first step was to produce a sales forecast. This was used to schedule the production runs, to determine the number of staff needed, and to order materials, parts, services, and operating supplies.

In the past, Dave's sales forecast had been based on the sales representatives' estimates of sales in their territories for the coming year. The sales estimates, however, always were too low: people underestimated their sales so they would exceed a quota based on their own estimates.

This year, Dave decided to use time series decomposition to generate the sales forecast. The company's sales were continuing to grow each year and Dave noticed that there were seasonal variations over the year. He obtained the sales figures (dollar amounts) for each month of the last six years.

Month	Year 1	Year 2	Year 3	Year 4	Year 5	Year 6
Jan	887	1088	1263	1391	1586	1720
Feb	1375	1544	1653	1693	1740	1860
Mar	1831	1909	1907	1830	1890	1950
Apr	1768	1963	2093	2145	2272	2340
May	1523	1805	2052	2239	2410	2676
Jun	1152	1473	1793	2089	2272	2509
Jul	749	1047	1381	1732	2094	2387
Aug	413	632	917	1255	1504	1893
Sep	229	333	515	775	992	1174
Oct	226	246	277	412	508	682
Nov	258	265	340	464	572	694
Dec	354	485	652	832	1004	1192

Case Study Questions

1. How is this data set used to generate a table of centered moving averages?
2. What information is contained in the centered moving averages?
3. How are the centered moving averages used to generate seasonal information?
4. What are the seasonal indexes for each forecast month?
5. What are the trend components for this set of data?
6. What effect does the cyclical component have on the forecast?
7. Make a monthly forecast for the next year.
8. Write a brief memo setting forth the advantages and disadvantages of this forecast. Do you recommend it in preference to the old salesforce estimates? State why or why not.

CHAPTER 17

Quantitative Business Forecasting

A Look Back/Introduction

We have introduced you to methods of capturing the behavior of a dependent variable, Y. The first procedure was linear regression, which used a set of predictor (independent) variables to explain the observed values of this variable. In *simple* linear regression, a single predictor is used. When we had two or more predictor variables, we used a multiple linear regression model to attempt to account for the variation within the observed values of the dependent variable. The calculations were considerably more complex, and a computer solution was used to estimate the linear relationship between the dependent variable (Y) and the predictor variables ($X_1, X_2, \ldots$).

The success or failure of this technique lies in your ability to arrive at a set of predictor variables that can accurately predict past (and future) values of the dependent variable. Suppose your model fails to fit adequately the observed values of Y, with a resulting large sum of squares for error (SSE) and a low value of R^2 (coefficient of determination). Does this imply that multiple linear regression is not a reliable method of prediction for this situation? This could be the case, but it is just as likely that you omitted one or more key variables that would have significantly improved your prediction accuracy.

The time series decomposition technique, presented in the previous chapter, uses a different approach. This procedure attempts to explain each observed value by means of the various components that make up this observation. These include trend (long-term growth or decline in the time series), seasonality (predictable variation within each year) and cyclical activity (generally due to unpredictable swings in the national or international economy).

The key distinction between these two procedures is that the time series approach does not search for explanatory (predictor) variables. Rather, it seeks to capture the past behavior of the time series by analyzing the various components. More complex times series techniques, which were not discussed, use past observations to predict the value for the future. You can use a time series approach to forecast future values by "extending" the pattern into the future. For example, if your company sales have been increasing approximately 150,000 units each year over the past 6 years, a reasonable forecast for next year would be a sales volume of 150,000 more than the present year's value.

Statistical forecasting is, in one sense, an extension of the prediction of a dependent variable. However, we now enter a more uncertain world—that of extrapolation. In previous chapters, we warned you of the dangers of this procedure, because outside the range of your data, the predicted values become less reliable. We can only hope that tomorrow's world will be similar to today's and that patterns observed over the past will continue. This makes forecasting fascinating. We live in an uncertain world, and a reasonably accurate forecast can be extremely valuable for a marketing or production strategy.

This chapter will introduce many (certainly not all) methods of using quantitative techniques for predicting future values for the variable of interest. We will demonstrate how to forecast future values by using the past observations (the time series approach) as well as by using the multiple linear regression method. By applying the proper forecast method, you often can make the future considerably less uncertain.

17.1

Time Series Forecasting

A time series forecast is made by capturing the patterns that exist in the past observations and extending them into the future. Consider the annual data reflecting the sales of the Clayton Corporation between 1970 and 1984, represented in Figure 17.1. The data reflect a strong linear trend, as shown by the line passing through the points.

Figure 17.1

Sales for Clayton Corporation.

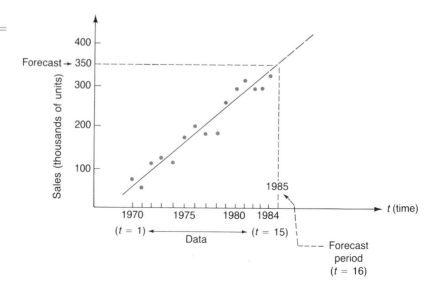

To estimate the sales for 1985, one simple method would be to extend this line into 1985, as illustrated in Figure 17.1. By graphically extending this line and observing the estimated value, we obtain

$$\hat{y}_{16} = \text{forecast for 1985 is approximately 350}$$

that is, 350,000 units.

This procedure, and methods of dealing with trend *and* seasonality, will be discussed later in the chapter.

As in Chapter 16, we will not put any statistical bounds (such as a 95% CI) on the predicted values. Rather, we will suggest alternative methods of forecasting and demonstrate a way of determining the "best" forecasting procedure for a particular set of data. Of course, all forecasts are subject to error and are based on the assumption that the past historical patterns (such as the straight line in Figure 17.1) continue into the future.

At first glance, it might appear that time series forecasting is easier to apply than are multiple regression models. After all, there is no need to search for a reliable set of predictor variables. It *is* true that time series predictors can be simple and straightforward, as is the so-called naive forecast discussed in the next section. Frequently, however, extracting the complex and interrelated structure of an observed time series requires sophisticated and complex prediction equations.

17.2

The Naive Forecast

Simply put, the naive forecast procedure states that the estimate of Y for tomorrow is the actual value from today. In general,

$$\hat{y}_{t+1} = y_t \tag{17-1}$$

for any time period, t.

Once again, the "hat" notation is used to denote an estimate. Equation 17-1 reads: "y hat for time period $t + 1$ is y for time, t." Here, $\hat{y}_{t+1}$ represents the *forecast* for time period $t + 1$.

This method of forecasting often works well for data that are recorded for smaller time intervals (such as daily or weekly) and contain no apparent upward or downward trend among the observed values. Data of this type are not apt to shift direction suddenly from one day to the next, and the naive forecast can provide a simple, yet fairly reliable, estimate of the next day's value. On more than one occasion, this predictor has outperformed much more complex forecasting equations—particularly when applied to a difficult-to-predict time series, such as an individual stock market price. It provides an inexpensive, easy method of forecasting.

Example 17.1

The weekly closing price for a share of Keller Toy Company stock was recorded over a 12-week period. Using the following data, determine a forecast for week 13.

Week	Price	Week	Price	Week	Price
1	60	5	$64\frac{1}{2}$	9	$63\frac{1}{4}$
2	$62\frac{1}{4}$	6	62	10	$62\frac{1}{2}$
3	$61\frac{3}{4}$	7	$63\frac{1}{2}$	11	61
4	63	8	64	12	$61\frac{1}{2}$

Solution The observed value for the last time period is $y_{12} = 61\frac{1}{2}$, so your forecast for the next time period is

$$\hat{y}_{13} = y_{12} = 61\frac{1}{2}$$

Notice that we are careful to distinguish between a *forecast*, such as $\hat{y}_{13}$, and an *observed* value, such as y_{12}.

One method of checking to see whether a particular forecasting technique is appropriate for your time series involves applying this procedure to each period of the observed data. For example, in example 17.1, what would we have predicted for the fifth week using the naive forecasting equation 17-1? In other words, suppose we are at the end of the fourth week and need a forecast for $t = 5$. Using the naive predictor,

$$\hat{y}_5 = y_4 = 63$$

The actual value turned out to be $y_5 = 64\frac{1}{2}$, providing a **residual** of

$$\text{residual} = y_5 - \hat{y}_5 = 64\frac{1}{2} - 63 = 1\frac{1}{2}$$

●

Example 17.2 Apply the naive forecasting procedure to the 12 time periods in example 17.1 and determine the residual for each week.

Solution The procedure cannot be applied during the first time period ($t = 1$) because $\hat{y}_1 = y_0$, where y_0 is the closing price for the week preceding the observations in the table. If this value is available, then the forecast value for $t = 1$ can be determined; it is equal to this value. Otherwise, the forecast for this time period is left blank. (Refer to Table 17.1.)

●

When we first introduced the concept of a residual (or error) in the chapters dealing with linear regression, we stressed that small residuals were desirable. When the residuals were near zero for regression applications, this meant that the model did a good job of "fitting" the sample observations.

The same idea applies to evaluating the effectiveness of a forecasting procedure. Small residuals indicate that this particular forecast technique would have done a good job of predicting the past values of this time series. A method of combining these residuals into a single measure (much like the SSE in linear regression) will be introduced in a later section.

Table 17.1

Residuals for naive forecasts

Week	y_t	$\hat{y}_t$	Residual ($y_t - \hat{y}_t$)
1	60	—	—
2	$62\frac{1}{4}$	60	$2.25 (= 62\frac{1}{4} - 60)$
3	$61\frac{3}{4}$	$62\frac{1}{4}$	$-.5 (= 61\frac{3}{4} - 62\frac{1}{4})$
4	63	$61\frac{3}{4}$	1.25 (and so on)
5	$64\frac{1}{2}$	63	1.5
6	62	$64\frac{1}{2}$	-2.5
7	$63\frac{1}{2}$	62	1.5
8	64	$63\frac{1}{2}$	.5
9	$63\frac{1}{4}$	64	$-.75$
10	$62\frac{1}{2}$	$63\frac{1}{4}$	$-.75$
11	61	$62\frac{1}{2}$	-1.5
12	$61\frac{1}{2}$	61	.5

Exercises

17.1 Explain the distinction between the technique of time series analysis and that of multiple regression analysis.

17.2 If a regression or time series model fits a set of data well, would the model necessarily provide small forecasting errors for future observations?

17.3 The price of the stock of Intersecond Bank has been cyclical over the years. From the following data, calculate the forecasted price of the stock using the naive model for the years 1975 to 1984. Also, calculate the residual for each forecast.

Year	Price of Stock
1974	28.50
1975	29.25
1976	31.75
1977	29.50
1978	28.00
1979	27.50
1980	28.25
1981	29.75
1982	32.50
1983	31.50
1984	30.00

17.4 Sullivan's Mutual Fund invests primarily in technology stocks. The net asset value of the fund at the end of each month for the 12 months of 1984 is given below. Find the forecasted value of the mutual fund for each month, starting with February, by using the naive model. Calculate the residuals.

Month	Mutual Fund Price
Jan	8.43
Feb	8.10
Mar	7.15
Apr	6.95
May	7.25
Jun	7.95
Jul	8.35
Aug	9.45
Sep	9.01
Oct	10.31
Nov	10.25
Dec	11.04

17.5 What advantages and disadvantages can you think of in using the naive model to forecast?

17.3
Projecting the Least Squares Trend Equation

For data containing a strong linear or curvilinear trend, a method of predicting future values of the time series is to extend the trend line (or curve) into the forecast periods. This was illustrated in Figure 17.1, in which the data from 1970 to 1984 demonstrated a very strong linear growth over these 15 years.

Suppose that a simple linear regression analysis is performed on these data, using the 15 sales values as the dependent variable and $t = 1, 2, \ldots, 15$ as the predictor variable (as discussed in Chapter 16). The resulting least squares line, shown in Figure 17.1, turns out to be

$$\hat{y}_t = 32 + 20t$$

The estimated forecast for 1985 in the earlier discussion was $\hat{y}_{16} = 350$. This was determined simply by extending the least squares line into this time period and "eye-balling" the estimate for 1985. The actual forecast is

$$\hat{y}_{16} = 32 + 20(16) = 352$$

So, our estimate of sales for 1985 is 352,000 units, based on the linear trend equation.

A Time Series Containing Trend and Seasonality

The previous procedure can be adapted to situations in which the time series contains significant trend *and* seasonality. Such a situation can occur when the data are monthly or quarterly, with seasonal fluctuations about a linear or curvilinear trend.

The quarterly sales for Video-Comp over a four-year period (1981 to 1984) are contained in Table 16.3 on page 597 and are illustrated in Figure 17.2.

The deseasonalized sales figures (often called *seasonally adjusted* sales) are summarized in Table 16.6 on page 602 and also are graphed in Figure 17.2. Notice that the extreme seasonal fluctuations of the original time series have been removed when these values were divided by the appropriate seasonal index. The indexes for this application were derived in example 16.8, indicating low sales for the first two quarters, above-average sales for the third quarter, and extremely high sales during the fourth (Christmas) quarter. The corresponding indexes were

$$S_1 = .852$$
$$S_2 = .692$$
$$S_3 = 1.166$$
$$S_4 = 1.290$$

Figure 17.2

Quarterly sales at Video-Comp.

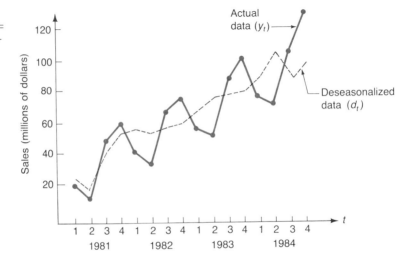

To forecast future values when using seasonal data, you once again determine the least squares line (or curve), except that now you use the *deseasonalized data* (say, d_t) as your dependent variable. Once you have calculated the trend forecast, you obtain your final forecast by multiplying this deseasonalized estimate by the corresponding seasonal index. So the procedure for extending trend and seasonal components is:

1. Calculate the deseasonalized (seasonally adjusted) data from the original time series $(y_1, y_2, \ldots, y_T)$. Call these values $d_1, d_2, \ldots, d_T$.
2. Construct a least squares line through the deseasonalized data, where $(t = 1, 2, \ldots, T)$

$$\hat{d}_T = b_0 + b_1 t$$

3. Calculate the forecast for time period $T + 1$ using

$$\hat{y}_{T+1} = \hat{d}_{T+1} (\text{seasonal index for } t = T + 1)$$
$$= [b_0 + b_1(T + 1)](\text{seasonal index for } t = T + 1)$$

Example 17.3

Using the Video-Comp data, what would be your forecast for the first-quarter sales of 1985? Second-quarter sales?

Solution The deseasonalized data and corresponding least squares line are shown in Figure 17.3. The MINITAB solution for the least squares line is shown in Figure 17.4, where

$$\hat{d}_t = 19.372 + 5.0375t$$

This equation tells us that, apart from seasonal variation, the sales at Video-Comp are increasing by approximately $5 million each quarter. Using this equation and Figure 17.3, your deseasonalized forecast for the first quarter of 1985 (time period 17) is

$$\hat{d}_{17} = 19.372 + 5.0375(17)$$
$$= 105.01$$

Figure 17.3

Trend line through deseasonalized data (quarterly sales, Video-Comp).

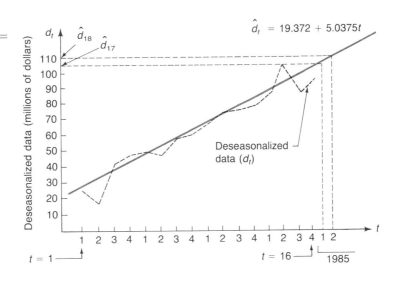

Figure 17.4

MINITAB solution for
deseasonalized trend
line.

```
MTB > SET INTO C1
DATA> 1:16
DATA> END
MTB > SET INTO C2
DATA> 23.47 17.34 40.31 46.51 46.95 46.24 55.75 58.91
DATA> 65.73 72.25 72.90 77.52 88.03 101.16 86.62 95.35
DATA> END
MTB > REGRESS Y IN C2 USING 1 PREDICTOR IN C1

The regression equation is
C2 = 19.4 + 5.04 C1

Predictor        Coef         Stdev      t-ratio
Constant       19.372         3.111         6.23
C1              5.0375        0.3217       15.66

s = 5.932       R-sq = 94.6%      R-sq(adj) = 94.2%

Analysis of Variance

SOURCE          DF          SS            MS
Regression       1        8627.9        8627.9
Error           14         492.6          35.2
Total           15        9120.5
```

Now, the sales for the first quarter of each year are lower than the yearly average, as reflected in the seasonal index of $S_1 = .852$ (from example 16.8). Consequently, your actual forecast for this time period is

$$\hat{y}_{17} = \hat{d}_{17} \cdot \text{(seasonal index for quarter 1)}$$

$$= 105.01 \cdot .852$$

$$= 89.5 \text{ (million dollars)}$$

This procedure can be used to forecast any future time period. For the second quarter of 1985, the estimated sales will be

$$\hat{y}_{18} = \hat{d}_{18} \cdot \text{(seasonal index for quarter 2)}$$

$$= [19.372 + 5.0375(18)] \cdot .692$$

$$= (110.05)(.692) = 76.2 \text{ (million dollars)}$$

Do these estimates seem reasonable? Look at the values for the first and second quarters. (The forecast values are those for 1985.)

Year	First-Quarter Sales	Second-Quarter Sales
1981	20	12
1982	40	32
1983	56	50
1984	75	70
1985	89.5	76.2

The forecast for the first quarter of 1985 seems to be about what we would expect, based on the past first-quarter sales. The predicted sales value for the second quarter of 1985 seems to be on the low side, with an increase of only 6.2 from the second quarter of 1984. Remember, however, that this forecasting technique contains the effect of *all* the quarters observed over the four years. By examining the past sales during the second quarter only, we are ignoring the remaining quarters, and perhaps an explanation for this seemingly low forecast lies in these values. ●

It is possible that this forecasting procedure is not a good one for the application in example 17.3. There may be a better way to obtain a forecast for this situation. We will show you several ways to forecast a time series and then determine which of these does the best job for a particular set of observed values. No one procedure always performs well for all applications.

Comments

Remember that any quantitative forecasting technique can never replace the forecast of an individual (or team of people) who uses his or her expertise and knowledge of unpredictable future events (such as strikes, wars, or market shifts) to make forecasts. Rather, the quantitative forecast is a tool the forecaster uses. A forecast offers an excellent baseline, which can be modified by informed judgment.

Exercises

17.6 A set of quarterly data has been gathered for 3 years. The seasonal indexes are found to be $S_1 = .81$, $S_2 = .93$, $S_3 = 1.19$, $S_4 = 1.07$. The least squares line through the deseasonalized data is found to be

$$\hat{d}_t = 10.1 + 1.3t$$

from 12 quarterly periods. Find the forecast for quarterly periods 13, 14, 15, and 16.

17.7 Sands Motel, which usually has a busy summer season on the beaches of Atlantic City in New Jersey, would like to obtain a forecast of future business. Business (in thousands of dollars) for each month from 1976 to 1982 is given below:

Year	Jan	Feb	Mar	Apr	May	Jun	Jul	Aug	Sep	Oct	Nov	Dec
1976	.4	.5	.7	.9	1.3	1.8	2.5	2.9	2.3	2.0	1.2	.7
1977	.5	.6	.8	1.1	1.2	1.9	2.8	3.1	2.7	2.1	.9	.8
1978	.7	.6	.9	1.1	1.4	2.1	2.8	3.3	2.9	2.4	1.5	.9
1979	.8	.7	.9	1.3	1.6	2.3	2.9	3.4	3.2	2.6	1.7	1.2
1980	1.0	.9	1.1	1.4	1.8	2.4	3.0	3.4	3.3	2.7	1.9	1.4
1981	1.1	.8	.9	1.3	1.9	2.5	3.2	3.6	3.2	2.6	2.0	1.5
1982	1.3	1.1	1.2	1.5	2.2	2.7	3.4	3.8	3.4	2.8	2.1	1.6

a. Find the seasonal indexes.

b. Find the least squares trend line for the deseasonalized data.

c. Find the forecast for March 1983, July 1983, and December 1983.

17.8 Slater Industries would like to cut costs on the amount of inventory it holds. Quarterly data have been gathered for 5 years from 1980 through 1984. The following table lists the dollar amount of inventory in units of 10,000.

Year	Quarter 1	Quarter 2	Quarter 3	Quarter 4
1980	.3	.5	.4	.2
1981	.4	.7	.5	.3
1982	.5	.9	.7	.4
1983	.7	1.1	.9	.8
1984	.8	1.5	1.0	.9

a. Find the seasonal indexes.

b. Find the least squares trend line for the deseasonalized data.

c. Find the forecast for each quarter of 1985.

17.9 Is the experience of the managers of a company necessary to use in aiding the forecasting process, if the model fits the past data very well?

17.10 Refer to exercise 16.45. What is the deseasonalized forecast for January of 1984 for the price per square foot of the typical three-bedroom, two-bath, two-car–garage house? What is the actual forecast?

17.4

Simple Exponential Smoothing

In Chapter 16, we introduced the concept of smoothing a time series by computing a set of centered *moving averages*. The moving averages were used to derive the various seasonal indexes, but they also provided a "new" time series with considerably less random variation (irregular activity) and no seasonality. Because the moving average series was much smoother, it provided a clearer picture of any existing trend or cyclical activity.

Another method of smoothing a time series, which also serves as a forecasting procedure, is **exponential smoothing.** Unlike the moving averages, this technique uses all of the preceding observations to determine a smoothed value for a particular time period. The method described in this section is called **simple** (or single) **exponential smoothing** and works well for a time series containing *no trend* (Figure 17.5). A time series (such as the one in this figure) is said to be **stationary** if the data exhibit no trend and the variance about the mean ($\bar{y}_t$) remains constant over time. Simple exponential smoothing generally will track the original time series well, provided this series is stationary. We will extend the simple exponential smoothing procedure for a series containing trend and seasonality in later sections.

The simplest way to determine a smoothed value for time period t using exponential smoothing is to find a weighted sum of the actual observation for this time period, y_t, and the previous smoothed value, S_{t-1}.

$$S_t = \text{smoothed value for time period, } t$$
$$= Ay_t + (1 - A)S_{t-1} \qquad (17\text{-}2)$$

where A is any number between 0 and 1.

The value of A is the **smoothing constant.** Small values of A produce smoothed values giving less weight to the corresponding observation, y_t. You should use such values (say $A \leqslant .1$) for a volatile time series containing considerable irregular activity (noise). In this way, you give more weight to the previous smoothed value, S_{t-1}, rather than to the original observation, y_t. You can use larger values of A for a more stable time series.

Figure 17.5

Illustration of a stationary time series.

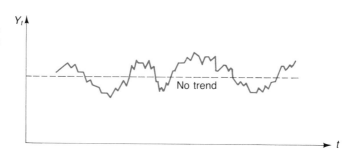

The smoothing procedure used here begins by setting the first smoothed value, S_1, equal to the first observation, y_1. So,

$$S_1 = y_1$$

Then,

$$S_2 = Ay_2 + (1 - A)S_1$$
$$\quad = Ay_2 + (1 - A)y_1$$
$$S_3 = Ay_3 + (1 - A)S_2$$
$$S_4 = Ay_4 + (1 - A)S_3$$

and so on.

The average attendance (in thousands—y_t) for major events held at the Jefferson County Civic Center for the past 13 years is contained in Table 17.2. We will determine the exponentially smoothed values using two smoothing constants, $A = .1$ and $A = .9$.

The actual time series and the two smoothed series are shown in Figure 17.6. For $A = .1$,

$$S_1 = y_1 = 5.0$$
$$S_2 = (.1)y_2 + (.9)S_1$$
$$\quad = (.1)(8.0) + (.9)(5.0) = 5.3$$
$$S_3 = (.1)y_3 + (.9)S_2$$
$$\quad = (.1)(2.1) + (.9)(5.3) = 4.98$$

and so on.

Notice that the average attendance, y_t, had a significant jump in 1980 when (it turns out) the facility was completely refurnished, providing better seating and more accessible snack booths. With the small value of $A = .1$, the smoothed values did not "track" the original series very well after this point. In general, when you use exponential smoothing with a small smoothing constant, the resulting series will be slow to detect any turning points or shifts in the observed values. However, such values of A provide considerable smoothing, as is evident from the values between the years 1972 and 1979.

Table 17.2

Actual and smoothed values for attendance at Jefferson County Civic Center

Year	t	y_t	$S_t (A = .1)$	$S_t (A = .9)$
1972	1	5.0	5.0	5.0
1973	2	8.0	5.3	7.7
1974	3	2.1	4.98	2.66
1975	4	7.1	5.19	6.66
1976	5	4.8	5.15	4.99
1977	6	2.0	4.84	2.30
1978	7	7.8	5.13	7.25
1979	8	5.0	5.12	5.23
1980	9	14.1	6.02	13.21
1981	10	13.0	6.72	13.02
1982	11	13.5	7.39	13.45
1983	12	14.2	8.07	14.12
1984	13	14.0	8.67	14.01

Figure 17.6

Smoothed values for
attendance data (Table
17.2).

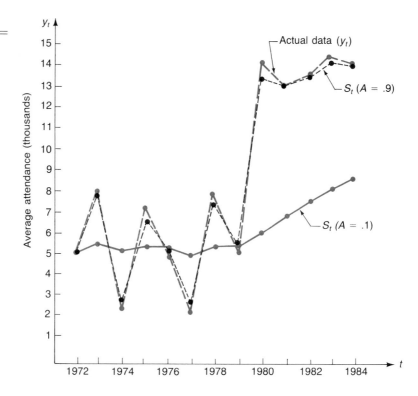

The large value of $A = .9$ provides much better tracking but not much smoothing. Larger smoothing constants are more useful for a time series that does not contain a great deal of random fluctuation. Later we will discuss methods of comparing the tracking ability for different values of A, in an effort to determine the "best" smoothing constant for a particular series.

To see why this procedure is called exponential smoothing, we will look at how each smoothed value is obtained. First, $S_1 = y_1$. Then,

$$S_2 = Ay_2 + (1 - A)S_1$$
$$= Ay_2 + (1 - A)y_1$$
$$S_3 = Ay_3 + (1 - A)S_2$$
$$= Ay_3 + (1 - A)[Ay_2 + (1 - A)y_1]$$
$$= Ay_3 + A(1 - A)y_2 + (1 - A)^2 y_1$$
$$S_4 = Ay_4 + (1 - A)S_3$$
$$= Ay_4 + (1 - A)[Ay_3 + A(1 - A)y_2 + \cdot(1 - A)^2 y_1]$$
$$= Ay_4 + A(1 - A)y_3 + A(1 - A)^2 y_2 + (1 - A)^3 y_1$$

In general,

$$S_t = Ay_t + A(1 - A)y_{t-1} + A(1 - A)^2 y_{t-2} + \ldots + A(1 - A)^{t-2} y_2 + (1 - A)^{t-1} y_1$$

For example, if $A = .3$, then

$$S_t = .3y_t + .21y_{t-1} + .15y_{t-2} + .10y_{t-3} + \ldots$$

Therefore, each smoothed value is actually a weighted sum of *all the previous obser-vations*. Because the more recent observations have the largest weight, they have a larger effect on the smoothed value. Notice that the weights on the observations are decreasing exponentially. That is, the weight given to a particular observation is some constant (namely, $1 - A$) *times* the weight given to the preceding observation. That is why this procedure is called exponential smoothing.

Forecasting Using Simple Exponential Smoothing

The naive forecasting procedure introduced earlier predicts the time series value for tomorrow using the actual value for today. In other words, $\hat{y}_{t+1} = y_t$. The exponential smoothing process is similar, except now the forecast for tomorrow is the *smoothed* value from today. In general,

$$\hat{y}_{t+1} = S_t \qquad\qquad (17\text{-}3)$$

For the special case where $A = 1$, we have

$$\hat{y}_{t+1} = S_t = 1y_t + (1 - 1)S_{t-1}$$
$$= y_t$$

and the exponential smoothing forecast is the same as that provided by the naive predictor. Because A is considerably less than one in practice, the smoothed forecast makes use of all the past observations, rather than only the most recent measurement.

Example 17.4

Using simple exponential smoothing with $A = .1$, what are the predicted values and residuals for the attendance data in Table 17.2?

Solution Suppose the year is 1972 ($t = 1$), and you want a forecast for 1973 ($t = 2$). This would be the smoothed value for 1972, so $\hat{y}_2 = S_1 = 5.0$. Next, the year is 1973, and you need a forecast for 1974. Here, $\hat{y}_3 = S_2 = 5.3$ (from Table 17.2). Continuing in this way, we obtain Table 17.3.

How well does this forecasting procedure perform here? We cannot use Figure 17.6 to compare the $\hat{y}$'s and the y's because, for each time period t, we have plotted y_t

Table 17.3

Forecasts and residuals using simple exponential smoothing on atten-dance data ($A = .1$)

Year	t	y_t	$\hat{y}_t$	Residual ($y_t - \hat{y}_t$)
1972	1	5.0	—	—
1973	2	8.0	5.0	3.00
1974	3	2.1	5.3	−3.20
1975	4	7.1	4.98	2.12
1976	5	4.8	5.19	− .39
1977	6	2.0	5.15	−3.15
1978	7	7.8	4.84	2.96
1979	8	5.0	5.13	− .13
1980	9	14.1	5.12	8.98
1981	10	13.0	6.02	6.98
1982	11	13.5	6.72	6.78
1983	12	14.2	7.39	6.81
1984	13	14.0	8.07	5.93

Figure 17.7

Predicted versus actual values for attendance data (Table 17.3).

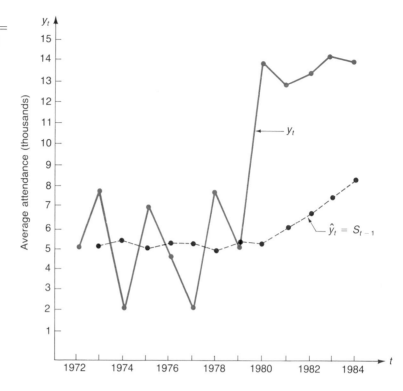

and S_t. The predicted value at t, however, is $\hat{y}_t = S_{t-1}$, not S_t. So we need to shift the smoothed values in Figure 17.6 one period to the right. This is shown in Figure 17.7, which contains a plot of the values in Table 17.3 for $A = .1$.

As we might expect from Figure 17.7, the residuals using this method are quite large from 1980 on because this value of A produces smoothed values that fail to adapt to the shift that occurred in 1980. This was not a good time series for simple exponential smoothing because of this sudden shift. However, between the years 1972 and 1979 (a relatively stationary set of observations), the smoothed time series contains much less noise using $A = .1$ and gives a clear indication of the lack of any trend. ●

This is a popular method of forecasting, particularly when there are hundreds, or perhaps thousands, of forecasts to be updated for each time period. Such is the case for many inventory-control systems, which are used to predict future demand levels for each item in inventory by means of a computerized forecasting procedure. Simple exponential smoothing often is used for such situations because each forecast, $\hat{y}_{t+1}$, requires only two values: the current observation (y_t) and the previous smoothed value, S_{t-1}. There is no need to store all of the previous observations. Computationally, the procedure is very simple and requires less computer time than do more sophisticated forecasting techniques.

Exercises

17.11 If the smoothed value for time period $t = 5$ is $S_5 = 10$, find the forecast using simple exponential smoothing for time period $t = 7$ assuming that $y_6 = 14$ and $A = 0.2$.

17.12 The Fitness and Health Center has been increasing its membership over the years and is considering opening a new center. The following table lists the quarterly membership for the past 4 years.

Year	Quarter 1	Quarter 2	Quarter 3	Quarter 4
1980	105	117	120	115
1981	110	125	130	126
1982	120	135	140	132
1983	131	141	145	141

Using simple exponential smoothing with $A = .3$, find the forecasted membership for the first quarter of 1984.

17.13 The yield on a general obligation bond for Harrisville county fluctuates with the market. The following are the monthly quotations for the past year.

Month	Yield
Jan	10.17
Feb	10.75
Mar	11.03
Apr	11.31
May	11.57
Jun	12.10
Jul	12.45
Aug	12.10
Sep	11.75
Oct	11.60
Nov	11.75
Dec	11.03

Using simple exponential smoothing with $A = .1$, find the forecasted yield for the months of October, November, and December using the data from the previous months. Calculate the residuals.

17.14 Refer to exercise 17.3. Using simple exponential smoothing with $A = .3$, calculate the forecasted price of the stock of Intersecond Bank for the years 1975 to 1984. Calculate the residuals. Compare the residuals from simple exponential smoothing with those from the naive model.

17.15 Refer to exercise 17.8. Using simple exponential smoothing with $A = .2$, calculate the forecasted amount of inventory for Slater Industries for the first quarter of 1985. Compare this to the forecasted value found in exercise 17.8.

17.5

Exponential Smoothing for a Time Series Containing Trend

The simple exponential smoothing technique discussed in the previous section always will lag behind a time series that contains a steadily increasing or decreasing trend. A procedure known as *Holt's two-parameter linear exponential smoothing* allows you to estimate separately the smoothed value of the time series as well as the average trend gain at each point in time. The resulting smoothed values track the past time series observations more accurately. We will refer to this procedure as **linear exponential smoothing.** There are two equations for this method. The first, for smoothing the observations, is

$$S_t = Ay_t + (1 - A)(S_{t-1} + b_{t-1}) \tag{17-4}$$

The second, for smoothing the trend, is

$$b_t = B(S_t - S_{t-1}) + (1 - B)b_{t-1} \qquad\qquad (17\text{-}5)$$

where (1) S_t is the smoothed value for time period t, (2) b_t is the smoothed *trend* estimate for this time period, and (3) A and B are smoothing constants between 0 and 1.

Smoothing the Observations (Equation 17-4)

Equation 17-4 is similar to the equation used for simple exponential smoothing, except that S_{t-1} is replaced by $(S_{t-1} + b_{t-1})$ to include the effect of the trend. The smoothing constant for this equation is $0 < A < 1$; typically, $A \leq .3$.

Smoothing the Trend (Equation 17-5)

Equation 17-5 is a new addition to the smoothing process, and represents the smoothed trend. It uses a separate smoothing constant, B, to smooth the trend values. This constant also is generally less than or equal to .3. This smoothed trend estimate is updated by using a weighted sum of (1) the difference between the last two smoothed values (an estimate of the current "trend") and (2) the previous smoothed trend estimate. Such a procedure significantly reduces any randomness (irregular activity) in the trend values across time.

Forecasting Using Linear Exponential Smoothing

This forecasting procedure uses both the smoothed observations and the smoothed trend estimates. The forecast for time period $t + 1$ is the current smoothed value plus the current smoothed trend value.

$$\hat{y}_{t+1} = S_t + b_t \qquad\qquad (17\text{-}6)$$

We also can use this procedure to forecast any number of time periods into the future; say, m periods. Here,

$$\hat{y}_{t+m} = S_t + mb_t \qquad\qquad (17\text{-}7)$$

The forecast using equation 17-6 is the **one-step ahead forecast** and the value from equation 17-7 is the **m-step ahead forecast**.

Summarizing the Results

To summarize the necessary calculations for linear exponential smoothing, you can use the format in Table 17.4. The initial year for this time series is 1972. As we did for simple exponential smoothing, we continue to set the first smoothed value, S_1, equal to the first observation, y_1. A new problem arises here, and this is an initial estimate of the trend, b_1. We will examine two procedures for estimating this value.

Table 17.4

Summary for linear exponential smoothing

Year	t	Actual Observation (y_t)	Smoothed Observation (S_t)	Smoothed trend (b_t)	Forecast $(\hat{y}_t)$	Residual $(y_t - \hat{y}_t)$
1972	1	y_1	$S_1 = y_1$	b_1	—	—
1973	2	y_2	S_2	b_2	$\hat{y}_2$	$y_2 - \hat{y}_2$
1974	3	y_3	S_3	b_3	$\hat{y}_3$	$y_3 - \hat{y}_3$
1975	4	y_4	S_4	b_4	$\hat{y}_4$	$y_4 - \hat{y}_4$

Procedure 1 Let $b_1 = 0$. Provided you have a large number of years in your observed time series, this procedure provides an adequate initial estimate for the trend. The smoothed trend value will soon "catch up" with the actual trend contained within the series.

Procedure 2 You can obtain a more accurate estimate of b_1 by using the first five (or so) time periods to estimate the initial trend. A least squares line is constructed through these five observations (exactly as discussed in Chapter 16), with the resulting equation $\hat{y} = a + bt$. The value of b provides an initial trend estimate.

We will demonstrate this technique in example 17.5, which uses both procedures to obtain the initial trend estimate, b_1.

Example 17.5

The time series contained in the following table contains the city taxes (in thousands of dollars) collected in Jackson City over the past 20 quarters. Using procedures 1 and 2 to calculate an initial trend estimate, obtain the smoothed values, S_t, for each time period. Also determine the predicted values, $\hat{y}_t$, using smoothing constants $A = .1$ and $B = .3$.

Year	Quarter	Taxes Collected
1980	1	76
	2	93
	3	108
	4	128
1981	1	196
	2	175
	3	141
	4	236
1982	1	256
	2	190
	3	227
	4	299
1983	1	403
	2	282
	3	288
	4	387
1984	1	484
	2	384
	3	330
	4	497

Table 17.5

Solution to example 17.5
using linear exponen-
tial smoothing ($A = .1$,
$B = .3$)

		PROCEDURE 1				PROCEDURE 2			
t	y_t	S_t	b_t	$\hat{y}_t$	$y_t - \hat{y}_t$	S_t	b_t	$\hat{y}_t$	$y_t - \hat{y}_t$
1	76.0	76.00	0.0	—	—	76.00	27.50	—	—
2	93.0	77.70	0.51	76.00	17.00	102.45	27.18	103.50	− 10.50
3	108.0	81.19	1.40	78.21	29.79	127.47	26.54	129.63	− 21.63
4	128.0	87.13	2.77	82.59	45.41	151.41	25.76	154.01	− 26.01
5	196.0	100.51	5.95	89.90	106.10	179.05	26.32	177.16	18.84
6	175.0	113.31	8.01	106.46	68.54	202.33	25.41	205.37	− 30.37
7	141.0	123.29	8.60	121.32	19.68	219.07	22.81	227.74	− 86.74
8	236.0	142.29	11.72	131.88	104.12	241.29	22.63	241.87	− 5.87
9	256.0	164.21	14.78	154.01	101.99	263.13	22.39	263.92	− 7.92
10	190.0	180.09	15.11	178.99	11.01	275.97	19.53	285.52	− 95.52
11	227.0	198.38	16.06	195.20	31.80	288.65	17.47	295.49	− 68.49
12	299.0	222.90	18.60	214.44	84.56	305.41	17.26	306.12	− 7.12
13	403.0	257.65	23.44	241.50	161.50	330.70	19.67	322.67	80.33
14	282.0	281.18	23.47	281.09	0.91	343.53	17.62	350.37	− 68.37
15	288.0	302.99	22.97	304.66	− 16.66	353.83	15.42	361.15	− 73.15
16	387.0	332.07	24.80	325.96	61.04	371.03	15.96	369.26	17.74
17	484.0	369.58	28.62	356.87	127.13	396.69	18.87	386.99	97.01
18	384.0	396.78	28.19	398.20	− 14.20	412.40	17.92	415.55	− 31.55
19	330.0	415.47	25.34	424.97	− 94.97	420.29	14.91	430.32	− 100.32
20	497.0	446.43	27.03	440.81	56.19	441.38	16.76	435.20	61.80

Solution A summary of the results using both initial trend estimates is shown in
Table 17.5. For procedure 1, $b_1 = 0$. For procedure 2, the first five years were used
to obtain an initial trend estimate. The least squares line through these five observations is $\hat{y}_t = 37.7 + 27.5t$, and so we use $b_1 = 27.5$ for procedure 2.

To illustrate the necessary calculations here, consider $t = 10$, using procedure 1.

1. $y_{10} = 190$

2. $S_{10} = .1y_{10} + .9(S_9 + b_9)$

    $= .1(190) + .9(164.21 + 14.78)$

    $= 180.09$

3. $b_{10} = .3(S_{10} - S_9) + .7(b_9)$

    $= .3(180.09 - 164.21) + .7(14.78)$

    $= 15.11$

4. $\hat{y}_{10} = S_9 + b_9$ (from equation 17-6)

    $= 164.21 + 14.78 = 178.99$

5. Residual for $t = 10$ is

    $y_{10} - \hat{y}_{10} = 190 - 178.99$

    $= 11.01$

Figure 17.8

Predicted values using
linear exponential
smoothing ($A = .1$,
$B = .3$).

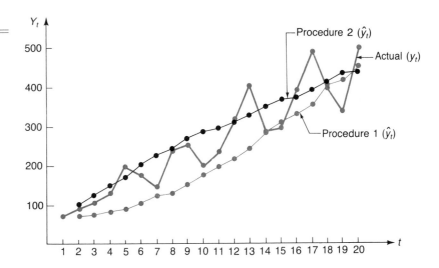

The values of y_t and $\hat{y}_t$ (the predicted value for that time period) are shown in Figure 17.8. For this particular example, procedure 2, which used the first five years to obtain the initial trend estimate, estimated (and smoothed) the past values more accurately.

●

Exercises

17.16 Using Holt's two-parameter linear exponential smoothing technique, find the smoothed value at time $t = 9$, using these values with $A = .1$ and $B = .2$.

$$Y_9 = 10.5$$
$$S_8 = 10.0$$
$$S_7 = 9.5$$
$$b_8 = 0.5$$

17.17 The number of employees at Computeron has fluctuated over the past 9 years. The table lists the number of employees on the payroll at Computeron at the end of each year for the years 1976 to 1984. The company would like you to forecast employment in 1985 by using the linear exponential smoothing technique.

Year	Employees
1976	1030
1977	1020
1978	1041
1979	1050
1980	1062
1981	1075
1982	1130
1983	1135
1984	1175

a. Using an initial estimate of the slope to be zero with $A = .2$ and $B = .2$, determine the predicted value for the employment at the end of 1985.

b. Using the least squares estimate for the slope, from the first 3 years, redo question a.

c. Compare the predicted values in questions a and b.

17.18 The amount of money in the money-market account at First Louisiana State Bank has fluctuated with the interest rate over the years. The bank would like to make a forecast using linear exponential smoothing.

Year	Amount in Money-Market Account
1974	390,121
1975	395,310
1976	416,432
1977	427,489
1978	443,560
1979	435,495
1980	440,370
1981	444,184
1982	458,543
1983	451,967

a. Using an initial estimate of the slope to be zero, find the predicted value for the amount of money in the money-market account at the end of 1984. Let $A = .1$ and $B = .2$.

b. Using the least squares estimate for the slope from the first 3 years, redo question a. What is the predicted value for the amount of money in the money-market account at the end of 1984?

17.19 Using the data in exercise 17.3, find the predicted value for the stock price of Intersecond Bank for 1985, using linear exponential smoothing. Let the initial value of the slope be zero, with $A = .09$ and $B = .15$.

17.20 Using the data in exercise 17.12, find the forecasted membership values for the 4 quarters of 1984. Use the least squares estimate of the slope of the first five observations for the initial value of the slope. Let $A = .3$ and $B = .2$. Compare these forecasted values with those obtained in exercise 17.12

17.6

Exponential Smoothing Method for Trend and Seasonality

As we discussed earlier, seasonality is present in a time series whenever certain months or quarters are consistently higher or lower than the yearly average. In such cases, an extension of Holt's method, **Winter's linear and seasonal exponential smoothing**, offers additional flexibility. This three-parameter technique (that is, there are three smoothing constants) not only smooths the past observation and trend estimates (as does linear exponential smoothing) but also provides smoothed seasonality factors for each time period.

The smoothing equations for Winter's method are, for smoothing the observations,

$$S_t = A\left(\frac{y_t}{F_{t-L}}\right) + (1 - A)(S_{t-1} + b_{t-1}) \qquad (17\text{-}8)$$

for smoothing the seasonality factors,

$$F_t = B\left(\frac{y_t}{S_t}\right) + (1 - B)F_{t-L} \qquad (17\text{-}9)$$

and for smoothing the trend estimates,

$$b_t = C(S_t - S_{t-1}) + (1 - C)b_{t-1} \qquad\qquad (17\text{-}10)$$

Here, (1) S_t is the smoothed observation for time period t; (2) F_t is the smoothed seasonality factor for this time period; (3) b_t is the smoothed estimate of trend; (4) L is the number of periods per year ($L = 4$ for quarterly data and $L = 12$ for monthly data); and (5) A, B, and C are the three smoothing constants.

Equations 17-8 and 17-10 are similar to the corresponding equations from the linear exponential smoothing procedure, except that S_t now consists of deseasonalized smoothed values. These are obtained by dividing each observation, y_t, by the smoothed seasonal factor of one year previous to that observation, F_{t-L}.

Forecasting Using Linear and Seasonal Exponential Smoothing

The procedure for forecasting using Winter's exponential smoothing method is similar to that used for Holt's. Here, the forecast for a particular quarter (month) includes the effect of all three smoothing equations. The forecast for m periods ahead is

$$\hat{y}_{t+m} = (S_t + mb_t) \cdot F_{t+m-L} \qquad\qquad (17\text{-}11)$$

The term $(S_t + mb_t)$ represents the smoothed *deseasonalized* estimate and includes the smoothed trend effect. The seasonality is included in the final estimate by multiplying by the smoothed seasonality factor belonging to the quarter (or month) one year previous to the forecast time period, namely, F_{t+m-L}. This procedure is much like that used in section 17.3, where the deseasonalized estimate was multiplied by the corresponding seasonal index to arrive at the final forecast.

When using this procedure on the past observations, you would, for example, determine $\hat{y}_{10}$ by assuming observations $y_1, y_2, \ldots, y_9$ are available. You would do a one-step ahead forecast ($m = 1$) using the smoothed seasonal value from the previous year; that is, $F_{10-4} = F_6$, assuming quarterly data. As a result,

$$\hat{y}_{10} = [S_9 + (1)b_9] \cdot F_6$$

Similarly,

$$\hat{y}_{11} = [S_{10} + (1)b_{10}] \cdot F_7$$
$$\hat{y}_{12} = [S_{11} + (1)b_{11}] \cdot F_8$$

and so on.

Forecasting *beyond* the range of your observations (extrapolating) will be illustrated in the next section.

When dealing with quarterly data, your first set of predicted values will be

$$\hat{y}_5 = [S_4 + (1)b_4] \cdot F_1$$
$$\hat{y}_6 = [S_5 + (1)b_5] \cdot F_2$$
$$\hat{y}_7 = [S_6 + (1)b_6] \cdot F_3$$

and so on. If the time series consists of monthly observations ($L = 12$), then you begin your predicted values with

$$\hat{y}_{13} = [S_{12} + (1)b_{12}] \cdot F_1$$

$$\hat{y}_{14} = [S_{13} + (1)b_{13}] \cdot F_2$$

$$\hat{y}_{15} = [S_{14} + (1)b_{14}] \cdot F_3$$

and so on.

Summarizing the Results

A method of summarizing the necessary calculations is shown in Table 17.6. Suppose that the original year of the observed time series is 1980, with quarterly observations. Initial estimates must be supplied for (1) the seasonal factors for each quarter of 1979, (2) the trend estimate for quarter 4, 1979, and (3) the smoothed value corresponding to quarter 4, 1979.

Once again, we will examine two procedures for this situation—one is quick and easy, and the other is more accurate but requires additional calculations. Procedure 1 is used in Table 17.6. Both procedures will be demonstrated in example 17.6. These are not the only procedures—can you think of one or two others?

Procedure 1

1. Set the initial seasonal factors equal to 1.
2. Set the initial trend estimate (b_0) equal to 0.
3. Set the initial smoothed value for quarter 4, 1979 (S_0) equal to the actual value for quarter 4, 1980 (y_4). This is also the *forecasted value* ($\hat{y}_t$) for each of the 4 quarters in 1980.

Table 17.6

Summary of linear and seasonal exponential smoothing (using procedure 1)

Year	Qtr.	t	Actual Observations (y_t)	Smoothed Observations (S_t)	Smoothed Seasonal Factors (F_t)	Smoothed Trend (b_t)	Forecast ($\hat{y}_t$)	Residual ($y_t - \hat{y}_t$)
1979	1				(1) 1.0			
(year 0)	2				1.0			
	3			(3)	1.0	(2)		
	4			$S_0 = y_4$	1.0	$b_0 = 0$		
1980	1	1	y_1	S_1	F_1	b_1	$\hat{y}_1 = S_0$	$y_1 - \hat{y}_1$
(year 1)	2	2	y_2	S_2	F_2	b_2	$\hat{y}_2 = S_0$	$y_2 - \hat{y}_2$
	3	3	y_3	S_3	F_3	b_3	$\hat{y}_3 = S_0$	$y_3 - \hat{y}_3$
	4	4	y_4	S_4	F_4	b_4	$\hat{y}_4 = S_0$	$y_4 - \hat{y}_4$
1981	1	5	y_5	S_5	F_5	b_5	$\hat{y}_5$	$y_5 - \hat{y}_5$
(year 2)	2	6	y_6	S_6	F_6	b_6	$\hat{y}_6$	$y_6 - \hat{y}_6$
	.							
	.							
	.							

Procedure 2

1. Use the first two years of data to determine the seasonal indexes. These are the four values for F_t in 1979. Actually, any number of years of data can be used here.
2. Deseasonalize the data for the first two years (or any number of years), and calculate the least squares line through these deseasonalized values, d_t. Call this line $\hat{d}_t = a + bt$. The initial trend estimate (b_0) is b.
3. The initial smoothed value for quarter 4, 1979 will be $S_0 = [a + b(0)]$ · (seasonal index for quarter 4 in step 1) $= a$ · (seasonal index), where a is the intercept of the least squares line in step 2. Also, S_0 is the *forecast value* ($\hat{y}_t$) for each of the 4 quarters in 1980.

Example 17.6 The quarterly taxes from Jackson City in example 17.5 indicated significant seasonality. In particular, the first-quarter taxes appeared to be considerably larger than those for the yearly average. Using the linear and seasonal exponential smoothing procedures, determine the smoothed value, S_t, and predicted value, $\hat{y}_t$, for each time period. Use smoothing constants $A = .1$, $B = .3$, and $C = .2$.

Solution The computed results using procedure 1 are summarized in Table 17.7, where $b_0 = 0$, $S_0 = y_4$, and the initial seasonal factors are each 1.

The procedure 2 solution is contained in Table 17.8. The first two years were used to obtain the initial seasonal factors by finding the four seasonal indexes as described in Chapter 16. These are

quarter 1 = 1.23   quarter 3 = .91
quarter 2 = .98   quarter 4 = .88

Table 17.7

Solution using linear and seasonal exponential smoothing, procedure 1 ($A = .1$, $B = .3$, $C = .2$)

	t	y_t	S_t	F_t	b_t	$\hat{y}_t$	$y_t - \hat{y}_t$
				1.0			
				1.0			
				1.0			
			128	1.0	0.0		
1980	1	76.0	122.80	0.89	−1.04	128.00	−52.00
	2	93.0	118.88	0.93	−1.62	128.00	−35.00
	3	108.0	116.34	0.98	−1.80	128.00	−20.00
	4	128.0	115.89	1.03	−1.53	128.00	0.0
1981	5	196.0	125.05	1.09	0.61	101.28	94.72
	6	175.0	131.81	1.05	1.84	117.45	57.55
	7	141.0	134.70	1.00	2.05	130.78	10.22
	8	236.0	145.95	1.21	3.89	141.03	94.97
1982	9	256.0	158.34	1.25	5.59	163.36	92.64
	10	190.0	165.59	1.08	5.92	172.55	17.45
	11	227.0	177.08	1.08	7.04	171.33	55.67
	12	299.0	190.48	1.32	8.31	222.23	76.77
1983	13	403.0	211.19	1.45	10.79	248.11	154.89
	14	282.0	225.87	1.13	11.57	239.97	42.03
	15	288.0	240.26	1.12	12.13	257.35	30.65
	16	387.0	256.57	1.37	12.97	332.12	54.88
1984	17	484.0	276.05	1.54	14.27	389.79	94.21
	18	384.0	295.23	1.18	15.25	328.43	55.57
	19	330.0	308.94	1.10	14.94	347.21	−17.21
	20	497.0	327.68	1.42	15.70	444.89	52.11

Table 17.8

Solution using linear and seasonal exponential smoothing, procedure 2 ($A = .1$, $B = .3$, $C = .2$)	t	y_t	S_t	F_t	b_t	$\hat{y}_t$	$y_t - \hat{y}_t$
				1.23			
				.98			
				.91			
			39	.88	23		
1980	1	76.0	61.98	1.23	23.00	39.00	37.00
	2	93.0	85.97	1.01	23.19	39.00	54.00
	3	108.0	110.11	0.93	23.38	39.00	69.00
	4	128.0	134.69	0.90	23.62	39.00	89.00
1981	5	196.0	158.44	1.23	23.65	194.55	1.45
	6	175.0	181.19	1.00	23.47	184.00	−9.00
	7	141.0	199.34	0.86	22.40	190.59	−49.59
	8	236.0	225.76	0.94	23.21	199.81	36.19
1982	9	256.0	244.86	1.18	22.39	306.56	−50.56
	10	190.0	259.57	0.92	20.85	266.48	−76.48
	11	227.0	278.65	0.85	20.50	242.31	−15.31
	12	299.0	300.90	0.96	20.85	282.51	16.49
1983	13	403.0	323.85	1.20	21.27	378.24	24.76
	14	282.0	341.34	0.89	20.51	316.67	−34.67
	15	288.0	359.58	0.83	20.06	307.30	−19.30
	16	387.0	382.02	0.98	20.53	364.14	22.86
1984	17	484.0	402.76	1.20	20.58	481.55	2.45
	18	384.0	424.14	0.89	20.74	376.83	7.17
	19	330.0	439.92	0.81	19.75	371.36	−41.36
	20	497.0	464.65	1.00	20.74	448.32	48.68

Next, the data from the first 2 years were deseasonalized by dividing by the corresponding seasonal index to obtain the deseasonalized values, d_t. A least squares line through these eight values using the simple linear regression procedure from Chapter 16 produced

$$\hat{d}_t = 44.03 + 23.02t$$

The value of 23.02 (rounded to 23) became the initial slope estimate, b_0. Finally, the initial smoothed value for quarter 4, 1979, is

$$S_0 = (44.03)(\text{initial seasonal index for quarter 4})$$

$$= (44.03)(.88) = 38.7 \text{ (rounded to 39)}$$

Also, $S_0 = 39$ becomes the forecast value ($\hat{y}_t$) for each of the quarters in 1980. The calculations required here can be illustrated using Table 17.7 and $t = 10$ for procedure 1.

1. $y_{10} = 190$

2. $S_{10} = .1\left(\dfrac{y_{10}}{F_{10-4}}\right) + .9(S_9 + b_9)$

$$= .1\left(\dfrac{y_{10}}{F_6}\right) + .9(S_9 + b_9)$$

$$= .1\left(\dfrac{190}{1.05}\right) + .9(158.34 + 5.59)$$

$$= 165.59$$

Figure 17.9

Forecasted values using linear and seasonal exponential smoothing ($A = .1$, $B = .3$, $C = .2$).

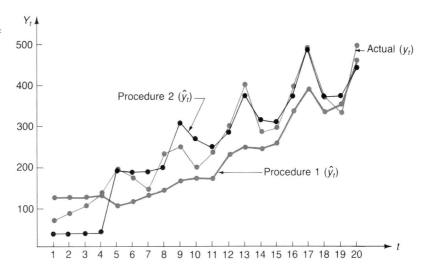

3. $F_{10} = .3\left(\dfrac{y_{10}}{S_{10}}\right) + .7F_6$

$= .3\left(\dfrac{190}{165.59}\right) + .7(1.05)$

$= 1.08$

4. $b_{10} = .2(S_{10} - S_9) + .8b_9$

$= .2(165.59 - 158.34) + .8(5.59)$

$= 5.92$

5. $\hat{y}_{10} = [(S_9 + (1)(b_9)]F_6$ (from equation 17-11)

$= (158.34 + 5.59)1.05$ (computer-stored value is 1.0526)

$= 172.55$

6. Residual for $t = 10$ is

$y_{10} - \hat{y}_{10} = 190 - 172.55$

$= 17.45$

A graphical illustration of the actual observations, y_t, and the predicted value for each time period, $\hat{y}_t$, is shown in Figure 17.9. Once again, the more complex procedure 2 performed better than did procedure 1; for the last ten quarters, procedure 2 tracked the actual time series extremely well. ●

Exercises

17.21 Using Winter's linear and seasonal smoothing technique, answer the following questions using these values:

$b_6 = 0.7$	$F_8 = 0.9$	$B = 0.1$
$S_7 = 15.7$	$F_4 = 0.75$	$C = 0.1$
$S_6 = 14.3$	$Y_8 = 15.0$	$L = 4$
$S_5 = 14.0$	$A = 0.2$	

a. Find the smoothed observation for time $t = 8$.

b. Find the forecasted value for time period 8.

17.22 Ektronics manufactures electronic testing and measuring instruments. The company has managed to capture a large share of the market over the past 4 years. Sales of its equipment (in ten thousands) is recorded monthly for 1982 to 1985.

Year	Jan	Feb	Mar	Apr	May	Jun	Jul	Aug	Sep	Oct	Nov	Dec
1982	1.0	1.1	1.2	1.7	1.9	2.3	2.7	3.1	2.5	2.3	2.0	1.9
1983	1.7	1.4	1.5	1.7	2.4	2.7	3.3	3.9	3.4	3.0	2.6	2.0
1984	1.9	2.0	2.1	2.3	3.1	3.5	4.1	4.7	4.3	3.4	2.9	2.8
1985	2.9	2.8	2.7	3.4	3.7	4.1	4.6	5.0	4.7	4.0	3.7	3.6

Use Winter's linear and seasonal smoothing technique to find the smoothed values for the first 4 months of 1985. Let $A = .2$, $B = .1$, and $C = .1$. Using procedure 1, set the initial estimates of the seasonal factors to 1.0 and let $b_0 = 0$.

17.23 The earnings per share of Mecta Mining, a large producer of silver, are:

Year	Quarter 1	Quarter 2	Quarter 3	Quarter 4
1979	0.25	0.20	0.27	0.30
1980	0.26	0.24	0.34	0.37
1981	0.30	0.27	0.38	0.45
1982	0.36	0.32	0.47	0.50

Using the linear and seasonal exponential smoothing procedure, determine the predicted value for each quarter of 1983. Use procedure 2 and the first two years of data to obtain b_0, S_0, and the four initial seasonal factors (F). Let $A = .3$, $B = .2$, and $C = .1$.

17.24 Refer to exercise 17.7. Find the predicted values of future business for Sands Motel for the 12 months of 1981, using the linear and seasonal exponential smoothing procedure. Use procedure 1 to obtain b_0, S_0, and the four initial seasonal factors (F). Let $A = .2$, $B = .1$, and $C = .1$.

17.25 Refer to exercise 17.8. Find the predicted amount of inventory for the 4 quarters of 1985 using the linear and seasonal exponential smoothing procedure. Use procedure 2 and the first two years of data to obtain b_0, S_0, and the four initial seasonal factors (F). Let $A = .05$, $B = .1$, and $C = .1$.

17.26 Refer to exercise 17.12. Find the forecasted memberships for the 4 quarters of 1984 using procedure 1 of the linear and seasonal exponential smoothing techniques. Compare these values to those obtained in exercise 17.12. Let $A = .05$, $B = .1$, and $C = .1$.

17.7

Choosing the Appropriate Forecasting Procedure

Our purpose in showing you several different forecasting techniques is to point out that, unfortunately, no one procedure works well all the time. One method may work well on a particular steadily increasing time series that has little random fluctuation but perform poorly on a series that has considerable seasonality or random fluctuation.

As you gain more experience in time series applications, you will be better able to choose an appropriate forecasting technique. One factor to consider is the length of your forecast. We classify the forecast period as

Short-term forecast: one to three months
Medium-range forecast: greater than three months but less than 2 years
Long-range forecast: two years or more

The exponential smoothing procedures are excellent for *short-term* forecasts, whereas the component decomposition method (in Section 17.3) is useful in medium- and long-range forecasting. The latter also is a popular procedure for many short-term applications, including inventory control and production planning.

One method of deciding whether a certain forecast technique is appropriate in a particular situation is to determine how well the procedure "fits" the observed time series. You accomplish this by pretending that, in each time period, the next observation is unknown, and letting the forecasting procedure "predict" the next value (the $\hat{y}_t$ values in the previous examples). Next, you compare the predicted ($\hat{y}_t$) values with the observed values (y_t).

The two most popular methods of comparing the predicted and observed values use measures involving the residuals. They are the mean absolute deviation and the predictive mean squared error. The **mean absolute deviation (MAD)** is the average of the absolute values of each residual. Let

$$e_t = \text{residual at time } t$$

$$= y_t - \hat{y}_t$$

The mean absolute deviation is defined as

$$\text{MAD} = \frac{\Sigma |e_t|}{n} \tag{17-12}$$

where n is the number of *predicted* values obtained from the past data. For example, when using linear exponential smoothing on 20 data values, you obtain 19 predicted values because $\hat{y}_1$ is unavailable. So $n = 19$ and not 20.

The **predictive mean squared error (MSE)** is similar to the MAD, except we find the average of the *squared* residuals.

$$(\text{predictive}) \text{ MSE} = \frac{\Sigma e_t^2}{n} \tag{17-13}$$

where, again, n is the number of predicted values.*

The MSE severely penalizes large residuals because it *squares* each value. Consequently, you use the MSE for situations in which you prefer several small residuals to one large value and wish to be warned if there is one larger residual.

To illustrate these measures, consider Table 17.9. For forecasting method 1, there are no large errors, whereas method 2 results in one large residual. So the MSE is smaller for method 1, but the MAD is smaller for method 2. When using either measure, the *smaller* this value, the *more accurate* your forecast procedure.

There is no consensus among statisticians as to which measure is preferable. Instead, it depends on the results of having large forecast residuals. If a large error is disastrous

---

*The MSE that we compute as a measure of how well a forecasting procedure fits the observed data is not the same as the MSE computed in a normal ANOVA table. The ANOVA MSE is equal to SSE/ (degrees of freedom for residual). In contrast, the predictive MSE is not used in any test of hypothesis and is merely the average of the squared deviations.

Table 17.9

Comparison of the mean absolute deviation (MAD) and the mean squared error (MSE)

Forecast	y_t	$\hat{y}_t$	$e_t = y_t - \hat{y}_t$	$|e_t|$	e_t^2
METHOD 1	36	32	4	4	16
	42	46	-4	4	16
	45	49	-4	4	16
				12	48

$$\text{MAD} = \frac{\Sigma|e_t|}{n} = \frac{12}{3} = 4.0$$

$$\text{MSE} = \frac{\Sigma e_t^2}{n} = \frac{48}{3} = 16.0$$

METHOD 2	36	34	2	2	4
	42	40	2	2	4
	45	52	-7	7	49
				11	57

$$\text{MAD} = \frac{11}{3} = 3.67$$

$$\text{MSE} = \frac{57}{3} = 19.0$$

(such as in predicting the inventory level of an expensive product), then using the MSE is preferable. On the other hand, if you can afford to overlook a single severe miss provided the general tracking is close, then the MAD serves better.

Example 17.7

We used two types of exponential smoothing to smooth (and predict) the city taxes collected in Jackson City over the past five years. Data from the past 20 quarters are contained in the table in example 17.5, in which we used linear exponential smoothing (with smoothing constants $A = .1$ and $B = .3$) to reduce randomness within the observations and trend values. The results are summarized in Table 17.5, using the two procedures for providing initial estimates.

Example 17.6 examined the same data using linear and seasonal exponential smoothing, with smoothing constants $A = .1$, $B = .3$, and $C = .2$. A much better fit was obtained using the more sophisticated method of providing initial smoothed estimates (procedure 2). These results are summarized in Tables 17.7 and 17.8 and are presented graphically in Figure 17.9.

Determine the predictive MSE for each of these four methods. Using the appropriate procedure, determine the forecasted tax revenue for each quarter of 1985.

Solution

1. *Linear Exponential Smoothing (Procedure 1).* The residuals from this forecasting procedure are contained in Table 17.5. The computed predictive mean squared error is

$$\text{MSE} = \frac{(17.00)^2 + (29.79)^2 + \ldots + (56.19)^2}{19}$$

$$= 5670.11$$

2. *Linear Exponential Smoothing (Procedure 2).* Based on Figure 17.8, we would expect a much smaller predictive MSE here. There are no surprises because

$$MSE = \frac{(-10.50)^2 + (-21.63)^2 + \ldots + (61.80)^2}{19}$$

$$= 3426.46$$

3. *Linear and Seasonal Exponential Smoothing (Procedure 1).* These residuals are listed in Table 17.7, with a corresponding predictive mean squared error of

$$MSE = \frac{(-52.00)^2 + (-35.00)^2 + \ldots + (52.11)^2}{20}$$

$$= 4414.95$$

(Note that we divide by 20 here, because 20 predicted values are available using this procedure.)

A warning: it is not valid to conclude, based on the large MSE value, that this forecasting method is less appropriate than linear exponential smoothing. Remember that we are at the mercy of the particular values of the smoothing constants, *A, B,* and *C.* Perhaps a different set of constants would have resulted in a significantly smaller MSE. Finding the "best" set of constants for any one application involves finding the set of values for *A, B,* and *C* that *minimize* the resulting predictive MSE. This (not insignificant) computational burden is one of the drawbacks to using Holt's and Winter's exponential smoothing techniques.

4. *Linear and Seasonal Exponential Smoothing (Procedure 2).* Based on Figure 17.9, we observe excellent agreement between the actual time series, y_t, and the predicted series, $\hat{y}_t$, using the smoothed estimates. A very small predictive MSE value would be expected here, and such is the case.

$$MSE = \frac{(37.00)^2 + (54.00)^2 + \ldots + (48.68)^2}{20}$$

$$= 1828.89$$

We conclude that the best choice of these four alternatives is the linear and seasonal exponential smoothing method using procedure 2 to derive the original estimates.

5. *Forecasted Tax Revenue.* Using equation 17-11 and the results in Table 17.8, the forecasts for 1985 would be as follows.

For the first quarter (one-step ahead): $t = 20, L = 4, m = 1$

$$\hat{y}_{21} = [S_{20} + (1)b_{20}] \cdot F_{17}$$

$$= [464.65 + (1)(20.74)](1.20)$$

$$= 582$$

For the second quarter (two-step ahead): $t = 20, L = 4, m = 2$

$$\hat{y}_{22} = [S_{20} + (2)b_{20}] \cdot F_{18}$$

$$= [464.65 + (2)(20.74)] \cdot (.89)$$

$$= 450$$

For the third quarter (three-step ahead): $t = 20$, $L = 4$, $m = 3$

$$\hat{y}_{23} = [S_{20} + (3)b_{20}] \cdot F_{19}$$
$$= [464.65 + (3)(20.74)] \, (.81)$$
$$= 427$$

For the fourth quarter (four-step ahead): $t = 20$, $L = 4$, $m = 4$

$$\hat{y}_{24} = [S_{20} + (4)b_{20}] \cdot F_{20}$$
$$= [464.65 + (4)(20.74)] \cdot (1.00)$$
$$= 548$$

Selecting the Smoothing Constants

As mentioned earlier, the computed MSE (or MAD) value for any exponential smoothing procedure is determined not only by the procedure itself but also by the value of the necessary smoothing constants. In example 17.6, the smoothing constants were $A = .1$, $B = .3$, and $C = .2$, with a corresponding MSE value of 1828.89, using procedure 2. By changing these constants, you might improve the fit (lower the MSE), or you might obtain a less desirable solution (a larger MSE).

To illustrate this point, using example 17.6 and procedure 2, for

$A = .1$, $B = .4$, $C = .3 :$ MSE $= 1748.10$ (an improvement)

$A = .2$, $B = .2$, $C = .2 :$ MSE $= 2127.67$

To arrive at the smallest possible predictive MSE, you must examine a variety of values, compute the MSE for each combination, and select the set of values that provides the smallest MSE. For example, if you consider all nonzero values of A, B, and C between 0 and .4, in increments of .05, this results in $(.4/.05)^3 = 8^3 = 512$ different passes through the procedure to determine the corresponding 512 MSE values. The set of A, B, and C values that provides the smallest MSE is the one you should use in forecasting future values of the time series.

This procedure is not extremely difficult to perform with the help of a computer, but it takes away one main advantage of exponential smoothing—namely, the computational simplicity of this procedure in calculating and updating smoothed estimates. If you are using this method to perform a small number of forecasts, then this poses no problem. On the other hand, if the technique is being used to forecast future demand levels continuously for thousands of inventory items, then this added complexity is a cause for concern. You will have to consider complexity versus cost on an individual application basis.

We can increase the computational burden (but also improve the accuracy) even more by using different values of the smoothing constant(s) at different times in the analysis of a time series. Such techniques are computer controlled. The constant(s) are changed automatically to adapt the process to shifts in the structure of the time series, using **adaptive control procedures.** An excellent discussion of these methods is contained in the text by Johnson and Montgomery, referenced at the end of this chapter.

We have showed you several forecasting procedures and methods for comparing the predictive accuracy of these techniques. Our purpose is to give you an arsenal of methodologies that will allow you to apply each procedure to a particular time series and then summarize and compare the resulting residuals. In this way, you can determine the most accurate procedure for a particular time series and use this method to arrive at a forecast.

Next we turn to another forecasting model, the autoregressive model. With this procedure, we again use the past observations to predict future values but in a slightly different way: we use the past values as variables in a regression equation.

Exercises

17.27 Consider the following forecasts for the yearly sales of Dentroff Wholesale Plumbing Supplies. Sales are given in units of 100,000.

Year	Actual	Forecast
1972	1.1	—
1973	1.2	1.0
1974	1.5	1.3
1975	1.9	1.6
1976	2.3	1.8
1977	2.1	2.0
1978	2.0	2.2
1979	2.5	2.3
1980	2.7	2.5
1981	3.4	2.9

a. Compute the MAD and predictive MSE for the forecasts.

b. Compute the MAD and predictive MSE using the naive forecasts of sales.

c. Compare the forecasts in questions a and b.

17.28 The advertising expenditure for a local supermarket (in thousands of dollars) is:

Year	Jan	Feb	Mar	Apr	May	Jun	Jul	Aug	Sep	Oct	Nov	Dec
1982	.3	.4	.4	.5	.5	.6	.7	.7	.8	.7	.7	.6
1983	.5	.6	.6	.7	.6	.8	.9	1.0	1.2	1.1	1.1	1.0
1984	.7	.8	.9	.9	.9	.8	.9	1.0	1.1	1.4	1.3	1.2
1985	.9	1.0	1.0	1.2	1.1	1.3	1.4	1.6	1.6	1.4	1.5	1.3

a. Using the naive model, obtain a forecast for the 47 time periods, omitting the first time period. Find the MAD and the predictive MSE.

b. Obtain a forecast for the 47 time periods, omitting the first time period, by using a least squares line that represents just trend. Find the MAD and predictive MSE.

c. Obtain a forecast for the 47 time periods, omitting the first time period, using only the trend and seasonal components to forecast. Find the MAD and predictive MSE.

d. Compare the forecasts obtained in questions a, b and c.

17.29 Two forecasting procedures produce the following set of forecast errors:

Year	Month	Procedure 1	Procedure 2	Year	Month	Procedure 1	Procedure 2
1984	Jan	+5	+1		Nov	+6	+2
	Feb	+7	−2		Dec	+1	+1
	Mar	+6	+3	1985	Jan	−3	−3
	Apr	+2	−1		Feb	−5	+1
	May	−1	+2		Mar	−4	0
	Jun	−2	0		Apr	+3	−2
	Jul	−3	+1		May	+2	−19
	Aug	+2	+1		Jun	−1	−20
	Sep	+4	0				
	Oct	+7	−1				

Compute the predictive MSE and MAD for each forecasting procedure. Comment on the adequacy of the forecasting procedure.

17.30 The following data represent the number of single-family housing starts in a certain sector of the state of California. The units are in 10,000.

Year	Quarter 1	Quarter 2	Quarter 3	Quarter 4
1982	.6	.8	1.4	.8
1983	.9	1.1	1.7	1.3
1984	1.2	1.4	2.1	1.6
1985	1.4	1.7	2.6	1.9

a. Using the simple exponential procedure with $A = 0.3$, find the predicted number of housing starts for each time period, omitting the first time period. Find the predictive MSE and MAD.

b. Use Holt's two-parameter linear exponential smoothing technique to obtain a forecast for each time period, omitting the first time period. Let $A = .3$ and $B = .2$. Use the least squares estimate of the slope for the initial value of the slope from the first 5 periods. Find the predictive MSE and MAD.

c. Compare the forecasts obtained in questions a and b.

17.31 If an investor invested $10,000 into the T. Krow long-term–growth mutual fund, the investor would have realized a gain of 93% after 5 years. The following table shows the performance of the fund over this period of time.

Year	Quarter 1	Quarter 2	Quarter 3	Quarter 4
1981	10,031	9,638	12,591	12,480
1982	12,691	11,745	13,721	13,980
1983	13,043	12,680	15,376	15,860
1984	14,932	14,280	17,035	17,210
1985	16,830	15,923	18,671	19,300

a. Use Winter's linear and seasonal smoothing technique to find the forecasted value of the original $10,000 invested for each of the quarters of 1983, 1984, and 1985. Let $A = .2$, $B = .1$, and $C = .1$. Using procedure 1 and Winter's technique, set the initial estimates of the seasonal factors to 1.0 and $b_0 = 0$. Find the predictive MSE.

b. Redo question a with $A = .1$, $B = .2$, and $C = .2$. Find the predictive MSE.

c. Compare the forecasts found in questions a and b using the predictive MSEs.

17.32 Explain how the MAD and predictive MSE differ in what they measure. Why should the sum of the forecast errors divided by the number of forecasts not be used to compare two forecasting procedures?

17.33 Find the predictive MSE and MAD for the forecasts of the amount of money in the money-market account at First Louisiana State Bank in exercise 17.18b for the years 1975 to 1983 using the linear exponential smoothing technique asked for in that exercise.

17.34 Find the predictive MSE and MAD for the forecast of monthly sales of Ektronics in exercise 17.22 for the months of 1984 and 1985 using the linear and seasonal technique asked for in that exercise.

17.8

Autoregressive Forecasting Techniques

So far, the forecasting procedures have used either a member of the exponential smoothing family or the method of time series decomposition. The exponential smoothing technique greatly reduces the randomness (irregular activity) within the observed time series, as well as smoothing any existing trend or seasonal effects.

For the case of simple exponential smoothing, the forecast for the next time period

$(\hat{y}_{t+1})$ is the smoothed value for the current period (S_t). When you use the other exponential smoothing procedures, your forecast includes the effect of the smoothed seasonality or trend.

The time series decomposition method determines the various components in each observation, including seasonality, trend, cycles, and random activity. Forecasts are derived by extending the trend and seasonal components into the future. Unlike exponential smoothing, this method can provide reliable long-range forecasts. Naturally, the longer this forecast period is, the less reliable your forecasted value becomes.

This section examines yet another method of forecasting, which can be used when the time series variable is related to past values of itself. By regressing y_t on some combination of its past values, we are able to derive a forecasting equation. So we return to multiple linear regression, except now the dependent variable is y_t, and the predictor variables are the past values, $y_{t-1}, y_{t-2}, \ldots$. This forecasting technique is **autoregression;** we are essentially regressing the time series variable on itself.

We can expect the autoregressive forecast technique to perform reasonably well for a time series that (1) is not extremely volatile, and does not contain extreme amounts of random movement, and (2) requires a short-term or medium-range forecast (that is, less than 2 years). The fact that the autoregressive procedure does not perform well on a time series containing a great deal of irregular activity is not a serious disadvantage; practically all forecasting techniques perform poorly in this situation.

Suppose we attempt to predict the values of y_t using the previous two observations. The prediction equation is

$$\hat{y}_t = b_0 + b_1 y_{t-1} + b_2 y_{t-2} \qquad (17\text{-}14)$$

The values of b_0, b_1, and b_2 are the least squares regression estimates, obtained from any multiple linear regression computer package. There are two predictor variables here: the **lagged variables,** y_{t-1} and y_{t-2}. Equation 17-14 is a **second-order** autoregressive equation because it uses the first two lagged terms. In general, a pth order autoregressive equation is written

$$\hat{y}_t = b_0 + b_1 y_{t-1} + b_2 y_{t-2} + \ldots + b_p y_{t-p} \qquad (17\text{-}15)$$

We will illustrate the computer-input procedure for the second-order equation with an example. Earlier, we used the naive forecasting procedure (forecast for tomorrow is the observed value for today) to predict the closing price of Keller Toy Company stock. The closing prices for a 12-week period are shown on page 631; the predicted values are summarized in Table 17.1.

Suppose we use the second-order autoregressive equation (17-14) to predict these values. The input data required by the linear regression routine consists of the actual time series data and the two columns of lagged data, as illustrated in Table 17.10. The ten input rows are below the line. Notice that we lose the first two observations due to the missing values for the lagged variables. If these data are available from the two weeks prior to week 1, they can be used to fill in the missing values, providing 12 rows of data.

A computer solution to this problem using MINITAB is in Figure 17.10. The prediction equation is

Figure 17.10

MINITAB procedure for second-order autoregression.

```
MTB > SET INTO C1
DATA> 60 62.25 61.75 63 64.5 62 63.5 64 63.25 62.5 61 61.5
DATA> END
MTB > LAG BY 1 OF C1, PUT INTO C2
MTB > LAG BY 2 OF C1, PUT INTO C3
MTB > REGRESS Y IN C1 USING 2 PREDICTORS IN C2,C3

The regression equation is
C1 = 45.5 + 0.278 C2 - 0.004 C3

10 cases used 2 cases contain missing values

Predictor        Coef         Stdev       t-ratio
Constant         45.50        29.35          1.55
C2                0.2775       0.3923        0.71
C3               -0.0035       0.3285       -0.01

s = 1.249       R-sq = 6.8%       R-sq(adj) = 0.0%

Analysis of Variance

SOURCE          DF            SS             MS
Regression       2          0.799         0.400
Error            7         10.926         1.561
Total            9         11.725
```

SSE — Predictive MSE
= $\dfrac{10.926}{10}$
= 1.09

$$\hat{y}_t = 45.5 + .278y_{t-1} - .004y_{t-2}$$

Also, $R^2 = .068$, indicating that the two lagged variables account for only 7% of the total variation in the ten time series values used as input (y_3 through y_{12}).

To determine whether this is the best way to forecast a particular time series, we can use the procedure discussed in the previous section. This involves calculating an MSE (or MAD), using the autoregressive technique on the past observations, and comparing this MSE with the MSE using other forecasting methods. For example, we obtain an improvement over the naive forecasting procedure here because, from Figure 17.10,

$$\text{(predictive) MSE} = \frac{10.926}{10} = 1.09 \text{ (for autoregressive forecaster)}$$

Table 17.10

Input for the second order autoregressive predictor

y_t	y_{t-1}	y_{t-2}
60	—	—
62.25	60	—
61.75	62.25	60
63	61.75	62.25
64.5	63	61.75
62	64.5	63
63.5	62	64.5
64	63.5	62
63.25	64	63.5
62.5	63.25	64
61	62.5	63.25
61.5	61	62.5

and from Table 17.1,

$$\text{(predictive) MSE} = \frac{(2.25)^2 + (-.5)^2 + \ldots + (.5)^2}{11}$$

$$= \frac{21.5}{11}$$

$$= 1.95 \text{ (for naive forecaster)}$$

So, despite the low value of R^2, we obtain a better fit to the observed data using the second-order autoregressive technique. This value of R^2, however, does indicate that the search for a more accurate forecasting procedure should continue.

Determining Autocorrelations

There are several methods of calculating the correlation between a time series, y_t, and its past values. For example, in Table 17.10,

y_t	y_{t-1}	y_{t-2}
61.75	62.25	60
63	61.75	62.25
.	.	.
.	.	.
61.5	61	62.5

To find the correlation between y_t and y_{t-1}, we could use the equation for a sample correlation coefficient, r, defined in Chapters 4 and 14. We also could find the correlation between y_t and y_{t-2} using the same procedure.

There is, however, a computationally more efficient way to find each of these correlations, which also helps us to identify a time series that is not stationary. This equation for the correlation between y_t and y_{t-k} (for any lag k) is

$$r_k = \frac{\sum_{t=1}^{T-k} (y_t - \bar{y})(y_{t+k} - \bar{y})}{\sum_{t=1}^{T} (y_t - \bar{y})^2} \tag{17-16}$$

where (1) k is the lag under consideration, (2) r_k is the **autocorrelation** for lag k, (3) $\bar{y}$ is the average of the observed time series; that is,

$$\bar{y} = \frac{1}{T} \sum_{t=1}^{T} y_t$$

and (4) T is the number of observations in the time series.

Example 17.8 Determine r_1 and r_2 using the following time series:

t	y_t
1	5
2	12
3	20
4	15
5	13

Figure 17.11

Correlogram for example 17.8.

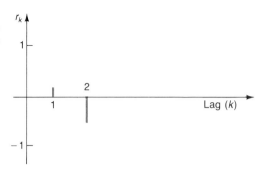

Solution Here $T = 5$ and

$$\bar{y} = \frac{1}{5} (5 + 12 + 20 + 15 + 13) = 13$$

Consequently,

r_1 = correlation between y_t and y_{t-1}

$$= \frac{(y_1 - \bar{y})(y_2 - \bar{y}) + (y_2 - \bar{y})(y_3 - \bar{y}) + (y_3 - \bar{y})(y_4 - \bar{y}) + (y_4 - \bar{y})(y_5 - \bar{y})}{(y_1 - \bar{y})^2 + (y_2 - \bar{y})^2 + \ldots + (y_5 - \bar{y})^2}$$

$$= \frac{(-8)(-1) + (-1)(7) + (7)(2) + (2)(0)}{(-8)^2 + (-1)^2 + (7)^2 + (2)^2 + (0)^2}$$

$$= 15/118 = .13$$

Also,

$$r_2 = \frac{(y_1 - \bar{y})(y_3 - \bar{y}) + (y_2 - \bar{y})(y_4 - \bar{y}) + (y_3 - \bar{y})(y_5 - \bar{y})}{118}$$

$$= \frac{(-8)(7) + (-1)(2) + (7)(0)}{118}$$

$$= \frac{-58}{118} = -.49$$

A graphical representation of these autocorrelations is a **correlogram.** The correlogram for example 17.8 contains the values of r_1 and r_2, as illustrated in Figure 17.11. By inspecting a correlogram, you can determine which lagged variables appear to contribute to the prediction of your time series variable. The autoregressive equation would include those lagged variables the corresponding autocorrelation of which is large. There are statistical procedures for identifying significantly large autocorrelations. These are discussed in Bowerman and O'Connell and also Makridakis and Wheelright (see references on page 690).

Detecting Seasonality

The autoregressive forecasting approach does allow you to detect seasonality in your time series data. If seasonality is present in quarterly data, we expect a significant positive correlation between y_t and y_{t-4}; that is, r_4 will be large. This implies that the y value of one year ago is a good predictor of the y value today. Similarly, for monthly data, we can expect r_{12} to be large if there is significant seasonality present.

Table 17.11

Quarterly profits of Ken's Auto Paint Shop (in thousands of dollars)

QUARTER	1981	1982	1983	1984	1985
Spring	5.56	5.11	4.12	6.31	4.81
Summer	16.36	15.21	14.33	15.02	16.82
Fall	2.12	5.72	5.25	2.83	4.75
Winter	3.15	2.65	6.75	4.56	8.54

Example 17.9

Table 17.11 contains data for the quarterly profits from Ken's Auto Paint Shop. Which lagged variables appear to be correlated with y_t = profit during time period t?

Solution The MINITAB output for the autocorrelation equation (17-16) is shown in Figure 17.12. Here the *autocorrelation function* (called ACF by MINITAB) computes the first $10 + \sqrt{T}$ autocorrelations, where T (20, here) is the number of observations in the time series. If $10 + \sqrt{T}$ is not an integer, it is rounded *down* to the nearest integer, which is 14 in this case.

The seasonality pattern of four-quarter duration can be seen from the resulting autocorrelations in Figure 17.12. The large r_k values are $r_4 = .678$, $r_8 = .512$, and $r_{12} = .388$. Notice that $r_4 > r_8 > r_{12}$, which is typical in the presence of strong four-period seasonality. The large value of r_4 is your clue that such seasonality exists, and the large values of r_8 and r_{12} confirm this suspicion.

Using y_{t-4} as the predictor variable, we find from Figure 17.13 that the autoregression equation is

$$\hat{y}_t = 1.42 + .87 y_{t-4}$$

The corresponding predictive MSE using this model is

$$\text{(predictive) MSE} = \frac{\text{SSE}}{\text{(number of observations used)}}$$

$$= \frac{64.40}{16}$$

$$= 4.025$$

Figure 17.12

Autocorrelations for example 17.9 using MINITAB.

```
MTB > SET INTO C1
DATA> 5.56 16.36 2.12 3.15 5.11 15.21 5.72 2.65 4.12 14.33 5.25 6.75
DATA> 6.31 15.02 2.83 4.56 4.81 16.82 4.75 8.54
DATA> END
MTB > ACF OF C1 ──────[Generates the autocorrelations, r₁, r₂, ...]

ACF of C1

             -1.0 -0.8 -0.6 -0.4 -0.2  0.0  0.2  0.4  0.6  0.8  1.0
             +----+----+----+----+----+----+----+----+----+----+
     1  -0.315                          XXXXXXXXX
     2  -0.260                          XXXXXXX
     3  -0.286                          XXXXXXX
    [4]  0.678                          XXXXXXXXXXXXXXXXXX◄─┐
     5  -0.213                          XXXXX             │
     6  -0.168                          XXXX              │
     7  -0.156                          XXXX              │
     8   0.512                          XXXXXXXXXXXXXX◄────┼── Large
     9  -0.235                          XXXXXXX           │
    10  -0.134                          XXXX              │
    11  -0.104                          XXXX              │
    12   0.388                          XXXXXXXXXXX◄───────┘
    13  -0.155                          XXXXX
    14  -0.060                          XX
```

Figure 17.13

MINITAB solution for
example 17.9.

See Figure 17.12

```
MTB > LAG BY 4 OF C1, PUT INTO C2
MTB > REGRESS Y IN C1 USING 1 PREDICTOR IN C2

The regression equation is
C1 = 1.42 + 0.870 C2

16 cases used 4 cases contain missing values

Predictor          Coef         Stdev       t-ratio
Constant         1.4198        0.9623          1.48
C2               0.8697        0.1111          7.83

s = 2.145        R-sq = 81.4%      R-sq(adj) = 80.1%

Analysis of Variance

SOURCE          DF          SS            MS
Regression       1       281.82        281.82
Error           14        64.40          4.60    ──SSE
Total           15       346.22
```

To decide whether this procedure performs well for this time series, we would need to compare this MSE with the MSE obtained using other forecasting techniques.

●

Removing Nonstationarity

The autoregressive procedures discussed so far are effective if the time series is **stationary,** that is, if it contains no trend and has constant variance about the mean, $\bar{y}$. One method of detecting nonstationarity in a time series is to examine the correlogram. If you notice that the autocorrelations in the correlogram do not die down rapidly (say after the second or third lag), then your time series *is not stationary.*

With such a time series, an autoregressive procedure is *not appropriate,* unless you modify the time series to make it more stationary. That is, the data should be transformed to a stationary series before attempting to determine seasonality. This can be achieved by using the **differencing** method, which replaces y_t by the first difference, defined by

$$y_t' = y_t - y_{t-1}$$

To illustrate this technique, consider the series

2, 5, 8, 11, 14, . . .

This series clearly contains a linear trend; each value is three more than the preceding value. The first differences are

$$y_2' = 5 - 2 = 3$$
$$y_3' = 8 - 5 = 3$$
$$y_4' = 11 - 8 = 3$$
$$y_5' = 14 - 11 = 3$$

and so on. These values contain no trend, and so the resulting series of first differences *is* stationary.

If this procedure has been successful in producing a stationary time series, the resulting correlogram (using the y_t' values) should die out quickly. If such is not the case, using the *second* differences of the original time series values ($y_1, y_2, . . . , y_T$)

often will produce a stationary series. Here, the second differences can be found by deriving first differences of the y'_t values, namely,

$$y''_t = y'_t - y'_{t-1} = y_t - 2y_{t-1} + y_{t-2}$$

You generally can achieve stationarity in your original time series by continuing to take differences until the autocorrelations of the "new" series drop to near zero after two or three time lags (except for possible large values, or *spikes*, due to seasonal effects). It usually is necessary to determine only first or second order differences when dealing with a nonstationary time series.

Example 17.10   In Chapter 16, we examined the quarterly sales data of Video-Comp, contained in Table 16.3 on page 597. These data contained a strong linear trend and a definite seasonal pattern, with low sales in the first two quarters and high sales in the final two quarters. A graph of the data is contained in Figure 17.2. Is the seasonal effect more apparent using the original data or the first differences?

Solution   The MINITAB autocorrelations using the original data are summarized and plotted in Figure 17.14. You can see the nonstationarity of this series—the autocorrelations fail to "die out" after two or three periods. Because of the strong trend component, the seasonal effect is not apparent.

The first differences are formed by subtracting adjacent y_t values. These are

y_t	First Differences $y'_t = y_t - y_{t-1}$
20	*
12	-8
47	35
60	13
40	-20
.	.
.	.
.	.

Figure 17.14

MINITAB autocorrelations using sales data (example 17.10).

```
MTB > SET INTO C1
DATA> 20 12 47 60 40 32 65 76 56 50 85 100 75 70 101 123
DATA> END
MTB > ACF C1

ACF of C1

                -1.0 -0.8 -0.6 -0.4 -0.2  0.0  0.2  0.4  0.6  0.8  1.0
                 +----+----+----+----+----+----+----+----+----+----+
      1   0.541                             XXXXXXXXXXXXXX
      2   0.105                             XXXX
      3   0.280                             XXXXXXXX
      4   0.473                             XXXXXXXXXXXXX
      5   0.122                             XXXX
      6  -0.232                      XXXXXXX
      7  -0.087                          XXX
      8   0.063                             XXX
      9  -0.176                        XXXXX
     10  -0.422                 XXXXXXXXXXXX
     11  -0.279                     XXXXXXXX
     12  -0.121                         XXXX
     13  -0.234                      XXXXXXX
     14  -0.343                  XXXXXXXXXX
```

Figure 17.15

MINITAB autocorrelations using first differences (example 17.10).

```
MTB > SET INTO C1
DATA> 20 12 47 60 40 32 65 76 56 50 85 100 75 70 101 123
DATA> END
MTB > DIFFERENCES OF LAG 1 FOR C1,PUT INTO C2
MTB > ACF C2

ACF of C2

             -1.0 -0.8 -0.6 -0.4 -0.2  0.0  0.2  0.4  0.6  0.8  1.0
              +----+----+----+----+----+----+----+----+----+----+
    1   0.001                                  X
    2  -0.821        XXXXXXXXXXXXXXXXXXXXXX
    3  -0.034                               XX
    4   0.698                                  XXXXXXXXXXXXXXXXXX
    5   0.001                                  X
    6  -0.546             XXXXXXXXXXXXXXX
    7  -0.024                               XX
    8   0.431                                  XXXXXXXXXXX
    9  -0.005                                  X
   10  -0.307                  XXXXXXXXX
   11  -0.019                                  X
   12   0.148                                  XXXXX
   13   0.010                                  X
```

The MINITAB autocorrelations using the first differences are computed in Figure 17.15. Now the seasonality pattern is much clearer, with large negative values for r_2, r_6, and r_{10} as well as large positive values for r_4, r_8, and r_{12}. The negative values are a result of a high (low) sales value in time period t followed by a low (high) sales figure two quarters later. Similarly, the large value of r_4 indicates a strong four-quarter seasonal effect; the large values of r_8 and r_{12} support this conclusion.

If you wished to use an autoregressive model for this application, you would use y_t' (not y_t) as your dependent variable because the y_t' values *are* stationary. An excellent set of predictor variables (using Figure 17.15) would be y_{t-2}' and y_{t-4}'. ●

Exercises

17.35 Malcom Chemicals manufactures 12 different speciality chemicals. The company's net profit from these speciality chemicals has been stable over the past 5 years, as the data indicate. The figures in the table are net profit per quarter in units of $10,000$.

Year	Quarter 1	Quarter 2	Quarter 3	Quarter 4
1980	4.3	5.7	8.3	2.4
1981	4.7	5.9	8.0	2.7
1982	4.4	5.5	7.6	2.5
1983	4.9	5.9	8.4	2.8
1984	5.3	6.2	8.6	2.9

Fit the following two autoregressive processes to the data:

$$y_t = b_0 + b_1 y_{t-1} + b_2 y_{t-2}$$
$$y_t = b_0 + b_1 y_{t-1} + b_2 y_{t-2} + b_3 y_{t-3} + b_4 y_{t-4}$$

Find the predictive MSE for each autoregressive process and compare the values. Use a computerized statistical package to find the coefficients of the autoregressive equations.

17.36 The debt-to-equity capitalization ratio for Dooper Industries, a maker of machinery parts, has never been above 20% for the past 6 years as a result of excellent management. These ratios (given as a percentage) for the past 6 years are as follows:

Year	Quarter 1	Quarter 2	Quarter 3	Quarter 4
1980	12	15	18	13
1981	11	14	16	12
1982	10	16	19	12
1983	11	17	20	14
1984	12	15	18	12
1985	11	14	17	13

a. Find the autocorrelations for lags of $k = 1, 2, 3$, and 4.

b. Using a computer package, find the coefficients for the autoregressive process

$$y_t = b_0 + b_1 y_{t-1} + b_2 y_{t-2} + b_3 y_{t-3} + b_4 y_{t-4}$$

17.37 The percent of Medical International's total revenue derived from free-standing centers for cardiac rehabilitation is given for the past 16 years.

Year	% of Revenue
1970	45
1971	47
1972	46
1973	43
1974	40
1975	36
1976	35
1977	39
1978	42
1979	43
1980	40
1981	37
1982	35
1983	37
1984	40
1985	43

a. Find the autocorrelations for lags $k = 1, 2, 3$, and 4.

b. From the autocorrelations in question a, determine an appropriate autoregressive model. Find the coefficients of the autoregressive model using a computerized statistical package.

17.38 How should the graph of a correlogram look if the time series is stationary?

17.39 Refer to exercise 17.7. Find the autocorrelations for the seasonal data for Sands Motel, using lags of $k = 1, 2, 3, \ldots, 12$. Do the data appear to be stationary?

17.40 Refer to exercise 17.18. Use a first-order autoregressive process to fit the data on the amount of money that First Louisiana State Bank has in its money-market accounts. Find the predictive MSE.

17.41 Determine whether the following data are stationary. If the data are not stationary, take differences until it becomes clear that the resulting time series is stationary. The data represent quarterly interest (in thousands of dollars) paid by a local savings and loan association to those of its depositors who have regular saving accounts.

Year	Quarter 1	Quarter 2	Quarter 3	Quarter 4
1981	25	38	15	21
1982	46	57	36	32
1983	65	80	54	49
1984	84	97	77	70
1985	104	109	96	90

17.42 The manager of a children's clothing store has tabulated a sales index of children's clothes sold each quarter. The sales of children's clothes has been in an upward trend over the past 5 years, but the sales are also affected by seasonal variation.

Year	Quarter 1	Quarter 2	Quarter 3	Quarter 4
1981	108	256	201	190
1982	185	380	290	320
1983	280	421	360	331
1984	300	504	432	450
1985	400	862	510	480

a. Calculate the autocorrelations through lag 12.

b. Calculate the first differences for the time series.

c. Calculate the autocorrelations for the data obtained by differencing in question b.

d. Compare the autocorrelations in questions a and c. Comment on whether the autocorrelations describe a stationary time series.

17.43 The following table represents the number of homes sold monthly in a growing community in California over the past 5 years:

Month	1980	1981	1982	1983	1984
Jan	48	83	117	156	192
Feb	51	85	121	158	195
Mar	65	98	133	170	208
Apr	67	102	134	173	209
May	69	105	139	176	214
Jun	78	114	149	184	221
Jul	81	118	153	187	224
Aug	85	123	155	191	227
Sep	67	105	132	173	210
Oct	71	109	142	175	213
Nov	72	113	145	179	217
Dec	75	115	148	184	220

a. Calculate the autocorrelations through lag 15.

b. Calculate the first differences for the time series.

c. Calculate the autocorrelations for the difference data obtained in question b.

d. Calculate the autocorrelations in questions a and c. Do the autocorrelations describe a stationary time series? Comment.

17.9

The Other Side of Forecasting: Linear Regression Using Time Series Data

We have already used linear regression procedures in many of the time series forecasting techniques we have discussed. For instance, simple linear regression was used to describe the *trend* present in time series data. Multiple linear regression was used in the previous section to predict a future time series value using the past one or more observations. This was the autoregressive forecasting method, where, for example,

$$\hat{y}_t = b_0 + b_1 y_{t-1} + b_2 y_{t-2}$$

Here the predictor variables are the *lagged* time series variables, y_{t-1} and y_{t-2}.

Often, you will wish to combine one or more autoregressive terms and several time related predictor variables into the regression equation, such as

$$\hat{y}_t = b_0 + b_1 y_{t-1} + b_2 y_{t-2} + b_3 X_{1,t} + b_4 X_{2,t} + b_5 X_{3,t}$$

Or you can omit the autoregressive terms and use an equation such as

$$\hat{y}_t = b_0 + b_1 X_{1,t} + b_2 X_{2,t} + b_3 X_{3,t}$$

The notation $X_{1,t}, X_{2,t}, \ldots$ is used (rather than $X_1, X_2, \ldots$) to denote values of the predictor variables during time period t. For example, $X_{2,5}$ represents the observed value of X_2 during the fifth time period. In this way, we can refer to *specific* values of these variables. There is nothing different about this model and the multiple regression model in Chapter 15, except for a slight change in notation because we are dealing with time series data.

Linear regression techniques on time series data offer a variety of opportunities for better forecasting precision, including (1) the use of dummy variables to capture *additive* seasonality and (2) the use of lagged independent variables to allow for time delay effects between the dependent and predictor variables. On the other hand, when this technique is used on time series data, it becomes increasingly difficult to satisfy the linear regression assumptions discussed in Chapter 15. In particular, the error term from one time period often is seriously affected by the previous errors, violating the assumption of independent errors. This means that we can expect to find that the *residuals* are *autocorrelated*. The degree of autocorrelation in the residuals can be measured and tested for significance by calculating the **Durbin–Watson statistic,** which is obtained from the residuals.

These matters will be discussed in the remaining sections of this chapter. We will look at how regression techniques expand the area of time series analysis but also present a new set of problems.

Use of Dummy Variables for Seasonality

We introduced the concept of *additive* seasonality previously. Essentially, this type of seasonal effect is present whenever the amount of the seasonal variation is unaffected by the underlying trend in the time series. This was illustrated in Figure 16.15 on page 589. Notice that even as the sales grow over time, the seasonal effect remains the same.

Ignoring any cyclical activity, each observation, y_t, can be described by

$$y_t = TR_t + S_t + I_t$$

where (1) TR_t is the trend component described by a straight line ($TR_t = \beta_0 + \beta_1 t$) or a quadratic curve ($TR_t = \beta_0 + \beta_1 t + \beta_2 t^2$), (2) S_t is the seasonal effect, and (3) I_t is the irregular activity component.

Both the trend and seasonal components can be obtained by using multiple linear regression. The seasonal effects are captured by including a set of *dummy variables* in the regression equation. This type of variable was first introduced in Chapter 15, where we used a set of dummy variables to represent the categories of a *qualitative* variable—such as seasons of the year, in this application.

We use the same procedure for defining dummy variables here—we define one less dummy variable than the number of seasons (categories), L. Because $L = 4$ for quarterly data, we will need $L - 1 = 3$ dummy variables. One possible scheme is to define

$$Q_1 = \begin{cases} 1 \text{ if quarter 1} \\ 0 \text{ otherwise} \end{cases} \quad Q_2 = \begin{cases} 1 \text{ if quarter 2} \\ 0 \text{ otherwise} \end{cases} \quad Q_3 = \begin{cases} 1 \text{ if quarter 3} \\ 0 \text{ otherwise} \end{cases} \quad (17\text{-}17)$$

With this procedure, no dummy variable is defined for the fourth quarter. The resulting coefficient of Q_1, Q_2, or Q_3 in the prediction equation will compare the effect of that quarter *against the fourth quarter*. For example, if the coefficient of Q_2 from your computer solution is -5, then, apart from any changes due to trend, quarter 2 produces a value of the dependent variable *five less* than during quarter 4. Quarter 4 is called the **base** quarter. Remember that the base period you select has absolutely *no effect* on the predicted values, $\hat{y}_t$.

For monthly data, you define $L - 1 = 12 - 1 = 11$ dummy variables. As before, you can omit the dummy variable for any one month, which then becomes the base month for all the computed dummy variable coefficients. If you omitted a variable for December, then December would be the base month, and your corresponding set of dummy variables would be

$$M_1 = \begin{cases} 1 \text{ if January} \\ 0 \text{ otherwise} \end{cases}$$

$$M_2 = \begin{cases} 1 \text{ if February} \\ 0 \text{ otherwise} \end{cases} \quad \cdots \quad M_{11} = \begin{cases} 1 \text{ if November} \\ 0 \text{ otherwise} \end{cases}$$

(17-18)

The quarterly sales at Video-Comp were examined in examples 16.10 and 16.11, assuming *multiplicative* seasonality. The vice-president of retail marketing, in reviewing this solution, thinks that the seasonal fluctuations do *not* appear to be increasing along with the trend, and so he believes that additive seasonality actually is present. We will use the dummy variable approach to model the seasonality and calculate the forecasts for the first four quarters of 1985. We want to know whether this approach appears to provide a good "fit" to the four years of observed sales.

The prediction equation will be

$$\hat{y}_t = \hat{TR}_t + \hat{S}_t$$

where (1) $\hat{TR}_t = b_0 + b_1 t$ (the trend appears to be nearly linear) and (2) $\hat{S}_t = b_2 Q_1 + b_3 Q_2 + b_4 Q_3$. Here, Q_1, Q_2, and Q_3 are the dummy variables defined in equation 17-17.

The input configuration used by the computer program consists of 16 rows and five columns:

y_t	t	Q_1	Q_2	Q_3
20	1	1	0	0
12	2	0	1	0
47	3	0	0	1
60	4	0	0	0
40	5	1	0	0
32	6	0	1	0
65	7	0	0	1
76	8	0	0	0
56	9	1	0	0
50	10	0	1	0
85	11	0	0	1
100	12	0	0	0
75	13	1	0	0
70	14	0	1	0
101	15	0	0	1
123	16	0	0	0

Figure 17.16

MINITAB solution using dummy variables to represent quarterly sales at Video-Comp.

```
MTB > READ INTO C1-C5
DATA> 20 1 1 0 0
DATA> 12 2 0 1 0
DATA> 47 3 0 0 1
DATA> 60 4 0 0 0
DATA> 40 5 1 0 0
DATA> 32 6 0 1 0
DATA> 65 7 0 0 1
DATA> 76 8 0 0 0
DATA> 56 9 1 0 0
DATA> 50 10 0 1 0
DATA> 85 11 0 0 1
DATA> 100 12 0 0 0
DATA> 75 13 1 0 0
DATA> 70 14 0 1 0
DATA> 101 15 0 0 1
DATA> 123 16 0 0 0
DATA> END
        16 ROWS READ
MTB > REGRESS Y IN C1 USING 4 PREDICTORS IN C2-C5
```

The regression equation is
C1 = 41.7 + 4.80 C2 - 27.6 C3 - 39.2 C4 - 10.4 C5

Predictor	Coef	Stdev	t-ratio
Constant	41.750	1.688	24.74
C2	4.8000	0.1258	38.16
C3	-27.600	1.635	-16.88
C4	-39.150	1.611	-24.30
C5	-10.450	1.596	-6.55

s = 2.250   R-sq = 99.6% ◀—R^2 R-sq(adj) = 99.4%

Analysis of Variance ┌─SSE

SOURCE	DF	SS	MS
Regression	4	13629.3	3407.3
Error	11	55.7	5.1
Total	15	13685.0	

The MINITAB solution for $b_0, b_1, \ldots, b_4$ is provided in Figure 17.16. The resulting equation is

$$\hat{y}_t = 41.75 + 4.8t - 27.6Q_1 - 39.15Q_2 - 10.45Q_3 \qquad (17\text{-}19)$$

Notice that $R^2 = .996$, which indicates a strong fit to the 16 observations. How does this method of forecasting compare to the one used in example 17.3, where we assumed *multiplicative* seasonality in the quarterly sales data? Comparing the two MSE's in Table 17.12, it appears that the seasonality effect is in fact additive, and the marketing vice-president was correct.

From equation 17-19, we find that

1. The sales are increasing at an average rate of 4.8 (million dollars) per quarter.
2. Apart from trend effects, sales for the first quarter are 27.6 (million dollars) less than the sales for the fourth quarter.
3. Apart from trend effects, sales for the second quarter are 39.15 less than for the fourth quarter.
4. Sales for the third quarter are 10.45 lower than those during the fourth quarter, ignoring trend effects.

After you have decided to use the additive seasonality equation, to determine the 1985 forecasts you use the appropriate value for t with the 0 or 1 values for the dummy variables.

Table 17.12

Summary of multiplicative versus additive seasonal forecasting (quarterly Sales of Video-Comp)

	MULTIPLICATIVE SEASONALITY				ADDITIVE SEASONALITY		
t	y_t	$\hat{y}_t$	$y_t - \hat{y}_t$	t	y_t	$\hat{y}_t$	$y_t - \hat{y}_t$
1	20	20.80	$-$.80	1	20	18.95	1.05
2	12	20.38	-8.38	2	12	12.20	$-$.20
3	47	40.21	6.79	3	47	45.70	1.30
4	60	50.98	9.02	4	60	60.95	$-$.95
5	40	37.96	2.04	5	40	38.15	1.85
6	32	34.32	-2.32	6	32	31.40	.60
7	65	63.70	1.30	7	65	64.90	.10
8	76	76.98	$-$.98	8	76	80.15	-4.15
9	56	55.13	.87	9	56	57.35	-1.35
10	50	48.26	1.74	10	50	50.60	$-$.60
11	85	87.20	-2.20	11	85	84.10	.90
12	100	102.97	-2.97	12	100	99.35	.65
13	75	72.30	2.70	13	75	76.55	-1.55
14	70	62.21	7.79	14	70	69.80	.20
15	101	110.69	-9.69	15	101	103.30	-2.30
16	123	128.96	-5.96	16	123	118.55	4.45

Forecasting equation: $\hat{y}_t = (19.372 + 5.0375t) \times S_t$

$S_1 = S_5 = S_9 = \ldots = .852$

$S_2 = S_6 = S_{10} = \ldots = .692$

$S_3 = S_7 = S_{11} = \ldots = 1.166$

$S_4 = S_8 = S_{12} = \ldots = 1.290$

predictive MSE $= \dfrac{\Sigma(y_t - \hat{y}_t)^2}{16}$

$\qquad = \dfrac{425.36}{16} = 26.58$

Forecasting equation: $\hat{y}_t = 41.75 + 4.8t - 27.6Q_1 - 39.15Q_2 - 10.45Q_3$

predictive MSE $= \dfrac{\Sigma(y_t - \hat{y}_t)^2}{16}$

$\qquad = \dfrac{55.7}{16} = 3.48$

Forecast for first quarter of 1985: Here, $Q_1 = 1$, $Q_2 = 0$, $Q_3 = 0$,

$\hat{y}_{17} = 41.75 + 4.8(17) - 27.6(1) - 39.15(0) - 10.45(0)$

$\qquad = 95.75$ (million dollars)

Forecast for second quarter of 1985: Here, $Q_2 = 1$ (all other Q's $= 0$), and

$\hat{y}_{18} = 41.75 + 4.8(18) - 27.6(0) - 39.15(1) - 10.45(0)$

$\qquad = 89$

Forecast for third quarter of 1985: Now, $Q_3 = 1$ (all other Q's $= 0$), and

$\hat{y}_{19} = 41.75 + 4.8(19) - 27.6(0) - 39.15(0) - 10.45(1)$

$\qquad = 122.5$

Forecast for the fourth quarter of 1985: Since $Q_1 = Q_2 = Q_3 = 0$,

$\hat{y}_{20} = 41.75 + 4.8(20) - 27.6(0) - 39.15(0) - 10.45(0)$

$\qquad = 137.75$

Exercises

17.44 The following multiple regression equation was used to fit quarterly sales data. The data are in units of 10,000.

$$Y_t = 0.5 + 1.8t + 3Q_1 - 0.6Q_2 + 1.1Q_3$$

where

$$Q_1 = \begin{cases} 1 \text{ if Quarter 1} \\ 0 \text{ otherwise} \end{cases}$$

$$Q_2 = \begin{cases} 1 \text{ if Quarter 2} \\ 0 \text{ otherwise} \end{cases}$$

$$Q_3 = \begin{cases} 1 \text{ if Quarter 3} \\ 0 \text{ otherwise} \end{cases}$$

a. Apart from seasonality, how fast are sales increasing each quarter?

b. Apart from trend, how much are sales for the first quarter ahead of sales for the fourth quarter?

c. Apart from trend, how much lower are sales for the second quarter than for the fourth quarter?

d. What is the forecasted sales for time period 12, which is a fourth quarter?

17.45 National Finance Company provides short-term loans to consumers to finance household goods. The amount of interest received quarterly is given below in units of 10,000.

Year	Quarter 1	Quarter 2	Quarter 3	Quarter 4
1981	20	31	39	42
1982	28	35	43	45
1983	31	38	45	49
1984	35	40	43	52
1985	38	44	48	56

Determine the multiple regression equation which takes into account trend and seasonality.

17.46 Quality Homes Inc. builds single-family houses in several large cities. The number of carpenters that it hires fluctuates with the demand for housing. For the 6 years shown, find a multiple regression equation to predict the number of carpenters on the payroll at Quality Homes. The multiple regression equation should take into account the trend and the monthly seasonality. What percentage of the total variation has been explained using these variables?

Year	Jan	Feb	Mar	Apr	May	Jun	Jul	Aug	Sep	Oct	Nov	Dec
1980	145	148	150	169	197	250	267	290	280	230	180	160
1981	155	150	166	178	220	290	320	325	300	270	200	190
1982	180	195	210	213	255	308	350	368	345	320	280	250
1983	230	245	258	290	330	342	394	405	380	350	310	290
1984	285	298	310	345	396	408	451	465	441	430	390	370
1985	350	361	372	395	420	439	480	495	483	450	420	410

17.47 Refer to exercise 17.7. Using a computerized statistical package, find the coefficients of a multiple regression model for the monthly data for Sands Motel that takes into account both the trend and the effect due to the particular month.

17.48 Explain the difference between multiplicative seasonality and additive seasonality. Which forecasting techniques are best suited for each of these situations?

17.49 Refer to exercise 17.36. Find the coefficients of the multiple regression model for the quarterly data from Dooper Industries that takes into account both the trend and seasonality.

Use of Lagged Independent Variables

When using multiple linear regression on time series data, we can represent the model as

$$y_t = \beta_0 + \beta_1 X_{1,t} + \beta_2 X_{2,t} + \ldots + \beta_k X_{k,t} + e_t$$

where each $X_{i,t}$ represents the value of predictor variable X_i in time period t, and e_t is the error component for this period.

Look at the data in Table 17.13. The object is to predict the number of home loans financed by Liberty Savings and Loan. The data in this table consist of semiannual figures from the past eight years. The predictor variables were chosen to be average interest rate (X_1), advertising expenditure (X_2), an election-year dummy variable $(X_3 = 1$ for an election year, and 0 otherwise), and a seasonal dummy variable, where $X_4 = 1$ for the first six months, and $X_4 = 0$ for the final six months.

A financial analyst at Liberty Savings saw two problems with the data in Table 17.13. First, she thought that the number of home loans during a particular six-month period should be more affected by the *previous* six-month interest rate, due to the time delay between loan application and actual funding. The value of y_t increases by 1 each time a loan is funded, not when the application is turned in. This time delay generally ran between three and six months. For the same reason, she believed that the effect of any increased (or decreased) advertising would be reflected in the loan amounts of the next period.

The procedure to follow in this situation is to *lag* the predictor variable by the corresponding time lag. For this example, we can lag X_1 and X_2 by one time period, which results in the following regression model

$$y_t = \beta_0 + \beta_1 X_{1,t-1} + \beta_2 X_{2,t-1} + \beta_3 X_{3,t} + \beta_4 X_{4,t} + e_t$$

The other problem she foresaw with using the regression variables in Table 17.13 is a common difficulty in applying regression techniques to a forecasting situation. If we had not lagged X_1 and X_2, then any forecast for 1985 would involve *specifying values for X_1 and X_2 for this future time period*. Because these values may be just as difficult to predict as the dependent variable, our model has little potential as a forecaster. By

Table 17.13

Housing data for Liberty Savings and Loan

Year	t	Number of Home Loans y_t	Average Interest Rate $(X_{1,t})$	Advertising Expenditure (thousands of $) $(X_{2,t})$	Election Year Variable $(X_{3,t})$	Seasonal Variable $(X_{4,t})$
1977	1	86	11.0	5.1	0	1
	2	96	10.1	6.8	0	0
1978	3	110	13.5	6.8	0	1
	4	76	15.1	9.1	0	0
1979	5	62	10.5	7.5	0	1
	6	104	9.8	5.1	0	0
1980	7	135	10.1	8.8	1	1
	8	120	10.8	4.3	1	0
1981	9	115	13.0	9.1	0	1
	10	84	14.7	9.5	0	0
1982	11	76	14.1	6.1	0	1
	12	81	12.0	8.2	0	0
1983	13	122	11.8	10.4	0	1
	14	118	12.4	6.7	0	0
1984	15	106	11.0	7.5	1	1
	16	140	14.5	7.8	1	0

lagging these variables, we have removed this problem for a one-period ahead forecast because now the lagged values for tomorrow are the actual values for today.

A portion of the input data using the lagged predictors is shown below.

y_t	$X_{1,t-1}$	$X_{2,t-1}$	$X_{3,t}$	$X_{4,t}$
86	12.5	7.6	0	1
96	11.0	5.1	0	0
110	10.1	6.8	0	1
76	13.5	6.8	0	0
62	15.1	9.1	0	1
104	10.5	7.5	0	0
135	9.8	5.1	1	1

.
.
.

Figure 17.17

MINITAB solution using lagged interest and advertising variables (data from Table 17.13).

```
MTB > READ INTO C1-C5
DATA> 86 11.0 5.1 0 1
DATA> 96 10.1 6.8 0 0
DATA> 110 13.5 6.8 0 1
DATA> 76 15.1 9.1 0 0
DATA> 62 10.5 7.5 0 1
DATA> 104 9.8 5.1 0 0
DATA> 135 10.1 8.8 1 1
DATA> 120 10.8 4.3 1 0
DATA> 115 13.0 9.1 0 1
DATA> 84 14.7 9.5 0 0
DATA> 76 14.1 6.1 0 1
DATA> 81 12.0 8.2 0 0
DATA> 122 11.8 10.4 0 1
DATA> 118 12.4 6.7 0 0
DATA> 106 11.0 7.5 1 1
DATA> 140 14.5 7.8 1 0
DATA> END
      16 ROWS READ
MTB > LAG BY 1 OF C2, PUT INTO C12
MTB > LAG BY 1 OF C3, PUT INTO C13
MTB > REGRESS Y IN C1 USING 4 PREDICTORS IN C12,C13 C4,C5;
SUBC> DW.

The regression equation is
C1 = 207 - 10.3 C12 + 1.87 C13 + 14.7 C4 + 4.47 C5

15 cases used 1 cases contain missing values

Predictor        Coef        Stdev      t-ratio
Constant        206.62       27.04         7.64
C12             -10.293       2.335       -4.41
C13               1.867       2.097        0.89
C4               14.694       8.122        1.81
C5                4.475       6.700        0.67

s = 12.57       R-sq = 78.9%       R-sq(adj) = 70.5%
```

R^2 (pointing to R-sq = 78.9%)

```
Analysis of Variance

SOURCE        DF         SS          MS
Regression     4      5924.2      1481.0
Error         10      1579.8       158.0
Total         14      7504.0
```

SSE (pointing to 1579.8)

```
Continue?
SOURCE        DF      SEQ SS
C12            1      5183.2
C13            1       113.6
C4             1       556.9
C5             1        70.5

Durbin-Watson statistic = 1.31
```

The resulting prediction equation, shown in Figure 17.17, is

$$\hat{y}_t = 206.62 - 10.29X_{1,t-1} + 1.867X_{2,t-1} + 14.69X_{3,t} + 4.475X_{4,t}$$ (17-20)

We can draw several conclusions from Figure 17.17:

1. Based on the t values, the lagged interest rate variable ($X_{1,t-1}$) and the election year variable ($X_{3,t}$) are the only significant predictors of the number of home loans financed by Liberty.
2. Because $R^2 = .789$, 78.9% of the total variation of the y_t values has been explained using these four predictors.
3. The predictive mean squared error (for comparison purposes) is

$$\text{(predictive) MSE} = \frac{\text{SSE}}{15} = \frac{1579.8}{15} = 105.3$$

To illustrate the effect of lagging the independent variables, Figure 17.18 contains the solution to this example where neither X_1 nor X_2 are lagged. Two things are striking. First, the R^2 value drops from .789 to .397. Second, the interest variable, X_1, is *no longer significant,* based on its small t value.

For each application, try lagging the independent variables that could possibly have a delayed action on the dependent variable. You also should vary the lag period to account for predictor effects that show up several time periods later.

What would be the forecast for the first half of 1985 using the prediction equation 17-20? Here, $X_{1,t-1} = X_{1,16} =$ interest rate for the last half of 1984 $= 14.5$, and

Figure 17.18

MINITAB solution without lagging the interest and advertising variables (data from Table 17.13).

```
MTB > REGRESS Y IN C1 USING 4 PREDICTORS IN C2-C5;
SUBC> DW.

The regression equation is
C1 = 89.7 - 0.91 C2 + 2.24 C3 + 31.4 C4 - 2.4 C5

Predictor        Coef         Stdev      t-ratio
Constant        89.72         40.08        2.24
C2             -0.912          3.361      -0.27      ← No longer
C3              2.245          3.437       0.65         significant
C4             31.39          12.14        2.59
C5             -2.44          10.73       -0.23

s = 20.65      R-sq = 39.7%      R-sq(adj) = 17.7%

Analysis of Variance

SOURCE        DF          SS          MS
Regression     4        3083.5       770.9
Error         11        4691.4       426.5
Total         15        7774.9

Continue?
SOURCE        DF        SEQ SS
C2             1          91.5
C3             1         108.3
C4             1        2861.6
C5             1          22.1


Durbin-Watson statistic = 2.19
```

$X_{2,t-1} = X_{2,16} = 7.8$. Also, $X_{3,17} = 0$ (1985 is not an election year) and $X_{4,17} = 1$ (this applies to the first half of 1985). So,

$$\hat{y}_{17} = 206.62 - 10.29(14.5) + 1.867(7.8) + 14.69(0) + 4.475(1)$$

$$= 76.45$$

This results in a large drop from the value for the last half of 1984 (140). This is primarily due to the large interest rate in the final half of 1984 (14.5%) and the fact that 1985 is not an election year.

Exercises

17.50 What is the importance of using lagged independent variables in a regression equation?

17.51 The following table list the food price index (FPI) and the per-capita income (PCI) index for a certain third world nation. The indexes are listed in 6-month increments.

Year	Month	Y: FPI	X: PCI
1977	Jun	109	104
	Dec	101	116
1978	Jun	104	124
	Dec	107	120
1979	Jun	105	167
	Dec	114	133
1980	Jun	108	188
	Dec	126	148
1981	Jun	112	101
	Dec	100	158
1982	Jun	114	115
	Dec	104	127
1983	Jun	107	112
	Dec	102	141
1984	Jun	110	124
	Dec	105	162
1985	Jun	113	184
	Dec	120	140

a. Find the simple regression equation

$$y_t = b_0 + b_1 X_t$$

b. Find the simple regression equation

$$y_t = b_0 + b_1 X_{t-1}$$

c. Compare the R^2 for the two equations found in questions a and b.

17.52 Credit Corp finances small home-improvement projects for 1 year or less. Usually, the company does not screen clients rigorously, because a mechanics lien is placed on the home. Credit Corp has found that a significant correlation exists between the interest rate on loans and the number of defaults. The following data give the average interest rate charged on a loan for that quarter and the number of times a loan holder has been more than 30 days behind on a payment.

Year	Quarter	Y: Average Interest Rate	X: Times Behind on a Loan Payment
1982	1	8.5	53
	2	8.0	45
	3	9.0	44
	4	9.5	47
1983	1	9.0	49
	2	10.0	46
	3	10.5	49
	4	10.0	52
1984	1	10.5	50
	2	11.25	51
	3	11.50	55
	4	11.00	57
1985	1	12.25	52
	2	12.50	60
	3	12.00	63
	4	11.50	58

a. Find the simple regression equation

$$y_t = b_0 + b_1 X_t$$

b. Find the simple regression equation

$$y_t = b_0 + b_1 X_{t-1}$$

c. Compare the R^2 for the two equations.

17.53 Refer to exercise 17.35. The following is the number of salespeople working for Malcom Chemical Company over the 5-year period 1980 through 1984.

Year	Quarter 1	Quarter 2	Quarter 3	Quarter 4
1980	30	41	13	23
1981	31	39	15	22
1982	27	37	12	25
1983	30	42	14	26
1984	32	43	15	25

Find the multiple regression equation to predict the net profit per quarter for Malcom Chemical. Use dummy variables to represent seasonality and the variable, number of salespeople, lagged by 1 time period. Also find the predictive MSE.

17.54 Refer to exercise 17.36. The following is the level of inventory for Dooper Industries in units of 10,000 for the years 1980 to 1985.

Year	Quarter 1	Quarter 2	Quarter 3	Quarter 4
1980	4.8	6.1	4.2	3.8
1981	4.2	5.2	4.1	3.3
1982	5.0	6.4	4.2	3.2
1983	5.5	6.8	4.2	3.1
1984	5.1	6.1	4.0	3.8
1985	4.2	5.9	4.1	3.7

Find the multiple regression equation to predict the debt-to-equity capitalization ratio for Dooper Industries using a variable to represent seasonality and the variable, level of inventory lagged by 1 quarter. Find the R^2.

17.55 A local used-car dealer believes that advertising has greatly increased sales at the used car lot. The sales (in hundreds of dollars) of cars for each month and also the corresponding advertising expenditure are:

Year	Month	Y: Sales	X: Advertising Expenditure
1984	Jan	19	250
	Feb	16	405
	Mar	20	308
	Apr	17	425
	May	21	550
	Jun	24	300
	Jul	16	450
	Aug	22	522
	Sep	23	630
	Oct	26	510
	Nov	23	320
	Dec	17	250
1985	Jan	16	300
	Feb	17	350
	Mar	19	401
	Apr	20	560
	May	23	630
	Jun	25	725
	Jul	28	630
	Aug	26	550
	Sep	23	430
	Oct	21	400
	Nov	21	350
	Dec	19	260

a. Find the simple regression equation

$$y_t = b_0 + b_1 X_t$$

b. Find the simple regression equation

$$y_t = b_0 + b_1 X_{t-1}$$

c. Compare the R^2 for the regression equations in questions a and b.

17.10

The Problem of Autocorrelation: The Durbin–Watson Statistic

A problem you will encounter frequently when using multiple linear regression on time series data is that the residual terms (e_t) are not independent. We discussed autoregressive forecasting, in which an observation (y_t) is related to its past values. For this situation, we said that significant autocorrelation was present in the *observations*.

When we have an autocorrelated time series, we simply regress y_t on the past values. However, when a particular model dealing with least squares estimates of the unknown parameters (such as multiple linear regression) results in **autocorrelated residuals,** problems do arise. In particular, all tests of hypothesis, including the t tests for individual predictors, become extremely suspect.

Detecting Autocorrelated Residuals

The Durbin–Watson statistic frequently is used to test for significant autocorrelation in the residuals. If its value is very small, significant *positive* autocorrelation exists. This means that each value of e_t is very close to its neighbors, e_{t-1} and e_{t+1}. A large value indicates high *negative* autocorrelation, where each e_t value is very different from the adjacent residual.

The value of the Durbin–Watson statistic (DW) is determined using each residual value, e_t, and its previous value, e_{t-1}.*

$$DW = \frac{\sum_{t=2}^{T} (e_t - e_{t-1})^2}{\sum_{t=1}^{T} e_t^2} \qquad (17\text{-}21)$$

where T is the number of observations in the time series.

The range of possible values for the Durbin–Watson statistic is from 0 to 4. The **ideal value of DW** is 2. For this situation, the errors are completely uncorrelated, and there is no violation of the independent errors assumption. As DW decreases from 2, positive autocorrelation of the errors increases. Values between 2 and 4 indicate various degrees of negative autocorrelation.

The common problem of autocorrelated errors has to do with *positive* correlation between neighboring errors. When this occurs, the errors are not independent of one another; instead, each error is largely determined by its previous value. This implies that a similar behavior will exist for the estimated residuals in the regression model— that is, we can expect the estimated residuals to be positively correlated. The test for autocorrelation using the DW statistic is unique, in that there is certain range of DW values for which we can neither reject H_0: no autocorrelation exists, nor fail to reject (FTR) it. The testing procedure uses Table A-9 on page 833; the value of k in Table A-9 represents the number of predictor variables in the regression equation. The hypotheses are

H_0: no autocorrelation exists

H_a: positive autocorrelation exists

The testing procedure, using the values of d_L and d_U from Table A-9, is

Reject H_0 if $DW < d_L$

FTR H_0 if $DW > d_U$

the test is inconclusive if $d_L \leqslant DW \leqslant d_U$

The assumption is that the errors follow a normal distribution.

Example 17.11

Determine the value of the Durbin–Watson statistic if equation 17-20 is used on the home-loan data in Table 17.13. Use $\alpha = .05$.

Solution Using Figure 17.17 to obtain the estimated values from equation 17-20, Table 17.14 shows the necessary calculations that make up the Durbin–Watson statistic. This is a standard portion of the MINITAB output, as indicated in Figure 17.17.

Using Table 17.14, the Durbin–Watson statistic for this situation is

$$DW = \frac{2071.2}{1579.8} = 1.31$$

---

*The Durbin–Watson statistic can be approximated using the autocorrelation of lag one (called r_1) discussed in section 17.8. This approximation is $DW \cong 2(1 - r_1)$.

Table 17.14

Calculating the Durbin–Watson statistic (example 17.11)

t	y_t	$\hat{y}_t$	$e_t = y_t - \hat{y}_t$	$e_t - e_{t-1}$	$(e_t - e_{t-1})^2$	e_t^2
1	86	—	—	—	—	—
2	96	102.92	− 6.92	—	—	47.92
3	110	119.83	− 9.83	− 2.91	8.48	96.72
4	76	80.37	− 4.37	5.47	29.91	19.06
5	62	72.67	− 10.67	− 6.30	39.71	113.78
6	104	112.55	− 8.55	2.12	4.48	73.11
7	135	134.44	.56	9.11	82.95	.31
8	120	133.79	− 13.79	− 14.35	205.82	190.14
9	115	107.96	7.04	20.83	433.78	49.54
10	84	89.81	− 5.81	− 12.84	164.98	33.72
11	76	77.53	− 1.53	4.28	18.28	2.34
12	81	72.88	8.12	9.65	93.08	65.89
13	122	102.89	19.11	10.99	120.77	365.07
14	118	104.58	13.42	− 5.69	32.40	179.96
15	106	110.67	− 4.67	− 18.08	327.06	21.81
16	140	122.10	17.90	22.57	509.47	320.47
					2071.2*	1579.8**

*Numerator for *DW*.
**Denominator for *DW* = SSE in Figure 17.17.

Using $\alpha = .05$, $n = 15$, $k = 4$ and Table A-9, $d_L = .69$ and $d_U = 1.97$. Notice that the value of n is 15 because only 15 values of y_t were estimated. Also, equation 17-20 uses four variables to predict y_t, and so $k = 4$. The test of hypothesis will be to

Reject H_0 if $DW < .69$

FTR H_0 if $DW > 1.97$,

the test is inconclusive if $.69 \leqslant DW \leqslant 1.97$

Because $DW = 1.31$ falls in the "gray area" between .69 and 1.97, the positive autocorrelation *could* exist, but this test is inconclusive. We need additional information before we can draw any conclusion concerning possible error autocorrelation. ●

Procedures for Correcting Autocorrelated Errors

All is not lost if the Durbin–Watson test concludes that significant autocorrelation is present in the residuals. We will not attempt to fully describe all the remedies for this situation. (For discussions of these methods, consult Bowerman and O'Connell, *Forecasting and Time Series,* and Makridakis and Wheelright, *Forecasting: Methods and Applications,* referenced at the end of this chapter.) However, the following procedures are often used to modify the model such that the "new" residuals are uncorrelated.

1. Replace y_t by the *first difference,* as discussed in section 17.8. The "new" dependent variable is

$$y_t' = y_t - y_{t-1}$$

2. Replace y_t by the *percentage change* during year t,

$$z_t = \left(\frac{y_t - y_{t-1}}{y_{t-1}} \right) 100$$

3. Include the lagged dependent variables, $y_{t-1}, y_{t-2}, \ldots$ as predictors of y_t in the regression equation. This is a modification of the autoregressive technique in section 17.8; now the lagged dependent variables are used with $X_{1,t}$, $X_{2,t}, \ldots$ (which might also be lagged) to predict the time series variable, y_t.

4. Improve the existing model by attempting to discover other significant predictor variables. Because the residuals include the effect of these missing variables, residual autocorrelation often can be improved by including these additional variables. This procedure offers the best solution to the autocorrelation problem but, unfortunately, is easier said than done.

5. Because the errors are autocorrelated, you can *model the error term* in much the same way as we handled the situation of autocorrelated observations. This involves describing each residual, e_t, by its previous values, such as

$$e_t = \phi_1 e_{t-1} + \phi_2 e_{t-2} + \ldots + \phi_j e_{t-j} + u_t$$

The value of j is arbitrary and represents the maximum period over which errors are correlated. Now the problem becomes to estimate not only the coefficients of the predictor variables ($\beta_0, \beta_1, \beta_2, \ldots$) but also those of ϕ_1, $\phi_2, \ldots$. The hope is that the "new" error term, u_t, will contain mostly noise with little autocorrelation.

Comment

Practically all computer packages automatically print out the Durbin–Watson statistic when performing multiple linear regression. When your data are *not* collected over time (but rather from different families, cities, companies, and so on), *this statistic is meaningless* and should be ignored.

Exercises

17.56 If autocorrelation is present in a data set, what procedure used in multiple regression analysis would possibly become invalid?

17.57 What type of correlation is indicated by a value of the Durbin–Watson statistic equal to zero? To two? To four?

17.58 Find the value of the Durbin–Watson statistic for the following yearly data.

Year	Data	Year	Data
1969	32	1977	42
1970	40	1978	48
1971	48	1979	54
1972	52	1980	64
1973	41	1981	42
1974	31	1982	35
1975	28	1983	32
1976	27	1984	27

a. Use the model $\hat{y}_t = b_0 + b_1 y_{t-1}$

b. Test for positive autocorrelation. Use a significance level of .05.

17.59 Test for positive autocorrelation in the residuals of the second-order process in exercise 17.35. Use a significance level of .05.

17.60 Test for positive autocorrelation in the residuals of the fourth-order autoregressive process in exercise 17.36. Use a significance level of .05.

17.61 Test for positive autocorrelation in the residuals of the multiple regression equation in exercise 17.46. Use a significance level of .05.

17.62 If significant correlations are present in the residuals, what procedures can be used to modify the model so that the "new" residuals are uncorrelated?

Summary

In this chapter, we have looked briefly at several popular forecasting techniques. To cover all aspects of time series forecasting would fill an entire textbook. It is a fascinating side of statistics because anyone having a reliable "crystal ball" technique for predicting the future definitely is one step ahead of the game. We hope that this chapter has whetted your appetite to pursue further reading in this area.

Forecasting methods can be divided into two (sometimes overlapping) sets of procedures, time series techniques and multiple linear regression on time series data. Time series procedures attempt to capture the past behavior of the time series and use this information to predict future values. No external predictors are considered; only the past observations are used to describe and predict the future value of the time series variable.

Time series methods include (1) the decomposition procedure, which extracts and extends the trend and seasonal components, (2) exponential smoothing, which reduces randomness and forecasts future values by using the smoothed values, and (3) autoregressive forecasting, which predicts future values by using a linear combination of past values.

There are various exponential smoothing procedures; the proper one to use depends on the nature of the time series. Single exponential smoothing works best when the time series contains neither trend nor seasonality. Linear exponential smoothing is better for a time series that does contain trend but has no seasonality, and linear and seasonal exponential smoothing should be used for a time series that has both components.

Exponential Smoothing

	STRUCTURE OF TIME SERIES	
TYPE	Contains Trend	Contains Seasonality
Single Exponential Smoothing	NO	NO
Linear Exponential Smoothing	YES	NO
Linear and Seasonal Exponential Smoothing	YES	YES

To measure the forecast accuracy of a particular method, you can calculate either the predictive mean squared error (MSE) or the mean absolute deviation (MAD). The MSE is found by squaring each of the residuals obtained by applying this technique to the past observations and then deriving the average of these squared residuals. This measure is very sensitive to one or two very large residuals. The MAD is calculated by averaging the absolute values of the residuals and is less sensitive to a single large residual.

The advantage of the time series methods is that there is no need to search for external predictors to explain the behavior of the dependent variable. One disadvantage is that the patterns within the observed values can be extremely complex and difficult to determine. Such methods often are hard to "sell" to managers, who may not be able to understand the technique.

Figure 17.19

A step-by-step proce-
dure for forecasting with
time series data.

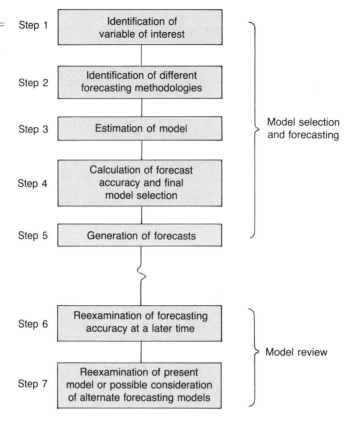

Multiple linear regression forecasting requires additional input data; for each time period, data are recorded for each predictor (independent) variable as well as for the dependent variable, y_t. The predictor variables can include lagged dependent or independent variables or dummy variables to represent seasonality or the occurrence (or nonoccurrence) of a particular event (such as an election year).

When you use multiple linear regression techniques on time series data, you often will violate the assumption of independent errors. The Durbin–Watson statistic can be used to test for significant autocorrelation in the regression residuals. If significant autocorrelation is present, the tests of hypothesis and CIs contained in the regression output are unreliable.

The advantages of multiple linear regression on time series data include: (1) it is a very flexible approach, in that a wide variety of explanatory variables can be included in the model; (2) it allows for lagging the predictor variables, including lagged values of the dependent variable; and (3) it is generally easier to explain to managers, who can see easily which variables are predicting the behavior of the dependent variable. On the other hand, residual autocorrelation often is a problem. This may be caused by missing variables in the prediction equation, which typically are extremely difficult to determine. Also, a very complex pattern within the observed time series may be difficult to capture using a linear combination of predictor variables. Finally, forecasting with this technique becomes extremely difficult unless lagged variables are used. Dummy variables can be included, provided that they can be predicted with certainty. A dummy variable representing an election year would be acceptable, whereas one representing the occurrence (or nonoccurrence) of an earthquake would not be.

The procedure for selecting a forecasting model is summarized in Figure 17.19. Steps 1 through 5 are the model selection and forecasting stage. Steps 6 and 7 are the model review phase, during which you reevaluate your forecasting procedure. This allows you to update your model using the latest observations or to consider changing your forecasting model by returning to step 2. Any forecasting technique should be reviewed; you must reexamine the forecast errors from the previous observations.

Review Exercises

17.63 A set of monthly data has been gathered over 3 years from January 1983 to December 1985. From these data, the seasonal indexes for the 12 months are found to be

$$S_1 = 0.75 \quad S_2 = 0.85 \quad S_3 = 0.95 \quad S_4 = 0.99 \quad S_5 = 0.90 \quad S_6 = 1.01$$
$$S_7 = 1.20 \quad S_8 = 1.10 \quad S_9 = 1.15 \quad S_{10} = 1.05 \quad S_{11} = 1.11 \quad S_{12} = 0.94$$

The least squares line through the deseasonalized data is found to be

$$\hat{d}_t = 2.73 + 0.62t$$

for the 36 monthly periods. Find the forecast for monthly periods 37, 38, 39, 40, and 41.

17.64 The total monthly volume of trade on the stock of Xcon Corp is given for a 4-year period. Units are in millions of shares.

Year	Jan	Feb	Mar	Apr	May	Jun	Jul	Aug	Sep	Oct	Nov	Dec
1982	1.1	1.2	1.4	1.3	1.2	1.5	1.9	1.8	1.3	1.1	0.9	0.8
1983	1.3	1.4	1.5	1.4	1.4	1.7	2.1	1.9	1.6	1.4	1.1	1.1
1984	1.4	1.4	1.6	1.7	1.6	1.9	2.3	2.2	1.8	1.7	1.4	1.2
1985	1.3	1.5	1.5	1.6	1.7	2.0	2.2	2.3	1.9	1.7	1.5	1.4

Using simple exponential smoothing with the parameter $A = .3$, find the forecasted membership for the first month of 1986.

17.65 The total number of cars, trucks, and buses (in millions) on the highways of the United States in each year from 1967 to 1983 is given in the following table:*

Year	Cars, Trucks, and Buses
1967	96.9
1968	100.9
1969	105.1
1970	108.4
1971	113.0
1972	118.8
1973	125.7
1974	129.9
1975	132.9
1976	138.5
1977	142.4
1978	148.4
1979	151.8
1980	155.8
1981	158.5
1982	159.5
1983	161.9

*Source: *United States Statistical Abstracts, 1985.*

a. Forecast the total number of cars, trucks, and buses for the year 1984. Use linear exponential smoothing with an initial estimate of zero for the slope with $A = .1$ and $B = .2$.

b. Rework question a using the least squares estimate of the slope from the first 4 years.

17.66 Two forecasting procedures were used to forecast the 12 quarters from 1983 to 1985. Compute the predictive MSE and MAD for each forecasting procedure. Interpret the results.

Year	Quarter	Procedure 1 Forecast Error	Procedure 2 Forecast Error
1983	1	−1.0	0.7
	2	0.5	−0.5
	3	−2.1	−0.2
	4	2.5	0.9
1984	1	0.9	0.1
	2	2.1	0.2
	3	−1.3	−0.3
	4	1.6	0.9
1985	1	2.7	11.2
	2	−1.9	−0.1
	3	2.4	0.2
	4	−1.2	−0.2

17.67 The amount of money spent on research and development by Energy Today in finding economical uses of alternative fuels for energy is given over a 4-year period. Units are in $\$10,000$.

Year	Quarter 1	Quarter 2	Quarter 3	Quarter 4
1981	4.2	4.5	4.8	4.0
1982	4.3	4.7	5.6	4.4
1983	4.6	4.9	5.7	4.5
1984	4.7	5.0	5.8	4.7

Use Holt's two-parameter linear exponential smoothing technique to obtain a forecast for each of the quarters, omitting the first time period. Let $A = .3$, and $B = .2$. Use the least squares estimate of the trend from the first 5 periods for the initial value of the slope. Calculate the predictive MSE.

17.68 The total number of stamps and stamped paper that the U.S. Postal Service sold in the years from 1970 to 1983 follows.* Fit a second-order autoregressive process to the data. Sales are in units of millions of dollars.

Year	Sales
1970	1936
1971	1999
1972	2371
1973	2399
1974	2504
1975	2819
1976	3155
1977	3658
1978	3943
1979	4382
1980	4287
1981	4625
1982	5559
1983	5709

*Source: *United States Statistical Abstracts, 1985.*

17.69 The total number of retail sales for the years 1967 to 1983 for the United States are given in the following table.* Units are in billions of dollars. Find the first and second order autoregressive models. Calculate the predictive MSE for each model.

Year	Sales
1967	293.0
1968	324.4
1969	346.7
1970	368.4
1971	406.2
1972	449.1
1973	509.5
1974	541.0
1975	588.1
1976	657.4
1977	725.2
1978	806.9
1979	899.4
1980	960.8
1981	1043.5
1982	1074.6
1983	1174.0

17.70 An independent gas station allows its customers to buy gasoline on credit. The amount of credit on the books for the 20 quarters of the years 1981 through 1985 follows. Find the multiple regression equation that takes into account trend and seasonality. The figures in the table are in units of $10,000.

Year	Quarter 1	Quarter 2	Quarter 3	Quarter 4
1981	2.3	2.7	3.4	3.0
1982	2.4	3.0	3.6	3.2
1983	2.6	3.1	3.8	3.4
1984	3.0	3.3	4.0	3.2
1985	3.2	3.4	4.4	3.5

17.71 Using Holt's two-parameter linear exponential smoothing technique, find the smoothed value at time $t = 12$, where the observed value at $t = 12$ is 13.6 and the observed value at $t = 11$ is 12.1. Also let $S_{11} = 7.4$, $S_{10} = 10.4$, $b_{11} = 0.6$, A $= .1$ and B $= .2$.

17.72 In Holt's two-parameter linear exponential smoothing technique, why do you think the values of A and B are typically less than or equal to .3?

17.73 Explain what one should look for in determining the appropriate forecasting procedure.

Case Study

Barton Industries

A major reason for Linda Lowe's success as product manager at Barton Industries is her ability to develop yearly plans and adjust those plans during the course of the year as new information relative to what was planned accrues. This approach allows her to oversee the entire scope of a product's life from ordering needed quantities to its sale at retail outlets.

Linda is a firm believer in using quantitative techniques to generate a wide variety of forecasts to make her product profitable for the company. Forecasts of what is going

*Source: *United States Statistical Abstracts, 1985.*

to happen under varying and ever-changing market/economic conditions make the use of statistical information essential in her job.

Linda's most recent task dealt with determining accurate estimates of consumer demand for a particular product produced by Barton Industries. Accurate forecasts of the demand for the product minimized the out-of-stock situation which leads customers to purchase a competitive substitute. The cost of having to store large quantities of inventory items was also a major consideration in Linda's inventory strategy.

As a first step, she collected data for the past eight years on the amount of the inventory remaining at the end of each quarter. Her intent was to analyze the data and arrive at a proper forecasting procedure which would accurately predict the inventory level for the first quarter of 1986. The data for end-of-quarter inventory levels (in units of 1,000) are shown below.

Year	Quarter 1	Quarter 2	Quarter 3	Quarter 4
1978	37.1	61.2	56.7	65.7
1979	42.5	41.4	40.3	45.1
1980	41.1	57.6	59.5	40.7
1981	62.5	42.7	36.4	56.6
1982	38.6	51.5	51.7	39.5
1983	67.1	37.2	40.8	48.8
1984	42.7	50.3	62.4	40.1
1985	53.6	45.1	42.8	65.3

Case Study Questions

1. Determine the quarterly seasonal indexes. Does there appear to be significant seasonality here?
2. Determine the trend line through the deseasonalized data. Comment on the presence of any trend.
3. Select several different forecasting models that seem appropriate for this situation.
4. Determine the predictive MSE for each model.
5. Would you suggest including the lagged inventory level (y_{t-1}) as a predictor in the equation? Discuss.
6. Prepare a forecast for the inventory level at the end of the first quarter in 1986.

Further Reading

Bowerman, B. L. and R. T. O'Connell, *Forecasting and Time Series,* North Scituate, MA: Duxbury, 1979.

Hanke, J., A. Reitsch, and J. P. Dickson, *Statistical Decision Models for Management,* Newton, MA: Allyn and Bacon, 1984.

Johnson, L. A. and D. C. Montgomery, *Forecasting and Time Series Analysis,* New York: McGraw-Hill, 1976.

Makridakis, S., S. C. Wheelright and V. E. McGee, *Forecasting: Methods and Applications,* 2nd edition New York: Wiley, 1978.

Mendenhall, W. and J. T. McClave, *A Second Course in Business Statistics: Regression Analysis,* San Francisco: Dellen, 1981.

Example Solution

Section 17.3

We used multiple linear regression on time series data to predict the number of home loans financed by Liberty Savings and Loan (Table 17.13). The predictor variables used were average interest rate, advertising expenditure, an election-year dummy variable, and a seasonal dummy variable. The SPSSX program listing in Figure 17.20 was used to compute the regression equation from the time series data. Each line represents one card image to be entered:

The TITLE command names the SPSSX run.

The DATA LIST command gives each variable a name and describes the data as being in free form.

The VARIABLE LABELS statement assigns a descriptive label to the variables. This descriptive label is substituted for the variable name when output is printed.

The COMPUTE X1TLAG = LAG(X1T, 1) command provides X1TLAG with the value of X1T for the case before the current one. For example, in the first half of 1977, the average interest rate (X1T) was 11.0%. Therefore, the value of X1TLAG for the second half of 1977 is also 11.0.

The COMPUTE X2TLAG = LAG(X2T, 1) command provides X2TLAG with the value of X2T for the case before the current one.

The BEGIN DATA command indicates to SPSSX that the input data immediately follow.

Figure 17.20

SPSSX program listing used to compute the regression equation from time series data using lagged variables.

```
TITLE    LIBERTY SAVINGS AND LOAN
DATA LIST FREE / YEAR TIME YT X1T X2T X3T X4T
VARIABLE LABELS    YT 'NUMBER OF HOME LOANS'
                   X1T 'AVERAGE INTEREST RATE'
                   X2T 'ADVERTISING EXPENDITURE'
                   X3T 'ELECTION YEAR VARIABLE'
                   X4T 'SEASONAL VARIABLE'
COMPUTE X1TLAG=LAG(X1T,1)
COMPUTE X2TLAG=LAG(X2T,1)
BEGIN DATA
1977 1 86 11.0 5.1 0 1
1977 2 96 10.1 6.8 0 0
1978 3 110 13.5 6.8 0 1
1978 4 76 15.1 9.1 0 0
1979 5 62 10.5 7.5 0 1
1979 6 104 9.8 5.1 0 0
1980 7 135 10.1 8.8 1 1
1980 8 120 10.8 4.3 1 0
1981 9 115 13.0 9.1 0 1
1981 10 84 14.7 9.5 0 0
1982 11 76 14.1 6.1 0 1
1982 12 81 12.0 8.2 0 0
1983 13 122 11.8 10.4 0 1
1983 14 118 12.4 6.7 0 0
1984 15 106 11.0 7.5 1 1
1984 16 140 14.5 7.8 1 0
END DATA
PRINT / YEAR TIME YT X1T X2T X3T X4T X1TLAG X2TLAG
REGRESSION VARIABLES=YT X1TLAG X2TLAG X3T X4T/
            DEPENDENT=YT/ENTER/RESID=DURBIN
```

```
                    * * * *   M U L T I P L E   R E G R E S S I O N   * * * *

LISTWISE DELETION OF MISSING DATA

EQUATION NUMBER 1   DEPENDENT VARIABLE..   YT   NUMBER OF HOME LOANS

BEGINNING BLOCK NUMBER  1.  METHOD:  ENTER

VARIABLE(S) ENTERED ON STEP NUMBER   1..   X4T      SEASONAL VARIABLE
                                     2..   X3T      ELECTION YEAR VARIABLE
                                     3..   X2TLAG
                                     4..   X1TLAG

MULTIPLE R            .88852        ANALYSIS OF VARIANCE
R SQUARE             .78917  — R²                       DF      SUM OF SQUARES     MEAN SQUARE
ADJUSTED R SQUARE    .70526        REGRESSION            4        5924.17109       1481.04277
STANDARD ERROR      12.56912        RESIDUAL            10        1579.82891        157.98289

                         F =     9.37470        SIGNIF F =   .0020

------------------ VARIABLES IN THE EQUATION ------------------

VARIABLE              B          SE B         BETA         T    SIG T

X4T            4.474719      6.700184     .099809      .668    .5193
X3T           14.694477      8.121511     .290528     1.809    .1005
X2TLAG         1.867273      2.096636     .144439      .891    .3941
X1TLAG       -10.292543      2.334529    -.774673    -4.409    .0013
(CONSTANT)   206.617343     27.041474                 7.641    .0000

END BLOCK NUMBER   1   ALL REQUESTED VARIABLES ENTERED.
```

$$\hat{y}_t = 206.62 - 10.29\,X_{1,\,t-1} + 1.867\,X_{2,\,t-1} + 14.694\,X_{3,\,t} + 4.475\,X_{4,\,t}$$

```
                    * * * *   M U L T I P L E   R E G R E S S I O N   * * * *

EQUATION NUMBER 1   DEPENDENT VARIABLE..   YT   NUMBER OF HOME LOANS

RESIDUALS STATISTICS:

                MIN          MAX      MEAN   STD DEV   N

*PRED        72.6669     134.4427  103.0000  20.5707   15
*RESID      -13.7891      19.1068     .0000  10.6228   15
*ZPRED       -1.4746       1.5285     .0000   1.0000   15
*ZRESID      -1.0971       1.5201     .0000    .8452   15

TOTAL CASES =      16

DURBIN-WATSON TEST =    1.31101
```

Figure 17.21

Output obtained by executing the SPSSX program listing in Figure 17.20.

The next 16 lines are card images that represent time series data over 16 time periods. The first line, for example, represents the first half of 1977, the first time period, 86 home loans, average interest rate of 11%, and so on.

The END DATA statement indicates the end of the data card images.

The PRINT command causes the printing of the values of YEAR, TIME, YT, X1T, X2T, X3T, X4T, X1TLAG, and X2TLAG.

The REGRESSION VARIABLES statement specifies that variables YT, X1TLAG, X2TLAG, X3T, and X4T are to be used in the regression equation and that YT is the dependent variable.

The ENTER option specifies that all independent variables are to be applied in the equation simultaneously.

The RESID option specifies that the Durbin–Watson statistic is to be computed.

Figure 17.21 shows the output obtained by executing the program listing in Figure 17.20.

Solution

Example 17.9

Example 17.9 is divided into two computer runs. In the first run, we use the autocorrelation function to determine the significant autocorrelations among the given lag periods. In the second run, the significant lag period (lag 4) is included in the autoregression equation. The SPSSX program listings in Figures 17.22 and 17.23 were used to perform the two procedures. Each line represents one card image to be entered:

The TITLE command names the SPSSX run.

The DATA LIST command gives each variable a name and describes the data as being in free form.

The VARIABLE LABELS statement assigns a descriptive label to the variables. This descriptive label is substituted for the variable name when output is printed.

The BEGIN DATA command indicates to SPSSX that the input data immediately follow.

The next 20 lines are card images that represent time series data over 20 time periods. For example, 1 5.56 represents the OBSERVED VALUE of 5.56 for time period 1.

The END DATA statement indicates the end of the data card images.

The PRINT command causes the printing of the variables T and YT.

The BOX-JENKINS VARIABLE = YT/IDENTIFY statement indicates that the YT time series is to be analyzed and that we wish to produce statistics for model identification.

Figure 17.22

SPSSX program listing used to determine significant autocorrelations.

```
TITLE     KEN'S AUTO PAINT SHOP - AUTOCORRELATION FUNCTION
DATA LIST FREE / T YT
VARIABLE LABELS T 'TIME'
                YT 'OBSERVED VALUES'
BEGIN DATA
1  5.56
2  16.36
3  2.12
4  3.15
5  5.11
6  15.21
7  5.72
8  2.65
9  4.12
10 14.33
11 5.25
12 6.75
13 6.31
14 15.02
15 2.83
16 4.56
17 4.81
18 16.82
19 4.75
20 8.54
END DATA
PRINT / T YT
BOX-JENKINS VARIABLE=YT/IDENTIFY
```

Figure 17.23

SPSSX program listing used to determine the autocorrelation equation using one lagged variable.

```
TITLE    KEN'S AUTO PAINT SHOP - AUTOREGRESSIVE MODEL
DATA LIST FREE / T YT
VARIABLE LABELS T 'TIME'
                YT 'OBSERVED VALUES'
BEGIN DATA
1 5.56
2 16.36
3 2.12
4 3.15
5 5.11
6 15.21
7 5.72
8 2.65
9 4.12
10 14.33
11 5.25
12 6.75
13 6.31
14 15.02
15 2.83
16 4.56
17 4.81
18 16.82
19 4.75
20 8.54
END DATA
COMPUTE YT4=LAG(YT,4)
PRINT / T YT YT4
REGRESSION VARIABLES=YT YT4/DEP=YT/ENTER/SAVE PRED(PREDX)
PRINT / YT PREDX
EXECUTE
```

Figure 17.24

Output obtained by executing the SPSSX program listing in Figure 17.22.

```
* * * * * * * * * * * * * * * * * * * * A R I M A    A N A L Y S I S * * * * * * * * * * * *

VARIABLE YT      CONTAINS THE TIME SERIES

DEGREE OF NONSEASONAL DIFFERENCING -   0

DEGREE OF SEASONAL DIFFERENCING -   0

SEASONAL SPAN -   1

MEAN VALUE OF THE PROCESS
   0.74985D+01

STANDARD DEVIATION OF THE PROCESS
   0.48828D+01

AUTOCORRELATION FUNCTION FOR VARIABLE YT
AUTOCORRELATIONS *
TWO STANDARD ERROR LIMITS

     AUTO. STAND.
LAG  CORR.  ERR.  -1 -.75 -.5 -.25  0  .25 .5  .75  1
                  ----:----:----:----:----:----:----:----:----
  1 -0.315  0.202                    *
  2 -0.260  0.197                   *
  3 -0.286  0.191                   *
  4  0.678  0.185                              *
  5 -0.213  0.178                 *
  6 -0.168  0.172                  *
  7 -0.156  0.165                  *
  8  0.512  0.158                           *
  9 -0.235  0.151                 *
 10 -0.134  0.143                  *
 11 -0.104  0.135                   *
 12  0.388  0.126                         *
 13 -0.155  0.117                  *
 14 -0.060  0.107                   *
 15 -0.123  0.095                  *
 16  0.206  0.083                    *
 17 -0.101  0.067                  *
 18  0.031  0.048                    *
                                   rₖ
*** BOX-JENKINS REQUIRES      3872 BYTES OF WORKSPACE FOR IDENTIFICATION ***
```

Use this lagged variable in the autoregressive equation

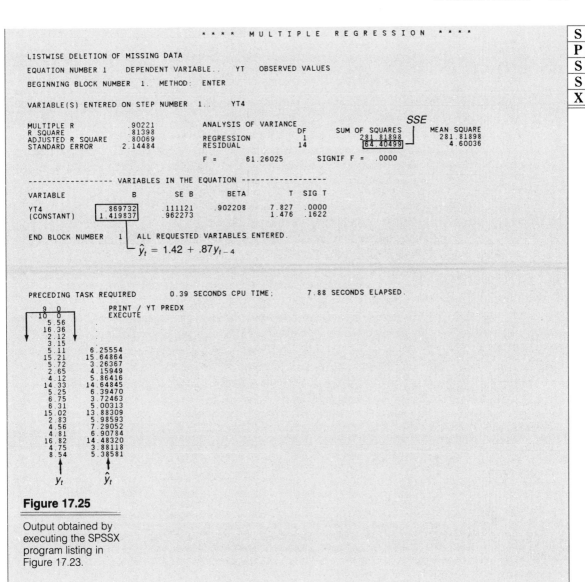

Figure 17.25

Output obtained by executing the SPSSX program listing in Figure 17.23.

The commands in Figure 17.23 are the same as those in Figure 17.22, with the following exceptions:

The COMPUTE YT4 = LAG(YT,4) command provides YT4 with the value of YT for the fourth case before the current one. For example, the value of YT in case 16 is 4.56. Therefore, the value of YT4 in case 20 is also 4.56.

The REGRESSION VARIABLES statement specifies that variables YT and YT4 are to be used in the regression equation and that YT is the dependent variable.

The ENTER option specifies that all independent variables are to be applied in the equation simultaneously.

The SAVE option saves the predicted values under the name PREDX.

Figures 17.24 and 17.25 show the outputs obtained by executing the program listings in Figures 17.22 and 17.23.

•	S
•	A
•	S

Example Solution

Section 17.3

We used multiple linear regression on time series data to predict the number of home loans financed by Liberty Savings and Loan (Table 17.13). The predictor variables used were average interest rate, advertising expenditure, an election year dummy variable, and a seasonal dummy variable. The SAS program listing in Figure 17.26 was used to compute the regression equation from the time series data. Each line represents one card image to be entered:

The TITLE command names the SAS run.

The DATA command gives the data a name.

The INPUT command names and gives the correct order for the different fields on the data cards.

The LABEL statement assigns labels for the variables YT, X1T, X2T, X3T, and X4T. These labels are substituted for the variable names when output is printed.

The X1TLAG = LAG1(X1T) command provides X1TLAG with the value of X1T for the case before the current one. For example, the average interest rate (X1T) in the first half of 1977 was 11.0%. Therefore, the value of X1TLAG for the second half of 1977 is also 11.0.

The X2TLAG = LAG1(X2T) command provides X2TLAG with the value of X2T for the case before the current one.

The CARDS command indicates to SAS that the input data immediately follow.

Figure 17.26

SAS program listing used to compute the regression equation from time series data using lagged variables.

```
TITLE     LIBERTY SAVINGS AND LOAN MODEL;
DATA AUTO;
 INPUT YEAR TIME YT X1T X2T X3T X4T;
 LABEL YT=NUMBER OF HOME LOANS
      X1T=AVERAGE INTEREST RATE
      X2T=ADVERTISING EXPENDITURE
      X3T=ELECTION YEAR VARIABLE
      X4T=SEASONAL VARIABLE;
 X1TLAG=LAG1(X1T);
 X2TLAG=LAG1(X2T);
CARDS;
1977 1 86 11.0 5.1 0 1
1977 2 96 10.1 6.8 0 0
1978 3 110 13.5 6.8 0 1
1978 4 76 15.1 9.1 0 0
1979 5 62 10.5 7.5 0 1
1979 6 104 9.8 5.1 0 0
1980 7 135 10.1 8.8 1 1
1980 8 120 10.8 4.3 1 0
1981 9 115 13.0 9.1 0 1
1981 10 84 14.7 9.5 0 0
1982 11 76 14.1 6.1 0 1
1982 12 81 12.0 8.2 0 0
1983 13 122 11.8 10.4 0 1
1983 14 118 12.4 6.7 0 0
1984 15 106 11.0 7.5 1 1
1984 16 140 14.5 7.8 1 0
PROC PRINT;
PROC REG;
 MODEL YT=X1TLAG X2TLAG X3T X4T/ DW;
```

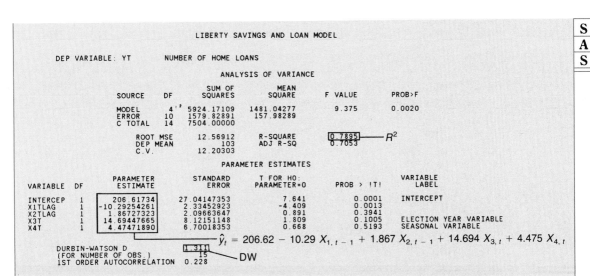

Figure 17.27

Output obtained by executing the SAS program listing in Figure 17.26.

The next 16 lines are card images that represent time series data over 16 time periods. The first line, for example, represents the first half of 1977, the first time period, 86 home loans, average interest rate of 11.0%, and so on.

The PROC PRINT command directs SAS to print the data that were just read in.

The PROC REG command and MODEL subcommand specify that variables YT, X1TLAG, X2TLAG, X3T, and X4T are to be used in the regression equation and that YT is the dependent variable.

The DW option requests that the Durbin–Watson statistic be computed.

Figure 17.27 shows the output obtained by executing the program listing in Figure 17.26.

Solution

Example 17.9

Example 17.9 is divided into two computer runs. In the first run, we use the autocorrelation function to determine the significant autocorrelations among the given lag periods. In the second run, the significant lag period (lag 4) is included in the autoregression equation. The SAS program listings in Figures 17.28 and 17.29 were used to perform the two procedures. Each line represents one card image to be entered:

The TITLE command names the SAS run.

The DATA command gives the data a name.

The INPUT command names and gives the correct order for the different fields on the data cards.

The LABELS statement assigns the labels TIME for variable T and OBSERVED VALUES for variable YT. These labels are substituted for the variable names when output is printed.

The CARDS command indicates to SAS that the input data immediately follow.

The next 20 lines are card images that represent time series data over 20 time periods. For example, 1 5.56 represents the OBSERVED VALUE of 5.56 housing starts for the first time period.

Figure 17.28

SAS program listing used to determine significant autocorrelations.

```
TITLE    KEN'S AUTO PAINT SHOP - AUTOCORRELATION FUNCTION;
DATA AUTO;
 INPUT T YT;
 LABEL T=TIME
        YT=OBSERVED VALUES;
 CARDS;
1 5.56
2 16.36
3 2.12
4 3.15
5 5.11
6 15.21
7 5.72
8 2.65
9 4.12
10 14.33
11 5.25
12 6.75
13 6.31
14 15.02
15 2.83
16 4.56
17 4.81
18 16.82
19 4.75
20 8.54
PROC PRINT;
PROC ARIMA;
 IDENTIFY VAR=YT;
```

Figure 17.29

SAS program listing used to determine the autocorrelation equation using one lagged variable.

```
TITLE    KEN'S AUTO PAINT SHOP - AUTOREGRESSIVE MODEL;
DATA AUTO;
 INPUT T YT;
 LABEL T=TIME
        YT=OBSERVED VALUES;
YT4=LAG4(YT);
 CARDS;
1 5.56
2 16.36
3 2.12
4 3.15
5 5.11
6 15.21
7 5.72
8 2.65
9 4.12
10 14.33
11 5.25
12 6.75
13 6.31
14 15.02
15 2.83
16 4.56
17 4.81
18 16.82
19 4.75
20 8.54
PROC PRINT;
PROC REG;
 MODEL YT=YT4;
 OUTPUT OUT=C PRED=P;
PROC PRINT;
 VAR YT P;
```

Figure 17.30

Output obtained by
executing the SAS
program listing in
Figure 17.29.

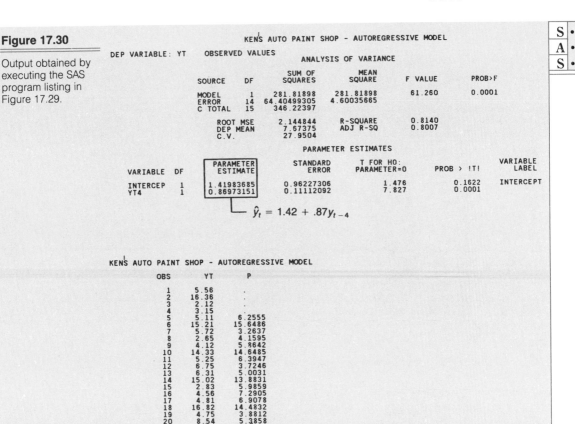

The PROC PRINT command directs SAS to print the data that were just read in.
The PROC ARIMA and IDENTIFY commands are used to analyze the time series
YT and identify the significant autocorrelations.

The commands in Figure 17.29 are the same as those in Figure 17.30, with the
following exceptions:

The YT4 = LAG4(YT) command provides YT4 with the value of YT for the fourth
case before the current one. For example, the value of YT in case 16 is
4.56. Therefore, the value of YT4 in case 20 is also 4.56.

The PROC REG command and MODEL subcommand specify that variables YT
and YT4 are to be used in the regression equation, and that YT is the
dependent variable.

The OUTPUT command specifies that the output from PROC REG is to be stored
in an output data set named C and that the predicting values in the data set
are named PRED.

Figure 17.30 shows the output obtained by executing the program listing in Figure
17.29.

18

Decision Making Under Uncertainty

A Look Back/Introduction

You have been exposed to decision making in which you use a statistical test of hypothesis. The final step for any test of hypothesis is to reject or fail to reject the null hypothesis, H_0. The previous chapters examined a number of such tests, ranging from a decision regarding two means (for example, is $\mu_1 > \mu_2$?) to selecting predictor variables for a multiple regression equation.

The previous tests of hypothesis concentrated on the *probabilistic* aspects of decision making. For example, if the probability of observing a t value as large as the computed sample value was less than a predetermined significance level α, we rejected H_0 and decided to keep a particular predictor variable in the regression equation. Such procedures are intended to help you make statistical decisions regarding certain population *parameters*, such as the mean (μ) or standard deviation (σ) of a normal population, the population coefficient (β) for a certain independent variable in a regression equation, or the proportion of successes (p) for a binomial situation.

We now examine a different side of decision making that is particularly useful when money is involved. This area of statistics allows the decision maker to consider the various benefits and losses associated with each possible alternative, in an effort to find the "best" decision. For example, if your aging car one day rolls over and goes to that great garage in the sky, you may be faced with the decision of buying a new car or leasing one. If you are lucky enough to have the option of buying a new car that runs well and will incur few repair bills, perhaps your best bet would be to purchase it. Other factors to consider would be the length of time that you intend to keep the car and the tax advantages for each alternative. The main problem, however, is that the future reliability of the new car is uncertain.

The problem of decision making in such a situation would be greatly simplified if you had a crystal ball. A perfect predictor would tell you whether the new car you are thinking of buying is a lemon. Unfortunately, no such device exists, so you need to develop various decision strategies to deal with future uncertainties. Certain strategies are *conservative;* you stand neither to gain nor to lose a large amount. Other procedures attempt to measure the likelihood of future events by using probabilities. If you are a gambler at heart, strategies exist that allow you to defy odds in hopes of a big payoff.

If your life savings are at stake, you may elect to use a more conservative strategy in your investment decisions; gambling with these funds could be too dangerous. On the other hand, you may have certain reserve funds that you would be willing to invest in more speculative ventures, hoping for a large return at the risk of losing your investment. The purchase of a lottery ticket is a small-scale example of such an investment.

This chapter will examine the various strategies available to the decision maker and illustrate these techniques for different business situations.

18.1

Defining the Decision Problem

Essentially, when confronted with making a decision in the face of uncertainty, you need to be concerned with two basic questions:

1. What are my possible **actions** (alternatives) for this problem?
2. What is it about the future that affects the desirability of each action?

For the buy versus lease example, you are faced with two possible actions,

Action	Description
A_1	Purchase the car
A_2	Lease the car

When you are trying to decide between these two options, what would you like to know? One possibility is to describe the future (as it applies to this decision) by means of three events, or **states of nature**.

S_1: the new car will have less-than-average repair costs

S_2: the new car will have average repair costs

S_3: the new car will have above-average repair costs

These future states of nature are **outcomes**. The key distinction between an action and a state of nature is that the action taken is *under your control,* whereas the state of nature that occurs is strictly a matter of chance. We will assume that *one and only one* of the states of nature will occur in the future; that is, they are *mutually exclusive.*

Other questions that require the decision maker to specify corresponding states of nature are ones such as

What will be the future demand for a new computer software package?
How long will it be until the newly purchased electrical pump breaks down and needs to be replaced?

Table 18.1

Payoff table

Action	S_1	S_2	S_3	S_n
		STATES OF NATURE		
A_1	π_{11}	π_{12}	π_{13}	π_{1n}
A_2	π_{21}	π_{22}	π_{23}	π_{2n}
A_3	π_{31}	π_{32}	π_{33}	π_{3n}
.				
.				
.				
A_k	π_{k1}	π_{k2}	π_{k3}	π_{kn}

Will the stock market turn up or down in the next three months?

Will this year's winter be milder or colder than the average for the past 20 years?

Associated with each action (A) and state of nature (S) is a corresponding **payoff** or **profit.** We will assume that the payoff associated with each particular state of nature and action is known with certainty. These payoffs can be summarized in a **payoff table,** shown in Table 18.1. The entry, for example, corresponding to action A_2 (row 2) and state of nature S_3 (column 3) is denoted as π_{23} and is the payoff associated with action A_2 should state of nature S_3 occur.

Mr. Larson is owner of Sailtown, a store in southern Minnesota specializing in the sale of small sailboats. Each spring he is forced to place an order for his entire stock of Bluefin sailboats to be sold during the summer months because the Bluefin manufacturer is unable to supply any additional boats once the summer has begun.

Mr. Larson's main concern when ordering his summer inventory is the demand for his product during the next five months. He has discovered that this demand seems to be largely dependent on economic conditions, in particular on the prevailing interest rate. He has four possible actions (order quantities)

A_1: purchase 50 boats,

A_2: purchase 75 boats,

A_3: purchase 100 boats,

A_4: purchase 150 boats

The states of nature for this problem are

S_1: the interest rate increases significantly (more than 1.5%) from the current rate

S_2: the interest rate holds steady

S_3: the interest rate drops significantly (more than 1.5%)

Based on his expected sales under each condition, the payoff table in Table 18.2

Table 18.2

Profit table for Sailtown (thousands of dollars)

Amount Ordered	Increases (S_1)	Steady (S_2)	Decreases (S_3)
		AVERAGE INTEREST RATE	
50 (A_1)	15	15	15
75 (A_2)	2.5	22.5	22.5
100 (A_3)	-10	30	30
150 (A_4)	-35	5	45

Table 18.3

Demand for sailboats for each state of nature

State of Nature	Interest Rate	Corresponding Demand
S_1	Increases	50
S_2	Holds steady	100
S_3	Decreases	150

was constructed. To demonstrate how the payoffs were determined, consider $\pi_{42} = 5$, which is the resulting profit if he orders 150 sailboats (action A_4) and if the interest rate remains basically unchanged (state of nature S_2). Mr. Larson believes that, for S_2, the resulting demand will be 100 sailboats. His profit per sale is $300, and his cost for holding and returning an unsold boat at the end of the fall season is $500. Consequently, if the demand is for 100 boats and he decides to stock 150, he ends up selling 100 boats and returning 50 of them to the manufacturer. The resulting dollar amounts are

$$\text{profit for selling 100 boats} = 100 \cdot \$300 = \$30,000$$
$$\text{loss for returning 50 boats} = 50 \cdot \$500 = \underline{\$25,000}$$
$$\text{net payoff} = \pi_{42} = \$5,000$$

So Mr. Larson calculates that the interest rate holding steady is equivalent to a demand for 100 sailboats. Similarly, he determines that an increase in the interest rate will result in a demand for 50 boats, whereas a decrease in the interest rate will produce a demand for 150 boats (Table 18.3).

Example 18.1

Using Table 18.3, determine the payoff for each of the four alternatives if the interest rate increases over the summer months. What would be the best action to take if you knew that this particular state of nature would occur?

Solution We are given that state of nature S_1 will occur. Mr. Larson thinks that, under this state of nature, 50 people will walk in his front door wanting to purchase a Bluefin sailboat. Under this assumption, the payoffs in Table 18.4 can be derived.

If we know that the interest rate will increase during the summer months, Table 18.4 tells us that the ideal action is to purchase 50 boats (action A_1).

Is action A_1 the ideal action for each state of nature? Given state of nature S_2 and using Table 18.2, the payoffs are $15,000 (for A_1), $22,500 (for A_2), $30,000 (for A_3), and $5000 (for A_4). In this case, you would achieve maximum profit by purchasing 100 boats (action A_3). The third column of Table 18.2 shows that action A_4 (purchasing 150 boats) provides the maximum profit in the event that the interest rate declines.

●

Table 18.4

Payoff for Sailtown under S_1 (example 18.1)

Action	Revenue for Boats Sold	Loss Due to Returned Boats	Net Payoff
A_1	$50 \cdot 300 = \$15,000$	$0 \cdot 500 = \$0$	$15,000
A_2	$50 \cdot 300 = \$15,000$	$25 \cdot 500 = \$12,500$	$2,500
A_3	$50 \cdot 300 = \$15,000$	$50 \cdot 500 = \$25,000$	$-$10,000
A_4	$50 \cdot 300 = \$15,000$	$100 \cdot 500 = \$50,000$	$-$35,000

This is an example of **decision making under certainty.** Although the decision maker will never have this luxury, the technique at least enables him or her to determine the maximum profit under each state of nature. Also, if the *same action* provides the maximum payoff regardless of the state of nature, then this particular action is the obvious choice for this situation. Such was not the case in Table 18.2. There is no obviously superior action here, so we need to consider more elaborate decision strategies.

Exercises

18.1 A stockbroker is trying to decide which of three possible actions to recommend to a client. One action (A_1) would be to invest 100% in a mutual fund that invests in stocks. Another action (A_2) would be to invest 50% in a fixed account yielding 10% per year and 50% in a stock market mutual fund. The third action (A_3) would be to invest 100% in the fixed account, yielding 10% per year. The stockbroker believes the following returns can be made in a particular mutual fund in 1 year with regard to the stock market's direction.

S_1: Stock Market Goes Up	S_2: Stock Market Has No Direction	S_3: Stock Market Goes Down
20%	5%	-10%

Using the three states of nature, S_1, S_2, and S_3 and the three actions A_1, A_2, and A_3 construct a payoff table if a client has $10,000 to invest for 1 year.

18.2 Would the following decisions be made under certainty or uncertainty?

a. Whether to buy or lease a new car.

b. Whether to accept a client who wants to pay you $40 per visit for five visits.

c. Whether to borrow $10,000 at 12% interest per year for 5 years.

d. Whether to switch jobs or stay at the same job.

18.3 A seminar on sales motivation is being given at a local hotel. The cost of handouts and materials per attendee is $10. The total cost of the hotel arrangements is $75. Each attendee pays $25 for the seminar. The coordinator of the seminar must plan the number of handouts and materials. The coordinator must plan for 7, 8, 9, 10, 11, 12, or 13 attendees. Construct the payoff table if the demand is 5, 6, 7, 8, 9, 10, 11, 12, or 13 attendees.

18.4 The Jones family has moved out of their house and now have it up for sale. They need to decide whether to price their house at the top of market, $88,000, at the market, $85,000, or below the market at $82,000. Each month that it takes to sell the house, the Jones family loses $700 from making the monthly payment. Construct a payoff table that shows the selling price of the home minus $700 for each month the house remains unsold. Use S_1 = sold in 1 month, S_2 = sold in 2 months, . . . , S_6 = sold in 6 months.

18.5 Mini-Super, a convenience food store, orders milk each week. The store pays $1.10 per gallon and sells the milk for $2.00 per gallon. Unsold milk at the end of the week is given to an orphanage. The manager must decide on ordering 100 gallons, 125 gallons, or 150 gallons per week. Construct the payoff table for this problem if demand is 100 gallons, 125 gallons, or 150 gallons a week.

18.2

Decision Strategies

When the action providing a maximum payoff depends on an uncertain state of nature, the decision maker is forced to consider all the values in the payoff table to choose the most attractive action. The various strategies discussed here will allow you to choose a procedure that best fits your style of making decisions. We will begin with a conservative strategy, the minimax procedure.

The Conservative (Minimax) Strategy

A conservative strategy is basically one that, when choosing between a savings account and an extremely risky venture, selects the savings account. It does this because, under the *worst* conditions, your loss is smaller with a savings account than with the high-risk venture.

We examined the ideal action for Mr. Larson to take in the event that he knew that the interest rate was going to increase (S_1 in Table 18.2). This action was to order 50 boats for a payoff of $\pi_{11} = 15$ (thousand). If he had taken action A_2 instead, his profit would be only $2500. For this situation, we say that the opportunity loss is $15,000 - 2500 = \$12,500$.

The **opportunity loss,** L_{ij}, is the difference between the payoff for action i and the payoff for the action that would have the largest payoff under state of nature j.

The opportunity loss is not a loss in the accounting sense; rather, it describes how much more profit you *would have made* had you chosen the best action for this state of nature. The opportunity loss for action A_3 (assuming state of nature S_1) is

$$\text{opportunity loss} = L_{31} = 15 - (-10)$$
$$= 25 \text{ (thousand dollars)}$$

and this value for action A_4 (under S_1) is

$$\text{opportunity loss} = L_{41} = 15 - (-35)$$
$$= 50 \text{ (thousand dollars)}$$

Example 18.2

Construct the remaining opportunity losses for Mr. Larson, and summarize them in an opportunity loss table.

Solution Keep in mind that opportunity losses are determined one *column* at a time in Table 18.2 by assuming that each individual state of nature occurs, and then looking for the best action under this condition. This is exactly the same procedure that we used when discussing the unrealistic situation of decision making under certainty.

If the interest rate holds steady (S_2 occurs), the best action is to stock 100 boats (action A_3) with a payoff of $\pi_{32} = 30$. Table 18.5 shows the opportunity loss for this situation.

Similarly, action A_4 (stock 150 boats) is your ideal action in the event the interest rate decreases (S_3) and sales increase, as shown in Table 18.6.

Table 18.5

Opportunity loss for assumption: S_2 occurs; best action: A_3; maximum payoff: 30

Action	Payoff	Opportunity Loss
A_1	15	$L_{12} = 30 - 15 = 15$
A_2	22.5	$L_{22} = 30 - 22.5 = 7.5$
A_3	30	$L_{32} = 30 - 30 = 0$
A_4	5	$L_{42} = 30 - 5 = 25$

Table 18.6

Opportunity loss for assumption: S_3 occurs; best action: A_4; maximum payoff: 45

Action	Payoff	Opportunity Loss
A_1	15	$L_{13} = 45 - 15 = 30$
A_2	22.5	$L_{23} = 45 - 22.5 = 22.5$
A_3	30	$L_{33} = 45 - 30 = 15$
A_4	45	$L_{43} = 45 - 45 = 0$

Table 18.7

Opportunity loss table for Sailtown decision problem (thousands of dollars)

	STATE OF NATURE		
Action	S_1	S_2	S_3
A_1	0	15	30
A_2	12.5	7.5	22.5
A_3	25	0	15
A_4	50	25	0

We format this as an **opportunity loss table** as shown in Table 18.7. Notice that each column of an opportunity loss table contains a zero, and all values in this table are nonnegative ($\geqslant 0$). ●

The Minimax Strategy The minimax strategy is to

1. Construct an opportunity loss table by using the maximum payoff for each state of nature.
2. Determine the maximum opportunity loss for each action.
3. Find the minimum value of those found in step 2; the corresponding action is the one selected by the minimax strategy.

This is a very conservative approach that does not search for large payoffs; rather, it selects the action that has the smallest "worst case" opportunity loss.

The minimax procedure begins by examining the worst possible situation for each action. So you examine Table 18.7 one *row* at a time and determine the largest opportunity loss for each action. Thus, we have

Action	Maximum Opportunity Loss
A_1	30
A_2	22.5
A_3	25
A_4	50

This is the *max* part of the minimax strategy. The *mini* side is finding the *minimum* of these four values. In this way, you attempt to offset the "worst possible situation" scenario. For this example, of 30, 22.5, 25, and 50, the minimum is 22.5, which belongs to action A_2, so the **minimax decision** is to order 75 sailboats.

Example 18.3

The owner of Foodway, a large supermarket, has decided to keep his store open on the fourth of July holiday. He has decided to use either two, three, or four clerks, but he is uncertain about the number of customers to expect on this holiday. If the traffic is below average, two clerks will be enough; if the traffic is above average, four will be needed. He has decided to consider three states of nature,

S_1 = number of customers is below average

S_2 = number of customers is average

S_3 = number of customers is above average

with three alternative actions,

A_1: employ 2 clerks

A_2: employ 3 clerks

A_3: employ 4 clerks

Table 18.8

Payoff table for Foodway (dollars)

	VOLUME OF CUSTOMERS		
Action	Below Average (S_1)	Average (S_2)	Above Average (S_3)
Employ 2 clerks (A_1)	350	400	450
Employ 3 clerks (A_2)	300	750	850
Employ 4 clerks (A_3)	250	500	1000

Table 18.9

Opportunity loss table for Foodway (dollars)

	STATE OF NATURE		
Action	S_1	S_2	S_3
A_1	0	350	550
A_2	50	0	150
A_3	100	250	0

Considering the cost of each clerk and the average purchase amount per customer, the payoff (profit) table in Table 18.8 was constructed. How many clerks should the owner employ using the minimax strategy?

Solution The first step is to construct an opportunity loss table. For example, if state of nature S_1 occurs, the best action is A_1, with a payoff of $350 and an opportunity loss of zero. Consequently, A_2 has an opportunity loss of 50 (350 − 300), and A_3 has an opportunity loss of 100(350 − 250). Continuing in this way, we can construct Table 18.9.

Next, we find the maximum opportunity loss for each action.

Action	Maximum Opportunity Loss
A_1	Maximum of 0, 350, 550 = 550
A_2	Maximum of 50, 0, 150 = 150
A_3	Maximum of 100, 250, 0 = 250

Finally, we select the minimum of these maximum values. This is 150, corresponding to A_2. The minimax decision is to employ three clerks for the fourth of July. This action is the one that minimizes the maximum difference between the profit received and the profit that *could* have been received if the state of nature (customer traffic) that occurred had been known in advance. ●

The Gambler (Maximax) Strategy

The maximax strategy is the opposite of the minimax procedure and appeals to those who are gamblers at heart. The **maximax strategy** is to choose that action having the largest possible payoff. It is not a recommended procedure for most business decisions because, by choosing that action with the largest payoff, it fails to consider the possibility of large accounting losses or opportunity losses.

Example 18.4

In Table 18.2, which action would you select using the maximax strategy?

Solution Of the 12 payoffs in Table 18.2, the largest is 45, which corresponds to action A_4. If Sailtown is desperate for a large payoff, the appropriate action using this strategy would be to order 150 sailboats for the summer months. Of course, the company also stands to lose the most using this action; the loss will be $35,000 if the interest rate increases. ●

Example 18.5

Based on the payoff table in Table 18.8 and the maximax strategy, how many clerks should the owner of Foodway employ for the fourth of July?

Solution The maximum payoff is $1000 in Table 18.8, and this corresponds to action A_3. So, if the owner wants to gamble for a large payoff, the corresponding action would be to hire four clerks for the holiday. This procedure ignores the effect of the ideal state of nature for this action (S_3) *not* occurring. ●

Exercises

18.6 Why is the following table not an opportunity loss table? Give two reasons.

Action	S_1	S_2	S_3
A_1	4	6	80
A_2	29	0	150
A_3	57	−1	0

18.7 The owner of a bookstand orders the local daily newspapers and charges 25 cents per copy. The owner pays 10 cents for each copy. Each day, the owner orders either 70, 80, 90, or 100 copies. At the end of the day, the leftover newspapers are discarded. Construct the payoff table and opportunity loss table if the demand is 50, 60, 70, 80, 90, or 100 copies. What is the minimax decision? What is the maximax decision?

18.8 The owner of a small commercial building can either pay $1000 per year to insure the $200,000 building or not insure and save a $1000 per year. If the states of nature are complete loss of the commercial building or no loss at all, what would the payoff table and opportunity loss table be for this situation? What is the minimax decision?

18.9 What would the opportunity loss table be using the following payoff table?

Action	S_1	S_2	S_3	S_4
A_1	150	2	89	5
A_2	−20	10	76	−10
A_3	0	15	94	−20

18.10 Refer to exercise 18.1. Construct the opportunity loss table for the actions of the stockbroker and the states of nature of the stock market. What is the minimax decision? What is the maximax decision?

The Strategist (Maximizing Expected Payoff)

In many respects, a more sensible approach to any decision problem is to consider the likelihood that each state of nature will occur. In this way, you can use any information you have to help evaluate the possibilities of each of the states of nature. If you believe strongly that the chance of the interest rate declining is small, a decision strategy that uses this information would be useful. The strategy discussed here differs from previous procedures, in that we begin by determining the *probability* associated with each state of nature.

Selecting the Probabilities The probability for each state of nature measures to what degree you believe this state of nature will occur in the future. One way to obtain these probabilities is from past experience—referred to as **empirical evidence.** For example, if, under similar conditions in the past, the stock market declined 15% of the time, we would set

$$P(\text{stock market declines}) = .15$$

In this way, you can determine the probability for each state of nature. Because we are assuming that one (and only one) of these states *must* occur, these probabilities must sum to 1.

Another method of selecting these probabilities is the **subjective approach.** With this procedure, an individual, or group of individuals, will select each probability such that (1) each value represents their confidence that each state of nature will occur, and (2) the probabilities sum to 1.

To someone unfamiliar with the concept of a probability, you can pose the question, "Given this set of circumstances 100 different times, how often do you think the stock market will decline?" If the answer is, "I'd say about 15 times," then once again you have

$$P(\text{stock market declines}) = .15$$

If the resulting probabilities do not sum to 1 on the first pass, you can say, "These probabilities are *all* a little too small (or large). Let's try it again." By continuing in this manner, you eventually will arrive at a set of probabilities for this situation.

The strength and weakness of using these probabilities in the decision process lie in the accuracy of their values. If they are inaccurate, you may well choose an action that incurs a small (or negative) payoff. As a result, this strategy can lead to poor decisions, particularly if the action chosen was based on unreliable subjective probabilities. Nevertheless, it continues to be a popular decision strategy because it allows the decision maker to place probabilities on the unknown future and consider the alternatives.

The Decision Strategy When using probabilities for each of the states of nature, you determine the *average* payoff for each action in the long run—the average payoff if you repeatedly took this action. This is the **expected payoff** for each action. The strategy in this case is to choose that action having the *largest* expected payoff.

Consider Table 18.2. Suppose that the owner of Sailtown believes that there is a 30% chance that the interest rate will increase over the summer months. This can be written as

$$P(S_1) = .3$$

The chance of the interest rate holding steady is believed to be 20%, whereas the value corresponding to a drop in the rate is 50% (Table 18.10).

Table 18.10

Probabilities for S_1, S_2, and S_3 from Table 18.2

State of Nature		Probability
S_1	Interest rate increases	$P(S_1) = .3$
S_2	Interest rate remains unchanged	$P(S_2) = .2$
S_3	Interest rate decreases	$P(S_3) = .5$

One of the alternatives for this problem was to stock 150 sailboats (action A_4). Using Table 18.2, the respective payoffs are a loss of \$35,000 should the interest rate increase (S_1), a profit of \$5000 if it holds steady (S_2), and a profit of \$45,000 if it decreases (S_3). So, if you repeatedly took this action (under the same conditions facing the owner of Sailtown), then you would

Lose \$35,000, 30% of the time (S_1 occurs)
Make \$5000, 20% of the time (S_2 occurs)
Make \$45,000, 50% of the time (S_3 occurs)

This is the situation discussed in Chapter 6, where we examined *discrete random variables*. The random variable for this situation is

X = payoff under action A_4

Based on the preceding discussion, we have

$$X = \begin{cases} -35 \text{ with probability} & .3 \\ 5 \text{ with probability} & .2 \\ 45 \text{ with probability} & \underline{.5} \\ & 1.0 \end{cases} \qquad (18\text{-}1)$$

The expected payoff for this action is simply the *mean of the random variable, X*. In Chapter 6, this was defined to be

expected payoff for A_4 = mean of X

$= \Sigma(\text{each value of } X)(\text{its probability})$

$= (-35)(.3) + (5)(.2) + (45)(.5)$

$= 13$

This implies that, if the owner of Sailtown repeatedly ordered 150 sailboats (under similar conditions), he would make a profit of \$13,000 on the average.

We next use these expected payoffs to form a decision strategy.

Example 18.6   Determine the expected payoff for each of the actions in Table 18.2. Using this procedure, how many sailboats should Mr. Larson order?

Solution Based on the four expected payoffs, the appropriate action is to order 100 sailboats (A_3) with an expected (average) payoff of \$18,000 (Table 18.11). If Mr. Larson chooses this alternative, his payoff for a one-time decision will be not a profit of \$18,000 but, rather, a loss of \$10,000 [with probability $P(S_1) = .3$] or a gain of \$30,000 [with probability $P(S_2) + P(S_3) = .7$]. Mr. Larson will select this action if

Table 18.11

Expected payoffs for
Sailtown (thousands of
dollars)

Action	Expected Payoff
A_1 Order 50 sailboats	$(15)(.3) + (15)(.2) + (15)(.5) = 15$
A_2 Order 75 sailboats	$(2.5)(.3) + (22.5)(.2) + (22.5)(.5) = 16.5$
A_3 Order 100 sailboats	$(-10)(.3) + (30)(.2) + (30)(.5) = 18$
A_4 Order 150 sailboats	$(-35)(.3) + (5)(.2) + (45)(.5) = 13$

he believes that his long-term gain under this alternative has been maximized. In a sense, he has measured the uncertainty of the future in order to select the best action.

●

Example 18.7

Omega is about to introduce a new line of microcomputers. Their main concern is what selling price they should charge for their computer. The managers can estimate accurately the demand at each price; they are primarily concerned about the time it will take their competitors to "catch up" and introduce a similar product. They intend to determine a selling price and then not change it for the next two years. They decide to structure the decision problem using four possible alternatives (actions),

A_1: set selling price at \$1500

A_2: set selling price at \$1750

A_3: set selling price at \$2000

A_4: set selling price at \$2500

The states of nature specify the amount of time until a similar product is introduced by one of their competitors. These are

S_1 = less than 6 months

S_2 = 6 to 12 months

S_3 = 12 to 18 months

S_4 = longer than 18 months

The next step for this decision problem is to construct a payoff table. This is *not* an easy step because the managers must consider price–demand, cost–volume and consumer-preference information in order to specify a payoff for each action under each state of nature. After many meetings between the production and marketing staffs, Table 18.12 was derived, showing projected profits over the next two years.

What is the appropriate action (selling price) if

1. The minimax strategy is used?
2. Omega decides to maximize the expected payoff?

Use

$$P(S_1) = .1 \qquad P(S_2) = .5 \qquad P(S_3) = .3 \qquad P(S_4) = .1$$

Solution 1 Using the minimax strategy, we first construct an opportunity loss table for this situation (Table 18.13). We do this by considering each state of nature and finding the action with the largest payoff under each state. The opportunity loss for each action is the maximum payoff under this state of nature minus the payoff for this particular action.

Next, we find the maximum opportunity loss *for each action* (row in Table 18.14).

Table 18.12

Profit table for Omega computer-price problem (millions of dollars)

Selling Price	< 6 months (S_1)	6–12 months (S_2)	12–18 months (S_3)	> 18 months (S_4)
A_1 \$1500	250	320	350	400
A_2 \$1750	150	260	300	370
A_3 \$2000	120	290	380	450
A_4 \$2500	80	280	410	550

Table 18.13

Opportunity loss table for Omega (example 18.7)

State of Nature	Action with Largest Payoff	Opportunity Loss
S_1	A_1	for A_1: 250 − 250 = 0 for A_2: 250 − 150 = 100 for A_3: 250 − 120 = 130 for A_4: 250 − 80 = 170
S_2	A_1	for A_1: 320 − 320 = 0 for A_2: 320 − 260 = 60 for A_3: 320 − 290 = 30 for A_4: 320 − 280 = 40
S_3	A_4	for A_1: 410 − 350 = 60 for A_2: 410 − 300 = 110 for A_3: 410 − 380 = 30 for A_4: 410 − 410 = 0
S_4	A_4	for A_1: 550 − 400 = 150 for A_2: 550 − 370 = 180 for A_3: 550 − 450 = 100 for A_4: 550 − 550 = 0

Action	Maximum Opportunity Loss
A_1	150
A_2	180
A_3	130
A_4	170

The minimum of these values is 130, belonging to A_3. The minimax strategy would be to select a selling price of \$2,000 for the next two years.*

Solution 2 The expected profit for each action is summarized in Table 18.15.

Table 18.14

Opportunity loss table for Omega computer-price problem (millions of dollars)

Selling Price	< 6 months (S_1)	6−12 months (S_2)	12−18 months (S_3)	> 18 months (S_4)
A_1 \$1500	0	0	60	150
A_2 \$1750	100	60	110	180
A_3 \$2000	130	30	30	100
A_4 \$2500	170	40	0	0

Table 18.15

Expected profits for Omega (example 18.7)

Action	Expected Profit
A_1	(.1)(250) + (.5)(320) + (.3)(350) + (.1)(400) = 330
A_2	(.1)(150) + (.5)(260) + (.3)(300) + (.1)(370) = 272
A_3	(.1)(120) + (.5)(290) + (.3)(380) + (.1)(450) = 316
A_4	(.1)(80) + (.5)(280) + (.3)(410) + (.1)(550) = 326

*The minimax procedure is often confused with the *maximin* strategy, which examines the minimum payoff for each action and selects that action having the maximum of these minimum payoffs. For this application, the minimum payoffs for each action are A_1: 250, A_2: 150, A_3: 120, and A_4: 80. The maximum value here is 250 (belonging to A_1), and the maximin strategy is to select action A_1. The resulting conclusions using minimax and maximin are not the same here because the minimax strategy (which selects that action minimizing the maximum opportunity loss) is to use action A_3. Both strategies are typically very conservative.

The maximum expected profit is 330, for action A_1. So the strategy here is to set the selling price at $1500, with an expected payoff of $330 million. Notice, however, that the three largest expected values are quite close to each other. The implications of this are that one of the other alternatives might surpass A_1 *if* the state of nature probabilities are *adjusted* slightly. The preference for A_1 may be very sensitive to these probabilities. This should concern a decision maker, especially if the probabilities are determined subjectively. ●

Example 18.7 suggests another important element of the decision process—a sensitivity analysis.

Sensitivity Analysis

Typically, there is no way to determine a state of nature probability with certainty. You can consider past observations and derive an empirical estimate or merely "make up" a value that measures your belief that this event will occur (the subjective approach). The next step when using the maximum expected payoff strategy is to examine what happens to this solution under other sets of realistic probabilities. This is a **sensitivity analysis.**

In example 18.6, the expected payoff procedure selected action A_3. By ordering 100 sailboats, Sailtown achieved a maximum expected profit of $18,000. The state of nature probabilities used here were

$P(S_1) = .3$ (interest rate increases)

$P(S_2) = .2$ (interest rate remains unchanged)

$P(S_3) = .5$ (interest rate decreases)

Although Mr. Larson and his financial advisor are uncertain as to the precise values of these probabilities, they believe that

1. There is no more than a 50% chance that the interest rate will increase $(P(S_1) \leqslant .5)$.
2. There is no more than a 30% chance that the rate will remain unchanged $(P(S_2) \leqslant .3)$.
3. The probability that the rate will decrease is between .3 and .5.

They decide to examine the expected payoffs under the probability conditions listed in Table 18.16. The expected payoffs under each set of probabilities are determined

Table 18.16

Summary of sensitivity analysis (values in color represent the action with the largest expected payoff)

			EXPECTED PAYOFF			
$P(S_1)$	$P(S_2)$	$P(S_3)$	A_1	A_2	A_3	A_4
.4	.2	.4	15	14.5	14	5
.4	.3	.3	15	14.5	14	1
.4	.1	.5	15	14.5	14	9
.5	.2	.3	15	12.5	10	−3
.5	.1	.4	15	12.5	10	1
.3	.3	.4	15	16.5	18	9
.3	.2	.5	15	16.5	18	13

as in example 18.6. As an illustration, using $P(S_1) = .4$ and $P(S_2) = P(S_3) = .3$, the expected payoff for action A_4 is $(.4)(-35) + (.3)(5) + (.3)(45) = 1$ (that is, $1000).

The sensitivity summary in Table 18.16 indicates that action A_1 (ordering 50 sailboats) may be much more attractive than we thought. In fact, if there is more than a 30% chance that the interest rate will increase $(P(S_1) > .3)$, this action produces the largest expected payoff. Under this decision, Mr. Larson can expect to sell all of his inventory, resulting in a profit of $15,000 *regardless of the state of nature*. Consequently, Sailtown would be seeking an expected gain of $3000 ($18,000 for A_3 minus $15,000 for A_1) by speculating on the uncertain future.

Without such a sensitivity analysis, Mr. Larson would not have noticed these results. In five of the six cases using probabilities other than those used in example 18.6, action A_1 produced the maximum expected payoff. If Mr. Larson is uncertain in his original determination of these probabilities, this action is a better solution to his decision problem.

Evaluating Risk

Using the preceding sensitivity analysis and the payoffs in Table 18.2, we noticed that the payoff for action A_1 was 15 (thousand dollars), regardless of the state of nature. Action A_4, on the other hand, has possible payoffs of -35, 5, and 45. This implies that you will encounter a higher *risk* using A_4 rather than A_1. In fact, action A_1 has *no risk* because its payoff is known with certainty.

Take a closer look at action A_4. In discussing equation 18-1, we remarked that the payoff for this action, X, is a random variable, where

$$X = \begin{cases} -35 \text{ with probability } .3 \\ 5 \text{ with probability } .2 \\ 45 \text{ with probability } .5 \end{cases}$$

The expected payoff for this action is the *mean* of X.

A risky alternative (action) is one that has larger probabilities attached to extremely large or small payoffs. A good measure of this risk is simply the *variance* of X; the variance of the possible payoffs for each action is a measure of the risk associated with this alternative. The larger the variance is, the more risk will be incurred using this action. The variance of this *discrete* random variable is found in the same way as it was in Chapter 6 and is summarized here.

Let X_i be the payoff associated with action A_i. Then

$$X_i = \begin{cases} x_1 \text{ with probability } p_1 \\ x_2 \text{ with probability } p_2 \\ . \\ . \\ . \\ x_n \text{ with probability } p_n \end{cases}$$

where n represents the number of states of nature.

The **expected payoff** for this action is the mean of X_i, where

$$\text{expected payoff} = \mu_i = \Sigma xp \qquad (18\text{-}2)$$

The **risk** associated with action A_i is the variance of X_i. So,

$$\text{risk} = \Sigma x^2 p - \mu_i^2 \qquad\qquad (18\text{-}3)$$

Example 18.8

Compute the risk for each of the actions in Table 18.2, using the state of nature probabilities from example 18.6. Based on these results and the sensitivity analysis in Table 18.16, which action appears to be the best one for this situation?

Solution Using equation 18-3, we can find the risk associated with each of the four alternatives, as shown in Table 18.17. The purpose of examining the risk for each action is that often the decision maker will prefer a less risky alternative over a riskier action with a larger expected payoff. In this example, action A_1 has no risk and also has a maximum expected payoff for most of the situations examined in the sensitivity analysis. On the other hand, action A_3 (the other suggested approach) carries the second-largest risk, as measured in Table 18.17. For these reasons, the soundest alternative appears to be action A_1, with a known payoff of $15,000. ●

Example 18.9

Which of the alternatives in Example 18.7 has the least amount of risk?

Solution As before, the risk associated with each action is the variance of the corresponding random variable, shown in Table 18.18. The most desirable action for Omega is A_1 because it wins on two counts. This action (selling price = $1500) not only has the largest expected profit, it also has the smallest risk. For a great many decision problems, this will not be the case, and so the decision maker will have to decide how much risk she or he is willing to assume in an effort to gain a higher expected profit. If a heavy loss would be devastating to a company, it may be forced into adopting strategies that select alternatives with reasonably attractive profits but considerably less risk. ●

Table 18.17

Risk calculations for Sail-town decision problem

Action	Expected Payoff (μ_i)	Risk (using equation 18-3)
A_1	15	$[(15)^2(.3) + (15)^2(.2) + (15)^2(.5)] - 15^2 = 0$
A_2	16.5	$[(2.5)^2(.3) + (22.5)^2(.2) + (22.5)^2(.5)] - 16.5^2 = 84$
A_3	18	$[(-10)^2(.3) + (30)^2(.2) + (30)^2(.5)] - 18^2 = 336$
A_4	13	$[(-35)^2(.3) + (5)^2(.2) + (45)^2(.5)] - 13^2 = 1216$

Table 18.18

Risk calculations for Omega decision problem

Action	Expected Payoff (μ_i)	Risk (using equation 18-3)
A_1	330	$[(250)^2(.1) + (320)^2(.5) + (350)^2(.3) + (400)^2(.1)] - 330^2 = 1,300$
A_2	272	$[(150)^2(.1) + (260)^2(.5) + (300)^2(.3) + (370)^2(.1)] - 272^2 = 2,756$
A_3	316	$[(120)^2(.1) + (290)^2(.5) + (380)^2(.3) + (450)^2(.1)] - 316^2 = 7,204$
A_4	326	$[(80)^2(.1) + (280)^2(.5) + (410)^2(.3) + (550)^2(.1)] - 326^2 = 14,244$

Exercises

18.11 The following table gives the payoff for four different states of nature and three different actions. If each state of nature is equally likely, find the decision resulting from maximizing expected payoff. What is the risk for each action?

Action	S_1	S_2	S_3	S_4
A_1	180	150	10	50
A_2	55	55	55	55
A_3	80	160	100	40

18.12 The manager of a hardware store orders several cords of split logs to be sold to customers for firewood. More wood typically is sold when a winter is colder than usual. The manager figures that the chance of an extremely cold winter (S_1) is 0.25, the chance of a normal winter (S_2) is 0.50, and the chance of a relatively mild winter (S_3) is 0.25. The manager must decide on ordering either 50, 40, 30, or 20 cords of wood. The payoff table follows.

Action	S_1	S_2	S_3
A_1 (50)	5000	3000	1000
A_2 (40)	4400	3200	1200
A_3 (30)	3200	2800	1400
A_4 (20)	3000	2500	2000

a. What is the minimax decision?

b. What is the decision based on the maximum expected payoff?

c. What is the risk of each action?

d. What is the decision based on minimum risk?

18.13 Programs need to be printed for a theatrical performance. The programs are sold at the entrance of the theater before the performance starts. The director of the theater believes that there is a 35% chance that there will be a heavy turnout (S_1). The director also believes that there is a 50% chance for a normal turnout (S_2) and a 15% chance for a low turnout (S_3). The director must decide to have 200 copies (A_1), 300 copies (A_2), 400 copies (A_3), or 500 copies (A_4) of the program printed. The payoff table follows. Unsold programs would result in a loss.

Action	S_1	S_2	S_3
A_1	100	100	100
A_2	150	140	110
A_3	200	160	75
A_4	250	120	-50

a. Find the minimax decision.

b. Find the decision based on the maximum expected payoff.

c. Find the risk associated with each decision.

18.14 In exercise 18.1, what is the decision based on the maximum expected payoff if the probability that the stock market goes up is 10%, the probability that the stock market has no direction is 50%, and the probability that the stock market goes down is 40%?

18.15 In exercise 18.7, what is the maximum expected payoff if the demand for newspapers has the following probabilities?

Demand	Probability	Demand	Probability
50	0.10	80	0.25
60	0.10	90	0.20
70	0.25	100	0.10

18.16 In exercise 18.8, what is the maximum expected payoff if the probability of a complete loss of the commercial building is .05? Assume that the probability of no loss is 0.95. Find the risk associated with each action.

Dominated Actions and the Value of a Crystal Ball

In a decision problem, we often can eliminate an action from consideration if another action in the problem has a larger payoff, regardless of the state of nature. Consider actions A_1 and A_2 from Table 18.12. Notice that the payoff for A_1 exceeds that for A_2 for all four states of nature. In this case, we say that A_1 **dominates** A_2. Action A_i **dominates** A_j if the payoff for A_i is greater than or equal to that for A_j under each state of nature. For at least one state of nature, the payoff for A_i must exceed that for A_j. In our example, there is no reason to consider A_2 for any decision strategy because A_1 produces a larger profit, regardless of what happens in the future. We say that action A_2 is inadmissible; it will not be included in the group of actions to be considered in the problem solution. Action A_i is **inadmissible** if it is dominated by any other action. Consequently, A_i is **admissible** if no other action under consideration dominates it.

Example 18.10

Which of the actions in Table 18.8 are admissible?

Solution The procedure here is to determine whether any of these actions are dominated by any other action. For example, for actions A_2 and A_3, A_2 has a larger payoff, given state of nature S_1, but A_3 produces a bigger profit, given S_3. Therefore, neither of these two actions dominates the other. Comparing A_1 with A_2 and A_1 with A_3 produces a similar argument; no one action produces a larger payoff for all states of nature. This implies that *all three* actions are admissible, and so they will all be considered in the search for the "best" action under the selected decision strategy.

Note that there is no serious harm in considering a dominated action; such an action never is selected by any of the decision strategies. By eliminating a dominated action from consideration, however, we simplify the decision process since we have fewer actions to consider.

Expected Value of Perfect Information When using the strategy of maximizing expected profit, one value of interest is how much you would be willing to pay for a predictor that could tell you the future state of nature correctly 100% of the time. For example, you might have the (very unrealistic) situation of a consulting firm that predicts the future correctly all of the time or, just as farfetched, a crystal ball. Because the future is in fact never perfectly predictable, any information about the future will be imperfect. Consequently, you use the value of a perfect predictor to evaluate any cost that you might incur for such imperfect information.

In example 18.6, what would Mr. Larson, the owner of Sailtown, expect to make if a perfect predictor existed? Referring to Table 18.2, because $P(S_1) = .3$, the crystal ball will predict state of nature S_1 30% of the time. In this case, Mr. Larson inspects this column of Table 18.2, realizes that action A_1 has the largest payoff, and so orders 50 sailboats. His profit for this decision will be 15 (thousand dollars).

Now suppose the crystal ball predicts that the interest rate will remain unchanged (S_2 occurs). In this event, Mr. Larson will order 100 sailboats (A_3), because this is the largest payoff in the column under S_2 in Table 18.2. His profit will be 30. Finally, if he is informed that S_3 will occur, he selects action A_4, with a payoff of 45, because this produces the largest profit given that the interest rate will decrease.

In the long run, with a perfect predictor, Mr. Larson would make

$15,000 30% of the time (when S_1 occurs)

$30,000 20% of the time (when S_2 occurs)

$45,000 50% of the time (when S_3 occurs)

This means that his *expected payoff with a perfect predictor* is

$(15,000)(.3) + (30,000)(.2) + (45,000)(.5) = \$33,000$

Finally, recall that the action that maximized the expected payoff (from example 18.6) was A_3, with a value of $18,000. So, Mr. Larson would make $33,000 on the average *with* a crystal ball. Conversely, he would earn $18,000 on the average *without* it by taking action A_3 each time. This means that the maximum price he should be willing to pay for a perfect predictor is

$33,000 - 18,000 = \$15,000$

This is the expected value of perfect information.

When you use expected payoffs in your decision strategy, you select that action (say, A') having the largest expected payoff. The **expected value of perfect information (EVPI)** is

$$EVPI = \frac{\text{(average payoff using a perfect predictor)} -}{\text{(average payoff for } A')} \qquad (18\text{-}4)$$

Example 18.11   In example 18.7, the managers of Omega attempted to choose a selling price for their new computer. The states of nature for this problem were concerned with the amount of time until a major competitor introduced a similar product. The payoffs for this situation are summarized in Table 18.12. Assuming that $P(S_1) = .1$, $P(S_2) = .5$, $P(S_3) = .3$, and $P(S_4) = .1$, determine the expected value of perfect information.

Solution The action having the largest expected profit (according to example 18.7) is A_1, with an expected value of 330. Consequently, the payoff with a selling price of $1500 would be $330 million on the average.

Given a perfect predictor, the following payoffs are available.

State of Nature (S_i)	Maximum Payoff	Probability $P(S_i)$
S_1	250 (for A_1)	.1
S_2	320 (for A_1)	.5
S_3	410 (for A_4)	.3
S_4	550 (for A_4)	.1

Consequently, the expected payoff using a perfect predictor is

$(.1)(250) + (.5)(320) + (.3)(410) + (.1)(550) = 363$ (million dollars)

From these results, the expected value of perfect information (from equation 18-4) is

$EVPI = 363 - 330 = 33$ (million dollars)

So what is the maximum amount that Omega Corporation should be willing to pay an outside consulting firm for information regarding the time until a competitor introduces a similar model into the market? This is what the *EVPI* represents—an upper limit for the price of *any* information regarding the future. If Omega elects to pay an outside firm for information, they realize that the predicted state of nature could be wrong (that is, this information will be imperfect). For this reason, this information is worth *considerably less* than the *EVPI* of $33 million. Its value will depend in part on the reliability of the consulting firm, as measured by the latter's past performance in similar situations. This topic will be pursued further in Section 18.4.   ●

Exercises

18.17 Consider the following payoff table, in which each state of nature is equally likely. Find the *EVPI*. Are all actions admissible?

Action	S_1	S_2	S_3	S_4
A_1	40	10	4	15
A_2	30	15	0	35
A_3	20	10	-5	30
A_4	35	20	10	10

18.18 A builder usually builds 20-, 50-, or 100-unit apartments. The builder is concerned with three states of nature: low demand (S_1), medium demand (S_2), and high demand (S_3). The builder believes that the probability of S_1 is 0.40, the probability of S_2 is 0.30, and the probability of S_3 is 0.30. From the following payoff table, what is the maximum amount that the builder would be willing to pay a consultant for advice regarding the market demand for apartments? Are all the actions admissible?

Action	S_1	S_2	S_3
A_1 (20 units)	10,000	13,000	16,000
A_2 (50 units)	8,000	23,000	25,000
A_3 (100 units)	8,000	20,000	40,000

18.19 Greetings card shop must decide on whether to order 1500, 2000, or 2500 Christmas cards before the Christmas season. The card shop makes a profit of 50 cents on each card it sells and loses 30 cents on each card that remains unsold. If the demand for Christmas cards is strong (S_1), 2500 cards should sell. If the demand is average (S_2), 2000 cards should sell. If the demand is weak (S_3), 1,500 cards should sell. The manager of Greetings believes that the following probabilities are representative of past sales: $P(S_1) = 0.40$, $P(S_2) = 0.40$, and $P(S_3) = 0.20$. What is the maximum amount that the manager of Greetings would be willing to pay for perfect information regarding the demand for Christmas cards?

18.20 If the *EVPI* for a certain company is $40,000 and the average payoff based on the decision from the maximum expected payoff is $25,000, what is the maximum payoff using a perfect market predictor?

18.21 Refer to exercise 18.1. What is the maximum that the stockbroker would be willing to pay a consultant regarding the direction of the stock market, assuming that all of the three states of nature are equally likely?

18.22 Refer to exercise 18.12. What is the maximum that the manager of the hardware store would be willing to pay to obtain perfect information regarding the type of winter for the current year?

18.23 Refer to exercise 18.13. What is the *EVPI* for the manager of the theater, regarding attendance turnout? Are any of the actions inadmissible?

18.3

The Concept of Utility

We have concentrated on choosing the best action under various decision strategies by using the values contained in the payoff table. For example, one strategy determines that action having the largest expected payoff. Another (the minimax procedure) examines opportunity losses derived from the payoff table. Still another strategy examines expected payoffs. In other words, each action is evaluated by the corresponding *dollar amount* resulting from a particular strategy.

There are many instances in which it is more advantageous *not* to use expected payoffs, particularly when large amounts of money are at stake. Anyone who purchases an insurance policy or buys a lottery ticket generally is trying neither to minimize expected losses nor maximize expected gains. Rather, such a person *gambles* his or her money, trying to guard against a heavy loss (insurance) or hoping to strike it rich (lottery).

There is something else besides money involved in the decision to purchase an insurance policy or lottery ticket. In the case of insurance, suppose you have a $100,000 home insured for the full amount. For most people, a gift of $100,000 would be nice— in fact, *very* nice—but a $100,000 loss would be totally devastating. This is the underlying concept behind the insurance philosophy. A gain of $100,000 does not have the same effect on the positive side as does a $100,000 loss on the negative one.

When you fail to purchase insurance, you are betting that your house will not go up in smoke. Your *risk* here is that the house may burn. When we look at expected payoffs *only,* we ignore risk. On the other hand, we also discussed a method of examining the risk of each action by finding the variance of the respective payoffs. What we need is a method that combines the decision maker's attitude toward the payoff with the corresponding risk of each alternative. An action with a possible higher payoff (or loss, in the case of insurance) often contains more risk. We measure the attractiveness of each outcome using utility values, which we will now develop.

> The **utility value** of a particular outcome is used to measure both the attractiveness and the risk associated with this dollar amount.

Constructing a Utility Value

Suppose you have $10,000 saved up for college expenses one year before you begin your freshman year. A friend of yours has offered you part interest in an oil-drilling venture for your $10,000. If the venture fails, you lose your entire investment, but if it succeeds, you stand to gain $40,000. According to the latest geological survey, the probability of hitting oil is .3. Also, if oil exists, the expected life of the venture is one year, with the payoff of $40,000.

Your other option is to invest the money for one year in a money-market account at an expected interest rate of 12%. If you choose to maximize your expected payoff (dollars on hand at the end of the year), which action should you select?

The decision problem involves two actions,

A_1: put the $10,000 into the money market (interest = 12%)

A_2: invest $10,000 in the oil venture

with two states of nature

S_1: oil does not exist on the site

S_2: oil does exist on the site

Your corresponding payoffs, should you select the oil investment, are

$0 if S_1 occurs (and you lose your investment)

$40,000 if S_2 occurs

The payoff table is shown below with the corresponding state of nature probabilities in parentheses.

The expected payoffs here are

	S_1 (.7)	S_2 (.3)
A_1	11,200	11,200
A_2	0	40,000

for action A_1: $11,200(.7) + 11,200(.3) = 11,200$

for action A_2: $(0)(.7) + (40,000)(.3) = 12,000$

The oil venture (A_2) has a larger expected payoff, so, using this decision strategy, you would elect to gamble your money in hopes of a large payoff. But is this a realistic strategy? Assume that the loss of your $10,000 would result in your not going to college. All things considered, this would be extremely disastrous. Although the large payoff would be terrific, the high probability of a heavy loss might make you wonder if the gamble is a good idea.

The problem in this illustration is that a large payoff often is very attractive, but it is offset by a risk associated with it. We say that the **utility** associated with a gain of, say, $100,000 without risk is *higher* than the utility of this amount with a high risk. For each decision problem, we ask the decision maker to determine the utility value associated with the various payoffs in the problem. In this way, the person can build in his or her attitudes regarding avoiding risk or preferring a gamble with a big payoff (a *risk taker*).

To illustrate the construction of a utility value, consider the payoff table we just constructed. There are many ways to proceed here, although all the various ways of assigning utility values produce the *same* decision when using these values to arrive at the best alternative. We will use a two-step procedure.

Step 1 Assign a utility value of zero to the smallest payoff amount (π_{min}) and a value of 100 to the largest (π_{max}). For this example, this would be written as $U(0) = 0$ and $U(40,000) = 100$, because $\pi_{min} = 0$ and $\pi_{max} = 40,000$. *All utility values range from 0 to 100*. Whether you assign utility values from 0 to 1, 0 to 100, 1 to 5, or any range does not matter. It is not the actual value of the utility that is important but rather its value *relative* to the range of all values.

There is one other payoff in the table to consider, namely, $11,200. What is the utility of this dollar amount to the decision maker—you, in this case? We will consider both the attractiveness and the risk involved with this payoff in the following situation.

Consider the largest payoff of $40,000 and the smallest of $0. You need to decide what the probability, P, would have to be before you would consider

$11,200 with certainty

to be as attractive as

$40,000 with probability P and $0 with probability $1 - P$

Suppose you decide that you would need at least a 50% chance of striking oil. So, $P = .5$. We next define the utility of the $11,200 payoff by using

$$\begin{aligned} \text{Utility value} &= P \cdot 100 \\ &= .5 \cdot 100 \\ &= 50 \end{aligned}$$

That is,

$$U(11,200) = 50$$

A graphical illustration of these utilities is shown in Figure 18.1. An easy way to measure your attitude toward risk is to connect the lower left (utility = 0) and upper right (utility = 100) corners. If the utility values you have assigned fall *above* this line, you tend to avoid risk. If they fall *below* the line, you are a risk taker. For this example, $U(11,200) = 50$ lies above the diagonal line, which indicates that, for this situation, you are a risk avoider. A summary of this procedure is step 2 of the utility value assignment.

Step 2 The utility value for any payoff (say, π_{ij}) under consideration is found by using

$$U(\pi_{ij}) = P \cdot 100$$

where P is the probability such that

$$\pi_{ij} \text{ with certainty}$$

is equally as attractive as

$$\pi_{max} \text{ with probability } P \text{ and } \pi_{min} \text{ with probability } 1 - P$$

and π_{max} and π_{min} are determined in step 1.

The resulting table of utility values for this example is shown below.

Action	S_1: Oil Venture Is Unsuccessful (.7)	S_2: Oil Venture Is Successful (.3)
A_1 money-market account	50	50
A_2 oil venture	0	100

Figure 18.1

Illustration of utility values for oil venture.

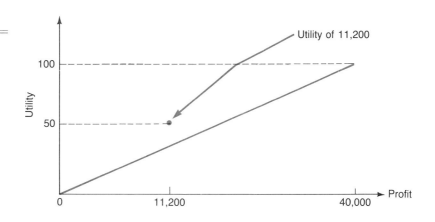

Notice that we return to the *original* probabilities for the states of nature (.7 and .3) when constructing this table. The values of .5 and .5 were used only to measure your willingness to take a risk. This does not change the fact that S_1 will occur 70% of the time (even though you may wish it would occur only 50% of the time).

To use the utility values in choosing one of the alternative actions, we proceed exactly as before, except that we select that action having the *largest expected utility* rather than the largest expected payoff.

expected utility for each action
$$= \sum \text{(each utility value)} \cdot \text{(its probability)} \qquad (18\text{-}5)$$

Example 18.12

Using the above table, which action, based on expected utility, is the more attractive of the two?

Solution

A_1: expected utility $= (50)(.7) + (50)(.3) = 50$

A_2: expected utility $= (0)(.7) + (100)(.3) = 30$

Because action A_1 (the money-market account) has a larger expected utility, we choose this action over the riskier oil venture, A_2. This was also suggested by Figure 18.1, which indicated that, for this application, you are a risk avoider. ●

Determining Utility Values for Large Decision Problems

Whenever your payoff table contains a large number of values, there is an alternative to the two-step procedure just described. The main problem here is the second step, which requires that the decision maker determine the utility of *each* payoff contained in the payoff table. This can be quite difficult, because there is a requirement. The requirement for step 2 is that, if

payoff π_{ij} < payoff π_{st}

then it is necessary that

$U(\pi_{ij}) < U(\pi_{st})$

This means that, if one payoff is larger than another, the corresponding utility values must be in the *same order.*

When forced to determine the utility of many payoffs, some of which are nearly the same, the decision maker may rate one payoff lower than another, but the utility values may be in the opposite order. One way to avoid this situation is *not* to use step 2 on every payoff involved in the problem; rather, you use this step on *between five and ten payoff values over the range of payoffs* for this problem. Consequently, you would examine π_{min} and π_{max} from step 1 and select, say, six payoffs between these values. These *need not* be actual payoff values from the payoff table. You then use the step 2 procedure to determine the utility value (U) for each of these six payoffs.

Your next step is to plot these values in a graph and connect them to form a **utility curve.** The utility of each value within the payoff table can be obtained by approximating it from the resulting graph. Because of the requirement for step 2, you need to make sure that the utility curve always *increases as the payoff increases.* We will demonstrate this technique in example 18.13.

Example 18.13 | Table 18.12 contains the various payoffs for the selling-price decision facing the Omega Corporation. The minimum payoff is π_{min} = 80 (million dollars), and the maximum is π_{max} = 550. So, for step 1, we have

$$U(80) = 0$$

and

$$U(550) = 100$$

Describe a procedure for determining the utility of the remaining 14 values.

Solution One method, of course, is to have the decision maker choose 14 corresponding utility values using step 2 on each payoff. An easier procedure is to request this information for payoffs of, say, 100, 150, 200, 300, 400, and 500. Notice that these payoffs are not necessarily contained in Table 18.12, but they do cover the range from 80 to 550. For a payoff of 200, we ask for that value of P such that a payoff of 200 (million dollars) with certainty is equally as attractive as a payoff of 500 with probability P and a payoff of 80 with probability $1 - P$. Suppose the decision maker's response is P = .55. Then the utility value of this payoff is

$$U(200) = .55 \cdot 100 = 55$$

Consider the set of probabilities (P) and corresponding utilities in Table 18.19. It will be much easier for the decision maker to supply these six values than to choose the 14 values remaining in Table 18.12. A key ingredient to making any quantitative procedure useable is to keep it reasonably simple!

The utilities for this problem are plotted in Figure 18.2; the curve through these points represents the decision maker's utility curve. Notice that the utility values *do* increase as the payoffs increase, so the requirement for step 2 is satisfied. As with Figure 18.1, the utility values lie *above* the line connecting the corners, indicating that this individual is a risk avoider. ●

Table 18.19

Utilities for example 18.13

	PAYOFF					
	100	150	200	300	400	500
Probability (P)	.20	.40	.55	.75	.90	.97
Utility [P (100)]	20	40	55	75	90	97

Figure 18.2

Utility curve for Omega computer-price decision (example 18.13).

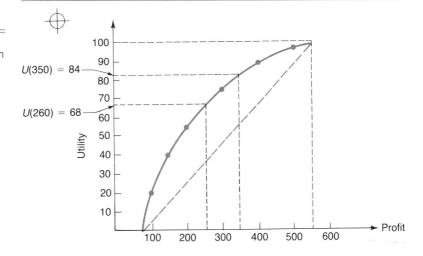

Table 18.20

Utility table for Omega computer-price decision problem (example 18.14)

Action	S_1 (.1)	S_2 (.5)	S_3 (.3)	S_4 (.1)	Expected Utility
A_1: price = $1500	67	79	84	90	80.4
A_2: price = $1750	40	68	75	87	69.2
A_3: price = $2000	30	74	88	94	75.8
A_4: price = $2500	0	72	91	100	73.3

Example 18.14   Using the utility curve in Figure 18.2, determine the utility for each payoff in Table 18.12. Which action (selling price) has the largest expected utility?

Solution From step 1, we have $U(80) = 0$ and $U(550) = 100$. The remaining utilities can be estimated from the utility curve constructed in example 18.13. This is illustrated for payoffs of 260 (action A_2, state of nature S_2) and 350 (action A_1, state of nature S_3) in Figure 18.2. Consequently,

$U(260) = 68$

$U(350) = 84$

Continuing this procedure results in Table 18.20. The expected utilities are, for example,

expected utility for $A_2 = (.1)(40) + (.5)(68) + (.3)(75) + (.1)(87) = 69.2$

If we choose that action with the largest expected utility, our decision is to select action A_1 (selling price $1500). For this application, A_1 maximizes both expected payoff (see example 18.7) and expected utility. ●

Shape of Utility Curves

The shape of a decision maker's utility curve indicates his or her preference for or aversion to risk. There are essentially three categories of people in regard to risk: (1) the risk avoider, (2) the risk neutral, and (3) the risk taker.

The basic shape of the utility curve for each of these classifications is contained in Figure 18.3. Notice that, in all three situations, the utility curves increase as the payoff increases. Variations of these curves also can occur; for example, a person may prefer a risk for small payoffs but then avoid a risk for large payoffs. A utility curve for such a person is S-shaped.

An individual who is **risk neutral** will have resulting utility values that lie close to the line connecting the corners. It makes no difference whether you maximize expected payoff or expected utility—the resulting best action for this person is the *same* in both cases. Very wealthy people often demonstrate this behavior because, for them, the utility of each dollar remains nearly constant.

Most people are **risk avoiders,** particularly when large payoffs or losses are involved. For two actions with equal expected payoffs, the risk avoider prefers the one with the smaller risk. This person also prefers a smaller expected payoff with a small risk over a larger expected payoff with a large risk. The **risk taker,** on the other hand, is the gambler; he or she prefers an action with a possible large payoff, even if the risk is more severe.

In summary, utility values allow the decision maker to combine both payoff and risk into a single measure. However, the assignment of these values is subjective and special care must be taken in their determination.

Figure 18.3

Three classes of utility curves. **A** The risk avoider. **B** The risk neutral. **C** The risk taker.

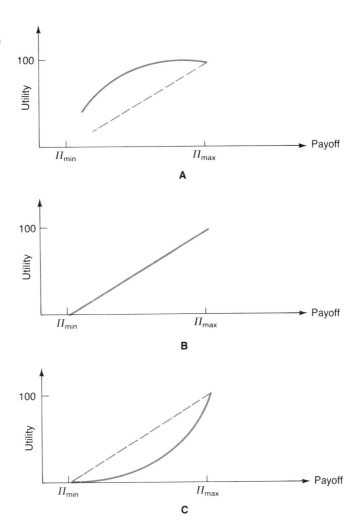

Exercises

18.24 A utility function is assigned the value 100 for the largest payoff, which is $20,000. Also, the utility function is assigned the value zero for the smallest payoff, which is $0. The following table gives the probability, P, that, if the amount in the left hand column were certain, it would be equivalent to having a payoff of $20,000 with probability P and a payoff of $0 with probability $1 - P$. Graph the utility function and determine the attitude toward risk of a person with this utility curve. From the graph, determine the approximate utility value for a payoff of $17,000.

Payoff	Probability
2,000	0.125
4,000	0.230
8,000	0.40
12,000	0.60
16,000	0.85
18,000	0.90

18.25 Suppose that a person has a utility function $U(x) = 2\sqrt{x}$, where x is assumed to be any value between 1 and 100. Consider the following payoff table in which all four states of nature are equally likely.

Action	S_1	S_2	S_3	S_4
A_1	1	100	50	10
A_2	80	30	40	25
A_3	90	20	30	10

a. Find the decision based on the maximum expected payoff.

b. Find the decision based on the maximum expected utility of the payoff.

18.26 Suppose that a person is risk neutral and has the utility function $U(x) = 3x$. In the following payoff table, $P(S_1) = 0.20$, $P(S_2) = 0.40$, $P(S_3) = 0.30$, and $P(S_4) = 0.10$. Show that the decision based on the maximum expected payoff is equivalent to the decision based on the maximum expected utility of the payoff.

Action	S_1	S_2	S_3	S_4
A_1	50	10	30	10
A_2	20	20	30	60
A_3	10	50	10	20

18.27 If a person has a utility function $U(x) = x$, what probability, P, would the person have to assign to a maximum payoff of $\$10,000$ and a $1 - P$ probability to a minimum payoff of $\$0$, assuming that the person could receive $\$8,100$ with certainty?

18.28 The utilities of the payoffs given in the table in exercise 18.11 are as follows:

Action	S_1	S_2	S_3	S_4
A_1	2.83	2.72	1.59	2.19
A_2	2.23	2.23	2.23	2.23
A_3	2.40	2.76	2.51	2.09

Find the decision based on the maximum expected utility of the payoff.

18.29 If the utility curve of the manager of the hardware store in exercise 18.12 is $U(x) = \log_{10}(x)$, find the decision based on the maximum expected utility. Is the manager a risk neutral, a risk taker, or a risk avoider?

18.30 If the utility function for the director of the theater in exercise 18.13 is $U(x) = \sqrt[3]{x}$, find the decision based on the maximum expected utility.

18.4

Decision Trees and Bayes' Rule

This section will describe a device useful for structuring and illustrating the uncertain outcomes associated with any decision problem. This is a decision tree, which graphically represents and offers you a "picture" of the entire decision problem, including a representation of

1. The possible actions facing the decision maker.
2. The outcomes (states of nature) that can occur.
3. The relationships between these actions and outcomes.

The decision tree makes it easier for you to compute the expected values and to understand the process of making a decision. We will demonstrate how to construct a tree diagram and discuss a procedure for using the diagram to examine the alternatives and arrive at a decision.

Constructing Decision Trees

A convenient way of representing a set of alternatives and states of nature is by means of a decision tree. A **decision tree** is a picture of the actions under consideration, as

Figure 18.4

Decision tree for the
Omega computer-price
problem.

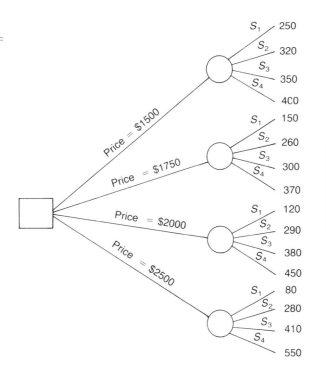

Time until
competitor response

S_1: < 6 months
S_2: 6–12 months
S_3: 12–18 months
S_4: > 18 months

well as of the states of nature that affect the profitability of each action. It is a convenient way of illustrating the entire decision problem, because you can tell at a glance exactly which alternatives are being considered and what the payoff is under each state of nature.

In example 18.7, Omega needed to make a decision regarding a selling price for their new computer. A decision tree for this situation is shown in Figure 18.4.

A decision tree represents a sequence of *decisions,* represented by a box, and *outcomes* left strictly to chance, represented by a circle. The boxes are decision nodes, and the circles are chance nodes.

When you reach a **decision node,** you need to make a decision at this point in the decision tree. The path you select reflects your choice of the best action to take at this point. This decision is under your control. The paths away from a **chance node** represent states of nature (S_1, S_2, . . .). There is no choice for you to make here; rather, each of these paths will occur with a certain probability, written as $P(S_1)$, $P(S_2)$, ...

The final step in completing a decision tree is to determine a dollar amount (or utility amount, if you are using utility values) within each chance node and decision node. The amount placed inside a chance node is the *expected payoff* at this point, using the probability for each state of nature. Consider the top chance node in Figure 18.4. Using the state of nature probabilities from example 18.7, the completed tree (Figure 18.5) contains the expected payoff for each selling price. To illustrate, the expected payoff for a selling price of $1500 is

$$(.1)(250) + (.5)(320) + (.3)(350) + (.1)(400) = 330$$

In Figure 18.5, the amount in each *decision* node is not an expected value, because there are no probabilities with the paths leading away from this point. Instead, the dollar (or utility) amount, or the expected dollar (or utility) amount, associated with

Figure 18.5

Completed decision tree for the Omega computer-price problem.

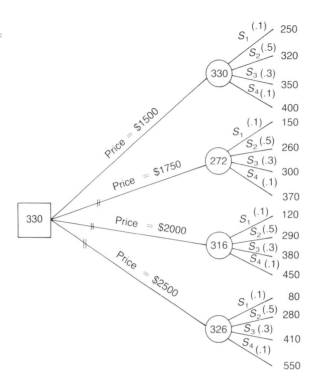

Figure 18.6

Decision tree for Sailtown decision problem (example 18.15).

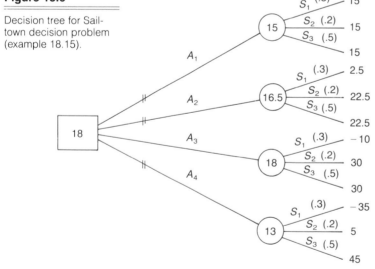

Actions
A_1: order 50 sailboats
A_2: order 75 sailboats
A_3: order 100 sailboats
A_4: order 150 sailboats
States of nature
S_1: interest rate increases
S_2: interest rate holds steady
S_3: interest rate decreases

the best action at this point is contained within the box. Of the four paths leading away from the decision node in Figure 18.5, action A_1 (price = $1500) has the largest expected payoff, so this amount goes into the box. On the remaining three paths at this node, a double vertical bar across the path indicates that we have "struck out" these alternatives because they are not the ones to use at this point in the decision path.

Our conclusion from reading this tree would be to select a selling price of $1500 for an expected payoff of 330 (million dollars).

Example 18.15   Structure the decision problem with the data from Table 18.2 as a decision tree.

Solution Once again, the decision path begins with a decision node (how many sailboats to purchase) followed by a sequence of chance nodes reflecting the change in the interest rate. Figure 18.6 contains the completed tree for this problem. As in the previous analysis, when you are maximizing expected payoffs, your best alternative is to order 100 sailboats (action A_3) with an expected payoff of 18 (thousand dollars).

●

Once again you should perform a follow-up *sensitivity analysis* to determine how sensitive this solution is to the state of nature probabilities. When you summarize the results of a sensitivity analysis, you can construct a decision tree for each set of probabilities under consideration, which will indicate the optimum path under this condition.

An Application of Decision Trees: Bayes' Rule

Thomas Bayes was an English clergyman who lived in the 1700s. He is credited with developing a procedure that allows you to *revise* the probabilities for each state of nature in light of sample results or outside information. For example, in Table 18.2, the probability that the interest rate will increase (S_1) was $P(S_1) = .3$. What if a reliable consulting firm using various economic indicators predicted that the interest rate would increase? The value of $P(S_1) = .3$ was a subjective estimate, measuring Mr. Larson's belief that the rate would increase. In light of the *new information* obtained from the consulting firm, we would expect the probability of S_1 to increase—if, in fact, the firm is reliable.

The initial probability of .3 was obtained *prior* to receiving the new information and is thus a **prior probability.**

prior probability: $P(S_1) = .3$

This was obtained by examining the existing conditions and did not take into account the new information provided by the consulting firm. The *revised* probability uses the consulting firm's information; hence, it is a *conditional* probability. Because it is obtained after receiving the new information, it is called a **posterior probability.**

posterior probability: $P(S_1 \mid$ firm predicts a rate increase$) = $ (to be determined using Bayes' Rule)

This section will discuss a method of determining these probabilities using the procedure developed by Thomas Bayes.

Bayes' rule states that, given the final event, B, the probability that this event was reached along the ith path corresponding to event E_i is

$$P(E_i \mid B) = \frac{P(E_i \text{ and } B)}{P(B)}$$

$$= \frac{i\text{th branch}}{\text{sum of the branches}}$$

(18-6)

where (1) ith branch is the product of all probabilities along this branch and (2) the sum of the branches is the sum of all such products for the tree diagram. This is the probability of event B, that is, $P(B)$.

We will illustrate the Bayes' procedure for revising probabilities in the following example. The Pine Bluff Credit Union obtains a credit rating for each person that applies for an automobile loan. This rating is either type A (the best), type B, or type C (the worst). The latest statistics released by the local credit bureau indicate that 50% of the residents are rated type A, 30% are type B, and 20% are type C.

The credit union also has determined from past experience that 5% of type A people will default on their car loan. The corresponding percentages for type B and type C are 15% and 35%, respectively. We wish to determine (1) the probability that an individual applying for a car loan at the credit union will default and (2) the probability that a person has a type A credit rating if it is *known* that this person has just defaulted on a car loan.

Although this is not a decision problem, we can construct a tree diagram for this situation. It consists of all chance nodes, as shown in Figure 18.7. Notice that we intentionally have left off a branch on each of the final chance nodes. The complete picture for the top node is shown in Figure 18.8. When you use a tree diagram to revise probabilities, we recommend that you omit these branches and end the tree with the *same event listed down the right side*. This event should be the "new information" provided in the problem. For this example, this information would be that a certain person defaulted on a car loan.

The probabilities on the first three branches represent the *prior* probabilities of having a type A, type B, or type C credit rating. The final three probabilities are conditional probabilities, representing the chances of each of these credit types defaulting. According to the information provided,

$$.05 = P(\text{person defaults} \mid \text{person is type A})$$
$$.15 = P(\text{person defaults} \mid \text{person is type B})$$
$$.35 = P(\text{person defaults} \mid \text{person is type C})$$

Figure 18.7

Tree diagram for Pine Bluff Credit Union.

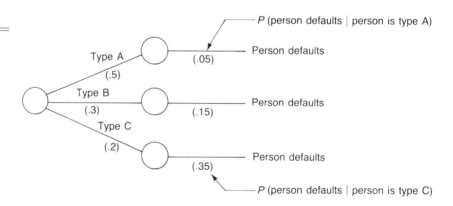

Figure 18.8

Top node for Figure 18.7.

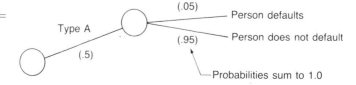

The advantage of constructing the tree as in Figure 18.7 is that the probability of the final event (person defaults) is simply the **sum of the branches.** So, when we use an incomplete tree,

the probability of the final event = sum of the branches (sum of the product of all probabilities along each branch)

To determine the probability that a person applying for a car loan will default, refer to Figure 18.7. Here,

$$\text{sum of the branches} = (.5)(.05) + (.3)(.15) + (.2)(.35)$$
$$= .14$$

Consequently,

$$P(\text{person defaults}) = .14$$

which means that 14% of all people applying for a car loan will default.

Now you are given the information that the person has defaulted on a car loan and are asked to find the probability that he or she has a type A credit rating, in light of this new information. That is, you are given that the final event occurred and are asked to find the probability that it occurred *along the first branch,* belonging to type A. This can be written as

$$P(\text{type A} \mid \text{person defaults})$$

Recalling from Chapter 5 that, for any events A and B,

$$P(A \mid B) = \frac{P(A \text{ and } B)}{P(B)} \qquad (18\text{-}7)$$

it follows that

$$P(\text{type A} \mid \text{person defaults}) = \frac{P(\text{type A and person defaults})}{P(\text{person defaults})}$$

Also from Chapter 5,

$$P(A \text{ and } B) = P(B)P(A \mid B)$$
$$= P(A)P(B \mid A)$$

for any events A and B. The first equation simply is a rearrangement of equation 18-7. Using the second equation,

$$P(\text{type A} \mid \text{person defaults}) = \frac{P(\text{type A and person defaults})}{P(\text{person defaults})}$$

$$= \frac{P(\text{type A})P(\text{person defaults} \mid \text{type A})}{P(\text{person defaults})}$$

$$= \frac{(.5)(.05)}{.14} = .18$$

.5 and .05 are from the tree diagram in Figure 18.7, and .14 was derived earlier in this discussion. We see that 18% of the people who default have a type A credit rating. The probabilities .5 and .05 lie along the first branch, so this can be written as

$$P(\text{type A} \mid \text{person defaults}) = \frac{\text{first branch}}{\text{sum of the branches}}$$

This example thus provided an illustration of Bayes' rule. You apply this rule whenever you are given that the final event in the tree diagram has occurred and you are asked to find the probability that you "traveled" along a particular branch.

Using Bayes' rule (equation 18-6) in our example, the probability that a person has a type C credit rating, given the information that the person defaulted, is

$$P(\text{type C} \mid \text{person defaults}) = \frac{\text{3rd branch}}{\text{sum of the branches}}$$

$$= \frac{(.2)(.35)}{.14} = .50$$

Consequently, once we know that a person has defaulted, the *revised probability* of this person having a type C rating goes from .2, which is the *prior* probability (before this information) to .5, which is the *posterior* or *revised* probability (in light of this information).

Using Bayes' Rule to Maximize Profits

An excellent opportunity to use Bayes' Rule arises when you want to update your prior probabilities based on recent information regarding the states of nature in your decision problem. This information can come from such sources as an outside consulting firm or a questionnaire developed by your company's marketing staff. Based on the new information, you can maximize your expected payoff (or utility) by replacing the prior probabilities with their corresponding posterior probabilities.

Example 18.16

Now take another look at the Sailtown example. Mr. Larson, the owner, has decided to purchase the services of an outside consultant in an effort to determine more accurately the movement of the interest rate over the summer months. The information supplied by the consultant will be one of the following:

I_1: consultant predicts an increase in the interest rate

I_2: consultant predicts no change in this rate

I_3: consultant predicts a drop in this rate

The information in Table 18.21 also was provided; it describes the past performance of this consultant when predicting interest rates. The values in the table contain conditional probabilities for the consultant's prediction under each state of nature. For example, $.7 = P(I_1 \mid S_1)$, $.4 = P(I_1 \mid S_2)$, and so forth. This means that, 70% of the time she predicted an increase when, in fact, it actually did increase, and 40% of the time she predicted an increase when there was no change in the interest rate. If the consultant is extremely reliable, the numbers from the upper left to the lower right (.7, .5 and .6) should be near 1. The remaining values should be small.

Table 18.21

Conditional probabilities for consultant $[= P(I \mid S)]$ (example 18.16)

Consultant Predicted	ACTUALLY OCCURRED		
	An Increase (S_1)	No Change (S_2)	A Decrease (S_3)
I_1 an increase	.7	.4	.2
I_2 no change	.2	.5	.2
I_3 a decrease	.1	.1	.6
	1.0	1.0	1.0

Figure 18.9

Decision tree, given information I_1.

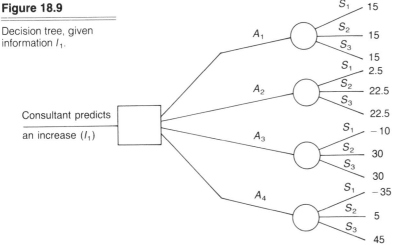

Actions
A_1: order 50 sailboats
A_2: order 75 sailboats
A_3: order 100 sailboats
A_4: order 150 sailboats

States of nature
S_1: interest rate increases
S_2: interest rate holds steady
S_3: interest rate decreases

The consultant predicts an increase (I_1) in the interest rate. What is the best action for Mr. Larson to take in light of this information? What is his expected profit?

Solution Figure 18.9 shows the new decision tree. Notice that Figures 18.6 and 18.9 are very similar, including the payoff amounts. The big difference is that the prior probabilities of $P(S_1) = .3$, $P(S_2) = .2$, and $P(S_3) = .5$ have been revised in light of the new information: $P(S_1)$ is replaced by $P(S_1 \mid I_1)$, $P(S_2)$ by $P(S_2 \mid I_1)$, and $P(S_3)$ by $P(S_3 \mid I_1)$.   ●

Deriving the Posterior Probabilities To derive the posterior probabilities, we begin by constructing a tree diagram with the *new* information as the event on the *far right*, as shown in Figure 18.10. We can then obtain the probabilities along the various branches from the prior probabilities and the information in Table 18.21.

Using Bayes' rule,

$$P(I_1) = \text{sum of the branches}$$
$$= (.3)(.7) + (.2)(.4) + (.5)(.2)$$
$$= .39$$

The posterior probabilities are given by

$$P(S_1 \mid I_1) = \frac{\text{1st branch}}{\text{sum of branches}}$$
$$= .21/.39 = .54$$

$$P(S_2 \mid I_1) = \frac{\text{2nd branch}}{\text{sum of branches}}$$
$$= .08/.39 = .20$$

Figure 18.10

Partial tree diagram for deriving posterior probabilities; new information is the event on the far right.

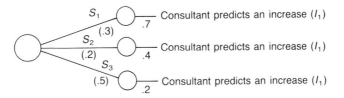

Figure 18.11

Completed decision tree using posterior probabilities.

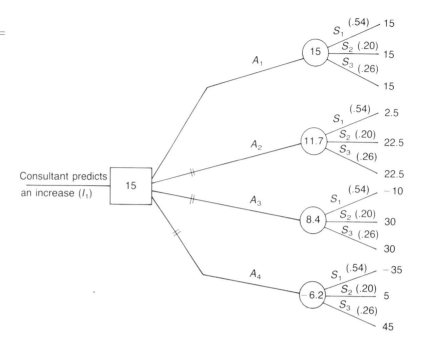

$$P(S_3 \mid I_1) = \frac{\text{3rd branch}}{\text{sum of branches}}$$

$$= .10/.39 = .26$$

Placing these values in the decision tree results in Figure 18.11. The expected payoffs using the posterior probabilities are found in the usual manner. For action A_2,

$$\text{expected payoff} = (.54)(2.5) + (.20)(22.5) + (.26)(22.5) = 11.7$$

Our conclusion is that, given the information that the consultant has predicted a rise in the interest rate, Mr. Larson's best alternative is to order 50 sailboats (action A_1) with an expected payoff of 15 (thousand dollars). Remember that, given no information at all, we use the *prior* probabilities to select that action having the largest expected payoff. These expected values were summarized in Table 18.11, where action A_3 (ordering 100 sailboats) provided the largest expected value. Notice also that, in Table 18.11, the expected payoff for action A_2, given no information from the consultant, is 16.5. In other words, our revised expected payoff for this action, given the consultant's forecast, drops from 16.5 to 11.7.

Evaluating Sample Information

By combining a decision tree with Bayes' rule for calculating posterior probabilities, the decision maker is able to determine whether purchasing new information is a good idea. We will refer to this new information as **sample information**. This may be collected from one of many sources, including a sample of questionnaires, a recently released government report, or, as in the previous example, an outside consultant. Typically, such information costs money; by using a decision-tree analysis, you will be able to decide between

1. Not purchasing any additional information and using the prior probabilities to determine that action with the maximum expected payoff (or utility).

2. Purchasing this information because the expected payoff (or utility) for this decision is larger than that obtained using prior probabilities only.

In example 18.16, the owner of Sailtown used information provided by a consultant to revise his prior probabilities regarding a possible change in the interest rate. Based on the information provided (the interest rate will increase), Mr. Larson derived the posterior probabilities and decided to purchase 50 sailboats (action A_1).

Was it a good idea for Mr. Larson to purchase the consultant's services in the first place? The cost of this information was $2500. We previously found the expected value of perfect information ($EVPI$) for this situation to be $15,000. The consultant's fee is considerably less than this amount, so Mr. Larson was willing to evaluate the alternative of purchasing this information.

To construct a decision tree for the full problem, we begin exactly as we did in Figure 18.6. Our next step is to include an additional branch for purchasing information from the consultant. To complete this branch, we can use a two-step procedure (refer to Figure 18.12).

Step 1 The next node will be a *chance node,* representing the possible information to be provided. In Figure 18.12, this is

I_1: consultant predicts an increase in the interest rate

I_2: consultant predicts no change in the interest rate

I_3: consultant predicts a decrease in the interest rate

Step 2 For each branch representing I_1, I_2, . . . in step 1, we reconstruct the decision tree in Figure 18.6 because the possible actions and states of nature from this point on are the *same as before.* However, the probabilities for S_1, S_2, . . . will be the *posterior* probabilities rather than the prior probabilities in Figure 18.6.

Having constructed the decision tree, you next need to calculate the posterior probabilities. This was illustrated in example 18.16, where I_1 occurred (the consultant predicted an increase in the interest rate). Notice that the tree for this situation in Figure 18.11 becomes a portion of the large tree in Figure 18.12. A summary of the posterior probabilities is contained in Figure 18.13.

Also contained in Figure 18.13 are the probabilities for each of the possible predictions by the consultant. Here, $P(I_1) = .39$, $P(I_2) = .26$, and $P(I_3) = .35$. Because this prediction is *not* under your control, step 1 constructs a chance node at this point, including these three probabilities.

We find the expected payoff given each consultant's prediction (15, 20.8, and 36.2) by using the posterior probabilities, as in example 18.16 and Figure 18.13. We then calculate the expected payoff when using the consultant, where

$$\text{expected payoff with consultant} = (.39)(15) + (.26)(20.8) + (.35)(36.2)$$
$$= 23.9$$

From this amount you need to subtract the cost of this information (2.5 thousand dollars), providing a net expected payoff of 21.4 (thousand dollars). Because this exceeds the four expected payoffs where no additional information is purchased, this action maximizes the expected payoff and provides the best alternative.

We thus conclude that the owner of Sailtown was right to purchase the services of the external consultant. The best action for him to take for each prediction is summarized in Table 18.22. The net profit is obtained for each case by subtracting the cost of information, 2.5 (thousand dollars).

Figure 18.12

Completed decision tree for Sailtown decision problem.

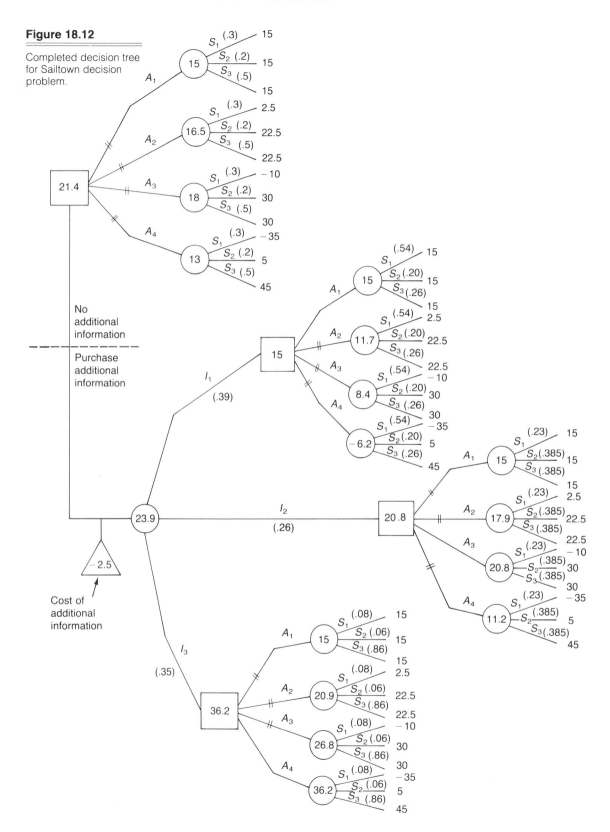

Figure 18.13

Deriving the posterior probabilities for the Sail-town decision problem.

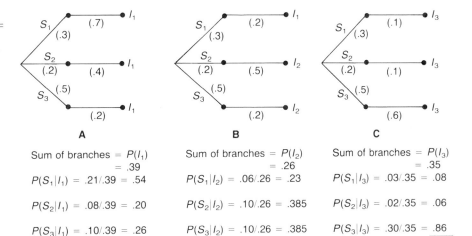

A

Sum of branches = $P(I_1)$
          = .39
$P(S_1|I_1)$ = .21/.39 = .54

$P(S_2|I_1)$ = .08/.39 = .20

$P(S_3|I_1)$ = .10/.39 = .26
                    1.0

B

Sum of branches = $P(I_2)$
          = .26
$P(S_1|I_2)$ = .06/.26 = .23

$P(S_2|I_2)$ = .10/.26 = .385

$P(S_3|I_2)$ = .10/.26 = .385
                    1.0

C

Sum of branches = $P(I_3)$
          = .35
$P(S_1|I_3)$ = .03/.35 = .08

$P(S_2|I_3)$ = .02/.35 = .06

$P(S_3|I_3)$ = .30/.35 = .86
                    1.0

Table 18.22

Best actions for Mr. Larson, given the consultant's advice

Consultant Predicts	Best Action
A rise in the interest rate (I_1)	Order 50 sailboats (A_1) Expected payoff: 15 Net profit: 12.5
No change in the interest rate (I_2)	Order 100 sailboats (A_3) Expected payoff: 20.8 Net profit: 18.3
A drop in the interest rate (I_3)	Order 150 sailboats (A_4) Expected payoff: 36.2 Net profit: 33.7

Exercises

18.31 Complete the following tree diagram and determine the decision based on the maximum expected payoff. Let $P(S_1) = 0.4$, $P(S_2) = 0.2$, $P(S_3) = 0.1$, and $P(S_4) = 0.3$.

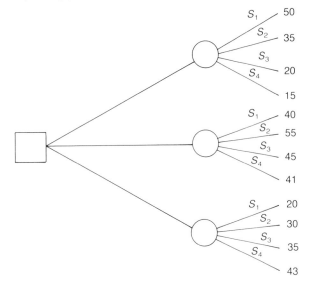

18.32 Security Designs sells alarm systems to businesses for protection against burglary and fire. If the number of small businesses continues to increase at a medium or fast rate, then Security Designs believes it should advertise more to increase its business. The manager at Security Designs believes that there is a 15% chance that the number of small businesses will decrease (S_1). He believes that there is a 25% chance that the number will stay the same (S_2), and a 25% chance and 35% chance that the number of small businesses will increase moderately (S_3) and rapidly (S_4), respectively. Construct a decision tree using the following payoff table to find the decision based on the maximum expected payoff. The payoff is the amount of monthly profit. A_1: no advertising; A_2: keep advertising at current period; A_3: increase advertising 15%; A_4: increase advertising 30%.

Advertising	S_1	S_2	S_3	S_4
A_1	1451	1840	2050	2300
A_2	−1091	1685	2430	2900
A_3	−2015	1100	3060	3561
A_4	−3460	−1350	3340	4300

18.33 Consider the following payoff table, which lists the utilities of the payoff to an investor who needs to decide on one of three different investment strategies: A_1, A_2, and A_3. The investor believes that there are four different states of nature that can affect the return on the investment. States S_1, S_2, S_3, and S_4 are believed to occur with probabilities .1, .3, .4, and .2, respectively.

Action	S_1	S_2	S_3	S_4
A_1	30	25	32	45
A_2	35	15	40	42
A_3	44	27	20	18

Construct a decision tree to find the decision based on the maximum expected utility of the payoff.

18.34 Using a decision tree, find the decision that the builder in exercise 18.18 should make, based on the maximum expected payoff.

18.35 Refer to exercise 18.25. Construct the decision tree to find the decision based on the maximum expected utility of the payoff.

18.36 Refer to exercise 18.26. Construct the decision tree to find the decision based on the maximum expected utility of the payoff.

18.37 Let A_1, A_2, A_3, and A_4 be a set of outcomes with $P(A_1) = 0.2$, $P(A_2) = 0.3$, $P(A_3) = 0.3$, and $P(A_4) = 0.2$. If it is given that $P(B \mid A_1) = 0.4$, $P(B \mid A_2) = 0.1$, $P(B \mid A_3) = 0.2$, and $P(B \mid A_4) = 0.1$, what are the probabilities $P(A_1 \mid B)$, $P(A_2 \mid B)$, $P(A_3 \mid B)$, and $P(A_4 \mid B)$?

18.38 A survey shows that 30% of the fashions that were found to be unprofitable were marketed by the major fashion clothes stores; 60% of the fashions found to be profitable were marketed by the major fashion clothes stores. If 70% of all fashions are profitable to market, find the probability that a fashion will be profitable if the major fashion clothes stores market it. What is the probability that the major fashion clothes stores market a particular fashion?

18.39 David, Harold, and Daniel are three salespeople at Southeast Insurance. David sells 40% of all insurance policies, Harold sells 33%, and Daniel sells 27%. The percent of policies sold by David that are whole-life insurance policies is 5%. That sold by Harold is 8% and that sold by Daniel is 10%. If a whole-life insurance policy at Southeast Insurance is selected at random, what is the probability that the insurance policy was sold by Harold?

18.40 Refer to exercise 18.32. Assume that the manager at Security Designs has obtained some additional information from a consultant who predicts that the number of small businesses will stay the same; that is, state of nature S_2 is predicted to occur. The consultant has the following record, letting I be the event that the consultant predicts the number of small businesses will stay the same: $P(I \mid S_1) = .2$, $P(I \mid S_2) = .7$, $P(I \mid S_3) = .2$, and $P(I \mid S_4) = .1$. Find the decision based on the maximum expected payoff using revised probabilities with the additional information.

18.41 The investor in exercise 18.33 subscribes to the stock market newsletter *Prudent Investor*. The newsletter forecasts state of nature S_1. Let I be the event that the newsletter forecasts S_1. The stock market newsletter has the following record: $P(I \mid S_1) = .6$, $P(I \mid S_2) = .2$, $P(I \mid S_3) = .3$, and $P(I \mid S_4) = .1$. Using revised probabilities based on this additional information, find the decision based on the maximum expected utility of the payoff.

18.42 Four legal secretaries type legal documents at a certain law firm. Secretary A types 15% of the work load, secretary B types 25%, secretary C types 20%, and secretary D types 40% of the work load. The secretaries produce the following proportions of the typographical errors:

Secretary	Performance
A	.04
B	.06
C	.08
D	.03

If a typographical error is found on a legal document, which secretary would have the highest probability of having typed the error?

18.43 A decision maker must determine whether to conduct an experiment that will give one of three predictions, I_1, I_2, or I_3. If the experiment indicates I_1 and the decision maker uses this information, the expected profit is $15,000. If I_2 is indicated, the expected profit is $5000. But if I_3 is indicated, the expected profit is only $1000. If the experiment is not performed, the maximum expected profit would be $4000. Assuming that each of the predictions I_1, I_2, and I_3 is equally likely, is it worthwhile to conduct an experiment that costs $2000?

18.44 Nutritious Cereals would like to market a new multigrain cereal. The manager is trying to decide whether to produce the cereal in large quantities (A_1), moderate quantities (A_2), or small quantities (A_3). The manager believes that the probability of strong demand (S_1) is 0.4, of moderate demand (S_2) is 0.4, and of weak demand (S_3) is 0.2. A survey that can be conducted would predict strong demand (I_1), moderate demand (I_2), or weak demand (I_3). Historical data show the following conditional probabilities with regard to the predictions of the survey $[P(I \mid S)]$:

Prediction	S_1	S_2	S_3
I_1	0.8	0.3	0.3
I_2	0.1	0.5	0.1
I_3	0.1	0.2	0.6

The profit resulting from the different actions of Nutritious Cereal with regard to marketing the product is given in the following payoff table in thousands of dollars.

Action	S_1	S_2	S_3
A_1	88	53	20
A_2	75	66	32
A_3	57	50	39

If the survey costs $20,000 to conduct, should the management of Nutritious Cereals undertake it?

18.45 The following table lists conditional probabilities for certain predictions that are made by the consultant in exercise 18.32, given the four states of nature of S_1, S_2, S_3, and S_4. Assume that I_1 represents the event that the consultant predicts the number of small businesses will decrease, I_2 that they will stay the same, I_3 that they will increase moderately, and I_4 that they will increase rapidly.

Prediction	S_1	S_2	S_3	S_4
I_1	0.80	0.10	0.20	0.10
I_2	0.10	0.70	0.20	0.20
I_3	0.05	0.10	0.50	0.30
I_4	0.05	0.10	0.10	0.40

Would the consultant's fee of $1200 be so high that Security Designs would not consider using the consultant's service?

18.46 Refer to exercise 18.18. Let I_1, I_2, and I_3 be the events that an economist forecasts states of nature S_1, S_2, and S_3, respectively. The following table lists the conditional probabilities that the consultant makes one of these predictions given a particular state of nature. Would it be worth paying $2000 for the economist's services?

Prediction	S_1	S_2	S_3
I_1	.8	.4	.2
I_2	.1	.4	.2
I_3	.1	.2	.6

Summary

This chapter presented a different approach to using probabilities—arriving at a decision when the future is uncertain. For example, should you lease a building or incur the extra expense of building one? Should your recently acquired inheritance be put in a money-market account or should you take advantage of a reliable (in the past, at least) stock market report and invest in a newly formed corporation?

When facing such a problem, the decision maker must define the possible actions or alternatives (such as lease versus purchase or invest in the money market versus invest in stocks) and states of nature that describe the uncertain future (such as company sales will be below expected, equal to expected, or greater than expected). For each action and state of nature, the decision maker must determine the corresponding payoff amount. These values can be summarized in a payoff table. This is certainly the most difficult and crucial step in the decision process because each payoff value must reflect such factors as future costs to the company and responses of competitors. Any action whose payoff is less than that belonging to another action *regardless of the state of nature* is said to be dominated and can be removed from consideration.

Different strategies exist for any decision problem. If you elect to describe the uncertain future by assigning a probability to each state of nature, then a popular strategy is to select the action that maximizes the expected payoff. Typically, these probabilities are subjective, so any decision based on this method always should be followed up by a sensitivity analysis that repeats the decision procedure under various sets of probabilities. In other words, it is a "what-if" process that says, "if the future is described by the following set of probabilities, then the best action using this strategy is . . . ."

The minimax and maximax procedures do not require state of nature probabilities. The minimax strategy is very conservative. It begins by constructing an opportunity loss table that summarizes, for each state of nature, the loss the decision maker incurs by failing to take the most profitable action, given that this state of nature occurs. The action to take using this strategy is the one that minimizes the maximum opportunity loss for each of the actions under consideration. The maximax strategy is suited to the gambler; it selects that action having the largest possible payoff. Because it fails to take into consideration any heavy losses, it is not appropriate for most business decisions.

When using the expected payoff strategy, you should examine not only the payoffs that you can expect in the long run from each action but also the risk associated with each action. Here you measure the variation in the possible payoffs corresponding to each alternative. You often will select a less risky alternative and sacrifice a small amount of expected payoff. When you use the expected payoff strategy, a useful piece of information is the expected value of perfect information (*EVPI*), which is how much a decision maker should be willing to pay for a perfect prediction of tomorrow's state of nature—for a crystal ball. Because any information about the future probably will be imperfect (for example, the consultant might be wrong), such information should cost considerably less than the *EVPI*.

It is not necessary to set up a decision problem by defining a payoff table in financial units. An alternative is to use utility values, which measure both the attractiveness and the risk associated with each dollar amount. For example, a $100,000 gain might be attractive, but a $100,000 loss may well be disastrous to a struggling company. The utility value for each dollar amount can be summarized in a utility curve. You use the shape of this curve to identify a decision maker as a risk avoider, a risk neutral, or a risk taker.

A complex decision problem can be summarized best using a decision tree. The tree identifies clearly the actions under consideration, the states of nature for the problem, and the expected payoffs for various segments of the decision analysis. Bayes' rule puts such a tree to good use by allowing the decision maker to revise the subjective probability for each state of nature (the prior probabilities) in light of new information about the future. This new information could be a recent stock-market analysis or predictions made by a consulting firm. The revised probabilities are posterior probabilities. Bayes' rule allows you to analyze a decision problem by determining the expected payoff of (1) not purchasing this information and using the prior probabilities or (2) purchasing this information and basing your decision on the results of this prediction.

Review Exercises

18.47 Pay-Lo drive-in grocery must decide how many loaves of bread to order each day. The demand per day is 29, 30, 31, 32, 33, 34, 35, or 36 loaves of bread. Given that 60 cents profit is made on each loaf of bread sold and a loss of 20 cents is incurred on each loaf not sold, construct the payoff table and the opportunity loss table, if any number of loaves between 29 and 36 are ordered for a particular day. What is the minimax decision? What is the maximax decision?

18.48 What would the opportunity loss table be using the following payoff table? What is the minimax decision?

Action	S_1	S_2	S_3	S_4
A_1	120	40	50	70
A_2	30	-20	60	90
A_3	-30	-30	80	40

18.49 Refer to example 18.7. The managers at Omega have decided that a sensitivity analysis should be made before making a decision. Rework example 18.7 using the following sets of probabilities. How sensitive is the decision based on the maximum expected payoff?

$P(S_1)$	$P(S_2)$	$P(S_3)$	$P(S_4)$
.1	.5	.2	.2
.1	.5	.1	.3
.1	.5	.3	.1
.1	.5	.2	.2
.2	.5	.2	.1

18.50 S & W Bookstore competes with the bookstore on a university campus for selling textbooks to students. *Introductory Statistics* is one of the textbooks that sells in large quantities. The manager of S & W Bookstore believes that there is a 30% chance that there will be a heavy enrollment (S_1) in this course. The probabilities for a normal enrollment (S_2) and a low enrollment (S_3) are 0.55 and 0.15, respectively. The manager must decide to order either 300, 400, or 500 copies of the textbooks. The payoff table follows.

Action	S_1	S_2	S_3
A_1 (300)	830	750	710
A_2 (400)	1230	1125	620
A_3 (500)	1850	910	330

a. Are all the actions admissible?

b. What is the minimax decision?

c. What is the decision based on the maximum expected payoff?

d. What is the risk of each action?

e. What is the decision based on minimum risk?

f. What is the *EVPI?*

18.51 Suppose you have $5000 that you would like to invest in either a no-load mutual fund that invests completely in stocks (A_1) or a fixed money-market account that yields 12% for 1 year (A_2). Assume that there are two states of nature: the stock market goes up (S_1), or the stock market goes down (S_2). An investment advisor gives you the following payoff table. Determine what value your personal utility function would have for the payoffs.

Action	S_1	S_2
A_1	1200	-575
A_2	600	600

18.52 You want to find several values of your utility for money from $0 to $2000. Find the value of your utility function at $0, $500, $1000, $1500, and $2000. Then, by graphing, approximate the value of your utility function at $700 and $1200.

18.53 Complete the tree diagram on the opposite page and determine the decision based on the maximum expected payoff. Assume $P(S_1) = .3$, $P(S_2) = .3$, $P(S_3) = .2$, and $P(S_4) = .2$. What is the *EVPI?*

18.54 Refer to exercise 18.50. Assume that the manager at S & W Bookstore has obtained additional information from a consultant that the enrollment in the introductory statistics course will be heavy (I_1). Evidence from the consultant's previous performance indicates the following probabilities: $P(I_1 \mid S_1) = .6$, $P(I_1 \mid S_2) = .2$, and $P(I_1 \mid S_3) = .2$. Determine the decision based on the maximum expected payoff, using revised probabilities.

18.55 Refer to exercise 18.54. Suppose that the consultant's predictions I_2 and I_3, which represent a normal enrollment and a low enrollment, respectively, have the following conditional probabilities: $P(I_2 \mid S_1) = .1$, $P(I_2 \mid S_2) = .5$, $P(I_3 \mid S_3) = .3$, $P(I_3 \mid S_1) = .3$, $P(I_3 \mid S_2) = .3$, $P(I_3 \mid S_3) = .5$. Would the consultant's fee of $350 make it worthwhile for S & W Bookstore to hire this consultant?

18.56 At JBM, a computer company, 30% of the employees are females. Of the female employees, 20% are in top management positions. Also, 25% of the male employees are in top management. What is the probability that a randomly selected person from top management is a female?

18.57 Thirty percent of the clients of an investment broker invest in only long-term–growth mutual funds. Of this group of clients, 60% are under the age of 40 years. Of those clients who do not invest solely in only long-term mutual funds, 15% are under the age of 40 years. What is the probability that a randomly selected client under 40 years of age invests only in long-term–growth mutual funds?

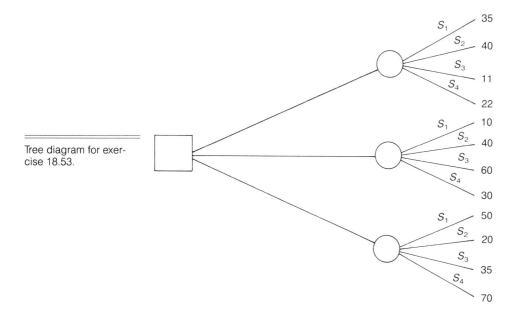

Tree diagram for exercise 18.53.

Nonparametric Statistics

A Look Back/Introduction

Although last, this chapter is far from the least in importance. **Nonparametric** statistical techniques are used extensively for a variety of business-related applications.

In the previous chapters, we introduced a large assortment of tests of hypothesis. These tests generally were concerned with things such as the mean or variance of a population. A mean, variance, or proportion is referred to as a *parameter* in statistics, and so these tests are called *parametric* tests of hypothesis. The common underlying assumption in testing a parameter from a continuous population is that this population has a *normal* distribution. *Any* time you use a t statistic, you assume a normal population distribution. When you test more than two means using the ANOVA procedure, you also assume that the shape of the populations is normal.

What can you do if you have reason to believe that the populations under study are not normally distributed? For example, suppose that data collected previously from these populations have been extremely skewed (not symmetric). One option when dealing with means or proportions is to collect large samples. In such a situation, the central limit theorem (CLT) assures us that the distribution of the sample estimators is approximately normal *regardless* of the population distribution. The other alternative, particularly for small or moderate sample sizes, is to use a nonparametric statistical procedure that deals with cases in which the assumptions of normality are not true.

Many of the nonparametric statistical tests try to answer the same sorts of questions as do those tests discussed previously. With these tests, however, the assumptions can be relaxed considerably. In earlier chapters, means and medians were referred to as *measures of central tendency*. A nonparametric test concerning such a measure does not assume an underlying normal population—unlike its parametric counterpart. Consequently, nonparametric methods are used for situations that violate the assumptions of the parametric procedures.

A common method for practically all nonparametric techniques is the use of **ranks.** Given a set of data, we obtain a set of ranks by replacing each data value by its relative *position*. To illustrate this idea, consider the following eight observations.

10.8, 6.4, 11.7, 5.3, 9.5, 2.5, 15.1, 10.4

Arranged in order, these are

Position	1	2	3	4	5	6	7	8
Value	2.5	5.3	6.4	9.5	10.4	10.8	11.7	15.1

We say that the rank of the value 2.5 is 1, the rank of the value 5.3 is 2, and so forth. Replacing each value by its rank and maintaining the original position produces

6, 3, 7, 2, 4, 1, 8, 5

Most nonparametric procedures use the eight *ranks* rather than the original data values. By using ranks, we are able to relax the assumptions regarding the underlying populations and develop tests that apply to a wider variety of situations.

You often will encounter an application in which a numeric measurement is extremely difficult to obtain, but a rank value is not. One example of this is a consumer taste test; each participant finds it much easier to rank several different brands of soft drinks than to assign a numeric value to each one. The data for analysis consist of the rank assigned to each brand.

Such data are said to be *ordinal* because only the relative position of each value has any meaning (see Chapter 1). This is a "weaker" form of data than is the *interval* form, for which not only the position but also the *difference* between data values is meaningful. In this text, we have dealt mostly with interval data. Data consisting of temperatures, for example, are interval data; the difference between 60°F and 70°F is the same as that between 65°F and 75°F (10°F). When dealing with ranks, this is not the case; there is no reason to assume that the difference between ranks 1 and 3 is the same as that between ranks 3 and 5.

In Chapter 13, we introduced one nonparametric procedure, which used the chi-square statistic to test for goodness-of-fit or independence between two classifications. In this chapter, we will examine other popular nonparametric methods used in a business setting. These tests of hypothesis by no means constitute all of the nonparametric techniques used in practice, but they should provide you with a basis for knowing how and when to apply such a method to a particular set of sample data.

19.1

A Test for Randomness: The Runs Test

A crucial assumption behind a great many statistical procedures is based on the concept of *randomness*. In the earlier chapters, all samples were assumed to be random. The reliability of any statistical test—even if run on a high-powered computer—is suspect if the sample was not obtained in a random manner. Similarly, the *t* and *F* tests in linear regression contain the assumption that the resulting sample residuals are *inde-*

pendent, with no observable pattern. This means that the *signs* of these errors should be random.

When you examine a sequence of observations or residuals, one method of detecting a lack of randomness is to observe the number of runs contained in the sequence. For a sequence containing two possible values (A and B, $+$ and $-$, and so on) a **run** consists of a string of identical values.

Suppose we flip a coin ten times, where each flip results in a head (H) or a tail (T). Consider the following three outcomes, each containing five heads and five tails.

Sequence 1	H	H	H	H	H	T	T	T	T	T
Sequence 2	H	T	H	T	H	T	H	T	H	T
Sequence 3	H	H	T	H	T	T	H	T	T	H

Only sequence 3 exhibits a random pattern. To see why, we will examine each sequence.

Sequence 1 These ten observations contain only two runs:

$$\underline{\text{H H H H H}}\qquad\underline{\text{T T T T T}}$$

Run 1   Run 2

The small number of runs indicates that this sequence was not generated in a random manner.

Sequence 2 At first glance, this pattern may appear to be random, but there is an excessive number (ten) of runs.

$$\underline{\text{H}}\ \ \underline{\text{T}}\ \ \underline{\text{H}}\ \ \underline{\text{T}}\ \ \underline{\text{H}}\ \ \underline{\text{T}}\ \ \underline{\text{H}}\ \ \underline{\text{T}}\ \ \underline{\text{H}}\ \ \underline{\text{T}}$$

Run 1   Run 10

Once again, the process that generated this sequence is not random, as indicated by the large number of runs.

Sequence 3 This sequence seems to be a compromise between the first two, exhibiting neither too few runs nor too many.

$$\underline{\text{H H}}\ \ \underline{\text{T}}\ \ \underline{\text{H}}\ \ \underline{\text{T T}}\ \ \underline{\text{H}}\ \ \underline{\text{T T}}\ \ \underline{\text{H}}$$

Run 1   Run 7

It appears that the sequence was generated in a random manner.

In this section, we will use the runs test statistical procedure to test for randomness using the number of observed runs.

The Runs Test (Small Samples)

Consider a sequence of n observations, containing n_1 symbols of the first type (H, in our example) and n_2 symbols of the second type (T). So, $n = n_1 + n_2$. Let

R = number of runs within these n observations

The situation we will consider here is for small samples, where $n_1 \leq 10$ and $n_2 \leq 10$. This provides a good method of demonstrating how this particular nonparametric technique is indeed distribution free; that is, it makes no assumptions about the population of H's and T's.

Table 19.1

Arrangements when n_1 = 2, n_2 = 3	Arrangement	Number of Runs (R)
	H H T T T	2
	H T H T T	4
	H T T H T	4
	H T T T H	3
	T H H T T	3
	T H T H T	5
	T H T T H	4
	T T H H T	3
	T T H T H	4
	T T T H H	2

Consider the case where $n_1 = 2$ and $n_2 = 3$. In this section, we will assume (without any loss of generality) that $n_1 \leq n_2$. So we have two H's and three T's. How many such arrangements (permutations) of these five symbols are there?* There are ten, provided in Table 19.1. This value in general can be found using

$$\text{number of arrangements} = A = \frac{n!}{n_1! \, n_2!} \tag{19-1}$$

where $n = n_1 + n_2$. For this illustration, this would be

$$A = \frac{5!}{2! \, 3!} = \frac{\overset{2}{(5)(\cancel{4})(3)(\cancel{2})}}{(\cancel{2})(\cancel{3})(\cancel{2})} = 10$$

Each of the ten arrangements in Table 19.1 is equally likely to occur *providing* the process generating this sequence is *random,* so each has probability .1. Some conclusions we can draw from Table 19.1 include

1. For two of these sequences, there are two runs, and so $P(R = 2) = .2$.
2. For three of the sequences, there are three runs, and so $P(R = 3) = .3$.
3. For four of the sequences, there are four runs, and so $P(R = 4) = .4$.
4. For one of the sequences, there are five runs, and so $P(R = 5) = .1$.

Notice that these probabilities sum to 1, as they should.

Consequently, for this situation, we can make the following statements:

$$P(R \leq 2) = P(R = 2) = .2$$
$$P(R \leq 3) = P(R = 2) + P(R = 3) = .2 + .3 = .5$$
$$P(R \leq 4) = .2 + .3 + .4 = .9$$
$$P(R \leq 5) = .2 + .3 + .4 + .1 = 1.0$$

This means that, for example, the probability of observing three or less runs if H_0: the sequence has been produced in a random manner, is true will be .5. What we are seeing here is that these probabilities are obtained *without* assuming any probability distribution for the underlying population (process) that generated a sequence of $n_1 = 2$ values of H and $n_2 = 3$ values of T. This is the beauty of nonparametric methods.

---

*The formulas for the number of permutations given in Chapter 5 do not apply here because the n objects (symbols) are not all different (distinct).

Table 19.2

A portion of Table A-15 for the runs test. Each entry is $P(R \leq a)$ where the values of a run across the table.

(n_1, n_2)	2	3	4	5	6	7	8	9	10
(2,3)	.200	.500	.900	1.000					
(2,4)	.133	.400	.800	1.000					
(2,5)	.095	.333	.714	1.000					
(2,6)	.071	.286	.643	1.000					
(2,7)	.056	.250	.583	1.000					
(2,8)	.044	.222	.533	1.000					
(2,9)	.036	.200	.491	1.000					
(2,10)	.030	.182	.455	1.000					
(3,3)	.100	.300	.700	.900	1.000				
(3,4)	.057	.200	.543	.800	.971	1.000			
(3,5)	.036	.143	.429	.714	.929	1.000			
(3,6)	.024	.107	.345	.643	.881	1.000			
(3,7)	.017	.083	.283	.583	.833	1.000			
(3,8)	.012	.067	.236	.533	.788	1.000			
(3,9)	.009	.055	.200	.491	.745	1.000			
(3,10)	.007	.045	.171	.455	.706	1.000			
(4,4)	.029	.114	.371	.629	.886	.971	1.000		
(4,5)	.016	.071	.262	.500	.786	.929	.992	1.000	
(4,6)	.010	.048	.190	.405	.690	.881	.976	1.000	
(4,7)	.006	.033	.142	.333	.606	.833	.954	1.000	
(4,8)	.004	.024	.109	.279	.533	.788	.929	1.000	
(4,9)	.003	.018	.085	.236	.471	.745	.902	1.000	
(4,10)	.002	.014	.068	.203	.419	.706	.874	1.000	
(5,5)	.008	**.040**	.167	.357	.643	.833	**.960**	.992	1.000
(5,6)	.004	.024	.110	.262	.522	.738	.911	.976	.998

Probabilities such as those just discussed are summarized in Table A-15 on page 844. The top portion of this table is reproduced in Table 19.2. The table entries contain the probability that $R \leq a$ for the possible values of a. Notice that the first row of this table is identical to the $\leq$ probabilities (called *cumulative* probabilities) that we just derived.

The hypotheses under investigation here are

H_0: the sequence was generated in a random manner

H_a: the sequence was not generated in a random manner

As we mentioned earlier, we will reject H_0 whenever the number of runs is too *small* (say, whenever $R \leq k_1$) or too *large* (say, whenever $R \geq k_2$).

To illustrate the testing procedure here, consider our original sequences for the ten coins with $n_1 = 5$ and $n_2 = 5$. According to equation 19-1, there are $A = 10!/5!\ 5! = 252$ possible arrangements here—sequences 1, 2, and 3 are three of these. We are looking for some "cut-off number" of runs, k_1, where we are fairly sure that $\leq k_1$ are "too few" and $\geq k_2$ are "too many." Using Table 19.2 with $n_1 = 5$ and $n_2 = 5$, we find, for example, that (assuming H_0 is true)

$$P(R \leq 3) = .04$$
$$P(R \leq 8) = .96.$$

Consequently, $P(R > 8) = P(R \geq 9) = 1 - .96 = .04$. In other words, the event of observing three or less runs is very unlikely (with probability .04) if H_0 is true, so a value of $R \leq 3$ indicates that H_0 is not true and should be rejected. The same reasoning applies to $R \geq 9$.

This means that, with a significance level of $\alpha = .04 + .04 = .08$, the values of k_1 and k_2 are $k_1 = 3$ and $k_2 = 9$. The corresponding testing procedure will be to

Reject H_0 if $R \leqslant 3$ or $R \geqslant 9$

We will formalize the procedure for using this information.

The overall significance level of this test is $.04 + .04 = .08$. One disadvantage of small-sample nonparametric procedures is that you cannot derive a test for *any* specified significance level (such as $\alpha = .05$ here). Rather, you are at the mercy of the available values in this table. We can summarize this testing procedure as follows.

Hypotheses:

H_0: pattern was generated in a random manner

H_a: pattern was not generated in a random manner

Test statistic (for small samples): R, where R denotes the number of runs in the sequence.

Procedure:

Reject H_0 if $R \leqslant k_1$ or $R \geqslant k_2$

where (1) k_1 is the value from Table A-15 such that $P(R \leqslant k_1) = \alpha/2$, and (2) k_2 is the value from Table A-15 such that $P(R \geqslant k_2) = \alpha/2$.

Example 19.1

Using a significance level between .05 and .10 and as close to .05 as possible, determine which of the three sequences of five H's and five T's in the earlier discussion were generated in a random manner.

Solution Using Table 19.2 (or Table A-15), the three smallest available significance levels for this test are

$.008 + (1 - .992) = .008 + .008 = .016 \ (k_1 = 2, \ k_2 = 10)$

$.040 + (1 - .960) = .040 + .040 = .08 \ (k_1 = 3, \ k_2 = 9)$

$.167 + (1 - .833) = .167 + .167 = .334 \ (k_1 = .4, \ k_2 = 8)$

Because $\alpha = .08$ comes closest to satisfying our desired significance level, we will

Reject H_0 if $R \leqslant 3$ or $R \geqslant 9$

The results are

for sequence 1: $R = 2$ reject H_0

for sequence 2: $R = 10$ reject H_0

for sequence 3: $R = 7$ fail to reject H_0

So, for the first two sequences we conclude that these arrangements were not the result of a random process. For the third sequence, we have no reason to suspect the presence of a nonrandom process.   ●

The Runs Test (Large Samples)

For large samples ($n_1 > 10$ and $n_2 > 10$), the approximate distribution for R, if the generating process *is* random, will be approximately *normal* with mean

$$\mu_R = 1 + \frac{2n_1n_2}{n_1 + n_2} \qquad\qquad (19\text{-}2)$$

and standard deviation

$$\sigma_R = \sqrt{\frac{2n_1n_2(2n_1n_2 - n_1 - n_2)}{(n_1 + n_2)^2(n_1 + n_2 - 1)}} \qquad\qquad (19\text{-}3)$$

By standardizing R in the usual way, we obtain the following summary.
Hypotheses:

H_0: pattern was generated in a random manner

H_a: pattern was not generated in a random manner

Test statistic (for large samples):

$$Z = \frac{R - \mu_R}{\sigma_R} \qquad\qquad (19\text{-}4)$$

where (1) R denotes the number of runs in the data sequence, and (2) μ_R and σ_R are the mean and standard deviation of this random variable, defined in equations 19-2 and 19-3.

The testing procedure using the standard normal random variable is the same as in previous tests using Z. For the randomness test, a nonrandom pattern is indicated by a Z value in the right tail (too many runs) or in the left tail (too few runs).

Example 19.2

The president of Northside National Bank requested the savings-account balance for 45 randomly selected accounts of nonmarried customers. When she examined the data, she began to question the randomness of the procedure used to select the accounts. Letting M denote a male account and F a female account, the following sequence was obtained, listed in the order in which they were selected for the supposedly random sample.

M M F F F F F M F F M M M M M M F F F F M M F
M M F F M F F F F F M M M M M F F F F M M M

Based upon this sequence, would you conclude that this sample consists of 45 randomly selected males and females? Use $\alpha = .05$.

Solution The preceding sequence contains $R = 15$ runs. Also,

$n_1 = $ number of males $= 22$

$n_2 = $ number of females $= 23$

For these values of n_1 and n_2, the mean number of runs if H_0 is true is

$$\mu_R = 1 + \frac{(2)(22)(23)}{45} = 23.49$$

This implies that, on the average, whenever $n_1 = 22$ and $n_2 = 23$, you will obtain 23.49 runs.

The sample contains only 15 runs, so it could be that this sequence exhibits a nonrandom pattern, due to insufficient runs. However, this depends heavily on the standard deviation of R; therefore, to complete the analysis, we next find

$$\sigma_R = \sqrt{\frac{(2)(22)(23)[(2)(22)(23) - 45]}{(45)^2(44)}}$$
$$= \sqrt{10.9832} = 3.314$$

To determine whether $R = 15$ is sufficiently small to reject the random sequence hypothesis, we calculate the test statistic.

$$Z^* = \frac{15 - 23.49}{3.314} = -2.56$$

The test procedure here (using $\alpha = .05$) is to

Reject H_0 if $|Z| > 1.96$

The computed Z value does have an absolute value larger than 1.96, and so we reject H_0. There is evidence that the male–female sequence is nonrandom, indicating a lack of randomness in the sampling procedure used in selecting the individual accounts from the bank records. ●

We encounter another application of the runs test when we examine the residuals from a linear regression analysis. A key assumption when using linear regression is that the residuals are *independent*. Consequently, you should observe a random pattern in the sample residuals. If the observations in your data set are recorded across time (say, 24 consecutive months), this often results in residuals that are *not* independent. In this case, we would say that the errors are correlated—more precisely, they are *autocorrelated*: they are correlated with each other. In Chapter 17, we computed the Durbin–Watson (DW) statistic to measure the degree of autocorrelation.

The DW statistic assumes that the errors follow a normal distribution, as do all of the tests of hypothesis when using a linear regression equation. The nonparametric runs test also can be used to examine the residuals, by recording the *sign* ($+$ or $-$) of each residual and counting the number of runs. This test will be valid regardless of the distribution of the residuals and can be used for any model that assumes the residuals are uncorrelated.

Example 19.3

In example 15.4, a multiple linear regression model was used to predict $Y =$ the number of houses sold per month using $X_1 =$ the number of houses shown for this month and $X_2 =$ average interest rate for the month. Figure 15.6 on page 510 contains the MINITAB solution for this problem, which includes a calculation of the $n = 50$ residuals. These values are repeated in Table 19.3. Using $\alpha = .05$, is there any evidence that the residuals are not random?

Solution We begin by forming a sequence containing the sign of each residual.

```
  -   +    - -   +   - - - - -     +    - - - - -
+ + +    - -   +   -   + + + + +    -   +   - - - -
+ +   -   + + +   -   + +   - - - - - -   + +
```

Table 19.3

Residuals for multiple regression in example 19.3

− .40	1.94	− 3.39	− 3.84	6.03	− 1.47	− 1.71	− 1.52
− .12	− 2.09	2.63	− 4.20	.72	− 3.91	.66	− 3.21
7.68	.48	4.17	− 1.91	− .67	3.43	− .41	.54
.48	.49	4.38	1.46	− .68	1.20	− 2.49	− 4.34
− 4.51	5.73	5.07	− 2.15	1.24	2.90	2.02	− .90
3.40	2.88	− 1.87	− .65	− 1.33	− 4.15	− 2.26	− 5.70
2.18	.92						

The number of runs here is $R = 22$. Also, there are $n_1 = 22$ pluses and $n_2 = 28$ minuses. So the expected number of runs for this situation, if H_0 is true, is

$$\mu_R = 1 + \frac{(2)(22)(28)}{50} = 25.64$$

Also,

$$\sigma_R = \sqrt{\frac{(2)(22)(28)(1232 - 50)}{(50)^2(49)}} = 3.45$$

Using $\alpha = .05$, the test procedure here is to

Reject H_0 if $|Z| > 1.96$

The computed test statistic for this example is

$$Z^* = \frac{22 - 25.64}{3.45} = -1.06$$

This value does not lie in the rejection region, so we fail to reject H_0. There is not enough evidence to indicate that the residuals are autocorrelated. Incidentally, the value of the Durbin–Watson statistic for this example is $DW = 2.01$. As we pointed out in Chapter 17, a value of 2.0 is ideal because it indicates that no correlation is present in the residuals. Here, both procedures agree that the assumption of independent errors is met. ●

A computer solution using MINITAB is contained in Figure 19.1. This solution contains the number of runs, as well as the mean of the runs statistic if H_0 is true. The MINITAB procedure also could be used for the male–female sequence in example 19.2 by using − 1 for male and + 1 for female in the computer input. Also contained in Figure 19.1 is the p-value for this test, $p = .2913$. Because this value is larger than the significance level of $\alpha = .05$, we once again fail to reject H_0 and conclude that there is insufficient evidence to indicate that the errors are autocorrelated. When you perform a one-tailed runs test, you should divide this value by two and then compare it to the level of significance (α) before making the decision. Also be sure that the sign of the Z value is compatible with your one-tailed alternative hypothesis; that is, it should be positive when testing H_a: too many runs, and negative when testing H_a: too few runs.

Figure 19.1

MINITAB solution for
runs test.

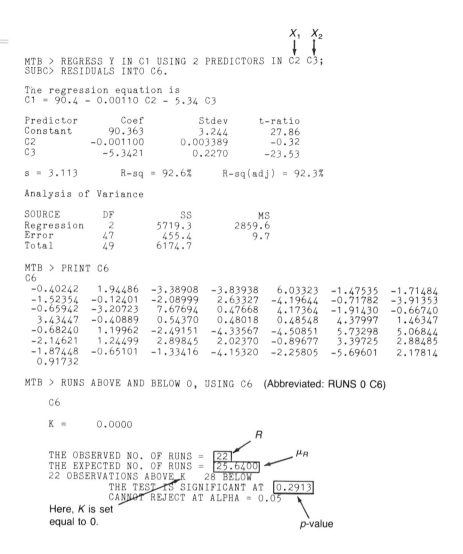

X_1 X_2

```
MTB > REGRESS Y IN C1 USING 2 PREDICTORS IN C2 C3;
SUBC> RESIDUALS INTO C6.

The regression equation is
C1 = 90.4 - 0.00110 C2 - 5.34 C3

Predictor        Coef        Stdev       t-ratio
Constant        90.363       3.244         27.86
C2             -0.001100     0.003389      -0.32
C3             -5.3421       0.2270       -23.53

s = 3.113       R-sq = 92.6%     R-sq(adj) = 92.3%

Analysis of Variance

SOURCE          DF          SS            MS
Regression       2        5719.3        2859.6
Error           47         455.4           9.7
Total           49        6174.7

MTB > PRINT C6
C6
 -0.40242    1.94486   -3.38908   -3.83938    6.03323   -1.47535   -1.71484
 -1.52354   -0.12401   -2.08999    2.63327   -4.19644   -0.71782   -3.91353
 -0.65942   -3.20723    7.67694    0.47668    4.17364   -1.91430   -0.66740
  3.43447   -0.40889    0.54370    0.48018    4.37997    1.46347
 -0.68240    1.19962   -2.49151   -4.33567   -4.50851    5.73298    5.06844
 -2.14621    1.24499    2.89845    2.02370   -0.89677    3.39725    2.88485
 -1.87448   -0.65101   -1.33416   -4.15320   -2.25805   -5.69601    2.17814
  0.91732

MTB > RUNS ABOVE AND BELOW 0, USING C6   (Abbreviated: RUNS 0 C6)

   C6

   K =      0.0000
```

R

```
   THE OBSERVED NO. OF RUNS =   22
   THE EXPECTED NO. OF RUNS =  25.6400
   22 OBSERVATIONS ABOVE K    28 BELOW
            THE TEST IS SIGNIFICANT AT   0.2913
            CANNOT REJECT AT ALPHA = 0.05
```
μ_R

Here, K is set
equal to 0.

p-value

Exercises

19.1   What assumptions need to be made about the data when using the runs test?

19.2   A jar contains two balls, a red one and a blue one. A person is asked to draw a ball at random. The ball is then replaced in the jar and the experiment is repeated. The results of repeating the experiment 17 times follow, where R represents the red ball and B represents the blue ball. At the 0.05 level of significance is there any evidence that the sequence is not randomly generated?

   R B B R R B R R B B B R B R R B R

19.3   Are the negative and positive numbers randomly ordered in the following sequence? Use a 0.10 level of significance.

   $-1, 2, -5, 4, -10, 3, -1, 4, 6, 9, -7, 8, -3, 5$

19.4   Ozark County Bank is taking applications for the position of loan officer. The following sequence lists the order in which either a male (M) or a female (F) applied for the position. Is there evidence to indicate that the sequence is not randomly generated? Use a .05 significance level.

   M M M F M M F M M F M F F M M F M M M F F F F M M F F F

19.5 After a television debate between two political candidates, a telephone line is open to viewers wishing to express their opinion on whether the democratic (D) or the republican (R) candidate won the debate. The following sequence represents 19 opinions of viewers in the order in which they telephoned. Using a runs test and a significance level of 5%, does the sequence indicate a nonrandom order?

R R D D R D D R R R R D D R D R D D D

19.6 Conduct a runs test on the following sequence of 3's and 4's to see if there is evidence that the sequence is not randomly generated. Use a 5% significance level.

3 3 3 4 4 3 4 3 4 3 3 3 4 4 3 4 4 3 3 3 3 3 4 3

19.7 A certain computer program generates a sequence of random digits. Test whether there is any evidence that the following sequence of numbers is nonrandom by considering the sequence of odd and even numbers. Use a 10% significance level.

4 8 7 9 3 2 1 6 7 9 4 1 8 3 2 5

19.8 The following sequence lists the residuals from fitting a multiple regression equation to a set of data. Does the sequence of positive and negative numbers appear to be randomly generated? Use a 10% significance level in performing a runs test.

$0.4, 0.8, 1.2, -0.9, -2.1, -0.1, 1.3, 1.8, 0.2, 0.8, 1.1, 0.9, -0.3, -0.4, -1.7, -1.2, -1.9, -2.1$

19.9 Thirty-five true-or-false questions were given on a history test. The following sequence contains the answers to the questions in the order in which they appeared. At the 5% level, is there evidence that the true and false answers are not randomly assigned?

F F F F T T F T T F F F F T F T F F T T T T F F T T F F T F T T T T F

19.10 Toss a coin 30 times. Record the sequence of heads and tails. Using a runs test, determine whether there is evidence at the 5% significance level that this sequence is nonrandom.

19.2

Nonparametric Tests of Central Tendency

Chapter 3 introduced you to measures of central tendency. The more commonly used measures are the mean and median, which attempt to identify the "middle" of a set of sample data. In Chapter 10, we introduced two populations, where the question of interest was whether the two means were the same (a two-tailed test) or whether one mean exceeded the other (a one-tailed test). This is illustrated in Figure 19.2, where the variable of interest is height.

The main assumption in Figure 19.2 is that the two populations are normally distributed. When you sample from these populations, if both sample sizes (n_1 and n_2) are *large*, you can remove this assumption. However, there is a need for a nonparametric technique for this two-population situation, when (1) you have small samples and you suspect that one or both populations do not follow a normal distribution, or (2) your data are such that only the relative ranks are available within each sample, such as in a consumer taste test. In other words, you are dealing with *ordinal data*.

Figure 19.2

Two-population test of hypothesis for means.

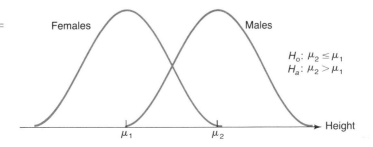

The *t* tests from Chapter 10 assumed that the measurement scale of the data was at least interval, and so these tests are inappropriate for data consisting of ranks.

Also in Chapter 10, when dealing with samples from two populations, we looked at two situations.

1. The two samples are *independent.* In Figure 19.2, this would mean that a sample of n_1 female heights is obtained independently of the n_2 male heights. There is no reason to match up the first male height with the first female height, the second male height with the second female height, and so on in your two samples.
2. The two samples are *dependent* or *paired.* This might occur in Figure 19.3 if the question were "Are husbands taller than wives?" The data would then consist of n_1 wives and $n_2 = n_1$ husbands.

This portion of the chapter discusses the nonparametric counterparts to these two parametric tests of hypothesis. The assumptions behind the application of these methods are considerably weaker than those for the *t* tests in Chapter 10. These nonparametric techniques, named after the people responsible for their development, are the Mann–Whitney *U* test—a nonparametric procedure for situation 1 (two independent samples)—and the Wilcoxon signed rank test—a nonparametric procedure for situation 2 (two paired samples).

The Mann–Whitney *U* Test for Independent Samples

The **Mann–Whitney *U* test** for two means is named after H. B. Mann and R. Whitney, who developed this test in the 1940s. The purpose of this procedure is to provide a test for two means (or medians) that does not require the assumption of normal populations. The test is an alternative to the *t* tests from Chapter 10, which do contain this assumption.

The hypotheses for the Mann–Whitney test are the same as for the *t* tests:

H_0: $\mu_1 = \mu_2$

H_a: $\mu_1 \neq \mu_2$ (or $\mu_1 > \mu_2$ or $\mu_1 < \mu_2$)

When using this nonparametric procedure, we typically make little distinction between means and medians, and so often H_0 and H_a are written in terms of the two population *medians.*

Figure 19.3

Illustration of dependent (paired) samples.

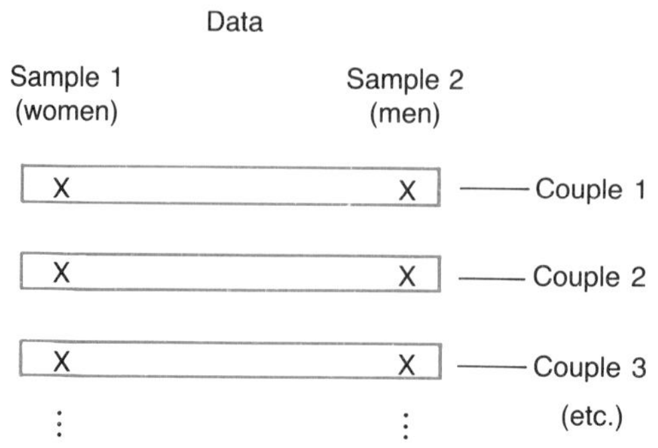

Data

Sample 1 (women)   Sample 2 (men)

X	X	—— Couple 1
X	X	—— Couple 2
X	X	—— Couple 3
⋮	⋮	(etc.)

To use the Mann–Whitney nonparametric technique, we begin by combining (pooling) the two samples into one large sample, and then determining the rank of each observation in the pooled sample. Next, let

T_1 = sum of the ranks of the observations from the first sample in this pooled sample

T_2 = sum of the ranks of the observations from the second sample

The procedure is

Reject H_0 if T_1 is "too much different" than T_2.

To illustrate this, consider the following pooled sample, where the pooled observations have been arranged in order from smallest to largest. Here A represents a value from population A and B is a value from population B.

Value	A	A	A	A	A	B	B	B	B	B
Rank	1	2	3	4	5	6	7	8	9	10

For this pooled sample, we have

$n_1 = 5$

T_1 = sum of ranks of the five A observations in the pooled sample

$= 1 + 2 + 3 + 4 + 5$

$= 15$

$n_2 = 5$

T_2 = sum of the ranks of the B observations

$= 6 + 7 + 8 + 9 + 10$

$= 40$

Now consider another pooled sample:

Value	A	B	B	A	B	A	A	A	B	B
Rank	1	2	3	4	5	6	7	8	9	10

For this situation, the values are $T_1 = 1 + 4 + 6 + 7 + 8 = 26$ and $T_2 = 2 + 3 + 5 + 9 + 10 = 29$.

In the first pooled sample, there is clear evidence that the mean of the second population is *larger* than that for the first population, as indicated by the large difference between $T_1 = 15$ and $T_2 = 40$. This also was evident when you examined this pooled sample, because the values from population A are all less than those from population B. The Mann–Whitney procedure will result in rejecting H_0: $\mu_1 = \mu_2$ in favor of H_a: $\mu_1 \neq \mu_2$ (or H_a: $\mu_1 < \mu_2$ had we used a one-tailed test). For the second set of ten pooled observations, there is no indication of a difference in the population means; the A and B values are fairly well mixed in the combined sample. This is evidenced by the values of $T_1 = 26$ and $T_2 = 29$, which are nearly equal here. The Mann–Whitney test will lead to a failure to reject H_0: $\mu_1 = \mu_2$.

Mann–Whitney Test for Small Samples For this test of hypothesis, small samples are defined as both n_1 and $n_2 \leq 10$. *Regardless* of the sample sizes, the procedure begins by finding T_1 and T_2 as described previously, and then letting

$$U_1 = n_1 n_2 + \frac{n_1(n_1 + 1)}{2} - T_1 \qquad (19\text{-}5)$$

and

$$U_2 = n_1 n_2 + \frac{n_2(n_2 + 1)}{2} - T_2 \qquad (19\text{-}6)$$

The Mann–Whitney test is summarized in the accompanying box.

The Mann–Whitney Test for Small Samples

Hypotheses:

H_0: $\mu_1 = \mu_2$

H_a: $\mu_1 \neq \mu_2$ (or $\mu_1 > \mu_2$ or $\mu_1 < \mu_2$)

where μ_1 and μ_2 represent the means, or medians, for the two populations of interest.

Assumptions:

1. Random samples are obtained from each population.
2. The two samples are independent of one another—respective observations are not paired.
3. The sample data are at least ordinal.

Procedure:

1. Assume that $n_1 \leq n_2$ (if this is not the case, reverse your populations, so that n_1 is the smaller sample size).
2. Determine U_1 and U_2 from equations 19-5 and 19-6.
3. Use the value from Table A-10 on page 835 to test H_0 versus H_a where, once again, small p-values lead to rejecting H_0.

TWO-SIDED TEST　　　　**ONE-SIDED TEST**

H_a: $\mu_1 \neq \mu_2$　　　　H_a: $\mu_1 > \mu_2$　　　　H_a: $\mu_1 < \mu_2$

Reject H_0 if Table A-10 value for U is $< \alpha/2$, where U = minimum of U_1 and U_2.

Reject H_0 if Table A-10 value for U is $< \alpha$, where $U = U_1$.

Reject H_0 if Table A-10 value for U is $< \alpha$, where $U = U_2$.

Example 19.4

A local auto dealer wants to know whether single male buyers purchase the same amount of "extras" (such as air conditioning, power steering, exterior trim) as do single females when ordering a new car. A sample of eight males and nine females was obtained; the data consist of the dollar amounts of the ordered extras.

| Male purchases | 2450 | 1436 | 850 | 1240 | 3645 | 1766 | 1226 | 2840 | |
| Female purchases | 1742 | 3146 | 2740 | 2160 | 3436 | 2750 | 562 | 1290 | 2060 |

Use $\alpha = .05$ to test for a difference between the amounts purchased by the male and female buyers.

Solution The hypotheses are

$$H_0: \mu_M = \mu_F$$

$$H_a: \mu_M \neq \mu_F$$

The pooled sample here is

562, 850, 1226, 1240, 1290, 1436, 1742, 1766, 2060, 2160, 2450, 2740, 2750, 2840, 3146, 3436, 3645

Next, we indicate which sample each value came from in the pooled sample.

Rank	Male Sample	Female Sample	Ranks for Male Sample	Ranks for Female Sample
1		562		1
2	850		2	
3	1226		3	
4	1240		4	
5		1290		5
6	1436		6	
7		1742		7
8	1766		8	
9		2060		9
10		2160		10
11	2450		11	
12		2740		12
13		2750		13
14	2840		14	
15		3146		15
16		3436		16
17	3645		17	
			$T_1 = 65$	$T_2 = 88$

Using equations 19-5 and 19-6,

$$U_1 = (8)(9) + \frac{(8)(9)}{2} - 65 = 43$$

$$U_2 = (8)(9) + \frac{(9)(10)}{2} - 88 = 29$$

Because this is a two-sided alternative, we let $U =$ the minimum of 29 and 43, so $U = 29$.

For $n_1 = 8$, $n_2 = 9$, and $U = 29$, the value in Table A-10 is .2707. Because this is $> \alpha/2 = .025$, we fail to reject H_0. Based on these data, there is insufficient evidence to indicate a difference between male and female purchase amounts.

The p-value for this test is $(2)(.2707) = .5414$, which is extremely large. For a one-sided test, the p-value would be obtained by finding the value from Table A-10 and *not* doubling it.

Ties When the pooled sample contains two or more identical observations, each is assigned a rank equal to the *average* of the ranks of the tied observations. For example, if there are two observations tied for sixth and seventh place, each is assigned a rank of 6.5. The rank of the next largest sample value will be 8. We will illustrate this procedure in the next section.

Mann–Whitney Test for Large Samples Whenever n_1 *or* n_2 is greater than ten, a large sample approximation can be used for the distribution of the Mann–Whitney U statistic. For this case, we can use either U_1 or U_2 in the test statistic for both one-sided *and* two-sided tests. The following discussion will use U_2.

In the event that $\mu_1 = \mu_2$, the U_2 statistic is approximately *normally* distributed with mean

$$\mu_{U_2} = \frac{n_1 n_2}{2}$$

and standard deviation

$$\sigma_{U_2} = \sqrt{\frac{n_1 n_2 (n_1 + n_2 + 1)}{12}} \qquad (19\text{-}7)$$

The rejection region for the various alternative hypotheses are defined in the accompanying box.

The corresponding test statistic here is

$$Z = \frac{U_2 - \mu_{U_2}}{\sigma_{U_2}} \qquad (19\text{-}8)$$

The Mann–Whitney Test for Large Samples

Hypotheses:

H_0: $\mu_1 = \mu_2$

H_a: $\mu_1 \neq \mu_2$ (or $\mu_1 > \mu_2$ or $\mu_1 < \mu_2$)

Assumptions: Same as for small samples.

Procedure: Determine

$$U_2 = n_1 n_2 + \frac{n_2(n_2 + 1)}{2} - T_2$$

where T_2 = sum of the ranks for the second sample in the pooled sample.

TWO-SIDED TEST	**ONE-SIDED TEST**	
H_a: $\mu_1 \neq \mu_2$	H_a: $\mu_1 > \mu_2$	H_a: $\mu_1 < \mu_2$
Reject H_0 if $|Z| > Z_{\alpha/2}$ where (1) Z is defined in equation 19-8 and (2) $Z_{\alpha/2}$ is the value from Table A-4 having a right-tail area of $\alpha/2$.	Reject H_0 if $Z > Z_\alpha$	Reject H_0 if $Z < -Z_\alpha$

Example 19.5

Food World operates two supermarkets in a large metropolitan area. One of their services to customers is to cash personal checks at no charge. The owner of Food World is concerned that one of the stores (store A), situated in a low-income neigh-

Table 19.4

Pooled sample for example 19.5

Rank	Store A Sample	Store B Sample	Ranks for Store A	Ranks for Store B
1		8		1
2		10		2
3		14		3
4		15		4
5		17		
				5.5
7		19		
				5.5
9		22		7
10		24		8
11		28		9
12		35		10
13	38		13	11
14	42		15	12
15		42		
16	42		15	
17		45		15
18	47		18	
19		50		17
20	55		20	
21	57		21	19
22	59		22	
23	60		23	
24	65		24	
25	68		25	
26	71		26	
27	76		27	
			$T_1 = 249$	$T_2 = 129$

borhood, may have a greater number of checks returned due to insufficient funds in the customer's checking account than does store B, which is located in a higher-income area. Data were collected for 12 randomly selected six-month periods from store A, consisting of the number of returned checks over this period. This was repeated for 15 randomly selected six-month periods for store B.

Store A   42, 65, 38, 55, 71, 60, 47, 59, 68, 57, 76, 42
Store B   22, 17, 35, 19, 8, 24, 42, 14, 28, 17, 10, 15, 20, 45, 50

The pooled sample and corresponding ranks are summarized in Table 19.4. Notice that there are two values of 17, tied for fifth and sixth place. Consequently, each is given a rank of $(5 + 6)/2 = 5.5$. Similarly, there is a three-way tie for fourteenth, fifteenth, and sixteenth place, so a rank of $(14 + 15 + 16)/3 = 15$ is given to each.

Using $\alpha = .05$, is there sufficient evidence to indicate that store A has a larger number of returned checks that does store B?

Solution   The hypotheses for this situation are

H_0: $\mu_A \leq \mu_B$

H_a: $\mu_A > \mu_B$

The test procedure will be to

Reject H_0 if $Z > 1.645$

Figure 19.4

MINITAB procedure for
Mann–Whitney test
(example 19.5).

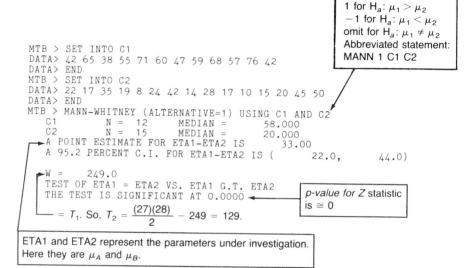

```
MTB > SET INTO C1
DATA> 42 65 38 55 71 60 47 59 68 57 76 42
DATA> END
MTB > SET INTO C2
DATA> 22 17 35 19 8 24 42 14 28 17 10 15 20 45 50
DATA> END
MTB > MANN-WHITNEY (ALTERNATIVE=1) USING C1 AND C2
    C1        N =  12      MEDIAN =      58.000
    C2        N =  15      MEDIAN =      20.000
  →A POINT ESTIMATE FOR ETA1-ETA2 IS      33.00
    A 95.2 PERCENT C.I. FOR ETA1-ETA2 IS (      22.0,      44.0)
  →W =     249.0
    TEST OF ETA1 = ETA2 VS. ETA1 G.T. ETA2
    THE TEST IS SIGNIFICANT AT 0.0000
    = T₁. So, T₂ = (27)(28)/2 - 249 = 129.
```

Alternative:
1 for H_a: $\mu_1 > \mu_2$
−1 for H_a: $\mu_1 < \mu_2$
omit for H_a: $\mu_1 \neq \mu_2$
Abbreviated statement:
MANN 1 C1 C2

p-value for Z statistic
is ≅ 0

ETA1 and ETA2 represent the parameters under investigation.
Here they are μ_A and μ_B.

where $1.645 = Z_{.05}$ is obtained from Table A-4. From Table 19.4, we find that

$$T_2 = \text{sum of ranks for store B}$$

$$= 1 + 2 + 3 + 4 + 5.5 + 5.5 + \ldots + 15 + 17 + 19$$

$$= 129$$

and so

$$U_2 = (12)(15) + \frac{(15)(16)}{2} - 129 = 171$$

Also, the mean and standard deviation of the U_2 statistic are

$$\mu_{U_2} = \frac{(12)(15)}{2} = 90$$

and

$$\sigma_{U_2} = \sqrt{\frac{(12)(15)(28)}{12}} = 20.49$$

The value of the resulting test statistic is

$$Z = \frac{U_2 - \mu_{U_2}}{\sigma_{U_2}} = \frac{171 - 90}{20.49} = 3.95$$

This exceeds 1.645, and so we reject H_0 and conclude that store A does in fact have a larger volume of returned checks than store B. ●

A MINITAB solution for example 19.5 is contained in Figure 19.4. The Mann–Whitney statistic is denoted as W, which is actually the sum of the first sample ranks, T_1. T_2 can be obtained by using the identity

$$T_1 + T_2 = \frac{n(n + 1)}{2}$$

where $n = $ pooled sample size $= n_1 + n_2$.

Wilcoxon Signed Rank Test for Paired Samples

When your sample data consist of *paired* observations from two populations, the Mann–Whitney procedure from the previous section does not apply; it assumes *independent* samples. By *paired observations,* we mean that respective observations from each sample are matched with one another. Examples include husband–wife, brother–sister, and before–after combinations.

A method of testing population means under this type of sampling procedure was introduced in Chapter 10, where we used a *t* test on the sample differences. However, as with all *t* tests, a key assumption using this method of testing two means is that the differences are *normally distributed.* When small samples from suspected nonnormal populations are used, or your data consist of ordinal rankings, a nonparametric technique is required. The **Wilcoxon signed rank test** is used for such situations.

The Wilcoxon test begins like its parametric counterpart, the paired-sample *t* test, by subtracting the data pairs and using the differences to perform a test on the means μ_1 and μ_2. As with the Mann–Whitney test, little distinction is made between the means and medians of the two populations; discussions of these procedures often define the hypotheses in terms of medians, rather than means. We will continue to define H_0 and H_a using μ_1 and μ_2.

The steps involved in applying the Wilcoxon test are:

1. Determine the difference for each sample pair.
2. Arrange the *absolute value* of these differences in order, assigning a rank to each.
3. Let T_+ = sum of the ranks having a positive difference and T_- = sum of the ranks for the negative differences.
4. T_+, T_-, or T = the minimum of T_+ and T_- to define a test of H_0 versus H_a.

To demonstrate the test, suppose we are interested in determining the effects of a vigorous six-month advertising campaign. Sales figures are collected before and after the campaign from ten different cities. The results are shown in Table 19.5.

We determine the paired differences and rank the corresponding absolute values in order. Ties are handled as before by assigning a rank equal to the average of the tied positions. Also, if a pair of observations has a difference equal to zero, then this pair should be *deleted* from the sample, and *n* is reduced by one. Other methods exist for handling ties, but this is the simplest procedure and works well provided there are only a few ties.

Table 19.5

Sales (thousands of $) for ten cities

City	Sales Before	Sales After
Denver	61	63
Boston	50	57
Salt Lake City	18	34
Seattle	56	48
Miami	29	44
Dallas	25	38
Atlanta	34	28
Baltimore	48	68
Topeka	37	57
Minneapolis	14	26

Table 19.6

Illustration of Wilcoxon signed rank procedure (example 19.6)

Sales Before	Sales After	Difference (After–Before)	|Difference|	Rank
61	63	2	2	1
50	57	7	7	3
18	34	16	16	8
56	48	−8	8	4(−)
29	44	15	15	7
25	38	13	13	6
34	28	−6	6	2(−)
48	68	20	20	9.5
37	57	20	20	9.5
14	26	12	12	5

According to Table 19.6, the negative differences are −6 and −8. Their corresponding ranks are 2 and 4. Therefore,

$$T_- = 2 + 4 = 6$$

A rule that can simplify the calculations here and serve as a check for arithmetic is that

$$T_+ + T_- = \frac{n(n + 1)}{2}$$

where n = the number of sample pairs. In our example, $n = 10$, so

$$T_+ + T_- = \frac{(10)(11)}{2} = 55$$

which means that $T_+ = 55 - T_- = 55 - 6 = 49$

The Wilcoxon Signed Rank Test for Small Samples (Paired) Once T_+ and T_- have been obtained, you can use the Wilcoxon signed rank test for testing hypotheses about the two population means.

The Wilcoxon Signed Rank Test for Small Samples (Paired)

Hypotheses:

H_0: $\mu_1 = \mu_2$

H_a: $\mu_1 \neq \mu_2$ (or $\mu_1 > \mu_2$ or $\mu_1 < \mu_2$)

Assumptions:

1. Each data pair is randomly selected.
2. The absolute values of the differences can be ranked.

Procedure:

1. Determine the n differences using each sample pair, where each difference is defined to be sample 1 − sample 2.
2. Assign a rank to the absolute value of each difference; define T_+ = sum of the ranks of the positive differences and T_- = sum of the ranks of the negative differences.

Table A-11 is used to define the rejection region for the following tests.

TWO-SIDED TEST	ONE-SIDED TEST	
$H_a: \mu_1 \neq \mu_2$	$H_a: \mu_1 > \mu_2$	$H_a: \mu_1 < \mu_2$
Using the two-sided value from Table A-11 on page 840, reject H_0 if T $\leq$ table value, where T $=$ minimum of T_+ and T_-.	Using the one-sided value from Table A-11, reject H_0 if $T_- \leq$ table value.	Using the one-sided value from Table A-11, reject H_0 if $T_+ \leq$ table value.

Example 19.6

Table 19.5 contains the sales results from ten cities before and after the six-month advertising campaign. Using $\alpha = .05$, are we able to conclude that there was a significant increase in sales after the advertising campaign?

Solution The hypotheses here can be stated as (A = after, B = before)

$$H_0: \mu_A \leq \mu_B$$

$$H_a: \mu_A > \mu_B$$

We refer to the "after" population as population 1 and the "before" population as population 2. This agrees with the difference column in Table 19.6 because our procedure assumes that each difference is sample 1 (A, here) − sample 2 (B).

The values of T_+ and T_- also are derived following Table 19.6, where

$$T_- = 6$$

and

$$T_+ = 49$$

The one-sided value in Table A-11 corresponding to $n = 10$, and $\alpha = .05$ is 11. Consequently, the test is to

Reject H_0 if $T_- \leq 11$

Because the value of T_- is smaller than 11, we reject H_0 and conclude that there is sufficient evidence of a sales increase after the advertising campaign. ●

The Wilcoxon Signed Rank Test for Large Samples (Paired) For samples consisting of $n > 15$ pairs, a large-sample approximation to the Wilcoxon test statistic can be used. An advantage to using this procedure is that p-values are much easier to determine. (A p-value is once again a measure of the strength of your conclusion.)

When using the large-sample procedure, we can define a test using either T_+ or T_-. The following hypothesis tests use T_+, the sum of the ranks for the positive differences. If the two population means are equal, then T_+ is approximately a normal random variable with mean

$$\mu_{T_+} = \frac{n(n + 1)}{4} \qquad (19\text{-}9)$$

and standard deviation

$$\sigma_{T_+} = \sqrt{\frac{n(n + 1)(2n + 1)}{24}} \tag{19-10}$$

The corresponding test statistic is

$$Z = \frac{T_+ - \mu_{T_+}}{\sigma_{T_+}} \tag{19-11}$$

The one- and two-sided large-sample procedures are summarized in the accompanying box.

The Wilcoxon Signed Rank Test for Large Samples (Paired)

Hypotheses:

$H_0: \mu_1 = \mu_2$

$H_a: \mu_1 \neq \mu_2$ (or $\mu_1 > \mu_2$ or $\mu_1 < \mu_2$)

Assumptions: Same as for small samples

Procedure: (1) and (2) are the same as for small samples. Each paired difference is defined to be sample 1 − sample 2.

TWO-SIDED TEST   **ONE-SIDED TEST**

$H_a: \mu_1 \neq \mu_2$ $H_a: \mu_1 > \mu_2$ $H_a: \mu_1 < \mu_2$

Reject H_0 if $|Z| > Z_{\alpha/2}$,   Reject H_0 if $Z > Z_\alpha$.   Reject H_0 if $Z < -Z_\alpha$.
where Z is defined as in
equation 19-11 and $Z_{\alpha/2}$
is the value from Table
A-4 having a right-tail
area of $\alpha/2$.

Example 19.7

The owner of Worldwide Travel Agency is interested in seeing whether her customers flew more miles in 1985 than in 1975. She randomly selects 20 customers who used her agency during 1975 *and* 1985, and she records the total number of passenger miles for each of the two years.

Customer	1975	1985	Customer	1975	1985
1	55	45	11	121	171
2	101	79	12	46	21
3	62	77	13	112	78
4	93	138	14	70	106
5	40	68	15	97	87
6	120	80	16	47	91
7	110	138	17	106	80
8	77	81	18	84	104
9	49	49	19	50	88
10	90	80	20	75	117

Use the Wilcoxon signed rank test to determine whether the owner's belief—that her customers flew more miles in 1985—is correct. Let $\alpha = .05$.

Solution If we let the 1975 population be population 1, then the correct hypotheses are

$$H_0: \mu_1 \geqslant \mu_2$$

$$H_a: \mu_1 < \mu_2$$

This agrees with Table 19.7, in which each difference is calculated using the 1975 value (sample 1) minus the 1985 value (sample 2). Because customer 9 had no change in the passenger miles for these 2 years, a difference of zero is the result, and so this customer is removed from the sample. This leaves $n = 19$ pairs in the sample.

Based on a significance level of $\alpha = .05$, the proper test is to

Reject H_0 if $Z < -1.645$

For a value of $n = 19$, the mean of T_+ (assuming $\mu_1 = \mu_2$) is

$$\mu_{T_+} = \frac{(19)(20)}{4} = 95$$

with a standard deviation of

$$\sigma_{T_+} = \sqrt{\frac{(19)(20)(39)}{24}} = 24.85$$

Table 19.7

Paired samples for example 19.7

Miles (thousands)		Difference:	Rank of		
1975	1985	1975–1985	Absolute Value	+ Ranks	− Ranks
55	45	10	3	3*	
101	79	22	7	7	
62	77	− 15	5(−)		5
93	138	− 45	18(−)		18
40	68	− 28	10.5(−)		10.5**
120	80	40	15	15	
110	138	− 28	10.5(−)		10.5**
77	81	− 4	1 (−)		1
[49	49	0	−	removed, so use $n = 19$ pairs]	
90	80	10	3	3*	
121	171	− 50	19(−)		19
46	21	25	8	8	
112	78	34	12	12	
70	106	− 36	13(−)		13
97	87	10	3	3*	
47	91	− 44	17(−)		17
106	80	26	9	9	
84	104	− 20	6(−)		6
50	88	− 38	14(−)		14
75	117	− 42	16(−)		16
				$T_+ = 60$	$T_- = 130$

*three-way tie; assigned rank = (2 + 3 + 4)/3 = 3.
**two-way tie; assigned rank = (10 + 11)/2 = 10.5.

Figure 19.5

p-value for example 19.7.

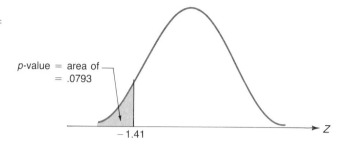

p-value = area of ⎯⎯
= .0793

-1.41

Z

Table 19.7 informs us that $T_+ = 60$, and so the value of the test statistic here is

$$Z^* = \frac{60 - 95}{24.85} = -1.41$$

This value is not less than -1.645, so there is insufficient evidence to conclude that her long-term customers flew more passenger miles in 1985 than in 1975.

The p-value for this test is obtained in the usual manner by finding, in this case, the area under a standard normal curve to the left of the calculated test statistic of $Z^* = -1.41$. According to Figure 19.5 and Table A-4, the p-value is .0793. Using our rule-of-thumb procedure from before, this p-value is neither large ($> .1$) nor small ($< .01$), but it *is* greater than $\alpha = .05$, which leads us to fail to reject H_0. ●

To use MINITAB for the Wilcoxon procedure, you begin by subtracting the two samples and then using the WTEST command on the differences, as illustrated in Figure 19.6. Note that the p-value in this figure is slightly different from our previous result because the MINITAB procedure includes a continuity adjustment (similar to that used in Chapter 7) and is slightly more accurate. If you have the MINITAB package available, use it to obtain more accurate p-values for this nonparametric test.

Figure 19.6

MINITAB commands for Wilcoxon signed rank test (example 19.7).

```
MTB > SET INTO C1
DATA> 55 101 62 93 40 120 110 77 49 90
DATA> 121 46 112 70 97 47 106 84 50 75
DATA> END
MTB > SET INTO C2
DATA> 45 79 77 138 68 80 138 81 49 80
DATA> 171 21 78 106 87 91 80 104 88 117
DATA> END
MTB > SUBTRACT C2 FROM C1 ,PUT INTO C3
MTB > WTEST USING C3;
SUBC> ALTER=-1.
```

Alternative:
1 for H_a: $\mu_1 > \mu_2$
-1 for H_a: $\mu_1 < \mu_2$
omit for H_a: $\mu_1 \neq \mu_2$

```
TEST OF MEDIAN = 0.00          VERSUS MEDIAN L.T. 0.00

                     N FOR    WILCOXON                  ESTIMATED
              N      TEST     STATISTIC   P-VALUE       MEDIAN
C3            20     19       60.0        0.083         -9.000
                                ↑
                               T_+
```

Exercises

19.11 What assumptions need to be made about the type and distribution of the data when the Mann–Whitney test is used?

19.12 If 15 observations are randomly selected from each of two populations and the sum of the ranks for the sample from population 1 (T_1) is 230, what is the sum of the ranks (T_2) for the sample from population 2?

19.13 Two groups of randomly selected students are given an aptitude test on understanding the financial markets. The first group has eight students, selected from second-semester freshmen, and the sum of the ranks (T_1) of these eight students is 65. If the second group has nine students selected from first-semester freshmen, test the null hypothesis that the aptitude of the second-semester freshmen is higher than the aptitude of the first-semester freshmen on understanding the financial markets. Use a 5% significance level.

19.14 A real estate agent claims that the homes in two neighborhoods have the same average value. A random sample from neighborhood A contains the following dollar values: 85,000, 70,000, 74,000, 69,000, 88,000, 89,000. A random sample from neighborhood B consists of the following values: 71,000, 64,000, 68,000, 73,000, 81,000, 69,000, 72,000. Test the alternative hypothesis that the average value of homes in neighborhood B is less than the average value of homes in neighborhood A. Use a 10% significance level.

19.15 An engineer is proposing a new manufacturing process to increase the tensile strength of a certain wire. Eleven samples of wire manufactured under the proposed process are collected, and 14 samples are collected from wire manufactured under the existing process. Use the following data and a 10% significance level, test the hypothesis that there is greater tensile strength in the proposed technique.

Proposed technique (psi)	Existing technique (psi)
1.4	1.2
2.1	1.6
1.8	1.7
1.7	1.7
1.6	2.0
1.9	1.3
1.4	1.4
2.2	1.8
2.0	1.7
1.9	2.0
2.0	1.8
	1.9
	1.6
	2.1

19.16 The head lawyer of the Brown and Smith firm would like to know whether there is a difference in the number of errors made by the two secretaries employed in the firm. Five randomly selected documents are given to secretary A to type, and five are given to secretary B. The number of errors per document is shown in the following table. Using a 5% level of significance, test the hypothesis that there is no difference in the number of errors made by each secretary.

Secretary A	Secretary B
3	2
5	0
4	4
2	3
0	1

19.17 A nursery is experimenting with two blends of fertilizer for fertilizing lawns in a certain area. Twenty-four randomly selected patches of grass are selected for experimenting with the fertilizer. Twelve patches are randomly assigned to fertilizer A and another 12 patches are randomly assigned to fertilizer B. The increase in the height of the grass after 2 weeks is given in the following table. Using a 10% level of significance, test the hypothesis that fertilizer B is more effective than fertilizer A.

Fertilizer A	Fertilizer B
1.2	1.0
0.9	1.1
1.3	1.0
0.5	0.9
0.3	0.7
0.9	0.8
0.8	1.2
1.4	1.3
0.7	0.8
0.9	1.0
0.8	0.8
0.7	1.1

19.18 Two samples of light bulbs are taken from the brands Everglo and Britelite. The following table gives the life of the bulbs for the collected sample. At the 1% level, is there sufficient evidence to indicate that Britelite bulbs last longer than do Everglo bulbs?

Everglo (hours)	Britelite (hours)
1134	1405
1255	1251
1313	1106
1012	1384
1265	1193
1375	1208
1102	1110
1107	1290
1095	1210
1401	1198
1109	1203
1150	1295
	1102
	1185

19.19 An economist wishes to compare the percent increase in personal income for two suburbs of Chicago. Using the data in the following table, test at the 5% significance level the hypothesis that there is no difference in the percent increase in personal income.

Suburb A (%)	Suburb B (%)
5.2	2.6
3.1	9.7
10.6	1.2
11.4	1.4
1.2	5.0
0.0	9.8
1.3	11.3
8.4	8.1
9.1	4.2
11.3	1.6
12.1	2.7
9.8	7.9

19.20 A supermarket manager was curious as to which of the two vending machines located at opposite ends of the store was used the most during peak hours. On 12 randomly selected days during the peak hours, the number of users were counted for machine A. On another randomly selected 12 days during the peak hours, the number of users were counted for machine B. From the following data, test at the 5% level of significance the hypothesis that there is no difference in the use of the two vending machines.

Vending Machine A	Vending Machine B
10	9
12	11
13	14
11	10
10	13
15	14
13	9
19	8
11	12
10	13
15	14
12	11

19.21 At the 5% significance level, test the hypothesis that there is no significant difference in the time for machine 1 and machine 2 to produce an item in exercise 10.34 on page 310, using the Mann–Whitney test. Compare to the results obtained using the t test.

19.22 For the data in exercise 10.40 on page 317, use the Mann–Whitney test in testing the null hypothesis that the means of the two parent populations are equal. Use a significance level of .05. When would you prefer the Mann–Whitney test to the t test?

19.23 What assumption needs to be made about the sample data used in the Wilcoxon signed rank test? What assumption needs to be made about the distributions of the population?

19.24 From 12 paired observations, it is found that by ranking the magnitude of the differences of the observations in each pair, T_+ (the sum of the ranks of the positive differences) is 27. Using a .05 significance level, can it be concluded that there is a difference in the mean of the two populations?

19.25 A psychologist conducts a seminar to increase a person's self-esteem. A before-and-after test that measures each person's self-esteem is given to nine individuals. Using the following scores and a 5% significance level, is there evidence to conclude that the scores after the seminar are greater than the scores before the seminar?

Before	After
70	74
72	88
75	71
61	62
82	89
55	58
43	41
51	63
84	80

19.26 An insurance company believes that employees who have a college degree when hired progress faster in the company than those who do not. Pairs of employees are randomly selected; each pair consists of two people hired at the same time, one person with a college degree and the other without a college degree. The percent increase in pay for the employees after 3 years is recorded below. At the 10% level of significance, can you conclude that employees who have a college degree when hired progress faster than those who do not?

Without College Degree (%)	With College Degree (%)
10	13
9	10
8	6
13	13
14	18
7	10
12	11
11	15
16	20
12	13
9	8
18	16
9	12
15	17
10	9
11	13
10	9

19.27 Seven randomly selected faculty members were asked to evaluate two research project proposals on a scale from 0 to 10, with a higher score indicating a more acceptable proposal. The scores follow. Using a 5% significance level, can you conclude that the proposal for research project 2 is more acceptable than the proposal for research project 1?

Research Project 1	Research Project 2
5	7
3	5
6	9
7	6
8	9
4	6
7	10

19.28 Martin's Weight Control Center claims that if a woman maintains her same diet but attends aerobic classes three times per week, she will definitely lose weight. Seventeen women who attended the program for three months were randomly selected. From the table, which gives the participants' weights before and after, test the claim of Martin's Weight Control Center. Use a 5% significance level.

Before	After	Before	After
119	117	110	114
131	130	130	132
135	125	118	110
125	121	114	108
140	143	122	114
119	114	125	111
148	140	120	118
152	138	112	113
180	171		

19.29 The manager of a calculator-assembly plant wanted to know whether machine operators with little experience produced more defective calculators than did the experienced machine operators. The number of defective calculators produced by 20 randomly selected experienced machine operators in 1 week was recorded. Then, these 20 experienced operators were replaced by inexperienced machine operators and the number of defective calculators produced at these positions was recorded for 1 week. If the operators at each position can be considered to be a pair, use the Wilcoxon test to test that the experienced operators produced fewer defective calculators. Use a 5% significance level.

Experienced Employees	Inexperienced Employees	Experienced Employees	Inexperienced Employees
10	14	13	19
13	14	18	21
15	12	19	18
18	25	10	13
14	13	19	26
10	15	25	26
30	21	15	17
14	18	21	20
22	23	20	28
15	13	12	19

19.30 The manager of an insurance company sent ten randomly selected salespeople to a sales-motivation lecture given by several top selling insurance salespeople. The manager recorded the dollar amount (in hundreds of thousands) of insurance sold by the ten salespeople during the 4 months prior to attending the lecture and the 4 months after the lecture. At the 5% significance level, is there evidence to suggest that the sales-motivation lecture improved sales?

Before Lecture	After Lecture
1.2	1.9
1.8	3.4
3.8	3.1
1.9	4.5
5.8	5.0
6.2	6.3
1.5	1.4
3.3	4.9
2.4	3.5
3.1	3.0

19.31 A paired-difference experiment yielded a value of 280 for the sum of the ranks of the positive differences from 30 observations. Using a 5% significance level, is there evidence to suggest that there is a difference in the mean of the two populations?

19.32 A large discount department-store chain decided to rearrange the layout of its merchandise at six of its stores to encourage customers to buy more on impulse. Sales from the 6 months prior to the rearrangement and sales from the 6 months after the rearrangement are given below. Using a 5% significance level, can it be concluded that there is an increase in sales after the rearrangement.

Sales Before the Rearrangement ($\times$ \$100,000)	Sales After the Rearrangement ($\times$ \$100,000)
3.4	3.9
2.8	2.9
4.1	4.0
3.6	3.8
4.8	5.6
5.1	5.4

19.33 The following values are the differences from 17 pairs of observations. At the 10% level, test that there is no difference in the means of the two populations.

-1.1, -2.3, 4.5, 1.6, 2.3, -4.3, 1.9, -2.6, 1.8, 1.6, -2.7, 1.8, 2.1, -3.8, -1.0, 1.4, 2.5

19.34 For exercise 10.47 on page 324, test at the 5% significance level that the blood pressure is less after the drug is administered. Use the Wilcoxon signed rank test. Compare the results using the paired t test and a 5% significance level.

19.35 In exercise 10.50, use the Wilcoxon signed rank test to test the hypothesis that there is no difference in the weekly sales of the two restaurants. Use a 5% significance level. When would you prefer the Wilcoxon test to the paired t test?

19.3

Comparing More Than Two Populations: The Kruskal–Wallis Test

When comparing the means of more than two populations, a popular technique is the ANOVA procedure discussed in Chapter 12. The assumptions behind this technique include that you are dealing with normally distributed populations; the F test used in the ANOVA table is invalid unless all of the populations are nearly normally distributed.

The nonparametric counterpart to the one-way ANOVA method is the **Kruskal–Wallis test**. It is named after W. H. Kruskal and W. A. Wallis, who published their results in 1952. This test, like many other nonparametric procedures, is relatively young, unlike most of the parametric hypothesis tests, which were developed much earlier. The assumption of normal populations is *not necessary* for the Kruskal–Wallis test, which makes it an ideal technique for samples exhibiting a nonsymmetric (skewed) pattern. The test also is useful when the data consist of rankings within each sample.

The Kruskal–Wallis test is actually an extension of the Mann–Whitney U test discussed earlier for *two* independent samples. Both procedures require that the sample values have a measurement scale that is at least ordinal, which means that each sample can be ranked from smallest to largest.

The hypotheses for this situation can be written in terms of the population means or medians; once again, little distinction is made between these two parameters. The hypotheses are the same as they are for the ANOVA procedure:

H_0: $\mu_1 = \mu_2 = \ldots = \mu_k$

H_a: at least two of the μ's are different

Procedure You first obtain random samples of size $n_1, n_2, \ldots, n_k$ from each of the k populations. The total sample size is $n = n_1 + n_2 + \ldots + n_k$. As with the Mann–Whitney procedure, you next pool the samples and arrange them in order, assigning a rank to each. For ties, you assign the average rank to the tied positions.

Let T_i = the total of the ranks from the ith sample. The Kruskal–Wallis test statistic (KW) is

$$KW = \frac{12}{n(n+1)} \sum_{i=1}^{k} \frac{T_i^2}{n_i} - 3(n+1) \qquad (19\text{-}12)$$

The distribution of the KW statistic is approximately chi-square with $k - 1$ degrees of freedom (df). This approximation is good even if the sample sizes are small. To test H_0 versus H_a, the procedure will be to

Reject H_0 if KW is "large"

that is, if KW is in the right tail of the chi-square curve. This right-tail critical value is obtained from Table A-6, using a significance level = α and $df = k - 1$.

> ### The Kruskal–Wallis Test
>
> Hypotheses:
>
> H_0: $\mu_1 = \mu_2 = \ldots = \mu_k$
>
> H_a: the k means are not all equal
>
> where the μ's represent the means, or medians, of the k populations.
>
> Assumptions:
>
> **1.** Random samples are obtained from each of the k populations.
> **2.** The individual samples are obtained independently.
> **3.** Values within each sample can be ranked.
>
> Procedure: The individual samples are pooled and then ranked from smallest to largest. Letting T_i = the sum of the ranks of the ith sample, the KW statistic is determined using equation 19-12.
>   The null hypothesis, H_0, is rejected if
>
> $$KW > \chi^2_{\alpha, df}$$
>
> where $\chi^2_{\alpha, df}$ is the value from Table A-6 corresponding to $df = k - 1$, with a right-tail area = α.

Example 19.8

Drexton Industries has a number of different brands of copying machines at their main facility. A critical factor in the attractiveness of each brand is the amount of time that a machine is not working and is waiting for repair (down time). Management requested a study to be made on four different brands of machines to determine whether there is a difference in the amount of down time for these brands. Data were collected by finding the total down time per month for 20 randomly selected months. In this way, the down times for five randomly selected months were obtained for each of the four brands of machine. These results are shown in Table 19.8.

   Do these data indicate a difference in the amount of down time for the four brands? Use $\alpha = .05$.

Solution There are $k = 4$ populations here, so we need the $\chi^2_{.05, 3}$ value from Table A-6. Based on this value, the testing procedure is to

   Reject H_0 if $KW > \chi^2_{.05, 3} = 7.81$

Table 19.8

Amount of down time for copying machines (example 19.8)

Brand 1	Rank	Brand 2	Rank	Brand 3	Rand	Brand 4	Rank
28	12	5	1	10	3	45	18
41	17	16	6	8	2	30	13
34	15	20	8	18	7	49	19
52	20	24	9	14	4	32	14
25	10	15	5	26	11	36	16
	$T_1 = 74$		$T_2 = 29$		$T_3 = 27$		$T_4 = 80$

Figure 19.7

p-value for KW statistic; χ^2 curve with 3 df (example 19.8).

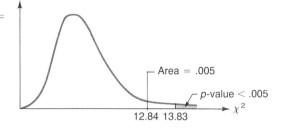

Area = .005

p-value $< .005$

χ^2

12.84 13.83

Figure 19.8

MINITAB procedure for Kruskal–Wallis test (example 19.8).

```
MTB > SET INTO C1
DATA> 28 41 34 52 25 5 16 20 24 15
DATA> 10 8 18 14 26 45 30 49 32 36
DATA> END
MTB > SET INTO C2
DATA> 1 1 1 1 1 2 2 2 2 2 3 3 3 3 3 4 4 4 4 4
DATA> END
MTB > KRUSKAL-WALLIS USING DATA IN C1,LEVELS IN C2

    LEVEL      NOBS     MEDIAN    AVE. RANK    Z VALUE
      1          5       34.00       14.8        1.88
      2          5       16.00        5.8       -2.05
      3          5       14.00        5.4       -2.23
      4          5       36.00       16.0        2.40
    OVERALL     20                   10.5
```

H = 13.83 $\longleftarrow$ KW

From Table 19.8, we are able to compute the value of the KW statistic using the ranks of the observations in the pooled sample

$$KW = \frac{12}{(20)(21)} \left[\frac{74^2}{5} + \frac{29^2}{5} + \frac{27^2}{5} + \frac{80^2}{5} \right] - 3(21)$$
$$= 13.83$$

As a check of your calculations at this point, make sure the ranks sum to $n(n + 1)/2$. For this example, $n =$ total number of observations $= 20$, and so the total of the ranks should be $(20)(21)/2 = 210$; here, $74 + 29 + 27 + 80 = 210$.

The calculated KW value exceeds 7.81, and so our conclusion is that there *is* a difference in average down time among the four brands. From the small values of T_2 and T_3, it appears that these two brands have much less down time and are superior in this respect to brands 1 and 4.

Finally, the p-value here is $< .005$, indicating a very strong conclusion. In other words, these data indicate a clear difference among the four brands. This p-value is illustrated in Figure 19.7. ●

The Kruskal–Wallis test statistic is computed using MINITAB in Figure 19.8. Notice that the down-time values are stored in column C1, whereas column C2 contains the sample number of each observation (1, 2, 3, or 4). The value of the Kruskal–Wallis statistic is called H, and agrees with the previous result.

Exercises

19.36 Samples of nine observations were taken from each of three populations, making a total of 27 observations. When the observations were pooled and then ranked from smallest to largest, the sum of the ranks for the first, second, and third samples were 120, 148, and 110, respectively.

At a significance level of .05, do the data indicate a difference in mean value of the three populations?

19.37 Ron, Ted, and James are three sales representatives covering three separate territories for a company that sells farm equipment at the wholesale level. To test the hypothesis that there is no difference in the mean monthly commission of the three salespeople, 8 months were chosen at random for each and their commissions were recorded in thousand-dollar units. Use the Kruskal–Wallis test on the data to test this hypothesis. Use a 1% significance level.

Month	Ron	Ted	James	Month	Ron	Ted	James
1	2.3	2.8	2.0	5	4.6	1.7	4.4
2	2.1	2.9	1.9	6	3.8	3.4	2.2
3	1.5	3.1	2.6	7	3.1	2.3	3.8
4	2.3	1.8	3.9	8	2.6	2.1	2.5

19.38 The following table lists observations from a sample of four populations. Is there reason to believe that the four populations have different means? Use a 1% significance level.

Population 1	Population 2	Population 3	Population 4
101	104	104	105
110	99	102	110
120	86	100	120
105	105	111	121
100	110	103	127
107	120	102	118
106	114		112
	110		

19.39 A survey was taken of the starting salaries of students who had completed a degree in business administration at either Oceanspray College, Stanton University, or Hillside College. Do the following data indicate, at the .05 level, a difference in the mean starting salaries of students with a degree in business administration from one of the three schools?

Oceanspray College	Stanton University	Hillside College
27,100	24,500	22,500
25,300	27,250	23,000
22,450	26,700	26,000
26.800	27,000	25,750
25,100	26,500	21,630
21,350	22,300	22,500
22,500	27,600	23,650
25,000	28,150	24,180
		22,750

19.40 Four machines are used to package 16-ounce bags of puffed wheat. Each machine is designed to package the bags so that the average bag has 16 ounces of cereal in it. From the data, in which samples of eight bags were randomly selected from each machine, is there an indication that the mean amount of puffed wheat packaged is not the same for all four machines? Use a .05 significance level.

Machine 1	Machine 2	Machine 3	Machine 4
15.9	16.1	15.8	16.4
15.8	16.3	15.9	16.5
16.0	16.0	16.0	16.0
15.7	15.9	16.1	16.1
16.1	16.4	16.0	16.4
16.2	15.8	16.4	16.3
15.6	16.2	16.1	16.1
15.8	16.1	15.7	16.4

19.41 Thirty new employees were selected to test two training programs. Ten of them (group A) were randomly selected for a self-paced training program. Another ten (group B) were randomly selected for a classroom training program. The remaining ten employees (group C) were not given any training. After the completion of the experiment, the manager evaluated the 30 employees on their productivity over a 2-week span. The following ranks were given by the manager, with the highest rankings being given to those who were not productive.

Program A	Program B	Program C
6	5	1
22	21	10
25	15	11
26	4	13
20	8	2
30	12	3
16	18	7
23	24	14
28	27	17
9	29	19

From the data, is there a significant difference in the productivity of the three groups? Use a .05 significance level.

19.42 Joe's Delicatessen sells cheese sandwiches, ham sandwiches, and roast-beef sandwiches. Joe would like to know if there is a significant difference in the number of sandwiches of each type sold. On 30 randomly selected days, the following number of sandwiches of each type were sold. Ten days were therefore selected for each type of sandwich sold. Is there a significant difference at the 10% level?

Cheese	Ham	Roast Beef	Cheese	Ham	Roast Beef
27	30	33	26	22	34
24	21	25	25	24	31
23	20	23	24	21	30
29	31	22	25	22	30
21	32	27	28	20	27

19.43 The management of a company that markets Soft and Fresh Detergent would like to increase sales of detergent by including a free drinking glass in the box, including a coupon worth 50 cents toward the next purchase, or using a colorful see-through plastic container for the detergent. Ten stores in different cities were randomly selected to market the detergent in one of the three ways, providing a total of 30 stores in the sample. The number of boxes sold over a 1-month period at the stores using each of the three marketing strategies follows. Do the data indicate a difference in the mean number of boxes sold for each of the marketing strategies? Use a 5% significance level.

Free Glass	Coupon	See-through Plastic Container
350	320	374
310	315	371
250	300	332
380	315	361
290	390	356
270	311	349
340	318	331
310	330	322
290	340	368
375	314	351

19.44 The number of hours it takes three workers to complete a task is given in the following table. The task is assigned to each worker four times. Do the data indicate a significant difference in the time it takes each worker to complete the task? Use a significance level of .05.

Worker 1	Worker 2	Worker 3
3.1	3.4	3.5
3.4	3.3	3.2
3.0	3.4	3.3
3.1	3.2	3.1

19.45 The number of cars passing each of three different intersections in Crossroads City between 5:00 P.M. and 5:30 P.M. is given in the following table for randomly selected days. Fifteen days were randomly selected and then the amount of traffic was recorded for 5 of the 15 days at each intersection. Test the null hypothesis that there is no difference in the amount of traffic at each intersection between 5:00 P.M. and 5:30 P.M. Use a 10% significance level.

Intersection 1	Intersection 2	Intersection 3
440	480	433
420	392	406
530	386	427
401	456	338
454	427	397

19.46 A manager believes that the higher-salaried employees in a certain company are more satisfied with their job than are the lower-salaried employees. A sample of ten employees from each of the salary levels indicated by the following table was taken. Is there a significant difference in the satisfaction level, measured on a scale of 1 to 10 (10 being a perfectly satisfied employee), for the three groups? Use a significance level of 5%.

$25,000 to $40,000	$40,001 to $60,000	Over $60,000	$25,000 to $40,000	$40,001 to $60,000	Over $60,000
4	7	8	9	3	9
3	8	7	1	4	10
7	6	6	8	9	3
6	7	7	7	6	8
5	9	5	6	7	7

19.47 For the data in exercise 12.1, use the Kruskal–Wallis test statistic to test that there is no difference in the amount of wear on three different designs of rubber soles. Use a significance level of .05. Compare with the results obtained from the ANOVA procedure.

19.48 In exercise 12.7, can you conclude that there is a significant difference in the monthly sales of the three salespeople using the Kruskal–Wallis test statistic? Use a 5% significance level. When would you prefer the Kruskal–Wallis test to the usual ANOVA procedure?

19.4

A Measure of Association: Spearman's Rank Correlation

Whenever you encounter data describing two variables (say, X and Y), one measure of interest is the degree of **association** between X and Y. Are large values of X associated with large values of Y (a *positive* relationship)? Or do you observe smaller values of Y with larger values of X (a *negative* relationship)? Another possibility is that no relationship is observed between these two variables.

Consider the following data, in which a sample of ten families is used to determine the relationship (if any) that exists between X = market value of the family's home and Y = their total indebtedness (excluding the home mortgage; in thousands of dollars). Included in Y are any charge accounts, automobile loans, and other current liabilities.

	X	**Y**
Family	**(market value of home)**	**(total indebtedness)**
1	85	12
2	147	27
3	340	45
4	94	10
5	120	17
6	105	4
7	135	20
8	162	25
9	480	35
10	88	14

The president of Metro Savings and Loan believes that larger home values are associated with larger indebtedness; that is, a positive relationship exists between these two variables. This is confirmed in the scatter plot contained in Figure 19.9.

One method of measuring the association between two variables is the Pearson product moment correlation, r, introduced in Chapters 4 and 14. The equation used to determine this measure is

$$r = \frac{\Sigma xy - (\Sigma x)(\Sigma y)/n}{\sqrt{\Sigma x^2 - (\Sigma x)^2/n} \, \sqrt{\Sigma y^2 - (\Sigma y)^2/n}} \tag{19-13}$$

where n represents the number of observations (pairs).

The value of r, often called the *sample correlation coefficient,* measures the amount of linearity that exists between the sample values of X and Y. It is used to measure ρ (rho), the *population* correlation coefficient. The value of ρ can be thought of as the correlation between *all* possible X, Y pairs, not just those contained in the sample.

In the previous discussions, a significant relationship between X and Y existed if we were able to reject H_0: $\rho = 0$. The test statistic here was a t statistic, so this test assumes a normal distribution for the X, Y variables.

Figure 19.9

MINITAB scatter plot of home value versus debt.

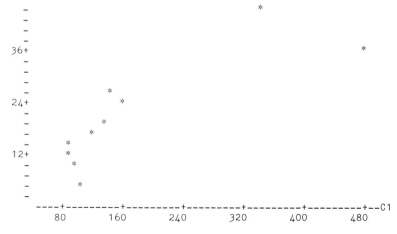

```
MTB > SET INTO C1
DATA> 85 147 340 94 120 105 135 162 480 88
DATA> END
MTB > SET INTO C2
DATA> 12 27 45 10 17 4 20 25 35 14
DATA> END
MTB > PLOT Y IN C2 VS X IN C1
```

An alternative to this procedure is a measure of association derived from the *ranks* of the X and Y variables. This nonparametric measure does *not* assume a normal distribution; it assumes only that the values within the X and Y samples can be ranked. For data such as the home price versus debt values, each of the X and Y values also are replaced by their ranks. If we use these ranks in place of the actual data in equation 19-13, we obtain another measure of association, called the **Spearman rank correlation coefficient, r_s:**

$$r_s = \frac{\Sigma R(x)R(y) - [\Sigma R(x)][\Sigma R(y)]/n}{\sqrt{\Sigma R^2(x) - [\Sigma R(x)]^2/n} \sqrt{\Sigma R^2(y) - [\Sigma R(y)]^2/n}} \qquad (19\text{-}14)$$

where $R(x) = $ rank of the X observation, and $R(y) = $ rank of the Y observation.

If there are no ties, a second formula provides a much easier method of finding r_s. If there are a few ties, this still serves as a very good approximation to r_s. The shortcut method of finding r_s is

$$r_s = 1 - \frac{6\Sigma d^2}{n(n^2 - 1)} \qquad (19\text{-}15)$$

where, for each observation, d is the difference between the X and Y ranks; that is, $d = R(x) - R(y)$.

The Pearson product moment correlation, r, measures the amount of the *linear* relationship between X and Y and ranges from -1 to 1. Also, $r = 1$ or -1 only if all of the points fall exactly on a straight line. Similarly, the range for the Spearman rank correlation is

$$-1 \leq r_s \leq 1$$

One difference here is that r_s will equal 1 provided Y increases every time X does in the sample observations. This rate of increase need not be linear. This is illustrated in Figure 19.10 for a sample of five observations that do not lie on a straight line. Consequently, r is less than one but, as the following table shows, $r_s = 1$.

X	Rank R(X)	Y	Rank R(Y)	Difference of Ranks (d)	d^2
3	1	4	1	$1 - 1 = 0$	0
5	2	7	2	$2 - 2 = 0$	0
7	3	8	3	$3 - 3 = 0$	0
9	4	10	4	$4 - 4 = 0$	0
11	5	16	5	$5 - 5 = 0$	0
				$\Sigma d^2 =$	0

You can also see this in Figure 19.10, where the pairwise ranks *are* perfectly linear, which is why $r_s = 1$.

$$r_s = 1 - \frac{6\Sigma d^2}{n(n^2 - 1)}$$

$$= 1 - \frac{(6)(0)}{(5)(24)} = 1$$

Figure 19.10

Measure of association. Pearson product moment correlation, r, and Spearman rank correlation, r_s.

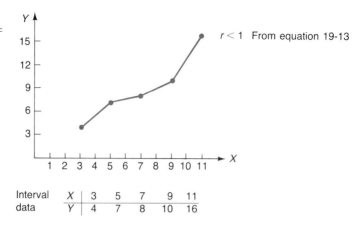

Interval data	X	3	5	7	9	11
	Y	4	7	8	10	16

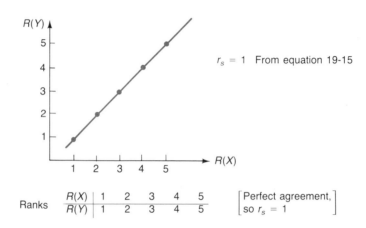

Ranks	R(X)	1	2	3	4	5
	R(Y)	1	2	3	4	5

$$\begin{bmatrix} \text{Perfect agreement,} \\ \text{so } r_s = 1 \end{bmatrix}$$

When it is possible to calculate both, the values of r and r_s are generally not the same, although they are usually quite close. They will have the same sign. A positive value indicates a *positive* relationship between the two variables. Similarly, if r_s and r are negative, then a *negative* relationship exists (Y decreases as X increases). If the values of r and r_s are nearly the same, this usually indicates high linearity between the two variables.

As we discussed earlier, nonparametric methods are well suited for situations in which (1) the data are *ordinal* or (2) the distribution of the population(s) from which the data are obtained is suspected to be nonnormal. When using data of the ordinal type, it is no longer appropriate to use the Pearson coefficient of correlation (r) for performing a t test to determine whether a significant linear relationship exists. This procedure requires interval or ratio data.

Similarly, when dealing with nonnormal populations, the t test is no longer valid because the normality assumption is a vital part of this procedure.

In Chapter 4 (many moons ago), when we first introduced rank correlation, we examined a situation in which Mr. Roberts and Mr. Clauson each evaluated eight brands of television sets by inspecting eight different sets. After inspecting the sets, rather than assigning each of them a "score" of some kind, they merely ranked them from 1 (best) to 8 (worst). The results were

Brand	X (Roberts)	Y (Clauson)	Difference
A	1	2	−1
B	4	3	1
C	2	1	1
D	6	6	0
E	8	7	1
F	3	5	−2
G	7	8	−1
H	5	4	1

Notice that each set of rankings consists of ordinal data because the only meaningful information contained within these values is the *order*, not the difference between them. For example, Mr. Robert's three favorite brands were brands A (first), C (second), and F (third). We have no way of knowing whether brand A was "much" better than brand C or only "slightly" better; the same is true for brand C versus brand F. Consequently, there is no way of knowing if the "distances" between ranks 1 and 2 and between ranks 2 and 3 are the same, and so these differences are meaningless.

A measure of how well the two people agree is the Spearman rank correlation, r_s. The larger this value is, the more agreement there is between the two sets of rankings. A value of $r_s = 1$ would indicate perfect agreement, whereas perfect disagreement would result in a value of $r_s = -1$. Here the rank correlation is

$$r_s = 1 - \frac{6\Sigma d^2}{n(n^2 - 1)}$$

$$= 1 - \frac{6[(-1)^2 + (1)^2 + \ldots + (-1)^2 + (1)^2]}{8(64 - 1)}$$

$$= 1 - \frac{(6)(10)}{(8)(63)} = .881$$

This value appears to be quite large, although we will need a formal testing procedure to determine whether there is significant agreement between the two testers.

Example 19.9

Refer to the table for the home values and debt data. The president of Metro Savings and Loan would like a measure of association between these two variables. Based on past experience, he is reluctant to assume that the home values are normally distributed; they usually are skewed right. There generally are enough homes with an extremely large market value (two, here) to produce a skewed distribution (see Figure 19.9). He asks you to use the Spearman measure of correlation and determine the value of r_s.

Solution The ranks are calculated as follows:

Family	X	Rank R(X)	Y	Rank R(Y)	Difference (d)	d^2
1	85	(1)	12	(3)	−2	4
2	147	(7)	27	(8)	−1	1
3	340	(9)	45	(10)	−1	1
4	94	(3)	10	(2)	1	1
5	120	(5)	17	(5)	0	0
6	105	(4)	4	(1)	3	9
7	135	(6)	20	(6)	0	0
8	162	(8)	25	(7)	1	1
9	480	(10)	35	(9)	1	1
10	88	(2)	14	(4)	−2	4

$$\Sigma d^2 = 22$$

Figure 19.11

MINITAB procedure for finding the Spearman rank correlation (example 19.9).

```
MTB > SET INTO C1
DATA> 85 147 340 94 120 105 135 162 480 88
DATA> END
MTB > SET INTO C2
DATA> 12 27 45 10 17 4 20 25 35 14
DATA> END
MTB > RANK C1,PUT INTO C11
MTB > RANK C2,PUT INTO C12
MTB > CORRELATION BETWEEN C11 AND C12          $r_s$

Correlation of C11 and C12 = 0.867
```

Then,

$$r_s = 1 - \frac{(6)(22)}{(10)(99)} = .867$$

Based on this value, it appears that a significant positive relationship exists between the market value of a family's home and their total debts.

To determine whether a derived value of r_s is "large enough" to support a conclusion, as in example 19.9, we will develop a test of hypothesis that uses the rank correlation, r_s, as the test statistic.

To obtain a computer solution for Spearman's rank correlation, you ask MINITAB to rank the X and Y values and to compute r for the ranks. Recall that equation 19-15 was a shortcut for determining the rank correlation. This is illustrated in Figure 19.11, where, as before, $r_s = .867$.

A Test of Hypothesis Using the Rank Correlation

In Chapter 4, we introduced a table of significant values of r_s, with a vague disclaimer that there was a 5% chance of concluding that there was a significant relationship between these two variables when, in fact, there was not. We were really performing a test of hypothesis using a significance level of $\alpha = .05$.

In Chapter 14, we used the Pearson correlation coefficient, r, to determine whether a linear relationship existed between two variables, X and Y. This relationship could be either positive (Y increases as X increases) or negative (Y decreases as X increases). When using Spearman's rank correlation, r_s, we drop the "linear" term in the hypotheses and test

H_0: no association exists between the X and Y variables

H_a: association does exist between the X and Y variables

You can also perform one-sided tests, as summarized in the accompanying box. In this way, you can test for a significant positive or negative relationship between the two variables.

The Spearman Test for Rank Correlation		
TWO-SIDED TEST	**ONE-SIDED TEST**	
H_0: no association exists between X and Y	H_0: no association exists between X and Y	H_0: no association exists between X and Y
H_a: association does exist between X and Y	H_a: a positive relationship exists between X and Y	H_a: a negative relationship exists between X and Y

Assumption: Sample values for each variable can be ranked.		
Procedure: Determine the value from Table A-12 using the sample size, n, and the column corresponding to $\alpha/2$.	Use the column in Table A-12 corresponding to α.	Use the column in Table A-12 corresponding to α.
Reject H_0 if $|r_s| >$ (table value)	Reject H_0 if $r_s >$ (table value)	Reject H_0 if $r_s <$ (table value)

Example 19.10   In the television-ranking example, is there sufficient evidence to indicate that there was general agreement between the rankings made by Mr. Roberts and those made by Mr. Clauson? Use $\alpha = .05$.

Solution   The appropriate hypotheses here are

H_0: no association exists between the two ranks

H_a: a positive association exists between the two ranks

According to Table A-12, using $\alpha = .05$ and $n = 8$, the testing procedure is to

Reject H_0 if $r_s > .643$

Because the computed value of r_s is .881 (as we derived previously), we reject H_0 and conclude that there *was* significant agreement between the two sets of rankings.

The p-value for this result can be obtained by looking across the row in Table A-12 corresponding to $n = 8$. Here we find that .881 corresponds to $\alpha = .005$. Consequently, the p-value here is .005.   ●

Example 19.11   The president of Metro Savings and Loan is attempting to demonstrate that a positive relationship exists between $X =$ market value of a family's home and $Y =$ their total indebtedness (excluding the home mortgage). Using the results of Example 19.9, is there sufficient evidence of a positive relationship between these two variables? Use $\alpha = .05$.

Solution   In example 19.9, the sample rank correlation was found to be $r_s = .867$. Using Table A-12 for $\alpha = .05$ and $n = 10$, we test

H_0: no association exists between the home market value and total indebtedness

H_a: a positive relationship exists

using

Reject H_0 if $r_s > .564$

The computed value of .867 exceeds the table value, so we reject H_0 and conclude that there *is* a tendency for larger values of $X =$ home value and $Y =$ family indebtedness to be paired together. This large value of r_s also is off the right side of Table A-12, indicating that for this test the p-value is $< .005$. This extremely small value is strong evidence of a positive relationship between these two variables.   ●

Exercises

19.49 A market stand sells watermelons each week at different prices, depending on the supply of watermelons. Calculate the Pearson product moment correlation and the Spearman rank correlation of the quantity sold and the price.

Price	Quantity Sold
1.80	53
2.00	45
1.50	60
1.25	75
1.75	50
2.25	48
2.50	46
2.10	46
1.50	70
1.75	65
1.90	47

19.50 The rank correlation coefficient between 15 pairs of observations is 0.31. Using a significance level of .05, test the null hypothesis that there is no positive relationship between the two variables sampled.

19.51 The following data represent the high temperature of the day (°F) and the number of sno-cones sold at Dairy Freeze. Using a nonparametric procedure and a 5% significance level, test the hypothesis that there is a positive relationship between the two variables.

Daily High Temperature	Number of Sno-cones Sold
90	49
91	48
86	40
85	38
84	40
93	55
92	51
90	52
88	46

19.52 A factory wants to know what the relationship is between the age of its machines and the number of breakdowns per year. Ten machines were selected at random and the following table was constructed. Using the Spearman test for rank correlation, is there a relationship between the age of the machine and the number of breakdowns per year? Use a 10% significance level.

Age (years)	Breakdowns per Year
2	6
4	10
5	12
8	24
6	17
7	20
5	16
6	15
3	10
4	12

19.53 A physician would like to know the relationship between a person's diastolic blood pressure and the average number of hours spent exercising each week. Twenty people of age 30 years were selected randomly. Is there an indication from the data that there may be a negative relationship between exercise and blood pressure? Test with the Spearman test for rank correlation and use a 1% significance level.

Diastolic Blood Pressure	Hours Exercised	Diastolic Blood Pressure	Hours Exercised
74	9	80	8
70	10	64	18
62	16	56	20
58	15	68	10
82	6	72	11
84	3	78	8
90	0	84	7
84	4	88	4
72	12	70	12
70	9	66	15

19.54 Two taste testers were asked to rank ten beers in order of taste preference, with the best tasting beers receiving the highest ranks.

Beer	Taste Tester 1	Taste Tester 2
1	5	7
2	3	3
3	6	6
4	1	2
5	8	10
6	7	5
7	2	4
8	10	9
9	4	1
10	9	8

Using a .05 significance level, is there a significant agreement between the first beer tester's rankings and the second beer tester's ranking?

19.55 The manager of Sales Unlimited wanted to know whether there was a significant positive relationship between a salesperson's travel expenses (in thousands of dollars) and his or her sales (in tens of thousands of dollars). Using the following data, test that there is a positive relationship at the .05 significance level.

Travel Expenses	Sales
1.5	3.4
2.0	3.9
3.5	6.1
1.6	2.5
1.8	3.4
2.5	4.1
2.2	3.6
3.8	5.7
4.1	4.3
2.6	4.6

19.56 A psychologist wanted to determine whether a relationship existed between the level of satisfaction (measured from 1 to 10) of two married people and the number of years the couple had been married. Test the null hypothesis that there is no relationship and use a 10% significance level.

Level of Satisfaction	Number of Years Married
6	1
3	5
7	10
5	12
8	6
4	5
3	2
9	10
7	7
8	12
7	16

19.57 The management of a firm wishes to know whether there is a positive relationship between the length of time a certain product has been on the market and the percent of market that the product has captured. Do the data indicate that a positive relationship exists? Use a 5% significance level.

Time on Market (years)	Percent of Market
1	1.2
2	2.6
3	1.8
4	2.7
5	2.9
6	3.9
7	3.2
8	4.1
9	3.8
10	4.6

19.58 The owner of a used car lot believes that there is a negative relationship between the number of cars sold monthly and the average monthly interest rate used for financing the cars. Twelve months were randomly selected to obtain the following data. Use a 5% significance level to determine whether the owner's belief is correct.

Number of Cars Sold Monthly	Average Monthly Interest Rate (%)
35	12
25	15
28	16
31	12
40	11.5
48	11
50	11
20	15
35	11.5
42	12.5
46	12
28	15

19.59 The manager of a small-town savings and loan association is interested in finding out whether there is a relationship between the average monthly balance of a savings account and the age of the savings account. Fifteen accounts were selected at random. Do the data indicate a relationship at the .05 significance level?

Average Monthly Balance	Age of Account (years)	Average Monthly Balance	Age of Account (years)
2510	1.5	6148	3.8
3612	2.6	5134	4.7
5634	3.5	2614	1.1
3698	1.8	2581	1.9
3978	2.1	2501	0.5
6751	4.3	3986	4.2
5869	10.1	6645	4.1
		3582	2.3

Summary

A key step in applying any statistical technique correctly is to make sure that it is appropriate for the type of data that is involved. For example, performing a t test using a small sample containing ordinal data (such as a set of consumer rankings) never is correct. For situations in which your data are ordinal or from populations that you suspect are nonnormally distributed, a nonparametric technique is often preferable. This chapter has introduced some (certainly not all) of the more popular nonparametric procedures.

The runs test examines a sequence containing an arrangement of two symbols (M or F, yes or no, $+$ or $-$, and so on) to determine whether the sequence was generated in a random manner. We defined tests for both small samples (using Table A-15) and large samples (using a test statistic having an approximate normal distribution and Table A-4).

The Mann–Whitney U test is a nonparametric procedure for testing the means (or medians) of two populations using two independent samples. Unlike its counterpart, the t test, this test does not require that the populations be normally distributed. By combining (pooling) the samples and finding the ranks of the combined sample, you can calculate a value of the test statistic. This method can be applied to both small samples (using Table A-10) and large samples (using an approximate normal distribution and Table A-4).

The Wilcoxon signed rank test is a nonparametric procedure used for testing the means (or medians) of two populations when dealing with two dependent (paired) samples. The Wilcoxon technique determines the differences of the paired observations and then calculates a value of the test statistic using the ranks of these differences. Both small samples (using Table A-11) and large samples (using an approximate normal distribution and Table A-4) can be used.

The Kruskal–Wallis test is an extension of the Mann–Whitney test. It is used to test the equality of more than two population means (or medians) when using independent samples. As in the Mann–Whitney procedure, the samples are pooled and then the values are ranked from smallest to largest. The resulting ranks are then used to define a test statistic. This statistic has an approximate chi-square distribution (tabulated in Table A-6), even for fairly small sample sizes.

These tests are summarized in Figure 19.12.

The final nonparametric technique, the Spearman rank correlation, allows you to measure the association between sample values on two variables that consist of ordinal data. If the data are of the interval or ratio type, they can be converted to ordinal data by using the ranks of these values. The Spearman rank correlation coefficient, denoted as r_s, is a nonparametric measure of association between the observations of these two variables. This statistic is computed using the ranks of the observations and can be used to test for a significant relationship between the two variables.

Figure 19.12

Summary of nonpara-
metric tests of central
tendency.

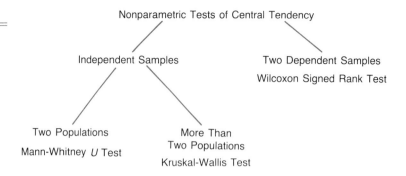

Review
Exercises

19.60 Using the runs test, is there evidence that the following sequence of A's and B's is not randomly generated? Use a 10% significance level.

A A B A B B A A B B B A A B A B A A B B A A B A B A A A A B

19.61 A radio station requests that people telephone the station to express their opinion on the new property tax that the city is levying. An F represents a person telephoning in who is for the tax, and an A represents one against it. Test whether the following sequence of people telephoning the radio station is a nonrandom sample. Use a 10% significance level.

F A F A A A F A A F A A A F F A F A F A F A A A F A A

19.62 The following list of numbers represents the residuals from fitting an autoregressive model to a set of data. Use the sequence of positive and negative numbers to perform a runs test and determine whether the data indicate that the residuals are nonrandomly generated. Use a 5% significance level.

0.5, −2.6, −1.5, 0.6, 0.9, 0.3, −1.7, −2.6, −1.0, 0.4, 0.8, −1.6, 0.7, −1.8, −2.0, 1.0, 1.5, −3.1

19.63 Explain the differences in the assumptions necessary to perform parametric tests and nonparametric tests on two population means.

19.64 A statistician wants to test the difference between the average values of two different populations. After collecting a sample of size eight from each population, the statistician finds that the sum of the ranks of the observations in population 1 is 60. Is there evidence to indicate that there is a difference between the average value of the two populations? Use a 5% significance level.

19.65 An economist believes that the cost of a typical basket of goods bought by a family of four costs more in Atlanta, Georgia, than it does in Houston, Texas. Seven grocery stores were randomly selected in each of the two cities to collect the following data (cost of basket of goods, in dollars). Test that there is no difference in the costs of the basket of goods for the two cities. Use a 10% significance level.

Atlanta	Houston
30	37
33	36
41	39
43	40
37	32
39	36
41	32

19.66 Jeff's Auto Parts store special orders parts from either warehouse A or warehouse B. Warehouse A claims that it delivers parts faster than any other warehouse. Jeff special ordered

18 auto parts—nine from warehouse A and nine from warehouse B—and noted the number of days it took to receive them. Using the following data, test warehouse A's claim. Use a 5% significance level.

Warehouse A	Warehouse B
2.50	3.00
2.25	3.25
3.50	2.50
2.00	2.75
2.75	3.00
2.25	2.00
3.00	2.25
2.50	2.75
2.50	2.25

19.67 Vulcan Construction believes that a minicourse in safety to increase the employees' awareness of potential accidents would reduce the incidence of on-the-job accidents. The following data represent the number of accidents reported at 15 construction sites for the month before and the month after the workers attended the minicourse. Do the data indicate that the minicourse reduced accidents? Use a 5% significance level.

Before	After
4	3
5	6
7	6
8	5
7	8
10	3
12	2
9	8
11	6
7	7
8	5
5	3
10	11
9	4
11	9

19.68 A cooking contest was conducted; two top chefs baked chicken and then asked 12 tasters to judge the quality of the cooking on a scale from 1 to 10, 10 being the highest score. Test the null hypothesis that there was no difference between the taster's judgment of the quality of cooking for the two chefs at a significance level of .05.

Taster	Chef A	Chef B
1	8	7
2	6	10
3	5	9
4	10	4
5	5	8
6	3	7
7	9	9
8	10	7
9	9	10
10	8	6
11	4	9
12	7	3

19.69 Paint A, paint B, and paint C were painted on metallic surfaces and then subjected to high temperatures. Nine replications of the experiment were made. A measure of the cohesiveness of the paint was then taken. The following coded data represent the cohesiveness of the individual paints. Test the hypothesis that there was no difference in the average measure of cohesiveness for the three paints. Use a 10% significance level.

Paint A	Paint B	Paint C
1.3	2.1	3.4
1.6	2.7	2.8
3.1	1.6	1.9
2.6	1.9	2.0
4.3	1.6	2.8
1.6	1.9	2.5
2.6	2.3	2.4
2.7	1.8	1.9
1.9	1.6	1.7

19.70 A chemist was interested in knowing whether three different drugs used for insomnia were equally effective. Three groups of mice, with ten mice to a group, were used. Each group of mice was given the adult-equivalent dosage for one of the three drugs. The time in minutes it took for the mice to fall asleep was recorded. Using the following data, test the null hypothesis that each drug is equally effective in reducing sleep latency. Use a significance level of .05.

Drug 1	Drug 2	Drug 3	Drug 1	Drug 2	Drug 3
32	38	31	41	35	30
35	37	33	28	39	28
40	42	29	34	40	33
30	44	34	39	41	37
33	37	31	28	42	35

19.71 An automobile worker would like to know whether there is any difference in the comfort of three different cars. Three groups of five drivers were selected to judge the riding comfort of the three cars; one of the three cars was assigned to each group. The drivers rated the comfort of each car on a scale from 1 to 5, 5 being the most comfortable. Test that there is no difference in the comfort of the three cars from these data. Use a .05 significance level.

Car 1	Car 2	Car 3
2	5	4
4	3	1
4	4	2
3	3	5
5	2	4

19.72 A microbiologist wants to know whether there is any difference in the time in hours it takes to make yogurt from three different starters. Seven batches of yogurt were made with each of the starters. The following data give the times it took to make each batch. At the .05 significance level, do the data indicate a difference in the time it takes to make yogurt from the three starters?

Lactobacillus Acidophilus	Bulgarius	Mixture of Acidophilus and Bulgarius
6.8	6.1	7.3
6.3	6.4	6.1
7.4	5.7	6.4
6.1	6.5	7.2
8.2	6.9	7.4
7.3	6.3	6.5
6.9	6.7	6.8

19.73 A company uses four advertising methods to increase sales: newspaper, mailers, television, and radio. Four 6-months periods were randomly selected, and sales (in thousands of dollars) were recorded monthly for one of the 6-month periods for each advertising method. Do the following data indicate a difference in sales promotion for the four advertising methods? Use a .05 significance level.

Newspaper	Mailers	Television	Radio
2.1	4.1	5.1	4.2
5.6	2.6	4.2	4.3
6.2	2.1	3.7	4.0
3.4	3.3	2.0	3.1
3.1	3.0	3.6	3.8
4.1	3.1	3.1	3.7

19.74 The following data represent the years of job-related experience and last year's salary (in thousands of dollars) for ten randomly selected realtors. Do the data indicate a positive relationship? Use a 5% significance level.

Years of Experience	Annual Salary
13.2	42.5
10.1	36.8
4.6	15.9
5.7	27.6
6.7	34.3
7.8	38.4
5.4	29.6
3.8	21.6
9.6	33.7
8.4	35.3

19.75 The owner of a convenience food store is interested in whether there is a positive relationship between the number of cars that pass the store weekly (given in thousands) and the weekly sales of the store (in thousands of dollars). Test the hypothesis that there is a positive relationship using a 5% significance level.

Week	Number of Cars	Sales
1	24.6	1.3
2	29.7	2.6
3	22.6	1.4
4	30.4	2.8
5	20.1	1.1
6	24.6	1.2
7	32.7	2.9
8	35.1	3.4
9	29.9	3.9

Solution

Example 19.2

Example 19.2 used the nonparametric runs test to determine whether a sample of savings accounts at the Northside National Bank was determined in a random manner. The runs test was used to see if the sample consisted of 45 randomly selected males and females. The SPSSX program listing in Figure 19.13 was used to compute the number of runs and the Z value. Each line represents one card image to be entered:

S
P
S
S
X

Figure 19.13

SPSSX program listing used to compute the number of runs and Z value for example 19.2.

```
TITLE    RUNS TEST FOR NORTHSIDE NATIONAL BANK
DATA LIST FREE/SEX
VALUE LABELS SEX -1 'FEMALE' 1 'MALE'/
PRINT / SEX
BEGIN DATA
1
1
1                              1
-1                            -1
-1                            -1
-1                             1
-1                            -1
-1                            -1
1                             -1
-1                            -1
-1                            -1
1                              1
1                              1
1                              1
1                              1
1                              1
1                             -1
-1                            -1
-1                            -1
-1                            -1
-1                             1
1                              1
1                              1
-1             END DATA
1              NPAR TESTS RUNS(1)=SEX/
```

The TITLE command names the SPSSX run.

The DATA LIST command gives each variable a name and describes the data as being in free form.

The VALUE LABELS statement assigns labels to the values of the variable SEX. The value -1 is assigned the label FEMALE, whereas the value $+1$ is assigned the label MALE.

The PRINT command prints the value of variable SEX.

The BEGIN DATA command indicates to SPSSX that the input data immediately follow.

The next 45 lines are card images; each line represents either a -1 for a female or a $+1$ for a male.

The END DATA statement indicates the end of the data card images.

The NPAR TESTS command indicates that we wish to perform a nonparametric test. In this case, it is the runs test. We are testing for runs that are greater than zero and less than zero—in other words, runs of females (-1) or males $(+1)$.

Figure 19.14 shows the output obtained by executing the program listing in Figure 19.13.

Figure 19.14

Output obtained by executing the SPSSX program listing in Figure 19.13.

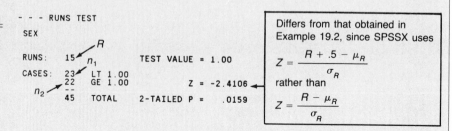

```
- - - RUNS TEST

SEX
                    R
RUNS:    15      n₁           TEST VALUE = 1.00
CASES:   23      LT 1.00
         22      GE 1.00              Z = -2.4106
   n₂    --
         45      TOTAL    2-TAILED P =   .0159
```

Differs from that obtained in Example 19.2, since SPSSX uses

$$Z = \frac{R + .5 - \mu_R}{\sigma_R}$$

rather than

$$Z = \frac{R - \mu_R}{\sigma_R}$$

Solution

Example 19.5

Example 19.5 used the nonparametric Mann–Whitney U test to determine whether there was sufficient evidence to indicate that Food World's store A had a larger number of returned checks than did their store B. The SPSSX program listing in Figure 19.15 was used to compute the Mann–Whitney test statistic. Each line represents one card image to be entered:

The TITLE command names the SPSSX run.

The DATA LIST command gives each variable a name and describes the data as being in free form.

The PRINT command prints the values of variables STORE and GROUP.

The BEGIN DATA command indicates to SPSSX that the input data immediately follow.

The next 27 lines are card images; each line represents the number of returned checks per month per store and the group in which the specific store belongs (0 = store A, 1 = store B).

The END DATA statement indicates the end of the data card images.

The NPAR TESTS command indicates that we wish to perform a nonparametric Mann–Whitney test, comparing the number of returned checks (variable STORE) by the store category (variable GROUP).

Figure 19.16 shows the output obtained by executing the program listing in Figure 19.15.

Figure 19.15

SPSSX program listing used to determine the Mann–Whitney test statistic.

```
TITLE    FOOD WORLD SUPERMARKETS
DATA LIST FREE/STORE GROUP
PRINT /STORE GROUP
BEGIN DATA
42  0
65  0
38  0
55  0
71  0
60  0
47  0
59  0
68  0
57  0
76  0
42  0
22  1
17  1
35  1
19  1
8   1
24  1
42  1
14  1
28  1
17  1
10  1
15  1
20  1
45  1
50  1
END DATA
NPAR TESTS M-W = STORE BY GROUP (0,1)
```

Figure 19.16

Output obtained by executing the SPSSX program listing in Figure 19.15.

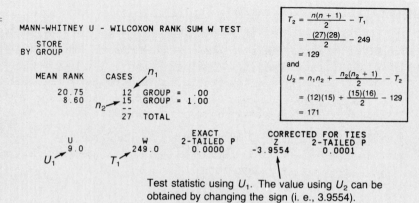

MANN-WHITNEY U - WILCOXON RANK SUM W TEST

```
       STORE
    BY GROUP

     MEAN RANK      CASES      n₁

       20.75          12  GROUP =  .00
        8.60          15  GROUP = 1.00
                      --
                      27  TOTAL
```

$$T_2 = \frac{n(n+1)}{2} - T_1$$
$$= \frac{(27)(28)}{2} - 249$$
$$= 129$$
and
$$U_2 = n_1 n_2 + \frac{n_2(n_2+1)}{2} - T_2$$
$$= (12)(15) + \frac{(15)(16)}{2} - 129$$
$$= 171$$

```
                             EXACT         CORRECTED FOR TIES
         U           W     2-TAILED P       Z      2-TAILED P
        9.0       249.0     0.0000      -3.9554     0.0001
```

U_1 T_1

Test statistic using U_1. The value using U_2 can be obtained by changing the sign (i. e., 3.9554).

Solution

Example 19.7

Example 19.7 used the nonparametric Wilcoxon signed ranks test to determine whether customers at Worldwide Travel flew more miles in 1985 than they did in 1975. The SPSSX program listing in Figure 19.17 was used to compute the Wilcoxon Z statistic for the two time periods. Each line represents one card image to be entered:

The TITLE command names the SPSSX run.

The DATA LIST command gives each variable a name and describes the data as being in free form.

The VARIABLE LABELS statement assigns a descriptive label to the variables. This descriptive label is substituted for the variable name when output is printed.

The PRINT command prints the values of variables YEAR75 and YEAR85.

The BEGIN DATA command indicates to SPSSX that the input data immediately follow.

The next 20 lines are card images; each line represents the number of miles flown by continuing customers in both 1975 and 1985.

Figure 19.17

SPSSX program listing used to determine the Wilcoxon Z statistic for example 19.7.

```
TITLE    WORLDWIDE TRAVEL CUSTOMER MILEAGE COMPARISON
DATA LIST FREE/YEAR75 YEAR85
VARIABLE LABELS
         YEAR75 'MILES FLOWN IN 1975'
         YEAR85 'MILES FLOWN IN 1985'
PRINT / YEAR75 YEAR85
BEGIN DATA
55    45
101   79
62    77
93   138
40    68
120   80
110  138
77    81
49    49
90    80
121  171
46    21
112   78
70   106
97    87
47    91
106   80
84   104
50    88
75   117
END DATA
NPAR TESTS  WILCOXON=ALL
```

Figure 19.18

Output obtained by executing the SPSSX program listing in Figure 19.17.

```
- - - - - WILCOXON MATCHED-PAIRS SIGNED-RANKS TEST

        YEAR75    MILES FLOWN IN 1975
WITH YEAR85    MILES FLOWN IN 1985

     MEAN RANK      CASES

        7.50          8   - RANKS (YEAR85 LT YEAR75)
       11.82         11   + RANKS (YEAR85 GT YEAR75)
                      1     TIES (YEAR85 EQ YEAR75)
                     --
                     20     TOTAL
```

```
Z =    -1.4085                  2-TAILED P =   .1590
```

p-value for a one-tailed
test (see example 19.7) is
.1590/2 = .0795

The END DATA statement indicates the end of the data card images.

The NPAR TESTS command indicates that we wish to perform the nonparametric Wilcoxon test as well as generate both the *Z* value and two-tailed *p*-value.

Figure 19.18 shows the output obtained by executing the program listing in Figure 19.17.

Solution

Example 19.8

Example 19.8 used the nonparametric Kruskal–Wallis one-way test to determine whether there was a difference in the amount of down time among four different copying machines. Data were collected by observing the down time for 20 randomly selected months. In this way, five randomly selected months were observed for each of the four brands of machines. The SPSSX program listing in Figure 19.19 was used to compute the Kruskal–Wallis statistic and the *p*-value. Each line represents one card image to be entered:

The TITLE command names the SPSSX run.

The DATA LIST command gives each variable a name and describes the data as being in free form.

Figure 19.19

SPSSX program listing used to determine the Kruskal–Wallis statistic and the *p*-value in example 19.8.

```
TITLE    DREXTON INDUSTRIES COPYING MACHINES
DATA LIST FREE/DOWNTIME GROUP
PRINT / DOWNTIME GROUP
BEGIN DATA
28 1
41 1
34 1
52 1
25 1
5   2
16 2
20 2
24 2
15 2
10 3
8   3
18 3
14 3
26 3
45 4
30 4
49 4
32 4
36 4
END DATA
NPAR TESTS  K-W = DOWNTIME BY GROUP (1,4)
```

Figure 19.20

Output obtained by executing the SPSSX program listing in Figure 19.19.

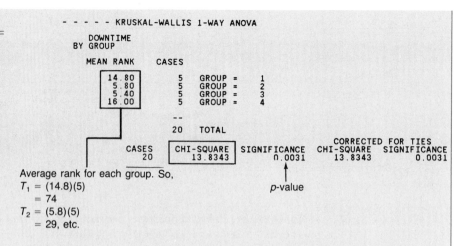

```
- - - - - KRUSKAL-WALLIS 1-WAY ANOVA

        DOWNTIME
      BY GROUP

      MEAN RANK    CASES
         14.80        5    GROUP =    1
          5.80        5    GROUP =    2
          5.40        5    GROUP =    3
         16.00        5    GROUP =    4
                     --
                     20    TOTAL

                                                  CORRECTED FOR TIES
            CASES    CHI-SQUARE   SIGNIFICANCE   CHI-SQUARE   SIGNIFICANCE
              20       13.8343       0.0031        13.8343       0.0031
```

Average rank for each group. So,

$T_1 = (14.8)(5)$
$\quad = 74$
$T_2 = (5.8)(5)$
$\quad = 29$, etc.

p-value

The PRINT command prints the values of variables DOWNTIME and GROUP.

The BEGIN DATA command indicates to SPSSX that the input data immediately follow.

The next 20 lines are card images; each line represents the down time, in hours, of each machine and the machine type (1, 2, 3, or 4).

The END DATA statement indicates the end of the data card images.

The NPAR TESTS command indicates that we wish to perform a Kruskal–Wallis test, analyzing DOWNTIME by GROUP.

Figure 19.20 shows the output obtained by executing the program listing in Figure 19.19.

Solution

Examples 19.9 and 19.11

Examples 19.9 and 19.11 used the nonparametric Spearman rank correlation coefficient to determine the relationship between the market value of homes and the personal indebtedness of the homeowner. The SPSSX program listing in Figure 19.21 was used to compute the Spearman rank correlation coefficient, r_s. Each line represents one card image to be entered:

The TITLE command names the SPSSX run.

The DATA LIST command gives each variable a name and describes the data as being in free form.

Figure 19.21

SPSSX program listing used to determine the Spearman rank correlation coefficient, r_s, in examples 19.9 and 19.11.

```
TITLE  HOME VALUE AND FAMILY INDEBTEDNESS ANALYSIS
DATA LIST FREE/MKTVALUE DEBT
VARIABLE LABELS
     MKTVALUE 'MARKET VALUE OF HOME'
     DEBT     'TOTAL INDEBTEDNESS'
PRINT / MKTVALUE DEBT
BEGIN DATA
85    12
147   27
340   45
94    10
120   17
105   4
135   20
162   25
480   35
88    14
END DATA
NONPAR CORR MKTVALUE WITH DEBT
```

Figure 19.22

Output obtained by
executing the SPSSX
program listing in
Figure 19.21.

```
- - -   S P E A R M A N     C O R R E L A T I O N     C O E F F I C I E N T S   - - -

                         DEBT

MKTVALUE             .8667  ←——— rₛ
                 N(   10)
                 SIG .001  ←——— p-value for Hₒ: no association exists between X and Y

  "   " IS PRINTED IF A COEFFICIENT CANNOT BE COMPUTED.
```

The VARIABLE LABEL statement assigns a descriptive label to the variables. This descriptive label is substituted for the variable name when the output is printed.

The PRINT command prints the values of variables MKTVALUE and DEBT.

The BEGIN DATA command indicates to SPSSX that the input data immediately follow.

The next ten lines are card images; each line represents the total market value of the home and the total indebtedness of the homeowner.

The END DATA statement indicates the end of the data card images.

The NONPAR CORR statement requests that MKTVALUE be correlated with DEBT.

Figure 19.22 shows the output obtained by executing the program listing in Figure 19.21.

Solution

Example 19.5

Example 19.5 used the nonparametric Mann–Whitney U test to determine whether there was sufficient evidence to indicate that Food World's store A had a larger number of returned checks than did their store B. The SAS program listing in Figure 19.23 was used to compute the Mann–Whitney test statistic. Each line represents one card image to be entered:

The TITLE command names the SAS run.

The DATA command gives the data a name.

The INPUT command names and gives the correct order for the different fields on the data cards.

The CARDS command indicates to SAS that the input data immediately follow.

The next 27 lines are card images; each line represents the number of returned checks per month per store and the group in which the store belongs (0 = store A, 1 = store B).

The PROC PRINT command directs SAS to print the data that were just read in.

The Mann–Whitney test is a version of the Wilcoxon test. The following command set was used to obtain the statistics:

PROC NPAR1WAY WILCOXON

VAR STORE

CLASS GROUP

Figure 19.23

SAS program listing used to compute the Mann–Whitney test statistic in example 19.5.

```
TITLE    FOOD WORLD SUPERMARKETS;
DATA STORES;
  INPUT STORE GROUP;
CARDS;
42 0
65 0
38 0
55 0
71 0
60 0
47 0
59 0
68 0
57 0
76 0
42 0
22 1
17 1
35 1
19 1
8 1
24 1
42 1
14 1
28 1
17 1
10 1
15 1
20 1
45 1
50 1
PROC PRINT;
PROC NPAR1WAY WILCOXON;
 VAR STORE;
 CLASS GROUP;
```

Using the above command set, we are able to compare the number of returned checks (variable STORE) by the store category (variable GROUP).

Figure 19.24 shows the output obtained by executing the program listing in Figure 19.23.

Figure 19.24

Output obtained by executing the SAS program listing in Figure 19.23.

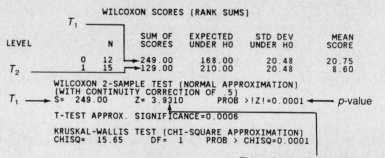

This value is slightly different from the Z value in Example 19.5, since SAS adds .5 to the numerator of Z as well as adjusting this Z value for any ties obtained in the pooled sample.

Figure 19.25

SAS program listing used to compute the Kruskal–Wallis statistic and *p*-value in example 19.8.

```
TITLE   DREXTON INDUSTRIES COPYING MACHINES;
DATA MACHINES;
 INPUT DOWNTIME BRAND;
CARDS;
28 1
41 1
34 1
52 1
25 1
5  2
16 2
20 2
24 2
15 2
10 3
8  3
18 3
14 3
26 3
45 4
30 4
49 4
32 4
36 4
PROC PRINT;
PROC NPAR1WAY WILCOXON;
 VAR DOWNTIME;
 CLASS BRAND;
```

Solution

Example 19.8

Example 19.8 used the nonparametric Kruskal–Wallis one-way test to determine whether there was a difference in the amount of down time among four different copying machines. Data were collected by observing the down time for 20 randomly selected months. In this way, five randomly selected months were observed for each of the four brands of machines. The SAS program listing in Figure 19.25 was used to compute the Kruskal–Wallis statistic and the *p*-value. Each line represents one card image to be entered:

The TITLE command names the SAS run.

The DATA command gives the data a name.

The INPUT command names and gives the correct order for the different fields on the data cards.

The CARDS command indicates to SAS that the input data immediately follow.

The next 20 lines are card images; each line represents the down time, in hours, of each machine and machine type (1, 2, 3, or 4).

The PROC PRINT command directs SAS to print the data that were just read in.

The following command set was used to obtain the Kruskal–Wallis statistic:

```
PROC NPAR1WAY WILCOXON
VAR DOWNTIME
CLASS BRAND
```

Using the above command set, we analyze the difference in average down time for each of the four brands of copiers.

Figure 19.26 shows the output obtained by executing the program listing in Figure 19.25.

Figure 19.26

Output obtained by executing the SAS program listing in Figure 19.25.

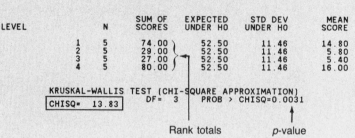

DREXTON INDUSTRIES COPYING MACHINES

ANALYSIS FOR VARIABLE DOWNTIME CLASSIFIED BY VARIABLE BRAND

WILCOXON SCORES (RANK SUMS)

LEVEL	N	SUM OF SCORES	EXPECTED UNDER H0	STD DEV UNDER H0	MEAN SCORE
1	5	74.00	52.50	11.46	14.80
2	5	29.00	52.50	11.46	5.80
3	5	27.00	52.50	11.46	5.40
4	5	80.00	52.50	11.46	16.00

KRUSKAL-WALLIS TEST (CHI-SQUARE APPROXIMATION)
DF= 3   PROB > CHISQ=0.0031
CHISQ= 13.83

Rank totals   *p*-value

Solution

Examples 19.9 and 19.11

Examples 19.9 and 19.11 used the nonparametric Spearman rank correlation coefficient to determine the relationship between the market value of homes and the personal indebtedness of the homeowner. The SAS program listing in Figure 19.27 was used to compute the Spearman rank correlation coefficient, r_s. Each line represents one card image to be entered:

The TITLE command names the SAS run.

The DATA command gives the data a name.

The INPUT command names and gives the correct order for the different fields on the data cards.

The LABEL statements assign a descriptive label to the variables. This descriptive label is substituted for the variable name when output is printed.

The CARDS command indicates to SAS that the input data immediately follow.

The next ten lines are card images; each line represents the market value of a home and the personal indebtedness of the homeowner.

The PROC PRINT command directs SAS to print the data that were just read in.

Figure 19.27

SAS program listing used to compute the Spearman rank correlation coefficient r_s in examples 19.9 and 19.11.

```
TITLE   HOME VALUE AND FAMILY INDEBTEDNESS ANALYSIS;
DATA HOMES;
 INPUT MKTVALUE DEBT;
 LABEL MKTVALUE=MARKET VALUE OF HOMES
       DEBT=TOTAL INDEBTEDNESS;
CARDS;
85   12
147  27
340  45
94   10
120  17
105  4
135  20
162  25
480  35
88   14
PROC PRINT;
PROC CORR NOSIMPLE SPEARMAN;
 VAR MKTVALUE DEBT;
```

Figure 19.28

Output obtained by executing the SAS program listing in Figure 19.27.

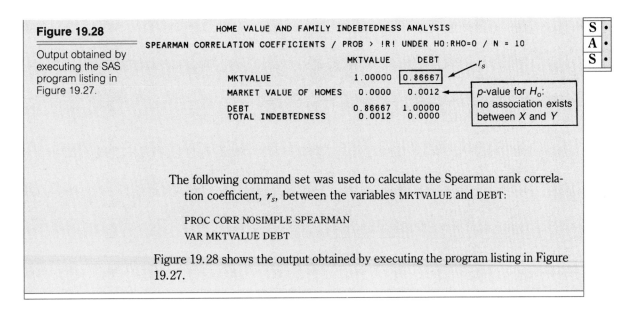

The following command set was used to calculate the Spearman rank correlation coefficient, r_s, between the variables MKTVALUE and DEBT:

PROC CORR NOSIMPLE SPEARMAN
VAR MKTVALUE DEBT

Figure 19.28 shows the output obtained by executing the program listing in Figure 19.27.

Appendixes

APPENDIX A

Tables

Table A-1 Binomial Probabilities $[_nC_x p^x (1-p)^{n-x}]$

								P							
n	x	0.01	0.05	0.10	0.20	0.30	0.40	0.50	0.60	0.70	0.80	0.90	0.95	0.99	x
2	0	980	902	810	640	490	360	250	160	090	040	010	002	0+	0
	1	020	095	180	320	420	480	500	480	420	320	180	095	020	1
	2	0+	002	010	040	090	160	250	360	490	640	810	902	980	2
3	0	970	857	729	512	343	216	125	064	027	008	001	0+	0+	0
	1	029	135	243	384	441	432	375	288	189	096	027	007	0+	1
	2	0+	007	027	096	189	288	375	432	441	384	243	135	029	2
	3	0+	0+	001	008	027	064	125	216	343	512	729	857	970	3
4	0	961	815	656	410	240	130	062	026	008	002	0+	0+	0+	0
	1	039	171	292	410	412	346	250	154	076	026	004	0+	0+	1
	2	001	014	049	154	265	346	375	346	265	154	049	014	001	2
	3	0+	0+	004	026	076	154	250	346	412	410	292	171	039	3
	4	0+	0+	0+	002	008	026	062	130	240	410	656	815	961	4
5	0	951	774	590	328	168	078	031	010	002	0+	0+	0+	0+	0
	1	048	204	328	410	360	259	156	077	028	006	0+	0+	0+	1
	2	001	021	073	205	309	346	312	230	132	051	008	001	0+	2
	3	0+	001	008	051	132	230	312	346	309	205	073	021	001	3
	4	0+	0+	0+	006	028	077	156	259	360	410	328	204	048	4
	5	0+	0+	0+	0+	002	010	031	078	168	328	590	774	951	5
6	0	941	735	531	262	118	047	016	004	001	0+	0+	0+	0+	0
	1	057	232	354	393	303	187	094	037	010	002	0+	0+	0+	1
	2	001	031	098	246	324	311	234	138	060	015	001	0+	0+	2
	3	0+	002	015	082	185	276	312	276	185	082	015	002	0+	3
	4	0+	0+	001	015	060	138	234	311	324	246	098	031	001	4
	5	0+	0+	0+	002	010	037	094	187	303	393	354	232	057	5
	6	0+	0+	0+	0+	001	004	016	047	118	262	531	735	941	6
7	0	932	698	478	210	082	028	008	002	0+	0+	0+	0+	0+	0
	1	066	257	372	367	247	131	055	017	004	0+	0+	0+	0+	1
	2	002	041	124	275	318	261	164	077	025	004	0+	0+	0+	2
	3	0+	004	023	115	227	290	273	194	097	029	003	0+	0+	3
	4	0+	0+	003	029	097	194	273	290	227	115	023	004	0+	4

From Mosteller, Rourke, & Thomas, *Probability with Statistical Applications*, © 1970. Addison-Wesley, Reading, Mass. Reprinted with permission.

Table A-1 (continued)

n	x	0.01	0.05	0.10	0.20	0.30	0.40	0.50	0.60	0.70	0.80	0.90	0.95	0.99	x
	5	0+	0+	0+	004	025	077	164	261	318	275	124	041	002	5
	6	0+	0+	0+	0+	004	017	055	131	247	367	372	257	066	6
	7	0+	0+	0+	0+	0+	002	008	028	082	210	478	698	932	7
8	0	923	663	430	168	058	017	004	001	0+	0+	0+	0+	0+	0
	1	075	279	383	336	198	090	031	008	001	0+	0+	0+	0+	1
	2	003	051	149	294	296	209	109	041	010	001	0+	0+	0+	2
	3	0+	005	033	147	254	279	219	124	047	009	0+	0+	0+	3
	4	0+	0+	005	046	136	232	273	232	136	046	005	0+	0+	4
	5	0+	0+	0+	009	047	124	219	279	254	147	033	005	0+	5
	6	0+	0+	0+	001	010	041	109	209	296	294	149	051	003	6
	7	0+	0+	0+	0+	001	008	031	090	198	336	383	279	075	7
	8	0+	0+	0+	0+	0+	001	004	017	058	168	430	663	923	8
9	0	914	630	387	134	040	010	002	0+	0+	0+	0+	0+	0+	0
	1	083	299	387	302	156	060	018	004	0+	0+	0+	0+	0+	1
	2	003	063	172	302	267	161	070	021	004	0+	0+	0+	0+	2
	3	0+	008	045	176	267	251	164	074	021	003	0+	0+	0+	3
	4	0+	001	007	066	172	251	246	167	074	017	001	0+	0+	4
9	5	0+	0+	001	017	074	167	246	251	172	066	007	001	0+	5
	6	0+	0+	0+	003	021	074	164	251	267	176	045	008	0+	6
	7	0+	0+	0+	0+	004	021	070	161	267	302	172	063	003	7
	8	0+	0+	0+	0+	0+	004	018	060	156	302	387	299	083	8
	9	0+	0+	0+	0+	0+	0+	002	010	040	134	387	630	914	9
10	0	904	599	349	107	028	006	001	0+	0+	0+	0+	0+	0+	0
	1	091	315	387	268	121	040	010	002	0+	0+	0+	0+	0+	1
	2	004	075	194	302	233	121	044	011	001	0+	0+	0+	0+	2
	3	0+	010	057	201	267	215	117	042	009	001	0+	0+	0+	3
	4	0+	001	011	088	200	251	205	111	037	006	0+	0+	0+	4
	5	0+	0+	001	026	103	201	246	201	103	026	001	0+	0+	5
	6	0+	0+	0+	006	037	111	205	251	200	088	011	001	0+	6
	7	0+	0+	0+	001	009	042	117	215	267	201	057	010	0+	7
	8	0+	0+	0+	0+	001	011	044	121	233	302	194	075	004	8
	9	0+	0+	0+	0+	0+	002	010	040	121	268	387	315	091	9
	10	0+	0+	0+	0+	0+	0+	001	006	028	107	349	599	904	10
11	0	895	569	314	086	020	004	0+	0+	0+	0+	0+	0+	0+	0
	1	099	329	384	236	093	027	005	001	0+	0+	0+	0+	0+	1
	2	005	087	213	295	200	089	027	005	001	0+	0+	0+	0+	2
	3	0+	014	071	221	257	177	081	023	004	0+	0+	0+	0+	3
	4	0+	001	016	111	220	236	161	070	017	002	0+	0+	0+	4
	5	0+	0+	002	039	132	221	226	147	057	010	0+	0+	0+	5
	6	0+	0+	0+	010	057	147	226	221	132	039	002	0+	0+	6
	7	0+	0+	0+	002	017	070	161	236	220	111	016	001	0+	7
	8	0+	0+	0+	0+	004	023	081	177	257	221	071	014	0+	8
	9	0+	0+	0+	0+	001	005	027	089	200	295	213	087	005	9
	10	0+	0+	0+	0+	0+	001	005	027	093	236	384	329	099	10
	11	0+	0+	0+	0+	0+	0+	0+	004	020	086	314	569	895	11
12	0	886	540	282	069	014	002	0+	0+	0+	0+	0+	0+	0+	0
	1	107	341	377	206	071	017	003	0+	0+	0+	0+	0+	0+	1
	2	006	099	230	283	168	064	016	002	0+	0+	0+	0+	0+	2
	3	0+	017	085	236	240	142	054	012	001	0+	0+	0+	0+	3
	4	0+	002	021	133	231	213	121	042	008	001	0+	0+	0+	4

Table A-1 (continued)

n	x	0.01	0.05	0.10	0.20	0.30	0.40	P 0.50	0.60	0.70	0.80	0.90	0.95	0.99	x
12	5	0+	0+	004	053	158	227	193	101	029	003	0+	0+	0+	5
	6	0+	0+	0+	016	079	177	226	177	079	016	0+	0+	0+	6
	7	0+	0+	0+	003	029	101	193	227	158	053	004	0+	0+	7
	8	0+	0+	0+	001	008	042	121	213	231	133	021	002	0+	8
	9	0+	0+	0+	0+	001	012	054	142	240	236	085	017	0+	9
	10	0+	0+	0+	0+	0+	002	016	064	168	283	230	099	006	10
	11	0+	0+	0+	0+	0+	0+	003	017	071	206	377	341	107	11
	12	0+	0+	0+	0+	0+	0+	0+	002	014	069	282	540	886	12
13	0	878	513	254	055	010	001	0+	0+	0+	0+	0+	0+	0+	0
	1	115	351	367	179	054	011	002	0+	0+	0+	0+	0+	0+	1
	2	007	111	245	268	139	045	010	001	0+	0+	0+	0+	0+	2
	3	0+	021	100	246	218	111	035	006	001	0+	0+	0+	0+	3
	4	0+	003	028	154	234	184	087	024	003	0+	0+	0+	0+	4
	5	0+	0+	006	069	180	221	157	066	014	001	0+	0+	0+	5
	6	0+	0+	001	023	103	197	209	131	044	006	0+	0+	0+	6
	7	0+	0+	0+	006	044	131	209	197	103	023	001	0+	0+	7
	8	0+	0+	0+	001	014	066	157	221	180	069	006	0+	0+	8
	9	0+	0+	0+	0+	003	024	087	184	234	154	028	003	0+	9
	10	0+	0+	0+	0+	001	006	035	111	218	246	100	021	0+	10
	11	0+	0+	0+	0+	0+	001	010	045	139	268	245	111	007	11
	12	0+	0+	0+	0+	0+	0+	002	011	054	179	367	351	115	12
	13	0+	0+	0+	0+	0+	0+	0+	001	010	055	254	513	878	13
14	0	869	488	229	044	007	001	0+	0+	0+	0+	0+	0+	0+	0
	1	123	359	356	154	041	007	001	0+	0+	0+	0+	0+	0+	1
	2	008	123	257	250	113	032	006	001	0+	0+	0+	0+	0+	2
	3	0+	026	114	250	194	085	022	003	0+	0+	0+	0+	0+	3
	4	0+	004	035	172	229	155	061	014	001	0+	0+	0+	0+	4
	5	0+	0+	008	086	196	207	122	041	007	0+	0+	0+	0+	5
	6	0+	0+	001	032	126	207	183	092	023	002	0+	0+	0+	6
	7	0+	0+	0+	009	062	157	209	157	062	009	0+	0+	0+	7
	8	0+	0+	0+	002	023	092	183	207	126	032	001	0+	0+	8
	9	0+	0+	0+	0+	007	041	122	207	196	086	008	0+	0+	9
	10	0+	0+	0+	0+	001	014	061	155	229	172	035	004	0+	10
	11	0+	0+	0+	0+	0+	003	022	085	194	250	114	026	0+	11
	12	0+	0+	0+	0+	0+	001	006	032	113	250	257	123	008	12
	13	0+	0+	0+	0+	0+	0+	001	007	041	154	356	359	123	13
	14	0+	0+	0+	0+	0+	0+	0+	001	007	044	229	488	869	14
15	0	860	463	206	035	005	0+	0+	0+	0+	0+	0+	0+	0+	0
	1	130	366	343	132	031	005	0+	0+	0+	0+	0+	0+	0+	1
	2	009	135	267	231	092	022	003	0+	0+	0+	0+	0+	0+	2
	3	0+	031	129	250	170	063	014	002	0+	0+	0+	0+	0+	3
	4	0+	005	043	188	219	127	042	007	001	0+	0+	0+	0+	4
	5	0+	001	010	103	206	186	092	024	003	0+	0+	0+	0+	5
	6	0+	0+	002	043	147	207	153	061	012	001	0+	0+	0+	6
	7	0+	0+	0+	014	081	177	196	118	035	003	0+	0+	0+	7
	8	0+	0+	0+	003	035	118	196	177	081	014	0+	0+	0+	8
	9	0+	0+	0+	001	012	061	153	207	147	043	002	0+	0+	9
	10	0+	0+	0+	0+	003	024	092	186	206	103	010	001	0+	10
	11	0+	0+	0+	0+	001	007	042	127	219	188	043	005	0+	11
	12	0+	0+	0+	0+	0+	002	014	063	170	250	129	031	0+	12

Table A-1 (continued)

n x	0.01	0.05	0.10	0.20	0.30	0.40	P 0.50	0.60	0.70	0.80	0.90	0.95	0.99	x
13	0+	0+	0+	0+	0+	0+	003	022	092	231	267	135	009	13
14	0+	0+	0+	0+	0+	0+	001	005	031	132	343	366	130	14
15	0+	0+	0+	0+	0+	0+	0+	0+	005	035	206	463	860	15
16 0	852	440	185	028	003	0+	0+	0+	0+	0+	0+	0+	0+	0
1	138	371	329	113	023	003	0+	0+	0+	0+	0+	0+	0+	1
2	010	146	274	211	073	015	002	0+	0+	0+	0+	0+	0+	2
3	0+	036	142	246	146	047	008	001	0+	0+	0+	0+	0+	3
4	0+	006	051	200	204	101	028	004	0+	0+	0+	0+	0+	4
5	0+	001	014	120	210	162	067	014	001	0+	0+	0+	0+	5
6	0+	0+	003	055	165	198	122	039	006	0+	0+	0+	0+	6
7	0+	0+	0+	020	101	189	175	084	018	001	0+	0+	0+	7
8	0+	0+	0+	006	049	142	196	142	049	006	0+	0+	0+	8
9	0+	0+	0+	001	018	084	175	189	101	020	0+	0+	0+	9
10	0+	0+	0+	0+	006	039	122	198	165	055	003	0+	0+	10
11	0+	0+	0+	0+	001	014	067	162	210	120	014	001	0+	11
12	0+	0+	0+	0+	0+	004	028	101	204	200	051	006	0+	12
13	0+	0+	0+	0+	0+	001	008	047	146	246	142	036	0+	13
14	0+	0+	0+	0+	0+	0+	002	015	073	211	274	146	010	14
15	0+	0+	0+	0+	0+	0+	0+	003	023	113	329	371	138	15
16	0+	0+	0+	0+	0+	0+	0+	0+	003	028	185	440	852	16
17 0	843	418	167	022	002	0+	0+	0+	0+	0+	0+	0+	0+	0
1	145	374	315	096	017	002	0+	0+	0+	0+	0+	0+	0+	1
2	012	158	280	191	058	010	001	0+	0+	0+	0+	0+	0+	2
3	001	042	156	239	124	034	005	0+	0+	0+	0+	0+	0+	3
4	0+	008	060	209	187	080	018	002	0+	0+	0+	0+	0+	4
5	0+	001	018	136	208	138	047	008	001	0+	0+	0+	0+	5
6	0+	0+	004	068	178	184	094	024	003	0+	0+	0+	0+	6
7	0+	0+	001	027	120	193	148	057	010	0+	0+	0+	0+	7
8	0+	0+	0+	008	064	161	186	107	028	002	0+	0+	0+	8
9	0+	0+	0+	002	028	107	186	161	064	008	0+	0+	0+	9
10	0+	0+	0+	0+	010	057	148	193	120	027	001	0+	0+	10
11	0+	0+	0+	0+	003	024	094	184	178	068	004	0+	0+	11
12	0+	0+	0+	0+	001	008	047	138	208	136	018	001	0+	12
13	0+	0+	0+	0+	0+	002	018	080	187	209	060	008	0+	13
14	0+	0+	0+	0+	0+	0+	005	034	124	239	156	042	001	14
15	0+	0+	0+	0+	0+	0+	001	010	058	191	280	158	012	15
16	0+	0+	0+	0+	0+	0+	0+	002	017	096	315	374	145	16
17	0+	0+	0+	0+	0+	0+	0+	0+	002	022	167	418	843	17
18 0	834	397	150	018	002	0+	0+	0+	0+	0+	0+	0+	0+	0
1	152	376	300	081	013	001	0+	0+	0+	0+	0+	0+	0+	1
2	013	168	284	172	046	007	001	0+	0+	0+	0+	0+	0+	2
3	001	047	168	230	105	025	003	0+	0+	0+	0+	0+	0+	3
4	0+	009	070	215	168	061	012	001	0+	0+	0+	0+	0+	4
5	0+	001	022	151	202	115	033	004	0+	0+	0+	0+	0+	5
6	0+	0+	005	082	187	166	071	014	001	0+	0+	0+	0+	6
7	0+	0+	001	035	138	189	121	037	005	0+	0+	0+	0+	7
8	0+	0+	0+	012	081	173	167	077	015	001	0+	0+	0+	8
9	0+	0+	0+	003	039	128	186	128	039	003	0+	0+	0+	9

Table A-1 (continued)

n	x	0.01	0.05	0.10	0.20	0.30	0.40	0.50	0.60	0.70	0.80	0.90	0.95	0.99	x
	10	0+	0+	0+	001	015	077	167	173	081	012	0+	0+	0+	10
	11	0+	0+	0+	0+	005	037	121	189	138	035	001	0+	0+	11
	12	0+	0+	0+	0+	001	014	071	166	187	082	005	0+	0+	12
	13	0+	0+	0+	0+	0+	004	033	115	202	151	022	001	0+	13
	14	0+	0+	0+	0+	0+	001	012	061	168	215	070	009	0+	14
	15	0+	0+	0+	0+	0+	0+	003	025	105	230	168	047	001	15
	16	0+	0+	0+	0+	0+	0+	001	007	046	172	284	168	013	16
	17	0+	0+	0+	0+	0+	0+	0+	001	013	081	300	376	152	17
	18	0+	0+	0+	0+	0+	0+	0+	0+	002	018	150	397	834	18
19	0	826	377	135	014	001	0+	0+	0+	0+	0+	0+	0+	0+	0
	1	159	377	285	068	009	001	0+	0+	0+	0+	0+	0+	0+	1
	2	014	179	285	154	036	005	0+	0+	0+	0+	0+	0+	0+	2
	3	001	053	180	218	087	018	002	0+	0+	0+	0+	0+	0+	3
	4	0+	011	080	218	149	047	007	0+	0+	0+	0+	0+	0+	4
	5	0+	002	027	164	192	093	022	002	0+	0+	0+	0+	0+	5
	6	0+	0+	007	096	192	145	052	008	0+	0+	0+	0+	0+	6
	7	0+	0+	001	044	152	180	096	024	002	0+	0+	0+	0+	7
	8	0+	0+	0+	017	098	180	144	053	008	0+	0+	0+	0+	8
	9	0+	0+	0+	005	051	146	176	098	022	001	0+	0+	0+	9
	10	0+	0+	0+	001	022	098	176	146	051	005	0+	0+	0+	10
	11	0+	0+	0+	0+	008	053	144	180	098	017	0+	0+	0+	11
	12	0+	0+	0+	0+	002	024	096	180	152	044	001	0+	0+	12
	13	0+	0+	0+	0+	0+	008	052	145	192	096	007	0+	0+	13
	14	0+	0+	0+	0+	0+	002	022	093	192	164	027	002	0+	14
	15	0+	0+	0+	0+	0+	0+	007	047	149	218	080	011	0+	15
	16	0+	0+	0+	0+	0+	0+	002	018	087	218	180	053	001	16
	17	0+	0+	0+	0+	0+	0+	0+	005	036	154	285	179	014	17
	18	0+	0+	0+	0+	0+	0+	0+	001	009	068	285	377	159	18
	19	0+	0+	0+	0+	0+	0+	0+	0+	001	014	135	377	826	19
20	0	818	358	122	012	001	0+	0+	0+	0+	0+	0+	0+	0+	0
	1	165	377	270	058	007	0+	0+	0+	0+	0+	0+	0+	0+	1
	2	016	189	285	137	028	003	0+	0+	0+	0+	0+	0+	0+	2
	3	001	060	190	205	072	012	001	0+	0+	0+	0+	0+	0+	3
	4	0+	013	090	218	130	035	005	0+	0+	0+	0+	0+	0+	4
	5	0+	002	032	175	179	075	015	001	0+	0+	0+	0+	0+	5
	6	0+	0+	009	109	192	124	037	005	0+	0+	0+	0+	0+	6
	7	0+	0+	002	054	164	166	074	015	001	0+	0+	0+	0+	7
	8	0+	0+	0+	022	114	180	120	036	004	0+	0+	0+	0+	8
	9	0+	0+	0+	007	065	160	160	071	012	0+	0+	0+	0+	9
	10	0+	0+	0+	002	031	117	176	117	031	002	0+	0+	0+	10
	11	0+	0+	0+	0+	012	071	160	160	065	007	0+	0+	0+	11
	12	0+	0+	0+	0+	004	036	120	180	114	022	0+	0+	0+	12
	13	0+	0+	0+	0+	001	015	074	166	164	054	002	0+	0+	13
	14	0+	0+	0+	0+	0+	005	037	124	192	109	009	0+	0+	14
	15	0+	0+	0+	0+	0+	001	015	075	179	175	032	002	0+	15
	16	0+	0+	0+	0+	0+	0+	005	035	130	218	090	013	0+	16
	17	0+	0+	0+	0+	0+	0+	001	012	072	205	190	060	001	17
	18	0+	0+	0+	0+	0+	0+	0+	003	028	137	285	189	016	18
	19	0+	0+	0+	0+	0+	0+	0+	0+	007	058	270	377	165	19
	20	0+	0+	0+	0+	0+	0+	0+	0+	001	012	122	358	818	20

Table A-2 Values of e^{-a}

a	e^{-a}	a	e^{-a}	a	e^{-a}	a	e^{-a}
0.00	1.000000	2.60	.074274	5.10	.006097	7.60	.000501
0.10	.904837	2.70	.067206	5.20	.005517	7.70	.000453
0.20	.818731	2.80	.060810	5.30	.004992	7.80	.000410
0.30	.740818	2.90	.055023	5.40	.004517	7.90	.000371
0.40	.670320	3.00	.049787	5.50	.004087	8.00	.000336
0.50	.606531	3.10	.045049	5.60	.003698	8.10	.000304
0.60	.548812	3.20	.040762	5.70	.003346	8.20	.000275
0.70	.496585	3.30	.036883	5.80	.003028	8.30	.000249
0.80	.449329	3.40	.033373	5.90	.002739	8.40	.000225
0.90	.406570	3.50	.030197	6.00	.002479	8.50	.000204
1.00	.367879	3.60	.027324	6.10	.002243	8.60	.000184
1.10	.332871	3.70	.024724	6.20	.002029	8.70	.000167
1.20	.301194	3.80	.022371	6.30	.001836	8.80	.000151
1.30	.272532	3.90	.020242	6.40	.001661	8.90	.000136
1.40	.246597	4.00	.018316	6.50	.001503	9.00	.000123
1.50	.223130	4.10	.016573	6.60	.001360	9.10	.000112
1.60	.201897	4.20	.014996	6.70	.001231	9.20	.000101
1.70	.182684	4.30	.013569	6.80	.001114	9.30	.000091
1.80	.165299	4.40	.012277	6.90	.001008	9.40	.000083
1.90	.149569	4.50	.011109	7.00	.000912	9.50	.000075
2.00	.135335	4.60	.010052	7.10	.000825	9.60	.000068
2.10	.122456	4.70	.009095	7.20	.000747	9.70	.000061
2.20	.110803	4.80	.008230	7.30	.000676	9.80	.000056
2.30	.100259	4.90	.007447	7.40	.000611	9.90	.000050
2.40	.090718	5.00	.006738	7.50	.000553	10.00	.000045
2.50	.082085						

Table A-3 Poisson Probabilities $\left[\dfrac{e^{-\mu}\mu^{x}}{x!} \right]$

x	0.005	0.01	0.02	0.03	0.04	0.05	0.06	0.07	0.08	0.09
0	0.9950	0.9900	0.9802	0.9704	0.9608	0.9512	0.9418	0.9324	0.9231	0.9139
1	0.0050	0.0099	0.0192	0.0291	0.0384	0.0476	0.0565	0.0653	0.0738	0.0823
2	0.0000	0.0000	0.0002	0.0004	0.0008	0.0012	0.0017	0.0023	0.0030	0.0037
3	0.0000	0.0000	0.0000	0.0000	0.0000	0.0000	0.0000	0.0001	0.0001	0.0001

x	0.1	0.2	0.3	0.4	0.5	0.6	0.7	0.8	0.9	1.0
0	0.9048	0.8187	0.7408	0.6703	0.6065	0.5488	0.4966	0.4493	0.4066	0.3679
1	0.0905	0.1637	0.2222	0.2681	0.3033	0.3293	0.3476	0.3595	0.3659	0.3679
2	0.0045	0.0164	0.0333	0.0536	0.0758	0.0988	0.1217	0.1438	0.1647	0.1839
3	0.0002	0.0011	0.0033	0.0072	0.0126	0.0198	0.0284	0.0383	0.0494	0.0613
4	0.0000	0.0001	0.0002	0.0007	0.0016	0.0030	0.0050	0.0077	0.0111	0.0153

Source: Robert Parsons, *Statistical Analysis: A Decision Making Approach*, 2d ed. (New York: Harper & Row, 1978). Reproduced with permission.

Table A-3 (continued)

x	0.1	0.2	0.3	0.4	0.5	0.6	0.7	0.8	0.9	1.0
5	0.0000	0.0000	0.0000	0.0001	0.0002	0.0004	0.0007	0.0012	0.0020	0.0031
6	0.0000	0.0000	0.0000	0.0000	0.0000	0.0000	0.0001	0.0002	0.0003	0.0005
7	0.0000	0.0000	0.0000	0.0000	0.0000	0.0000	0.0000	0.0000	0.0000	0.0001

x	1.1	1.2	1.3	1.4	1.5	1.6	1.7	1.8	1.9	2.0
0	0.3329	0.3012	0.2725	0.2466	0.2231	0.2019	0.1827	0.1653	0.1496	0.1353
1	0.3662	0.3614	0.3543	0.3452	0.3347	0.3230	0.3106	0.2975	0.2842	0.2707
2	0.2014	0.2169	0.2303	0.2417	0.2510	0.2584	0.2640	0.2678	0.2700	0.2707
3	0.0738	0.0867	0.0998	0.1128	0.1255	0.1378	0.1496	0.1607	0.1710	0.1804
4	0.0203	0.0260	0.0324	0.0395	0.0471	0.0551	0.0636	0.0723	0.0812	0.0902
5	0.0045	0.0062	0.0084	0.0111	0.0141	0.0176	0.0216	0.0260	0.0309	0.0361
6	0.0008	0.0012	0.0018	0.0026	0.0035	0.0047	0.0061	0.0078	0.0098	0.0120
7	0.0001	0.0002	0.0003	0.0005	0.0008	0.0011	0.0015	0.0020	0.0027	0.0034
8	0.0000	0.0000	0.0001	0.0001	0.0001	0.0002	0.0003	0.0005	0.0006	0.0009
9	0.0000	0.0000	0.0000	0.0000	0.0000	0.0000	0.0001	0.0001	0.0001	0.0002

x	2.1	2.2	2.3	2.4	2.5	2.6	2.7	2.8	2.9	3.0
0	0.1225	0.1108	0.1003	0.0907	0.0821	0.0743	0.0672	0.0608	0.0050	0.0498
1	0.2572	0.2438	0.2306	0.2177	0.2052	0.1931	0.1815	0.1703	0.1596	0.1494
2	0.2700	0.2681	0.2652	0.2613	0.2565	0.2510	0.2450	0.2384	0.2314	0.2240
3	0.1890	0.1966	0.2033	0.2090	0.2138	0.2176	0.2205	0.2225	0.2237	0.2240
4	0.0992	0.1082	0.1169	0.1254	0.1336	0.1414	0.1488	0.1557	0.1622	0.1680
5	0.0417	0.0476	0.0538	0.0602	0.0668	0.0735	0.0804	0.0872	0.0940	0.1008
6	0.0146	0.0174	0.0206	0.0241	0.0278	0.0319	0.0362	0.0407	0.0455	0.0504
7	0.0044	0.0055	0.0068	0.0083	0.0099	0.0118	0.0139	0.0163	0.0188	0.0216
8	0.0011	0.0015	0.0019	0.0025	0.0031	0.0038	0.0047	0.0057	0.0068	0.0081
9	0.0003	0.0004	0.0005	0.0007	0.0009	0.0011	0.0014	0.0018	0.0022	0.0027
10	0.0001	0.0001	0.0001	0.0002	0.0002	0.0003	0.0004	0.0005	0.0006	0.0008
11	0.0000	0.0000	0.0000	0.0000	0.0000	0.0001	0.0001	0.0001	0.0002	0.0002
12	0.0000	0.0000	0.0000	0.0000	0.0000	0.0000	0.0000	0.0000	0.0000	0.0001

x	3.1	3.2	3.3	3.4	3.5	3.6	3.7	3.8	3.9	4.0
0	0.0450	0.0408	0.0369	0.0334	0.0302	0.0273	0.0247	0.0224	0.0202	0.0183
1	0.1397	0.1304	0.1217	0.1135	0.1057	0.0984	0.0915	0.0850	0.0789	0.0733
2	0.2165	0.2087	0.2008	0.1929	0.1850	0.1771	0.1692	0.1615	0.1539	0.1465
3	0.2237	0.2226	0.2209	0.2186	0.2158	0.2125	0.2087	0.2046	0.2001	0.1954
4	0.1734	0.1781	0.1823	0.1858	0.1888	0.1912	0.1931	0.1944	0.1951	0.1954
5	0.1075	0.1140	0.1203	0.1264	0.1322	0.1377	0.1429	0.1477	0.1522	0.1563
6	0.0555	0.0608	0.0662	0.0716	0.0771	0.0826	0.0881	0.0936	0.0989	0.1042
7	0.0246	0.0278	0.0312	0.0348	0.0385	0.0425	0.0466	0.0508	0.0551	0.0595
8	0.0095	0.0111	0.0129	0.0148	0.0169	0.0191	0.0215	0.0241	0.0269	0.0298
9	0.0033	0.0040	0.0047	0.0056	0.0066	0.0076	0.0089	0.0102	0.0116	0.0132
10	0.0010	0.0013	0.0016	0.0019	0.0023	0.0028	0.0033	0.0039	0.0045	0.0053
11	0.0003	0.0004	0.0005	0.0006	0.0007	0.0009	0.0011	0.0013	0.0016	0.0019
12	0.0001	0.0001	0.0001	0.0002	0.0002	0.0003	0.0003	0.0004	0.0005	0.0006
13	0.0000	0.0000	0.0000	0.0000	0.0001	0.0001	0.0001	0.0001	0.0002	0.0002
14	0.0000	0.0000	0.0000	0.0000	0.0000	0.0000	0.0000	0.0000	0.0000	0.0001

Table A-3 (continued)

					μ					
x	4.1	4.2	4.3	4.4	4.5	4.6	4.7	4.8	4.9	5.0
0	0.0166	0.0150	0.0136	0.0123	0.0111	0.0101	0.0091	0.0082	0.0074	0.0067
1	0.0679	0.0630	0.0583	0.0540	0.0500	0.0462	0.0427	0.0395	0.0365	0.0337
2	0.1393	0.1323	0.1254	0.1188	0.1125	0.1063	0.1005	0.0948	0.0894	0.0842
3	0.1904	0.1852	0.1798	0.1743	0.1687	0.1631	0.1574	0.1517	0.1460	0.1404
4	0.1951	0.1944	0.1933	0.1917	0.1898	0.1875	0.1849	0.1820	0.1789	0.1755
5	0.1600	0.1633	0.1662	0.1687	0.1708	0.1725	0.1738	0.1747	0.1753	0.1755
6	0.1093	0.1143	0.1191	0.1237	0.1281	0.1323	0.1362	0.1398	0.1432	0.1462
7	0.0640	0.0686	0.0732	0.0778	0.0824	0.0869	0.0914	0.0959	0.1002	0.1044
8	0.0328	0.0360	0.0393	0.0428	0.0463	0.0500	0.0537	0.0575	0.0614	0.0653
9	0.0150	0.0168	0.0188	0.0209	0.0232	0.0255	0.0280	0.0307	0.0334	0.0363
10	0.0061	0.0071	0.0081	0.0092	0.0104	0.0118	0.0132	0.0147	0.0164	0.0181
11	0.0023	0.0027	0.0032	0.0037	0.0043	0.0049	0.0056	0.0064	0.0073	0.0082
12	0.0008	0.0009	0.0011	0.0014	0.0016	0.0019	0.0022	0.0026	0.0030	0.0034
13	0.0002	0.0003	0.0004	0.0005	0.0006	0.0007	0.0008	0.0009	0.0011	0.0013
14	0.0001	0.0001	0.0001	0.0001	0.0002	0.0002	0.0003	0.0003	0.0004	0.0005
15	0.0000	0.0000	0.0000	0.0000	0.0001	0.0001	0.0001	0.0001	0.0001	0.0002

x	5.1	5.2	5.3	5.4	5.5	5.6	5.7	5.8	5.9	6.0
0	0.0061	0.0055	0.0050	0.0045	0.0041	0.0037	0.0033	0.0030	0.0027	0.0025
1	0.0311	0.0287	0.0265	0.0244	0.0225	0.0207	0.0191	0.0176	0.0162	0.0149
2	0.0793	0.0746	0.0701	0.0659	0.0618	0.0580	0.0544	0.0509	0.0477	0.0446
3	0.1348	0.1293	0.1239	0.1185	0.1133	0.1082	0.1033	0.0985	0.0938	0.0892
4	0.1719	0.1681	0.1641	0.1600	0.1558	0.1515	0.1472	0.1428	0.1383	0.1339
5	0.1753	0.1748	0.1740	0.1728	0.1714	0.1697	0.1678	0.1656	0.1632	0.1606
6	0.1490	0.1515	0.1537	0.1555	0.1571	0.1584	0.1594	0.1601	0.1605	0.1606
7	0.1086	0.1125	0.1163	0.1200	0.1234	0.1267	0.1298	0.1326	0.1353	0.1377
8	0.0692	0.0731	0.0771	0.0810	0.0849	0.0887	0.0925	0.0962	0.0998	0.1033
9	0.0392	0.0423	0.0454	0.0486	0.0519	0.0552	0.0586	0.0620	0.0654	0.0688
10	0.0200	0.0220	0.0241	0.0262	0.0285	0.0309	0.0334	0.0359	0.0386	0.0413
11	0.0093	0.0104	0.0116	0.0129	0.0143	0.0157	0.0173	0.0190	0.0207	0.0225
12	0.0039	0.0045	0.0051	0.0058	0.0065	0.0073	0.0082	0.0092	0.0102	0.0113
13	0.0015	0.0018	0.0021	0.0024	0.0028	0.0032	0.0036	0.0041	0.0046	0.0052
14	0.0006	0.0007	0.0008	0.0009	0.0011	0.0013	0.0015	0.0017	0.0019	0.0022
15	0.0002	0.0002	0.0003	0.0003	0.0004	0.0005	0.0006	0.0007	0.0008	0.0009
16	0.0001	0.0001	0.0001	0.0001	0.0001	0.0002	0.0002	0.0002	0.0003	0.0003
17	0.0000	0.0000	0.0000	0.0000	0.0000	0.0001	0.0001	0.0001	0.0001	0.0001

x	6.1	6.2	6.3	6.4	6.5	6.6	6.7	6.8	6.9	7.0
0	0.0022	0.0020	0.0018	0.0017	0.0015	0.0014	0.0012	0.0011	0.0010	0.0009
1	0.0137	0.0126	0.0116	0.0106	0.0098	0.0090	0.0082	0.0076	0.0070	0.0064
2	0.0417	0.0390	0.0364	0.0340	0.0318	0.0296	0.0276	0.0258	0.0240	0.0223
3	0.0848	0.0806	0.0765	0.0726	0.0688	0.0652	0.0617	0.0584	0.0552	0.0521
4	0.1294	0.1249	0.1205	0.1162	0.1118	0.1076	0.1034	0.0992	0.0952	0.0912
5	0.1579	0.1549	0.1519	0.1487	0.1454	0.1420	0.1385	0.1349	0.1314	0.1277
6	0.1605	0.1601	0.1595	0.1586	0.1575	0.1562	0.1546	0.1529	0.1511	0.1490

Table A-3 (continued)

					μ					
x	6.1	6.2	6.3	6.4	6.5	6.6	6.7	6.8	6.9	7.0
7	0.1399	0.1418	0.1435	0.1450	0.1462	0.1472	0.1480	0.1486	0.1489	0.1490
8	0.1066	0.1099	0.1130	0.1160	0.1188	0.1215	0.1240	0.1263	0.1284	0.1304
9	0.0723	0.0757	0.0791	0.0825	0.0858	0.0891	0.0923	0.0954	0.0985	0.1014
10	0.0441	0.0469	0.0498	0.0528	0.0558	0.0588	0.0618	0.0649	0.0679	0.0710
11	0.0245	0.0265	0.0285	0.0307	0.0330	0.0353	0.0377	0.0401	0.0426	0.0452
12	0.0124	0.0137	0.0150	0.0164	0.0179	0.0194	0.0210	0.0227	0.0245	0.0264
13	0.0058	0.0065	0.0073	0.0081	0.0089	0.0098	0.0108	0.0119	0.0130	0.0142
14	0.0025	0.0029	0.0033	0.0037	0.0041	0.0046	0.0052	0.0058	0.0064	0.0071
15	0.0010	0.0012	0.0014	0.0016	0.0018	0.0020	0.0023	0.0026	0.0029	0.0033
16	0.0004	0.0005	0.0005	0.0006	0.0007	0.0008	0.0010	0.0011	0.0013	0.0014
17	0.0001	0.0002	0.0002	0.0002	0.0003	0.0003	0.0004	0.0004	0.0005	0.0006
18	0.0000	0.0001	0.0001	0.0001	0.0001	0.0001	0.0001	0.0002	0.0002	0.0002
19	0.0000	0.0000	0.0000	0.0000	0.0000	0.0000	0.0000	0.0001	0.0001	0.0001

x	7.1	7.2	7.3	7.4	7.5	7.6	7.7	7.8	7.9	8.0
0	0.0008	0.0007	0.0007	0.0006	0.0006	0.0005	0.0005	0.0004	0.0004	0.0003
1	0.0059	0.0054	0.0049	0.0045	0.0041	0.0038	0.0035	0.0032	0.0029	0.0027
2	0.0208	0.0194	0.0180	0.0167	0.0156	0.0145	0.0134	0.0125	0.0116	0.0107
3	0.0492	0.0464	0.0438	0.0413	0.0389	0.0366	0.0345	0.0324	0.0305	0.0286
4	0.0874	0.0836	0.0799	0.0764	0.0729	0.0696	0.0663	0.0632	0.0602	0.0573
5	0.1241	0.1204	0.1167	0.1130	0.1094	0.1057	0.1021	0.0986	0.0951	0.0916
6	0.1468	0.1445	0.1420	0.1394	0.1367	0.1339	0.1311	0.1282	0.1252	0.1221
7	0.1489	0.1486	0.1481	0.1474	0.1465	0.1454	0.1442	0.1428	0.1413	0.1396
8	0.1321	0.1337	0.1351	0.1363	0.1373	0.1382	0.1388	0.1392	0.1395	0.1396
9	0.1042	0.1070	0.1096	0.1121	0.1144	0.1167	0.1187	0.1207	0.1224	0.1241
10	0.0740	0.0770	0.0800	0.0829	0.0858	0.0887	0.0914	0.0941	0.0967	0.0993
11	0.0478	0.0504	0.0531	0.0558	0.0585	0.0613	0.0640	0.0667	0.0695	0.0722
12	0.0283	0.0303	0.0323	0.0344	0.0366	0.0388	0.0411	0.0434	0.0457	0.0481
13	0.0154	0.0168	0.0181	0.0196	0.0211	0.0227	0.0243	0.0260	0.0278	0.0296
14	0.0078	0.0086	0.0095	0.0104	0.0113	0.0123	0.0134	0.0145	0.0157	0.0169
15	0.0037	0.0041	0.0046	0.0051	0.0057	0.0062	0.0069	0.0075	0.0083	0.0090
16	0.0016	0.0019	0.0021	0.0024	0.0026	0.0030	0.0033	0.0037	0.0041	0.0045
17	0.0007	0.0008	0.0009	0.0010	0.0012	0.0013	0.0015	0.0017	0.0019	0.0021
18	0.0003	0.0003	0.0004	0.0004	0.0005	0.0006	0.0006	0.0007	0.0008	0.0009
19	0.0001	0.0001	0.0001	0.0002	0.0002	0.0002	0.0003	0.0003	0.0003	0.0004
20	0.0000	0.0000	0.0001	0.0001	0.0001	0.0001	0.0001	0.0001	0.0001	0.0002
21	0.0000	0.0000	0.0000	0.0000	0.0000	0.0000	0.0000	0.0000	0.0001	0.0001

x	8.1	8.2	8.3	8.4	8.5	8.6	8.7	8.8	8.9	9.0
0	0.0003	0.0003	0.0002	0.0002	0.0002	0.0002	0.0002	0.0002	0.0001	0.0001
1	0.0025	0.0023	0.0021	0.0019	0.0017	0.0016	0.0014	0.0013	0.0012	0.0011
2	0.0100	0.0092	0.0086	0.0079	0.0074	0.0068	0.0063	0.0058	0.0054	0.0050
3	0.0269	0.0252	0.0237	0.0222	0.0208	0.0195	0.0183	0.0171	0.0160	0.0150
4	0.0544	0.0517	0.0491	0.0466	0.0443	0.0420	0.0398	0.0377	0.0357	0.0337
5	0.0882	0.0849	0.0816	0.0784	0.0752	0.0722	0.0692	0.0663	0.0635	0.0607
6	0.1191	0.1160	0.1128	0.1097	0.1066	0.1034	0.1003	0.0972	0.0941	0.0911
7	0.1378	0.1358	0.1338	0.1317	0.1294	0.1271	0.1247	0.1222	0.1197	0.1171
8	0.1395	0.1392	0.1388	0.1382	0.1375	0.1366	0.1356	0.1344	0.1332	0.1318
9	0.1256	0.1269	0.1280	0.1290	0.1299	0.1306	0.1311	0.1315	0.1317	0.1318

Table A-3 (continued)

					μ					
x	8.1	8.2	8.3	8.4	8.5	8.6	8.7	8.8	8.9	9.0
10	0.1017	0.1040	0.1063	0.1084	0.1104	0.1123	0.1140	0.1157	0.1172	0.1186
11	0.0749	0.0776	0.0802	0.0828	0.0853	0.0878	0.0902	0.0925	0.0948	0.0970
12	0.0505	0.0530	0.0555	0.0579	0.0604	0.0629	0.0654	0.0679	0.0703	0.0728
13	0.0315	0.0334	0.0354	0.0374	0.0395	0.0416	0.0438	0.0459	0.0481	0.0504
14	0.0182	0.0196	0.0210	0.0225	0.0240	0.0256	0.0272	0.0289	0.0306	0.0324
15	0.0098	0.0107	0.0116	0.0126	0.0136	0.0147	0.0158	0.0169	0.0182	0.0194
16	0.0050	0.0055	0.0060	0.0066	0.0072	0.0079	0.0086	0.0093	0.0101	0.0109
17	0.0024	0.0026	0.0029	0.0033	0.0036	0.0040	0.0044	0.0048	0.0053	0.0058
18	0.0011	0.0012	0.0014	0.0015	0.0017	0.0019	0.0021	0.0024	0.0026	0.0029
19	0.0005	0.0005	0.0006	0.0007	0.0008	0.0009	0.0010	0.0011	0.0012	0.0014
20	0.0002	0.0002	0.0002	0.0003	0.0003	0.0004	0.0004	0.0005	0.0005	0.0006
21	0.0001	0.0001	0.0001	0.0001	0.0001	0.0002	0.0002	0.0002	0.0002	0.0003
22	0.0000	0.0000	0.0000	0.0000	0.0001	0.0001	0.0001	0.0001	0.0001	0.0001

x	9.1	9.2	9.3	9.4	9.5	9.6	9.7	9.8	9.9	10.0
0	0.0001	0.0001	0.0001	0.0001	0.0001	0.0001	0.0001	0.0001	0.0001	0.0000
1	0.0010	0.0009	0.0009	0.0008	0.0007	0.0007	0.0006	0.0005	0.0005	0.0005
2	0.0046	0.0043	0.0040	0.0037	0.0034	0.0031	0.0029	0.0027	0.0025	0.0023
3	0.0140	0.0131	0.0123	0.0115	0.0107	0.0100	0.0093	0.0087	0.0081	0.0076
4	0.0319	0.0302	0.0285	0.0269	0.0254	0.0240	0.0226	0.0213	0.0201	0.0189
5	0.0581	0.0555	0.0530	0.0506	0.0483	0.0460	0.0439	0.0418	0.0398	0.0378
6	0.0881	0.0851	0.0822	0.0793	0.0764	0.0736	0.0709	0.0682	0.0656	0.0631
7	0.1145	0.1118	0.1091	0.1064	0.1037	0.1010	0.0982	0.0955	0.0928	0.0901
8	0.1302	0.1286	0.1269	0.1251	0.1232	0.1212	0.1191	0.1170	0.1148	0.1126
9	0.1317	0.1315	0.1311	0.1306	0.1300	0.1293	0.1284	0.1274	0.1263	0.1251
10	0.1198	0.1210	0.1219	0.1228	0.1235	0.1241	0.1245	0.1249	0.1250	0.1251
11	0.0991	0.1012	0.1031	0.1049	0.1067	0.1083	0.1098	0.1112	0.1125	0.1137
12	0.0752	0.0776	0.0799	0.0822	0.0844	0.0866	0.0888	0.0908	0.0928	0.0948
13	0.0526	0.0549	0.0572	0.0594	0.0617	0.0640	0.0662	0.0685	0.0707	0.0729
14	0.0342	0.0361	0.0380	0.0399	0.0419	0.0439	0.0459	0.0479	0.0500	0.0521
15	0.0208	0.0221	0.0235	0.0250	0.0265	0.0281	0.0297	0.0313	0.0330	0.0347
16	0.0118	0.0127	0.0137	0.0147	0.0157	0.0168	0.0180	0.0192	0.0204	0.0217
17	0.0063	0.0069	0.0075	0.0081	0.0088	0.0095	0.0103	0.0111	0.0119	0.0128
18	0.0032	0.0035	0.0039	0.0042	0.0046	0.0051	0.0055	0.0060	0.0065	0.0071
19	0.0015	0.0017	0.0019	0.0021	0.0023	0.0026	0.0028	0.0031	0.0034	0.0037
20	0.0007	0.0008	0.0009	0.0010	0.0011	0.0012	0.0014	0.0015	0.0017	0.0019
21	0.0003	0.0003	0.0004	0.0004	0.0005	0.0006	0.0006	0.0007	0.0008	0.0009
22	0.0001	0.0001	0.0002	0.0002	0.0002	0.0002	0.0003	0.0003	0.0004	0.0004
23	0.0000	0.0001	0.0001	0.0001	0.0001	0.0001	0.0001	0.0001	0.0002	0.0002
24	0.0000	0.0000	0.0000	0.0000	0.0000	0.0000	0.0000	0.0001	0.0001	0.0001

Table A-4 Areas of the Standard Normal Distribution

The entries in this table are the probabilities that a standard normal random variable is between 0 and z (the shaded area).

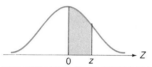

z	0.00	0.01	0.02	0.03	0.04	0.05	0.06	0.07	0.08	0.09
					Second Decimal Place in z					
0.0	0.0000	0.0040	0.0080	0.0120	0.0160	0.0199	0.0239	0.0279	0.0319	0.0359
0.1	0.0398	0.0438	0.0478	0.0517	0.0557	0.0596	0.0636	0.0675	0.0714	0.0753
0.2	0.0793	0.0832	0.0871	0.0910	0.0948	0.0987	0.1026	0.1064	0.1103	0.1141
0.3	0.1179	0.1217	0.1255	0.1293	0.1331	0.1368	0.1406	0.1443	0.1480	0.1517
0.4	0.1554	0.1591	0.1628	0.1664	0.1700	0.1736	0.1772	0.1808	0.1844	0.1879
0.5	0.1915	0.1950	0.1985	0.2019	0.2054	0.2088	0.2123	0.2157	0.2190	0.2224
0.6	0.2257	0.2291	0.2324	0.2357	0.2389	0.2422	0.2454	0.2486	0.2517	0.2549
0.7	0.2580	0.2611	0.2642	0.2673	0.2704	0.2734	0.2764	0.2794	0.2823	0.2852
0.8	0.2881	0.2910	0.2939	0.2967	0.2995	0.3023	0.3051	0.3078	0.3106	0.3133
0.9	0.3159	0.3186	0.3212	0.3238	0.3264	0.3289	0.3315	0.3340	0.3365	0.3389
1.0	0.3413	0.3438	0.3461	0.3485	0.3508	0.3531	0.3554	0.3577	0.3599	0.3621
1.1	0.3643	0.3665	0.3686	0.3708	0.3729	0.3749	0.3770	0.3790	0.3810	0.3830
1.2	0.3849	0.3869	0.3888	0.3907	0.3925	0.3944	0.3962	0.3980	0.3997	0.4015
1.3	0.4032	0.4049	0.4066	0.4082	0.4099	0.4115	0.4131	0.4147	0.4162	0.4177
1.4	0.4192	0.4207	0.4222	0.4236	0.4251	0.4265	0.4279	0.4292	0.4306	0.4319
1.5	0.4332	0.4345	0.4357	0.4370	0.4382	0.4394	0.4406	0.4418	0.4429	0.4441
1.6	0.4452	0.4463	0.4474	0.4484	0.4495	0.4505	0.4515	0.4525	0.4535	0.4545
1.7	0.4554	0.4564	0.4573	0.4582	0.4591	0.4599	0.4608	0.4616	0.4625	0.4633
1.8	0.4641	0.4649	0.4656	0.4664	0.4671	0.4678	0.4686	0.4693	0.4699	0.4706
1.9	0.4713	0.4719	0.4726	0.4732	0.4738	0.4744	0.4750	0.4756	0.4761	0.4767
2.0	0.4772	0.4778	0.4783	0.4788	0.4793	0.4798	0.4803	0.4808	0.4812	0.4817
2.1	0.4821	0.4826	0.4830	0.4834	0.4838	0.4842	0.4846	0.4850	0.4854	0.4857
2.2	0.4861	0.4864	0.4868	0.4871	0.4875	0.4878	0.4881	0.4884	0.4887	0.4890
2.3	0.4893	0.4896	0.4898	0.4901	0.4904	0.4906	0.4909	0.4911	0.4913	0.4916
2.4	0.4918	0.4920	0.4922	0.4925	0.4927	0.4929	0.4931	0.4932	0.4934	0.4936
2.5	0.4938	0.4940	0.4941	0.4943	0.4945	0.4946	0.4948	0.4949	0.4951	0.4952
2.6	0.4953	0.4955	0.4956	0.4957	0.4959	0.4960	0.4961	0.4962	0.4963	0.4964
2.7	0.4965	0.4966	0.4967	0.4968	0.4969	0.4970	0.4971	0.4972	0.4973	0.4974
2.8	0.4974	0.4975	0.4976	0.4977	0.4977	0.4978	0.4979	0.4979	0.4980	0.4981
2.9	0.4981	0.4982	0.4982	0.4983	0.4984	0.4984	0.4985	0.4985	0.4986	0.4986
3.0	0.4987	0.4987	0.4987	0.4988	0.4988	0.4989	0.4989	0.4989	0.4990	0.4990
3.1	0.4990	0.4991	0.4991	0.4991	0.4992	0.4992	0.4992	0.4992	0.4993	0.4993
3.2	0.4993	0.4993	0.4994	0.4994	0.4994	0.4994	0.4994	0.4995	0.4995	0.4995
3.3	0.4995	0.4995	0.4995	0.4996	0.4996	0.4996	0.4996	0.4996	0.4996	0.4997
3.4	0.4997	0.4997	0.4997	0.4997	0.4997	0.4997	0.4997	0.4997	0.4997	0.4998
3.5	0.4998									
4.0	0.49997									
4.5	0.499997									
5.0	0.4999997									

Reprinted with permission from *Standard Mathematical Tables*, 15th ed., © CRC Press, Inc., Boca Raton, FL.

Table A-5 Critical Values of t

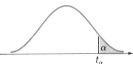

DEGREES OF FREEDOM	$t_{.100}$	$t_{.050}$	$t_{.025}$	$t_{.010}$	$t_{.005}$
1	3.078	6.314	12.706	31.821	63.657
2	1.886	2.920	4.303	6.965	9.925
3	1.638	2.353	3.182	4.541	5.841
4	1.533	2.132	2.776	3.747	4.604
5	1.476	2.015	2.571	3.365	4.032
6	1.440	1.943	2.447	3.143	3.707
7	1.415	1.895	2.365	2.998	3.499
8	1.397	1.860	2.306	2.896	3.355
9	1.383	1.833	2.262	2.821	3.250
10	1.372	1.812	2.228	2.764	3.169
11	1.363	1.796	2.201	2.718	3.106
12	1.356	1.782	2.179	2.681	3.055
13	1.350	1.771	2.160	2.650	3.012
14	1.345	1.761	2.145	2.624	2.977
15	1.341	1.753	2.131	2.602	2.947
16	1.337	1.746	2.120	2.583	2.921
17	1.333	1.740	2.110	2.567	2.898
18	1.330	1.734	2.101	2.552	2.878
19	1.328	1.729	2.093	2.539	2.861
20	1.325	1.725	2.086	2.528	2.845
21	1.323	1.721	2.080	2.518	2.831
22	1.321	1.717	2.074	2.508	2.819
23	1.319	1.714	2.069	2.500	2.807
24	1.318	1.711	2.064	2.492	2.797
25	1.316	1.708	2.060	2.485	2.787
26	1.315	1.706	2.056	2.479	2.779
27	1.314	1.703	2.052	2.473	2.771
28	1.313	1.701	2.048	2.467	2.763
29	1.311	1.699	2.045	2.462	2.756
30	1.310	1.697	2.042	2.457	2.750
40	1.303	1.684	2.021	2.423	2.704
60	1.296	1.671	2.000	2.390	2.660
120	1.289	1.658	1.980	2.358	2.617
∞	1.282	1.645	1.960	2.326	2.576

From M. Merrington, "Table of Percentage Points of the t-Distribution," *Biometrika*, 1941, *32*, 300. Reproduced by permission of the *Biometrika* trustees.

Table A-6 Critical Values of χ^2

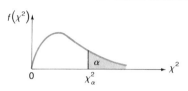

DEGREES OF FREEDOM	$\chi^2_{.995}$	$\chi^2_{.990}$	$\chi^2_{.975}$	$\chi^2_{.950}$	$\chi^2_{.900}$
1	0.0000393	0.0001571	0.0009821	0.0039321	0.0157908
2	0.0100251	0.0201007	0.0506356	0.102587	0.210720
3	0.0717212	0.114832	0.215795	0.351846	0.584375
4	0.206990	0.297110	0.484419	0.710721	1.063623
5	0.411740	0.554300	0.831211	1.145476	1.61031
6	0.675727	0.872085	1.237347	1.63539	2.20413
7	0.989265	1.239043	1.68987	2.16735	2.83311
8	1.344419	1.646482	2.17973	2.73264	3.48954
9	1.734926	2.087912	2.70039	3.32511	4.16816
10	2.15585	2.55821	3.24697	3.94030	4.86518
11	2.60321	3.05347	3.81575	4.57481	5.57779
12	3.07382	3.57056	4.40379	5.22603	6.30380
13	3.56503	4.10691	5.00874	5.89186	7.04150
14	4.07468	4.66043	5.62872	6.57063	7.78953
15	4.60094	5.22935	6.26214	7.26094	8.54675
16	5.14224	5.81221	6.90766	7.96164	9.31223
17	5.69724	6.40776	7.56418	8.67176	10.0852
18	6.26481	7.01491	8.23075	9.39046	10.8649
19	6.84398	7.63273	8.90655	10.1170	11.6509
20	7.43386	8.26040	9.59083	10.8508	12.4426
21	8.03366	8.89720	10.28293	11.5913	13.2396
22	8.64272	9.54249	10.9823	12.3380	14.0415
23	9.26042	10.19567	11.6885	13.0905	14.8479
24	9.88623	10.8564	12.4011	13.8484	15.6587
25	10.5197	11.5240	13.1197	14.6114	16.4734
26	11.1603	12.1981	13.8439	15.3791	17.2919
27	11.8076	12.8786	14.5733	16.1513	18.1138
28	12.4613	13.5648	15.3079	16.9279	18.9392
29	13.1211	14.2565	16.0471	17.7083	19.7677
30	13.7867	14.9535	16.7908	18.4926	20.5992
40	20.7065	22.1643	24.4331	26.5093	29.0505
50	27.9907	29.7067	32.3574	34.7642	37.6886
60	35.5346	37.4848	40.4817	43.1879	46.4589
70	43.2752	45.4418	48.7576	51.7393	55.3290
80	51.1720	53.5400	57.1532	60.3915	64.2778
90	59.1963	61.7541	65.6466	69.1260	73.2912
100	67.3276	70.0648	74.2219	77.9295	82.3581

Table A-6 (continued)

DEGREES OF FREEDOM	$\chi^2_{.100}$	$\chi^2_{.050}$	$\chi^2_{.025}$	$\chi^2_{.010}$	$\chi^2_{.005}$
1	2.70554	3.84146	5.02389	6.63490	7.87944
2	4.60517	5.99147	7.37776	9.21034	10.5966
3	6.25139	7.81473	9.34840	11.3449	12.8381
4	7.77944	9.48773	11.1433	13.2767	14.8602
5	9.23635	11.0705	12.8325	15.0863	16.7496
6	10.6446	12.5916	14.4494	16.8119	18.5476
7	12.0170	14.0671	16.0128	18.4753	20.2777
8	13.3616	15.5073	17.5346	20.0902	21.9550
9	14.6837	16.9190	19.0228	21.6660	23.5893
10	15.9871	18.3070	20.4831	23.2093	25.1882
11	17.2750	19.6751	21.9200	24.7250	26.7569
12	18.5494	21.0261	23.3367	26.2170	28.2995
13	19.8119	22.3621	24.7356	27.6883	29.8194
14	21.0642	23.6848	26.1190	29.1413	31.3193
15	22.3072	24.9958	27.4884	30.5779	32.8013
16	23.5418	26.2962	28.8454	31.9999	34.2672
17	24.7690	27.5871	30.1910	33.4087	35.7185
18	25.9894	28.8693	31.5264	34.8053	37.1564
19	27.2036	30.1435	32.8523	36.1908	38.5822
20	28.4120	31.4104	34.1696	37.5662	39.9968
21	29.6151	32.6705	35.4789	38.9321	41.4010
22	30.8133	33.9244	36.7807	40.2894	42.7956
23	32.0069	35.1725	38.0757	41.6384	44.1813
24	33.1963	36.4151	39.3641	42.9798	45.5585
25	34.3816	37.6525	40.6465	44.3141	46.9278
26	35.5631	38.8852	41.9232	45.6417	48.2899
27	36.7412	40.1133	43.1944	46.9630	49.6449
28	37.9159	41.3372	44.4607	48.2782	50.9933
29	39.0875	42.5569	45.7222	49.5879	52.3356
30	40.2560	43.7729	46.9792	50.8922	53.6720
40	51.8050	55.7585	59.3417	63.6907	66.7659
50	63.1671	67.5048	71.4202	76.1539	79.4900
60	74.3970	79.0819	83.2976	88.3794	91.9517
70	85.5271	90.5312	95.0231	100.425	104.215
80	96.5782	101.879	106.629	112.329	116.321
90	107.565	113.145	118.136	124.116	128.229
100	118.498	124.342	129.561	135.807	140.169

Table A-7 Percentage Points of the F Distribution

(a) $\alpha = .10$

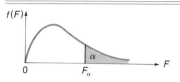

ν_2 \ ν_1	NUMERATOR DEGREES OF FREEDOM								
	1	2	3	4	5	6	7	8	9
1	39.86	49.50	53.59	55.83	57.24	58.20	58.91	59.44	59.86
2	8.53	9.00	9.16	9.24	9.29	9.33	9.35	9.37	9.38
3	5.54	5.46	5.39	5.34	5.31	5.28	5.27	5.25	5.24
4	4.54	4.32	4.19	4.11	4.05	4.01	3.98	3.95	3.94
5	4.06	3.78	3.62	3.52	3.45	3.40	3.37	3.34	3.32
6	3.78	3.46	3.29	3.18	3.11	3.05	3.01	2.98	2.96
7	3.59	3.26	3.07	2.96	2.88	2.83	2.78	2.75	2.72
8	3.46	3.11	2.92	2.81	2.73	2.67	2.62	2.59	2.56
9	3.36	3.01	2.81	2.69	2.61	2.55	2.51	2.47	2.44
10	3.29	2.92	2.73	2.61	2.52	2.46	2.41	2.38	2.35
11	3.23	2.86	2.66	2.54	2.45	2.39	2.34	2.30	2.27
12	3.18	2.81	2.61	2.48	2.39	2.33	2.28	2.24	2.21
13	3.14	2.76	2.56	2.43	2.35	2.28	2.23	2.20	2.16
14	3.10	2.73	2.52	2.39	2.31	2.24	2.19	2.15	2.12
15	3.07	2.70	2.49	2.36	2.27	2.21	2.16	2.12	2.09
16	3.05	2.67	2.46	2.33	2.24	2.18	2.13	2.09	2.06
17	3.03	2.64	2.44	2.31	2.22	2.15	2.10	2.06	2.03
18	3.01	2.62	2.42	2.29	2.20	2.13	2.08	2.04	2.00
19	2.99	2.61	2.40	2.27	2.18	2.11	2.06	2.02	1.98
20	2.97	2.59	2.38	2.25	2.16	2.09	2.04	2.00	1.96
21	2.96	2.57	2.36	2.23	2.14	2.08	2.02	1.98	1.95
22	2.95	2.56	2.35	2.22	2.13	2.06	2.01	1.97	1.93
23	2.94	2.55	2.34	2.21	2.11	2.05	1.99	1.95	1.92
24	2.93	2.54	2.33	2.19	2.10	2.04	1.98	1.94	1.91
25	2.92	2.53	2.32	2.18	2.09	2.02	1.97	1.93	1.89
26	2.91	2.52	2.31	2.17	2.08	2.01	1.96	1.92	1.88
27	2.90	2.51	2.30	2.17	2.07	2.00	1.95	1.91	1.87
28	2.89	2.50	2.29	2.16	2.06	2.00	1.94	1.90	1.87
29	2.89	2.50	2.28	2.15	2.06	1.99	1.93	1.89	1.86
30	2.88	2.49	2.28	2.14	2.05	1.98	1.93	1.88	1.85
40	2.84	2.44	2.23	2.09	2.00	1.93	1.87	1.83	1.79
60	2.79	2.39	2.18	2.04	1.95	1.87	1.82	1.77	1.74
120	2.75	2.35	2.13	1.99	1.90	1.82	1.77	1.72	1.68
∞	2.71	2.30	2.08	1.94	1.85	1.77	1.72	1.67	1.63

DENOMINATOR DEGREES OF FREEDOM

Table A-7 (a) (continued)

ν_1 / ν_2	NUMERATOR DEGREES OF FREEDOM									
	10	12	15	20	24	30	40	60	120	∞
1	60.19	60.71	61.22	61.74	62.00	62.26	62.53	62.79	63.06	63.33
2	9.39	9.41	9.42	9.44	9.45	9.46	9.47	9.47	9.48	9.49
3	5.23	5.22	5.20	5.18	5.18	5.17	5.16	5.15	5.14	5.13
4	3.92	3.90	3.87	3.84	3.83	3.82	3.80	3.79	3.78	3.76
5	3.30	3.27	3.24	3.21	3.19	3.17	3.16	3.14	3.12	3.10
6	2.94	2.90	2.87	2.84	2.82	2.80	2.78	2.76	2.74	2.72
7	2.70	2.67	2.63	2.59	2.58	2.56	2.54	2.51	2.49	2.47
8	2.54	2.50	2.46	2.42	2.40	2.38	2.36	2.34	2.32	2.29
9	2.42	2.38	2.34	2.30	2.28	2.25	2.23	2.21	2.18	2.16
10	2.32	2.28	2.24	2.20	2.18	2.16	2.13	2.11	2.08	2.06
11	2.25	2.21	2.17	2.12	2.10	2.08	2.05	2.03	2.00	1.97
12	2.19	2.15	2.10	2.06	2.04	2.01	1.99	1.96	1.93	1.90
13	2.14	2.10	2.05	2.01	1.98	1.96	1.93	1.90	1.88	1.85
14	2.10	2.05	2.01	1.96	1.94	1.91	1.89	1.86	1.83	1.80
15	2.06	2.02	1.97	1.92	1.90	1.87	1.85	1.82	1.79	1.76
16	2.03	1.99	1.94	1.89	1.87	1.84	1.81	1.78	1.75	1.72
17	2.00	1.96	1.91	1.86	1.84	1.81	1.78	1.75	1.72	1.69
18	1.98	1.93	1.89	1.84	1.81	1.78	1.75	1.72	1.69	1.66
19	1.96	1.91	1.86	1.81	1.79	1.76	1.73	1.70	1.67	1.63
20	1.94	1.89	1.84	1.79	1.77	1.74	1.71	1.68	1.64	1.61
21	1.92	1.87	1.83	1.78	1.75	1.72	1.69	1.66	1.62	1.59
22	1.90	1.86	1.81	1.76	1.73	1.70	1.67	1.64	1.60	1.57
23	1.89	1.84	1.80	1.74	1.72	1.69	1.66	1.62	1.59	1.55
24	1.88	1.83	1.78	1.73	1.70	1.67	1.64	1.61	1.57	1.53
25	1.87	1.82	1.77	1.72	1.69	1.66	1.63	1.59	1.56	1.52
26	1.86	1.81	1.76	1.71	1.68	1.65	1.61	1.58	1.54	1.50
27	1.85	1.80	1.75	1.70	1.67	1.64	1.60	1.57	1.53	1.49
28	1.84	1.79	1.74	1.69	1.66	1.63	1.59	1.56	1.52	1.48
29	1.83	1.78	1.73	1.68	1.65	1.62	1.58	1.55	1.51	1.47
30	1.82	1.77	1.72	1.67	1.64	1.61	1.57	1.54	1.50	1.46
40	1.76	1.71	1.66	1.61	1.57	1.54	1.51	1.47	1.42	1.38
60	1.71	1.66	1.60	1.54	1.51	1.48	1.44	1.40	1.35	1.29
120	1.65	1.60	1.55	1.48	1.45	1.41	1.37	1.32	1.26	1.19
∞	1.60	1.55	1.49	1.42	1.38	1.34	1.30	1.24	1.17	1.00

DENOMINATOR DEGREES OF FREEDOM

Table A-7 Percentage Points of the *F* Distribution

(b) $\alpha = .05$

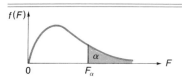

ν_2 \ ν_1	NUMERATOR DEGREES OF FREEDOM								
	1	2	3	4	5	6	7	8	9
1	161.4	199.5	215.7	224.6	230.2	234.0	236.8	238.9	240.5
2	18.51	19.00	19.16	19.25	19.30	19.33	19.35	19.37	19.38
3	10.13	9.55	9.28	9.12	9.01	8.94	8.89	8.85	8.81
4	7.71	6.94	6.59	6.39	6.26	6.16	6.09	6.04	6.00
5	6.61	5.79	5.41	5.19	5.05	4.95	4.88	4.82	4.77
6	5.99	5.14	4.76	4.53	4.39	4.28	4.21	4.15	4.10
7	5.59	4.74	4.35	4.12	3.97	3.87	3.79	3.73	3.68
8	5.32	4.46	4.07	3.84	3.69	3.58	3.50	3.44	3.39
9	5.12	4.26	3.86	3.63	3.48	3.37	3.29	3.23	3.18
10	4.96	4.10	3.71	3.48	3.33	3.22	3.14	3.07	3.02
11	4.84	3.98	3.59	3.36	3.20	3.09	3.01	2.95	2.90
12	4.75	3.89	3.49	3.26	3.11	3.00	2.91	2.85	2.80
13	4.67	3.81	3.41	3.18	3.03	2.92	2.83	2.77	2.71
14	4.60	3.74	3.34	3.11	2.96	2.85	2.76	2.70	2.65
15	4.54	3.68	3.29	3.06	2.90	2.79	2.71	2.64	2.59
16	4.49	3.63	3.24	3.01	2.85	2.74	2.66	2.59	2.54
17	4.45	3.59	3.20	2.96	2.81	2.70	2.61	2.55	2.49
18	4.41	3.55	3.16	2.93	2.77	2.66	2.58	2.51	2.46
19	4.38	3.52	3.13	2.90	2.74	2.63	2.54	2.48	2.42
20	4.35	3.49	3.10	2.87	2.71	2.60	2.51	2.45	2.39
21	4.32	3.47	3.07	2.84	2.68	2.57	2.49	2.42	2.37
22	4.30	3.44	3.05	2.82	2.66	2.55	2.46	2.40	2.34
23	4.28	3.42	3.03	2.80	2.64	2.53	2.44	2.37	2.32
24	4.26	3.40	3.01	2.78	2.62	2.51	2.42	2.36	2.30
25	4.24	3.39	2.99	2.76	2.60	2.49	2.40	2.34	2.28
26	4.23	3.37	2.98	2.74	2.59	2.47	2.39	2.32	2.27
27	4.21	3.35	2.96	2.73	2.57	2.46	2.37	2.31	2.25
28	4.20	3.34	2.95	2.71	2.56	2.45	2.36	2.29	2.24
29	4.18	3.33	2.93	2.70	2.55	2.43	2.35	2.28	2.22
30	4.17	3.32	2.92	2.69	2.53	2.42	2.33	2.27	2.21
40	4.08	3.23	2.84	2.61	2.45	2.34	2.25	2.18	2.12
60	4.00	3.15	2.76	2.53	2.37	2.25	2.17	2.10	2.04
120	3.92	3.07	2.68	2.45	2.29	2.17	2.09	2.02	1.96
∞	3.84	3.00	2.60	2.37	2.21	2.10	2.01	1.94	1.88

DENOMINATOR DEGREES OF FREEDOM

Table A-7 (b) (continued)

ν_1 / ν_2	NUMERATOR DEGREES OF FREEDOM									
	10	12	15	20	24	30	40	60	120	∞
1	241.9	243.9	245.9	248.0	249.1	250.1	251.1	252.2	253.3	254.3
2	19.40	19.41	19.43	19.45	19.45	19.46	19.47	19.48	19.49	19.50
3	8.79	8.74	8.70	8.66	8.64	8.62	8.59	8.57	8.55	8.53
4	5.96	5.91	5.86	5.80	5.77	5.75	5.72	5.69	5.66	5.63
5	4.74	4.68	4.62	4.56	4.53	4.50	4.46	4.43	4.40	4.36
6	4.06	4.00	3.94	3.87	3.84	3.81	3.77	3.74	3.70	3.67
7	3.64	3.57	3.51	3.44	3.41	3.38	3.34	3.30	3.27	3.23
8	3.35	3.28	3.22	3.15	3.12	3.08	3.04	3.01	2.97	2.93
9	3.14	3.07	3.01	2.94	2.90	2.86	2.83	2.79	2.75	2.71
10	2.98	2.91	2.85	2.77	2.74	2.70	2.66	2.62	2.58	2.54
11	2.85	2.79	2.72	2.65	2.61	2.57	2.53	2.49	2.45	2.40
12	2.75	2.69	2.62	2.54	2.51	2.47	2.43	2.38	2.34	2.30
13	2.67	2.60	2.53	2.46	2.42	2.38	2.34	2.30	2.25	2.21
14	2.60	2.53	2.46	2.39	2.35	2.31	2.27	2.22	2.18	2.13
15	2.54	2.48	2.40	2.33	2.29	2.25	2.20	2.16	2.11	2.07
16	2.49	2.42	2.35	2.28	2.24	2.19	2.15	2.11	2.06	2.01
17	2.45	2.38	2.31	2.23	2.19	2.15	2.10	2.06	2.01	1.96
18	2.41	2.34	2.27	2.19	2.15	2.11	2.06	2.02	1.97	1.92
19	2.38	2.31	2.23	2.16	2.11	2.07	2.03	1.98	1.93	1.88
20	2.35	2.28	2.20	2.12	2.08	2.04	1.99	1.95	1.90	1.84
21	2.32	2.25	2.18	2.10	2.05	2.01	1.96	1.92	1.87	1.81
22	2.30	2.23	2.15	2.07	2.03	1.98	1.94	1.89	1.84	1.78
23	2.27	2.20	2.13	2.05	2.01	1.96	1.91	1.86	1.81	1.76
24	2.25	2.18	2.11	2.03	1.98	1.94	1.89	1.84	1.79	1.73
25	2.24	2.16	2.09	2.01	1.96	1.92	1.87	1.82	1.77	1.71
26	2.22	2.15	2.07	1.99	1.95	1.90	1.85	1.80	1.75	1.69
27	2.20	2.13	2.06	1.97	1.93	1.88	1.84	1.79	1.73	1.67
28	2.19	2.12	2.04	1.96	1.91	1.87	1.82	1.77	1.71	1.65
29	2.18	2.10	2.03	1.94	1.90	1.85	1.81	1.75	1.70	1.64
30	2.16	2.09	2.01	1.93	1.89	1.84	1.79	1.74	1.68	1.62
40	2.08	2.00	1.92	1.84	1.79	1.74	1.69	1.64	1.58	1.51
60	1.99	1.92	1.84	1.75	1.70	1.65	1.59	1.53	1.47	1.39
120	1.91	1.83	1.75	1.66	1.61	1.55	1.50	1.43	1.35	1.25
∞	1.83	1.75	1.67	1.57	1.52	1.46	1.39	1.32	1.22	1.00

DENOMINATOR DEGREES OF FREEDOM

Table A-7 Percentage Points of the *F* Distribution

(c) α = .025

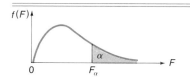

ν_2 \ ν_1	NUMERATOR DEGREES OF FREEDOM								
	1	2	3	4	5	6	7	8	9
1	647.8	799.5	864.2	899.6	921.8	937.1	948.2	956.7	963.3
2	38.51	39.00	39.17	39.25	39.30	39.33	39.36	39.37	39.39
3	17.44	16.04	15.44	15.10	14.88	14.73	14.62	14.54	14.47
4	12.22	10.65	9.98	9.60	9.36	9.20	9.07	8.98	8.90
5	10.01	8.43	7.76	7.39	7.15	6.98	6.85	6.76	6.68
6	8.81	7.26	6.60	6.23	5.99	5.82	5.70	5.60	5.52
7	8.07	6.54	5.89	5.52	5.29	5.12	4.99	4.90	4.82
8	7.57	6.06	5.42	5.05	4.82	4.65	4.53	4.43	4.36
9	7.21	5.71	5.08	4.72	4.48	4.32	4.20	4.10	4.03
10	6.94	5.46	4.83	4.47	4.24	4.07	3.95	3.85	3.78
11	6.72	5.26	4.63	4.28	4.04	3.88	3.76	3.66	3.59
12	6.55	5.10	4.47	4.12	3.89	3.73	3.61	3.51	3.44
13	6.41	4.97	4.35	4.00	3.77	3.60	3.48	3.39	3.31
14	6.30	4.86	4.24	3.89	3.66	3.50	3.38	3.29	3.21
15	6.20	4.77	4.15	3.80	3.58	3.41	3.29	3.20	3.12
16	6.12	4.69	4.08	3.73	3.50	3.34	3.22	3.12	3.05
17	6.04	4.62	4.01	3.66	3.44	3.28	3.16	3.06	2.98
18	5.98	4.56	3.95	3.61	3.38	3.22	3.10	3.01	2.93
19	5.92	4.51	3.90	3.56	3.33	3.17	3.05	2.96	2.88
20	5.87	4.46	3.86	3.51	3.29	3.13	3.01	2.91	2.84
21	5.83	4.42	3.82	3.48	3.25	3.09	2.97	2.87	2.80
22	5.79	4.38	3.78	3.44	3.22	3.05	2.93	2.84	2.76
23	5.75	4.35	3.75	3.41	3.18	3.02	2.90	2.81	2.73
24	5.72	4.32	3.72	3.38	3.15	2.99	2.87	2.78	2.70
25	5.69	4.29	3.69	3.35	3.13	2.97	2.85	2.75	2.68
26	5.66	4.27	3.67	3.33	3.10	2.94	2.82	2.73	2.65
27	5.63	4.24	3.65	3.31	3.08	2.92	2.80	2.71	2.63
28	5.61	4.22	3.63	3.29	3.06	2.90	2.78	2.69	2.61
29	5.59	4.20	3.61	3.27	3.04	2.88	2.76	2.67	2.59
30	5.57	4.18	3.59	3.25	3.03	2.87	2.75	2.65	2.57
40	5.42	4.05	3.46	3.13	2.90	2.74	2.62	2.53	2.45
60	5.29	3.93	3.34	3.01	2.79	2.63	2.51	2.41	2.33
120	5.15	3.80	3.23	2.89	2.67	2.52	2.39	2.30	2.22
∞	5.02	3.69	3.12	2.79	2.57	2.41	2.29	2.19	2.11

DENOMINATOR DEGREES OF FREEDOM

Table A-7 (c) (continued)

ν_1 / ν_2	NUMERATOR DEGREES OF FREEDOM									
	10	12	15	20	24	30	40	60	120	∞
1	968.6	976.7	984.9	993.1	997.2	1001	1006	1010	1014	1018
2	39.40	39.41	39.43	39.45	39.46	39.46	39.47	39.48	39.49	39.50
3	14.42	14.34	14.25	14.17	14.12	14.08	14.04	13.99	13.95	13.90
4	8.84	8.75	8.66	8.56	8.51	8.46	8.41	8.36	8.31	8.26
5	6.62	6.52	6.43	6.33	6.28	6.23	6.18	6.12	6.07	6.02
6	5.46	5.37	5.27	5.17	5.12	5.07	5.01	4.96	4.90	4.85
7	4.76	4.67	4.57	4.47	4.42	4.36	4.31	4.25	4.20	4.14
8	4.30	4.20	4.10	4.00	3.95	3.89	3.84	3.78	3.73	3.67
9	3.96	3.87	3.77	3.67	3.61	3.56	3.51	3.45	3.39	3.33
10	3.72	3.62	3.52	3.42	3.37	3.31	3.26	3.20	3.14	3.08
11	3.53	3.43	3.33	3.23	3.17	3.12	3.06	3.00	2.94	2.88
12	3.37	3.28	3.18	3.07	3.02	2.96	2.91	2.85	2.79	2.72
13	3.25	3.15	3.05	2.95	2.89	2.84	2.78	2.72	2.66	2.60
14	3.15	3.05	2.95	2.84	2.79	2.73	2.67	2.61	2.55	2.49
15	3.06	2.96	2.86	2.76	2.70	2.64	2.59	2.52	2.46	2.40
16	2.99	2.89	2.79	2.68	2.63	2.57	2.51	2.45	2.38	2.32
17	2.92	2.82	2.72	2.62	2.56	2.50	2.44	2.38	2.32	2.25
18	2.87	2.77	2.67	2.56	2.50	2.44	2.38	2.32	2.26	2.19
19	2.82	2.72	2.62	2.51	2.45	2.39	2.33	2.27	2.20	2.13
20	2.77	2.68	2.57	2.46	2.41	2.35	2.29	2.22	2.16	2.09
21	2.73	2.64	2.53	2.42	2.37	2.31	2.25	2.18	2.11	2.04
22	2.70	2.60	2.50	2.39	2.33	2.27	2.21	2.14	2.08	2.00
23	2.67	2.57	2.47	2.36	2.30	2.24	2.18	2.11	2.04	1.97
24	2.64	2.54	2.44	2.33	2.27	2.21	2.15	2.08	2.01	1.94
25	2.61	2.51	2.41	2.30	2.24	2.18	2.12	2.05	1.98	1.91
26	2.59	2.49	2.39	2.28	2.22	2.16	2.09	2.03	1.95	1.88
27	2.57	2.47	2.36	2.25	2.19	2.13	2.07	2.00	1.93	1.85
28	2.55	2.45	2.34	2.23	2.17	2.11	2.05	1.98	1.91	1.83
29	2.53	2.43	2.32	2.21	2.15	2.09	2.03	1.96	1.89	1.81
30	2.51	2.41	2.31	2.20	2.14	2.07	2.01	1.94	1.87	1.79
40	2.39	2.29	2.18	2.07	2.01	1.94	1.88	1.80	1.72	1.64
60	2.27	2.17	2.06	1.94	1.88	1.82	1.74	1.67	1.58	1.48
120	2.16	2.05	1.94	1.82	1.76	1.69	1.61	1.53	1.43	1.31
∞	2.05	1.94	1.83	1.71	1.64	1.57	1.48	1.39	1.27	1.00

DENOMINATOR DEGREES OF FREEDOM

Table A-7 Percentage Points of the *F* Distribution

(d) $\alpha = .01$

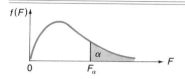

ν_1				NUMERATOR DEGREES OF FREEDOM					
ν_2	1	2	3	4	5	6	7	8	9
1	4,052	4,999.5	5,403	5,625	5,764	5,859	5,928	5,982	6,022
2	98.50	99.00	99.17	99.25	99.30	99.33	99.36	99.37	99.39
3	34.12	30.82	29.46	28.71	28.24	27.91	27.67	27.49	27.35
4	21.20	18.00	16.69	15.98	15.52	15.21	14.98	14.80	14.66
5	16.26	13.27	12.06	11.39	10.97	10.67	10.46	10.29	10.16
6	13.75	10.92	9.78	9.15	8.75	8.47	8.26	8.10	7.98
7	12.25	9.55	8.45	7.85	7.46	7.19	6.99	6.84	6.72
8	11.26	8.65	7.59	7.01	6.63	6.37	6.18	6.03	5.91
9	10.56	8.02	6.99	6.42	6.06	5.80	5.61	5.47	5.35
10	10.04	7.56	6.55	5.99	5.64	5.39	5.20	5.06	4.94
11	9.65	7.21	6.22	5.67	5.32	5.07	4.89	4.74	4.63
12	9.33	6.93	5.95	5.41	5.06	4.82	4.64	4.50	4.39
13	9.07	6.70	5.74	5.21	4.86	4.62	4.44	4.30	4.19
14	8.86	6.51	5.56	5.04	4.69	4.46	4.28	4.14	4.03
15	8.68	6.36	5.42	4.89	4.56	4.32	4.14	4.00	3.89
16	8.53	6.23	5.29	4.77	4.44	4.20	4.03	3.89	3.78
17	8.40	6.11	5.18	4.67	4.34	4.10	3.93	3.79	3.68
18	8.29	6.01	5.09	4.58	4.25	4.01	3.84	3.71	3.60
19	8.18	5.93	5.01	4.50	4.17	3.94	3.77	3.63	3.52
20	8.10	5.85	4.94	4.43	4.10	3.87	3.70	3.56	3.46
21	8.02	5.78	4.87	4.37	4.04	3.81	3.64	3.51	3.40
22	7.95	5.72	4.82	4.31	3.99	3.76	3.59	3.45	3.35
23	7.88	5.66	4.76	4.26	3.94	3.71	3.54	3.41	3.30
24	7.82	5.61	4.72	4.22	3.90	3.67	3.50	3.36	3.26
25	7.77	5.57	4.68	4.18	3.85	3.63	3.46	3.32	3.22
26	7.72	5.53	4.64	4.14	3.82	3.59	3.42	3.29	3.18
27	7.68	5.49	4.60	4.11	3.78	3.56	3.39	3.26	3.15
28	7.64	5.45	4.57	4.07	3.75	3.53	3.36	3.23	3.12
29	7.60	5.42	4.54	4.04	3.73	3.50	3.33	3.20	3.09
30	7.56	5.39	4.51	4.02	3.70	3.47	3.30	3.17	3.07
40	7.31	5.18	4.31	3.83	3.51	3.29	3.12	2.99	2.89
60	7.08	4.98	4.13	3.65	3.34	3.12	2.95	2.82	2.72
120	6.85	4.79	3.95	3.48	3.17	2.96	2.79	2.66	2.56
∞	6.63	4.61	3.78	3.32	3.02	2.80	2.64	2.51	2.41

DENOMINATOR DEGREES OF FREEDOM

Table A-7 (d) (continued)

ν_2 \ ν_1	NUMERATOR DEGREES OF FREEDOM									
	10	12	15	20	24	30	40	60	120	∞
1	6,056	6,106	6,157	6,209	6,235	6,261	6,287	6,313	6,339	6,366
2	99.40	99.42	99.43	99.45	99.46	99.47	99.47	99.48	99.49	99.50
3	27.23	27.05	26.87	26.69	26.60	26.50	26.41	26.32	26.22	26.13
4	14.55	14.37	14.20	14.02	13.93	13.84	13.75	13.65	13.56	13.46
5	10.05	9.89	9.72	9.55	9.47	9.38	9.29	9.20	9.11	9.02
6	7.87	7.72	7.56	7.40	7.31	7.23	7.14	7.06	6.97	6.88
7	6.62	6.47	6.31	6.16	6.07	5.99	5.91	5.82	5.74	5.65
8	5.81	5.67	5.52	5.36	5.28	5.20	5.12	5.03	4.95	4.86
9	5.26	5.11	4.96	4.81	4.73	4.65	4.57	4.48	4.40	4.31
10	4.85	4.71	4.56	4.41	4.33	4.25	4.17	4.08	4.00	3.91
11	4.54	4.40	4.25	4.10	4.02	3.94	3.86	3.78	3.69	3.60
12	4.30	4.16	4.01	3.86	3.78	3.70	3.62	3.54	3.45	3.36
13	4.10	3.96	3.82	3.66	3.59	3.51	3.43	3.34	3.25	3.17
14	3.94	3.80	3.66	3.51	3.43	3.35	3.27	3.18	3.09	3.00
15	3.80	3.67	3.52	3.37	3.29	3.21	3.13	3.05	2.96	2.87
16	3.69	3.55	3.41	3.26	3.18	3.10	3.02	2.93	2.84	2.75
17	3.59	3.46	3.31	3.16	3.08	3.00	2.92	2.83	2.75	2.65
18	3.51	3.37	3.23	3.08	3.00	2.92	2.84	2.75	2.66	2.57
19	3.43	3.30	3.15	3.00	2.92	2.84	2.76	2.67	2.58	2.49
20	3.37	3.23	3.09	2.94	2.86	2.78	2.69	2.61	2.52	2.42
21	3.31	3.17	3.03	2.88	2.80	2.72	2.64	2.55	2.46	2.36
22	3.26	3.12	2.98	2.83	2.75	2.67	2.58	2.50	2.40	2.31
23	3.21	3.07	2.93	2.78	2.70	2.62	2.54	2.45	2.35	2.26
24	3.17	3.03	2.89	2.74	2.66	2.58	2.49	2.40	2.31	2.21
25	3.13	2.99	2.85	2.70	2.62	2.54	2.45	2.36	2.27	2.17
26	3.09	2.96	2.81	2.66	2.58	2.50	2.42	2.33	2.23	2.13
27	3.06	2.93	2.78	2.63	2.55	2.47	2.38	2.29	2.20	2.10
28	3.03	2.90	2.75	2.60	2.52	2.44	2.35	2.26	2.17	2.06
29	3.00	2.87	2.73	2.57	2.49	2.41	2.33	2.23	2.14	2.03
30	2.98	2.84	2.70	2.55	2.47	2.39	2.30	2.21	2.11	2.01
40	2.80	2.66	2.52	2.37	2.29	2.20	2.11	2.02	1.92	1.80
60	2.63	2.50	2.35	2.20	2.12	2.03	1.94	1.84	1.73	1.60
120	2.47	2.34	2.19	2.03	1.95	1.86	1.76	1.66	1.53	1.38
∞	2.32	2.18	2.04	1.88	1.79	1.70	1.59	1.47	1.32	1.00

DENOMINATOR DEGREES OF FREEDOM

Table A-8 Confidence Interval for a Population Proportion, Small Sample

$n = 5$	$\alpha = .05$		$\alpha = .10$	
	P_L	P_U	P_L	P_U
$x = 1$	0.005	0.716	0.010	0.657
2	0.053	0.853	0.076	0.811
3	0.147	0.947	0.189	0.924
4	0.284	0.995	0.343	0.990

$n = 6$	$\alpha = .05$		$\alpha = .10$	
	P_L	P_U	P_L	P_U
$x = 1$	0.004	0.641	0.009	0.582
2	0.043	0.777	0.063	0.729
3	0.118	0.882	0.153	0.847
4	0.223	0.957	0.271	0.937
5	0.359	0.996	0.418	0.991

$n = 7$	$\alpha = .05$		$\alpha = .10$	
	P_L	P_U	P_L	P_U
$x = 1$	0.004	0.579	0.007	0.521
2	0.037	0.710	0.053	0.659
3	0.099	0.816	0.129	0.775
4	0.184	0.901	0.225	0.871
5	0.290	0.963	0.341	0.947
6	0.421	0.996	0.479	0.993

$n = 8$	$\alpha = .05$		$\alpha = .10$	
	P_L	P_U	P_L	P_U
$x = 1$	0.003	0.527	0.006	0.471
2	0.032	0.651	0.046	0.600
3	0.085	0.755	0.111	0.711
4	0.157	0.843	0.193	0.807
5	0.245	0.915	0.289	0.889
6	0.349	0.968	0.400	0.954
7	0.473	0.997	0.529	0.994

$n = 9$	$\alpha = .05$		$\alpha = .10$	
	P_L	P_U	P_L	P_U
$x = 1$	0.003	0.482	0.006	0.429
2	0.028	0.600	0.041	0.550
3	0.075	0.701	0.098	0.655
4	0.137	0.788	0.169	0.749
5	0.212	0.863	0.251	0.831
6	0.299	0.925	0.345	0.902
7	0.400	0.972	0.450	0.959
8	0.518	0.997	0.571	0.994

$n = 10$	$\alpha = .05$		$\alpha = .10$	
	P_L	P_U	P_L	P_U
$x = 1$	0.003	0.445	0.005	0.394
2	0.025	0.556	0.037	0.507
3	0.067	0.652	0.087	0.607
4	0.122	0.738	0.150	0.696
5	0.187	0.813	0.222	0.778
6	0.262	0.878	0.304	0.850
7	0.348	0.933	0.393	0.913
8	0.444	0.975	0.493	0.963
9	0.555	0.997	0.606	0.995

$n = 11$	$\alpha = .05$		$\alpha = .10$	
	P_L	P_U	P_L	P_U
$x = 1$	0.002	0.413	0.005	0.364
2	0.023	0.518	0.033	0.470
3	0.060	0.610	0.079	0.564
4	0.109	0.692	0.135	0.650
5	0.167	0.766	0.200	0.729
6	0.234	0.833	0.271	0.800
7	0.308	0.891	0.350	0.865
8	0.390	0.940	0.436	0.921
9	0.482	0.977	0.530	0.967
10	0.587	0.998	0.636	0.995

$n = 12$	$\alpha = .05$		$\alpha = .10$	
	P_L	P_U	P_L	P_U
$x = 1$	0.002	0.385	0.004	0.339
2	0.021	0.484	0.030	0.438
3	0.055	0.572	0.072	0.527
4	0.099	0.651	0.123	0.609
5	0.152	0.723	0.181	0.685
6	0.211	0.789	0.245	0.755
7	0.277	0.848	0.315	0.819
8	0.349	0.901	0.391	0.877
9	0.428	0.945	0.473	0.928
10	0.516	0.979	0.562	0.970
11	0.615	0.998	0.661	0.996

$n = 13$	$\alpha = .05$		$\alpha = .10$	
	P_L	P_U	P_L	P_U
$x = 1$	0.002	0.360	0.004	0.316
2	0.019	0.454	0.028	0.410
3	0.050	0.538	0.066	0.495
4	0.091	0.614	0.113	0.573
5	0.139	0.684	0.166	0.645
6	0.192	0.749	0.224	0.713
7	0.251	0.808	0.287	0.776
8	0.316	0.861	0.355	0.834
9	0.386	0.909	0.427	0.887
10	0.462	0.950	0.505	0.934
11	0.546	0.981	0.590	0.972
12	0.640	0.998	0.684	0.996

$n = 14$	$\alpha = .05$		$\alpha = .10$	
	P_L	P_U	P_L	P_U
$x = 1$	0.002	0.339	0.004	0.297
2	0.018	0.428	0.026	0.385
3	0.047	0.508	0.061	0.466
4	0.084	0.581	0.104	0.540
5	0.128	0.649	0.153	0.610
6	0.177	0.711	0.206	0.675
7	0.230	0.770	0.264	0.736
8	0.289	0.823	0.325	0.794
9	0.351	0.872	0.390	0.847
10	0.419	0.916	0.460	0.896
11	0.492	0.953	0.534	0.939
12	0.572	0.982	0.615	0.974
13	0.661	0.998	0.703	0.996

Table A-8 (continued)

$n = 15$	$\alpha = .05$		$\alpha = .10$	
$x =$	P_L	P_U	P_L	P_U
1	0.002	0.319	0.003	0.279
2	0.017	0.405	0.024	0.363
3	0.043	0.481	0.057	0.440
4	0.078	0.551	0.097	0.511
5	0.118	0.616	0.142	0.577
6	0.163	0.677	0.191	0.640
7	0.213	0.734	0.244	0.700
8	0.266	0.787	0.300	0.756
9	0.323	0.837	0.360	0.809
10	0.384	0.882	0.423	0.858
11	0.449	0.922	0.489	0.903
12	0.519	0.957	0.560	0.943
13	0.595	0.983	0.637	0.976
14	0.681	0.998	0.721	0.997

$n = 16$	$\alpha = .05$		$\alpha = .10$	
$x =$	P_L	P_U	P_L	P_U
1	0.002	0.302	0.003	0.264
2	0.016	0.383	0.023	0.344
3	0.040	0.456	0.053	0.417
4	0.073	0.524	0.090	0.484
5	0.110	0.587	0.132	0.548
6	0.152	0.646	0.178	0.609
7	0.198	0.701	0.227	0.667
8	0.247	0.753	0.279	0.721
9	0.299	0.802	0.333	0.773
10	0.354	0.848	0.391	0.822
11	0.413	0.890	0.452	0.868
12	0.476	0.927	0.516	0.910
13	0.544	0.960	0.583	0.947
14	0.617	0.984	0.656	0.977
15	0.698	0.998	0.736	0.997

$n = 17$	$\alpha = .05$		$\alpha = .10$	
$x =$	P_L	P_U	P_L	P_U
1	0.001	0.287	0.003	0.250
2	0.015	0.364	0.021	0.326
3	0.038	0.434	0.050	0.396
4	0.068	0.499	0.085	0.461
5	0.103	0.560	0.124	0.522
6	0.142	0.617	0.166	0.580
7	0.184	0.671	0.212	0.636
8	0.230	0.722	0.260	0.689
9	0.278	0.770	0.311	0.740
10	0.329	0.816	0.364	0.788
11	0.383	0.858	0.420	0.834
12	0.440	0.897	0.478	0.876
13	0.501	0.932	0.539	0.915
14	0.566	0.962	0.604	0.950
15	0.636	0.985	0.674	0.979
16	0.713	0.999	0.750	0.997

$n = 18$	$\alpha = .05$		$\alpha = .10$	
$x =$	P_L	P_U	P_L	P_U
1	0.001	0.273	0.003	0.238
2	0.014	0.347	0.020	0.310
3	0.036	0.414	0.047	0.377
4	0.064	0.476	0.080	0.439
5	0.097	0.535	0.116	0.498
6	0.133	0.590	0.156	0.554
7	0.173	0.643	0.199	0.608
8	0.215	0.692	0.244	0.659
9	0.260	0.740	0.291	0.709
10	0.308	0.785	0.341	0.756
11	0.357	0.827	0.392	0.801
12	0.410	0.867	0.446	0.844
13	0.465	0.903	0.502	0.884
14	0.524	0.936	0.561	0.920
15	0.586	0.964	0.623	0.953
16	0.653	0.986	0.690	0.980
17	0.727	0.999	0.762	0.997

$n = 19$	$\alpha = .05$		$\alpha = .10$	
$x =$	P_L	P_U	P_L	P_U
1	0.001	0.260	0.003	0.226
2	0.013	0.331	0.019	0.296
3	0.034	0.396	0.044	0.359
4	0.061	0.456	0.075	0.419
5	0.091	0.512	0.110	0.476
6	0.126	0.565	0.147	0.530
7	0.163	0.616	0.188	0.582
8	0.203	0.665	0.230	0.632
9	0.244	0.711	0.274	0.680
10	0.289	0.756	0.320	0.726
11	0.335	0.797	0.368	0.770
12	0.384	0.837	0.418	0.812
13	0.435	0.874	0.470	0.853
14	0.488	0.909	0.524	0.890
15	0.544	0.939	0.581	0.925
16	0.604	0.966	0.641	0.956
17	0.669	0.987	0.704	0.981
18	0.740	0.999	0.774	0.997

$n = 20$	$\alpha = .05$		$\alpha = .10$	
$x =$	P_L	P_U	P_L	P_U
1	0.001	0.249	0.003	0.216
2	0.012	0.317	0.018	0.283
3	0.032	0.379	0.042	0.344
4	0.057	0.437	0.071	0.401
5	0.087	0.491	0.104	0.456
6	0.119	0.543	0.140	0.508
7	0.154	0.592	0.177	0.558
8	0.191	0.639	0.217	0.606
9	0.231	0.685	0.259	0.653
10	0.272	0.728	0.302	0.698
11	0.315	0.769	0.347	0.741
12	0.361	0.809	0.394	0.783
13	0.408	0.846	0.442	0.823
14	0.457	0.881	0.492	0.860
15	0.509	0.913	0.544	0.896
16	0.563	0.943	0.599	0.929
17	0.621	0.968	0.656	0.958
18	0.683	0.988	0.717	0.982
19	0.751	0.999	0.784	0.997

Construction of Table A-8

Confidence limits for the binomial parameter can be determined using the incomplete beta distribution. A beta distribution has two parameters, say A and B. Consider a 95% confidence interval ($\alpha = .05$) for the binomial parameter, p. To find the lower confidence limit, P_L, for a given sample size (n) and observed number of successes (x), set

$$A = x \quad \text{and} \quad B = n - x + 1.$$

Then, P_L is that value of the beta random variable for which

$$\left(\begin{array}{l} \text{area under the beta distribution} \\ \text{with parameters A and B to the} \\ \text{left of } P_L \end{array} \right) = \frac{\alpha}{2}$$

$$= .025.$$

This can be determined by using a computerized incomplete beta function, as shown below.

Similarly, to find the upper limit, P_U, for a given sample size (n) and observed number of successes (x), set

$$A = x + 1 \quad \text{and} \quad B = n - x.$$

Then P_U is that value of the beta random variable for which

$$\left(\begin{array}{l} \text{area under the beta distribution} \\ \text{with parameters A and B to the} \\ \text{left of } P_U \end{array} \right) = 1 - \frac{\alpha}{2}$$

$$= .975.$$

Again, this can be determined by using a computerized incomplete beta function.

The listing of FORTRAN statements used to generate the values in Table A-8 is shown below. To change the starting value of n (= 5, here), the final value of n (= 20, here), or the two significance levels to be considered (.05 and .10, here), change one or more of the first four lines of code. The incomplete beta function subroutine used here is MDBETI, available through International Mathematical and Statistical Libraries, Inc. (IMSL), Sixth Floor, NBC Building, 7500 Bellaire Boulevard, Houston, Texas 77036.

```
0001          NST=5
0002          NEND=20
0003          ALPHA1=.05
0004          ALPHA2=.10
0005          DO 10 N=NST,NEND
0006          PRINT 500 , N,ALPHA1,ALPHA2
0007          NP1 = N + 1
0008          DO 10 J=2,N
0009          JX = J - 1
0010          T2 = ALPHA1/2.0
0011          T1 = 1.0 - T2
0012          A1 = JX + 1
0013          A2 = JX
0014          B1 = N - JX
0015          B2 = N - JX + 1
0016          CALL MDBETI (T1,A1,B1,P2,IER1)
0017          CALL MDBETI (T2,A2,B2,P1,IER2)
```

```
0018          IF(IER1.GT.0) PRINT 100 , ALPHA1,IER1
0019          IF(IER2.GT.0) PRINT 150 , ALPHA1,IER2
0020          TT2 = ALPHA2/2.0
0021          TT1 = 1.0 - TT2
0022          CALL MDBETI(TT1,A1,B1,PP2,IER1)
0023          CALL MDBETI(TT2,A2,B2,PP1,IER2)
0024          IF(IER1.GT.0) PRINT 100 , ALPHA2, IER1
0025          IF(IER2.GT.0) PRINT 150 , ALPHA2, IER2
0026          IF(J.EQ.2) PRINT 200 , JX,P1,P2,PP1,PP2
0027          IF(J.NE.2) PRINT 250 , JX,P1,P2,PP1,PP2
       C
0028       10 CONTINUE
0029      100 FORMAT('0FOR ALPHA = ',F5.2,' ERROR NUMBER',I3,
              *' OCCURRED WHEN FINDING P2')
0030      150 FORMAT('0FOR ALPHA = ',F5.2,' ERROR NUMBER',I3,
              *' OCCURRED WHEN FINDING P1')
0031      200 FORMAT('0 X = ',I2,4(4X,F5.3))
0032      250 FORMAT('0',5X,I2,4(4X,F5.3))
0033      500 FORMAT('1',///' N = ',I2,8X,'ALPHA = ',F3.2,8X,'ALPHA = ',
              *F3.2,//,13X,' P1',6X,' P2',6X,' P1',6X,' P2')
0034          STOP
0035          END
```

Table A-9 Critical Values for the Durbin–Watson DW Statistic

(a) $\alpha = .05$

n	$k = 1$		$k = 2$		$k = 3$		$k = 4$		$k = 5$	
	d_L	d_U	d_L	d_U	d_L	d_U	d_L	d_U	d_L	d_U
15	1.08	1.36	0.95	1.54	0.82	1.75	0.69	1.97	0.56	2.21
16	1.10	1.37	0.98	1.54	0.86	1.73	0.74	1.93	0.62	2.15
17	1.13	1.38	1.02	1.54	0.90	1.71	0.78	1.90	0.67	2.10
18	1.16	1.39	1.05	1.53	0.93	1.69	0.82	1.87	0.71	2.06
19	1.18	1.40	1.08	1.53	0.97	1.68	0.86	1.85	0.75	2.02
20	1.20	1.41	1.10	1.54	1.00	1.68	0.90	1.83	0.79	1.99
21	1.22	1.42	1.13	1.54	1.03	1.67	0.93	1.81	0.83	1.96
22	1.24	1.43	1.15	1.54	1.05	1.66	0.96	1.80	0.86	1.94
23	1.26	1.44	1.17	1.54	1.08	1.66	0.99	1.79	0.90	1.92
24	1.27	1.45	1.19	1.55	1.10	1.66	1.01	1.78	0.93	1.90
25	1.29	1.45	1.21	1.55	1.12	1.66	1.04	1.77	0.95	1.89
26	1.30	1.46	1.22	1.55	1.14	1.65	1.06	1.76	0.98	1.88
27	1.32	1.47	1.24	1.56	1.16	1.65	1.08	1.76	1.01	1.86
28	1.33	1.48	1.26	1.56	1.18	1.65	1.10	1.75	1.03	1.85
29	1.34	1.48	1.27	1.56	1.20	1.65	1.12	1.74	1.05	1.84
30	1.35	1.49	1.28	1.57	1.21	1.65	1.14	1.74	1.07	1.83
31	1.36	1.50	1.30	1.57	1.23	1.65	1.16	1.74	1.09	1.83
32	1.37	1.50	1.31	1.57	1.24	1.65	1.18	1.73	1.11	1.82
33	1.38	1.51	1.32	1.58	1.26	1.65	1.19	1.73	1.13	1.81
34	1.39	1.51	1.33	1.58	1.27	1.65	1.21	1.73	1.15	1.81
35	1.40	1.52	1.34	1.58	1.28	1.65	1.22	1.73	1.16	1.80
36	1.41	1.52	1.35	1.59	1.29	1.65	1.24	1.73	1.18	1.80
37	1.42	1.53	1.36	1.59	1.31	1.66	1.25	1.72	1.19	1.80
38	1.43	1.54	1.37	1.59	1.32	1.66	1.26	1.72	1.21	1.79
39	1.43	1.54	1.38	1.60	1.33	1.66	1.27	1.72	1.22	1.79

Table A-9 (a) (continued)

n	k = 1 d_L	k = 1 d_U	k = 2 d_L	k = 2 d_U	k = 3 d_L	k = 3 d_U	k = 4 d_L	k = 4 d_U	k = 5 d_L	k = 5 d_U
40	1.44	1.54	1.39	1.60	1.34	1.66	1.29	1.72	1.23	1.79
45	1.48	1.57	1.43	1.62	1.38	1.67	1.34	1.72	1.29	1.78
50	1.50	1.59	1.46	1.63	1.42	1.67	1.38	1.72	1.34	1.77
55	1.53	1.60	1.49	1.64	1.45	1.68	1.41	1.72	1.38	1.77
60	1.55	1.62	1.51	1.65	1.48	1.69	1.44	1.73	1.41	1.77
65	1.57	1.63	1.54	1.66	1.50	1.70	1.47	1.73	1.44	1.77
70	1.58	1.64	1.55	1.67	1.52	1.70	1.49	1.74	1.46	1.77
75	1.60	1.65	1.57	1.68	1.54	1.71	1.51	1.74	1.49	1.77
80	1.61	1.66	1.59	1.69	1.56	1.72	1.53	1.74	1.51	1.77
85	1.62	1.67	1.60	1.70	1.57	1.72	1.55	1.75	1.52	1.77
90	1.63	1.68	1.61	1.70	1.59	1.73	1.57	1.75	1.54	1.78
95	1.64	1.69	1.62	1.71	1.60	1.73	1.58	1.75	1.56	1.78
100	1.65	1.69	1.63	1.72	1.61	1.74	1.59	1.76	1.57	1.78

Table A-9 Critical Values for the Durbin–Watson DW Statistic

(b) $\alpha = .01$

n	k = 1 d_L	k = 1 d_U	k = 2 d_L	k = 2 d_U	k = 3 d_L	k = 3 d_U	k = 4 d_L	k = 4 d_U	k = 5 d_L	k = 5 d_U
15	0.81	1.07	0.70	1.25	0.59	1.46	0.49	1.70	0.39	1.96
16	0.84	1.09	0.74	1.25	0.63	1.44	0.53	1.66	0.44	1.90
17	0.87	1.10	0.77	1.25	0.67	1.43	0.57	1.63	0.48	1.85
18	0.90	1.12	0.80	1.26	0.71	1.42	0.61	1.60	0.52	1.80
19	0.93	1.13	0.83	1.26	0.74	1.41	0.65	1.58	0.56	1.77
20	0.95	1.15	0.86	1.27	0.77	1.41	0.68	1.57	0.60	1.74
21	0.97	1.16	0.89	1.27	0.80	1.41	0.72	1.55	0.63	1.71
22	1.00	1.17	0.91	1.28	0.83	1.40	0.75	1.54	0.66	1.69
23	1.02	1.19	0.94	1.29	0.86	1.40	0.77	1.53	0.70	1.67
24	1.04	1.20	0.96	1.30	0.88	1.41	0.80	1.53	0.72	1.66
25	1.05	1.21	0.98	1.30	0.90	1.41	0.83	1.52	0.75	1.65
26	1.07	1.22	1.00	1.31	0.93	1.41	0.85	1.52	0.78	1.64
27	1.09	1.23	1.02	1.32	0.95	1.41	0.88	1.51	0.81	1.63
28	1.10	1.24	1.04	1.32	0.97	1.41	0.90	1.51	0.83	1.62
29	1.12	1.25	1.05	1.33	0.99	1.42	0.92	1.51	0.85	1.61
30	1.13	1.26	1.07	1.34	1.01	1.42	0.94	1.51	0.88	1.61
31	1.15	1.27	1.08	1.34	1.02	1.42	0.96	1.51	0.90	1.60
32	1.16	1.28	1.10	1.35	1.04	1.43	0.98	1.51	0.92	1.60
33	1.17	1.29	1.11	1.36	1.05	1.43	1.00	1.51	0.94	1.59
34	1.18	1.30	1.13	1.36	1.07	1.43	1.01	1.51	0.95	1.59
35	1.19	1.31	1.14	1.37	1.08	1.44	1.03	1.51	0.97	1.59
36	1.21	1.32	1.15	1.38	1.10	1.44	1.04	1.51	0.99	1.59
37	1.22	1.32	1.16	1.38	1.11	1.45	1.06	1.51	1.00	1.59
38	1.23	1.33	1.18	1.39	1.12	1.45	1.07	1.52	1.02	1.58

Table A-9 (b) (continued)

n	k = 1 d_L	d_U	k = 2 d_L	d_U	k = 3 d_L	d_U	k = 4 d_L	d_U	k = 5 d_L	d_U
39	1.24	1.34	1.19	1.39	1.14	1.45	1.09	1.52	1.03	1.58
40	1.25	1.34	1.20	1.40	1.15	1.46	1.10	1.52	1.05	1.58
45	1.29	1.38	1.24	1.42	1.20	1.48	1.16	1.53	1.11	1.58
50	1.32	1.40	1.28	1.45	1.24	1.49	1.20	1.54	1.16	1.59
55	1.36	1.43	1.32	1.47	1.28	1.51	1.25	1.55	1.21	1.59
60	1.38	1.45	1.35	1.48	1.32	1.52	1.28	1.56	1.25	1.60
65	1.41	1.47	1.38	1.50	1.35	1.53	1.31	1.57	1.28	1.61
70	1.43	1.49	1.40	1.52	1.37	1.55	1.34	1.58	1.31	1.61
75	1.45	1.50	1.42	1.53	1.39	1.56	1.37	1.59	1.34	1.62
80	1.47	1.52	1.44	1.54	1.42	1.57	1.39	1.60	1.36	1.62
85	1.48	1.53	1.46	1.55	1.43	1.58	1.41	1.60	1.39	1.63
90	1.50	1.54	1.47	1.56	1.45	1.59	1.43	1.61	1.41	1.64
95	1.51	1.55	1.49	1.57	1.47	1.60	1.45	1.62	1.42	1.64
100	1.52	1.56	1.50	1.58	1.48	1.60	1.46	1.63	1.44	1.65

Table A-10 Distribution Function for the Mann–Whitney U Statistic

This table contains the value of $P(U \leq U_0)$ where $n_1 \leq n_2$.

$n_2 = 3$	U_0	n_1 1	2	3
	0	.25	.10	.05
	1	.50	.20	.10
	2		.40	.20
	3		.60	.35
	4			.50

$n_2 = 4$	U_0	n_1 1	2	3	4
	0	.2000	.0667	.0286	.0143
	1	.4000	.1333	.0571	.0286
	2	.6000	.2667	.1143	.0571
	3		.4000	.2000	.1000
	4		.6000	.3143	.1714
	5			.4286	.2429
	6			.5714	.3429
	7				.4429
	8				.5571

Computed by M. Pagano, Dept. of Statistics, University of Florida. Reprinted by permission from *Statistics for Management and Economics*, 4th ed., by William Mendenhall and James E. Reinmuth. Copyright © 1982 by PWS Publishers, Boston.

Table A-10 (continued)

$n_2 = 5$	U_0	n_1				
		1	2	3	4	5
	0	.1667	.0476	.0179	.0079	.0040
	1	.3333	.0952	.0357	.0159	.0079
	2	.5000	.1905	.0714	.0317	.0159
	3		.2857	.1250	.0556	.0278
	4		.4286	.1964	.0952	.0476
	5		.5714	.2857	.1429	.0754
	6			.3929	.2063	.1111
	7			.5000	.2778	.1548
	8				.3651	.2103
	9				.4524	.2738
	10				.5476	.3452
	11					.4206
	12					.5000

$n_2 = 6$	U_0	n_1					
		1	2	3	4	5	6
	0	.1429	.0357	.0119	.0048	.0022	.0011
	1	.2857	.0714	.0238	.0095	.0043	.0022
	2	.4286	.1429	.0476	.0190	.0087	.0043
	3	.5714	.2143	.0833	.0333	.0152	.0076
	4		.3214	.1310	.0571	.0260	.0130
	5		.4286	.1905	.0857	.0411	.0206
	6		.5714	.2738	.1286	.0628	.0325
	7			.3571	.1762	.0887	.0465
	8			.4524	.2381	.1234	.0660
	9			.5476	.3048	.1645	.0898
	10				.3810	.2143	.1201
	11				.4571	.2684	.1548
	12				.5429	.3312	.1970
	13					.3961	.2424
	14					.4654	.2944
	15					.5346	.3496
	16						.4091
	17						.4686
	18						.5314

$n_2 = 7$	U_0	n_1						
		1	2	3	4	5	6	7
	0	.1250	.0278	.0083	.0030	.0013	.0006	.0003
	1	.2500	.0556	.0167	.0061	.0025	.0012	.0006
	2	.3750	.1111	.0333	.0121	.0051	.0023	.0012
	3	.5000	.1667	.0583	.0212	.0088	.0041	.0020
	4		.2500	.0917	.0364	.0152	.0070	.0035
	5		.3333	.1333	.0545	.0240	.0111	.0055
	6		.4444	.1917	.0818	.0366	.0175	.0087
	7		.5556	.2583	.1152	.0530	.0256	.0131
	8			.3333	.1576	.0745	.0367	.0189
	9			.4167	.2061	.1010	.0507	.0265
	10			.5000	.2636	.1338	.0688	.0364

Table A-10 (continued)

$n_2 = 7$	U_0	n_1						
		1	2	3	4	5	6	7
	11				.3242	.1717	.0903	.0487
	12				.3939	.2159	.1171	.0641
	13				.4636	.2652	.1474	.0825
	14				.5364	.3194	.1830	.1043
	15					.3775	.2226	.1297
	16					.4381	.2669	.1588
	17					.5000	.3141	.1914
	18						.3654	.2279
	19						.4178	.2675
	20						.4726	.3100
	21						.5274	.3552
	22							.4024
	23							.4508
	24							.5000

$n_2 = 8$	U_0	n_1							
		1	2	3	4	5	6	7	8
	0	.1111	.0222	.0061	.0020	.0008	.0003	.0002	.0001
	1	.2222	.0444	.0121	.0040	.0016	.0007	.0003	.0002
	2	.3333	.0889	.0242	.0081	.0031	.0013	.0006	.0003
	3	.4444	.1333	.0424	.0141	.0054	.0023	.0011	.0005
	4	.5556	.2000	.0667	.0242	.0093	.0040	.0019	.0009
	5		.2667	.0970	.0364	.0148	.0063	.0030	.0015
	6		.3556	.1394	.0545	.0225	.0100	.0047	.0023
	7		.4444	.1879	.0768	.0326	.0147	.0070	.0035
	8		.5556	.2485	.1071	.0466	.0213	.0103	.0052
	9			.3152	.1414	.0637	.0296	.0145	.0074
	10			.3879	.1838	.0855	.0406	.0200	.0103
	11			.4606	.2303	.1111	.0539	.0270	.0141
	12			.5394	.2848	.1422	.0709	.0361	.0190
	13				.3414	.1772	.0906	.0469	.0249
	14				.4040	.2176	.1142	.0603	.0325
	15				.4667	.2618	.1412	.0760	.0415
	16				.5333	.3108	.1725	.0946	.0524
	17					.3621	.2068	.1159	.0652
	18					.4165	.2454	.1405	.0803
	19					.4716	.2864	.1678	.0974
	20					.5284	.3310	.1984	.1172
	21						.3773	.2317	.1393
	22						.4259	.2679	.1641
	23						.4749	.3063	.1911
	24						.5251	.3472	.2209
	25							.3894	.2527
	26							.4333	.2869
	27							.4775	.3227
	28							.5225	.3605
	29								.3992
	30								.4392
	31								.4796
	32								.5204

Table A-10 (continued)

$n_2 = 9$	U_0	n_1 1	2	3	4	5	6	7	8	9
	0	.1000	.0182	.0045	.0014	.0005	.0002	.0001	.0000	.0000
	1	.2000	.0364	.0091	.0028	.0010	.0004	.0002	.0001	.0000
	2	.3000	.0727	.0182	.0056	.0020	.0008	.0003	.0002	.0001
	3	.4000	.1091	.0318	.0098	.0035	.0014	.0006	.0003	.0001
	4	.5000	.1636	.0500	.0168	.0060	.0024	.0010	.0005	.0002
	5		.2182	.0727	.0252	.0095	.0038	.0017	.0008	.0004
	6		.2909	.1045	.0378	.0145	.0060	.0026	.0012	.0006
	7		.3636	.1409	.0531	.0210	.0088	.0039	.0019	.0009
	8		.4545	.1864	.0741	.0300	.0128	.0058	.0028	.0014
	9		.5455	.2409	.0993	.0415	.0180	.0082	.0039	.0020
	10			.3000	.1301	.0559	.0248	.0115	.0056	.0028
	11			.3636	.1650	.0734	.0332	.0156	.0076	.0039
	12			.4318	.2070	.0949	.0440	.0209	.0103	.0053
	13			.5000	.2517	.1199	.0567	.0274	.0137	.0071
	14				.3021	.1489	.0723	.0356	.0180	.0094
	15				.3552	.1818	.0905	.0454	.0232	.0122
	16				.4126	.2188	.1119	.0571	.0296	.0157
	17				.4699	.2592	.1361	.0708	.0372	.0200
	18				.5301	.3032	.1638	.0869	.0464	.0252
	19					.3497	.1942	.1052	.0570	.0313
	20					.3986	.2280	.1261	.0694	.0385
	21					.4491	.2643	.1496	.0836	.0470
	22					.5000	.3035	.1755	.0998	.0567
	23						.3445	.2039	.1179	.0680
	24						.3878	.2349	.1383	.0807
	25						.4320	.2680	.1606	.0951
	26						.4773	.3032	.1852	.1112
	27						.5227	.3403	.2117	.1290
	28							.3788	.2404	.1487
	29							.4185	.2707	.1701
	30							.4591	.3029	.1933
	31							.5000	.3365	.2181
	32								.3715	.2447
	33								.4074	.2729
	34								.4442	.3024
	35								.4813	.3332
	36								.5187	.3652
	37									.3981
	38									.4317
	39									.4657
	40									.5000

Table A-10 (continued)

$n_2 = 10$	U_0	1	2	3	4	5	6	7	8	9	10
	0	.0909	.0152	.0035	.0010	.0003	.0001	.0001	.0000	.0000	.0000
	1	.1818	.0303	.0070	.0020	.0007	.0002	.0001	.0000	.0000	.0000
	2	.2727	.0606	.0140	.0040	.0013	.0005	.0002	.0001	.0000	.0000
	3	.3636	.0909	.0245	.0070	.0023	.0009	.0004	.0002	.0001	.0000
	4	.4545	.1364	.0385	.0120	.0040	.0015	.0006	.0003	.0001	.0001
	5	.5455	.1818	.0559	.0180	.0063	.0024	.0010	.0004	.0002	.0001
	6		.2424	.0804	.0270	.0097	.0037	.0015	.0007	.0003	.0002
	7		.3030	.1084	.0380	.0140	.0055	.0023	.0010	.0005	.0002
	8		.3788	.1434	.0529	.0200	.0080	.0034	.0015	.0007	.0004
	9		.4545	.1853	.0709	.0276	.0112	.0048	.0022	.0011	.0005
	10		.5455	.2343	.0939	.0376	.0156	.0068	.0031	.0015	.0008
	11			.2867	.1199	.0496	.0210	.0093	.0043	.0021	.0010
	12			.3462	.1518	.0646	.0280	.0125	.0058	.0028	.0014
	13			.4056	.1868	.0823	.0363	.0165	.0078	.0038	.0019
	14			.4685	.2268	.1032	.0467	.0215	.0103	.0051	.0026
	15			.5315	.2697	.1272	.0589	.0277	.0133	.0066	.0034
	16				.3177	.1548	.0736	.0351	.0171	.0086	.0045
	17				.3666	.1855	.0903	.0439	.0217	.0110	.0057
	18				.4196	.2198	.1099	.0544	.0273	.0140	.0073
	19				.4725	.2567	.1317	.0665	.0338	.0175	.0093
	20				.5275	.2970	.1566	.0806	.0416	.0217	.0116
	21					.3393	.1838	.0966	.0506	.0267	.0144
	22					.3839	.2139	.1148	.0610	.0326	.0177
	23					.4296	.2461	.1349	.0729	.0394	.0216
	24					.4765	.2811	.1574	.0864	.0474	.0262
	25					.5235	.3177	.1819	.1015	.0564	.0315
	26						.3564	.2087	.1185	.0667	.0376
	27						.3962	.2374	.1371	.0782	.0446
	28						.4374	.2681	.1577	.0912	.0526
	29						.4789	.3004	.1800	.1055	.0615
	30						.5211	.3345	.2041	.1214	.0716
	31							.3698	.2299	.1388	.0827
	32							.4063	.2574	.1577	.0952
	33							.4434	.2863	.1781	.1088
	34							.4811	.3167	.2001	.1237
	35							.5189	.3482	.2235	.1399
	36								.3809	.2483	.1575
	37								.4143	.2745	.1763
	38								.4484	.3019	.1965
	39								.4827	.3304	.2179

Table A-10 (continued)

$n_2 = 10$	U_0	1	2	3	4	5	6	7	8	9	10
										n_1	
	40								.5173	.3598	.2406
	41									.3901	.2644
	42									.4211	.2894
	43									.4524	.3153
	44									.4841	.3421
	45									.5159	.3697
	46										.3980
	47										.4267
	48										.4559
	49										.4853
	50										.5147

Table A-11 Critical Values of the Wilcoxon Signed Rank Test ($n = 5, \ldots, 50$)

1-sided	2-sided	$n = 5$	$n = 6$	$n = 7$	$n = 8$	$n = 9$	$n = 10$
$\alpha = .05$	$\alpha = .10$	1	2	4	6	8	11
$\alpha = .025$	$\alpha = .05$		1	2	4	6	8
$\alpha = .01$	$\alpha = .02$			0	2	3	5
$\alpha = .005$	$\alpha = .01$				0	2	3
1-sided	2-sided	$n = 11$	$n = 12$	$n = 13$	$n = 14$	$n = 15$	$n = 16$
$\alpha = .05$	$\alpha = .10$	14	17	21	26	30	36
$\alpha = .025$	$\alpha = .05$	11	14	17	21	25	30
$\alpha = .01$	$\alpha = .02$	7	10	13	16	20	24
$\alpha = .005$	$\alpha = .01$	5	7	10	13	16	19
1-sided	2-sided	$n = 17$	$n = 18$	$n = 19$	$n = 20$	$n = 21$	$n = 22$
$\alpha = .05$	$\alpha = .10$	41	47	54	60	68	75
$\alpha = .025$	$\alpha = .05$	35	40	46	52	59	66
$\alpha = .01$	$\alpha = .02$	28	33	38	43	49	56
$\alpha = .005$	$\alpha = .01$	23	28	32	37	43	49
1-sided	2-sided	$n = 23$	$n = 24$	$n = 25$	$n = 26$	$n = 27$	$n = 28$
$\alpha = .05$	$\alpha = .10$	83	92	101	110	120	130
$\alpha = .025$	$\alpha = .05$	73	81	90	98	107	117
$\alpha = .01$	$\alpha = .02$	62	69	77	85	93	102
$\alpha = .005$	$\alpha = .01$	55	61	68	76	84	92
1-sided	2-sided	$n = 29$	$n = 30$	$n = 31$	$n = 32$	$n = 33$	$n = 34$
$\alpha = .05$	$\alpha = .10$	141	152	163	175	188	201
$\alpha = .025$	$\alpha = .05$	127	137	148	159	171	183
$\alpha = .01$	$\alpha = .02$	111	120	130	141	151	162
$\alpha = .005$	$\alpha = .01$	100	109	118	128	138	149

From F. Wilcoxon and R. A. Wilcox, "Some Rapid Approximate Statistical Procedures," 1964. Reprinted by permission of Lederle Labs, a division of the American Cyanamid Co.

1-sided	2-sided	n = 35	n = 36	n = 37	n = 38	n = 39	
α = .05	α = .10	214	228	242	256	271	
α = .025	α = .05	195	208	222	235	250	
α = .01	α = .02	174	186	198	211	224	
α = .005	α = .01	160	171	183	195	208	

1-sided	2-sided	n = 40	n = 41	n = 42	n = 43	n = 44	n = 45
α = .05	α = .10	287	303	319	336	353	371
α = .025	α = .05	264	279	295	311	327	344
α = .01	α = .02	238	252	267	281	297	313
α = .005	α = .01	221	234	248	262	277	292

1-sided	2-sided	n = 46	n = 47	n = 48	n = 49	n = 50	
α = .05	α = .10	389	408	427	446	466	
α = .025	α = .05	361	379	397	415	434	
α = .01	α = .02	329	345	362	380	398	
α = .005	α = .01	307	323	339	356	373	

Table A-12 Critical Values of Spearman's Rank Correlation Coefficient

n	α = .05	α = .025	α = .01	α = .005
5	0.900	—	—	—
6	0.829	0.886	0.943	—
7	0.714	0.786	0.893	—
8	0.643	0.738	0.833	0.881
9	0.600	0.683	0.783	0.833
10	0.564	0.648	0.745	0.794
11	0.523	0.623	0.736	0.818
12	0.497	0.591	0.703	0.780
13	0.475	0.566	0.673	0.745
14	0.457	0.545	0.646	0.716
15	0.441	0.525	0.623	0.689
16	0.425	0.507	0.601	0.666
17	0.412	0.490	0.582	0.645
18	0.399	0.476	0.564	0.625
19	0.388	0.462	0.549	0.608
20	0.377	0.450	0.534	0.591
21	0.368	0.438	0.521	0.576
22	0.359	0.428	0.508	0.562
23	0.351	0.418	0.496	0.549
24	0.343	0.409	0.485	0.537
25	0.336	0.400	0.475	0.526
26	0.329	0.392	0.465	0.515
27	0.323	0.385	0.456	0.505
28	0.317	0.377	0.448	0.496
29	0.311	0.370	0.440	0.487
30	0.305	0.364	0.432	0.478

From E. G. Olds, "Distribution of Sums of Squares of Rank Differences for Small Samples," *Annals of Mathematical Statistics*, Vol. 9 (1938). Reprinted with permission of the Institute of Mathematical Statistics.

Table A-13 Random Numbers

12651	61646	11769	75109	86996	97669	25757	32535	07122	76763
81769	74436	02630	72310	45049	18029	07469	42341	98173	79260
36737	98863	77240	76251	00654	64688	09343	70278	67331	98729
82861	54371	76610	94934	72748	44124	05610	53750	95938	01485
21325	15732	24127	37431	09723	63529	73977	95218	96074	42138
74146	47887	62463	23045	41490	07954	22597	60012	98866	90959
90759	64410	54179	66075	61051	75385	51378	08360	95946	95547
55683	98078	02238	91540	21219	17720	87817	41705	95785	12563
79686	17969	76061	83748	55920	83612	41540	86492	06447	60568
70333	00201	86201	69716	78185	62154	77930	67663	29529	75116
14042	53536	07779	04157	41172	36473	42123	43929	50533	33437
59911	08256	06596	48416	69770	68797	56080	14223	59199	30162
62368	62623	62742	14891	39247	52242	98832	69533	91174	57979
57529	97751	54976	48957	74599	08759	78494	52785	68526	64618
15469	90574	78033	66885	13936	42117	71831	22961	94225	31816
18625	23674	53850	32827	81647	80820	00420	63555	74489	80141
74626	68394	88562	70745	23701	45630	65891	58220	35442	60414
11119	16519	27384	90199	79210	76965	99546	30323	31664	22845
41101	17336	48951	53674	17880	45260	08575	49321	36191	17095
32123	91576	84221	78902	82010	30847	62329	63898	23268	74283
26091	68409	69704	82267	14751	13151	93115	01437	56945	89661
67680	79790	48462	59278	44185	29616	76531	19589	83139	28454
15184	19260	14073	07026	25264	08388	27182	22557	61501	67481
58010	45039	57181	10238	36874	28546	37444	80824	63981	39942
56425	53996	86245	32623	78858	08143	60377	42925	42815	11159
82630	84066	13592	60642	17904	99718	63432	88642	37858	25431
14927	40909	23900	48761	44860	92467	31742	87142	03607	32059
23740	22505	07489	85986	74420	21744	97711	36648	35620	97949
32990	97446	03711	63824	07953	85965	87089	11687	92414	67257
05310	24058	91946	78437	34365	82469	12430	84754	19354	72745
21839	39937	27534	88913	49055	19218	47712	67677	51889	70926
08833	42549	93981	94051	28382	83725	72643	64233	97252	17133
58336	11139	47479	00931	91560	95372	97642	33856	54825	55680
62032	91144	75478	47431	52726	30289	42411	91886	51818	78292
45171	30557	53116	04118	58301	24375	65609	85810	18620	49198
91611	62656	60128	35609	63698	78356	50682	22505	01692	36291
55472	63819	86314	49174	93582	73604	78614	78849	23096	72825
18573	09729	74091	53994	10970	86557	65661	41854	26037	53296
60866	02955	90288	82136	83644	94455	06560	78029	98768	71296
45043	55608	82767	60890	74646	79485	13619	98868	40857	19415
17831	09737	79473	75945	28394	79334	70577	38048	03607	06932
40137	03981	07585	18128	11178	32601	27994	05641	22600	86064
77776	31343	14576	97706	16039	47517	43300	59080	80392	63189
69605	44104	40103	95635	05635	81673	68657	09559	23510	95875
19916	52934	26499	09821	97331	80993	61299	36979	73599	35055
02606	58552	07678	56619	65325	30705	99582	53390	46357	13244
65183	73160	87131	35530	47946	09854	18080	02321	05809	04893
10740	98914	44916	11322	89717	88189	30143	52687	19420	60061
98642	89822	71691	51573	83666	61642	46683	33761	47542	23551
60139	25601	93663	25547	02654	94829	48672	28736	84994	13071

Table A-14 Critical Values of Hartley's *H*-statistic, α = .05

n = **number of observations in each sample**
k = **number of samples**

n	2	3	4	5	6	7	8	9	10	11	12
						k					
3	39.0	87.5	142	202	266	333	403	475	550	626	704
4	15.4	27.8	39.2	50.7	62.0	72.9	83.5	93.9	104	114	124
5	9.60	15.5	20.6	25.2	29.5	33.6	37.5	41.1	44.6	48.0	51.4
6	7.15	10.8	13.7	16.3	18.7	20.8	22.9	24.7	26.5	28.2	29.9
7	5.82	8.38	10.4	12.1	13.7	15.0	16.3	17.5	18.6	19.7	20.7
8	4.99	6.94	8.44	9.70	10.8	11.8	12.7	13.5	14.3	15.1	15.8
9	4.43	6.00	7.18	8.12	9.03	9.78	10.5	11.1	11.7	12.2	12.7
10	4.03	5.34	6.31	7.11	7.80	8.41	8.95	9.45	9.91	10.3	10.7
11	3.72	4.85	5.67	6.34	6.92	7.42	7.87	8.28	8.66	9.01	9.34
13	3.28	4.16	4.79	5.30	5.72	6.09	6.42	6.72	7.00	7.25	7.48
16	2.86	3.54	4.01	4.37	4.68	4.95	5.19	5.40	5.59	5.77	5.93
21	2.46	2.95	3.29	3.54	3.76	3.94	4.10	4.24	4.37	4.49	4.59
31	2.07	2.40	2.61	2.78	2.91	3.02	3.12	3.21	3.29	3.36	3.39
61	1.67	1.85	1.96	2.04	2.11	2.17	2.22	2.26	2.30	2.33	2.36
∞	1.00	1.00	1.00	1.00	1.00	1.00	1.00	1.00	1.00	1.00	1.00

Table A-15 Distribution Function for the Number of Runs R, in Samples of Size (n_1, n_2)
Each entry is $P(R \leq a)$.

(n_1, n_2)	2	3	4	5	6	7	8	9	10
(2, 3)	.200	.500	.900	1.000					
(2, 4)	.133	.400	.800	1.000					
(2, 5)	.095	.333	.714	1.000					
(2, 6)	.071	.286	.643	1.000					
(2, 7)	.056	.250	.583	1.000					
(2, 8)	.044	.222	.533	1.000					
(2, 9)	.036	.200	.491	1.000					
(2, 10)	.030	.182	.455	1.000					
(3, 3)	.100	.300	.700	.900	1.000				
(3, 4)	.057	.200	.543	.800	.971	1.000			
(3, 5)	.036	.143	.429	.714	.929	1.000			
(3, 6)	.024	.107	.345	.643	.881	1.000			
(3, 7)	.017	.083	.283	.583	.833	1.000			
(3, 8)	.012	.067	.236	.533	.788	1.000			
(3, 9)	.009	.055	.200	.491	.745	1.000			
(3, 10)	.007	.045	.171	.455	.706	1.000			
(4, 4)	.029	.114	.371	.629	.886	.971	1.000		
(4, 5)	.016	.071	.262	.500	.786	.929	.992	1.000	
(4, 6)	.010	.048	.190	.405	.690	.881	.976	1.000	
(4, 7)	.006	.033	.142	.333	.606	.833	.954	1.000	
(4, 8)	.004	.024	.109	.279	.533	.788	.929	1.000	
(4, 9)	.003	.018	.085	.236	.471	.745	.902	1.000	
(4, 10)	.002	.014	.068	.203	.419	.706	.874	1.000	
(5, 5)	.008	.040	.167	.357	.643	.833	.960	.992	1.000
(5, 6)	.004	.024	.110	.262	.522	.738	.911	.976	.998
(5, 7)	.003	.015	.076	.197	.424	.652	.854	.955	.992
(5, 8)	.002	.010	.054	.152	.347	.576	.793	.929	.984
(5, 9)	.001	.007	.039	.119	.287	.510	.734	.902	.972
(5, 10)	.001	.005	.029	.095	.239	.455	.678	.874	.958
(6, 6)	.002	.013	.067	.175	.392	.608	.825	.933	.987
(6, 7)	.001	.008	.043	.121	.296	.500	.733	.879	.966
(6, 8)	.001	.005	.028	.086	.226	.413	.646	.821	.937
(6, 9)	.000	.003	.019	.063	.175	.343	.566	.762	.902
(6, 10)	.000	.002	.013	.047	.137	.288	.497	.706	.864
(7, 7)	.001	.004	.025	.078	.209	.383	.617	.791	.922
(7, 8)	.000	.002	.015	.051	.149	.296	.514	.704	.867
(7, 9)	.000	.001	.010	.035	.108	.231	.427	.622	.806
(7, 10)	.000	.001	.006	.024	.080	.182	.355	.549	.743
(8, 8)	.000	.001	.009	.032	.100	.214	.405	.595	.786
(8, 9)	.000	.001	.005	.020	.069	.157	.319	.500	.702
(8, 10)	.000	.000	.003	.013	.048	.117	.251	.419	.621
(9, 9)	.000	.000	.003	.012	.044	.109	.238	.399	.601
(9, 10)	.000	.000	.002	.008	.029	.077	.179	.319	.510
(10, 10)	.000	.000	.001	.004	.019	.051	.128	.242	.414

From F. Swed and C. Eisenhart, "Tables for Testing Randomness of Grouping in a Sequence of Alternatives," *Annals of Mathematical Statistics*, Vol. 14 (1943). Reproduced with permission of the Institute of Mathematical Statistics.

Table A-15 (continued)

(n_1, n_2)					a					
	11	12	13	14	15	16	17	18	19	20
(2, 3)										
(2, 4)										
(2, 5)										
(2, 6)										
(2, 7)										
(2, 8)										
(2, 9)										
(2, 10)										
(3, 3)										
(3, 4)										
(3, 5)										
(3, 6)										
(3, 7)										
(3, 8)										
(3, 9)										
(3, 10)										
(4, 4)										
(4, 5)										
(4, 6)										
(4, 7)										
(4, 8)										
(4, 9)										
(4, 10)										
(5, 5)										
(5, 6)	1.000									
(5, 7)	1.000									
(5, 8)	1.000									
(5, 9)	1.000									
(5, 10)	1.000									
(6, 6)	.998	1.000								
(6, 7)	.992	.999	1.000							
(6, 8)	.984	.998	1.000							
(6, 9)	.972	.994	1.000							
(6, 10)	.958	.990	1.000							
(7, 7)	.975	.996	.999	1.000						
(7, 8)	.949	.988	.998	1.000	1.000					
(7, 9)	.916	.975	.994	.999	1.000					
(7, 10)	.879	.957	.990	.998	1.000					
(8, 8)	.900	.968	.991	.999	1.000	1.000				
(8, 9)	.843	.939	.980	.996	.999	1.000	1.000			
(8, 10)	.782	.903	.964	.990	.998	1.000	1.000			
(9, 9)	.762	.891	.956	.988	.997	1.000	1.000	1.000		
(9, 10)	.681	.834	.923	.974	.992	.999	1.000	1.000	1.000	
(10, 10)	.586	.758	.872	.949	.981	.996	.999	1.000	1.000	1.000

Derivation of Minimum Total Sample Size

Claim: When obtaining two independent samples, the maximum error for the difference of the two population means, $\mu_1 - \mu_2$, is

$$E = Z_{\alpha/2}\sqrt{\frac{\sigma_1^{\,2}}{n_1} + \frac{\sigma_2^{\,2}}{n_2}} \qquad (\sigma_1, \sigma_2 \text{ known})$$

or estimated using

$$E = Z_{\alpha/2}\sqrt{\frac{s_1^2}{n_1} + \frac{s_2^2}{n_2}} \qquad (\sigma_1, \sigma_2 \text{ unknown})$$

For a specific value of E, the sample sizes, n_1 and n_2, that minimize the total sample size, $n = n_1 + n_2$, are given by

$$n_1 = \frac{Z_{\alpha/2}^2 s_1(s_1 + s_2)}{E^2}$$

and

$$n_2 = \frac{Z_{\alpha/2}^2 s_2(s_1 + s_2)}{E^2}$$

Proof: For ease of notation, define

$$Z = Z_{\alpha/2}$$
$$a = s_1$$
$$b = s_2$$
$$x = n_1$$
$$y = n_2$$

(For the case where the σ's are known, then $a = \sigma_1$ and $b = \sigma_2$.) Now,

$$E = Z\sqrt{\frac{a^2}{x} + \frac{b^2}{y}}$$

is fixed. Solving for y yields

$$y = \frac{Z^2 b^2 x}{E^2 x - Z^2 a^2}$$

The total sample size is $n = x + y$, and so

$$n = f(x) = x + \frac{Z^2 b^2 x}{E^2 x - Z^2 a^2}$$

To determine the value of x that minimizes $n = f(x)$, the procedure will be to find $f'(x)$, set it to zero, and solve for x.

$$f'(x) = 1 + \frac{(E^2 x - Z^2 a^2)(Z^2 b^2) - Z^2 b^2 x(E^2)}{(E^2 x - Z^2 a^2)^2}$$

$$= 1 - \frac{Z^4 a^2 b^2}{(E^2 x - Z^2 a^2)^2}$$

Now,

$$f'(x) = 0$$

iff $x^2(E^4) + x(-2Z^2 E^2 a^2) + (Z^4 a^4 - Z^4 a^2 b^2) = 0$

iff $x = \dfrac{2Z^2 E^2 a^2 \mp \sqrt{4Z^4 E^4 a^4 - 4Z^4 E^4 a^2(a^2 - b^2)}}{2E^4}$

$$= \frac{Z^2 a^2 \mp Z^2 ab}{E^2}$$

Now,

$$f''(x) = \frac{2Z^4 E^2 a^2 b^2(E^2 x - Z^2 a^2)}{(E^2 x - Z^2 a^2)^4}$$

Consequently,

$$f''(x) > 0 \quad \text{iff } (E^2 x - Z^2 a^2) > 0$$

Letting

$$x = \frac{Z^2 a^2 + Z^2 ab}{E^2}$$

then

$$E^2 x - Z^2 a^2 = Z^2 ab > 0$$

because a and b are > 0. Letting

$$x = \frac{Z^2 a^2 - Z^2 ab}{E^2}$$

then

$$E^2 x - Z^2 a^2 = -Z^2 ab < 0$$

Conclusion:

1. $f(x)$ has a local minimum at

$$x = \frac{Z^2 a(a + b)}{E^2}$$

2. $f(x)$ has a local maximum at

$$x = \frac{Z^2 a(a - b)}{E^2}$$

Because we are restricted to values of x (that is, n_1) such that $f(x)$ = total sample size is positive, and because $f(x)$ approaches ∞ as x approaches ∞, for the admissible values of x, $f(x)$ has a global minimum at

$$x = n_1 = \frac{Z^2 a(a + b)}{E^2}$$
$$= \frac{Z^2 s_1(s_1 + s_2)}{E^2}$$

Solving for n_2, we previously stated that

$$y = \frac{Z^2 b^2 x}{E^2 x - Z^2 a^2}$$

Substituting

$$x = \frac{Z^2 s_1(s_1 + s_2)}{E^2}$$

into this expression produces

$$y = n_2 = \frac{Z^2 s_2(s_1 + s_2)}{E^2}$$

Introduction to MINITAB

MINITAB is an easy-to-use, flexible statistical package. It was originally designed for students; over the years, it has been constantly improved. It is one of the more powerful statistical systems currently available. MINITAB will allow you to "speak" to the computer using commands that are similar to English sentences. The sequence of steps in a typical problem solution resembles the same steps you would take if solving the problem by hand.

MINITAB consists of a worksheet containing rows and columns. The data for each variable are stored in a particular *column*. The following discussion will provide a brief introduction of data entry and use of MINITAB commands.

Entering the Data

Data for each of the variables in your data set are stored in columns. For example, suppose you have four test scores (80, 75, 43, and 91) that you want to enter as one variable. These can be entered as shown in Figure C.1 using the SET command. Here, the four test scores are stored in column C1. Notice that (1) the data values are separated by blanks (commas are OK) and (2) at the end of the data string, the word END is entered on the next line. If your data will not fit on a single line, type as many values as you wish, enter these, continue typing on the next line, enter another line of data, and so forth until you have entered all of your data. Your last line always will be END.

Figure C.1

Commands to enter four test scores.

```
MTB > SET INTO C1
DATA> 80 75 43 91
DATA> END
```

Suppose that you have test scores for three people (Joe, Mary, and Al), each of whom has four scores. The previous four test scores (80, 75, 43, and 91) belong to Joe. The other method of entering data is to read in your data one *row* at a time using the READ command. Each line contains a single row of data on each of the variables (three variables, here). This is shown in Figure C.2.

Figure C.2

Commands to enter four test scores for each of three students.

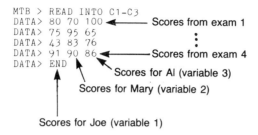

These steps will input the 12 test scores one row (exam) at a time. Note that C1-C3 means C1 through C3.

Output of the Data

To display (or print, if using a hard-copy terminal) the data, you should use the PRINT command, as shown in Figure C.3.

Figure C.3

Commands to display (or print) data.

```
MTB > PRINT C1
C1
    80      75      43      91

MTB > PRINT C1-C3
  ROW     C1      C2      C3

    1      80      70     100
    2      75      95      65
    3      43      83      76
    4      91      90      86
```

MINITAB Shorthand

One exceptionally nice feature of MINITAB is that most of the commands can be shortened to save time and effort. You are able to do this because the MINITAB system does not process the entire line that you enter—it reads only those pieces of information that it needs to know and ignores everything else! Consequently, you can misspell words or leave out unnecessary words and MINITAB will still execute your command. For example, in Figure C.1, you could have used the command

```
MTB > SET C1
```

That is, the word "into" was not necessary. We used it originally because it makes the statement easier to comprehend for someone who wants to know what we are doing at this step.

Many of the MINITAB commands are illustrated on the inside front cover of this book. Only those portions of each statement that are colored must be included. What you put between the colored portions is up to you—you can leave them blank (the shorthand version) or put in any words you wish to make the statement easier to understand. For example, In Figure C.1, we could have used

```
MTB > SET THE EXAM SCORES FOR JOE INTO C1
```

Here, all MINITAB needs to see is SET and C1. What you put in between is your decision.

In addition, for the commands on the inside front cover, any portion of the statement enclosed in brackets [   ] need not be included in the statement. If you want to omit this portion of the statement, you may do so. The information in the brackets generally allows you to be more specific in your input to MINITAB or informs MINITAB in which columns you would like certain information from the output to be stored.

MINITAB Subcommands

Some of the more sophisticated MINITAB commands allow you to specify further information by using one or more *subcommands*. For those commands that allow subcommands (not all of them do), you should end the main command line with a *semicolon, ;*. This informs MINITAB that subcommands will follow. Each subcommand line should end with a semicolon unless it is the last subcommand—the last one ends with a *period*. If you forget to type the period at the end of the last subcommand, simply type a period on the next line.

An example of a command utilizing subcommands (called REGRESS, discussed in Chapters 14 and 15) is shown in Figure C.4. The MINITAB solutions contained throughout the text will clarify what commands allow the use of subcommands and what these possible subcommands are.

Figure C.4

The REGRESS command, with subcommands.

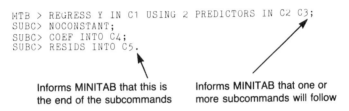

```
MTB > REGRESS Y IN C1 USING 2 PREDICTORS IN C2 C3;
SUBC> NOCONSTANT;
SUBC> COEF INTO C4;
SUBC> RESIDS INTO C5.
```

Informs MINITAB that this is the end of the subcommands

Informs MINITAB that one or more subcommands will follow

Introduction to SPSSX

Computer packages often are used to perform various statistical analysis procedures. When used properly, these computer packages can save time and decrease the probability of human error. The purpose of this appendix is to provide a basic overview of one such package, the Statistical Package for the Social Sciences (SPSSX).

To solve a statistical problem using SPSSX, you must define the data and the format in which it is to be interpreted, and specify the statistical procedure to be performed. For example, the data in Figure D.1 are test grades for three students. If you wish to find the mean grade for each of the students, you define, to SPSSX, each individual test score and specify the SPSSX procedure to obtain mean values (CONDESCRIPTIVE). Figure D.2 shows the statements and data required to perform this task under SPSSX.

Figure D.1

Test grades for three students.

80	70	100
75	95	65
43	83	76
91	90	86

Figure D.2

Statements and data to find mean grades for three students.

```
TITLE           SPSSX-APPENDIX
DATA LIST FREE /JOE MARY AL
CONDESCRIPTIVE  ALL
BEGIN DATA
80   70   100
75   95   65
43   83   76
91   90   86
END DATA
FINISH
```

Analysis of Statements

The following is an analysis of each of the statements used to obtain the mean grades for each student:

TITLE SPSSX-APPENDIX   Defines the name of the SPSSX run.

DATA LIST FREE / JOE MARY AL   Defines three variables (students) named Joe, Mary, and Al. FREE specifies the data is not in any format, other than it is to be read sequentially, starting at column one.

CONDESCRIPTIVE ALL	Specifies the SPSSX procedure to be performed. In this program, the mean, as well as other statistics, will be calculated for all variables.
BEGIN DATA	Specifies that the following lines are input data lines.
80 70 100	Gives the test-score values for the first test (Joe scored 80, Mary scored 70, and Al scored 100).
75 95 65	Gives the test-score values for the second test.
43 83 76	Gives the test-score values for the third test.
91 90 86	Gives the test-score values for the fourth test.
	As shown, the values must be separated by one or more spaces, and there must be a value for all four tests for each of the three students.
END DATA	Indicates the end of the data card images.
FINISH	Indicates the end of the SPSSX program.

Figure D.3

Results of running listing in Figure D.2.

Figure D.3 shows the printed results of running this procedure under SPSSX.

VARIABLE	N	MEAN	STANDARD DEVIATION	MINIMUM VALUE	MAXIMUM VALUE	STD ERROR OF MEAN	SUM	VARIANCE	C.V.
JOE	4	72.25000000	20.61350690	43.00000000	91.00000000	10.30675345	289.00000000	424.91666667	28.531
MARY	4	84.50000000	10.84742673	70.00000000	95.00000000	5.42371337	338.00000000	117.66666667	12.837
AL	4	81.75000000	14.88567544	65.00000000	100.00000000	7.44283772	327.00000000	221.58333333	18.209

Most SPSSX procedures require additional statements, either to describe the problem or to request different options for solving the problem in different ways. All procedures, statements, and options necessary for solving the problems in this text are discussed in the end-of-chapter appendixes. For further information on SPSSX, refer to the *SPSSX Introductory Statistics Guide* (Marija Norusis, New York: McGraw-Hill, 1983).

Basic SPSSX Rules

As with all computer packages, you must observe certain rules when running SPSSX programs. The following is a list of the basic rules for SPSSX:

1. All commands must begin in column 1 and cannot exceed column 15.
2. Any additional information must appear in columns 16 through 80.
3. All command keywords must be separated by only one blank.
4. Multiple blanks are allowed beyond column 15.
5. Include the decimal point when entering decimal data (such as 38.95).

Additional rules concerning individual procedures are contained in the *SPSSX Introductory Statistics Guide*.

JCL Statements

Job Control Language (JCL) statements must be included with SPSSX statements in order for the SPSSX program to execute properly. These statements identify the user and the procedure to be performed. Typically, you need only a job statement, an execute statement (EXEC SPSSX), and a card image input statement (SYSIN DD *). The format and order of these statements may differ, so consult your computer center before attempting to run your first program.

Introduction to SAS

Computer packages often are used to perform various statistical analysis procedures. When used properly, these computer packages can save time and decrease the probability of human error. The purpose of this appendix is to provide a basic overview of one such package, the Statistical Analysis System (SAS).

To solve a statistical problem using SAS, you must define the data to be used and specify the statistical procedure to be performed. For example, the data in Figure E.1 lists test grades for three students. If you wish to find the mean grade for each of the students, you define, to SAS, each individual test score and specify the SAS procedure to obtain mean values (PROC MEANS). Figure E.2 shows the statements and data required to perform this task under SAS.

Figure E.1

Test grades for three students.

```
80   70   100
75   95   65
43   83   76
91   90   86
```

Figure E.2

Statements and data to find mean grades for three students.

```
TITLE      SAS-APPENDIX;
DATA       GRADES;
INPUT      JOE MARY AL;
CARDS;
80   70   100
75   95   65
43   83   76
91   90   86
;
PROC PRINT;
PROC  MEANS;
```

Analysis of Statements

The following is an analysis of each of the statements used to obtain the mean grades for each student:

TITLE SAS-APPENDIX;   Defines the name of the SAS run.

DATA GRADES;   Defines a dataset named grades.

INPUT JOE MARY AL;   Defines three variables (students) named Joe, Mary, and Al.

CARDS;   Defines the input medium as card images.

80 70 100	Gives the test-score values for the first test (Joe scored 80, Mary scored 70, and Al scored 100).
75 95 65	Gives the test-score values for the second test.
43 83 76	Gives the test-score values for the third test.
91 90 86	Gives the test-score values for the fourth test.
	As shown, the values must be separated by one or more spaces, and there must be a value for all four tests for each of the three students.
	Indicates the end of the data set.
PROC PRINT	Specifies that the input data values are to be printed.
PROC MEANS	Specifies the SAS procedure to be performed.

Figure E.3 shows the printed results of running this procedure under SAS.

Figure E.3

Results of running listing in Figure E.2.

```
NUMBER OF VALID OBSERVATIONS (LISTWISE) =        4.00

VARIABLE        MEAN      STD DEV      MINIMUM     MAXIMUM VALID N    LABEL
JOE           72.250      20.614        43.00       91.00     4
MARY          84.500      10.847        70.00       95.00     4
AL            81.750      14.886        65.00      100.00     4
```

Most SAS procedures require additional statements, either to describe the problem or to request different options for solving the problem in different ways. All procedures, statements, and options necessary for solving the problems in this text are discussed in the end-of-chapter appendices. For further information on SAS, refer to the *SAS User's Guide: Statistics Version,* 5th ed. (SAS Institute, Inc., Cary, NC, 1985).

Basic SAS Rules

As with all computer packages, you must observe certain rules when running SAS programs. The following is a list of the basic rules for SAS:

1. SAS statements must begin in column 1 and cannot exceed column 72. Any SAS statement longer than 72 columns may be continued on the next line.
2. All SAS statements must end with a semicolon (;).
3. All data must be defined before a procedure can be run.
4. More than one procedure can be performed by adding more procedure cards.
5. You must include the decimal point when entering decimal data (such as 38.95).

Additional rules concerning individual procedures are contained in the *User's Guide.*

JCL Statements

Job Control Language (JCL) statements must be included with SAS statements in order for the SAS program to execute properly. These statements identify the user and the procedure to be performed. Typically, you need only a job statement, an execute statement (EXEC SAS), and a data input statement (SYSIN DD *). The format and order of these statements may differ, so consult your computer center before attempting to run your first program.

APPENDIX F

Data Base Using Household Financial Variables

1140 Observations Using 8 Variables

X_1 Income of principle wage earner

X_2 Income of secondary wage earner

X_3 Family size

X_4 Own or Rent (1 = own, 0 = rent)

X_5 Total indebtedness (excluding home mortgage)

X_6 House payment or apartment/house rent

X_7 Monthly utility expenditure

X_8 Location of residence (1 = NE sector, 2 = NW sector, 3 = SW sector, 4 = SE sector)

OBS	X1	X2	X3	X4	X5	X6	X7	X8
1	36741	20691	4	1	14340	1138	295	1
2	27242	25454	5	1	13160	1108	260	2
3	43633		6	1	9746	1012	274	1
4	41076	25396	3	1	10391	867	211	1
5	32980	24302	3	1	14577	1026	245	1
6	44143	25715	4	0	14422	1200	261	2
7	32082		5	1	17042	1105	281	1
8	44534	22739	2	1	16042	926	288	2
9	41073	32128	5	0	18027	1494	384	3
10	31603	15136	4	0	18075	1312	3	1
11	45092		5	1	15042	362	346	1
12	29857	23431	5	0	14986	1246	95	2
13	36937	20418	2	0	11821	460	281	1
14	35066		2	1	17637	965	148	1
15	46632	23135	3	1	15400	9037	80	1
16	45319	25028	3	0	17566	935	213	1
17	51952		4	1	13973	1646	259	1
18	55899		6	1	79986	757	228	2
19	31989		1	1	9209	803	193	3
20	36222	17720	7	1	11413	906	107	1
21	45321	19045	4	1	13542	555	273	1
22	28002		2	0	88075	943	183	2
23	35210	22311	4	0	14233	1018	160	1
24	55730	16511	2	0	13008	679	277	1
25	34732		1	1	10382	1139	273	2
26	35864		5	1	18067	775	269	1
27	41230	15323	4	0	10066	505	133	1
28	30993	23054	2	0	10449	579	159	3
29	42080		2	0	15948	1624	160	1
30	39816		3	1	5948	527	136	2
31	28864	2223	2	0	7197	648	168	1
32	31882	13937	2	0	7955	527	266	1
33	30607	13865	3	1	15195	648	232	1
34	31876	18500	2	0	11624	894	212	2
35	29438		5	0	10810	1114	293	1
36	37141		3	1	14191	1816	247	2
37	40966	23413	5	0	9271	1372	273	1
38	39926		3	0	15965	1157	245	4
39	38312	25335	2	1	10203	1097	269	1
40	41204	16904	3	1	16378	1007	296	2
41	44604	15424	3	1	14134	1176	272	3
42	37954	23670	4	1	17053	1160	247	2

OBS	X1	X2	X3	X4	X5	X6	X7	X8
55	26882	24519	5	0	12832	1442	353	1
56	50224	5008	4	1	15078	3622	76	4
57	35449	14458	2	1	12456	7380	222	2
58	47275	19396	3	1	12447	918	203	1
59	28205	14486	1	1	10803	612	134	1
60	43304		2	1	10803	892	156	1
61	40497	15729	6	0	11822	1209	307	2
62	26922	17879	4	1	15742	1409	269	1
63	30071	31060	3	1	12683	1104	221	2
64	31637	31741	2	1	14559	585	156	1
65	26583	26655	1	1	12175	9561	249	4
66	38847	22201	5	1	9689	737	273	2
67	34981		3	1	88182	952	142	1
68	41107	11982	1	0	14763	207	229	1
69	27980	24140	5	0	10938	1357	190	2
70	31397	17739	2	1	13331	799	272	1
71	34079	15961	1	1	14105	894	116	1
72	31890	23477	4	1	7463	1138	459	1
73	21000	24656	2	1	15767	1877	211	1
74	41779	21196	7	1	14291	1657	207	4
75	38300	22843	2	1	10146	399	385	1
76	34404		6	1	9746	1156	118	2
77	39044	16284	4	1	121189	722	249	1
78	32559		1	1	7957	317	175	1
79	31905	21302	5	0	7224	429	120	2
80	15800	18313	2	0	11651	1192	315	1
81	28990		1	0	85811	372	87	1
82	21374	13286	2	0	9861	1289	162	1
83	34402	19533	1	1	13993	359	295	2
84	36540		5	1	5278	1058	134	1
85	33935		1	0	16494	763	272	1
86	37872	24913	2	0	15394	1511	235	2
87	32444	19149	5	1	13905	1283	379	1
88	46140	23785	2	1	10706	904	211	1
89	29707	10439	5	1	7403	606	181	4
90	32049	1273	1	0	11175	349	122	1
91	31715		1	1	14628	477	123	1
92	33182	13275	2	0	17903	1640	146	1
93	22264	26546	2	1	13672	612	166	4
94	30757		5	0	9830	859	163	2
95	30467	21576	3	0	7668	894	201	3
96	20464	17153	4	1	5829	1457	336	1
97	25922		3	0	7601	1251	278	1
98	37858	12108	4	1	9477			
99	36812	27812	4	1	16399			
100		14429	3	1	12787			

OBS	X1	X2	X3	X4	X5	X6	X7	X8
163	22397	18529	7	1	10216	1386	343	1
164	29995	20112	3	0	12507	1820	207	1
165	36582	22969	4	0	14866	1250	283	1
166	54131		4	1	13512	1174	256	1
167	39248	32401	4	1	9793	655	241	2
168	42107		2	1	18610	766	161	4
169	22401		3	0	18630	1040	187	4
170	22041	18159	3	0	5486	7660	156	4
171	38947		4	1	14263	821	233	1
172	24531	24830	3	0	6117	1387	193	1
173	47566	19247	4	1	18076	1635	362	4
174	36022		6	1	13795	643	353	1
175	26068	21342	2	1	9029	430	352	1
176	25143	22518	4	0	12122	980	110	2
177	36501		5	0	9118	813	225	1
178	36554	18405	1	1	11578	1204	178	4
179	27972	22958	4	1	12023	1826	283	2
180	35161		2	1	8837	1536	369	1
181	34495		6	0	9521	767	160	3
182	32118	14081	3	0	10604	4780	167	2
183	38171		2	1	8601	720	126	4
184	32418		1	0	9521	576	246	3
185	35304		3	1	8081	382	151	2
186	28707		2	1	13016	925	277	2
187	46646	20902	4	1	17363	960	224	1
188	47800	22870	2	0	15753	1038	264	1
189	27047	15209	2	1	11248	553	161	2
190	27047	20777	1	0	13266	822	213	1
191	33675	17637	4	1	10046	777	184	1
192	40282	19462	2	1	14506	783	254	2
193	36118		2	1	7496	1240	157	1
194	30809	21965	6	0	8802	672	326	1
195	35259		1	1	10236	746	152	2
196	43146		7	1	14574	969	196	1
197	29937		3	0	10154	443	294	1
198	54284	15224	2	1	108350	9805	113	2
199	33663	18774	5	1	13350	548	218	1
200	31934	13631	1	1	16746	774	178	1
201	42438		2	1	13968	320	165	1
202	29301	17601	2	0	16311	474	118	1
203	32861	21740	3	1	10378	651	204	2
204	30301	24023	2	0	15012	442	137	4
205	32467	22873	1	1	13868	991	302	2
206	35247		2	0	14768	11922	218	1
207	33106	12300	1	0	10341	9221	185	1
208	32861	15263	4	1	10378	856	135	1
209	33247	25263	2	1	14768	625	184	1
210	33775	23216	4	0	8284			
211	41441	23904	2	0	10742			
212	33235	2336	3	1				
213	43058		3	1				

OBS	X1	X2	X3	X4	X5	X6	X7	X8
109	30782		2	1	7668	430	103	2
110	40463	12267	2	1	13163	312	112	1
111	45213		5	1	11287	1297	299	2
112	40003		3	0	9984	799	192	2
113	26590	9836	4	1	9091	840	203	2
114	54553		2	1	136114	872	225	2
115	27727		6	0	6908	716	234	3
116	27400		2	1	8075	1163	247	1
117	47121	18619	2	1	11762	8852	216	2
118	39123	27820	3	0	9764	1339	335	2
119	36065	19829	2	1	13652	578	143	2
120	29265		1	0	14250	542	138	3
121	39397		6	1	14787	10225	265	1
122	32988	26966	2	0	8228	6810	230	2
123	35568	23240	4	0	8871	9609	258	2
124	23605	15555	2	1	5971	651	200	3
125	44452		5	0	17835	959	211	1
126	27949		2	1	11272	689	173	1
127	43379	16231	3	0	10831	1244	214	2
128	41722	16917	4	1	10407	972	189	4
129	21292	23540	4	1	9358	869	195	1
130	23426		3	1	10066	651	199	1
131	32964	20091	3	0	14102	859	223	1
132	34485	17543	3	0	8599	808	168	2
133	37026		3	0	12505	1030	269	2
134	33325	15012	2	1	13627	1472	219	2
135	31418	22205	5	0	8563	616	382	4
136	31486		2	1	12005	743	119	1
137	51868		2	1	13392	972	159	2
138	33239		3	0	14695	616	255	2
139	31957		2	1	16291	820	467	2
140	67301		5	0	16803	673	182	4
141	35258	25137	2	1	8789	1724	236	1
142	36992	19970	2	0	15511	604	142	2
143	31626		2	1	12879	531	187	4
144	61344	20728	4	1	11695	718	199	4
145	26188	20080	2	1	8873	7358	112	1
146	40260	14213	2	0	10361	564	106	2
147	35143		2	1	6764	707	107	4
148	21344		1	1	8234	550	237	4
149	27814	13969	2	1	12482	967	221	2
150	21432	25059	2	1	17442	355	181	4
151	29519	20009	1	0	9013	9517	179	2
152	33028		2	1	5271	775	236	4
153	44939	16455	1	1	17778	860	181	3
154	36028		4	1		751	202	2
155	36103	15952	4	0	14644	703		1
156	32662	13408	3	1				
157	35626	25857	4	1				
158	36167		2	0				
159	31226		2	1				
160	17796							
161	32822							

Top block (OBS 271–324):

OBS	X1	X2	X3	X4	X5	X6	X7	X8
271	24514	0	4	0	61100	1072	235	3
272	37021	22935	2	1	49720	634	193	2
273	49514	25880	3	0	148300	662	241	4
274	32562	0	2	1	108115	457	114	2
275	46698	16114	1	1	156860	659	184	1
276	28347	22908	1	1	127960	522	198	1
277	33472	21377	2	1	122810	846	867	1
278	32777	20626	3	1	136990	1020	252	2
279	28653	24350	3	0	132320	936	169	1
280	29796	28762	2	0	108483	7462	200	4
281	43599	0	1	1	122440	1297	329	2
282	30264	1881	3	1	66307	1286	127	1
283	35176	0	5	0	128161	660	286	4
284	23237	16174	5	1	57781	1307	217	4
285	19611	0	2	1	130999	1063	289	1
286	31215	20905	3	1	134240	1080	152	3
287	35061	18840	5	0	134240	524	229	3
288	37428	18836	2	1	121561	501	125	2
289	40800	17934	4	1	12403	488	144	2
290	49655	13903	3	0	38643	1060	259	2
291	15514	0	2	1	69050	1410	328	2
292	32162	0	2	0	125068	583	142	3
293	30132	0	4	1	58025	752	108	1
294	33001	19985	4	1	83083	668	204	4
295	36411	0	7	0	96330	1233	163	3
296	33633	0	3	0	93130	1602	305	2
297	38594	0	2	1	117185	763	201	4
298	26208	15983	1	1	126920	939	228	1
299	36533	19536	3	1	90448	1010	375	4
300	33732	0	2	0	64448	1364	206	2
301	20305	17125	5	0	108380	317	94	4
302	25878	0	3	1	132200	902	235	4
303	34325	15882	4	1	126890	866	271	2
304	28749	0	4	1	15813	1154	259	2
305	27356	19701	1	1	10679	305	271	1
306	48700	0	2	0	12287	1045	100	1
307	25758	22975	5	0	11016	702	240	1
308	31209	23441	3	1	1208	570	202	2
309	51209	0	4	1	7076	1191	149	2
310	26318	14630	4	1	15458	394	249	1
311	28392	17049	1	1		996	111	1
312	34088	16453	2	0		610	252	2
313		0	3	1		806	138	1
314		23814	3				186	3
315		0	2					1
316		27849	1					

Bottom block (OBS 217–270):

OBS	X1	X2	X3	X4	X5	X6	X7	X8
217	30669	21252	2	0	12961	491	146	1
218	37471	23504	3	1	16217	925	232	1
219	25162	9894	3	0	10193	497	101	4
220	30981	11841	4	1	10728	633	163	4
221	28992	14419	5	1	10199	725	317	1
222	30974	26251	2	1	11327	125	229	1
223	39019	0	6	1	16299	1263	223	1
224	40418	24547	1	1	16741	873	312	1
225	28564	0	2	0	17114	542	188	2
226	31634	0	5	1	7025	740	105	3
227	57203	24125	4	0	14278	1195	209	2
228	35192	19066	2	1	16679	367	295	1
229	38649	21859	7	0	10387	1043	89	3
230	31197	0	3	1	15106	1899	214	4
231	24988	24539	7	0	18286	1583	414	1
232	49379	22825	4	1	13894	1453	336	1
233	32810	19283	4	0	11113	858	193	1
234	26130	21413	2	1	11935	1136	251	2
235	38210	20260	4	1	9084	663	294	3
236	36167	26843	4	1	17149	1138	236	4
237	40159	0	3	1	13545	1805	211	1
238	41630	0	2	0	15442	1056	265	1
239	34467	23149	4	1	9432	730	246	1
240	42285	12384	2	1	6553	1007	162	1
241	32998	22385	4	0	12231	1097	275	2
242	41630	0	1	0	13946	883	279	1
243	44612	30462	4	1	15667	600	229	3
244	42788	19681	3	0	15316	736	253	1
245	24021	23097	2	1	14868	861	186	1
246	42998	14967	4	1	14854	1137	212	2
247	37490	0	4	1	11760	549	209	1
248	41606	19333	3	1	8232	1078	182	2
249	37784	2308	1	0	9346	714	179	2
250	25213	0	2	0	9429	979	241	1
251	51727	16438	5	1	11679	683	253	3
252	43322	21605	4	0	12791	771	117	1
253	21716	0	3	1	16507	849	139	2
254	39236	22758	1	0	14561	802	304	4
255	27413	19323	2	1	17040	740		
256	23203	16558	3	0	10233	936		
257	30473	29001	3	1	4741	951		
258		8361	2	0	6841	419		
259		23209	4	1	7865	579		
260					13400	1328		

OBS	X1	X2	X3	X4	X5	X6	X7	X8
379	17339	12077	5	0	7331	1006	258	4
380	24063	22366	4	1	11592	1008	237	2
381	356819	0	3	0	8896	581	123	2
382	45819	23533	1	1	11432	471	172	1
383	24319	21516	2	1	11951	619	113	1
384	26594	17507	5	1	6631	570	149	3
385	37897	0	3	1	14919	11167	294	1
386	38269	13560	5	1	13919	663	166	2
387	23146	0	6	0	5766	853	227	4
388	26057	21368	5	0	9891	1727	432	3
389	27988	0	2	0	6971	1009	274	4
390	23878	17888	1	1	9942	757	164	4
391	25745	15579	1	1	11758	447	102	2
392	20903	19562	3	1	6533	349	97	4
393	26195	0	7	1	10470	1046	225	3
394	21763	0	2	1	8410	1580	385	1
395	33715	21433	2	1	11903	616	137	2
396	47693	0	2	1	8309	800	94	3
397	28316	22743	5	0	7052	510	205	2
398	28280	0	2	0	16473	561	212	4
399	38932	0	3	0	7781	698	117	3
400	34556	0	2	0	14586	352	327	1
401	31217	18010	6	1	8236	440	107	2
402	33043	23321	1	1	6421	880	105	3
403	25740	0	1	0	13434	704	194	1
404	32605	15888	3	1	13939	708	244	3
405	35828	17882	3	0	9219	927	230	3
406	36947	0	1	1	15936	817	101	2
407	47932	0	2	0	10207	791	236	1
408	32981	0	3	1	13003	1251	148	1
409	29817	0	1	0	7928	762	291	3
410	31788	0	5	1	10304	1420	237	1
411	41289	20948	4	0	11272	3810	342	2
412	44220	18987	5	1	16803	977	230	2
413	26952	11034	3	1	8933	555	147	2
414	29441	0	5	1	10601	1394	309	1
415	42508	0	2	1	7899	561	145	1
416	31468	0	5	1	11612	1250	283	3
417	46503	0	1	0	7314	1243	132	3
418	29316	20171	1	0	14672	1036	256	2
419	29115	16062	4	1	15060	531	182	1
420	39303	20962	3	1	14728	915	191	3
421	35574	0	2	0	14724	829	141	3
422	36347	23429	2	1	14065	1036		2
423	36433	22725	2	1	14969	470		
424	34737		2		8662			

OBS	X1	X2	X3	X4	X5	X6	X7	X8
325	30079	23441	3	1	13431	777	207	1
326	39557	0	6	0	9867	1579	343	1
327	44281	23696	1	1	11047	512	112	2
328	24612	0	5	1	12060	1705	381	3
329	29969	26902	3	0	11951	812	159	1
330	27484	0	2	0	13573	872	209	3
331	29375	0	1	1	7327	458	108	2
332	38188	20769	2	0	9529	1885	132	3
333	37304	22058	4	0	93113	6081	209	2
334	34501	0	4	1	17543	1930	249	3
335	24260	26538	3	1	11359	595	145	2
336	22260	0	2	1	5543	7118	168	2
337	33949	29146	2	1	15045	420	191	1
338	35455	0	4	1	15898	123	155	1
339	34898	28424	1	0	14282	4605	100	3
340	28761	0	3	1	13698	5585	123	2
341	45234	19722	4	1	15682	420	162	4
342	35134	2099	5	1	11635	1123	263	1
343	44571	19991	2	1	7795	1547	149	1
344	42837	17096	4	1	10125	12188	208	2
345	31250	0	2	1	13856	530	194	1
346	29544	0	2	1	7970	711	201	1
347	40570	0	6	0	11359	810	222	4
348	31795	13727	2	1	13113	755	222	2
349	31941	21663	4	1	13219	1324	101	4
350	30852	14933	1	1	13807	934	180	3
351	39863	19336	3	1	7142	9612	207	1
352	32975	14002	4	0	11876	866	146	4
353	33090	26124	4	0	14384	750	176	1
354	30227	22726	2	0	5721	662	147	2
355	28649	15120	6	0	15721	590	325	4
356	25720	0	2	0	17648	568	257	4
357	57626	21857	3	0	10740	1298	214	3
358	35364	0	4	0	15517	886	197	1
359	30695	27583	4	0	14461	736	300	4
360	27416	15628	1	0	12332	802	116	4
361	62146	23107	3	0	11775	1643	260	2
362	29767	16190	3	1	8573	332	303	3
363	34354	22227	4	1	63441	869	98	4
364	29783	0	4	1	88553	1224	244	2
365	25461	17399	3	0	13785	578	209	4
366	21700	13346	2	0	13588	858		3
367	35507	21732	5	1	12959	780		1
368	29519	22336	4	0	12726			
369	29671	21018	1	1				
370	29969							

Observations 487–540:

OBS	X1	X2	X3	X4	X5	X6	X7	X8
487	204430	18115	7	0	9615	1060	295	1
488	244571	21329	1	1	11430	993	270	3
489	351371	0	2	1	8763	369	93	2
490	372388	14201	1	0	9305	983	253	2
491	263180	21380	4	0	10009	339	292	2
492	446342	0	2	1	16484	1341	327	1
493	403640	14775	3	1	10072	1024	145	1
494	299594	0	6	0	7472	737	203	2
495	307519	0	4	0	11352	806	101	3
496	244760	22913	3	1	6091	450	143	2
497	318100	0	1	1	7940	675	270	4
498	453053	13109	2	1	11308	398	94	2
499	351470	0	3	0	14994	1068	208	1
500	351913	29326	2	1	8094	3227	258	1
501	369890	19766	2	1	9457	697	337	2
502	324500	23537	4	1	12480	1031	245	1
503	272293	1627	1	1	16633	535	297	1
504	349800	0	5	1	12114	1371	168	3
505	352690	0	1	0	12609	605	103	1
506	348910	19743	3	0	18699	9605	169	1
507	306909	18563	7	0	5549	744	279	2
508	400597	13212	3	0	7651	363	290	1
509	335800	2247	4	1	14933	1918	198	2
510	365540	0	1	1	8377	1505	120	1
511	422050	18309	2	1	13769	554	257	1
512	371120	19914	5	1	13061	788	193	2
513	231510	20107	3	1	9261	603	186	3
514	340771	26948	1	1	10348	714	122	1
515	314320	14452	1	0	15151	3061	313	1
516	364680	0	2	0	12866	1534	130	1
517	270850	27421	2	0	10364	1572	340	3
518	411820	20803	4	0	8768	1733	103	1
519	417260	0	5	1	17113	903	208	1
520	535266	11717	2	0	15631	1025	213	4
521	255420	0	3	1	13296	1130	275	2
522	264810	0	6	0	9261	823	217	2
523	280690	18477	1	0	6144	475	297	1
524	286150	27082	5	1	6171	5136	211	2
525	354570	23159	5	1	11763	956	103	1
526	237780	0	4	1	15615	1329	235	3
527	158730	20657	3	0	11713	1409	324	1
528	619580	23271	4	1	3949	904	253	1
529	498230	9643	4	1	15472	771	372	1
530	326280	0	7	1	17599		210	3
531	445490	21745	3	0	16938		203	2
532	326028				10537			
533	501380				12517			
534	244320				11527			

Observations 433–486:

OBS	X1	X2	X3	X4	X5	X6	X7	X8
433	316115	27183	6	1	14670	1421	358	1
434	448705	11808	2	0	15635	1095	277	1
435	448150	25967	4	1	13114	1014	246	1
436	269650	15864	4	0	13085	1347	314	3
437	347180	22668	6	1	13750	903	207	1
438	322165	21483	1	0	13394	817	227	1
439	321650	20311	1	1	19749	1204	99	1
440	258550	18233	1	6	9749	1053	305	2
441	225855	17882	2	0	11550	717	207	1
442	272247	25727	2	1	10576	887	203	1
443	346110	0	2	1	9631	1457	373	2
444	338180	0	3	1	9622	1534	301	1
445	345790	0	8	1	8620	700	193	2
446	292367	12357	7	0	8591	3100	116	1
447	221850	21001	2	0	10771	1090	264	2
448	271585	22862	4	0	15051	623	173	1
449	322035	0	4	1	7983	506	349	4
450	338718	23018	4	1	12542	1401	86	1
451	466723	14978	2	0	12450	636	233	2
452	261230	15228	1	1	15440	976	259	2
453	263900	12140	1	1	10469	1104	353	2
454	305500	0	3	1	16610	1312	323	2
455	180890	0	5	1	6576	1513	304	1
456	333620	1594	1	1	10469	1441	364	1
457	311120	0	5	1	4495	1260	86	1
458	267240	21647	2	0	16976	777	233	2
459	267240	18430	6	0	12479	853	265	2
460	309240	27114	6	1	10542	957	230	2
461	346110	15547	6	1	8206	707	157	3
462	203580	12215	3	0	7710	852	266	1
463	285350	0	4	1	13538	382	101	2
464	285350	20711	4	1	8649	0	210	2
465	361960	0	5	0	7591	1159	85	1
466	239820	10108	4	0	12094	469	109	2
467	196470	19915	2	1	11476	975	239	2
468	284890	0	1	1	9390	859	377	3
469	203580	21786	3	1	8573	632	228	1
470	285350	0	1	0	48899	403	159	1
471	458160	12847	5	1	6749	1150	106	2
472	376600	0	5	1	7103	469	149	1
473	239820	0	2	0	16884	975	259	3
474	196470	21154	6	1	14275	859		2
475	284890	17174	4	1	15739	632		1
476	203580	23859	3	1	10305	403		3
477	285350	0	2	0	13816	700		4
478	361960	0	1	1		978		

OBS	X1	X2	X3	X4	X5	X6	X7	X8
595	41690	0	7	1	10406	1278	313	1
596	19114		2	1	4762	767	180	3
597	54478	18623	2	1	13590	767	171	1
598	206713	15923	3	1	13418	774	215	1
599	378123		7	1	13418	1368	405	1
600	33523	0	5	1	8359	1168	317	3
601	32613	1967	4	0	8135	772	143	2
602	32489		4	0	15512	1259	289	1
603	35996	19389	4	1	15512	1504	283	2
604	21566	13984	2	1	10223	1346	141	2
605	44106	25892	1	1	14502	1410	256	1
606	49294	0	4	0	18780	1025	115	1
607	27936	0	3	0	5567	797	187	4
608	27450	0	2	1	5567	639	112	1
609	29517	0	1	0	6842	956	271	2
610	38234	0	6	1	7360	569	121	4
611	45802	23252	2	0	9538	602	162	2
612	38046	0	4	1	11430	601	242	4
613	40454	1657	3	0	9651	1147	319	2
614	30154	0	5	1	7991	1218	286	1
615	32901	20112	7	1	13333	523	126	3
616	39035	0	4	1	9750	348	136	4
617	30224	16662	1	0	12354	648	211	3
618	24619	26216	2	1	9734	873	134	2
619	32043	13467	2	1	14565	577	125	2
620	41238	22753	0	1	6133	591	136	1
621	26444	0	3	1	12688	1489	314	1
622	33064	0	1	1	9999	609	316	1
623	35004	25874	5	0	12612	647	299	1
624	40856	21643	2	1	14477	1288	264	1
625	33290	0	6	1	9984	966	166	1
626	42574	30505	5	0	16162	1345	324	2
627	32947	0	4	1	8214	1091	366	1
628	41002	24689	3	1	17895	1291	296	1
629	60047	0	3	1	14980	1079	224	2
630	30119	8487	2	0	13638	667	217	1
631	30119	0	5	0	10958	738	217	1
632	43896	16880	2	1	13216	1296	313	3
633	36779	26354	3	1	14477	890	247	2
634	411808	19248	4	0	12288	957	261	4
635	33550	28249	4	1	13181	1032	229	1
636	283882	23325	4	1	14138	658	197	4
637	281873	0	3	1	16244	819	354	1
638	42633	27404	3	1	15170	1466	240	2
639	30749	20631	5	1	14060	1269	236	4
640	35980	15427	5	1	10334	947	132	1
641	25980	23069	3	1	15903	1029	236	2
642	40730	0	2	0	8408	1690	132	1
643	33701	0	5	1	10601	981	202	2
644	42478			0				

OBS	X1	X2	X3	X4	X5	X6	X7	X8
541	21042	19298	5	1	10062	967	269	3
542	26080	18208	1	1	11049	673	135	2
543	34516	23336	2	1	14443	935	261	1
544	26741	13614	7	1	10767	15548	353	2
545	32811	18337	2	0	12767	567	185	1
546	51580	0	1	0	12876	469	130	4
547	36610	26312	4	0	9126	452	111	1
548	32478	0	2	1	14680	1016	290	1
549	33276	16361	2	1	8304	885	151	3
550	25713	21575	1	1	10504	725	189	1
551	23548	0	1	1	11265	1067	230	1
552	34416	18895	4	1	8553	1060	234	1
553	27416	25748	1	0	11553	826	308	2
554	39376	17875	3	0	11797	1283	362	1
555	28712	17473	4	0	9126	1333	295	4
556	18712	21887	4	1	17402	1113	266	2
557	42208	0	4	1	14954	915	310	3
558	38004	18371	2	1	8388	1045	115	2
559	33597	14487	4	0	12911	857	258	1
560	51770	0	6	0	11049	1236	392	3
561	29713	21364	3	0	11387	1601	150	1
562	30772	0	4	0	4795	458	260	1
563	20109	0	3	0	5015	1098	260	2
564	24995	24517	1	0	17554	1637	189	3
565	48858	14152	5	1	9614	554	293	2
566	28884	0	5	1	12976	1157	287	1
567	50386	0	4	1	13873	872	257	2
568	31062	17886	4	0	12809	841	238	1
569	12801	13463	1	0	12556	1181	104	1
570	35181	0	6	1	16585	1094	267	3
571	38882	18284	1	1	11485	1118	301	1
572	48554	20735	5	1	7662	448	372	1
573	39066	0	4	0	9947	321	105	1
574	37324	26150	2	0	13463	1210	263	2
575	25228	21040	6	1	9352	1343	212	1
576	39835	0	1	0	9087	1253	1964	3
577	39882	17719	1	0	13025	792	262	2
578	27782	19521	5	1	13544	819	162	1
579	34170	19812	4	1	9620	971	229	4
580	18729	0	2	1	13030	1014	246	3
581	43236	18257	6	1	10944	1243	197	1
582	32369	0	2	1	10333	909	163	1
583	46759	21831	3	0	14415	669	166	3
584	35981	0	1	1	9230	648		
585	30359	0	2	1				
586	30383	21380	4	1				
587	43139	0	4	0				
588	41396		3	1				
589	36365		1	1				
590	36986		1	0				

OBS	X1	X2	X3	X4	X5	X6	X7	X8
649	42141	23873	1	0	16486	626	172	3
650	41539	17380	5	1	12210	1086	262	3
651	31675		3	1	15145	1009	131	4
652	33800	13096	2	1	83287	406	143	2
653	36148		4	1	12287	459	236	1
654	29240	12295	3	0	11593	873	190	4
655	33920	8865	2	1	10316	915	161	1
656	32455	16043	4	0	9048	956	193	1
657	36265	24238	2	1	9044	740	180	1
658	34790	22004	2	0	14388	615	150	2
659	36866		2	1	14699	670	199	2
660	36996	20166	4	0	5718	366	145	1
661	24490	17508	1	1	5608	785	175	4
662	36673	21348	3	1	10793	563	107	2
663	24275	20479	2	1	10095	527	168	4
664	25750	20953	1	1	11903	208	136	2
665	26315		2	1	12573	738	214	4
666	29879	22437	4	1	14257	7149	199	2
667	36223	12541	2	0	16037	3889	116	3
668	24243		5	0	12230	1389	340	1
669	36463	19890	3	1	5914	1000	128	1
670	33723		3	1	12536	773	244	2
671	35611		2	0	7099	837	157	4
672	30311	26647	2	0	9418	525	164	2
673	28511	17399	1	0	13186	788	201	3
674	30313	25952	4	1	5392	923	191	1
675	37961	1857	3	1	14343	863	210	4
676	29761		5	0	11552	948	204	2
677	52803	12698	3	0	18933	489	297	1
678	21653	13581	2	0	10581	1698	178	3
679	31014	26363	1	1	9326	699	390	1
680	28808	14323	4	1	9336	1727	288	1
681	49380		4	1	12120	1264	187	1
682	37402	19377	3	1	13411	807	139	1
683	35881	19991	5	1	12146	1091	242	2
684	40395	17126	3	1	14699	335	202	4
685	29980		2	1	9204	835	232	1
686	39515	25083	6	0	14698	802	214	1
687	39155	16937	3	0	15773	678	244	1
688	20608	19825	2	0	7838	1558	247	3
689	36915	15582	4	1	11594	814	234	3
690	31444		3	1	14283	1356	294	1
691	31023	20979	2	1	11997	1054	227	2
692	37396		4	1	7466	791	257	2
693	30469		2	1	12102	899	280	1
694	32498		5	1		1111		
695	29951		4					
696	27535							

OBS	X1	X2	X3	X4	X5	X6	X7	X8
703	33945	16302	5	1	12541	1281	302	1
704	28252	20262	5	1	17046	912	217	4
705	20766	24078	1	1	10239	301	94	2
706	50812	16639	3	0	12686	1032	223	1
707	36381	20289	3	1	15094	9101	186	1
708	38818	17002	1	1	14042	662	162	1
709	41817		5	1	14603	519	107	1
710	25405	21739	3	0	10549	1239	309	1
711	42256		2	1	127799	6616	185	1
712	29530		2	1	107364	645	135	4
713	34257	28272	3	1	107730	653	172	2
714	43264	11833	2	0	13522	485	112	1
715	31033	22473	2	1	13078	962	202	1
716	52481	19663	3	1	9850	16804	414	2
717	39467	25737	1	1	15296	837	130	1
718	39758	14602	2	1	9676	907	214	1
719	32079	11793	7	0	10203	625	192	2
720	55065	20277	3	1	14362	1350	352	1
721	35065	11557	1	0	12698	897	266	1
722	32219	21908	2	0	10996	7764	186	2
723	25682	1914	5	0	15645	627	295	1
724	28300		2	0	10793	1123	255	1
725	25440	14550	5	0	9431	977	247	2
726	38763	13585	2	0	14037	1295	337	1
727	37184		4	1	13537	1180	160	1
728	36144	9830	2	0	11070	1140	301	1
729	26785		2	1	11573	5814	292	2
730	29313		5	0	16229	1074	267	1
731	44004	14568	5	1	11199	1276	384	2
732	29804		3	1	13347	1704	375	1
733	53346		7	1	13472	1548	316	1
734	53395		7	1	14767	1167	176	1
735	44605	22554	2	0	11324	540	245	1
736	47827	19196	4	0	15324	715	159	1
737	54527	17906	3	0	13614	452	182	4
738	21434		6	0	9492	1275	341	2
739	22811		4	1	5322	330	203	1
740	41222		1	1	102887	687	101	1
741	20822	11439	2	1	5187	1101	229	1
742	21528	13522	2	0	10153	4600	127	2
743	21888		5	1	10513	882	204	1
744	27355		2	0	11524	7002	293	3
745	42138		3	1	10316	1176	174	2
746	35249		5	0	11623	781	252	1
747	36723		2	1	10163	992	174	2
748	28835		2	0	10567	677	188	2

OBS	X1	X2	X3	X4	X5	X6	X7	X8
8111	22586	0	3	0	5625	534	112	4
8112	40246	25086	3	1	16313	687	182	1
8113	29770	22230	2	1	12971	634	167	1
8114	28263	0	5	0	17046	1016	257	2
8115	23227	0	4	0	5785	1632	1154	3
8116	29916	15863	1	0	9908	473	155	2
8117	29418	22220	4	1	11416	1245	2806	1
8118	42873	0	2	0	11393	477	126	2
8119	20131	14218	3	1	10697	900	2207	1
8120	25752	19992	2	0	5034	8104	205	3
8121	38967	15554	1	1	9971	844	157	3
8122	34012	0	2	1	9728	641	154	3
8123	34093	25698	4	1	15881	681	177	2
8124	52262	0	3	0	12371	6119	193	1
8125	25903	14048	2	0	13039	6142	209	1
8126	26034	17930	2	1	6461	1110	267	2
8127	42451	20891	3	0	6563	255	110	4
8128	29208	0	5	0	10010	596	166	2
8129	51233	0	1	1	15080	9501	234	2
8130	31030	30226	2	0	10577	460	301	1
8131	50616	0	7	1	12814	5687	149	1
8132	33444	28758	2	0	7894	817	93	3
8133	31441	24560	2	0	15292	1392	215	1
8134	25471	0	1	1	8352	584	368	1
8135	33763	23151	1	1	15034	5844	127	4
8136	24838	16384	2	0	8416	412	170	3
8137	29204	30055	6	1	6193	850	97	4
8138	28391	0	3	0	13065	1158	244	1
8139	35463	20987	2	1	11329	1601	372	3
8140	30927	22810	2	0	16363	839	217	1
8141	32189	24734	5	0	7713	894	235	3
8142	42393	25522	1	1	13257	510	144	1
8143	46093	0	1	1	16277	1073	102	1
8144	30557	18797	6	0	13252	1277	256	2
8145	29580	14798	3	1	17683	786	208	1
8146	30068	0	2	0	14003	388	110	1
8147	30024	0	2	1	13595	1286	370	2
8148	41303	17055	1	1	10997	709	192	3
8149	28005	24299	4	0	9491	713	195	1
8150	27974	24243	2	0	7490	456	1125	1
8151	21408	15630	6	1	8230	589	174	2
8152	34746	18630	2	0	14573	1109	124	1
8153	47463	20236	3	1	13059	733	271	4
8154	28751	24052	1	1	13384	1214	168	1
8155			4	1	9304	1339	333	2
8156			6	0	13322	879	282	2
8157			2	1	16902	919	225	2
8158			3	1	13184		233	1

OBS	X1	X2	X3	X4	X5	X6	X7	X8
7757	34311	23194	3	1	14355	659	216	1
7758	32429	24114	2	1	14134	527	169	1
7759	32229	0	4	1	8039	788	215	2
7760	34632	0	2	0	8646	444	195	3
7761	27443	0	4	1	10148	1109	282	1
7762	43191	13230	1	1	10134	1726	198	4
7763	43152	26422	5	1	12007	1568	403	2
7764	35201	20987	3	1	11871	1069	1000	1
7765	32505	0	2	1	16931	934	212	1
7766	44170	13196	4	1	8110	1363	180	4
7767	32516	23647	4	1	14471	7415	3707	2
7768	32517	0	4	1	6273	1466	207	3
7769	25156	28218	4	0	7475	845	209	4
7770	29887	0	4	0	14155	1026	333	3
7771	56814	0	4	1	12235	3997	179	2
7772	37116	11311	5	1	11857	3542	2007	1
7773	31563	14358	1	1	11464	845	2307	2
7774	37937	26466	3	1	13583	5116	231	4
7775	26202	0	3	1	9032	1258	1107	3
7776	35126	0	2	1	8768	1127	2164	2
7777	35204	0	5	1	11189	1598	294	1
7778	52703	0	4	1	13119	1605	289	2
7779	28765	25073	2	0	7168	1101	1159	1
7780	37356	13573	2	0	10835	5162	246	4
7781	23996	17733	4	0	10410	752	3883	1
7782	50996	0	7	1	15708	978	396	1
7783	41763	21161	6	1	15702	1101	278	2
7784	24467	17610	2	1	14002	1010	1190	1
7785	32567	26353	6	1	13922	1647	226	4
7786	35723	0	1	0	8894	654	4311	2
7787	30137	22205	3	0	11876	573	353	4
7788	21200	16737	2	1	11676	459	122	4
7789	35535	21527	7	1	15667	362	139	1
7790	34916	17016	5	1	12617	847	217	1
7791	32911	0	3	0	12609	991	92	2
7792	52104	0	2	1	12960	1582	2116	2
7793	28104	0	4	1	13998	336	2029	1
7794	28190	22357	4	1	10359	953	372	1
7795	32291	16005	5	0	6692	631	103	4
7796	36371	0	2	1	15882		162	1
7797	36891	19732	3	1	14904		241	1
7798	26833	2434	6	1			177	2
7808	24193							
7810	37141	22564	3	1				

OBS	X1	X2	X3	X4	X5	X6	X7	X8
919	45779		2	1	11424	689	164	1
920	28768		2	0	17169	807	209	2
921	34406	16866	2	1	8595	806	229	1
922	39587	28236	3	1	14092	1191	299	1
923	43406	24736	3	1	10833	815	214	4
924	41536	16840	2	1	17423	899	257	1
925	33080		2	1	14436	1077	228	1
926	30616		2	1	9341	908	145	3
927	20610	17592	3	1	9079	703	191	1
928	31808	21061	3	1	7929	703	222	2
929	36578	12441	4	1	9128	1021	274	1
930	33153		5	1	7758	1082	302	2
931	31102		4	1	12657	1071	307	1
932	42265	23615	2	1	15086	1214	96	2
933	41211	11830	7	0	13656	1275	131	2
934	28031	18183	3	0	10280	1114	325	2
935	32324	29927	2	1	7167	335	221	1
936	28224	20889	6	0	9681	620	224	1
937	37057	12851	5	1	9064	1089	224	3
938	26135	12860	2	0	12937	847	317	2
939	32241		3	1	9242	462	290	4
940	31840	16214	4	1	11290	946	260	2
941	45769	11337	5	1	6520	521	176	1
942	42431		3	1	15518	1258	329	4
943	31388	22881	2	0	17943	918	296	2
944	40778	16683	2	0	13798	1040	64	1
945	26750	1557	2	0	11988	1095	122	4
946	37089		4	1	7829	632	304	3
947	46241		2	1	14230	1291	1994	3
948	28122	7204	4	1	6488	505	161	1
949	22064	2010	2	0	9252	1116	177	1
950	29439	26322	2	0	17256	855	88	2
951	32203	21053	3	1	14545	747	314	1
952	42486	20375	2	1	10901	806	261	4
953	42431		4	1	5499	651	308	2
954	41631		2	1	9138	1354	143	2
955	43817		4	1	8039	1091	320	4
956	26014	11908	4	0	16999	957	117	3
957	35584	19500	3	1	16971	594	166	1
958	29152		2	1	10934	494	217	3
959	28452		4	1	11748	1263	266	1
960	37698		4	1	12371	1129	417	4
961	38958		3	1	8801	1402	105	4
962	30894		4	0	7087	733	355	3
963	33846	17196	7	1	9404	709		1
964	33582		5	1	10680	1076		
965					13068	1793		
966					12676	1485		

OBS	X1	X2	X3	X4	X5	X6	X7	X8
865	25211	24836	2	1	12493	858	242	1
866	29807	18783	2	0	12120	861	211	1
867	33357		4	0	10831	889	226	2
868	30178	13791	5	1	10991	1388	321	1
869	32067	20688	2	1	11914	1907	1183	1
870	27034	14309	2	1	11574	761	905	2
871	28710		2	0	71156	4519	285	3
872	38111	17290	5	1	7583	1196	1139	1
873	45114		1	1	13831	642	246	2
874	55451		4	1	11025	1589	127	1
875	26405	25434	4	1	113834	1129	1483	1
876	27711	17709	2	0	13203	4538	243	1
877	31460	20240	3	0	6575	559	132	4
878	41165	19202	1	0	14870	657	1287	1
879	28130		2	1	12076	10498	257	2
880	39868	21128	5	0	9993	490	2088	1
881	31878		4	1	17948	8491	119	2
882	45795	12432	2	0	16256	5319	1337	1
883	25099	24195	2	1	5728	9557	125	1
884	29999	23651	4	0	9351	1557	1267	4
885	30882	24011	7	0	13747	548	225	3
886	27432	1965	3	1	12748	8561	3362	2
887	37794		2	0	16179	1116	207	1
888	22551	2061	1	0	9443	480	2119	2
889	25499	17994	4	1	12909	1632	249	2
890	32211	13624	2	0	6356	985	99	2
891	32706	16730	4	1	6036	1296	149	3
892	36201	14753	1	0	5785	475	379	1
893	31968		3	1	13314	804	1603	1
894	23555		3	0	7259	993	363	2
895	47237	28651	2	1	9027	412	173	2
896	28530	17298	6	1	11794	7345	2061	1
897	48208	20998	3	1	6039	1614	207	3
898	25288		4	0	11799	1398	1011	4
899	43590		4	0	17579	616	316	2
900	33020	17225	4	1	10866	9844	244	2
901	28686	24944	1	0	14898	10118	124	3
902	29628	19085	3	0	12399	1487	293	4
903	41730		7	1	14761	9983	2004	2
904	34298		3	0	13569	6800	209	1
905	25443		7	0	14810	15965	139	1
906	19315		3	0	8550	1076	251	2

OBS	X1	X2	X3	X4	X5	X6	X7	X8
1027	44433	0	2	1	11085	982	244	4
1028	208544	0	2	0	51190	530	90	2
1029	463842	14564	6	1	152011	1529	389	1
1030	36142	0	1	0	9020	15205	153	2
1031	30398	0	6	0	7581	1209	314	1
1032	39436	23298	3	1	15661	11140	295	2
1033	427602	14177	2	1	14194	899	180	1
1034	266042	15553	3	1	10519	887	205	1
1035	323177	16497	1	1	11471	308	92	1
1036	30968	15000	3	0	10823	610	154	2
1037	245321	18841	4	1	10668	947	209	3
1038	271597	15718	6	1	12521	1370	334	2
1039	265981	23581	1	1	9623	444	104	1
1040	311515	0	2	1	13276	869	217	4
1041	293397	22067	4	1	6570	610	151	3
1042	219339	0	1	0	7316	785	228	3
1043	219081	18150	4	1	10001	529	121	2
1044	21925	0	1	1	7622	862	197	4
1045	276114	21866	2	1	54607	478	115	2
1046	306341	12863	2	1	12347	650	280	4
1047	394801	15453	7	1	12270	992	294	2
1048	448914	0	3	1	11502	1096	184	4
1049	357187	16718	4	0	9847	625	326	2
1050	328400	14335	2	1	11206	641	145	3
1051	34053	0	1	1	8906	702	338	3
1052	51582	18397	4	1	12366	751	175	4
1053	357476	0	2	1	12073	1064	164	1
1054	357914	20924	3	1	10349	392	227	1
1055	231214	23057	2	1	9349	620	143	3
1056	264380	20057	3	1	13526	440	87	1
1057	273082	19615	2	0	11099	655	186	3
1058	313077	0	2	1	12357	7100	172	1
1059	257717	12582	4	1	11187	846	185	2
1060	456012	23761	2	1	12471	843	225	4
1061	283739	0	4	1	16424	1006	219	4
1062	423120	33693	2	0	14526	548	255	2
1063	446211	0	6	1	13683	1435	266	1
1064	324040	17673	4	1	17170	873	155	3
1065	466100	22319	5	1	18976	1124	336	1
1066	270400	14805	3	1	11134	1066	220	1
1067	404440	22724	1	1	12493	561	161	3
1068	38060	0	5	0	12315	1329	267	2
1069	286050	0	2	1	15335	763	99	4
1070	353800	25869	2	1	15779	756	207	1
1071	640285	0	3	1	6994	500	208	1
1072	427800	0	2	1	9626	481	99	3
1073	435500	0	1	0	15293	626	129	2
1074	44601	0	3	1	15986	642	169	1

OBS	X1	X2	X3	X4	X5	X6	X7	X8
973	30786	19922	1	1	12655	816	191	3
974	246022	17954	2	0	106220	722	165	2
975	338932	18744	7	1	84522	1273	283	2
976	206324	22188	1	1	9822	742	308	1
977	419194	17870	5	1	16020	1101	146	3
978	327006	18447	2	1	12619	1612	209	1
979	375062	0	4	1	12379	642	336	2
980	495824	20628	4	0	12148	1564	286	1
981	280040	0	2	1	13439	1106	199	2
982	538564	15143	4	1	8490	794	165	1
983	340034	0	2	1	13435	680	212	4
984	38678	23524	2	1	11765	790	189	2
985	280562	0	3	0	6991	760	14	3
986	236154	24573	1	0	6978	387	101	1
987	279802	2147	1	1	12667	439	354	4
988	322924	0	5	1	9947	14105	292	2
989	343802	20933	3	1	14360	990	256	1
990	501927	0	1	0	13945	426	96	2
991	338670	20373	2	0	12530	301	104	1
992	285302	17761	3	0	8447	728	176	2
993	320962	17230	3	0	7992	830	69	4
994	309360	0	5	1	5078	810	203	3
995	293722	0	2	1	12421	109	178	2
996	315902	23963	4	0	10616	1180	235	1
997	321596	18347	2	1	12193	578	248	4
998	329291	24775	4	1	8116	898	137	3
999	245394	22000	2	0	12325	858	214	4
1000	254089	0	4	0	14854	1228	206	4
1001	411660	25869	3	0	13170	825	214	3
1002	277920	19453	1	1	10965	690	269	2
1003	439012	18071	4	1	9132	683	183	1
1004	366372	15900	2	1	12277	956	149	1
1005	257099	0	2	1	11440	1312	178	2
1006	489303	23509	2	1	14509	1574	277	4
1007	277632	17276	5	1	86450	438	357	4
1008	421962	19460	1	1	15268	1056	264	2
1009	338680	0	3	1	15526	677	245	1
1010	393103	12900	2	0	11941	1157	293	3
1011	450034	0	2	1	14562	544	180	1
1012	263587	18157	4	0	13510	723	181	2
1013	283872	15100	4	1	14931	736	196	2
1014	183172	0	3	0	8274	717	291	4
1015	412082	16518	3	1	14931	1259	81	1
1016	359393	0	2	0	8427	846	14	4
1017	416079	0	5	1	11523	320	129	1
1018	348054	0	3	1	8031	315	114	2

OBS	X1	X2	X3	X4	X5	X6	X7	X8
1135	28467	17792	2	0	11543	799	210	1
1136	36615	23158	3	0	14924	904	138	2
1137	32908	21289	2	1	13535	454	123	2
1138	27762	21946	3	1	12401	827	215	2
1139	72709	0	7	1	18159	1911	457	1
1140	32168	0	3	1	8021	1121	251	3

OBS	X1	X2	X3	X4	X5	X6	X7	X8
1081	48358	0	1	1	12070	402	132	1
1082	55404	0	3	1	13831	721	201	1
1083	28804	0	6	0	17186	470	128	4
1084	28855	21194	3	0	11741	1390	348	1
1085	34847	0	6	1	8687	567	128	4
1086	36397	0	2	1	9081	1225	293	1
1087	30998	0	5	1	7731	860	172	1
1088	29228	0	2	0	7292	475	131	3
1089	29522	0	2	1	12715	827	119	1
1090	50959	0	2	1	15178	635	232	1
1091	38032	22766	1	1	9087	455	106	2
1092	36420	0	2	1	9201	833	90	3
1093	25866	11015	4	1	15198	390	210	1
1094	37051	23830	2	1	8314	1145	116	1
1095	33335	1737	4	0	12381	382	296	3
1096	33230	0	2	1	12311	470	129	3
1097	32010	18524	3	1	7628	802	137	1
1098	26804	0	2	0	9614	1109	236	1
1099	38543	14399	1	1	13219	312	277	2
1100	38550	22640	5	0	13829	869	99	1
1101	32774	810	1	0	6997	1060	216	2
1102	27843	0	4	1	8977	1027	256	2
1103	28047	0	5	1	11167	1231	208	2
1104	44780	0	4	0	15420	462	252	1
1105	61755	17660	3	1	12805	980	309	1
1106	33648	18725	2	0	13145	913	150	1
1107	33953	0	2	1	6334	478	225	4
1108	31635	0	3	0	7409	718	101	2
1109	46937	17187	5	0	8938	1123	295	3
1110	31309	21234	1	1	11263	910	188	3
1111	28667	19687	4	0	10883	822	244	1
1112	43630	0	4	1	12488	799	237	1
1113	25060	13551	2	1	11900	881	214	2
1114	29876	10370	2	0	13870	554	114	1
1115	37670	22838	1	1	9733	839	199	3
1116	42012	0	1	0	12029	653	165	1
1117	27062	26629	4	1	6747	951	216	1
1118	31635	0	1	0	14543	495	149	2
1119	46937	19914	3	0	11707	839	227	1
1120	31309	18617	2	1	17806	653	192	1
1121	28667	0	2	1	10234	951	241	2
1122	43630	23440	3	1	11799	495	179	1
1123	25060	1217	1	1	10892	803	198	1
1124	29876	0	2	1	12108	903	257	1
1125	37033	0	4	1	10491	688	265	4
1126	39514	23227	1	0	9333	777	166	1
1127	29036	14827	3	1	9243	904	313	1
1128	26095	23789	2	1	15665	598	226	2
1129	30833	11256	5	1	10500	595	257	3
1130	39540	0	4	1	10947	976	198	2
1131	35355	0	3	1	9867	1115	265	3
1132	45305	14040	4	1	12335	1088	313	2
1133		23138	2	1	17085	702	166	2
1134						1354	226	

Answers to Odd-Numbered Exercises

Chapter 1

1.1 The population of interest is the group of tourists who visit the city. The sample is the group of 100 randomly selected tourists.

1.3 a. Represents the population of employees at General Motors **b.** Represents a sample of students on the university campus **c.** Represents a sample of people listed in the telephone directory **d.** Represents the population of all possible ways of choosing 2 cards from a deck of 52 cards

1.5 Inferential statistics uses a sample to form conclusions about a population. A census obtains information about everyone in a population.

1.7 Age is ratio. Sex is nominal. Grade point average is interval. Classification is nominal.

1.9 Answers on a marketing survey that indicate strongly agree to strongly disagree

Chapter 2

2.1 b. There is no "correct" number of classes. Consider using $K = 8$ classes. **c.** $CW = (100 - 18) / 8 = 10.25$ (round to 10). **e.** Relative frequency is equal to the frequency divided by the total number of values in the data set. Cumulative frequency is the total of the frequencies up to, and including, a particular class.

2.3 a. Relative frequencies are 0.38, 0.31, 0.21, 0.06, 0.03, 0.01. **b.** Lower class limits are 0, 2, 4, 6, 8 and the upper class limits are 2, 4, 6, 8, 10. **c.** Class midpoints are 1, 3, 5, 7, 9. **d.** No

2.5 a. Discrete data

2.7 a. $CW = (17.1 - 2.2) / 5 = 2.98$ (round to 3) **b.** Determine the basic shape of the data. **c.** Consider $K = 6$ classes, 2 and under 5, 5 and under 8, etc.

2.13 b. The shape indicates that only one class has a low frequency and that most of the data fell in the larger class intervals **c.** No, the shape would not change.

2.19 a. Classes are 0–3, 4–7, 8–11, 12–15, 16–19; frequencies are 12, 10, 7, 1, 1; cumulative relative frequencies are .39, .71, .94, .97, 1.00. **b.** 6%

2.23 c. The distribution peaks between 70 and 80, and nearly 90% of the distribution is between 40 and 100.

2.25 b. $X = 12$ (approximately)

2.27 d. A "typical" return on sales is between 3 and 6 **e.** Yes, IBM, Kaiser Steel, Aluminum Company of America, and Standard Oil have much higher returns.

2.29 Proprietorships are 76.97% (277 degrees), partnerships are 7.82% (28 degrees), and corporations are 15.21% (55 degrees).

2.31 The class 10,000–14,999 is 17.5% (63 degrees); the class 15,000–19,999 is 10.0% (36 degrees); the class 20,000–24,999 is 32.5% (117 degrees); the class 25,000–29,999 is 15.0% (54 degrees); and the class 30,000–34,999 is 25.0% (90 degrees).

2.33 c. Yes, consumption varies between 8 and 17 kilowatt-hours.

2.35 c. The suicide frequencies are somewhat uniformly distributed between ages 20 to 60 with small frequencies for ages less than 20.

2.39 a. The data can be considered to be continuous.

2.49 c. Nearly 35% of the loan officers are between 45 and 55 years of age with another 35% between 35 and 45.

2.51 c. 75% of the boxes contain less than 15 defective fuses.

2.53 b. For 15 days out of 30 there are at least 11 workers absent.

Chapter 3

3.1 Mean is 93.13, median is 92, mode is 88

3.3 Mean is 3.227, median is 2.96, no mode

3.5 The median would be close to $25,000

3.7 Mean is 7.153, median is 5.3, no mode

3.9 Mean is 74.35, median is 57.5, mode is 130

3.11 Mean is 20,521.375, median is 16,671

3.13 a. Range is 87 **b.** MAD is 24.09 **c.** Variance is 794.08 **d.** s is 28.18 **e.** CV is 56.27

3.15 s is 10.045

3.17 Variance is 1811.86 and standard deviation is 42.566

3.19 a. Player A is better (on the average). **b.** Player B is more consistent.

3.21 Variance is 1742.13

3.23 Approximately the 39th percentile

3.25 a. 32 **b.** 19

3.27 a. $Z = 0.78$ **b.** $X = 63$ is 0.78 standard deviation to the right of the sample mean.

3.29 s is 2.5

3.31 $(X - \bar{X}) = 14.24$

3.33 a. Mean is 1356.86, median is 1369.7, variance is 27,571.24, s is 166.046 **b.** 858.72 to 1855.00

3.35 $17,710 to $19,490

3.37 Near zero

3.39 a. No **b.** 8,578.57 to 32,464.19

3.41 15.8 to 40.6

3.43 0 to 134.62

3.45 $200 to $360

3.47 Median is approximately $26,833.33

3.49 Median is approximately 29.98 years

3.51 a. Mean is 75.96, variance is 162.8049 **b.** s is 12.76

3.53 Mean is 412.125, s is 7.53

3.55 Mean is 1760, s is 2932

3.57 Mean is 0.0013271, s is 0.0001555

3.59 a. Range is 6.8 **b.** Mean is 5.57 **c.** Median is 5.6 **d.** Mode is 5.6 **e.** s is 1.75 **f.** 31.5 **g.** 4.3 **h.** 7.7

3.61 a. The data are skewed slightly to the right **b.** Sk = 0.564 **c.** 8.173 to 15.531 **d.** Actual percentage is 60%

3.63 $45 to $105

3.65 a. $Z = -4.0$ **b.** $X = 45$ is 4 standard deviations to the left of the mean

3.67 Mean is 53.756, s is 2.78

3.69 a. Mean is 167.758 **b.** Median is 164.9 **c.** no mode **d.** variance is 3263.08 **e.** s is 57.123 **f.** MAD is 37.2925 **g.** Range is 280.8 **h.** CV is 34% **i.** Sk is 0.150 **j.** 139.8 **k.** 221.5 **l.** $Z = -0.381$ **m.** 53.512 to 282.004 **n.** approximately 68%

Chapter 4

4.1 a. Positive **b.** No relationship **c.** Positive **d.** No relationship

4.3 Nearly a perfect negative linear relationship

4.5 Low positive relationship

4.7 Negative relationship

4.9 a. Significant **b.** Not significant **c.** Not significant **d.** Significant **e.** Not significant

4.11 a. $r = -0.983$ **b.** Yes **c.** Significant

4.13 a. $r = 0.383$ **b.** No **c.** Not significant

4.15 b. $r = 0.982$ **c.** Positive relationship **d.** Significant

4.17 a. Rank correlation is -0.857 **b.** Negative relationship **c.** Significant

4.19 a. Rank correlation is -0.964 **b.** Negative relationship **c.** Significant **d.** Yes

4.21 a. Rank correlation is 0.588 **b.** Not significant

4.23 a. Rank correlation is 0.429 **b.** Positive relationship **c.** Not significant **d.** Yes

4.25 b. It is linear with a negative slope. **c.** $r = -0.991$

4.27 a. Moderately positive **b.** Highly positive **c.** No relationship **d.** Moderately positive **e.** Low positive

4.29 b. $r = -0.949$ **c.** Significant

4.31 a. Rank correlation is -0.921 **b.** Significant **c.** The values are both negative and nearly equal.

4.33 a. $r = 0.924$ **b.** $r = 0.8845$

4.35 a. $r = -0.964$ **b.** Significant

4.37 a. Rank correlation is 0.952 **b.** Significant

Chapter 5

5.1 a. Outcomes are red, blue, and green. Each outcome is equally likely with probability 1/3.

5.3 0.75

5.5 c

5.7 a. 0.16 **b.** 0.45 **c.** 0.676 **d.** 0.84

5.9 a. 0.541 **b.** 0.015 **c.** 0.5 **d.** 0.607 **e.** Yes

5.11 a. 0.776 **b.** 0.403 **c.** 0.263 **d.** They are mutually exclusive but not independent.

5.13 a. 0.703 **b.** 0.228 **c.** 0.638 **d.** 0.768

5.17 0.58

5.19 P(both) $= 0.36$, P(at least one) $= 0.84$

5.21 No

5.23 0.4, they are independent

5.25 0.25

5.27 0.24

5.29 a. 0.054 **b.** 0.86 **c.** 0.675

5.31 0.3858, assuming they are independent

5.33 0.167

5.35 0.75

5.37 a. Yes **b.** 0.343 **c.** zero

5.39 Yes

5.41 0.00148

5.43 0.86

5.45 20,000

5.47 120

5.49 210

5.51 90

5.53 24

5.55 60

5.57 45

5.59 1/595

5.61 Probability is 1/495. This does constitute a random sample.

5.63 1/45

5.65 0.075

5.67 a. 0.091 **b.** 0.125 **c.** 0.273

5.69 a. 0.857 **b.** 0.857 **c.** one **d.** 0.286

5.71 a. 0.55 **b.** 0.85 **c.** one **d.** 0.15 **e.** zero **f.** 0.4706

5.73 847,660,528

5.75 a. 0.8 **b.** 0.2

5.77 0.75

Chapter 6

6.1 The number of customers or daily account size of its customers

6.3 a. Discrete **b.** Discrete **c.** Continuous **d.** Continuous **e.** Continuous

6.5 12 outcomes, each with probability 1/12

6.7 0.25

6.9 a. $P(X = x) = 1/6$

6.11 $P(X = 0) = 9/49, P(X = 1) = 24/49, P(X = 2) = 16/49$

6.13 Yes

6.15 $P(X = x) = 1/3$ for $x = 1, 2, 3$

6.17 $P(X = x) = 1/3$ for $x = 2, 4, 6$

6.21 Mean is 0.2, variance is 0.18

6.23 Mean is 3, variance is 3

6.25 Mean is 1.1428, standard deviation is 0.6999

6.27 Mean is 3, standard deviation is 1.4142

6.29 0.2963

6.31 a. 0.991 **b.** 0.913 **c.** 0.275

6.33 0.506

6.35 0.404

6.37 a. 0.001 **b.** 3 **c.** 1.55

6.39 Mean is 2.16, standard deviation is 1.38

6.41 0.816

6.43 0.8

6.45 0.6353

6.47 0.9286

6.49 a. 0.86 **b.** 0.599 **c.** 0.673

6.51 Mean is 3, probability is 0.5768

6.53 a. 0.9577 **b.** 2.83

6.55 0.2378

6.57 Mean is 1/3 and the standard deviation is 0.7454

6.59 Mean is 3.5 and the variance is 18.85

6.61 a. 0.029 **b.** 0.237 **c.** 0.117 **d.** 0.085

6.63 0.560

6.65 Mean is 2.8, probability is 0.5305

6.67 0.3658

6.69 Probability is 0.224, standard deviation is 1.73

Chapter 7

7.1 The mean and variance indicate where the curve is centered and how wide the curve is, respectively.

7.3 a. 0.3413 **b.** 0.0919 **c.** 0.6826 **d.** 0.0606

7.5 a. 0.9439 **b.** 0.0179 **c.** 0.1986 **d.** 0.9010

7.7 a. $z = 0.35$ **b.** $z = 0.67$ **c.** $z = 1.57$ **d.** $z = -1.62$

7.9 $z = 0.64$ and $z = 1.57$

7.11 a. 0.3632 **b.** 0.2119 **c.** 0.3842 **d.** 0.1791

7.13 8.08%

7.15 0.0228

7.17 101 is the passing score

7.19 0.1587

7.21 Value is $82.80

7.23 Mean is 9.45

7.25 Mean is 1.29 and standard deviation is 0.556

7.27 a. 0.668 **b.** 0.692

7.29 0.9612

7.31 0.8564

7.33 0.0314

7.35 a. 0.5 **b.** Value is 1.8

7.37 a. 0.524 **b.** 23.15 **c.** 1.819

7.39 0.3

7.41 0.2997

7.43 0.3836

7.45 0.4541

7.47 a. 0.0133 **b.** 0.8664 **c.** 0.2734

7.49 0.1539

7.51 Values are -7.025 and 7.025

7.53 Value is 87.12

7.55 Probability is 0.3442, standard deviation is 30

7.57 58.89%

7.59 0.0668

7.61 0.4168

7.63 a. Mean is 1.0, standard deviation is 0.289 **b.** 0.3

7.65 50%

7.67 a. 0.6826 **b.** 0.3811 **c.** 0.3446 **d.** 0.1587

7.69 Variance is 4.30

Chapter 8

8.1 b. $\overline{X}$ | 0 | 0.5 | 1.0 | 1.5 | 2.0 | 2.5 | 3.0 | 3.5 | 4.0

P | 1/16 | 2/16 | 1/16 | 2/16 | 4/16 | 2/16 | 1/16 | 2/16 | 1/16

8.3 a. 0.3085 **b.** 0.1314

8.5 a. 0.017 **b.** 0.1446 **c.** 0.2974 **d.** 0.7108

8.7 0.7482, assuming the population is normally distributed

8.9 Without replacement: 0.0020; with replacement: 0.0031

8.11 0.7960, assuming the population of electric bill amounts follows a normal distribution

8.13 0.0823

8.15 0.0268

8.17 approximately zero

8.19 19.86 to 21.34

8.21 92.41 to 107.59

8.23 70.62 to 443.67

8.25 22.24 to 23.36

8.27 12.72 to 13.68

8.29 7.86 to 8.74

8.31 a. 1.311 **b.** 2.160 **c.** 1.7341 **d.** -1.325 **e.** -1.708 **f.** 1.282

8.33 27.78 to 32.22

8.35 a. 62.25 to 73.75 **b.** 63.34 to 72.66

8.37 302.55 to 317.45

8.39 9.79 to 12.11

8.41 92.54 to 99.66, assuming a normal population for the tensile strengths

8.43 89

8.45 16

8.47 6.1033

8.49 24

8.51 57

8.53 601

8.55 Estimate is 0.80, CI is 0.716 to 0.884 (in thousands)

8.57 Estimate is 5.0422, CI is 4.47 to 5.61

8.59 Estimate is 3.3923, CI is 2.54 to 4.25

8.61 a. 0.2266 **b.** 0.0329

8.63 28.71 to 30.09

8.65 59

8.67 a. 0.0344 **b.** 0.0455

8.69 Estimate is 50.36, CI is 48.94 to 51.79

Chapter 9

9.1 a. When failing to reject the null hypothesis, the possible outcomes are: (1) the loan is made and paid back and (2) the loan is made and not paid back. When rejecting the null hypothesis, the possible outcomes are: (1) the loan is not made and would not have been paid back had it been granted and (2) the loan is not made and would have been paid back had it been granted. **b.** Type II **c.** No, a Type I error may have been made.

9.3 a. False **b.** False **c.** True **d.** False

9.5 $Z^* = 4.65$, reject H_0

9.7 $Z^* = -3.486$, reject H_0

9.9 Reject H_0 since the 95% confidence interval does not contain 2.0

9.11 a. 12.7274 to 12.7326 **b.** Reject H_0

9.13 a. 0.9732 **b.** approximately one **c.** 0.9131

9.15 $P(Z < -15.29) + P(Z > -11.37) = 1$

9.17 a. $Z > 1.645$ **b.** $Z < -1.645$ or $Z > 1.645$ **c.** $Z < -2.33$

9.19 $Z^* = -2.93$, reject H_0

9.21 $Z^* = -14.14$, reject H_0

9.23 $Z^* = 3.64$, reject H_0

9.25 $Z^* = 2.795$, reject H_0

9.27 a. FTR H_0 **b.** Reject H_0 **c.** Reject H_0 **d.** FTR H_0

9.31 $Z^* = 1.03$, p-value is .1515, FTR H_0

9.33 $Z^* = -1.29$, p-value is .0985, FTR H_0 for a significance level of .05 and .01

9.35 $Z^* = 2.80$, p-value is .0026

9.37 a. $t < -1.729$ **b.** $t > 1.318$ **c.** $t > 2.145$ or $t < -2.145$

9.39 $t^* = 0.59$, FTR H_0

9.41 $Z^* = -5.46$, reject H_0

9.43 $t^* = 3.0$, p-value $< .005$, reject H_0

9.45 $t^* = -6.56$, p-value $< .005$, reject H_0

9.47 a. 15.987 **b.** 46.979 **c.** 7.261 **d.** 45.642

9.49 a. 7.612 to 27.439 **b.** 2.76 to 5.24 **c.** FTR H_0

9.51 Chi-square $= 19.81$, FTR H_0

9.53 Chi-square $= 21.39$, p-value $> .10$, FTR H_0

9.55 Chi-square $= 12.05$, FTR H_0

9.57 a. Increasing (decreasing) the significance level will increase (decrease) the rejection region. **b.** Increasing (decreasing) the significance level will decrease (increase) the probability of a Type II error.

9.59 $Z^* = -2.99$, p-value $= .0028$, reject H_0

9.61 a. $P(Z < -.75) + P(Z > 3.17) = .2274$ **b.** $P(Z < -2.77) + P(Z > 1.15) = .1279$ **c.** $P(Z < -6.04) + P(Z > -2.12) = .9830$

9.63 $Z^* = -3.5$, p-value $= .0004$, reject H_0

9.65 $t^* = -9.25$, reject H_0

9.67 a. 14.193 to 14.807 **b.** $Z^* = 3.19$, reject H_0

9.69 a. $t^* = 10.55$, reject H_0 **b.** p-value $< .005$

9.71 a. .047 to .162 **b.** .217 to .403 **c.** FTR H_0

9.73 Chi-square $= 14.37$, FTR H_0

9.75 Chi-square $= 27.22$, FTR H_0

Chapter 10

10.1 a. Paired **b.** Independent **c.** Independent

10.3 Dependent samples

10.5 No, the samples are dependent.

10.7 The samples are independent.

10.9 a. $Z^* = 1.77$, p-value $= .0384$ **b.** $Z^* = -0.19$, p-value $= .8494$ **c.** $Z^* = -0.06$, p-value $= .4761$

10.11 7.485 to 8.171

10.13 -4.849 to -2.951

10.15 $Z^* = 0.697$, FTR H_0

10.17 $Z^* = 0.405$, FTR H_0

10.19 $Z^* = -3.2$, reject H_0

10.21 $Z^* = -2.66$, reject H_0

10.23 $Z^* = 2.19$, reject H_0

10.25 $t^* = 1.53$, FTR H_0

10.27 $df = 13$, $t'^* = 0.4595$, FTR H_0

10.29 $t^* = 0.4595$, FTR H_0

10.31 -48.364 to -1.636

10.33 $t^* = -0.80$, FTR H_0

10.35 $df = 14$, CI is -4.026 to -0.934

10.37 $F^* = 1.746$, FTR H_0

10.39 .1273 to .3983

10.41 .511 to 12.753

10.43 .70 to 3.91

10.45 $F^* = 2.0$, FTR H_0

10.47 $t^* = 3.5355$, reject H_0

10.49 $t^* = 0.707$, FTR H_0

10.51 p-value $> .10$

10.53 a. $t^* = 0.638$, FTR H_0 **b.** The samples are dependent.

10.55 -110.28 to 1047.43

10.57 The samples are dependent since both brands of tires are placed on the same car.

10.59 $t^* = 3.8443$, reject H_0

10.61 $t^* = 2.01$, reject H_0

10.63 73.76 to 204.24

10.65 1.944 to 6.055

10.67 $t* = 3.90$, reject H_0

Chapter 11

11.1 .394 to .783

11.3 601

11.5 .363 to .748

11.7 655

11.9 8141

11.11 1168

11.13 .001 to .069

11.15 1068

11.17 p-value $= .2296$, FTR H_0

11.19 $Z* = -1.834$, reject H_0, p-value $= .0336$

11.21 Sample size must be at least 167

11.23 $Z* = 0.3985$, FTR H_0

11.25 p-value $= .3015$

11.27 p-value $= .121$, FTR H_0

11.29 $Z* = 1.59$, FTR H_0

11.31 $Z* = 2.38$, reject H_0

11.33 There is no change.

11.35 $-.097$ to .107

11.37 $-.0987$ to .2387

11.39 $-.21677$ to .40236

11.41 a. Critical value is .003, FTR H_0 **b.** .003 to .226

11.43 .213 to .734

11.45 $Z* = 2.68$, p-value $= .0037$, reject H_0

11.47 $Z* = 1.3488$, reject H_0

11.49 a. .23 **b.** .13 **c.** 41

11.51 No

11.53 p-value $= .3557$, FTR H_0

11.55 $Z* = -0.512$, FTR H_0

11.57 p-value $= .6100$

Chapter 12

12.1 a. H_0: $\mu_1 = \mu_2 = \mu_3$; H_a: not all three means are equal **b.** The samples are taken from normal populations with a common variance. **c.** for μ_1: 4.533, for μ_2: 5.333, for μ_3: 4.633 **d.** 1.29

e.

Source	df	SS	MS	F
Factor	2	2.28	1.14	0.88
Error	15	19.38	1.29	
Total	17	21.66		

$F^* = 0.88$, FTR H_0

12.3

Source	df	SS	MS	F
Factor	1	6.5334	6.5334	2.2603
Error	28	80.9343	2.8905	
Total	29	87.4677		

$F^* = 2.2603$, FTR H_0

12.5 $t^* = -2.792$, reject H_0. The F value is the square of the t value.

12.7 a.

Source	df	SS	MS	F
Factor	2	74026.1	37013.05	8.7670
Error	21	88659.2	4221.8667	
Total	23	162685.3		

$F^* = 8.7670$, reject H_0 **b.** p-value $< .01$ **c.** John: 834.15 to 929.61; Randy: 716.52 to 811.98; Ted: 716.15 to 811.16 **d.** 50.07 to 185.19 **e.** -67.19 to 67.93

12.9

Source	df	SS	MS	F
Factor	2	11.6667	5.8335	1.232
Error	27	127.8	4.7333	
Total	29	139.4667		

$F^* = 1.232$, FTR H_0, p-value $> .10$

12.11 The samples are from normal populations with a common variance.

12.13

Source	df	SS	MS	F
Factor	2	23.1111	11.5555	12.5302
Error	15	13.8333	.9222	
Total	17	36.9444		

$F^* = 12.5302$, reject H_0

12.15 $H^* = 4.611$, reject H_0

12.17 a.

Source	df	SS	MS	F
Factor	2	1.2381	0.61905	0.07359
Error	18	151.4286	8.4127	
Total	20	152.6667		

$F^* = 0.07359$, FTR H_0, p-value $> .10$ **b.** Right eye: 0.6968 to 5.5032; left eye: 1.1254 to 5.7318; both eyes: 1.2682 to 5.8746

12.19 a. $t^* = -.8355$, FTR H_0

b.

Source	df	SS	MS	F
Factor	1	517,750	517,750	.70
Blocks	10	1,730,841,990	173,084,199	
Error	10	7,349,590	734,959	
Total	21	1,738,709,330		

$F^* = 0.70$, FTR H_0 **c.** The F value is the square of the t value.

12.21

Source	df	SS	MS	F
Factor	3	1998	666	57.61
Blocks	3	734	244.67	21.16
Error	9	104	11.56	
Total	15	2836		

12.25 The sum of squares and conclusions are the same.

12.27 $b = 5$, $F^* = 4.7273$

12.29

Source	df	SS	MS	F
Factor	2	0.8184	0.4092	13.4605
Blocks	12	5.5225	0.4602	
Error	24	0.7283	0.0304	
Total	38	7.0692		

$F^* = 13.4605$, reject H_0

12.31

Source	df	SS	MS	F
Factor	3	293.1	97.7	15.4988
Blocks	9	5160.2	573.3550	90.955
Error	27	170.2	6.3037	
Total	39	5623.5		

Both F values are significant.

12.33

Source	df	SS	MS	F
Factor	2	77.0556	38.5278	16.8582
Blocks	11	42.2223	3.8384	1.6795
Error	22	50.2777	2.2854	
Total	35	169.5556		

The factor F value is significant. The block F value is not significant.

12.35 a. H_0: $\mu_1 = \mu_2 = \mu_3$; H_a: The means are not equal **b.** 14.0952 **c.** 53.1429

d.

Source	df	SS	MS	F
Factor	2	14.0952	7.0476	2.3871
Error	18	53.1429	2.9524	
Total	20	67.2381		

$F^* = 2.3871$, FTR H_0, p-value > 0.1

12.37

Source	df	SS	MS	F
Factor	2	1.0747	0.5374	7.4227
Error	27	1.955	0.0724	
Total	29	3.0297		

$F^* = 7.4227$, reject H_0

12.39 a.

Source	df	SS	MS	F
Factor	2	0.8889	0.4445	17.5
Blocks	11	7.3922	0.6720	26.4567
Error	22	0.5578	0.0254	
Total	35	8.8389		

$F^* = 17.5$, significant **b.** $F^* = 26.4567$, significant

12.41

Source	df	SS	MS	F
Factor	3	217.9	72.6333	706.549
Error	36	3.7	0.1028	
Total	39	221.6		

$F* = 706.549$, reject H_0, p-value $< .01$

12.43

Source	df	SS	MS	F
Factor	9	190	21.111	2.5503
Blocks	2	250	125	15.1006
Error	18	149	8.2778	
Total	29	589		

12.45

Source	df	SS	MS	F
Factor	2	58.3333	29.1667	2.8824
Blocks	7	74	10.5714	
Error	14	141.6667	10.1191	
Total	23	274		

12.47 $H* = 2.64$, FTR H_0

12.49 -0.4512 to 0.1512

12.51

Source	df	SS	MS	F
Designs	2	61.6	30.8	1.98
Error	21	327.4	15.6	
Total	23	389.0		

$F* = 1.98$, FTR H_0

Chapter 13

13.1 a. $Z* = -0.8386$, FTR H_0 **b.** Chi-square $= 0.7033$, FTR H_0 **c.** The chi-square value is the square of the Z value.

13.5 Chi-square $= 0.8125$, FTR H_0

13.7 Pool the last three groups. Chi-square $= 1.2$, FTR H_0

13.9 Using classes ≤ 1, 2, 3, ≥ 4, chi-square $= 1.2579$, FTR H_0

13.11 Estimate of proportion $= .02$. Using the classes ≤ 1, 2, 3, ≥ 4, chi-square $= 0.4184$, FTR H_0

13.13 Chi-square $= 2.24$, FTR H_0

13.15 Chi-square $= 8.9839$, reject H_0

13.17 Pool SATISFIED and NOT SATISFIED. Chi-square $= 0.5641$, FTR H_0

13.19 Chi-square $= 6.8458$, reject H_0, $.005 < p$-value $< .01$

13.21 Chi-square $= 95.739$, p-value $< .005$, reject H_0

13.23 Chi-square $= 6.06514$, FTR H_0

13.25 Chi-square $= 8.8571$, reject H_0

13.27 Using $E_1 = 50$, $E_2 = 27$, $E_3 = 12$, $E_4 = 11$, chi-square $= 2.276$, FTR H_0

13.29 Chi-square $= 1.72$, FTR H_0

13.31 Estimate of mean = 3. Using the classes $\leqslant 1$, 2, 3, 4, $\geqslant 5$, chi-square = 0.829, FTR H_0

13.33 Estimate of proportion = .70. Using the classes $\leqslant 5$, 6, 7, 8, $\geqslant 9$, chi-square = 2.148, FTR H_0

13.35 Chi-square = 10.9603, p-value < .005, reject H_0

13.37 Chi-square = 1267.09, reject H_0

13.39 Chi-square = 0.4144, FTR H_0

13.41 Chi-square = 15.89, reject H_0

13.43 Chi-square = 3.2511, reject H_0

Chapter 14

14.1 b. $r = 0.9726$

14.3 b. $\hat{Y} = 544.5516 + 3.084X$

14.7 a. $\hat{Y} = 0.4543 + 4.0615X$ **b.** $\hat{Y} = 19.5434$ (thousand)

14.9 a. $r = 0.8024$ **b.** $\hat{Y} = 9.4761 + 0.2989X$ **c.** SSE = 1.3890

14.11 $\hat{Y} = 1.5823 + 0.7659X$. For $X = 9.67$, $\hat{Y} = 8.9886$.

14.13 a. $\hat{Y} = 6.662 + 2.984X$

b.

Y :	10.125	10.000	10.250	10.750	10.500	14.000	14.250
$Y - \hat{Y}$:	0.210	0.055	0.246	-1.283	-1.981	1.370	1.321

Y :	14.370	15.000	14.550
$Y - \hat{Y}$:	0.248	-0.167	-0.020

c. The error terms do not appear to be correlated.

14.15 0.3158

14.17 SSE = 155.94, $s = 2.6624$, all the sample residuals are within two standard deviations

14.19 Yes, the variance of the error component is not constant.

14.21 No

14.23 a. SSE = 15.7775, $t^* = 9.9296$, there is a positive relationship **b.** p-value < .005, there is a positive relationship

14.25 Using log Y as the dependent variable, SSE = 0.0285, $t^* = 27.1601$, there is a positive relationship between X and log Y

14.27 SSE = 296.9413, $t^* = 14.7230$, reject H_0. CI is 3.3346 to 4.5238

14.29 0.8665 to 1.8001

14.31 0.2080 to 0.3898

14.33 $r = 0.8371$, $t^* = 5.5172$, there is a linear relationship

14.35 $r = 0.9742$, $t^* = 15.5525$, there is a linear relationship

14.37 a. No **b.** $r = -0.1225$, r-squared = .015, $t^* = -0.4450$, FTR H_0

14.39 $r = -0.93167$, $t^* = -10.8799$, reject H_0 (the same result as before)

14.41 $t^* = 2.9344$, reject H_0

14.43 a. $\hat{Y} = -201.7469 + 25.9865X$. For $X = 30$, $\hat{Y} = 577.8481$, CI is 520.9389 to 634.7573. **b.** Prediction interval is 317.9274 to 837.7688

14.45 $\hat{Y} = 9.1036$, prediction interval is 7.4260 to 10.7812

ANSWERS TO ODD-NUMBERED EXERCISES **885**

14.47 The prediction interval is wider. Both intervals are the narrowest for $X = \bar{x}$.

14.49 a. $\hat{Y} = 0.29255 + 0.0909X$. For $X = 75$, $\hat{Y} = 7.1101$, CI is 6.3529 to 7.8673 **b.** Prediction interval is 4.3343 to 9.8859 **c.** 69.07

14.51 $\hat{Y} = -0.0267 + 1.2233(0.30) = 0.3403$, prediction interval is 0.2098 to 0.4708

14.53 a. $\hat{Y} = 39.5106 - 0.15566X$ **b.** 0.8688 **c.** SSE $= 23.3391$, CI is -0.252 to -0.108 **d.** $\hat{Y} = 20.8314$, CI is 19.427 to 22.236 **e.** Prediction interval is 16.750 to 24.913

14.55 a. $\hat{Y} = 568.696 + 0.9664X$ **b.** 0.5613 **c.** SSE $= 149.8681$ **d.** 8.3260 **e.** $t^* = 4.7990$, reject H_0 **f.** $\hat{Y} = 684.664$, prediction interval is 677.15 to 692.18

14.57 $\hat{Y} = 3.5118 + 3.9292(29) = 117.4586$, CI is 113.936 to 120.981. The narrowest CI is at $X = 28.4167$

14.59 a. $\hat{Y} = 219.2880 - 1.2342X$ **b.** $r = -0.7253$, $t^* = -6.5794$, reject H_0 **c.** SSE $= 154.1407$, CI is -1.543 to -0.926

14.61 0.6438

14.63 SSE $= 80.75$, $s = 2.06155$, one of the sample residuals lies outside two standard deviations, the histogram appears to be nearly symmetric

Chapter 15

15.1 a. $\hat{Y} = 13.85$ **b.** 2.8

15.3 SSE $= 191.6$, $s = 3.4565$, all the residuals lie within two standard deviations, empirical rule approximately holds

15.5 a. $\hat{Y} = 0.0090 + 1.1102X_1 + 0.13855X_2$ **b.** SSE $= 4.7289$

15.7 6.6646

15.9 a. $F^* = 196.5126$, reject H_0

15.11 a. $t^* = 2.7678$, reject H_0 **b.** $t^* = 6.496$, reject H_0

15.13 a. $t^* = 5.593$, X_2 contributes **b.** 3.4056 to 7.7944

15.15

Source	df	SS	MS	F
Regression	7	200	28.5714	10.3896
Residual	20	55	2.75	
Total	27	255		

15.17

Source	df	SS	MS	F
Regression	2	97.12	48.56	1.9994
Residual	17	412.88	24.287	
Total	19	510		

$F^* = 1.9994$, FTR H_0

15.19 $F^* = 68.84$, reject H_0, CI is 0.7092 to 1.5112

15.21 one

15.23 $F^* = 14.056$, X_2 and X_3 contribute

15.25 $F^* = 2.718$, X_2 and X_3 do not contribute

15.27 $F^* = 2.6367$, the three variables do not contribute

15.29 $F^* = 27.554$, X_3 contributes

15.31 Presence of multicollinearity

15.33 Correlation $= 0.8625$, multicollinearity may be present

15.35 a. 0.955 **b.** Using X_1, 0.951; using X_2, 0.993 **c.** No, due to the high correlation between X_1 and X_2

15.37 No

15.39 a. $\hat{Y} = 7630$ **b.** $F^* = 10.0$, the dummy variables contribute

15.41 $Y = \beta_0 + \beta_1 X_1 + \beta_2 X_2 + \beta_3 X_3 + \beta_4 X_4 + \beta_5 X_5 + \beta_6 X_6 + \beta_7 X_7 + \beta_8 X_8 + e$

Y = total amount of compensation paid for a claim
X_1 = age of employee (years)

$X_2 = \begin{cases} 1 \text{ if male} \\ 0 \text{ if female} \end{cases}$

$X_3 = \begin{cases} 1 \text{ if employee is single} \\ 0 \text{ if not} \end{cases}$

X_4 = length of employment (years)

$X_5 = \begin{cases} 1 \text{ if injury is to head} \\ 0 \text{ if not} \end{cases}$

$X_6 = \begin{cases} 1 \text{ if injury is to a limb} \\ 0 \text{ if not} \end{cases}$

$X_7 = \begin{cases} 1 \text{ if employee works for} \\ \quad \text{manufacturer \#1} \\ 0 \text{ if not} \end{cases}$

$X_8 = \begin{cases} 1 \text{ if employee works for} \\ \quad \text{manufacturer \#2} \\ 0 \text{ if not} \end{cases}$

15.43 a. X_3 **b.** X_3

15.45 Stepwise regression can remove variables previously included.

15.47 Equal variance for error terms

15.49 a. $\hat{Y} = 14.9$, CI is 8.984 to 20.816 **b.** 4.895 to 24.905

15.51 The prediction interval is always wider than the corresponding confidence interval.

15.53 a. $\hat{Y} = 25.1434$, CI is 22.9139 to 27.3729 **b.** 18.7494 to 31.5374

15.55 a. Yes, since the predictor variables will quite likely be highly correlated. **b.** 4.14 billion dollars. This is not a valid conclusion if multicollinearity is present.

15.57 a. $F^* = 37.16$, reject H_0 **b.** $F^* = 1.48$, X_2 does not contribute **c.** 0.0192 to 0.1465 **d.** 1.4757 to 2.3519 **e.** $\hat{Y} = 11.5657$

15.59 a. $\hat{Y} = 18.62 + 0.1380X_1 - 0.984X_2 + 11.808X_3 - 1.097X_4$ **b.** $.299$, 29.9% of the total variation is explained using this model **c.** $.073$ **d.** Use X_3 only **e.** Use X_3 only **g.** $\hat{Y} = 36.152$, CI is 22.94 to 49.36 **h.** 9.7973 to 62.5067

15.61 a. $\hat{Y} = 15.24 + 4.8676X_1 - 5.802 \ X_2 - 2.248X_3$ **b.** 0.987 **c.** $F^* = 18.1538$, X_2 and X_3 contribute **d.** $t^* = 22.778$, X_1 contributes **e.** The residuals appear to be random.

Chapter 16

16.3 Due to seasonal effects, there may be a decline in demand.

16.5 a. Cyclical **b.** Seasonal **c.** Trend **d.** Irregular

16.7 a. $\hat{y}_t = -45424.479 + 23.0303t$ **b.** $\hat{y}_t = 37.333 + 23.0303t$ **c.** The predicted values are the same.

16.9 The nature of the quadratic curve is unknown outside the range of the time series data.

16.11 $\hat{y}_t = -24.418 + 6.2429t$

16.13 a. $\hat{y}_t = 32.696970 + .213287t$ **b.** $\hat{y}_{14} = 32.696970 + .213287(14) = 35.68$

16.15 a. $\hat{y}_t = 557.68 + 192.044t$ **b.** $\hat{y}_t = 896.44 + 72.48t + 7.4728t^2$ **c.** $\hat{y}_{16} = 896.44 + 72.48(16) + 7.47(16)^2 = 3968.44$

16.17 $C_{11} = .9811$, $C_{12} = .9152$, $C_{13} = .9344$, $C_{14} = .9833$, $C_{15} = 1.033$. The period of the cycle appears to be longer than five years.

16.19 a. $\hat{y}_t = 8.417 + 0.5833t$, where $t = 1$ corresponds to 1975 **b.** $C_t = y_t/\hat{y}_t$. These components are 0.778, 1.565, 0.984, 0.465, 0.971, 1.427, 0.96, 0.612, 1.244. **c.** Approximately four years.

16.21 The trend equation is $\hat{y}_t = 74.654 + 0.5220t$. The cyclical components are 1.062, 0.991, 0.932, . . . , 0.958, 0.976, 1.031.

16.23 a. The trend equation is $\hat{y}_t = 105.153 + 0.1940t$. **b.** The cyclical components are 0.997, 1.004, 0.993, 0.990, 0.995, 1.021, 1.011, 1.009, 0.992, 0.988.

16.25 The trend equation is $\hat{y}_t = 164.0 + 2.6t$. The cyclical components are 0.906, 1.147, 1.030, 0.900, 1.062, 0.908, 0.939, 1.077, 1.142, 0.890.

16.29 65.4, 78.9, 87.1, 84.1

16.31 9.9, 16.24, 12.48, 27.69, 23.98, 31.22, 54.72, 72.23, 7.14, 4.86, 4.96, 2.53

16.33 53, 83, 99, 8, 13, 3, 9, 9, 65, 76, 71, 67

16.35 Centered moving averages are 6.88, 7.75, 8.88, . . . , 19.13, 20.13, 21.00.

16.39 Seasonal indexes are 0.8710, 0.8256, 0.8458, 0.9291, 1.0280, 1.0503, 1.0730, 1.1614, 1.1411, 1.0629, 1.0452, 0.9670.

16.41 Seasonal indexes are 1.0918, 1.2155, 0.8573, 0.8358.

16.43 Seasonal indexes are 0.87, 0.61, 0.86, 1.65.

16.45 a. Seasonal indexes ared 0.94, 0.97, 1.01, 1.02, 1.07, 1.06, 1.04, 1.02, 0.99, 0.98, 0.96, 0.94. **b.** The deseasonalized trend line is $\hat{d}_t = 27.1648 + .1773t$. **c.** The cyclical components are 0.9888, 0.9825, 0.9694, 0.9711, 0.9817, 0.9932, 0.9937, 0.9959, 0.9992, 1.0019, 1.0053, 1.0048. **d.** The irregular components are 1.0113, 1.0138, 0.9878.

16.47 The trend equation is $\hat{y}_t = 1.552 + 0.0263t$. The cyclical components for $t = 2, 3, 4$, . . . , 17, 18, 19 are 1.103, 1.063, 1.026, . . . , 1.059, 1.053, 1.043.

16.49 a. Seasonal indexes are 0.89, 0.94, 0.94, 1.04, 0.98, 1.02, 1.08, 1.10, 1.10, 1.02, 0.97, 0.93. **b.** $\hat{d}_t = 3.7214 + .0836t$ **c.** Cyclical components are 1.0358, 1.0005, 0.9829, 0.9771, 0.9800, 0.9812, 0.9930, 0.9941, 0.9987, 0.9958, 0.9913, 1.0047. **d.** Irregular components are 0.9850, 0.9800, 1.0122.

16.51 Cyclical components are 0.9465, 0.9879, 1.0627, 1.0356. Irregular components are 0.7508, 1.1694, 1.0340, 0.9012.

16.53 Index numbers are 100.0, 101.6, 109.4, 132.9, 156.5, 187.8.

16.55 a. 120.6 **b.** 119.0 **c.** 118.7

16.57 a. 135.6 **b.** 136.11 **c.** 135.9

16.61 a. 114.64

16.63 a. Trend **b.** Irregular **c.** Seasonal **d.** Irregular

16.65 a. Seasonal indexes are 1.20, 1.15, 1.07, 0.92, 0.91, 0.95, 0.96, 0.96, 0.92, 0.93, 0.99, 1.05 **b.** $\hat{d}_t = 151.8064 + 1.0940t$ for $t = 1, 2, \ldots$ **c.** 1.0223, 1.0094, 1.0014, 0.9898, 0.9709, 0.9781, 0.9832, 0.9892, 0.9382, 0.9975, 0.9972, 1.0076 **d.** For June 1983 irregular component is 0.9978; for July 1983 irregular component is 1.0006.

16.67 a. Seasonal indexes are 0.97, 0.97, 0.97, 0.97, 0.97, 1.04, 1.05, 1.05, 1.02, 1.01, 0.98, 0.99 **b.** $\hat{d}_t = 51.7404 + .4391t$ for $t = 1, 2, \ldots$ **c.** 0.9897, 1.0028, 1.0074, 1.0084, 1.0087, 1.0084, 1.0104, 1.0097, 1.0137, 1.0174, 1.0143, 1.0152, **d.** For September 1984 irregular component is 1.0017; for October 1984 irregular component is 0.9984.

16.69 The deseasonalized trend equation is $\hat{d}_t = 3.8255 + 0.0215t$. The cyclical components for 1982 and 1983 are 1.0082, 0.9928, 0.9953, 0.9979, 0.9985, 0.9823, 0.9880, 0.9907.

16.71 Index for 1975 is 154.7, index for 1980 is 271.9, index for 1983 is 313.1

16.73 a. Seasonal indexes are 0.99, 1.02, 1.00, 0.98 **b.** $\hat{d}_t = 144.7426 + .8401t$ **c.** 0.9719, 0.9444, 0.9435, 0.9426 **d.** Irregular components for the first two quarters are 0.9909 and 1.0050.

Chapter 17

17.3 Estimates for 1975–1984 are 28.50, 29.25, 31.75, 29.50, 28.00, 27.50, 28.25, 29.75, 32.50, 31.50

17.7 a. 0.48, 0.42, 0.52, 0.68, 0.88, 1.21, 1.62, 1.84, 1.63, 1.33, 0.83, 0.58 **b.** $\hat{d}_t = 1.2595 + 0.0137t$ **c.** $\hat{y}_{87} = 1.275$, $\hat{y}_{91} = 4.060$, $\hat{y}_{96} = 1.493$

17.11 10.8

17.13 Estimated values are 11.06, 11.11, 11.18. Residuals are 0.54, 0.64, -0.15

17.15 Forecast $= S_{20} = 0.91$

17.17 a. 1123.2 **b.** 1135.78

17.19 29.79

17.21 a. 17.176 **b.** 12.35

17.23 Initial seasonal factors are 0.95, 0.83, 1.07 and 1.16. Least squares line is $0.2287 + 0.0109t$. Forecasts for each quarter are 0.404, 0.361, 0.491, 0.538.

17.25 Initial seasonal factors are 0.91, 1.50, 1.09 and 0.50. Least squares line is $0.2709 + 0.0342t$. Forecasts for each quarter are 1.05, 1.78, 1.29, 0.72.

17.27 a. MAD $= 0.267$, MSE $= 0.089$ **b.** MAD $= 0.32$, MSE $= 0.14$

17.29 Procedure 1: MAD $= 3.556$, MSE $= 3.333$; procedure 2: MAD $= 16.556$, MSE $= 44.556$. Procedure 1 is superior overall, and procedure 2 is superior if the last two observations are ignored.

17.31 a. Predicted values for 1983–1985 are 12500.97, 12564.44, 13096.19, . . . , 15940.29, 17151.46, 17656.35. MSE $= 2,049,098.2$ **b.** Predicted values are 12067.43, 11996.72, 13013.65, . . . , 15160.85, 17268.70, 17738.42. MSE $= 2,694,686.4$ **c.** The procedure in part **a** is better.

17.33 MAD $= 16,931.80$, MSE $= 472,762,368$

17.35 Second-order equation is

$$\hat{y}_t = 10.919 - 0.4813y_{t-1} - 0.5393y_{t-2}$$

Fourth-order equation is

$$\hat{y}_t = -0.483 + 0.0171y_{t-1} + 0.0515y_{t-2} + 0.0376y_{t-3} + 1.0115y_{t-4}$$

MSE for second-order equation is 2.9641. MSE for fourth-order equation is 0.1155

17.37 a. $r_1 = 0.693$, $r_2 = 0.108$, $r_3 = -0.355$, $r_4 = -0.428$ **b.** One possible model is

$$\hat{y}_t = b_0 + b_1 y_{t-1} = 11.542 + 0.7105y_{t-1}$$

17.39 $r_1 = 0.848$, $r_2 = 0.500$, $r_3 = 0.066$, $r_4 = -0.334$, $r_5 = -0.599$, $r_6 = -0.688$, $r_7 = -0.590$, $r_8 = -0.320$, $r_9 = 0.046$, $r_{10} = 0.435$, $r_{11} = 0.726$, $r_{12} = 0.832$. The data do not appear to be stationary.

17.41 The series of second differences appears to be stationary with two period seasonal spikes.

17.43 d. The first differences appear to be stationary.

17.45 Let $Q_1 = 1$ for quarter 1, $Q_2 = 1$ for quarter 2, $Q_3 = 1$ for quarter 3. The regression equation is

$$\hat{y}_t = 39.275 - 16.019Q_1 - 9.613Q_2 - 4.406Q_3 + 0.79375t$$

17.47 Let $M_1 = 1$ for Jan., $M_2 = 1$ for Feb., . . . , $M_{11} = 1$ for Nov. The regression equation is

$$\hat{y}_t = 0.6143 - 0.2042M_1 - 0.3012M_2 - 0.1268M_3 + 0.1619M_4 + 0.5506M_5 + 1.5355M_6$$
$$+ 1.8422M_7 + 2.2452M_8 + 1.8768M_9 + 1.3226M_{10} + 0.4685M_{11} + 0.01131t$$

17.49 $\hat{y}_t = 12.617 - 1.489Q_1 + 2.507Q_2 + 5.337Q_3 + .0036t$

17.51 a. $\hat{y}_t = 108.52 + .0031x_t$ **b.** $\hat{y}_t = 74.454 + 0.252x_{t-1}$ **c.** R^2 for part **a** is approximately 0.0, R^2 for part **b** is .957

17.53 $\hat{y}_t = 0.5134 + 0.1555x_{t-1} + 0.5783Q_1 + 0.6600Q_2 + 1.3822Q_3$
MSE $= .0091$

17.55 a. $\hat{y}_t = 14.532 + 0.01459x_t$ **b.** $\hat{y}_t = 9.5539 + 0.02569x_{t-1}$ **c.** R^2 for part **a** is .334, R^2 for part **b** is .972

17.57 positive autocorrelation, no autocorrelation, negative autocorrelation

17.59 DW $= 2.66$, FTR H_0

17.61 DW $= 0.56$, possible positive autocorrelation

17.63 $\hat{y}_{37} = 19.25$, $\hat{y}_{38} = 22.35$, $\hat{y}_{39} = 25.56$, $\hat{y}_{40} = 27.25$, $\hat{y}_{41} = 25.34$

17.65 a. 161.68 **b.** 171.11

17.67 MSE $= 0.32$

17.69 First-order model is

$$\hat{y}_t = 15.46 + 1.0634y_{t-1}$$

Second-order model is

$$\hat{y}_t = 17.99 + 0.9583y_{t-1} + 0.1103y_{t-2}$$

First-order model: predictive MSE $= 5418/16 = 338.6$
Second-order model: predictive MSE $= 5354/15 = 356.9$

17.71 8.56

Chapter 18

18.1

States of Nature

Action	S_1	S_2	S_3
A_1	2,000	500	$-1,000$
A_2	1,500	750	0
A_3	1,000	1,000	1,000

18.3

States of Nature

Action	5	6	7	8	9	10	11	12	13
7	-20	5	30	30	30	30	30	30	30
8	-30	-5	20	45	45	45	45	45	45
9	-40	-15	10	35	60	60	60	60	60
10	-50	-25	0	25	50	75	75	75	75
11	-60	-35	-10	15	40	65	90	90	90
12	-70	-45	-20	5	30	55	80	105	105
13	-80	-55	-30	-5	20	45	70	95	120

18.5

States of Nature

Action	$S_1(100)$	$S_2(125)$	$S_3(150)$
$A_1(100)$	90	90	90
$A_2(125)$	62.5	112.5	112.5
$A_3(150)$	35	85	135

18.7 a.

States of Nature

Action	50	60	70	80	90	100
70	5.5	8	10.5	10.5	10.5	10.5
80	4.5	7	9.5	12	12	12
90	3.5	6	8.5	11	13.5	13.5
100	2.5	5	7.5	10	12.5	12.5

b.

States of Nature

Action	50	60	70	80	90	100
70	0	0	0	1.5	3.5	4.5
80	1	1	1	0	1.5	3
90	2	2	2	1	0	1.5
100	3	3	3	2	1	0

Minimax decision is to order 90 copies. Maximax decision is to order 100 copies.

18.9

States of Nature

Action	S_1	S_2	S_3	S_4
A_1	0	13	5	0
A_2	170	5	18	15
A_3	150	0	0	25

18.11 a. $E(A_1) = 97.5$, $E(A_2) = 55$, $E(A_3) = 95$; expected payoff is maximized using A_1 **b.** risk $(A_1) = 4868.75$, risk $(A_2) = 0$, risk $(A_3) = 1875$

18.13 a. A_3 **b.** A_3 **c.** risk $(A_1) = 0$, risk $(A_2) = 169$, risk $(A_3) = 1642.1875$, risk $(A_4) = 9850$

18.15 Maximum expected payoff is 10.125

18.17 $EVPI = 6.25$; action A_3 is inadmissible

18.19 Expected payoff by ordering 2000 cards is $840; expected payoff with a perfect predictor is $950; maximum amount is $110.

18.21 Expected payoff using A_3 is 1000; expected payoff with a perfect predictor is 1333.33; maximum amount is 333.33.

18.23 $EVPI = 22.75$, A_1 is inadmissible

18.25 a. A_2 **b.** Table of utility values:

States of Nature

Action	S_1	S_2	S_3	S_4
A_1	2	20	14.14	6.32
A_2	17.89	10.95	12.65	10
A_3	18.97	8.94	10.95	6.32

$E(A_1) = 10.615$, $E(A_2) = 12.873$, $E(A_3) = 11.295$; the decision is A_2.

18.27 $p = 0.81$

18.29 $E(A_1) = 3.413$, $E(A_2) = 3.433$, $E(A_3) = 3.386$, $E(A_4) = 3.394$. Because the decision is A_2, the manager is a risk avoider.

18.31

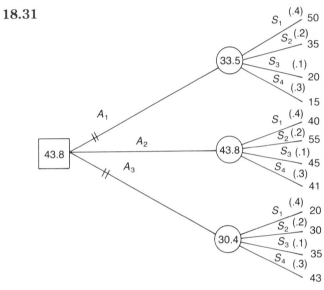

18.33

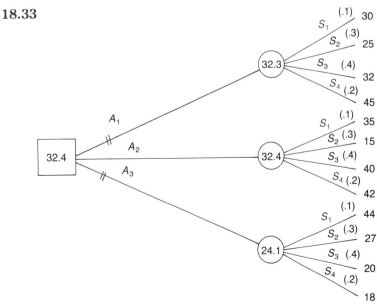

18.35

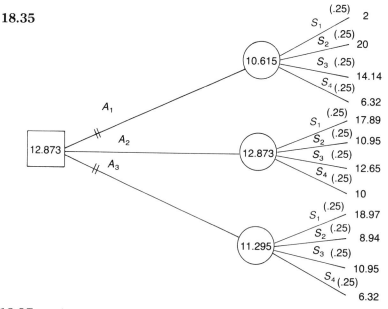

18.37 $P(A_1|B) = 0.421$, $P(A_2|B) = 0.158$, $P(A_3|B) = 0.316$, $P(A_4|B) = 0.105$

18.39 $0.0264/0.0734 = 0.3597$

18.41 $P(B) = 0.26$, $P(S_1|B) = 0.2308$, $P(S_2|B) = 0.2308$, $P(S_3|B) = 0.4615$, $P(S_4|B) = 0.0769$; maximum expected utility of 33.23 occurs for A_2.

18.43 $= 3000$; yes

18.45 $EVPI = 2442.27 - 1995.15 = 447.12$. It is not worthwhile to hire the consultant.

18.47 Minimax decision is to order 34 or 35 loaves; maximax decision is to order 36 loaves.

18.49 The change of probabilities will not affect the minimax decision. Using the expected payoffs, action A_4 is the optimal action for sets 1, 2, and 4, and action A_1 is optimal for sets 3 and 5.

18.51 One example would be to let $U(x) = 0$ for $x < 0$, $U(x) = 2x$ for $0 \leqslant x \leqslant 1000$, and $U(x) = 2000 + (x - 1000)^2$ for $x > 1000$.

18.53

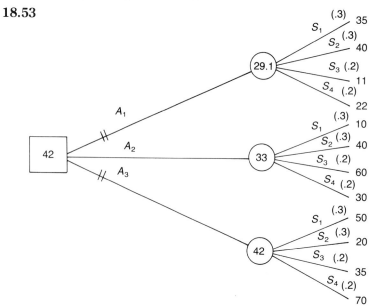

18.55 The maximum payoff with the consultant is 1157.08. The maximum payoff without the consultant is 1105 using A_3. Since $1157.08 - 1105 = 52.08$, which is less than 350, it is not worthwhile to have the consultant's service.

18.57 $P(\text{long} \mid \text{under } 40) = 0.632$

Chapter 19

19.1 The only assumption needed is that you have a sequence of n observations containing n_1 symbols of the first type and n_2 symbols of the second type.

19.3 $R = 12$, reject H_0

19.5 $R = 10$, FTR H_0

19.7 $R = 12$, FTR H_0

19.9 $R = 17$, $Z^* = (17 - 18.486) / 2.91 = -0.51$, FTR H_0

19.13 $U = U_1 = 43$, FTR H_0

19.15 $Z^* = (97 - 77) / 18.267 = 1.09$, FTR H_0

19.17 $Z^* = (53.5 - 72) / 17.32 = -1.068$, FTR H_0

19.19 $Z^* = (88.5 - 72) / 17.32 = 0.953$, FTR H_0

19.21 $U = 14$, reject H_0

19.25 $T_+ = 12$, FTR H_0

19.27 $T_- = 26.5$, reject H_0

19.29 $Z^* = (48 - 105) / 26.786 = -2.13$, reject H_0

19.31 $Z^* = (280 - 232.5) / 48.618 = 0.9769$, FTR H_0

19.33 $Z^* = (81.5 - 76.5) / 21.12 = 0.24$, FTR H_0

19.35 $T = 6$, FTR H_0

19.37 $KW = 0.485$, FTR H_0

19.39 $KW = 6.167$, reject H_0

19.41 $KW = 7.649$, reject H_0

19.43 $KW = 6.83$, reject H_0

19.45 $KW = 2.105$, FTR H_0

19.47 $KW = 1.51$, FTR H_0

19.49 $r = -0.83$, rank correlation $= -0.865$

19.51 rank correlation $= 0.874$, reject H_0

19.53 rank correlation $= -0.944$, reject H_0

19.55 rank correlation $= 0.88$, reject H_0

19.57 rank correlation $= 0.93$, reject H_0

19.59 rank correlation $= 0.84$, reject H_0

19.61 $R = 16$, $Z^* = (16 - 12.52) / 2.25 = 1.55$, FTR H_0

19.65 $U = 16$, FTR H_0

19.67 $T_- = 10.5$, reject H_0

19.69 $KW = 2.93$, FTR H_0

19.71 $KW = 0.14$, FTR H_0

19.73 $KW = 4.10$, FTR H_0

19.75 rank correlation $= 0.845$, reject H_0

Index

895